TOWER HAMLETS
D0488629

EFERENCE

Dictionary of

Synonyms and Antonyms

idea
Library Learning Information
To renew this item call:
0115 929 3388
or visit
www.ideastore.co.uk
TOWER HAMLETS
Created and managed by Tower Hamlets Council

Oxford
Paperback
Reference

The most authoritative and up-to-date reference books for both students and the general reader.

Accounting
Animal Behaviour
Archaeology
Architecture and Landscape Architecture
Art and Artists
Art Terms
Arthurian Literature and Legend
Astronomy
Battles
Bible
Biology
Biomedicine
British History
British Place-Names
Business and Management
Card Games
Chemistry
Christian Church
Classical Literature
Classical World
Computing
Construction, Surveying, and Civil Engineering
Cosmology
Countries of the World
Critical Theory
Dance
Dentistry
Earth Sciences
Ecology
Economics
Education
English Etymology
English Grammar
English Literature
English Surnames
Environment and Conservation
Everyday Grammar
Film Studies
Finance and Banking
Foreign Words and Phrases
Forensic Science
Geography
Hinduism
Human Geography
Humorous Quotations
Idioms
Irish History
Islam
Kings and Queens of Britain
Law
Law Enforcement
Linguistics
Literary Terms
London Place-Names
Mathematics
Marketing
Mechanical Engineering
Media and Communication
Medical
Modern Slang
Music
Musical Terms
Nursing
Opera Characters
Philosophy
Physics
Plant Sciences
Plays
Pocket Fowler's Modern English Usage
Political Quotations
Politics
Popes
Proverbs
Psychology
Quotations
Quotations by Subject
Reference and Allusion
Rhymes
Rhyming Slang
Saints
Science
Scottish History
Shakespeare
Slang
Social Work and Social Care
Sociology
Statistics
Superstitions
Synonyms and Antonyms
Theatre & Performance
Weather
Weights, Measures, and Units
Word Origins
Zoology

Many of these titles are also available online at www.oxfordreference.com

The Oxford Dictionary of

Synonyms and Antonyms

THIRD EDITION

OXFORD
UNIVERSITY PRESS

OXFORD
UNIVERSITY PRESS

Great Clarendon Street, Oxford, OX2 6DP
United Kingdom

Oxford University Press is a department of the University of Oxford.
It furthers the University's objective of excellence in research, scholarship, and education by publishing worldwide. Oxford is a registered trade mark of Oxford University Press in the UK and in certain other countries

© Oxford University Press 1999, 2007, 2014

The moral rights of the author have been asserted

Database right Oxford University Press (maker)

First Edition published in 1999
Second Edition published in 2007
Third Edition published in 2014

Impression: 1

All rights reserved. No part of this publication may be reproduced, stored in a retrieval system, or transmitted, in any form or by any means, without the prior permission in writing of Oxford University Press, or as expressly permitted by law, by licence or under terms agreed with the appropriate reprographics rights organization. Enquiries concerning reproduction outside the scope of the above should be sent to the Rights Department, Oxford University Press, at the address above

You must not circulate this work in any other form
and you must impose this same condition on any acquirer

Published in the United States of America by Oxford University Press
198 Madison Avenue, New York, NY 10016, United States of America

British Library Cataloguing in Publication Data
Data available

Library of Congress Control Number: 2013951374

ISBN 978-0-19-870518-5

Printed in Great Britain by Clays Ltd, St Ives plc

TOWER HAMLETS LIBRARIES

91000004326864

Bertrams	24/04/2014
423.12	£9.99
THISBO	TH13002031

Contents

Introduction vii

Guide to the dictionary ix

Labels xi

Abbreviations xiii

The Oxford Dictionary of Synonyms and Antonyms 1

Commonly confused words *Centre section*

Wordfinder *Centre section*

Introduction

A dictionary of synonyms and antonyms contains lists of words that have a similar meaning to another word. It can help you to express yourself more clearly, find a word that is on the tip of your tongue, or avoid repeating a word that you have already used. It can also be a very useful resource for crossword puzzles and other word games.

Extra help is provided by the boxed Word Links—words related in different ways to a selection of key entries. Under **bird**, for example, you will find the words **avian** (meaning 'relating to birds') and **ornithology** (meaning 'the study of birds').

New to this Third Edition are words such as **podcast**, **staycation**, **redact**, **chilled**, **coruscating**, **nemesis**, and **disruptive** (in the sense of 'innovative').

In addition, there is a useful centre section designed to improve your knowledge of the English language even further: a supplement of commonly confused words explains the crucial differences between similar words that are often mixed up, and a Wordfinder section offers more sources of vocabulary in the form of thematic lists—from chemical elements and clothing to phobias and flowers.

To explore language further, visit Oxford Dictionaries Online at www.oxforddictionaries.com. This free site, which is regularly updated, allows you to search our largest dictionary of current English, as well as dictionaries of French, German, Italian, and Spanish. It also offers fascinating information on usage, grammar, and writing, a Word of the Day, a language blog, and more.

Guide to the dictionary

Here is an explanation of the main features that you will find in this dictionary.

Entry word (known as a *headword*)

Numbered sense of the entry word

Example of use

Word closest in meaning to the entry word (in **bold** type)

Words meaning the opposite of the entry word

colourful *adjective* **1 bright**, vivid, vibrant, brilliant, radiant, gaudy, garish, multicoloured, psychedelic; *informal* jazzy. **2** *a colourful account* **vivid**, graphic, lively, animated, dramatic, fascinating, interesting, stimulating, scintillating, evocative.
– OPPOSITES drab, dull.

Label showing the level of English in which the following synonym is used

Labels showing the region of the world in which the following synonyms are used

horse *noun* **mount**, charger, cob, nag, hack, colt, stallion, mare, filly; *N. Amer.* bronco; *Austral./NZ* moke; *informal* gee-gee.

WORD LINKS
equine relating to horses
equestrian relating to horse riding

Word links providing extra vocabulary related to the entry word

Different parts of speech of the entry word

Phrase for which synonyms are given

root *noun* **1 source**, origin, cause, reason, basis, foundation, bottom, seat. **2** *his Irish roots* **origins**, beginnings, family, birth, heritage.
● *verb* **rummage**, hunt, search, rifle, delve, forage, dig, poke.
□ **root out** eradicate, eliminate, weed out, destroy, wipe out, stamp out, abolish, end, put a stop to.

Labels

Most of the synonyms in this dictionary are part of standard English, but some are used only in certain contexts or types of writing. These are grouped at the end of their sense, preceded by one of the following labels, as appropriate:

informal	normally used only in speech or informal writing or email (e.g. **barmy** or **gawp**)
formal	normally used only in writing, especially in official documents (e.g. **dwelling**)
dated	no longer used by most people (e.g. **navvy**)
old use	not in ordinary use today, though sometimes used to give an old-fashioned effect (e.g. **comely**)
historical	only used today to refer to things that are no longer part of modern life (e.g. **alms**)
literary	found only or mainly in works of literature (e.g. **plenteous**)
technical:	normally used only in technical language (e.g. **occlude**)
derogatory	meant to convey a low opinion or to insult someone (e.g. **pleb**)

Geographical labels

English is spoken throughout the world, and while most of the words used in standard British English are also used in other varieties, there are some words which are only found in one type of English. If a word has the geographical label *Brit.* in this dictionary, this means that it is used in standard British English but not in American English, although it may be found in other varieties such as Australian English. The labels *US* and *N. Amer.*, on the other hand, mean that the word is typically American and is not standard in British English, though it may be found elsewhere.

Subject labels

These are used to show that a word or sense is connected with a particular subject or specialist activity such as *Medicine* or *Computing*.

Abbreviations used in this dictionary

Austral.	Australian
Brit.	British
Canad.	Canadian
N. Amer.	North American
NZ	New Zealand
US	United States

Trademarks

This dictionary includes some words which have, or are asserted to have, proprietary status as trademarks or otherwise. Their inclusion does not imply that they have acquired for legal purposes a non-proprietary or general significance, nor any other judgement concerning their legal status. In cases where the editorial staff have some evidence that a word has proprietary status this is indicated in the entry for that word by the label *trademark*, but no judgement concerning the legal status of such words is made or implied thereby.

Aa

abandon *verb* **1** *he abandoned his wife* **desert**, leave, turn your back on, cast aside, finish with, jilt, throw over; *informal* walk/run out on, dump, ditch; *literary* forsake. **2** *she had abandoned painting* **give up**, stop, have done with; *informal* pack in, quit; *Brit.* jack in. **3** *they abandoned the car* **leave (behind)**, vacate, dump, quit, evacuate, discard, jettison. **4** *the party abandoned those policies* **renounce**, relinquish, dispense with, discard, give up, drop; *informal* ditch, scrap, junk; *formal* forswear.
- OPPOSITES keep.
● *noun* **uninhibitedness**, recklessness, lack of restraint, lack of inhibition.
- OPPOSITES self-control.

abate *verb* **subside**, die down/away/out, lessen, ease (off), let up, decrease, diminish, fade, weaken.
- OPPOSITES intensify.

abbreviate *verb* **shorten**, reduce, cut, contract, condense, compress, abridge, summarize, precis.
- OPPOSITES lengthen, expand.

abbreviation *noun* **short form**, contraction, acronym, initialism.

abdicate *verb* **resign**, retire, stand down, step down, renounce the throne.

abdomen *noun* **stomach**, belly, gut, middle; *informal* tummy, guts.

WORD LINKS
abdominal, **ventral** relating to the abdomen

abdominal *adjective* **gastric**, intestinal, stomach, duodenal, visceral, coeliac, ventral.

abduct *verb* **kidnap**, carry off, seize, capture, run away/off with, take hostage; *informal* snatch.

aberration *noun* **anomaly**, deviation, abnormality, irregularity, variation, freak, oddity, peculiarity, curiosity, mistake.

abhor *verb* **hate**, detest, loathe, despise, shudder at; *formal* abominate.
- OPPOSITES love, admire.

abhorrent *adjective* **hateful**, detestable, loathsome, abominable, repellent, repugnant, repulsive, revolting, vile, odious, disgusting, horrible, horrid, horrifying, awful, heinous.
- OPPOSITES admirable.

abide *verb* **1** *(informal) I can't abide smoke* **stand**, bear; *Brit. informal* stick. **2** *one memory will abide* **continue**, remain, survive, last, persist, live on.
□ **abide by** comply with, obey, observe, follow, keep to, adhere to, stick to, go along with, heed, accept.

abiding *adjective* **enduring**, lasting, everlasting, perpetual, eternal, unending, permanent.

ability *noun* **1 capacity**, capability, power, potential, faculty, facility, wherewithal, means. **2 talent**, skill, aptitude, expertise, savoir faire, prowess, accomplishment, competence, proficiency, flair, gift, knack, genius; *informal* know-how.
- OPPOSITES inability.

able *adjective* **intelligent**, clever, talented, skilful, skilled, expert, accomplished, gifted, proficient, apt, adroit, adept, capable, competent; *informal* genius.
- OPPOSITES incompetent.

abnormal *adjective* **unusual**, uncommon, atypical, untypical, unexpected, unrepresentative, irregular, anomalous, deviant, aberrant, freak, strange, odd, peculiar, eccentric, bizarre, weird, unnatural, perverted, twisted, warped; *informal* funny, freaky, kinky.
- OPPOSITES normal.

a

abnormality *noun* **deformity**, defect, malformation, oddity, strangeness, irregularity, anomaly, deviation, aberration.

abolish *verb* **put an end to**, get rid of, scrap, cancel, end, remove, dissolve, stop, ban; *informal* do away with, axe, ditch.

abominable *adjective* **loathsome**, detestable, hateful, obnoxious, despicable, contemptible, disgusting, revolting, repellent, repulsive, repugnant, abhorrent, reprehensible, atrocious, execrable, foul, vile, wretched, horrible, awful, dreadful, appalling, nauseating; *informal* terrible, shocking, God-awful; *Brit. informal* beastly.
- OPPOSITES good, admirable.

abort *verb the crew aborted the take-off* **halt**, stop, end, call off, abandon, discontinue, terminate; *informal* pull the plug on.

abortion *noun* **termination**, miscarriage.

abortive *adjective* **unsuccessful**, failed, vain, ineffective, ineffectual, unproductive, futile, useless, unavailing.
- OPPOSITES successful.

abound *verb* **be plentiful**, be abundant, be numerous, be thick on the ground; *informal* grow on trees, be two/ten a penny.

about *preposition* **regarding**, concerning, referring to, with regard to, with respect to, relating to, on, dealing with, on the subject of.
● *adverb* **approximately**, roughly, around, in the region of, circa, of the order of, or so, or thereabouts, more or less; *Brit.* getting on for; *N. Amer. informal* in the ballpark of.

above *preposition* **1 over**, higher (up) than, on top of, on. **2 superior to**, senior to, over, higher (up) than, more powerful than, in charge of, commanding.
- OPPOSITES below.
● *adverb* **overhead**, on/at the top, high up, on high, up above, (up) in the sky.
□ **above all** most importantly, most of all, chiefly, primarily, first and foremost, essentially, in essence, at bottom; *informal* at the end of the day, when all is said and done.

abrasion *noun* **1 graze**, cut, scrape, scratch, gash, laceration. **2 erosion**, wearing away/down.

abrasive *adjective* **1 rough**, coarse, harsh, scratchy, chafing. **2 curt**, brusque, sharp, harsh, caustic, grating.
- OPPOSITES gentle.

abridge *verb* **shorten**, cut (down), edit, abbreviate, condense, compress, truncate, prune, summarize, precis, synopsize; (**abridged**) concise.
- OPPOSITES extend.

abridgement *noun* **summary**, synopsis, precis, abstract, outline, résumé, digest, cut-down version.

abroad *adverb* **overseas**, out of the country, to/in foreign parts, to/in a foreign country/land.

abrupt *adjective* **1 sudden**, rapid, quick, hasty, unexpected, unanticipated, unforeseen, precipitate. **2 curt**, brusque, blunt, short, rude, sharp, terse, brisk, unceremonious.
- OPPOSITES gradual, gentle.

abscond *verb* **run away**, run off, escape, bolt, flee, make off, take flight, take off, decamp; *informal* scarper, vamoose, do a bunk, do a runner.

absence *noun* **1 non-attendance**, absenteeism, truancy, leave, holiday, vacation, sabbatical. **2 lack**, want, non-existence, unavailability, scarcity, shortage, dearth.
- OPPOSITES presence.

absent *adjective* **1 away**, off, out, elsewhere, off duty, on holiday, on leave, playing truant; *informal* AWOL. **2 non-existent**, lacking, missing. **3 distracted**, preoccupied, inattentive, vague, absorbed, dreamy, faraway, blank, empty, vacant.
- OPPOSITES present.
□ **absent yourself** stay away, be absent, go away, leave, withdraw.

absent-minded *adjective* **forgetful**, distracted, scatterbrained, preoccupied, inattentive, vague; *informal* with a mind/memory like a sieve.

absolute *adjective* **1** *absolute silence* | *an absolute disgrace* **complete**, total, utter, out-and-out, outright, perfect, pure, thorough, unqualified, unreserved, downright, unmitigated, sheer, unadulterated. **2** *absolute power* **unlimited**, unrestricted, unrestrained, infinite, total, supreme, unconditional. **3** *an absolute ruler* **autocratic**, dictatorial, all-powerful, omnipotent, supreme.
- OPPOSITES partial, qualified, limited.

absolutely *adverb* **completely**, totally, utterly, perfectly, entirely, wholly, fully, quite, thoroughly, unreservedly, definitely, certainly, unquestionably, undoubtedly, without (a) doubt, without question, in every way/respect, one hundred per cent.

absorb *verb* **1 soak up**, suck up, draw up/in, take up/in, mop up. **2 engross**, captivate, occupy, preoccupy, engage, rivet, grip, hold, immerse, involve, enthral, spellbind, fascinate.

absorbent *adjective* **spongy**, sponge-like, porous, permeable.

absorbing *adjective* **fascinating**, interesting, captivating, gripping, engrossing, compelling, compulsive, enthralling, riveting, spellbinding; *informal* unputdownable.
- OPPOSITES boring.

absorption *noun* **1 soaking up**, sucking up. **2 involvement**, immersion, raptness, preoccupation, captivation, fascination, enthralment.

abstain *verb* **refrain**, desist, forbear, give up, renounce, avoid, eschew, forgo, go/do without, refuse, decline; *informal* cut out.

abstemious *adjective* **moderate**, restrained, temperate, self-disciplined, self-restrained, self-denying, sober, austere, ascetic, puritanical, spartan.
- OPPOSITES self-indulgent.

abstinence *noun* **self-denial**, self-restraint, teetotalism, temperance, sobriety, abstemiousness.

abstract *adjective* **theoretical**, conceptual, intellectual, metaphysical, philosophical, academic.
- OPPOSITES actual, concrete.
● *noun* **summary**, synopsis, precis, résumé, outline, abridgement; *N. Amer.* wrap-up.

abstruse *adjective* **obscure**, arcane, esoteric, rarefied, recondite, difficult, hard, cryptic, over/above your head, incomprehensible, unfathomable, impenetrable.

absurd *adjective* **irrational**, illogical, inappropriate, ridiculous, ludicrous, farcical, comical, stupid, idiotic, asinine, hare-brained, foolish, silly, pointless, senseless, preposterous; *informal* crazy, cockeyed; *Brit. informal* barmy, daft.
- OPPOSITES sensible.

abundance *noun* **plenty**, plentifulness, plethora, profusion, exuberance, riot, cornucopia, superabundance.
- OPPOSITES scarcity.

abundant *adjective* **plentiful**, copious, ample, profuse, large, huge, great, bumper, prolific, overflowing, teeming, superabundant; *informal* galore.
- OPPOSITES scarce.

abuse *verb* **1 misuse**, exploit, take advantage of. **2 mistreat**, maltreat, ill-treat, hurt, harm, beat, molest, interfere with. **3 insult**, be rude to, swear at, shout at, vilify, curse.
● *noun* **1 misuse**, exploitation. **2 mistreatment**, maltreatment, ill-treatment, molestation. **3 insults**, expletives, swear words, swearing, name-calling, invective, vilification, curses.

abusive *adjective* **1 insulting**, rude, offensive, derogatory, defamatory, slanderous, libellous. **2 violent**, brutal, cruel, harsh, oppressive.
- OPPOSITES polite.

abysmal *adjective* **terrible**, dreadful, awful, appalling, frightful, atrocious, disgraceful, deplorable, lamentable;

informal rotten, pathetic, pitiful, woeful, useless, lousy, dire, poxy, the pits; *Brit. informal* chronic, shocking.

abyss *noun* **chasm**, crevasse, gulf, pit, void.

academic *adjective* **1 educational**, scholastic. **2 scholarly**, learned, literary, intellectual, erudite, high-brow, bookish, studious. **3 theoretical**, hypothetical, notional, speculative, conjectural, irrelevant, beside the point.
● *noun* **scholar**, intellectual, don, professor, man/woman of letters, thinker; *informal* egghead; *Brit. informal* boffin.

academy *noun* **college**, school, university, institute.

accelerate *verb* **1 speed up**, go faster, gain momentum, increase speed, pick up speed, gather speed. **2 hasten**, quicken, speed up, further, advance, expedite; *informal* crank up.
- OPPOSITES decelerate, delay.

accent *noun* **1 pronunciation**, intonation, enunciation, articulation, inflection. **2 emphasis**, stress, priority, importance, prominence.

accentuate *verb* **focus attention on**, draw attention to, point up, underline, underscore, accent, highlight, spotlight, foreground, bring to the fore, emphasize, stress.

accept *verb* **1 receive**, take, get, obtain, acquire, pick up. **2 agree to**, accede to, consent to, acquiesce in, concur with, endorse, comply with, go along with, defer to, put up with, recognize, acknowledge, admit. **3 believe**, trust, credit, be convinced of, have faith in; *informal* buy, swallow.
- OPPOSITES reject.

acceptable *adjective* **satisfactory**, adequate, reasonable, fair, good enough, sufficient, tolerable, passable.

acceptance *noun* **1 receipt**, receiving, taking. **2 respect**, acknowledgement, belief, toleration, consent, agreement, assent, compliance, acquiescence.

accepted *adjective* **recognized**, acknowledged, established, traditional, orthodox, agreed, approved, customary, normal, standard.
- OPPOSITES unorthodox.

access *noun* **1** *a side access* **entrance**, entry, approach, path, drive, way in. **2** *they were denied access* **admission**, admittance, entry.

accessible *adjective* **approachable**, attainable, reachable, obtainable, available, understandable, comprehensible, intelligible; *informal* get-at-able.

accessory *noun* **1 extra**, add-on, addition, supplement, attachment, fitment. **2 accomplice**, abetter, collaborator, co-conspirator, henchman, associate.

accident *noun* **1 mishap**, misadventure, disaster, tragedy, catastrophe, calamity. **2 crash**, collision, smash, bump, derailment; *N. Amer.* wreck; *informal* smash-up, pile-up; *Brit. informal* shunt. **3 chance**, fate, fortune, luck, good luck, fluke, coincidence.

accidental *adjective* **1 chance**, coincidental, unexpected, incidental, fortuitous, serendipitous. **2 unintentional**, unintended, unplanned, inadvertent, unwitting, unpremeditated.
- OPPOSITES intentional.

acclaim *verb* **praise**, applaud, cheer, commend, approve, welcome, hail, celebrate, eulogize; *formal* laud.
- OPPOSITES criticize.
● *noun* **praise**, applause, tributes, plaudits, approval, admiration, congratulations, commendation, eulogies.
- OPPOSITES criticism.

acclimatize *verb* **adjust**, adapt, get used, familiarize yourself, find your feet, get your bearings; *N. Amer.* acclimate.

accommodate *verb* **1** *refugees were accommodated in army camps* **lodge**, house, put up, billet, board. **2** *the cottages accommodate six people* **hold**, take, have room for, sleep, seat. **3** *we tried to accommodate her* **help**, assist, oblige, cater for, fit in with, satisfy, meet the needs of.

accommodating *adjective* **obliging**, cooperative, helpful, amenable, hospitable, flexible.

accommodation *noun* **housing**, homes, lodging(s), (living) quarters, rooms, billet, shelter, a roof over your head; *informal* digs, pad; *formal* residence, dwelling, abode.

accompaniment *noun* **1** *a musical accompaniment* **backing**, support, background, soundtrack. **2** *wine is a good accompaniment to cheese* **complement**, addition, adjunct, accessory, companion.

accompany *verb* **1 escort**, go with, travel with, keep someone company, chaperone, partner, show, see, usher, conduct. **2 occur with**, go along with with, go together with, attend, be linked with, go hand in hand with. **3** *he accompanied the choir on the piano* **back**, play along with, support.

accomplice *noun* **partner in crime**, abetter, accessory, collaborator, co-conspirator, henchman, associate; *informal* sidekick.

accomplish *verb* **achieve**, succeed in, realize, attain, manage, bring off, carry through, execute, effect, perform, complete.

accomplished *adjective* **expert**, skilled, skilful, masterly, virtuoso, master, proficient, polished, practised, consummate, talented, gifted, able, capable; *informal* mean, nifty, crack, ace.

accomplishment *noun* **1 achievement**, success, act, deed, exploit, effort, feat, coup. **2 talent**, skill, gift, ability.

accord *verb* **1 give**, grant, present, award, confer on, bestow on. **2 correspond**, agree, tally, match, concur, be in harmony, be in tune.
– OPPOSITES disagree, differ.
● *noun* **1** *a peace accord* **pact**, treaty, agreement, settlement, deal, entente, protocol. **2** *the two sides failed to reach accord* **agreement**, consensus, unanimity, harmony.
– OPPOSITES disagreement.
□ **of your own accord** voluntarily, of your own free will, of your own volition, by choice, willingly, freely, readily.

account *noun* **1 description**, report, version, story, statement, explanation, tale, chronicle, narrative, history, record, log. **2 financial record**, ledger, balance sheet, financial statement; (**accounts**) books. **3** *his background is of no account* **importance**, import, significance, consequence, value.
□ **account for 1** explain, answer for, give reasons for, justify. **2** constitute, make up, comprise, represent, be responsible for, produce.

accountability *noun* **responsibility**, liability, answerability.

accountable *adjective* **responsible**, liable, answerable, to blame.

accumulate *verb* **gather**, collect, amass, stockpile, pile up, build up, store (up), hoard, lay in/up, increase, accrue, run up.
– OPPOSITES disperse.

accumulation *noun* **mass**, build-up, pile, collection, stock, store, stockpile, hoard.

accuracy *noun* **correctness**, precision, exactness, fidelity, truth, truthfulness, authenticity, realism.

accurate *adjective* **1 correct**, precise, exact, right, factual, literal, faithful, true, truthful, on the mark, authentic, realistic; *Brit. informal* spot on, bang on; *N. Amer. informal* on the money, on the button. **2 well aimed**, on target, unerring, deadly, true.

accusation *noun* **allegation**, charge, indictment, impeachment, claim, assertion, imputation.

accuse *verb* **1 charge**, indict, impeach, prefer charges against, arraign.
2 blame, hold responsible, condemn, criticize, denounce; *informal* point the finger at.

accustom *verb* **adapt**, adjust, acclimatize, habituate, familiarize, become reconciled, get used to, come to terms with, learn to live with; *N. Amer.* acclimate.

a

accustomed *adjective* **customary**, established, habitual, usual, normal, regular, routine; *literary* wonted.

ache *noun* **pain**, twinge, pang, soreness, tenderness, irritation, discomfort, burning, throbbing, cramp.
● *verb* **hurt**, be sore, be painful, be tender, burn, be in pain, throb.

achieve *verb* **attain**, reach, realize, bring off, pull off, accomplish, carry through, fulfil, complete, succeed in, manage, effect; *informal* wrap up, swing.

achievement *noun* **1 attainment**, realization, accomplishment, fulfilment, implementation, completion. **2 feat**, exploit, triumph, coup, accomplishment, act, action, deed, effort, work, handiwork.

acid *adjective* **1 sour**, acidic, tart, sharp, vinegary. **2 sharp**, sharp-tongued, catty, sarcastic, scathing, cutting, biting, stinging, caustic; *informal* bitchy.
– OPPOSITES sweet.

acknowledge *verb* **1 admit**, accept, grant, agree, own, allow, concede, confess, recognize. **2 greet**, salute, address, nod to, wave to, say hello to. **3 answer**, reply to, respond to.
– OPPOSITES deny, ignore.

acquaint *verb* **familiarize**, make aware of, inform of, advise of, brief; *informal* fill in on, clue in on.

acquaintance *noun* **1** *a business acquaintance* **contact**, associate, colleague. **2** *my acquaintance with George* **association**, relationship. **3** *some acquaintance with the language* **familiarity with**, knowledge of, experience of, awareness of, understanding of, grasp of.

acquire *verb* **get**, obtain, come by, receive, collect, gain, buy, earn, win, come into, secure, pick up, procure; *informal* get your hands on, get hold of, land, bag, score.
– OPPOSITES lose.

acquisition *noun* **purchase**, addition, investment, possession, accession; *informal* buy.

acquit *verb* **1 clear**, exonerate, find innocent, absolve, discharge, free, release; *informal* let off (the hook). **2** *the boys acquitted themselves well* **behave**, conduct yourself, perform, act.
– OPPOSITES convict.

acrid *adjective* **pungent**, bitter, sharp, harsh, stinging, burning.

acrimonious *adjective* **bitter**, angry, rancorous, harsh, vicious, nasty, bad-tempered, ill-natured.

act *verb* **1 take action**, take steps, take measures, move. **2 behave**, conduct yourself, react. **3** *I'll act as lookout* **function**, work, serve, operate. **4 perform**, play, appear; *informal* tread the boards.
● *noun* **1 deed**, action, step, move, gesture, feat, exploit. **2 law**, decree, statute, bill, edict, ruling, order. **3 performance**, turn, routine, number, sketch. **4 pretence**, show, front, facade, masquerade, charade, pose; *informal* put-on.

acting *adjective* **temporary**, interim, caretaker, pro tem, provisional, stopgap; *N. Amer. informal* pinch-hitting.
– OPPOSITES permanent.

action *noun* **1 deed**, act, undertaking, feat, exploit, behaviour, conduct, activity. **2 measures**, steps, initiatives, activism, campaigning, pressure. **3 operation**, working, effect, influence, process, power. **4 battle**, combat, hostilities, fighting, conflict, active service. **5 lawsuit**, suit, case, prosecution, litigation, proceedings.

activate *verb* **start (up)**, switch on, turn on, set going, trigger (off), set off, energize.

active *adjective* **1 busy**, lively, dynamic, vigorous, sprightly, spry, mobile; *informal* on the go, full of beans. **2 hard-working**, industrious, tireless, energetic, diligent, enthusiastic, keen, committed, devoted, zealous. **3 working**, operative, functioning, operational, in action, in operation, in force; *informal* (up and) running.
– OPPOSITES inactive.

activity *noun* **1 action**, bustle, movement, life, hurly-burly; *informal* toing and froing, comings and goings. **2 pursuit**, occupation, hobby, pastime, recreation, diversion, venture, undertaking, enterprise, project, scheme.

actor, **actress** *noun* **performer**, player, thespian, star, starlet; *Brit. informal* luvvy.

actual *adjective* **real**, true, genuine, authentic, bona fide, confirmed, definite, hard, concrete; *informal* real live.
- OPPOSITES imaginary.

actually *adverb* **really**, in (actual) fact, in point of fact, as a matter of fact, in reality, in truth, if truth be told, to tell the truth.

acute *adjective* **1 severe**, dire, terrible, grave, serious, desperate, urgent, pressing. **2 excruciating**, sharp, severe, stabbing, agonizing, racking, searing. **3 quick**, astute, shrewd, sharp, keen, penetrating, razor-sharp, quick-witted, agile, nimble, intelligent, canny, discerning, perceptive.
- OPPOSITES mild, dull.

adamant *adjective* **unshakeable**, unwavering, unswerving, immovable, resolute, resolved, determined, firm, dead set.

adapt *verb* **1** *the policy can be adapted* **modify**, alter, change, adjust, remodel, reorganize, customize, tailor; *informal* tweak. **2** *he adapts well to new surroundings* **adjust**, conform, acclimatize, accommodate, get used, get accustomed, habituate yourself.

add *verb* **1 attach**, append, tack on, join on. **2** *they added the figures up* **total**, count (up), reckon up, tally; *Brit.* tot up.
- OPPOSITES subtract.
□ **add to** increase, augment, magnify, amplify, enhance, intensify, heighten, deepen, exacerbate, aggravate, compound, reinforce. **add up to** amount to, come to, run to, make, total, equal, number.

addict *noun* **1 abuser**; *informal* junkie, druggy, -head, freak; *N. Amer. informal* hophead. **2** *(informal)* **enthusiast**, fan, lover, devotee, aficionado; *informal* buff, freak, nut, fanatic.

addicted *adjective* **dependent**, obsessed, fixated, fanatical, passionate, a slave to; *informal* hooked.

addiction *noun* **dependency**, dependence, habit, obsession, infatuation, passion, love, mania, enslavement.

addictive *adjective* **habit-forming**, compulsive; *Brit. informal* moreish.

addition *noun* **1 adding**, inclusion, incorporation, introduction. **2 add-on**, extra, adjunct, appendage, supplement, rider, addendum, postscript, appendix.
- OPPOSITES subtraction.
□ **in addition** see **additionally**.

additional *adjective* **extra**, added, supplementary, further, more, spare, other, new, fresh.

additionally *adverb* **also**, in addition, besides, too, as well, on top (of that), furthermore, moreover, into the bargain, to boot, to say nothing of.

address *noun* **1 house**, flat, apartment, home, location, whereabouts; *formal* residence, dwelling, domicile. **2 speech**, lecture, talk, presentation, dissertation, sermon, oration.
● *verb* **speak to**, talk to, give a talk to, lecture, make a speech to, hold forth to.

adept *adjective* **expert**, proficient, accomplished, skilful, practised, masterly, consummate.
- OPPOSITES inept.

adequate *adjective* **1** *he has adequate financial resources* **sufficient**, enough. **2** *an adequate service* **satisfactory**, acceptable, passable, reasonable, tolerable, fair, average, not bad, all right, middling; *informal* OK.
- OPPOSITES insufficient, inadequate.

adhere *verb* **stick**, cling, bond, hold.
□ **adhere to** abide by, stick to, hold to, comply with, conform to, follow, obey, heed, observe, respect, uphold, fulfil.

adherent *noun* **follower**, supporter, upholder, defender, advocate, disciple,

devotee, member.
- OPPOSITES opponent.

adjacent *adjective* **adjoining**, neighbouring, next-door, abutting; *formal* contiguous.
□ **adjacent to** next to, by the side of, bordering on, beside, alongside, touching.

adjoining *adjective* **connecting**, connected, interconnecting, bordering, abutting, attached, adjacent, neighbouring, next-door.

adjourn *verb* **suspend**, break off, discontinue, interrupt, recess, postpone, put off/back, defer, delay, hold over.

adjust *verb* **1 modify**, alter, regulate, tune, fine-tune, balance, tailor, customize, rearrange, change, reshape; *informal* tweak. **2** *she adjusted to her new life* **adapt**, become accustomed, get used, accommodate, acclimatize, habituate yourself, assimilate, come to terms with, fit in with; *N. Amer.* acclimate.

adjustable *adjective* **alterable**, adaptable, modifiable, variable, convertible, multiway, versatile.

administer *verb* **1 manage**, direct, control, operate, regulate, coordinate, conduct, handle, run, organize, govern, steer. **2 dispense**, issue, give out, provide, apply, offer, distribute, deliver, hand out, deal out, dole out.

administration *noun* **1 management**, direction, control, conduct, operation, running, coordination, governance, supervision, regulation. **2 government**, regime, executive, cabinet, authority, directorate, council, leadership, management, incumbency, term of office.

administrative *adjective* **managerial**, executive, operational, organizational, supervisory, directorial, governmental, regulatory.

administrator *noun* **manager**, director, executive, controller, official, coordinator, supervisor.

admirable *adjective* **commendable**, praiseworthy, laudable, creditable, exemplary, worthy, deserving, respectable, worthwhile, good, sterling, fine, excellent.
- OPPOSITES deplorable.

admiration *noun* **respect**, approval, appreciation, (high) regard, esteem, recognition.
- OPPOSITES scorn.

admire *verb* **1 respect**, think highly of, look up to, have a high opinion of, hold in high regard, rate highly, esteem, prize, approve of. **2 adore**, love, worship, be taken with, be attracted to, idolize, hero-worship; *informal* carry a torch for, have a thing about.
- OPPOSITES despise.

admirer *noun* **fan**, devotee, enthusiast, aficionado, supporter, adherent, follower, disciple.

admission *noun* **1 confession**, acknowledgement, acceptance, concession, disclosure, divulgence. **2 admittance**, entry, entrance, access, entrée, acceptance, initiation.

admit *verb* **1** *Paul admitted that he was angry* **confess**, acknowledge, concede, grant, accept, allow, own, reveal, disclose, divulge. **2** *he admitted the offence* **confess (to)**, plead guilty to, own up to. **3 let in**, accept, receive, initiate, take on.
- OPPOSITES deny.

admittance *noun* **entry**, admission, entrance, access, entrée.
- OPPOSITES exclusion.

adolescence *noun* **teenage years**, teens, youth, later childhood.

adolescent *noun* **teenager**, youth, juvenile; *informal* teen, teeny-bopper.
● *adjective* **teenage**, young, pubescent, immature, childish, juvenile, infantile, puerile; *informal* teen.
- OPPOSITES mature.

adopt *verb* **take on**, embrace, take up, espouse, assume, follow, choose, endorse, approve.
- OPPOSITES abandon.

adore *verb* **love**, be devoted to, dote on, cherish, treasure, prize, think the world

of, admire, look up to, revere, worship.
- OPPOSITES hate.

adorn *verb* **decorate**, embellish, array, ornament, bedeck, trim, enhance.
- OPPOSITES disfigure.

adrift *adjective* **1 lost**, off course, drifting, disorientated, confused, (all) at sea, rootless, unsettled. **2** *(informal)* **loose**, free, detached, unsecured, unfastened.

adult *adjective* **mature**, grown-up, fully grown, fully developed, of age.
- OPPOSITES immature.

advance *verb* **1 move forward**, press on, push on, attack, make progress, make headway, gain ground, forge ahead. **2** *the move advanced his career* **promote**, further, forward, help, aid, assist, boost. **3** *technology has advanced* **progress**, develop, evolve, make strides, move forward (in leaps and bounds), move on. **4 lend**, loan, put up, come up with; *Brit. informal* sub.
- OPPOSITES retreat.
● *noun* **1 progress**, (forward) movement, attack. **2 breakthrough**, development, step forward, (quantum) leap.
● *adjective* **early**, prior.
□ **in advance** beforehand, before, ahead of time, earlier, previously, in readiness.

advanced *adjective* **1 state-of-the-art**, modern, sophisticated, up to date, up to the minute, cutting-edge, new, the latest, pioneering, innovative, progressive, trendsetting. **2 higher-level**, higher, tertiary.
- OPPOSITES primitive, elementary.

advantage *noun* **1 upper hand**, edge, lead, sway, whip hand, superiority, dominance, supremacy. **2 benefit**, value, good/strong point, asset, plus, bonus, boon, blessing, virtue, profit, good.
- OPPOSITES disadvantage.

advantageous *adjective* **1 superior**, dominant, powerful, fortunate, lucky, favourable. **2 beneficial**, of benefit, helpful, of assistance, useful, of value, profitable, in someone's interests.
- OPPOSITES disadvantageous.

adventure *noun* **1 exploit**, escapade, undertaking, experience, incident. **2 excitement**, thrills, action, stimulation, risk, danger.

adventurous *adjective* **1 intrepid**, daring, daredevil, bold, fearless, brave; *informal* gutsy. **2 risky**, dangerous, perilous, hazardous, exciting.
- OPPOSITES cautious, safe.

adversary *noun* **opponent**, rival, enemy, nemesis, antagonist, challenger, contender, competitor, opposition, competition; *literary* foe.
- OPPOSITES ally.

adverse *adjective* **1** *adverse weather* **unfavourable**, inclement, bad, poor, untoward, inauspicious, unpropitious. **2** *adverse side effects* **harmful**, dangerous, injurious, detrimental, deleterious, inimical. **3** *an adverse response* **hostile**, unfavourable, antagonistic, unfriendly, negative.
- OPPOSITES favourable, beneficial.

adversity *noun* **misfortune**, bad luck, trouble, difficulty, hardship, disaster, suffering, sorrow, misery, woe, trials and tribulations.

advertise *verb* **publicize**, make public, announce, broadcast, proclaim, trumpet, promote, market; *informal* push, plug, hype; *N. Amer. informal* ballyhoo, flack.

advertisement *noun* **announcement**, commercial, promotion, blurb, write-up; *informal* ad, push, plug; *Brit. informal* advert.

advice *noun* **guidance**, counselling, counsel, help, direction, recommendations, guidelines, suggestions, hints, tips, pointers.

advisable *adjective* **wise**, sensible, prudent, expedient, politic, in your (best) interests.

advise *verb* **1 counsel**, give guidance, guide, offer suggestions, give hints/tips/pointers. **2 recommend**, advocate, suggest, urge. **3 inform**, notify, give notice, apprise, warn.

a

adviser *noun* **counsellor**, aide, mentor, guide, consultant, confidant, confidante, guru.

advocate *noun* **champion**, upholder, supporter, apologist, backer, promoter, proponent, campaigner, lobbyist; *N. Amer.* booster.
- OPPOSITES critic.
● *verb* **recommend**, champion, uphold, support, back, promote, campaign for, urge, subscribe to, speak for, argue for, lobby for.
- OPPOSITES oppose.

affair *noun* **1 event**, incident, episode, case, matter, business. **2 business**, concern, matter, responsibility, problem; *Brit. informal* lookout. **3** (**affairs**) **transactions**, activities, dealings, undertakings, ventures, business. **4 relationship**, romance, fling, dalliance, liaison, involvement, amour; *informal* hanky-panky; *Brit. informal* carry-on.

affect[1] *verb* **1 influence**, have an effect on, have an impact on, act on, change, alter, modify. **2 move**, touch, hit (hard), make an impression on, upset, trouble, distress, disturb, shake (up).

affect[2] *verb* **put on**, assume, take on, adopt, feign.

affectation *noun* **pretension**, pretentiousness, affectedness, artificiality, posturing, airs (and graces); *Brit. informal* side.

affection *noun* **fondness**, love, liking, soft spot, tenderness, warmth, devotion, caring, attachment, friendship.

affectionate *adjective* **fond**, loving, adoring, devoted, caring, tender, warm, friendly, demonstrative; *informal* touchy-feely, lovey-dovey.
- OPPOSITES cold.

affiliate *verb* **associate**, unite, combine, join (up), join forces, link up, ally, align, amalgamate, merge.

affinity *noun* **empathy**, rapport, sympathy, accord, harmony, similarity, relationship, bond, closeness, understanding; *informal* chemistry.
- OPPOSITES aversion.

affirm *verb* **declare**, state, assert, proclaim, pronounce, attest, swear, maintain, avow.
- OPPOSITES deny.

affirmative *adjective* **positive**, assenting, consenting, approving, favourable.
- OPPOSITES negative.

afflict *verb* **trouble**, burden, distress, beset, harass, worry, oppress, torment, plague, bedevil.

affluent *adjective* **wealthy**, rich, prosperous, well off, well-to-do, of means; *informal* well heeled, rolling in it, made of money, loaded.
- OPPOSITES poor.

afford *verb* **1 pay for**, find the money for, run to, stretch to, stand, manage, spare. **2 give**, offer, supply, provide, furnish, yield.

afraid *adjective* **1 frightened**, scared, terrified, fearful, nervous, petrified, intimidated, cowardly, faint-hearted; *informal* scared stiff, chicken; *N. Amer. informal* spooked. **2 reluctant**, hesitant, unwilling, slow, shy. **3** *I'm afraid I'm late* **sorry**.
- OPPOSITES brave, confident.

after *preposition* **following**, subsequent to, at the end of, in the wake of.

aftermath *noun* **consequences**, aftereffects, results, repercussions, upshot.

afterwards *adverb* **later**, later on, subsequently, then, next, after this/that, in due course.

again *adverb* **once more**, another time, afresh, anew.

against *preposition* **opposed to**, in opposition to, hostile to, antagonistic towards, unsympathetic to, at odds with, in disagreement with; *informal* anti.

age *noun* **1 old age**, maturity, advancing years, elderliness, seniority, senescence. **2 era**, epoch, period, time, generation.
● *verb* **1 mature**, mellow, ripen, soften, season, weather. **2 grow old**, decline, wither, fade.

agency *noun* **business**, organization, company, firm, office, bureau.

agenda *noun* **programme**, schedule, to-do list, timetable, plan.

agent *noun* **1 representative**, intermediary, middleman, negotiator, go-between, proxy, broker, emissary, envoy, spokesperson, delegate; *informal* rep. **2 spy**, secret agent, operative, mole; *N. Amer. informal* spook, G-man.

aggravate *verb* **1 worsen**, make worse, exacerbate, inflame, compound. **2** *(informal)* **annoy**, antagonize, irritate, exasperate, nettle, provoke, get on someone's nerves; *Brit.* rub up the wrong way; *informal* needle, hack off, get someone's goat; *Brit. informal* wind up; *N. Amer. informal* tick off.
- OPPOSITES alleviate, improve.

aggregate *noun* **total**, sum, grand total, combined score.

aggression *noun* **hostility**, belligerence, force, violence, attack.

aggressive *adjective* **1** *aggressive behaviour* **violent**, confrontational, antagonistic, combative, pugnacious. **2** *aggressive foreign policy* **warmongering**, warlike, warring, belligerent, bellicose, hawkish, militaristic, expansionist; *informal* gung-ho. **3** *an aggressive campaign* **assertive**, forceful, pushy, vigorous, energetic, dynamic, audacious; *informal* in-your-face, feisty.
- OPPOSITES peaceable, peaceful.

agile *adjective* **1 nimble**, lithe, supple, graceful, fit, acrobatic, sprightly, spry. **2 alert**, sharp, acute, shrewd, astute, perceptive, quick.
- OPPOSITES clumsy.

agitate *verb* **1 upset**, fluster, ruffle, disconcert, unnerve, disquiet, disturb, distress, unsettle, worry, perturb, trouble; *informal* rattle, faze. **2 shake**, whisk, beat, stir.

agonizing *adjective* **excruciating**, painful, acute, searing, severe, harrowing, torturous.

agony *noun* **suffering**, torture, pain, torment, anguish.

agree *verb* **1 concur**, see eye to eye, be in sympathy, be as one, be unanimous. **2** *they agreed to a ceasefire* **consent**, assent, acquiesce, allow, approve; *formal* accede. **3 match (up)**, correspond, conform, coincide, fit, tally, be consistent; *informal* square. **4 decide on**, settle, arrive at, negotiate, shake hands on.
- OPPOSITES disagree.

agreeable *adjective* **1** *an agreeable atmosphere* **pleasant**, pleasing, enjoyable, pleasurable, nice, appealing, relaxing, friendly, congenial. **2** *an agreeable man* **likeable**, amiable, affable, pleasant, nice, friendly, good-natured, sociable, genial. **3 willing**, amenable, in agreement.
- OPPOSITES unpleasant.

agreement *noun* **1 accord**, concurrence, consensus, assent, acceptance, consent, acquiescence. **2 contract**, treaty, pact, concordat, accord, settlement, understanding, bargain. **3 correspondence**, consistency, compatibility, accord, similarity, resemblance, likeness.
- OPPOSITES discord, dissimilarity.

agricultural *adjective* **farm**, farming, agrarian, rural, rustic, countryside.
- OPPOSITES urban.

agriculture *noun* **farming**, cultivation, husbandry, agribusiness, agronomy.

> WORD LINKS
> **agrarian** relating to agriculture

aid *noun* **1** *with the aid of his colleagues* **assistance**, support, help, backing, cooperation, a helping hand. **2** *humanitarian aid* **relief**, assistance, support, subsidy, funding, donations, grants; *historical* alms.
- OPPOSITES hindrance.

● *verb* **help**, assist, be of service, support, encourage, further, boost, promote, facilitate.
- OPPOSITES hinder.

aide *noun* **assistant**, helper, adviser, supporter, right-hand man/woman, adjutant, deputy, second (in command), lieutenant.

a

ailing *adjective* **1 ill**, sick, unwell, sickly, poorly, weak, in poor/bad health, infirm. **2 failing**, weak, poor, fragile, unstable.
- OPPOSITES healthy.

ailment *noun* **illness**, disease, disorder, affliction, malady, complaint, infirmity; *informal* bug, virus.

aim *verb* **1** *he aimed the rifle* **point**, direct, train, sight, line up. **2** *she aimed at the target* **take aim**, fix on, zero in on, draw a bead on. **3** *this food is aimed at children* **target**, intend, direct, design, tailor, market, pitch. **4 intend**, mean, hope, want, plan, propose.
● *noun* **objective**, object, goal, end, target, design, desire, intention, intent, plan, purpose, ambition, aspiration, wish, dream, hope.

aimless *adjective* **purposeless**, pointless, directionless, undirected, random.
- OPPOSITES purposeful.

air *noun* **1 breeze**, draught, wind, gust/puff of wind; *literary* zephyr. **2** *an air of defiance* **look**, appearance, impression, aspect, manner, tone, feel, atmosphere, mood.
● *verb* **1 express**, voice, make public, articulate, give vent to, state, declare. **2 ventilate**, freshen, refresh, cool.

WORD LINKS
aerial relating to air

airless *adjective* **stuffy**, close, muggy, humid, stifling, suffocating, oppressive, unventilated.
- OPPOSITES airy.

airy *adjective* **spacious**, uncluttered, light, bright, well ventilated, fresh.
- OPPOSITES airless, stuffy.

aisle *noun* **passage**, passageway, lane, path, gangway, walkway.

akin *adjective* **similar**, related, close, near, comparable, equivalent, connected, alike, analogous.
- OPPOSITES unlike.

alarm *noun* **1 fear**, anxiety, apprehension, distress, agitation, consternation, fright, panic, trepidation. **2 warning**, danger signal, siren, bell, detector, sensor.
- OPPOSITES calmness, composure.
● *verb* **frighten**, scare, panic, unnerve, distress, agitate, upset, disconcert, shock, disturb; *informal* rattle, spook; *Brit. informal* put the wind up.

alcoholic *adjective* **intoxicating**, strong, hard, stiff, fermented, brewed, distilled.
● *noun* **drunkard**, dipsomaniac, drunk, heavy drinker, problem drinker, alcohol-abuser; *informal* lush, alky, dipso, soak, wino; *Austral./NZ informal* hophead.

alert *adjective* **1 vigilant**, watchful, attentive, observant, wide awake, on the lookout, on your guard/toes; *informal* keeping your eyes open/peeled. **2 quick-witted**, sharp, bright, quick, perceptive, on your toes; *informal* on the ball, quick on the uptake, all there, with it.
- OPPOSITES inattentive.
● *noun* **1 vigilance**, watchfulness, attentiveness, alertness. **2 warning**, notification, notice, siren, alarm, signal.
● *verb* **warn**, notify, inform, apprise, forewarn, put on your guard; *informal* tip off.

alien *adjective* **foreign**, unfamiliar, unknown, peculiar, exotic, strange.
- OPPOSITES native, familiar.
● *noun* **1 foreigner**, foreign national, non-native, immigrant, émigré, stranger. **2 extraterrestrial**, ET; *informal* little green man.

alienate *verb* **isolate**, distance, estrange, cut off, turn away, drive apart, set at variance/odds, drive a wedge between.

alienation *noun* **isolation**, detachment, estrangement, distance, separation.

alight *adjective* **burning**, ablaze, on fire, in flames, blazing, lit.

align *verb* **1 line up**, range, rank, straighten, even up, arrange, coordinate. **2** *he aligned himself with the workers* **ally**, affiliate, associate, side, join forces, team up, band together, throw in your lot.

alike *adjective* **similar**, (much) the same, analogous, corresponding, indistinguishable, identical, uniform, interchangeable; *informal* much of a muchness.
- OPPOSITES different.
● *adverb great minds think alike* **similarly**, the same, correspondingly, analogously, identically.
- OPPOSITES differently.

alive *adjective* **1 active**, in existence, functioning, in operation, operative, on the map. **2 alert**, awake, aware, conscious, mindful, heedful, sensitive.
- OPPOSITES dead, unaware.

allay *verb* **reduce**, diminish, decrease, lessen, alleviate, assuage, ease, relieve, soothe, soften, calm.
- OPPOSITES increase, intensify.

allegation *noun* **claim**, assertion, charge, accusation, contention.

allege *verb* **claim**, assert, accuse, contend, state, declare, maintain.

alleged *adjective* **reported**, supposed, so-called, claimed, professed, purported, ostensible, unproven.
- OPPOSITES confirmed.

allegiance *noun* **loyalty**, faithfulness, fidelity, obedience, adherence, devotion; *historical* fealty.
- OPPOSITES disloyalty, treachery.

alleviate *verb* **ease**, relieve, take the edge off, deaden, dull, lessen, reduce, moderate, allay, assuage, soothe, help, soften.
- OPPOSITES aggravate.

alley *noun* **passage**, passageway, alleyway, backstreet, lane, path, pathway, walk.

alliance *noun* **association**, union, league, confederation, federation, syndicate, consortium, cartel, coalition, partnership, relationship, marriage, cooperation.

allied *adjective* **associated**, united, related, connected, interconnected, linked, cooperating, in league, affiliated, combined, coupled, married.
- OPPOSITES unrelated, independent.

allocate *verb* **allot**, assign, set aside, earmark, consign, distribute, apportion, share out, dole out, give out.

allocation *noun* **1 allotment**, assignment, distribution, sharing out, doling out, giving out. **2 allowance**, allotment, consignment, quota, share, ration; *informal* cut; *Brit. informal* whack.

allow *verb* **1 permit**, let, enable, authorize, give leave, license, entitle, consent to, assent to, acquiesce in, agree to, approve; *informal* give the go-ahead to, give the thumbs up to, OK, give the green light to; *formal* accede to. **2 set aside**, allocate, allot, earmark, designate, reserve.
- OPPOSITES prevent, forbid.

allowance *noun* **1 allocation**, allotment, quota, share, ration, grant, limit. **2 payment**, contribution, grant, handout, subsidy, maintenance.

all right *adjective* **1 satisfactory**, acceptable, adequate, passable, reasonable; *informal* so-so, OK. **2 unhurt**, uninjured, unharmed, in one piece, safe (and sound), alive and well; *informal* OK. **3 permissible**, permitted, allowed, acceptable, legal, lawful, authorized, approved, in order; *informal* OK, legit, cool.
- OPPOSITES unsatisfactory.
● *adverb* **satisfactorily**, adequately, fairly well, passably, acceptably, reasonably, well, fine; *informal* OK.

allude *verb* **refer**, touch on, suggest, hint, imply, mention (in passing), intimate.

allusion *noun* **reference**, mention, suggestion, intimation, hint.

ally *noun* **associate**, colleague, friend, confederate, partner, supporter.
- OPPOSITES enemy, opponent.
● *verb* **unite**, combine, join (up), join forces, band together, team up, collaborate, side, align yourself.

almost *adverb* **nearly**, (just) about, practically, virtually, all but, as good as, close to, not quite; *informal* pretty nearly/much/well; *literary* well nigh, nigh on.

alone *adjective* & *adverb* **by yourself**, on your own, unaccompanied, solo, single, isolated, solitary, lonely, deserted, abandoned, friendless; *Brit. informal* on your tod.
- OPPOSITES accompanied.

aloof *adjective* **distant**, detached, unfriendly, remote, unapproachable, reserved, unforthcoming, uncommunicative; *informal* stand-offish.
- OPPOSITES friendly.

also *adverb* **too**, as well, besides, in addition, additionally, furthermore, further, moreover, into the bargain, on top (of that), what's more, to boot.

alter *verb* **change**, make/become different, adjust, adapt, amend, modify, revise, rework, redo, transform; *informal* tweak.

alteration *noun* **change**, adjustment, adaptation, modification, amendment, transformation.

alternate *verb* **1 be interspersed**, follow one another, take turns, take it in turns, oscillate, see-saw. **2 rotate**, swap, exchange, interchange.
● *adjective* **every other**, every second, alternating.

alternative *adjective* **1 different**, other, second, substitute, replacement, standby, emergency, reserve, backup, auxiliary, fallback; *N. Amer.* alternate. **2 unorthodox**, unconventional, nonconformist, radical, revolutionary, avant-garde; *informal* offbeat, way-out, edgy.
● *noun* **(other) option**, (other) choice, substitute, replacement.

altogether *adverb* **1 completely**, totally, entirely, absolutely, wholly, fully, thoroughly, utterly, perfectly, one hundred per cent, in all respects. **2 in all**, all told, in total.

always *adverb* **1** *he's always late* **every time**, all the time, without fail, consistently, invariably, regularly, habitually, unfailingly. **2** *she's always complaining* **continually**, continuously, constantly, forever, all the time, day and night; *informal* 24-7. **3** *the place will always be dear to me* **forever**, for good, for evermore, for ever and ever, until the end of time, eternally.
- OPPOSITES never, seldom.

amalgamate *verb* **combine**, merge, unite, join, fuse, blend, meld, mix, incorporate.
- OPPOSITES separate.

amass *verb* **gather**, collect, assemble, accumulate, stockpile, hoard.

amateur *noun* **non-professional**, non-specialist, layman, layperson, dilettante, dabbler.
● *adjective* **non-professional**, unpaid, non-specialist, lay, unqualified, inexperienced.
- OPPOSITES professional, expert.

amateurish *adjective* **incompetent**, inept, inexpert, unprofessional, amateur, clumsy, crude, second-rate; *Brit. informal* bodged.

amaze *verb* **astonish**, astound, surprise, stun, stagger, nonplus, shock, startle, stop someone in their tracks, leave open-mouthed, dumbfound; *informal* bowl over, flabbergast; *Brit. informal* knock for six; (**amazed**) thunderstruck, at a loss for words, speechless; *informal* gobsmacked.

amazement *noun* **astonishment**, surprise, shock, speechlessness, awe, wonder.

amazing *adjective* **astonishing**, astounding, surprising, stunning, staggering, breathtaking, awesome, awe-inspiring, sensational, remarkable, spectacular, stupendous, phenomenal, extraordinary, incredible, unbelievable; *informal* mind-blowing; *literary* wondrous.

ambassador *noun* **envoy**, emissary, representative, diplomat, minister, consul, attaché.

ambiguous *adjective* **vague**, unclear, ambivalent, double-edged, equivocal, inconclusive, enigmatic, cryptic.
- OPPOSITES clear.

ambition *noun* **1 drive**, determination, enterprise, initiative, eagerness, motivation, a sense of purpose; *informal* get-up-and-go. **2 aspiration**, desire, dream, intention, goal, aim, objective, plan.

ambitious *adjective* **1 aspiring**, determined, motivated, driven, energetic, committed, purposeful, power-hungry; *informal* go-ahead, go-getting. **2 challenging**, exacting, demanding, formidable, difficult, hard, tough.

ambush *verb* **surprise**, waylay, trap, ensnare, attack, jump on, pounce on; *N. Amer.* bushwhack.

amend *verb* **revise**, alter, change, modify, adapt, adjust, edit, rewrite, redraft, rephrase, reword.

amends *plural noun*
▫ **make amends for** make up for, atone for, pay for, make good.
▫ **make amends to** compensate, recompense, indemnify, make it up to.

amenity *noun* **facility**, service, resource, convenience, comfort.

amiable *adjective* **friendly**, affable, amicable, cordial, good-natured, nice, pleasant, agreeable, likeable, genial, good-humoured, companionable.
– OPPOSITES unfriendly, disagreeable.

amnesty *noun* **pardon**, reprieve, forgiveness, release, discharge; *informal* let-off.

amount *noun* **quantity**, number, total, aggregate, sum, quota, size, mass, weight, volume.
▫ **amount to 1** add up to, come to, run to; *Brit.* tot up to. **2** constitute, comprise, be tantamount to.

ample *adjective* **1 enough**, sufficient, adequate, plenty of, more than enough, abundant, copious, profuse, lavish, liberal, generous; *informal* galore. **2 spacious**, full, capacious, roomy, voluminous, loose-fitting, baggy, sloppy.
– OPPOSITES insufficient.

amplify *verb* **1 make louder**, turn up, increase, raise. **2 expand**, enlarge on, elaborate on, develop, flesh out.

amuse *verb* **1 make someone laugh**, entertain, delight, divert, cheer (up), please, charm, tickle; *Brit. informal* crack up, crease up. **2 occupy**, engage, busy, absorb, engross, entertain.
– OPPOSITES bore.

amusement *noun* **1 mirth**, merriment, hilarity, glee, delight. **2 entertainment**, pleasure, leisure, relaxation, fun, enjoyment, interest. **3 activity**, entertainment, diversion, pastime, recreation, game, sport.

amusing *adjective* **funny**, comical, humorous, light-hearted, jocular, witty, droll, entertaining, diverting.

analogy *noun* **similarity**, parallel, correspondence, likeness, resemblance, correlation, relation, comparison.
– OPPOSITES dissimilarity.

analyse *verb* **examine**, inspect, survey, study, scrutinize, investigate, probe, explore, evaluate, break down.

analysis *noun* **examination**, inspection, study, scrutiny, breakdown, investigation, exploration, evaluation.

analytical, **analytic** *adjective* **systematic**, logical, scientific, methodical, precise, meticulous, rigorous, investigative, enquiring.

anarchy *noun* **lawlessness**, disorder, chaos, pandemonium, mayhem, riot, revolution.
– OPPOSITES order.

anatomy *noun* **structure**, make-up, composition, constitution, form, body, physique.

ancestor *noun* **forefather**, forebear, predecessor, antecedent, progenitor, parent, grandparent.
– OPPOSITES descendant.

ancestry *noun* **ancestors**, forebears, forefathers, progenitors, antecedents, family tree, lineage, genealogy, parentage, blood.

ancient *adjective* **1** *ancient civilizations* **early**, prehistoric, primeval, primordial, primitive, bygone. **2** *an ancient custom* **old**, age-old, venerable, time-worn, time-honoured, archaic, antique, obsolete. **3** *I feel ancient* **antiquated**, antediluvian, geriatric; *informal* out of

the ark; *Brit. informal* past its/your sell-by date, superannuated.
- OPPOSITES contemporary, recent.

anecdote *noun* **story**, tale, urban myth, narrative, reminiscence; *informal* yarn.

angelic *adjective* **innocent**, pure, virtuous, saintly, cherubic, adorable.

anger *noun* **annoyance**, vexation, temper, indignation, rage, fury, wrath, outrage; *literary* ire.
● *verb* **annoy**, irk, vex, enrage, incense, infuriate, rile, provoke, outrage.
- OPPOSITES pacify, placate.

angle *noun* **1 gradient**, slope, slant, inclination. **2 corner**, point, fork, nook, crook, edge. **3 perspective**, point of view, viewpoint, standpoint, position, aspect, slant, direction, approach, tack.
● *verb* **tilt**, slant, twist, swivel, lean, tip, turn.

angry *adjective* **furious**, irate, vexed, wrathful, irked, enraged, incensed, seething, infuriated, in a temper, fuming, apoplectic, outraged, cross; *informal* (hopping) mad, up in arms, foaming at the mouth, steamed up, in a paddy; *Brit. informal* shirty; *N. Amer. informal* sore.
- OPPOSITES pleased.
□ **get angry** lose your temper, go berserk, flare up; *informal* hit the roof, go through the roof, go up the wall, see red, go off the deep end, fly off the handle, blow your top, blow a fuse/gasket, lose your rag, flip (your lid), have a fit, foam at the mouth, go ballistic; *Brit. informal* go spare, do your nut.

anguish *noun* **agony**, pain, torment, torture, suffering, distress, woe, misery, sorrow, heartache.
- OPPOSITES happiness.

animal *noun* **1 creature**, beast, (living) thing; (**animals**) wildlife, fauna. **2** *the man was an animal* **beast**, brute, monster, devil, fiend; *informal* swine, bastard, pig.

WORD LINKS
zoological relating to animals
zoology study of animals

animate *verb* **enliven**, energize, invigorate, liven up, inspire, fire, rouse, stir, galvanize, stimulate, excite, move, revitalize, revive, rejuvenate.
● *adjective* **living**, alive, live, breathing, sentient.
- OPPOSITES inanimate.

animated *adjective* **lively**, spirited, energetic, full of life, excited, enthusiastic, eager, alive, vigorous, vibrant, vivacious, exuberant, ebullient, bouncy, bubbly, perky; *informal* bright-eyed and bushy-tailed, full of beans, bright and breezy, chirpy, chipper.
- OPPOSITES lethargic, lifeless.

animosity *noun* **hostility**, antipathy, antagonism, rancour, enmity, resentment, hatred, loathing, ill feeling/will, dislike, bad blood, animus.
- OPPOSITES goodwill, friendship.

annihilate *verb* **destroy**, obliterate, eradicate, wipe out, wipe off the face of the earth; *informal* rub out, snuff out.
- OPPOSITES create.

announce *verb* **make public**, make known, report, declare, state, give out, publicize, broadcast, publish, advertise, circulate, proclaim, release, disclose, divulge.

announcement *noun* **1 statement**, declaration, proclamation, pronouncement, bulletin, communiqué; *N. Amer.* advisory. **2 declaration**, notification, reporting, publishing, broadcasting, disclosure.

annoy *verb* **irritate**, bother, vex, make cross, exasperate, irk, anger, antagonize, nettle, rankle with; *Brit.* rub up the wrong way; *informal* aggravate, peeve, miff, rile, needle, get (to), bug, hack off, wind up; *Brit. informal* nark, get on someone's wick; *N. Amer. informal* tee off, tick off.
- OPPOSITES please.

annoyance *noun* **irritation**, exasperation, vexation, indignation, anger, displeasure, chagrin.

annoyed *adjective* **irritated**, cross, angry, vexed, exasperated, irked, piqued, displeased, put out, disgruntled, nettled; *informal* aggravated, peeved, miffed, riled, hacked off, hot under the collar, narked, shirty; *Brit. informal* not best pleased; *N. Amer. informal* teed off, ticked off, sore.

annoying *adjective* **irritating**, infuriating, exasperating, maddening, trying, tiresome, troublesome, irksome, vexing, galling; *informal* aggravating.

annual *adjective* **yearly**, once-a-year, year-long, twelve-month.

annually *adverb* **yearly**, once a year, each year, per annum.

annul *verb* **declare invalid**, declare null and void, nullify, invalidate, void, repeal, revoke.

anomaly *noun* **oddity**, peculiarity, abnormality, irregularity, inconsistency, aberration, quirk.

anonymous *adjective* **unnamed**, nameless, unidentified, unknown, incognito, unsigned.

answer *noun* **1 reply**, response, rejoinder, reaction, retort, riposte; *informal* comeback. **2 solution**, remedy, way out, explanation.
- OPPOSITES question.
● *verb* **reply**, respond, rejoin, retort, riposte.
□ **answer for** pay for, be punished for, suffer for, make amends for.

answerable *adjective* **accountable**, responsible, liable.

antagonistic *adjective* **hostile**, opposed, antipathetic, ill-disposed, resistant, in disagreement; *informal* anti.

antagonize *verb* **provoke**, intimidate, alienate, anger, annoy, irritate.
- OPPOSITES pacify.

anthem *noun* **hymn**, song, chorale, chant, psalm, canticle.

anthology *noun* **collection**, selection, compendium, compilation, miscellany, treasury.

anticipate *verb* **1 expect**, foresee, predict, be prepared for, bargain on, reckon on; *N. Amer. informal* figure on. **2 look forward to**, await, long for, can't wait for.

anticipation *noun* **expectation**, expectancy, prediction, hope, excitement, suspense.

anticlimax *noun* **let-down**, disappointment, comedown, non-event, disillusionment, bathos; *Brit.* damp squib; *informal* washout.

antics *plural noun* **capers**, pranks, larks, high jinks, skylarking, horseplay, clowning; *Brit. informal* monkey tricks.

antidote *noun* **remedy**, cure, solution, countermeasure, corrective.

antipathy *noun* **hostility**, antagonism, animosity, aversion, animus, distaste, dislike, hatred, abhorrence, loathing.
- OPPOSITES affinity, liking.

antiquated *adjective* **outdated**, outmoded, outworn, behind the times, old, old-fashioned, anachronistic, antediluvian; *informal* out of the ark, superannuated, clunky.
- OPPOSITES modern.

antique *noun* **collector's item**, museum piece, period piece, antiquity.
● *adjective* **antiquarian**, old, collectable, vintage, classic.
- OPPOSITES modern.

antisocial *adjective* **1** *antisocial behaviour* **objectionable**, offensive, unacceptable, disruptive, rowdy. **2** *I'm feeling a bit antisocial* **unsociable**, unfriendly, uncommunicative, reclusive, misanthropic.
- OPPOSITES acceptable, sociable.

anxiety *noun* **worry**, concern, apprehension, unease, fear, disquiet, doubts, nervousness, nerves, tension, stress, angst; *informal* butterflies (in your stomach), the jitters, collywobbles.

anxious *adjective* **1 worried**, concerned, apprehensive, fearful, uneasy, disturbed, fretful, agitated, nervous, on edge, worked up, jumpy, tense, distraught; *informal* uptight, with butterflies in your stomach, jittery, twitchy; *N. Amer. informal* antsy. **2** *she was anxious for news* **eager**, keen,

itching, impatient, desperate.
- OPPOSITES unconcerned.

apart *adverb*
▫ **apart from** except for, but for, aside from, with the exception of, excepting, excluding, bar, barring, besides, other than; *informal* outside of.

apartment *noun* **1 flat**, suite, penthouse; *Austral.* home unit.
2 suite (of rooms), rooms, quarters, accommodation.

apathetic *adjective* **uninterested**, indifferent, unenthusiastic, unconcerned, unmoved, uninvolved, unemotional, lukewarm, half-hearted, unresponsive, lethargic; *informal* couldn't-care-less.
- OPPOSITES enthusiastic.

aperture *noun* **opening**, hole, gap, slit, slot, vent, crevice, chink, crack; *technical* orifice.

apologetic *adjective* **sorry**, regretful, contrite, remorseful, penitent, repentant.
- OPPOSITES unrepentant.

apologize *verb* **say sorry**, express regret, ask forgiveness, ask for pardon, eat humble pie.

apology *noun* **regrets**, expression of regret.
▫ **apology for** travesty of, poor imitation of, poor substitute for, pale shadow of; *informal* excuse for.

appal *verb* **horrify**, shock, dismay, distress, outrage, scandalize, disgust, revolt, sicken, nauseate, offend, make someone's blood run cold.

appalling *adjective* **1** *an appalling crime* **horrific**, shocking, horrible, terrible, awful, dreadful, ghastly, hideous, horrendous, frightful, atrocious, abominable, outrageous. **2** *your schoolwork is appalling* **dreadful**, terrible, atrocious, deplorable, hopeless, lamentable; *informal* rotten, crummy, woeful, useless, lousy, abysmal, dire; *Brit. informal* chronic, shocking.

apparatus *noun* **equipment**, gear, kit, tackle, mechanism, appliance, device, instrument, machine, tool.

apparent *adjective* **1 evident**, plain, obvious, clear, manifest, visible, discernible, noticeable, perceptible, unmistakable, patent. **2 seeming**, ostensible, outward, superficial.
- OPPOSITES unclear, real.

appeal *verb* **ask**, request, call, petition, plead, entreat, beg, implore, beseech.
▫ **appeal to** attract, interest, fascinate, please, tempt, lure, draw; *informal* float someone's boat.
● *noun* **1 plea**, request, petition, entreaty, cry, call, cri de coeur.
2 attraction, allure, charm, fascination, magnetism, pull.

appealing *adjective* **attractive**, engaging, alluring, enchanting, captivating, bewitching, fascinating, tempting, enticing, irresistible, charming; *Brit. informal* tasty.

appear *verb* **1 become visible**, come into view, materialize, turn up, show up. **2** *differences were beginning to appear* **be revealed**, emerge, surface, manifest itself, become apparent/evident, come to light, arrive, arise, crop up, show up. **3** *they appeared completely devoted* **seem**, look, give the impression of being, come across as, strike someone as.
- OPPOSITES vanish.

appearance *noun* **1** *her dishevelled appearance* **look**, air, aspect, looks, mien, expression, behaviour. **2** *an appearance of respectability* **impression**, air, (outward) show, semblance, illusion, facade, front, pretence. **3 occurrence**, manifestation, emergence, arrival, development, materialization.

appease *verb* **placate**, conciliate, pacify, mollify, reconcile, win over; *informal* sweeten.
- OPPOSITES provoke.

appendix *noun* **supplement**, addendum, postscript, codicil, coda, epilogue, afterword, tailpiece.

appetite *noun* **1 hunger**, taste, palate, stomach. **2** *my appetite for learning* **desire**, liking, hunger, thirst, longing, yearning, passion, enthusiasm, keenness, eagerness; *informal* yen.

appetizing *adjective* **mouth-watering**, inviting, tempting, tasty, delicious, flavoursome, toothsome, delectable; *informal* scrumptious, scrummy, yummy, moreish.

applaud *verb* **1 clap**, give a standing ovation, put your hands together; *informal* give someone a big hand. **2 praise**, congratulate, commend, salute, welcome, celebrate, approve of.
- OPPOSITES boo, criticize.

appliance *noun* **device**, machine, instrument, gadget, tool, contraption, apparatus, mechanism, contrivance, labour-saving device; *informal* gizmo.

applicable *adjective* **relevant**, appropriate, pertinent, apposite, material, fitting, suitable, apt.
- OPPOSITES inappropriate, irrelevant.

applicant *noun* **candidate**, interviewee, contender, entrant, claimant, petitioner, prospective student/employee, job-seeker.

application *noun* **1 request**, appeal, petition, approach, claim, demand. **2 implementation**, use, exercise, employment, execution, enactment. **3 hard work**, diligence, industry, effort, commitment, dedication, devotion, perseverance, persistence, concentration.

apply *verb* **1** *300 people applied for the job* **put in**, bid, try, audition, seek, solicit, claim, request, ask, petition. **2** *the Act did not apply to Scotland* **be relevant**, pertain, appertain, relate, concern, affect, involve, cover, touch, deal with, have a bearing on. **3 implement**, put into practice, introduce. **4 put on**, rub in/on, work in, spread, smear on, slap on. **5 exert**, administer, use, exercise, employ, utilize, bring to bear.
□ **apply yourself** work hard, exert yourself, make an effort, be industrious, show dedication, buckle down, persevere, persist, concentrate; *informal* put your back into it, knuckle down, get stuck in.

appoint *verb* **nominate**, name, designate, install, commission, engage, co-opt, select, choose, elect, vote in.

appointed *adjective* **1 scheduled**, arranged, prearranged, specified, agreed, designated, set, allotted, fixed. **2 furnished**, decorated, fitted out, supplied.

appointment *noun* **1 meeting**, engagement, interview, consultation, rendezvous, date, assignation; *literary* tryst. **2 nomination**, naming, designation, installation, commissioning, engagement, co-option, selection, election. **3 job**, post, position, situation, place, office.

appraisal *noun* **assessment**, evaluation, estimation, judgement, summing-up, consideration.

appreciate *verb* **1 value**, admire, respect, think highly of, think much of, be grateful for, be glad of. **2 recognize**, realize, know, be aware of, be conscious of, be sensitive to, understand, sympathize with. **3 increase**, gain, grow, rise, go up, soar.
- OPPOSITES disparage, depreciate.

appreciation *noun* **1 knowledge**, awareness, enjoyment, love, feeling, discrimination, sensitivity. **2 gratitude**, thanks, gratefulness. **3 acknowledgement**, recognition, realization, knowledge, awareness, consciousness, understanding. **4 review**, critique, criticism, analysis, assessment, evaluation, judgement; *Brit. informal* crit. **5 increase**, gain, growth, rise, inflation, escalation.
- OPPOSITES ingratitude, depreciation.

appreciative *adjective* **1** *we are appreciative of your support* **grateful**, thankful, obliged, indebted. **2** *an appreciative audience* **admiring**, enthusiastic, approving, complimentary.

apprehension *noun* **1 anxiety**, worry, unease, nervousness, nerves, misgivings, disquiet, concern, trepidation. **2 arrest**, capture, seizure, detention.
- OPPOSITES confidence.

a

apprehensive *adjective* **anxious**, worried, uneasy, nervous, concerned, fearful.
- OPPOSITES confident.

apprentice *noun* **trainee**, learner, probationer, novice, beginner, tyro, starter, pupil, student; *informal* rookie; *N. Amer. informal* tenderfoot, greenhorn.
- OPPOSITES veteran.

approach *verb* **1 move towards**, near, come near, close in on, close with, gain on. **2 speak to**, talk to, sound out, make a proposal to, proposition, appeal to. **3 tackle**, address, manage, set about, go about, start work on.
- OPPOSITES leave.
● *noun* **1 method**, procedure, technique, modus operandi, style, way, strategy, tactic, system, means, line of action. **2 proposal**, submission, application, appeal, plea, request, overture, proposition. **3 advance**, arrival, appearance. **4 driveway**, drive, road, path, entry, way.

approachable *adjective* **1 friendly**, welcoming, pleasant, agreeable, affable, sympathetic, congenial. **2 accessible**, reachable, attainable; *informal* get-at-able.
- OPPOSITES aloof, inaccessible.

appropriate *adjective* **suitable**, proper, fitting, seemly, apt, right, convenient, opportune, relevant, apposite.
- OPPOSITES inappropriate.
● *verb* **seize**, commandeer, requisition, expropriate, usurp, take over, hijack, steal; *informal* swipe, nab; *Brit. informal* pinch, nick.

approval *noun* **1 acceptance**, agreement, consent, assent, permission, rubber stamp, sanction, blessing, endorsement, ratification, authorization; *informal* the go-ahead, the green light, the OK, the thumbs up. **2 favour**, liking, appreciation, admiration, regard, esteem, respect.
- OPPOSITES refusal, disapproval.

approve *verb* **agree to**, accept, consent to, assent to, give your blessing to, bless, ratify, sanction, endorse, authorize, validate, pass, rubber-stamp; *informal* give the go-ahead to, give the green light to, give the OK to, give the thumbs-up to.
- OPPOSITES refuse.
□ **approve of** agree with, hold with, endorse, support, be in favour of, favour, think well of, like, take kindly to, admire.

approximate *adjective* **estimated**, rough, imprecise, inexact, broad, loose; *N. Amer. informal* ballpark.
- OPPOSITES precise.
□ **approximate to** roughly equal, come near/close to, approach, border on, verge on, resemble, be similar to.

approximately *adverb* **roughly**, about, around, circa, round about, more or less, nearly, almost, approaching; *Brit.* getting on for; *informal* pushing; *N. Amer. informal* in the ballpark of.

apt *adjective* **1 suitable**, fitting, appropriate, relevant, apposite, felicitous; *Brit. informal* spot on. **2 inclined**, given, likely, liable, prone. **3 clever**, quick, bright, sharp, smart, able, gifted, talented; *informal* genius.
- OPPOSITES inappropriate.

aptitude *noun* **talent**, gift, flair, bent, skill, knack, facility, ability, capability, potential, capacity, faculty.

arbitrary *adjective* **random**, unpredictable, capricious, subjective, whimsical, wanton, motiveless, irrational, groundless, unjustified.

arbitration *noun* **adjudication**, judgement, mediation, conciliation, intervention.

arbitrator *noun* **adjudicator**, arbiter, judge, referee, umpire, mediator, go-between.

arc *noun* **curve**, arch, bow, curl, crescent, semicircle, half-moon.

arch *noun* **archway**, vault, span.
● *verb* **curve**, arc, bend, bow, crook, hunch.

architect *noun* **designer**, planner, originator, author, creator, founder, inventor.

architecture *noun* **building**, planning, design, construction.

archive *noun* **1** *the family archives* **records**, papers, documents, files, annals, chronicles, history. **2** *the National Sound Archive* **record office**, registry, repository, museum, library. ● *verb* **file**, log, catalogue, document, record, register, store.

ardent *adjective* **passionate**, fervent, zealous, wholehearted, intense, fierce, enthusiastic, keen, eager, avid, committed, dedicated.
- OPPOSITES apathetic.

arduous *adjective* **tough**, difficult, hard, heavy, laborious, onerous, taxing, strenuous, back-breaking, demanding, challenging, punishing, gruelling; *informal* killing; *Brit. informal* knackering.
- OPPOSITES easy.

area *noun* **1 district**, zone, region, sector, quarter, locality, neighbourhood; *informal* neck of the woods; *Brit. informal* manor; *N. Amer. informal* turf. **2** *the dining area* **space**, section, part, place, room, footprint. **3** *specific areas of knowledge* **field**, sphere, realm, domain, sector, province, territory.

arena *noun* **1 stadium**, amphitheatre, ground, field, ring, rink, pitch, court; *N. Amer.* bowl, park. **2 scene**, sphere, realm, province, domain, forum, territory, world.

argue *verb* **1 claim**, maintain, insist, contend, assert, hold, reason, allege. **2 quarrel**, disagree, dispute, row, squabble, bicker, have words, cross swords, fight, wrangle.

argument *noun* **1 quarrel**, disagreement, difference of opinion, squabble, dispute, altercation, fight, wrangle; *Brit.* row; *informal* slanging match, tiff, set-to; *Brit. informal* barney. **2 reasoning**, justification, explanation, case, defence, vindication, evidence, reasons, grounds.

arid *adjective* **dry**, waterless, parched, scorched, desiccated, desert, barren, infertile.
- OPPOSITES wet, fertile.

arise *verb* **1** *many problems arose* **come about**, happen, occur, come into being, emerge, crop up, come to light, become apparent, appear, turn up, surface, spring up. **2** *injuries arising from defective products* **result**, stem, originate, proceed, follow, ensue, be caused by.

aristocrat *noun* **nobleman**, noblewoman, lord, lady, peer (of the realm), patrician; *informal* aristo; *Brit. informal* toff, nob.
- OPPOSITES commoner.

aristocratic *adjective* **noble**, titled, upper-class, blue-blooded, high-born, patrician; *informal* upper crust, top drawer; *Brit. informal* posh.
- OPPOSITES common.

arm *verb* **equip**, provide, supply, furnish, issue, fit out.

armaments *plural noun* **arms**, weapons, weaponry, firearms, guns, ordnance, artillery, munitions, materiel.

armistice *noun* **truce**, ceasefire, peace, suspension of hostilities.

armoured *adjective* **armour-plated**, steel-plated, ironclad, bulletproof, bombproof, reinforced, toughened.

arms *plural noun* **weapons**, weaponry, firearms, guns, ordnance, artillery, armaments, munitions.

army *noun* **1 armed force**, military force, land force(s), military, soldiery, infantry, militia, troops, soldiers. **2** *an army of tourists* **crowd**, swarm, horde, mob, gang, throng, mass, flock, herd, pack.

WORD LINKS
military, **martial** relating to armies

aroma *noun* **smell**, odour, fragrance, scent, perfume, bouquet, nose.

aromatic *adjective* **fragrant**, scented, perfumed, fragranced.

around *preposition* **1 surrounding**, enclosing, on all sides of. **2 approximately**, about, round about, circa, roughly, more or less, nearly, almost, approaching; *Brit.* getting on for; *N. Amer. informal* in the ballpark of.

arouse *verb* **1 provoke**, trigger, stir up, engender, cause, whip up, rouse, inflame, agitate, incite, galvanize, electrify, stimulate, inspire, fire up. **2 wake (up)**, awaken, bring to/round, rouse.
- OPPOSITES allay.

arrange *verb* **1 set out**, (put in) order, lay out, align, position, present, display, exhibit, group, sort, organize, tidy. **2 organize**, fix (up), plan, schedule, contrive, determine, agree. **3** *he arranged the piece for a full orchestra* **adapt**, set, score, orchestrate.

arrangement *noun* **1 positioning**, presentation, grouping, organization, alignment. **2 preparation**, plan, provision, planning. **3 agreement**, deal, understanding, bargain, settlement, pact. **4** *an arrangement of Beethoven's symphonies* **adaptation**, orchestration, scoring, interpretation.

array *noun* **range**, collection, selection, assortment, variety, arrangement, line-up, display, exhibition.
● *verb* **arrange**, assemble, group, order, range, place, position, set out, lay out, spread out, display, exhibit.

arrest *verb* **1 detain**, apprehend, seize, capture, take into custody; *informal* pick up, pull in, collar; *Brit. informal* nick. **2 stop**, halt, check, block, curb, prevent, obstruct, stem, slow, interrupt, delay.
- OPPOSITES release.
● *noun* **detention**, apprehension, seizure, capture.

arresting *adjective* **striking**, eye-catching, conspicuous, impressive, imposing, spectacular, dramatic, breathtaking, stunning, awe-inspiring.
- OPPOSITES inconspicuous.

arrival *noun* **coming**, appearance, entrance, entry, approach, advent.
- OPPOSITES departure.

arrive *verb* **come**, turn up, get here/there, make it, appear; *informal* show (up), roll in/up, blow in.
- OPPOSITES depart, leave.

arrogant *adjective* **haughty**, conceited, self-important, cocky, supercilious, condescending, full of yourself, overbearing, imperious, proud; *informal* high and mighty, too big for your boots.
- OPPOSITES modest.

art *noun* **1 fine art**, design, artwork, aesthetics. **2 skill**, craft, technique, knack, facility, aptitude, talent, flair, mastery, expertise.

article *noun* **1 object**, thing, item, piece, artefact, device, implement. **2 report**, account, story, essay, feature, item, piece (of writing), column. **3 clause**, section, paragraph, point, item.

articulate *adjective* **eloquent**, fluent, effective, persuasive, lucid, expressive, silver-tongued, clear, coherent.
- OPPOSITES unintelligible.
● *verb* **express**, voice, vocalize, put in words, communicate, state.

artificial *adjective* **1 synthetic**, fake, imitation, mock, ersatz, man-made, manufactured, plastic, simulated, faux; *informal* pretend. **2 insincere**, feigned, false, unnatural, contrived, put-on, forced, laboured, hollow; *informal* pretend, phoney.
- OPPOSITES natural, genuine.

artistic *adjective* **1 creative**, imaginative, inventive, sensitive, perceptive, discerning. **2 attractive**, aesthetic, beautiful, stylish, ornamental, decorative, graceful, subtle, expressive.

ascent *noun* **1** *the ascent of the Matterhorn* **climbing**, scaling, conquest. **2** *the ascent grew steeper* **slope**, incline, gradient, hill, climb.
- OPPOSITES descent, drop.

ascertain *verb* **find out**, discover, get to know, work out, make out, fathom (out), learn, deduce, divine, establish, determine; *informal* figure out.

ashamed *adjective* **1 sorry**, shamefaced, sheepish, guilty, contrite, remorseful, regretful, apologetic, mortified, red-faced, repentant, penitent, rueful, chagrined. **2 reluctant**, loath, unwilling, afraid, embarrassed.
- OPPOSITES proud.

ask *verb* **1 enquire**, want to know, question, interrogate, quiz. **2** *they'll ask a few questions* **put (forward)**, pose, raise, submit. **3 request**, demand, seek, solicit, apply, petition, call, appeal.
- OPPOSITES answer.

asleep *adjective* **sleeping**, napping, dozing, drowsing; *informal* snoozing, dead to the world; *humorous* in the land of Nod.
- OPPOSITES awake.

aspect *noun* **1 feature**, facet, side, characteristic, particular, detail. **2 point of view**, position, standpoint, viewpoint, perspective, angle, slant. **3** *his face had a sinister aspect* **appearance**, look, air, mien, demeanour, expression.

aspiration *noun* **desire**, hope, dream, wish, longing, yearning, aim, ambition, expectation, goal, target.

aspire *verb*
▫ **aspire to** desire, aim for, hope for, dream of, long for, yearn for, set your heart on, wish for, want, seek, set your sights on.

aspiring *adjective* **would-be**, hopeful, budding, potential, prospective; *informal* wannabe.

assassin *noun* **murderer**, killer, gunman, executioner; *informal* hit man.

assassinate *verb* **murder**, kill, eliminate, liquidate, execute; *N. Amer.* terminate; *informal* hit.

assault *verb* **attack**, hit, strike, beat up; *informal* lay into, rough up, do over.
● *noun* **1 violence**, battery; *Brit.* grievous bodily harm, GBH, actual bodily harm, ABH. **2 attack**, strike, onslaught, offensive, charge, push, thrust, raid.

assemble *verb* **1 gather**, collect, get together, congregate, convene, meet, muster, rally, round up, marshal.
2 construct, build, erect, set up, make, manufacture, fabricate, put together, connect.
- OPPOSITES disperse, dismantle.

assembly *noun* **1 gathering**, meeting, congregation, convention, council, rally, group, crowd; *informal* get-together. **2 construction**, manufacture, building, fabrication, erection.

assert *verb* **1 declare**, state, maintain, contend, argue, claim, insist. **2** *you should assert your rights* **insist on**, stand up for, uphold, defend, press/push for.

assertion *noun* **declaration**, contention, statement, claim, opinion, protestation.

assertive *adjective* **confident**, self-confident, bold, decisive, forceful, insistent, emphatic, determined, strong-willed, commanding, pushy; *informal* feisty.
- OPPOSITES timid.

assess *verb* **evaluate**, judge, gauge, rate, estimate, appraise, weigh up, calculate, value, work out, determine; *informal* size up.

asset *noun* **1 benefit**, advantage, blessing, good/strong point, strength, forte, virtue, recommendation, attraction, resource. **2** *the seizure of all their assets* **property**, resources, estate, holdings, funds, valuables, possessions, effects, belongings.
- OPPOSITES liability.

assign *verb* **1 allocate**, give, set, charge with, entrust with. **2 appoint**, promote, delegate, nominate, commission, post, co-opt; *Military* detail. **3 earmark**, designate, set aside, reserve, appropriate, allot, allocate.

assignation *noun* **rendezvous**, date, appointment, meeting; *literary* tryst.

assignment *noun* **task**, job, duty, responsibility, mission, errand, undertaking, commission.

assist *verb* **1 help**, aid, lend a (helping) hand to, support, back (up), work with, cooperate with. **2** *the aim was to assist cashflow* **facilitate**, aid, ease, promote, boost, speed, benefit, encourage, further.
- OPPOSITES hinder.

assistance *noun* **help**, aid, a (helping) hand, support, backing, reinforcement.
- OPPOSITES hindrance.

assistant *noun* **helper**, aide, deputy, lieutenant, second (in command), number two, right-hand man/woman, PA, auxiliary, attendant, henchman; *informal* sidekick, gofer; *Brit. informal* dogsbody, skivvy.

associate *verb* **1 link**, connect, relate, bracket, identify, equate. **2 mix**, keep company, mingle, socialize, go around, have dealings; *informal* hobnob, hang out/around/round.
- OPPOSITES avoid.
● *noun* **partner**, colleague, co-worker, workmate, collaborator, comrade, ally; *informal* crony.

associated *adjective* **related**, connected, linked, similar, corresponding, attendant, accompanying, incidental.
- OPPOSITES unrelated.

association *noun* **1 alliance**, consortium, coalition, union, league, guild, syndicate, federation, confederation, cartel, cooperative, partnership. **2 relationship**, relation, interrelation, connection, interconnection, interdependence, link, bond.

assorted *adjective* **various**, miscellaneous, mixed, varied, diverse, different, sundry.
- OPPOSITES uniform.

assortment *noun* **variety**, mixture, array, mix, miscellany, selection, medley, melange, ragbag, potpourri.

assume *verb* **1 presume**, suppose, take it (as given), take for granted, take as read, conclude, infer, think, fancy, imagine, surmise, believe, understand, gather, suspect; *N. Amer.* figure. **2 affect**, adopt, put on. **3 accept**, shoulder, bear, undertake, take on/up. **4 seize**, take (over), appropriate, wrest, usurp.

assumed *adjective* **false**, fictitious, fake, bogus, invented, made-up; *informal* pretend, phoney.
- OPPOSITES genuine.

assumption *noun* **supposition**, presumption, inference, conjecture, belief, surmise, hypothesis, theory, suspicion, guess.

assurance *noun* **1 promise**, word (of honour), pledge, vow, oath, undertaking, guarantee, commitment. **2 confidence**, self-confidence, self-assurance, self-possession, nerve, poise; *informal* cool. **3 insurance**, indemnity, protection, security, cover.

assure *verb* **1 reassure**, convince, satisfy, persuade. **2 promise**, guarantee, swear, confirm, certify, vow, give your word. **3 ensure**, secure, guarantee, seal, clinch; *informal* sew up.

assured *adjective* **1 confident**, self-confident, self-assured, self-possessed, poised, composed, imperturbable, unruffled; *informal* unflappable, together. **2 guaranteed**, certain, sure, secure, reliable, dependable; *informal* sure-fire.
- OPPOSITES nervous, uncertain.

astonish *verb* **amaze**, astound, stagger, startle, stun, surprise, confound, dumbfound, nonplus, take aback, leave open-mouthed; *informal* flabbergast, bowl over; *Brit. informal* knock for six.

astonishing *adjective* **amazing**, astounding, staggering, surprising, breathtaking, remarkable, extraordinary, incredible, unbelievable, phenomenal; *informal* mind-boggling.
- OPPOSITES unremarkable.

astound *verb* **amaze**, astonish, stagger, surprise, startle, stun, confound, dumbfound, take aback, leave open-mouthed; *informal* flabbergast, bowl over; *Brit. informal* knock for six.

astounding *adjective* **amazing**, astonishing, staggering, surprising, breathtaking, remarkable, extraordinary, incredible, unbelievable, phenomenal; *informal* mind-boggling.
- OPPOSITES unremarkable.

astute *adjective* **shrewd**, sharp, acute, quick, clever, intelligent, bright, smart, canny, perceptive, perspicacious; *informal* quick on the uptake.
- OPPOSITES stupid.

asylum *noun* **refuge**, sanctuary, shelter, protection, immunity, a safe haven.

athletic *adjective* **muscular**, fit, strapping, well built, strong, sturdy, powerful, brawny, burly.

atmosphere *noun* **1 air**, sky; *literary* the heavens, the ether. **2** *a relaxed atmosphere* **ambience**, spirit, air, mood, feel, feeling, character, tone, aura, quality, environment, climate; *informal* vibe.

WORD LINKS
meteorology study of the atmosphere

atrocious *adjective* **1 wicked**, cruel, brutal, barbaric, vicious, monstrous, vile, inhuman, fiendish. **2 appalling**, awful, dreadful, terrible, miserable; *informal* abysmal, dire, rotten, lousy; *Brit. informal* shocking.
– OPPOSITES admirable, superb.

atrocity *noun* **1** *a number of atrocities* **outrage**, horror, violation, abuse, crime. **2** *scenes of hardship and atrocity* **wickedness**, cruelty, brutality, barbarity, viciousness, savagery, inhumanity.

attach *verb* **1 fasten**, fix, affix, join, secure, stick, connect, tie, link, couple, pin, hitch. **2** *they attach importance to research* **ascribe**, assign, attribute, accredit, impute. **3** *the medical officer attached to HQ* **assign**, appoint, allocate, second.
– OPPOSITES detach.

attached *adjective*
□ **attached to** fond of, devoted to, keen on; *informal* mad about, crazy about.

attachment *noun* **1 bond**, closeness, devotion, loyalty, fondness for, love for, affection for, feeling for, sympathy for. **2 accessory**, fitting, extension, add-on.

attack *verb* **1 assault**, beat up, set upon, mug, charge, pounce on, raid, rush, storm; *informal* lay into, do over, work over, rough up; *Brit. informal* duff up. **2 criticize**, censure, condemn, denounce, revile, vilify, impugn, disparage; *informal* knock, slam, lay into; *Brit. informal* slate, slag off, rubbish.
– OPPOSITES defend, praise.
● *noun* **1 assault**, onslaught, offensive, strike, blitz, raid, incursion, sortie, foray, charge, invasion. **2 criticism**, censure, condemnation, vilification, disparagement; *Brit. informal* slating. **3 fit**, seizure, spasm, convulsion, paroxysm, bout, episode.
– OPPOSITES defence, praise.

attacker *noun* **assailant**, assaulter, mugger, aggressor, raider, invader.
– OPPOSITES victim.

attain *verb* **achieve**, accomplish, reach, obtain, gain, secure, get, win, earn, realize, fulfil; *informal* clinch, bag, wrap up.

attempt *verb* **try**, strive, aim, venture, endeavour, seek, have a go, bid.
● *noun* **try**, effort, endeavour, venture, bid, go; *informal* crack, shot, stab.

attend *verb* **1 be present at**, sit in on, take part in, appear at, turn up at, visit, go to; *informal* show up at. **2 pay attention**, listen, be attentive, concentrate.
□ **attend to 1** deal with, see to, look after, manage, organize, sort out, handle, take care of, tackle. **2** care for, look after, minister to, see to, tend, treat, help.

attendance *noun* **1 presence**, appearance, attention. **2 audience**, turnout, house, gate, crowd.
– OPPOSITES absence.

attendant *noun* **assistant**, aide, companion, escort, steward, equerry, servant, retainer, valet, maid.
● *adjective* **accompanying**, associated, concomitant, related, connected, resulting, consequent.

attention *noun* **1 consideration**, contemplation, deliberation, thought, study, observation, mind, investigation, action. **2 awareness**, notice, scrutiny, eye, gaze. **3** *medical attention* **care**, ministrations, treatment, therapy, relief, aid, assistance.

attentive *adjective* **1** *an attentive pupil* **alert**, perceptive, observant, acute, aware, heedful, focused, studious, diligent, conscientious, earnest. **2** *the most attentive of husbands* **considerate**, conscientious, thoughtful, kind, caring,

a

solicitous, understanding, sympathetic.
- OPPOSITES inattentive.

attic *noun* **loft**, roof space, garret.

attitude *noun* **1 view**, viewpoint, outlook, perspective, stance, standpoint, position, frame of mind, approach, opinion. **2** *an attitude of prayer* **posture**, position, pose, stance.

attract *verb* **1 appeal to**, fascinate, charm, captivate, interest, tempt, entice, lure, bewitch, beguile, seduce. **2 draw**, pull, magnetize.
- OPPOSITES repel.

attraction *noun* **1 appeal**, attractiveness, pull, desirability, fascination, allure, charisma, charm. **2** *the town's main attractions* **entertainment**, activity, diversion, amenity, service. **3** *magnetic attraction* **pull**, draw, force.
- OPPOSITES repulsion.

attractive *adjective* **1 good-looking**, beautiful, pretty, handsome, lovely, stunning, striking, desirable, gorgeous, prepossessing, fetching; *Scottish & N. English* bonny; *informal* drop-dead gorgeous, hunky; *Brit. informal* fit; *N. Amer. informal* cute; *old use* comely. **2 appealing**, inviting, tempting, pleasing, interesting.
- OPPOSITES unattractive, ugly.

attribute *verb* **ascribe**, assign, accredit, credit, put down, chalk up, pin on.
● *noun* **quality**, characteristic, trait, feature, element, aspect, property, sign, hallmark, mark.

audible *adjective* **perceptible**, discernible, detectable, distinct, clear.
- OPPOSITES inaudible, faint.

audience *noun* **1 spectators**, **listeners**, viewers, onlookers, concertgoers, theatregoers, crowd, public, throng, gallery, congregation, turnout. **2 meeting**, interview, consultation, conference, hearing, reception.

augment *verb* **increase**, add to, supplement, enhance, build up, raise, boost, up, hike up, enlarge, swell, expand, extend.
- OPPOSITES decrease, reduce.

august *adjective* **distinguished**, respected, eminent, venerable, illustrious, prestigious, renowned, celebrated, honoured, acclaimed, esteemed.

aura *noun* **atmosphere**, ambience, air, quality, character, mood, feeling; *informal* vibe.

auspicious *adjective* **favourable**, promising, encouraging, fortunate, opportune, timely, advantageous, good.
- OPPOSITES inauspicious, unfavourable.

austere *adjective* **1 severe**, stern, strict, harsh, dour, grim, cold, frosty, unfriendly. **2 spartan**, frugal, ascetic, puritanical, abstemious, strict, simple, hard. **3** *an austere building* **plain**, simple, basic, functional, unadorned, bleak, bare, clinical.
- OPPOSITES easy-going, ornate.

authentic *adjective* **1 genuine**, real, bona fide, true, legitimate; *informal* pukka, kosher; *Austral./NZ informal* dinkum. **2 accurate**, factual, true, truthful, reliable, trustworthy, honest, faithful.
- OPPOSITES fake, unreliable.

authenticate *verb* **verify**, validate, prove, substantiate, corroborate, confirm, support, back up.
- OPPOSITES disprove.

author *noun* **1 writer**, novelist, poet, playwright, dramatist, columnist, reporter, wordsmith; *informal* scribe, scribbler. **2 creator**, originator, founder, father, architect, designer, producer.

authoritarian *adjective* **strict**, autocratic, dictatorial, despotic, tyrannical, domineering, imperious, illiberal, undemocratic; *informal* bossy.
- OPPOSITES democratic, liberal.
● *noun* **disciplinarian**, autocrat, dictator, despot, tyrant.
- OPPOSITES democrat, liberal.

authoritative *adjective* **1 reliable**, dependable, trustworthy, accurate, authentic, valid, definitive, classic. **2 commanding**, masterful, assertive, self-assured, self-confident.
- OPPOSITES unreliable.

authority *noun* **1** *a rebellion against those in authority* **power**, command, control, charge, dominance, jurisdiction, rule; *informal* clout. **2** *the authority to arrest drug traffickers* **right**, authorization, power, mandate, prerogative, licence. **3** *they need parliamentary authority* **permission**, authorization, consent, sanction, assent, agreement, approval, clearance; *informal* the go-ahead. **4** (**the authorities**) **officials**, officialdom, government, administration, establishment, police; *informal* the powers that be. **5 expert**, specialist, professional, master, connoisseur, pundit, doyen(ne), guru.

authorize *verb* **1** *they authorized further action* **permit**, sanction, allow, approve, consent to, assent to; *informal* give the go-ahead to, OK. **2** *the troops were authorized to fire* **empower**, give authority, mandate, commission, entitle.
- OPPOSITES forbid.

authorized *adjective* **approved**, sanctioned, accredited, recognized, licensed, certified, official, legal, legitimate.
- OPPOSITES unauthorized, unofficial.

automatic *adjective* **1 mechanized**, powered, mechanical, automated, computerized, electronic, robotic. **2 instinctive**, involuntary, unconscious, reflex, knee-jerk, subconscious, spontaneous, impulsive, unthinking, mechanical; *informal* gut. **3 inevitable**, unavoidable, inescapable, certain.
- OPPOSITES manual, conscious, deliberate.

autonomous *adjective* **self-governing**, independent, sovereign, free.
- OPPOSITES dependent.

autonomy *noun* **self-government**, self-rule, home rule, self-determination, independence, sovereignty, freedom.
- OPPOSITES dependence.

auxiliary *adjective* **additional**, supplementary, extra, reserve, backup, emergency, fallback, second.

available *adjective* **obtainable**, accessible, to/at hand, to be had, on sale, untaken, unsold, free, vacant, unoccupied; *informal* up for grabs, on tap.

avalanche *noun an avalanche of enquiries* **barrage**, flood, deluge, torrent, wave, onslaught.

avant-garde *adjective* **experimental**, modern, cutting-edge, progressive, unorthodox, unconventional; *informal* edgy, offbeat, way-out.
- OPPOSITES conservative, traditional.

avarice *noun* **greed**, acquisitiveness, covetousness, materialism.
- OPPOSITES generosity.

average *noun* **mean**, median, mode, norm, standard, rule, par.
● *adjective* **1** *the average temperature* **mean**, median. **2** *a woman of average height* **normal**, standard, typical, ordinary, common, regular.
- OPPOSITES abnormal, unusual.
□ **on average** normally, usually, ordinarily, generally, typically, for the most part, as a rule, by and large, overall, on the whole.

averse *adjective* **opposed**, hostile, antagonistic, resistant, disinclined, reluctant, loath; *informal* anti.
- OPPOSITES keen.

aversion *noun* **dislike**, hatred, loathing, abhorrence, distaste, antipathy, hostility, reluctance, disinclination.
- OPPOSITES liking.

avert *verb* **1 turn aside**, turn away, shift, redirect. **2 prevent**, avoid, stave off, ward off, head off, forestall.

avid *adjective* **keen**, eager, enthusiastic, ardent, passionate, zealous, devoted.
- OPPOSITES apathetic.

avoid *verb* **1 keep away from**, steer clear of, give a wide berth to. **2 evade**, dodge, sidestep, escape, run away from; *informal* duck, wriggle out of, get out of. **3** *book early to avoid disappointment* **prevent**, preclude, stave off, forestall, head off, ward off. **4** *avoid alcohol* **refrain from**, abstain from, desist from, steer clear of, eschew.
- OPPOSITES confront, face.

await *verb* **1 wait for**, expect, look forward to, anticipate. **2 be in store for**, lie ahead of, be waiting for, be round the corner.

awake *verb* **wake up**, wake, awaken, waken, stir, come to, come round, rouse, call.
● *adjective* **1 sleepless**, wide awake, restless, insomniac. **2** *too few are awake to the dangers* **aware of**, conscious of, mindful of, alert to.
- OPPOSITES asleep, oblivious.

awaken *verb* **1** see **awake** (verb). **2 arouse**, kindle, bring out, trigger, stir up, stimulate, revive.

award *verb* **give**, grant, accord, confer on, bestow on, present to, decorate with.
● *noun* **1 prize**, trophy, medal, decoration, reward; *informal* gong. **2 grant**, scholarship, endowment; *Brit.* bursary.

aware *adjective* **1** *she is aware of the dangers* **conscious of**, mindful of, informed about, acquainted with, familiar with, alive to, alert to; *informal* wise to, in the know about. **2** *environmentally aware* **sensitive**, enlightened, knowledgeable, (well) informed; *informal* clued up; *Brit. informal* switched-on.
- OPPOSITES ignorant.

awareness *noun* **consciousness**, recognition, realization, perception, understanding, grasp, appreciation, knowledge, familiarity.

away *adverb* **elsewhere**, abroad, gone, off, out, absent, on holiday, on vacation.

awe *noun* **wonder**, wonderment, admiration, reverence, respect, fear, dread.

awesome *adjective* **breathtaking**, awe-inspiring, magnificent, amazing, stunning, staggering, imposing, formidable, intimidating; *informal* mind-boggling, mind-blowing, brilliant.
- OPPOSITES unimpressive.

awful *adjective* **1** *the place smells awful* **disgusting**, terrible, dreadful, ghastly, horrible, vile, foul, revolting, repulsive, repugnant, sickening, nauseating; *informal* gross; *Brit. informal* beastly. **2** *an awful book* **dreadful**, terrible, frightful, atrocious, lamentable; *informal* crummy, pathetic, rotten, woeful, lousy, appalling, abysmal, dismal, dire; *Brit. informal* rubbish. **3** *I feel awful* **ill**, unwell, sick, nauseous, off colour, poorly; *Brit. informal* grotty, ropy; *Austral./NZ informal* crook.
- OPPOSITES delightful, excellent, well.

awfully *adverb* **1** *(informal) an awfully nice man* **very**, extremely, really, immensely, exceedingly, thoroughly, dreadfully, terrifically, terribly, exceptionally, remarkably, extraordinarily; *N. English* right; *informal* seriously; *Brit. informal* jolly, dead, well; *N. Amer. informal* real, mighty; *informal, dated* frightfully. **2** *we played awfully* **terribly**, dreadfully, atrociously, appallingly; *informal* abysmally, diabolically.

awkward *adjective* **1 difficult**, tricky, cumbersome, unwieldy; *Brit. informal* fiddly. **2 unreasonable**, uncooperative, unhelpful, difficult, obstructive, contrary, perverse, obstinate, stubborn; *Brit. informal* bloody-minded, bolshie; *N. Amer. informal* balky. **3** *an awkward time* **inconvenient**, inappropriate, inopportune, difficult. **4** *he put her in an awkward position* **embarrassing**, uncomfortable, unenviable, delicate, tricky, problematic, troublesome, humiliating, compromising; *informal* sticky. **5** *she felt awkward* **uncomfortable**, uneasy, tense, nervous, edgy, self-conscious, embarrassed. **6** *his awkward movements* **clumsy**, ungainly, uncoordinated, graceless, inelegant, gauche, gawky, stiff, unskilful, inept, blundering; *informal* ham-fisted, cack-handed; *Brit. informal* all (fingers and) thumbs.
- OPPOSITES easy, amenable, convenient, graceful.

axe *noun* **hatchet**, chopper, cleaver; *historical* battleaxe.
● *verb* **1 cancel**, withdraw, drop, scrap, cut, discontinue, end; *informal* ditch, dump, pull the plug on. **2 dismiss**, make redundant, lay off, get rid of; *informal* sack, fire.

axle *noun* **shaft**, spindle, rod.

Bb

babble *verb* **prattle**, rattle on, gabble, chatter, jabber, twitter, burble, blather; *informal* yatter, blabber, jaw, gas, shoot your mouth off; *Brit. informal* witter, rabbit, chunter, natter, waffle.

baby *noun* **infant**, newborn, child; *Scottish & N. English* bairn; *technical* neonate; *informal* sprog, tot, bundle of joy; *literary* babe.
● *adjective* **miniature**, mini, little, toy, pocket, fun-size, midget, dwarf; *Scottish* wee; *N. Amer.* vest-pocket; *informal* teeny, teensy, tiddly, bite-sized; *Brit. informal* titchy.

babyish *adjective* **childish**, infantile, juvenile, puerile, immature.
- OPPOSITES mature.

back *noun* **1 spine**, backbone, spinal column, vertebral column. **2 rear**, end, rear end, tail end; *Nautical* stern. **3 reverse**, other side, underside; *informal* flip side.
- OPPOSITES front.
● *verb* **1 sponsor**, finance, fund, subsidize, underwrite; *informal* pick up the bill for. **2 support**, endorse, sanction, approve of, give your blessing to, smile on, favour, advocate, promote, champion; *informal* throw your weight behind. **3 bet on**, gamble on, stake money on. **4 reverse**, draw back, step back, pull back, retreat, withdraw.
- OPPOSITES oppose, advance.
● *adjective* **1 rear**, rearmost, hind, hindmost, posterior. **2 past**, old, previous, earlier.
- OPPOSITES front, future.
□ **back down** give in, concede defeat, surrender, yield, submit, climb down. **back out of** renege on, withdraw from, pull out of, fail to honour. **back up 1** substantiate, corroborate, confirm, support, bear out, endorse, lend weight to. **2** support, stand by, side with, take someone's part.

WORD LINKS
dorsal, **lumbar** relating to the back
supine lying on your back

backbone *noun* **1 spine**, spinal column, vertebral column, vertebrae. **2 mainstay**, cornerstone, foundation. **3 strength of character**, strength of will, firmness, resolution, resolve, grit, determination, fortitude, mettle, spirit.

backer *noun* **1 sponsor**, investor, underwriter, financier, patron, benefactor; *informal* angel. **2 supporter**, defender, advocate, promoter; *N. Amer.* booster.

backfire *verb* **rebound**, boomerang, come back, fail; *informal* blow up in someone's face.

background *noun* **1 backdrop**, backcloth, surrounding(s), setting, scene, framework. **2 social circumstances**, family circumstances, environment, class, culture, tradition. **3 experience**, record, history, past, training, education.
- OPPOSITES foreground.

backing *noun* **1 support**, endorsement, approval, blessing, assistance, aid, help. **2 sponsorship**, finance, funding, subsidy, patronage.

backlash *noun* **adverse reaction**, counterblast, repercussion, comeback, retaliation, reprisal.

backup *noun* **help**, support, assistance, aid, reserve, reinforcements.
● *adjective* **reserve**, spare, substitute, replacement, standby, fallback, emergency.

backward *adjective* **1 rearward**, towards the rear, behind you, reverse. **2 retrograde**, regressive, for the worse, in the wrong direction, downhill, negative. **3 underdeveloped**, undeveloped, primitive. **4 hesitant**, reticent, reluctant, shy, diffident, timid,

self-effacing, unassertive.
– OPPOSITES forward, advanced.

backwards *adverb* **towards the rear**, rearwards, behind you.
– OPPOSITES forwards.

bad *adjective* **1** *bad workmanship* **unsatisfactory**, substandard, poor, inferior, second-rate, second-class, inadequate, deficient, imperfect, defective, faulty, shoddy, negligent, disgraceful, awful, terrible, appalling, dreadful, frightful, atrocious, abysmal; *informal* crummy, rotten, pathetic, useless, woeful, lousy, diabolical; *Brit. informal* duff, rubbish. **2** *the alcohol had a bad effect* **harmful**, damaging, detrimental, injurious, hurtful, destructive, deleterious, inimical. **3** *the bad guys* **wicked**, evil, sinful, criminal, immoral, corrupt, villainous; *informal* crooked, bent. **4** *you bad girl!* **naughty**, badly behaved, disobedient, wayward, wilful, defiant, unruly, undisciplined. **5** *bad news* **unpleasant**, disagreeable, unwelcome, unfavourable, unfortunate, grim, distressing, gloomy. **6** *a bad time to arrive* **unfavourable**, inauspicious, unpropitious, inopportune, unfortunate, disadvantageous, inappropriate, unsuitable. **7** *a bad accident* **serious**, severe, grave, critical, acute. **8** *the meat's bad* **rotten**, off, decayed, putrid, rancid, curdled, sour, mouldy. **9** *a bad knee* **injured**, wounded, diseased; *informal* gammy; *Brit. informal* knackered; *Austral./NZ informal* crook.
– OPPOSITES good, beneficial, virtuous, favourable.

badge *noun* **1 brooch**, pin, emblem, crest, insignia; *N. Amer.* button. **2** *a badge of success* **sign**, symbol, indication, signal, mark, hallmark, trademark.

badger *verb* **pester**, harass, hound, harry, nag, bother, go on at; *informal* hassle, bug.

badly *adverb* **1 poorly**, unsatisfactorily, inadequately, incorrectly, faultily, defectively, shoddily, amateurishly, carelessly, incompetently, inexpertly. **2 unfavourably**, ill, critically, disapprovingly. **3 naughtily**, disobediently, wilfully, mischievously. **4 cruelly**, wickedly, unkindly, harshly, shamefully, unfairly, unjustly, wrongly. **5 unfavourably**, unsuccessfully, adversely, unfortunately. **6 severely**, seriously, gravely, acutely, critically.
– OPPOSITES well.

bad-tempered *adjective* **irritable**, irascible, tetchy, testy, grumpy, grouchy, crotchety, in a (bad) mood, cantankerous, curmudgeonly, ill-tempered, ill-humoured, peevish, cross, fractious, petulant, pettish, crabby, quarrelsome, dyspeptic; *informal* snappish, on a short fuse; *Brit. informal* shirty, stroppy, ratty; *N. Amer. informal* cranky, ornery.
– OPPOSITES good-humoured, affable.

baffle *verb* **puzzle**, perplex, bewilder, mystify, confuse; *informal* flummox, stump, beat, fox.

bag *noun* **suitcase**, case, valise, holdall, grip, rucksack, haversack, satchel, handbag.
● *verb* **1 catch**, land, capture, trap, net, snare. **2 get**, secure, obtain, acquire, pick up, win, achieve; *informal* land, net.

baggage *noun* **luggage**, suitcases, cases, bags, belongings.

baggy *adjective* **loose**, roomy, generously cut, sloppy, voluminous, full.
– OPPOSITES tight.

bail *noun* **surety**, security, indemnity, bond, guarantee, pledge.
□ **bail out 1** eject, parachute to safety. **2** rescue, save, relieve, finance, help (out), aid.

bait *noun* **enticement**, lure, decoy, snare, trap, inducement, siren, carrot, attraction; *informal* come-on.
● *verb* **taunt**, tease, goad, pick on, torment, persecute, harass; *informal* needle; *Brit. informal* wind up.

balance *noun* **1 stability**, equilibrium, steadiness, footing. **2 fairness**, justice, impartiality, parity, equity, evenness, uniformity, comparability. **3 remainder**, outstanding amount, rest, residue, difference.

- OPPOSITES instability, bias.
● *verb* **1 steady**, stabilize, poise, level. **2 counterbalance**, balance out, offset, counteract, compensate for, make up for. **3 correspond**, agree, tally, match up, coincide. **4 weigh (up)**, compare, evaluate, consider, assess.

bald *adjective* **1 hairless**, smooth, shaven, depilated. **2 plain**, simple, direct, blunt, unadorned, unvarnished, unembellished, stark; *informal* upfront.
- OPPOSITES hairy.

ball *noun* **sphere**, globe, orb, globule, spheroid.

ballot *noun* **vote**, poll, election, referendum, show of hands, plebiscite.

ban *verb* **prohibit**, forbid, veto, proscribe, outlaw, make illegal, bar, debar, prevent, exclude, banish.
- OPPOSITES permit, admit.
● *noun* **prohibition**, embargo, veto, boycott, bar, proscription, moratorium, injunction.

banal *adjective* **unoriginal**, unimaginative, uninspired, trite, hackneyed, clichéd, platitudinous, commonplace, stereotyped, overused, stale, boring, dull, obvious, predictable, tired, pedestrian; *informal* corny, old hat.
- OPPOSITES original.

band[1] *noun* **1 loop**, wristband, headband, ring, hoop, circlet, belt, sash, girdle, strap, strip, tape, circle. **2 stripe**, strip, line, belt, bar, streak, border, swathe.

band[2] *noun* **1 gang**, group, mob, pack, troop, troupe, company, set, party, crew, body, team; *informal* bunch. **2 pop group**, ensemble, group, orchestra; *informal* combo.

bandage *noun* **dressing**, covering, plaster, compress, gauze, lint.
● *verb* **bind**, dress, cover, strap (up).

bandit *noun* **robber**, thief, raider, mugger, pirate, outlaw, hijacker, looter, marauder, gangster; *literary* brigand; *historical* rustler, highwayman, footpad.

bang *noun* **1 crash**, crack, thud, thump, bump, boom, blast, clap, report, explosion. **2 blow**, bump, knock, hit, smack, crack, thump; *informal* bash, whack.
● *verb* **1 hit**, strike, beat, thump, hammer, knock, rap, pound, thud, punch, bump, smack, crack, slap, slam; *informal* bash, whack, clobber, clout, wallop. **2 crash**, boom, pound, explode, detonate, burst, blow up.

banish *verb* **1 exile**, expel, deport, eject, repatriate, transport, extradite, evict, throw out, exclude, shut out, ban. **2 dispel**, dismiss, disperse, scatter, dissipate, drive away, chase away, shut out.

bank[1] *noun* **1 edge**, shore, side, embankment, levee, margin, verge, brink. **2 slope**, rise, incline, gradient, ramp, mound, pile, heap, ridge, hillock, knoll, bar, shoal, mass, drift. **3 array**, row, line, tier, group, series.
● *verb* **1 pile up**, heap up, stack up, amass. **2 tilt**, lean, tip, slant, incline, angle, list, camber, pitch.

bank[2] *noun* **store**, reserve, stock, stockpile, supply, pool, fund, cache, hoard, deposit.
● *verb* **deposit**, pay in, save.

bankrupt *adjective* **insolvent**, ruined; *Brit.* in administration, in receivership; *informal* bust, broke, belly up, wiped out.
- OPPOSITES solvent.

banner *noun* **1 placard**, sign, poster, notice. **2 flag**, standard, ensign, colour(s), pennant, pennon, banderole.

banquet *noun* **feast**, dinner; *informal* spread, blowout; *Brit. informal* nosh-up, slap-up meal.

banter *noun* **repartee**, witty conversation, raillery, wordplay, cut and thrust, badinage, persiflage.
● *verb* **joke**, jest; *informal* josh, wisecrack.

baptize *verb* **1 christen**. **2** *they were baptized into the church* **admit**, initiate, enrol, recruit. **3 name**, call, dub.

bar *noun* **1 rod**, stick, pole, batten, shaft, rail, spar, strut, crosspiece, beam. **2 block**, slab, cake, tablet, wedge,

ingot. **3 counter**, table, buffet. **4 inn**, tavern, hostelry; *Brit.* pub, public house; *Brit. informal* local, boozer. **5 obstacle**, impediment, hindrance, obstruction, block, hurdle, barrier.
- OPPOSITES aid.
● *verb* **1 bolt**, lock, fasten, secure, block, barricade, obstruct. **2 prohibit**, debar, preclude, forbid, ban, exclude, obstruct, prevent, hinder, block, stop.

barbarian *noun* **savage**, heathen, brute, beast, philistine, boor, yahoo, oaf, lout, vandal; *Brit. informal* yob.

barbaric *adjective* **1 cruel**, brutal, barbarous, brutish, savage, vicious, wicked, ruthless, vile, inhuman. **2 uncultured**, uncivilized, barbarian, philistine, boorish, loutish; *Brit. informal* yobbish.
- OPPOSITES civilized.

bare *adjective* **1 naked**, unclothed, undressed, uncovered, stripped, with nothing on, nude; *informal* without a stitch on, in the altogether; *Brit. informal* starkers; *Scottish informal* in the scud; *N. Amer. informal* buck naked. **2 empty**, unfurnished, clear, undecorated, unadorned, bleak, austere. **3 basic**, essential, bare-bones, fundamental, plain, straightforward, simple, unembellished, pure, stark, bald, cold, hard.
- OPPOSITES dressed.

barely *adverb* **hardly**, scarcely, only just, narrowly, by the skin of your teeth, by a hair's breadth; *informal* by a whisker; *Brit. informal* at a push.

bargain *noun* **1 agreement**, arrangement, understanding, deal, contract, pact. **2 good value**; *informal* good buy, cheap buy, snip, steal, giveaway.
● *verb* **haggle**, negotiate, discuss terms, deal, barter.
□ **bargain for/on** expect, anticipate, be prepared for, allow for, plan for, reckon with, envisage, foresee, predict, count on, reckon on; *N. Amer. informal* figure on. **into the bargain** in addition, as well, also, moreover, besides, on top, to boot, for good measure.

bark[1] *verb* **1 woof**, yap. **2 shout**, snap, bawl, yell, roar, bellow, thunder; *informal* holler.
- OPPOSITES whisper.

bark[2] *noun* **rind**, skin, peel, covering.

barracks *plural noun* **garrison**, camp, encampment, depot, billet, quarters, fort, cantonment.

barrage *noun* **1 bombardment**, gunfire, shelling, salvo, volley, fusillade; *historical* broadside. **2 deluge**, stream, storm, torrent, onslaught, flood, spate, tide, avalanche, hail, blaze. **3 dam**, barrier, weir, dyke, embankment, wall.

barrel *noun* **cask**, keg, butt, vat, tun, drum, hogshead, firkin.

WORD LINKS
cooper person who makes barrels

barren *adjective* **unproductive**, infertile, unfruitful, sterile, arid, desert, waste, lifeless, empty.
- OPPOSITES fertile.

barricade *noun* **barrier**, roadblock, blockade, obstacle, obstruction.
● *verb* **seal up**, close up, block off, shut off/up, defend, protect, fortify, occupy.

barrier *noun* **1 fence**, railing, barricade, hurdle, bar, blockade, roadblock. **2** *a barrier to international trade* **obstacle**, obstruction, hurdle, stumbling block, bar, impediment, hindrance, curb.

barter *verb* **1 swap**, trade, exchange, sell. **2 haggle**, bargain, negotiate, deal.

base[1] *noun* **1 foundation**, bottom, foot, support, stand, pedestal, plinth, rest. **2 basis**, foundation, bedrock, starting point, source, origin, root(s), core, key component. **3 headquarters**, camp, site, station, settlement, post, centre.
- OPPOSITES top.
● *verb* **1 found**, build, construct, form, ground; (**be based on**) derive from, spring from, stem from, depend on. **2 locate**, situate, position, install, station, site.

base[2] *adjective* **sordid**, ignoble, low, mean, immoral, unscrupulous, unprincipled, dishonest, dishonourable,

shameful, shabby, contemptible, despicable.
- OPPOSITES noble.

bashful *adjective* **shy**, reserved, diffident, inhibited, retiring, reticent, reluctant, shrinking, self-effacing, unassertive, timid, nervous, self-conscious.
- OPPOSITES bold, confident.

basic *adjective* **1 fundamental**, essential, bare-bones, vital, primary, principal, cardinal, elementary, intrinsic, central, pivotal, critical, key, focal. **2 plain**, simple, unsophisticated, straightforward, adequate, spartan, stark, severe, austere, limited, meagre, rudimentary, patchy, sketchy, minimal, crude, makeshift; *informal* bog-standard.
- OPPOSITES unimportant, luxurious.

basically *adverb* **fundamentally**, essentially, first and foremost, primarily, at heart, at bottom, intrinsically, inherently, principally, chiefly, above all, mostly, mainly, on the whole, by and large; *informal* at the end of the day.

basics *plural noun* **fundamentals**, essentials, first principles, foundations, preliminaries, groundwork, essence, basis, core; *informal* nitty-gritty, brass tacks, nuts and bolts, ABC.

basin *noun* **bowl**, dish, pan, container, receptacle, vessel.

basis *noun* **1** *the basis of his method* **foundation**, support, base, reasoning, rationale, defence, reason, grounds, justification. **2** *the basis of discussion* **starting point**, base, point of departure, beginning, premise, fundamental point/principle, cornerstone, core, heart. **3** *on a part-time basis* **footing**, condition, status, position, arrangement.

bask *verb* **1 laze**, lie, lounge, relax, sprawl, loll, luxuriate. **2 revel**, wallow, delight, take pleasure, enjoy, relish, savour.

bass *adjective* **low**, deep, resonant, sonorous, rumbling, booming, resounding.
- OPPOSITES high.

batch *noun* **group**, quantity, lot, bunch, cluster, raft, set, collection, bundle, pack, consignment, shipment.

bathe *verb* **1 swim**, take a dip. **2 clean**, wash, rinse, wet, soak, steep. **3 envelop**, cover, flood, fill, wash, pervade, suffuse.

baton *noun* **stick**, rod, staff, wand, truncheon, club, mace.

batter *verb* **beat up**, hit repeatedly, pummel, pound, rain blows on, buffet, belabour, thrash; *informal* knock about/around, lay into, do over.

battle *noun* **1** *he was killed in the battle* **fight**, engagement, armed conflict, clash, struggle, skirmish, fray, war, campaign, crusade, warfare, combat, action, hostilities; *informal* scrap, dogfight, shoot-out. **2** *a legal battle* **conflict**, clash, struggle, disagreement, argument, dispute, tussle.
● *verb* **fight**, combat, contend with, resist, withstand, stand up to, confront, war, feud, struggle, strive, work.

battlefield *noun* **battleground**, field of battle, field of operations, combat zone, lines, front, theatre of war.

bawdy *adjective* **ribald**, indecent, risqué, racy, earthy, rude, suggestive, titillating, naughty, improper, indelicate, vulgar, crude, smutty; *informal* raunchy.

bawl *verb* **1 shout**, yell, roar, bellow, screech, scream, shriek, bark, thunder; *informal* yammer, holler. **2 cry**, sob, weep, wail, whine, howl; *Scottish informal* greet.
- OPPOSITES whisper.

bay[1] *noun* **cove**, inlet, gulf, sound, bight, basin, fjord.

bay[2] *noun* **alcove**, recess, niche, nook, opening, inglenook.

bazaar *noun* **1 market**, marketplace, souk, mart. **2 fete**, fair, fund-raiser; *Brit.* jumble sale, bring-and-buy sale, car boot sale; *N. Amer.* rummage sale, tag sale.

be *verb* **1 exist**, live, be alive, breathe, be extant. **2 occur**, happen, take place, come about, arise, fall; *literary* come to

b

pass, befall, betide. **3 be situated**, be located, be found, be present, be set, be positioned, be placed, be installed, sit, lie.

beach *noun* **sands**, seaside, seashore, coast; *literary* strand, littoral.
● *verb* **land**, ground, strand, run ashore.

beached *adjective* **stranded**, run aground, ashore, marooned, high and dry, stuck.
- OPPOSITES afloat.

beacon *noun* **signal**, light, fire, danger signal, bonfire, lighthouse.

bead *noun* **1 ball**, pellet, pill, globule, sphere, spheroid, orb, round; (**beads**) necklace, rosary, chaplet. **2** *beads of sweat* **droplet**, drop, drip, blob, pearl, dot.

beaker *noun* **cup**, tumbler, glass, mug, drinking vessel.

beam *noun* **1 plank**, timber, joist, rafter, lintel, spar, girder, support. **2 ray**, shaft, stream, streak, pencil, flash, gleam, glint. **3 grin**, smile.
- OPPOSITES frown.
● *verb* **1 broadcast**, transmit, relay, disseminate, direct, send, aim. **2 shine**, radiate, glare, gleam. **3 grin**, smile.
- OPPOSITES frown.

bear[1] *verb* **1 carry**, bring, transport, move, convey, take, fetch; *informal* tote. **2 display**, be marked with, show, carry, exhibit. **3 withstand**, support, sustain, stand, take, carry, hold up, cope with, handle. **4 harbour**, foster, entertain, cherish, nurse. **5** *I can't bear sport* **endure**, tolerate, put up with, stand, abide, countenance, stomach; *informal* hack, swallow; *Brit. informal* stick, wear; *formal* brook. **6 give birth to**, bring forth, deliver, have, produce, spawn. **7 produce**, yield, give, provide, supply.
□ **bear fruit** yield results, succeed, be effective, be profitable, work; *informal* pay off, do the trick. **bear out** confirm, corroborate, substantiate, endorse, vindicate, give credence to, support, justify, prove. **bear up** remain cheerful, cope, manage, get by, muddle through. **bear with** be patient with, make allowances for, tolerate, put up with, endure.

bear[2] *noun*

WORD LINKS
ursine relating to bears

bearable *adjective* **tolerable**, endurable, supportable, sustainable.

bearer *noun* **1 carrier**, porter. **2 bringer**, messenger, agent, conveyor, emissary.

bearing *noun* **1 posture**, stance, carriage, gait, demeanour, manner, mien, air, aspect, attitude, style; *Brit.* deportment. **2** *this has no bearing on the matter* **relevance**, pertinence, connection, relation, relationship, import, significance, application. **3 direction**, orientation, course, trajectory, heading, tack, path. **4** *I lost my bearings* **orientation**, sense of direction, whereabouts, location, position.
- OPPOSITES irrelevance.

beast *noun* **1 creature**, animal; *N. Amer. informal* critter. **2 monster**, brute, savage, barbarian, animal, swine, ogre, fiend, sadist, demon, devil.

beat *verb* **1 hit**, strike, batter, thump, bang, hammer, punch, knock, thrash, pound, pummel, slap, rain blows on, assault; *informal* wallop, belt, bash, whack, clout, clobber. **2 throb**, pulse, pulsate, pump, palpitate, pound, thump, thud, hammer, drum. **3 flap**, flutter, thrash, wave, vibrate. **4 whisk**, mix, blend, whip. **5 defeat**, conquer, vanquish, trounce, rout, overpower, overcome; *informal* lick, thrash, whip; *US informal* own. **6 exceed**, surpass, better, improve on, eclipse, transcend, top, trump, cap.
● *noun* **1 rhythm**, pulse, metre, time, measure, cadence, stress, accent. **2 pounding**, banging, thumping, thudding, hammering, crashing. **3 pulse**, pulsation, vibration, throb, palpitation, reverberation, pounding, thump, thud, hammering, drumming. **4 circuit**, round, route, path.

□ **beat off** repel, fight off, fend off, stave off, repulse, drive away/back, push back. **beat up** assault, attack, mug; *informal* knock about/around, do over, work over, rough up; *Brit. informal* duff up.

beautiful *adjective* **attractive**, pretty, handsome, good-looking, fetching, lovely, charming, graceful, elegant, appealing, winsome, ravishing, gorgeous, stunning, glamorous; *Scottish & N. English* bonny; *informal* tasty, knockout, drop-dead gorgeous; *Brit. informal* smashing; *N. Amer. informal* cute, foxy; *Austral./NZ informal* beaut, spunky; *old use* comely.
- OPPOSITES ugly.

beautify *verb* **adorn**, embellish, enhance, decorate, ornament, prettify, glamorize; *informal* do up, tart up.

beauty *noun* **1 attractiveness**, prettiness, good looks, loveliness, appeal, winsomeness, charm, grace, elegance, exquisiteness, glamour; *literary* pulchritude. **2 belle**, vision, goddess, picture, Venus; *informal* babe, looker, lovely, stunner, knockout, bombshell, bit of all right.
- OPPOSITES ugliness.

because *conjunction* **since**, as, seeing that, in view of the fact that, in that.
□ **because of** on account of, as a result of, as a consequence of, owing to, due to, thanks to, by virtue of; *formal* by reason of.

beckon *verb* **1 gesture**, signal, wave, gesticulate, motion. **2 entice**, invite, tempt, lure, charm, attract, draw, call.

become *verb* **1** *she became rich* **grow**, get, turn, come to be, get to be. **2** *he became a tyrant* **turn into**, change into, be transformed into, be converted into. **3** *he became Foreign Secretary* **be appointed**, be assigned as, be nominated, be elected. **4 suit**, flatter, look good on, set off; *informal* do something for.
□ **become of** happen to, be the fate of, be the lot of, overtake.

becoming *adjective* **flattering**, fetching, attractive, pretty, elegant, handsome, well chosen, stylish, fashionable, tasteful.

bed *noun* **1 couch**, berth, billet, cot; *informal* the sack. **2** *a flower bed* **patch**, plot, border, strip. **3 base**, foundation, footing, support, basis.
● *verb* **embed**, set, fix, insert, inlay, implant, bury, plant.
□ **go to bed** retire; *informal* hit the sack, hit the hay, turn in.

bedraggled *adjective* **dishevelled**, disordered, untidy, unkempt, tousled; *N. Amer. informal* mussed.
- OPPOSITES neat.

before *preposition* **1 prior to**, previous to, earlier than, preparatory to, in advance of, ahead of, pre-. **2 in front of**, in the presence of. **3 in preference to**, rather than, sooner than.
- OPPOSITES after.
● *adverb* **previously**, before now/then, until now/then, up to now/then, earlier, formerly, hitherto, in the past.
- OPPOSITES afterwards, later.

beforehand *adverb* **in advance**, in readiness, ahead of time, before, before now/then, earlier (on), previously, already, sooner.
- OPPOSITES afterwards.

beg *verb* **1 ask for money**, seek charity; *informal* sponge, cadge, scrounge, bum. **2** *we begged for mercy* **plead for**, request, ask for, appeal for, call for, sue for, solicit, seek. **3** *he begged her not to go* **implore**, entreat, plead with, appeal to, pray to, call on, petition; *literary* beseech.

beggar *noun* **tramp**, vagrant, vagabond, mendicant; *N. Amer.* hobo; *informal* scrounger, sponger, cadger, freeloader; *Brit. informal* dosser; *N. Amer. informal* bum; *Austral./NZ informal* bagman.

begin *verb* **1 start**, commence, set about, go about, embark on, launch into, get down to, take up, initiate, set in motion, get going, get off the ground, lead off, institute, inaugurate,

open; *informal* get cracking on, kick off. **2 appear**, arise, become apparent, spring up, crop up, turn up, come into existence, originate, start, commence, develop.
- OPPOSITES finish, end.

beginner *noun* **novice**, learner, starter, (raw) recruit, newcomer, tyro, fresher, probationer, apprentice, trainee; *N. Amer. informal* rookie, new kid (on the block), tenderfoot, greenhorn.
- OPPOSITES expert, veteran.

beginning *noun* **1 start**, commencement, creation, birth, inception, conception, origination, origin, genesis, germ, emergence, rise, dawn, launch, onset, outset, day one; *informal* kick-off. **2 opening**, start, commencement, first part, introduction, preamble.
- OPPOSITES end, conclusion.

begrudge *verb* **envy**, resent, grudge, be jealous of, be envious of, mind, object to.

behalf *noun*
▫ **on behalf of 1** representing, as a representative of, as a spokesperson for, for, in the name of, in place of, on the authority of. **2** in the interests of, in support of, for, for the benefit of, for the good of, for the sake of.

behave *verb* **1** *she behaved badly* **act**, conduct yourself, acquit yourself. **2** *the children behaved themselves* **act correctly**, be good, be well behaved, mind your manners; *informal* mind your Ps and Qs.
- OPPOSITES misbehave.

behaviour *noun* **conduct**, actions, manners, ways, deportment, bearing, etiquette.

behind *preposition* **1 at the back of**, at the rear of, beyond, on the far side of; *N. Amer.* in back of. **2 after**, following, at the back/rear of, hard on the heels of, in the wake of. **3 responsible for**, at the bottom of, the cause of, the perpetrator of, the organizer of, to blame for, guilty of. **4 supporting**, backing, for, on the side of, in agreement with; *informal* rooting for.

being *noun* **1 existence**, living, life, reality, lifeblood, vital force. **2 soul**, spirit, nature, essence, psyche, heart, bosom, breast. **3 creature**, life form, organism, living thing, individual, person, human.

belated *adjective* **late**, overdue, behindhand, delayed, tardy, unpunctual.
- OPPOSITES early.

beleaguered *adjective* **1 besieged**, blockaded, surrounded, encircled, hemmed in, under attack. **2 troubled**, harassed, hard-pressed, in difficulties, under pressure, in a tight corner; *informal* up against it.

belief *noun* **1 opinion**, view, conviction, judgement, thinking, idea, theory, thought, feeling. **2 faith**, trust, reliance, confidence, credence. **3 ideology**, principle, ethic, tenet, doctrine, teaching, dogma, creed, credo.
- OPPOSITES disbelief, doubt.

believe *verb* **1** *I don't believe you* **trust**, have confidence in, consider honest, consider truthful. **2** *do you believe that story?* **accept**, be convinced by, give credence to, credit, trust, put confidence in; *informal* swallow, buy, go for. **3 think**, be of the opinion that, have an idea that, imagine, assume, presume, take it, understand, gather; *informal* reckon, figure.
- OPPOSITES doubt.
▫ **believe in** have faith in, trust in, have every confidence in, cling to, set (great) store by, value, be convinced by, be persuaded by; *informal* swear by, rate.

believer *noun* **disciple**, follower, supporter, adherent, devotee, upholder, worshipper.
- OPPOSITES infidel, sceptic.

belittle *verb* **disparage**, denigrate, run down, deprecate, play down, trivialize, minimize; *informal* do down, pooh-pooh.

belligerent *adjective* **1 hostile**, aggressive, threatening, antagonistic, pugnacious, bellicose, truculent, confrontational, contentious, militant, combative, argumentative; *informal*

spoiling for a fight; *Brit. informal* stroppy, bolshie; *N. Amer. informal* scrappy. **2** *the belligerent states* **warring**, combatant, fighting, battling.
- OPPOSITES peaceable.

bellow *verb* **roar**, shout, bawl, thunder, boom, bark, yell, shriek, howl, scream; *informal* holler.
- OPPOSITES whisper.

belly *noun* **stomach**, abdomen, paunch, middle, midriff, girth; *informal* tummy, gut, insides.

belong *verb* **1 be owned by**, be the property of, be held by, be in the hands of. **2 be a member of**, be in, be affiliated to, be allied to, be associated with. **3 be part of**, be attached to, go with. **4 fit in**, be suited to; *informal* go, click.

belongings *plural noun* **possessions**, effects, worldly goods, chattels, property; *informal* gear, tackle, kit, things, stuff, bits and pieces; *Brit. informal* clobber.

beloved *adjective* **darling**, dear, precious, adored, cherished, treasured, prized, valued, idolized.
● *noun* **sweetheart**, love, darling, dearest, lover, girlfriend, boyfriend; *informal* steady, baby, angel, honey, pet.

below *preposition* **1 beneath**, under, underneath, lower than. **2 less than**, lower than, under, not as much as, smaller than. **3 inferior to**, subordinate to, under, beneath.
- OPPOSITES above, over.

belt *noun* **1 sash**, girdle, band, strap, cummerbund. **2 region**, strip, stretch, zone, area, district, sector, territory.

bemused *adjective* **bewildered**, confused, puzzled, perplexed, baffled, mystified, nonplussed, dumbfounded, at sea, at a loss; *informal* flummoxed, bamboozled, fazed.

bench *noun* **1 seat**, form, pew, stall, settle. **2 workbench**, worktop, counter.

benchmark *noun* **standard**, point of reference, guide, guideline, norm, touchstone, yardstick, barometer, model, gauge, criterion, specification.

bend *verb* **1 curve**, crook, flex, angle, hook, bow, arch, buckle, warp, contort, distort, deform, twist. **2 turn**, curve, incline, swing, veer, fork, change course, curl, loop. **3 stoop**, bow, crouch, hunch, lean down/over.
- OPPOSITES straighten.
● *noun* **curve**, turn, corner, kink, angle, arc, twist.

beneath *preposition* **1 under**, underneath, below, at the foot of, at the bottom of, lower than. **2 inferior to**, below, lower than, subordinate to. **3 unworthy of**, unbecoming to, degrading to.
- OPPOSITES above.
● *adverb* **underneath**, below, further down, lower down.
- OPPOSITES above.

benefactor *noun* **patron**, supporter, backer, sponsor, donor, contributor, subscriber; *informal* angel.

beneficial *adjective* **advantageous**, favourable, helpful, useful, of assistance, valuable, salutary, worthwhile, fruitful, productive, profitable, rewarding, gainful.
- OPPOSITES disadvantageous.

beneficiary *noun* **recipient**, payee, heir, heiress, inheritor.

benefit *noun* **1 good**, sake, welfare, well-being, advantage, comfort, ease, convenience, help, aid, assistance, service. **2 advantage**, profit, plus point, boon, blessing, reward; *informal* perk. **3 social security payment**, welfare, charity; *informal* the dole.
- OPPOSITES detriment, disadvantage.
● *verb* **1 help**, be advantageous to, be beneficial to, profit, do good to, be of service to, serve, be useful to, be helpful to, aid, assist. **2 profit**, gain, reap reward, make the most of, exploit, turn to your advantage, put to good use.
- OPPOSITES disadvantage, harm.

benevolent *adjective* **kind**, kindly, kind-hearted, good-natured, compassionate, caring, altruistic, humanitarian, philanthropic, beneficent, well meaning, benign.
- OPPOSITES unkind.

b

benign *adjective* **1 kindly**, kind, warm-hearted, good-natured, friendly, genial, tender-hearted, gentle, sympathetic, compassionate, caring, well disposed, benevolent. **2 mild**, temperate, gentle, balmy, soft, pleasant, favourable, healthy. **3** *(Medicine)* **harmless**, non-malignant, non-cancerous.
- OPPOSITES unkind, malignant.

bent *adjective* **1 twisted**, crooked, warped, contorted, deformed, misshapen, out of shape, bowed, arched, curved, angled, hooked, kinked; *N. Amer. informal* pretzeled. **2 corrupt**, dishonest, fraudulent, criminal, untrustworthy.
- OPPOSITES straight.
● *noun* **inclination**, leaning, tendency, talent, gift, flair, aptitude, facility, skill.
□ **bent on** intent on, determined on, set on, insistent on, resolved on.

bequeath *verb* **leave**, will, hand down, pass on, entrust, make over, grant, transfer, give, bestow on, confer on.

bequest *noun* **legacy**, estate, inheritance, endowment, settlement.

bereavement *noun* **death in the family**, loss, passing (away), demise; *formal* decease.

berserk *adjective* **mad**, crazy, insane, out of your mind, hysterical, frenzied, crazed, demented, maniacal, manic, frantic, raving, wild, out of control, amok, on the rampage; *informal* off your head, off the deep end, ape, bananas, bonkers; *Brit. informal* spare; *N. Amer. informal* postal.

berth *noun* **1 bunk**, bed, cot, couch, hammock. **2 mooring**, dock, pier, jetty, quay.
● *verb* **dock**, moor, land, tie up, make fast.

beseech *verb* **implore**, beg, entreat, plead with, appeal to, call on, importune, pray to, ask, petition.

beside *preposition* **alongside**, by/at the side of, next to, parallel to, abreast of, adjacent to, next door to, neighbouring.
□ **beside yourself** distraught, overcome, out of your mind, frantic, desperate, distracted, at your wits' end, frenzied, hysterical.

besides *preposition* **in addition to**, as well as, over and above, on top of, apart from, other than, aside from, not counting, excluding, leaving aside; *N. Amer. informal* outside of.

besiege *verb* **1 lay siege to**, beleaguer, blockade. **2 surround**, mob, harass, pester, badger. **3 overwhelm**, bombard, inundate, deluge, flood, swamp, snow under.

best *adjective* **finest**, premier, greatest, top, foremost, leading, pre-eminent, supreme, superlative, unrivalled, second to none, without equal, unsurpassed, unparalleled, unbeatable, optimum, ultimate, incomparable, record-breaking; *informal* star, number-one, a cut above the rest, top-drawer.
● *noun only the best will do* **finest**, choicest, top, cream, choice, prime, elite, crème de la crème, flower, jewel in the crown; *informal* tops, pick of the bunch.
- OPPOSITES worst.

bestow *verb* **confer on**, grant, accord, afford, endow with, present, award, give, donate, entrust with, vouchsafe.

bet *verb* **1 wager**, gamble, stake, risk, venture, hazard, chance; *Brit. informal* punt, have a flutter. **2** *(informal)* **be certain**, be sure, be convinced, be confident, expect, predict, guess.
● *noun* **1 wager**, gamble, stake, ante; *Brit. informal* punt, flutter. **2** *(informal) your best bet is to go early* **option**, choice, alternative, course of action, plan.

betray *verb* **1 be disloyal to**, be unfaithful to, break faith with, play someone false, inform on/against, give away, denounce, sell out, stab in the back; *informal* split on, rat on, stitch up, do the dirty on, sell down the river; *Brit. informal* grass on, shop, sneak on; *N. Amer. informal* rat out, drop a/the dime on, finger; *Austral./NZ informal* dob in, point the bone at. **2 reveal**, disclose, divulge, tell, give away, leak, bring out into the open.

betrayal *noun* **disloyalty**, treachery, bad faith, breach of faith, breach of trust, faithlessness, duplicity, deception, double-dealing, stab in the back, double-cross, sell-out.
- OPPOSITES loyalty.

better *adjective* **1 superior**, finer, of higher quality, preferable; *informal* a cut above, streets ahead, head and shoulders above, ahead of the pack/field. **2 healthier**, fitter, stronger, well again, cured, healed, recovered, recovering, on the road to recovery, on the mend.
- OPPOSITES worse, inferior.
● *verb* **1 surpass**, improve on, beat, exceed, top, cap, trump, eclipse. **2 improve**, ameliorate, raise, advance, further, lift, upgrade, enhance.
- OPPOSITES worsen.

between *preposition* **1 in the middle of**, with one on either side, among; *old use* betwixt. **2 connecting**, linking, joining, uniting, allying.

beware *verb* **watch out**, look out, mind out, be alert, be on your guard, keep your eyes open/peeled, keep an eye out, take care, be careful, be cautious, watch your step, guard against.

bewilder *verb* **baffle**, mystify, bemuse, perplex, puzzle, confuse; *informal* flummox, faze, stump, beat.

bewildered *adjective* **baffled**, mystified, bemused, perplexed, puzzled, confused, nonplussed, at sea, at a loss, disorientated; *informal* flummoxed, bamboozled; *N. Amer. informal* discombobulated.

bewitch *verb* **captivate**, enchant, entrance, enrapture, charm, beguile, delight, fascinate, enthral, cast a spell on.

beyond *preposition* **1 on the far side of**, on the other side of, further away than, behind, past, after. **2 later than**, past, after. **3 greater than**, more than, exceeding, in excess of, above, upwards of.

bias *noun* **prejudice**, partiality, favouritism, partisanship, unfairness, one-sidedness, discrimination, leaning, tendency, inclination.
- OPPOSITES impartiality.
● *verb* **prejudice**, influence, colour, sway, predispose, distort, skew, slant.

biased *adjective* **prejudiced**, partial, partisan, one-sided, bigoted, discriminatory, distorted, warped, twisted, skewed.
- OPPOSITES impartial.

bid *verb* **offer**, put up, tender, proffer, propose.
● *noun* **1 offer**, tender, proposal. **2 attempt**, effort, endeavour, try; *informal* crack, go, shot, stab.

bidding *noun* **command**, order, direction, instruction, decree, injunction, demand, beck and call.

big *adjective* **1 large**, sizeable, substantial, considerable, great, huge, immense, enormous, extensive, colossal, massive, mammoth, vast, gigantic, cosmic, giant, spacious; *informal* jumbo, whopping, thumping, bumper, mega; *Brit. informal* whacking, ginormous; *formal* commodious. **2 well built**, sturdy, brawny, burly, broad-shouldered, muscular, bulky, hulking, strapping, hefty, tall, huge, fat, stout; *informal* hunky, beefy. **3 elder**, older, grown-up, adult, mature, grown. **4 important**, significant, major, momentous, weighty, far-reaching, key, vital, crucial. **5** *that was big of you* **generous**, kind, kindly, caring, compassionate, loving.
- OPPOSITES small, minor.

bigoted *adjective* **prejudiced**, biased, partial, one-sided, sectarian, discriminatory, opinionated, dogmatic, intolerant, narrow-minded, blinkered, illiberal.
- OPPOSITES open-minded.

bill *noun* **1 invoice**, account, statement, list of charges; *humorous* the damage; *N. Amer.* check; *informal* tab. **2 draft law**, proposal, measure. **3 programme**, line-up; *N. Amer.* playbill. **4** *(N. Amer.)* **banknote**, note;

US informal greenback. **5 poster**, advertisement, notice, announcement, flyer, leaflet, handbill; *informal* ad; *Brit. informal* advert.

● *verb* **1 invoice**, charge, debit. **2 advertise**, announce, schedule, programme, timetable; *N. Amer.* slate. **3** *he was billed as the new Sean Connery* **describe**, call, style, label, dub, promote, talk up; *informal* hype.

billow *verb* **1 puff out**, balloon (out), swell, fill (out). **2 swirl**, spiral, roll, undulate, eddy, pour, flow.

bind *verb* **1 tie up**, fasten together, secure, make fast, attach, rope, lash, tether. **2 bandage**, dress, cover, wrap, strap up, tape up. **3 trim**, hem, edge, border, fringe.

- OPPOSITES untie.

binding *adjective* **irrevocable**, unalterable, inescapable, unbreakable, contractual, compulsory, obligatory, mandatory, incumbent.

binge *noun (informal)* **bout**, spell, fling, spree, orgy, drinking bout; *informal* bender, session; *Scottish informal* skite; *N. Amer. informal* jag.

bird *noun* fowl, chick, fledgling, nestling.

> WORD LINKS
> **avian** relating to birds
> **ornithology** study of birds

birth *noun* **1 childbirth**, delivery, nativity. **2 beginning(s)**, emergence, genesis, dawn, dawning, rise, start. **3 ancestry**, lineage, blood, descent, parentage, family, extraction, origin, stock.

- OPPOSITES death, end.

□ **give birth to** have, bear, produce, be delivered of, bring into the world; *informal* drop.

> WORD LINKS
> **antenatal** before birth
> **post-natal** after birth
> **obstetrics** branch of medicine concerned with birth

bit *noun* **piece**, portion, section, part, chunk, lump, hunk, fragment, scrap, shred, crumb, grain, speck, spot, drop, pinch, dash, morsel, mouthful, bite, sample, iota, jot, whit, atom, particle, trace, touch, suggestion, hint, tinge; *informal* smidgen, tad.

bite *verb* **1 chew**, sink your teeth into, munch, crunch, champ. **2 grip**, hold, get a purchase. **3 take effect**, work, act, have results.

● *noun* **1 chew**, munch, nibble, gnaw, nip, snap. **2 mouthful**, piece, bit, morsel, snack. **3 piquancy**, pungency, spiciness, tang, zest; *informal* kick, punch, zing.

biting *adjective* **1 vicious**, harsh, cruel, savage, cutting, sharp, bitter, scathing, caustic, acerbic, acid, acrimonious, spiteful, venomous, vitriolic; *informal* bitchy, catty. **2 freezing**, icy, arctic, bitter, piercing, penetrating, raw.

- OPPOSITES mild.

bitter *adjective* **1 sharp**, acid, acrid, tart, sour, vinegary. **2 acrimonious**, hostile, angry, rancorous, spiteful, vicious, vitriolic, savage, ferocious, nasty. **3** *a bitter woman* **resentful**, embittered, aggrieved, spiteful, jaundiced, sullen, sour. **4 freezing**, icy, arctic, biting, piercing, penetrating, raw.

- OPPOSITES sweet, mild.

bizarre *adjective* **strange**, peculiar, odd, funny, fantastic, extraordinary, curious, outlandish, eccentric, unconventional, unorthodox, weird, outré, surreal; *informal* wacky, oddball, way out, freaky; *N. Amer. informal* wacko.

- OPPOSITES normal.

black *adjective* **1 dark**, pitch-black, coal-black, jet-black, ebony, inky, sable. **2** *a black day* **tragic**, dark, disastrous, calamitous, catastrophic, cataclysmic, fateful. **3** *a black mood* **miserable**, unhappy, sad, wretched, heartbroken, grief-stricken, sorrowful, anguished, desolate, despairing, disconsolate, downcast, dejected, gloomy; *informal* blue. **4 macabre**, cynical, unhealthy, ghoulish, weird, morbid, gruesome; *informal* sick.

- OPPOSITES white, bright.

□ **black out** faint, lose consciousness, pass out, swoon.

blacklist *verb* **boycott**, ostracize, avoid, embargo, ignore, refuse to employ.

blackmail *noun* **extortion**, demanding money with menaces, threats, intimidation.
● *verb* **1 extort money from**, threaten, hold to ransom, intimidate. **2 coerce**, pressure, force, dragoon; *informal* lean on, twist someone's arm.

blame *verb* **1 hold responsible**, hold accountable, condemn, accuse, find/consider guilty. **2** *they blame youth crime on unemployment* **attribute to**, ascribe to, impute to, lay at the door of, put down to; *informal* pin.
- OPPOSITES absolve.
● *noun* **responsibility**, guilt, accountability, liability, culpability, fault.

blameless *adjective* **innocent**, guiltless, above reproach, irreproachable, unimpeachable, in the clear, exemplary, impeccable, unblemished; *informal* squeaky clean.
- OPPOSITES guilty.

bland *adjective* **1 uninteresting**, dull, boring, tedious, monotonous, ordinary, run-of-the-mill, drab, dreary, unexciting, lacklustre, flat, stale, trite. **2 tasteless**, flavourless, plain, insipid, weak, watery, thin, wishy-washy.
- OPPOSITES interesting, tangy.

blank *adjective* **1 empty**, unmarked, unused, clear, free, bare, clean, plain. **2 expressionless**, deadpan, wooden, stony, impassive, inscrutable, glazed, fixed, lifeless.
- OPPOSITES expressive.
● *noun* **space**, gap, void.

blanket *noun a blanket of cloud* **covering**, layer, coating, carpet, cloak, mantle, veil, pall, shroud.
● *verb* **cover**, coat, carpet, cloak, shroud, swathe, envelop.

blasé *adjective* **indifferent**, unconcerned, casual, nonchalant, offhand, uninterested, unimpressed, unmoved, uncaring; *informal* laid-back.

blasphemous *adjective* **sacrilegious**, profane, irreligious, irreverent, impious, ungodly, godless.
- OPPOSITES reverent.

blasphemy *noun* **profanity**, sacrilege, irreligion, irreverence, taking the Lord's name in vain, impiety, desecration.
- OPPOSITES reverence.

blast *noun* **1 explosion**, detonation, discharge, burst. **2 gust**, rush, gale, squall, flurry. **3** *the shrill blast of the trumpets* **blare**, wail, roar, screech, shriek, hoot, honk, beep.
● *verb* **1 blow up**, bomb, blow (to pieces), dynamite, explode, fire, shoot, blaze, let fly, discharge. **2 blare**, boom, roar, thunder, bellow, shriek, screech.

blatant *adjective* **flagrant**, glaring, obvious, undisguised, open, overt, outright, naked, shameless, barefaced, unashamed, brazen.
- OPPOSITES discreet, inconspicuous.

blaze *noun* **1 fire**, flames, conflagration, inferno, holocaust. **2** *a blaze of light* **glare**, flash, burst, flare, streak, radiance, brilliance, beam, glitter.
● *verb* **1 burn**, be alight, be on fire, be in flames. **2 shine**, flash, flare, glare, gleam, glitter, glisten. **3 fire**, shoot, blast, let fly.

bleach *verb* **turn white**, whiten, turn pale, blanch, lighten, fade.
- OPPOSITES darken.

bleak *adjective* **1 bare**, exposed, desolate, stark, desert, lunar, open, empty, windswept. **2 unpromising**, unfavourable, dim, gloomy, black, grim, discouraging, disheartening, depressing, dismal.
- OPPOSITES lush, promising.

bleary *adjective* **blurry**, unfocused, fogged, clouded, misty, watery, rheumy.
- OPPOSITES clear.

blemish *noun* **imperfection**, flaw, defect, fault, discoloration, stain, scar, mark, spot.
● *verb* **mar**, spoil, impair, disfigure, deface, mark, stain, scar, blight, tarnish.
- OPPOSITES enhance.

b

blend *verb* **1 mix**, mingle, combine, merge, fuse, amalgamate, stir, whisk, fold in. **2 harmonize**, go (well), fit (in), be in tune, be compatible, coordinate, match, complement, suit.
● *noun* **mixture**, mix, melange, combination, synthesis, compound, amalgam, fusion, alloy.

bless *verb* **1 consecrate**, sanctify, dedicate to God, make holy; *formal* hallow. **2 endow**, bestow, furnish, give, favour, confer on. **3 sanction**, consent to, endorse, agree to, approve, back, support; *informal* give the green light to, OK.
– OPPOSITES curse, oppose.

blessed *adjective* **holy**, sacred, hallowed, consecrated, sanctified, ordained, canonized, beatified.
– OPPOSITES cursed.

blessing *noun* **1 benediction**, dedication, consecration, grace, invocation, intercession. **2 sanction**, endorsement, approval, consent, assent, agreement, backing, support; *informal* the green light, OK. **3 advantage**, godsend, boon, benefit, help, bonus, plus, stroke of luck, windfall.
– OPPOSITES condemnation.

blight *noun* **1** *potato blight* **disease**, canker, infestation, fungus, mildew, mould. **2** *the blight of aircraft noise* **curse**, scourge, affliction, plague, menace, misfortune, bane, trouble, nuisance, pest.
● *verb* **ruin**, wreck, spoil, mar, frustrate, disrupt, undo, scotch, destroy, shatter, devastate, demolish; *informal* mess up, foul up, put paid to, put the kibosh on, stymie; *Brit. informal* scupper.

blind *adjective* **1 sightless**, unsighted, visually impaired, unseeing. **2 uncritical**, unreasoned, unthinking, unquestioning, mindless, undiscerning, indiscriminate. **3** *blind to the realities of the situation* **unaware of**, oblivious to, ignorant of, unmindful of, heedless of, insensible to, indifferent to.
● *noun* **screen**, shade, sunshade, curtain, awning, canopy, louvre, jalousie, shutter.

blindly *adverb* **1 impetuously**, impulsively, recklessly, heedlessly. **2 uncritically**, unquestioningly, unthinkingly, mindlessly, indiscriminately.

bliss *noun* **joy**, happiness, pleasure, delight, ecstasy, elation, rapture, euphoria, seventh heaven.
– OPPOSITES misery.

blitz *noun* **bombing**, air raid, air strike, bombardment, barrage, attack, assault.

bloated *adjective* **swollen**, distended, bulging, puffed out, inflated, dilated.

blob *noun* **drop**, droplet, globule, bead, bubble, spot, dab, blotch, blot, dot, smudge; *informal* splodge.

bloc *noun* **group**, alliance, coalition, federation, confederation, league, union, axis, association.

block *noun* **1 chunk**, hunk, lump, wedge, cube, brick, ingot, slab, piece. **2 building**, complex, structure, development. **3 obstacle**, bar, barrier, impediment, hindrance, check, hurdle.
● *verb* **1 clog**, stop up, choke, plug, bung up, obstruct, gum up, dam up, congest, jam. **2 hinder**, hamper, obstruct, impede, inhibit, halt, stop, bar, check, prevent, fend off, hold off, repel.
– OPPOSITES clear, aid.
□ **block out** keep out, exclude, stop, conceal, blot out, blank out, obliterate.

blockage *noun* **obstruction**, stoppage, block, jam, congestion, bottleneck.

blonde, **blond** *adjective* **fair**, light, yellow, flaxen, golden.
– OPPOSITES dark.

blood *noun* **1 lifeblood**, gore, vital fluid. **2 ancestry**, lineage, descent, parentage, family, birth, extraction, origin, stock.

WORD LINKS
haematology branch of medicine concerned with blood

bloodshed *noun* **slaughter**, massacre, killing, wounding, carnage, butchery, bloodletting, bloodbath.

bloodthirsty *adjective* **murderous**, homicidal, violent, vicious, barbarous, barbaric, savage, brutal, cut-throat.

bloody *adjective* **1 bloodstained**, blood-soaked, gory, bleeding. **2 vicious**, ferocious, savage, fierce, brutal, cruel, murderous, gory.

bloom *verb* **1 flower**, blossom, open, mature. **2 flourish**, thrive, prosper, progress, burgeon; *informal* be in the pink.
- OPPOSITES wither, decline.

blossom *noun* **flower**, bloom, bud.
● *verb* **1 bloom**, flower, open, mature. **2 develop**, grow, mature, progress, evolve, burgeon, flourish, thrive, prosper, bloom.
- OPPOSITES wither, decline.

blot *noun* **1 patch**, dab, smudge, blotch, mark, dot, spot; *Brit. informal* splodge. **2 blemish**, taint, stain, blight, flaw, fault. **3** *a blot on the landscape* **eyesore**, monstrosity, carbuncle, mess; *informal* sight.
□ **blot out 1** conceal, hide, obscure, exclude, obliterate, shadow, eclipse. **2** erase, blank out, wipe out, eradicate.

blow[1] *verb* **1 gust**, puff, flurry, blast, roar, bluster, rush, storm. **2 sweep**, carry, toss, drive, push, force, drift, flutter, waft, float, glide, whirl. **3** *he blew the trumpet* **sound**, blast, toot, play, pipe, trumpet.
□ **blow out** extinguish, put out, snuff, douse, quench, smother. **blow up 1** explode, detonate, go off, ignite, erupt, bomb, blast, destroy. **2** inflate, pump up, fill up, puff up, swell, expand, distend.

blow[2] *noun* **1 stroke**, knock, bang, hit, punch, thump, smack, crack, rap; *informal* whack, bash, clout, wallop. **2 upset**, disaster, setback, misfortune, disappointment, calamity, catastrophe, thunderbolt, bombshell, shock, surprise, jolt.

blue *adjective* azure, cobalt, sapphire, navy, indigo, sky-blue, ultramarine, aquamarine, turquoise, cyan.

blueprint *noun* **plan**, design, diagram, drawing, sketch, layout, model, template, pattern, example, guide, prototype, pilot.

bluff[1] *noun* **trick**, deception, fraud, ruse, pretence, sham, fake, hoax, charade; *informal* put-on.
● *verb* **pretend**, sham, fake, feign, lie, deceive, delude, mislead, trick, fool, hoodwink, dupe, hoax; *informal* con, kid, have on.

bluff[2] *adjective* **plain-spoken**, straightforward, blunt, direct, no-nonsense, frank, open, candid, forthright, unequivocal; *informal* upfront.
- OPPOSITES guarded.

blunder *noun* **mistake**, error, gaffe, slip, oversight, faux pas; *informal* slip-up, boo-boo; *Brit. informal* clanger, boob, howler; *N. Amer. informal* blooper.
● *verb* **1 make a mistake**, err, miscalculate, bungle, trip up; *informal* slip up, screw up, blow it, goof; *Brit. informal* boob. **2 stumble**, lurch, stagger, flounder, grope.

blunt *adjective* **1** *a blunt knife* **dull**, worn. **2** *a broad leaf with a blunt tip* **rounded**, flat, stubby. **3 straightforward**, frank, plain-spoken, candid, direct, bluff, forthright, unequivocal, brusque, abrupt, curt, bald, brutal, harsh, stark; *informal* upfront.
- OPPOSITES sharp, subtle.
● *verb* **dull**, deaden, dampen, numb, take the edge off, weaken, allay, diminish, lessen.
- OPPOSITES intensify.

blur *verb* **cloud**, fog, obscure, dim, make hazy, make fuzzy, soften, dull, numb, deaden, mute.

blurred *adjective* **indistinct**, fuzzy, hazy, misty, foggy, clouded, cloudy, faint, unclear, vague, indefinite, unfocused.
- OPPOSITES sharp, clear.

blurt *verb*
□ **blurt out** burst out with, exclaim, call out, divulge, disclose, reveal, betray, let slip, give away; *informal* blab, let on, spill the beans.

blush *verb* **redden**, go pink, go red, flush, colour, burn up.

● *noun* **flush**, rosiness, redness, pinkness, bloom, high colour, glow.

b

blustery *adjective* **stormy**, gusty, blowy, windy, squally, wild.
- OPPOSITES calm.

board *noun* **1 plank**, beam, panel, slat, batten, timber. **2 committee**, council, panel, directorate, commission.
● *verb* **1 get on**, go aboard, enter, mount, ascend, embark, catch. **2 lodge**, live, reside, stay, be housed; *N. Amer.* room; *informal* put up.

boast *verb* **1 brag**, crow, swagger, swank, show off, blow your own trumpet, sing your own praises; *informal* talk big, lay it on thick; *Austral./NZ informal* skite. **2** *the hotel boasts a fine restaurant* **have**, possess, own, enjoy, pride yourself/itself on, offer.
● *noun* **1 brag**, exaggeration, overstatement; *informal* swank; *Austral./NZ informal* skite. **2 pride**, joy, pride and joy, apple of someone's eye, wonder, delight.

boastful *adjective* **bragging**, swaggering, bumptious, swollen-headed, puffed up, full of yourself, cocky, conceited, arrogant; *informal* swanky, big-headed.
- OPPOSITES modest.

bob *verb* **move up and down**, bounce, toss, skip, dance, wobble, jiggle, joggle, jolt, jerk.

bodily *adjective* **physical**, corporeal, corporal, mortal, material, tangible, concrete, real, actual, incarnate.
- OPPOSITES spiritual, mental.
● *adverb* **forcefully**, forcibly, violently, completely, entirely.

body *noun* **1 figure**, frame, form, physique, anatomy, skeleton. **2 torso**, trunk. **3 corpse**, carcass, skeleton, remains; *informal* stiff; *Medicine* cadaver. **4 main part**, core, heart, hub. **5 association**, organization, assembly, delegation, committee, executive, company, society, corporation, group.

WORD LINKS
corporal, **corporeal** relating to the body

bog *noun* **marsh**, swamp, mire, quagmire, morass, slough, fen, wetland.
□ **bog down** mire, stick, entangle, ensnare, embroil, hamper, hinder, impede, obstruct, swamp, overwhelm.

bogus *adjective* **fake**, spurious, false, fraudulent, sham, counterfeit, forged, feigned; *informal* phoney, pretend.
- OPPOSITES genuine.

boil[1] *verb* **simmer**, bubble, stew, seethe, froth, foam.

boil[2] *noun* **swelling**, spot, pimple, blister, gathering, pustule, carbuncle, abscess.

boisterous *adjective* **lively**, animated, exuberant, spirited, noisy, loud, rowdy, unruly, wild, uproarious, unrestrained, uninhibited, uncontrolled, rough, disorderly, riotous; *informal* rumbustious.
- OPPOSITES restrained.

bold *adjective* **1 daring**, intrepid, brave, courageous, valiant, valorous, fearless, dauntless, audacious, daredevil, adventurous, heroic, plucky; *informal* gutsy, spunky. **2 striking**, vivid, bright, strong, eye-catching, prominent, gaudy, lurid, garish.
- OPPOSITES timid, faint.

bolster *verb* **strengthen**, reinforce, boost, fortify, support, prop up, buoy up, shore up, buttress, maintain, help, augment, increase.

bolt *noun* **1** *the bolt on the door* **bar**, lock, catch, latch, fastener. **2** *nuts and bolts* **pin**, rivet, peg, screw.
● *verb* **1** *he bolted the door* **lock**, bar, latch, fasten, secure. **2** *the lid was bolted down* **pin**, rivet, peg, screw, fasten, fix. **3 dash**, dart, run, sprint, hurtle, rush, fly, shoot; *informal* tear, scoot, leg it. **4 gobble**, gulp, wolf, guzzle, devour; *informal* demolish, polish off, shovel down; *N. Amer. informal* scarf, snarf.

bomb *noun* **explosive**, incendiary (device), missile, projectile.
● *verb* **blow up**, blast, shell, blitz, strafe, pound, bombard, attack, assault, destroy, demolish.

bombard *verb* **1 shell**, pound, blitz, strafe, bomb, batter, blast, pelt. **2 swamp**, inundate, flood, deluge, snow under, overwhelm.

bombardment *noun* **assault**, attack, bombing, shelling, strafing, blitz, air raid, cannonade, fusillade, barrage, broadside.

bonanza *noun* **windfall**, godsend, blessing, bonus, stroke of luck; *informal* jackpot.

bond *noun* **1 friendship**, relationship, fellowship, partnership, association, affiliation, alliance, attachment, tie, connection, link. **2 promise**, pledge, vow, oath, word (of honour), guarantee, assurance, agreement, contract, pact, deal.
● *verb* **join**, fasten, fix, affix, attach, secure, bind, stick, fuse.

bonus *noun* **1 advantage**, plus, benefit, extra, boon, blessing, godsend, stroke of luck, attraction. **2 gratuity**, handout, gift, present, reward, prize, incentive; *informal* perk, sweetener.
- OPPOSITES disadvantage.

bony *adjective* **skinny**, thin, lean, gaunt, scrawny, spare, skin and bone, skeletal, emaciated, underweight.
- OPPOSITES plump.

book *noun* **1 volume**, tome, publication, title, novel, treatise, manual. **2 notepad**, notebook, pad, exercise book, logbook, ledger, journal, diary; *Brit.* jotter, pocketbook; *N. Amer.* scratch pad.
● *verb* **reserve**, prearrange, order; *informal* bag.
□ **book in** register, check in, enrol.

WORD LINKS
bibliography list of books

booklet *noun* **pamphlet**, brochure, leaflet, tract; *N. Amer.* folder, mailer.

boom *noun* **1 roar**, rumble, thunder, crashing, drumming, pounding, echoing, resonance, reverberation. **2 increase**, growth, advance, boost, escalation, improvement, upsurge, upturn.
- OPPOSITES slump.
● *verb* **1 roar**, rumble, thunder, crash, roll, clap, explode, bang, resound, blare, echo, resonate, reverberate. **2 shout**, yell, bellow, roar, thunder, bawl; *informal* holler. **3 flourish**, thrive, prosper, burgeon, progress, improve, pick up, expand.

boorish *adjective* **coarse**, uncouth, rude, vulgar, uncivilized, unrefined, oafish, ignorant, uncultured, philistine, rough, thuggish, loutish, Neanderthal; *Brit. informal* yobbish; *Austral. informal* ocker.
- OPPOSITES refined.

boost *verb* **increase**, raise, escalate, improve, strengthen, inflate, push up, promote, advance, foster, stimulate, encourage, facilitate, help, assist, aid; *informal* hike, bump up.
- OPPOSITES decrease.
● *noun* **1** *a boost to your morale* **uplift**, lift, spur, encouragement, help, inspiration, stimulus, fillip; *informal* shot in the arm. **2** *a boost in sales* **increase**, expansion, upturn, upsurge, rise, escalation, improvement, advance, growth, boom; *informal* hike.
- OPPOSITES decrease.

boot *verb* **kick**, punt, tap, propel, drive, knock.

booth *noun* **1 stall**, stand, kiosk. **2** *a phone booth* **cubicle**, kiosk, box, compartment, enclosure, cabin.

booty *noun* **loot**, plunder, haul, spoils, ill gotten gains, pickings; *informal* swag.

border *noun* **1 edge**, margin, perimeter, circumference, periphery, rim, fringe, verge, sides. **2 frontier**, boundary, borderline, perimeter.
● *verb* **1 surround**, enclose, encircle, edge, fringe, bound, flank. **2 edge**, fringe, hem, trim, pipe, finish. **3 adjoin**, abut, be next to, be adjacent to, touch.
□ **border on** verge on, approach, come close to, be comparable to, approximate to, be tantamount to.

bore[1] *verb* **drill**, pierce, perforate, puncture, punch, tunnel, burrow, mine, dig, gouge, sink.

b

bore[2] *verb* **weary**, pall on, tire, fatigue, send to sleep, leave cold; *informal* turn off.
- OPPOSITES interest.
● *noun* **tedious person/thing**, tiresome person/thing, bother, nuisance, pest, annoyance, trial, thorn in your flesh/side; *informal* drag, pain (in the neck), headache, hassle.

boredom *noun* **tedium**, ennui, apathy, weariness, dullness, monotony, repetitiveness, flatness, dreariness.
- OPPOSITES interest, excitement.

boring *adjective* **tedious**, dull, dreary, monotonous, repetitive, uneventful, unimaginative, characterless, featureless, colourless, lifeless, uninteresting, unexciting, lacklustre, humdrum, mind-numbing, soul-destroying, wearisome, tiresome; *informal* deadly; *Brit. informal* samey; *N. Amer. informal* dullsville.
- OPPOSITES interesting, exciting.

borrow *verb* **1 loan**, lease, hire; *informal* cadge, scrounge, bum, touch someone for; *N. Amer. informal* mooch; *Austral./NZ informal* bludge. **2 adopt**, take on, acquire, embrace, copy, imitate.
- OPPOSITES lend.

boss *(informal) noun* **head**, chief, principal, director, president, chief executive, chair, manager, supervisor, foreman, overseer, controller, employer, owner, proprietor; *Brit. informal* gaffer, governor; *N. Amer. informal* head honcho.
● *verb* **order around**, dictate to, bully, push around/about, call the shots, lay down the law; *informal* bulldoze, walk all over, railroad.

bossy *adjective (informal)* **domineering**, pushy, overbearing, imperious, officious, high-handed, authoritarian, dictatorial, autocratic; *informal* high and mighty.
- OPPOSITES submissive.

bother *verb* **1** *no one bothered her* **disturb**, trouble, inconvenience, pester, badger, harass, molest, plague; *informal* hassle, bug; *N. English informal* mither; *N. Amer. informal* ride. **2** *don't bother about me* **mind**, care, worry, concern yourself, trouble yourself. **3** *something was bothering him* **worry**, trouble, concern, perturb, disturb, disquiet; *informal* rattle.
● *noun* **1 trouble**, effort, exertion, inconvenience, fuss, pains; *informal* hassle. **2 nuisance**, pest, palaver, rigmarole, job, trial, bind, bore, drag, inconvenience, trouble; *informal* hassle, headache, pain (in the neck). **3** *a spot of bother in the public bar* **disorder**, fighting, trouble, disturbance, commotion, uproar; *informal* hoo-ha, aggro, argy-bargy, kerfuffle.

bottle *noun* **flask**, carafe, decanter, pitcher, flagon, magnum, demijohn, phial.
□ **bottle up** suppress, repress, restrain, hold in, smother, contain, conceal, hide; *informal* keep a lid on.

bottom *noun* **1 foot**, lowest part, base, foundation. **2 underside**, underneath, undersurface, underbelly. **3 floor**, bed, depths. **4 farthest point**, extremity, far end. **5** *(Brit.)* **buttocks**, rear (end), rump, seat, derrière; *informal* behind, backside; *Brit. informal* bum, jacksie; *N. Amer. informal* butt, fanny; *humorous* posterior.
- OPPOSITES top, surface.
● *adjective* **lowest**, last, bottommost.
- OPPOSITES top.

bounce *verb* **1 rebound**, spring back, ricochet; *N. Amer.* carom. **2 bound**, leap, jump, spring, bob, hop, skip, gambol, trip, prance.
● *noun* **1 springiness**, resilience, elasticity, give. **2 vitality**, vigour, energy, vivacity, liveliness, animation, sparkle, verve, spirit; *informal* get-up-and-go, pep, zing.

bound[1] *adjective* **1 tied**, restrained, fixed, fastened, secured. **2 certain**, sure, very likely, destined. **3** *bound by the Official Secrets Act* **constrained**, obliged, compelled, required, obligated.
- OPPOSITES free.

bound[2] *verb* **leap**, jump, spring, vault, bounce, hop, skip, dance, prance, gambol, gallop.

bound[3] *verb* **1 limit**, restrict, confine, circumscribe, demarcate, delimit. **2 enclose**, surround, encircle, circle, border, close in/off, hem in.

boundary *noun* **1 border**, frontier, borderline, partition, dividing line. **2** *the boundary of his estate* **limits**, confines, bounds, margins, edges, fringes, border, periphery, perimeter.

boundless *adjective* **limitless**, untold, immeasurable, abundant, inexhaustible, endless, infinite, interminable, unfailing, ceaseless, everlasting.
– OPPOSITES limited.

bouquet *noun* **1 posy**, nosegay, spray, corsage, buttonhole, garland, wreath, arrangement. **2 aroma**, nose, smell, fragrance, perfume, scent, odour.

bourgeois *adjective* **middle-class**, conservative, conformist, conventional, propertied, provincial, suburban, small-town.
– OPPOSITES proletarian.

bout *noun* **1 spell**, period, stretch, stint, session, burst, flurry, spurt. **2 attack**, fit, spasm. **3 contest**, fight, match, round, competition, meeting, encounter; *Brit.* clash.

bow[1] *verb* **1 incline your head**, bend, stoop, bob, curtsy, kneel, genuflect. **2** *the mast bowed in the wind* **bend**, buckle, curve, flex. **3** *the government bowed to foreign pressure* **give in**, submit, yield, surrender, succumb, capitulate.
● *noun* **nod**, bob, obeisance, curtsy, genuflection, salaam.

bow[2] *noun* **prow**, front, stem, nose, head.

bowels *plural noun* **1 intestines**, entrails, viscera, innards, digestive system; *Medicine* gut; *informal* guts, insides. **2 interior**, inside, core, belly, depths, recesses; *informal* innards.

bowl[1] *verb* **throw**, pitch, hurl, toss, lob, fling, roll, launch, propel; *informal* chuck, sling, bung.

bowl[2] *noun* **dish**, basin, pot, crock, vessel, receptacle.

box[1] *noun* **1 carton**, pack, packet, case, crate, chest, coffer, casket. **2** *a telephone box* **booth**, kiosk, cubicle, compartment, cabin, hut.
● *verb* **pack**, package, parcel, encase, bundle, crate.

box[2] *verb* **fight**, spar, battle, brawl; *informal* scrap.

boxer *noun* **fighter**, pugilist, prizefighter; *informal* bruiser, scrapper.

boy *noun* **lad**, youth, young man, stripling; *Scottish & N. English* laddie.

boycott *verb* **shun**, snub, spurn, avoid, ostracize, blacklist, blackball, reject, veto, send to Coventry.
● *noun* **ban**, veto, embargo, prohibition, moratorium, sanction, restriction, avoidance, rejection.

boyfriend *noun* **lover**, sweetheart, beloved, darling, partner; *informal* fella, fancy man; *N. Amer. informal* squeeze; *dated* beau; *literary* swain.

brace *noun* **prop**, strut, stay, support, bracket.
● *verb* **1 support**, shore up, prop up, hold up, buttress, reinforce. **2 steady**, secure, stabilize, poise, fix. **3** *brace yourself for disappointment* **prepare**, get ready, gear up, nerve, steel, fortify; *informal* psych yourself up.

bracing *adjective* **invigorating**, refreshing, stimulating, energizing, exhilarating, restorative, rejuvenating.

bracket *noun* **1 support**, prop, stay, batten, rest, mounting, rack, frame. **2 group**, category, grade, classification, division.

brag *verb* **boast**, crow, swagger, swank, show off, blow your own trumpet, sing your own praises; *informal* talk big.

brain *noun* **intelligence**, intellect, brainpower, cleverness, wit(s), reasoning, wisdom, judgement, understanding, sense; *informal* nous, grey matter; *N. Amer. informal* smarts.

WORD LINKS
cerebral relating to the brain

b

brake *noun* **curb**, check, restraint, constraint, control, limit.
● *verb* **slow (down)**, decelerate, reduce speed.
- OPPOSITES accelerate.

branch *noun* **1 bough**, limb, arm, offshoot, twig. **2 division**, subdivision, section, subsection, department, unit, sector, wing, office, bureau, agency, subsidiary.
● *verb* **1 fork**, divide, split, bifurcate. **2** *narrow paths branched off the road* **diverge**, split off, fan out, radiate.

brand *noun* **1 make**, line, label, marque, trade name, trademark, proprietary name. **2 type**, kind, sort, variety, class, category, genre, style, ilk; *N. Amer.* stripe.
● *verb* **1 mark**, stamp, burn, sear. **2 stigmatize**, characterize, label, mark out, denounce, discredit, vilify.

brandish *verb* **flourish**, wave, shake, wield, swing, swish.

brash *adjective* **1 self-assertive**, pushy, cocky, self-confident, arrogant, bold, audacious, brazen. **2 garish**, gaudy, loud, flamboyant, showy, tasteless; *informal* flashy, tacky.
- OPPOSITES meek.

brave *adjective* **courageous**, intrepid, bold, plucky, heroic, fearless, daring, audacious, dauntless, valiant, valorous, doughty, indomitable, stout-hearted; *informal* game, gutsy.
- OPPOSITES cowardly.
● *verb* **endure**, put up with, bear, withstand, weather, suffer, face, confront, defy.

bravery *noun* **courage**, boldness, heroism, intrepidity, nerve, daring, fearlessness, audacity, pluck, valour; *informal* guts; *Brit. informal* bottle.

brawl *noun* **fight**, skirmish, scuffle, tussle, fray, melee, fracas, fisticuffs; *informal* scrap, set-to; *Brit. informal* punch-up.

brawny *adjective* **strong**, muscular, muscly, well built, powerful, strapping, burly, sturdy; *informal* beefy, hulking.
- OPPOSITES puny, weak.

brazen *adjective* **bold**, shameless, unashamed, unrepentant, unabashed, defiant, impudent, impertinent, cheeky, barefaced, blatant, flagrant.

breach *noun* **1 contravention**, violation, infringement, infraction, transgression. **2 break**, rupture, split, crack, fracture, opening, gap, hole, fissure. **3 rift**, severance, estrangement, parting, parting of the ways, split, falling-out, schism.
● *verb* **1 break (through)**, burst, rupture. **2 contravene**, break, violate, infringe, defy, disobey, flout.

breadth *noun* **1 width**, broadness, thickness, span, diameter. **2 range**, extent, scope, depth, reach, compass, scale.

break *verb* **1 shatter**, smash, crack, snap, fracture, fragment, splinter, split, burst; *informal* bust. **2 stop working**, break down, give out, go wrong, malfunction, crash; *informal* go kaput, conk out; *Brit. informal* pack up. **3 violate**, contravene, infringe, breach, defy, flout, disobey. **4** *the film broke box-office records* **beat**, surpass, exceed, better, cap, top, outdo, outstrip. **5** *he tried to break the news gently* **reveal**, disclose, divulge, impart, tell, announce, release.
- OPPOSITES repair, obey.
● *noun* **1 interval**, interruption, gap, disruption, stoppage, cessation, halt, stop. **2 rest**, respite, recess, pause, intermission; *informal* breather, time out. **3 gap**, opening, space, hole, breach, chink, crack, fracture, fissure, tear, split.
□ **break down 1** stop working, give out, go wrong, malfunction, crash; *informal* go kaput, conk out; *Brit. informal* pack up. **2** fail, collapse, founder, fall through. **3** burst into tears, lose control, be overcome, go to pieces; *informal* crack up, lose it. **4** analyse, categorize, classify, sort, itemize, organize, divide, separate, split. **break off 1** snap

off, pull off, sever, detach. **2** end, terminate, stop, cease, call a halt to, suspend, discontinue; *informal* pull the plug on. **break out 1** escape, abscond, flee, get free. **2** flare up, start suddenly, erupt, burst out. **break up 1** end, finish, stop, terminate, adjourn; *N. Amer.* recess. **2** disperse, scatter, disband, part company. **3** split up, separate, part (company), divorce.

breakdown *noun* **1 failure**, collapse, disintegration, foundering. **2 nervous breakdown**, collapse. **3 malfunction**, failure, crash. **4 analysis**, itemization, classification, examination, investigation, explanation.

break-in *noun* **burglary**, robbery, theft, raid, breaking and entering; *informal* smash-and-grab.

breakthrough *noun* **advance**, development, step forward, success, improvement, discovery, innovation, revolution, quantum leap.
– OPPOSITES setback.

breast *noun* **chest**, bosom, bust; *informal* boobs, knockers.

breath *noun* **inhalation**, exhalation, gulp of air, puff, gasp; *Medicine* respiration.

breathe *verb* **1 inhale**, exhale, respire, draw breath, puff, pant, blow, gasp, wheeze; *Medicine* inspire, expire. **2 whisper**, murmur, purr, sigh.

WORD LINKS
respiratory relating to breathing

breathless *adjective* **1 out of breath**, panting, puffing, gasping, wheezing, winded; *informal* out of puff. **2 eager**, agog, open-mouthed, excited, on the edge of your seat, on tenterhooks.

breathtaking *adjective* **spectacular**, magnificent, awe-inspiring, awesome, astonishing, amazing, stunning, thrilling; *informal* sensational, out of this world.

breed *verb* **1 reproduce**, produce offspring, procreate, multiply, mate. **2 bring up**, rear, raise, nurture. **3 cause**, produce, bring about, give rise to, occasion, arouse, stir up, generate, foster.
● *noun* **1** *a breed of cow* **variety**, stock, strain, race, species. **2** *a new breed of journalist* **type**, kind, sort, variety, class, genre, generation.

breeding *noun* **(good) manners**, gentility, refinement, cultivation, polish, urbanity; *informal* class.

breeze *noun* **gentle wind**, puff of air, gust, draught; *literary* zephyr.

breezy *adjective* **1 windy**, fresh, brisk, blowy, blustery, gusty. **2 jaunty**, cheerful, cheery, brisk, carefree, easy, casual, relaxed, informal, light-hearted, upbeat.

brevity *noun* **conciseness**, concision, succinctness, pithiness, incisiveness, shortness, compactness.

brew *verb* **1 ferment**, make, prepare, infuse; *Brit. informal* mash. **2 develop**, loom, be imminent, be on the horizon, be in the offing, be just around the corner.
● *noun* **1** *home brew* **beer**, ale. **2** *a hot reviving brew* **drink**, beverage, infusion. **3 mixture**, mix, blend, combination, amalgam, cocktail.

bribe *verb* **buy off**, pay off, suborn; *informal* grease someone's palm, keep someone sweet, square; *Brit. informal* nobble.
● *noun* **inducement**; *informal* bung, backhander, pay-off, kickback, sweetener.

bribery *noun* **corruption**; *N. Amer.* payola; *informal* palm-greasing, graft, hush money.

WORD LINKS
venal susceptible to bribery

bridge *noun* **1 viaduct**, flyover, overpass, aqueduct. **2 link**, connection, bond, tie.
● *verb* **span**, cross (over), extend across, traverse, arch over, straddle.

WORD LINKS
pontine relating to bridges

b

brief *adjective* **1 concise**, succinct, short, pithy, compact, thumbnail, potted, condensed, to the point, terse, summary. **2 short**, flying, fleeting, hasty, hurried, quick, cursory, perfunctory, temporary, short-lived, ephemeral, transient, transitory.
- OPPOSITES long.
● *noun* **1** *my brief is to reorganize the project* **instructions**, directions, directive, remit, mandate. **2** *a barrister's brief* **case**, summary, argument, contention, dossier.
● *verb* **inform**, tell, update, notify, advise, prepare, prime, instruct; *informal* fill in, put in the picture.

briefly *adverb* **1 concisely**, succinctly, tersely. **2 momentarily**, temporarily, fleetingly. **3** *briefly, the plot is as follows* **in short**, to cut a long story short, in brief, in a word, in a nutshell, in essence.

briefs *plural noun* **underpants**, pants, knickers, bikini briefs; *N. Amer.* shorts; *informal* panties; *Brit. informal* kecks.

brigade *noun* **squad**, team, group, band, party, crew, force, outfit.

bright *adjective* **1 shining**, brilliant, dazzling, glaring, sparkling, flashing, glittering, gleaming, glistening, coruscating, shimmering, radiant, glowing, luminous, shiny, glossy, lustrous. **2 sunny**, cloudless, clear, fair, fine. **3** *bright colours* **vivid**, brilliant, intense, strong, vibrant, bold, gaudy, lurid, garish. **4 clever**, intelligent, quick-witted, smart, canny, astute, perceptive, ingenious; *informal* brainy, genius.
- OPPOSITES dull, cloudy, dark, stupid.

brighten *verb* **1 illuminate**, light up, lighten. **2 cheer up**, perk up, liven up, rally, feel heartened; *informal* buck up.

brilliance *noun* **1 brightness**, vividness, intensity, sparkle, glitter, blaze, luminosity, radiance. **2 genius**, intelligence, talent, ability, prowess, skill, expertise, aptitude, flair, wisdom, intellect. **3 splendour**, magnificence, grandeur, resplendence, glory.
- OPPOSITES dullness, stupidity.

brilliant *adjective* **1 bright**, shining, sparkling, blazing, coruscating, dazzling, vivid, intense, glaring, luminous, radiant. **2 clever**, bright, intelligent, smart, able, talented, gifted, skilful, astute; *informal* brainy, genius. **3** *her brilliant career* **superb**, glorious, illustrious, successful, impressive, remarkable, exceptional, excellent, outstanding, distinguished.
- OPPOSITES dim, stupid, undistinguished.

brim *noun* **1** peak, visor, shield. **2 rim**, lip, brink, edge.
● *verb* **be full (up)**, overflow, run over, well over.

bring *verb* **1 fetch**, carry, bear, take, convey, transport, shift. **2 escort**, conduct, guide, lead, usher. **3 cause**, produce, create, bring about, generate, precipitate, occasion, provoke, lead to, give rise to, result in.
□ **bring in** introduce, launch, inaugurate, initiate, institute. **bring off** achieve, accomplish, bring about, succeed in, pull off, carry off, manage. **bring out** launch, establish, begin, start, found, set up, market, publish, issue. **bring up 1** rear, raise, nurture, look after. **2** mention, raise, broach, introduce, air, suggest.

brink *noun* **1 edge**, verge, margin, rim, lip, border, boundary. **2** *on the brink of war* **verge**, threshold, point, edge.

brisk *adjective* **1 quick**, rapid, fast, swift, speedy, hurried, energetic, lively; *informal* nippy. **2 no-nonsense**, businesslike, decisive, brusque, abrupt, short, sharp, curt, blunt, terse; *informal* snappy.
- OPPOSITES leisurely.

bristle *noun* **1 hair**, whisker; (**bristles**) stubble, five o'clock shadow. **2 spine**, prickle, quill, barb.
● *verb* **1 rise**, stand up, stand on end. **2 take offence**, bridle, take umbrage, be offended. **3 be crowded**, be full, be packed, be jammed, be covered, overflow; *informal* be thick, be chockfull.

brittle *adjective* **breakable**, fragile, crisp, crumbly, delicate.
– OPPOSITES flexible.

broach *verb* **bring up**, raise, introduce, mention, touch on, air.

broad *adjective* **1 wide**, extensive, vast, immense, great, spacious, expansive, sizeable, sweeping. **2 comprehensive**, inclusive, extensive, wide, all-embracing, unlimited. **3** *a broad outline* **general**, non-specific, rough, approximate, basic, loose, vague.
– OPPOSITES narrow, limited.

broadcast *verb* **1 transmit**, relay, air, beam, show, televise, screen, telecast, videocast, podcast. **2 report**, announce, publicize, advertise, make public, proclaim, spread, circulate, promulgate.
● *noun* **transmission**, programme, show, telecast, videocast, podcast, production.

broaden *verb* **1** *her smile broadened* **widen**, expand, stretch (out), spread. **2** *the government tried to broaden its political base* **expand**, enlarge, extend, widen, swell, increase, add to, develop.
– OPPOSITES narrow, restrict.

broad-minded *adjective* **liberal**, tolerant, freethinking, indulgent, progressive, permissive, unshockable, unprejudiced, unbiased.
– OPPOSITES intolerant.

brochure *noun* **booklet**, prospectus, catalogue, pamphlet, leaflet, circular, mailshot; *N. Amer.* folder.

broken *adjective* **1 smashed**, shattered, fragmented, splintered, crushed, snapped, in bits, in pieces, cracked, split, fractured; *informal* in smithereens. **2 faulty**, damaged, defective, not working, malfunctioning, out of order, broken down, down; *informal* kaput, bust, acting up; *Brit. informal* knackered. **3 interrupted**, disturbed, fitful, disrupted, discontinuous, intermittent. **4 halting**, hesitating, disjointed, faltering, imperfect.

broken-hearted *adjective* **heartbroken**, grief-stricken, desolate, devastated, inconsolable, miserable, wretched, forlorn, heavy-hearted, woeful.
– OPPOSITES overjoyed.

broker *noun* **dealer**, agent, middleman, intermediary, mediator, factor, liaison, stockbroker.
● *verb* **arrange**, organize, orchestrate, work out, settle, clinch, negotiate, mediate.

brood *noun* **offspring**, young, family, litter, clutch, progeny.
● *verb* **think**, ponder, contemplate, meditate, ruminate, muse, worry, dwell on, fret, agonize.

brook *noun* **stream**, rill; *N. English* beck; *Scottish & N. English* burn; *N. Amer. & Austral./NZ* creek.

brotherly *adjective* **fraternal**, friendly, comradely, affectionate, amicable, kind, devoted, loyal.

brow *noun* **1 forehead**, temple. **2 summit**, peak, top, crest, crown, head, pinnacle, apex.

browbeat *verb* **bully**, intimidate, force, coerce, compel, dragoon, bludgeon, pressure, pressurize, tyrannize, terrorize; *informal* bulldoze, railroad.

brown *adjective* **1** hazel, chestnut, chocolate, coffee, brunette, sepia, mahogany, tan, café au lait, caramel. **2 tanned**, suntanned, bronzed, swarthy.
● *verb* **grill**, toast, singe, sear, barbecue, sauté.

browse *verb* **look through**, scan, skim, glance, peruse, thumb, leaf, flick, dip into.

bruise *noun* **contusion**, bump, swelling, lump, mark, injury, welt.
● *verb* **contuse**, injure, mark, discolour, make black and blue, blemish, damage, spoil.

brush[1] *noun* **1 broom**, sweeper, besom, whisk. **2 clean**, sweep, wipe, dust. **3** *a brush with the law* **encounter**, clash, confrontation, conflict, altercation, incident; *informal* run-in, to-do; *Brit. informal* spot of bother.

● *verb* **1 sweep**, clean, buff, polish, scrub. **2 groom**, comb, neaten, tidy, smooth, arrange. **3** *his lips brushed her cheek* **touch**, stroke, caress, skim, sweep, graze, contact, kiss.
□ **brush aside** disregard, ignore, dismiss, shrug off, wave aside, reject, spurn, laugh off, make light of; *informal* pooh-pooh. **brush up (on)** revise, read up, go over, improve, polish up, enhance, hone, perfect; *informal* bone up on; *Brit. informal* swot up (on).

brush[2] *noun* **undergrowth**, scrub, brushwood, shrubs, bushes; *N. Amer.* underbrush, chaparral.

brusque *adjective* **curt**, abrupt, blunt, short, sharp, brisk, peremptory, gruff, discourteous, impolite, rude.
- OPPOSITES polite.

brutal *adjective* **savage**, violent, cruel, vicious, ferocious, barbaric, wicked, murderous, bloodthirsty, cold-blooded, callous, ruthless, heartless, merciless, sadistic, inhuman.
- OPPOSITES gentle.

bubbly *adjective* **1 fizzy**, sparkling, effervescent, gassy, aerated, carbonated, frothy, foamy. **2 vivacious**, animated, ebullient, lively, high-spirited, bouncy, merry, happy, cheerful, sunny; *informal* chirpy.
- OPPOSITES still.

buckle *noun* **clasp**, clip, catch, hasp, fastener.
● *verb* **1 fasten**, do up, hook, secure, clasp, clip. **2 bend**, warp, twist, distort, contort, deform, crumple, collapse, give way.

budding *adjective* **promising**, up-and-coming, rising, in the making, aspiring, future, fledgling, developing.

budge *verb* **1 move**, shift, stir, go. **2 persuade**, convince, influence, sway, bend.

budget *noun* **1 financial plan**, forecast. **2** *the defence budget* **allowance**, allocation, quota, funds, resources, capital.
● *verb* **allocate**, allot, allow, earmark, designate, set aside.

buff[1] *verb* **polish**, burnish, shine, smooth, rub.

buff[2] *noun (informal)* **enthusiast**, fan, devotee, lover, admirer, expert, aficionado, authority; *informal* freak, nut, addict.

buffer *noun* **cushion**, bulwark, shield, barrier, guard, safeguard.

buffet[1] *noun* **1 cold table**, self-service meal, smorgasbord. **2 cafe**, cafeteria, snack bar, canteen, restaurant.

buffet[2] *verb* **batter**, pound, lash, strike, hit, beat.

bug *noun* **1** *(informal)* **illness**, disease, sickness, disorder, upset, ailment, infection, virus; *Brit. informal* lurgy. **2 insect**, minibeast; *informal* creepy-crawly, beastie. **3 listening device**, hidden microphone, wire, wiretap, tap. **4 fault**, error, defect, flaw, virus; *informal* glitch, gremlin.
● *verb* **eavesdrop on**, spy on, tap, monitor.

build *verb* **construct**, erect, put up, assemble, make, create, fashion, model, shape.
- OPPOSITES demolish, dismantle.
● *noun* **physique**, frame, body, figure, form, shape, stature, proportions; *informal* vital statistics.
□ **build up 1** increase, grow, mount up, intensify, strengthen. **2** boost, strengthen, increase, improve, augment, raise, enhance, swell. **3** accumulate, amass, collect, gather.

building *noun* **structure**, construction, edifice, pile, property, premises, establishment.

WORD LINKS
architectural relating to building

build-up *noun* **increase**, growth, expansion, enlargement, escalation, accumulation, development.

bulbous *adjective* **bulging**, round, fat, rotund, swollen, distended, bloated.

bulge *noun* **swelling**, bump, lump, hump, protrusion, protuberance.
● *verb* **swell**, stick out, project, protrude, stand out, puff out, balloon (out), fill out, distend.

bulk *noun* **1 size**, volume, dimensions, proportions, mass, scale. **2 majority**, mass, generality, main part, lion's share, preponderance.

bulky *adjective* **unwieldy**, cumbersome, unmanageable, awkward, ponderous, outsize, oversized; *informal* hulking.

bullet *noun* **ball**, shot, pellet; *informal* slug; (**bullets**) lead.

bulletin *noun* **1 report**, dispatch, story, newsflash, statement, announcement, message, communication, communiqué. **2 newsletter**, news-sheet, proceedings, newspaper, magazine, gazette, review.

bully *noun* **persecutor**, oppressor, tyrant, tormentor, intimidator, bully boy, thug, attack dog.
● *verb* **1** *the others bully him* **persecute**, oppress, tyrannize, browbeat, intimidate, dominate, terrorize; *informal* push around/about. **2** *she was bullied into helping* **coerce**, pressure, press, push, prod, browbeat, dragoon, strong-arm; *informal* bulldoze, railroad, lean on.

bump *noun* **1 jolt**, crash, smash, smack, crack, bang, thud, thump, clang, knock, clunk, boom; *informal* whack, wallop. **2 swelling**, lump, bulge, injury, contusion, hump, knob.
● *verb* **1 hit**, crash into, smash into, slam into, bang, knock, run into, plough into, ram, collide with, strike; *N. Amer.* impact. **2 bounce**, jolt, jerk, rattle, shake.

bumper *adjective* **exceptional**, large, abundant, rich, bountiful, good, plentiful, record, successful; *informal* whopping.
– OPPOSITES meagre.

bumpy *adjective* **1 uneven**, rough, rutted, pitted, potholed, lumpy, rocky. **2 bouncy**, rough, uncomfortable, jolting, lurching, jerky, jarring, bone-shaking.
– OPPOSITES smooth.

bunch *noun* **1 bouquet**, posy, nosegay, spray, wreath, garland. **2 cluster**, clump, knot, group, bundle.
● *verb* **cluster**, huddle, gather, congregate, collect, amass, group, crowd.

bundle *noun* **collection**, roll, clump, wad, parcel, sheaf, bale, pile, stack, heap, mass, bunch; *informal* load, wodge.
● *verb* **1 tie**, parcel, wrap, swathe, roll, fold, bind, pack. **2** *he was bundled into a van* **push**, shove, thrust, throw, propel, jostle, manhandle.

bungle *verb* **mishandle**, mismanage, mess up, spoil, ruin; *informal* blow, botch, fluff, make a hash of, screw up; *Brit. informal* make a pig's ear of; *N. Amer. informal* goof up.

bungling *adjective* **incompetent**, blundering, amateurish, inept, unskilful, clumsy, awkward, bumbling; *informal* ham-fisted, cack-handed.

buoy *noun* **float**, marker, beacon.

buoyant *adjective* **1 floating**, floatable. **2 cheerful**, cheery, happy, light-hearted, carefree, joyful, bubbly, bouncy, sunny, upbeat.
– OPPOSITES gloomy.

burden *noun* **responsibility**, onus, obligation, duty, liability, trouble, care, problem, difficulty, worry, strain.
● *verb* **oppress**, trouble, worry, weigh down, overload, encumber, saddle, tax, afflict.

bureau *noun* **1 desk**, writing table, secretaire. **2 department**, agency, office, division, branch, section, station, unit.

bureaucracy *noun* **1 red tape**, rules and regulations, protocol, officialdom, paperwork. **2 civil service**, government, administration, establishment, system, powers that be, authorities.

bureaucrat *noun* **official**, administrator, civil servant, minister, functionary, mandarin; *derogatory* apparatchik.

burgeon *verb* **grow**, increase, rocket, mushroom, expand, escalate, swell, boom, flourish, thrive, prosper.

burglar *noun* **housebreaker**, thief, intruder, robber, raider, looter.

burglary *noun* **housebreaking**, breaking and entering, break-in, theft, raid, stealing, robbery, larceny, looting; *informal* smash-and-grab; *N. Amer. informal* heist.

burgle *verb* **rob**, loot, steal from, raid.

burial *noun* **funeral**, interment, committal, inhumation, entombment, obsequies, exequies.
- OPPOSITES exhumation.

burly *adjective* **strapping**, well built, strong, muscular, muscly, hefty, sturdy, brawny; *informal* hunky, beefy.
- OPPOSITES puny.

burn *verb* **1 be on fire**, be alight, blaze, go up (in smoke), be in flames, smoulder, glow. **2 set fire to**, set alight, set light to, kindle, ignite, touch off, incinerate, cremate; *informal* torch. **3 scorch**, singe, sear, char, blacken, brand.

burning *adjective* **1 on fire**, blazing, flaming, fiery, glowing, red-hot, smouldering. **2** *a burning desire* **intense**, passionate, deep-seated, profound, strong, ardent, fervent, urgent, fierce, consuming. **3** *burning issues* **important**, crucial, critical, vital, essential, pivotal, urgent, pressing, compelling.

burrow *noun* **warren**, tunnel, hole, dugout, lair, set, den, earth.
● *verb* **tunnel**, dig, excavate, mine, bore, channel.

burst *verb* **1** *one balloon burst* **split (open)**, rupture, break, tear. **2** *a shell burst* **explode**, blow up, detonate, go off. **3** *smoke burst through the hole* **gush**, erupt, surge, rush, stream, flow, pour, spurt, jet. **4** *he burst into the room* **charge**, plunge, barge, plough, hurtle, career, rush, dash, tear.
● *noun* **1 rupture**, puncture, breach, split, blowout. **2 explosion**, detonation, blast, eruption, bang. **3** *a burst of gunfire* **volley**, salvo, barrage, hail, rain. **4** *a burst of activity* **outbreak**, eruption, flare-up, blaze, attack, fit, rush, storm, surge, spurt.

bury *verb* **1 inter**, lay to rest, entomb. **2 hide**, conceal, cover, enfold, sink. **3** *the bullet buried itself in the wood* **embed**, sink, implant, submerge, lodge.
- OPPOSITES exhume.

bush *noun* **1 shrub**, thicket; (**bushes**) undergrowth, shrubbery. **2** *the bush* **wilds**, wilderness, backwoods; *N. Amer.* backcountry; *Austral./NZ* outback, backblocks; *N. Amer. informal* boondocks.

bushy *adjective* **thick**, shaggy, curly, fuzzy, bristly, fluffy, woolly.

business *noun* **1 work**, occupation, profession, career, employment, job, position. **2 trade**, commerce, dealing, traffic, dealings, transactions, negotiations. **3 firm**, company, concern, enterprise, venture, organization, operation, undertaking; *informal* outfit. **4** *it's none of your business* **concern**, affair, responsibility, duty. **5** *an odd business* **affair**, matter, case, circumstance, situation, event, incident.

businesslike *adjective* **professional**, efficient, organized, slick, methodical, systematic, orderly, structured, disciplined, practical, pragmatic.

businessman, **businesswoman** *noun* **executive**, entrepreneur, industrialist, merchant, dealer, trader, manufacturer, tycoon, employer, broker, buyer, seller, tradesman, retailer, supplier.

bust *noun* **1 bosom**, breasts, chest; *informal* boobs, knockers. **2 sculpture**, carving, effigy, statue, head and shoulders.

bustle *verb* **rush**, dash, hurry, scurry, scuttle, scamper, scramble; *informal* scoot, beetle, buzz.
● *noun* **activity**, action, liveliness, excitement, tumult, commotion, hubbub, hurly-burly, whirl; *informal* toing and froing.

bustling *adjective* **busy**, crowded, swarming, teeming, humming, buzzing, hectic, lively.

busy *adjective* **1** *I'm very busy* **hard at work**, involved, rushed off your feet, hard-pressed, pushed; *informal* on the go, hard at it; *Brit. informal* on the hop. **2** *I'm sorry, she's busy* **unavailable**, engaged, occupied, absorbed, engrossed, immersed, preoccupied,

working; *informal* tied up. **3** *a busy day* **hectic**, active, lively, full, eventful, energetic, tiring.
- OPPOSITES idle, free, quiet.
● *verb* **occupy**, involve, engage, concern, absorb, engross, immerse, distract.

but *conjunction* **1 however**, nevertheless, nonetheless, even so, yet, still. **2 whereas**, conversely.
● *preposition* **except (for)**, apart from, other than, besides, aside from, with the exception of, bar.
□ **but for** except for, if it were not for, notwithstanding, barring.

butt[1] *verb* **ram**, headbutt, bump, poke, prod, push, shove, thrust.
□ **butt in** interrupt, intrude, break in, cut in, interfere, put your oar in; *informal* poke your nose in; *Brit. informal* chip in.

butt[2] *noun* **target**, victim, object, dupe, laughing stock.

butt[3] *noun* **1 stock**, end, handle, hilt, haft. **2 stub**, end, stump; *informal* fag end, dog end.

buttocks *plural noun* **bottom**, rear (end), rump, seat, derrière, cheeks; *informal* behind, backside; *Brit. informal* bum; *N. Amer. informal* butt, fanny; *humorous* posterior.

buttress *verb* **strengthen**, shore up, reinforce, fortify, support, bolster, underpin, cement, uphold, defend, back up.

buy *verb* **purchase**, acquire, obtain, get, pick up, snap up, invest in; *informal* get hold of, score.
- OPPOSITES sell.
● *noun (informal)* **purchase**, deal, bargain, investment, acquisition.

buyer *noun* **purchaser**, customer, consumer, shopper, investor; (**buyers**) clientele, market.

buzz *noun* **hum**, murmur, drone, whirr.

bypass *noun* **ring road**, detour, diversion, alternative route; *Brit.* relief road.
● *verb* **1 go round**, go past, make a detour round, avoid. **2 ignore**, sidestep, avoid, evade, escape, elude, skirt, dodge, circumvent, get round, go over the head of, pass over; *informal* short-circuit, duck.

bystander *noun* **onlooker**, passer-by, observer, spectator, eyewitness.

Cc

cab *noun* **taxi**, taxi cab; *Brit.* minicab, hackney carriage; *N. Amer.* hack.

cabin *noun* **1 berth**, stateroom, compartment. **2 hut**, log cabin, shanty, shack, chalet; *Scottish* bothy; *N. Amer.* cabana.

cabinet *noun* **cupboard**, bureau, chest of drawers.

cable *noun* **1** *a thick cable moored the ship* **rope**, cord, line, guy; *Nautical* hawser. **2** *electric cables* **wire**, lead, cord, power line; *Brit.* flex.

cache *noun* **hoard**, store, stockpile, stock, supply, reserve, arsenal; *informal* stash.

cadence *noun* **rhythm**, tempo, metre, beat, pulse, intonation, modulation, lilt.

cafe *noun* **snack bar**, cafeteria, coffee bar/shop, tea room/shop, bistro, brasserie; *N. Amer.* diner, lunchroom.

cafeteria *noun* **self-service restaurant**, canteen, cafe, buffet, refectory, mess hall.

cage *noun* **enclosure**, pen, pound, coop, hutch, birdcage, aviary.
● *verb* **confine**, shut in/up, pen, coop up, enclose.

cagey *adjective (informal)* **secretive**, guarded, tight-lipped, reticent, evasive; *informal* playing your cards close to your chest.

cajole *verb* **persuade**, wheedle, coax, talk into, prevail on; *informal* sweet-talk, soft-soap.

cake *noun* **1 bun**, pastry, gateau, slice. **2 bar**, tablet, block, slab, lump, wedge.
● *verb boots caked with mud* **coat**, encrust, plaster, cover.

calamity *noun* **disaster**, catastrophe, tragedy, cataclysm, accident, misfortune, misadventure.

calculate *verb* **1 compute**, work out, reckon, figure, add up/together, count up, tally, total; *Brit.* tot up. **2 intend**, mean, design.

calculated *adjective* **deliberate**, premeditated, planned, pre-planned, preconceived, intentional, intended.
– OPPOSITES unintentional.

calculating *adjective* **cunning**, crafty, wily, sly, scheming, devious, disingenuous.

calculation *noun* **1 computation**, reckoning, adding up, counting up, working out; *Brit.* totting up. **2 assessment**, judgement, forecast, projection, prediction.

calendar *noun* **schedule**, diary, programme, timetable, agenda.

calibre *noun* **1 quality**, standard, level, merit, distinction, stature, excellence, ability, expertise, talent, capability. **2 bore**, diameter, gauge.

call *verb* **1 cry**, cry out, shout, yell, sing out, exclaim, shriek, scream, roar; *informal* holler. **2 wake (up)**, awaken, rouse; *Brit. informal* knock up. **3 phone**, telephone, give someone a call; *Brit.* ring (up), give someone a ring; *informal* call up, give someone a buzz; *Brit. informal* give someone a bell. **4 summon**, send for, order. **5 pay a visit to**, visit, call/drop/look in on, drop/stop by, pop into, nip over to. **6 convene**, summon, assemble. **7 name**, christen, baptize, designate, style, term, dub. **8 describe as**, regard as, look on as, think of as, consider to be.
● *noun* **1 cry**, shout, yell, exclamation, shriek, scream, roar; *informal* holler. **2** *the call of the barn owl* **cry**, song. **3 phone call**, telephone call; *Brit.* ring; *informal* buzz; *Brit. informal* bell. **4 appeal**, plea, request. **5** *there's no call for that kind of language* **need**, necessity, reason, justification, excuse. **6** *there's no call for expensive wine*

demand, desire, market. **7 attraction**, appeal, lure, allure, pull, draw.
□ **call for 1** require, need, necessitate, make necessary, demand, be grounds for, justify, warrant. **2** ask for, request, seek, apply for, appeal for, demand, insist on, order. **call off** cancel, abandon, scrap, drop, axe; *informal* scrub; *N. Amer. informal* redline. **call up** enlist, recruit, conscript; *US* draft.

calling *noun* **profession**, occupation, job, vocation, career, métier, work, line of work, employment, trade, craft.

callous *adjective* **heartless**, unfeeling, uncaring, cold, cold-hearted, hard, hardbitten, as hard as nails, hard-hearted, insensitive, unsympathetic.
– OPPOSITES kind, compassionate.

calm *adjective* **1 relaxed**, composed, self-possessed, serene, tranquil, unruffled, unperturbed, unflustered, untroubled, unexcitable, level-headed, unemotional, phlegmatic, imperturbable; *informal* unflappable, laid-back, chilled. **2 windless**, still, quiet, tranquil, smooth.
– OPPOSITES excited, nervous, stormy.
● *noun* **1** *his usual calm deserted him* **composure**, coolness, calmness, self-possession, sangfroid, serenity, tranquillity; *informal* cool, unflappability. **2** *calm prevailed* **tranquillity**, stillness, quiet, peace.
□ **calm down 1** soothe, pacify, placate, mollify; *Brit.* quieten (down). **2** compose yourself, regain your composure, control yourself, pull yourself together, simmer down, cool down/off, take it easy; *Brit.* quieten down; *informal* get a grip, keep your shirt on; *N. Amer. informal* decompress.

camouflage *noun* **disguise**, mask, screen, cover, cloak, front, facade, blind, concealment, subterfuge.
● *verb* **disguise**, hide, conceal, mask, screen, cover (up).

camp *noun* **1 campsite**, encampment, camping ground, bivouac, base, settlement. **2 faction**, wing, group, lobby, caucus, bloc.

campaign *noun* **1** *Napoleon's Russian campaign* **operation(s)**, manoeuvre(s), offensive, attack, war, battle, crusade. **2** *the campaign to reduce vehicle emissions* **effort**, drive, push, struggle, movement, crusade, operation, strategy.
● *verb* **fight**, battle, push, press, strive, struggle, lobby, agitate.

cancel *verb* **1 call off**, abandon, scrap, drop, axe; *informal* scrub; *N. Amer. informal* redline. **2 annul**, invalidate, declare null and void, void, revoke, rescind, retract, withdraw.
□ **cancel out** neutralize, negate, nullify, wipe out, balance (out), make up for, compensate for, offset.

cancer *noun* **(malignant) growth**, tumour, malignancy; *technical* carcinoma, sarcoma.

WORD LINKS
carcinogenic causing cancer
oncology branch of medicine concerned with cancer

candid *adjective* **frank**, forthright, direct, blunt, outspoken, plain-spoken, open, honest, truthful, sincere; *informal* upfront; *N. Amer. informal* on the up and up.
– OPPOSITES guarded.

candidate *noun* **applicant**, contender, competitor, entrant, claimant, nominee, interviewee, examinee, possible; *Brit. informal* runner.

canny *adjective* **shrewd**, astute, smart, sharp, discerning, discriminating, perceptive, clever, judicious, wise.
– OPPOSITES foolish.

canopy *noun* **awning**, shade, sunshade, covering.

canvass *verb* **1 campaign**, electioneer. **2 poll**, question, survey, interview, consult.

canyon *noun* **ravine**, gorge, gully, chasm, abyss, gulf; *N. Amer.* gulch, coulee.

cap *noun* **1 lid**, top, stopper, cork, bung; *N. Amer.* stopple. **2 limit**, ceiling, curb, check.

● *verb* **1 top**, crown, cover, coat, tip. **2 limit**, restrict, curb, control, peg.

capability *noun* **ability**, capacity, power, potential, competence, aptitude, faculty, skill, talent, flair; *informal* know-how.
- OPPOSITES inability.

capable *adjective* **able**, competent, effective, proficient, accomplished, experienced, skilful, talented, gifted; *informal* useful.
- OPPOSITES incapable, incompetent.

capacity *noun* **1 volume**, size, dimensions, measurements, proportions. **2 ability**, capability, power, potential, competence, aptitude, faculty, skill, talent, flair. **3 role**, function, position, post, job, office.

cape[1] *noun* **cloak**, mantle, shawl, poncho, pashmina.

cape[2] *noun* **headland**, promontory, point, head, horn, mull, peninsula.

capital *noun* **money**, finance(s), funds, cash, wherewithal, means, assets, wealth, resources, deep pockets.

capitalism *noun* **private enterprise**, free enterprise, the free market, private ownership.
- OPPOSITES communism.

capitalize *verb*
□ **capitalize on** take advantage of, profit from, make the most of, exploit, develop; *informal* cash in on.

capitulate *verb* **surrender**, give in, yield, concede defeat, give up (the struggle), submit, lay down your arms, throw in the towel/sponge.
- OPPOSITES resist.

capricious *adjective* **fickle**, volatile, unpredictable, temperamental, mercurial, impulsive, changeable, unreliable, erratic, wayward, whimsical, flighty.
- OPPOSITES consistent.

capsize *verb* **overturn**, turn over, turn upside down, upend, flip/tip over, keel over, turn turtle.

capsule *noun* **1 pill**, tablet, lozenge, pastille; *informal* tab. **2 module**, craft, probe.

captain *noun* **1** *the ship's captain* **commander**, master; *informal* skipper. **2** *the team captain* **leader**, head, chief; *informal* boss, skipper.

caption *noun* **title**, heading, legend, description.

captivate *verb* **enthral**, charm, enchant, bewitch, fascinate, beguile, entrance, delight, attract, allure.
- OPPOSITES bore.

captive *noun* **prisoner**, convict, detainee, hostage, prisoner of war, internee.
● *adjective* **confined**, caged, incarcerated, locked up, jailed, imprisoned, interned, detained.
- OPPOSITES free.

captivity *noun* **imprisonment**, incarceration, confinement, detention, internment.
- OPPOSITES freedom.

capture *verb* **1 catch**, apprehend, seize, arrest, take prisoner, take into custody, detain. **2 occupy**, invade, conquer, seize, take.
- OPPOSITES release, liberate.
● *noun* **arrest**, apprehension, detention, seizure.

car *noun* **1 motor**, motor car, automobile; *informal* wheels; *N. Amer. informal* auto. **2 carriage**, coach; *Brit.* saloon.

carcass *noun* **corpse**, dead body, remains; *Medicine* cadaver; *informal* stiff.

care *noun* **1 safe keeping**, supervision, custody, charge, protection, responsibility, guardianship. **2 discretion**, caution, sensitivity, thought, regard, consideration. **3 worry**, anxiety, trouble, concern, stress, pressure, strain.
- OPPOSITES neglect, carelessness.
● *verb* **be concerned**, worry (yourself), trouble/concern yourself, bother, mind, be interested; *informal* give a damn/hoot.
□ **care for 1** love, be fond of, be devoted to, treasure, adore, dote on, think the world of, worship. **2** look after, take care of, tend, attend to, minister to, nurse.

career *noun* **profession**, occupation, vocation, calling, life's work, employment.
● *verb* **hurtle**, rush, shoot, race, speed, charge, hare, fly; *informal* belt, tear; *Brit. informal* bucket.

carefree *adjective* **unworried**, untroubled, blithe, nonchalant, happy-go-lucky, free and easy, easy-going, relaxed; *informal* laid-back.
– OPPOSITES troubled.

careful *adjective* **1** *be careful on the stairs* **cautious**, alert, attentive, watchful, vigilant, wary, on your guard, circumspect. **2** *careful with money* **prudent**, thrifty, economical, sparing, frugal. **3** *careful consideration of the facts* **attentive**, conscientious, painstaking, meticulous, diligent, assiduous, scrupulous, methodical.
– OPPOSITES careless.

careless *adjective* **1** *careless motorists* **inattentive**, negligent, heedless, irresponsible, impetuous, reckless. **2** *careless work* **shoddy**, slapdash, slipshod, scrappy, slovenly, sloppy, negligent, lax, slack, disorganized, hasty, hurried. **3** *a careless remark* **thoughtless**, insensitive, indiscreet, unguarded, incautious, inadvertent.
– OPPOSITES careful.

caress *verb* **stroke**, touch, fondle, brush, feel, skim.

caretaker *noun* **janitor**, attendant, porter, custodian, concierge; *N. Amer.* superintendent.
● *adjective* **temporary**, acting, provisional, substitute, interim, stand-in, fill-in, stopgap; *N. Amer. informal* pinch-hitting.

cargo *noun* **freight**, load, haul, consignment, delivery, shipment, goods, merchandise.

caricature *noun* **cartoon**, parody, satire, lampoon, burlesque; *informal* send-up, take-off.
● *verb* **parody**, satirize, lampoon, make fun of, mock, ridicule; *informal* send up, take off.

carnage *noun* **slaughter**, massacre, murder, butchery, bloodbath, bloodletting, holocaust.

carnival *noun* **festival**, fiesta, fete, fair, gala, Mardi Gras.

carp *verb* **complain**, find fault, quibble, grumble, grouse, whine; *informal* nit-pick, gripe, moan, bitch, whinge.

carpenter *noun* **woodworker**, joiner, cabinetmaker; *Brit. informal* chippy.

carriage *noun* **1** *a railway carriage* **coach**, car; *Brit.* saloon. **2** *a horse and carriage* **wagon**, coach. **3 posture**, bearing, gait; *Brit.* deportment.

carry *verb* **1 convey**, transfer, transport, move, take, bring, bear, fetch; *informal* cart, hump, lug. **2 transmit**, conduct, relay, communicate, convey, beam, send. **3 approve**, pass, accept, endorse, ratify. **4 be audible**, travel, reach, be heard.
□ **carry on** continue, keep (on), go on, persist in; *informal* stick with/at. **carry out 1** conduct, perform, execute, implement. **2** keep, honour, fulfil, observe, abide by, comply with, adhere to, stick to.

carton *noun* **box**, package, cardboard box, case, container, pack, packet.

cartoon *noun* **1 animation**, animated film, comic strip, graphic novel. **2 caricature**, parody, lampoon, satire; *informal* take-off, send-up.

cartridge *noun* **cassette**, magazine, canister, case, container.

carve *verb* **1 sculpt**, cut, hew, whittle, chisel, shape, fashion. **2 engrave**, incise, score, cut. **3 slice**, cut up, chop.
□ **carve up** divide, break up, partition, apportion, subdivide, split up, share out.

cascade *noun* **waterfall**, cataract, falls, rapids, white water, flood, torrent.
● *verb* **pour**, gush, surge, spill, stream, flow, issue, spurt, jet.

case[1] *noun* **1** *a classic case of overreaction* **instance**, example, occurrence, occasion, demonstration, illustration. **2** *is that the case?* **situation**, position, state of affairs, circumstances, conditions, facts; *Brit.* state of play; *informal* score. **3 assignment**, job, project, investigation, exercise. **4** *he lost his case* **lawsuit**, legal action, trial, legal proceedings, litigation. **5** *the case against animal testing* **argument**, defence, justification, vindication, exposition, thesis.

case[2] *noun* **1 container**, box, canister, holder. **2 casing**, cover, sheath, envelope, sleeve, jacket, shell. **3** *(Brit.)* **suitcase**, travel bag, valise; (**cases**) luggage, baggage. **4 cabinet**, cupboard.

cash *noun* **1 money**, currency, bank notes, coins, change; *N. Amer.* bills; *informal* dough, loot; *Brit. informal* dosh, brass; *N. Amer. informal* dinero. **2 finance**, money, resources, funds, assets, means, wherewithal.

cashier *noun* **clerk**, teller, banker, treasurer, bursar, purser.

cask *noun* **barrel**, keg, butt, tun, vat, drum, hogshead; *historical* firkin.

cast *verb* **1 throw**, toss, fling, pitch, hurl, lob; *informal* chuck, sling, bung. **2 direct**, shoot, throw, fling, send. **3 register**, record, enter, file. **4 emit**, give off, throw, send out, radiate. **5 mould**, fashion, form, shape, forge.
● *noun* **1 mould**, die, matrix, shape, casting, model. **2 actors**, performers, players, company, troupe, dramatis personae, characters.

caste *noun* **class**, rank, level, order, stratum, echelon, status.

castle *noun* **fortress**, fort, stronghold, fortification, keep, citadel, palace, chateau, tower.

casual *adjective* **1** *a casual attitude* **unconcerned**, uncaring, indifferent, lackadaisical, nonchalant, offhand, flippant, easy-going, free and easy, blithe, carefree, devil-may-care; *informal* laid-back. **2** *a casual remark* **offhand**, spontaneous, unthinking, unconsidered, impromptu, throwaway, unguarded; *informal* off-the-cuff. **3** *a casual glance* **cursory**, perfunctory, superficial, passing, fleeting. **4** *casual work* **temporary**, freelance, irregular, occasional. **5** *a casual meeting* **chance**, accidental, unplanned, unintended, unexpected, unforeseen. **6** *a casual atmosphere* **relaxed**, friendly, informal, easy-going, free and easy; *informal* laid-back.
– OPPOSITES serious, deliberate, formal.

casualty *noun* **victim**, sufferer, fatality, death, loss, wounded person, injured person.

cat *noun* **feline**, tomcat, tom, kitten; *informal* pussy (cat), puss, kitty; *Brit. informal* moggie, mog.

> WORD LINKS
> **feline** relating to cats

catalogue *noun* **directory**, register, index, list, listing, record, schedule, archive, inventory.
● *verb* **classify**, categorize, index, list, archive, record, itemize.

catastrophe *noun* **disaster**, calamity, cataclysm, ruin, tragedy, fiasco, debacle.

catch *verb* **1 seize**, grab, snatch, grasp, grip, clutch, intercept, trap, receive, get. **2 capture**, apprehend, seize, arrest, take prisoner, trap, snare, net; *informal* nab, collar; *Brit. informal* nick. **3 become trapped**, become entangled, snag, jam, wedge, lodge, get stuck. **4 discover**, find, come across, stumble on, chance on, surprise. **5 contract**, go/come down with, be taken ill with, develop, pick up, succumb to.
– OPPOSITES drop, release.
● *noun* **1 haul**, net, bag, yield. **2 latch**, lock, fastener, clasp, hasp. **3 snag**, disadvantage, drawback, stumbling block, hitch, complication, problem, trap, trick.
□ **catch on** *(informal)* **1** become popular, take off, boom, flourish, thrive. **2** understand, comprehend, learn, see the light; *informal* cotton on, latch on.

catching *adjective (informal)* **infectious**, contagious, communicable; *dated* infective.

catchy *adjective* **memorable**, unforgettable, haunting, appealing, popular.
– OPPOSITES forgettable.

categorical *adjective* **unqualified**, unconditional, unequivocal, absolute, explicit, unambiguous, definite, direct, emphatic, positive, out-and-out.

category *noun* **class**, classification, group, grouping, bracket, heading, set, type, sort, kind, grade, order, rank.

cater *verb*
□ **cater for 1** provide (food) for, feed, serve, cook for. **2** *a resort catering for older holidaymakers* serve, provide for, meet the needs/wants of, accommodate. **3** *we cater for all tastes* take into account, take into consideration, allow for, consider, bear in mind, make provision for, have regard for.

cattle *plural noun* **cows**, oxen, herd, livestock.

WORD LINKS
bovine relating to cattle

cause *noun* **1** *the cause of the fire* **source**, root, origin, beginning(s), starting point, originator, author, creator, agent. **2** *there is no cause for alarm* **reason**, grounds, justification, call, need, necessity, occasion, excuse. **3** *raising money for good causes* **principle**, ideal, belief, conviction, object, aim, objective, purpose, charity.
● *verb* **bring about**, give rise to, lead to, result in, create, produce, generate, engender, spawn, bring on, precipitate, prompt, provoke, trigger, make happen, induce, inspire, promote, foster.

caustic *adjective* **1 corrosive**, acid, burning. **2 sarcastic**, cutting, biting, mordant, sharp, scathing, sardonic, scornful, trenchant, acerbic, vitriolic.

caution *noun* **1 care**, attention, alertness, circumspection, discretion, prudence. **2 warning**, admonishment, injunction, reprimand, rebuke; *informal* telling-off, dressing-down; *Brit. informal* ticking-off.
● *verb* **1** *advisers cautioned against tax increases* **advise**, warn, counsel, urge. **2** *he was cautioned by the police* **warn**, admonish, reprimand; *informal* tell off; *Brit. informal* tick off.

cautious *adjective* **careful**, attentive, alert, judicious, circumspect, prudent, tentative, guarded.
– OPPOSITES reckless.

cave *noun* **cavern**, grotto, pothole, chamber, gallery, hollow.

WORD LINKS
speleology, **potholing** exploration of caves
spelunking (N. Amer.)

cavity *noun* **space**, chamber, hollow, hole, pocket, gap, crater, pit.

cease *verb* **stop**, come/bring to an end, come/bring to a halt, end, halt, conclude, terminate, finish, wind up, discontinue, suspend, break off.
– OPPOSITES start, continue.

ceaseless *adjective* **continual**, constant, continuous, incessant, unending, endless, never-ending, interminable, non-stop, unremitting, relentless, unrelenting, sustained, persistent, eternal, perpetual.
– OPPOSITES intermittent.

celebrate *verb* **1 commemorate**, observe, mark, keep, honour, remember. **2 enjoy yourself**, make merry, have fun, have a good time, have a party; *N. Amer.* step out; *informal* party, whoop it up, have a ball. **3 perform**, observe, officiate at, preside at.

celebrated *adjective* **acclaimed**, admired, highly rated, esteemed, exalted, vaunted, eminent, great, distinguished, prestigious, illustrious, notable.
– OPPOSITES unsung.

celebration *noun* **1 commemoration**, observance, marking, keeping. **2 merrymaking**, jollification, revelry, revels, festivities; *informal* partying. **3 party**, function, gathering, festivities, festival, fete, carnival, jamboree; *informal* do, bash, rave; *Brit. informal* rave-up. **4 performance**, observance, officiation, solemnization.

celebrity *noun* **1 fame**, prominence, renown, stardom, popularity, distinction, prestige, stature, repute,

reputation. **2 famous person**, VIP, personality, big name, household name, star, superstar; *informal* celeb, megastar.
- OPPOSITES obscurity.

celestial *adjective* **1 (in) space**, heavenly, astronomical, extraterrestrial, stellar, planetary. **2 heavenly**, holy, saintly, divine, godly, godlike, ethereal, angelic.

celibate *adjective* **unmarried**, single, chaste, pure, virginal.

cell *noun* **1 room**, cubicle, chamber, dungeon, compartment, lock-up. **2 unit**, squad, detachment, group.

cellar *noun* **basement**, vault, crypt.

cement *noun* **adhesive**, glue, fixative, gum, paste.

cemetery *noun* **graveyard**, churchyard, burial ground, necropolis, garden of remembrance, mass grave; *Scottish* kirkyard.

censor *verb* **cut**, edit, expurgate, redact, sanitize, clean up, ban, delete.

censorious *adjective* **critical**, overcritical, hypercritical, disapproving, condemnatory, judgemental, moralistic, fault-finding, reproachful.

censure *verb* **condemn**, criticize, attack, reprimand, rebuke, admonish, upbraid, reproach.
- OPPOSITES defend, praise.
● *noun* **condemnation**, criticism, attack, reprimand, rebuke, admonishment, reproof, disapproval, reproach.
- OPPOSITES approval, praise.

central *adjective* **1** *a central position* **middle**, centre, halfway, midway, mid. **2** *central London* **inner**, innermost, middle, mid. **3 main**, chief, principal, primary, foremost, key, crucial, vital, essential, basic, fundamental, core; *informal* number-one.
- OPPOSITES side, outer.

centralize *verb* **concentrate**, consolidate, amalgamate, condense, unify, focus.
- OPPOSITES devolve.

centre *noun* **middle**, nucleus, heart, core, hub.
- OPPOSITES edge.
● *verb the story centres on a doctor* **focus**, concentrate, pivot, revolve, be based.

ceremonial *adjective* **formal**, official, state, public, ritual, ritualistic, stately, solemn.
- OPPOSITES informal.

ceremony *noun* **1 rite**, ritual, observance, service, event, function. **2 pomp**, protocol, formality, formalities, niceties, decorum, etiquette, pageantry, ceremonial.

certain *adjective* **1** *I'm certain he's guilty* **sure**, confident, positive, convinced, in no doubt, satisfied. **2** *it is certain that more changes are in the offing* **unquestionable**, sure, definite, beyond question, indubitable, undeniable, indisputable. **3** *they are certain to win* **sure**, bound, destined. **4** *certain defeat* **inevitable**, assured, unavoidable, inescapable, inexorable. **5** *there is no certain cure* **reliable**, dependable, foolproof, guaranteed, sure, infallible; *informal* sure-fire.
- OPPOSITES doubtful, unlikely, possible.

certainly *adverb* **definitely**, surely, assuredly, unquestionably, beyond/without question, undoubtedly, without doubt, indubitably, undeniably, irrefutably, indisputably.

certainty *noun* **1 confidence**, sureness, conviction, assurance. **2 inevitability**, foregone conclusion; *informal* sure thing; *Brit. informal* (dead) cert.
- OPPOSITES doubt, possibility.

certificate *noun* **guarantee**, document, authorization, authentication, accreditation, credentials, testimonial.

certify *verb* **1 verify**, guarantee, attest, validate, confirm, endorse. **2 accredit**, recognize, license, authorize, approve.

cessation *noun* **end**, termination, halt, finish, stoppage, conclusion, winding up, pause, suspension.
- OPPOSITES start, resumption.

chain *noun* **1 fetters**, shackles, irons, manacles, handcuffs; *informal* cuffs, bracelets. **2 series**, succession, string, sequence, train, course.
● *verb* **secure**, fasten, tie, tether, hitch, restrain, shackle, fetter, manacle, handcuff.

chairman, **chairwoman** *noun* **chair**, chairperson, president, chief executive, leader, master of ceremonies, MC.

challenge *noun* **1 dare**, provocation, offer. **2 problem**, difficult task, test, trial.
● *verb* **1 question**, dispute, take issue with, call into question, protest against, oppose. **2 dare**, defy, invite, throw down the gauntlet to. **3 test**, tax, strain, make demands on, stretch.

challenging *adjective* **demanding**, testing, taxing, exacting, hard, difficult, stimulating.
- OPPOSITES easy.

champion *noun* **1 winner**, title-holder, gold medallist, prizewinner; *informal* champ, number one. **2 advocate**, proponent, promoter, supporter, defender, upholder, backer; *N. Amer.* booster.
● *verb* **advocate**, promote, defend, uphold, support, espouse, stand up for, campaign for, lobby for, fight for.
- OPPOSITES oppose.

chance *noun* **1 possibility**, prospect, probability, likelihood, risk, threat, danger. **2** *I gave her a chance to answer* **opportunity**, opening, occasion, window; *N. Amer. & Austral./NZ* show; *Brit. informal* look-in. **3** *he took an awful chance* **risk**, gamble, leap in the dark. **4 coincidence**, accident, fate, destiny, providence, happenstance, good fortune, luck, fluke.
- OPPOSITES certainty.
● *adjective* **accidental**, fortuitous, fluky, coincidental.
□ **by chance** by accident, fortuitously, accidentally, coincidentally, unintentionally, inadvertently.

change *verb* **1 alter**, make/become different, adjust, adapt, amend, modify, revise, vary, transform, metamorphose, evolve. **2 exchange**, substitute, swap, switch, replace, alternate.
● *noun* **1 alteration**, modification, variation, revision, amendment, adjustment, adaptation, metamorphosis, transformation, evolution. **2 replacement**, exchange, substitution, swap, switch.

changeable *adjective* **variable**, varying, changing, fluctuating, irregular, erratic, inconsistent, unstable, unsettled, inconstant, fickle, capricious, temperamental, volatile, mercurial, unpredictable.
- OPPOSITES constant.

channel *noun* **1 strait(s)**, sound, narrows, passage. **2 duct**, gutter, conduit, trough, sluice, drain. **3 means**, medium, instrument, mechanism, agency, vehicle, route, avenue.
● *verb* **convey**, transmit, conduct, direct, relay, pass on, transfer.

chant *noun* **shout**, cry, call, slogan, chorus, refrain.
● *verb* **shout**, chorus, repeat, call.

chaos *noun* **disorder**, disorganization, confusion, mayhem, bedlam, pandemonium, havoc, turmoil, anarchy, lawlessness; *Brit.* a shambles; *informal* all hell broken loose; *Brit. informal* an omnishambles.
- OPPOSITES order.

chaotic *adjective* **disorderly**, disorganized, in confusion, in turmoil, topsy-turvy, anarchic, lawless; *Brit. informal* shambolic.

chap *noun (Brit.)* **man**, boy, individual, character; *informal* fellow, guy, geezer; *Brit. informal* bloke, lad; *N. Amer. informal* dude, hombre.

chapter *noun* **1 section**, part, division, topic, stage, episode. **2 period**, phase, page, stage, epoch, era.

character *noun* **1 personality**, nature, quality, disposition, temperament, mentality, make-up, spirit, identity, tone, feel. **2 integrity**, honour, moral strength/fibre, strength, backbone, resolve, grit, will power; *informal* guts; *Brit. informal* bottle. **3 reputation**, (good) name, standing, position, status. **4 eccentric**, oddity, crank, original, individualist, madcap, nonconformist; *informal* oddball. **5 person**, man, woman, soul, creature, individual, customer; *informal* cookie; *Brit. informal* bod, guy. **6 letter**, figure, symbol, mark, device, sign, hieroglyph.

characteristic *noun* **attribute**, feature, quality, property, trait, aspect, idiosyncrasy, peculiarity, quirk.
● *adjective* **typical**, usual, normal, distinctive, representative, particular, special, peculiar, idiosyncratic.
- OPPOSITES abnormal.

characterize *verb* **1 distinguish**, mark, typify, set apart. **2 portray**, depict, present, represent, describe, categorize, class, brand.

charade *noun* **pretence**, act, masquerade, show, facade, pantomime, farce, travesty, mockery, parody.

charge *verb* **1 ask**, demand, bill, invoice. **2 accuse**, indict, arraign, prosecute, try, put on trial; *N. Amer.* impeach. **3 entrust**, burden, encumber, saddle, tax. **4 attack**, storm, assault, assail, descend on; *informal* lay into, tear into. **5 rush**, storm, stampede, push, plough, launch yourself, go headlong; *informal* steam; *N. Amer. informal* barrel. **6** *charge your glasses!* **fill (up)**, top up, load (up), arm.
● *noun* **1 fee**, payment, price, rate, tariff, fare, levy. **2 accusation**, allegation, indictment, arraignment; *N. Amer.* impeachment. **3 attack**, assault, offensive, onslaught, drive, push. **4** *the child was in her charge* **care**, protection, safe keeping, control, custody, hands.

charisma *noun* **charm**, presence, (force of) personality, strength of character, (animal) magnetism, appeal, allure.

charismatic *adjective* **charming**, magnetic, compelling, inspiring, captivating, mesmerizing, appealing, alluring, glamorous.

charitable *adjective* **1 philanthropic**, generous, open-handed, giving, munificent, benevolent, altruistic, unselfish, public-spirited, humanitarian, non-profit-making. **2 magnanimous**, generous, liberal, tolerant, sympathetic, understanding, lenient, indulgent, forgiving.
- OPPOSITES commercial, mean.

charity *noun* **1 voluntary organization**, charitable institution, fund, trust, foundation. **2 aid**, financial assistance, welfare, relief, donations, handouts, gifts, largesse; *historical* alms. **3 philanthropy**, humanitarianism, altruism, public-spiritedness, social conscience, benevolence. **4 goodwill**, compassion, consideration, concern, kindness, sympathy, indulgence, tolerance, leniency.

charm *noun* **1 appeal**, attraction, fascination, beauty, loveliness, allure, seductiveness, magnetism, charisma; *informal* pulling power. **2 spell**, incantation, formula; *N. Amer.* mojo, hex. **3 talisman**, trinket, amulet, mascot, fetish.
● *verb* **1 delight**, please, win (over), attract, captivate, lure, fascinate, enchant, beguile. **2 coax**, cajole, wheedle; *informal* sweet-talk, soft-soap.

charming *adjective* **delightful**, pleasing, endearing, lovely, adorable, appealing, attractive, good-looking, alluring, winning, fetching, captivating, enchanting, entrancing.

chart *noun* **graph**, table, diagram, plan, map; *Computing* graphic.
● *verb* **1 plot**, tabulate, graph, record, register, represent. **2 follow**, trace, outline, describe, detail, record, document.

charter *noun* **1** *a Royal charter* **authority**, authorization, sanction, dispensation, permit, licence, warrant. **2** *the UN Charter* **constitution**, code, principles.
● *verb* **hire**, lease, rent, book.

chase *verb* **1 pursue**, run after, follow, hunt, track, trail; *informal* tail. **2** *she chased away the dogs* **drive**, send, scare; *informal* send packing. **3** *she chased away all thoughts of him* **dispel**, banish, dismiss, drive away, shut out, put out of your mind.

● *noun* **pursuit**, hunt, trail.

chat *noun* **talk**, conversation, gossip; *informal* jaw, gas, confab; *Brit. informal* natter, chinwag; *Austral. informal* convo.
● *verb* **talk**, gossip; *informal* gas, jaw, chew the rag/fat; *Brit. informal* natter, have a chinwag; *N. Amer. informal* shoot the breeze/bull.

chatter *verb* **prattle**, chat, gossip, jabber, babble; *informal* yatter; *Brit. informal* natter, chunter, rabbit on.
● *noun* **prattle**, chat, gossip, patter, jabber, babble; *informal* chit-chat, yattering; *Brit. informal* nattering, chuntering, rabbiting on.

chatty *adjective* **talkative**, communicative, effusive, gossipy, loquacious, voluble; *informal* mouthy, gabby.
– OPPOSITES taciturn.

cheap *adjective* **1 inexpensive**, low-priced, low-cost, economical, competitive, affordable, reasonable, budget, economy, bargain, cut-price, reduced, discounted; *informal* dirt cheap. **2 poor-quality**, second-rate, substandard, inferior, vulgar, shoddy, trashy, tawdry; *informal* tacky; *Brit. informal* naff. **3 despicable**, contemptible, immoral, unscrupulous, unprincipled, cynical.
– OPPOSITES expensive.

cheat *verb* **swindle**, defraud, deceive, trick, dupe, hoodwink, double-cross, gull; *informal* rip off, diddle, con, pull a fast one on; *N. Amer. informal* sucker.
● *noun* **swindler**, fraudster, confidence trickster, double-dealer, double-crosser, fraud, fake, charlatan; *informal* con artist.

check *verb* **1 examine**, inspect, look at/over, scrutinize, study, investigate, probe, look into, enquire into; *informal* check out, give something a/the once-over. **2 make sure**, confirm, verify. **3 halt**, stop, arrest, bar, obstruct, foil, thwart, curb, block.
● *noun* **1 examination**, inspection, scrutiny, perusal, study, investigation, test, check-up; *informal* once-over. **2 control**, restraint, constraint, curb, limitation.
□ **check in** register, book in, report.
check out pay the bill, settle up, leave.

cheek *noun* **impudence**, impertinence, insolence, rudeness, disrespect; *informal* brass neck, lip, mouth, chutzpah; *Brit. informal* backchat; *N. Amer. informal* sass, back talk.

cheeky *adjective* **impudent**, impertinent, insolent, rude, disrespectful; *informal* brass-necked, lippy, mouthy, fresh; *N. Amer. informal* sassy, nervy.
– OPPOSITES respectful, polite.

cheer *verb* **1 applaud**, hail, salute, shout for, clap, put your hands together for, bring the house down; *informal* holler for, give someone a big hand; *N. Amer. informal* ballyhoo. **2 please**, raise/lift someone's spirits, brighten, buoy up, hearten, gladden, perk up, encourage; *informal* buck up.
– OPPOSITES boo, depress.
● *noun* **hurrah**, hurray, whoop, bravo, shout; (**cheers**) acclaim, applause, ovation.
– OPPOSITES boo.
□ **cheer up** perk up, brighten up, rally, revive, bounce back, take heart; *informal* buck up.

cheerful *adjective* **1 happy**, jolly, merry, bright, sunny, joyful, in good/high spirits, buoyant, cheery, animated, smiling, good-humoured; *informal* chipper, chirpy, full of beans. **2 pleasant**, attractive, agreeable, bright, sunny, friendly, welcoming.
– OPPOSITES sad, gloomy.

cheerless *adjective* **gloomy**, dreary, dull, dismal, bleak, drab, sombre, dark, dim, dingy, funereal, austere, stark, unwelcoming, uninviting, depressing.

chemist *noun* **pharmacist**, dispenser; *N. Amer.* druggist; *old use* apothecary.

cherish *verb* **1 adore**, love, dote on, be devoted to, revere, think the world of, care for, look after, protect, keep safe. **2 treasure**, prize, hold dear. **3 harbour**, entertain, nurse, cling to, foster.
– OPPOSITES hate.

chest *noun* **1 breast**, upper body, torso, trunk, front. **2 box**, case, casket, crate, trunk, coffer, strongbox.

> WORD LINKS
> **pectoral**, **thoracic** relating to the chest

chew *verb* **munch**, champ, chomp, crunch, gnaw, bite, masticate.

chic *adjective* **stylish**, smart, elegant, sophisticated, fashionable; *informal* trendy; *Brit. informal* swish; *N. Amer. informal* kicky, tony.
- OPPOSITES unfashionable.

chief *noun* **1** *a Highland chief* **leader**, chieftain, head, ruler, master, commander. **2** *the chief of the central bank* **head**, chief executive, chief executive officer, CEO, president, chairman, chairwoman, principal, governor, director, manager; *informal* boss, (head) honcho; *Brit. informal* gaffer, guv'nor.
● *adjective* **1 head**, leading, principal, premier, highest, supreme, arch. **2 main**, principal, primary, prime, first, cardinal, central, key, crucial, essential; *informal* number-one.
- OPPOSITES subordinate, minor.

chiefly *adverb* **mainly**, in the main, primarily, principally, predominantly, mostly, for the most part, usually, typically, commonly, generally, on the whole, largely.

child *noun* **youngster**, baby, infant, toddler, minor, juvenile, junior, descendant; *Scottish & N. English* bairn; *informal* kid, kiddie, nipper, tiny, tot; *derogatory* brat.

> WORD LINKS
> **paediatrics** branch of medicine concerned with children

childbirth *noun* **labour**, delivery, birthing; *old use* confinement.

childhood *noun* **youth**, early years/life, infancy, babyhood, boyhood, girlhood, minority.
- OPPOSITES adulthood.

childish *adjective* **immature**, babyish, infantile, juvenile, puerile, silly.
- OPPOSITES mature.

childlike *adjective* **youthful**, innocent, unsophisticated, naive, trusting, artless, unaffected, uninhibited, natural, spontaneous.
- OPPOSITES adult.

chill *noun* **1 coldness**, chilliness, coolness, nip. **2 cold**, dose of flu, fever. **3 shiver**, frisson.
- OPPOSITES warmth.
● *verb* **scare**, frighten, petrify, terrify, alarm, make someone's blood run cold; *informal* scare the pants off; *Brit. informal* put the wind up.
- OPPOSITES warm.
● *adjective* **cold**, chilly, cool, fresh, wintry, frosty, icy, arctic, bitter, freezing; *informal* nippy; *Brit. informal* parky.

chilly *adjective* **1 cold**, cool, crisp, fresh, wintry, frosty, icy; *informal* nippy; *Brit. informal* parky. **2 unfriendly**, unwelcoming, cold, cool, frosty; *informal* stand-offish.
- OPPOSITES warm.

china *noun* **crockery**, dishes, plates, cups and saucers, tableware, porcelain, dinnerware, dinner service, tea service.

chink *noun* **gap**, crack, space, hole, aperture, fissure, cranny, cleft, split, slit.

chip *noun* **1 fragment**, sliver, splinter, shaving, shard, flake. **2 nick**, crack, scratch. **3 counter**, token; *N. Amer.* check.
● *verb* **1 nick**, crack, scratch. **2** *chip off the old plaster* **cut**, hack, chisel, carve, hew, whittle.

chivalrous *adjective* **gallant**, gentlemanly, honourable, respectful, considerate, courteous, polite, gracious, well mannered.
- OPPOSITES rude.

choice *noun* **1** *freedom of choice* **selection**, choosing, picking, pick, preference, decision, say, vote. **2** *you have no other choice* **option**, alternative, course of action. **3** *an extensive choice* **range**, variety, selection, assortment.
● *adjective* **superior**, first-class, first-rate, prime, premier, grade A, best, finest, select, quality, top, top-quality,

high-grade, prize; *informal* A1, top-notch.
- OPPOSITES inferior.

choke *verb* **1 gag**, retch, cough, fight for breath. **2 suffocate**, asphyxiate, smother, stifle, strangle, throttle; *informal* strangulate. **3 clog (up)**, bung up, stop up, block, obstruct.

choose *verb* **1 select**, pick (out), opt for, plump for, settle on, prefer, decide on, fix on, elect, adopt. **2 wish**, want, desire, please, like.

choosy *adjective (informal)* **fussy**, finicky, fastidious, over-particular, hard to please; *informal* picky, pernickety; *N. Amer. informal* persnickety.

chop *verb* **cut (up)**, cube, dice, hew, split, fell; *N. Amer.* hash.
□ **chop off** cut off, sever, lop, shear.

choppy *adjective* **rough**, turbulent, heavy, heaving, stormy, tempestuous, squally.
- OPPOSITES calm.

chore *noun* **task**, job, duty, errand, burden; *informal* hassle.

christen *verb* **1** *she was christened Sara* **baptize**, name, give the name of, call. **2** *a group christened 'The Magic Circle'* **call**, name, dub, style, term, label, nickname.

chronic *adjective* **1** *a chronic illness* **persistent**, long-standing, long-term, incurable. **2** *chronic economic problems* **constant**, continuing, persistent, long-lasting, severe, serious, acute, grave, dire. **3** *a chronic liar* **inveterate**, hardened, dyed-in-the-wool, incorrigible, compulsive; *informal* pathological.
- OPPOSITES acute, temporary.

chronicle *noun* **record**, account, history, annals, archive(s), log, diary, journal.
● *verb* **record**, write down, set down, document, report.

chubby *adjective* **plump**, tubby, flabby, rotund, portly, chunky; *Brit. informal* podgy; *N. Amer. informal* zaftig, corn-fed.
- OPPOSITES skinny.

chuck *verb (informal)* **1 throw**, toss, fling, hurl, pitch, cast, lob; *informal* sling, bung. **2 throw away**, throw out, discard, dispose of, get rid of, dump, bin, jettison; *informal* ditch, junk; *N. Amer. informal* trash. **3 give up**, leave, resign from; *informal* quit, pack in; *Brit. informal* jack in. **4 jilt**, finish with, break off with, leave; *informal* dump, ditch, give someone the elbow; *Brit. informal* give someone the push.

chuckle *verb* **laugh**, chortle, giggle, titter, snigger.

chum *noun (informal)* **friend**, companion, playmate, classmate, schoolmate, workmate; *informal* pal, crony; *Brit. informal* mate; *N. Amer. informal* buddy.
- OPPOSITES enemy.

chunk *noun* **lump**, hunk, wedge, block, slab, square, nugget, brick, cube; *informal* wodge; *N. Amer. informal* gob.

churlish *adjective* **rude**, ill-mannered, discourteous, ungracious, impolite, inconsiderate, surly, sullen.
- OPPOSITES polite.

churn *verb* **disturb**, stir up, agitate, beat.

cinema *noun* **1 the movies**, the pictures, multiplex; *informal* the flicks. **2** *British cinema* **films**, film, movies, pictures, motion pictures.

circa *preposition* **approximately**, (round) about, around, in the region of, roughly, something like, or so, or thereabouts, more or less; *informal* as near as dammit; *N. Amer. informal* in the ballpark of.
- OPPOSITES exactly.

circle *noun* **1 ring**, band, hoop, circlet, halo, disc. **2 group**, set, crowd, band, company, clique, coterie, club, society; *informal* gang, bunch.
● *verb* **1** *seagulls circled above* **wheel**, revolve, rotate, whirl, spiral. **2** *satellites circling the earth* **go round**, travel round, circumnavigate, orbit. **3** *the abbey was circled by a wall* **surround**, encircle, ring, enclose.

circuit *noun* **1** *two circuits of the track* **lap**, turn, round, circle. **2** *(Brit.) a racing circuit* **track**, racetrack, course, route, stadium.

circuitous *adjective* **roundabout**, indirect, winding, meandering, twisting, tortuous.
– OPPOSITES direct.

circular *adjective* **round**, ring-shaped.
● *noun* **leaflet**, pamphlet, handbill, flyer, advertisement, notice.

circulate *verb* **1 spread**, communicate, disseminate, make known, make public, broadcast, publicize, distribute. **2 socialize**, mingle, mix, wander, stroll.

circumspect *adjective* **cautious**, wary, careful, chary, guarded, on your guard; *informal* cagey.
– OPPOSITES unguarded.

circumstances *plural noun* **situation**, conditions, state of affairs, position, the lie of the land, (turn of) events, factors, facts, background, environment, context.

cite *verb* **quote**, mention, refer to, allude to, instance, specify, name.

citizen *noun* **1** *a British citizen* **subject**, national, passport holder. **2** *the citizens of Edinburgh* **inhabitant**, resident, native, townsman, townswoman, taxpayer; *formal* denizen.

city *noun* **town**, municipality, metropolis, conurbation, urban area; *Scottish* burgh; *informal* big smoke; *N. Amer. informal* burg.

WORD LINKS
urban, **civic**, **metropolitan** relating to cities

civic *adjective* **municipal**, city, town, urban, metropolitan, public, community.

civil *adjective* **1 secular**, non-religious, lay. **2 non-military**, civilian. **3 polite**, courteous, well mannered, gentlemanly, chivalrous, ladylike.
– OPPOSITES religious, military, rude.

civilization *noun* **1 human development**, advancement, progress, enlightenment, culture, refinement, sophistication. **2 culture**, society, nation, people.

civilize *verb* **enlighten**, improve, educate, instruct, refine, cultivate, socialize.

civilized *adjective* **1** *civilized society* **advanced**, developed, sophisticated, enlightened, educated, cultured, cultivated. **2** *civilized behaviour* **polite**, courteous, well mannered, civil, refined, polished.
– OPPOSITES unsophisticated, rude.

claim *verb* **1 assert**, declare, profess, protest, maintain, insist, contend, allege. **2 request**, ask for, apply for, demand.
● *noun* **1 assertion**, declaration, profession, protestation, insistence, contention, allegation. **2 application**, request, demand.

clamour *noun* **noise**, din, racket, rumpus, uproar, shouting, commotion, hubbub; *Brit.* row; *informal* hullabaloo.

clamp *verb* **fasten**, secure, fix, attach, clench, grip, hold, press, clasp, screw, bolt.

clan *noun* **family**, house, dynasty, tribe.

clandestine *adjective* **secret**, covert, furtive, surreptitious, stealthy, cloak-and-dagger, underhand; *Military* black; *informal* hush-hush.

clap *verb* **applaud**, give someone a round of applause, put your hands together; *informal* give someone a (big) hand; *N. Amer. informal* give it up.
● *noun* **1 round of applause**, handclap; *informal* hand. **2 crack**, peal, crash, bang, boom.

clarify *verb* **make clear**, shed/throw light on, illuminate, elucidate, explain, interpret, spell out, clear up.
– OPPOSITES confuse.

clarity *noun* **1** *the clarity of his explanation* **lucidity**, precision, coherence, transparency, simplicity. **2** *the clarity of the image* **sharpness**, clearness, crispness, definition. **3** *the clarity of the water* **transparency**, clearness, limpidity, translucence.

clash *noun* **1 fight**, battle, confrontation, skirmish, engagement, encounter, conflict. **2 argument**, altercation, confrontation, quarrel, disagreement, dispute; *informal* run-in, slanging match. **3 crash**, clang, bang, clatter, clangour.
● *verb* **1 fight**, battle, confront, skirmish, contend, come to blows. **2 disagree**, differ, wrangle, dispute, cross swords, lock horns, be at loggerheads. **3 conflict**, coincide, overlap. **4 bang**, strike, clang, crash.

clasp *verb* **grasp**, grip, clutch, hold, squeeze, seize, grab, embrace, hug.
● *noun* **1 fastener**, catch, clip, pin, buckle. **2 grasp**, grip, squeeze, embrace, hug.

class *noun* **1 kind**, sort, type, variety, genre, category, grade, rating, classification. **2 group**, grouping, rank, stratum, level, echelon, status, caste.
● *verb* **classify**, categorize, group, grade, order, rate, bracket, designate, label, rank.

classic *adjective* **1 definitive**, authoritative, outstanding, first-rate, first-class, best, finest, excellent, superior, masterly. **2 typical**, archetypal, quintessential, model, representative, perfect, prime, textbook. **3 timeless**, traditional, simple, elegant, understated.
● *noun* **definitive example**, model, epitome, paradigm, exemplar, masterpiece, master work.

classification *noun* **categorization**, classifying, grouping, grading, ranking, organization, sorting, codification.

classify *verb* **categorize**, group, grade, rank, order, organize, sort, type, codify, bracket.

classy *adjective (informal)* **stylish**, high-class, superior, exclusive, chic, elegant, smart, sophisticated; *Brit.* upmarket; *N. Amer.* high-toned; *informal* posh, ritzy, plush, swanky; *Brit. informal* swish.

clause *noun* **section**, paragraph, article, passage, subsection, chapter, condition, proviso, rider.

claw *noun* **talon**, nail, pincer.
● *verb* **scratch**, lacerate, tear, rip, scrape, dig into.

clean *adjective* **1 washed**, scrubbed, cleansed, cleaned, laundered, spotless, unstained, unsullied, unblemished, immaculate, pristine, disinfected, sterilized, sterile, aseptic, decontaminated. **2 blank**, empty, clear, plain, unused, new, pristine, fresh, unmarked. **3 pure**, clear, fresh, unpolluted, uncontaminated.
– OPPOSITES dirty, polluted.
● *verb* **wash**, cleanse, wipe, sponge, scrub, mop, rinse, scour, swab, shampoo, launder, dry-clean.
– OPPOSITES dirty.

cleanse *verb* **1 clean (up)**, wash, bathe, rinse, disinfect. **2** *cleansing the environment of traces of lead* **rid**, clear, free, purify, purge.

clear *adjective* **1 understandable**, comprehensible, intelligible, plain, uncomplicated, explicit, lucid, coherent, simple, straightforward, unambiguous, clear-cut. **2 obvious**, evident, plain, sure, definite, unmistakable, manifest, indisputable, unambiguous, patent, incontrovertible, visible, conspicuous, overt, blatant, glaring. **3 transparent**, limpid, translucent, crystal clear, pellucid. **4 bright**, cloudless, unclouded, blue, sunny, starry. **5 unobstructed**, passable, open, unrestricted, unhindered.
– OPPOSITES incoherent, vague, cloudy.
● *verb* **1 disappear**, go away, stop, die away, fade, wear off, lift, settle, evaporate, dissipate, decrease, lessen, shift. **2 unblock**, unstop, clean out. **3 evacuate**, vacate, empty, leave. **4 remove**, strip, take away, carry away, tidy away/up. **5 go over**, pass over, sail over, jump (over), vault (over), leap (over). **6 acquit**, declare innocent, find not guilty, absolve, exonerate; *informal* let off (the hook).
□ **clear up 1** tidy (up), put in order, straighten up, clean up, fix. **2** solve, resolve, straighten out, find an/the

answer to, get to the bottom of, explain; *informal* crack, figure out, suss out.

clearance *noun* **1 removal**, clearing, demolition. **2 authorization**, permission, consent, approval, leave, sanction, licence, dispensation; *informal* the go-ahead. **3 space**, room (to spare), headroom, margin, leeway.

clear-cut *adjective* **definite**, distinct, precise, specific, explicit, unambiguous, unequivocal, black and white.
- OPPOSITES vague.

clearly *adverb* **1 intelligibly**, plainly, distinctly, comprehensibly, legibly, audibly. **2 obviously**, evidently, patently, unquestionably, undoubtedly, without doubt, plainly, undeniably.

cleft *noun* **split**, crack, fissure, crevice.

clench *verb* **grip**, grasp, grab, clutch, clasp, clamp, hold tightly, seize, squeeze.

clergyman, **clergywoman** *noun* **priest**, cleric, minister, preacher, chaplain, padre, father, pastor, vicar, rector, parson, curate; *Scottish* kirkman.

clerical *adjective* **1 office**, desk, administrative, secretarial, white-collar. **2 ecclesiastical**, church, priestly, religious, spiritual, holy.

clever *adjective* **1 intelligent**, bright, smart, astute, quick-witted, shrewd, talented, gifted, capable, able, competent; *informal* brainy, genius. **2** *a clever scheme* **ingenious**, canny, cunning, crafty, artful, slick, neat. **3** *she was clever with her hands* **skilful**, dexterous, adroit, adept, deft, nimble, handy, skilled, talented, gifted.
- OPPOSITES stupid.

cliché *noun* **platitude**, hackneyed phrase, commonplace, banality, truism, stock phrase; *informal* old chestnut.

click *verb* **1 clack**, snick, snap, clink. **2 become clear**, fall into place, make sense, dawn on someone, register, get through, sink in. **3 take to each other**, get along, be compatible, be like-minded, see eye to eye, be on the same wavelength; *informal* hit it off. **4 go down well**, prove popular, be a hit, succeed, resonate, work, take off.

client *noun* **customer**, buyer, purchaser, shopper, patient, patron; *Brit. informal* punter.

cliff *noun* **precipice**, rock face, crag, bluff, ridge, escarpment, scar, scarp.

climate *noun* **1 (weather) conditions**, weather. **2 atmosphere**, mood, spirit, ethos, feeling, ambience, environment.

climax *noun* **peak**, pinnacle, height, high point, top, zenith, culmination.
- OPPOSITES anticlimax, nadir.

climb *verb* **1 ascend**, mount, scale, scramble up, clamber up, shin up, conquer. **2 rise**, ascend, go up, gain height, soar, rocket. **3** *the road climbs steeply* **slope (upwards)**, rise, go uphill, incline.
- OPPOSITES descend.
□ **climb down** back down, retreat, give in, backtrack, eat your words, eat humble pie, do a U-turn, row back; *N. Amer. informal* eat crow.

clinch *verb* **1** *he clinched the deal* **secure**, settle, conclude, close, confirm, seal, finalize, wrap up; *informal* sew up. **2** *these findings clinched the matter* **settle**, decide, determine, resolve.

cling *verb* **stick**, adhere, hold.
□ **cling (on) to** hold on, clutch, grip, grasp, clasp, hang on, embrace, hug.

clinical *adjective* **1 detached**, impersonal, dispassionate, indifferent, uninvolved, distant, remote, aloof, cold. **2 plain**, stark, austere, spartan, bleak, bare, functional, basic, institutional.
- OPPOSITES emotional.

clip[1] *noun* **fastener**, clasp, hasp, catch, hook, buckle, lock.
● *verb* **fasten**, attach, fix, join, pin, staple, tack.

clip[2] *verb* **1 trim**, prune, cut, snip, crop, shear, lop. **2 hit**, strike, graze, glance off, nudge, scrape.
● *noun* **1 extract**, excerpt, snippet, fragment, trailer. **2 trim**, cut, crop, haircut.

clique *noun* **coterie**, set, circle, ring, in-crowd, group, gang, fraternity.

cloak *noun* **1 cape**, robe, wrap, mantle. **2** *a cloak of secrecy* **cover**, veil, mantle, shroud, screen, blanket.
● *verb* **conceal**, hide, cover, veil, shroud, mask, obscure, cloud, envelop, swathe, surround.

clog *verb* **block**, obstruct, congest, jam, choke, bung up, plug, stop up.

close[1] *adjective* **1 near**, nearby, adjacent, neighbouring, adjoining, abutting, at hand. **2 neck and neck**, even, nip and tuck. **3 intimate**, dear, bosom, close-knit, inseparable, devoted, faithful, special, firm. **4** *a close resemblance* **noticeable**, marked, distinct, pronounced, strong. **5 careful**, detailed, thorough, minute, searching, painstaking, meticulous, rigorous. **6 humid**, muggy, stuffy, airless, heavy, sticky, sultry, stifling.
- OPPOSITES far, distant.

close[2] *verb* **1** *she closed the door* **shut**, pull to, push to, slam. **2** *close the hole* **block**, stop up, plug, seal, bung up, clog up, choke, obstruct. **3 end**, conclude, finish, terminate, wind up. **4 shut down**, close down, cease production, cease trading, be wound up, go out of business; *informal* fold, go to the wall, go bust. **5 clinch**, settle, secure, seal, confirm, pull off, conclude, finalize; *informal* wrap up.
- OPPOSITES open, start.
● *noun* **end**, finish, conclusion.
- OPPOSITES beginning.

closet *noun* **cupboard**, wardrobe, cabinet, locker.
● *adjective* **secret**, covert, private, surreptitious, clandestine.
● *verb* **shut away**, sequester, seclude, cloister, confine, isolate.

clot *noun* **lump**, clump, mass, thrombosis; *informal* glob; *Brit. informal* gob.
● *verb* **coagulate**, set, congeal, thicken, solidify.

cloth *noun* **1 fabric**, material, textile(s), stuff. **2 rag**, wipe, duster, flannel; *Austral.* washer.

clothe *verb* **dress**, attire, robe, garb, costume, swathe, deck (out), turn out, fit out, rig (out); *informal* get up.

clothes *plural noun* **clothing**, garments, attire, garb, dress, wear, costume, wardrobe; *informal* gear, togs; *Brit. informal* clobber; *N. Amer. informal* threads; *formal* apparel.

> WORD LINKS
> **sartorial** relating to clothes
> **clothier**, **couturier**, **tailor** person who sells or makes clothes

clothing *noun* see **clothes**.

cloud *noun a cloud of exhaust smoke* **mass**, billow, mantle, blanket, pall.
● *verb* **confuse**, muddle, obscure.

cloudy *adjective* **1 overcast**, dark, grey, black, leaden, murky, gloomy, sunless, starless. **2 murky**, muddy, milky, dirty, turbid.
- OPPOSITES clear, sunny.

clown *noun* **1 joker**, comedian, comic, wag, wit, jester. **2 fool**, idiot, buffoon, dolt, ignoramus; *informal* moron, ass, numbskull, halfwit, fathead; *Brit. informal* prat, berk, twit, twerp.

club[1] *noun* **1 society**, association, group, circle, league, guild, union. **2 nightclub**, bar; *informal* disco. **3 team**, squad, side.

club[2] *noun* **stick**, cudgel, truncheon, bludgeon, baton, mace, bat; *N. Amer.* blackjack, nightstick; *Brit. informal* cosh.
● *verb* **hit**, beat, strike, cudgel, bludgeon, batter; *informal* clout, clobber; *Brit. informal* cosh.

clue *noun* **hint**, indication, sign, signal, pointer, lead, tip, evidence.

clump *noun* **1** *a clump of trees* **cluster**, thicket, group, bunch. **2** *a clump of earth* **lump**, clod, mass, chunk.

clumsy *adjective* **1 awkward**, uncoordinated, ungainly, graceless, lumbering, inelegant, inept, unskilful, accident-prone, all fingers and thumbs; *informal* cack-handed, ham-fisted, butterfingered; *N. Amer. informal* klutzy.

2 unwieldy, cumbersome, bulky, awkward.
- OPPOSITES graceful.

cluster *noun* **bunch**, clump, mass, knot, group, clutch, huddle, crowd.
● *verb* **congregate**, gather, collect, group, assemble, huddle, crowd.

clutch *verb* **grip**, grasp, clasp, cling to, hang on to, clench, hold, grab, snatch.

clutter *noun* **disorder**, chaos, mess, disarray, untidiness, confusion, litter, rubbish, junk.
● *verb* **litter**, mess up, be strewn, be scattered, cover, bury.

coach[1] *noun* **1** *a journey by coach* **bus**; *dated* omnibus, charabanc. **2** *a railway coach* **carriage**, wagon; *N. Amer.* car.

coach[2] *noun* **instructor**, trainer, teacher, tutor, mentor, guru.
● *verb* **instruct**, teach, tutor, school, educate, drill, train.

coagulate *verb* **congeal**, clot, thicken, solidify, harden, set, dry.

coalition *noun* **alliance**, union, partnership, bloc, federation, league, association, confederation, consortium, syndicate, amalgamation, merger.

coarse *adjective* **1 rough**, scratchy, prickly, wiry, harsh. **2** *coarse manners* **uncouth**, oafish, loutish, boorish, rude, impolite, ill-mannered, vulgar, common, rough. **3** *a coarse remark* **vulgar**, crude, rude, off colour, lewd, smutty, indelicate.
- OPPOSITES soft, refined, polite.

coast *noun* **shore**, coastline, seashore, seaboard, shoreline, seaside; *literary* strand.
● *verb* **freewheel**, cruise, taxi, drift, glide, sail.

WORD LINKS
littoral relating to a coast or seashore

coat *noun* **1 fur**, hair, wool, fleece, hide, pelt, skin. **2 layer**, covering, coating, skin, film, deposit.
● *verb* **cover**, surface, plate, spread, daub, smear, plaster, cake.

coax *verb* **persuade**, wheedle, cajole, get round, inveigle, manoeuvre; *informal* sweet-talk, soft-soap, twist someone's arm.

cocky *adjective* **arrogant**, conceited, overconfident, swollen-headed, self-important, full of yourself, egotistical, presumptuous, boastful; *informal* too big for your boots.
- OPPOSITES modest.

code *noun* **1 cipher**. **2 convention**, etiquette, protocol, ethic. **3 law(s)**, rules, regulations, constitution, system.

coerce *verb* **pressure**, press, push, constrain, force, compel, oblige, browbeat, bully, threaten, intimidate, dragoon, twist someone's arm; *informal* railroad, steamroller, lean on.

cogent *adjective* **convincing**, persuasive, compelling, strong, forceful, powerful, potent, effective, sound, telling, coherent, clear, lucid, logical, well argued.

coherent *adjective* **logical**, reasoned, rational, sound, cogent, consistent, clear, lucid, articulate, intelligible.
- OPPOSITES muddled.

coil *verb* **wind**, loop, twist, curl, spiral, twine, wrap.

coin *verb* **invent**, create, make up, conceive, originate, think up, dream up.

WORD LINKS
numismatic relating to coins

coincide *verb* **1 occur simultaneously**, happen together, co-occur, coexist. **2 tally**, correspond, agree, accord, match up, be compatible, dovetail, mesh; *informal* square.
- OPPOSITES differ.

coincidence *noun* **accident**, chance, providence, happenstance, fate, luck, fortune, fluke.

coincidental *adjective* **accidental**, chance, fluky, random, fortuitous, unintentional, unplanned.

cold *adjective* **1 chilly**, chill, cool, freezing, icy, wintry, frosty, raw, bitter; *informal* nippy; *Brit. informal* parky.

2 unfriendly, inhospitable, unwelcoming, cool, frigid, frosty, distant, formal, stiff.
- OPPOSITES hot, warm.

collaborate *verb* **1 cooperate**, join forces, work together, combine, pool resources, club together. **2 fraternize**, conspire, collude, cooperate, consort.

collaborator *noun* **1 co-worker**, partner, associate, colleague, confederate, assistant. **2 sympathizer**, traitor, quisling, fifth columnist.

collapse *verb* **1 cave in**, fall in, subside, fall down, give (way), crumple, crumble, disintegrate. **2 faint**, pass out, black out, lose consciousness. **3 go to pieces**, break down, be overcome; *informal* crack up. **4 fail**, break down, fall through, fold, founder; *informal* flop, fizzle out, flatline.
● *noun* **1 cave-in**, disintegration. **2 breakdown**, failure.

colleague *noun* **co-worker**, fellow worker, workmate, teammate, associate, partner, collaborator, ally, confederate.

collect *verb* **1** *he collected up the rubbish* **gather**, accumulate, assemble, amass, stockpile, pile up, heap up, store (up), hoard, save. **2** *a crowd soon collected* **gather**, assemble, meet, muster, congregate, convene, converge. **3 fetch**, pick up, go/come and get, call for, meet.
- OPPOSITES distribute, disperse.

collected *adjective* **calm**, cool, self-possessed, self-controlled, composed, poised, serene, tranquil, relaxed; *informal* laid-back.
- OPPOSITES excited.

collection *noun* **1 hoard**, pile, heap, stock, store, stockpile, accumulation, reserve, supply, bank, pool, fund; *informal* stash. **2 group**, crowd, body, gathering, knot, cluster. **3 anthology**, selection, compendium, compilation, miscellany, treasury. **4 appeal**; *informal* whip-round.

collective *adjective* **common**, shared, joint, combined, mutual, communal, pooled, united, allied, cooperative, collaborative.
- OPPOSITES individual.

collide *verb* **crash**, hit, strike, run into, bump into.

collision *noun* **crash**, accident, smash; *N. Amer.* wreck; *informal* pile-up; *Brit. informal* shunt, prang.

colloquial *adjective* **informal**, conversational, everyday, familiar, popular, casual, idiomatic, slangy, vernacular.
- OPPOSITES formal.

colonize *verb* **settle (in)**, people, populate, occupy, take over, invade.

colony *noun* **territory**, dependency, protectorate, satellite, settlement, outpost, province.

colossal *adjective* **huge**, massive, enormous, gigantic, giant, mammoth, vast, cosmic, immense, monumental, mountainous; *informal* monster, whopping, humongous; *Brit. informal* ginormous.
- OPPOSITES tiny.

colour *noun* **1 hue**, shade, tint, tone, coloration. **2 paint**, pigment, colourant, dye, stain.
● *verb* **1 tint**, dye, stain, tinge. **2 influence**, affect, taint, warp, skew, distort.

WORD LINKS
chromatic relating to colour

colourful *adjective* **1 bright**, vivid, vibrant, brilliant, radiant, gaudy, garish, multicoloured, psychedelic; *informal* jazzy. **2** *a colourful account* **vivid**, graphic, lively, animated, dramatic, fascinating, interesting, stimulating, scintillating, evocative.
- OPPOSITES drab, dull.

column *noun* **1 pillar**, post, support, upright, pier, pile. **2 article**, piece, feature. **3 line**, file, queue, procession, convoy; *informal* crocodile.

comb *verb* **1 groom**, brush, untangle, smooth, straighten, neaten, tidy, arrange. **2 search**, scour, explore, sweep.

combat *noun* **battle**, fighting, action, hostilities, conflict, war, warfare.

● *verb* **fight**, battle, tackle, attack, counter, resist.

combative *adjective* **aggressive**, pugnacious, antagonistic, quarrelsome, argumentative, hostile, truculent, belligerent; *informal* spoiling for a fight.
- OPPOSITES conciliatory.

combination *noun* **mixture**, mix, blend, fusion, amalgamation, amalgam, merger, marriage, synthesis.

combine *verb* **1 mix**, blend, fuse, amalgamate, integrate, merge, marry. **2 unite**, collaborate, join forces, get together, team up.

come *verb* **1** *come and listen* **approach**, advance, draw close/closer, draw near/nearer. **2** *they came last night* **arrive**, get here/there, make it, appear, turn up, materialize; *informal* show (up), roll up. **3** *they came to a stream* **reach**, arrive at, get to, come across, run across, happen on, chance on, come upon, stumble on, end up at; *informal* wind up at. **4** *she comes from Belgium* **be from**, be a native of, hail from, live in, reside in. **5 happen**, occur, take place, come about, fall, crop up.
- OPPOSITES go, leave.
□ **come about** happen, occur, take place, transpire, fall, arise. **come across** meet, run into, run across, come upon, chance on, stumble on, happen on, discover, encounter, find; *informal* bump into. **come on** progress, develop, shape up, take shape, come along, turn out, improve.

comeback *noun* **return**, recovery, resurgence, rally, upturn; *Brit.* fightback.

comedian *noun* **1 comic**, comedienne, funny man/woman, humorist, stand-up; *N. Amer.* tummler. **2 joker**, wit, wag, comic, clown; *informal* laugh, hoot.

comedy *noun* **humour**, fun, hilarity, funny side, laughs, jokes.
- OPPOSITES tragedy.

comfort *noun* **1 ease**, repose, luxury, prosperity. **2 consolation**, condolence, sympathy, commiseration, support, reassurance, cheer.
- OPPOSITES discomfort.
● *verb* **console**, support, reassure, soothe, calm, cheer, hearten.
- OPPOSITES distress, depress.

comfortable *adjective* **1 affluent**, prosperous, well-to-do, pleasant, luxurious, opulent. **2 cosy**, snug, warm, pleasant, agreeable, homely; *informal* comfy. **3 loose**, loose-fitting, roomy, casual; *informal* comfy.

comforting *adjective* **soothing**, reassuring, calming, heartening, cheering.
- OPPOSITES upsetting.

comic *adjective* **humorous**, funny, amusing, hilarious, comical, zany, witty, droll.
- OPPOSITES serious.
● *noun* **comedian**, comedienne, funny man/woman, humorist, wit, joker.

comical *adjective* **1 funny**, humorous, droll, witty, comic, amusing, entertaining; *informal* wacky. **2 absurd**, silly, ridiculous, laughable, ludicrous, preposterous, foolish; *informal* crazy.
- OPPOSITES serious.

coming *adjective* **forthcoming**, imminent, impending, approaching.
● *noun* **approach**, advance, advent, arrival, appearance, emergence.

command *verb* **1 order**, tell, direct, instruct, call on, require, charge, enjoin, ordain; *old use* bid. **2 be in charge of**, be in command of, head, lead, control, direct, manage, supervise, oversee; *informal* head up.
● *noun* **1 order**, instruction, direction, directive, injunction, decree, edict, dictate, mandate, commandment, fiat. **2** *he had 160 men under his command* **authority**, control, charge, power, direction, dominion, guidance, leadership, rule, government, management, supervision, jurisdiction. **3 knowledge**, mastery, grasp, comprehension, understanding.

commander *noun* **leader**, head, chief, overseer, director, controller; *informal* boss, skipper, head honcho; *Brit. informal* gaffer, guv'nor.

commanding *adjective* **dominant**, controlling, superior, powerful, advantageous, favourable.

commemorate *verb* **celebrate**, remember, recognize, acknowledge, observe, mark, pay tribute to, pay homage to, honour, salute.

commence *verb* **begin**, inaugurate, start, initiate, launch into, open, get the ball rolling, get going, get under way, get off the ground, set about, embark on; *informal* kick off.
– OPPOSITES conclude.

commend *verb* **1 praise**, compliment, congratulate, applaud, salute, honour, sing the praises of, pay tribute to. **2 recommend**, endorse, vouch for, speak for, support, back.
– OPPOSITES criticize.

commendable *adjective* **admirable**, praiseworthy, creditable, laudable, meritorious, exemplary, honourable, respectable.
– OPPOSITES reprehensible.

comment *noun* **1 remark**, observation, statement, pronouncement, judgement, reflection, opinion, view. **2 discussion**, debate, interest. **3 note**, annotation, commentary, footnote, gloss, explanation.
● *verb* **remark**, observe, say, state, note, point out, mention, interject; *formal* opine.

commentary *noun* **1 narration**, description, report, review, voice-over. **2 explanation**, elucidation, interpretation, analysis, assessment, review, criticism, notes, comments.

commentator *noun* **1 reporter**, narrator, journalist, newscaster. **2 analyst**, pundit, critic, columnist, leader-writer, opinion-former, monitor, observer.

commerce *noun* **trade**, trading, business, dealing, buying and selling, traffic, trafficking.

commercial *adjective* **1 trade**, trading, business, mercantile, sales. **2 profit-making**, materialistic, mercenary.

commission *noun* **1 percentage**, share, premium, fee, bonus, royalty; *informal* cut, rake-off, slice; *Brit. informal* whack. **2 contract**, engagement, assignment, booking, job. **3 committee**, board, council, panel, body.
● *verb* **1 engage**, contract, book, employ, hire, recruit, take on, retain, appoint. **2 order**, place an order for, pay for.

commit *verb* **1 carry out**, do, perpetrate, engage in, execute, accomplish, be responsible for; *informal* pull off. **2 entrust**, consign, assign, deliver, hand over. **3 consign**, send, confine.

commitment *noun* **1 responsibility**, obligation, duty, liability, engagement, tie. **2 dedication**, devotion, allegiance, loyalty. **3 promise**, vow, pledge, undertaking.

committed *adjective* **devoted**, dedicated, motivated, driven, staunch, loyal, faithful, devout, firm, steadfast, unwavering, passionate, ardent, sworn.
– OPPOSITES apathetic.

common *adjective* **1** *a common occurrence* **frequent**, regular, everyday, normal, usual, ordinary, familiar, standard, commonplace, average, unexceptional, typical. **2** *a common belief* **widespread**, general, universal, popular, mainstream, prevalent, rife, established, conventional, accepted. **3 collective**, communal, shared, community, public, popular, general. **4 uncouth**, vulgar, coarse, rough, uncivilized, unsophisticated, unrefined, inferior, plebeian; *informal* plebby.
– OPPOSITES unusual, rare.

commonplace *adjective* see **normal** (sense 1).

common sense *noun* **good sense**, native wit, good judgement, level-headedness, prudence, wisdom; *informal* horse sense, nous; *Brit. informal* common; *N. Amer. informal* smarts.
– OPPOSITES stupidity.

commotion *noun* **disturbance**, uproar, disorder, confusion, rumpus, fuss, furore, hue and cry, stir, storm, chaos, havoc, pandemonium.

communal *adjective* **1** *a communal kitchen* **shared**, joint, common, public, general. **2** *they farm on a communal basis* **collective**, cooperative, community.
- OPPOSITES private, individual.

communicate *verb* **1 liaise**, be in touch, be in contact, have dealings, talk, speak, interface. **2 convey**, tell, relay, transmit, impart, pass on, report, recount, relate. **3 transmit**, spread, transfer, pass on.

communication *noun* **1 contact**, dealings, relations, connection, correspondence, dialogue, conversation. **2 message**, statement, announcement, report, dispatch, bulletin, disclosure, communiqué, letter, correspondence.

communicative *adjective* **forthcoming**, expansive, expressive, unreserved, vocal, outgoing, frank, open, candid, talkative, chatty.

communist *noun* & *adjective* **collectivist**, Bolshevik, Marxist, Maoist, Soviet; *informal, derogatory* red, Commie.

community *noun* **society**, population, populace, people, public, residents, inhabitants, citizens.

compact[1] *adjective* **1 dense**, tightly packed, compressed, thick, tight, firm, solid. **2 neat**, small, handy, portable, fun-size. **3 concise**, succinct, condensed, brief, pithy, to the point, short and sweet; *informal* snappy.
- OPPOSITES loose, bulky, lengthy.
● *verb* **compress**, condense, pack down, tamp (down), flatten.

compact[2] *noun* **treaty**, pact, accord, agreement, contract, bargain, deal, settlement.

companion *noun* **comrade**, fellow, partner, associate, escort, compatriot, confederate, friend; *informal* pal, chum, crony; *Brit. informal* mate; *N. Amer. informal* buddy.

company *noun* **1 firm**, business, corporation, establishment, agency, office, house, institution, concern, enterprise, consortium, syndicate; *informal* outfit. **2 companionship**, fellowship, society, presence. **3 unit**, section, detachment, corps, squad, platoon.

comparable *adjective* **1 similar**, close, near, approximate, equivalent, proportionate. **2** *nobody is comparable with him* **equal to**, as good as, in the same league as, on a level with, a match for.
- OPPOSITES incomparable.

compare *verb* **1 contrast**, balance, set against, weigh up. **2 liken**, equate, class with, bracket with. **3 be as good as**, be comparable to, bear comparison with, be the equal of, match up to, be on a par with, be in the same league as, come close to, rival.

comparison *noun* **resemblance**, likeness, similarity, correspondence.

compartment *noun* **bay**, locker, recess, alcove, cell, cubicle, pod, pigeonhole, cubbyhole.

compass *noun* **scope**, range, extent, reach, span, breadth, ambit, limits, parameters, bounds.

compassion *noun* **sympathy**, empathy, understanding, fellow feeling, pity, care, concern, sensitivity, kindness.
- OPPOSITES indifference, cruelty.

compassionate *adjective* **sympathetic**, understanding, pitying, caring, sensitive, warm, loving, kind.
- OPPOSITES unsympathetic, uncaring.

compatible *adjective* **well matched**, (well) suited, like-minded, in tune, in harmony, in keeping, consistent, consonant; *informal* on the same wavelength.

compel *verb* **force**, pressure, coerce, dragoon, press, push, oblige, require, make; *informal* lean on, railroad, put the screws on.

compelling *adjective* **1 enthralling**, captivating, gripping, riveting, spellbinding, mesmerizing, absorbing. **2 convincing**, persuasive, cogent, irresistible, powerful, strong.
- OPPOSITES boring, weak.

compensate *verb* **1 recompense**, repay, pay back, reimburse, remunerate, indemnify. **2 balance (out)**, counterbalance, counteract, offset, make up for, cancel out.

compensation *noun* **recompense**, repayment, reimbursement, remuneration, redress, amends, damages; *N. Amer. informal* comp.

compete *verb* **1 take part**, participate, be a contestant, play, enter, go in for. **2** *they had to compete with other firms* **contend**, vie, battle, jockey, go head to head, pit yourself against, challenge, take on.

competence *noun* **1** *my technical competence* **ability**, capability, proficiency, accomplishment, expertise, skill, prowess; *informal* know-how. **2** *the competence of the system* **adequacy**, suitability, fitness.

competent *adjective* **1 able**, capable, proficient, adept, accomplished, skilful, skilled, expert. **2 fit**, suitable, suited, appropriate, qualified, empowered, authorized.

competition *noun* **1 contest**, tournament, championship, match, game, heat; *Brit.* clash. **2 rivalry**, competitiveness, conflict; *informal* keeping up with the Joneses. **3 opposition**, rivals, other side, field, enemy.

competitive *adjective* **1** *a competitive player* **ambitious**, zealous, keen, combative, aggressive, driven, motivated; *informal* go-ahead. **2** *a highly competitive industry* **ruthless**, aggressive, fierce, cut-throat; *informal* dog-eat-dog. **3** *competitive prices* **reasonable**, moderate, keen, low, cheap, budget, bargain, rock-bottom, bargain-basement.

competitor *noun* **1 contestant**, contender, challenger, participant, entrant, player. **2 rival**, challenger, opponent, competition, opposition.

compile *verb* **assemble**, put together, make up, collate, compose, organize, arrange, gather, collect.

complacency *noun* **smugness**, self-satisfaction, self-congratulation, self-regard.

complacent *adjective* **smug**, self-satisfied, self-congratulatory, resting on your laurels, pleased with yourself.

complain *verb* **protest**, grumble, whine, bleat, carp, cavil, grouse, make a fuss, object, find fault; *informal* whinge, gripe, moan, bitch.

complaint *noun* **1 protest**, objection, grievance, grouse, grumble, criticism; *informal* gripe, whinge. **2 disorder**, disease, illness, sickness, ailment, infection, condition, problem, upset, trouble.

complement *noun* **1 accompaniment**, companion, addition, supplement, accessory, finishing touch. **2 amount**, contingent, capacity, allowance, quota.
● *verb* **accompany**, go with, round off, set off, suit, harmonize with, enhance, complete.

complementary *adjective* **harmonious**, compatible, corresponding, matching, reciprocal.

complete *adjective* **1 entire**, whole, full, total, uncut, unabridged, unexpurgated. **2 finished**, ended, concluded, completed; *informal* wrapped up, sewn up. **3 absolute**, utter, out-and-out, total, downright, prize, perfect, unqualified, unmitigated, sheer; *N. Amer.* full-bore.
– OPPOSITES partial, unfinished.
● *verb* **1 finish**, end, conclude, finalize, wind up, clinch; *informal* wrap up. **2 finish off**, round off, top off, crown, cap, add the finishing touch.

completely *adverb* **totally**, entirely, wholly, thoroughly, fully, utterly, absolutely, perfectly, downright.

complex *adjective* **1 compound**, composite, multiplex. **2 complicated**, involved, intricate, convoluted, elaborate, difficult; *Brit. informal* fiddly.
– OPPOSITES simple.
● *noun* **1 network**, system, nexus, web. **2** *(informal)* **obsession**, fixation, preoccupation, neurosis; *informal* hang-up, thing.

complexion *noun* **1 skin**, skin colour/tone, colouring. **2 kind**, nature, character, colour, persuasion, outlook.

complicate *verb* **make (more) difficult**, make complicated, mix up, confuse, muddle, obscure.
- OPPOSITES simplify.

complicated *adjective* **complex**, involved, intricate, convoluted, elaborate, difficult, knotty, tortuous, labyrinthine, Byzantine; *Brit. informal* fiddly.
- OPPOSITES simple, straightforward.

complication *noun* **difficulty**, problem, issue, obstacle, hurdle, stumbling block, snag, catch, hitch; *Brit.* spanner in the works; *informal* headache.

compliment *noun* **tribute**, accolade, commendation, pat on the back; (**compliments**) praise, acclaim, admiration, flattery, congratulations; *N. Amer. informal* kudos.
- OPPOSITES criticism, insult.
● *verb* **praise**, pay tribute to, flatter, commend, acclaim, applaud, salute, congratulate.
- OPPOSITES criticize.

complimentary *adjective* **1 flattering**, appreciative, congratulatory, admiring, approving, favourable, glowing. **2 free (of charge)**, gratis; *informal* on the house.
- OPPOSITES critical.

comply *verb* **obey**, observe, abide by, adhere to, conform to, follow, respect, go along with.
- OPPOSITES disobey.

component *noun* **part**, piece, bit, element, constituent, ingredient, unit, module.

compose *verb* **1 write**, devise, make up, think up, produce, invent, pen, author. **2 organize**, arrange, construct, set out. **3 make up**, constitute, form, comprise.
□ **compose yourself** calm down, control yourself, regain your composure, pull yourself together, steady yourself; *informal* get a grip.

composed *adjective* **calm**, collected, cool (as a cucumber), self-possessed, poised, serene, relaxed, at ease, unruffled, unperturbed; *informal* unflappable, together, laid-back, chilled.

composition *noun* **1 make-up**, constitution, configuration, structure, formation, anatomy, organization. **2 work (of art)**, creation, opus, piece. **3 writing**, creation, formulation, compilation. **4 essay**, paper, study, piece of writing; *N. Amer.* theme. **5 arrangement**, layout, proportions, balance, symmetry.

composure *noun* **self-control**, self-possession, calm, equanimity, equilibrium, serenity, tranquillity, poise, presence of mind, sangfroid, placidness, impassivity; *informal* cool.

compound *noun* **amalgam**, blend, mixture, mix, alloy.
● *adjective* **composite**, complex, multiple.
- OPPOSITES simple.
● *verb* **1 mix**, combine, blend. **2 aggravate**, exacerbate, worsen, add to, augment, intensify, heighten, increase.

comprehend *verb* **understand**, grasp, see, take in, follow, make sense of, fathom; *informal* work out, figure out, get.

comprehensible *adjective* **intelligible**, understandable, lucid, coherent, accessible, self-explanatory, clear, plain, straightforward.
- OPPOSITES incomprehensible.

comprehension *noun* **understanding**, grasp, mastery, conception, knowledge, awareness.
- OPPOSITES ignorance.

comprehensive *adjective* **inclusive**, all-inclusive, complete, full, thorough, extensive, all-embracing, blanket, exhaustive, detailed, sweeping, wholesale, broad, wide-ranging.
- OPPOSITES limited.

compress *verb* **1 squeeze**, press, squash, crush, compact. **2 shorten**, abridge, condense, abbreviate, contract, telescope, summarize, precis.
- OPPOSITES expand, pad out.

comprise *verb* **1** *the country comprises twenty states* **consist of**, be made up of, be composed of, contain. **2** *this breed comprises half the herd* **make up**, constitute, form, account for.

compromise *noun* **agreement**, understanding, settlement, terms, deal, trade-off, bargain, middle ground. ● *verb* **1 meet each other halfway**, come to an understanding, make a deal, make concessions, find a happy medium, strike a balance. **2 undermine**, weaken, damage, harm, jeopardize, prejudice.

compulsion *noun* **1** *he is under no compulsion to go* **obligation**, pressure, coercion. **2 urge**, impulse, need, desire, drive, obsession, fixation, addiction.

compulsive *adjective* **1** *a compulsive desire* **irresistible**, uncontrollable, compelling, overwhelming. **2** *compulsive eating* **obsessive**, obsessional, addictive, uncontrollable. **3 inveterate**, chronic, incorrigible, incurable, hopeless, persistent, habitual; *informal* pathological. **4 fascinating**, compelling, gripping, riveting, engrossing, enthralling, captivating.

compulsory *adjective* **obligatory**, mandatory, required, requisite, necessary, binding, enforced, prescribed.
- OPPOSITES optional.

compute *verb* **calculate**, work out, reckon, determine, evaluate, add up, total.

comrade *noun* **companion**, friend, colleague, associate, partner, ally; *Brit. informal* mate; *N. Amer. informal* buddy.

conceal *verb* **1** *clouds concealed the sun* **hide**, screen, cover, obscure, block out, blot out, mask. **2** *he concealed his true feelings* **keep secret**, hide, disguise, mask, veil, bottle up; *informal* keep a/the lid on.
- OPPOSITES reveal, confess.

concede *verb* **1 admit**, acknowledge, accept, allow, grant, recognize, own, confess, agree. **2 surrender**, yield, give up, relinquish, hand over.
- OPPOSITES deny.

conceit *noun* **vanity**, pride, arrogance, egotism, self-importance, narcissism, self-admiration.
- OPPOSITES humility.

conceited *adjective* **vain**, proud, arrogant, egotistic, self-important, narcissistic, full of yourself, swollen-headed, boastful, cocky, self-satisfied, smug; *informal* big-headed, stuck-up.

conceivable *adjective* **imaginable**, possible, plausible, credible, believable, feasible.

conceive *verb* **1 think up**, think of, dream up, devise, formulate, design, create, develop; *informal* cook up. **2 imagine**, envisage, visualize, picture.

concentrate *verb* **1 focus on**, pay attention to, give your attention to, put your mind to, keep your mind on, be absorbed in, be engrossed in, be immersed in. **2 collect**, gather, congregate, converge, mass, rally.

concentrated *adjective* **1 strenuous**, concerted, intensive, all-out, intense. **2 condensed**, reduced, undiluted, strong.
- OPPOSITES half-hearted, diluted.

concentration *noun* **close attention**, attentiveness, application, single-mindedness, absorption.
- OPPOSITES inattention.

concept *noun* **idea**, notion, conception, abstraction, theory, hypothesis.

conception *noun* **1 pregnancy**, fertilization, impregnation, insemination. **2 inception**, genesis, origination, creation, invention, beginning, origin. **3 plan**, idea, notion, scheme, project, proposal, intention, aim.

concern *verb* **1 be about**, deal with, cover, relate to, pertain to. **2 affect**, involve, be relevant to, apply to, have a bearing on, impact on. **3 worry**, disturb, trouble, bother, perturb, unsettle. ● *noun* **1 anxiety**, worry, disquiet, apprehensiveness, unease, misgiving, issue. **2 care**, consideration, solicitude, sympathy. **3 responsibility**, business, affair, duty, job; *informal* bailiwick; *Brit. informal* lookout. **4** *issues of concern to women* **interest**, importance, relevance, significance. **5 firm**, business, company, enterprise, operation,

corporation; *informal* outfit.
- OPPOSITES indifference.

concerned *adjective* **1 worried**, anxious, upset, troubled, uneasy, bothered. **2 interested**, involved, affected, implicated.
- OPPOSITES unconcerned.

concerning *preposition* **about**, regarding, relating to, with reference to, referring to, with regard to, as regards, touching, in connection with, re, apropos.

concerted *adjective* **1** *a concerted effort* **strenuous**, vigorous, intensive, all-out, intense, concentrated. **2** *concerted action* **joint**, united, collaborative, collective, combined, cooperative.

concession *noun* **1 compromise**, accommodation, trade-off, sop. **2 reduction**, cut, discount, deduction, rebate; *informal* break. **3 right**, privilege, licence, permit, franchise, warrant.

concise *adjective* **succinct**, pithy, brief, abridged, condensed, abbreviated, compact, potted.
- OPPOSITES lengthy.

conclude *verb* **1 finish**, end, come/bring to an end, draw to a close, close, wind up, terminate, stop, cease; *informal* wrap up. **2 settle**, clinch, finalize, tie up; *informal* sew up. **3 deduce**, infer, gather, judge, decide, surmise; *N. Amer.* figure.
- OPPOSITES begin.

conclusion *noun* **1 end**, ending, finish, close. **2 settlement**, clinching, completion, arrangement. **3 deduction**, inference, interpretation, judgement, verdict.
- OPPOSITES beginning.

conclusive *adjective* **incontrovertible**, undeniable, indisputable, irrefutable, unquestionable, convincing, certain, decisive, definitive, definite, positive, categorical, unequivocal.
- OPPOSITES unconvincing.

concoct *verb* **make up**, dream up, fabricate, invent, devise, formulate, hatch, brew; *informal* cook up.

concrete *adjective* **1 solid**, material, real, physical, tangible. **2 definite**, specific, firm, positive, conclusive, definitive.
- OPPOSITES abstract, imaginary.

concur *verb* **agree**, be in agreement, accord, be in sympathy, see eye to eye, be of the same mind, be of the same opinion.
- OPPOSITES disagree.

condemn *verb* **1 censure**, criticize, denounce, deplore, decry; *informal* slam; *Brit. informal* slate, slag off. **2** *his illness condemned him to a lonely childhood* **doom**, destine, damn, sentence.
- OPPOSITES praise.

condense *verb* **abridge**, compress, summarize, shorten, cut, abbreviate, edit.
- OPPOSITES expand.

condescend *verb* **1 patronize**, talk down to, look down your nose at, look down on. **2** *he condescended to see us* **deign**, stoop, lower yourself, demean yourself, consent.

condescending *adjective* **patronizing**, supercilious, superior, disdainful, lofty, haughty; *informal* snooty, stuck-up; *Brit. informal* toffee-nosed.

condition *noun* **1 state**, shape, order, fitness, health, form; *Brit. informal* nick, fettle. **2 circumstances**, surroundings, environment, situation, state of affairs, position. **3 disorder**, problem, complaint, illness, disease, ailment, malady. **4 stipulation**, constraint, prerequisite, precondition, requirement, term, proviso.
● *verb* **train**, teach, educate, guide, accustom, adapt, habituate, mould.

conditional *adjective* **qualified**, dependent, contingent, with reservations, limited, provisional, provisory.

condone *verb* **disregard**, accept, allow, let pass, turn a blind eye to, overlook, forget, forgive, pardon, excuse.
- OPPOSITES condemn.

conducive *adjective* **favourable**, beneficial, advantageous, opportune,

encouraging, promising, convenient, good, helpful, instrumental.
- OPPOSITES unfavourable.

conduct *noun* **1 behaviour**, actions, deeds, doings, exploits. **2 management**, running, direction, control, supervision, regulation, administration, organization, coordination, handling.
● *verb* **1 manage**, direct, run, administer, organize, coordinate, orchestrate, handle, carry out/on. **2 escort**, guide, lead, usher, steer. **3 transmit**, convey, carry, channel.
□ **conduct yourself** behave, act, acquit yourself, bear yourself.

confer *verb* **1 bestow**, present, grant, award, honour with. **2 consult**, talk, speak, converse, have a chat, deliberate, compare notes.

conference *noun* **meeting**, congress, convention, seminar, discussion, council, forum, summit.

confess *verb* **1 admit**, acknowledge, reveal, disclose, divulge, own up, plead guilty, accept the blame; *informal* come clean. **2** *I confess I don't know* **acknowledge**, admit, concede, grant, allow, own.
- OPPOSITES deny.

confide *verb* **reveal**, disclose, divulge, impart, declare, vouchsafe, tell, confess.

confidence *noun* **1 trust**, belief, faith, credence. **2 self-assurance**, self-confidence, self-possession, assertiveness, self-belief, conviction.
- OPPOSITES distrust, doubt.

confident *adjective* **1 sure**, certain, positive, convinced, in no doubt, satisfied. **2 self-assured**, assured, self-confident, positive, assertive, self-possessed.

confidential *adjective* **private**, personal, intimate, quiet, secret, sensitive, classified, restricted; *informal* hush-hush.

confine *verb* **1 enclose**, incarcerate, imprison, intern, hold captive, cage, lock up, coop up, kettle. **2 restrict**, limit.

confirm *verb* **1 corroborate**, verify, prove, substantiate, justify, vindicate, bear out. **2 affirm**, reaffirm, assert, assure someone, repeat. **3 ratify**, approve, endorse, validate, sanction, authorize.
- OPPOSITES contradict, deny.

confiscate *verb* **impound**, seize, commandeer, requisition, appropriate, expropriate, take, sequestrate.

conflict *noun* **1 dispute**, quarrel, squabble, disagreement, clash, feud, discord, friction, strife, antagonism, hostility. **2 war**, campaign, fighting, engagement, struggle, hostilities, warfare, combat. **3** *a conflict between work and home life* **clash**, incompatibility, friction, mismatch, variance, contradiction.
- OPPOSITES agreement, peace, harmony.
● *verb* **clash**, be incompatible, be at odds, differ, diverge, disagree, collide.

conflicting *adjective* **contradictory**, incompatible, inconsistent, irreconcilable, contrary, opposite, opposing, clashing.

conform *verb* **1** *visitors have to conform to our rules* **comply with**, abide by, obey, observe, follow, keep to, stick to, adhere to, uphold, heed, accept, go along with. **2 fit in**, behave (yourself), toe the line, obey the rules; *informal* play by the rules.
- OPPOSITES flout, rebel.

confound *verb* **baffle**, bewilder, mystify, bemuse, perplex, puzzle, confuse, dumbfound, throw; *informal* flabbergast, flummox.

confront *verb* **1 challenge**, square up to, face (up to), come face to face with, meet, accost, stand up to, tackle. **2 face**, bedevil, beset, plague, bother, trouble, threaten. **3** *they must confront these issues* **tackle**, address, face (up to), get to grips with, grapple with, deal with, sort out.
- OPPOSITES evade.

confrontation *noun* **conflict**, clash, fight, battle, encounter, head-to-head;

informal set-to, run-in, dust-up, showdown.

confuse *verb* **1 bewilder**, baffle, mystify, bemuse, perplex, puzzle, nonplus; *informal* flummox, faze. **2** *the authors have confused the issue* **complicate**, muddle, blur, obscure, cloud. **3** *some confuse strokes with heart attacks* **mix up**, muddle up, mistake for.
- OPPOSITES enlighten, simplify.

confused *adjective* **1 puzzled**, bemused, bewildered, perplexed, baffled, mystified; *informal* flummoxed. **2 disorientated**, bewildered, muddled, addled, befuddled, demented, senile. **3** *a confused recollection* **vague**, unclear, indistinct, imprecise, blurred, hazy, dim. **4 disorderly**, disorganized, untidy, jumbled, mixed up, chaotic, topsy-turvy, tangled; *informal* higgledy-piggledy; *Brit. informal* shambolic.
- OPPOSITES clear, lucid.

confusion *noun* **1 bewilderment**, bafflement, perplexity, puzzlement, bemusement, mystification, befuddlement, disorientation, uncertainty. **2 disorder**, disarray, muddle, mess, chaos, mayhem, pandemonium, turmoil; *informal* a shambles; *Brit. informal* an omnishambles.
- OPPOSITES clarity, order.

congeal *verb* **coagulate**, clot, thicken, cake, set, gel.

congenial *adjective* **agreeable**, pleasant, friendly, amicable, amiable, nice.
- OPPOSITES unfriendly, unpleasant.

congested *adjective* **blocked**, clogged, choked, jammed, obstructed, crowded, overcrowded, overflowing, packed; *informal* snarled up, gridlocked.
- OPPOSITES clear.

congratulate *verb* **compliment**, wish someone happiness, pay tribute to, pat on the back, take your hat off to, praise, applaud, salute, honour.
- OPPOSITES criticize.

congratulations *plural noun* **best wishes**, compliments, greetings, felicitations; *N. Amer. informal* kudos.

congregate *verb* **assemble**, gather, collect, come together, convene, rally, muster, meet, cluster, group.
- OPPOSITES disperse.

conjure *verb* **1 produce**, magic, summon. **2** *the picture that his words conjured up* **bring to mind**, call to mind, evoke, summon up, suggest.

connect *verb* **1 attach**, join, fasten, fix, link, hook (up), secure, hitch, stick. **2 associate**, link, couple, identify, relate to.
- OPPOSITES detach.

connection *noun* **1 link**, relationship, relation, interconnection, interdependence, association, bond, tie, tie-in, correspondence. **2** *he has the right connections* **contact**, friend, acquaintance, ally, colleague, associate, relation.

connive *verb* **1 ignore**, overlook, disregard, pass over, take no notice of, turn a blind eye to. **2 conspire**, collude, collaborate, plot, scheme.

conniving *adjective* **scheming**, cunning, calculating, devious, wily, sly, artful, manipulative, Machiavellian, deceitful.

connotation *noun* **overtone**, undertone, undercurrent, implication, nuance, hint, echo, association.

conquer *verb* **1 defeat**, beat, vanquish, triumph over, overcome, overwhelm, overpower, overthrow, subdue, subjugate. **2** *Peru was conquered by Spain* **seize**, take (over), appropriate, capture, occupy, invade, annex, overrun. **3 overcome**, get the better of, control, master, deal with, cope with, rise above; *informal* lick; *US informal* own.

conquest *noun* **1 defeat**, overthrow, subjugation. **2 seizure**, takeover, capture, occupation, invasion, annexation.

conscience *noun* **moral sense**, morals, sense of right and wrong, standards, values, principles, ethics, beliefs, scruples, qualms.

conscientious *adjective* **diligent**, industrious, punctilious, painstaking, dedicated, careful, meticulous,

thorough, attentive, hard-working, rigorous, scrupulous.
- OPPOSITES casual.

conscious *adjective* **1 aware**, awake, responsive; *informal* with us. **2 deliberate**, purposeful, knowing, considered, calculated, wilful, premeditated.
- OPPOSITES unaware, unconscious.

consecutive *adjective* **successive**, succeeding, in succession, running, in a row, straight; *informal* on the trot.

consensus *noun* **1 agreement**, unanimity, harmony, accord, unity, solidarity. **2** *the consensus was that they should act* **general opinion**, common view.
- OPPOSITES disagreement.

consent *noun* **agreement**, assent, acceptance, approval, permission, authorization, sanction; *informal* go-ahead, green light, OK.
- OPPOSITES dissent.
● *verb* **agree**, assent, submit, allow, sanction, approve, go along with.
- OPPOSITES forbid, refuse.

consequence *noun* **1 result**, upshot, outcome, effect, repercussion, ramification, product, end result. **2** *the past is of no consequence* **importance**, import, significance, account, value, concern.
- OPPOSITES cause.

consequent *adjective* **resulting**, resultant, ensuing, consequential, following, subsequent.

consequently *adverb* **as a result**, as a consequence, so, thus, therefore, accordingly, hence, for this/that reason, because of this/that.

conservation *noun* **preservation**, protection, safe keeping, husbandry, upkeep, maintenance, repair, restoration.

conservative *adjective* **1 right-wing**, reactionary, traditionalist, old-fashioned, dyed-in-the-wool, hidebound, unadventurous, set in your ways; *informal* stick-in-the-mud. **2 conventional**, sober, modest, sensible, restrained; *informal* square.
- OPPOSITES socialist, radical.

conserve *verb* **preserve**, protect, save, safeguard, keep, look after, sustain, husband.
- OPPOSITES squander.

consider *verb* **1 think about**, contemplate, reflect on, mull over, ponder, deliberate on, chew over, meditate on, ruminate on, evaluate, weigh up, appraise, take account of, bear in mind; *informal* size up. **2 deem**, think, believe, judge, rate, count, find, regard as, hold to be, reckon to be, view as, see as.

considerable *adjective* **sizeable**, substantial, appreciable, significant, plentiful, goodly; *informal* tidy.
- OPPOSITES paltry.

considerably *adverb* **greatly**, (very) much, a great deal, a lot, lots, significantly, substantially, appreciably, markedly, noticeably; *informal* plenty.

considerate *adjective* **attentive**, thoughtful, solicitous, kind, unselfish, caring, polite, sensitive.

consideration *noun* **1 thought**, deliberation, reflection, contemplation, examination, inspection, scrutiny, analysis, discussion, attention. **2 factor**, issue, matter, concern, aspect, feature. **3 attentiveness**, concern, care, thoughtfulness, solicitude, understanding, respect, sensitivity.

considering *preposition* **bearing in mind**, taking into consideration, taking into account, in view of, in the light of.

consist *verb*
□ **consist of** be composed of, be made up of, be formed of, comprise, include, contain.

consistent *adjective* **1 constant**, regular, uniform, steady, stable, even, unchanging. **2** *her injuries were consistent with a knife attack* **compatible**, in tune, in line, corresponding to, conforming to, consonant with.
- OPPOSITES irregular, incompatible.

consolation *noun* **comfort**, solace, sympathy, pity, commiseration, relief, encouragement, reassurance.

console *verb* **comfort**, sympathize with, commiserate with, show compassion for, help, support, cheer (up), hearten, encourage, reassure, soothe.
- OPPOSITES upset.

consolidate *verb* **1 strengthen**, secure, stabilize, reinforce, fortify. **2 combine**, unite, merge, integrate, amalgamate, fuse, synthesize.

consort *verb*
□ **consort with** associate with, keep company with, mix with, socialize with, fraternize with, have dealings with.

conspicuous *adjective* **obvious**, evident, apparent, visible, noticeable, clear, plain, marked, patent, blatant.
- OPPOSITES inconspicuous.

conspiracy *noun* **plot**, scheme, intrigue, plan, collusion.

conspire *verb* **1 plot**, scheme, intrigue, manoeuvre, plan. **2 combine**, unite, join forces, work together.

constant *adjective* **1** *constant noise* **continuous**, persistent, sustained, ceaseless, unceasing, perpetual, incessant, never-ending, eternal, endless, non-stop. **2** *a constant speed* **consistent**, regular, steady, uniform, even, invariable, unvarying, unchanging. **3 faithful**, loyal, devoted, true, fast, firm, unswerving.
- OPPOSITES intermittent, variable, fickle.

consternation *noun* **dismay**, distress, disquiet, discomposure, surprise, alarm, fear, fright, shock.

constitute *verb* **1 comprise**, make up, form, account for. **2 amount to**, be tantamount to, be equivalent to, represent. **3 establish**, inaugurate, found, create, set up.

constitution *noun* **1 composition**, make-up, structure, construction, arrangement, configuration, formation, anatomy. **2 health**, condition, strength, stamina, build, physique.

constraint *noun* **1 restriction**, limitation, curb, check, restraint, control. **2 inhibition**, uneasiness, embarrassment, self-consciousness, awkwardness.
- OPPOSITES freedom, ease.

constrict *verb* **narrow**, tighten, compress, contract, squeeze, strangle.
- OPPOSITES expand, dilate.

construct *verb* **1 build**, erect, put up, set up, assemble, fabricate. **2 formulate**, create, form, put together, devise, compose, work out, frame.
- OPPOSITES demolish.

construction *noun* **1 structure**, building, edifice, work. **2 interpretation**, explanation, analysis, reading, meaning; *informal* take.

constructive *adjective* **useful**, helpful, productive, positive, practical, valuable, profitable, worthwhile.

consult *verb* **1 seek advice from**, ask, call (on), turn to; *informal* pick someone's brains. **2 confer**, talk things over, communicate, deliberate, compare notes. **3 refer to**, look at, check.

consultant *noun* **adviser**, expert, specialist, authority.

consultation *noun* **1 discussion**, talk(s), dialogue, debate, negotiation, deliberation. **2 meeting**, talk, discussion, interview, audience, hearing.

consume *verb* **1 eat**, devour, swallow, gobble up, wolf down, guzzle, drink. **2 use (up)**, expend, deplete, exhaust, spend. **3 destroy**, demolish, lay waste, raze, devastate, gut, ruin, wreck. **4 eat up**, devour, grip, overwhelm, absorb, obsess, preoccupy.

consumer *noun* **buyer**, purchaser, customer, shopper, user.

contact *noun* **1 communication**, correspondence, connection, relations, dealings, touch. **2 connection**, link, acquaintance, associate, friend.
● *verb* **get in touch with**, communicate with, approach, notify, speak to, write to, come forward; *informal* get hold of.

contagious *adjective* **infectious**, communicable, transmittable, transmissible; *informal* catching.

contain *verb* **1 hold**, carry, enclose, accommodate, have room for. **2 include**, comprise, incorporate, involve, consist of, be made up of, be composed of. **3 restrain**, control, curb, rein in, suppress, stifle, swallow, bottle up, keep in check.

container *noun* **receptacle**, vessel, holder, repository.

contaminate *verb* **pollute**, taint, poison, stain, adulterate, defile, debase, corrupt.
- OPPOSITES purify.

contemplate *verb* **1 look at**, gaze at, stare at, view, regard, examine, inspect, observe, survey, study, eye. **2 think about**, ponder, reflect on, consider, mull over, muse on, dwell on, deliberate over, meditate on, ruminate on, chew over. **3 envisage**, consider, think about, have in mind, intend, plan, propose.

contemplative *adjective* **thoughtful**, pensive, reflective, meditative, ruminative, introspective, brooding, deep/lost in thought.

contemporary *adjective* **1** *contemporary sources* **of the time**, contemporaneous, concurrent, coexisting, coeval. **2** *contemporary society* **modern**, present-day, present, current. **3** *a very contemporary design* **modern**, up to date, up to the minute, fashionable, recent; *informal* trendy.
- OPPOSITES former, old-fashioned.

contempt *noun* **scorn**, disdain, derision, disgust, disrespect.
- OPPOSITES respect.

contemptible *adjective* **despicable**, detestable, beneath contempt, reprehensible, deplorable, unspeakable, disgraceful, shameful, ignominious, abject, low, mean, cowardly, discreditable, worthless, shabby, cheap.
- OPPOSITES admirable.

contemptuous *adjective* **scornful**, disdainful, derisive, mocking, sneering, scoffing, condescending, dismissive.
- OPPOSITES respectful.

contend *verb* **1 compete**, vie, battle, tussle, struggle, jostle, strive. **2 assert**, maintain, hold, claim, argue, insist, allege.
□ **contend with** cope with, struggle with, grapple with, deal with, take on, handle.

content[1] *adjective* **satisfied**, contented, pleased, gratified, fulfilled, happy, glad, cheerful, at ease, at peace, relaxed, comfortable, untroubled.
- OPPOSITES dissatisfied.
● *verb* **satisfy**, comfort, gratify, gladden, please, soothe, placate, appease, mollify.

content[2] *noun* **1 amount**, proportion, level. **2 constituents**, ingredients, components. **3 subject matter**, theme, argument, thesis, message, substance, material, ideas.

contented *adjective* see **content**[1] (adjective).

contentious *adjective* **controversial**, debatable, disputed, open to debate, moot, vexed.

contentment *noun* **contentedness**, content, satisfaction, fulfilment, happiness, pleasure, cheerfulness, ease, comfort, well-being, peace.

contest *noun* **1 competition**, match, tournament, rally, race, game, bout. **2 fight**, battle, tussle, struggle, competition, race.
● *verb* **1** *he will contest the seat* **compete for**, contend for, vie for, fight for. **2** *the parties contesting the election* **compete in**, take part in, fight, enter. **3 oppose**, challenge, take issue with, question, call into question, object to.
- OPPOSITES accept.

contestant *noun* **competitor**, participant, player, contender, candidate, entrant.

context *noun* **circumstances**, conditions, frame of reference, factors, state of affairs, situation, background, scene, setting.

contingency *noun* **eventuality**, possibility, chance event, incident, occurrence, accident, emergency.

continual *adjective* **1** *continual breakdowns* **frequent**, regular, repeated, constant, recurrent, recurring, habitual. **2** *continual pain* **constant**, continuous, unremitting, unrelenting, non-stop, sustained, chronic, uninterrupted, incessant, ceaseless, unceasing, never-ending, unbroken, perpetual.
- OPPOSITES occasional, temporary.

continue *verb* **1 carry on**, go on, keep on, persist, persevere, proceed, pursue, keep at; *informal* stick at. **2** *we hope to continue this relationship* **maintain**, keep up, sustain, keep going, keep alive, preserve, perpetuate. **3** *his willingness to continue in office* **remain**, stay, carry on, keep going. **4** *we continued our conversation* **resume**, pick up, take up, carry on with, return to, revisit.
- OPPOSITES stop.

continuous *adjective* **continual**, persistent, sustained, ceaseless, unceasing, unremitting, unrelenting, perpetual, incessant, never-ending, eternal, endless, non-stop, unbroken, uninterrupted.
- OPPOSITES intermittent.

contort *verb* **twist**, bend out of shape, distort, misshape, warp, buckle, deform.

contract *noun* **agreement**, arrangement, commitment, settlement, understanding, compact, covenant, deal, bargain.
● *verb* **1 shrink**, diminish, reduce, decrease, dwindle, decline. **2 tighten**, tense, flex, constrict, draw in. **3 engage**, take on, hire, commission, employ. **4 catch**, pick up, come/go down with, develop.
- OPPOSITES expand, relax, lengthen.

contraction *noun* **1 shrinking**, shrinkage, decline, decrease, diminution, dwindling. **2 tightening**, tensing, flexing. **3 abbreviation**, short form, shortening.

contradict *verb* **1 deny**, refute, rebut, dispute, challenge, counter. **2 argue with**, go against, challenge, oppose.
- OPPOSITES confirm, agree with.

contradiction *noun* **1 conflict**, clash, disagreement, inconsistency, mismatch. **2 denial**, refutation, rebuttal, countering.
- OPPOSITES agreement, confirmation.

contradictory *adjective* **inconsistent**, incompatible, irreconcilable, opposed, opposite, contrary, conflicting, at variance.

contraption *noun* **device**, gadget, apparatus, machine, appliance, mechanism, invention, contrivance; *informal* gizmo, widget; *Brit. informal* gubbins.

contrary *adjective* **1 opposite**, opposing, contradictory, clashing, conflicting, antithetical, incompatible, irreconcilable. **2 perverse**, awkward, difficult, uncooperative, obstinate, pig-headed, intractable; *Brit. informal* bloody-minded, stroppy; *N. Amer. informal* balky.
- OPPOSITES compatible, accommodating.
● *noun* **opposite**, reverse, converse, antithesis.

contrast *noun* **1 difference**, dissimilarity, disparity, divergence, variance, distinction, comparison. **2 opposite**, antithesis, foil, complement.
- OPPOSITES similarity.
● *verb* **1 differ**, be at variance, be contrary, conflict, be at odds, disagree, clash. **2 compare**, juxtapose, measure, distinguish, differentiate.
- OPPOSITES resemble, liken.

contribute *verb* **give**, donate, put up, grant, provide, supply; *informal* chip in; *Brit. informal* stump up.
□ **contribute to** play a part in, be instrumental in, have a hand in, be conducive to, make for.

contribution *noun* **gift**, donation, offering, present, handout, grant, subsidy.

contributor *noun* **donor**, benefactor, supporter, backer, patron, sponsor.

contrite *adjective* **remorseful**, repentant, penitent, regretful, sorry, apologetic, rueful, sheepish, hangdog, ashamed, shamefaced.

contrive *verb* **1 create**, engineer, manufacture, devise, concoct, construct, fabricate, hatch. **2 manage**, find a way, engineer a way, arrange.
- OPPOSITES fail.

contrived *adjective* **forced**, strained, laboured, overdone, unnatural, artificial, false, affected.
- OPPOSITES natural.

control *noun* **1 power**, authority, command, dominance, sway, management, direction, leadership, rule, government, sovereignty, supremacy. **2 limit**, limitation, restriction, restraint, check, curb, regulation. **3 self-control**, self-restraint, composure, calm; *informal* cool.
● *verb* **1 run**, manage, direct, preside over, supervise, command, rule, govern, lead, dominate. **2** *she struggled to control her temper* **restrain**, keep in check, curb, hold back, suppress, repress. **3** *public spending was controlled* **limit**, restrict, curb, cap.

controversial *adjective* **disputed**, contentious, moot, debatable, arguable, vexed.

controversy *noun* **dispute**, disagreement, argument, debate, contention, quarrel, war of words, storm; *Brit.* row.

convalesce *verb* **recuperate**, get better, recover, get well, get back on your feet.

convene *verb* **1** *he convened a meeting* **summon**, call, order. **2** *the committee convened* **assemble**, gather, meet, come together; *formal* foregather.

convenience *noun* **1 advantage**, benefit, expedience, suitability. **2 ease of use**, usefulness, utility, accessibility, availability.
- OPPOSITES inconvenience.

convenient *adjective* **1 suitable**, favourable, advantageous, appropriate, opportune, timely, expedient. **2 nearby**, handy, well situated, practical, useful, accessible.

convention *noun* **1 custom**, usage, practice, tradition, etiquette, protocol. **2 agreement**, accord, protocol, pact, treaty. **3 conference**, meeting, congress, assembly, gathering.

conventional *adjective* **1 orthodox**, traditional, established, accepted, customary, received, prevailing, normal, standard, regular, ordinary, usual, typical. **2 conservative**, traditional, conformist, old-fashioned; *informal* square, stick-in-the-mud. **3 unoriginal**, formulaic, predictable, unadventurous, run-of-the-mill, routine, pedestrian.
- OPPOSITES unorthodox, original.

converge *verb* **meet**, intersect, cross, connect, link up, join, merge.
- OPPOSITES diverge.
□ **converge on** meet at, arrive at, close in on, bear down on, descend on, approach, move towards.

conversation *noun* **discussion**, talk, chat, gossip, tête-à-tête, exchange, dialogue; *Brit. informal* chinwag, natter; *Austral. informal* convo.

conversion *noun* **change**, transformation, metamorphosis, alteration, adaptation, modification, redevelopment, rebuilding, remodelling.

convert *verb* **1 change**, transform, alter, adapt, turn, modify, redevelop, remodel, rebuild, reorganize, metamorphose. **2 win over**, convince, persuade, claim, redeem, save, reform, re-educate, proselytize, evangelize.

convey *verb* **1 transport**, carry, bring, take, fetch, move. **2 communicate**, pass on, impart, relate, relay, transmit, send. **3 express**, get across/over, put across/over, communicate, indicate.

convict *verb* **find guilty**, sentence.
- OPPOSITES acquit.
● *noun* **prisoner**, inmate, criminal, offender, felon; *informal* jailbird, con, (old) lag.

conviction *noun* **1 beliefs**, opinions, views, persuasion, ideals, position, stance, values. **2 assurance**, confidence, certainty.
- OPPOSITES diffidence.

convince *verb* **1** *he convinced me I was wrong* **assure**, persuade, satisfy, prove to. **2** *I convinced her to marry me* **persuade**, induce, prevail on, talk into, talk round, win over, coax, cajole.

convincing *adjective* **1 persuasive**, powerful, strong, forceful, compelling, cogent, plausible, irresistible, telling. **2** *a convincing win* **resounding**, emphatic, decisive, conclusive.
- OPPOSITES unconvincing.

convivial *adjective* **friendly**, genial, affable, amiable, congenial, agreeable, cordial, warm, sociable, outgoing, gregarious, cheerful.

convoy *noun* **group**, fleet, cavalcade, motorcade, cortège, caravan, line.

cook *verb* **prepare**, make, put together; *informal* fix, rustle up; *Brit. informal* knock up.

WORD LINKS
culinary relating to cooking

cool *adjective* **1 chilly**, chill, bracing, cold, brisk, crisp, fresh; *informal* nippy; *Brit. informal* parky. **2 unenthusiastic**, lukewarm, tepid, indifferent, uninterested, apathetic. **3 unfriendly**, distant, remote, aloof, cold, chilly, frosty, unwelcoming; *informal* stand-offish. **4 calm**, collected, composed, self-possessed, poised, serene, relaxed, at ease, unruffled, unperturbed; *informal* unflappable, together, laid-back, chilled.
- OPPOSITES warm, enthusiastic, friendly.

● *noun* **1 chill**, chilliness, coldness, coolness. **2** *(informal)* **self-control**, control, composure, self-possession, calmness, aplomb, poise.
- OPPOSITES warmth.

● *verb* **chill**, refrigerate, freeze.
- OPPOSITES warm.

cooperate *verb* **1 collaborate**, work together, pull together, join forces, team up, unite, combine, pool resources. **2 assist**, help, lend a hand, be of service, do your bit; *informal* play ball.

cooperation *noun* **1 collaboration**, joint action, combined effort, teamwork, give and take, compromise. **2 assistance**, help.

cooperative *adjective* **1 collaborative**, collective, combined, joint, shared, united, concerted. **2 helpful**, eager to help, obliging, accommodating, willing.

coordinate *verb* **organize**, arrange, order, synchronize, bring together, orchestrate.

cope *verb* **1 manage**, survive, look after yourself, fend for yourself, shift for yourself, get by/through, hold your own. **2** *his inability to cope with the situation* **deal with**, handle, manage, address, face (up to), confront, tackle, get to grips with.

copious *adjective* **abundant**, plentiful, ample, profuse, extensive, generous, lavish, liberal, overflowing, in abundance, numerous, many; *informal* galore; *literary* plenteous.
- OPPOSITES sparse.

copy *noun* **1 duplicate**, facsimile, photocopy; *trademark* Xerox. **2 replica**, reproduction, imitation, likeness, forgery, fake, counterfeit.

● *verb* **1 duplicate**, photocopy, xerox, photostat, reproduce. **2 reproduce**, replicate, forge, fake, counterfeit. **3 imitate**, reproduce, emulate, mimic; *informal* rip off.

cord *noun* **string**, thread, line, rope, cable, wire, twine, yarn.

cordon *noun* **barrier**, line, chain, ring, circle.

□ **cordon off** close off, seal off, fence off, separate off, isolate, enclose, encircle, surround.

core *noun* **1** *the earth's core* **centre**, interior, middle, nucleus. **2** *the core of the argument* **heart**, nucleus, nub, kernel, meat, essence, crux, pith, substance; *informal* nitty-gritty.

corner *noun* **1 bend**, curve, turn, junction; *Brit.* hairpin bend. **2 district**, region, area, quarter; *informal* neck of the woods.

● *verb* **1 surround**, trap, hem in, pen in, kettle, cut off. **2 gain control of**, take over, dominate, monopolize, capture; *informal* sew up.

corporation *noun* **company**, firm, business, concern, operation, conglomerate, group, chain, multinational.

corpse *noun* **dead body**, carcass, remains; *informal* stiff; *Medicine* cadaver.

correct *adjective* **1 right**, accurate, exact, true, perfect; *informal* spot on. **2 proper**, decent, right, respectable, decorous, seemly, suitable, appropriate, accepted.
- OPPOSITES wrong, improper.
● *verb* **rectify**, right, put right, set right, amend, remedy, repair, reform, cure.

correction *noun* **rectification**, righting, amendment, repair, remedy, cure.

correctly *adverb* **1 accurately**, right, perfectly, exactly, precisely. **2 properly**, decorously, with decorum, decently, fittingly, appropriately, well.

correspond *verb* **1 be consistent**, correlate, agree, accord, coincide, tally, tie in, match; *informal* square. **2** *a rank corresponding to a British sergeant* **be equivalent**, be analogous, be comparable, equate. **3 exchange letters**, write, communicate.

correspondence *noun* **1 parallel**, correlation, agreement, consistency, conformity, similarity, resemblance, comparability. **2 letters**, messages, mail, post, communication.

correspondent *noun* **reporter**, journalist, columnist, writer, contributor, commentator.

corresponding *adjective* **equivalent**, related, parallel, matching, comparable, analogous.

corrupt *adjective* **1 dishonest**, unscrupulous, criminal, fraudulent, illegal, unlawful; *informal* crooked; *Brit. informal* bent. **2 immoral**, depraved, degenerate, debauched, vice-ridden, perverted, dissolute.
- OPPOSITES honest, ethical, pure.
● *verb* **deprave**, pervert, lead astray, debauch, defile, pollute, sully.

corruption *noun* **1 dishonesty**, unscrupulousness, double-dealing, fraud, misconduct, bribery, venality; *N. Amer.* payola; *informal* graft, sleaze. **2 immorality**, depravity, vice, degeneracy, perversion, debauchery, wickedness, evil, sin.
- OPPOSITES honesty, morality.

cosmetic *adjective* **superficial**, surface, skin-deep, outward, external.
- OPPOSITES fundamental.

cosmopolitan *adjective* **1 multicultural**, multiracial, international, worldwide, global. **2 sophisticated**, cultivated, cultured, worldly, suave, urbane.

cost *noun* **1 price**, fee, tariff, fare, toll, levy, charge, payment, value, rate, outlay; *humorous* damage. **2 sacrifice**, loss, toll, harm, damage, price. **3** *we need to cover our costs* **expenses**, outgoings, overheads, expenditure, spend, outlay.
● *verb* **1 be priced at**, sell for, be valued at, fetch, come to, amount to; *informal* set someone back, go for. **2 price**, value, put a price/value/figure on.

costly *adjective* **1 expensive**, dear, high-cost, overpriced; *informal* steep, pricey. **2 catastrophic**, disastrous, calamitous, ruinous, damaging, harmful, deleterious.
- OPPOSITES cheap.

costume *noun* **clothes**, garments, outfit, ensemble, dress, clothing, attire, garb, uniform, livery; *formal* apparel.

cosy *adjective* **1 snug**, comfortable, warm, homely, welcoming, safe, sheltered, secure; *informal* comfy. **2 intimate**, relaxed, informal, friendly.

cottage *noun* **lodge**, chalet, cabin, shack, shanty; *(in Russia)* dacha; *Scottish* bothy; *Austral. informal* weekender.

cough *verb* **hack**, hawk, bark, clear your throat.
● *noun* **bark**, hack; *informal* frog in your throat.

council *noun* **1** *the town council* **authority**, government, administration, executive, chamber, assembly; *Brit.* corporation. **2** *the Schools Council* **committee**, board, commission, assembly, panel, synod.

counsel *noun* **1 advice**, guidance, counselling, recommendations, suggestions, direction. **2 barrister**, lawyer; *Scottish* advocate; *N. Amer.* attorney, counselor(-at-law).
● *verb* **advise**, recommend, advocate, encourage, warn, caution, guide.

count *verb* **1 add up**, reckon up, total, tally, calculate, compute; *Brit.* tot up. **2 include**, take into account/consideration, take account of, allow for. **3 consider**, think, feel, regard, look on as, view as, hold to be, judge, deem. **4 matter**, be important, be of consequence, be significant, signify, carry weight, rate.
□ **count on** rely on, depend on, bank on, be sure of, have confidence in, believe in, put your faith in, take for granted, take as read.

counter *verb* **1 respond to**, parry, hit back at, answer. **2 oppose**, dispute, argue against/with, contradict, challenge, contest.
– OPPOSITES support.
□ **counter to** against, in opposition to, contrary to, at variance with, in defiance of, in conflict with, at odds with.

counteract *verb* **offset**, counterbalance, balance (out), cancel out, work against, countervail, neutralize, nullify, prevent.

counterfeit *adjective* **fake**, pirate, bogus, forged, imitation; *informal* phoney.
– OPPOSITES genuine.
● *noun* **fake**, forgery, copy, reproduction, imitation, fraud, sham; *informal* phoney.
– OPPOSITES original.
● *verb* **fake**, forge, copy, reproduce, imitate, falsify.

counterpart *noun* **equivalent**, opposite number, peer, equal, parallel, complement, analogue, match, twin, mate, fellow.

countless *adjective* **innumerable**, numerous, untold, legion, numberless, limitless, incalculable; *informal* umpteen; *N. Amer. informal* gazillions of.
– OPPOSITES few.

country *noun* **1 nation**, state, kingdom, realm, land, territory, province. **2 people**, public, population, populace, citizens, nation; *Brit. informal* Joe Public. **3 terrain**, land, territory, landscape, countryside, scenery, surroundings, environment. **4 countryside**, provinces, rural areas, backwoods, hinterland; *Austral./NZ* outback, bush, back country; *informal* sticks.

countryside *noun* see **country** (sense 3), **country** (sense 4).

county *noun* **shire**, province, territory, region, district, area.

coup *noun* **1 takeover**, coup d'état, overthrow, palace revolution, rebellion, uprising. **2 success**, triumph, feat, masterstroke, accomplishment, achievement, scoop.

couple *noun* **1 pair**, duo, twosome, two, brace. **2 husband and wife**, twosome, partners, lovers; *informal* item.
● *verb* **1 combine**, accompany, ally, mix, incorporate, add to. **2 connect**, attach, join, fasten, fix, link, secure, hook (up).
– OPPOSITES detach.

coupon *noun* **voucher**, token, ticket, slip.

courage *noun* **bravery**, pluck, valour, fearlessness, nerve, daring, audacity, boldness, grit, heroism, gallantry; *informal* guts; *Brit. informal* bottle.
– OPPOSITES cowardice.

courageous *adjective* **brave**, plucky, fearless, intrepid, valiant, heroic, undaunted, dauntless; *informal* gutsy, have-a-go.
– OPPOSITES cowardly.

course *noun* **1 route**, way, track, path, line, trail, trajectory, bearing, heading. **2 procedure**, plan (of action), course

of action, practice, approach, technique, policy, strategy, tactic. **3 racecourse**, racetrack, track. **4 course of study**, curriculum, syllabus, classes, lectures, studies. **5 programme**, series, sequence, system, schedule, regime.
● *verb* **flow**, pour, stream, run, rush, gush, cascade, flood, roll.
□ **of course** naturally, as you would expect, needless to say, as a matter of course, obviously, it goes without saying.

court *noun* **1 court of law**, law court, bench, bar, tribunal, assizes. **2 household**, retinue, entourage, train, courtiers, attendants.
● *verb* **1 cultivate**, flatter, curry favour with, wine and dine; *informal* butter up. **2 seek**, pursue, go after, strive for, solicit. **3 risk**, invite, attract, bring on yourself. **4** *(dated)* **woo**, go out with, date, go steady with.

WORD LINKS
forensic relating to a court of law

courteous *adjective* **polite**, well mannered, civil, respectful, well behaved, gracious, obliging, considerate.
– OPPOSITES rude.

courtesy *noun* **politeness**, good manners, civility, respect, grace, consideration, thought.

cove *noun* **bay**, inlet, fjord.

cover *verb* **1 protect**, shield, shelter, hide, conceal, mask, screen, veil, obscure, spread over, extend over, overlay. **2 cake**, coat, encrust, plaster, smother, blanket, carpet, shroud. **3 deal with**, consider, take in, include, involve, incorporate, embrace.
– OPPOSITES reveal.
● *noun* **1** *a protective cover* **covering**, sleeve, wrapping, wrapper, envelope, sheath, housing, jacket, casing, cowling, canopy. **2** *a manhole cover* **lid**, top, cap. **3** *a book cover* **binding**, jacket, dust jacket, dust cover, wrapper. **4 coating**, coat, covering, layer, carpet, blanket, film, sheet, veneer, crust, skin, cloak, mantle, veil, pall, shroud. **5 shelter**, protection, refuge, sanctuary.

covert *adjective* **secret**, furtive, clandestine, surreptitious, stealthy, cloak-and-dagger, backstairs, hidden, concealed, private, undercover, underground; *Military* black; *informal* hush-hush.
– OPPOSITES overt.

covet *verb* **desire**, yearn for, crave, have your heart set on, long for, hanker after/for, hunger after/for, thirst for.

coward *noun* **mouse**, baby; *informal* chicken, scaredy-cat, yellow-belly, sissy; *Brit. informal* big girl's blouse; *N. Amer. informal* pantywaist.

cowardly *adjective* **faint-hearted**, lily-livered, spineless, craven, timid, timorous, fearful; *informal* yellow, chicken, gutless, yellow-bellied.
– OPPOSITES brave.

cower *verb* **cringe**, shrink, flinch, crouch, blench.

coy *adjective* **demure**, shy, modest, bashful, diffident, self-effacing, shrinking.
– OPPOSITES brazen.

crack *noun* **1** *a crack in the glass* **split**, break, chip, fracture, rupture. **2** *a crack between two rocks* **space**, gap, crevice, fissure, cleft, cranny, chink. **3 bang**, report, explosion, detonation, clap, crash. **4** *a crack on the head* **blow**, bang, hit, knock, rap, bump, smack, slap; *informal* bash, whack, clout.
● *verb* **1 break**, split, fracture, rupture, snap. **2 break down**, give way, cave in, go to pieces, give in, yield, succumb. **3 hit**, strike, smack, slap, beat, thump, knock, rap; *informal* bash, whack, clobber, clout, clip. **4** *(informal)* **decipher**, interpret, decode, break, solve.

cradle *noun* **1 crib**, Moses basket, cot, carrycot. **2 birthplace**, fount, fountainhead, source, spring, origin.
● *verb* **hold**, support, cushion, pillow, nurse, rest.

craft *noun* **1 activity**, occupation, trade, profession, work, line of work, job. **2 cunning**, craftiness, guile, wiliness, artfulness, deviousness, slyness, trickery, duplicity, dishonesty, deceit, deceitfulness, deception, intrigue, subterfuge, wiles, ploys, ruses, schemes, tricks. **3 vessel**, ship, boat, aircraft, spacecraft.

craftsman, **craftswoman** *noun* **artisan**, artist, skilled worker, technician, expert, master.

crafty *adjective* **cunning**, wily, sly, artful, devious, tricky, scheming, calculating, shrewd, canny, dishonest, deceitful.
– OPPOSITES honest.

cram *verb* **1** *wardrobes crammed with clothes* **fill**, stuff, pack, jam, fill to overflowing, overload, crowd, throng. **2** *he crammed his clothes into a case* **push**, thrust, shove, force, ram, jam, stuff, pack, pile, squash, squeeze, compress. **3 revise**, study; *informal* swot, mug up, bone up.

cramp *noun* **spasm**, pain, shooting pain, twinge, pang, convulsion.
● *verb* **hinder**, impede, inhibit, hamper, constrain, hamstring, interfere with, restrict, limit, slow.

cramped *adjective* **1 poky**, uncomfortable, confined, restricted, constricted, small, tiny, narrow, crowded, congested. **2 small**, crabbed, illegible, unreadable, indecipherable.
– OPPOSITES spacious.

crash *verb* **1** *the car crashed into a tree* **smash into**, collide with, be in collision with, hit, strike, ram, cannon into, plough into, meet head-on; *N. Amer.* impact. **2** *he crashed his car* **smash**, wreck; *Brit.* write off; *Brit. informal* prang; *N. Amer. informal* total. **3 fall**, drop, plummet, plunge, sink, dive, tumble. **4** *(informal)* **fail**, fold, collapse, go under, go bankrupt; *informal* go bust, go to the wall, flatline.
● *noun* **1 accident**, collision, smash; *N. Amer.* wreck; *informal* pile-up; *Brit. informal* shunt, prang. **2 bang**, smash, smack, crack, bump, thud, explosion. **3 failure**, collapse, liquidation, bankruptcy.

crate *noun* **packing case**, chest, tea chest, box, container.

crater *noun* **hollow**, bowl, basin, hole, cavity, depression, dip; *Geology* caldera.

crave *verb* **long for**, yearn for, hanker after, desire, want, hunger for, thirst for, pine for; *informal* be dying for.

craving *noun* **longing**, yearning, desire, hankering, hunger, thirst, appetite.

crawl *verb* **1 creep**, worm your way, go on all fours, wriggle, slither, squirm. **2** *(informal)* **grovel**, kowtow, pander, toady, bow and scrape, fawn; *informal* suck up, lick someone's boots.

craze *noun* **fad**, fashion, trend, vogue, enthusiasm, mania, passion, rage; *informal* thing.

crazy *adjective (informal)* **1 mad**, insane, out of your mind, deranged, demented, crazed, lunatic, unbalanced, unhinged; *Brit.* sectionable; *informal* mental, off your head, round the bend; *Brit. informal* barmy, crackers, barking (mad), potty, round the twist. **2** *a crazy idea* **stupid**, foolish, idiotic, silly, absurd, ridiculous, ludicrous, preposterous, asinine; *informal* cockeyed, half-baked; *Brit. informal* barmy, daft. **3** *he's crazy about her* **passionate**, very keen, enamoured, infatuated, smitten, enthusiastic, fanatical; *informal* wild, mad, nuts; *Brit. informal* potty.
– OPPOSITES sane, sensible.

cream *noun* **1 lotion**, ointment, moisturizer, cosmetic, salve, rub. **2 best**, finest, pick, flower, crème de la crème, elite, A-list.
– OPPOSITES dregs.
● *adjective* **off-white**, creamy, ivory.

creamy *adjective* **smooth**, thick, velvety, rich, buttery.

crease *noun* **fold**, line, crinkle, ridge, furrow, groove, corrugation, wrinkle, crow's foot.
● *verb* **crumple**, wrinkle, crinkle, line, scrunch up, rumple, ruck up, pucker.

create *verb* **1 produce**, generate, bring into being, make, fashion, build, construct. **2 bring about**, give rise to, lead to, result in, cause, breed, generate, engender, produce. **3 establish**, found, initiate, institute, constitute, inaugurate, launch, set up, form.
– OPPOSITES destroy, abolish.

creation *noun* **1 establishment**, formation, foundation, initiation, institution, inauguration, constitution, setting up. **2 the world**, the universe, the cosmos, nature, the natural world. **3 work**, work of art, production, opus, oeuvre, achievement, concoction, invention; *informal* brainchild.
- OPPOSITES abolition, destruction.

creative *adjective* **inventive**, imaginative, innovative, experimental, original, artistic, inspired, visionary.
- OPPOSITES unimaginative.

creator *noun* **maker**, producer, author, designer, deviser, originator, inventor, architect.

creature *noun* **animal**, beast, brute, living thing, living being; *N. Amer. informal* critter.

credentials *plural noun* **1 suitability**, eligibility, attributes, qualifications, record, experience, background. **2 documents**, identity papers, ID, passport, testimonial, reference, certification.

credibility *noun* **plausibility**, believability, credence, trustworthiness, reliability, dependability, integrity.

credible *adjective* **believable**, plausible, conceivable, persuasive, convincing, tenable, probable, possible, feasible, reasonable.

credit *noun* **praise**, commendation, acclaim, acknowledgement, recognition, kudos, glory, respect, appreciation.
● *verb* **1** *(Brit.) you wouldn't credit it!* **believe**, accept, give credence to, trust, have faith in. **2 ascribe to**, attribute to, put down to.

credulous *adjective* **gullible**, naive, easily taken in, impressionable, unsuspecting, unsuspicious, innocent, inexperienced, unsophisticated, wide-eyed.
- OPPOSITES suspicious.

creed *noun* **1** *people of many creeds* **faith**, religion, belief, religious persuasion. **2** *his political creed* **beliefs**, principles, articles of faith, tenets, ideology, credo, doctrines, teachings.

creek *noun* **inlet**, bay, estuary, fjord; *Scottish* firth.

creep *verb* **tiptoe**, steal, sneak, slink, edge, inch, skulk, prowl.

creepy *adjective (informal)* **frightening**, eerie, disturbing, sinister, weird, menacing, threatening; *informal* spooky, scary.

crest *noun* **1 tuft**, comb, plume, crown. **2 summit**, peak, top, ridge, pinnacle, brow, crown, apex. **3 insignia**, emblem, coat of arms, arms, badge, device, regalia.

crestfallen *adjective* **downhearted**, downcast, despondent, disappointed, disconsolate, disheartened, discouraged, dispirited, dejected, sad, dismayed, unhappy, forlorn.
- OPPOSITES cheerful.

crevice *noun* **crack**, fissure, interstice, cleft, chink, cranny, slit, split.

crew *noun* **1** *the ship's crew* **company**, complement, sailors, hands. **2** *a film crew* **team**, squad, company, unit, party, gang.

crime *noun* **1 offence**, unlawful act, illegal act, felony, violation, misdemeanour. **2 lawbreaking**, delinquency, wrongdoing, criminality, misconduct, illegality, villainy, vice.

criminal *noun* **lawbreaker**, felon, offender, malefactor, villain, delinquent, culprit, miscreant, wrongdoer; *informal* crook.
● *adjective* **1 unlawful**, illegal, illicit, lawless, delinquent, corrupt, felonious, nefarious; *informal* crooked; *Brit. informal* bent. **2** *(informal)* **deplorable**, shameful, reprehensible, disgraceful, inexcusable, outrageous, scandalous.
- OPPOSITES lawful.

cringe *verb* **1 cower**, shrink, recoil, shy away, flinch, quail, blench, tremble, quiver, quake. **2 wince**, shudder, squirm, feel embarrassed/mortified.

cripple *verb* **1 disable**, paralyse, immobilize, incapacitate, handicap. **2 damage**, weaken, hamper, paralyse, ruin, destroy, wipe out, bring to a standstill, put out of action, put out of business.

crippled *adjective* **disabled**, paralysed, incapacitated, physically handicapped, lame, immobilized, bedridden, confined to a wheelchair; *euphemistic* physically challenged.

crisis *noun* **1 emergency**, disaster, catastrophe, calamity, meltdown, predicament, plight, dire straits. **2 critical point**, turning point, crossroads, head, point of no return, moment of truth; *informal* crunch.

crisp *adjective* **1 crunchy**, crispy, brittle, breakable, dry. **2 invigorating**, brisk, cool, fresh, refreshing, exhilarating.
- OPPOSITES soft.

criterion *noun* **standard**, measure, gauge, test, benchmark, yardstick, touchstone, barometer.

critic *noun* **1 reviewer**, commentator, analyst, judge, pundit, expert. **2 detractor**, attacker, fault-finder.

critical *adjective* **1 disapproving**, disparaging, scathing, fault-finding, judgemental, negative, unfavourable, censorious; *informal* nit-picking, picky. **2 serious**, grave, precarious, touch-and-go, in the balance, desperate, dire, acute, life-and-death. **3 crucial**, vital, essential, all-important, paramount, fundamental, key, pivotal.
- OPPOSITES complimentary.

criticism *noun* **1 fault-finding**, censure, condemnation, disapproval, disparagement; *informal* flak, a bad press, panning; *Brit. informal* stick. **2 evaluation**, assessment, appraisal, appreciation, analysis, critique, judgement, commentary.
- OPPOSITES praise.

criticize *verb* **find fault with**, censure, condemn, attack, disparage, denigrate, run down; *informal* knock, pan, pull to pieces; *Brit. informal* slag off, slate, rubbish; *N. Amer. informal* trash.
- OPPOSITES praise.

crook *noun* see **criminal** (noun).

crooked *adjective* **1 winding**, twisting, zigzag, meandering, tortuous, serpentine. **2 bent**, twisted, misshapen, deformed, malformed, contorted, warped, bowed, distorted. **3 lopsided**, askew, awry, off-centre, out of true, at an angle, slanting, squint; *Scottish* agley; *Brit. informal* skewwhiff, wonky. **4** *(informal)* **dishonest**, criminal, illegal, unlawful, nefarious, fraudulent, corrupt; *informal* shady; *Brit. informal* bent.
- OPPOSITES straight.

crop *noun* **harvest**, yield, fruits, produce, vintage.
● *verb* **1 cut**, clip, trim, shear, shave, lop off, chop off, hack off, dock. **2 graze on**, browse on, feed on, nibble, eat.
□ **crop up** happen, occur, arise, turn up, pop up, emerge, materialize, surface, appear, come to light.

cross *noun* **1** *we all have our crosses to bear* **burden**, trouble, worry, trial, tribulation, affliction, curse, misfortune, woe; *informal* hassle, headache. **2** *a cross between a yak and a cow* **mixture**, blend, combination, amalgam, hybrid, cross-breed, mongrel.
● *verb* **1 travel across**, traverse, negotiate, navigate, cover. **2 intersect**, meet, join, connect. **3 oppose**, resist, defy, obstruct, contradict, argue with, stand up to. **4 hybridize**, cross-breed, interbreed, cross-fertilize, cross-pollinate.
● *adjective* **angry**, annoyed, irate, vexed, irritated, in a bad mood, put out, exasperated; *informal* hot under the collar, peeved; *Brit. informal* shirty, ratty, not best pleased; *N. Amer. informal* sore, ticked off.
- OPPOSITES pleased.
□ **cross out** delete, strike out, score out, cancel, obliterate.

crossing *noun* **1 junction**, crossroads, intersection, interchange, level crossing. **2 journey**, passage, voyage.

crouch *verb* **squat**, bend (down), hunker down, hunch over, stoop, duck, cower.

crow *verb* **boast**, brag, blow your own trumpet, swagger, swank, gloat.

crowd *noun* **1 horde**, throng, mass, multitude, host, army, herd, swarm,

troop, mob, rabble; *informal* gaggle. **2** *they're a nice crowd* **group**, set, circle, clique; *informal* gang, bunch, crew, lot. **3** *a capacity crowd* **audience**, spectators, listeners, viewers, house, turnout, attendance, gate, congregation.
● *verb* **1 cluster**, flock, swarm, mill, throng, huddle, gather, assemble, congregate, converge. **2 surge**, throng, push, jostle, elbow your way, squeeze, pile, cram.

crowded *adjective* **packed**, full, filled to capacity, full to bursting, congested, overflowing, teeming, swarming, thronged, populous, overpopulated, busy; *informal* jam-packed, stuffed, chock-a-block, chock-full, bursting at the seams, full to the gunwales, wall-to-wall, mobbed; *Austral./NZ informal* chocker.
– OPPOSITES deserted.

crown *noun* **1 coronet**, diadem, tiara, circlet. **2 monarch**, sovereign, king, queen, emperor, empress, monarchy, royalty. **3 top**, crest, summit, peak, pinnacle, tip, brow, apex.
● *verb the post at Harvard crowned his career* **round off**, cap, be the climax of, be the culmination of, top off, complete, perfect.

crucial *adjective* **1 pivotal**, critical, key, decisive, life-and-death. **2 all-important**, of the utmost importance, of the essence, critical, paramount, essential, vital.
– OPPOSITES insignificant, unimportant.

crude *adjective* **1 unrefined**, unpurified, unprocessed, untreated, coarse, raw, natural. **2 primitive**, simple, basic, homespun, rudimentary, rough and ready, makeshift, improvised, unsophisticated. **3 vulgar**, rude, dirty, naughty, smutty, indecent, obscene, coarse; *informal* blue.
– OPPOSITES refined.

cruel *adjective* **1** *a cruel man* **brutal**, savage, inhuman, barbaric, vicious, sadistic, monstrous, callous, ruthless, merciless, heartless, pitiless, implacable, unkind, inhumane. **2** *her death was a cruel blow* **harsh**, severe, bitter, heartbreaking, heart-rending, painful, agonizing, traumatic.
– OPPOSITES compassionate.

cruise *noun* **(boat) trip**, voyage, sail.
● *verb* **1 sail**, voyage. **2 drive slowly**, drift; *informal* mosey, tootle; *Brit. informal* pootle.

crumb *noun* **fragment**, bit, morsel, particle, speck, scrap, shred, atom, trace, mite, jot, ounce; *informal* smidgen, tad.

crumble *verb* **1 disintegrate**, fall apart, fall to pieces, collapse, decompose, break up, decay, become dilapidated, deteriorate, degenerate. **2 break up**, crush, fragment, pulverize.

crumple *verb* **1 crush**, scrunch up, screw up, squash, squeeze. **2 crease**, wrinkle, crinkle, rumple. **3 collapse**, give way, cave in, go to pieces, break down, crumble.

crunch *verb* **munch**, chomp, champ, bite into, crush, grind.

crusade *noun* **campaign**, drive, push, movement, effort, struggle, battle, war, offensive.
● *verb* **campaign**, fight, battle, do battle, strive, struggle, agitate, lobby.

crush *verb* **1 squash**, squeeze, press, pulp, mash, mangle, pulverize. **2 crease**, crumple, rumple, wrinkle, scrunch up. **3 suppress**, put down, quell, stamp out, repress, subdue, extinguish. **4 demoralize**, deflate, flatten, squash, devastate, shatter, mortify, humiliate.
● *noun* **crowd**, throng, horde, swarm, press, mob.

crust *noun* **covering**, layer, coating, surface, topping, sheet, film, skin, shell, scab.

cry *verb* **1 weep**, shed tears, sob, wail, snivel, whimper; *Scottish* greet; *informal* blub, blubber; *Brit. informal* grizzle. **2 call**, shout, exclaim, sing out, yell, bawl, bellow, roar; *informal* holler.
– OPPOSITES laugh.
● *noun* **call**, shout, exclamation, yell, bawl, bellow, roar; *informal* holler.
□ **cry off** *(informal)* back out, pull out,

cancel, withdraw, change your mind; *informal* get cold feet, cop out.

crypt *noun* **tomb**, vault, burial chamber, sepulchre, catacomb.

cryptic *adjective* **enigmatic**, mysterious, mystifying, puzzling, obscure, abstruse, arcane, unintelligible.
– OPPOSITES clear.

cuddle *verb* **1 hug**, embrace, clasp, hold in your arms, caress, pet, fondle; *informal* canoodle, smooch. **2 snuggle**, nestle, curl, nuzzle.

cudgel *noun* **club**, truncheon, bludgeon, baton, shillelagh, mace; *N. Amer.* blackjack, nightstick; *Brit. informal* cosh.
● *verb* **club**, bludgeon, beat, batter, bash; *Brit. informal* cosh.

cue *noun* **signal**, sign, indication, prompt, reminder.

culminate *verb* **come to a climax**, come to a head, climax, end, finish, conclude, build up to, lead up to.

culmination *noun* **climax**, peak, pinnacle, high point, height, summit, zenith, apotheosis, apex, apogee.

culpable *adjective* **to blame**, guilty, at fault, in the wrong, answerable, accountable, responsible.
– OPPOSITES innocent.

culprit *noun* **guilty party**, offender, wrongdoer, miscreant, criminal, lawbreaker, felon, delinquent; *informal* baddy, crook.

cult *noun* **1 sect**, group, movement. **2 obsession**, fixation, idolization, devotion, worship, veneration.

cultivate *verb* **1 farm**, work, till, plough, dig. **2 grow**, raise, rear, tend, plant, sow. **3 woo**, court, curry favour with, ingratiate yourself with; *informal* get in someone's good books. **4 improve**, better, refine, educate, develop, enrich.

cultivated *adjective* see **cultured**.

cultural *adjective* **1 social**, lifestyle, sociological, anthropological, racial, ethnic. **2 aesthetic**, artistic, intellectual, educational, civilizing.

culture *noun* **1** *a lover of culture* **the arts**, high art. **2** *a man of culture* **education**, cultivation, enlightenment, discernment, discrimination, taste, refinement, sophistication. **3 civilization**, society, way of life, lifestyle, customs, traditions, heritage, values. **4 philosophy**, ethic, outlook, approach, rationale.

cultured *adjective* **cultivated**, artistic, enlightened, civilized, educated, well read, learned, discerning, discriminating, refined, sophisticated; *informal* arty.
– OPPOSITES ignorant.

cunning *adjective* **1 crafty**, wily, artful, devious, Machiavellian, sly, scheming, canny, dishonest, deceitful. **2 clever**, shrewd, astute, canny, ingenious, imaginative, enterprising, inventive, resourceful, creative, original, inspired, brilliant.
– OPPOSITES honest, stupid.
● *noun* **1 guile**, craftiness, deviousness, trickery, duplicity. **2 ingenuity**, imagination, inventiveness, enterprise, resourcefulness.

curator *noun* **custodian**, keeper, conservator, guardian, caretaker.

curb *noun* **restraint**, restriction, check, brake, control, limit.
● *verb* **restrain**, hold back, keep in check, control, rein in, contain; *informal* keep a lid on.

cure *verb* **1 heal**, restore to health, make well/better. **2 rectify**, remedy, put/set right, right, fix, mend, repair, solve, sort out, eliminate, end. **3 preserve**, smoke, salt, dry, pickle.
● *noun* **remedy**, medicine, medication, antidote, treatment, therapy.

curiosity *noun* **1 interest**, inquisitiveness, attention, spirit of enquiry; *informal* nosiness. **2 oddity**, curio, novelty, rarity.

curious *adjective* **1 intrigued**, interested, eager, inquisitive. **2 strange**, odd, peculiar, funny, unusual, queer, bizarre, weird, eccentric, extraordinary, abnormal, anomalous.

– OPPOSITES uninterested, normal.

curl *verb* **spiral**, coil, wreathe, twirl, swirl, wind, curve, twist (and turn), snake, corkscrew, twine, entwine, wrap.
● *noun* **1 ringlet**, corkscrew, kink, lock. **2** *a curl of smoke* **spiral**, coil, twirl, swirl, twist, corkscrew.

curly *adjective* **wavy**, curling, curled, frizzy, kinky, corkscrew.
– OPPOSITES straight.

currency *noun* **1 money**, legal tender, cash, banknotes, notes, coins; *N. Amer.* bills. **2 popularity**, circulation, exposure, acceptance, prevalence.

current *adjective* **1 contemporary**, present-day, modern, topical, live, burning. **2 prevalent**, common, accepted, in circulation, popular, widespread. **3 valid**, usable, up to date. **4 incumbent**, present, in office, in power, reigning.
– OPPOSITES past, former.
● *noun* **1 flow**, stream, draught, jet, tide. **2 course**, progress, progression, flow, tide, movement.

curse *noun* **1 jinx**, malediction; *N. Amer.* hex; *formal* imprecation, anathema. **2 affliction**, burden, misery, ordeal, evil, scourge. **3 swear word**, expletive, oath, profanity, four-letter word, dirty word, obscenity; *informal* cuss word.
● *verb* **1 afflict**, trouble, plague, bedevil. **2 swear**, take the Lord's name in vain, blaspheme; *informal* cuss, turn the air blue, eff and blind.

cursed *adjective* **damned**, doomed, ill-fated, ill-starred, jinxed.

cursory *adjective* **brief**, hasty, hurried, quick, rapid, passing, perfunctory, desultory, casual.
– OPPOSITES thorough.

curt *adjective* **terse**, brusque, abrupt, clipped, blunt, short, sharp, rude, ungracious; *informal* snappy.
– OPPOSITES expansive.

curtail *verb* **reduce**, shorten, cut, cut down, decrease, trim, restrict, limit, curb, rein in/back, cut short, truncate; *informal* slash.
– OPPOSITES increase, extend.

curve *noun* **bend**, turn, loop, arc, arch, bow, curvature.
● *verb* **bend**, turn, loop, wind, meander, snake, arc, arch.

curved *adjective* **bent**, arched, bowed, rounded, crescent.
– OPPOSITES straight.

cushion *noun a cushion against inflation* **protection**, buffer, shield, defence, bulwark.
● *verb* **1** *cushioned from the outside world* **protect**, shield, shelter, cocoon. **2** *cushion the blow* **soften**, lessen, diminish, mitigate, alleviate, take the edge off, dull, deaden.

custody *noun* **care**, guardianship, charge, supervision, safe keeping, responsibility, protection.
□ **in custody** in prison, in jail, imprisoned, incarcerated, under lock and key, on remand; *informal* behind bars, doing time, inside; *Brit. informal* banged up.

custom *noun* **1** *local customs* **tradition**, practice, usage, way, convention, formality, ritual, mores. **2** *it was his custom to sleep in a chair* **habit**, practice, routine, way; *formal* wont.

customary *adjective* **usual**, traditional, normal, conventional, habitual, familiar, accepted, accustomed, routine, established, time-honoured, prevailing.
– OPPOSITES unusual.

customer *noun* **consumer**, buyer, purchaser, patron, client, shopper; *Brit. informal* punter.

cut *verb* **1 gash**, slash, lacerate, slit, wound, scratch, graze, nick. **2 slice**, chop, dice, cube, carve; *N. Amer.* hash. **3 carve**, engrave, incise, etch, score, chisel, whittle. **4 reduce**, cut back/down on, decrease, lessen, mark down, discount, lower; *informal* slash. **5 shorten**, abridge, condense, abbreviate, truncate, edit, censor. **6 delete**, remove, take out, excise.
● *noun* **1 gash**, slash, laceration, incision, wound, scratch, graze, nick. **2 piece**, joint, fillet, section. **3** *(informal)* **share**, portion, quota, percentage;

informal slice (of the cake). **4 reduction**, cutback, decrease, lessening; *N. Amer.* rollback. **5 style**, design, line, fit.

cutback *noun* **reduction**, cut, decrease, economy, saving; *N. Amer.* rollback.
- OPPOSITES increase.

cute *adjective* **endearing**, adorable, lovable, sweet, lovely, appealing, engaging, delightful, dear; *informal* twee; *Brit. informal* dinky.

cutting *noun* **clipping**, article, piece, column, paragraph.
● *adjective* **hurtful**, wounding, barbed, sharp, scathing, caustic, sarcastic, snide, spiteful, malicious, vicious, cruel; *informal* bitchy.

cycle *noun* **1** *the cycle of birth, death, and rebirth* **circle**, round, pattern, rhythm, loop. **2** *a cycle of three plays* **series**, sequence, set, succession, run.

cynic *noun* **sceptic**, doubter, doubting Thomas, pessimist, prophet of doom.
- OPPOSITES idealist, optimist.

cynical *adjective* **sceptical**, doubtful, distrustful, suspicious, disbelieving, pessimistic, negative, world-weary, disillusioned, disenchanted, jaundiced.
- OPPOSITES idealistic, optimistic.

Dd

dab *verb* **pat**, press, touch, blot, swab, daub, wipe.
● *noun* **drop**, spot, smear, splash, bit.

dabble *verb* **toy with**, dip into, flirt with, tinker with, play with.

daft *adjective (Brit. informal)* **absurd**, preposterous, ridiculous, ludicrous, idiotic, stupid, foolish, asinine, senseless, inane; *informal* crazy, cockeyed, half-baked; *Brit. informal* barmy.
– OPPOSITES sensible.

daily *adjective* **everyday**, day-to-day; *formal* quotidian.
● *adverb* **every day**, once a day, day after day.

dainty *adjective* **1 delicate**, fine, elegant, exquisite, graceful. **2 fastidious**, fussy, particular, finicky; *informal* choosy, picky; *Brit. informal* faddy.
– OPPOSITES unwieldy.

dam *noun* **barrage**, barrier, wall, embankment, barricade, obstruction.
● *verb* **block (up)**, obstruct, bung up, close, hold back.

damage *noun* **1 harm**, destruction, vandalism, injury, ruin, devastation. **2** *she won £4,000 damages* **compensation**, recompense, restitution, redress, reparation(s); *N. Amer. informal* comp.
● *verb* **harm**, injure, deface, spoil, impair, vandalize, ruin, destroy, wreck; *N. Amer. informal* trash.
– OPPOSITES repair.

damaging *adjective* **harmful**, detrimental, injurious, hurtful, destructive, environmentally unfriendly, ruinous, deleterious.
– OPPOSITES beneficial.

damn *verb* **condemn**, censure, criticize, attack, denounce.
– OPPOSITES praise.

damning *adjective* **incriminating**, damaging, condemnatory, conclusive, irrefutable.

damp *adjective* **moist**, humid, muggy, clammy, sweaty, dank, wet, rainy, drizzly, showery, misty, foggy, dewy.
– OPPOSITES dry.
● *noun* **moisture**, liquid, wet, wetness, dampness, humidity.

dampen *verb* **1 moisten**, damp, wet, soak. **2 lessen**, decrease, diminish, reduce, moderate, cool, suppress, stifle, inhibit.
– OPPOSITES dry, heighten.

dance *verb* **1 trip**, sway, twirl, whirl, pirouette, gyrate, jive; *informal* bop, trip the light fantastic; *N. Amer. informal* get down. **2** *the girls danced round me* **caper**, cavort, frolic, skip, prance, gambol, leap, hop, jig, bounce.
● *noun* **ball**; *N. Amer.* prom, hoedown; *informal* disco, rave, hop, bop.

danger *noun* **1 peril**, hazard, risk, jeopardy, endangerment, menace. **2 possibility**, chance, risk, probability, likelihood, threat.
– OPPOSITES safety.

dangerous *adjective* **1 menacing**, threatening, treacherous. **2 hazardous**, perilous, risky, unsafe, unpredictable, precarious, insecure; *informal* dicey, hairy; *Brit. informal* dodgy.
– OPPOSITES harmless, safe.

dangle *verb* **hang**, swing, droop, wave, trail, stream.

dank *adjective* **damp**, musty, chilly, clammy.
– OPPOSITES dry.

dapper *adjective* **smart**, spruce, trim, debonair, neat, well dressed, elegant; *informal* snappy, natty; *N. Amer. informal* spiffy, fly.
– OPPOSITES scruffy.

dare *verb* **1 be brave enough**, have the courage, venture, have the nerve, risk, take the liberty of; *N. Amer.* take a flyer; *informal* stick your neck out.

2 challenge, defy, invite, bid, provoke, goad.
● *noun* **challenge**, invitation, wager, bet.

daring *adjective* **bold**, audacious, intrepid, fearless, brave, heroic, dashing; *informal* gutsy.
- OPPOSITES cowardly, timid.
● *noun* **boldness**, audacity, temerity, fearlessness, bravery, courage, pluck; *informal* nerve, guts; *Brit. informal* bottle; *N. Amer. informal* moxie.
- OPPOSITES cowardice.

dark *adjective* **1** *a dark room* **dingy**, gloomy, shadowy, murky, grey, poorly lit, inky, black. **2** *dark hair* **brunette**, dark brown, sable, jet-black, ebony. **3** *dark skin* **swarthy**, dusky, olive, black, ebony. **4** *dark thoughts* **gloomy**, dismal, negative, downbeat, bleak, grim, fatalistic, black. **5** *a dark look* **angry**, forbidding, threatening, ominous, moody, brooding, sullen, scowling, glowering. **6** *dark deeds* **evil**, wicked, sinful, bad, iniquitous, ungodly, vile, foul, monstrous; *informal* dirty, shady, crooked.
- OPPOSITES bright, light, blonde, pale.
● *noun* **night**, night-time, darkness, nightfall, blackout.

darken *verb* **grow dark**, make dark, blacken, grow dim, cloud over, lour.
- OPPOSITES lighten.

darkness *noun* **1** *lights shone in the darkness* **dark**, blackness, gloom, dimness, murk, shadow, shade. **2** *darkness fell* **night**, night-time, dark. **3** *the forces of darkness* **evil**, wickedness, sin, ungodliness, the Devil.

darling *noun* **1 dear**, dearest, love, sweetheart, beloved; *informal* honey, angel, pet, sweetie, baby, poppet. **2 favourite**, idol, hero, heroine; *Brit. informal* blue-eyed boy/girl.
● *adjective* **1 dear**, dearest, precious, beloved. **2 adorable**, charming, cute, sweet, enchanting, dear, delightful; *Scottish & N. English* bonny.

dart *verb* **1 dash**, rush, tear, shoot, sprint, bound, scurry, scamper; *informal* scoot, whip. **2 direct**, cast, throw, shoot, send, flash.

dash *verb* **1 rush**, race, run, sprint, career, charge, shoot, hurtle, hare, fly, speed, zoom; *informal* tear, belt; *Brit. informal* bomb; *N. Amer. informal* barrel. **2 hurl**, smash, fling, slam, throw, toss, cast; *informal* chuck, sling. **3 shatter**, destroy, wreck, ruin, demolish, scotch, frustrate, thwart; *informal* put paid to; *Brit. informal* scupper.
- OPPOSITES dawdle.
● *noun* **1 rush**, race, run, sprint, bolt, dart, leap, charge, bound. **2 pinch**, touch, sprinkle, taste, spot, drop, dab, splash; *informal* smidgen, tad.

dashing *adjective* **debonair**, stylish, dapper, devil-may-care, raffish, flamboyant, swashbuckling.

data *noun* **facts**, figures, statistics, details, particulars, information.

date *noun* **1 day**, occasion, time, year, age, period, era, epoch. **2 appointment**, meeting, engagement, rendezvous, commitment, assignation; *literary* tryst. **3** *(informal)* **partner**, escort, girlfriend, boyfriend.
● *verb* **1 age**, grow old, become dated, show its age, be of its time. **2** *(informal)* **go out with**, take out, go with, see; *informal* go steady with; *dated* court, woo.
□ **date from** be from, originate in, come from, belong to, go back to.

WORD LINKS
chronological relating to dates

dated *adjective* **old-fashioned**, outdated, outmoded, unfashionable, passé, behind the times, archaic, obsolete, antiquated; *informal* old hat, out of the ark.
- OPPOSITES modern.

daunt *verb* **discourage**, deter, demoralize, put off, dishearten, intimidate, overawe, awe.

daunting *adjective* **intimidating**, forbidding, challenging, formidable, unnerving, disconcerting, discouraging, disheartening, demoralizing, dismaying, scary, frightening, alarming.

dawdle *verb* **linger**, take your time, be slow, waste time, dally, amble, stroll, trail, move at a snail's pace; *informal* dilly-dally.
- OPPOSITES hurry.

dawn *noun* **1 daybreak**, sunrise, first light, daylight, cockcrow, first thing; *N. Amer.* sunup. **2 beginning**, start, birth, inception, genesis, emergence, advent, appearance, arrival, rise, origin.
- OPPOSITES dusk.
● *verb* **1** *Thursday dawned crisp and sunny* **begin**, break, arrive, emerge. **2** *a bright new future has dawned* **begin**, start, commence, be born, appear, arrive, emerge, arise, rise, unfold, develop. **3** *the reality dawned on him* **become evident**, register, cross someone's mind, suggest itself, occur to, come to, strike, hit.

day *noun* **1 daytime**, daylight (hours), waking hours. **2 period**, time, date, age, era, generation.
- OPPOSITES night.

WORD LINKS
diurnal relating to the day

daze *verb* **dumbfound**, stupefy, stun, shock, stagger, bewilder, take aback, nonplus; *informal* flabbergast; *Brit. informal* knock for six.
● *noun* **stupor**, trance, haze, spin, whirl, muddle, jumble.

dazzle *verb* **1 blind**, confuse, disorient. **2 overwhelm**, overcome, impress, move, stir, touch, awe, overawe; *informal* bowl over, blow away, knock out.

dead *adjective* **1 passed on**, passed away, departed, late, lost, perished, fallen, killed, lifeless, extinct; *informal* six feet under, pushing up daisies; *formal* deceased. **2 obsolete**, extinct, defunct, disused, abandoned, superseded, vanished, archaic, ancient. **3 not working**, out of order, inoperative, inactive, broken, defective; *informal* kaput, conked out, on the blink, bust; *Brit. informal* knackered. **4 boring**, uninteresting, unexciting, uninspiring, dull, flat, quiet, sleepy, slow, lifeless; *informal* one-horse; *N. Amer. informal* dullsville.
- OPPOSITES alive, living, lively.
● *adverb* **1 completely**, absolutely, totally, utterly, deadly, perfectly, entirely, quite, thoroughly. **2 directly**, exactly, precisely, immediately, right, straight, due.

deaden *verb* **1 numb**, dull, blunt, alleviate, mitigate, diminish, reduce, lessen, ease, soothe, relieve, assuage. **2 muffle**, mute, smother, stifle, damp (down), soften, cushion.
- OPPOSITES intensify, amplify.

deadline *noun* **time limit**, finishing date, target date, cut-off point.

deadlock *noun* **stalemate**, impasse, checkmate, stand-off, standstill, gridlock.

deadly *adjective* **1 fatal**, lethal, mortal, life-threatening, noxious, toxic, poisonous. **2** *deadly enemies* **mortal**, irreconcilable, implacable, bitter, sworn. **3** *his aim is deadly* **unerring**, unfailing, perfect, true, accurate; *Brit. informal* spot on.
- OPPOSITES harmless.

deafening *adjective* **ear-splitting**, thunderous, crashing, uproarious, almighty, booming.
- OPPOSITES low, soft.

deal *noun* **agreement**, understanding, pact, bargain, covenant, contract, treaty, arrangement, compromise, settlement, terms.
● *verb* **1 trade in**, buy and sell, purvey, supply, market, traffic in. **2 distribute**, give out, share out, divide out, hand out, pass out, pass round, dispense, allocate.
□ **deal with 1** cope with, handle, manage, treat, take care of, take charge of, take in hand, sort out, tackle, take on, control. **2** concern, be about, have to do with, discuss, consider, cover, tackle, explore, investigate, examine.

dealer *noun* **trader**, merchant, salesman/woman, seller, vendor, purveyor, pedlar, distributor, supplier, shopkeeper, retailer, wholesaler, tradesman, tradesperson; *Brit.* stockist.

dear *adjective* **1** *a dear friend* **beloved**, precious, close, intimate, bosom. **2** *her pictures were too dear to part with* **precious**, treasured, valued, prized, cherished, special. **3 endearing**, adorable, lovable, appealing, engaging, charming, captivating, lovely, delightful, sweet, darling. **4 expensive**, costly, high-priced, overpriced, exorbitant, extortionate; *Brit.* over the odds; *informal* pricey.
- OPPOSITES disagreeable, cheap.
● *noun* **darling**, dearest, love, beloved, sweetheart, precious; *informal* sweetie, sugar, honey, baby, pet, poppet.

dearly *adverb* **very much**, a great deal, greatly, profoundly, deeply.

dearth *noun* **lack**, scarcity, shortage, shortfall, deficiency, insufficiency, inadequacy, absence.
- OPPOSITES surfeit.

death *noun* **1 dying**, demise, end, passing, loss of life; *formal* decease. **2 end**, finish, termination, extinction, extinguishing, collapse, destruction.
- OPPOSITES life, birth.

WORD LINKS
fatal, **lethal**, **mortal** causing death

deathly *adjective* **deathlike**, ghostly, ghastly, ashen, white, pale, pallid.

debacle *noun* **fiasco**, failure, catastrophe, disaster; *informal* fail.

debase *verb* **degrade**, devalue, demean, cheapen, prostitute, discredit, drag down, tarnish, blacken, disgrace, dishonour, shame.
- OPPOSITES enhance.

debatable *adjective* **arguable**, questionable, open to question, disputable, controversial, contentious, doubtful, dubious, uncertain, borderline, moot.

debate *noun* **discussion**, argument, dispute, talks.
● *verb* **1 discuss**, talk over/through, talk about, thrash out, argue, dispute. **2 consider**, think over/about, chew over, mull over, weigh up, ponder, deliberate.

debauched *adjective* **dissolute**, dissipated, degenerate, decadent, profligate, immoral, lecherous, lewd, licentious.
- OPPOSITES wholesome.

debris *noun* **ruins**, remains, rubble, wreckage, detritus, refuse, rubbish, waste, scrap, flotsam and jetsam.

debt *noun* **1 bill**, account, dues, arrears, charges. **2 indebtedness**, obligation, gratitude, appreciation.

decay *verb* **1 decompose**, rot, putrefy, go bad, go off, spoil, fester, perish. **2 deteriorate**, degenerate, decline, go downhill, slump, slide, go to rack and ruin, go to seed; *informal* go to the dogs.
● *noun* **1 decomposition**, putrefaction, rot. **2 deterioration**, degeneration, decline, weakening, crumbling, disintegration, collapse.

deceit *noun* **deception**, deceitfulness, duplicity, double-dealing, lies, fraud, cheating, trickery.
- OPPOSITES honesty.

deceitful *adjective* **dishonest**, untruthful, insincere, false, disingenuous, untrustworthy, unscrupulous, unprincipled, two-faced, duplicitous, fraudulent, double-dealing; *informal* sneaky, tricky, crooked; *Brit. informal* bent.
- OPPOSITES honest.

deceive *verb* **trick**, cheat, defraud, swindle, hoodwink, hoax, dupe, take in, mislead, delude, fool; *informal* con, pull the wool over someone's eyes; *N. Amer. informal* sucker, goldbrick.

decency *noun* **1 propriety**, decorum, good taste, respectability, morality, virtue, modesty. **2 courtesy**, politeness, good manners, civility, consideration, thoughtfulness.

decent *adjective* **1** *a decent burial* **proper**, correct, right, appropriate, suitable, respectable, decorous, modest, seemly, accepted; *informal* pukka. **2** *a job with decent pay* **satisfactory**, reasonable, fair, acceptable, adequate,

sufficient, not bad, all right, tolerable, passable, suitable; *informal* OK. **3** *(Brit. informal)* **kind**, generous, thoughtful, considerate, obliging, courteous, polite, well mannered, neighbourly, hospitable, pleasant, agreeable, amiable.
– OPPOSITES improper, unsatisfactory.

deception *noun* **1 deceit**, duplicity, double-dealing, fraud, cheating, trickery, guile, bluff, lying, pretence, treachery. **2 trick**, sham, fraud, pretence, hoax, ruse, scheme, dodge, cheat, swindle; *informal* con, set-up, scam.

deceptive *adjective* **misleading**, confusing, illusory, distorted, ambiguous.

decide *verb* **1 resolve**, determine, make up your mind, choose, opt, plan, aim, intend, have in mind, set your sights on. **2 settle**, resolve, determine, work out, answer; *informal* sort out. **3 adjudicate**, arbitrate, judge, pronounce on, give a verdict on, rule on.

decidedly *adverb* **distinctly**, clearly, markedly, obviously, noticeably, unmistakably, patently, manifestly, definitely, positively.

decision *noun* **1 resolution**, conclusion, settlement, choice, option, selection. **2 verdict**, finding, ruling, judgement, adjudication, sentence.

decisive *adjective* **1 resolute**, firm, strong-minded, strong-willed, determined, purposeful. **2 deciding**, conclusive, determining, key, pivotal, critical, crucial.

declaration *noun* **1 announcement**, statement, communication, pronouncement, proclamation; *N. Amer.* advisory. **2 assertion**, profession, affirmation, acknowledgement, revelation, disclosure, confirmation, testimony, avowal, protestation.

declare *verb* **1 announce**, proclaim, state, reveal, air, voice, articulate, express, vent, set forth, publicize, broadcast. **2 assert**, profess, affirm, maintain, state, contend, claim, argue, insist, avow.

decline *verb* **1 turn down**, reject, brush aside, refuse, rebuff, spurn, repulse, dismiss, pass up, say no; *informal* give something a miss. **2 decrease**, reduce, lessen, diminish, dwindle, contract, shrink, fall off, tail off, drop, fall, go down. **3 deteriorate**, degenerate, decay, crumble, collapse, slump, slip, slide, go downhill, worsen; *informal* go to the dogs.
– OPPOSITES accept, increase, improve.
● *noun* **1 reduction**, decrease, downturn, downswing, diminution, ebb, drop, slump, plunge. **2 deterioration**, degeneration, degradation, shrinkage, erosion.
– OPPOSITES rise, improvement.

decompose *verb* **decay**, rot, putrefy, go bad, go off, spoil, perish, deteriorate, degrade, break down.

decor *noun* **decoration**, furnishing, colour scheme.

decorate *verb* **1 ornament**, adorn, trim, embellish, garnish, furnish, enhance. **2 paint**, wallpaper, paper, refurbish, renovate, redecorate; *informal* do up, give something a facelift, give something a makeover. **3 give a medal to**, honour, cite, reward.

decoration *noun* **1 ornamentation**, adornment, trimming, embellishment, beautification. **2 ornament**, bauble, trinket, knick-knack. **3 medal**, award, prize; *Brit. informal* gong.

decorative *adjective* **ornamental**, fancy, ornate, attractive, pretty, showy.
– OPPOSITES functional.

decorum *noun* **1 propriety**, seemliness, decency, good taste, correctness, politeness, good manners. **2 etiquette**, protocol, good form, custom, convention.
– OPPOSITES impropriety.

decrease *verb* **lessen**, reduce, drop, diminish, decline, dwindle, fall off, plummet, plunge.
– OPPOSITES increase.
● *noun* **reduction**, drop, decline, downturn, cut, cutback, diminution.
– OPPOSITES increase.

decree *noun* **1** *a presidential decree* **order**, command, commandment, edict, proclamation, law, statute, act. **2** *a court decree* **judgement**, verdict, adjudication, finding, ruling, decision. ● *verb* **order**, direct, command, rule, dictate, pronounce, proclaim, ordain.

decrepit *adjective* **dilapidated**, rickety, run down, tumbledown, ramshackle, derelict, ruined, in (a state of) disrepair, gone to rack and ruin, on its last legs, decayed, crumbling.

dedicate *verb* **1 commit**, devote, pledge, give (up), sacrifice, set aside. **2 inscribe**, address, offer. **3 devote**, assign, bless, consecrate, sanctify.

dedicated *adjective* **1 committed**, devoted, enthusiastic, keen, staunch, firm, steadfast, loyal, faithful. **2 specialized**, custom-built, customized, purpose-built, exclusive.
- OPPOSITES half-hearted.

dedication *noun* **1 commitment**, devotion, loyalty, allegiance, application, resolve, conscientiousness, perseverance, persistence. **2 inscription**, message.
- OPPOSITES apathy.

deduce *verb* **conclude**, reason, work out, infer, understand, assume, presume, surmise, reckon; *informal* figure out, put two and two together; *Brit. informal* suss out.

deduct *verb* **subtract**, take away, take off, debit, dock, stop; *informal* knock off.
- OPPOSITES add.

deduction *noun* **1 subtraction**, removal, debit. **2 stoppage**, tax, expenses, rebate, discount, concession. **3 conclusion**, inference, supposition, hypothesis, assumption, presumption, suspicion.

deed *noun* **1 act**, action, feat, exploit, achievement, accomplishment, endeavour. **2 document**, contract, instrument.

deep *adjective* **1 cavernous**, yawning, gaping, huge, extensive, bottomless, fathomless. **2 intense**, heartfelt, wholehearted, deep-seated, sincere, genuine, earnest, enthusiastic, great. **3 profound**, serious, intelligent, intellectual, learned, wise, scholarly. **4** *he was deep in concentration* **rapt**, absorbed, engrossed, preoccupied, intent, immersed, lost, gripped. **5 obscure**, complex, mysterious, unfathomable, opaque, abstruse, esoteric, enigmatic. **6 low-pitched**, low, bass, rich, resonant, booming, sonorous. **7 dark**, intense, rich, strong, vivid.
- OPPOSITES shallow, superficial, high.

deeply *adverb* **profoundly**, greatly, enormously, extremely, very, strongly, intensely, keenly, acutely, thoroughly, completely, entirely, seriously.

deface *verb* **vandalize**, disfigure, spoil, ruin, damage; *N. Amer. informal* trash.

defeat *verb* **1 beat**, conquer, win against, triumph over, get the better of, vanquish, rout, trounce, overcome, overpower; *informal* lick, thrash; *US informal* own. **2 thwart**, frustrate, foil, ruin, scotch, derail; *informal* put paid to, stymie; *Brit. informal* scupper. ● *noun* **loss**, conquest, rout; *informal* thrashing, hiding, drubbing, licking.
- OPPOSITES victory.

defect *noun* **fault**, flaw, imperfection, deficiency, deformity, blemish, mistake, error.

defective *adjective* **faulty**, flawed, imperfect, unsound, inoperative, malfunctioning, out of order, broken; *informal* on the blink; *Brit. informal* duff.
- OPPOSITES perfect.

defence *noun* **1 protection**, guarding, security, fortification, resistance. **2 armaments**, weapons, weaponry, arms, the military, the armed forces. **3 justification**, vindication, explanation, mitigation, excuse, alibi, denial, rebuttal, plea, pleading, argument, case.
- OPPOSITES attack, prosecution.

defenceless *adjective* **vulnerable**, helpless, powerless, weak, undefended, unprotected, unguarded, unarmed, exposed, open to attack.

defend *verb* **1 protect**, guard, safeguard, secure, shield, fortify, watch over. **2 justify**, vindicate, explain, argue for, support, back, stand by, make a case for, stick up for.
– OPPOSITES attack, criticize.

defender *noun* **1 protector**, guardian, guard, custodian. **2 supporter**, upholder, backer, champion, advocate, apologist.

defensive *adjective* **1 defending**, protective. **2 self-justifying**, oversensitive, prickly, paranoid, neurotic; *informal* twitchy.

defer *verb* **postpone**, put off, delay, hold over/off, put back, shelve, suspend; *N. Amer.* table; *informal* put on ice, put on the back burner.

defiance *noun* **resistance**, opposition, non-compliance, disobedience, insubordination, rebellion, disregard, contempt, insolence.
– OPPOSITES obedience.

defiant *adjective* **disobedient**, resistant, obstinate, uncooperative, non-compliant, recalcitrant, insubordinate; *Brit. informal* stroppy, bolshie.
– OPPOSITES cooperative.

deficiency *noun* **1 lack**, insufficiency, shortage, inadequacy, deficit, shortfall, scarcity, dearth. **2 defect**, fault, flaw, failing, weakness, shortcoming, limitation.
– OPPOSITES surplus, strength.

deficit *noun* **shortfall**, deficiency, shortage, debt, arrears, loss.
– OPPOSITES surplus.

define *verb* **1 explain**, give the meaning of, spell out, expound, interpret, describe. **2 determine**, establish, fix, specify, designate, decide, stipulate, set out.

definite *adjective* **specific**, explicit, express, precise, exact, clear, clear-cut, unambiguous, certain, sure, positive, conclusive, decisive, firm, unequivocal, unmistakable, proven, decided, marked, distinct, identifiable.
– OPPOSITES vague, ambiguous.

definitely *adverb* **certainly**, surely, for sure, unquestionably, without doubt, undoubtedly, undeniably, clearly, positively, absolutely, unmistakably.

definition *noun* **1 meaning**, sense, interpretation, explanation, description. **2 clarity**, sharpness, focus, crispness, resolution.

definitive *adjective* **1 conclusive**, final, unqualified, absolute, categorical, positive, definite. **2 authoritative**, best, ultimate, classic, standard, recognized, accepted, exhaustive.

deflect *verb* **divert**, turn away, draw away, distract, fend off, parry, stave off.

deformed *adjective* **misshapen**, distorted, malformed, contorted, out of shape, twisted, crooked, warped, buckled, gnarled, disfigured, mutilated, mangled.

defraud *verb* **swindle**, cheat, rob, deceive, dupe, hoodwink, double-cross, trick; *informal* con, do, sting, diddle, rip off, shaft, pull a fast one on, put one over on, sell a pup to; *N. Amer. informal* sucker, snooker, stiff; *Austral. informal* pull a swifty on.

deft *adjective* **skilful**, adept, adroit, dexterous, agile, nimble, handy, able, capable, skilled, proficient, accomplished, expert, polished, slick, professional.
– OPPOSITES clumsy.

defy *verb* **disobey**, flout, disregard, ignore, break, violate, contravene, breach, challenge, fly in the face of, confront.
– OPPOSITES obey.

degenerate *adjective* **corrupt**, perverted, decadent, dissolute, dissipated, debauched, immoral, unprincipled, disreputable.
● *verb* **deteriorate**, decline, worsen, slip, slide, go downhill; *informal* go to the dogs.
– OPPOSITES improve.

degrade *verb* **demean**, debase, humiliate, humble, belittle, mortify, dehumanize, brutalize.
– OPPOSITES dignify.

degree *noun* **level**, standard, grade, stage, mark, amount, extent, measure, intensity, strength, proportion.

deign *verb* **condescend**, stoop, lower yourself, demean yourself, humble yourself, consent.

d

dejected *adjective* **downcast**, downhearted, despondent, disconsolate, dispirited, crestfallen, disheartened, depressed; *informal* down in the mouth, down in the dumps.
- OPPOSITES cheerful.

delay *verb* **1 detain**, hold up, make late, slow up/down, bog down, hinder, hamper, impede, obstruct. **2 linger**, drag your feet, hold back, dawdle, waste time, stall, hesitate, dither, shilly-shally; *informal* dilly-dally. **3 postpone**, put off, defer, hold over, adjourn, reschedule.
- OPPOSITES hurry, advance.
● *noun* **1 hold-up**, wait, interruption, stoppage. **2** *the delay of his trial* **postponement**, deferral, adjournment.

delegate *noun* **representative**, envoy, emissary, commissioner, agent, deputy.
● *verb* **assign**, entrust, pass on, hand on/over, turn over, devolve.

delegation *noun* **deputation**, mission, commission, contingent, legation.

delete *verb* **remove**, cut (out), take out, edit out, excise, cancel, cross out, strike out, obliterate, rub out, erase.
- OPPOSITES add.

deliberate *adjective* **1 intentional**, calculated, conscious, intended, planned, wilful, premeditated. **2 careful**, cautious, measured, regular, even, steady. **3 methodical**, systematic, careful, painstaking, meticulous, thorough.
- OPPOSITES accidental, hasty.
● *verb* **think**, think about/over, ponder, consider, contemplate, reflect on, muse on, meditate on, ruminate on, mull over; *N. Amer.* think on.

deliberately *adverb* **1 intentionally**, on purpose, purposely, by design, knowingly, wittingly, consciously, wilfully. **2 carefully**, cautiously, slowly, steadily, evenly.

deliberation *noun* **thought**, consideration, reflection, contemplation, discussion.

delicacy *noun* **1 fineness**, delicateness, fragility, thinness, lightness, flimsiness. **2 difficulty**, trickiness, sensitivity, ticklishness, awkwardness. **3 care**, sensitivity, tact, discretion, diplomacy, subtlety. **4 treat**, luxury, titbit, speciality.

delicate *adjective* **1** *delicate embroidery* **fine**, intricate, dainty, exquisite, graceful. **2** *a delicate shade of blue* **subtle**, soft, pale, muted, pastel, light. **3** *delicate china cups* **fragile**, dainty. **4** *his wife is very delicate* **sickly**, unhealthy, frail, feeble, weak. **5** *a delicate issue* **difficult**, tricky, sensitive, ticklish, awkward, touchy, embarrassing; *informal* sticky, dicey. **6** *the matter needs delicate handling* **careful**, sensitive, tactful, diplomatic, discreet, kid-glove, subtle. **7** *a delicate mechanism* **sensitive**, light, precision.
- OPPOSITES coarse, strong, robust.

delicious *adjective* **delectable**, mouth-watering, appetizing, tasty, flavoursome; *informal* scrumptious, moreish; *N. Amer. informal* finger-licking.
- OPPOSITES unpalatable.

delight *verb* **charm**, enchant, captivate, entrance, thrill, entertain, amuse, divert; *informal* send, tickle pink, bowl over.
- OPPOSITES dismay, disgust.
● *noun* **pleasure**, happiness, joy, glee, excitement, amusement, bliss, ecstasy.
- OPPOSITES displeasure.
□ **delight in** love, relish, savour, adore, lap up, take pleasure in, enjoy, revel in.

delighted *adjective* **pleased**, glad, happy, thrilled, overjoyed, ecstatic, elated, on cloud nine, walking on air, in seventh heaven, jumping for joy, gleeful, cock-a-hoop; *informal* over the moon, tickled pink, as pleased as Punch, on top of the world, as happy as Larry; *Brit. informal* chuffed; *N. English informal* made up; *Austral. informal* wrapped.

delightful *adjective* **1** *a delightful evening* **lovely**, enjoyable, amusing, entertaining, pleasant, pleasurable. **2** *a delightful girl* **charming**, enchanting, captivating, bewitching, appealing, sweet, endearing, cute, adorable, delectable.

deliver *verb* **1 bring**, take, convey, carry, transport, send, distribute, dispatch, ship. **2 state**, utter, give, read, broadcast, pronounce, announce, declare, proclaim, hand down, return. **3 administer**, deal, inflict, give; *informal* land.

delivery *noun* **1 conveyance**, carriage, transportation, transport, distribution, dispatch, shipping. **2 consignment**, load, shipment. **3 speech**, pronunciation, enunciation, articulation, elocution.

delusion *noun* **misapprehension**, misconception, false impression, misunderstanding, mistake, error, misconstruction, illusion, fantasy, fancy.

delve *verb* **1 rummage**, search, hunt, scrabble about, root about, ferret, fish about, dig, rifle through. **2 investigate**, enquire, probe, explore, research, look into, go into.

demand *noun* **1** *I gave in to her demands* **request**, call, command, order, dictate. **2** *the demands of a young family* **requirement**, need, claim, commitment, imposition. **3 market**, call, appetite, desire.

● *verb* **1 call for**, ask for, request, push for, press for, seek, claim, insist on. **2 order**, command, enjoin, require. **3 ask**, enquire, question, query. **4 require**, need, necessitate, call for, involve, entail. **5 insist on**, stipulate, expect, look for.

demanding *adjective* **1 difficult**, challenging, taxing, exacting, tough, hard, onerous, formidable, arduous, gruelling, back-breaking, punishing. **2 nagging**, trying, tiresome, hard to please, high-maintenance.

– OPPOSITES easy.

demeaning *adjective* **degrading**, humiliating, shameful, undignified, menial; *informal* infra dig.

demeanour *noun* **manner**, air, attitude, appearance, look, mien, bearing, carriage, behaviour, conduct.

demise *noun* **1 death**, dying, passing, end. **2 end**, break-up, disintegration, fall, downfall, collapse, overthrow.

– OPPOSITES birth.

democratic *adjective* **elected**, representative, parliamentary, popular, egalitarian, self-governing.

demolish *verb* **1 knock down**, pull down, tear down, destroy, flatten, raze to the ground, dismantle, level, bulldoze, blow up. **2 destroy**, ruin, wreck, overturn, explode, drive a coach and horses through; *informal* shoot full of holes.

– OPPOSITES build.

demonstrate *verb* **1 indicate**, prove, show, establish, confirm, verify. **2 reveal**, manifest, indicate, illustrate, signify, signal, denote, show, display, exhibit. **3 protest**, march, parade, picket, strike.

demonstration *noun* **1 exhibition**, presentation, display. **2 manifestation**, indication, sign, mark, proof, testimony. **3 protest**, march, rally, mass lobby, sit-in; *informal* demo.

demonstrative *adjective* **expressive**, open, forthcoming, communicative, unreserved, emotional, effusive, affectionate, loving, warm, friendly, approachable; *informal* touchy feely.

– OPPOSITES reserved.

demoralized *adjective* **dispirited**, disheartened, downhearted, dejected, downcast, low, depressed, dismayed, daunted, discouraged.

demure *adjective* **modest**, reserved, shy, unassuming, decorous, decent, proper.

– OPPOSITES brazen.

den *noun* **1 lair**, burrow, hole, shelter, hiding place, hideout. **2 study**, studio, workshop, retreat, sanctuary, hideaway; *informal* hidey-hole.

denial *noun* **1 contradiction**, rebuttal, repudiation, refutation, disclaimer. **2 refusal**, withholding.

denomination *noun* **1 religious group**, sect, cult, movement, persuasion, order, creed, school, church. **2 value**, unit, size.

denote *verb* **indicate**, be a mark of, signify, signal, designate, symbolize, represent.

denounce *verb* **1 condemn**, attack, censure, decry, stigmatize, deprecate, disparage, revile, damn. **2 expose**, betray, inform on, incriminate, implicate, cite, accuse.

dense *adjective* **1** *a dense forest* **thick**, crowded, compact, solid, tight, overgrown, impenetrable, impassable. **2** *dense smoke* **thick**, heavy, opaque, murky. **3** *(informal)* **stupid**, brainless, foolish, slow, simple-minded, empty-headed, obtuse; *informal* thick, dim, dopey.
- OPPOSITES sparse, thin.

dent *noun* **knock**, indentation, dint, depression, hollow, crater, pit; *N. Amer. informal* ding.
● *verb* **knock**, dint, mark; *N. Amer. informal* ding.

deny *verb* **1 contradict**, rebut, repudiate, refute, challenge, contest. **2 refuse**, turn down, reject, rebuff, decline, veto, dismiss; *informal* give the thumbs down to.
- OPPOSITES confirm, allow, accept.

depart *verb* **1 leave**, go away, withdraw, absent yourself, quit, exit, decamp, retreat, retire, make off; *informal* make tracks, take off, split; *Brit. informal* sling your hook. **2 deviate**, diverge, digress, stray, veer, differ, vary.
- OPPOSITES arrive.

department *noun* **division**, section, sector, unit, branch, wing, office, bureau, agency, ministry.

departure *noun* **1 leaving**, going, leave-taking, withdrawal, exit. **2 deviation**, divergence, digression, shift, variation. **3 change**, innovation, novelty.

depend *verb* **1** *her career depends on this* **be dependent on**, hinge on, hang on, rest on, rely on. **2** *my family depends on me* **rely on**, lean on, count on, bank on, trust (in), pin your hopes on.

dependable *adjective* **reliable**, trustworthy, trusty, faithful, loyal, stable, sensible, responsible.

dependent *adjective* **1 addicted**, reliant; *informal* hooked. **2 reliant**, needy, helpless, infirm, invalid, incapable, debilitated, disabled.
- OPPOSITES independent.
□ **dependent on 1** conditional on, contingent on, based on, subject to, determined by, influenced by. **2** reliant on, relying on, counting on, sustained by.

depict *verb* **1 portray**, show, represent, picture, illustrate, reproduce, render. **2 describe**, detail, relate, present, set forth, set out, outline.

deplete *verb* **reduce**, decrease, diminish, exhaust, use up, consume, expend, drain, empty.
- OPPOSITES augment.

deplore *verb* **1 abhor**, find unacceptable, frown on, disapprove of, take a dim view of, take exception to, condemn, denounce. **2 regret**, lament, mourn, bemoan, bewail, complain about, grieve over, sigh over.
- OPPOSITES applaud.

deploy *verb* **1 position**, station, post, place, install, locate, base. **2 use**, utilize, employ, take advantage of, exploit, call on.

deport *verb* **expel**, banish, extradite, repatriate.
- OPPOSITES admit.

depose *verb* **overthrow**, unseat, dethrone, topple, remove, supplant, displace, oust.

deposit *noun* **1 layer**, covering, coating, blanket, accumulation, sediment. **2 seam**, vein, lode, layer, stratum, bed. **3 down payment**, advance payment, prepayment, instalment, retainer, security.

● *verb* **1 put down**, place, set down, unload, rest, drop; *informal* dump, park, plonk; *N. Amer. informal* plunk. **2 leave (behind)**, precipitate, dump, wash up, cast up. **3 lodge**, bank, house, store, stow.

depot *noun* **1 terminal**, terminus, station, garage, headquarters, base. **2 storehouse**, warehouse, store, repository, depository, cache, arsenal, armoury, dump.

depress *verb* **1 sadden**, dispirit, cast down, get down, dishearten, demoralize, crush, weigh down on. **2 slow down**, weaken, impair, inhibit, restrict. **3 reduce**, lower, cut, cheapen, discount, deflate, diminish, depreciate, devalue. **4 press**, push, hold down.
- OPPOSITES cheer, boost, raise.

depressed *adjective* **1 sad**, unhappy, miserable, gloomy, dejected, downhearted, downcast, down, despondent, dispirited, low, morose, dismal, desolate; *informal* blue, down in the dumps, down in the mouth. **2 weak**, inactive, flat, slow, slack, sluggish, stagnant. **3 poverty-stricken**, poor, disadvantaged, deprived, needy, distressed, run down.
- OPPOSITES cheerful.

depressing *adjective* **dismal**, sad, unhappy, sombre, gloomy, grave, bleak, black, melancholy, dreary, grim, cheerless.

depression *noun* **1 unhappiness**, sadness, melancholy, melancholia, misery, sorrow, gloom, despondency, low spirits. **2 recession**, slump, decline, downturn. **3 hollow**, indentation, dent, cavity, dip, pit, crater, basin, bowl.

deprivation *noun* **1 poverty**, impoverishment, privation, hardship, destitution, need, want. **2 dispossession**, withholding, withdrawal, removal, seizure.
- OPPOSITES prosperity.

deprive *verb* **dispossess**, strip, divest, relieve, rob, cheat out of.

deprived *adjective* **disadvantaged**, underprivileged, poverty-stricken, impoverished, poor, destitute, needy.
- OPPOSITES privileged.

depth *noun* **1 deepness**, drop, height. **2 extent**, range, scope, breadth, width. **3 profundity**, wisdom, understanding, intelligence, discernment, penetration, insight, awareness. **4 intensity**, richness, vividness, strength, brilliance.

deputize *verb* **stand in**, sit in, fill in, cover, substitute, replace, take someone's place, take over, hold the fort, step into the breach.

deputy *noun* **second in command**, number two, assistant, aide, lieutenant, proxy, stand-in, replacement, substitute, representative, reserve.

derelict *adjective* **dilapidated**, ramshackle, run down, tumbledown, in ruins, falling down, disused, abandoned, deserted.
● *noun* **tramp**, vagrant, down and out, homeless person, drifter, beggar; *informal* dosser, bag lady.

derision *noun* **mockery**, ridicule, jeers, sneers, taunts, disdain, disparagement, denigration, insults.

derogatory *adjective* **disparaging**, disrespectful, demeaning, critical, pejorative, negative, unfavourable, uncomplimentary, unflattering, insulting, defamatory, slanderous, libellous.
- OPPOSITES complimentary.

descend *verb* **1 go down**, come down, drop, fall, sink, dive, plummet, plunge, nosedive. **2 slope**, dip, slant, go down, fall away. **3 alight**, disembark, get down, get off, dismount.
- OPPOSITES climb, board.
□ **descend on** flock to, besiege, surround, take over, invade, swoop on, occupy.

descent *noun* **1 dive**, drop, fall, plunge, nosedive. **2 slope**, incline, dip, drop, gradient. **3 decline**, slide, fall, degeneration, deterioration. **4 ancestry**, parentage, ancestors, family, extraction, origin, derivation, birth, lineage, stock, blood, roots, origins.

describe *verb* **1 report**, recount, relate, narrate, tell of, set out, detail, give a rundown of. **2 portray**, depict, paint, define, characterize, call, label, class, brand. **3 mark out**, delineate, outline, trace, draw.

description *noun* **1 account**, report, narrative, story, portrayal, portrait, sketch, details. **2 designation**, labelling, naming, dubbing, characterization, definition, classification, branding. **3 sort**, variety, kind, type.

desert[1] *verb* **1 abandon**, leave, jilt, leave high and dry, leave in the lurch, leave behind, strand, maroon; *informal* walk/run out on, dump, ditch; *literary* forsake. **2 abscond**, defect, run away, decamp, flee, turn tail, take French leave; *Military* go AWOL.

desert[2] *noun* **wasteland**, wastes, wilderness, dust bowl.

deserted *adjective* **1 abandoned**, jilted, cast aside, neglected, stranded, marooned, forlorn; *literary* forsaken. **2 empty**, uninhabited, unoccupied, abandoned, evacuated, desolate, lonely, godforsaken.
- OPPOSITES populous.

deserve *verb* **merit**, earn, warrant, rate, justify, be worthy of, be entitled to.

deserved *adjective* **well earned**, merited, warranted, justified, rightful, due, fitting, just, proper.

deserving *adjective* **worthy**, commendable, praiseworthy, admirable, estimable, creditable.

design *noun* **1 plan**, blueprint, drawing, sketch, outline, map, plot, diagram, draft. **2 pattern**, motif, device, style, theme, layout.
● *verb* **1 invent**, create, think up, come up with, devise, formulate, conceive; *informal* dream up. **2 intend**, aim, mean.

designate *verb* **1 appoint**, nominate, delegate, select, choose, pick, elect, name, identify, assign. **2 classify**, class, label, tag, name, call, term, dub.

desirable *adjective* **1 attractive**, sought-after, in demand, popular, enviable; *informal* to die for, must-have. **2 advantageous**, advisable, wise, sensible, recommended, beneficial, preferable. **3 (sexually) attractive**, beautiful, pretty, appealing, seductive, alluring, irresistible; *informal* sexy.
- OPPOSITES unattractive.

desire *noun* **1 wish**, want, aspiration, yearning, longing, craving, hankering, hunger; *informal* yen, itch. **2 lust**, passion, sensuality, sexuality, libido, lasciviousness.
● *verb* **want**, wish for, long for, yearn for, crave, hanker after, be desperate for, be bent on, covet, aspire to.

desolate *adjective* **1 bleak**, stark, bare, dismal, grim, wild, inhospitable, deserted, uninhabited, empty, abandoned, godforsaken, isolated, remote. **2 miserable**, unhappy, despondent, depressed, disconsolate, devastated, despairing, inconsolable, wretched, broken-hearted.

despair *noun* **desperation**, anguish, unhappiness, despondency, depression, misery, wretchedness, hopelessness.
- OPPOSITES hope, joy.
● *verb* **lose hope**, give up, lose heart, be discouraged, be despondent, be demoralized.

despatch *verb* & *noun* see **dispatch**.

desperate *adjective* **1 despairing**, hopeless, anguished, distressed, wretched, desolate, forlorn, distraught, at your wits' end, at the end of your tether. **2 last-ditch**, last-gasp, eleventh-hour, do-or-die, final, frantic, frenzied, wild. **3 grave**, serious, critical, acute, urgent, pressing, drastic, extreme.

desperation *noun* **hopelessness**, despair, distress, anguish, agony, torment, misery.

despise *verb* **detest**, hate, loathe, abhor, deplore, scorn, disdain, deride, sneer at, revile, spurn, shun.
- OPPOSITES adore, respect.

despite *preposition* **in spite of**, notwithstanding, regardless of, in the face of, in the teeth of, undeterred by, for all, even with.

destined *adjective* **1 fated**, ordained, predestined, doomed, meant, intended. **2** *computers destined for Pakistan* **heading**, bound, en route, scheduled, headed.

destiny *noun* **1 future**, fate, fortune, doom, lot, nemesis. **2 providence**, fate, God, the stars, luck, fortune, chance, karma, kismet.

destitute *adjective* **penniless**, poor, impoverished, poverty-stricken, impecunious, indigent, down and out; *Brit.* on the breadline; *informal* (flat) broke, on your uppers; *Brit. informal* stony broke, skint; *formal* penurious.
- OPPOSITES rich.

destroy *verb* **1 demolish**, knock down, level, raze to the ground, fell, blow up. **2 spoil**, ruin, wreck, blight, devastate, wreak havoc on. **3 kill**, put down, put to sleep, slaughter, cull. **4 annihilate**, wipe out, obliterate, eliminate, eradicate, liquidate, exterminate; *informal* take out; *N. Amer. informal* waste.
- OPPOSITES build.

destruction *noun* **1 devastation**, carnage, ruin, chaos, wreckage. **2** *the destruction of the countryside* **wrecking**, ruining, annihilation, obliteration, elimination, eradication, devastation. **3 killing**, slaughter, extermination, culling.
- OPPOSITES preservation.

destructive *adjective* **devastating**, ruinous, damaging, harmful, environmentally unfriendly, detrimental, injurious, hurtful, deleterious.

detach *verb* **disconnect**, separate, unfasten, disengage, uncouple, isolate, remove, loose, unhitch, unhook, free, pull off, cut off, break off, split off, sever.
- OPPOSITES attach, join.

detached *adjective* **1 disconnected**, separated, separate, unfastened, disengaged, uncoupled, isolated, loosened, unhitched, unhooked, free, severed, cut off. **2 dispassionate**, disinterested, objective, outside, neutral, unbiased, impartial.

detachment *noun* **1 objectivity**, dispassion, disinterest, neutrality, impartiality. **2 unit**, squad, detail, troop, contingent, task force, party, platoon.

detail *noun* **1 feature**, respect, particular, characteristic, specific, aspect, fact, point, element. **2 triviality**, technicality, nicety, fine point. **3 unit**, detachment, squad, troop, contingent, outfit, task force, party, platoon.
● *verb* **describe**, relate, catalogue, list, spell out, itemize, identify, specify.

detailed *adjective* **comprehensive**, full, complete, thorough, exhaustive, all-inclusive, elaborate, minute, precise, itemized, blow-by-blow.
- OPPOSITES general.

detain *verb* **1 hold**, take into custody, confine, imprison, intern, arrest, apprehend, seize; *informal* pick up; *Brit. informal* nick. **2 delay**, hold up, make late, keep, slow up/down, hinder.
- OPPOSITES release.

detect *verb* **1 notice**, perceive, discern, become aware of, note, make out, spot, recognize, identify, catch, sense. **2 discover**, uncover, turn up, unearth, dig up, root out, expose. **3 catch**, hunt down, track down, find out, expose, reveal, unmask, smoke out.

detective *noun* **investigator**, police officer; *informal* private eye, sleuth; *N. Amer. informal* gumshoe.

detention *noun* **custody**, imprisonment, incarceration, internment, captivity, remand, arrest, quarantine.
- OPPOSITES release.

deter *verb* **1 discourage**, dissuade, put off, scare off, dishearten, demoralize, daunt, intimidate. **2 prevent**, stop, avert, stave off, ward off.
- OPPOSITES encourage.

deteriorate *verb* **worsen**, decline, degenerate, fail, go downhill, wane.
- OPPOSITES improve.

determination *noun* **resolution**, resolve, will power, strength of character, dedication, single-mindedness, perseverance, persistence, tenacity, staying power, doggedness; *informal* guts.

determine *verb* **1 control**, decide, regulate, direct, dictate, govern. **2 resolve**, decide, make up your mind, choose, elect, opt. **3 specify**, set, fix, decide on, settle, establish, ordain, prescribe, decree. **4 ascertain**, find out, discover, learn, establish, calculate, work out; *informal* figure out.

determined *adjective* **resolute**, purposeful, adamant, single-minded, unswerving, unwavering, persevering, persistent, tenacious, dedicated, dogged.
- OPPOSITES irresolute.

deterrent *noun* **disincentive**, discouragement, damper, curb, check, restraint, inhibition.
- OPPOSITES incentive.

detest *verb* **hate**, abhor, loathe, regard with disgust, be unable to bear, have an aversion to, find intolerable, disdain, despise.
- OPPOSITES love.

detrimental *adjective* **harmful**, damaging, injurious, hurtful, inimical, deleterious, destructive, pernicious, undesirable, unfavourable, environmentally unfriendly.
- OPPOSITES beneficial.

devastate *verb* **1 destroy**, ruin, wreck, lay waste, ravage, demolish, raze to the ground, level, flatten. **2 shatter**, shock, stun, daze, dumbfound, traumatize, distress; *informal* knock sideways; *Brit. informal* knock for six.

devastation *noun* **destruction**, ruin, desolation, wreckage, ruins.

develop *verb* **1 grow**, expand, spread, advance, progress, evolve, mature. **2 initiate**, instigate, set in motion, originate, invent, form. **3 expand**, augment, broaden, supplement, reinforce, enhance, refine, improve, polish, perfect. **4 start**, begin, emerge, erupt, break out, arise, break, unfold.

development *noun* **1 evolution**, growth, expansion, enlargement, spread, progress. **2 event**, change, circumstance, incident, occurrence. **3 estate**, complex, site.

deviate *verb* **diverge**, digress, drift, stray, veer, swerve, get sidetracked, branch off, differ, vary.

device *noun* **1 implement**, gadget, utensil, tool, appliance, apparatus, instrument, machine, mechanism, contrivance, contraption; *informal* gizmo. **2 ploy**, tactic, move, stratagem, scheme, manoeuvre, plot, trick, ruse.

devil *noun* **1 Satan**, Beelzebub, Lucifer, the Prince of Darkness; *informal* Old Nick. **2 evil spirit**, demon, fiend. **3 brute**, beast, monster, fiend, villain, sadist, barbarian, ogre.

WORD LINKS
diabolical, **diabolic**, **satanic** relating to the Devil

devious *adjective* **1 underhand**, dishonest, crafty, cunning, conniving, scheming, sneaky, furtive; *informal* crooked, shady; *Brit. informal* dodgy. **2 circuitous**, roundabout, indirect, meandering, tortuous.
- OPPOSITES honest, direct.

devise *verb* **conceive**, think up, dream up, work out, formulate, concoct, hatch, contrive, design, invent, coin; *informal* cook up.

devoid *adjective*
▫ **devoid of** empty of, free of, bereft of, lacking, deficient in, without, wanting in; *informal* minus.

devote *verb* **dedicate**, allocate, assign, allot, commit, give (over), consign, pledge, set aside, earmark, reserve.

devoted *adjective* **dedicated**, committed, devout, loyal, faithful, true, staunch, steadfast, fond, loving.

devotee *noun* **enthusiast**, fan, lover, aficionado, admirer, supporter, disciple; *informal* buff, freak, nut, fanatic.

devotion *noun* **1 loyalty**, fidelity, commitment, allegiance, dedication, fondness, love, care. **2 piety**, spirituality, godliness, holiness, sanctity.

devour *verb* **1 gobble**, guzzle, gulp down, bolt, wolf; *informal* polish off; *Brit. informal* scoff. **2 consume**, engulf, envelop.

devout *adjective* **dedicated**, devoted, committed, loyal, sincere, fervent, pious, reverent, God-fearing, dutiful, churchgoing.

diagnose *verb* **identify**, determine, distinguish, recognize, interpret, detect, pinpoint.

diagnosis *noun* **1 identification**, detection, recognition, determination, discovery, pinpointing. **2 opinion**, judgement, verdict, conclusion.

diagonal *adjective* **crosswise**, crossways, slanting, slanted, oblique, angled, cornerways, cornerwise.

diagram *noun* **drawing**, representation, plan, outline, figure, chart, graph.

dialogue *noun* **conversation**, talk, discussion, chat, tête-à-tête, exchange, debate, conference, consultation; *informal* confab; *Austral. informal* convo.

diary *noun* **1 appointment book**, engagement book, personal organizer; *trademark* Filofax. **2 journal**, memoir, chronicle, log, logbook, history, annal, record, weblog, blog; *N. Amer.* daybook.

dictate *verb* **1 prescribe**, lay down, impose, set down, order, command, decree, ordain, direct. **2 determine**, control, govern, decide, influence, affect.
□ **dictate to** give orders to, order about/around, lord it over; *informal* boss about/around, push about/around.

dictator *noun* **autocrat**, despot, tyrant, absolute ruler.
- OPPOSITES democrat.

dictatorial *adjective* **domineering**, autocratic, authoritarian, oppressive, imperious, overweening, overbearing, peremptory; *informal* bossy, high-handed.

dictionary *noun* **lexicon**, glossary, vocabulary.

WORD LINKS
lexicography writing of dictionaries

die *verb* **1 pass away**, pass on, perish; *informal* give up the ghost, kick the bucket, croak, bite the dust, flatline; *Brit. informal* snuff it, peg out, pop your clogs; *N. Amer. informal* buy the farm. **2 lessen**, subside, drop, ease (off), let up, moderate, abate, fade, peter out, wane, ebb. **3** *(informal) the engine died* **fail**, cut out, give out, break down, stop; *informal* conk out, go kaput; *Brit. informal* pack up.
- OPPOSITES live.

diet *noun* **1** *a healthy diet* **food**, nutrition, eating habits. **2** *she's on a diet* **dietary regime**, regimen, restricted diet, fast.
● *verb* **be on a diet**, slim, lose weight, watch your weight; *N. Amer.* reduce; *N. Amer. informal* slenderize.

differ *verb* **1** *the second set of data differed from the first* **contrast with**, be different to, vary from, deviate from, conflict with, run counter to, be at odds with, contradict. **2 disagree**, conflict, be at variance/odds, be in dispute, not see eye to eye.
- OPPOSITES resemble, agree.

difference *noun* **1 dissimilarity**, contrast, distinction, differentiation, variance, variation, divergence, disparity, contradiction. **2 disagreement**, difference of opinion, dispute, argument, quarrel; *Brit.* row. **3** *I'll pay the difference* **balance**, remainder, rest.
- OPPOSITES similarity.

different *adjective* **1 dissimilar**, unlike, contrasting, differing, varying, disparate, poles apart, incompatible, mismatched; *informal* like chalk and cheese. **2 changed**, altered, transformed, new, unfamiliar, unknown, strange. **3 distinct**, separate, individual, independent. **4** *(informal)* **unusual**, out of the ordinary, unfamiliar, novel, new, fresh, original, unconventional, exotic.
- OPPOSITES similar, ordinary.

difficult *adjective* **1** *a difficult job* **laborious**, strenuous, arduous, hard, tough, demanding, punishing, gruelling, back-breaking, exhausting, tiring; *informal* hellish, killing, no picnic. **2** *a difficult problem* **hard**, complicated, complex, puzzling, perplexing, baffling, problematic, thorny, ticklish. **3** *a difficult child* **troublesome**, tiresome, trying, exasperating, awkward, demanding, contrary, recalcitrant, uncooperative, fussy.
- OPPOSITES easy, simple, cooperative.

difficulty *noun* **1 strain**, stress, trouble, problems, struggle; *informal* hassle. **2 problem**, complication, snag, hitch, issue, obstacle, hurdle, stumbling block, pitfall; *Brit.* spanner in the works; *informal* headache. **3** *he got into difficulties* **trouble**, predicament, plight, hard times; *informal* fix, scrape, jam.
- OPPOSITES ease.

diffident *adjective* **shy**, bashful, modest, self-effacing, unassuming, meek, unconfident, insecure, unassertive, timid, shrinking, reticent.
- OPPOSITES confident.

dig *verb* **1** *she began to dig the soil* **turn over**, work, break up. **2** *he dug a hole* **excavate**, dig out, quarry, hollow out, scoop out, bore, burrow, mine. **3 poke**, prod, jab, stab, shove, ram, push, thrust, drive, stick. **4 delve**, probe, search, enquire, look, investigate, research.
● *noun* **1 poke**, prod, jab, stab, shove, push. **2** *(informal)* **snide remark**, cutting remark, jibe, taunt, sneer, insult; *informal* wisecrack, put-down.
□ **dig up** exhume, disinter, unearth.

digest *verb* **assimilate**, absorb, take in, understand, comprehend, grasp.
● *noun* **summary**, synopsis, abstract, precis, résumé, summation.

dignified *adjective* **stately**, noble, majestic, distinguished, regal, imposing, impressive, grand, solemn, formal, ceremonious, decorous, sedate.

dignity *noun* **1 stateliness**, nobility, majesty, impressiveness, grandeur, magnificence, ceremoniousness, formality, decorum, propriety, respectability, worthiness, integrity, solemnity, gravitas. **2 self-respect**, pride, self-esteem, self-worth.

dilapidated *adjective* **run down**, tumbledown, ramshackle, in disrepair, shabby, battered, rickety, crumbling, in ruins, ruined, decaying, decrepit, neglected, uncared-for, gone to rack and ruin.

dilemma *noun* **quandary**, predicament, catch-22, vicious circle, plight, conflict; *informal* fix, tight spot/corner; (**in a dilemma**) between the devil and the deep blue sea, between a rock and a hard place.

diligent *adjective* **industrious**, hard-working, assiduous, conscientious, particular, punctilious, meticulous, painstaking, rigorous, careful, thorough, sedulous.
- OPPOSITES lazy.

dilute *verb* **1** *dilute the bleach with water* **make weaker**, water down, thin, doctor, adulterate; *informal* cut. **2** *the original plans have been diluted* **tone down**, moderate, weaken, water down, compromise.

dim *adjective* **1** *the dim light* **faint**, weak, feeble, soft, pale, dull, subdued, muted. **2** *long dim corridors* **dark**, badly lit, dingy, dismal, gloomy, murky. **3** *a dim figure* **indistinct**, ill-defined, vague, shadowy, nebulous, blurred, fuzzy. **4** *dim memories* **vague**, imprecise, imperfect, unclear, indistinct, sketchy, hazy. **5** see **stupid** (sense 1).
- OPPOSITES bright, distinct, clear.
● *verb* **1 turn down**, lower, soften, subdue. **2 fade**, dwindle, dull.
- OPPOSITES brighten.

dimension *noun* **1 size**, measurements, proportions, extent, length, width, breadth, depth. **2 aspect**, feature, element, angle, facet, side.

diminish *verb* **1 subside**, lessen, decline, reduce, decrease, dwindle, fade, slacken off, let up. **2** *new laws diminished the courts' authority* **reduce**,

decrease, lessen, curtail, cut, limit, curb.
- OPPOSITES increase.

din *noun* **noise**, racket, rumpus, cacophony, hubbub, uproar, commotion, clangour, clatter, clamour; *Brit.* row; *informal* hullabaloo.
- OPPOSITES silence.

dine *verb* **eat**, have dinner, have lunch.

dingy *adjective* **gloomy**, dark, dull, dim, dismal, dreary, drab, sombre, grim, cheerless, dirty, grimy, shabby, seedy, run down.
- OPPOSITES bright.

dinner *noun* **main meal**, lunch, evening meal, supper, feast, banquet; *Brit.* tea.

dip *verb* **1 immerse**, submerge, plunge, dunk, bathe, sink. **2 sink**, set, drop, fall, descend. **3 decrease**, fall, drop, fall off, decline, diminish, dwindle, slump, plummet, plunge. **4 slope down**, descend, go down, drop (away), fall away.
- OPPOSITES rise, increase.
● *noun* **1 swim**, bathe, paddle. **2 slope**, incline, decline, descent, hollow, depression, basin. **3 decrease**, fall, drop, downturn, decline, falling-off, slump, reduction.
□ **dip into 1** draw on, use, spend. **2** browse through, skim through, look through, flick through.

diplomacy *noun* **1 statesmanship**, statecraft, negotiation(s), discussion(s), talks. **2 tact**, tactfulness, sensitivity, discretion, soft skills.

diplomat *noun* **ambassador**, attaché, consul, chargé d'affaires, envoy, emissary.

diplomatic *adjective* **tactful**, sensitive, subtle, delicate, polite, discreet, judicious, politic.
- OPPOSITES tactless.

dire *adjective* **terrible**, dreadful, appalling, frightful, awful, grim, sore, alarming, acute, grave, serious, urgent, pressing, wretched, desperate, parlous.

direct *adjective* **1 straight**, short, quick. **2 non-stop**, through, unbroken, uninterrupted. **3 frank**, candid, straightforward, open, blunt, plain-spoken, outspoken, forthright, no-nonsense, matter-of-fact; *informal* upfront.
● *verb* **1 manage**, govern, run, administer, control, conduct, handle, be in charge of, preside over, lead, head, rule. **2 aim**, target, address to, intend for, mean for, design for. **3 give directions**, show the way, point someone in the direction of. **4 instruct**, tell, command, order, require; *old use* bid.

direction *noun* **1 way**, route, course, line, bearing, orientation. **2 running**, management, administration, conduct, handling, supervision, superintendence, command, rule, leadership. **3 instruction**, order, command, rule, regulation, requirement.

directive *noun* **instruction**, direction, command, order, injunction, decree, dictum, edict.

directly *adverb* **1** *they flew directly to New York* **straight**, as the crow flies. **2** *directly after breakfast* **immediately**, right (away), straight (away), without delay, promptly. **3** *the houses directly opposite* **exactly**, right, immediately, diametrically; *informal* bang. **4 frankly**, candidly, openly, bluntly, forthrightly, without beating about the bush.

director *noun* **manager**, head, chief, principal, leader, governor, president, chair, chief executive; *informal* boss, gaffer.

dirt *noun* **1 grime**, filth, muck, dust, mud, pollution; *Brit. informal* gunge. **2** *a dirt road* **earth**, soil, clay, loam.

dirty *adjective* **1 soiled**, grimy, grubby, filthy, mucky, stained, unwashed, greasy, muddy, dusty, polluted, contaminated, foul, unhygienic; *Brit. informal* manky, grotty. **2 obscene**, indecent, rude, naughty, vulgar, smutty, coarse, crude, filthy, off colour, pornographic, explicit, X-rated; *informal* blue; *euphemistic* adult. **3 malevolent**, hostile, black, angry, disapproving.
- OPPOSITES clean.

● *verb* **soil**, stain, muddy, blacken, mess (up), mark, spatter, smudge, smear, splatter, sully, pollute, foul.

disability *noun* **handicap**, incapacity, impairment, infirmity, defect, abnormality, condition, disorder, affliction.

d

disable *verb* **1 incapacitate**, put out of action, debilitate, handicap, cripple, lame, maim, immobilize, paralyse. **2 deactivate**, defuse, disarm, make safe.

disabled *adjective* **handicapped**, incapacitated, infirm, crippled, lame, paralysed, immobilized, bedridden; *euphemistic* physically challenged, differently abled.
- OPPOSITES able-bodied.

disadvantage *noun* **1 drawback**, snag, downside, fly in the ointment, catch, nuisance, handicap, trouble; *informal* minus. **2 detriment**, prejudice, harm, loss, hurt.
- OPPOSITES advantage.

disagree *verb* **1 be of a different opinion**, not see eye to eye, take issue, challenge, contradict, differ, dissent, be in dispute, clash. **2 differ**, be dissimilar, be different, be at variance/odds, vary, contradict each other, conflict. **3** *the food disagreed with her* **make ill**, make unwell, upset, nauseate.
- OPPOSITES agree.

disagreeable *adjective* **unpleasant**, distasteful, off-putting, unpalatable, nasty, objectionable, disgusting, horrible, offensive, repulsive, obnoxious, odious, repellent, revolting, vile, foul.
- OPPOSITES pleasant.

disagreement *noun* **dissent**, difference of opinion, controversy, discord, division, dispute, quarrel.
- OPPOSITES agreement.

disappear *verb* **1 vanish**, be lost to view/sight, recede, fade away, melt away, clear. **2 die out**, cease to exist, end, go, pass away, pass into oblivion, vanish, perish.
- OPPOSITES materialize.

disappoint *verb* **let down**, fail, dissatisfy, upset, dismay, sadden, disenchant, disillusion, shatter someone's illusions.

disappointed *adjective* **upset**, saddened, let down, displeased, dissatisfied, disheartened, downhearted, discouraged, crestfallen, disenchanted, disillusioned; *informal* choked, cut up; *Brit. informal* gutted, as sick as a parrot.
- OPPOSITES delighted.

disappointment *noun* **1 sadness**, sorrow, regret, dismay, displeasure, dissatisfaction, disenchantment, disillusionment. **2 let-down**, non-event, anticlimax; *Brit.* damp squib; *informal* washout.
- OPPOSITES delight.

disapproval *noun* **disfavour**, objection, dislike, dissatisfaction, distaste, displeasure, criticism, censure, condemnation, denunciation.
- OPPOSITES approval.

disapprove *verb*
▫ **disapprove of** object to, have a poor opinion of, take exception to, dislike, take a dim view of, look askance at, frown on, be against, not believe in, deplore, censure, condemn, denounce.

disarm *verb* **1 lay down your arms**, demobilize, disband, demilitarize. **2 defuse**, disable, deactivate, make safe. **3 win over**, charm, persuade, soothe, mollify, appease, placate.
- OPPOSITES arm, antagonize.

disarmament *noun* **demilitarization**, demobilization, disbandment, decommissioning, arms reduction, arms limitation.

disarming *adjective* **winning**, charming, irresistible, persuasive, soothing, conciliatory, mollifying.

disarray *noun* **disorder**, confusion, chaos, untidiness, disorganization, a mess, a muddle; *informal* a shambles; *Brit. informal* an omnishambles.
- OPPOSITES tidiness.

disaster *noun* **1 catastrophe**, calamity, cataclysm, tragedy, act of God, accident. **2 misfortune**, mishap, misadventure, setback, reversal, stroke of bad luck, blow. **3 failure**, fiasco, catastrophe; *informal* flop, washout,

dead loss, fail.
- OPPOSITES success.

disastrous *adjective* **catastrophic**, calamitous, cataclysmic, tragic, devastating, ruinous, terrible, awful.

disbelief *noun* **incredulity**, incredulousness, scepticism, doubt, cynicism, suspicion, distrust.

discard *verb* **dispose of**, throw away/out, get rid of, toss out, jettison, dispense with, scrap, reject, drop; *informal* ditch, bin, junk; *Brit. informal* get shot of; *N. Amer. informal* trash.
- OPPOSITES keep.

discharge *verb* **1 dismiss**, eject, expel, throw out, make redundant, release, let go; *Military* cashier; *informal* sack, fire. **2 free**, set free, release, let out, liberate. **3 emit**, give off, let out, send out, exude, leak, secrete, excrete, release. **4 fire**, shoot, let off, set off, loose off, trigger, launch. **5 unload**, offload, put off, remove. **6 carry out**, perform, execute, conduct, fulfil, complete.
- OPPOSITES recruit, imprison.
● *noun* **1 dismissal**, release, removal, ejection, expulsion; *Military* cashiering; *informal* the sack, the boot. **2 leak**, leakage, emission, secretion, excretion, suppuration, pus. **3 carrying out**, performance, execution, conduct, fulfilment, accomplishment, completion.

disciple *noun* **follower**, adherent, believer, admirer, devotee, acolyte, apostle, supporter, advocate.

discipline *noun* **1 control**, regulation, direction, order, authority, strictness. **2 good behaviour**, order, control, obedience. **3 field (of study)**, branch of knowledge, subject, area, speciality.
● *verb* **1 train**, drill, teach, school, coach. **2 punish**, penalize, bring to book, reprimand, rebuke; *Brit. informal* carpet.

disclose *verb* **reveal**, make known, divulge, tell, impart, communicate, pass on, release, make public, broadcast, publish.
- OPPOSITES conceal.

discolour *verb* **stain**, mark, soil, dirty, streak, smear, tarnish, spoil.

discomfort *noun* **1 pain**, aches and pains, soreness, aching, twinge, pang, throb, cramp. **2 inconvenience**, difficulty, problem, trial, tribulation, hardship. **3 embarrassment**, discomfiture, unease, awkwardness, discomposure, confusion, nervousness, distress, anxiety.

disconnect *verb* **1 detach**, disengage, uncouple, unhook, unhitch, undo, unfasten, unyoke. **2 separate**, cut off, divorce, sever, isolate, dissociate, remove. **3 deactivate**, shut off, turn off, switch off, unplug.
- OPPOSITES attach, connect.

discontent *noun* **dissatisfaction**, disaffection, grievances, unhappiness, displeasure, resentment, envy, restlessness, unrest, unease.
- OPPOSITES satisfaction.

discontented *adjective* **dissatisfied**, disgruntled, disaffected, unhappy, aggrieved, displeased, resentful, envious, restless, frustrated; *informal* fed up.
- OPPOSITES satisfied.

discordant *adjective* **tunelesss**, inharmonious, off-key, dissonant, harsh, jarring, grating, jangly, jangling, strident, shrill, cacophonous.
- OPPOSITES harmonious.

discount *noun* **reduction**, deduction, markdown, price cut, concession, rebate.
● *verb* **1 disregard**, pay no attention to, take no notice of, dismiss, ignore, overlook; *informal* pooh-pooh. **2 reduce**, mark down, cut, lower; *informal* knock down.

discourage *verb* **1 dissuade**, deter, put off, talk out of. **2 dishearten**, dispirit, demoralize, disappoint, put off, unnerve, daunt, intimidate. **3 prevent**, deter, stop, avert, inhibit, curb.
- OPPOSITES encourage.

discover *verb* **1 find**, locate, come across/upon, stumble on, chance on, uncover, unearth, turn up. **2 find out**, learn, realize, ascertain, work out, recognize; *informal* figure out; *Brit. informal* twig.

discovery *noun* **1 finding**, location, uncovering, unearthing. **2 realization**, recognition, revelation, disclosure. **3 breakthrough**, finding, find, innovation.

discredit *verb* **1 bring into disrepute**, disgrace, dishonour, blacken the name of, put/show in a bad light, compromise, smear, tarnish; *N. Amer.* slur. **2 disprove**, invalidate, explode, refute; *informal* debunk.
- OPPOSITES honour, prove.
● *noun* **dishonour**, disgrace, shame, humiliation, ignominy.

discreet *adjective* **tactful**, circumspect, diplomatic, judicious, sensitive, careful, cautious, strategic.

discrepancy *noun* **difference**, disparity, variation, deviation, divergence, disagreement, inconsistency, mismatch, conflict.
- OPPOSITES correspondence.

discretion *noun* **1 tact**, diplomacy, delicacy, sensitivity, good sense, prudence, circumspection. **2** *at the discretion of the council* **choice**, option, preference, disposition, pleasure, will, inclination.

discriminate *verb* **1 differentiate**, distinguish, draw a distinction, tell the difference, tell apart, separate. **2** *policies that discriminate against women* **be biased**, be prejudiced, treat differently, treat unfairly, put at a disadvantage, victimize, pick on.

discriminating *adjective* **discerning**, perceptive, judicious, selective, tasteful, refined, sensitive, cultivated, cultured.
- OPPOSITES indiscriminate.

discrimination *noun* **1 prejudice**, bias, bigotry, intolerance, favouritism, partisanship. **2 discernment**, judgement, perceptiveness, (good) taste, refinement, sensitivity, cultivation.
- OPPOSITES impartiality.

discuss *verb* **1 talk over**, talk about, talk through, debate, confer about. **2 examine**, explore, study, analyse, go into, deal with, consider, tackle.

discussion *noun* **1 conversation**, talk, chat, dialogue, conference, debate, exchange of views, consultation, deliberation; *informal* confab; *Austral. informal* convo. **2 examination**, exploration, study, analysis, treatment, consideration.

disdain *noun* **contempt**, scorn, derision, disrespect, condescension, superciliousness, hauteur, haughtiness.
- OPPOSITES respect.
● *verb* **scorn**, deride, regard with contempt, sneer at, look down your nose at, look down on, despise.

disease *noun* **illness**, sickness, ill health, infection, ailment, malady, disorder, condition, problem; *informal* bug, virus; *Brit. informal* lurgy.

WORD LINKS
pathological relating to disease

diseased *adjective* **unhealthy**, ill, sick, unwell, ailing, infected, septic, rotten, bad.

disgrace *noun* **1 dishonour**, shame, discredit, ignominy, disrepute, infamy, scandal, stigma, humiliation, loss of face. **2 scandal**, discredit, reproach, stain, blemish, blot, black mark, outrage, affront.
- OPPOSITES honour, credit.
● *verb* **shame**, bring shame on, dishonour, discredit, stigmatize, taint, sully, tarnish, stain, blacken.
- OPPOSITES honour.

disgraceful *adjective* **shameful**, scandalous, contemptible, dishonourable, discreditable, disreputable, reprehensible, blameworthy, unworthy, ignoble.
- OPPOSITES admirable.

disgruntled *adjective* **dissatisfied**, discontented, fed up, put out, aggrieved, resentful, displeased, unhappy, disappointed, annoyed; *informal* hacked off, browned off; *Brit. informal* cheesed off, narked, not best pleased; *N. Amer. informal* sore, ticked off.
- OPPOSITES contented.

disguise *verb* **camouflage**, conceal, hide, cover up, mask, screen, veil, paper over.
- OPPOSITES expose.

disgust *noun* **revulsion**, repugnance, aversion, distaste, abhorrence, loathing, hatred.
- OPPOSITES delight.
● *verb* **revolt**, repel, repulse, sicken, nauseate, horrify, appal, shock, turn someone's stomach, scandalize, outrage, offend, affront; *N. Amer. informal* gross out.
- OPPOSITES delight.

disgusting *adjective* **1** *the food was disgusting* **revolting**, repulsive, sickening, nauseating, stomach-turning, off-putting; *N. Amer.* vomitous; *informal* gross, sick-making. **2** *I find racism disgusting* **outrageous**, objectionable, abhorrent, repellent, loathsome, offensive, appalling, shocking, horrifying, scandalous, monstrous, detestable; *informal* sick.
- OPPOSITES delightful.

dish *noun* **1 bowl**, plate, platter, salver, pot. **2 recipe**, meal, course, fare.
□ **dish out** distribute, dispense, issue, hand out/round, give out, pass round, deal out, dole out, allocate.

dishevelled *adjective* **untidy**, unkempt, scruffy, messy, disarranged, rumpled, bedraggled, tousled, tangled, windswept; *N. Amer. informal* mussed (up).
- OPPOSITES tidy.

dishonest *adjective* **fraudulent**, cheating, underhand, devious, treacherous, unfair, dirty, criminal, illegal, unlawful, false, untruthful, deceitful, lying, corrupt, dishonourable, untrustworthy, unscrupulous; *informal* crooked, shady, sharp; *Brit. informal* bent; *Austral./NZ informal* shonky.
- OPPOSITES honest.

dishonourable *adjective* **disgraceful**, shameful, discreditable, ignoble, reprehensible, shabby, shoddy, despicable, contemptible, base, low.

disintegrate *verb* **break up**, crumble, break apart, fall apart, fall to pieces, collapse, fragment, shatter, splinter.

disinterested *adjective* **unbiased**, unprejudiced, impartial, neutral, detached, objective, dispassionate, non-partisan.

dislike *verb* **find distasteful**, regard with distaste, be averse to, have an aversion to, disapprove of, object to, take exception to, have no taste for, hate, despise.
- OPPOSITES like.
● *noun* **distaste**, aversion, disfavour, antipathy, disgust, abhorrence, hatred.
- OPPOSITES liking.

disloyal *adjective* **unfaithful**, faithless, false, untrue, inconstant, two-faced, double-dealing, double-crossing, deceitful, treacherous, subversive, seditious, unpatriotic; *informal* back-stabbing, two-timing; *literary* perfidious.

dismal *adjective* **1** *a dismal look* **gloomy**, glum, melancholy, morose, doleful, woebegone, forlorn, dejected, downcast. **2** *a dismal hall* **dim**, dingy, dark, gloomy, dreary, drab, dull.
- OPPOSITES cheerful, bright.

dismantle *verb* **take apart**, take to pieces/bits, pull to pieces, disassemble, break up, strip (down).
- OPPOSITES build.

dismay *noun* **alarm**, distress, concern, consternation, disquiet.
- OPPOSITES pleasure, relief.
● *verb* **concern**, distress, disturb, worry, alarm, disconcert, take aback, unnerve, unsettle.
- OPPOSITES encourage.

dismiss *verb* **1 give someone their notice**, discharge, lay off, make redundant; *informal* sack, fire. **2 send away**, let go, release, disband, discharge. **3 banish**, set aside, put out of your mind, brush aside, reject, repudiate, spurn; *informal* pooh-pooh.

disobedient *adjective* **naughty**, insubordinate, defiant, unruly, wayward, badly behaved, delinquent, rebellious, mutinous, troublesome, wilful.
- OPPOSITES obedient.

disobey *verb* **defy**, go against, flout, contravene, infringe, transgress, violate, disregard, ignore, pay no heed to.

disorder *noun* **1 untidiness**, mess, disarray, chaos, confusion, clutter, jumble, a muddle; *informal* a shambles; *Brit. informal* an omnishambles. **2 unrest**, disturbance, turmoil, mayhem, violence, fighting, fracas, rioting, lawlessness, anarchy, breach of the peace. **3 disease**, infection, complaint, condition, affliction, malady, sickness, illness, ailment.
- OPPOSITES tidiness, peace.

disorderly *adjective* **1 untidy**, disorganized, topsy-turvy, at sixes and sevens, messy, jumbled, cluttered, in disarray, chaotic; *informal* like a bomb's hit it, higgledy-piggledy; *Brit. informal* shambolic. **2 unruly**, riotous, disruptive, troublesome, disobedient, lawless.
- OPPOSITES tidy, peaceful.

disorganized *adjective* **unmethodical**, unsystematic, undisciplined, unstructured, haphazard, chaotic, muddled, hit-or-miss, sloppy, slapdash, slipshod; *Brit. informal* shambolic.
- OPPOSITES organized.

disown *verb* **reject**, cast off/aside, abandon, renounce, repudiate, deny, turn your back on, wash your hands of, disinherit.

dispatch *verb* **1 send (off)**, post, mail, forward. **2 deal with**, finish, conclude, settle, discharge, perform. **3 kill**, put to death, massacre, wipe out, exterminate, eliminate, murder, assassinate, execute.
● *noun* **message**, report, communication, communiqué, bulletin, statement, letter, news, intelligence.

dispel *verb* **banish**, drive away/off, chase away, scatter, eliminate, dismiss, allay, ease, quell.

dispense *verb* **1 distribute**, pass round, hand out, dole out, dish out, share out. **2 administer**, deliver, issue, deal out, mete out. **3** *dispensing medicines* **prepare**, make up, supply, provide.
□ **dispense with 1** waive, omit, drop, leave out, forgo, do away with; *informal* give something a miss. **2** get rid of, throw away/out, dispose of, discard; *informal* ditch, scrap, dump, chuck out/away; *Brit. informal* get shot of.

disperse *verb* **1 break up**, split up, disband, scatter, leave, go their separate ways, drive away/off, chase away. **2 dissipate**, dissolve, melt away, fade away, clear, lift. **3 scatter**, distribute, spread, disseminate.
- OPPOSITES assemble, gather.

displace *verb* **1 dislodge**, dislocate, move out of place/position, shift. **2 replace**, take the place of, supplant, supersede, oust, remove, depose.

display *verb* **1 exhibit**, show, arrange, array, present, lay out, set out. **2 show off**, parade, highlight, reveal, showcase. **3 manifest**, be evidence of, reveal, demonstrate, show.
- OPPOSITES conceal.
● *noun* **1 exhibition**, exposition, array, arrangement, presentation, demonstration, spectacle, show, parade. **2 manifestation**, expression, show, proof, demonstration, evidence.

displease *verb* **annoy**, irritate, anger, incense, irk, vex, nettle, put out, upset, exasperate.

dispose *verb*
□ **dispose of** throw away, throw out, get rid of, discard, jettison, scrap; *informal* dump, junk, ditch, chuck (out/away); *Brit. informal* get shot of; *N. Amer. informal* trash.

disposition *noun* **1 temperament**, nature, character, constitution, make-up, mentality. **2 arrangement**, positioning, placement, configuration, set-up, line-up, layout.

disprove *verb* **refute**, prove false, rebut, debunk, give the lie to, demolish; *informal* shoot full of holes, blow out of the water.

dispute *noun* **1 debate**, discussion, argument, controversy, disagreement, dissent, conflict. **2 quarrel**, argument, altercation, squabble, falling-out,

disagreement, difference of opinion, clash; *Brit.* row.
- OPPOSITES agreement.
● *verb* **1 debate**, discuss, exchange views, quarrel, argue, disagree, clash, fall out, wrangle, bicker, squabble. **2 challenge**, contest, question, call into question, quibble over, contradict, argue about, disagree with, take issue with.
- OPPOSITES accept.

disqualify *verb* **rule out**, bar, exclude, prohibit, debar, preclude.

disregard *verb* **ignore**, take no notice of, pay no attention to, discount, overlook, turn a blind eye to, shut your eyes to, gloss over, brush off/aside, shrug off.
- OPPOSITES heed.
● *noun* **indifference**, non-observance, inattention, heedlessness, neglect, contempt.
- OPPOSITES attention.

disrupt *verb* **interrupt**, disturb, interfere with, play havoc with, upset, unsettle, obstruct, impede, hold up, delay.

disruptive *adjective* **1 troublesome**, disturbing, upsetting, unsettling, unruly, badly behaved, rowdy, disorderly, undisciplined, unmanageable, uncontrollable, uncooperative, attention-seeking.
- OPPOSITES well behaved. **2 innovative**, groundbreaking, inventive, ingenious, pioneering, revolutionary, radical, experimental, original, new, novel, fresh, unusual; *informal* edgy.

dissatisfied *adjective* **discontented**, disappointed, disaffected, displeased, disgruntled, aggrieved, unhappy.
- OPPOSITES contented.

dissent *verb* **disagree**, differ, demur, be at variance/odds, take issue, protest, object.
- OPPOSITES agree, conform.
● *noun* **disagreement**, difference of opinion, argument, dispute, resistance, objection, protest, opposition.
- OPPOSITES agreement, conformity.

dissident *noun* **dissenter**, objector, protester, rebel, revolutionary, subversive, agitator, refusenik.
- OPPOSITES conformist.
● *adjective* **dissenting**, opposing, objecting, protesting, rebellious, revolutionary, subversive, nonconformist.
- OPPOSITES conformist.

dissimilar *adjective* **different**, differing, unalike, variant, diverse, divergent, heterogeneous, disparate, unrelated, distinct, contrasting.

dissociate *verb* **separate**, detach, disconnect, sever, cut off, divorce, isolate, alienate.
- OPPOSITES associate.

dissolve *verb* **1 break down**, liquefy, melt, deliquesce, disintegrate. **2 disband**, disperse, bring to an end, end, terminate, discontinue, break up, close down, wind up/down, suspend, adjourn. **3 annul**, nullify, void, invalidate, revoke.

dissuade *verb* **discourage**, deter, prevent, stop, talk out of, persuade against, advise against, argue out of.
- OPPOSITES encourage.

distance *noun* **1 interval**, space, span, gap, extent, length, range, reach. **2 aloofness**, remoteness, detachment, unfriendliness, reserve, reticence, formality; *informal* stand-offishness.
- OPPOSITES proximity.

distant *adjective* **1 faraway**, far-off, far-flung, remote, out of the way, outlying. **2 bygone**, remote, ancient, prehistoric. **3 vague**, faint, dim, indistinct, sketchy, hazy. **4 aloof**, reserved, remote, detached, unapproachable, unfriendly; *informal* stand-offish. **5 distracted**, absent, faraway, detached, vague.
- OPPOSITES near, close, recent.

distasteful *adjective* **unpleasant**, disagreeable, displeasing, undesirable, objectionable, offensive, unsavoury, unpalatable.
- OPPOSITES agreeable.

distinct *adjective* **1** *two distinct categories* **discrete**, separate, different, unconnected, distinctive, contrasting.

2 *the tail has distinct black tips* **clear**, well defined, unmistakable, easily distinguishable, recognizable, visible, obvious, pronounced, prominent, striking.
- OPPOSITES similar.

d

distinction *noun* **1 difference**, contrast, variation, division, differentiation, discrepancy. **2 merit**, worth, greatness, excellence, quality, repute, renown, honour, credit.
- OPPOSITES similarity.

distinctive *adjective* **distinguishing**, characteristic, typical, individual, particular, peculiar, unique, exclusive, special.
- OPPOSITES common.

distinctly *adverb* **1 decidedly**, markedly, definitely, unmistakably, manifestly, patently. **2 clearly**, plainly, intelligibly, audibly.

distinguish *verb* **1 differentiate**, tell apart, discriminate between, tell the difference between. **2 discern**, see, perceive, make out, detect, recognize, identify. **3 separate**, set apart, make distinctive, make different, single out, mark off.

distinguished *adjective* **eminent**, famous, renowned, prominent, well known, great, esteemed, respected, notable, illustrious, acclaimed, celebrated.
- OPPOSITES unknown, obscure.

distorted *adjective* **1 twisted**, warped, contorted, buckled, deformed, malformed, misshapen, disfigured, crooked, out of shape. **2 misrepresented**, perverted, twisted, falsified, misreported, misstated, garbled, inaccurate, biased, prejudiced.

distract *verb* **divert**, sidetrack, draw away, lead astray, disturb, put off.

distracted *adjective* **preoccupied**, inattentive, vague, abstracted, absent-minded, faraway, in a world of your own, troubled, harassed, worried; *informal* miles away, not with it.
- OPPOSITES attentive.

distraction *noun* **1 diversion**, interruption, disturbance, interference. **2 amusement**, entertainment, diversion, recreation, pastime, leisure pursuit.

distraught *adjective* **distressed**, frantic, fraught, overcome, overwrought, beside yourself, out of your mind, desperate, hysterical, worked up, at your wits' end; *informal* in a state.
- OPPOSITES calm.

distress *noun* **1 anguish**, suffering, pain, agony, torment, heartache, heartbreak, sorrow, sadness, unhappiness. **2** *a ship in distress* **danger**, peril, difficulty, trouble, jeopardy, risk.
- OPPOSITES happiness.

● *verb* **upset**, pain, trouble, worry, perturb, disturb, disquiet, agitate, torment.
- OPPOSITES comfort.

distribute *verb* **1 give out**, deal out, dole out, dish out, hand out/round, share out, divide out/up, parcel out, apportion, allocate, allot. **2** *the newsletter is distributed free* **circulate**, issue, deliver, disseminate, publish.
- OPPOSITES collect.

distribution *noun* **1** *the distribution of aid* **giving out**, dealing out, doling out, handing out/round, issuing, allocation, sharing out, dividing up/out, parcelling out. **2** *centres of food distribution* **supply**, delivery, dispersal, transportation.

district *noun* **area**, region, quarter, sector, zone, territory, locality, neighbourhood, community.

distrust *noun* **mistrust**, suspicion, wariness, scepticism, doubt, cynicism, misgivings, qualms.
- OPPOSITES trust.

● *verb* **mistrust**, be suspicious of, be wary of, be chary of, regard with suspicion, suspect, be sceptical of, doubt, be unsure of/about, have misgivings about.
- OPPOSITES trust.

disturb *verb* **1 interrupt**, intrude on, butt in on, barge in on, distract, disrupt, bother, trouble, pester, harass. **2 move**, rearrange, mix up, interfere with, mess up. **3 perturb**, trouble,

concern, worry, upset, fluster, disconcert, dismay, alarm, distress, unsettle.
- OPPOSITES calm, reassure.

disturbance *noun* **1 disruption**, distraction, interference, inconvenience, upset, annoyance, irritation, intrusion. **2 riot**, fracas, brawl, street fight, free-for-all, commotion, disorder.
- OPPOSITES order.

disturbed *adjective* **1 disrupted**, interrupted, fitful, intermittent, broken. **2 troubled**, distressed, upset, distraught, unbalanced, unstable, disordered, dysfunctional, maladjusted, neurotic, unhinged; *informal* screwed up.
- OPPOSITES uninterrupted.

ditch *noun* **trench**, trough, channel, dyke, drain, gutter, gully, watercourse.

dive *verb* **1 plunge**, plummet, nosedive, jump, fall, drop, pitch. **2 leap**, jump, lunge, throw/fling yourself, go headlong.
● *noun* **1 plunge**, nosedive, jump, fall, drop, swoop. **2 lunge**, spring, jump, leap.

diverge *verb* **1 separate**, part, fork, divide, split, bifurcate, go in different directions. **2 differ**, be different, be dissimilar, disagree, be at variance/odds, conflict, clash.
- OPPOSITES converge, agree.

diverse *adjective* **various**, sundry, varied, varying, miscellaneous, assorted, mixed, diversified, divergent, different, differing, distinct, unlike, dissimilar.
- OPPOSITES similar.

diversion *noun* **1 detour**, deviation, alternative route, re-routing, redirection. **2 distraction**, disturbance, smokescreen; *informal* red herring. **3 entertainment**, amusement, pastime, delight, fun, recreation, pleasure.

diversity *noun* **variety**, miscellany, assortment, mixture, mix, range, array, multiplicity, variation, difference.
- OPPOSITES uniformity.

divert *verb* **1 re-route**, redirect, change the course of, deflect, channel. **2 distract**, sidetrack, disturb, draw away, put off. **3 amuse**, entertain, distract, delight, enchant, interest, fascinate, absorb, engross, rivet, grip.

divide *verb* **1** *he divided his kingdom into four* **split (up)**, cut up, carve up, dissect, bisect, halve, quarter. **2** *a curtain divided her cabin from the galley* **separate**, segregate, partition, screen off, section off, split off. **3 diverge**, separate, part, branch (off), fork, split (in two). **4 share out**, ration out, parcel out, deal out, dole out, dish out, distribute. **5 disunite**, drive apart, drive a wedge between, break up, split (up), separate, isolate, alienate.
- OPPOSITES unify, converge, unite.

divine[1] *adjective* **godly**, angelic, heavenly, celestial, holy, sacred.
- OPPOSITES mortal.

divine[2] *verb* **guess**, surmise, deduce, infer, discern, discover, perceive; *informal* figure (out); *Brit. informal* suss.

division *noun* **1** *the division of the island* **dividing (up)**, breaking up, breakup, carving up, splitting, dissection, partitioning, separation, segregation. **2** *the division of his estates* **sharing out**, dividing up, parcelling out, dishing out, allocation, allotment, splitting up, carving up. **3 dividing line**, divide, boundary, border, demarcation line, gap, gulf. **4 section**, subsection, subdivision, category, class, group, grouping, set. **5 department**, branch, arm, wing. **6 disunity**, disunion, conflict, discord, disagreement, alienation, isolation.
- OPPOSITES unification.

divorce *noun* **1 dissolution**, annulment, decree nisi, separation. **2** *the divorce between the church and people* **separation**, division, split, gulf, disunity, alienation, schism.
- OPPOSITES marriage.
● *verb* **1 split up**, get a divorce, separate. **2** *religion cannot be divorced from morality* **separate**, divide, detach, isolate, alienate, set apart, cut off.

divulge *verb* **disclose**, reveal, tell, communicate, pass on, publish, give away, let slip.
- OPPOSITES conceal.

dizzy *adjective* **giddy**, light-headed, faint, unsteady, shaky, muzzy, wobbly; *informal* woozy.

do *verb* **1** *she does most of the work* **carry out**, undertake, discharge, execute, perform, accomplish, achieve, bring about, engineer; *informal* pull off. **2** *they can do as they please* **act**, behave, conduct yourself. **3 suffice**, be adequate, be satisfactory, fill/fit the bill, serve. **4** *a portrait I am doing* **make**, create, produce, work on, design, manufacture.
□ **do away with** abolish, get rid of, eliminate, discontinue, stop, end, terminate, drop, abandon, give up; *informal* scrap. **do without** forgo, dispense with, abstain from, refrain from, eschew, give up, cut out, renounce, manage without.

docile *adjective* **compliant**, obedient, pliant, submissive, deferential, unassertive, cooperative, amenable, accommodating, biddable.
- OPPOSITES disobedient, wilful.

dock[1] *noun* **harbour**, marina, port, wharf, quay, pier, jetty, landing stage.
● *verb* **moor**, berth, put in, tie up, anchor.

dock[2] *verb* **1 deduct**, subtract, remove, debit, take off/away; *informal* knock off. **2 reduce**, cut, decrease. **3 cut off**, cut short, shorten, crop, lop.

doctor *noun* **physician**, medical practitioner, general practitioner, GP, clinician, consultant; *informal* doc, medic; *Brit. informal* quack.
● *verb* **1 adulterate**, tamper with, lace; *informal* spike. **2 falsify**, tamper with, interfere with, alter, change, forge, fake; *Brit. informal* fiddle.

doctrine *noun* **creed**, credo, dogma, belief, teaching, ideology, tenet, maxim, canon, principle.

document *noun* **paper**, certificate, deed, form, contract, agreement, report, record.
● *verb* **record**, register, report, log, chronicle, authenticate, verify.

dodge *verb* **1** *he dodged the police* **elude**, evade, avoid, escape, run away from, lose, shake (off); *informal* give someone the slip. **2** *the minister tried to dodge the debate* **avoid**, evade, get out of, back out of, sidestep; *informal* duck, wriggle out of. **3 dart**, duck, dive, swerve, veer.
● *noun a clever dodge | a tax dodge* **ruse**, scheme, tactic, stratagem, ploy, subterfuge, trick, hoax, cheat, deception, fraud; *informal* scam; *Brit. informal* wheeze.

dog *noun* **hound**, canine, man's best friend, mongrel; *informal* pooch, mutt; *Austral. informal* bitzer.
● *verb* **plague**, beset, bedevil, blight, trouble.

WORD LINKS
canine relating to dogs

dogged *adjective* **tenacious**, determined, resolute, stubborn, obstinate, purposeful, persistent, persevering, single-minded, tireless.
- OPPOSITES half-hearted.

dogmatic *adjective* **opinionated**, assertive, insistent, emphatic, adamant, doctrinaire, authoritarian, imperious, dictatorial, uncompromising.

dole *verb*
□ **dole out** deal out, share out, divide up, allocate, distribute, dispense, hand out, give out, dish out.

domain *noun* **1 realm**, kingdom, empire, dominion, province, territory, land. **2 field**, area, sphere, discipline, province, world.

domestic *adjective* **1 family**, home, household. **2 domesticated**, homely, home-loving. **3 tame**, pet, domesticated; *Brit.* house-trained. **4 national**, state, home, internal.

dominant *adjective* **1 ruling**, governing, controlling, presiding, commanding. **2 assertive**, authoritative, forceful, domineering, commanding, controlling, pushy. **3 main**, principal, prime, chief, primary, central, key, crucial, core.
- OPPOSITES subservient, subsidiary.

dominate *verb* **1 control**, influence, command, be in charge of, rule, govern, direct. **2 overlook**, command, tower above/over, loom over.

domination *noun* **control**, power, command, authority, dominion, rule, supremacy, superiority, ascendancy, sway, mastery.

domineering *adjective* **overbearing**, authoritarian, imperious, high-handed, peremptory, autocratic, dictatorial, despotic, strict, harsh; *informal* bossy.

don *verb* **put on**, get dressed in, dress (yourself) in, get into, slip into/on, change into.

donate *verb* **give**, contribute, gift, subscribe, grant, present, endow; *informal* chip in, stump up.

donation *noun* **gift**, contribution, subscription, present, handout, grant, offering.

donor *noun* **giver**, contributor, benefactor, benefactress, subscriber, supporter, backer, patron, sponsor.
- OPPOSITES beneficiary.

doom *noun* **destruction**, downfall, ruin, extinction, annihilation, death, nemesis.
● *verb* **destine**, fate, predestine, preordain, mean, condemn, sentence.

doomed *adjective* **ill-fated**, ill-starred, cursed, jinxed, damned; *literary* star-crossed.

dose *noun* **measure**, portion, draught, dosage.

dot *noun* **spot**, speck, fleck, speckle, full stop, decimal point.
● *verb* **1 spot**, fleck, mark, spatter. **2 scatter**, pepper, sprinkle, strew, spread.

dote *verb*
□ **dote on** adore, love dearly, be devoted to, idolize, treasure, cherish, worship.

double *adjective* **dual**, duplex, twin, binary, duplicate, coupled, matching, twofold, in pairs.
- OPPOSITES single.
● *noun* **lookalike**, twin, clone, duplicate, exact likeness, replica, copy, facsimile, doppelgänger; *informal* spitting image, dead ringer.

doubt *noun* **1 uncertainty**, indecision, hesitation, irresolution, hesitancy, vacillation, lack of conviction. **2 scepticism**, distrust, mistrust, suspicion, cynicism, wariness, reservations, misgivings, suspicions.
- OPPOSITES certainty, trust.
● *verb* **disbelieve**, distrust, mistrust, suspect, be suspicious of, have misgivings about.
□ **in doubt 1** doubtful, uncertain, unconfirmed, unknown, undecided, unresolved, in the balance, up in the air; *informal* iffy. **2** irresolute, hesitant, doubtful, unsure, uncertain, in two minds, undecided, in a quandary/dilemma. **no doubt** doubtless, undoubtedly, indubitably, without (a) doubt, unquestionably, undeniably, clearly, plainly, obviously, patently.

doubtful *adjective* **1 hesitant**, in doubt, unsure, uncertain, in two minds, in a quandary, in a dilemma. **2 in doubt**, uncertain, open to question, unsure, debatable, up in the air, inconclusive, unconfirmed. **3 unlikely**, improbable. **4 distrustful**, mistrustful, sceptical, suspicious, having reservations, wary, chary, leery. **5 questionable**, dubious, suspect, suspicious.
- OPPOSITES confident, certain.

doubtless *adverb* **undoubtedly**, no doubt, unquestionably, indisputably, undeniably, certainly, surely, of course.

douse *verb* **1 drench**, soak, saturate, wet. **2 extinguish**, put out, quench, smother.

dowdy *adjective* **unfashionable**, frumpy, old-fashioned, shabby, frowzy; *Brit. informal* mumsy.
- OPPOSITES fashionable.

downfall *noun* **ruin**, ruination, undoing, defeat, overthrow, nemesis, destruction, annihilation, end, collapse, fall, crash, failure.
- OPPOSITES rise.

downgrade *verb* **demote**, reduce, relegate.
- OPPOSITES promote.

downright *adjective* **complete**, total, absolute, utter, thorough, out-and-out, outright, sheer, arrant, pure.
● *adverb* **thoroughly**, utterly, positively, profoundly, really, completely, totally, entirely.

drab *adjective* **1 colourless**, grey, dull, washed out, dingy, dreary, dismal, cheerless, gloomy, sombre. **2 uninteresting**, dull, boring, tedious, monotonous, dry, dreary.
- OPPOSITES bright, interesting.

draft *noun* **1 version**, sketch, attempt, effort, outline, plan. **2 cheque**, order, money order, bill of exchange.

drag *verb* **haul**, pull, tug, heave, lug, draw, trail.
● *noun* **1 pull**, resistance, tug. **2** *(informal)* **bore**, nuisance, bother, trouble, pest, annoyance, trial; *informal* pain (in the neck), bind, headache, hassle.

drain *verb* **1** *a valve for draining the tank* **empty (out)**, void, clear (out), evacuate, unload. **2** *drain off any surplus liquid* **draw off**, extract, siphon off, pour out, pour off, bleed, tap, filter, discharge. **3** *the water drained away* **flow**, pour, trickle, stream, run, rush, gush, flood, surge, leak, ooze, seep, dribble. **4 use up**, exhaust, deplete, consume, expend, get through, sap, milk, bleed. **5 drink**, gulp (down), guzzle, quaff, swallow, finish off, toss off; *informal* sink, down, swig, swill (down), knock back.
- OPPOSITES fill.
● *noun* **1 sewer**, channel, ditch, culvert, duct, pipe, gutter. **2 strain**, pressure, burden, load, demand.

drama *noun* **1 play**, show, piece, theatrical work, stage show, dramatization. **2 acting**, the theatre, the stage, dramatic art, stagecraft, dramaturgy. **3 incident**, scene, spectacle, crisis, disturbance, row, commotion, excitement, thrill, sensation, dramatics, theatrics, histrionics.

dramatic *adjective* **1 theatrical**, thespian, dramaturgical. **2 considerable**, substantial, significant, remarkable, extraordinary, exceptional, phenomenal. **3 exciting**, stirring, action-packed, sensational, spectacular, startling, unexpected, tense, gripping, riveting, thrilling, hair-raising, lively. **4 striking**, impressive, imposing, spectacular, breathtaking, dazzling, sensational, awesome, awe-inspiring, remarkable. **5 exaggerated**, theatrical, ostentatious, actressy, stagy, showy, melodramatic.
- OPPOSITES unremarkable, boring.

dramatize *verb* **1 adapt**, turn into a play/film. **2 exaggerate**, overdo, overstate, magnify, amplify, inflate, sensationalize, embroider, colour, aggrandize, embellish, elaborate; *informal* blow up (out of all proportion).

drape *verb* **wrap**, cover, envelop, shroud, wind, swathe, festoon, hang.

drastic *adjective* **extreme**, serious, desperate, radical, far-reaching, momentous, substantial.
- OPPOSITES moderate.

draught *noun* **1 current of air**, wind, breeze, gust, puff, waft. **2 gulp**, drink, swallow, mouthful; *informal* swig.

draw *verb* **1 sketch**, outline, rough out, illustrate, render, represent, trace, portray, depict. **2 pull**, haul, drag, tug, heave, lug, tow; *informal* yank. **3 move**, go, come, proceed, progress, pass, drive, inch, roll, glide, cruise, sweep. **4 pull out**, take out, produce, fish out, extract, withdraw, unsheathe. **5 attract**, win, capture, catch, engage, lure, entice, bring in.
● *noun* **1 raffle**, lottery, sweepstake, sweep, tombola, ballot. **2 tie**, dead heat, stalemate. **3 attraction**, lure, allure, pull, appeal, temptation, charm, fascination.
□ **draw on** call on, have recourse to, turn to, look to, exploit, use, employ, utilize, bring into play. **draw out** prolong, protract, drag out, spin out, string out, extend, lengthen. **draw up**

compose, formulate, frame, write down, draft, prepare, think up, devise, work out, create, invent, design.

drawback *noun* **disadvantage**, snag, downside, stumbling block, catch, hitch, pitfall, issue, fly in the ointment, weak spot/point, weakness, imperfection; *informal* minus.
– OPPOSITES benefit.

drawing *noun* **sketch**, picture, illustration, representation, portrayal, depiction, diagram, outline.

WORD LINKS
graphic relating to drawing

dread *verb* **fear**, be afraid of, worry about, be anxious about, shudder at the thought of.
● *noun* **fear**, apprehension, trepidation, anxiety, panic, alarm, terror, disquiet, unease.

dreadful *adjective* **1** *a dreadful accident* **terrible**, frightful, horrible, grim, awful, horrifying, shocking, distressing, appalling, harrowing, ghastly, gruesome, fearful, horrendous, tragic. **2** *a dreadful meal* **very bad**, frightful, shocking, awful, abysmal, dire, atrocious, disgraceful, deplorable; *informal* woeful, rotten, lousy, ropy; *Brit. informal* duff, rubbish. **3** *a dreadful flirt* **outrageous**, shocking, real, awful, terrible, inordinate, incorrigible.
– OPPOSITES wonderful, excellent.

dream *noun* **1 daydream**, reverie, trance, daze, stupor. **2 ambition**, aspiration, hope, goal, aim, objective, intention, desire, wish, daydream, fantasy. **3 delight**, joy, marvel, wonder, gem, treasure.
– OPPOSITES nightmare.
● *verb* **1 fantasize**, daydream, wish, hope, long, yearn, hanker. **2 daydream**, be in a trance, be lost in thought, be preoccupied, be abstracted, stare into space, be in cloud cuckoo land.
□ **dream up** think up, invent, concoct, devise, hatch, come up with.

dreary *adjective* **dull**, uninteresting, tedious, boring, unexciting, unstimulating, uninspiring, soul-destroying, monotonous, uneventful.
– OPPOSITES exciting.

drench *verb* **soak**, saturate, wet through, douse, steep, flood, drown.

dress *noun* **1** *a long blue dress* **frock**, gown, robe, shift. **2** *full evening dress* **clothes**, clothing, garments, garb, attire, costume, outfit; *informal* get-up, gear; *Brit. informal* clobber; *formal* apparel.
● *verb* **1 clothe**, attire, deck out, garb; *informal* get up. **2 decorate**, trim, adorn, arrange, prepare. **3 bandage**, cover, bind, wrap.
– OPPOSITES undress.

WORD LINKS
sartorial relating to dress

dribble *verb* **1 drool**, slaver, slobber. **2 trickle**, drip, roll, run, drizzle, ooze, seep, leak.

drift *verb* **1 be carried**, be borne, float, bob, glide, coast, waft. **2 wander**, meander, stray, stroll, dawdle, float, roam. **3 stray**, digress, wander, deviate, get sidetracked. **4 pile up**, bank up, heap up, accumulate, gather, amass.
● *noun* **1 movement**, shift, flow, transfer, gravitation. **2 gist**, meaning, sense, significance, thrust, import, tenor, intention, direction. **3 pile**, heap, bank, mound, mass, accumulation.

drill *noun* **1 training**, instruction, coaching, teaching, (physical) exercises; *informal* square-bashing. **2 procedure**, routine, practice, programme, schedule, method, system.
● *verb* **1 bore**, pierce, puncture, perforate. **2 train**, instruct, coach, teach, discipline, exercise.

drink *verb* **1 swallow**, gulp (down), quaff, guzzle, imbibe, sip, drain; *informal* swig, down, knock back. **2 drink alcohol**, tipple, indulge, carouse; *informal* hit the bottle, booze; *Brit. informal* bevvy.
● *noun* **1 beverage**, liquid refreshment; *Brit. informal* bevvy. **2 alcohol**, intoxicating liquor, spirits; *informal*

booze, the hard stuff, the bottle, grog. **3 swallow**, gulp, mouthful, draught, sip; *informal* swig, slug.

drip *verb* **drop**, dribble, leak, trickle, run, splash, sprinkle.
● *noun* **drop**, dribble, spot, trickle, splash, bead.

drive *verb* **1 operate**, handle, manage, pilot, steer, work. **2 go by car**, motor. **3 run**, chauffeur, give someone a lift, take, ferry, transport, convey. **4 power**, propel, move, push. **5 hammer**, screw, ram, sink, plunge, thrust, knock. **6 force**, compel, prompt, precipitate, oblige, coerce, pressure, spur, prod.
● *noun* **1 excursion**, outing, trip, jaunt, tour, ride, run, journey; *informal* spin. **2 motivation**, ambition, single-mindedness, determination, will power, dedication, doggedness, tenacity, enthusiasm, zeal, commitment, energy, vigour; *informal* get-up-and-go. **3 campaign**, crusade, movement, effort, push, initiative.

droop *verb* **hang down**, wilt, dangle, sag, flop, sink, slump, drop.

drop *verb* **1 let fall**, let go of, release. **2 fall**, descend, plunge, plummet, dive, sink, dip, tumble. **3 decrease**, lessen, reduce, fall, decline, dwindle, sink, slump. **4 abandon**, give up, discontinue, finish with, renounce, reject, forgo, relinquish, dispense with, leave out; *informal* dump, pack in, quit.
- OPPOSITES rise, increase.
● *noun* **1 droplet**, blob, globule, bead. **2 small amount**, little, bit, dash, spot, dribble, sprinkle, trickle, splash, mouthful; *informal* smidgen, tad. **3 decrease**, reduction, decline, fall-off, downturn, slump. **4 cliff**, precipice, slope, descent, incline.
□ **drop off** fall asleep, doze (off), nap, drowse; *informal* nod off, drift off, snooze, take forty winks. **drop out** leave, give up, withdraw, retire, pull out, abandon something, fall by the wayside; *informal* quit, pack in, jack in.

drug *noun* **1 medicine**, medication, remedy, cure, antidote. **2 narcotic**, stimulant, hallucinogen; *informal* dope, gear.
● *verb* **1 anaesthetize**, poison, knock out; *informal* dope. **2 tamper with**, lace, poison; *informal* dope, spike, doctor.

WORD LINKS
pharmacology branch of medicine concerned with drugs
pharmacy (*Brit.* **chemist**; *N. Amer.* **drugstore**) shop selling drugs

drum *noun* **canister**, barrel, cylinder, tank, bin, can.
● *verb* **1 tap**, beat, rap, thud, thump, tattoo, thrum. **2 instil**, drive, din, hammer, drill, implant, ingrain, inculcate.
□ **drum up** round up, gather, collect, summon, attract, canvass, solicit, petition.

drunk *adjective* **intoxicated**, inebriated, drunken, tipsy, under the influence; *informal* tight, merry, plastered, sloshed, pickled, tanked (up), ratted, three sheets to the wind, squiffy; *Brit. informal* legless, paralytic, Brahms and Liszt, tiddly; *N. Amer. informal* loaded.
- OPPOSITES sober.
● *noun* **drunkard**, alcoholic, dipsomaniac, inebriate; *informal* boozer, soak, wino, alky.

dry *adjective* **1 arid**, parched, waterless, dehydrated, desiccated, withered, shrivelled, wizened. **2 dull**, uninteresting, boring, unexciting, tedious, dreary, monotonous, unimaginative, sterile; *informal* deadly. **3 wry**, subtle, laconic, ironic, sardonic, sarcastic, cynical.
- OPPOSITES wet, moist.
● *verb* **1 parch**, scorch, bake, sear, dehydrate, desiccate, wither, shrivel. **2 wipe**, towel, rub dry, drain.
- OPPOSITES wet, moisten.

dual *adjective* **double**, twofold, duplex, binary, twin, matching, paired, coupled.
- OPPOSITES single.

dub *verb* **name**, call, nickname, label, christen, term, tag.

dubious *adjective* **1 doubtful**, uncertain, unsure, hesitant, sceptical, suspicious; *informal* iffy. **2 suspicious**, suspect, untrustworthy, unreliable, questionable; *informal* shady; *Brit. informal* dodgy.
– OPPOSITES certain, trustworthy.

duck *verb* **1 bob down**, bend down, stoop, crouch, squat, hunch down, hunker down. **2** *(informal)* **shirk**, dodge, evade, avoid, elude, escape, sidestep.

duct *noun* **tube**, channel, canal, vessel, conduit, pipe, outlet, inlet, flue, shaft, vent.

due *adjective* **1** *their fees were due* **owing**, owed, payable, outstanding, overdue, unpaid, unsettled. **2** *the chancellor's statement is due today* **expected**, anticipated, scheduled, awaited, required. **3 deserved**, merited, warranted, justified, owing, appropriate, fitting, right, rightful, proper. **4 proper**, correct, suitable, appropriate, adequate, sufficient.
● *noun* **fee**, subscription, charge, payment, contribution, levy.
● *adverb* **directly**, straight, exactly, precisely, dead.
□ **due to 1** *her death was due to an infection* attributable to, caused by, because of, down to. **2** *the train was cancelled due to staff shortages* because of, owing to, on account of, as a consequence of, as a result of, thanks to.

duel *noun* **1 single combat**, fight, confrontation, head-to-head; *informal* shoot-out. **2 contest**, match, game, meet, encounter, clash.

dull *adjective* **1 uninteresting**, boring, tedious, monotonous, unimaginative, uneventful, featureless, colourless, lifeless, unexciting, uninspiring, flat, bland, stodgy, dreary; *informal* deadly; *N. Amer. informal* dullsville. **2 overcast**, cloudy, gloomy, dark, dismal, dreary, sombre, grey, murky, sunless. **3 drab**, dreary, sombre, dark, subdued, muted. **4 muffled**, muted, quiet, soft, faint, indistinct, stifled. **5 unintelligent**, stupid, slow, brainless, mindless, foolish, idiotic; *informal* dense, dim, half-witted, thick.
– OPPOSITES interesting, bright.
● *verb* **lessen**, decrease, diminish, reduce, dampen, blunt, deaden, allay, ease.
– OPPOSITES intensify.

duly *adverb* **1 properly**, correctly, appropriately, suitably, fittingly. **2 at the right time**, on time, punctually.

dumb *adjective* **1 mute**, speechless, tongue-tied, silent, at a loss for words. **2** *(informal)* **stupid**, unintelligent, ignorant, dense, brainless, foolish, slow, dull, simple; *informal* thick, dim; *Brit. informal* daft.
– OPPOSITES talkative, clever.

dummy *noun* **mannequin**, model, figure.
● *adjective* **simulated**, practice, trial, mock, make-believe; *informal* pretend.

dump *noun* **1 tip**, rubbish dump, dumping ground. **2** *(informal)* **hovel**, slum; *informal* hole, pigsty.
● *verb* **1 put down**, set down, deposit, place, shove, unload, drop, throw down; *informal* stick, park, plonk; *Brit. informal* bung. **2 dispose of**, get rid of, throw away/out, discard, bin, jettison; *informal* ditch, junk.

dune *noun* **bank**, mound, hillock, hummock, knoll, ridge, heap, drift.

duplicate *noun* **copy**, photocopy, facsimile, reprint, replica, reproduction, clone; *trademark* Xerox, photostat.
● *adjective* **matching**, identical, twin, corresponding, equivalent.
● *verb* **1 copy**, photocopy, photostat, xerox, reproduce, replicate, reprint, run off. **2 repeat**, do again, redo, replicate.

durable *adjective* **1 hard-wearing**, wear-resistant, heavy-duty, tough, long-lasting, strong, sturdy, robust, utilitarian. **2 lasting**, long-lasting, long-term, enduring, persistent, abiding, permanent, undying, everlasting.
– OPPOSITES delicate, short-lived.

duration *noun* **length**, time, period, term, span, extent, stretch.

dusk *noun* **twilight**, nightfall, sunset, sundown, evening, close of day, semi-darkness, gloom; *literary* gloaming.
- OPPOSITES dawn.

dust *noun* **dirt**, grime, grit, powder, particles.
● *verb* **1 wipe**, clean, brush, sweep. **2** *dust the cake with icing sugar* **sprinkle**, scatter, powder, dredge, sift, cover.

dusty *adjective* **1 dirty**, grimy, grubby. **2 powdery**, crumbly, chalky, granular, soft, gritty.

dutiful *adjective* **conscientious**, responsible, dedicated, devoted, attentive, obedient, deferential.
- OPPOSITES remiss.

duty *noun* **1** *a sense of duty* **responsibility**, obligation, commitment, allegiance, loyalty. **2** *it was his duty to attend the king* **job**, task, assignment, mission, function, role. **3 tax**, levy, tariff, excise, toll, rate.

dwarf *verb* **1 dominate**, tower over, loom over, overshadow. **2 overshadow**, outshine, surpass, exceed, outclass, outstrip, outdo, top.

dwell *verb (formal)* **reside**, live, be housed, lodge, stay; *informal* put up; *formal* abide.
□ **dwell on** linger over, mull over, muse on, brood about/over, think about, be preoccupied by, obsess about, harp on about.

dwindle *verb* **diminish**, decrease, reduce, lessen, shrink, wane.
- OPPOSITES increase.

dye *noun* **colouring**, dyestuff, pigment, tint, stain, wash.
● *verb* **colour**, tint, pigment, stain, wash.

dying *adjective* **1 terminally ill**, at death's door, on your deathbed, fading fast, not long for this world, moribund, in extremis. **2 declining**, vanishing, fading, waning; *informal* on the way out.

dynamic *adjective* **energetic**, spirited, active, lively, vigorous, forceful, high-powered, aggressive, enterprising; *informal* go-getting, go-ahead.

dynasty *noun* **family**, house, line, lineage, regime, empire.

Ee

each *adverb* **apiece**, per person, per head, per capita.

eager *adjective* **1 keen**, enthusiastic, avid, ardent, zealous, highly motivated, committed, earnest. **2** *we were eager for news* **anxious**, impatient, agog, longing, yearning, wishing, hoping; *informal* itching, dying, raring.
- OPPOSITES apathetic.

ear *noun he has an ear for a good song* **appreciation**, feel, instinct, intuition, sense.

WORD LINKS
aural relating to the ear

early *adjective* **1 advance**, initial, preliminary, first. **2 untimely**, premature, unseasonable. **3 primitive**, ancient, prehistoric, primeval. **4 prompt**, timely, quick, speedy.
- OPPOSITES late, overdue.
● *adverb* **1 in advance**, in good time, ahead of schedule, with time to spare, before the last moment. **2 prematurely**, before the usual time, too soon, ahead of schedule.
- OPPOSITES late.

earmark *verb* **set aside**, keep (back), reserve, designate, assign, allocate.

earn *verb* **1 be paid**, take home, gross, receive, get, make, collect, bring in; *informal* pocket, bank. **2 deserve**, merit, warrant, justify, be worthy of, gain, win, secure, obtain.
- OPPOSITES lose.

earnest *adjective* **1 serious**, solemn, grave, sober, humourless, staid, intense. **2 devout**, heartfelt, wholehearted, sincere, impassioned, fervent, intense.
- OPPOSITES frivolous, half-hearted.

earnings *plural noun* **income**, pay, wages, salary, stipend, remuneration, fees, revenue, yield, profit, takings, proceeds.

earth *noun* **1 world**, globe, planet. **2 land**, ground, terra firma, floor. **3 soil**, clay, dust, dirt, loam, ground, turf.

WORD LINKS
terrestrial relating to the earth
geography, **geology** study of the earth

earthly *adjective* **worldly**, temporal, mortal, human, material, carnal, fleshly, bodily, physical, corporeal, sensual.
- OPPOSITES spiritual, heavenly.

earthquake *noun* **(earth) tremor**, shock, convulsion; *informal* quake.

WORD LINKS
seismic relating to earthquakes
seismology study of earthquakes

earthy *adjective* **1 down-to-earth**, unsophisticated, unrefined, simple, plain, unpretentious, natural. **2 bawdy**, ribald, racy, rude, crude, coarse, indelicate, indecent; *informal* raunchy; *Brit. informal* fruity.

ease *noun* **1 effortlessness**, no trouble, simplicity. **2 naturalness**, casualness, informality, composure, nonchalance, insouciance. **3 affluence**, wealth, prosperity, luxury, plenty, comfort, enjoyment, well-being.
- OPPOSITES difficulty.
● *verb* **1 relieve**, alleviate, soothe, moderate, dull, deaden, numb. **2** *the rain eased off* **let up**, abate, subside, die down, slacken off, diminish, lessen. **3 calm**, quieten, pacify, soothe, comfort, console. **4 slide**, slip, squeeze, guide, manoeuvre, inch, edge.
- OPPOSITES aggravate, intensify.

easily *adverb* **effortlessly**, comfortably, simply, without difficulty, readily, without a hitch.

easy *adjective* **1 uncomplicated**, undemanding, effortless, painless, trouble-free, simple, straightforward, elementary, plain sailing; *informal* a piece of cake, child's play, a cinch. **2 natural**, casual, informal, unceremonious, unreserved, unaffected, easy-going, amiable, affable, genial, good-humoured, carefree, nonchalant, unconcerned; *informal* laid-back. **3 quiet**, tranquil, serene, peaceful, untroubled, contented, relaxed, comfortable, secure, safe; *informal* cushy. **4** *an easy pace* **leisurely**, unhurried, comfortable, undemanding, easy-going, gentle, sedate, moderate, steady.
- OPPOSITES difficult, demanding.

easy-going *adjective* **relaxed**, even-tempered, placid, happy-go-lucky, carefree, imperturbable, undemanding, patient, tolerant, lenient, broad-minded, understanding; *informal* laid-back, unflappable.
- OPPOSITES intolerant.

eat *verb* **1 consume**, devour, swallow, partake of, munch, chomp; *informal* tuck into, put away. **2 have a meal**, feed, snack, breakfast, lunch, dine; *informal* graze.

eavesdrop *verb* **listen in**, spy, overhear; *informal* snoop, earwig.

ebb *verb* **1 recede**, go out, retreat. **2 diminish**, dwindle, wane, fade (away), peter out, decline, flag.
- OPPOSITES flow, increase.

ebullient *adjective* **exuberant**, buoyant, cheerful, cheery, merry, jolly, sunny, jaunty, animated, sparkling, vivacious, irrepressible; *informal* bubbly, bouncy, upbeat, chirpy, full of beans.
- OPPOSITES depressed.

eccentric *adjective* **unconventional**, abnormal, anomalous, odd, strange, peculiar, weird, bizarre, outlandish, idiosyncratic, quirky; *informal* oddball, kooky, cranky.
- OPPOSITES conventional.
● *noun* **oddity**, free spirit, misfit; *informal* oddball, weirdo.

echo *noun* **reverberation**, reflection, ringing, repetition, repeat.
● *verb* **1 reverberate**, resonate, resound, reflect, ring, vibrate. **2 repeat**, restate, reiterate, imitate, parrot, mimic, reproduce, recite.

eclipse *verb* **outshine**, overshadow, surpass, exceed, outclass, outstrip, outdo, transcend.

economic *adjective* **1 financial**, monetary, budgetary, commercial, fiscal. **2 profitable**, moneymaking, lucrative, remunerative, fruitful, productive.
- OPPOSITES unprofitable.

economical *adjective* **1 cheap**, inexpensive, low-cost, budget, economy, cut-price, bargain. **2 thrifty**, provident, prudent, sensible, frugal.
- OPPOSITES expensive, spendthrift.

economize *verb* **save (money)**, cut costs, cut back, make cutbacks, retrench, scrimp.

economy *noun* **1 wealth**, financial resources, financial management. **2 thrift**, thriftiness, prudence, careful budgeting, economizing, saving, restraint, frugality.
- OPPOSITES extravagance.

ecstasy *noun* **rapture**, bliss, joy, elation, euphoria, rhapsodies.
- OPPOSITES misery.

ecstatic *adjective* **enraptured**, elated, euphoric, rapturous, joyful, overjoyed, blissful; *informal* over the moon, on top of the world.

eddy *noun* **swirl**, whirlpool, vortex.
● *verb* **swirl**, whirl, spiral, wind, twist.

edge *noun* **1 border**, boundary, extremity, fringe, margin, side, lip, rim, brim, brink, verge, perimeter. **2 sharpness**, severity, bite, sting, sarcasm, malice, spite, venom. **3 advantage**, lead, head start, the whip hand, the upper hand, dominance.
- OPPOSITES middle.
● *verb* **1 border**, fringe, skirt, surround, enclose, encircle, bound. **2 trim**, decorate, finish, border, fringe. **3 creep**, inch, work your way, ease yourself, sidle, steal.

edgy *adjective* **tense**, nervous, on edge, anxious, apprehensive, uneasy, unsettled, twitchy, jumpy, nervy, keyed up, restive; *informal* uptight, wired.
- OPPOSITES calm.

edit *verb* **correct**, check, copy-edit, improve, polish, modify, adapt, revise, rewrite, reword, shorten, condense, cut, abridge; censor, redact, suppress.

edition *noun* **issue**, number, volume, printing, impression, publication, programme, version.

educate *verb* **teach**, school, tutor, instruct, coach, train, inform, enlighten.

educated *adjective* **informed**, literate, schooled, tutored, well read, learned, knowledgeable, enlightened, intellectual, academic, erudite, scholarly, cultivated, cultured.
- OPPOSITES uneducated.

education *noun* **1 teaching**, schooling, tuition, tutoring, instruction, coaching, training, guidance, enlightenment. **2 learning**, knowledge, literacy, scholarship, enlightenment.

educational *adjective* **1 academic**, scholastic, learning, teaching, pedagogic. **2 instructive**, instructional, educative, informative, illuminating, enlightening; *formal* edifying.

eerie *adjective* **uncanny**, sinister, ghostly, unnatural, unearthly, supernatural, other-worldly, strange, abnormal, weird, freakish; *informal* creepy, scary, spooky.

effect *noun* **1** *the effect of these changes* **result**, consequence, upshot, outcome, repercussions, end result, aftermath, footprint. **2** *the effect of the drug* **impact**, action, effectiveness, power, potency, strength, success. **3** *the dead man's effects* **belongings**, possessions, worldly goods, chattels, property; *informal* things, stuff; *Brit. informal* clobber.
- OPPOSITES cause.
● *verb* **achieve**, accomplish, carry out, manage, bring off, execute, conduct, engineer, perform, do, cause, bring about, produce.

effective *adjective* **1 successful**, effectual, potent, powerful, helpful, beneficial, advantageous, valuable, useful. **2 convincing**, compelling, strong, forceful, persuasive, plausible, credible, logical, reasonable, cogent. **3 operative**, in force, in effect, valid, official, legal, binding. **4 virtual**, practical, essential, actual.
- OPPOSITES ineffective.

effervescent *adjective* **fizzy**, sparkling, carbonated, aerated, gassy, bubbly.
- OPPOSITES still.

efficiency *noun* **1 economy**, productivity, cost-effectiveness, organization, order, orderliness, regulation. **2 competence**, capability, ability, proficiency, expertise, skill, effectiveness.
- OPPOSITES inefficiency, incompetence.

efficient *adjective* **1 economic**, productive, effective, cost-effective, streamlined, organized, methodical, systematic, orderly. **2 competent**, capable, able, proficient, skilful, skilled, effective, productive, organized, businesslike.
- OPPOSITES inefficient, incompetent.

effort *noun* **1 attempt**, try, endeavour; *informal* shot, stab, bash. **2 achievement**, accomplishment, feat, undertaking, enterprise, work, result, outcome. **3 exertion**, energy, work, application; *informal* elbow grease; *Brit. informal* graft.

egg *noun* **ovum**, gamete; (**eggs**) roe, spawn.
□ **egg on** urge, goad, incite, provoke, push, drive, spur on, prod.

WORD LINKS
ovoid egg-shaped

egotistic, **egoistic** *adjective* **self-centred**, selfish, egocentric, self-interested, self-seeking, self-absorbed, self-obsessed, narcissistic, vain, conceited, self-important, boastful.

eject *verb* **1 emit**, spew out, discharge, disgorge, give off, send out, belch, vent. **2 expel**, throw out, remove, oust, evict, banish; *informal* kick out, turf out, boot out.

elaborate *adjective* **1 complicated**, complex, intricate, involved, detailed. **2 ornate**, decorated, embellished, adorned, ornamented, fancy, fussy, busy.
- OPPOSITES simple, plain.
● *verb* **expand on**, enlarge on, add to, flesh out, develop, fill out, amplify.

elastic *adjective* **1 stretchy**, elasticated, springy, flexible, pliable, supple. **2 adaptable**, flexible, adjustable, accommodating, variable, fluid, versatile.
- OPPOSITES rigid.

elated *adjective* **thrilled**, delighted, overjoyed, ecstatic, euphoric, jubilant, rapturous, in raptures, walking on air, on cloud nine, in seventh heaven; *informal* on top of the world, over the moon, tickled pink.
- OPPOSITES miserable.

elder *adjective* **older**, senior.
● *noun* **leader**, patriarch, father.

elderly *adjective* **aged**, old, ageing, long in the tooth, grey-haired, in your dotage; *informal* getting on, over the hill.
- OPPOSITES youthful.

elect *verb* **1 vote in**, vote for, return, cast your vote for, choose, pick, select. **2 choose**, decide, opt, prefer, vote.

election *noun* **ballot**, vote, poll; *Brit.* by-election; *US* primary.

WORD LINKS
psephology study of elections

electric *adjective the atmosphere was electric* **exciting**, charged, electrifying, thrilling, dramatic, dynamic, stimulating, galvanizing.

electrify *verb* **excite**, thrill, stimulate, arouse, rouse, inspire, stir (up), exhilarate, galvanize, fire (with enthusiasm), fire someone's imagination, invigorate, animate; *N. Amer.* light a fire under.

elegance *noun* **1 style**, grace, taste, sophistication, refinement, dignity, poise. **2 neatness**, simplicity, aptness.

elegant *adjective* **1 stylish**, graceful, tasteful, sophisticated, classic, chic, smart, poised, cultivated, polished, cultured. **2** *an elegant solution* **neat**, simple, apt.
- OPPOSITES inelegant.

element *noun* **1 component**, constituent, part, section, portion, piece, segment, aspect, factor, feature, facet, ingredient, strand, detail, member. **2 trace**, touch, hint, smattering, soupçon. **3** (**elements**) **weather**, climate, weather conditions.

elementary *adjective* **1** *an elementary astronomy course* **basic**, rudimentary, preparatory, introductory. **2** *a lot of the work is elementary* **easy**, simple, straightforward, uncomplicated, undemanding, painless, child's play, plain sailing; *informal* a piece of cake.
- OPPOSITES advanced, difficult.

elevate *verb* **1 raise**, lift (up), raise up/aloft, hoist, hike up, haul up. **2 promote**, upgrade, move up, raise; *informal* kick upstairs.
- OPPOSITES lower, demote.

elevated *adjective* **1 raised**, overhead, in the air, high up. **2 lofty**, grand, fine, sublime, inflated, pompous, bombastic. **3 high**, high-ranking, lofty, exalted, grand, noble.

elicit *verb* **obtain**, draw out, extract, bring out, evoke, induce, prompt, generate, trigger, provoke.

eligible *adjective* **1 entitled**, permitted, allowed, qualified, able. **2 desirable**, suitable, available, single, unmarried, unattached.

eliminate *verb* **1 remove**, get rid of, put an end to, do away with, end, stop, eradicate, destroy, stamp out. **2 knock out**, exclude, rule out, disqualify.

elite *noun* **best**, pick, cream, crème de la crème, A-list, flower, high society, beautiful people, aristocracy, ruling class.
- OPPOSITES dregs.

eloquent *adjective* **articulate**, fluent, expressive, persuasive, well expressed,

effective, lucid, vivid.
- OPPOSITES inarticulate.

elude *verb* **evade**, avoid, get away from, dodge, escape from, lose, shake off, give the slip to, slip away from, throw off the scent.

elusive *adjective* **1 difficult to find**, evasive, slippery. **2 indefinable**, intangible, impalpable, fugitive, fleeting, transitory, ambiguous.

emaciated *adjective* **thin**, skeletal, bony, gaunt, wasted, thin as a rake, scrawny, skinny, scraggy, skin and bone, starved, cadaverous, shrivelled, shrunken, withered.
- OPPOSITES fat.

embargo *noun* **ban**, bar, prohibition, stoppage, veto, moratorium, restriction, block, boycott.
● *verb* **ban**, bar, prohibit, stop, outlaw, blacklist, restrict, block, boycott.
- OPPOSITES allow.

embark *verb* **board (ship)**, go on board, go aboard; *informal* hop on, jump on.
- OPPOSITES disembark.
□ **embark on** begin, start, undertake, set out on, take up, turn your hand to, get down to, enter into, venture into, launch into, plunge into, engage in.

embarrass *verb* **humiliate**, shame, put someone to shame, abash, mortify, fluster, discomfit; *informal* show up.

embarrassed *adjective* **humiliated**, mortified, red-faced, blushing, abashed, shamed, ashamed, shamefaced, self-conscious, uncomfortable, discomfited, disconcerted, flustered; *informal* with egg on your face.

embarrassing *adjective* **humiliating**, shameful, mortifying, ignominious, awkward, uncomfortable, compromising; *informal* cringeworthy, cringe-making, toe-curling.

embarrassment *noun* **1 humiliation**, mortification, shame, shamefacedness, awkwardness, self-consciousness, discomfort, discomfiture. **2 difficulty**, predicament, plight, problem, mess; *informal* bind, pickle, fix.

embellish *verb* **decorate**, adorn, ornament, beautify, enhance, trim, garnish, gild, deck, bedeck, festoon, emblazon.

embezzle *verb* **misappropriate**, steal, thieve, pilfer, purloin, appropriate, siphon off, pocket; *informal* filch; *Brit. informal* pinch, nick.

emblem *noun* **symbol**, representation, token, image, figure, mark, sign, crest, badge, device, insignia, coat of arms, shield, logo, trademark.

embody *verb* **1 personify**, manifest, symbolize, represent, express, epitomize, stand for, typify, exemplify. **2 incorporate**, include, contain.

embrace *verb* **1 hug**, take/hold in your arms, hold, cuddle, clasp to your bosom, squeeze, clutch, enfold. **2 welcome**, welcome with open arms, accept, take on board, take up, take to your heart, adopt, espouse. **3 include**, take in, comprise, contain, incorporate, encompass, cover, subsume.
● *noun* **hug**, cuddle, squeeze, clinch, caress.

emerge *verb* **1 appear**, come out, come into view, become visible, surface, materialize, issue, come forth. **2 become known**, become apparent, be revealed, come to light, come out, turn up, transpire, unfold, turn out, prove to be the case.

emergence *noun* **appearance**, arrival, coming, materialization, advent, inception, dawn, birth, origination, start, development.

emergency *noun* **crisis**, disaster, catastrophe, calamity, plight; *informal* panic stations.
● *adjective* **1 urgent**, crisis, extraordinary. **2 reserve**, standby, backup, fallback.

emigrate *verb* **move abroad**, move overseas, leave your country, migrate, relocate, resettle.
- OPPOSITES immigrate.

eminent *adjective* **illustrious**, distinguished, renowned, esteemed, pre-eminent, notable, noted, noteworthy,

great, prestigious, important, outstanding, celebrated, prominent, well known, acclaimed, exalted.
- OPPOSITES unknown.

emission *noun* **discharge**, release, outpouring, outflow, outrush, leak.

emit *verb* **1 discharge**, release, give out/off, pour out, radiate, leak, ooze, disgorge, eject, belch, spew out, exude. **2 utter**, voice, let out, produce, give vent to, come out with.

emotion *noun* **1 feeling**, sentiment, reaction, response, instinct, intuition. **2 passion**, strength of feeling, heart.

emotional *adjective* **1 passionate**, hot-blooded, ardent, fervent, warm, responsive, excitable, temperamental, demonstrative, sensitive. **2 poignant**, moving, touching, affecting, powerful, stirring, emotive, impassioned, dramatic; *informal* tear-jerking.
- OPPOSITES cold, clinical.

emphasis *noun* **1 prominence**, importance, significance, value, stress, weight, accent, attention, priority. **2** *the emphasis is on the word 'little'* **stress**, accent, weight, beat.

emphasize *verb* **stress**, underline, highlight, focus attention on, point up, lay stress on, draw attention to, spotlight, foreground.
- OPPOSITES understate.

emphatic *adjective* **forceful**, firm, vehement, wholehearted, energetic, vigorous, direct, insistent, certain, definite, out-and-out, decided, categorical, unqualified, unconditional, unequivocal, unambiguous, absolute, explicit, downright, outright, clear.

empire *noun* **1 kingdom**, realm, domain, territory, commonwealth, power. **2 business**, firm, company, corporation, multinational, conglomerate, group, consortium, operation.

WORD LINKS
imperial relating to an empire

employ *verb* **1 hire**, engage, recruit, take on, sign up, appoint, retain. **2 occupy**, engage, involve, keep busy, tie up. **3 use**, utilize, make use of, apply, exercise, practise, put into practice, exert, bring into play, bring to bear, draw on, resort to, turn to, have recourse to.
- OPPOSITES dismiss.

employed *adjective* **working**, in work, in employment, holding down a job, earning, salaried, waged.
- OPPOSITES unemployed.

employee *noun* **worker**, member of staff, blue-collar worker, white-collar worker, workman, labourer, hand; (**employees**) personnel, staff, workforce.

employment *noun* **work**, labour, service, job, post, position, situation, occupation, profession, trade, business, line of work.

empower *verb* **1 authorize**, entitle, permit, allow, license, enable. **2 emancipate**, unshackle, set free, liberate, enfranchise.
- OPPOSITES forbid.

empty *adjective* **1 vacant**, unoccupied, uninhabited, bare, clear, free. **2 meaningless**, hollow, idle, vain, futile, worthless, useless, ineffectual. **3 futile**, pointless, purposeless, worthless, meaningless, fruitless, valueless, of no value, senseless.
- OPPOSITES full, occupied.
● *verb* **1 unload**, unpack, clear, evacuate, drain. **2 remove**, take out, extract, tip out, pour out.
- OPPOSITES fill, replace.

emulate *verb* **imitate**, copy, mirror, echo, follow, model yourself on, take a leaf out of someone's book.

enable *verb* **allow**, permit, let, equip, empower, make able, fit, authorize, entitle, qualify.
- OPPOSITES prevent.

enact *verb* **1 make law**, pass, approve, ratify, validate, sanction, authorize. **2 act out**, perform, appear in, stage, mount, put on, present.
- OPPOSITES repeal.

enchanting *adjective* **captivating**, charming, delightful, adorable, lovely, attractive, appealing, engaging, fetching, irresistible, fascinating.

enclose *verb* **1 surround**, circle, ring, encircle, bound, close in, wall in. **2 include**, insert, put in, send.

WORD LINKS
claustrophobia fear of enclosed spaces

enclosure *noun* **compound**, pen, fold, stockade, ring, paddock, yard, run, coop; *N. Amer.* corral.

encompass *verb* **include**, cover, embrace, incorporate, take in, contain, comprise, involve, deal with.

encounter *verb* **1 experience**, run into, meet, come up against, face, be faced with, confront, suffer. **2 meet**, run into, come across/upon, stumble across/on, chance on, happen on; *informal* bump into.
● *noun* **1 meeting**, chance meeting. **2 battle**, fight, skirmish, clash, scuffle, confrontation, struggle; *informal* run-in, set-to, scrap.

encourage *verb* **1 hearten**, cheer, buoy up, uplift, inspire, motivate, spur on, stir, fire up, stimulate, embolden; *informal* buck up. **2** *she encouraged him to go* **persuade**, coax, urge, press, push, pressure, prod, egg on. **3 support**, back, promote, further, foster, nurture, cultivate, strengthen, stimulate.
- OPPOSITES discourage.

encouragement *noun* **1 support**, cheering up, inspiration, motivation, stimulation, morale-boosting; *informal* a shot in the arm. **2 persuasion**, coaxing, urging, prodding, prompting, inducement, incentive, carrot. **3 backing**, sponsorship, support, promotion, furtherance, fostering, nurture, cultivation, stimulation.

encouraging *adjective* **1 promising**, hopeful, auspicious, favourable, heartening, reassuring, cheering, comforting, welcome, pleasing, gratifying. **2 supportive**, understanding, helpful, positive, enthusiastic.

end *noun* **1 conclusion**, termination, ending, finish, close, resolution, climax, finale, culmination, denouement. **2 extremity**, limit, edge, border, boundary, periphery, point, tip, head, top, bottom. **3 aim**, goal, purpose, objective, object, target, intention, aspiration, wish, desire, ambition.
- OPPOSITES beginning, means.
● *verb* **1 finish**, conclude, terminate, close, stop, cease, culminate, climax. **2 break off**, call off, bring to an end, put an end to, stop, finish, terminate, discontinue, cancel.
- OPPOSITES begin.

endanger *verb* **jeopardize**, risk, put at risk, put in danger, be a danger to, threaten, compromise, imperil.
- OPPOSITES safeguard.

endearing *adjective* **charming**, appealing, attractive, engaging, winning, captivating, enchanting, cute, sweet, delightful, lovely.

endeavour *verb* **try**, attempt, seek, strive, struggle, labour, toil, work.
● *noun* **1 attempt**, try, bid, effort. **2 undertaking**, enterprise, venture, exercise, activity, exploit, deed, act, action, move.

ending *noun* **end**, finish, close, conclusion, resolution, summing-up, denouement, finale.
- OPPOSITES beginning.

endless *adjective* **1 unlimited**, limitless, infinite, inexhaustible, boundless, unbounded, ceaseless, unending, everlasting, constant, continuous, interminable, unfailing, perpetual, eternal, never-ending. **2 countless**, innumerable, numerous, a multitude of; *informal* umpteen, no end of; *literary* myriad.
- OPPOSITES limited, few.

endorse *verb* **support**, back, agree with, approve (of), favour, subscribe to, recommend, champion, uphold, sanction.
- OPPOSITES oppose.

endorsement *noun* **support**, backing, approval, seal of approval, agreement, recommendation, patronage, sanction.

endow *verb* **1 finance**, fund, pay for, subsidize, sponsor. **2** *he was endowed with great strength* **provide**, supply, furnish, equip, favour, bless, grace.

endowment *noun* **gift**, present, grant, funding, award, donation, contribution, subsidy, sponsorship, bequest, legacy.

endurance *noun* **1 toleration**, tolerance, forbearance, patience, acceptance, resignation, stoicism. **2 resistance**, durability, permanence, longevity, strength, toughness, stamina, staying power, fortitude.

endure *verb* **1 undergo**, go through, live through, experience, cope with, deal with, face, suffer, tolerate, put up with, brave, bear, withstand. **2 last**, live, live on, go on, survive, abide, continue, persist, remain.

enemy *noun* **opponent**, adversary, rival, nemesis, antagonist, combatant, challenger, competitor, opposition, competition, the other side; *literary* foe.
- OPPOSITES friend, ally.

energetic *adjective* **1** *an energetic woman* **active**, lively, dynamic, spirited, animated, bouncy, bubbly, sprightly, tireless, indefatigable, enthusiastic; *informal* full of beans. **2** *energetic exercises* **vigorous**, strenuous, brisk, hard, arduous, demanding, taxing, tough, rigorous. **3** *an energetic advertising campaign* **forceful**, vigorous, aggressive, hard-hitting, high-powered, all-out, determined, bold, intensive; *informal* in-your-face.
- OPPOSITES lethargic.

energy *noun* **vitality**, vigour, strength, stamina, animation, spirit, verve, enthusiasm, zest, exuberance, dynamism, drive; *informal* punch, bounce, oomph, go, get-up-and-go.

enforce *verb* **1 impose**, apply, administer, carry out, implement, bring to bear, put into effect. **2 force**, compel, coerce, exact.

engage *verb* **1 capture**, catch, arrest, grab, draw, attract, gain, hold, grip, absorb, occupy. **2 employ**, hire, recruit, take on, enrol, appoint. **3** *the chance to engage in a wide range of pursuits* **participate in**, join in, take part in, partake in/of, enter into, embark on. **4 attack**, fall on, take on, clash with, encounter, meet, fight, do battle with.
- OPPOSITES lose, dismiss.

engagement *noun* **1 appointment**, meeting, arrangement, commitment, date, assignation, rendezvous. **2 participation**, involvement. **3 battle**, fight, clash, confrontation, encounter, conflict, skirmish, action, hostilities.

engaging *adjective* **charming**, attractive, appealing, pleasing, pleasant, agreeable, likeable, lovable, sweet, winning, fetching; *Scottish & N. English* bonny.
- OPPOSITES unappealing.

engender *verb* **cause**, give rise to, bring about, occasion, lead to, result in, produce, create, generate, arouse, rouse, inspire, provoke, kindle, trigger, spark, stir up, whip up.

engine *noun* **motor**, generator, machine, turbine.

engineer *noun* **1** *a structural engineer* **designer**, planner, builder. **2** *a repair engineer* **mechanic**, repairer, technician, maintenance man, operator, driver.
● *verb* **bring about**, arrange, pull off, bring off, contrive, manoeuvre, negotiate, organize, orchestrate, plan, mastermind.

engraving *noun* **etching**, print, plate, picture, illustration, inscription.

engrossed *adjective* **absorbed**, involved, interested, occupied, preoccupied, immersed, caught up, riveted, gripped, rapt, fascinated, intent, captivated, enthralled.

engulf *verb* **swamp**, inundate, flood, deluge, immerse, swallow up, submerge, bury, envelop, overwhelm.

enhance *verb* **improve**, add to, strengthen, boost, increase, intensify, heighten, magnify, amplify, inflate, build up, supplement, augment.
- OPPOSITES diminish.

enjoy *verb* **1 like**, be fond of, take pleasure in, be keen on, delight in, relish, revel in, adore, lap up, savour, luxuriate in, bask in; *informal* get a thrill out of. **2 benefit from**, be blessed with, be favoured with, be endowed with, possess, own, boast.
- OPPOSITES dislike, lack.
□ **enjoy yourself** have fun, have a good time, make merry, celebrate, revel; *informal* party, have a whale of a time, let your hair down.

enjoyable *adjective* **entertaining**, amusing, delightful, pleasant, congenial, convivial, agreeable, pleasurable, satisfying.
- OPPOSITES disagreeable.

enjoyment *noun* **pleasure**, fun, entertainment, amusement, recreation, relaxation, happiness, merriment, joy, satisfaction, liking.

enlarge *verb* **1 extend**, expand, grow, add to, amplify, augment, magnify, build up, stretch, widen, broaden, lengthen, elongate, deepen, thicken. **2 swell**, distend, bloat, bulge, dilate, blow up, puff up.
- OPPOSITES reduce, shrink.
□ **enlarge on** elaborate on, expand on, add to, flesh out, add detail to, develop, fill out, embellish, embroider.

enlighten *verb* **inform**, tell, make aware, open someone's eyes, illuminate; *informal* put someone in the picture.

enlightened *adjective* **informed**, aware, sophisticated, liberal, open-minded, broad-minded, educated, knowledgeable, civilized, refined, cultured.
- OPPOSITES benighted.

enlightenment *noun* **insight**, understanding, awareness, education, learning, knowledge, illumination, awakening, instruction, teaching, open-mindedness, broad-mindedness, culture, refinement, cultivation, civilization.

enlist *verb* **1 join up**, enrol, sign up for, volunteer, register. **2 recruit**, call up, enrol, sign up, conscript, mobilize; *US* draft. **3 obtain**, engage, secure, win, get.
- OPPOSITES discharge, demobilize.

enormity *noun* **1 wickedness**, vileness, heinousness, baseness, depravity, outrageousness. **2 immensity**, hugeness, size, extent, magnitude.

enormous *adjective* **huge**, vast, immense, gigantic, giant, massive, colossal, mammoth, tremendous, extensive, mighty, monumental, mountainous, cosmic; *informal* mega, monster, whopping; *Brit. informal* ginormous.
- OPPOSITES tiny.

enough *determiner* **sufficient**, adequate, ample, abundant, the necessary; *informal* plenty of.
- OPPOSITES insufficient.
● *pronoun* **sufficient**, plenty, an adequate amount, as much as necessary, a sufficiency, an ample supply, your fill.

enquire *verb* **1 ask**, query, question. **2 investigate**, probe, look into, make enquiries, research, examine, explore, delve into; *informal* check out.

enquiry *noun* **1 question**, query. **2 investigation**, probe, examination, exploration, inquest, hearing.

enrage *verb* **anger**, infuriate, incense, madden, inflame, antagonize, provoke; *informal* drive mad/crazy, make someone see red, make someone's blood boil.
- OPPOSITES placate.

enraged *adjective* **furious**, infuriated, irate, incensed, raging, incandescent, fuming, seething, beside yourself; *informal* mad, livid, foaming at the mouth.

enrich *verb* **enhance**, improve, better, add to, augment, supplement, complement, refine.

enrol *verb* **1 register**, sign on/up, put your name down, apply, volunteer, enter, join. **2 accept**, admit, take on, sign on/up, recruit, engage.

ensemble *noun* **1 group**, band, company, troupe, cast, chorus, corps;

informal combo. **2 whole**, unit, body, set, collection, combination, composite, package. **3 outfit**, costume, suit; *informal* get-up.

ensue *verb* **result**, follow, develop, succeed, emerge, arise, proceed, stem.

ensure *verb* **1 make sure**, make certain, see to it, check, confirm, establish, verify. **2 secure**, guarantee, assure, certify.

entail *verb* **involve**, necessitate, require, need, demand, call for, mean, imply, cause, give rise to, occasion.

enter *verb* **1 go into**, come into, get into, set foot in, gain access to. **2 penetrate**, pierce, puncture, perforate. **3 join**, enrol in/for, enlist in, volunteer for, sign up for. **4 go in for**, register for, enrol for, sign on/up for, compete in, take part in, participate in. **5 record**, write, put down, take down, note, jot down, register, log. **6 key (in)**, type (in), tap in.
– OPPOSITES leave.

enterprise *noun* **1 undertaking**, endeavour, venture, exercise, activity, operation, task, business, project, scheme. **2 initiative**, resourcefulness, imagination, ingenuity, inventiveness, originality, creativity. **3 business**, company, firm, venture, organization, operation, concern, establishment; *informal* outfit.

enterprising *adjective* **resourceful**, entrepreneurial, imaginative, ingenious, inventive, creative, adventurous, bold; *informal* go-ahead.

entertain *verb* **1 amuse**, please, charm, cheer, interest, engage, occupy. **2 receive**, play host/hostess to, throw a party for, wine and dine, feed, fete. **3 consider**, contemplate, think of, hear of, countenance.
– OPPOSITES bore, reject.

entertainment *noun* **amusement**, pleasure, leisure, recreation, relaxation, fun, enjoyment, diversion, interest.

enthralling *adjective* **fascinating**, entrancing, enchanting, bewitching, captivating, delightful, absorbing, engrossing, compelling, riveting, gripping, exciting; *informal* unputdownable.

enthusiasm *noun* **keenness**, eagerness, passion, fervour, zeal, zest, gusto, energy, vigour, fire, spirit, interest, commitment, devotion; *informal* get-up-and-go.
– OPPOSITES apathy.

enthusiast *noun* **fan**, devotee, supporter, follower, aficionado, lover, admirer; *informal* buff.

enthusiastic *adjective* **keen**, eager, avid, ardent, fervent, passionate, zealous, excited, wholehearted, committed, devoted, fanatical, earnest.
– OPPOSITES apathetic.

entice *verb* **tempt**, lure, attract, appeal to, invite, persuade, beguile, coax, woo, lead on, seduce; *informal* sweet-talk.

entire *adjective* **whole**, complete, total, full.

entirely *adverb* **1 absolutely**, completely, totally, wholly, utterly, quite, altogether, thoroughly. **2 solely**, only, exclusively, purely, merely, just, alone.

entitle *verb* **1 qualify**, make eligible, authorize, allow, permit, enable, empower. **2 name**, title, call, label, designate, dub.

entity *noun* **being**, creature, individual, organism, life form, body, object, article, thing.

entrance[1] *noun* **1 entry**, way in, access, approach, door, portal, gate, opening, mouth, foyer, lobby, porch; *N. Amer.* entryway. **2 appearance**, arrival, entry, coming. **3 admission**, admittance, (right of) entry, entrée, access.
– OPPOSITES exit, departure.

entrance[2] *verb* **enchant**, bewitch, beguile, captivate, mesmerize, hypnotize, spellbind, transfix, enthral, engross, absorb, fascinate, stun, electrify, charm, delight; *informal* bowl over, knock out.

entrant *noun* **competitor**, contestant, contender, participant, candidate, applicant.

entreat *verb* **implore**, beg, plead with, pray, ask, request, bid, enjoin, appeal to, call on; *literary* beseech.

entrenched, **intrenched** *adjective* **ingrained**, established, fixed, firm, deep-seated, deep-rooted, unshakeable, ineradicable.

entrust *verb* **1 charge**, give someone the responsibility for, present. **2 assign**, confer on, bestow on, vest in, delegate, give, grant, vouchsafe.

entry *noun* **1 appearance**, arrival, entrance, coming. **2 entrance**, way in, access, approach, door, portal, gate, entrance hall, foyer, lobby; *N. Amer.* entryway. **3 admission**, admittance, entrance, access. **4 item**, record, note, memo, memorandum. **5 submission**, application, entry form.
– OPPOSITES departure, exit.

envelop *verb* **surround**, cover, enfold, engulf, encircle, cocoon, sheathe, swathe, enclose, cloak, veil, shroud.

envious *adjective* **jealous**, covetous, desirous, grudging, begrudging, resentful; *informal* green with envy.

environment *noun* **1 situation**, setting, milieu, background, backdrop, context, conditions, ambience, atmosphere. **2 the natural world**, nature, the earth, the ecosystem, the biosphere, Mother Nature, wildlife, flora and fauna, the countryside.

WORD LINKS
ecology study of the environment

environmentalist *noun* **conservationist**, ecologist, nature-lover, green; *informal* eco-warrior, tree-hugger.

envisage *verb* **1 foresee**, predict, forecast, anticipate, expect, think likely. **2 imagine**, contemplate, picture, conceive of, think of.

envoy *noun* **ambassador**, emissary, diplomat, representative, delegate, spokesperson, agent, intermediary, mediator; *informal* go-between.

envy *noun* **jealousy**, covetousness, resentment, bitterness.
● *verb* **1 be envious of**, be jealous of, be resentful of. **2 covet**, desire, aspire to, wish for, want, long for, yearn for, hanker after, crave.

ephemeral *adjective* **transitory**, transient, fleeting, passing, short-lived, momentary, brief, short, temporary, impermanent, short-term.
– OPPOSITES permanent.

epidemic *noun* **1 outbreak**, plague, pandemic. **2 spate**, rash, wave, eruption, plague, outbreak, craze, upsurge.

episode *noun* **1 incident**, event, occurrence, chapter, experience, occasion, interlude, adventure, exploit. **2 instalment**, chapter, passage, part, portion, section, programme, show. **3 period**, spell, bout, attack, phase; *informal* dose.

epitome *noun* **personification**, embodiment, incarnation, essence, quintessence, archetype, paradigm, exemplar, model.

epoch *noun* **era**, age, period, time, aeon.

equal *adjective* **1 identical**, uniform, alike, like, the same, matching, equivalent, corresponding. **2 impartial**, non-partisan, fair, just, equitable, unprejudiced, non-discriminatory. **3 evenly matched**, even, balanced, level, nip and tuck, neck and neck; *informal* level pegging.
– OPPOSITES different, unequal.
● *noun* **equivalent**, peer, fellow, like, counterpart, match, parallel.
● *verb* **1 be equal to**, be equivalent to, be the same as, come to, amount to, make, total, add up to. **2 match**, reach, parallel, be level with.

equality *noun* **fairness**, equal rights, equal opportunities, impartiality, even-handedness, justice.

equanimity *noun* **composure**, calm, level-headedness, self-possession, presence of mind, serenity, tranquillity, imperturbability, equilibrium, poise, aplomb, sangfroid, nerve; *informal* cool.
– OPPOSITES anxiety.

equate *verb* **1** *he equates criticism with treachery* **identify**, compare, bracket, class, associate, connect, link, relate. **2 equalize**, balance, even out/up, level, square, tally, match.

equilibrium *noun* **balance**, stability, poise, symmetry, harmony.
- OPPOSITES imbalance.

e

equip *verb* **1** *the boat was equipped with a flare gun* **provide**, furnish, supply, issue, kit out, stock, provision, arm. **2** *the course will equip them for the workplace* **prepare**, qualify, ready, suit, train.

equipment *noun* **apparatus**, kit, paraphernalia, tools, utensils, implements, hardware, gadgetry, things; *informal* stuff, gear.

equivalent *adjective* **comparable**, corresponding, commensurate, similar, parallel, analogous.
● *noun* **counterpart**, parallel, alternative, analogue, twin, opposite number.

equivocal *adjective* **ambiguous**, indefinite, non-committal, vague, imprecise, inexact, inexplicit, hazy, unclear, ambivalent, uncertain, unsure.
- OPPOSITES definite.

era *noun* **age**, epoch, period, time, date, day, generation.

eradicate *verb* **eliminate**, get rid of, remove, obliterate, extinguish, exterminate, destroy, annihilate, kill, wipe out.

erase *verb* **delete**, rub out, wipe off, blank out, expunge, excise, remove, obliterate, redact.

erect *adjective* **upright**, straight, vertical, perpendicular, standing (on end), bristling, stiff.
● *verb* **build**, construct, put up, assemble, put together, fabricate, raise.
- OPPOSITES demolish, dismantle.

erode *verb* **wear away**, abrade, grind down, crumble, weather, undermine, weaken, deteriorate, destroy.

erosion *noun* **wearing away**, abrasion, attrition, weathering, dissolution, deterioration, disintegration, destruction.

erotic *adjective* **sexually arousing**, sexually stimulating, titillating, suggestive, pornographic, sexually explicit; *informal* blue, X-rated; *euphemistic* adult.

errand *noun* **task**, job, chore, assignment, mission.

erratic *adjective* **unpredictable**, inconsistent, changeable, variable, inconstant, irregular, fitful, unstable, varying, fluctuating, unreliable.
- OPPOSITES consistent.

error *noun* **mistake**, inaccuracy, miscalculation, blunder, slip, oversight, misconception, delusion, misprint; *Brit. informal* boob.

erupt *verb fighting erupted* **break out**, flare up, blow up, explode, burst out.

eruption *noun* **1 discharge**, explosion, lava flow, pyroclastic flow. **2 outbreak**, flare-up, upsurge, outburst, explosion, wave, spate.

escalate *verb* **1 increase rapidly**, soar, rocket, shoot up, spiral; *informal* go through the roof. **2 grow**, develop, mushroom, increase, heighten, intensify, accelerate.
- OPPOSITES plunge, subside.

escape *verb* **1 run away**, run off, get away, break out, break free, bolt, make your getaway, slip away, abscond; *informal* vamoose, skedaddle, fly the coop; *Brit. informal* do a runner, do a bunk. **2** *he escaped his pursuers* **get away from**, elude, avoid, dodge, shake off; *informal* give someone the slip. **3** *they cannot escape their duties* **avoid**, evade, elude, cheat, sidestep, circumvent, steer clear of, shirk. **4 leak (out)**, spill (out), seep (out), discharge, flow (out), pour (out).
● *noun* **1 getaway**, breakout, flight. **2 leak**, spill, seepage, discharge, outflow, outpouring.

escort *noun* **guard**, bodyguard, protector, minder, attendant, chaperone, entourage, retinue, protection, convoy.
● *verb* **1 conduct**, accompany, guide, usher, shepherd, take, lead. **2 partner**, accompany, chaperone.

esoteric *adjective* **abstruse**, obscure, arcane, rarefied, recondite, abstract, enigmatic, cryptic, complex, complicated, incomprehensible, impenetrable, mysterious.

especially *adverb* **1 mainly**, mostly, chiefly, particularly, principally, largely, primarily. **2** *a committee formed especially for the purpose* **expressly**, specially, specifically, exclusively, just, particularly, explicitly. **3** *he is especially talented* **exceptionally**, particularly, unusually, extraordinarily, uncommonly, uniquely, remarkably, outstandingly.

essay *noun* **article**, composition, paper, dissertation, thesis, discourse, study, assignment, treatise, piece, feature; *N. Amer.* theme.

essence *noun* **1 nature**, heart, core, substance, basis, principle, quintessence, soul, spirit, reality; *informal* nitty-gritty. **2 extract**, concentrate, elixir, juice, oil.

essential *adjective* **1 crucial**, key, vital, indispensable, all-important, critical, imperative. **2 basic**, bare-bones, inherent, fundamental, quintessential, intrinsic, underlying, characteristic, innate, primary.
- OPPOSITES unimportant, incidental.
● *noun* **1 necessity**, prerequisite; *informal* must. **2** (**essentials**) **fundamentals**, basics, rudiments, first principles, foundations, essence, basis, core, kernel, crux; *informal* nitty-gritty, nuts and bolts.

establish *verb* **1 set up**, start, initiate, institute, found, create, inaugurate. **2 prove**, demonstrate, show, indicate, determine, confirm.

established *adjective* **accepted**, traditional, orthodox, set, fixed, official, usual, customary, common, normal, general, prevailing, accustomed, familiar, expected, conventional, standard.

establishment *noun* **1 foundation**, institution, formation, inception, creation, installation, inauguration. **2 business**, firm, company, concern, enterprise, venture, organization, operation; *informal* outfit. **3 institution**, place, premises, institute. **4** *criticism of the Establishment* **the authorities**, the powers that be, the system, the ruling class.

estate *noun* **1 property**, grounds, garden(s), park, parkland, land(s), territory. **2** *an industrial estate* **area**, development, complex. **3 plantation**, farm, holding, forest, vineyard; *N. Amer.* ranch. **4 assets**, capital, wealth, riches, holdings, fortune, property, effects, possessions, belongings.

esteem *noun* **respect**, admiration, acclaim, appreciation, recognition, honour, reverence, estimation, regard.
● *verb* **respect**, admire, value, regard highly, appreciate, like, prize, treasure, revere.

estimate *verb* **1 calculate**, approximate, guess, evaluate, judge, assess, weigh up. **2 consider**, believe, reckon, deem, judge, rate.
● *noun* **calculation**, approximation, estimation, guess, assessment, evaluation, costing, quotation, valuation; *informal* guesstimate.

estrangement *noun* **alienation**, disaffection, parting, separation, divorce, break-up, split, breach.

etch *verb* **engrave**, carve, inscribe, incise, score, mark, scratch.

etching *noun* **engraving**, print, plate.

eternal *adjective* **everlasting**, never-ending, endless, perpetual, undying, immortal, abiding, permanent, enduring, constant, continual, continuous, sustained, uninterrupted, unbroken, non-stop, round-the-clock.

eternity *noun* **1 ever**, all time, perpetuity. **2** *(informal)* **a long time**, an age, ages, a lifetime, hours, years, forever.

ethical *adjective* **moral**, morally correct, right-minded, principled, good, just, honourable, fair.

ethics *plural noun* **morals**, morality, values, principles, ideals, standards (of behaviour).

ethnic *adjective* **racial**, race-related, national, cultural, folk, tribal, ethnological.

euphoria *noun* **elation**, happiness, joy, delight, glee, excitement, exhilaration, jubilation, exultation, ecstasy, bliss, rapture.
- OPPOSITES misery.

evacuate *verb* **1 remove**, move out, take away. **2 leave**, vacate, abandon, move out of, quit, withdraw from, retreat from, flee. **3** *police evacuated the area* **clear**, empty.

evade *verb* **1 elude**, avoid, dodge, escape (from), steer clear of, sidestep, lose, leave behind, shake off; *informal* give someone the slip. **2 avoid**, dodge, sidestep, bypass, skirt round, fudge; *informal* duck, cop out of.
- OPPOSITES confront.

evaluate *verb* **assess**, judge, gauge, rate, estimate, appraise, weigh up; *informal* size up.

evaporate *verb* **1 vaporize**, dry up. **2 end**, pass (away), fizzle out, peter out, wear off, vanish, fade, disappear, melt away.
- OPPOSITES condense, materialize.

evasive *adjective* **equivocal**, prevaricating, elusive, ambiguous, non-committal, vague, unclear, oblique.

even *adjective* **1 flat**, smooth, uniform, level, plane. **2 uniform**, constant, steady, stable, consistent, unvarying, unchanging, regular. **3 all square**, drawn, tied, level, neck and neck, nip and tuck; *Brit.* level pegging; *informal* even-steven(s).
- OPPOSITES bumpy, irregular, unequal.

evening *noun* **dusk**, twilight, nightfall, sunset, sundown, night.

event *noun* **1 occurrence**, happening, incident, affair, occasion, phenomenon, function, gathering; *informal* do. **2 competition**, contest, tournament, match, fixture, tie, race, game, sport, discipline; *Brit.* clash.

eventful *adjective* **busy**, action-packed, full, lively, active, hectic.
- OPPOSITES dull.

eventual *adjective* **final**, ultimate, resulting, ensuing, consequent, subsequent.

eventually *adverb* **in the end**, in due course, by and by, in time, after a time, finally, at last, ultimately, in the long run, at the end of the day, one day, some day, sometime, sooner or later.

ever *adverb* **1 at any time**, at any point, on any occasion, under any circumstances, on any account, until now. **2 always**, forever, eternally, continually, constantly, endlessly, perpetually, incessantly.

everlasting *adjective* **eternal**, endless, never-ending, perpetual, undying, abiding, enduring, infinite.
- OPPOSITES transient, occasional.

everybody *pronoun* **everyone**, every person, each person, all, one and all, all and sundry, the whole world, the public.
- OPPOSITES nobody.

everyday *adjective* **1 daily**, day-to-day, ongoing; *formal* quotidian. **2 commonplace**, ordinary, common, usual, regular, familiar, conventional, routine, run-of-the-mill, standard, stock, household, domestic; *Brit.* common or garden.
- OPPOSITES unusual.

everyone *pronoun* see **everybody**.

everywhere *adverb* **all over**, all around, in every nook and cranny, far and wide, near and far, high and low, [here, there, and everywhere], the world over, worldwide; *informal* all over the place; *Brit. informal* all over the shop; *N. Amer. informal* all over the map.
- OPPOSITES nowhere.

evict *verb* **expel**, eject, remove, dislodge, turn out, throw out, drive out, dispossess; *informal* chuck out, kick out, boot out, throw someone out on their ear; *Brit. informal* turf out.

evidence *noun* **1 proof**, confirmation, verification, substantiation, corroboration. **2 testimony**, witness statement, declaration, submission; *Law* deposition, affidavit. **3 signs**, indications, marks, traces, suggestions, hints.

evident *adjective* **obvious**, apparent, noticeable, conspicuous, visible, discernible, clear, plain, manifest, patent; *informal* as clear as day.

evidently *adverb* **1 obviously**, clearly, plainly, unmistakably, manifestly, patently. **2 seemingly**, apparently, as far as you can tell, from all appearances, on the face of it, it seems, it appears.

evil *adjective* **1** *an evil deed* **wicked**, bad, wrong, immoral, sinful, vile, iniquitous, villainous, vicious, malicious, malevolent, demonic, diabolical, fiendish, dark, monstrous. **2** *an evil spirit* **harmful**, bad, malign. **3 unpleasant**, disagreeable, nasty, horrible, foul, filthy, vile.
- OPPOSITES good, virtuous.
● *noun* **1** *the evil in our midst* **wickedness**, badness, wrongdoing, sin, sinfulness, immorality, vice, iniquity, corruption, villainy. **2** *nothing but evil will result* **harm**, pain, misery, sorrow, suffering, trouble, disaster, misfortune, woe.
- OPPOSITES good.

evoke *verb* **bring to mind**, put someone in mind of, conjure up, summon (up), invoke, elicit, induce, kindle, awaken, arouse.

evolution *noun* **1 development**, progress, rise, expansion, growth. **2 natural selection**, Darwinism, adaptation, development.

evolve *verb* **develop**, progress, advance, grow, expand, spread.

exacerbate *verb* **aggravate**, worsen, inflame, compound, intensify, increase, heighten, magnify, add to.
- OPPOSITES reduce.

exact *adjective* **1** *an exact description* **precise**, accurate, correct, faithful, close, true, literal, strict, perfect. **2** *an exact record keeper* **careful**, meticulous, painstaking, punctilious, conscientious, scrupulous.
- OPPOSITES inaccurate, careless.
● *verb* **1 demand**, require, impose, extract, compel, force, wring. **2 inflict**, impose, administer, mete out, wreak.

exacting *adjective* **demanding**, stringent, testing, challenging, arduous, laborious, hard, taxing, gruelling, punishing, tough.
- OPPOSITES easy, easy-going.

exactly *adverb* **1 precisely**, entirely, absolutely, completely, totally, just, quite, in every respect. **2 accurately**, precisely, unerringly, faultlessly, perfectly, faithfully.

exaggerate *verb* **overstate**, overemphasize, overestimate, inflate, embellish, embroider, elaborate, overplay, dramatize; *Brit. informal* blow out of all proportion.
- OPPOSITES understate.

examination *noun* **1** *items spread out for examination* **scrutiny**, inspection, perusal, study, investigation, consideration, analysis. **2** *a medical examination* **inspection**, check-up, assessment, appraisal, test, scan. **3** *a school examination* **test**, exam, assessment; *N. Amer.* quiz.

examine *verb* **1 inspect**, scrutinize, investigate, look at, study, appraise, analyse, review, survey; *informal* check out. **2 test**, quiz, question, assess, appraise.

example *noun* **1 specimen**, sample, instance, case, illustration. **2 precedent**, lead, model, pattern, ideal, standard. **3 warning**, lesson, deterrent, disincentive.

exasperate *verb* **infuriate**, anger, annoy, irritate, madden, provoke, irk, vex, gall, get on someone's nerves; *Brit.* rub up the wrong way; *informal* aggravate, rile, bug, hack off; *Brit. informal* nark, get on someone's wick; *N. Amer. informal* tee off, tick off.

excavate *verb* **unearth**, dig up, uncover, reveal, disinter, exhume, dig out, quarry, mine.

exceed *verb* **be more than**, be greater than, be over, go beyond, top, surpass.

excel *verb* **shine**, be excellent, be outstanding, be skilful, be talented, stand out, be second to none.

excellence *noun* **distinction**, quality, superiority, brilliance, greatness, calibre, eminence.

excellent *adjective* **very good**, outstanding, superb, exceptional, marvellous, wonderful, splendid; *informal* terrific, fantastic.
- OPPOSITES inferior.

e

except *preposition* **excluding**, not including, excepting, except for, omitting, not counting, but, besides, apart from, aside from, barring, bar, other than; *informal* outside of.

exception *noun* **anomaly**, irregularity, deviation, special case, peculiarity, abnormality, oddity.

exceptional *adjective* **1** *the drought was exceptional* **unusual**, abnormal, atypical, out of the ordinary, rare, unprecedented, unexpected, surprising. **2** *her exceptional ability* **outstanding**, extraordinary, remarkable, special, phenomenal, prodigious.
- OPPOSITES normal, average.

excerpt *noun* **extract**, part, section, piece, portion, snippet, clip, citation, quotation, quote, line, passage, fragment.

excess *noun* **1 surplus**, surfeit, overabundance, superabundance, superfluity, glut. **2 remainder**, leftovers, extra, rest, residue. **3 overindulgence**, intemperance, immoderation, profligacy, extravagance, self-indulgence.
- OPPOSITES lack, restraint.
● *adjective excess oil* **surplus**, superfluous, redundant, unwanted, unneeded, excessive, extra.

excessive *adjective* **1 immoderate**, intemperate, overindulgent, unrestrained, uncontrolled, extravagant. **2 exorbitant**, extortionate, unreasonable, outrageous, uncalled for, inordinate, unwarranted, disproportionate; *informal* over the top.

exchange *noun* **1 interchange**, trade, trading, swapping, traffic, trafficking. **2 conversation**, dialogue, chat, talk, discussion.
● *verb* **trade**, swap, switch, change.

excitable *adjective* **temperamental**, volatile, mercurial, emotional, sensitive, highly strung, tempestuous, hot-headed, fiery.
- OPPOSITES placid.

excite *verb* **1 thrill**, exhilarate, animate, enliven, rouse, stir, stimulate, galvanize. **2 provoke**, stir up, rouse, arouse, kindle, trigger, spark off, incite, cause.
- OPPOSITES bore.

excitement *noun* **1** *the excitement of seeing a leopard in the wild* **thrill**, pleasure, delight, joy; *informal* kick, buzz. **2** *the excitement in her eyes* **exhilaration**, elation, animation, enthusiasm, eagerness, anticipation.

exciting *adjective* **thrilling**, exhilarating, stirring, rousing, stimulating, intoxicating, electrifying, invigorating, gripping, compelling, powerful, dramatic.

exclaim *verb* **cry out**, declare, proclaim, blurt out, call out, shout, yell.

exclude *verb* **1 keep out**, deny access to, shut out, bar, ban, prohibit. **2 rule out**, preclude. **3 be exclusive of**, not include.
- OPPOSITES admit, include.

exclusive *adjective* **1 select**, chic, high-class, elite, fashionable, stylish, elegant, premier; *Brit.* upmarket; *informal* posh, classy; *Brit. informal* swish. **2 sole**, unshared, unique, individual, personal, private. **3** *prices exclusive of VAT* **not including**, excluding, leaving out, omitting, excepting.
- OPPOSITES inclusive.

excruciating *adjective* **agonizing**, severe, acute, intense, violent, racking, searing, piercing, stabbing, unbearable, unendurable; *informal* splitting, killing.

excursion *noun* **outing**, trip, jaunt, expedition, journey, tour, day out, drive, run; *informal* spin.

excuse *verb* **1 forgive**, pardon. **2 justify**, defend, condone, forgive, overlook, disregard, ignore, tolerate, explain, mitigate. **3 let off**, release, relieve, exempt, absolve, free.
- OPPOSITES punish, condemn.

● *noun* **1 justification**, defence, reason, explanation, mitigating circumstances, mitigation. **2 pretext**, pretence; *Brit.* get-out; *informal* story, alibi.

execute *verb* **1 carry out**, accomplish, bring off/about, implement, achieve, complete, engineer; *informal* pull off. **2 put to death**, kill, hang, behead, electrocute, shoot.

execution *noun* **1 implementation**, carrying out, performance, accomplishment, bringing off/about, attainment, realization. **2 killing**, capital punishment, the death penalty.

executive *adjective* **administrative**, managerial, decision-making, law-making, governing, controlling.
● *noun* **1 director**, manager, senior official, administrator; *informal* boss, exec, suit. **2 administration**, management, directorate, government, authority.

exemplary *adjective* **perfect**, ideal, model, faultless, flawless, impeccable, irreproachable.
– OPPOSITES deplorable.

exemplify *verb* **typify**, epitomize, be an example of, be representative of, symbolize, illustrate, demonstrate.

exempt *adjective* **free**, not liable, not subject, immune, excepted, excused, absolved.
● *verb* **excuse**, free, release, exclude, grant immunity, spare, absolve; *informal* let off.

exemption *noun* **immunity**, exception, dispensation, indemnity, exclusion, freedom, release, relief, absolution.

exercise *noun* **1 physical activity**, a workout, working out, movement, training. **2 task**, piece of work, problem, assignment, practice. **3 manoeuvre**, operation, deployment.
● *verb* **1 work out**, do exercises, train. **2 use**, employ, make use of, utilize, practise, apply. **3 concern**, occupy, worry, trouble, bother, disturb, prey on someone's mind.

exert *verb* **bring to bear**, apply, use, utilize, deploy.
□ **exert yourself** work hard, labour, toil, make an effort, endeavour, slog away, push yourself.

exhaust *verb* **1 tire out**, wear out, overtire, fatigue, weary, drain; *informal* take it out of someone, shatter; *Brit. informal* knacker; *N. Amer. informal* poop, tucker out. **2 use up**, get through, consume, finish, deplete, spend, empty, drain; *informal* blow.
– OPPOSITES invigorate, replenish.

exhausting *adjective* **tiring**, wearying, taxing, wearing, draining, arduous, strenuous, onerous, demanding, gruelling; *informal* killing; *Brit. informal* knackering.

exhaustion *noun* **tiredness**, fatigue, weariness, debility, enervation.

exhibit *verb* **1 put on display**, show, display, unveil, present. **2 show**, reveal, display, manifest, indicate, demonstrate, express, evince, evidence.
● *noun* **item**, piece, artefact, display, collection.

exhibition *noun* **1 exposition**, display, show, showing, presentation. **2 display**, show, demonstration, manifestation, expression.

exhilarating *adjective* **thrilling**, exciting, invigorating, stimulating, intoxicating, electrifying.

exhort *verb* **urge**, encourage, call on, enjoin, charge, press, bid, appeal to, entreat, implore; *literary* beseech.

exile *noun* **1 banishment**, expulsion, deportation, eviction, isolation. **2 expatriate**, émigré, deportee, displaced person, refugee.

exist *verb* **1 live**, be alive, be, be present. **2 prevail**, occur, be found, be in existence, be the case; *formal* obtain. **3 survive**, subsist, live, support yourself, manage, make do, get by, scrape by, make ends meet, eke out a living.

existence *noun* **1 survival**, continuation. **2 way of life**, life, lifestyle, situation.

□ **in existence** existing, alive, surviving, remaining, extant, existent, in circulation, current.

exit *noun* **1 way out**, door, escape route, egress. **2 turning**, turn-off, junction. **3 departure**, leaving, withdrawal, going, retreat, flight, exodus, escape.
- OPPOSITES entrance, arrival.
● *verb* **leave**, go out, depart, withdraw, retreat.
- OPPOSITES enter.

exonerate *verb* **absolve**, clear, acquit, find innocent, discharge; *formal* exculpate.
- OPPOSITES convict.

exorbitant *adjective* **extortionate**, excessive, prohibitive, outrageous, unreasonable, inflated; *Brit.* over the odds; *informal* steep, stiff, a rip-off; *Brit. informal* daylight robbery.
- OPPOSITES cheap.

exotic *adjective* **1** *exotic birds* **foreign**, non-native, alien, tropical. **2** *exotic places* **foreign**, faraway, far-off, far-flung, distant. **3 striking**, colourful, eye-catching, unusual, unconventional, extravagant, outlandish.

expand *verb* **1** *metals expand when heated* **enlarge**, increase in size, swell, lengthen, stretch, spread, thicken, fill out. **2** *the company is expanding* **grow**, enlarge, increase in size, extend, augment, broaden, widen, develop, diversify, build up, branch out, spread.
- OPPOSITES contract.
□ **expand on** elaborate on, enlarge on, go into detail about, flesh out, develop.

expanse *noun* **area**, stretch, sweep, tract, swathe, belt, region, sea, carpet, blanket, sheet.

expansion *noun* **1** *expansion and contraction* **enlargement**, swelling, lengthening, elongation, stretching, thickening. **2** *the expansion of the company* **growth**, increase in size, enlargement, extension, development, diversification, spread.
- OPPOSITES contraction.

expect *verb* **1 suppose**, presume, imagine, assume, surmise; *informal* guess, reckon; *N. Amer. informal* figure. **2 anticipate**, envisage, await, look for, hope for, look forward to, contemplate, bargain for/on, predict, forecast. **3 require**, ask for, call for, want, insist on, demand.

expectation *noun* **1 supposition**, assumption, presumption, conjecture, calculation, prediction, hope. **2 anticipation**, expectancy, eagerness, excitement, suspense.

expedient *adjective* **convenient**, advantageous, useful, beneficial, helpful, practical, pragmatic, politic, prudent, judicious.
● *noun* **measure**, means, method, stratagem, scheme, plan, solution, move, tactic, manoeuvre, device, contrivance, ploy, ruse.

expedition *noun* **journey**, voyage, tour, safari, trek, mission, quest, hike, trip.

expel *verb* **throw out**, bar, ban, debar, drum out, banish, exile, deport, evict; *informal* chuck out.
- OPPOSITES admit.

expense *noun* **cost**, expenditure, spending, outlay, outgoings, payment, price, charge, fees, overheads, tariff, bill.
- OPPOSITES income, profit.

expensive *adjective* **costly**, dear, high-priced, overpriced, exorbitant, extortionate; *informal* steep, stiff, pricey.
- OPPOSITES cheap.

experience *noun* **1 skill**, practical knowledge, understanding, familiarity, involvement, participation, contact, acquaintance, exposure, background, track record, history; *informal* know-how. **2 incident**, occurrence, event, happening, episode, adventure.
● *verb* **undergo**, go through, encounter, face, meet, come across, come up against, come into contact with.

experienced *adjective* **knowledgeable**, skilful, skilled, expert, proficient, trained, competent, capable, seasoned, practised, mature, veteran.

experiment *noun* **test**, investigation, trial, examination, observation, research, assessment, evaluation,

appraisal, analysis, study.
● *verb* **carry out experiments**, test, trial, try out, assess, appraise, evaluate.

experimental *adjective* **1 exploratory**, investigational, trial, test, pilot, speculative, tentative, preliminary. **2 new**, innovative, creative, radical, avant-garde, alternative, unorthodox, unconventional, cutting-edge; *informal* edgy.

expert *noun* **specialist**, authority, professional, pundit, maestro, virtuoso, master, wizard, connoisseur, aficionado; *informal* ace, pro, hotshot; *Brit. informal* dab hand; *N. Amer. informal* maven.
- OPPOSITES amateur.
● *adjective* **skilful**, skilled, adept, accomplished, experienced, practised, knowledgeable, talented, masterly, virtuoso; *informal* ace, crack, mean, genius.
- OPPOSITES incompetent.

expertise *noun* **skill**, prowess, proficiency, competence, knowledge, ability, aptitude, capability; *informal* know-how.

expire *verb* **1 run out**, become invalid, become void, lapse, end, finish, stop, terminate. **2 die**, pass away, breathe your last; *informal* kick the bucket, croak; *Brit. informal* snuff it, peg out; *N. Amer. informal* buy the farm.

explain *verb* **1 describe**, make clear, spell out, put into words, define, elucidate, expound, clarify, throw light on. **2 account for**, give a reason for, excuse.

explanation *noun* **1 clarification**, description, statement, interpretation, definition, commentary. **2 account**, reason, justification, answer, excuse, defence, vindication.

explicit *adjective* **1 clear**, plain, straightforward, crystal clear, precise, exact, specific, unequivocal, unambiguous, detailed. **2 graphic**, candid, full-frontal, uncensored.
- OPPOSITES vague.

explode *verb* **1 blow up**, detonate, go off, burst, erupt. **2 lose your temper**, blow up; *informal* fly off the handle, hit the roof, blow your top; *Brit. informal* go spare; *N. Amer. informal* blow your lid/stack. **3 increase rapidly**, mushroom, snowball, escalate, burgeon, rocket. **4 disprove**, refute, rebut, repudiate, debunk, give the lie to; *informal* shoot full of holes, blow out of the water.

exploit *verb* **1 utilize**, make use of, turn/put to good use, make the most of, capitalize on, benefit from; *informal* cash in on. **2 take advantage of**, abuse, impose on, treat unfairly, misuse, ill-treat; *informal* walk (all) over.
● *noun* **feat**, deed, act, adventure, stunt, escapade, achievement.

exploration *noun* **investigation**, study, survey, research, inspection, examination, scrutiny, observation.

explore *verb* **1 travel through**, tour, survey, scout, reconnoitre. **2 investigate**, look into, consider, examine, research, survey, scrutinize, study, review; *informal* check out.

explosion *noun* **1 detonation**, eruption, bang, blast, boom. **2 outburst**, flare-up, outbreak, eruption, storm, rush, surge, fit, paroxysm. **3 sudden increase**, mushrooming, snowballing, escalation, multiplication, burgeoning, rocketing.

explosive *adjective* **1 volatile**, inflammable, flammable, combustible, incendiary. **2 fiery**, stormy, violent, volatile, passionate, tempestuous, turbulent, touchy, irascible. **3 tense**, highly charged, overwrought, dangerous, perilous, hazardous, sensitive, delicate, unstable, volatile.
● *noun* **bomb**, charge, incendiary (device).

expose *verb* **1** *at low tide the rocks are exposed* **reveal**, uncover, lay bare. **2** *he was exposed to radiation* **lay open**, subject, put at risk of, put in jeopardy of, leave unprotected from. **3** *they were exposed to new ideas* **introduce to**, bring into contact with, make aware of, familiarize with, acquaint with.

4 uncover, reveal, unveil, unmask, detect, find out, denounce, condemn; *informal* blow the whistle on.
- OPPOSITES cover, protect.

exposure *noun* **1 frostbite**, cold, hypothermia. **2 uncovering**, revelation, disclosure, unveiling, unmasking, discovery, detection. **3 publicity**, advertising, public attention, media interest; *informal* hype.

express[1] *verb* **communicate**, convey, indicate, show, demonstrate, reveal, put across/over, get across/over, articulate, put into words, voice, give voice to, state, air, give vent to.

express[2] *adjective* **rapid**, swift, fast, high-speed, non-stop, direct.

express[3] *adjective* **1 explicit**, clear, direct, plain, distinct, unambiguous, categorical. **2 sole**, specific, particular, special, specified.
- OPPOSITES vague.

expression *noun* **1 utterance**, uttering, voicing, declaration, articulation. **2 indication**, demonstration, show, exhibition, token, illustration. **3 look**, appearance, air, manner, countenance, mien. **4 idiom**, phrase, turn of phrase, term, proverb, saying, adage, maxim. **5 emotion**, feeling, spirit, passion, intensity, style.

expressive *adjective* **1 eloquent**, meaningful, demonstrative, suggestive. **2 emotional**, passionate, poignant, moving, stirring, emotionally charged, lyrical.
- OPPOSITES undemonstrative.

expulsion *noun* **1 removal**, debarment, dismissal, exclusion, ejection, banishment, eviction. **2 discharge**, ejection, excretion, voiding, evacuation, elimination, passing.
- OPPOSITES admission.

exquisite *adjective* **1 beautiful**, lovely, elegant, fine, delicate, fragile, dainty, subtle. **2** *exquisite taste* **discriminating**, discerning, sensitive, fastidious, refined.

extend *verb* **1 expand**, enlarge, increase, lengthen, widen, broaden. **2 continue**, carry on, stretch, reach. **3 widen**, expand, broaden, augment, supplement, increase, add to, enhance, develop. **4 prolong**, lengthen, increase, stretch out, protract, spin out, string out. **5 hold out**, reach out, hold forth, stretch out, outstretch, offer, give, proffer.
- OPPOSITES reduce, shorten.
□ **extend to** include, take in, incorporate, encompass.

extension *noun* **1 addition**, add-on, adjunct, annex, wing. **2 expansion**, increase, enlargement, widening, broadening, deepening, augmentation, enhancement, development, growth. **3 prolongation**, lengthening, increase.

extensive *adjective* **1 large**, sizeable, substantial, considerable, ample, great, vast. **2 comprehensive**, thorough, exhaustive, broad, wide, wide-ranging, catholic.

extent *noun* **1 area**, size, expanse, length, proportions, dimensions. **2 degree**, scale, level, magnitude, scope, size, reach, range.

exterior *adjective* **outer**, outside, outermost, outward, external.
- OPPOSITES interior.
● *noun* **outside**, external surface, outward appearance, facade.
- OPPOSITES interior.

external *adjective* **outer**, outside, outermost, outward, exterior.
- OPPOSITES internal.

extinct *adjective* **1 vanished**, lost, gone, died out, wiped out, destroyed. **2 inactive**.
- OPPOSITES living, dormant.

extinction *noun* **dying out**, disappearance, vanishing, extermination, destruction, elimination, eradication, annihilation.

extinguish *verb* **douse**, quench, put out, stamp out, smother, snuff out.
- OPPOSITES light.

extol *verb* **praise**, wax lyrical about, sing the praises of, acclaim, applaud, celebrate, eulogize, rave about, enthuse over; *formal* laud.

- OPPOSITES criticize.

extort *verb* **extract**, exact, wring, wrest, screw, squeeze.

extortionate *adjective* **exorbitant**, excessive, outrageous, unreasonable, inordinate, inflated; *Brit. informal* daylight robbery.

extra *adjective* **additional**, more, added, supplementary, further, auxiliary, ancillary, subsidiary, secondary.
● *adverb* **exceptionally**, particularly, specially, especially, extremely.
● *noun* **addition**, supplement, bonus, adjunct, addendum, add-on.

extract *verb* **1 take out**, draw out, pull out, remove, withdraw, release, extricate. **2 wrest**, exact, wring, screw, squeeze, obtain by force, extort. **3 squeeze out**, press out, obtain.
- OPPOSITES insert.
● *noun* **1 excerpt**, passage, citation, quotation. **2 distillation**, distillate, concentrate, essence, juice.

extraordinary *adjective* **1** *an extraordinary coincidence* **remarkable**, exceptional, amazing, astonishing, astounding, sensational, stunning, incredible, unbelievable, phenomenal; *informal* fantastic. **2** *extraordinary speed* **very great**, tremendous, enormous, immense, prodigious, stupendous, monumental.
- OPPOSITES unremarkable.

extravagant *adjective* **1 spendthrift**, profligate, wasteful, prodigal, lavish. **2 excessive**, immoderate, exaggerated, gushing, unrestrained, effusive, fulsome. **3 ornate**, elaborate, fancy, over-elaborate, ostentatious, exaggerated; *informal* flashy.
- OPPOSITES thrifty, moderate.

extreme *adjective* **1** *extreme danger* **utmost**, (very) great, greatest (possible), maximum, great, acute, enormous, severe, serious. **2** *extreme measures* **drastic**, serious, desperate, dire, radical, far-reaching, draconian; *Brit.* swingeing. **3 radical**, extremist, immoderate, fanatical, revolutionary, subversive, militant. **4 dangerous**, hazardous, risky, high-risk; *informal* white-knuckle. **5 furthest**, farthest, utmost, remotest, ultra-.
- OPPOSITES slight, moderate.
● *noun* **opposite**, antithesis, side of the coin, (opposite) pole, limit, extremity, contrast.

extremely *adverb* **very**, exceptionally, especially, extraordinarily, tremendously, immensely, hugely, supremely, highly, mightily; *informal* awfully, terribly, seriously; *Brit. informal* jolly; *N. Amer. informal* mighty.
- OPPOSITES slightly.

extremist *noun* **fanatic**, radical, zealot, fundamentalist, hardliner, militant, activist.
- OPPOSITES moderate.

extrovert *adjective* **outgoing**, extroverted, sociable, gregarious, lively, ebullient, exuberant, uninhibited, unreserved.
- OPPOSITES introverted.

exuberant *adjective* **ebullient**, buoyant, cheerful, high-spirited, cheery, lively, vivacious, enthusiastic, irrepressible, energetic, animated, full of life, sparkling; *informal* bubbly, bouncy, full of beans.

eye *verb* **look at**, observe, view, gaze at, stare at, regard, contemplate, survey, scrutinize, consider, glance at, watch; *informal* check out, size up; *N. Amer. informal* eyeball.

> WORD LINKS
> **ocular**, **ophthalmic**, **optic** relating to the eye
> **ophthalmology** branch of medicine dealing with the eye

eyewitness *noun* **observer**, onlooker, witness, bystander, passer-by.

Ff

fable *noun* **parable**, allegory, myth, legend, story, tale.

fabric *noun* **1 cloth**, material, textile, stuff. **2 structure**, construction, make-up, organization, framework, essence.

fabricate *verb* **falsify**, fake, counterfeit, invent, make up.

fabulous *adjective* **1 stupendous**, prodigious, phenomenal, exceptional, fantastic, breathtaking, staggering, unthinkable, unimaginable, incredible, undreamed of. **2** *(informal) a fabulous time*. see **excellent**.

facade *noun* **1 front**, frontage, face, elevation, exterior, outside. **2 show**, front, appearance, pretence, simulation, affectation, act, charade, mask, veneer.

face *noun* **1 countenance**, physiognomy, features, profile; *literary* visage, lineaments. **2 expression**, look, appearance, mien, air. **3** *he made a face* **grimace**, scowl, wince, frown, pout. **4 side**, aspect, surface, plane, facet, wall, elevation.
● *verb* **1 look out on**, front on to, look towards, look over/across, overlook, be opposite (to). **2 accept**, get used to, adjust to, learn to live with, cope with, deal with, come to terms with, become resigned to. **3 beset**, worry, trouble, confront, torment, plague, bedevil. **4 brave**, face up to, encounter, meet (head-on), confront. **5 cover**, clad, veneer, surface, dress, laminate, coat, line.

facelift *noun* **renovation**, redecoration, refurbishment, revamp, makeover.

facet *noun* **aspect**, feature, factor, side, dimension, strand, component, element.

facetious *adjective* **flippant**, flip, glib, frivolous, tongue-in-cheek, joking, jokey, jocular, playful.
– OPPOSITES serious.

facilitate *verb* **make easier**, ease, make possible, smooth the way for, enable, assist, help (along), aid, promote, hasten, speed up.
– OPPOSITES impede.

facility *noun* **1** *a wealth of local facilities* **amenity**, resource, service, benefit, convenience, equipment. **2** *a medical facility* **establishment**, centre, station, location, premises, site, post, base. **3 ease**, effortlessness, skill, adroitness, smoothness, fluency, slickness.

fact *noun* **1** *a fact we cannot ignore* **reality**, actuality, certainty, truth, verity, gospel. **2** *every fact was double-checked* **detail**, particular, finding, point, factor, feature, characteristic, aspect; (**facts**) information, data.
– OPPOSITES lie, fiction.

faction *noun* **1 clique**, coterie, caucus, bloc, camp, group, grouping, splinter group. **2 infighting**, dissent, dispute, discord, strife, conflict, friction, argument, disagreement, disunity, schism.

factor *noun* **element**, part, component, ingredient, strand, constituent, feature, facet, aspect, characteristic, consideration, influence, circumstance.

factory *noun* **works**, plant, yard, mill, facility, workshop, shop.

factual *adjective* **truthful**, true, accurate, authentic, historical, genuine, true-to-life, correct, exact.
– OPPOSITES fictitious.

faculty *noun* **1 power**, capability, capacity, facility; (**faculties**) senses, wits, reason, intelligence. **2 department**, school.

fad *noun* **craze**, vogue, trend, fashion, mode, mania, rage.

fade *verb* **1 grow pale**, become bleached, become washed out, lose colour, discolour, blanch. **2 (grow) dim**, grow faint, fail, dwindle, die away,

wane, disappear, vanish, decline, melt away. **3 decline**, die out, diminish, decay, crumble, collapse, fail.
- OPPOSITES brighten.

fail *verb* **1 be unsuccessful**, fall through, fall flat, collapse, founder, backfire, miscarry, come unstuck; *informal* flop, bomb, flatline. **2 be unsuccessful in**, not make the grade; *informal* flunk. **3 let down**, disappoint, desert, abandon, betray, be disloyal to. **4 break (down)**, stop working, cut out, crash, malfunction, go wrong; *informal* conk out; *Brit. informal* pack up. **5 deteriorate**, degenerate, decline, fade. **6 collapse**, crash, go under, go bankrupt, cease trading, be wound up; *informal* fold, go bust.
- OPPOSITES succeed, pass, improve.

failing *noun* **fault**, shortcoming, weakness, imperfection, deficiency, defect, flaw, frailty.
- OPPOSITES strength.

failure *noun* **1 lack of success**, defeat, collapse, foundering. **2 fiasco**, debacle, catastrophe, disaster; *informal* flop, washout, dead loss. **3 loser**, underachiever, ne'er-do-well, disappointment; *informal* no-hoper, dud. **4 negligence**, dereliction, omission, oversight. **5 breakdown**, malfunction, crash. **6 collapse**, crash, bankruptcy, insolvency, liquidation, closure.
- OPPOSITES success.

faint *adjective* **1 indistinct**, vague, unclear, indefinite, ill-defined, imperceptible, pale, light, faded. **2 quiet**, muted, muffled, stifled, feeble, weak, low, soft, gentle. **3 slight**, slender, slim, small, tiny, remote, vague. **4 dizzy**, giddy, light-headed, unsteady; *informal* woozy.
- OPPOSITES clear, loud, strong.
● *verb* **pass out**, lose consciousness, black out, keel over, swoon.
● *noun* **blackout**, fainting fit, loss of consciousness, coma, swoon.

faintly *adverb* **1 indistinctly**, softly, gently, weakly, in a whisper. **2 slightly**, vaguely, somewhat, quite, fairly, rather, a little, a bit, a touch, a shade.

fair[1] *adjective* **1 just**, equitable, honest, impartial, unbiased, unprejudiced, neutral, even-handed. **2 fine**, dry, bright, clear, sunny, cloudless. **3 blond(e)**, yellow, golden, flaxen, light. **4 pale**, light, pink, white, creamy. **5 reasonable**, passable, tolerable, satisfactory, acceptable, respectable, decent, all right, good enough, pretty good.
- OPPOSITES inclement, dark, poor.

fair[2] *noun* **1 fete**, gala, festival, carnival. **2 market**, bazaar, exchange, sale. **3 exhibition**, display, show, exposition.

fairly *adverb* **1 justly**, equitably, impartially, without bias, without prejudice, even-handedly, equally. **2 reasonably**, passably, tolerably, adequately, moderately, quite, relatively, comparatively; *informal* pretty. **3 positively**, really, simply, absolutely.

fairy *noun* **sprite**, pixie, elf, imp, brownie, puck, leprechaun.

faith *noun* **1 trust**, belief, confidence, conviction, reliance. **2 religion**, belief, creed, church, persuasion, ideology, doctrine.
- OPPOSITES mistrust.

faithful *adjective* **1 loyal**, constant, true, devoted, staunch, steadfast, dedicated, committed, trusty, dependable, reliable. **2 accurate**, precise, exact, true, strict, realistic, authentic.
- OPPOSITES disloyal, treacherous.

fake *noun* **1 forgery**, counterfeit, copy, sham, fraud, hoax, imitation; *informal* phoney, rip-off. **2 charlatan**, quack, sham, fraud, impostor; *informal* phoney.
● *adjective* **1 counterfeit**, forged, fraudulent, sham, pirated, false, bogus; *informal* phoney, dud. **2 imitation**, artificial, synthetic, simulated, reproduction, replica, ersatz, man-made, dummy, false, mock; *informal* pretend. **3 feigned**, faked, put-on, assumed, invented, affected.
- OPPOSITES genuine, real, authentic.
● *verb* **1 forge**, counterfeit, falsify, copy, pirate. **2 feign**, pretend, simulate, put on, affect.

fall *verb* **1 drop**, descend, plummet, plunge, sink, dive, tumble, cascade. **2 topple over**, tumble over, fall down/over, collapse. **3 subside**, recede, drop, retreat, fall away, go down, sink. **4 decrease**, decline, diminish, fall off, drop off, lessen, dwindle, plummet, plunge, slump, sink. **5 die**, perish, lose your life, be killed, be slain, be lost; *informal* bite the dust, buy it. **6 surrender**, yield, submit, give in, capitulate, succumb, be taken, be overwhelmed. **7 occur**, take place, happen, come about.
- OPPOSITES rise.
● *noun* **1 tumble**, trip, spill, topple. **2 decline**, fall-off, drop, decrease, cut, dip, reduction, slump; *informal* crash. **3 downfall**, collapse, failure, decline, destruction, overthrow, demise. **4 surrender**, capitulation, yielding, submission, defeat. **5 descent**, slope, slant.
- OPPOSITES rise.
□ **fall back** retreat, withdraw, back off, draw back, pull back, move away. **fall back on** resort to, turn to, look to, call on, have recourse to. **fall for** *(informal)* **1** fall in love with, take a fancy to, be smitten by, be attracted to. **2** be deceived by, be duped by, be fooled by, be taken in by; *informal* go for, buy, swallow. **fall out** quarrel, argue, fight, squabble, bicker; *Brit.* row. **fall through** fail, be unsuccessful, come to nothing, miscarry, go awry, collapse, founder, come to grief.

false *adjective* **1 incorrect**, untrue, wrong, inaccurate, untruthful, fictitious, fabricated, invented, made up, trumped up, counterfeit, forged, fraudulent. **2 disloyal**, faithless, unfaithful, untrue, inconstant, treacherous, double-crossing, deceitful, dishonest, duplicitous. **3 fake**, artificial, imitation, synthetic, simulated, reproduction, replica, ersatz, man-made, dummy, mock; *informal* pretend.
- OPPOSITES correct, faithful, genuine.

falsify *verb* **forge**, fake, counterfeit, fabricate, alter, change, doctor, tamper with, manipulate, misrepresent, misreport, distort.

falter *verb* **hesitate**, delay, drag your feet, stall, waver, vacillate, be indecisive, be irresolute; *Brit.* hum and haw; *informal* sit on the fence.

fame *noun* **renown**, celebrity, stardom, popularity, prominence, distinction, esteem, eminence, repute.
- OPPOSITES obscurity.

familiar *adjective* **1 well known**, recognized, accustomed, everyday, day-to-day, habitual, customary, routine. **2** *are you familiar with the subject?* **acquainted**, conversant, versed, knowledgeable, well informed, au fait; *informal* well up on. **3 overfamiliar**, presumptuous, disrespectful, forward, bold, impudent, impertinent.

familiarity *noun* **1** *a familiarity with politics* **acquaintance**, awareness, knowledge, experience, insight, understanding, comprehension. **2 overfamiliarity**, presumption, forwardness, boldness, cheek, impudence, impertinence, disrespect. **3 closeness**, intimacy, friendliness, friendship.

family *noun* **1 relatives**, relations, (next of) kin, clan, tribe; *informal* folks. **2 children**, little ones, youngsters; *informal* kids. **3 species**, order, class, genus, phylum.

famine *noun* **1 food shortage**, hunger, starvation, malnutrition. **2 shortage**, scarcity, lack, dearth, deficiency, insufficiency, shortfall.
- OPPOSITES plenty.

famished *adjective* **ravenous**, hungry, starving, starved, empty, unfed; *informal* peckish.
- OPPOSITES replete.

famous *adjective* **well known**, prominent, famed, popular, renowned, noted, eminent, distinguished, celebrated, illustrious, legendary.
- OPPOSITES unknown.

fan *noun* **enthusiast**, devotee, admirer, lover, aficionado, supporter, follower, disciple, adherent; *informal* buff.

fanatic *noun* **extremist**, militant, dogmatist, bigot, zealot, radical, diehard; *informal* maniac.

fanatical *adjective* **1 zealous**, extremist, extreme, militant, gung-ho, dogmatic, radical, diehard, intolerant, single-minded, blinkered, inflexible, uncompromising. **2 enthusiastic**, eager, keen, fervent, passionate, obsessive, obsessed, fixated, compulsive; *informal* wild, nuts, crazy; *Brit. informal* potty.

fancy *verb* **1** *(Brit. informal)* **wish for**, want, desire, long for, yearn for, crave, thirst for, hanker after, dream of, covet. **2** *(Brit. informal)* **be attracted to**, find attractive, be infatuated with, be taken with; *informal* have a crush on, carry a torch for. **3 imagine**, believe, think, be under the impression; *informal* reckon.
● *adjective* **elaborate**, ornate, ornamental, decorative, embellished, intricate, ostentatious, showy, flamboyant, lavish, expensive; *informal* flashy, snazzy, posh, classy; *Brit. informal* swish.
– OPPOSITES plain.
● *noun* **1 whim**, foible, urge, whimsy, fascination, fad, craze, enthusiasm, passion, caprice. **2 fantasy**, dreaming, imagination, creativity.

fantastic *adjective* **1 fanciful**, extravagant, extraordinary, irrational, wild, absurd, far-fetched, unthinkable, implausible, improbable, unlikely; *informal* crazy. **2 strange**, weird, bizarre, outlandish, grotesque, surreal, exotic. **3** *(informal)* **marvellous**, wonderful, sensational, outstanding, superb, excellent; *informal* terrific, fabulous; *Brit. informal* brilliant; *Austral./NZ informal* bonzer.
– OPPOSITES ordinary.

fantasy *noun* **1 imagination**, fancy, invention, make-believe, creativity, vision, daydreaming, reverie. **2 dream**, daydream, pipe dream, fanciful notion, wish, fond hope, delusion; *informal* pie in the sky.
– OPPOSITES realism.

far *adverb* **1 a long way**, a great distance, a good way, afar. **2 much**, considerably, markedly, greatly, significantly, substantially, appreciably, by a long way, by a mile, easily.
● *adjective* **1 distant**, faraway, far-off, remote, out of the way, far-flung, outlying. **2 further**, opposite.
– OPPOSITES near.

farce *noun* **mockery**, travesty, parody, sham, pretence, charade, joke; *informal* shambles.
– OPPOSITES tragedy.

fare *noun* **1 price**, cost, charge, fee, toll, tariff. **2 food**, meals, cooking, cuisine.
● *verb* **get on**, get along, cope, manage, do, survive; *informal* make out.

farewell *exclam.* **goodbye**, so long, adieu, au revoir, ciao; *informal* bye, cheerio, see you (later); *Brit. informal* ta-ta, cheers.
● *noun* **goodbye**, adieu, leave-taking, parting, departure, send-off.

farm *noun* **smallholding**, farmstead, plantation, estate, farmland; *Brit.* grange, croft; *Scottish* steading; *N. Amer.* ranch; *Austral./NZ* station.
● *verb* **breed**, rear, keep, raise, tend.
□ **farm out** contract out, outsource, subcontract, delegate.

farming *noun* **agriculture**, cultivation, husbandry; *Brit.* crofting.

fascinating *adjective* **interesting**, captivating, engrossing, absorbing, enchanting, enthralling, spellbinding, riveting, engaging, compelling, compulsive, gripping, charming, attractive, intriguing, diverting, entertaining.
– OPPOSITES boring.

fascination *noun* **interest**, preoccupation, passion, obsession, compulsion, allure, lure, charm, attraction, appeal, pull, draw.

fashion *noun* **1 vogue**, trend, craze, rage, mania, fad, style, look, convention, mode; *informal* thing. **2 clothes**, clothing design, couture; *informal* the rag trade. **3 manner**, way, method, style, approach, mode.
● *verb* **construct**, build, make,

manufacture, cast, shape, form, mould, sculpt, forge, hew, carve.

fashionable *adjective* **in vogue**, in fashion, popular, up to date, up to the minute, modern, all the rage, trendsetting, stylish, chic, modish; *informal* trendy, classy, cool; *N. Amer. informal* tony.

fast[1] *adjective* **1 speedy**, quick, swift, rapid, high-speed, accelerated, express, blistering, breakneck, hasty, hurried; *informal* nippy, scorching, supersonic; *Brit. informal* cracking. **2 secure**, fastened, tight, firm, closed, shut, immovable. **3 loyal**, devoted, faithful, firm, steadfast, staunch, true, boon, bosom, inseparable.
- OPPOSITES slow, loose.
● *adverb* **1 quickly**, rapidly, swiftly, speedily, briskly, at full tilt, hastily, hurriedly, in a hurry; *informal* double quick, nippily; *N. Amer. informal* lickety-split. **2 securely**, firmly, tight. **3** *he's fast asleep* **deeply**, sound, completely.

fast[2] *verb* **eat nothing**, go without food, go hungry, starve yourself, go on hunger strike.

fasten *verb* **1 bolt**, lock, secure, make fast, chain, seal. **2 attach**, fix, affix, clip, pin, tack, stick, join. **3 tie (up)**, tether, hitch, truss, fetter, lash, anchor, strap, rope.
- OPPOSITES unlock, untie.

fat *adjective* **1 obese**, overweight, plump, stout, chubby, portly, flabby, paunchy, pot-bellied, corpulent; *informal* tubby; *Brit. informal* podgy. **2 fatty**, greasy, oily. **3 thick**, big, chunky, substantial, sizeable.
- OPPOSITES thin, slim, lean.
● *noun* **1 blubber**, fatty tissue, adipose tissue, cellulite. **2 oil**, grease, lard, suet, butter, margarine.

fatal *adjective* **1 deadly**, lethal, mortal, death-dealing, terminal, incurable, untreatable, inoperable. **2 disastrous**, devastating, ruinous, catastrophic, calamitous, dire.
- OPPOSITES harmless, beneficial.

fate *noun* **1 destiny**, providence, the stars, chance, luck, serendipity, fortune, karma, kismet. **2 future**, destiny, outcome, end, lot. **3 death**, demise, end, sentence, nemesis.
● *verb* **predestine**, preordain, destine, mean, doom.

father *noun* **1** *informal* **dad**, daddy, pop, pa, old man; *informal, dated* pater. **2 originator**, initiator, founder, inventor, creator, author, architect.
● *verb* **sire**, spawn, breed, give life to.

WORD LINKS
paternal relating to a father
patricide killing of your father

fatigue *noun* **tiredness**, weariness, exhaustion.
- OPPOSITES energy.
● *verb* **tire out**, exhaust, wear out, drain, weary, overtire; *informal* knock out, take it out of; *Brit. informal* knacker.

fatty *adjective* **greasy**, fat, oily, creamy, rich.

fault *noun* **1** *he has his faults* **defect**, failing, imperfection, blemish, flaw, shortcoming, weakness, weak point, vice. **2** *engineers have located the fault* **defect**, flaw, imperfection, bug, error, mistake, inaccuracy, oversight; *informal* glitch. **3 responsibility**, liability, culpability, guilt.
- OPPOSITES strength.
● *verb* **find fault with**, criticize, attack, condemn; *informal* knock; *Brit. informal* slag off.
□ **at fault** to blame, blameworthy, culpable, responsible, guilty, in the wrong.

faultless *adjective* **perfect**, flawless, without fault, error-free, impeccable, accurate, precise, exact, correct, exemplary.
- OPPOSITES flawed.

faulty *adjective* **1 malfunctioning**, broken, damaged, defective, not working, out of order; *informal* on the blink, acting up; *Brit. informal* playing up. **2 flawed**, unsound, defective, inaccurate, incorrect, erroneous, wrong.
- OPPOSITES working, sound.

favour *noun* **1 good turn**, service, good deed, act of kindness, courtesy. **2 approval**, approbation, goodwill, kindness, benevolence.
- OPPOSITES disservice, disapproval.
● *verb* **1 advocate**, recommend, approve of, be in favour of, support, back, champion, campaign for, press for, lobby for, promote; *informal* push for. **2 prefer**, go for, choose, opt for, select, pick, plump for, like better, be biased towards. **3 benefit**, be to the advantage of, help, assist, aid, advance, be of service to.
- OPPOSITES oppose.
□ **in favour of** on the side of, pro, for, giving support to, approving of, sympathetic to.

favourable *adjective* **1 approving**, positive, complimentary, full of praise, flattering, glowing, enthusiastic, kind, good; *informal* rave. **2 advantageous**, beneficial, in your favour, good, right, suitable, appropriate, auspicious, promising, encouraging. **3 positive**, affirmative, assenting, approving, encouraging, reassuring.
- OPPOSITES critical, unfavourable.

favourite *adjective* **favoured**, preferred, chosen, choice, best-loved, dearest, pet.
● *noun* **first choice**, pick, preference, pet, darling, the apple of your eye; *informal* golden boy, teacher's pet; *Brit. informal* blue-eyed boy/girl; *N. Amer. informal* fair-haired boy/girl.

fear *noun* **1 terror**, fright, fearfulness, horror, alarm, panic, trepidation, dread, anxiety, angst, apprehension, nervousness. **2 phobia**, aversion, antipathy, dread, nightmare, horror, terror; *informal* hang-up.
● *verb* **1 be afraid of**, be fearful of, be scared of, be apprehensive of, dread, live in fear of, be terrified of. **2 suspect**, be afraid, have a sneaking suspicion, be inclined to think, have a hunch.

fearful *adjective* **1 afraid**, scared, frightened, scared stiff, scared to death, terrified, petrified, nervous, apprehensive, uneasy, anxious, timid; *informal* jittery. **2 terrible**, dreadful, awful, appalling, frightful, ghastly, horrific, horrible, shocking, gruesome.
- OPPOSITES unafraid.

fearless *adjective* **brave**, courageous, bold, audacious, intrepid, valiant, plucky, heroic, daring, unafraid; *informal* gutsy.
- OPPOSITES timid, cowardly.

feasible *adjective* **practicable**, practical, workable, achievable, attainable, realizable, viable, realistic, possible; *informal* doable.
- OPPOSITES impracticable.

feast *noun* **banquet**, dinner, treat; *informal* spread; *Brit. informal* beanfeast, slap-up meal.
● *verb* **gorge**, dine, binge; (**feast on**) devour, consume, partake of, eat your fill of; *informal* stuff your face with, pig out on.

feat *noun* **achievement**, accomplishment, coup, triumph, undertaking, enterprise, venture, exploit, operation, exercise, endeavour, effort.

feather *noun* **plume**, quill; (**feathers**) plumage, down.

feature *noun* **1 characteristic**, attribute, quality, property, trait, hallmark, aspect, facet, factor, ingredient, component, element. **2** *her delicate features* **face**, countenance, physiognomy; *informal* mug; *Brit. informal* mush, phizog; *literary* lineaments, visage. **3 centrepiece**, special attraction, highlight, focal point, focus, conversation piece. **4 article**, piece, item, report, story, column.
● *verb* **1 present**, promote, make a feature of, spotlight, highlight, showcase, foreground. **2 star**, appear, participate.

federation *noun* **confederation**, confederacy, association, league, alliance, coalition, union, syndicate, guild, consortium.

fee *noun* **payment**, wage, salary, price, charge, bill, tariff, rate; (**fees**) remuneration, dues, earnings, pay; *formal* emolument.

feeble *adjective* **1 weak**, weakened, debilitated, enfeebled, frail, decrepit, infirm, delicate, sickly, ailing, unwell, poorly. **2 ineffective**, unconvincing, implausible, unsatisfactory, poor, weak, flimsy, lame. **3 cowardly**, faint-hearted, spineless, timid, timorous, fearful, unassertive, weak, ineffectual; *informal* sissy, chicken; *Brit. informal* wet. **4 faint**, dim, weak, pale, soft, subdued, muted.
– OPPOSITES strong.

feed *verb* **1 cater for**, provide for, cook for, dine, nourish. **2 eat**, graze, browse, crop. **3 supply**, provide, give, deliver.
● *noun* **fodder**, food, provender.

feel *verb* **1 touch**, stroke, caress, fondle, finger, paw, handle. **2** *she felt a breeze on her back* **perceive**, sense, detect, discern, notice, be aware of, be conscious of. **3** *he will not feel any pain* **experience**, undergo, go through, bear, endure, suffer. **4 grope**, fumble, scrabble. **5 believe**, think, consider it right, be of the opinion, hold, maintain, judge; *informal* reckon, figure.
● *noun* **1 texture**, finish, touch, consistency. **2 atmosphere**, ambience, aura, mood, feeling, air, impression, spirit; *informal* vibes. **3 aptitude**, knack, flair, bent, talent, gift, ability.

feeling *noun* **1 sensation**, sense, perception, awareness, consciousness. **2 (sneaking) suspicion**, notion, inkling, hunch, impression, intuition, instinct, funny feeling, fancy, idea. **3 love**, affection, fondness, tenderness, warmth, emotion, passion, desire. **4 mood**, (tide of) opinion, attitude, sentiment, emotion, belief, views, consensus. **5 compassion**, sympathy, empathy, fellow feeling, concern, pity, sorrow, commiseration. **6** *he hurt her feelings* **sensibilities**, sensitivities, self-esteem, pride. **7 atmosphere**, ambience, aura, air, mood, impression, spirit; *informal* vibes. **8 aptitude**, knack, flair, bent, talent, feel, gift, ability.

felicitous *adjective* **apt**, well chosen, fitting, suitable, appropriate, apposite, pertinent, germane, relevant.
– OPPOSITES inappropriate.

fell *verb* **1 cut down**, chop down, hack down, saw down, clear. **2 knock down**, knock to the ground, floor, rugby-tackle, strike down, knock out; *informal* deck, flatten, lay out.

fellow *noun* **1** *(informal)* **man**, boy, person, individual, character; *informal* guy, lad; *Brit. informal* chap, bloke; *N. Amer. informal* dude. **2 companion**, friend, comrade, partner, associate, co-worker, colleague; *informal* pal, buddy; *Brit. informal* mate.

fellowship *noun* **1 companionship**, comradeship, camaraderie, friendship, sociability, solidarity. **2 association**, organization, society, club, league, union, guild, alliance, fraternity, brotherhood.

feminine *adjective* **womanly**, ladylike, soft, gentle, tender, delicate, pretty.
– OPPOSITES masculine.

fence *noun* **barrier**, paling, railing, enclosure, barricade, stockade.
● *verb* **1 enclose**, surround, encircle. **2 confine**, pen in, coop up, shut in/up, kettle; *N. Amer.* corral.

fend *verb*
□ **fend off** ward off, head off, stave off, hold off, repel, repulse, resist, fight off. **fend for yourself** take care of yourself, look after yourself, shift for yourself, cope alone, stand on your own two feet, get by.

ferocious *adjective* **1** *ferocious animals* **fierce**, savage, wild, predatory, ravening, aggressive, dangerous. **2** *a ferocious attack* **brutal**, vicious, violent, bloody, barbaric, savage, frenzied.
– OPPOSITES gentle, mild.

ferry *verb* **transport**, convey, carry, run, ship, shuttle.

fertile *adjective* **1 productive**, fruitful, fecund, rich, lush. **2 creative**, inventive, innovative, visionary, original, ingenious, prolific.
– OPPOSITES barren.

fertilizer *noun* **plant food**, dressing, manure, muck, guano, compost.

fervent *adjective* **impassioned**, passionate, intense, vehement, ardent, sincere, heartfelt, enthusiastic, zealous, fanatical, wholehearted, avid, eager, keen, committed, dedicated, devout.
- OPPOSITES apathetic.

fervour *noun* **passion**, ardour, intensity, zeal, vehemence, emotion, warmth, avidity, eagerness, keenness, enthusiasm, excitement, animation, vigour, energy, fire, spirit.
- OPPOSITES apathy.

festival *noun* **celebration**, festivity, fete, fair, gala, carnival, fiesta, jamboree, feast day, holiday, holy day.

festive *adjective* **jolly**, merry, joyous, joyful, happy, jovial, light-hearted, cheerful, jubilant, celebratory.

festoon *verb* **decorate**, adorn, ornament, trim, deck (out), hang, loop, drape, swathe, garland, wreathe, bedeck; *informal* do up/out, get up.

fetch *verb* **1 go and get**, go for, call for, summon, pick up, collect, bring, carry, convey, transport. **2 sell for**, bring in, raise, realize, yield, make, command; *informal* go for.

fetching *adjective* **attractive**, appealing, sweet, pretty, lovely, delightful, charming, captivating, enchanting; *Scottish & N. English* bonny; *Brit. informal* fit.

feud *noun* **vendetta**, conflict, quarrel, row, rivalry, hostility, strife.
● *verb* **quarrel**, fight, clash, argue, squabble, dispute.

fever *noun* **1 feverishness**, high temperature; *Medicine* pyrexia; *informal* temperature. **2 excitement**, mania, frenzy, agitation, passion.

WORD LINKS
febrile having a fever

feverish *adjective* **1 febrile**, fevered, hot, burning. **2 frenzied**, frenetic, hectic, agitated, excited, restless, nervous, worked up, overwrought, frantic, furious, hysterical, wild, uncontrolled, unrestrained.

few *determiner* **not many**, hardly any, scarcely any, a small number of, a handful of, a couple of, one or two.
- OPPOSITES many.
● *adjective* **scarce**, scant, meagre, sparse, in short supply, thin on the ground, few and far between.
- OPPOSITES plentiful.

fiasco *noun* **failure**, disaster, catastrophe, debacle, farce, mess; *informal* flop, washout, fail, shambles; *Brit. informal* cock-up.
- OPPOSITES success.

fibre *noun* **thread**, strand, filament, wisp, yarn.

fickle *adjective* **capricious**, flighty, giddy, changeable, volatile, mercurial, erratic, unpredictable, unreliable, unsteady.
- OPPOSITES constant.

fiction *noun* **1 novels**, stories, literature, creative writing. **2 fabrication**, invention, lie, fib, tall story, untruth, falsehood, fantasy, nonsense.
- OPPOSITES fact.

fictitious *adjective* **false**, fake, fabricated, bogus, spurious, assumed, affected, adopted, invented, made up; *informal* pretend, phoney.
- OPPOSITES genuine.

fiddle *noun* **fraud**, swindle, confidence trick; *informal* racket, scam.
● *verb* **1 fidget**, play, toy, finger, handle. **2 adjust**, tinker, play about/around, fool about/around, meddle, interfere, tamper; *informal* tweak, mess about/around; *Brit. informal* muck about/around. **3 falsify**, manipulate, massage, rig, distort, misrepresent, doctor, tamper with, interfere with; *informal* fix, cook (the books).

fidelity *noun* **1 faithfulness**, loyalty, constancy, allegiance, commitment, devotion. **2 accuracy**, exactness, precision, correctness, strictness, closeness, authenticity.
- OPPOSITES disloyalty.

fidget *verb* **1 wriggle**, squirm, twitch, jiggle, shuffle, be agitated; *informal* be jittery. **2 play**, fuss, toy, twiddle, fool about/around; *informal* fiddle, mess about/around.

fidgety *adjective* **restless**, restive, on edge, uneasy, nervous, nervy, keyed up, anxious, agitated; *informal* jittery, twitchy.

field *noun* **1 meadow**, pasture, paddock, grassland; *literary* lea, mead, greensward. **2 pitch**, ground; *Brit. informal* park. **3 area**, sphere, discipline, province, department, domain, territory, branch, subject. **4 scope**, range, sweep, reach, extent. **5 competitors**, entrants, competition, applicants, candidates, runners.
● *verb* **1 catch**, stop, retrieve, return, throw back. **2 deal with**, handle, cope with, answer, reply to, respond to.

fiendish *adjective* **1 wicked**, cruel, vicious, evil, malevolent, villainous, brutal, savage, barbaric, barbarous, inhuman, murderous, ruthless, merciless. **2 cunning**, clever, ingenious, crafty, canny, wily, devious. **3 difficult**, complex, challenging, complicated, intricate.

fierce *adjective* **1 ferocious**, savage, vicious, aggressive. **2 aggressive**, cutthroat, keen, intense, strong, relentless, dog-eat-dog. **3 intense**, powerful, vehement, passionate, impassioned, fervent, ardent. **4 powerful**, strong, violent, forceful, stormy, howling, raging, tempestuous.
- OPPOSITES gentle, mild.

fiery *adjective* **1 burning**, blazing, on fire, flaming, ablaze. **2 bright**, brilliant, vivid, intense, rich. **3 passionate**, impassioned, excitable, spirited, quick-tempered, volatile, explosive, impetuous.

fight *verb* **1 brawl**, exchange blows, scuffle, grapple, wrestle, tussle, spar; *informal* scrap; *Brit. informal* have a punch-up; *N. Amer. informal* rough-house. **2 do battle**, serve your country, go to war, take up arms, engage, meet, clash, skirmish. **3 wage**, engage in, conduct, prosecute, undertake. **4 quarrel**, argue, bicker, squabble, fall out, feud, wrangle; *Brit.* row; *informal* scrap. **5 campaign**, strive, battle, struggle, crusade, agitate, lobby, push, press. **6 oppose**, contest, confront, challenge, appeal against, take a stand against, dispute, resist. **7 repress**, restrain, suppress, stifle, smother, hold back, fight back, keep in check, curb, choke back; *informal* keep the lid on, cork up.
● *noun* **1 brawl**, scuffle, disturbance, fisticuffs, fracas, melee, skirmish, clash, tussle; *informal* scrap, dust-up; *Brit. informal* punch-up; *N. Amer. informal* rough house; *dated* affray. **2 boxing match**, bout, match, contest. **3 battle**, engagement, conflict, struggle, war, campaign, crusade, action, hostilities. **4 argument**, quarrel, squabble, wrangle, disagreement, falling-out, dispute, feud; *Brit.* row; *informal* tiff, spat, scrap; *Brit. informal* barney, ding-dong. **5 struggle**, battle, campaign, push, effort. **6** *she had no fight left in her* **will**, resistance, spirit, pluck, grit, strength, backbone, determination, resolution, resolve.

fighter *noun* **1 soldier**, fighting man/woman, warrior, combatant, serviceman, servicewoman; (**fighters**) troops, personnel, militia. **2 boxer**, pugilist, prizefighter, wrestler.

figurative *adjective* **metaphorical**, non-literal, symbolic, allegorical, representative, emblematic.
- OPPOSITES literal.

figure *noun* **1 statistic**, number, quantity, amount, level, total, sum; (**figures**) data, statistics. **2 digit**, numeral, character, symbol. **3 price**, cost, amount, value, valuation. **4 shape**, outline, form, silhouette, proportions, physique, build, frame. **5 person**, personage, individual, character, personality, celebrity. **6 shape**, pattern, design, motif. **7 diagram**, illustration, drawing, picture, plate.
● *verb he figures in many myths* **feature**, appear, be featured, be mentioned, be referred to.

□ **figure out** *(informal)* work out, fathom, puzzle out, decipher, make sense of, think through, get to the bottom of, understand, comprehend, see, grasp, get the hang of; *informal* twig, crack; *Brit. informal* suss out.

file[1] *noun* **1 folder**, portfolio, binder. **2 dossier**, document, record, report, data, information, documentation, archives.
● *verb* **1 categorize**, classify, organize, put in order, order, arrange, catalogue, store, archive. **2 bring**, press, lodge.

file[2] *noun* **line**, column, row, queue, string, chain, procession; *Brit. informal* crocodile.
● *verb* **walk in a line**, queue, march, parade, troop.

file[3] *verb* **smooth**, buff, rub down, polish, shape, scrape, abrade, rasp, manicure.

fill *verb* **1 fill up**, top up, charge. **2 crowd into**, throng, pack (into), occupy, squeeze into, cram (into). **3 stock**, pack, load, supply, replenish. **4 block up**, stop (up), plug, seal, caulk. **5 pervade**, permeate, suffuse, penetrate, infuse. **6 occupy**, hold, take up.
– OPPOSITES empty, clear, leave.

filling *noun* **stuffing**, padding, wadding, filler, contents.
● *adjective* **substantial**, hearty, ample, satisfying, square, heavy, stodgy.

film *noun* **1 layer**, coat, coating, covering, cover, skin, patina, tissue. **2 movie**, picture, feature film, motion picture, video, DVD. **3 cinema**, movies, the pictures, films, the silver screen, the big screen.
● *verb* **1 photograph**, record on film, shoot, capture on film, video. **2 cloud**, mist, haze, blur.

filter *noun* **strainer**, sifter, sieve, gauze, mesh, net.
● *verb* **1 sieve**, strain, sift, clarify, purify, refine, treat. **2 seep**, percolate, leak, trickle, ooze, leach.

filth *noun* **dirt**, muck, grime, mud, sludge, slime, excrement, excreta, ordure, sewage, pollution.

filthy *adjective* **1 dirty**, mucky, grimy, foul, squalid, sordid, soiled, stained, polluted, contaminated, unwashed. **2 obscene**, rude, vulgar, dirty, smutty, improper, coarse, bawdy, lewd; *informal* blue. **3 bad**, foul, irritable, grumpy, grouchy, cross; *informal* snappy; *Brit. informal* shirty, stroppy; *N. Amer. informal* cranky, ornery.
– OPPOSITES clean, pleasant.

final *adjective* **1 last**, closing, concluding, finishing, end, ultimate, eventual. **2 irrevocable**, unalterable, absolute, conclusive, irrefutable, incontrovertible, indisputable, unchallengeable, binding.
– OPPOSITES first, provisional.

finale *noun* **climax**, culmination, end, ending, finish, close, conclusion, termination, denouement.
– OPPOSITES opening.

finally *adverb* **1 eventually**, ultimately, in the end, after a long time, at (long) last, in the long run, in the fullness of time. **2 lastly**, last, in conclusion. **3 conclusively**, irrevocably, decisively, definitively, for ever, for good, once and for all.

finance *noun* **1 financial affairs**, money matters, economics, commerce, business, investment. **2 funds**, money, capital, cash, resources, assets, reserves, funding.
● *verb* **fund**, pay for, back, capitalize, endow, subsidize, invest in, sponsor; *N. Amer. informal* bankroll.

financial *adjective* **monetary**, money, economic, pecuniary, fiscal, banking, commercial, business, investment.

find *verb* **1 locate**, spot, pinpoint, unearth, obtain, search out, track down, root out, come across/upon, run across/into, chance on, happen on, stumble on, encounter; *informal* bump into. **2 discover**, invent, come up with, hit on. **3 realize**, become aware, discover, observe, notice, note, learn. **4 consider**, think, feel to be, look on as, view as, see as, judge, deem, regard as. **5 judge**, deem, rule, declare, pronounce.

- OPPOSITES lose.
● *noun* **1 discovery**, acquisition. **2 bargain**, godsend, boon, catch, asset; *informal* good buy.
□ **find out** discover, become aware of, learn, detect, discern, observe, notice, note, get/come to know, realize, bring to light; *informal* figure out, cotton on, tumble; *Brit. informal* twig, suss.

fine[1] *adjective* **1** *fine wines* **good**, choice, select, excellent, first-class, first-rate, great, exceptional, outstanding, splendid, magnificent, exquisite, superb, wonderful, superlative, prime, quality, special, superior, of distinction, premium, classic, vintage; *informal* A1, top-notch. **2** *a fine fellow* **worthy**, admirable, praiseworthy, laudable, upright, upstanding, respectable. **3 all right**, acceptable, suitable, good (enough), passable, satisfactory, adequate, reasonable, tolerable; *informal* OK. **4 healthy**, well, good, all right, (fighting) fit, blooming, thriving, in good shape/condition; *informal* OK, in fine fettle, in the pink. **5 fair**, dry, bright, clear, sunny, cloudless, balmy. **6 keen**, quick, alert, sharp, razor-sharp, acute, bright, brilliant, astute, clever, intelligent. **7 elegant**, stylish, expensive, smart, chic, fashionable, fancy, sumptuous, lavish, opulent; *informal* flashy. **8 flyaway**, wispy, delicate, thin, light. **9 sheer**, light, lightweight, thin, flimsy, diaphanous, filmy, see-through. **10 subtle**, ultra-fine, nice, hair-splitting.

fine[2] *noun* **penalty**, forfeit, damages, fee, excess charge.

finger *noun* **digit**.
● *verb* **touch**, feel, handle, stroke, rub, caress, fondle, toy with, play (about/around) with, fiddle with.

finish *verb* **1 complete**, end, conclude, close, terminate, wind up, round off, achieve, accomplish, fulfil; *informal* wrap up, sew up. **2 consume**, eat, devour, drink, finish off, polish off, use (up), exhaust, empty, drain, get through; *informal* down. **3 end**, come to an end, stop, conclude, come to a close, cease.
- OPPOSITES start.
● *noun* **1 end**, ending, completion, conclusion, close, termination, finale, denouement. **2 surface**, texture, coating, covering, lacquer, glaze, veneer, gloss, patina, sheen, lustre.
- OPPOSITES start.
□ **finish off 1** kill, execute, terminate, exterminate, liquidate, get rid of; *informal* wipe out, bump off, dispose of; *N. Amer. informal* waste. **2** overwhelm, overcome, defeat, get the better of, bring down; *informal* drive to the wall.

finite *adjective* **limited**, restricted, determinate, fixed.
- OPPOSITES infinite.

fire *noun* **1 blaze**, conflagration, inferno, flames, burning, combustion. **2 dynamism**, energy, vigour, animation, vitality, exuberance, zest, elan, passion, zeal, spirit, verve, vivacity, enthusiasm; *informal* go, get-up-and-go, oomph. **3 gunfire**, firing, shooting, bombardment, shelling, volley, salvo, hail.
● *verb* **1 launch**, shoot, discharge, let fly with. **2 shoot**, discharge, let off, set off. **3** *(informal)* **dismiss**, discharge, give someone their notice, lay off, let go; *informal* sack. **4 stimulate**, stir up, excite, awaken, rouse, inflame, animate, inspire, motivate.
□ **catch fire** ignite, catch light, burst into flames, go up in flames. **set on fire** ignite, light, set fire to, set alight.

WORD LINKS
arson crime of setting fire to property
pyromania obsessive desire to set fire to things

firm[1] *adjective* **1 hard**, solid, unyielding, resistant, compacted, compressed, dense, stiff, rigid, set. **2 secure**, stable, steady, strong, fixed, fast, tight, immovable, rooted, stationary, motionless. **3 resolute**, determined, decided, resolved, steadfast, adamant, emphatic, insistent, single-minded, wholehearted, unfaltering, unwavering, unflinching, unswerving, unbending, committed. **4 close**, good, boon, intimate, inseparable, dear, special,

constant, devoted, loving, faithful, long-standing, steady, steadfast. **5 definite**, fixed, settled, decided, cut-and-dried, established, confirmed, agreed.
- OPPOSITES soft, unstable.

firm[2] *noun* **business**, company, concern, enterprise, organization, corporation, conglomerate, office, bureau, agency, consortium; *informal* outfit, operation.

first *adjective* **1 earliest**, initial, opening, introductory. **2 fundamental**, basic, rudimentary, primary, key, cardinal, central, chief, vital, essential. **3 foremost**, principal, highest, greatest, paramount, top, main, overriding, central, core; *informal* number-one. **4 top**, best, prime, premier, winning, champion.
- OPPOSITES last.
● *adverb* **at first**, to begin with, first of all, at the outset, initially.
● *noun* **novelty**, innovation, departure, break with tradition.

fish *verb* **1 go fishing**, angle, trawl. **2 search**, delve, look, hunt, grope, fumble, ferret, rummage.
□ **fish out** pull out, haul out, remove, extricate, extract, retrieve, rescue, save.

WORD LINKS
piscine relating to fish
ichthyology study of fish

fit[1] *adjective* **1 suitable**, appropriate, suited, apposite, fitting, good enough, apt. **2 competent**, able, capable, ready, prepared, equipped. **3 healthy**, well, in good health, in (good) shape, in trim, in good condition, fighting fit, athletic, muscular, strapping, strong, robust, hale and hearty.
- OPPOSITES unsuitable, incapable.
● *verb* **1 lay**, install, put in, position, place, fix, arrange. **2 equip**, provide, supply, fit out, furnish. **3 join**, connect, piece together, attach, unite, link. **4 be appropriate to**, suit, match, correspond to, tally with, go with, accord with. **5 qualify**, prepare, make ready, train.
□ **fit in** conform, be in harmony, blend in, be in line, be assimilated.

fit[2] *noun* **1 convulsion**, spasm, paroxysm, seizure, attack. **2 outbreak**, outburst, attack, bout, spell. **3 tantrum**, frenzy; *informal* paddy.

fitness *noun* **1 good health**, strength, robustness, vigour, athleticism, toughness, stamina. **2 suitability**, capability, competence, ability, aptitude, readiness, preparedness.

fitting *noun* **1 attachment**, part, piece, component, accessory, apparatus. **2 furnishings**, furniture, fixtures, fitments, equipment.
● *adjective* **apt**, appropriate, suitable, apposite, fit, proper, right, seemly, correct.
- OPPOSITES unsuitable.

fix *verb* **1 fasten**, attach, affix, secure, connect, couple, link, install, stick, glue, pin, nail, screw, bolt, clamp, clip. **2 lodge**, stick, embed. **3 focus**, direct, level, point, train. **4 repair**, mend, put right, get working, restore. **5 arrange**, organize, contrive, manage, engineer; *informal* swing, wangle. **6** *(informal)* **arrange**, put in order, adjust, style, groom, comb, brush; *informal* do. **7** *(informal)* **prepare**, cook, make, get; *informal* rustle up; *Brit. informal* knock up. **8 decide on**, select, choose, settle, set, arrange, establish, allot, designate, name, appoint, specify. **9** *(informal)* **rig**, tamper with, skew, influence; *informal* fiddle.
● *noun (informal)* **1 predicament**, plight, difficulty, awkward situation, corner, tight spot, mess; *informal* pickle, jam, hole, scrape, bind. **2 fraud**, swindle, trick, charade, sham; *informal* set-up, fiddle.

fixation *noun* **obsession**, preoccupation, mania, addiction, compulsion; *informal* thing, bug, bee in your bonnet.

fixed *adjective* **predetermined**, set, established, arranged, specified, decided, agreed, determined, confirmed, prescribed, definite, defined, explicit, precise.

fizz *verb* **bubble**, sparkle, effervesce, froth.
● *noun* **1 bubbles**, sparkle, fizziness, effervescence, gassiness, froth. **2 crackle**, buzz, hiss, white noise.

fizzy *adjective* **sparkling**, effervescent, carbonated, gassy, bubbly, frothy.
– OPPOSITES still, flat.

flag[1] *noun* **banner**, standard, ensign, pennant, streamer, colours; *Brit.* pendant.
● *verb* **indicate**, identify, point out, mark, label, tag, highlight.
□ **flag down** hail, wave down, stop, halt.

flag[2] *verb* **1 tire**, grow tired, wilt, weaken, grow weak, droop. **2 fade**, decline, wane, ebb, diminish, decrease, lessen, dwindle.
– OPPOSITES revive.

flagrant *adjective* **blatant**, glaring, obvious, conspicuous, barefaced, shameless, brazen, undisguised.

flair *noun* **1 aptitude**, talent, gift, instinct, ability, facility, knack, skill. **2 style**, elegance, panache, dash, elan, poise, taste; *informal* class.

flake *noun* **sliver**, wafer, shaving, paring, chip, fragment, scrap, shred.
● *verb* **peel (off)**, chip, blister, come off.

flamboyant *adjective* **1 ostentatious**, exuberant, confident, lively, animated, vibrant, vivacious. **2 colourful**, bright, vibrant, vivid, dazzling, bold, showy, gaudy, garish, loud; *informal* jazzy, flashy.
– OPPOSITES restrained.

flame *noun* **1 fire**, blaze, conflagration, inferno. **2** *(informal)* **sweetheart**, boyfriend, girlfriend, lover, partner.
□ **in flames** on fire, burning, alight, flaming, blazing.

flank *noun* **1 side**, haunch, quarter, thigh. **2 side**, wing, sector, face, aspect.
● *verb* **edge**, bound, line, border, fringe.

flap *verb* **1** *ducks flapped their wings* **beat**, flutter, agitate, vibrate, wag, thrash, flail. **2** *the flag flapped in the breeze* **flutter**, wave, fly, blow, swing, ripple, stir.
● *noun* **1 beat**, stroke, flutter, movement. **2** *(informal)* **panic**, fluster; *informal* state, stew, tizzy; *N. Amer. informal* twit.

flare *noun* **1 blaze**, flame, flash, burst, flicker. **2 signal**, beacon, rocket, light, torch.
● *verb* **1 blaze**, flash, flare up, flame, burn, flicker. **2 spread**, splay, broaden, widen, dilate.

flash *verb* **1 shine**, flare, blaze, gleam, glint, sparkle, burn, blink, wink, flicker, shimmer, twinkle, glimmer, glisten. **2** *(informal)* **show off**, flaunt, flourish, display, parade. **3 zoom**, streak, tear, shoot, dash, dart, fly, whistle, hurtle, rush, bolt, race, speed, career; *informal* belt, zap; *Brit. informal* bomb; *N. Amer. informal* barrel.
● *noun* **flare**, blaze, burst, gleam, glint, sparkle, flicker, shimmer, twinkle, glimmer.

flashy *adjective* *(informal)* **ostentatious**, flamboyant, showy, conspicuous, extravagant, expensive, vulgar, tasteless, brash, garish, loud, gaudy; *informal* snazzy, fancy, swanky, flash, glitzy.
– OPPOSITES understated.

flat[1] *adjective* **1 level**, horizontal, smooth, even, plane. **2 calm**, still, glassy, smooth, placid, like a millpond. **3 stretched out**, prone, spreadeagled, prostrate, supine, recumbent. **4 monotonous**, toneless, lifeless, droning, boring, dull, tedious, uninteresting, unexciting. **5 inactive**, slow, sluggish, slack, quiet, depressed. **6** *(Brit.)* **run down**, dead, used up, expired. **7 deflated**, punctured, burst, blown. **8 fixed**, set, invariable, regular, constant. **9 outright**, direct, absolute, definite, positive, straight, plain, explicit, categorical.
– OPPOSITES sloping, rough, uneven.
● *adverb* **stretched out**, outstretched, spreadeagled, sprawling, prone, prostrate.

flat[2] *noun* **apartment**, suite, penthouse, rooms.

flatten *verb* **1 level**, even out, smooth out, make/become flat. **2 squash**, compress, press down, crush, compact, trample. **3 demolish**, raze (to the ground), tear down, knock down, destroy, wreck, devastate.
- OPPOSITES crumple.

flatter *verb* **1 compliment**, praise, express admiration for, fawn on, humour, wheedle, blarney; *informal* sweet-talk, soft-soap, butter up, play up to. **2 honour**, gratify, please, delight; *informal* tickle pink. **3 suit**, become, look good on, go well with; *informal* do something for.
- OPPOSITES insult, offend.

flattering *adjective* **1 complimentary**, praising, favourable, admiring, appreciative, fulsome, honeyed, obsequious, ingratiating, sycophantic. **2 pleasing**, gratifying, an honour. **3 becoming**, enhancing.
- OPPOSITES unflattering.

flattery *noun* **praise**, adulation, compliments, blandishments, honeyed words, fawning, blarney; *informal* sweet talk, soft soap, buttering up.

flaunt *verb* **show off**, display, make a great show of, put on show/display, parade, draw attention to, brag about, crow about, vaunt; *informal* flash.

flavour *noun* **1 taste**, savour, tang, smack. **2 flavouring**, seasoning, taste, tang, relish, bite, piquancy, spice. **3 character**, quality, feel, feeling, ambience, atmosphere, air, mood, tone, spirit. **4 impression**, suggestion, hint, taste.
● *verb* **season**, spice (up), add piquancy to, ginger up, enrich, infuse.

flaw *noun* **defect**, blemish, fault, imperfection, deficiency, weakness, weak spot/point, failing; *Computing* bug; *informal* glitch.
- OPPOSITES strength.

flawed *adjective* **1 faulty**, defective, unsound, imperfect, blemished, broken, cracked, scratched; *Brit. informal* duff. **2 unsound**, distorted, inaccurate, incorrect, erroneous, fallacious, wrong.
- OPPOSITES flawless.

flawless *adjective* **perfect**, unblemished, unmarked, unimpaired, whole, intact, sound, unbroken, undamaged, mint, pristine, impeccable, immaculate, accurate, correct, faultless, error-free, exemplary, model, ideal, copybook.
- OPPOSITES flawed.

flee *verb* **run away**, run off, run for it, make off, take off, take to your heels, make a break for it, bolt, beat a (hasty) retreat, make a quick exit, escape; *informal* beat it, clear off/out, skedaddle, scram; *Brit. informal* scarper.

fleet *noun* **navy**, naval force, (naval) task force, armada, flotilla, squadron, convoy.

fleeting *adjective* **brief**, short-lived, quick, momentary, cursory, transient, ephemeral, passing, transitory.
- OPPOSITES lasting.

flesh *noun* **1 tissue**, skin, muscle, fat, meat, body. **2 pulp**, marrow, meat. **3** *the pleasures of the flesh* **the body**, human nature, physicality, sensuality, sexuality.

flexibility *noun* **1 pliability**, suppleness, elasticity, stretchiness, springiness, spring, resilience, bounce; *informal* give. **2 adaptability**, adjustability, versatility, open-endedness, freedom, latitude. **3 willingness to compromise**, give and take, amenability, cooperation, tolerance.
- OPPOSITES rigidity.

flexible *adjective* **1 bendy**, pliable, supple, pliant, plastic, elastic, stretchy, springy, resilient, bouncy. **2 adaptable**, adjustable, variable, versatile, open-ended, open. **3 accommodating**, amenable, willing to compromise, cooperative, tolerant.
- OPPOSITES rigid, inflexible.

flick *noun* **jerk**, snap, flip, whisk.
● *verb* **1 click**, snap, flip, jerk, throw. **2 swish**, twitch, wave, wag, waggle, shake.
□ **flick through** thumb through, leaf

f

through, flip through, skim, scan, look through, browse through, dip into, glance at/through.

flicker *verb* **1 glimmer**, flare, dance, gutter, twinkle, sparkle, wink, flash. **2 flutter**, quiver, tremble, shiver, shudder, jerk, twitch.

flight *noun* **1 aviation**, flying, air transport, aeronautics. **2 flock**, swarm, cloud, throng. **3 escape**, getaway, hasty departure, exit, exodus, breakout, bolt, disappearance; *Brit. informal* flit.

flimsy *adjective* **1 insubstantial**, fragile, frail, rickety, ramshackle, makeshift, jerry-built, shoddy. **2 thin**, light, fine, filmy, floaty, diaphanous, sheer, delicate, gossamer, gauzy. **3 weak**, feeble, poor, inadequate, insufficient, thin, unsubstantial, unconvincing, implausible.
- OPPOSITES sturdy.

flinch *verb* **1 wince**, start, shudder, quiver, jerk. **2** *he never flinched from his duty* **shrink from**, recoil from, shy away from, dodge, evade, avoid, duck, baulk at.

fling *verb* **throw**, hurl, toss, sling, launch, pitch, lob; *informal* chuck, heave.
● *noun* **1 good time**, party, spree, fun and games; *informal* binge, bash, night on the town. **2 affair**, love affair, relationship, romance, liaison, entanglement, involvement.

flip *verb* **1 overturn**, turn over, tip over, roll (over), upturn, capsize, upend, invert, knock over, keel over, topple over, turn turtle. **2 flick**, click, throw, push, pull.
□ **flip through** thumb through, leaf through, flick through, skim through, scan, look through, browse through, dip into, glance at/through, peruse, run your eye over.

flippant *adjective* **frivolous**, facetious, tongue-in-cheek, disrespectful, irreverent, cheeky; *informal* flip, saucy; *N. Amer. informal* sassy.
- OPPOSITES serious.

flirt *noun* **tease**, coquette, heartbreaker.
□ **flirt with 1** tease, lead on, toy with. **2** dabble in, toy with, trifle with, play with, tinker with, dip into, scratch the surface of.

float *verb* **1 stay afloat**, stay on the surface, be buoyant, be buoyed up. **2 hover**, levitate, be suspended, hang, defy gravity. **3 drift**, glide, sail, slip, slide, waft. **4 launch**, offer, sell, introduce.
- OPPOSITES sink.

floating *adjective* **1 uncommitted**, undecided, undeclared, wavering; *informal* sitting on the fence. **2 unsettled**, transient, temporary, migrant, wandering, nomadic, migratory, itinerant.

flock *noun* **1 herd**, drove. **2 flight**, swarm, cloud, gaggle, skein.
● *verb* **1** *people flocked around her* **gather**, collect, congregate, assemble, converge, mass, crowd, throng, cluster, swarm. **2** *tourists flock to the place* **stream**, go in large numbers, swarm, crowd, troop.

flog *verb* **whip**, thrash, lash, scourge, birch, cane, beat.

flood *noun* **1 inundation**, deluge, torrent, overflow, flash flood; *Brit.* spate. **2 gush**, outpouring, torrent, rush, stream, surge, cascade. **3 succession**, series, string, barrage, volley, battery, avalanche, torrent, stream, storm.
● *verb* **1** *the town was flooded* **inundate**, swamp, deluge, immerse, submerge, drown, engulf. **2** *the river could flood* **overflow**, burst its banks, brim over, run over. **3 glut**, swamp, saturate, oversupply. **4 pour**, stream, flow, surge, swarm, pile, crowd.

floor *noun* **1 ground**, flooring. **2 storey**, level, deck, tier, stage.
● *verb* **1 knock down**, knock over, fell, rugby-tackle; *informal* deck, lay out. **2** *(informal)* **baffle**, defeat, confound, perplex, puzzle, disconcert; *informal* throw, beat, stump.

flop *verb* **1 collapse**, slump, crumple, sink, drop. **2 hang (down)**, dangle, droop, sag, loll. **3** *(informal)*

be unsuccessful, fail, fall flat, founder; *informal* bomb, flatline; *N. Amer. informal* tank.
● *noun (informal)* **failure**, disaster, fiasco, debacle, catastrophe; *Brit.* damp squib; *informal* washout, fail, also-ran.
- OPPOSITES success.

floppy *adjective* **limp**, flaccid, slack, flabby, relaxed, drooping, droopy, loose, flowing.
- OPPOSITES erect, stiff.

flounder *verb* **1** *floundering in the water* **struggle**, thrash, flail, twist and turn, splash, stagger, stumble, reel, lurch, blunder. **2** *she floundered, not knowing what to say* **struggle**, be out of your depth, be confused; *informal* scratch your head, be flummoxed, be fazed, be floored.

flourish *verb* **1** *ferns flourish in the shade* **grow**, thrive, prosper, do well, burgeon, increase, multiply, proliferate, run riot. **2** *the arts flourished* **thrive**, prosper, bloom, be in good health, be vigorous, be in its heyday, make progress, advance, expand; *informal* go places. **3 brandish**, wave, shake, wield, swing, display, show off.
- OPPOSITES wither, decline.

flout *verb* **defy**, refuse to obey, disobey, break, violate, fail to comply with, fail to observe, contravene, infringe, breach, commit a breach of, transgress against, ignore, disregard; *informal* cock a snook at.
- OPPOSITES observe.

flow *verb* **1 pour**, run, course, circulate, stream, swirl, surge, sweep, gush, cascade, roll, rush, trickle, seep, ooze, dribble. **2 result**, proceed, arise, follow, ensue, stem, originate, emanate, spring.
● *noun* **movement**, motion, current, circulation, stream, swirl, surge, gush, rush, spate, tide, trickle, ooze.

flower *noun* & *verb* **bloom**, blossom.

WORD LINKS
floral relating to flowers
florist person who sells flowers

fluctuate *verb* **vary**, change, shift, alter, waver, swing, oscillate, alternate, rise and fall.

fluent *adjective* **articulate**, eloquent, silver-tongued, communicative, natural, effortless.
- OPPOSITES inarticulate.

fluid *noun* **liquid**, solution, liquor, gas, vapour.
● *adjective* **1 free-flowing**, runny, liquid, liquefied, melted, molten, gaseous. **2 smooth**, fluent, flowing, effortless, easy, continuous, graceful, elegant.
- OPPOSITES solid.

flurry *noun* **1 swirl**, whirl, eddy, shower, gust. **2 burst**, outbreak, spurt, fit, spell, bout, rash, eruption.

flush *verb* **1 blush**, redden, go pink, go red, go crimson, go scarlet, colour (up). **2 rinse**, wash, sluice, swill, cleanse, clean; *Brit. informal* sloosh. **3 chase**, force, drive, dislodge, expel.
● *noun* **blush**, colour, rosiness, pinkness, ruddiness, bloom.
- OPPOSITES pallor.

flutter *verb* **1** *butterflies fluttered around* **flit**, hover, dance. **2** *a robin fluttered its wings* **flap**, beat, quiver, agitate, vibrate, ruffle. **3** *she fluttered her eyelashes* **flicker**, bat. **4** *flags fluttered* **flap**, wave, ripple, undulate, quiver, fly.

fly *verb* **1 wing**, glide, soar, wheel, take wing, take to the air, hover, swoop. **2 pilot**, operate, control, manoeuvre, steer. **3** *the ship flew a French flag* **display**, show, exhibit, hoist, raise, wave. **4 dash**, race, rush, bolt, zoom, dart, speed, hurry, career, hurtle; *informal* tear.

foam *noun* **froth**, spume, surf, spray, fizz, effervescence, bubbles, head, lather, suds.
● *verb* **froth**, fizz, effervesce, bubble, lather, ferment, boil, seethe.

focus *noun* **1 centre**, focal point, central point, centre of attention, hub, pivot, nucleus, heart, cornerstone, linchpin. **2 subject**, theme, concern, subject matter, topic, point, essence, gist.

● *verb* **bring into focus**, aim, point, turn.
□ **focus on** concentrate, centre, zero in, zoom in, address yourself to, pay attention to, pinpoint, revolve around.

fog *noun* **mist**, smog, murk, haze; *informal* pea-souper.

foggy *adjective* **1 misty**, smoggy, hazy, murky. **2** *a foggy memory* **muddled**, confused, dim, hazy, shadowy, cloudy, blurred, obscure, vague, indistinct, unclear.
- OPPOSITES clear.

foil[1] *verb* **thwart**, frustrate, stop, defeat, block, prevent, obstruct, hinder, snooker, scotch; *informal* put paid to; *Brit. informal* scupper.
- OPPOSITES assist.

foil[2] *noun* **contrast**, complement, antithesis.

fold *verb* **1 double**, crease, turn, bend, tuck, pleat. **2 fail**, collapse, founder, go bankrupt, cease trading, be wound up, be shut (down); *informal* crash, go bust, go under, go to the wall, go belly up, flatline.
● *noun* **crease**, knife-edge, wrinkle, crinkle, pucker, furrow, pleat.

folk *noun (informal)* **1 people**, individuals, {men, women, and children}, (living) souls, citizenry, inhabitants, residents, populace, population. **2 relatives**, relations, family, people; *informal* peeps.

follow *verb* **1 come behind**, come after, go behind, go after, walk behind. **2 accompany**, go along with, go around with, travel with, escort, attend; *informal* tag along with. **3 shadow**, trail, stalk, track; *informal* tail. **4 obey**, comply with, conform to, adhere to, stick to, keep to, act in accordance with, abide by, observe. **5 understand**, comprehend, take in, grasp, fathom, see; *informal* make head or tail of, figure out; *Brit. informal* suss out. **6 be a fan of**, be a supporter of, support, watch, keep up with.
- OPPOSITES lead, flout.

follower *noun* **1 disciple**, apostle, defender, champion, believer, worshipper. **2 fan**, enthusiast, admirer, devotee, lover, supporter, adherent.
- OPPOSITES leader, opponent.

following *noun* **admirers**, supporters, backers, fans, adherents, devotees, public, audience.
- OPPOSITES opposition.
● *adjective* **next**, ensuing, succeeding, subsequent, successive.
- OPPOSITES preceding.

folly *noun* **foolishness**, foolhardiness, stupidity, idiocy, lunacy, madness, rashness, recklessness, irresponsibility.
- OPPOSITES wisdom.

fond *adjective* **1** *she was fond of dancing* **keen on**, partial to, enthusiastic about, attached to; *informal* into. **2 adoring**, devoted, doting, loving, caring, affectionate, indulgent. **3 unrealistic**, naive, foolish, over-optimistic, absurd, vain.
- OPPOSITES indifferent, uncaring.

fondle *verb* **caress**, stroke, pat, pet, finger, tickle, play with.

food *noun* **nourishment**, sustenance, nutriment, fare, cooking, cuisine, foodstuffs, refreshments, meals, provisions, rations; *informal* eats, grub, nosh; *literary* viands; *dated* victuals.

WORD LINKS
alimentary relating to food

fool *noun* **1 idiot**, ass, halfwit, blockhead, dunce, simpleton; *informal* nincompoop, clod, dimwit, dummy, fathead, numbskull; *Brit. informal* nitwit, twit, clot, berk, prat, pillock, wally, dork, twerp, charlie; *N. Amer. informal* schmuck; *Austral./NZ informal* drongo. **2** *she made a fool of me* **laughing stock**, dupe, gull; *informal* stooge, sucker, mug, fall guy; *N. Amer. informal* sap.
- OPPOSITES genius.
● *verb* **1 deceive**, trick, hoax, dupe, take in, mislead, delude, hoodwink, bluff, gull; *informal* bamboozle, take for a ride, have on; *N. Amer. informal* sucker; *Austral. informal* pull a swifty

on. **2 pretend**, make believe, put on an act, act, sham, fake, joke, jest; *informal* kid; *Brit. informal* have on.

foolish *adjective* **stupid**, idiotic, senseless, mindless, unintelligent, thoughtless, imprudent, unwise, ill-advised, rash, reckless, foolhardy; *informal* dumb, dim, dim-witted, half-witted, moronic, thick, hare-brained; *Brit. informal* barmy, daft, potty.
- OPPOSITES sensible, wise.

foolproof *adjective* **infallible**, dependable, reliable, trustworthy, certain, sure, guaranteed, safe, sound, tried and tested, watertight, airtight, flawless, perfect; *informal* sure-fire.

foot *noun* **1 paw**, hoof, trotter, pad. **2 bottom**, base, lowest part, end, foundation.

> WORD LINKS
> **chiropody**, **podiatry** medical treatment of the feet

footing *noun* **1** *a solid financial footing* **basis**, base, foundation. **2** *on an equal footing* **standing**, status, position, condition, arrangement, basis, relationship, terms.

forbid *verb* **prohibit**, ban, outlaw, make illegal, veto, proscribe, embargo, bar, debar, rule out.
- OPPOSITES permit.

forbidden *adjective* **prohibited**, verboten, taboo, illegal, illicit, against the law.

forbidding *adjective* **threatening**, ominous, menacing, sinister, daunting, off-putting.

force *noun* **1 strength**, power, energy, might, effort. **2 coercion**, compulsion, constraint, duress, pressure, oppression, harassment, intimidation, violence; *informal* arm-twisting. **3 power**, potency, weight, effectiveness, persuasiveness, validity, strength, significance, influence, authority; *informal* punch. **4 body**, group, outfit, party, team, detachment, unit, squad.
● *verb* **1 compel**, coerce, make, constrain, oblige, impel, drive, pressure, pressurize, press-gang, bully; *informal* lean on, twist someone's arm. **2 break open**, knock/smash/break down, kick in. **3 propel**, push, thrust, shove, drive, press, pump.
□ **in force** effective, in operation, operative, valid, current, binding.

forced *adjective* **1 enforced**, compulsory, obligatory, mandatory, involuntary, imposed, required. **2 strained**, unnatural, artificial, false, feigned, simulated, contrived, laboured, affected, hollow; *informal* phoney, pretend, put on.
- OPPOSITES voluntary, natural.

forceful *adjective* **1 dynamic**, energetic, assertive, authoritative, vigorous, powerful, strong, pushy; *informal* in-your-face, go-ahead, feisty. **2 convincing**, cogent, compelling, strong, powerful, persuasive, coherent.
- OPPOSITES weak.

forecast *verb* **predict**, prophesy, foretell, foresee.
● *noun* **prediction**, prophecy, prognostication, prognosis.

foreign *adjective* **alien**, overseas, non-native, imported, distant, external, far-off, exotic, strange.
- OPPOSITES domestic, native.

foreigner *noun* **alien**, foreign national, non-native, stranger, outsider, immigrant, settler, newcomer, incomer.
- OPPOSITES native, national.

> WORD LINKS
> **xenophobia** irrational dislike or fear of foreigners

foremost *adjective* **leading**, principal, premier, prime, top, greatest, best, supreme, pre-eminent, outstanding, most important, most notable; *N. Amer.* ranking; *informal* number-one.
- OPPOSITES minor.

foresee *verb* **anticipate**, expect, envisage, predict, forecast, foretell, prophesy.

foresight *noun* **forethought**, planning, far-sightedness, vision, anticipation,

prudence, care, caution; *N. Amer.* forehandedness.
- OPPOSITES hindsight.

foretell *verb* **predict**, forecast, prophesy, foresee, anticipate, envisage, warn of.

forever *adverb* **1 for always**, evermore, for ever and ever, for good, for all time, until the end of time, eternally; *N. Amer.* forevermore; *informal* until the cows come home. **2 always**, continually, constantly, perpetually, incessantly, endlessly, persistently, repeatedly, regularly; *informal* 24-7.

forfeit *verb* **lose**, be deprived of, surrender, relinquish, sacrifice, give up, renounce, forgo.
● *noun* **penalty**, sanction, punishment, penance, fine, confiscation, loss, forfeiture, surrender.

forge *verb* **1 hammer out**, beat out, fashion. **2 build**, construct, form, create, establish, set up. **3 fake**, falsify, counterfeit, copy, imitate, pirate.

forged *adjective* **fake**, false, counterfeit, imitation, copied, pirate, bogus; *informal* phoney, dud.
- OPPOSITES genuine.

forgery *noun* **fake**, counterfeit, fraud, imitation, replica, copy, pirate copy; *informal* phoney.

forget *verb* **1 fail to remember**, be unable to remember. **2 leave behind**, fail to take/bring, travel/leave home without. **3** *I forgot to close the door* **neglect**, fail, omit.
- OPPOSITES remember.

forgetful *adjective* **1 absent-minded**, amnesiac, vague, scatterbrained, disorganized, dreamy, abstracted, with a mind/memory like a sieve; *informal* scatty. **2** *forgetful of the time* **heedless**, careless, inattentive to, negligent about, oblivious to, unconcerned about, indifferent to.

forgive *verb* **1 pardon**, excuse, exonerate, absolve. **2 excuse**, overlook, disregard, ignore, make allowances for, turn a blind eye to, condone, indulge, tolerate.
- OPPOSITES blame, resent.

forgiveness *noun* **pardon**, absolution, exoneration, indulgence, clemency, mercy, reprieve, amnesty; *informal* let-off.
- OPPOSITES punishment.

forgiving *adjective* **merciful**, lenient, compassionate, magnanimous, humane, soft-hearted, forbearing, tolerant, indulgent, understanding.
- OPPOSITES merciless, vindictive.

forgo, forego *verb* **do without**, go without, give up, waive, renounce, surrender, relinquish, part with, drop, sacrifice, abstain from, refrain from, eschew, cut out; *informal* swear off; *formal* forswear, abjure.

fork *verb* **split**, branch, divide, separate, part, diverge, go in different directions, bifurcate.

forlorn *adjective* **1 unhappy**, sad, miserable, sorrowful, dejected, despondent, disconsolate, wretched, down, downcast, dispirited, downhearted, crestfallen, depressed, melancholy, gloomy, glum, mournful, despairing, doleful, woebegone; *informal* blue, down in the mouth, down in the dumps, fed up. **2 hopeless**, useless, futile, pointless, purposeless, vain, unavailing.
- OPPOSITES happy.

form *noun* **1 shape**, configuration, formation, structure, construction, arrangement, appearance, exterior, outline, format, layout, design. **2 body**, shape, figure, frame, physique, anatomy; *informal* vital statistics. **3 manifestation**, appearance, embodiment, incarnation, semblance, shape, guise. **4 kind**, sort, type, class, category, variety, genre, brand, style. **5 questionnaire**, document, coupon, slip. **6 class**, year; *N. Amer.* grade. **7 condition**, fettle, shape, health; *Brit. informal* nick.
● *verb* **1 make**, construct, build, manufacture, fabricate, assemble, put together, create, fashion, shape. **2 formulate**, devise, conceive, work out, think up, lay, draw up, put together, produce, fashion, concoct, forge, hatch; *informal* dream up. **3 set**

up, establish, found, launch, create, institute, start, inaugurate. **4 materialize**, come into being/existence, emerge, develop, take shape, gather, accumulate, collect, amass. **5 arrange**, draw up, line up, assemble, organize, sort, order. **6 comprise**, make, make up, constitute, compose, add up to.
- OPPOSITES dissolve, disappear.

formal *adjective* **1 ceremonial**, ritualistic, ritual, official, conventional, traditional, stately, solemn, ceremonious. **2 aloof**, reserved, remote, detached, unapproachable, stiff, stuffy, correct, proper; *informal* stand-offish. **3 official**, legal, authorized, approved, certified, endorsed, sanctioned, licensed, recognized.
- OPPOSITES informal, casual, unofficial.

formality *noun* **1 ceremony**, ritual, protocol, decorum, solemnity. **2 aloofness**, reserve, remoteness, detachment, unapproachability, stiffness, stuffiness, correctness; *informal* stand-offishness.
- OPPOSITES informality.

format *noun* **design**, style, appearance, look, form, shape, size, arrangement, plan, structure, scheme, composition, configuration.

formation *noun* **1** *the formation of the island* **emergence**, genesis, development, evolution, shaping, origin. **2** *the formation of a new government* **establishment**, setting up, institution, foundation, creation, inauguration. **3 configuration**, arrangement, grouping, pattern, array, alignment, order.
- OPPOSITES destruction, dissolution.

former *adjective* **1 one-time**, erstwhile, sometime, as was, ex-, previous, preceding, earlier, prior, last; *formal* quondam. **2 earlier**, old, past, bygone, olden, long ago, gone by, long past, of old. **3 first-mentioned**, first.
- OPPOSITES future, current, latter.

formerly *adverb* **previously**, earlier, before, until now/then, once, once upon a time, at one time, in the past, as was.

formidable *adjective* **1 intimidating**, daunting, indomitable, forbidding, alarming, frightening, awesome, fearsome; *humorous* redoubtable. **2 accomplished**, masterly, virtuoso, expert, impressive, powerful, terrific, superb; *informal* tremendous, nifty, crack, ace, wizard, magic, mean, wicked, deadly.

formula *noun* **1 form of words**, set expression, rubric, phrase, saying. **2 recipe**, prescription, blueprint, plan, policy, method, procedure.

formulate *verb* **1 devise**, conceive, work out, think up, lay, draw up, form, concoct, contrive, forge, hatch, prepare, develop. **2 express**, phrase, word, define, specify, put into words, frame, couch, put, articulate, say.

fort *noun* **fortress**, castle, citadel, bunker, stronghold, fortification, bastion.

forte *noun* **strength**, strong point, speciality, strong suit, talent, skill, gift; *informal* thing.

forthcoming *adjective* **1 coming**, upcoming, approaching, imminent, impending, future. **2 communicative**, talkative, chatty, informative, expansive, expressive, frank, open, candid.
- OPPOSITES past, current, reticent.

forthright *adjective* **frank**, direct, straightforward, honest, candid, open, sincere, outspoken, straight, blunt, plain-spoken, no-nonsense, bluff, matter-of-fact, to the point; *informal* upfront.
- OPPOSITES secretive, evasive.

fortify *verb* **1 strengthen**, secure, barricade, protect, buttress, shore up. **2 invigorate**, strengthen, energize, enliven, animate, vitalize, buoy up; *informal* pep up, buck up.
- OPPOSITES weaken.

fortitude *noun* **courage**, bravery, endurance, resilience, mettle, strength of character, backbone, grit; *informal* guts; *Brit. informal* bottle.

fortress *noun* **fort**, castle, citadel, bunker, stronghold, fortification.

fortunate *adjective* **1 lucky**, favoured, blessed, leading a charmed life, in luck; *Brit. informal* born with a silver spoon in your mouth, jammy. **2 favourable**, advantageous, happy.
- OPPOSITES unfavourable, unlucky.

fortunately *adverb* **luckily**, as luck would have it, happily, mercifully, thankfully.

fortune *noun* **1 chance**, accident, coincidence, serendipity, destiny, providence; *N. Amer.* happenstance. **2 luck**, fate, destiny, predestination, the stars, karma, kismet, lot. **3** *an upswing in their fortunes* **circumstances**, state of affairs, condition, position, situation. **4 wealth**, money, riches, assets, resources, means, deep pockets, possessions, property, estate.

forum *noun* **meeting**, assembly, gathering, rally, conference, seminar, convention, symposium.

forward *adverb* **1 ahead**, forwards, onwards, onward, on, further. **2 towards the front**, out, forth, into view, up.
- OPPOSITES backwards, back.
● *adjective* **1 onward**, advancing. **2 front**, advance, foremost, leading. **3 future**, forward-looking, for the future, anticipatory. **4 bold**, brazen, cheeky, shameless, familiar, overfamiliar, presumptuous; *informal* fresh.
- OPPOSITES backward, rear.
● *verb* **1 send on**, post on, redirect, readdress, pass on. **2 send**, dispatch, transmit, carry, convey, deliver, ship.

foster *verb* **1 encourage**, promote, further, nurture, help, aid, assist, support, back. **2 bring up**, rear, raise, care for, take care of, look after, provide for.

foul *adjective* **1 disgusting**, revolting, repulsive, repugnant, abhorrent, loathsome, offensive, sickening, nauseating; *informal* ghastly, gruesome, gross. **2 contaminated**, polluted, infected, tainted, impure, filthy, dirty, unclean. **3 vulgar**, crude, coarse, filthy, dirty, obscene, indecent, naughty, offensive; *informal* blue.
- OPPOSITES pleasant.
● *verb* **1 dirty**, pollute, contaminate, poison, taint, sully. **2 tangle up**, entangle, snarl, catch, entwine.

found *verb* **establish**, set up, start, begin, get going, institute, inaugurate, launch.

foundation *noun* **1 footing**, foot, base, substructure, underpinning. **2 justification**, grounds, evidence, basis. **3 institution**, establishment, charitable body, agency.

founder[1] *noun* **originator**, creator, (founding) father, architect, developer, pioneer, author, inventor, mastermind.

founder[2] *verb* **1 sink**, go to the bottom, go down, be lost at sea. **2 fail**, be unsuccessful, fall flat, fall through, collapse, backfire, meet with disaster; *informal* flop, bomb, flatline.
- OPPOSITES succeed.

fountain *noun* **1 jet**, spray, spout, spurt, cascade, water feature. **2 source**, fount, well, reservoir, fund, mine.

foyer *noun* **entrance hall**, hallway, entry, porch, reception area, atrium, concourse, lobby, anteroom; *N. Amer.* entryway.

fracas *noun* **disturbance**, brawl, melee, rumpus, skirmish, struggle, scuffle, scrum, clash, fisticuffs, altercation; *informal* scrap, dust-up, set-to, shindy, shindig; *Brit. informal* punch-up, bust-up, ruck; *N. Amer. informal* rough house; *Law, dated* affray.

fraction *noun* **1** *a fraction of the population* **tiny part**, fragment, snippet, snatch. **2** *he moved a fraction closer* **bit**, little, touch, soupçon, trifle, mite, shade, jot; *informal* smidgen, tad.
- OPPOSITES whole.

fractious *adjective* **grumpy**, bad-tempered, irascible, irritable, crotchety, grouchy, cantankerous, tetchy, testy, ill-tempered, peevish, cross, pettish, waspish, crabby, crusty; *Brit. informal* shirty, stroppy, narky, ratty; *N. Amer. informal* cranky, ornery.

fracture *noun* **break**, crack, split, rupture, fissure.
● *verb* **break**, crack, split, rupture, snap, shatter, fragment, splinter.

fragile *adjective* **1 breakable**, delicate, brittle, flimsy, dainty, fine. **2 tenuous**, shaky, insecure, vulnerable, flimsy. **3 weak**, delicate, frail, debilitated, ill, unwell, poorly, sickly.
– OPPOSITES sturdy, robust.

fragment *noun* **1 piece**, bit, particle, speck, chip, shard, sliver, splinter, flake. **2 snatch**, snippet, scrap, bit.
● *verb* **break up**, crack open, shatter, splinter, fracture, disintegrate, fall to pieces, fall apart.

fragrance *noun* **1 sweet smell**, scent, perfume, bouquet, aroma, nose. **2 perfume**, scent, eau de toilette.

fragrant *adjective* **sweet-scented**, sweet-smelling, scented, perfumed, aromatic.
– OPPOSITES smelly.

frail *adjective* **1** *a frail old lady* **weak**, delicate, feeble, infirm, ill, unwell, sickly, poorly. **2** *a frail structure* **fragile**, easily damaged, delicate, flimsy, insubstantial, unsteady, unstable, rickety.
– OPPOSITES strong, robust.

frame *noun* **1 framework**, structure, substructure, skeleton, casing, chassis, shell. **2 body**, figure, form, shape, physique, anatomy, build.
● *verb* **1 mount**, set in a frame. **2 formulate**, draw up, draft, shape, compose, put together, form, devise.
□ **frame of mind** mood, state of mind, humour, temper, disposition.

framework *noun* **1 frame**, structure, skeleton, chassis, support, scaffolding. **2 structure**, shape, fabric, order, scheme, system, organization, anatomy; *informal* make-up.

frank *adjective* **1 candid**, direct, forthright, plain, plain-spoken, straight, to the point, matter-of-fact, open, honest; *informal* upfront. **2 undisguised**, open, unconcealed, naked, unmistakable, clear, obvious, transparent, patent, evident.
– OPPOSITES evasive.

frankly *adverb* **1 to be frank**, to be honest, to tell the truth, in all honesty. **2 candidly**, directly, plainly, straightforwardly, forthrightly, openly, honestly, without beating about the bush, bluntly.

frantic *adjective* **panic-stricken**, panicky, beside yourself, at your wits' end, distraught, overwrought, worked up, frenzied, frenetic, fraught, feverish, desperate; *informal* in a state, tearing your hair out; *Brit. informal* having kittens, in a flat spin.
– OPPOSITES calm.

fraternity *noun* **1 brotherhood**, fellowship, kinship, friendship, mutual support, solidarity, community. **2 profession**, community, trade, set, circle. **3** *(N. Amer.)* **society**, club, association, group.

fraud *noun* **1 deception**, sharp practice, cheating, swindling, trickery, embezzlement, deceit, double-dealing, chicanery. **2 swindle**, racket, deception, trick, cheat, hoax; *informal* scam, con, rip-off, sting, fiddle; *N. Amer. informal* hustle. **3 impostor**, fake, sham, charlatan, swindler, fraudster, confidence trickster; *informal* phoney.

fraudulent *adjective* **dishonest**, cheating, swindling, corrupt, criminal, deceitful, double-dealing, duplicitous; *informal* crooked, shady, dirty; *Brit. informal* bent, dodgy; *Austral./NZ informal* shonky.
– OPPOSITES honest.

fraught *adjective* **1** *a world fraught with danger* **full of**, filled with, rife with. **2 anxious**, worried, stressed, upset, distraught, overwrought, worked up, agitated, distressed, desperate, frantic, panic-stricken, panicky, beside yourself, at your wits' end, at the end of your tether.

frayed *adjective* **1 worn**, threadbare, tattered, ragged, the worse for wear; *informal* tatty; *N. Amer. informal* raggedy. **2 strained**, fraught, tense, edgy, stressed.

freak *noun* **1 aberration**, abnormality, oddity, monster, monstrosity, mutant, chimera. **2 anomaly**, aberration, rarity, oddity, one-off, fluke, twist of fate. **3** *(informal)* **eccentric**, misfit, oddity, crank; *informal* oddball, weirdo, nut; *Brit. informal* nutter; *N. Amer. informal* wacko, kook. **4** *(informal)* **enthusiast**, fan, devotee, lover, aficionado; *informal* nut, fanatic, addict, maniac.
● *adjective* **unusual**, anomalous, aberrant, atypical, unrepresentative, irregular, exceptional, isolated.

free *adjective* **1 free of charge**, without charge, for nothing, complimentary, gratis; *informal* for free, on the house. **2** *free of any pressures* **without**, unencumbered by, unaffected by, clear of, rid of, exempt from, not liable to, safe from, immune to, excused. **3 unoccupied**, not busy, available, off duty, off work, on holiday, on leave, at leisure, with time to spare. **4 vacant**, empty, available, unoccupied, not in use. **5 independent**, self-governing, self-determining, sovereign, autonomous, democratic. **6 on the loose**, at liberty, at large, loose, unrestrained. **7** *you are free to leave* **able**, in a position, allowed, permitted. **8 unobstructed**, unimpeded, unrestricted, unhampered, clear, open. **9** *she was free with her money* **generous**, liberal, open-handed, unstinting.
- OPPOSITES busy, occupied, confined.
● *verb* **1 release**, set free, let go, liberate, set loose, untie. **2 extricate**, release, get out, cut free, pull free, rescue.
- OPPOSITES confine, trap.

freedom *noun* **1 liberty**, liberation, release, deliverance. **2 independence**, self-government, self-determination, self-rule, home rule, sovereignty, autonomy, democracy. **3** *freedom from political accountability* **exemption**, immunity, dispensation, impunity. **4 right**, entitlement, privilege, prerogative, discretion, latitude, elbow room, licence, free rein, a free hand, carte blanche.
- OPPOSITES captivity, obligation.

freely *adverb* **1 openly**, candidly, frankly, directly, without beating about the bush, without mincing your words. **2 voluntarily**, willingly, readily, of your own accord, of your own free will, without being told to.

freeze *verb* **1 ice over**, ice up, solidify. **2 stand still**, stop dead in your tracks, go rigid, become motionless, become paralysed. **3 fix**, hold, peg, set, limit, restrict, cap.
- OPPOSITES thaw.

freezing *adjective* **1 icy**, bitter, chill, frosty, glacial, arctic, wintry, sub-zero, raw, biting. **2 frozen**, numb with cold, chilled to the bone/marrow.
- OPPOSITES balmy, hot.

freight *noun* **goods**, cargo, merchandise.

frenzied *adjective* **frantic**, wild, frenetic, hectic, feverish, fevered, mad, crazed, manic, furious, uncontrolled.
- OPPOSITES calm.

frenzy *noun* **hysteria**, madness, mania, delirium, wild excitement, fever, lather, passion, panic, fury, rage.

frequent *adjective* **recurrent**, recurring, repeated, periodic, continual, habitual, regular, successive, numerous, several.
- OPPOSITES occasional.
● *verb* **visit**, patronize, spend time in, visit regularly, haunt; *informal* hang out at.
- OPPOSITES avoid.

frequently *adverb* **often**, all the time, habitually, regularly, customarily, routinely, again and again, repeatedly, recurrently, continually; *N. Amer.* oftentimes.

fresh *adjective* **1 new**, modern, original, novel, different, innovative. **2 recently made**, just picked, crisp, raw, natural, unprocessed. **3 refreshed**, rested, restored, energetic, vigorous, invigorated, lively, sprightly, bright, alert, bouncing, perky; *informal* full of beans, bright-eyed and bushy-tailed. **4 bracing**, brisk, strong, invigorating, chilly, cool; *informal* nippy; *Brit. informal*

parky. **5 cool**, crisp, refreshing, invigorating, pure, clean, clear. **6** *(informal)* **impudent**, impertinent, insolent, presumptuous, forward, cheeky, disrespectful, rude; *informal* mouthy, saucy, lippy; *N. Amer. informal* sassy.
- OPPOSITES stale, old.

fret *verb* **worry**, be anxious, distress yourself, upset yourself, concern yourself, agonize, lose sleep.

friction *noun* **1 rubbing**, chafing, grating, rasping, scraping, resistance, drag, abrasion. **2 discord**, disagreement, dissension, dispute, conflict, hostility, animosity, antipathy, antagonism, resentment, acrimony, bitterness, bad feeling.
- OPPOSITES harmony.

friend *noun* **companion**, comrade, confidant, confidante, familiar, intimate, soul mate, playmate, playfellow, ally, associate; *informal* pal, chum; *Brit. informal* mate; *N. Amer. informal* buddy, amigo, compadre, homeboy.
- OPPOSITES enemy.

friendly *adjective* **1** *a friendly woman* **amiable**, companionable, sociable, gregarious, comradely, neighbourly, hospitable, easy to get on with, affable, genial, cordial, warm, affectionate, convivial; *informal* chummy, pally; *Brit. informal* matey. **2** *friendly conversation* **amicable**, cordial, pleasant, easy, relaxed, casual, informal, close, intimate, familiar.
- OPPOSITES hostile.

friendship *noun* **1** *lasting friendships* **relationship**, attachment, association, bond, tie, link, union. **2** *ties of friendship* **friendliness**, affection, camaraderie, comradeship, companionship, fellowship, closeness, affinity, unity, intimacy.
- OPPOSITES hostility.

fright *noun* **1 fear**, terror, horror, alarm, panic, dread, trepidation, dismay, nervousness. **2 scare**, shock, surprise, turn, jolt, start.

frighten *verb* **scare**, startle, alarm, terrify, petrify, shock, chill, panic, unnerve, intimidate; *informal* spook; *Brit. informal* put the wind up.

frightening *adjective* **terrifying**, horrifying, alarming, startling, chilling, spine-chilling, hair-raising, blood-curdling, disturbing, unnerving, intimidating, daunting, eerie, sinister, fearsome, nightmarish, menacing; *informal* scary, spooky, creepy.

frightful *adjective* **horrible**, horrific, ghastly, horrendous, awful, dreadful, terrible, nasty; *informal* horrid.

fringe *noun* **1 edge**, border, margin, extremity, perimeter, periphery, rim, limits, outskirts. **2 edging**, border, trimming, frill, flounce, ruffle.
- OPPOSITES middle.
● *adjective* **alternative**, avant-garde, experimental, innovative, left-field, radical.
- OPPOSITES mainstream.

frisky *adjective* **lively**, bouncy, bubbly, perky, active, energetic, animated, playful, coltish, skittish, spirited, high-spirited, in high spirits, exuberant; *informal* full of beans.

frivolous *adjective* **flippant**, glib, facetious, joking, jokey, light-hearted, fatuous, inane; *informal* flip.
- OPPOSITES serious.

front *noun* **1 fore**, foremost part, forepart, nose, head, bow, prow, foreground. **2 frontage**, face, facing, facade. **3 head**, beginning, start, top, lead. **4 appearance**, air, face, manner, exterior, veneer, (outward) show, act, pretence. **5 cover**, blind, disguise, facade, mask, cloak, screen, smokescreen, camouflage.
- OPPOSITES back.
● *adjective* **leading**, lead, first, foremost.
- OPPOSITES back, last.
□ **in front** ahead, to/at the fore, at the head, up ahead, in the lead, leading, coming first, at the head of the queue; *informal* up front.

frontier *noun* **border**, boundary, borderline, dividing line, perimeter, limit, edge.

frosty *adjective* **1 cold**, freezing, frozen, icy, bitter, chill, wintry, arctic; *informal* nippy; *Brit. informal* parky. **2 unfriendly**, cold, frigid, icy, glacial, inhospitable, unwelcoming, forbidding, hostile, stony.
- OPPOSITES warm, friendly.

froth *noun* **foam**, head, bubbles, frothiness, fizz, effervescence, lather, suds.
● *verb* **bubble**, fizz, effervesce, foam, lather, churn, seethe.

f

frown *verb* **scowl**, glower, glare, lour, make a face, look daggers, give someone a black look, knit your brows; *informal* give someone a dirty look.
- OPPOSITES smile.
□ **frown on** disapprove of, take a dim view of, take exception to, object to, look askance at, not take kindly to.

frugal *adjective* **1 thrifty**, economical, careful, cautious, prudent, provident, sparing, abstemious, austere, self-denying, ascetic, spartan. **2 meagre**, scanty, scant, paltry, skimpy, plain, simple, spartan, inexpensive, cheap, economical.
- OPPOSITES extravagant, lavish.

fruitful *adjective* **productive**, constructive, useful, worthwhile, helpful, beneficial, valuable, rewarding, profitable, advantageous.
- OPPOSITES barren, futile.

fruition *noun* **fulfilment**, realization, actualization, materialization, achievement, attainment, accomplishment, success, completion, consummation, conclusion, close, finish, perfection, maturity.

fruitless *adjective* **futile**, vain, in vain, to no avail, to no effect, idle, pointless, useless, worthless, hollow, ineffectual, ineffective, unproductive, unrewarding, profitless, unsuccessful, unavailing, abortive.
- OPPOSITES fruitful, productive.

frustrate *verb* **1 thwart**, defeat, foil, block, stop, counter, spoil, check, forestall, scotch, derail, snooker; *informal* stymie; *Brit. informal* scupper. **2 exasperate**, infuriate, discourage, dishearten, disappoint.
- OPPOSITES further, satisfy.

fudge *verb* **evade**, avoid, dodge, skirt, duck, gloss over, cloud, hedge, beat about the bush, equivocate.

fuel *verb* **1 power**, fire, drive, run. **2 fan**, feed, stoke up, inflame, intensify, stimulate, encourage, provoke, incite, sustain.

fugitive *noun* **escapee**, runaway, deserter, absconder, refugee.

fulfil *verb* **1 achieve**, attain, realize, make happen, succeed in, bring to completion, bring to fruition, satisfy. **2 carry out**, perform, accomplish, execute, do, discharge, conduct. **3 meet**, satisfy, comply with, conform to, fill, answer.

fulfilled *adjective* **satisfied**, content, contented, happy, pleased, at peace.
- OPPOSITES discontented.

full *adjective* **1 filled**, brimming, brimful, packed, loaded, crammed, crowded, bursting, overflowing, congested; *informal* jam-packed, wall-to-wall, chock-a-block, chock-full, awash. **2 replete**, full up, satisfied, sated, satiated; *informal* stuffed. **3 eventful**, interesting, exciting, lively, action-packed, busy, active. **4 comprehensive**, thorough, exhaustive, all-inclusive, all-encompassing, all-embracing, in-depth, complete, entire, whole, unabridged, uncut. **5 plump**, rounded, buxom, shapely, ample, curvaceous, voluptuous; *informal* busty, curvy, well endowed; *N. Amer. informal* zaftig. **6 loose-fitting**, loose, baggy, voluminous, roomy, capacious, billowing.
- OPPOSITES empty.

fully *adverb* **completely**, entirely, wholly, totally, perfectly, quite, altogether, thoroughly, in all respects, (up) to the hilt.
- OPPOSITES partly.

fumble *verb* **grope**, fish, scrabble, feel.

fume *noun* **smoke**, vapour, gas, exhaust, pollution.
● *verb* **be furious**, seethe, be livid, be incensed, boil, be beside yourself, spit;

informal foam at the mouth, see red.

fumigate *verb* **disinfect**, purify, sterilize, sanitize, decontaminate, cleanse, clean out.

fun *noun* **1 enjoyment**, entertainment, amusement, pleasure, jollification, merrymaking, recreation, leisure, relaxation, a good time; *informal* living it up, a ball. **2 merriment**, cheerfulness, jollity, joviality, high spirits, mirth, laughter, hilarity, light-heartedness, levity. **3** *he became a figure of fun* **ridicule**, derision, mockery, scorn, contempt.
- OPPOSITES boredom.
● *adjective (informal)* **enjoyable**, entertaining, amusing, pleasurable, pleasant, agreeable, convivial.
□ **make fun of** tease, poke fun at, ridicule, mock, laugh at, parody, caricature, satirize; *informal* take the mickey out of, send up; *N. Amer. informal* goof on.

function *noun* **1 purpose**, task, use, role. **2 responsibility**, duty, role, province, activity, assignment, task, job, mission. **3 social event**, party, social occasion, affair, gathering, reception, soirée; *N. Amer.* levee; *informal* do, bash.
● *verb* **1 work**, go, run, be in working/running order, operate. **2 act**, serve, operate, perform, do duty.

functional *adjective* **1 practical**, useful, utilitarian, workaday, serviceable, no-frills. **2 working**, in working order, functioning, in service, in use, going, running, operative; *Informal* up and running.

fund *noun* **1 collection**, kitty, reserve, pool, purse, savings, coffers. **2 money**, cash, wealth, means, assets, resources, savings, capital, reserves, deep pockets, the wherewithal; *informal* dosh; *Brit. informal* lolly.
● *verb* **finance**, pay for, back, capitalize, subsidize, endow, invest in, sponsor; *N. Amer. informal* bankroll.

fundamental *adjective* **basic**, underlying, core, rudimentary, root, primary, prime, cardinal, principal, chief, key, central, vital, essential.
- OPPOSITES secondary, incidental.

fundamentally *adverb* **essentially**, in essence, basically, at heart, at bottom, deep down, profoundly, primarily, above all.

funeral *noun* **burial**, interment, entombment, committal, laying to rest, cremation.

funny *adjective* **1 amusing**, humorous, witty, comic, comical, hilarious, hysterical, riotous, uproarious, farcical; *informal* rib-tickling, priceless. **2 strange**, peculiar, odd, weird, bizarre, curious, freakish, quirky, unusual. **3 suspicious**, suspect, dubious, untrustworthy, questionable; *informal* fishy; *Brit. informal* dodgy.
- OPPOSITES serious.

furious *adjective* **1 very angry**, enraged, infuriated, irate, incensed, fuming, ranting, raving, seething, beside yourself, outraged; *informal* hopping mad, wild, livid. **2 fierce**, heated, passionate, fiery, tumultuous, turbulent, tempestuous, violent, stormy, acrimonious.
- OPPOSITES pleased, calm.

furnish *verb* **1 fit out**, appoint, equip; *Brit. informal* do out. **2** *they furnished us with waterproofs* **supply**, provide, equip, issue, kit out; *informal* fix up.

furore *noun* **commotion**, uproar, outcry, fuss, upset, brouhaha, stir; *informal* to-do, hoo-ha, hullabaloo.

further *adverb* see **furthermore**.
● *adjective* **additional**, more, extra, supplementary, new, fresh.
● *verb* **promote**, advance, forward, develop, facilitate, aid, assist, help, boost, encourage.
- OPPOSITES impede.

furthermore *adverb* **moreover**, further, what's more, also, additionally, in addition, besides, as well, too, on top of that, into the bargain.

furthest *adjective* **most distant**, remotest, farthest, furthermost, farthermost, outer, outermost, extreme.
- OPPOSITES nearest.

furtive *adjective* **surreptitious**, secretive, secret, clandestine, hidden, covert, conspiratorial, cloak-and-dagger, sneaky; *Military* black; *informal* shifty.
– OPPOSITES open.

fury *noun* **1 rage**, anger, wrath, outrage; *literary* ire. **2 ferocity**, violence, turbulence, tempestuousness, savagery, severity, intensity, vehemence, force.

fuss *noun* **1 commotion**, excitement, stir, confusion, disturbance, brouhaha, uproar, furore, storm in a teacup; *informal* hoo-ha, to-do, song and dance, performance. **2 protest**, complaint, objection, argument; *Brit.* row. **3 trouble**, bother, inconvenience, effort, exertion, labour; *informal* hassle.
● *verb* **worry**, fret, be agitated, be worked up, make a big thing out of it, make a mountain out of a molehill; *informal* flap, be in a tizzy.

fussy *adjective* **1 particular**, finicky, fastidious, hard to please, faddish; *informal* pernickety, choosy, picky; *Brit. informal* faddy; *N. Amer. informal* persnickety. **2 over-elaborate**, ornate, fancy, busy, cluttered.

futile *adjective* **fruitless**, vain, pointless, useless, ineffectual, forlorn, hopeless.
– OPPOSITES useful.

future *noun* **1** *plans for the future* **time to come**, what lies ahead, the hereafter. **2** *her future lay in acting* **destiny**, fate, fortune, prospects, chances.
– OPPOSITES past.
● *adjective* **1 later**, to come, following, forthcoming, ensuing, succeeding, subsequent, coming, impending, approaching. **2** *her future husband* **to be**, destined, intended, planned, prospective.
– OPPOSITES previous, past.

fuzzy *adjective* **1 frizzy**, fluffy, woolly, downy. **2 blurred**, indistinct, unclear, out of focus, misty. **3 unclear**, imprecise, unfocused, nebulous, vague, hazy, loose, woolly.
– OPPOSITES smooth, sharp, clear.

Gg

gadget *noun* **device**, appliance, apparatus, instrument, implement, tool, utensil, contrivance, contraption, machine, mechanism, invention; *informal* gizmo.

gaffe *noun* **blunder**, mistake, error, slip, faux pas, indiscretion, solecism; *informal* slip-up, howler, boo-boo; *Brit. informal* boob, clanger; *N. Amer. informal* blooper.

gag[1] *verb* **1 silence**, muzzle, suppress, stifle, censor, curb, restrain. **2 retch**, heave.

gag[2] *noun (informal)* **joke**, quip, jest, witticism; *informal* crack, wisecrack, one-liner.

gain *verb* **1 obtain**, get, secure, acquire, come by, procure, attain, achieve, earn, win, capture; *informal* land. **2** *they stood to gain from the deal* **profit**, make money, benefit, do well out of. **3** *she gained weight* **put on**, increase in, build up. **4** *they're gaining on us* **catch up (with)**, catch, reduce someone's lead, narrow the gap.
- OPPOSITES lose.
● *noun* **1 profit**, earnings, income, yield, return, reward, advantage, benefit; *informal* take. **2 increase**, addition, rise, increment, advance.
- OPPOSITES loss.

gainful *adjective* **profitable**, paid, well paid, remunerative, lucrative, money-making, rewarding, fruitful, worthwhile, useful, productive, constructive, beneficial, advantageous, valuable.

gait *noun* **walk**, step, stride, pace, tread, way of walking, bearing, carriage; *Brit.* deportment.

gala *noun* **festival**, fair, fete, carnival, pageant, jubilee, jamboree, celebration.

gale *noun* **1 high wind**, blast, squall, storm, tempest, hurricane, tornado, cyclone, whirlwind, typhoon. **2 peal**, howl, hoot, shriek, roar, fit, paroxysm.

gallant *adjective* **1 brave**, courageous, valiant, bold, plucky, daring, fearless, intrepid, heroic, stout-hearted; *informal* gutsy, spunky. **2 chivalrous**, gentlemanly, courteous, polite, attentive, respectful, gracious, considerate, thoughtful.
- OPPOSITES cowardly, discourteous.

gamble *verb* **1 bet**, place a bet, wager, hazard; *Brit. informal* punt, have a flutter. **2 take a chance**, take a risk; *N. Amer.* take a flyer; *informal* stick your neck out; *Brit. informal* chance your arm.
● *noun I took a gamble* **risk**, chance, leap in the dark, speculation, lottery, pot luck.

game *noun* **1 pastime**, diversion, entertainment, amusement, distraction, recreation, sport, activity. **2 match**, contest, fixture, meeting, tie; *Brit.* clash.
● *adjective* **willing**, prepared, ready, disposed, interested, eager, keen, enthusiastic.

gang *noun* **band**, group, crowd, pack, horde, throng, mob, herd, swarm, troop; *informal* bunch, gaggle, load.

gangster *noun* **hoodlum**, racketeer, thug, villain, criminal, Mafioso; *informal* mobster, crook, tough; *N. Amer. informal* hood.

gaol *noun* & *verb* see **jail**.

gap *noun* **1 opening**, aperture, space, breach, chink, slit, crack, crevice, cleft, cavity, hole, interstice. **2 pause**, intermission, interval, interlude, break, breathing space, breather, respite, hiatus, lull; *N. Amer.* recess. **3 omission**, blank, lacuna. **4** *the gap between rich and poor* **chasm**, gulf, separation, contrast, difference, disparity, divergence, imbalance.

gape *verb* **1 stare**, goggle, gaze, ogle; *informal* rubberneck; *Brit. informal* gawp. **2 open**, yawn, part, split.

gaping *adjective* **wide**, broad, vast, yawning, cavernous.

garbage *(N. Amer.) noun* **1 waste**, refuse, rubbish, detritus, litter, junk, scrap, scraps, leftovers, remains; *N. Amer.* trash. **2 nonsense**, rubbish, balderdash, claptrap, twaddle, dross; *informal* hogwash, baloney, tripe, bilge, bull, bunk, poppycock, rot, piffle; *Brit. informal* tosh, codswallop.

g

garble *verb* **mix up**, muddle, jumble, confuse, obscure, distort.

garden *noun* park, estate, grounds.

WORD LINKS
horticultural relating to gardens

garish *adjective* **gaudy**, lurid, loud, harsh, showy, glittering, brash, tasteless, vulgar; *informal* flashy.
– OPPOSITES drab, tasteful.

garments *plural noun* **clothes**, clothing, dress, garb, wardrobe, costume, attire; *informal* gear, togs; *Brit. informal* clobber; *N. Amer. informal* threads; *formal* apparel.

garnish *verb* **decorate**, adorn, ornament, trim, dress, embellish.
● *noun* **decoration**, adornment, ornament, embellishment, enhancement, finishing touch.

garrison *noun* **1 troops**, forces, militia, soldiers, force, detachment, unit. **2 base**, camp, station, barracks, fort, command post.
● *verb* **station**, post, deploy, base, site, place, billet.

garrulous *adjective* **talkative**, loquacious, voluble, verbose, chatty, gossipy, effusive, expansive, forthcoming, conversational, communicative; *informal* mouthy, having the gift of the gab.
– OPPOSITES taciturn.

gash *noun* **cut**, laceration, slash, slit, split, wound, injury.
● *verb* **cut**, lacerate, slash, slit, split, wound, injure.

gasp *verb* **1 catch your breath**, gulp, draw in your breath. **2 pant**, puff, puff and blow, wheeze, breathe hard/heavily, choke, fight for breath.
● *noun* **gulp**, pant, puff.

gate *noun* **barrier**, turnstile, gateway, doorway, entrance, exit, door, portal; *N. Amer.* entryway.

gather *verb* **1 congregate**, assemble, meet, collect, get together, convene, muster, rally, converge. **2 summon**, call together, bring together, assemble, convene, rally, round up, muster, marshal. **3 harvest**, reap, crop, pick, pluck, collect. **4 understand**, believe, be led to believe, conclude, infer, assume, take it, surmise, hear, learn, discover. **5 pleat**, pucker, tuck, fold, ruffle.
– OPPOSITES disperse.

gathering *noun* **assembly**, meeting, convention, rally, council, congress, congregation, audience, crowd, group, throng, mass; *informal* get-together.

gauche *adjective* **awkward**, gawky, inelegant, graceless, ungraceful, clumsy, ungainly, maladroit, inept, unsophisticated.
– OPPOSITES elegant, sophisticated.

gaudy *adjective* **garish**, lurid, loud, glaring, harsh, showy, glittering, ostentatious, tasteless; *informal* flashy, tacky.
– OPPOSITES drab, tasteful.

gauge *noun* **meter**, measure, indicator, dial, scale, display.
● *verb* **1 measure**, calculate, compute, work out, determine, ascertain, count, weigh, quantify, put a figure on. **2 assess**, evaluate, determine, estimate, form an opinion of, appraise, weigh up, judge, guess; *informal* size up.

gaunt *adjective* **haggard**, drawn, thin, lean, skinny, spindly, spare, bony, angular, raw-boned, pinched, hollow-cheeked, scrawny, scraggy, as thin as a rake, cadaverous, skeletal, emaciated, skin and bone, wasted, withered; *informal* like a bag of bones.
– OPPOSITES plump.

gaze *verb* **stare**, gape, look fixedly, goggle, eye, scrutinize, ogle; *informal* rubberneck; *Brit. informal* gawp; *N. Amer. informal* eyeball.
● *noun* **stare**, gape, fixed look, regard, scrutiny.

gear *noun* **1 equipment**, apparatus, paraphernalia, tools, utensils, implements, instruments, rig, tackle; *Brit. informal* clobber. **2** *(informal)* **belongings**, possessions, effects, paraphernalia, bits and pieces; *informal* things, stuff, kit; *Brit. informal* clobber, gubbins. **3** *(informal)* **clothes**, clothing, garments, outfits, attire, garb, wardrobe; *informal* togs; *Brit. informal* clobber, kit; *N. Amer. informal* threads; *formal* apparel.

gem *noun* **1 jewel**, precious stone, semi-precious stone; *informal* rock, sparkler. **2 masterpiece**, classic, treasure, prize, find; *informal* one in a million, the bee's knees.

genealogy *noun* **lineage**, line (of descent), family tree, bloodline, pedigree, ancestry, heritage, parentage, family, stock, blood, roots.

general *adjective* **1** *suitable for general use* **widespread**, common, extensive, universal, wide, popular, public, mainstream. **2** *a general pay increase* **comprehensive**, overall, across the board, blanket, global, universal, mass, wholesale. **3 usual**, customary, habitual, traditional, normal, conventional, typical, standard, regular, accepted, prevailing, routine, established, everyday. **4** *a general description* **broad**, rough, loose, approximate, unspecific, vague, imprecise, inexact.
– OPPOSITES restricted, unusual, detailed.

generally *adverb* **1 normally**, in general, as a rule, by and large, mainly, mostly, for the most part, predominantly, on the whole, usually. **2 widely**, commonly, extensively, universally, popularly.

generate *verb* **create**, make, produce, engender, spawn, precipitate, prompt, provoke, trigger, spark off, stir up, induce.

generation *noun* **1 age**, age group, peer group. **2 crop**, batch, wave, range.

generosity *noun* **liberality**, lavishness, magnanimity, bounty, munificence, open-handedness, largesse, unselfishness, altruism, charity.
– OPPOSITES meanness, selfishness.

generous *adjective* **1 liberal**, lavish, magnanimous, giving, open-handed, bountiful, unselfish, ungrudging, free, unstinting, munificent; *literary* bounteous. **2 plentiful**, copious, ample, liberal, large, abundant, rich.
– OPPOSITES mean, selfish, meagre.

genesis *noun* **origin**, source, root, beginning, start.

genial *adjective* **friendly**, affable, cordial, amiable, warm, easy-going, approachable, sympathetic, good-natured, good-humoured, cheerful, hospitable, companionable, sociable, convivial, outgoing, gregarious; *informal* chummy, pally; *Brit. informal* matey.
– OPPOSITES unfriendly.

genius *noun* **1 brilliance**, intelligence, intellect, ability, cleverness, brains. **2 talent**, gift, flair, aptitude, facility, knack, ability, expertise, capacity, faculty. **3 brilliant person**, mastermind, Einstein, intellectual, brain, prodigy; *informal* egghead, bright spark; *Brit. informal* brainbox, clever clogs; *N. Amer. informal* brainiac.
● *adjective (informal)* **ingenious**, clever, canny, cunning, crafty, artful, slick, neat.

genre *noun* **category**, class, classification, group, set, type, sort, kind, variety.

genteel *adjective* **refined**, respectable, well mannered, courteous, polite, proper, correct, seemly, well bred, ladylike, gentlemanly, dignified, gracious.
– OPPOSITES uncouth.

gentle *adjective* **1 kind**, tender, sympathetic, considerate, understanding, compassionate, humane, mild, placid, serene. **2 light**, soft, quiet, low. **3 gradual**, slight, easy, slow, imperceptible.
– OPPOSITES brutal, strong, loud, steep.

genuine *adjective* **1 authentic**, real, actual, original, bona fide, true; *informal* pukka, the real McCoy, the real thing, kosher; *Austral./NZ informal* dinkum. **2 sincere**, honest, truthful, straightforward, direct, frank, candid, open, natural; *informal* straight, upfront.
- OPPOSITES bogus, insincere.

germ *noun* **1 microbe**, microorganism, bacillus, bacterium, virus; *informal* bug. **2** *the germ of an idea* **start**, beginnings, seed, embryo, bud, root, origin, source.

g

gesture *noun* **1 signal**, sign, motion, indication, gesticulation. **2 action**, act, deed, move.
● *verb* **signal**, motion, gesticulate, wave, indicate, give a sign.

get *verb* **1 obtain**, acquire, come by, receive, gain, earn, win, be given; *informal* get hold of, score. **2 become**, grow, turn, go. **3 fetch**, collect, go/come for, call for, pick up, bring, deliver, convey. **4 capture**, catch, arrest, apprehend, seize; *informal* collar, grab, pick up; *Brit. informal* nick. **5 contract**, develop, go down with, catch, fall ill with. **6 hear**, catch, make out, follow, take in. **7 understand**, comprehend, grasp, see, fathom, follow. **8 arrive**, reach, make it, turn up, appear, present yourself, come along; *informal* show up. **9 persuade**, induce, prevail on, influence, talk into. **10 prepare**, get ready, cook, make; *informal* fix, rustle up; *Brit. informal* knock up.
- OPPOSITES give.
□ **get across** communicate, get over, impart, convey, transmit, make clear, express. **get along** be friendly, be compatible, get on, agree, see eye to eye; *informal* hit it off. **get away** escape, run away/off, break free, bolt, flee, make off, take off, decamp; *informal* skedaddle, scarper; *Brit. informal* do a bunk, do a runner. **get by** manage, cope, survive, exist, subsist, muddle through/along, scrape by, make ends meet, make do; *informal* make out. **get out of** evade, dodge, shirk, avoid, escape, sidestep; *informal* wriggle out of. **get round** cajole, persuade, wheedle, coax, prevail on, win over, bring round, sway, inveigle; *informal* sweet-talk, butter up. **get up** get out of bed, rise, stir, rouse yourself; *informal* surface.

ghastly *adjective* **1 terrible**, frightful, horrible, grim, awful, horrifying, shocking, appalling, gruesome, horrendous, monstrous. **2** *(informal)* **unpleasant**, objectionable, disagreeable, distasteful, awful, terrible, dreadful, frightful, detestable, vile; *informal* horrible, horrid.
- OPPOSITES pleasant.

ghost *noun* **spectre**, phantom, wraith, spirit, presence, apparition; *informal* spook.

WORD LINKS
spectral relating to a ghost

ghostly *adjective* **supernatural**, unearthly, spectral, phantom, unnatural, eerie, weird, uncanny; *informal* spooky.

giant *noun* **colossus**, mammoth, monster, leviathan, ogre.
- OPPOSITES dwarf.
● *adjective* **huge**, colossal, massive, enormous, gigantic, mammoth, vast, immense, monumental, mountainous, titanic, towering, gargantuan; *informal* mega, monster, whopping; *Brit. informal* ginormous.
- OPPOSITES miniature.

giddy *adjective* **1 dizzy**, light-headed, faint, unsteady, wobbly, reeling; *informal* woozy. **2 flighty**, silly, frivolous, skittish, irresponsible, scatty; *informal* dizzy.

gift *noun* **1 present**, handout, donation, offering, bonus, award, endowment; *informal* prezzie. **2 talent**, flair, aptitude, facility, knack, bent, ability, skill, capacity, faculty.

gifted *adjective* **talented**, skilled, accomplished, expert, able, proficient, intelligent, clever, bright, brilliant, precocious; *informal* crack, ace, genius.
- OPPOSITES inept.

gigantic *adjective* **huge**, enormous, vast, giant, massive, colossal, mammoth, immense, monumental, mountainous, cosmic, gargantuan; *informal* mega, monster, whopping, humongous; *Brit. informal* ginormous.
– OPPOSITES tiny.

giggle *verb* & *noun* **titter**, snigger, chuckle, chortle, laugh.

girl *noun* **young woman**, young lady, miss; *Scottish & N. English* lass, lassie; *Irish* colleen; *informal* chick; *Brit. informal* bird; *N. Amer. informal* gal, broad, dame, babe; *Austral./NZ informal* sheila.

girlfriend *noun* **sweetheart**, lover, partner, significant other, girl, woman; *informal* steady; *Brit. informal* bird; *N. Amer. informal* squeeze.

give *verb* **1 donate**, contribute, present with, award, grant, bestow, hand (over), bequeath, leave, make over. **2 convey**, pass on, impart, communicate, transmit, send, deliver, relay. **3 sacrifice**, give up, relinquish, devote, dedicate. **4 organize**, arrange, lay on, throw, host, hold, have. **5 perform**, execute, make, do. **6 utter**, let out, emit, produce, make.
– OPPOSITES receive, take.
▫ **give away** betray, inform on; *informal* split on, rat on; *Brit. informal* grass on, shop; *N. Amer. informal* finger; *Austral./NZ informal* dob in. **give in/up** capitulate, concede defeat, admit defeat, give up, surrender, yield, submit. **give off** emit, produce, send out, throw out, discharge, release. **give up** stop, cease, discontinue, desist from, abstain from, cut out, renounce, forgo; *informal* quit; *Brit. informal* jack in.

glad *adjective* **1 pleased**, happy, gratified, delighted, thrilled, overjoyed; *informal* over the moon; *Brit. informal* chuffed; *N. English informal* made up. **2** *I'd be glad to help* **willing**, eager, happy, pleased, delighted, ready, prepared.
– OPPOSITES dismayed, reluctant.

gladly *adverb* **with pleasure**, happily, cheerfully, willingly, readily, eagerly, freely, ungrudgingly.

glamorous *adjective* **1 beautiful**, elegant, chic, stylish, fashionable. **2 exciting**, glittering, glossy, colourful, exotic; *informal* glitzy, jet-setting.
– OPPOSITES dowdy, dull.

glamour *noun* **1** *she had undeniable glamour* **beauty**, allure, elegance, chic, style, charisma, charm, magnetism. **2** *the glamour of TV* **allure**, attraction, fascination, charm, magic, romance, excitement, thrill; *informal* glitz, glam.

glance *verb* **1 look briefly**, look quickly, peek, peep, glimpse, catch a glimpse. **2** *I glanced through the report* **read quickly**, scan, skim, leaf, flick, flip, thumb, browse.

glare *verb* **scowl**, glower, look daggers, frown, lour; *informal* give someone a dirty look.
● *noun* **1 scowl**, glower, angry stare, frown, black look; *informal* dirty look. **2 blaze**, dazzle, shine, beam, brilliance.

glaring *adjective* **1 dazzling**, blinding, blazing, strong, harsh. **2 obvious**, conspicuous, unmistakable, inescapable, unmissable, striking, flagrant, blatant.

glaze *verb* **cover**, coat, varnish, lacquer, polish.
● *noun* **coating**, topping, varnish, lacquer, polish.

gleam *verb* **shine**, glint, glitter, shimmer, glimmer, sparkle, twinkle, flicker, wink, glisten, flash.
● *noun* **flash**, glimmer, glint, shimmer, twinkle, sparkle, flicker, beam, ray, shaft.

glide *verb* **1** *a gondola glided past* **slide**, slip, sail, float, drift, flow. **2** *seagulls gliding over the waves* **soar**, wheel, plane, fly.

glimpse *noun* **glance**, brief/quick look, sight, sighting, peek, peep.
● *verb* **catch sight of**, sight, spot, notice, discern, spy, pick out, make out.

glitter *verb* **sparkle**, twinkle, glint, shimmer, glimmer, wink, flash, shine.
● *noun* **sparkle**, twinkle, glint, shimmer, glimmer, flicker, flash.

global *adjective* **1 worldwide**, international, world, intercontinental, universal. **2 comprehensive**, overall, general, all-inclusive, all-encompassing, universal, broad.

gloom *noun* **1 darkness**, dark, murk, shadows, shade. **2 despondency**, depression, dejection, melancholy, unhappiness, sadness, misery, woe, despair.
- OPPOSITES light, happiness.

gloomy *adjective* **1 dark**, shadowy, murky, sunless, dim, dingy. **2 despondent**, depressed, downcast, downhearted, dejected, dispirited, disheartened, demoralized, crestfallen, glum, melancholy; *informal* down in the mouth, down in the dumps. **3 pessimistic**, depressing, downbeat, disheartening, disappointing, unfavourable, bleak, black.
- OPPOSITES bright, cheerful.

glorious *adjective* **wonderful**, marvellous, magnificent, superb, sublime, spectacular, lovely, fine, delightful; *informal* stunning, fantastic, terrific, tremendous, sensational, heavenly, divine, gorgeous, fabulous, awesome.
- OPPOSITES undistinguished.

glory *noun* **1 honour**, distinction, prestige, fame, renown, kudos, eminence, acclaim, celebrity, praise, recognition. **2 magnificence**, splendour, grandeur, majesty, greatness, nobility, opulence, beauty, elegance.
- OPPOSITES shame.
● *verb we gloried in our independence* **delight**, triumph, revel, rejoice, exult, relish, savour, be proud of; *informal* get a kick out of.

gloss *noun* **shine**, sheen, lustre, gleam, patina, polish, brilliance, shimmer.
□ **gloss over** conceal, cover up, hide, disguise, mask, veil, play down, minimize, understate.

glossy *adjective* **shiny**, gleaming, lustrous, brilliant, glistening, glassy, polished, lacquered, glazed.
- OPPOSITES dull.

glow *verb* **1 shine**, gleam, glimmer, flicker, flare. **2 smoulder**, burn.
● *noun* **radiance**, light, gleam, glimmer.

glowing *adjective* **1 bright**, radiant, incandescent, luminous, smouldering; *literary* lambent. **2 rosy**, pink, red, ruddy, flushed, blushing, burning. **3 vivid**, vibrant, bright, brilliant, rich, intense, radiant. **4 complimentary**, favourable, enthusiastic, admiring, rapturous, fulsome; *informal* rave.

glue *noun* **adhesive**, gum, paste, cement; *N. Amer.* mucilage; *N. Amer. informal* stickum.
● *verb* **stick**, gum, paste, fix, seal, cement.

glum *adjective* **gloomy**, downcast, dejected, despondent, crestfallen, disheartened, depressed, doleful, miserable, woebegone; *informal* fed up, down in the dumps, down in the mouth.
- OPPOSITES cheerful.

go *verb* **1** *he's gone into town* **travel**, move, proceed, make your way, journey, advance, progress, pass. **2** *the road goes to London* **lead**, stretch, reach, extend. **3 leave**, depart, take yourself off, go away, withdraw, absent yourself, exit, set off, start out, get under way, be on your way; *Brit.* make a move; *informal* make tracks. **4 be used up**, be spent, be exhausted, be consumed. **5 become**, get, turn, grow. **6 turn out**, work out, develop, progress, result, end (up); *informal* pan out. **7 match**, harmonize, blend, be complementary, coordinate, be compatible. **8 function**, work, run, operate.
● *noun (informal)* **1** *here, have a go* **try**, attempt, effort, bid; *informal* shot, stab, crack. **2 turn**, opportunity, chance, stint, spell, time.
□ **go down 1** sink, founder. **2** decrease, fall, drop, decline, plummet, plunge, slump. **go in for** take part in, participate in, engage in, get involved in, join in, enter into, undertake, practise, pursue, espouse, adopt, embrace. **go into** investigate, examine, enquire into, look into, research, probe,

explore, delve into, consider, review, analyse. **go off 1** explode, detonate, blow up. **2** *(Brit.)* go bad, go stale, go sour, turn, spoil, go rancid. **go on 1** last, continue, carry on, run on, proceed, endure, persist, take. **2** talk at length, ramble, rattle on, chatter, prattle; *Brit. informal* witter, rabbit. **3** happen, take place, occur, transpire; *N. Amer. informal* go down. **go out 1** be turned off, be extinguished, stop burning. **2** see, take out, be someone's boyfriend/girlfriend, be in a relationship with; *informal* date, go with. **go through 1** undergo, experience, face, suffer, live through, endure. **2** search, look, hunt, rummage, rifle. **3** examine, study, scrutinize, inspect, look over, scan, check.

goal *noun* **objective**, aim, end, target, intention, plan, purpose, ambition, aspiration.

gobble *verb* **guzzle**, bolt, gulp, devour, wolf; *informal* tuck into, put away, demolish; *Brit. informal* scoff; *N. Amer. informal* scarf (down/up).

god *noun* **deity**, goddess, divine being, divinity, immortal.

WORD LINKS
divine relating to God or a god
theology study of God

golden *adjective* **blonde**, yellow, fair, flaxen.
– OPPOSITES dark.

gone *adjective* **1 away**, absent, off, out, missing. **2 past**, over (and done with), no more, done, finished, ended, forgotten. **3 used up**, consumed, finished, spent, depleted.

good *adjective* **1 fine**, superior, excellent, superb, outstanding, magnificent, exceptional, marvellous, wonderful, first-rate, first-class, quality; *informal* great, ace, terrific, fantastic, fabulous, class, awesome, wicked; *Brit. informal* brilliant. **2 virtuous**, righteous, upright, upstanding, moral, ethical, principled, law-abiding, blameless, honourable, decent, respectable, trustworthy; *informal* squeaky clean. **3 well behaved**, obedient, dutiful, polite, courteous, respectful. **4 capable**, able, proficient, adept, adroit, accomplished, skilful, talented, masterly, expert; *informal* mean, wicked, nifty; *N. Amer. informal* crackerjack. **5 close**, intimate, dear, bosom, special, best, firm, loyal. **6 enjoyable**, pleasant, agreeable, pleasurable, delightful, lovely, amusing. **7** *it was good of you to come* **kind**, generous, charitable, gracious, noble, altruistic, unselfish. **8 convenient**, suitable, appropriate, fitting, fit, opportune, timely, favourable. **9** *milk is good for you* **wholesome**, healthy, nourishing, nutritious, beneficial. **10 tasty**, appetizing, flavoursome, palatable, succulent; *informal* scrumptious, scrummy, yummy; *Brit. informal* moreish. **11 valid**, genuine, authentic, legitimate, sound, bona fide, convincing, compelling. **12 fine**, fair, dry, bright, clear, sunny, cloudless, calm, warm, mild.
– OPPOSITES bad, wicked, naughty.
● *noun* **1 virtue**, righteousness, goodness, morality, integrity, honesty, truth, honour. **2** *it's for your own good* **benefit**, advantage, profit, gain, interest, welfare, well-being.
– OPPOSITES wickedness, disadvantage.
□ **for good** forever, permanently, for always, (for) evermore, for ever and ever; *N. Amer.* forevermore; *informal* for keeps.

goodbye *exclam.* **farewell**, adieu, au revoir, ciao, adios; *informal* bye, bye-bye, so long, see you (later); *Brit. informal* cheerio, cheers, ta-ta.

good-looking *adjective* **attractive**, beautiful, pretty, handsome, lovely, stunning, striking, arresting, gorgeous, prepossessing, fetching; *Scottish & N. English* bonny; *informal* tasty, easy on the eye; *Brit. informal* fit; *N. Amer. informal* cute, foxy; *old use* comely.
– OPPOSITES ugly.

goodness *noun* **1 virtue**, good, righteousness, morality, integrity, rectitude, honesty, honour, decency, respectability, nobility, worth, merit. **2 kindness**, humanity, benevolence, tenderness, warmth, affection, love, goodwill, sympathy, compassion, care, concern, understanding, generosity, charity.

goods *plural noun* **merchandise**, wares, stock, commodities, produce, products, articles.

goodwill *noun* **kindness**, compassion, goodness, benevolence, consideration, charity, decency, neighbourliness.
– OPPOSITES hostility.

gorge *noun* **ravine**, canyon, gully, defile, couloir, chasm, gulf; *S. English* chine; *N. English* gill; *N. Amer.* gulch, coulee.
□ **gorge yourself** stuff yourself, guzzle, overindulge; *informal* pig yourself, pig out, stuff your face.

gorgeous *adjective* **1 good-looking**, attractive, beautiful, pretty, handsome, lovely, stunning; *Scottish & N. English* bonny; *informal* fanciable, tasty, hot; *Brit. informal* fit; *N. Amer. informal* cute, foxy; *old use* comely. **2 spectacular**, splendid, superb, wonderful, grand, impressive, awe-inspiring, awesome, stunning, breathtaking; *informal* sensational, fabulous, fantastic. **3 resplendent**, magnificent, sumptuous, luxurious, elegant, dazzling, brilliant.
– OPPOSITES ugly, drab.

gossip *noun* **1 news**, rumours, scandal, hearsay, tittle-tattle; *informal* dirt, buzz; *N. Amer. informal* scuttlebutt. **2 chat**, talk, conversation, chatter, heart-to-heart, tête-à-tête; *informal* jaw, gas; *Brit. informal* natter, chinwag; *N. Amer. informal* gabfest. **3 gossipmonger**, busybody, scandalmonger, rumourmonger, muckraker.
● *verb* **1 talk**, whisper, tell tales, spread rumours; *informal* dish the dirt. **2** *people sat around gossiping* **chat**, talk, converse; *informal* gas, chew the fat, chew the rag, jaw; *Brit. informal* natter, chinwag; *N. Amer. informal* shoot the breeze.

gourmet *noun* **gastronome**, epicure, epicurean, connoisseur; *informal* foodie.

govern *verb* **1 rule**, preside over, control, be in charge of, command, run, head, manage, oversee, supervise. **2 determine**, decide, control, constrain, regulate, direct, rule, dictate, shape, affect.

government *noun* **administration**, executive, regime, authority, council, powers that be, cabinet, ministry.

governor *noun* **leader**, ruler, chief, head, administrator, principal, director, chairman, chairwoman, chair, superintendent, commissioner, controller; *informal* boss.

gown *noun* **dress**, frock, robe, habit, costume.

grab *verb* **seize**, grasp, snatch, take hold of, grip, clasp, clutch, catch.

grace *noun* **1 elegance**, poise, finesse, polish, fluency, smoothness, suppleness. **2** *he had the grace to apologize* **courtesy**, decency, (good) manners, politeness, respect. **3** *he fell from grace* **favour**, approval, approbation, acceptance, esteem, regard, respect.
– OPPOSITES awkwardness.
● *verb* **adorn**, embellish, decorate, ornament, enhance.

graceful *adjective* **elegant**, fluid, fluent, easy, polished, supple.

gracious *adjective* **courteous**, polite, civil, well mannered, tactful, diplomatic, kind, considerate, thoughtful, obliging, accommodating, hospitable.

grade *noun* **1** *hotels within the same grade* **category**, class, classification, ranking, quality, grouping, group, bracket. **2** *his job is of the lowest grade* **rank**, level, standing, position, class, status, order, echelon. **3 mark**, score, assessment, evaluation, appraisal. **4** *(N. Amer.)* **year**, form, class.
● *verb* **classify**, class, categorize, bracket, sort, group, arrange, pigeonhole, rank, evaluate, rate, value.

gradient *noun* **slope**, incline, hill, rise, ramp, bank; *N. Amer.* grade.

gradual *adjective* **1 slow**, steady, measured, unhurried, cautious, piecemeal,

step-by-step, bit-by-bit, progressive, continuous. **2 gentle**, moderate, slight, easy.
- OPPOSITES abrupt, steep.

gradually *adverb* **slowly**, steadily, slowly but surely, cautiously, gently, gingerly, piecemeal, bit by bit, by degrees, progressively, systematically.

graft *noun* **transplant**, implant.
● *verb* **1 splice**, join, insert, fix. **2 transplant**, implant.

grain *noun* **1 kernel**, seed. **2 granule**, particle, speck, bit, scrap, crumb, fragment, morsel. **3 trace**, hint, tinge, suggestion, shadow, soupçon, ounce, iota, jot, scrap, shred; *informal* smidgen. **4 texture**, weave, pattern, nap.

grand *adjective* **1 magnificent**, imposing, impressive, awe-inspiring, splendid, resplendent, majestic, monumental, palatial, stately; *Brit.* upmarket; *N. Amer.* upscale; *informal* fancy, posh; *Brit. informal* swish. **2 ambitious**, bold, epic, big, extravagant. **3 august**, distinguished, illustrious, eminent, venerable, dignified, proud. **4** *(informal)* **excellent**, marvellous, splendid, first-class, first-rate, wonderful, outstanding; *informal* superb, terrific, great, super; *Brit. informal* brilliant.
- OPPOSITES humble, poor.

grandeur *noun* **splendour**, magnificence, glory, resplendence, majesty, greatness, stateliness, pomp, ceremony.

grant *verb* **1** *he granted them leave of absence* **allow**, permit, agree to, accord, afford, vouchsafe. **2** *he granted them £20,000* **give**, award, bestow on, confer on, present with, endow with. **3 admit**, accept, concede, allow, appreciate, recognize, acknowledge, confess.
- OPPOSITES refuse, deny.
● *noun* **award**, bursary, endowment, scholarship, allowance, subsidy, contribution, handout, donation, gift.

graphic *adjective* **1 visual**, pictorial, illustrative, diagrammatic. **2 vivid**, explicit, detailed, realistic, descriptive, powerful, colourful, lurid, shocking.
- OPPOSITES vague.

grapple *verb* **1 wrestle**, struggle, tussle, scuffle, battle. **2 deal**, cope, get to grips, tackle, confront, face.

grasp *verb* **1 grip**, clutch, clasp, clench, squeeze, catch, seize, grab, snatch. **2 understand**, comprehend, take in, see, apprehend, assimilate, absorb; *informal* get, take on board; *Brit. informal* twig.
● *noun* **1 grip**, hold, squeeze. **2 reach**, scope, power, range, sights. **3 understanding**, comprehension, awareness, grip, knowledge, mastery, command.

grasping *adjective* **greedy**, acquisitive, avaricious, rapacious, mercenary, materialistic; *informal* tight-fisted, tight, money-grubbing.

grate *verb* **1 shred**, pulverize, mince, grind, crush, crumble. **2 grind**, rub, rasp, scrape, jar, creak.

grateful *adjective* **thankful**, appreciative, indebted, obliged, in someone's debt, beholden.

gratitude *noun* **thanks**, gratefulness, thankfulness, appreciation, indebtedness, recognition, acknowledgement.

grave[1] *noun* **tomb**, burial place, last resting place, vault, mausoleum, sepulchre.

grave[2] *adjective* **1 serious**, important, weighty, profound, significant, momentous, critical, urgent, pressing, dire, terrible, dreadful. **2 solemn**, serious, sober, unsmiling, grim, sombre, dour.
- OPPOSITES trivial, light-hearted.

graveyard *noun* **cemetery**, churchyard, burial ground, necropolis, garden of remembrance; *Scottish* kirkyard.

gravity *noun* **1 seriousness**, importance, significance, weight, consequence, magnitude, acuteness, urgency, dreadfulness. **2 solemnity**, seriousness, sobriety, severity, grimness, sombreness, dourness.

graze[1] *verb* **feed**, eat, crop, nibble, browse.

graze[2] *verb* **1 scrape**, skin, scratch, chafe, scuff, rasp. **2 touch**, brush, shave, skim, kiss, scrape, clip, glance off.
● *noun* **scratch**, scrape, abrasion.

grease *noun* **oil**, fat, lubricant.

greasy *adjective* **oily**, fatty, buttery, oleaginous, slippery, slick, slimy, slithery; *informal* slippy.

great *adjective* **1 considerable**, substantial, significant, serious, exceptional, extraordinary. **2 large**, big, extensive, expansive, broad, wide, vast, immense, huge, enormous, massive, cosmic; *informal* humongous, whopping; *Brit. informal* ginormous. **3 prominent**, eminent, distinguished, illustrious, celebrated, acclaimed, admired, esteemed, renowned, notable, famous, well known, leading, top, major. **4 magnificent**, imposing, impressive, awe-inspiring, grand, splendid, majestic. **5 expert**, skilful, skilled, adept, accomplished, talented, fine, masterly, master, brilliant, virtuoso, marvellous, outstanding, first-class, superb; *informal* crack, class. **6 keen**, eager, enthusiastic, devoted, ardent, fanatical, passionate, dedicated, committed. **7 enjoyable**, delightful, lovely, excellent, marvellous, wonderful, fine, splendid; *informal* terrific, fantastic, fabulous, super, cool; *Brit. informal* brilliant.
– OPPOSITES little, small, minor, modest.

greatly *adverb* **very much**, extremely, considerably, substantially, significantly, markedly, seriously, materially, enormously, vastly, immensely, tremendously, mightily.

greatness *noun* **1 eminence**, distinction, celebrity, fame, prominence, renown, importance. **2 brilliance**, genius, prowess, talent, expertise, mastery, artistry, skill, proficiency, flair.

greed *noun* **1 avarice**, acquisitiveness, covetousness, materialism, mercenariness; *informal* money-grubbing. **2 gluttony**, hunger, voracity, self-indulgence; *informal* piggishness. **3 desire**, appetite, hunger, thirst, craving, longing, yearning, hankering; *informal* itch.
– OPPOSITES generosity, temperance, indifference.

greedy *adjective* **1 gluttonous**, ravenous, voracious; *informal* piggish, piggy. **2 avaricious**, acquisitive, covetous, grasping, materialistic, mercenary; *informal* money-grubbing.

green *adjective* **1** olive green, pea green, emerald green, lime green, avocado, pistachio, bottle green, Lincoln green, jade. **2 verdant**, grassy, leafy. **3 environmental**, ecological, conservationist, eco-, eco-friendly. **4 inexperienced**, callow, raw, unseasoned, untried, naive, innocent, unworldly; *informal* wet behind the ears.

greet *verb* **1 say hello to**, address, salute, hail, welcome, meet, receive. **2** *the decision was greeted with outrage* **receive**, respond to, react to, take.

greeting *noun* **1 hello**, salutation, welcome, reception. **2 best wishes**, good wishes, congratulations, compliments, regards, respects.
– OPPOSITES farewell.

grey *adjective* **1** silvery, gunmetal, slate, charcoal, smoky. **2 cloudy**, overcast, dull, dark, sunless, murky, gloomy, cheerless. **3 pale**, wan, ashen, pasty, pallid, colourless, waxen. **4 characterless**, colourless, nondescript, flat, bland, dull, boring, tedious, monotonous. **5** *a grey area* **ambiguous**, doubtful, unclear, uncertain, indefinite, debatable.

grief *noun* **sorrow**, misery, sadness, anguish, pain, distress, heartache, heartbreak, agony, woe, desolation.
– OPPOSITES joy.

grievance *noun* **complaint**, objection, grumble, grouse, ill feeling, bad feeling, resentment; *informal* gripe.

grieve *verb* **1 mourn**, sorrow, cry, sob, weep. **2 sadden**, upset, distress, pain, hurt, wound, break someone's heart.
– OPPOSITES rejoice.

grim *adjective* **1 stern**, forbidding, uninviting, unsmiling, dour, formidable. **2 dreadful**, ghastly, horrible, terrible, awful, appalling, frightful, shocking, grisly, gruesome, depressing, distressing, upsetting. **3 bleak**, dismal, dingy, wretched, miserable, depressing, cheerless, joyless, gloomy, uninviting.
- OPPOSITES amiable, pleasant.

grin *verb* & *noun* **smile**, beam, smirk.

grind *verb* **1 crush**, pound, pulverize, mill, crumble. **2 rub**, grate, scrape. **3 sharpen**, whet, hone, put an edge on, mill, machine, polish, smooth.
● *noun* **drudgery**, toil, labour, donkey work, exertion, chores; *informal* slog.

grip *verb* **1 grasp**, clutch, clasp, take hold of, clench, cling to, grab, seize, squeeze. **2 engross**, enthral, absorb, rivet, spellbind, fascinate, mesmerize.
● *noun* **1 grasp**, hold. **2 traction**, purchase, friction, adhesion. **3 control**, power, hold, stranglehold, clutches, influence.

gripping *adjective* **engrossing**, enthralling, absorbing, riveting, captivating, spellbinding, fascinating, compelling, thrilling, exciting, action-packed, dramatic.
- OPPOSITES boring.

groan *verb* **1 moan**, cry. **2 complain**, grumble, moan, mutter; *informal* grouse, bellyache, bitch, whinge. **3 creak**, grate, rasp.
● *noun* **1 moan**, cry. **2 complaint**, grumble, grievance, moan, muttering; *informal* grouse, gripe, whinge. **3 creaking**, creak, grating, grinding.

groom *verb* **1 curry**, brush, clean, rub down. **2 brush**, comb, arrange, do; *informal* fix. **3 prepare**, prime, condition, coach, train, drill, teach, school.

groove *noun* **furrow**, channel, trench, trough, rut, gutter, canal, hollow, indentation.

grope *verb* **fumble**, scrabble, fish, ferret, rummage, feel, search, hunt.

gross *adjective* **1** *(informal)* **disgusting**, repulsive, revolting, foul, nasty, obnoxious, sickening, nauseating, stomach-churning. **2 thorough**, complete, utter, out and out, shameful, serious, unacceptable, flagrant, blatant, obvious, barefaced, shameless, brazen. **3 total**, full, overall, combined, before deductions, before tax.
- OPPOSITES pleasant, net.
● *verb* **earn**, make, bring in, take, get, receive; *informal* rake in.

grotesque *adjective* **1 misshapen**, deformed, distorted, twisted, monstrous, hideous, freakish, unnatural, abnormal, strange; *informal* weird. **2 outrageous**, monstrous, shocking, appalling, preposterous, ridiculous, ludicrous, unbelievable, incredible.

ground *noun* **1 floor**, earth, terra firma; *informal* deck. **2 earth**, soil, turf, land, terrain. **3 stadium**, pitch, field, arena, track; *Brit. informal* park. **4** *the mansion's grounds* **estate**, gardens, park, land, property, surroundings, territory. **5** *grounds for dismissal* **reason**, cause, basis, foundation, justification, rationale, argument, occasion, excuse, pretext.
● *verb* **1 base**, found, establish, root, build, form. **2** *she was well grounded in the classics* **teach**, instruct, coach, tutor, educate, school, train, drill.

group *noun* **1 category**, class, classification, grouping, cluster, set, batch, type, sort, kind, variety, family. **2 crowd**, party, body, band, company, gathering, conqreqation, assembly, collection, cluster, clump, knot, flock, pack, troop, gang; *informal* bunch. **3 band**, ensemble, act; *informal* line-up, combo, outfit.
● *verb* **1 categorize**, classify, class, catalogue, sort, bracket, pigeonhole. **2 assemble**, collect, organize, place, arrange, range, line up, lay out.

grovel *verb* **1 prostrate yourself**, lie, kneel, cringe. **2 be obsequious**, fawn on, kowtow, bow and scrape, toady, dance attendance on, ingratiate yourself with; *informal* crawl, creep, suck up to, lick someone's boots.

grow *verb* **1 enlarge**, get bigger, get larger, get taller, expand, increase in size, extend, spread, swell, multiply, snowball, mushroom, balloon, build up, mount up, pile up. **2 sprout**, germinate, spring up, develop, bud, bloom, flourish, thrive, run riot. **3 cultivate**, produce, propagate, raise, rear, farm. **4 become**, get, turn, begin to be.
- OPPOSITES shrink, decline.

grown-up *adjective* **adult**, mature, of age, fully grown, independent.
● *noun* **adult**, woman, man, grown man/woman.
- OPPOSITES child.

growth *noun* **1 enlargement**, increase in size, expansion, extension, swelling, multiplication, mushrooming, snowballing, rise, escalation, build-up, development. **2 tumour**, malignancy, cancer, lump, swelling.

grubby *adjective* **dirty**, grimy, filthy, mucky, unwashed, stained, soiled; *informal* cruddy, yucky; *Brit. informal* manky.
- OPPOSITES clean.

grudge *noun* **grievance**, resentment, bitterness, rancour, ill will, animosity, antipathy, antagonism; *informal* a chip on your shoulder.

gruelling *adjective* **exhausting**, tiring, taxing, draining, demanding, exacting, difficult, arduous, strenuous, back-breaking, punishing, crippling; *informal* murderous; *Brit. informal* knackering.

gruesome *adjective* **grisly**, ghastly, frightful, horrid, horrifying, hideous, horrible, grim, awful, dreadful, terrible, horrific; *informal* sick, sick-making, gross.
- OPPOSITES pleasant.

grumble *verb* **complain**, grouse, whine, mutter, carp, make a fuss; *informal* moan, bellyache, bitch, whinge; *N. English informal* mither.
● *noun* **complaint**, grouse, grievance, protest; *informal* grouch, moan, whinge, beef, gripe.

grumpy *adjective* **bad-tempered**, crabby, tetchy, touchy, irascible, cantankerous, curmudgeonly, surly, fractious; *informal* grouchy; *Brit. informal* ratty; *N. Amer. informal* cranky, ornery.
- OPPOSITES good-humoured.

guarantee *noun* **1 warranty**. **2 promise**, assurance, word (of honour), pledge, vow, oath, commitment. **3 collateral**, security, surety, bond.
● *verb* **1 promise**, swear, pledge, vow, give your word, give an assurance, give an undertaking. **2 underwrite**, stand surety.

guard *verb* **protect**, defend, shield, secure, cover, mind, stand guard over, watch, keep an eye on.
● *noun* **1 sentry**, sentinel, nightwatchman, protector, defender, guardian, lookout, watch. **2 warder**, warden, keeper, jailer; *informal* screw. **3 cover**, shield, screen, fender, bumper, buffer.

guarded *adjective* **cautious**, careful, circumspect, wary, chary, reluctant, non-committal; *informal* cagey.

guardian *noun* **protector**, defender, preserver, custodian, warden, guard, keeper, curator, caretaker, steward, trustee.

WORD LINKS
tutelary relating to a guardian

guerrilla *noun* **rebel**, irregular, partisan, freedom fighter, revolutionary, terrorist.

guess *verb* **1 estimate**, reckon, judge, speculate, conjecture, hypothesize, surmise. **2** *(informal)* **suppose**, think, imagine, expect, suspect, dare say; *informal* reckon.
● *noun* **hypothesis**, theory, conjecture, surmise, estimate, belief, opinion, supposition, speculation, suspicion, impression, feeling.

guest *noun* **1 visitor**, caller, company. **2 client**, customer, resident, boarder, lodger, patron, diner, holidaymaker, tourist.
- OPPOSITES host.

guidance *noun* **1 advice**, counsel, instruction, suggestions, tips, hints, pointers, guidelines. **2 direction**, control, leadership, management, supervision.

guide *noun* **1 escort**, attendant, courier, leader, usher. **2 outline**, template, example, exemplar, model, pattern, guideline, yardstick, precedent. **3 guidebook**, travel guide, vade mecum, companion, handbook, manual, directory, A to Z, instructions, directions; *informal* bible.
● *verb* **1 lead**, conduct, show, usher, shepherd, direct, steer, pilot, escort. **2 direct**, steer, manage, conduct, run, be in charge of, govern, preside over, supervise, oversee. **3 advise**, counsel, direct.

guild *noun* **association**, society, union, league, organization, company, fellowship, club, order, lodge.

guilt *noun* **1 culpability**, blameworthiness, responsibility. **2 remorse**, shame, regret, contrition, self-reproach, a guilty conscience.
- OPPOSITES innocence.

guilty *adjective* **1 culpable**, to blame, at fault, in the wrong, responsible. **2 ashamed**, guilt-ridden, conscience-stricken, remorseful, sorry, contrite, repentant, penitent, regretful, rueful, shamefaced.
- OPPOSITES innocent.

gulf *noun* **1 bay**, inlet, cove, bight, fjord, estuary, sound; *Scottish* firth. **2 gap**, divide, separation, difference, contrast.

gullible *adjective* **credulous**, naive, easily deceived, impressionable, unsuspecting, ingenuous, innocent, inexperienced, green; *informal* wet behind the ears.
- OPPOSITES suspicious.

gulp *verb* **1 swallow**, quaff, swill down; *informal* swig, down, knock back. **2 gobble**, guzzle, devour, bolt, wolf; *informal* shovel down; *Brit. informal* scoff. **3** *she gulped back her tears* **choke back**, fight/hold back, suppress, stifle, smother.
● *noun* **mouthful**, swallow, draught; *informal* swig.

gum *noun* **glue**, adhesive, paste, cement; *N. Amer.* mucilage; *N. Amer. informal* stickum.
● *verb* **stick**, glue, paste, cement, attach.

gun *noun* **firearm**, side arm, handgun, weapon; *informal* shooter; *N. Amer. informal* piece, shooting iron.

gunman *noun* **armed criminal**, assassin, sniper, terrorist, gunfighter; *informal* hit man, gunslinger; *N. Amer. informal* shootist.

guru *noun* **1 spiritual teacher**, tutor, sage, mentor, spiritual leader, master. **2 expert**, authority, pundit, leading light, master, specialist.
- OPPOSITES disciple.

gush *verb* **surge**, stream, spout, spurt, jet, rush, pour, spill, cascade, flood; *Brit. informal* sloosh.
● *noun* **surge**, stream, spout, spurt, jet, rush, outpouring, spill, outflow, cascade, flood, torrent.

gushing *adjective* **effusive**, overenthusiastic, extravagant, fulsome, lavish, unrestrained; *informal* over the top.

gust *noun* **flurry**, blast, puff, blow, rush, squall.

gut *noun* **1 stomach**, belly, abdomen, paunch, intestines, viscera; *informal* tummy, insides, innards. **2** *(informal) he has a lot of guts* **courage**, bravery, backbone, nerve, pluck, spirit, daring, grit, fearlessness, determination; *Brit. informal* bottle; *N. Amer. informal* moxie.
● *adjective (informal)* **instinctive**, intuitive, deep-seated, involuntary, spontaneous, unthinking, knee-jerk.
● *verb* **1 clean (out)**, disembowel, draw; *formal* eviscerate. **2 strip**, empty, devastate, lay waste, ravage, ruin, wreck.

WORD LINKS
visceral relating to the gut

gutter *noun* **drain**, trough, trench, ditch, sluice, sewer, channel, conduit, pipe.

guy *noun (informal)* **man**, fellow; *informal* lad; *Brit. informal* chap, bloke, geezer; *N. Amer. informal* dude, hombre.

guzzle *verb* **1 gobble**, bolt, wolf, devour; *informal* tuck into, shovel down, hoover up; *Brit. informal* scoff; *N. Amer. informal* snarf, scarf. **2 gulp down**, quaff, swill; *informal* knock back, swig, slug, neck.

gyrate *verb* **rotate**, revolve, wheel, turn, whirl, circle, pirouette, twirl, swirl, spin, swivel.

Hh

habit *noun* **1 custom**, practice, routine, way; *formal* wont. **2** *(informal)* **addiction**, dependence, craving, fixation.

habitual *adjective* **1 constant**, persistent, continual, continuous, perpetual, non-stop, endless, never-ending; *informal* eternal. **2 inveterate**, confirmed, compulsive, incorrigible, hardened, ingrained, chronic, regular. **3 customary**, accustomed, regular, usual, normal, characteristic; *literary* wonted.
– OPPOSITES occasional.

hack *verb* **cut**, chop, hew, lop, saw, slash.

hackneyed *adjective* **overused**, overdone, overworked, worn out, time-worn, stale, tired, threadbare, trite, banal, clichéd.
– OPPOSITES original.

haggard *adjective* **drawn**, tired, exhausted, drained, careworn, gaunt, pinched, hollow-cheeked, hollow-eyed.

haggle *verb* **barter**, bargain, negotiate, wrangle.

hail[1] *noun* **barrage**, volley, shower, stream, salvo.

hail[2] *verb* **1 call out to**, shout to, address, greet, salute, say hello to. **2 flag down**, wave down. **3 acclaim**, praise, applaud. **4** *he hails from Australia* **come**, be, be a native of.

hair *noun* **1 head of hair**, shock of hair, mane, mop, locks, tresses, curls. **2 hairstyle**, haircut; *informal* hairdo. **3 fur**, wool, coat, fleece, pelt, mane.

hairdresser *noun* **hairstylist**, coiffeur, coiffeuse, barber.

hairy *adjective* **1 shaggy**, bushy, long-haired, woolly, furry, fleecy. **2 bearded**, unshaven, stubbly, bristly; *formal* hirsute. **3** *(informal)* **risky**, dangerous, perilous, hazardous, tricky; *informal* dicey; *Brit. informal* dodgy.

half-hearted *adjective* **unenthusiastic**, cool, lukewarm, tepid, apathetic.
– OPPOSITES enthusiastic.

halfway *adjective* **midway**, middle, mid, central, centre, intermediate.
● *adverb* **midway**, in the middle, in the centre, part of the way.

hall *noun* **1 entrance hall**, hallway, entry, entrance, lobby, foyer, vestibule, atrium. **2 assembly room**, meeting room, chamber, auditorium, theatre, house.

hallucination *noun* **delusion**, illusion, figment of the imagination, mirage, chimera, fantasy.

halt *verb* **1** *halt at the barrier* **stop**, come to a halt, come to a stop, come to a standstill, pull up, draw up. **2** *a strike halted production* **stop**, bring to a stop, put a stop to, suspend, arrest, check, curb, stem, staunch, block, stall.
● *noun* **1 stop**, standstill. **2 stoppage**, break, pause, interval, interruption.
– OPPOSITES start.

halting *adjective* **hesitant**, faltering, hesitating, stumbling, stammering, stuttering, broken, imperfect.
– OPPOSITES fluent.

hammer *verb* **beat**, batter, bang, pummel, pound, knock, thump.

hamper *verb* **hinder**, obstruct, impede, inhibit, delay, slow down, hold up, interfere with, handicap, hamstring.
– OPPOSITES help.

hand *noun* **1 fist**, palm; *informal* paw, mitt. **2 handwriting**, writing, script. **3 worker**, employee, workman, labourer, operative, craftsman.
● *verb* **pass**, give, present, let someone have.

WORD LINKS
manual relating to the hands

handbook *noun* **manual**, instructions, ABC, A to Z, companion, guide, guidebook, vade mecum.

handcuff *verb* **manacle**, shackle, clap/put someone in irons; *informal* cuff.
● *noun* (**handcuffs**) **manacles**, shackles, irons; *informal* cuffs, bracelets.

handful *noun* **few**, small number, small amount, small quantity, sprinkling, smattering, one or two, some, not many.
- OPPOSITES lot.

handicap *noun* **1 disability**, infirmity, defect, impairment, affliction. **2 impediment**, hindrance, obstacle, barrier, constraint, disadvantage, stumbling block.
- OPPOSITES benefit, advantage.
● *verb* **hamper**, impede, hinder, impair, hamstring, restrict, constrain.
- OPPOSITES help.

handle *verb* **1 hold**, pick up, grasp, grip, lift, finger. **2 control**, drive, steer, operate, manoeuvre. **3 deal with**, manage, tackle, take care of, look after, take charge of, attend to, see to, sort out. **4 trade in**, deal in, buy, sell, supply, peddle, traffic in.
● *noun* **grip**, haft, hilt, stock, shaft.

handsome *adjective* **1 good-looking**, attractive, striking; *informal* hunky, dishy, tasty, fanciable; *Brit. informal* fit; *N. Amer. informal* cute. **2 substantial**, considerable, sizeable, princely, generous, lavish, ample, bumper; *informal* tidy, whopping; *Brit. informal* ginormous.
- OPPOSITES ugly.

handy *adjective* **1 useful**, convenient, practical, neat, easy to use, user-friendly, helpful, functional. **2 ready**, to hand, within reach, accessible, readily available, nearby, at the ready. **3 skilful**, skilled, dexterous, deft, adept, proficient.

hang *verb* **1** *lights hung from the trees* **be suspended**, dangle, swing, sway, hover, float. **2** *hang the picture at eye level* **suspend**, put up, pin up, display. **3 decorate**, adorn, drape, festoon, deck out. **4 send to the gallows**, execute, lynch; *informal* string up.

hang-up *noun* **neurosis**, phobia, preoccupation, fixation, obsession, inhibition, mental block; *informal* complex, thing, issue, bee in your bonnet.

hanker *verb* **yearn**, long, wish, hunger, thirst, lust, ache; *informal* itch.

haphazard *adjective* **random**, disorderly, indiscriminate, chaotic, hit-and-miss, aimless, chance; *informal* higgledy-piggledy.
- OPPOSITES methodical.

hapless *adjective* **unfortunate**, unlucky, unhappy, wretched, miserable.
- OPPOSITES lucky.

happen *verb* **1 occur**, take place, come about, arise, develop, result, transpire; *N. Amer. informal* go down; *literary* come to pass. **2** *I happened to be in London* **chance**, have the good/bad luck.

happening *noun* **occurrence**, event, incident, episode, affair.

happily *adverb* **1 cheerfully**, contentedly, cheerily, merrily, joyfully. **2 gladly**, willingly, readily, freely. **3 fortunately**, luckily, thankfully, mercifully, as luck would have it.

happiness *noun* **pleasure**, contentment, well-being, satisfaction, cheerfulness, good spirits, merriment, joy, joyfulness, delight, elation, jubilation.
- OPPOSITES sadness.

happy *adjective* **1 cheerful**, cheery, merry, joyful, jovial, jolly, carefree, in good spirits, in a good mood, pleased, contented, content, satisfied, gratified, delighted, sunny, radiant, elated, jubilant; *literary* blithe. **2 glad**, pleased, delighted, more than willing. **3 fortunate**, lucky, timely, convenient.
- OPPOSITES sad, unhappy, unfortunate.

harass *verb* **persecute**, intimidate, hound, pester, bother; *informal* hassle, bug; *N. Amer. informal* ride.

harassed *adjective* **stressed**, hard-pressed, careworn, worried, troubled; *informal* hassled.
- OPPOSITES carefree.

harassment *noun* **persecution**, intimidation, victimization, trouble, bother; *informal* hassle.

harbour *noun* **port**, dock, haven, marina, mooring, wharf, anchorage, waterfront.
● *verb* **1 shelter**, conceal, hide, shield, protect, give asylum to. **2 bear**, hold, nurse, foster.

hard *adjective* **1 firm**, solid, rigid, stiff, unbreakable, unyielding, compacted, compressed, tough, strong. **2 arduous**, strenuous, tiring, exhausting, back-breaking, gruelling, heavy, laborious, demanding, uphill; *Brit. informal* knackering. **3 industrious**, diligent, assiduous, conscientious, energetic, keen, enthusiastic, indefatigable. **4 difficult**, puzzling, complicated, complex, intricate, knotty, thorny, problematic. **5 harsh**, unpleasant, grim, austere, difficult, bad, bleak, tough. **6 forceful**, heavy, strong, sharp, violent, powerful.
– OPPOSITES soft, easy, gentle.
● *adverb* **1 forcefully**, roughly, heavily, sharply, violently. **2 diligently**, industriously, assiduously, conscientiously, energetically, doggedly; *informal* like mad, like crazy. **3 closely**, intently, critically, carefully, searchingly.

harden *verb* **1 solidify**, set, stiffen, thicken, cake, congeal. **2 toughen**, desensitize, inure, season, train, numb.
– OPPOSITES soften.

hardened *adjective* **inveterate**, seasoned, habitual, chronic, compulsive, confirmed, incorrigible.

hardly *adverb* **scarcely**, barely, only just, just.

hardship *noun* **difficulty**, privation, destitution, poverty, austerity, need, distress, suffering, adversity.
– OPPOSITES prosperity, ease.

hardware *noun* **equipment**, apparatus, gear, paraphernalia, tackle, kit, machinery.

hardy *adjective* **robust**, healthy, fit, strong, sturdy, tough, rugged.
– OPPOSITES delicate.

harm *noun* **injury**, damage, mischief, detriment, disservice.
– OPPOSITES good.
● *verb* **1 hurt**, injure, wound, lay a finger on, mistreat, ill-treat, maltreat. **2 damage**, spoil, affect, undermine, ruin.
– OPPOSITES heal, help.

harmful *adjective* **damaging**, injurious, detrimental, dangerous, unhealthy, unwholesome, environmentally unfriendly, hurtful, destructive, hazardous.
– OPPOSITES beneficial.

harmless *adjective* **1 safe**, innocuous, gentle, mild, non-toxic. **2 inoffensive**, innocuous, innocent, blameless, gentle.
– OPPOSITES harmful, objectionable.

harmonious *adjective* **1 melodious**, tuneful, musical, sweet-sounding, mellifluous, dulcet, euphonious. **2 friendly**, amicable, cordial, amiable, congenial, peaceful, in harmony, in tune. **3 balanced**, coordinated, pleasing, tasteful.
– OPPOSITES discordant, hostile.

harmonize *verb* **1 coordinate**, go together, match, blend, mix, balance, tone in, be compatible, be harmonious, suit each other, set each other off. **2 standardize**, coordinate, integrate, synchronize, make consistent, bring into line, systematize.
– OPPOSITES clash.

harmony *noun* **1 tunefulness**, euphony, melodiousness, unison. **2 accord**, agreement, peace, friendship, fellowship, cooperation, understanding, rapport, unity.
– OPPOSITES dissonance, disagreement.

harrowing *adjective* **distressing**, traumatic, upsetting, shocking, disturbing, painful, agonizing.

harry *verb* **harass**, hound, torment, pester, worry, badger, nag, plague; *informal* hassle, bug.

harsh *adjective* **1 grating**, rasping, strident, raucous, discordant, jarring, dissonant. **2 garish**, loud, glaring, gaudy, lurid. **3 cruel**, savage, barbarous, merciless, inhumane, ruthless, brutal,

hard-hearted, unfeeling, unrelenting. **4 severe**, stringent, firm, stiff, stern, rigorous, uncompromising, draconian. **5 rude**, discourteous, unfriendly, sharp, bitter, unkind, critical, disparaging. **6 austere**, grim, spartan, hard, inhospitable. **7 cold**, freezing, icy, bitter, hard, severe, bleak.
- OPPOSITES kind, mild, gentle.

harvest *noun* **crop**, yield, vintage, produce.
● *verb* **gather**, bring in, reap, pick, collect.

hassle *(informal) noun* **inconvenience**, bother, nuisance, trouble, annoyance, irritation, fuss; *informal* aggravation, headache, pain in the neck.
● *verb* **harass**, pester, be on at, badger, hound, bother, nag, torment; *informal* bug; *N. English informal* mither.

haste *noun* **speed**, hurriedness, swiftness, rapidity, quickness, briskness, alacrity; *old use* celerity.
- OPPOSITES delay.
□ **in haste** quickly, rapidly, fast, speedily, in a rush, in a hurry.

hasten *verb* **1 hurry**, rush, dash, race, fly, speed; *informal* zip, hare, scoot, hotfoot it; *N. Amer. informal* hightail. **2 speed up**, bring on, precipitate, advance.
- OPPOSITES dawdle, delay.

hasty *adjective* **hurried**, rash, impetuous, impulsive, reckless, precipitate, spur-of-the-moment.
- OPPOSITES considered.

hate *verb* **1 loathe**, detest, despise, dislike, abhor, shrink from, be unable to bear/stand; *formal* abominate. **2 be sorry**, be reluctant, be loath.
● *noun* **hatred**, loathing, abhorrence, abomination, aversion, disgust.
- OPPOSITES love.

hatred *noun* see **hate** (noun).

haul *verb* **drag**, pull, heave, lug, hump.
● *noun* **booty**, loot, plunder, spoils, stolen goods; *informal* swag.

haunt *verb* **torment**, disturb, trouble, worry, plague, prey on.
● *noun* **meeting place**, stamping ground, spot, venue; *informal* hangout; *N. Amer.* stomping ground.

haunted *adjective* **1 possessed**, cursed, jinxed, eerie. **2 tormented**, anguished, tortured, obsessed, troubled, worried.

haunting *adjective* **evocative**, affecting, stirring, powerful, poignant, memorable.

have *verb* **1 own**, be in possession of, be blessed with, boast, enjoy. **2 comprise**, consist of, contain, include, incorporate, be composed of, be made up of. **3 eat**, drink, take. **4 organize**, hold, give, throw, put on, lay on. **5** *I have to get up at six* **must**, be obliged to, be required to, be compelled to, be forced to, be bound to.
□ **have on 1** be wearing, be dressed in, be clothed in, be decked out in, sport. **2** *(Brit. informal)* play a trick on, play a joke on, pull someone's leg; *Brit. informal* wind up; *N. Amer. informal* put on.

haven *noun* **refuge**, retreat, shelter, sanctuary, oasis.

havoc *noun* **chaos**, mayhem, bedlam, pandemonium, a shambles.

hazard *noun* **danger**, risk, peril, menace, jeopardy, threat.

hazardous *adjective* **risky**, dangerous, unsafe, perilous, fraught with danger, high-risk; *informal* dicey; *Brit. informal* dodgy.
- OPPOSITES safe.

haze *noun* **mist**, fog, cloud, vapour.

hazy *adjective* **1 misty**, foggy, smoggy, murky. **2 vague**, dim, nebulous, blurred, fuzzy.

head *noun* **1 skull**, cranium; *informal* nut. **2 brain(s)**, brainpower, intellect, intelligence, grey matter; *Brit. informal* loaf; *N. Amer. informal* smarts. **3** *a head for business* **aptitude**, talent, gift, capacity. **4 leader**, chief, controller, governor, superintendent, commander, captain, director, manager, principal, president; *informal* boss; *Brit. informal* gaffer, guv'nor. **5 front**, beginning, start, top.
● *adjective* **chief**, principal, leading,

main, first, top, highest.
● *verb* **command**, control, lead, manage, direct, supervise, superintend, oversee, preside over.
□ **head off 1** intercept, divert, redirect, re-route, turn away. **2** forestall, avert, stave off, nip in the bud, prevent, avoid, stop.

headache *noun* **1 sore head**, migraine. **2** *(informal)* **problem**, worry, hassle, pain in the neck, bind.

heading *noun* **title**, caption, legend, rubric, headline.

headlong *adverb* **1 head first**, on your head. **2 without thinking**, precipitously, impetuously, rashly, recklessly, hastily.
- OPPOSITES cautiously.
● *adjective* **breakneck**, whirlwind, reckless, precipitous.

headquarters *plural noun* **head office**, HQ, base, nerve centre, mission control.

heady *adjective* **1 potent**, intoxicating, strong. **2 exhilarating**, exciting, stimulating, thrilling, intoxicating.

heal *verb* **1 cure**, make better, restore to health, treat. **2 get better**, be cured, recover, recuperate, mend, be on the mend. **3 put right**, repair, resolve, reconcile, settle; *informal* patch up.

health *noun* **1 well-being**, fitness, good condition, strength, robustness, vigour. **2** *her poor health forced her to retire* **condition**, state of health, physical shape, constitution.
- OPPOSITES illness.

WORD LINKS
salubrious good for the health

healthy *adjective* **1 well**, fit, in good shape, in fine fettle, in tip-top condition, strong, fighting fit; *informal* in the pink. **2 wholesome**, good for you, health-giving, nutritious, nourishing, invigorating, sanitary, hygienic.

heap *noun* **pile**, stack, mound, mountain.
● *verb* **pile (up)**, stack (up), make a mound of.

hear *verb* **1 make out**, catch, get, perceive, overhear. **2 learn**, find out, discover, gather, glean. **3 try**, judge, adjudicate on.

hearing *noun* **1 earshot**, hearing distance. **2 trial**, court case, enquiry, inquest, tribunal.

WORD LINKS
auditory, **aural** relating to hearing

heart *noun* **1 emotions**, feelings, sentiments, soul, mind. **2 compassion**, sympathy, humanity, fellow feeling(s), empathy, understanding, soul, goodwill. **3 enthusiasm**, spirit, determination, resolve, nerve; *Brit. informal* bottle. **4 centre**, middle, hub, core. **5 essence**, crux, core, nub, root, meat, substance, kernel; *informal* nitty-gritty.
□ **at heart** deep down, basically, fundamentally, essentially, in essence, intrinsically. **by heart** from memory, off pat, word for word, verbatim, parrot-fashion, word-perfect.

WORD LINKS
cardiac relating to the heart
coronary relating to the heart's arteries
cardiology branch of medicine concerning the heart

heartache *noun* **anguish**, suffering, distress, unhappiness, grief, misery, sorrow, sadness, heartbreak, pain, hurt, woe.
- OPPOSITES happiness.

heartbreaking *adjective* **distressing**, upsetting, disturbing, heart-rending, tragic, painful, sad, agonizing, harrowing.
- OPPOSITES comforting.

heartfelt *adjective* **sincere**, genuine, from the heart, earnest, profound, deep, wholehearted, honest.
- OPPOSITES insincere.

heartily *adverb* **1 wholeheartedly**, warmly, profoundly, eagerly, enthusiastically. **2 thoroughly**, completely, absolutely, exceedingly, downright; *N. Amer.* quite; *informal* seriously; *Brit.*

informal jolly; *N. Amer. informal* real, mighty.

heartless *adjective* **unfeeling**, unsympathetic, unkind, uncaring, hard-hearted, cold, callous, cruel, merciless, pitiless, inhuman.
- OPPOSITES compassionate.

hearty *adjective* **1 exuberant**, jovial, ebullient, cheerful, lively, loud, animated, vivacious, energetic, spirited. **2 wholehearted**, heartfelt, sincere, genuine, real. **3 robust**, healthy, hardy, fit, vigorous, sturdy, strong. **4 substantial**, large, ample, satisfying, filling, generous.

h

heat *noun* **1 warmth**, hotness, high temperature. **2 passion**, intensity, vehemence, fervour, excitement, agitation, anger.
- OPPOSITES cold, apathy.
● *verb* **1 warm (up)**, reheat, cook, keep warm. **2 get hot**, get warm, warm up; *Brit. informal* hot up.
- OPPOSITES cool.

WORD LINKS
thermal relating to heat

heated *adjective* **1 vehement**, passionate, impassioned, animated, lively, acrimonious, angry, bitter, furious, fierce. **2 excited**, animated, worked up, wound up, keyed up; *informal* het up.

heave *verb* **1 haul**, pull, drag, tug; *informal* yank. **2** *(informal)* **throw**, fling, cast, hurl, lob, pitch; *informal* chuck, sling. **3 let out**, breathe, give, emit, utter. **4 rise and fall**, roll, swell, surge, churn, seethe. **5 retch**, vomit, cough up; *Brit.* be sick; *N. Amer.* get sick; *informal* throw up, puke, chunder, chuck up, hurl, spew; *N. Amer. informal* barf.

heaven *noun* **1 paradise**, the hereafter, the next world, the afterworld, nirvana, Zion, Elysium. **2 bliss**, ecstasy, rapture, contentment, happiness, delight, joy, paradise.
- OPPOSITES hell.

WORD LINKS
celestial relating to heaven

heavenly *adjective* **1 divine**, angelic, holy, celestial. **2 celestial**, cosmic, stellar, sidereal. **3** *(informal)* **delightful**, wonderful, glorious, sublime, exquisite, beautiful, lovely, gorgeous, enchanting; *informal* divine, super, fantastic, fabulous.

heavily *adverb* **1 laboriously**, slowly, ponderously, awkwardly, clumsily. **2 decisively**, conclusively, roundly, soundly, utterly, completely, thoroughly. **3 excessively**, immoderately, copiously, intemperately. **4 densely**, closely, thickly. **5 deeply**, extremely, greatly, exceedingly, tremendously, profoundly.

heavy *adjective* **1 weighty**, hefty, substantial, ponderous, solid, dense, cumbersome, unwieldy. **2 forceful**, hard, strong, violent, powerful, mighty, sharp, severe. **3 strenuous**, hard, physical, difficult, arduous, demanding, back-breaking, gruelling. **4 intense**, fierce, relentless, severe, serious. **5 substantial**, filling, stodgy, rich, big.
- OPPOSITES light.

hectic *adjective* **frantic**, frenetic, frenzied, feverish, manic, busy, active, fast and furious.
- OPPOSITES leisurely.

heed *verb* **pay attention to**, take notice of, take note of, listen to, consider, take to heart, take into account, obey, adhere to, abide by, observe.
- OPPOSITES disregard.
● *noun* **attention**, notice, note, regard, thought.

hefty *adjective* **1 burly**, sturdy, strapping, bulky, strong, muscular, big, solid, well built; *informal* hulking, beefy. **2 powerful**, violent, hard, forceful, mighty. **3 substantial**, sizeable, considerable, stiff, large, heavy; *informal* whopping.
- OPPOSITES light.

height *noun* **1 tallness**, stature, elevation, altitude. **2** *mountain heights* **summit**, top, peak, crest, crown, tip, cap, pinnacle. **3** *the height of their fame* **highest point**, peak, zenith, pinnacle, climax.

- OPPOSITES width, nadir.

WORD LINKS
acrophobia fear of heights

heighten *verb* **intensify**, increase, enhance, add to, augment, boost, strengthen, deepen, magnify, reinforce.
- OPPOSITES reduce.

heinous *adjective* **odious**, wicked, evil, atrocious, monstrous, abominable, detestable, despicable, horrific, terrible, awful, abhorrent, loathsome, hideous, unspeakable, execrable.
- OPPOSITES admirable.

heir, **heiress** *noun* **successor**, next in line, inheritor, beneficiary, legatee.

hell *noun* **1 the underworld**, the netherworld, eternal damnation, perdition, hellfire, fire and brimstone, the Inferno, Hades. **2 misery**, torture, agony, purgatory, torment, a nightmare.
- OPPOSITES heaven, bliss.

WORD LINKS
infernal relating to hell

help *verb* **1 assist**, aid, abet, lend a hand, give assistance, come to the aid of, be of service, do someone a favour, do someone a service, do someone a good turn, rally round, pitch in. **2 support**, contribute to, give money to, donate to, promote, boost, back. **3 relieve**, soothe, ease, alleviate, improve, lessen. **4** *he could not help laughing* **resist**, avoid, refrain from, keep from, stop.
- OPPOSITES hinder, impede.
● *noun* **1 assistance**, aid, support, succour, benefit, use, advantage, service, solution. **2 relief**, alleviation, improvement, healing.
- OPPOSITES hindrance.

helper *noun* **assistant**, aide, deputy, auxiliary, supporter, second, mate, right-hand man/woman, attendant.

helpful *adjective* **1 obliging**, of assistance, supportive, accommodating, cooperative, neighbourly, eager to please. **2 useful**, beneficial, valuable, constructive, informative, instructive. **3 handy**, useful, convenient, practical, easy-to-use, serviceable; *informal* neat, nifty.
- OPPOSITES useless.

helping *noun* **portion**, serving, piece, slice, share, plateful; *informal* dollop.

helpless *adjective* **dependent**, incapable, powerless, paralysed, defenceless, vulnerable, exposed, unprotected.
- OPPOSITES independent.

hence *adverb* **consequently**, as a consequence, for this reason, therefore, so, accordingly, as a result, that being so.

herd *noun* **drove**, flock, pack, fold, swarm, mass, crowd, horde.

hereditary *adjective* **1 inherited**, bequeathed, handed down, passed down, family, ancestral. **2 genetic**, inborn, inherited, inbred, innate, in the family, in the blood, in the genes.

heritage *noun* **1 tradition**, history, past, background, culture, customs. **2 ancestry**, lineage, descent, extraction, parentage, roots, heredity, birth.

hermit *noun* **recluse**, loner, ascetic; *historical* anchorite, anchoress; *old use* eremite.

hero *noun* **1 star**, superstar, megastar, idol, celebrity, favourite, darling; *informal* celeb. **2 main character**, starring role, male protagonist, (male) lead, leading man; *informal* good guy.
- OPPOSITES villain.

heroic *adjective* **brave**, courageous, valiant, intrepid, bold, fearless, daring; *informal* gutsy, spunky.
- OPPOSITES cowardly.

heroine *noun* **1 star**, superstar, megastar, idol, celebrity, favourite, darling; *informal* celeb. **2 main character**, female protagonist, lead, leading lady, prima donna, diva.

heroism *noun* **bravery**, courage, valour, daring, fearlessness, pluck; *informal* guts, spunk; *Brit. informal* bottle; *N. Amer. informal* moxie.
- OPPOSITES cowardice.

hesitant *adjective* **1 uncertain**, undecided, unsure, doubtful, dubious, ambivalent, in two minds, wavering, vacillating, irresolute, indecisive; *Brit.* havering, humming and hawing; *informal* iffy. **2 timid**, diffident, shy, bashful, insecure, nervous.
- OPPOSITES certain, decisive, confident.

hesitate *verb* **1 pause**, delay, wait, stall, be uncertain, be unsure, be doubtful, be indecisive, vacillate, waver; *Brit.* haver, hum and haw; *informal* dilly-dally. **2** *don't hesitate to ask* **be reluctant**, be unwilling, be disinclined, scruple, have misgivings about, have qualms about, think twice about.

hidden *adjective* **1 concealed**, secret, invisible, unseen, camouflaged. **2 obscure**, unclear, concealed, cryptic, arcane, mysterious, secret, covert, abstruse, deep.
- OPPOSITES visible, obvious.

hide *verb* **1 conceal**, secrete, put out of sight, cache; *informal* stash. **2 conceal yourself**, secrete yourself, take cover, lie low, go to ground; *informal* hole up. **3 obscure**, block out, blot out, obstruct, cloud, shroud, veil, eclipse, camouflage. **4 keep secret**, conceal, cover up, keep quiet about, hush up, suppress, disguise, mask; *informal* keep a/the lid on.
- OPPOSITES reveal.

hideaway *noun* **retreat**, refuge, hiding place, hideout, safe house, den, bolthole; *informal* hidey-hole.

hideous *adjective* **1 ugly**, repulsive, repellent, unsightly, revolting, grotesque. **2 horrific**, terrible, appalling, awful, dreadful, frightful, horrible, horrendous, horrifying, shocking, sickening, gruesome, ghastly.
- OPPOSITES beautiful, pleasant.

hiding *noun (informal)* **beating**, thrashing, whipping, drubbing; *informal* licking, belting, pasting, walloping.

hierarchy *noun* **ranking**, order, pecking order, grading, ladder, scale.

high *adjective* **1 tall**, lofty, towering, giant, big, multi-storey, high-rise, elevated. **2 high-ranking**, leading, top, prominent, senior, influential, powerful, important, exalted; *N. Amer.* ranking. **3 inflated**, excessive, unreasonable, expensive, exorbitant, extortionate; *informal* steep, stiff. **4 high-pitched**, shrill, piercing, squeaky, penetrating, soprano, treble, falsetto.
- OPPOSITES low, deep.
● *adverb* **at a great height**, high up, way up, at altitude, in the sky, aloft, overhead, to a great height.
- OPPOSITES low.

highlight *noun* **high point**, climax, peak, pinnacle, height, zenith, summit, focus, feature.
● *verb* **spotlight**, call attention to, focus on, underline, show up, bring out, accentuate, accent, stress, emphasize.
- OPPOSITES play down.

hijack *verb* **commandeer**, seize, take over, appropriate, expropriate.

hike *noun* **1 walk**, trek, tramp, trudge, slog, march, ramble. **2 increase**, rise.
● *verb* **1 walk**, trek, tramp, trudge, slog, march, ramble, backpack. **2 increase**, raise, up, put up, push up; *informal* jack up, bump up.

hilarious *adjective* **very funny**, hysterical, uproarious, rib-tickling; *informal* side-splitting, priceless, a scream, a hoot.

hill *noun* **high ground**, hillock, hillside, rise, mound, knoll, hummock, fell, mountain; *Scottish* brae.

hinder *verb* **hamper**, impede, inhibit, thwart, foil, delay, interfere with, slow down, hold back, hold up, restrict, handicap, hamstring.
- OPPOSITES facilitate.

hindrance *noun* **impediment**, obstacle, barrier, obstruction, handicap, hurdle, restraint, restriction, encumbrance, complication, delay, drawback, setback, difficulty, inconvenience, hitch, stumbling block, fly in the ointment, hiccup; *Brit.* spanner in the works.
- OPPOSITES aid, help.

hint *noun* **1 clue**, inkling, suggestion, indication, sign, signal, intimation. **2 tip**, suggestion, pointer, guideline, recommendation. **3 trace**, touch, suspicion, suggestion, dash, soupçon; *informal* smidgen, tad.
● *verb* **imply**, insinuate, intimate, suggest, refer to, drive at, mean; *informal* get at.

hire *verb* **1 rent**, lease, charter. **2 employ**, engage, recruit, appoint, take on, sign up.
- OPPOSITES dismiss.

hiss *verb* **1 fizz**, whistle, wheeze. **2 jeer**, catcall, whistle, hoot.
- OPPOSITES cheer.
● *noun* **1 fizz**, whistle, wheeze. **2 jeer**, catcall, whistle, abuse, derision.
- OPPOSITES cheer.

historic *adjective* **significant**, notable, important, momentous, memorable, groundbreaking; *informal* earth-shattering.

historical *adjective* **1 documented**, recorded, chronicled, authentic, factual, actual. **2 past**, bygone, ancient, old, former.

history *noun* **1 the past**, former times, the olden days, yesterday, antiquity. **2 chronicle**, archive, record, report, narrative, account, study. **3 background**, past, life story, experiences, record.

hit *verb* **1 strike**, smack, slap, beat, punch, thump, thrash, batter, club, pummel, cuff, swat; *informal* whack, wallop, bash, clout, belt, clobber; *Brit. informal* slosh, stick one on; *N. Amer. informal* slug; *Austral./NZ informal* quilt. **2 crash into**, run into, smash into, knock into, bump into, plough into, collide with, meet head-on. **3 devastate**, affect badly, upset, shatter, crush, traumatize; *informal* knock sideways; *Brit. informal* knock for six.
● *noun* **1 blow**, slap, smack, thump, punch, knock, bang; *informal* whack, wallop, bash, clout, belt; *N. Amer. informal* slug. **2 success**, sell-out, winner, triumph, sensation, best-seller; *informal* smash hit, chart-topper, crowd-puller.
- OPPOSITES failure.
□ **hit back** retaliate, respond, reply, react, counter. **hit it off** *(informal)* get on (well), get along, be compatible, be on the same wavelength, see eye to eye, take to each other; *informal* click. **hit on** discover, come up with, think of, conceive of, dream up, invent, devise.

hitch *verb* **1 pull**, lift, raise; *informal* yank. **2 harness**, yoke, couple, fasten, connect, attach.
● *noun* **problem**, difficulty, issue, snag, setback, obstacle, complication; *informal* glitch, hiccup.

hoard *noun* **cache**, stockpile, store, collection, supply, reserve; *informal* stash.
● *verb* **stockpile**, store up, put aside, put by, lay by, set aside, cache, save, squirrel away; *informal* salt away.
- OPPOSITES squander.

hoarse *adjective* **rough**, harsh, croaky, throaty, gruff, husky, grating, rasping.

hoax *noun* **practical joke**, prank, trick, deception, fraud; *informal* con, spoof, wind-up, scam.

hobble *verb* **limp**, shamble, totter, dodder, stagger, stumble.

hobby *noun* **pastime**, leisure activity, sideline, diversion, relaxation, recreation, amusement.

hoist *verb* **raise**, lift, haul up, heave up, winch up, pull up, elevate.
● *noun* **crane**, winch, pulley, windlass.

hold *verb* **1 clasp**, clutch, grasp, grip, clench, cling to, hold on to, embrace, hug, squeeze. **2 detain**, imprison, lock up, keep behind bars, confine, intern, incarcerate. **3 take**, contain, accommodate, fit, have room for. **4 maintain**, consider, take the view, believe, think, feel, deem, be of the opinion, rule, decide; *informal* reckon. **5 convene**, call, summon, conduct, organize, run.
- OPPOSITES release.
● *noun* **1 grip**, grasp, clasp, clutch. **2 influence**, power, control, grip, dominance, authority, sway.

holder *noun* **1 bearer**, owner, possessor, keeper. **2 container**, receptacle, case, cover, housing, sheath.

hold-up *noun* **1 delay**, setback, hitch, snag, issue, difficulty, problem, glitch, hiccup, traffic jam, tailback; *informal* snarl-up. **2 robbery**, raid, armed robbery, mugging; *informal* stick-up; *N. Amer. informal* heist.

hole *noun* **1 opening**, aperture, orifice, gap, space, interstice, fissure, vent, chink, breach, crack, rupture, puncture. **2 pit**, crater, depression, hollow, cavern, cave, chamber. **3 burrow**, lair, den, earth, sett.

h

holiday *noun* **vacation**, break, rest, recess, time off, leave, day off, festival, feast day.

hollow *adjective* **1 empty**, hollowed out, void. **2 sunken**, deep-set, concave, depressed, recessed. **3 worthless**, meaningless, empty, profitless, fruitless, pointless, pyrrhic. **4 insincere**, false, deceitful, hypocritical, sham, untrue.
- OPPOSITES solid, convex.
● *noun* **1 hole**, pit, cavity, crater, trough, depression, indentation, dip. **2 valley**, vale, dale, dell.
● *verb* **gouge**, scoop, dig, cut, excavate, channel.

holy *adjective* **1 saintly**, godly, pious, religious, devout, God-fearing, spiritual. **2 sacred**, consecrated, hallowed, sanctified, venerated, revered.
- OPPOSITES sinful, irreligious.

homage *noun* **respect**, honour, reverence, worship, admiration, esteem, adulation, tribute.
- OPPOSITES contempt.

home *noun* **1 residence**, house, accommodation, property, quarters, lodgings, address, place; *informal* pad; *formal* abode, dwelling. **2 homeland**, native land, home town, birthplace, roots, fatherland, mother country, motherland. **3 institution**, hospice, shelter, refuge, retreat, asylum, hostel.
● *adjective* **domestic**, internal, local, national.
- OPPOSITES foreign, international.

homeless *adjective* **of no fixed abode**, without a roof over your head, on the streets, vagrant, sleeping rough, destitute.

homely *adjective* **1** *(Brit.)* **cosy**, comfortable, snug, welcoming, friendly; *informal* comfy. **2** *(N. Amer.)* **unattractive**, plain, unprepossessing, ugly; *Brit. informal* no oil painting.

homicide *noun* **murder**, manslaughter, killing, slaughter, butchery, assassination.

honest *adjective* **1** *an honest man* **upright**, honourable, principled, virtuous, good, decent, law-abiding, trustworthy, scrupulous, ethical, upstanding, right-minded. **2** *I haven't been honest with you* **truthful**, sincere, candid, frank, open, forthright, straight; *informal* upfront.
- OPPOSITES dishonest.

honestly *adverb* **1 fairly**, lawfully, legally, legitimately, honourably, decently, ethically; *informal* on the level. **2 sincerely**, genuinely, truthfully, truly, wholeheartedly, to be honest, to be frank, in all honesty, in all sincerity.

honesty *noun* **1 integrity**, uprightness, honour, righteousness, virtue, goodness, probity, trustworthiness. **2 sincerity**, candour, frankness, directness, truthfulness, truth, openness, straightforwardness.
- OPPOSITES dishonesty, insincerity.

honorary *adjective* **1 titular**, nominal, in name only, unofficial, token. **2** *(Brit.)* **unpaid**, unsalaried, voluntary, volunteer.

honour *noun* **1 integrity**, honesty, uprightness, morality, probity, principles, high-mindedness, decency, scrupulousness, fairness, justness. **2 distinction**, privilege, glory, kudos, cachet, prestige. **3 reputation**, good name, character, repute, image, standing, status. **4 privilege**, pleasure, compliment.
- OPPOSITES shame.

● *verb* **1 respect**, esteem, admire, look up to, value, cherish, revere, venerate. **2 applaud**, acclaim, praise, salute, recognize, celebrate, pay tribute to. **3 fulfil**, observe, keep, obey, heed, follow, carry out, keep to, abide by, adhere to, comply with, conform to, be true to.
- OPPOSITES disobey, break.

honourable *adjective* **1 honest**, moral, principled, righteous, decent, respectable, virtuous, good, upstanding, upright, noble, fair, trustworthy, law-abiding. **2 illustrious**, distinguished, eminent, great, glorious, prestigious.
- OPPOSITES dishonourable.

hook *noun* **1 peg**, nail. **2 fastener**, clasp, hasp, clip.
● *verb* **1 attach**, hitch, fasten, fix, secure, hang, clasp. **2 catch**, land, net, take, bag.

hooked *adjective* **curved**, hook-shaped, aquiline, angular, bent.
□ **hooked on** *(informal)* addicted to, dependent on, obsessed with, fanatical about, enthusiastic about; *informal* mad about.

hooligan *noun* **lout**, thug, tearaway, vandal, delinquent, ruffian, troublemaker; *Austral.* larrikin; *informal* tough, bruiser; *Brit. informal* yob, yobbo, lager lout; *Scottish informal* ned.

hoop *noun* **ring**, band, circle, wheel, circlet, loop.

hop *verb* & *noun* **jump**, bound, spring, bounce, skip, leap, prance, caper.

hope *noun* **1 aspiration**, desire, wish, expectation, ambition, aim, plan, dream. **2 optimism**, expectation, confidence, faith, belief.
- OPPOSITES pessimism.
● *verb* **1 expect**, anticipate, look for, be hopeful of, dream of. **2 aim**, intend, be looking, have the intention, have in mind, plan.

hopeful *adjective* **1 optimistic**, full of hope, confident, sanguine, positive, buoyant, bullish, upbeat. **2 promising**, encouraging, heartening, reassuring, favourable, optimistic.
- OPPOSITES pessimistic, discouraging.

hopefully *adverb* **1 optimistically**, full of hope, confidently, buoyantly, expectantly. **2 all being well**, if all goes well, God willing, with luck, touch wood, fingers crossed.

hopeless *adjective* **1 forlorn**, beyond hope, lost, irreparable, irreversible, incurable, impossible, futile. **2 bad**, poor, awful, terrible, dreadful, appalling, atrocious, incompetent; *informal* pathetic, useless, lousy, rotten; *Brit. informal* rubbish.
- OPPOSITES competent.

hopelessly *adverb* **utterly**, completely, irretrievably, impossibly, extremely, totally.

horde *noun* **crowd**, mob, pack, gang, troop, army, swarm, mass, throng.

horizontal *adjective* **level**, flat, parallel.
- OPPOSITES vertical.

horrible *adjective* **1 dreadful**, awful, terrible, shocking, appalling, horrifying, horrific, horrendous, grisly, ghastly, gruesome, harrowing, unspeakable, abhorrent. **2** *(informal)* **nasty**, horrid, disagreeable, obnoxious, disgusting, hateful, odious, objectionable, insufferable.
- OPPOSITES pleasant.

horrific *adjective* **dreadful**, horrendous, horrible, terrible, atrocious, horrifying, shocking, appalling, harrowing, hideous, grisly, ghastly, sickening.

horrify *verb* **shock**, appal, outrage, scandalize, offend, disgust, revolt, nauseate, sicken.

horror *noun* **1 terror**, fear, fright, alarm, panic. **2 dismay**, consternation, alarm, distress, disgust, shock.
- OPPOSITES delight, satisfaction.

horse *noun* **mount**, charger, cob, nag, hack, colt, stallion, mare, filly; *N. Amer.* bronco; *Austral./NZ* moke; *informal* gee-gee.

WORD LINKS
equine relating to horses
equestrian relating to horse riding

h

hospitable *adjective* **welcoming**, friendly, sociable, cordial, gracious, accommodating, warm.

hospital *noun* **infirmary**, clinic, sanatorium, hospice; *Brit.* cottage hospital; *Military* field hospital.

hospitality *noun* **friendliness**, neighbourliness, sociability, welcome, warmth, kindness, cordiality, generosity.

host *noun* **presenter**, compère, anchor, anchorman, anchorwoman, announcer.
- OPPOSITES guest.
● *verb* **present**, introduce, compère, front, anchor.

hostage *noun* **captive**, prisoner, detainee, internee.

hostile *adjective* **1 unfriendly**, unkind, unsympathetic, antagonistic, aggressive, confrontational, belligerent. **2 unfavourable**, adverse, bad, harsh, grim, inhospitable, forbidding. **3** *they are hostile to the idea* **opposed**, averse, antagonistic, ill-disposed, unsympathetic, antipathetic, against; *informal* anti.
- OPPOSITES friendly, favourable.

hostility *noun* **1 antagonism**, unfriendliness, malevolence, venom, hatred, aggression, belligerence. **2 opposition**, antagonism, animosity, antipathy. **3** *a cessation of hostilities* **fighting**, armed conflict, combat, warfare, war, bloodshed, violence.

hot *adjective* **1** *hot food* **heated**, sizzling, roasting, boiling, scorching, scalding, red-hot. **2** *a hot day* **very warm**, balmy, summery, tropical, scorching, searing, blistering, sweltering, torrid, sultry; *informal* boiling, baking, roasting. **3 spicy**, peppery, fiery, strong, piquant, powerful. **4 fierce**, intense, keen, competitive, cut-throat, ruthless, aggressive, violent. **5** *(informal) she's hot on local history* **knowledgeable**, well informed, au fait, well up, well versed; *informal* clued up.
- OPPOSITES cold, mild.

hotly *adverb* **vehemently**, vigorously, strenuously, fiercely, heatedly.

hound *verb* **pursue**, chase, stalk, harry, harass, pester, badger, torment.

house *noun* **1 residence**, home; *informal* pad; *Brit. informal* gaff; *formal* dwelling, abode, habitation, domicile. **2 family**, clan, tribe, dynasty, line, bloodline, lineage. **3 firm**, business, company, corporation, enterprise, establishment, institution, concern, organization, operation; *informal* outfit. **4 assembly**, legislative body, chamber, council, parliament, congress, senate.
● *verb* **1 accommodate**, give someone a roof over their head, lodge, quarter, board, billet, take in, sleep, put up. **2 contain**, hold, store, cover, protect, enclose.

household *noun* **family**, house, occupants, clan, tribe; *informal* brood.
● *adjective* **domestic**, family, everyday, workaday.

housing *noun* **1 accommodation**, houses, homes, living quarters; *formal* dwellings. **2 casing**, covering, case, cover, holder, fairing, sleeve.

hovel *noun* **shack**, slum, shanty, hut; *informal* dump, hole.

hover *verb* **1 hang**, be poised, be suspended, float, fly, drift. **2 wait**, linger, loiter.

however *adverb* **nevertheless**, nonetheless, even so, but, for all that, despite that, in spite of that.

howl *noun* **1 baying**, cry, bark, yelp, yowl. **2 wail**, cry, yell, yelp, bellow, roar, shout, shriek, scream, screech.
● *verb* **1 bay**, cry, bark, yelp, yowl. **2 wail**, cry, yell, bawl, bellow, shriek, scream, screech, caterwaul, ululate; *informal* holler.

hub *noun* **centre**, core, heart, focus, focal point, nucleus, kernel, nerve centre.
- OPPOSITES periphery.

huddle *verb* **1 crowd**, cluster, gather, bunch, throng, flock, collect, group, congregate. **2 curl up**, snuggle, nestle, hunch up.
- OPPOSITES disperse.

● *noun* **group**, cluster, bunch, collection; *informal* gaggle.

hue *noun* **colour**, shade, tone, tint, tinge.

hug *verb* **embrace**, cuddle, squeeze, clasp, clutch, hold tight.
● *noun* **embrace**, cuddle, squeeze, bear hug.

huge *adjective* **enormous**, vast, immense, massive, colossal, prodigious, gigantic, gargantuan, mammoth, monumental, giant, towering, mountainous, cosmic; *informal* mega, monster, astronomical; *Brit. informal* ginormous.
- OPPOSITES tiny.

hull *noun* **framework**, body, shell, frame, skeleton, structure.

hum *verb* **1 purr**, drone, murmur, buzz, whirr, throb. **2 be busy**, be active, be lively, buzz, bustle, be a hive of activity, throb.
● *noun* **murmur**, drone, purr, buzz.

human *adjective* **1 mortal**, flesh and blood, fallible, weak, frail, imperfect, vulnerable, physical, bodily, fleshly. **2 compassionate**, humane, kind, considerate, understanding, sympathetic.
● *noun* **person**, human being, Homo sapiens, man, woman, individual, mortal, (living) soul, earthling; (**humans**) the human race, humanity, humankind, mankind, people.

WORD LINKS
anthropology study of humankind

humane *adjective* **compassionate**, kind, considerate, understanding, sympathetic, tolerant, forbearing, forgiving, merciful, humanitarian, charitable.
- OPPOSITES cruel.

humanitarian *adjective* **1 compassionate**, humane, unselfish, altruistic, generous. **2 charitable**, philanthropic, public-spirited, socially concerned.
● *noun* **philanthropist**, altruist, benefactor, social reformer, good Samaritan, do-gooder.

humanity *noun* **1 humankind**, mankind, man, people, the human race, Homo sapiens. **2 compassion**, brotherly love, fellow feeling, humaneness, kindness, consideration, understanding, sympathy, tolerance.

humble *adjective* **1 meek**, deferential, respectful, submissive, self-effacing, unassertive, modest, unassuming, self-deprecating. **2 lowly**, poor, undistinguished, mean, common, ordinary, simple, modest.
- OPPOSITES proud, arrogant.
● *verb* **humiliate**, demean, lower, degrade, debase, mortify, shame.

humdrum *adjective* **mundane**, dull, dreary, boring, tedious, monotonous, prosaic, routine, ordinary, everyday, run-of-the-mill, workaday, pedestrian.

humid *adjective* **muggy**, close, sultry, sticky, steamy, clammy, heavy.
- OPPOSITES dry, fresh.

humiliate *verb* **embarrass**, mortify, humble, shame, disgrace, chasten, deflate, crush, squash, demean, take down a peg or two; *informal* show up, put down, cut down to size; *N. Amer. informal* make someone eat crow.
- OPPOSITES dignify.

humiliating *adjective* **embarrassing**, mortifying, humbling, ignominious, inglorious, shaming, undignified, chastening, demeaning, degrading, deflating.

humiliation *noun* **embarrassment**, mortification, shame, indignity, ignominy, disgrace, dishonour, degradation, discredit, loss of face, blow to your pride.

humility *noun* **modesty**, humbleness, meekness, respect, deference, diffidence.
- OPPOSITES pride.

humorous *adjective* **amusing**, funny, comic, comical, entertaining, diverting, witty, jocular, light-hearted, hilarious.
- OPPOSITES serious.

humour *noun* **1 comedy**, funny side, hilarity, absurdity, ludicrousness, satire,

irony. **2 jokes**, jests, quips, witticisms, funny remarks, wit, comedy; *informal* gags, wisecracks. **3 mood**, temper, disposition, spirits.
- OPPOSITES seriousness.
● *verb* **indulge**, accommodate, pander to, cater to, give in to, go along with, flatter, mollify, placate.

hunch *noun* **feeling**, guess, suspicion, impression, inkling, idea, notion, fancy, intuition; *informal* gut feeling.

hunger *noun* **1 lack of food**, starvation, malnutrition, undernourishment. **2 desire**, craving, longing, yearning, hankering, appetite, thirst; *informal* itch.
□ **hunger after/for** desire, crave, long for, yearn for, pine for, ache for, hanker after, thirst for, lust for; *informal* itch for, be dying for, be gagging for.

hungry *adjective* **1 ravenous**, famished, starving, starved, malnourished, undernourished, underfed; *informal* peckish. **2** *they are hungry for success* **eager**, keen, avid, longing, yearning, aching, greedy, craving, desirous of, hankering after; *informal* itching, dying, gagging.
- OPPOSITES full.

hunk *noun* **chunk**, wedge, block, slab, lump, square, gobbet; *Brit. informal* wodge.

hunt *verb* **1 chase**, stalk, pursue, course, track, trail. **2 search**, seek, look high and low, scour the area.
● *noun* **1 chase**, pursuit. **2 search**, quest.

hurdle *noun* **obstacle**, difficulty, problem, barrier, bar, snag, stumbling block, impediment, obstruction, complication, hindrance.

hurl *verb* **throw**, toss, fling, launch, pitch, cast, lob; *informal* chuck, sling, bung.

hurricane *noun* **cyclone**, typhoon, tornado, storm, windstorm, whirlwind, gale, tempest; *Austral.* willy-willy; *N. Amer. informal* twister.

hurried *adjective* **1 quick**, fast, swift, rapid, speedy, brisk, cursory, perfunctory, brief, short, fleeting. **2 hasty**, rushed, precipitate, spur-of-the-moment.
- OPPOSITES slow.

hurry *verb* **1 be quick**, hurry up, hasten, speed up, run, dash, rush, race, scurry, scramble, scuttle, sprint; *informal* get a move on, step on it, get a wiggle on, hightail it, hotfoot it; *Brit. informal* get your skates on. **2 hustle**, hasten, push, urge.
- OPPOSITES dawdle, delay.
● *noun* **rush**, haste, speed, urgency, hustle and bustle.

hurt *verb* **1 be painful**, ache, be sore, be tender, smart, sting, burn, throb; *informal* be agony. **2 injure**, wound, damage, disable, bruise, cut, gash, graze, scrape, scratch. **3 distress**, pain, wound, sting, upset, sadden, devastate, grieve, mortify.
● *noun* **distress**, pain, suffering, grief, misery, anguish, upset, sadness, sorrow.
● *adjective* **1 injured**, wounded, bruised, grazed, cut, gashed, sore, painful, aching. **2 pained**, aggrieved, offended, distressed, upset, sad, mortified; *informal* miffed.

hurtful *adjective* **upsetting**, distressing, wounding, unkind, cruel, nasty, mean, malicious, spiteful.

hush *verb* **silence**, quieten (down), shush, gag, muzzle; *informal* shut up.
● *noun* **silence**, quiet, stillness, peace, calm, tranquillity.
- OPPOSITES noise.
□ **hush up** keep secret, conceal, hide, suppress, cover up, keep quiet about, sweep under the carpet.

hut *noun* **shack**, shanty, cabin, shelter, shed, lean-to, hovel; *Scottish* bothy; *N. Amer.* cabana.

hybrid *noun* **cross**, cross-breed, mixture, blend, combination, composite, fusion, amalgam.
● *adjective* **composite**, cross-bred, interbred, mixed, blended, compound.

hygiene *noun* **cleanliness**, sanitation, sterility, purity, disinfection.

hygienic *adjective* **sanitary**, clean, germ-free, disinfected, sterilized, sterile, antiseptic, aseptic.
– OPPOSITES insanitary.

hypocritical *adjective* **sanctimonious**, pious, self-righteous, holier-than-thou, superior, insincere, two-faced.

hysteria *noun* **frenzy**, feverishness, hysterics, agitation, mania, panic, alarm, distress.
– OPPOSITES calm.

hysterical *adjective* **1 overwrought**, overemotional, out of control, frenzied, frantic, wild, beside yourself, manic, delirious; *informal* in a state. **2** *(informal)* **very funny**, hilarious, uproarious, rib-tickling; *informal* side-splitting, priceless, a scream, a hoot.
– OPPOSITES calm.

I

ice *noun* **1** icicles, black ice, frost, permafrost, hoar (frost); *literary* rime. **2 ice cream**, water ice, sorbet; *N. Amer.* sherbet. **3 coldness**, coolness, frostiness, iciness, hostility, unfriendliness.

WORD LINKS
glacial relating to ice

icy *adjective* **1 iced (over)**, frozen, frosty, slippery, treacherous; *literary* rimy. **2 freezing**, chill, biting, bitter, raw, arctic. **3 unfriendly**, hostile, forbidding, cold, chilly, frosty, stern.

idea *noun* **1 concept**, notion, conception, thought. **2 plan**, scheme, design, proposal, proposition, suggestion, aim, intention, objective, goal. **3 thought**, theory, view, opinion, feeling, belief. **4 sense**, feeling, suspicion, fancy, inkling, hunch, notion. **5 estimate**, approximation, guess, conjecture; *informal* guesstimate.

ideal *adjective* **perfect**, faultless, exemplary, classic, archetypal, quintessential, model, ultimate, utopian, fairy-tale.
● *noun* **1** *an ideal to aim at* **model**, pattern, archetype, exemplar, example, perfection, epitome, last word. **2** *liberal ideals* **principle**, standard, value, belief, conviction, ethos.

idealistic *adjective* **Utopian**, visionary, romantic, quixotic, unrealistic, impractical.

identical *adjective* **(exactly) the same**, indistinguishable, twin, duplicate, interchangeable, alike, matching.
– OPPOSITES different.

identification *noun* **1 recognition**, singling out, pinpointing, naming. **2 determination**, establishing, ascertainment, discovery, diagnosis. **3 ID**, papers, documents, credentials, card, pass, badge.

identify *verb* **1 recognize**, pick out, spot, point out, pinpoint, put your finger on, name. **2 determine**, establish, ascertain, make out, discern, distinguish. **3** *we identify sport with glamour* **associate**, link, connect, relate. **4** *he identified with the team captain* **empathize**, sympathize, understand, relate to, feel for.

identity *noun* **individuality**, self, personality, character, originality, distinctiveness, uniqueness.

ideology *noun* **belief**; doctrine, creed, theory.

idiomatic *adjective* **colloquial**, everyday, conversational, vernacular, natural.

idiosyncrasy *noun* **peculiarity**, oddity, eccentricity, mannerism, quirk, characteristic.

idiot *noun* **fool**, ass, halfwit, blockhead, dunce, simpleton; *informal* nincompoop, clod, dimwit, dummy, fathead, numbskull; *Brit. informal* nitwit, twit, clot, berk, prat, pillock, wally, dork, twerp, charlie, moron; *N. Amer. informal* schmuck; *Austral./NZ informal* drongo.
– OPPOSITES genius.

idle *adjective* **1 lazy**, indolent, slothful, shiftless, work-shy. **2 unemployed**, jobless, out of work, redundant, unoccupied; *Brit. informal* on the dole. **3 unoccupied**, spare, empty, unfilled. **4 frivolous**, trivial, trifling, minor, insignificant, unimportant, empty, meaningless, vain.
– OPPOSITES industrious, busy.

idol *noun* **1 icon**, effigy, statue, figurine, totem. **2 hero**, heroine, star, superstar, icon, celebrity, darling; *informal* pin-up, heart-throb.

idolize *verb* **hero-worship**, worship, revere, venerate, look up to, exalt; *informal* put on a pedestal.

if *conjunction* **provided**, providing, on condition that, presuming, supposing, assuming, as long as, in the event that.

ignite *verb* **1 catch fire**, burst into flames, explode. **2 light**, set fire to, set alight, kindle.
- OPPOSITES extinguish.

ignorance *noun* **1 lack of knowledge**, lack of education, unenlightenment. **2 unfamiliarity**, incomprehension, inexperience, innocence.
- OPPOSITES education, knowledge.

ignorant *adjective* **1 uneducated**, unschooled, illiterate, uninformed, unenlightened, inexperienced, unsophisticated. **2 unaware**, unconscious, unfamiliar, unacquainted, uninformed; *informal* in the dark.
- OPPOSITES educated, knowledgeable.

ignore *verb* **1 snub**, look right through, cold-shoulder, take no notice of, pay no attention to, cut (dead); *informal* blank. **2 disregard**, take no account of, fail to observe, disobey, defy, overlook, brush aside, turn a blind eye to.
- OPPOSITES acknowledge, obey.

ill *adjective* **1 unwell**, sick, poorly, peaky, indisposed, nauseous, queasy; *informal* rough, under the weather; *Brit. informal* grotty; *Austral./NZ informal* crook. **2** *ill effects* **harmful**, damaging, detrimental, deleterious, adverse, injurious, destructive, dangerous.
- OPPOSITES well, beneficial.
● *noun* **problem**, trouble, difficulty, misfortune, trial, tribulation; *informal* headache, hassle.
● *adverb* **1 barely**, scarcely, hardly, only just. **2 inadequately**, insufficiently, poorly, badly.

illegal *adjective* **unlawful**, illicit, illegitimate, criminal, fraudulent, corrupt, dishonest, outlawed, banned, forbidden, prohibited, proscribed, unlicensed, unauthorized; *informal* crooked, shady; *Brit. informal* bent, dodgy.
- OPPOSITES legal.

illegible *adjective* **unreadable**, indecipherable, unintelligible.

illegitimate *adjective* **illegal**, unlawful, illicit, criminal, felonious, fraudulent, corrupt, dishonest; *informal* crooked, shady; *Brit. informal* bent, dodgy.
- OPPOSITES legal, legitimate.

illicit *adjective* **illegal**, unlawful, criminal, outlawed, banned, forbidden, prohibited, proscribed, unlicensed, unauthorized, improper, disapproved of.
- OPPOSITES legal.

illness *noun* **sickness**, poor health, disease, ailment, disorder, complaint, indisposition, malady, affliction, infection; *informal* bug, virus.
- OPPOSITES health.

illogical *adjective* **irrational**, unreasonable, erroneous, invalid, spurious, fallacious, specious.

illuminating *adjective* **informative**, enlightening, revealing, explanatory, instructive, helpful, educational.
- OPPOSITES confusing.

illumination *noun* **light**, lighting, radiance, gleam, glow, glare.

illusion *noun* **1 delusion**, misapprehension, misconception, false impression, mistaken impression, fantasy, dream, fancy. **2 appearance**, impression, semblance. **3 mirage**, hallucination, apparition, figment of the imagination, trick of the light.

illusory *adjective* **false**, imagined, imaginary, fanciful, unreal, sham, fallacious.
- OPPOSITES genuine.

illustrate *verb* **1 decorate**, ornament, accompany, support. **2 explain**, elucidate, clarify, demonstrate, show, point up; *informal* get across/over.

illustration *noun* **1 picture**, drawing, sketch, figure, plate, image, print. **2 example**, sample, case, instance, exemplification, demonstration.

image *noun* **1 likeness**, depiction, portrayal, representation, painting, picture, portrait, drawing, photograph. **2 conception**, impression, perception, notion, idea. **3 persona**, profile, face.

WORD LINKS
iconography study of images

imaginary *adjective* **unreal**, non-existent, fictional, pretend, make-believe, invented, made-up, illusory.
- OPPOSITES real.

imagination *noun* **1 mind's eye**, fancy. **2 creativity**, vision, inventiveness, resourcefulness, ingenuity, originality.

imaginative *adjective* **creative**, visionary, inventive, resourceful, ingenious, original, innovative.

imagine *verb* **1 visualize**, envisage, picture, see in your mind's eye, dream up, think up/of, conceive. **2 assume**, presume, expect, take it (as read), suppose.

i

imbue *verb* **permeate**, saturate, suffuse, inject, inculcate, fill.

imitate *verb* **1 copy**, emulate, follow, echo, ape, parrot; *informal* rip off. **2 mimic**, do an impression of, impersonate, parody, caricature; *informal* take off, send up.

imitation *noun* **1 copy**, simulation, reproduction, replica, forgery. **2 emulation**, copying. **3 impersonation**, impression, parody, caricature; *informal* take-off, send-up, spoof.
● *adjective* **artificial**, synthetic, mock, fake, simulated, man-made, manufactured, substitute, ersatz.
- OPPOSITES real.

immaculate *adjective* **1 clean**, spotless, shining, shiny, gleaming, perfect, pristine, mint, flawless, faultless, unblemished; *informal* tip-top, A1. **2** *his immaculate record* **impeccable**, unsullied, spotless, unblemished, untarnished; *informal* squeaky clean.
- OPPOSITES dirty, damaged.

immature *adjective* **childish**, babyish, infantile, juvenile, puerile, callow.

immediate *adjective* **1 instant**, instantaneous, prompt, swift, speedy, rapid, quick. **2 current**, present, urgent, pressing. **3 nearest**, close, next-door, adjacent, adjoining.
- OPPOSITES delayed.

immediately *adverb* **1 straight away**, at once, right away, instantly, (right) now, directly, forthwith, there and then; *informal* pronto. **2 directly**, right, exactly, precisely, squarely, just, dead; *informal* slap bang; *N. Amer. informal* smack dab.
- OPPOSITES later.

immense *adjective* **huge**, massive, vast, enormous, gigantic, colossal, monumental, towering, giant, mammoth, cosmic; *informal* monster, whopping (great); *Brit. informal* ginormous.
- OPPOSITES tiny.

immerse *verb* **1 dip**, submerge, dunk, duck, sink. **2 absorb**, engross, occupy, engage, involve, bury, preoccupy; *informal* lose.

immigrant *noun* **newcomer**, settler, incomer, migrant, non-native, foreigner, foreign national, alien, expatriate.
- OPPOSITES native.

imminent *adjective* **near**, close (at hand), impending, approaching, coming, forthcoming, on the way, expected, looming.
- OPPOSITES distant.

immobile *adjective* **motionless**, still, stock-still, static, stationary, rooted to the spot, rigid, frozen, transfixed.

immodest *adjective* **indecorous**, improper, indecent, indelicate, immoral, forward, bold, brazen, shameless.

immoral *adjective* **wicked**, bad, wrong, unethical, unprincipled, unscrupulous, dishonest, corrupt, sinful, impure.
- OPPOSITES moral, ethical.

immortal *adjective* **1 undying**, deathless, eternal, everlasting, imperishable, indestructible. **2 timeless**, perennial, classic, time-honoured, enduring, evergreen.
- OPPOSITES mortal, ephemeral.

immovable *adjective* **1 fixed**, secure, set firm, set fast, stuck, jammed, stiff. **2 motionless**, unmoving, stationary, still, stock-still, rooted to the spot,

transfixed, paralysed, frozen.
- OPPOSITES mobile.

immune *adjective* **resistant**, not subject, not liable, not vulnerable, protected from, safe from, secure against.
- OPPOSITES susceptible, liable.

immunity *noun* **1 resistance**, protection, defence. **2 exemption**, exception, freedom, indemnity, privilege, prerogative, licence, impunity, protection.
- OPPOSITES susceptibility, liability.

immunize *verb* **vaccinate**, inoculate, inject.

impact *noun* **1 collision**, crash, smash, bump, knock. **2 effect**, influence, footprint, consequences, repercussions, ramifications.
● *verb* **1 crash into**, smash into, collide with, hit, strike, smack into, bang into. **2** *interest rates impacted on spending* **affect**, influence, hit, have an effect, make an impression.

impair *verb* **weaken**, damage, harm, undermine, diminish, reduce, lessen, decrease.
- OPPOSITES improve, enhance.

impart *verb* **communicate**, pass on, convey, transmit, relay, relate, tell, make known, report, announce.

impartial *adjective* **unbiased**, unprejudiced, neutral, non-partisan, disinterested, detached, dispassionate, objective.
- OPPOSITES biased, partisan.

impasse *noun* **deadlock**, dead end, stalemate, stand-off, standstill.

impatient *adjective* **1 restless**, agitated, nervous, anxious. **2 anxious**, eager, keen; *informal* itching, dying. **3 irritated**, annoyed, angry, tetchy, snappy, cross, curt, brusque.
- OPPOSITES patient.

impeccable *adjective* **flawless**, faultless, unblemished, spotless, stainless, perfect, exemplary, irreproachable; *informal* squeaky clean.
- OPPOSITES imperfect.

impede *verb* **hinder**, obstruct, hamper, hold back/up, delay, interfere with, disrupt, retard, slow (down).
- OPPOSITES facilitate.

impediment *noun* **1 hindrance**, obstruction, obstacle, barrier, bar, block, check, curb, restriction, problem, issue. **2 defect**, impairment, stammer, stutter, lisp.

impending *adjective* **imminent**, close (at hand), near, approaching, coming, brewing, looming, threatening.

impenetrable *adjective* **1 unbreakable**, indestructible, solid, thick, unyielding. **2 impassable**, dense, thick, overgrown. **3 incomprehensible**, unfathomable, unintelligible, baffling, bewildering, confusing, opaque.

imperative *adjective* **vital**, crucial, critical, essential, pressing, urgent.

imperceptible *adjective* **unnoticeable**, undetectable, indiscernible, invisible, inaudible, impalpable, slight, small, subtle, faint.

imperfect *adjective* **faulty**, flawed, defective, inferior, second-rate, shoddy, substandard, damaged, blemished, torn, broken, cracked, scratched; *Brit. informal* duff.

imperious *adjective* **peremptory**, high-handed, overbearing, domineering, authoritarian, dictatorial, authoritative, bossy, arrogant; *informal* pushy, high and mighty.

impersonal *adjective* **aloof**, distant, remote, detached, unemotional, unsentimental, cold, cool, indifferent, unconcerned, formal, stiff, business-like, matter-of-fact; *informal* starchy, stand-offish.

impersonate *verb* **imitate**, mimic, do an impression of, ape, parody, caricature, satirize, lampoon, masquerade as, pose as, pass yourself off as; *informal* take off, send up.

impertinent *adjective* **rude**, insolent, impolite, ill-mannered, disrespectful, impudent, cheeky, presumptuous, forward.
- OPPOSITES polite, respectful.

impetuous *adjective* **impulsive**, rash, hasty, reckless, foolhardy, imprudent, ill-considered, spontaneous, impromptu, spur-of-the-moment.

impetus *noun* **1 momentum**, drive, thrust, energy, force, power, push. **2 motivation**, stimulus, incentive, inspiration, driving force.

implant *verb* **1 insert**, embed, bury, inject, transplant, graft. **2 instil**, inculcate, introduce, plant, sow.

implausible *adjective* **unlikely**, improbable, questionable, doubtful, debatable, unconvincing, far-fetched.
- OPPOSITES convincing.

implement *noun* **tool**, utensil, instrument, device, apparatus, gadget, contraption, appliance; *informal* gizmo.
● *verb* **execute**, apply, put into effect, put into practice, carry out/through, perform, enact, fulfil.
- OPPOSITES abolish, cancel.

implicate *verb* **incriminate**, involve, connect, embroil, enmesh.

implication *noun* **1 suggestion**, inference, insinuation, innuendo, intimation, imputation. **2 consequence**, result, ramification, repercussion, reverberation, effect. **3 incrimination**, involvement, connection, entanglement, association.

implicit *adjective* **1 implied**, inferred, understood, hinted at, suggested, unspoken, unstated, tacit, taken for granted. **2 inherent**, latent, underlying, inbuilt, incorporated. **3 absolute**, complete, total, wholehearted, utter, unqualified, unconditional, unshakeable, unquestioning, firm.
- OPPOSITES explicit.

implore *verb* **plead with**, beg, entreat, appeal to, ask, request, call on, exhort, urge.

imply *verb* **1 insinuate**, suggest, infer, hint, intimate, give someone to understand, make out. **2 involve**, entail, mean, point to, signify, indicate, presuppose.

impolite *adjective* **rude**, bad-mannered, ill-mannered, discourteous, uncivil, disrespectful, insolent, impudent, impertinent, cheeky; *informal* lippy.

import *verb* **bring in**, buy in, ship in.
- OPPOSITES export.
● *noun* **1 importance**, significance, consequence, momentousness, magnitude, substance, weight, note, gravity, seriousness. **2 meaning**, sense, essence, gist, drift, message, thrust, substance, implication.
- OPPOSITES insignificance.

importance *noun* **1 significance**, momentousness, moment, import, consequence, note, weight, seriousness, gravity. **2 status**, eminence, prestige, worth, influence, power, authority.
- OPPOSITES insignificance.

important *adjective* **1 significant**, consequential, momentous, of great import, major, valuable, necessary, crucial, vital, essential, pivotal, decisive, far-reaching, historic. **2 powerful**, influential, well connected, high-ranking, prominent, eminent, notable, distinguished, esteemed, respected, great, prestigious.
- OPPOSITES insignificant.

impose *verb* **1** *he imposed his ideas on everyone* **foist**, force, inflict, press, saddle someone with. **2 levy**, charge, apply, enforce, set, establish, institute, introduce, bring into effect.
- OPPOSITES abolish.
□ **impose on** take advantage of, exploit, take liberties with, bother, trouble, disturb, inconvenience, put out, put to trouble.

imposing *adjective* **impressive**, spectacular, striking, dramatic, commanding, arresting, awesome, formidable, splendid, grand, majestic.
- OPPOSITES modest.

imposition *noun* **1 imposing**, foisting, forcing, inflicting. **2 levying**, charging, application, enforcement, enforcing, setting, establishment, introduction. **3 burden**, encumbrance, liberty, bother, worry; *informal* hassle.

impossible *adjective* **1 impracticable**, non-viable, unworkable, unattainable, unachievable, unobtainable, hopeless, out of the question; *informal* like herding cats. **2 unbearable**, intolerable, unendurable. **3** *(informal)* **unreasonable**, difficult, awkward, intolerable, unbearable, exasperating, maddening, infuriating.
- OPPOSITES possible.

impostor *noun* **impersonator**, deceiver, hoaxer, fraudster, fake, fraud; *informal* phoney.

impound *verb* **confiscate**, appropriate, take possession of, seize, commandeer, expropriate, requisition, take over.

impracticable *adjective* **unworkable**, unfeasible, non-viable, unachievable, unattainable, impractical; *informal* like herding cats.
- OPPOSITES practicable.

impractical *adjective* **1 unrealistic**, unworkable, unfeasible, non-viable, ill-thought-out, absurd, idealistic, fanciful, romantic, starry-eyed, pie-in-the-sky; *informal* cockeyed, crackpot, crazy. **2 unsuitable**, not sensible, inappropriate, unserviceable.
- OPPOSITES realistic, practical.

imprecise *adjective* **1 vague**, loose, indistinct, inaccurate, non-specific, sweeping, broad, general, hazy, fuzzy, woolly, nebulous, ambiguous, equivocal, uncertain. **2 inexact**, approximate, rough; *N. Amer. informal* ballpark.
- OPPOSITES exact.

impress *verb* **make an impression on**, have an impact on, influence, affect, move, stir, rouse, excite, inspire, dazzle, awe.
- OPPOSITES disappoint.
□ **impress on** emphasize to, stress to, bring home to, instil in, inculcate into, drum into.

impression *noun* **1 feeling**, sense, fancy, (sneaking) suspicion, inkling, intuition, hunch, notion, idea. **2 opinion**, view, image, picture, perception, reaction, judgement, verdict, estimation. **3 impact**, effect, influence. **4 indentation**, dent, mark, outline, imprint. **5 impersonation**, imitation, caricature; *informal* take-off.

impressionable *adjective* **easily influenced**, suggestible, susceptible, persuadable, pliable, malleable, pliant, ingenuous, trusting, naive, gullible.

impressive *adjective* **magnificent**, majestic, imposing, splendid, spectacular, grand, awe-inspiring, stunning, breathtaking.

imprint *verb* **stamp**, print, impress, mark, emboss.
● *noun* **impression**, print, mark, stamp, indentation.

imprison *verb* **incarcerate**, send to prison, jail, lock up, put away, intern, detain, hold prisoner, hold captive; *informal* send down; *Brit. informal* bang up.

imprisonment *noun* **custody**, incarceration, internment, confinement, detention, captivity; *informal* time; *Brit. informal* porridge.

improbable *adjective* **1 unlikely**, doubtful, dubious, debatable, questionable, uncertain. **2 unconvincing**, unbelievable, implausible, unlikely.

impromptu *adjective* **unrehearsed**, unprepared, unscripted, extempore, extemporized, improvised, spontaneous, unplanned; *informal* off-the-cuff.

improper *adjective* **1 unacceptable**, unprofessional, irregular, unethical, dishonest. **2 unseemly**, unfitting, unbecoming, unladylike, ungentlemanly, inappropriate, indelicate, indecent, immodest, indecorous, immoral. **3 indecent**, risqué, suggestive, naughty, dirty, filthy, vulgar, crude, rude, obscene, lewd; *informal* blue, raunchy, steamy.
- OPPOSITES proper, seemly.

improve *verb* **1 make better**, ameliorate, upgrade, refine, enhance, boost, build on, raise. **2 get better**, advance, progress, develop, make headway, make progress, pick up, look up, move forward. **3 recover**, get better,

recuperate, rally, revive, be on the mend.
- OPPOSITES worsen, deteriorate.

improvement *noun* **advance**, development, upgrade, refinement, enhancement, betterment, amelioration, boost, augmentation, rally, recovery, upswing.

improvise *verb* **1 extemporize**, ad-lib; *informal* speak off the cuff, play it by ear, busk it, wing it. **2 contrive**, devise, throw together, cobble together, rig up; *informal* whip up, rustle up; *Brit. informal* knock up.

impulse *noun* **1 urge**, instinct, drive, compulsion, itch, whim, desire, fancy, notion. **2 spontaneity**, impetuosity, recklessness, rashness.

impulsive *adjective* **1 hasty**, sudden, quick, precipitate, impetuous, impromptu, spontaneous, snap, unplanned, unpremeditated, thoughtless, rash, reckless. **2 impetuous**, instinctive, passionate, intuitive, emotional, devil-may-care.
- OPPOSITES cautious, premeditated.

inaccurate *adjective* **inexact**, imprecise, incorrect, wrong, erroneous, faulty, imperfect, defective, unreliable, false, mistaken, untrue; *Brit. informal* adrift.

inactivity *noun* **inaction**, inertia, idleness, non-intervention, negligence, apathy, indolence, laziness, slothfulness.
- OPPOSITES action.

inadequate *adjective* **1 insufficient**, deficient, poor, scant, scarce, sparse, in short supply, paltry, meagre. **2 incapable**, incompetent, ineffective, inefficient, inept, unfit; *informal* not up to scratch.

inadvertently *adverb* **accidentally**, by accident, unintentionally, by mistake, mistakenly, unwittingly.
- OPPOSITES intentionally.

inappropriate *adjective* **unsuitable**, unfitting, unseemly, unbecoming, improper, out of place/keeping, inapposite; *informal* out of order.

inaudible *adjective* **unclear**, indistinct, faint, muted, soft, low, muffled, whispered, muttered, murmured, mumbled.

inaugurate *verb* **1 initiate**, begin, start, institute, launch, get going, get under way, establish, bring in, usher in; *informal* kick off. **2 install**, instate, swear in, invest, ordain, crown.

incapable *adjective* **incompetent**, inept, inadequate, ineffective, ineffectual, unfit, unqualified; *informal* not up to it.
- OPPOSITES competent.

incense *verb* **enrage**, infuriate, anger, madden, outrage, exasperate, antagonize, provoke; *informal* make someone see red.
- OPPOSITES placate.

incensed *adjective* **enraged**, furious, infuriated, irate, raging, incandescent, fuming, seething, beside yourself, outraged; *informal* mad, hopping mad, wild, livid.

incentive *noun* **inducement**, motivation, motive, reason, stimulus, spur, impetus, encouragement, carrot; *informal* sweetener.
- OPPOSITES deterrent.

incident *noun* **1 event**, occurrence, episode, happening, affair, business, adventure, exploit, escapade. **2 disturbance**, commotion, clash, confrontation, scene, accident, fracas, contretemps; *Brit.* row. **3** *the journey was not without incident* **excitement**, adventure, drama, crisis, danger.

incidental *adjective* **1 secondary**, subsidiary, minor, peripheral, background, by-the-by, unimportant, insignificant, tangential. **2 chance**, accidental, random, fluky, fortuitous, serendipitous, coincidental, unlooked-for.
- OPPOSITES essential.

incidentally *adverb* **1 by the way**, by the by, in passing, speaking of which; *informal* as it happens. **2 by chance**, by accident, accidentally, fortuitously, by a fluke, by happenstance.

incite *verb* **1 stir up**, whip up, encourage, stoke up, fuel, kindle, inflame, instigate, provoke, excite, trigger, spark off. **2 provoke**, encourage, urge, goad, spur on, egg on, drive, prod, prompt; *informal* put up to.
- OPPOSITES discourage, deter.

inclination *noun* **tendency**, propensity, leaning, predisposition, predilection, impulse, bent, liking, taste, penchant, preference.
- OPPOSITES aversion.

incline *verb* **1 predispose**, lead, make, dispose, prejudice, prompt, induce. **2** *I incline to the opposite view* **tend**, lean, swing, veer, gravitate, be drawn, prefer, favour, go for. **3 bend**, bow, nod, bob, lower, dip.
● *noun* **slope**, gradient, pitch, ramp, bank, ascent, rise, hill, dip, descent; *N. Amer.* grade.

inclined *adjective* **1 disposed**, minded, of a mind. **2 prone**, given, in the habit of, liable, apt.

include *verb* **1 incorporate**, comprise, encompass, cover, embrace, take in, number, contain. **2 allow for**, count, take into account, take into consideration. **3 add**, insert, put in, append, enter.
- OPPOSITES exclude, leave out.

inclusive *adjective* **all-in**, comprehensive, overall, full, all-round, umbrella, catch-all, all-encompassing.
- OPPOSITES exclusive, limited.

income *noun* **earnings**, salary, wages, pay, remuneration, revenue, receipts, takings, profits, proceeds, yield, dividend; *N. Amer.* take.
- OPPOSITES expenditure, outgoings.

incoming *adjective* **1 arriving**, approaching, inbound, inward, returning, homeward. **2 new**, next, future, elect, designate.
- OPPOSITES outward, outgoing.

incompatible *adjective* **mismatched**, unsuited, poles apart, irreconcilable, inconsistent, conflicting, opposed, opposite, contradictory, at odds, at variance.
- OPPOSITES harmonious, consistent.

incompetent *adjective* **inept**, unskilled, inexpert, amateurish, unprofessional, bungling, blundering, clumsy; *informal* useless, not up to it.

incomplete *adjective* **1 unfinished**, uncompleted, partial, half-finished. **2 deficient**, insufficient, partial, sketchy, fragmentary, scrappy, bitty.
- OPPOSITES completed, full.

incomprehensible *adjective* **unintelligible**, impenetrable, unclear, indecipherable, unfathomable, abstruse, difficult, involved; *Brit. informal* double Dutch.
- OPPOSITES intelligible, clear.

inconsistent *adjective* **1 erratic**, changeable, unpredictable, variable, unstable, fickle, unreliable, volatile; *informal* up and down. **2 incompatible**, conflicting, at odds, at variance, irreconcilable, out of keeping, contrary.

inconvenience *noun* **trouble**, nuisance, bother, problem, disruption, difficulty, disturbance; *informal* aggravation, hassle, headache, pain, pain in the neck.
● *verb* **trouble**, bother, put out, put to any trouble, disturb, impose on.

inconvenient *adjective* **awkward**, difficult, inopportune, badly timed, unsuitable, inappropriate, unfortunate.

incorporate *verb* **1 absorb**, include, subsume, assimilate, integrate, swallow up. **2 include**, contain, embrace, build in, offer, boast. **3 blend**, mix, combine, fold in, stir in.

incorrect *adjective* **1 wrong**, erroneous, mistaken, untrue, false, fallacious, flawed; *informal* wide of the mark. **2 inappropriate**, unsuitable, unacceptable, improper, unseemly; *informal* out of order.
- OPPOSITES correct.

increase *verb* **1 grow**, get bigger, get larger, enlarge, expand, swell, rise, climb, mount, intensify, strengthen, extend, spread, widen. **2 add to**, make larger, make bigger, augment, supplement, top up, build up, extend,

raise, swell, inflate, intensify, heighten; *informal* up, bump up.
● *noun* **growth**, rise, enlargement, expansion, extension, increment, gain, addition, augmentation, surge; *informal* hike.
- OPPOSITES decrease.

incredible *adjective* **1 unbelievable**, unconvincing, far-fetched, implausible, improbable, inconceivable, unimaginable. **2 wonderful**, marvellous, spectacular, remarkable, phenomenal, prodigious, breathtaking; *informal* fantastic, terrific.

incur *verb* **bring on yourself**, expose yourself to, lay yourself open to, run up, earn, sustain, experience.

indecent *adjective* **1 obscene**, dirty, filthy, rude, naughty, vulgar, smutty, pornographic; *informal* blue; *euphemistic* adult. **2 unseemly**, improper, unbecoming, inappropriate.

independence *noun* **1 self-government**, self-rule, home rule, self-determination, sovereignty, autonomy. **2 impartiality**, neutrality, disinterestedness, detachment, objectivity.

independent *adjective* **1 self-governing**, self-ruling, self-determining, sovereign, autonomous, non-aligned, free. **2 separate**, different, unconnected, unrelated, discrete. **3 private**, non-state-run, private-sector, fee-paying, privatized, deregulated, denationalized. **4 impartial**, unbiased, unprejudiced, neutral, disinterested, uninvolved, detached, dispassionate, objective, non-partisan.
- OPPOSITES related, biased.

independently *adverb* **alone**, on your own, separately, individually, unaccompanied, solo, unaided, unassisted, without help, by your own efforts, under your own steam, single-handedly.

index *noun* **list**, listing, inventory, catalogue, register, directory, database.

indicate *verb* **1 point to**, be a sign of, be evidence of, demonstrate, show, testify to, be symptomatic of, denote, mark, signal, reflect, signify, suggest, imply. **2 state**, declare, make known, communicate, announce, put on record. **3 specify**, designate, stipulate, show.

indication *noun* **sign**, signal, indicator, symptom, mark, demonstration, pointer, guide, hint, clue, omen, warning.

indicator *noun* **measure**, gauge, meter, barometer, guide, index, mark, sign, signal.

indictment *noun* **charge**, accusation, arraignment, prosecution, citation, summons; *N. Amer.* impeachment.

indifference *noun* **detachment**, lack of concern, disinterest, lack of interest, nonchalance, boredom, unresponsiveness, impassivity, coolness.
- OPPOSITES concern.

indifferent *adjective* **1 detached**, unconcerned, uninterested, uncaring, casual, nonchalant, offhand, unenthusiastic, unimpressed, unmoved, impassive, cool. **2 mediocre**, ordinary, average, middle-of-the-road, uninspired, undistinguished, unexceptional, pedestrian, forgettable, amateurish; *informal* no great shakes, not up to much.
- OPPOSITES enthusiastic, brilliant.

indignant *adjective* **aggrieved**, affronted, displeased, resentful, angry, annoyed, offended, exasperated; *informal* peeved, irked, put out; *Brit. informal* narked, not best pleased; *N. Amer. informal* sore.

indirect *adjective* **1 incidental**, secondary, subordinate, ancillary, collateral, concomitant, contingent. **2 roundabout**, circuitous, meandering, winding, tortuous. **3 oblique**, implicit, implied.

individual *adjective* **1 single**, separate, discrete, independent, lone. **2 unique**, characteristic, distinctive, distinct, particular, idiosyncratic, peculiar, personal, special. **3 original**, exclusive, different, unusual, novel, unorthodox, out of the ordinary.
- OPPOSITES multiple, shared, ordinary.
● *noun* **person**, human being, soul,

creature, character; *informal* type, sort, customer.

individually *adverb* **separately**, singly, one by one, one at a time, independently.

induce *verb* **1 persuade**, convince, prevail on, get, make, prompt, encourage, cajole into, talk into. **2 bring about**, cause, produce, create, give rise to, generate, engender.
- OPPOSITES dissuade.

indulge *verb* **1 satisfy**, gratify, fulfil, feed, yield to, give in to, go along with. **2 pamper**, spoil, overindulge, coddle, mollycoddle, cosset, pander to, wait on hand and foot.

indulgence *noun* **1 satisfaction**, gratification, fulfilment. **2 self-gratification**, self-indulgence, overindulgence, intemperance, excess, extravagance, hedonism. **3 extravagance**, luxury, treat, non-essential, extra, frill. **4 pampering**, coddling, mollycoddling, cosseting. **5 tolerance**, forbearance, understanding, compassion, sympathy, leniency.
- OPPOSITES asceticism, intolerance.

indulgent *adjective* **generous**, permissive, easy-going, liberal, tolerant, forgiving, forbearing, lenient, kind, kindly, soft-hearted.
- OPPOSITES strict.

industrialist *noun* **manufacturer**, factory owner, captain of industry, magnate, tycoon.

industry *noun* **1 manufacturing**, production, construction, trade, commerce. **2 business**, trade, field, line of business, profession. **3 activity**, energy, effort, endeavour, hard work, industriousness, diligence, application.

ineffective *adjective* **1 unsuccessful**, unproductive, unprofitable, ineffectual, unavailing, to no avail, fruitless, futile. **2 ineffectual**, inefficient, inadequate, incompetent, incapable, unfit, inept; *informal* useless, hopeless.
- OPPOSITES effective.

inefficient *adjective* **1 ineffective**, ineffectual, incompetent, inept, disorganized. **2 uneconomical**, wasteful, unproductive, time-wasting, slow, unsystematic.

inequality *noun* **imbalance**, inequity, inconsistency, disparity, discrepancy, dissimilarity, difference, bias, prejudice, discrimination, unfairness.

inevitable *adjective* **unavoidable**, inescapable, inexorable, assured, certain, sure.
- OPPOSITES avoidable.

inevitably *adverb* **unavoidably**, necessarily, automatically, naturally, as a matter of course, of necessity, inescapably, certainly, surely; *informal* like it or not.

inexpensive *adjective* **cheap**, affordable, low-cost, economical, competitive, reasonable, budget, economy, bargain, cut-price, reduced.

inexperienced *adjective* **inexpert**, untrained, unqualified, unskilled, unseasoned, naive, new, callow, immature; *informal* wet behind the ears, wide-eyed.

infamous *adjective* **notorious**, disreputable, scandalous.
- OPPOSITES reputable.

infancy *noun* **beginnings**, early days, early stages, emergence, dawn, outset, birth, inception.
- OPPOSITES end.

infant *noun* **baby**, newborn, young child, tiny tot, little one; *Medicine* neonate; *Scottish & N. English* bairn, wean; *informal* tiny, sprog.

infect *verb* **contaminate**, pollute, taint, foul, poison, blight.

infection *noun* **1 disease**, virus, illness, ailment, disorder, sickness; *informal* bug. **2 contamination**, poison, bacteria, germs; *Medicine* sepsis.

infectious *adjective* **communicable**, contagious, transmittable, transmissible, transferable; *informal* catching.

inferior *adjective* **1 second-class**, lower-ranking, subordinate, junior, minor, lowly, humble, menial, beneath someone. **2 second-rate**, mediocre, substandard, low-grade, unsatisfactory, shoddy, poor; *informal* crummy, lousy.

- OPPOSITES superior.
● *noun* **subordinate**, junior, underling, minion.

infertility *noun* **barrenness**, sterility, childlessness.

infested *adjective* **overrun**, swarming, teeming, crawling, alive, plagued.

infiltrate *verb* **penetrate**, insinuate yourself into, worm your way into, sneak into, slip into, creep into, invade.

infiltrator *noun* **spy**, secret agent, plant, intruder, interloper, subversive, informer, mole, fifth columnist; *N. Amer. informal* spook.

infinite *adjective* **boundless**, unbounded, unlimited, limitless, never-ending, incalculable, untold, countless, uncountable, innumerable, numberless, immeasurable, cosmic.
- OPPOSITES limited.

inflame *verb* **1 enrage**, incense, anger, madden, infuriate, exasperate, provoke, antagonize; *informal* make someone see red. **2 aggravate**, exacerbate, intensify, worsen, compound.
- OPPOSITES placate.

inflamed *adjective* **swollen**, red, hot, burning, itchy, sore, painful, tender, infected.

inflate *verb* **1 blow up**, pump up, fill, puff up/out, dilate, distend, swell, bloat. **2 increase**, raise, boost, escalate, put up; *informal* hike up, jack up.
- OPPOSITES deflate, lower.

inflated *adjective* **1 high**, sky-high, excessive, unreasonable, outrageous, exorbitant, extortionate; *Brit.* over the odds; *informal* steep. **2 exaggerated**, immoderate, overblown, overstated.
- OPPOSITES low, modest.

inflict *verb* **1 give**, administer, deal out, mete out, exact, wreak. **2 impose**, force, thrust, foist.

influence *noun* **1 effect**, impact, control, spell, hold. **2** *a good influence on her* **example to**, role model for, inspiration to. **3 power**, authority, sway, leverage, weight, pull; *informal* clout.
● *verb* **1 affect**, have an impact on, determine, guide, control, shape, govern, decide, change, alter. **2 sway**, bias, prejudice, manipulate, persuade, induce.

influential *adjective* **powerful**, controlling, important, authoritative, leading, significant, instrumental, guiding.

inform *verb* **1 tell**, notify, apprise, advise, impart to, communicate to, let someone know, brief, enlighten, send word to. **2** *he informed on two colleagues* **betray**, give away, denounce, incriminate, report; *informal* rat, squeal, split, snitch, tell, blow the whistle; *Brit. informal* grass, shop; *N. Amer. informal* finger; *Austral./NZ informal* dob in.

informal *adjective* **1 unofficial**, casual, relaxed, easy-going, low-key. **2 colloquial**, vernacular, idiomatic, popular, familiar, everyday; *informal* slangy, chatty. **3 casual**, relaxed, comfortable, everyday; *informal* comfy.
- OPPOSITES formal.

information *noun* **facts**, particulars, details, figures, statistics, data, knowledge, intelligence; *informal* info, gen.

informative *adjective* **instructive**, illuminating, enlightening, revealing, explanatory, factual, educational, edifying.

informed *adjective* **knowledgeable**, enlightened, educated, briefed, up to date, up to speed, in the picture, in the know, au fait; *informal* clued up.
- OPPOSITES ignorant.

infuriate *verb* **enrage**, incense, provoke, anger, madden, exasperate; *informal* make someone see red; *Brit. informal* wind up.
- OPPOSITES please.

ingenious *adjective* **inventive**, creative, imaginative, original, innovative, pioneering, resourceful, enterprising, inspired, clever; *informal* genius.
- OPPOSITES unimaginative.

ingredient *noun* **constituent**, component, element, item, part, strand, unit, feature, aspect, attribute.

inhabit *verb* **live in**, occupy, settle, people, populate, colonize.

inhabitant *noun* **resident**, occupant, occupier, settler, local, native; (**inhabitants**) population, populace, people, public, community, citizenry, townsfolk, townspeople.

inhale *verb* **breathe in**, draw in, suck in, sniff in, drink in, gasp.
- OPPOSITES exhale.

inherit *verb* **be bequeathed**, be left, be willed, come into, succeed to, assume, take over.

inheritance *noun* **legacy**, bequest, endowment, birthright, heritage, patrimony.

WORD LINKS
hereditary relating to inheritance

inhibit *verb* **impede**, hinder, hamper, hold back, discourage, interfere with, obstruct, slow down, retard.
- OPPOSITES assist, allow.

inhibited *adjective* **reserved**, reticent, guarded, self-conscious, insecure, withdrawn, repressed, undemonstrative, shy, diffident, bashful; *informal* uptight.

initial *adjective* **beginning**, opening, commencing, starting, first, earliest, primary, preliminary, preparatory, introductory, inaugural.
- OPPOSITES final.

initially *adverb* **at first**, at the start, at the outset, in/at the beginning, to begin with, to start with, originally.

initiate *verb* **1 begin**, start (off), commence, institute, inaugurate, launch, instigate, establish, set up. **2** *he was initiated into a religious cult* **introduce**, admit, induct, install, swear in, ordain, invest.
- OPPOSITES end, expel.

initiative *noun* **1 enterprise**, resourcefulness, inventiveness, imagination, ingenuity, originality, creativity. **2 advantage**, upper hand, edge, lead, start. **3 scheme**, plan, strategy, measure, proposal, step, action.

inject *verb* **1 administer**, take; *informal* shoot (up), mainline, fix. **2 inoculate**, vaccinate. **3 insert**, introduce, feed, push, force, shoot. **4 introduce**, instil, infuse, imbue, breathe.

injection *noun* **1 inoculation**, vaccination, immunization, booster; *informal* jab, shot. **2 addition**, introduction, investment, dose, infusion, insertion.

injunction *noun* **order**, ruling, direction, directive, command, instruction, mandate.

injure *verb* **1 hurt**, wound, damage, harm, disable, break; *Medicine* traumatize. **2 damage**, mar, spoil, weaken, ruin, blight, blemish, tarnish, blacken.

injured *adjective* **1 hurt**, wounded, damaged, sore, bruised, broken, fractured; *Medicine* traumatized; *Brit. informal* gammy. **2 upset**, hurt, wounded, offended, reproachful, pained, aggrieved.
- OPPOSITES healthy.

injury *noun* **1 wound**, bruise, cut, gash, scratch, graze; *Medicine* trauma, lesion. **2 harm**, hurt, damage, pain, suffering. **3 offence**, abuse, injustice, disservice, affront, insult.

injustice *noun* **1 unfairness**, one-sidedness, inequity, bias, prejudice, discrimination, intolerance, exploitation, corruption. **2 wrong**, offence, crime, sin, outrage, scandal, disgrace, affront.

inland *adjective* **interior**, inshore, internal, upcountry.
- OPPOSITES coastal.

inlet *noun* **1 cove**, bay, bight, creek, estuary, fjord, sound; *Scottish* firth. **2 vent**, flue, shaft, duct, channel, pipe.

inmate *noun* **1 patient**, inpatient, resident, occupant. **2 prisoner**, convict, captive, detainee, internee.

inner *adjective* **1 central**, innermost; *N. Amer.* downtown. **2 internal**, interior, inside, innermost. **3 hidden**, secret, deep, underlying, veiled.
- OPPOSITES outer.

innocence *noun* **1 guiltlessness**, blamelessness. **2 naivety**, credulity, inexperience, gullibility, ingenuousness.

innocent *adjective* **1 guiltless**, blameless, clean, irreproachable, above reproach, honest, upright, law-abiding. **2 harmless**, innocuous, safe, inoffensive, unobjectionable. **3 naive**, ingenuous, trusting, credulous, impressionable, easily led, inexperienced, unsophisticated, artless.
- OPPOSITES guilty.

innovation *noun* **change**, alteration, upheaval, reorganization, restructuring, novelty, departure.

innovative *adjective* **original**, new, novel, fresh, unusual, experimental, inventive, disruptive, ingenious, pioneering, groundbreaking, revolutionary, radical; *informal* edgy.

inquest *noun* **enquiry**, investigation, probe, examination, review, hearing.

inquire see **enquire**.

inquiry see **enquiry**.

insane *adjective* **1 mad**, of unsound mind, certifiable, psychotic, schizophrenic, unhinged; *Brit.* sectionable; *informal* crazy, raving mad, bonkers, loony, round the bend; *Brit. informal* crackers, off your trolley; *N. Amer. informal* nutso. **2 stupid**, idiotic, nonsensical, absurd, ridiculous, ludicrous, preposterous; *informal* crazy, mad; *Brit. informal* daft, barmy.
- OPPOSITES sane.

insect *noun* **bug**; *informal* creepy-crawly; *Brit. informal* minibeast.

WORD LINKS
entomology study of insects

insecure *adjective* **1 unconfident**, uncertain, unsure, doubtful, diffident, hesitant, self-conscious, anxious, fearful. **2 unprotected**, unguarded, vulnerable, unsecured. **3 unstable**, rickety, wobbly, shaky, unsteady, precarious.
- OPPOSITES confident, stable.

insecurity *noun* **lack of confidence**, uncertainty, self-doubt, diffidence, hesitancy, nervousness, self-consciousness, anxiety, worry, unease.

insert *verb* **put**, place, push, thrust, slide, slip, load, fit, slot, install; *informal* pop, stick, bung.
- OPPOSITES extract, remove.

inside *noun* **1 interior**, centre, core, middle, heart. **2 (insides) stomach**, gut, bowels, intestines; *informal* tummy, belly, guts.
● *adjective* **1 inner**, interior, internal, innermost. **2 confidential**, classified, restricted, privileged, private, secret, exclusive; *informal* hush-hush.
- OPPOSITES outside.

insight *noun* **intuition**, perception, understanding, comprehension, appreciation, judgement, discernment, vision, imagination, wisdom; *informal* nous.

insignificant *adjective* **unimportant**, trivial, trifling, negligible, inconsequential, of no account, paltry, petty, insubstantial; *informal* piddling.

insincere *adjective* **false**, fake, hollow, artificial, feigned, pretended, put-on, disingenuous, hypocritical, cynical; *informal* phoney, pretend.

insist *verb* **1 stand firm**, stand your ground, be resolute, be determined, hold out, persist, be emphatic, lay down the law, not take no for an answer; *informal* stick to your guns, put your foot down. **2 demand**, command, order, require. **3 maintain**, assert, protest, swear, declare, repeat.

insistent *adjective* **persistent**, determined, tenacious, unyielding, dogged, unrelenting, importunate, relentless, inexorable.

inspect *verb* **examine**, check, scrutinize, investigate, vet, test, monitor, survey, study, look over; *informal* check out, give something a/the once-over.

inspection *noun* **examination**, check-up, survey, scrutiny, exploration, investigation; *informal* once-over, going-over.

inspector *noun* **examiner**, scrutineer, investigator, surveyor, assessor, supervisor, monitor, watchdog, ombudsman, auditor.

inspiration *noun* **1 stimulus**, motivation, encouragement, influence, spur, fillip; *informal* shot in the arm. **2 creativity**, invention, innovation, ingenuity, imagination, originality, insight, vision. **3 bright idea**, revelation; *informal* brainwave; *N. Amer. informal* brainstorm.

inspire *verb* **1 stimulate**, motivate, encourage, influence, move, spur, energize, galvanize. **2 give rise to**, lead to, bring about, prompt, spawn, engender. **3 arouse**, awaken, prompt, induce, ignite, trigger, kindle, produce, bring out.

inspired *adjective* **outstanding**, wonderful, marvellous, excellent, magnificent, coruscating, exceptional, first-class, virtuoso, superlative; *informal* tremendous, superb, awesome, out of this world, genius; *Brit. informal* brilliant.

inspiring *adjective* **inspirational**, encouraging, heartening, uplifting, stirring, rousing, electrifying, moving.

instability *noun* **unreliability**, uncertainty, unpredictability, insecurity, volatility, capriciousness, changeability, variability, inconsistency, mutability.
- OPPOSITES stability.

install *verb* **1 put**, place, station, site, insert. **2 swear in**, induct, inaugurate, invest, appoint, ordain, consecrate, anoint, enthrone, crown. **3 ensconce**, position, settle, seat, plant, sit (down); *informal* plonk, park.
- OPPOSITES remove.

instalment *noun* **1 payment**, repayment, tranche, portion. **2 part**, episode, chapter, issue, programme, section, segment, volume.

instance *noun* **example**, occasion, occurrence, case, illustration, sample.

instant *adjective* **1 immediate**, instantaneous, on-the-spot, prompt, swift, speedy, rapid, quick; *informal* snappy. **2 prepared**, pre-cooked, microwaveable.
- OPPOSITES delayed.
● *noun* **moment**, minute, second, split second, trice, twinkling of an eye, flash; *informal* jiffy.

instantly *adverb* **immediately**, at once, straight away, right away, instantaneously, forthwith, there and then, here and now, this/that minute, this/that second.

instead *adverb* **as an alternative**, in lieu, alternatively, rather, on second thoughts; *N. Amer.* alternately.

instinct *noun* **1 inclination**, urge, drive, compulsion, intuition, feeling, sixth sense, nose. **2 talent**, gift, ability, aptitude, skill, flair, feel, knack.

instinctive *adjective* **intuitive**, natural, instinctual, innate, inborn, inherent, unconscious, subconscious, automatic, reflex, knee-jerk; *informal* gut.

institute *noun* **organization**, establishment, institution, foundation, centre, academy, school, college, university, society, association, federation, body.
● *verb* **set up**, inaugurate, found, establish, organize, initiate, set in motion, get under way, get off the ground, start, launch.
- OPPOSITES abolish, end.

institution *noun* **1 establishment**, organization, institute, foundation, centre, academy, school, college, university, society, association, body. **2 (residential) home**, hospital, asylum, prison. **3** *the institution of marriage* **practice**, custom, convention, tradition.

institutional *adjective* **organized**, established, bureaucratic, conventional, procedural, formal, formalized, systematic, systematized, structured, regulated.

instruct *verb* **1 order**, direct, command, tell, mandate; *old use* bid. **2 teach**, coach, train, educate, tutor, guide, school, show.

instruction *noun* **1 order**, command, directive, direction, decree, injunction, mandate, commandment; *old use* bidding. **2** *read the instructions* **directions**, handbook, manual, guide, advice, guidance. **3 tuition**, teaching, coaching, schooling, lessons, classes, lectures, training, drill, guidance.

instructor *noun* **trainer**, coach, teacher, tutor, adviser, counsellor, guide.

instrument *noun* **1 implement**, tool, utensil, device, apparatus, gadget. **2 gauge**, meter, indicator, dial, display. **3 agent**, cause, agency, channel, medium, means, vehicle.

instrumental *adjective*
▫ **be instrumental in** play a part in, contribute to, be a factor in, have a hand in, promote, advance, further.

insufficient *adjective* **inadequate**, deficient, poor, scant, scanty, not enough, too little, too few.

insulate *verb* **1 wrap**, sheathe, cover, encase, enclose, lag, soundproof. **2 protect**, save, shield, shelter, screen, cushion, cocoon.

insult *verb* **abuse**, be rude to, call someone names, slight, disparage, discredit, malign, defame, denigrate, offend, hurt, humiliate; *informal* bad-mouth; *Brit. informal* slag off.
– OPPOSITES compliment.
● *noun* **jibe**, affront, slight, slur, barb, indignity, abuse, aspersions; *informal* dig, put-down.

insulting *adjective* **abusive**, rude, offensive, disparaging, belittling, derogatory, deprecating, disrespectful, uncomplimentary; *informal* bitchy, catty.

insurance *noun* **indemnity**, assurance, protection, security, cover, safeguard, warranty.

insure *verb* **provide insurance for**, indemnify, cover, assure, protect, underwrite, warrant.

intact *adjective* **whole**, entire, complete, unbroken, undamaged, unscathed, unblemished, unmarked, in one piece.
– OPPOSITES damaged.

integral *adjective* **1 essential**, fundamental, component, basic, intrinsic, inherent, vital, necessary. **2 built-in**, inbuilt, integrated, inboard, fitted. **3 unified**, integrated, comprehensive, holistic, joined-up, all-embracing.
– OPPOSITES peripheral, supplementary.

integrate *verb* **combine**, amalgamate, merge, unite, fuse, blend, consolidate, meld, mix, incorporate, assimilate, homogenize, desegregate.
– OPPOSITES separate.

integrity *noun* **1 honesty**, probity, rectitude, uprightness, fairness, honour, sincerity, truthfulness, trustworthiness. **2 unity**, coherence, cohesion, solidity. **3 soundness**, strength, sturdiness, solidity, durability, stability, rigidity.
– OPPOSITES dishonesty.

intellect *noun* **mind**, brain(s), intelligence, reason, judgement, grey matter, brain cells.

intellectual *adjective* **1 mental**, cerebral, rational, conceptual, theoretical, analytical, logical, cognitive. **2 learned**, academic, erudite, bookish, highbrow, scholarly, donnish.

intelligence *noun* **1 intellect**, cleverness, brainpower, judgement, reasoning, acumen, wit, insight, perception. **2 information**, facts, details, particulars, data, knowledge.

intelligent *adjective* **clever**, bright, quick-witted, smart, astute, sharp, insightful, perceptive, penetrating, educated, knowledgeable, enlightened; *informal* brainy, genius.

intelligible *adjective* **comprehensible**, understandable, accessible, digestible, user-friendly, clear, coherent, plain, unambiguous.

intend *verb* **plan**, mean, have in mind, aim, propose, hope, expect, envisage.

intense *adjective* **1 extreme**, great, acute, fierce, severe, high, exceptional, extraordinary, harsh, strong, powerful, violent; *informal* serious. **2 passionate**, impassioned, zealous, vehement, fervent, earnest, eager, committed.
– OPPOSITES mild, apathetic.

intensify *verb* **escalate**, increase, step up, raise, strengthen, reinforce, pick up, build up, heighten, deepen, extend, expand, amplify, magnify,

aggravate, exacerbate, worsen, inflame, compound.
– OPPOSITES abate.

intensity *noun* **1 strength**, power, force, severity, ferocity, fierceness, harshness, violence. **2 passion**, ardour, fervour, vehemence, fire, emotion, eagerness.

intensive *adjective* **thorough**, thoroughgoing, in-depth, rigorous, exhaustive, vigorous, detailed, minute, meticulous, painstaking, methodical, extensive.
– OPPOSITES cursory.

intent *noun* **aim**, intention, purpose, objective, goal.
● *adjective* **1** *he was intent on proving his point* **bent**, set, determined, insistent, resolved, hell-bent, keen, committed to, determined to. **2 attentive**, absorbed, engrossed, fascinated, enthralled, rapt, focused, concentrating, preoccupied.
– OPPOSITES distracted.

intention *noun* **aim**, purpose, intent, objective, goal.

intentional *adjective* **deliberate**, done on purpose, wilful, calculated, conscious, intended, planned, meant, knowing.

inter *verb* **bury**, lay to rest, consign to the grave, entomb.
– OPPOSITES exhume.

intercept *verb* **stop**, head off, cut off, catch, seize, block, interrupt.

intercourse *noun* **1 dealings**, relations, relationships, contact, interchange, communication, networking. **2 sexual intercourse**, sex, sexual relations, mating, copulation, fornication; *technical* coitus.

interdict *noun* **prohibition**, ban, bar, veto, embargo, moratorium, injunction.

interest *noun* **1 attentiveness**, attention, regard, notice, curiosity, enjoyment, delight. **2** *this will be of interest* **concern**, consequence, importance, import, significance, note, relevance, value. **3 hobby**, pastime, leisure pursuit, amusement, recreation, diversion, passion. **4 stake**, share, claim, investment, involvement, concern.
– OPPOSITES boredom.
● *verb* **appeal to**, be of interest to, attract, intrigue, amuse, divert, entertain, arouse someone's curiosity, whet someone's appetite; *informal* tickle someone's fancy.

interested *adjective* **1 attentive**, fascinated, riveted, gripped, captivated, agog, intrigued, curious, keen, eager. **2 concerned**, involved, affected.

interesting *adjective* **absorbing**, engrossing, fascinating, riveting, gripping, compelling, captivating, engaging, enthralling, appealing, entertaining, stimulating, diverting, intriguing.

interfere *verb* **butt in**, barge in, intrude, meddle, tamper, encroach; *informal* poke your nose in, stick your oar in.
□ **interfere with** impede, obstruct, stand in the way of, hinder, inhibit, restrict, constrain, hamper, handicap, disturb, disrupt, influence, affect, confuse.

interference *noun* **1 intrusion**, intervention, involvement, meddling, prying. **2 disruption**, disturbance, static, noise.

interior *adjective* **1 inside**, inner, internal, inland, upcountry, central. **2 internal**, home, domestic, national, state, civil, local. **3 inner**, mental, spiritual, psychological, private, personal, secret.
● *noun* **1 inside**, depths, recesses, bowels, belly, heart. **2 centre**, heartland.
– OPPOSITES exterior.

intermediary *noun* **mediator**, go-between, negotiator, arbitrator, peacemaker, middleman, broker.

intermediate *adjective* **halfway**, in-between, middle, mid, midway, intervening, transitional.

intermittent *adjective* **sporadic**, irregular, fitful, spasmodic, discontinuous, isolated, random, patchy, scattered, occasional, periodic.
– OPPOSITES continuous.

internal *adjective* **1 inner**, interior, inside, central. **2 domestic**, home, interior, civil, local, national, state.
- OPPOSITES external, foreign.

international *adjective* **global**, worldwide, world, intercontinental, universal, cosmopolitan, multiracial, multinational.
- OPPOSITES national, local.

interpret *verb* **1 explain**, elucidate, expound, clarify. **2 understand**, construe, take (to mean), see, regard. **3 decipher**, decode, translate, understand.

interpretation *noun* **1 explanation**, elucidation, exposition, clarification, analysis. **2 meaning**, understanding, explanation, inference. **3 rendition**, execution, presentation, performance, reading, playing, singing.

interrupt *verb* **1 cut in (on)**, break in (on), barge in (on), intrude, intervene; *informal* butt in (on), chime in (on); *Brit. informal* chip in (on). **2 suspend**, discontinue, adjourn, break off, stop, halt; *informal* put on ice.

interruption *noun* **1 cutting in**, barging in, interference, intervention, intrusion, disturbance; *informal* butting in. **2 suspension**, breaking off, discontinuance, stopping.

interval *noun* **intermission**, interlude, break, recess, time out.

intervene *verb* **intercede**, involve yourself, get involved, step in, interfere, intrude.

interview *noun* **meeting**, discussion, interrogation, cross-examination, debriefing, audience, talk, chat; *informal* grilling.
● *verb* **talk to**, question, quiz, interrogate, cross-examine, debrief, poll, canvass, sound out; *informal* grill, pump.

interviewer *noun* **questioner**, interrogator, examiner, assessor, journalist, reporter, inquisitor.

intimacy *noun* **closeness**, togetherness, rapport, attachment, familiarity, friendliness, affection, warmth.
- OPPOSITES formality.

intimate[1] *adjective* **1 close**, bosom, dear, cherished, fast, firm. **2 friendly**, warm, welcoming, hospitable, relaxed, informal, cosy, comfortable. **3 personal**, private, confidential, secret, inward. **4 detailed**, thorough, exhaustive, deep, in-depth, profound.
- OPPOSITES distant, formal, cold.

intimate[2] *verb* **1 announce**, state, make known, disclose, reveal, divulge, let it be known. **2 imply**, suggest, hint at, indicate, insinuate.

intimidate *verb* **frighten**, menace, scare, terrorize, threaten, browbeat, bully, harass, hound; *informal* lean on.

intricate *adjective* **complex**, complicated, convoluted, tangled, elaborate, ornate, detailed.
- OPPOSITES simple.

intrigue *verb* **interest**, fascinate, arouse someone's curiosity, attract, engage.
● *noun* **plotting**, conniving, scheming, machination, double-dealing, subterfuge.

intriguing *adjective* **interesting**, fascinating, absorbing, engaging.

introduce *verb* **1 institute**, initiate, launch, inaugurate, establish, found, bring in, set in motion, start, begin, get going. **2 present**, make known, acquaint with. **3 insert**, inject, put, force, shoot, feed. **4 instil**, infuse, inject, add.
- OPPOSITES end, remove.

introduction *noun* **1 institution**, establishment, initiation, launch, inauguration, foundation. **2 presentation**, meeting, audience. **3 foreword**, preface, preamble, prologue, prelude; *informal* intro.
- OPPOSITES ending, epilogue.

introductory *adjective* **1 opening**, initial, starting, initiatory, first, preliminary. **2 elementary**, basic, rudimentary, entry-level.
- OPPOSITES final, advanced.

intrude *verb* **encroach**, impinge, trespass, infringe, invade, violate, disturb, disrupt.

intruder *noun* **trespasser**, interloper, invader, infiltrator, burglar, housebreaker; *informal* gatecrasher.

intuition *noun* **1 instinct**, feeling, insight, sixth sense. **2 hunch**, feeling in your bones, inkling, sneaking suspicion, premonition; *informal* gut feeling.

intuitive *adjective* **instinctive**, innate, inborn, inherent, natural, unconscious, subconscious; *informal* gut.

invade *verb* **1 occupy**, conquer, capture, seize, take (over), annex, overrun, storm. **2 intrude on**, violate, encroach on, infringe on, trespass on, disturb, disrupt.
- OPPOSITES leave, liberate.

invader *noun* **attacker**, conqueror, raider, marauder, occupier, intruder, trespasser.

invalid[1] *adjective* **ill**, sick, ailing, infirm, incapacitated, bedridden, frail, sickly, poorly.
- OPPOSITES healthy.
● *verb* **disable**, incapacitate, hospitalize, put out of action, lay up.

invalid[2] *adjective* **1 void**, null and void, not binding, illegitimate, inapplicable. **2 false**, fallacious, spurious, unsound, wrong, untenable.

invaluable *adjective* **indispensable**, irreplaceable, all-important, crucial, vital, worth its weight in gold, priceless.
- OPPOSITES dispensable.

invariably *adverb* **always**, at all times, without fail, without exception, consistently, habitually, unfailingly.

invasion *noun* **1 occupation**, conquering, capture, seizure, annexation, takeover. **2 violation**, infringement, interruption, encroachment, disturbance, disruption, breach.
- OPPOSITES withdrawal.

invent *verb* **1 originate**, create, design, devise, develop. **2 make up**, fabricate, concoct, hatch, contrive, dream up; *informal* cook up.

invention *noun* **1 origination**, creation, development, design, discovery. **2 innovation**, contraption, contrivance, device, gadget. **3 fabrication**, concoction, (piece of) fiction, story, tale, lie, untruth, falsehood, fib.

inventive *adjective* **creative**, original, innovative, imaginative, resourceful, unusual, fresh, novel, new, groundbreaking, disruptive, unorthodox, unconventional.
- OPPOSITES unimaginative.

inventor *noun* **originator**, creator, designer, deviser, developer, author, architect, father.

inventory *noun* **list**, listing, catalogue, record, register, checklist, log, archive.

invest *verb* **put in**, plough in, put up, advance, expend, spend; *informal* lay out.
□ **invest in** put money into, sink money into, plough money into, fund, back, finance, underwrite.

investigate *verb* **enquire into**, look into, go into, probe, explore, scrutinize, analyse, study, examine; *informal* check out, suss out.

investigation *noun* **examination**, enquiry, study, inspection, exploration, analysis, research, scrutiny, probe, review.

investigator *noun* **researcher**, examiner, analyst, inspector, scrutineer, detective.

investment *noun* **1 investing**, speculation, outlay, funding, backing, financing, underwriting. **2 stake**, payment, outlay, venture, proposition.

invidious *adjective* **1 unpleasant**, awkward, difficult, undesirable, unenviable. **2 unfair**, unjust, unwarranted.

invigorate *verb* **revitalize**, energize, refresh, revive, enliven, liven up, perk up, wake up, animate, galvanize, fortify, rouse, exhilarate; *informal* buck up, pep up.
- OPPOSITES tire.

invincible *adjective* **invulnerable**, indestructible, unconquerable, unbeatable, indomitable, unassailable, impregnable.
- OPPOSITES vulnerable.

invisible *adjective* **unseen**, imperceptible, undetectable, inconspicuous, unnoticed, unobserved, hidden, out of sight.
- OPPOSITES visible.

invitation *noun* **request**, call, summons; *informal* invite.

invite *verb* **1 ask**, summon. **2 ask for**, request, call for, appeal for, solicit, seek. **3 cause**, induce, provoke, ask for, encourage, lead to, bring on yourself, arouse.

inviting *adjective* **tempting**, enticing, alluring, attractive, appealing, appetizing, mouth-watering, intriguing, seductive.
- OPPOSITES repellent.

invoke *verb* **1 cite**, refer to, resort to, have recourse to, turn to. **2 pray to**, call on, appeal to. **3 bring forth**, bring out, elicit, conjure up, generate.

involuntary *adjective* **1 reflex**, automatic, instinctive, unintentional, uncontrollable. **2 compulsory**, obligatory, mandatory, forced, prescribed.
- OPPOSITES deliberate, optional.

involve *verb* **1 entail**, require, necessitate, demand, call for. **2 include**, take in, incorporate, encompass, comprise, cover.
- OPPOSITES preclude, exclude.

involved *adjective* **1** *social workers involved in the case* **associated**, connected, concerned. **2** *he had been involved in burglaries* **implicated**, caught up, mixed up. **3 complicated**, intricate, complex, elaborate, convoluted, confusing. **4 engrossed**, absorbed, immersed, caught up, preoccupied, intent.

involvement *noun* **1 participation**, collaboration, collusion, complicity, association, connection, entanglement. **2 attachment**, friendship, intimacy, commitment.

inwards *adverb* **inside**, towards the inside, into the interior, inward, within.

iota *noun* **(little) bit**, mite, speck, scrap, shred, ounce, jot.

iron *adjective* **1 ferric**, ferrous. **2 uncompromising**, unrelenting, unyielding, unbending, rigid, steely.
- OPPOSITES flexible.

□ **iron out 1** resolve, straighten out, sort out, clear up, put right, solve, rectify; *informal* fix. **2** eliminate, eradicate, reconcile, resolve.

ironic *adjective* **1 sarcastic**, sardonic, satirical, dry, wry, double-edged, mocking, derisive, scornful; *Brit. informal* sarky. **2 paradoxical**, funny, strange.

irony *noun* **1 sarcasm**, mockery, ridicule, derision, scorn; *Brit. informal* sarkiness. **2 paradox**.

irrational *adjective* **unreasonable**, illogical, groundless, baseless, unfounded, unjustifiable.
- OPPOSITES rational, logical.

irrefutable *adjective* **indisputable**, undeniable, unquestionable, incontrovertible, incontestable, beyond question, beyond doubt, conclusive, definite, definitive, decisive.

irregular *adjective* **1 uneven**, crooked, misshapen, lopsided, asymmetrical, twisted. **2 rough**, bumpy, uneven, pitted, rutted, lumpy, knobbly, gnarled. **3 inconsistent**, unsteady, uneven, fitful, patchy, variable, varying, changeable, inconstant, erratic, unstable, spasmodic, intermittent. **4 improper**, illegitimate, unethical, unprofessional; *informal* shady, dodgy. **5 guerrilla**, underground, paramilitary, partisan, mercenary, terrorist.

● *noun* **guerrilla**, paramilitary, militiaman, resistance fighter, partisan, mercenary, terrorist.

irrelevant *adjective* **beside the point**, immaterial, unconnected, unrelated, peripheral, extraneous.

irreparable *adjective* **irreversible**, irrevocable, irrecoverable, unrepairable, beyond repair.

irrepressible *adjective* **ebullient**, exuberant, buoyant, breezy, jaunty, high-spirited, vivacious, animated, full of life, lively; *informal* bubbly, bouncy, peppy, chipper, chirpy, full of beans.

irresistible *adjective* **1 captivating**, enticing, alluring, enchanting, fascinating, seductive. **2 uncontrollable**, overwhelming, overpowering, ungovernable, compelling.

irresponsible *adjective* **reckless**, rash, careless, unwise, imprudent, ill-advised, injudicious, hasty, impetuous, foolhardy, foolish, unreliable, undependable, untrustworthy.

irreverent *adjective* **disrespectful**, impertinent, cheeky, flippant, rude, discourteous.
- OPPOSITES respectful.

irrevocable *adjective* **irreversible**, unalterable, unchangeable, immutable, final, binding, permanent, set in stone.

irritable *adjective* **bad-tempered**, short-tempered, irascible, tetchy, testy, grumpy, grouchy, crotchety, cantankerous, fractious, curmudgeonly.
- OPPOSITES good-humoured.

irritate *verb* **1 annoy**, bother, vex, make cross, exasperate, infuriate, anger, madden; *Brit.* rub up the wrong way; *informal* aggravate, peeve, rile, needle, get (to), bug, hack off; *Brit. informal* nark, get on someone's wick; *N. Amer. informal* tee off, tick off. **2 inflame**, hurt, chafe, scratch, scrape, rub.
- OPPOSITES delight, soothe.

irritation *noun* **annoyance**, exasperation, vexation, indignation, anger, displeasure, chagrin.
- OPPOSITES delight.

island *noun* **isle**, islet, atoll; *Brit.* holm; (**islands**) archipelago.

WORD LINKS
insular relating to an island

isolate *verb* **separate**, segregate, detach, cut off, shut away, alienate, distance, cloister, seclude, cordon off, seal off, close off, fence off.
- OPPOSITES integrate.

isolated *adjective* **1 remote**, out of the way, outlying, off the beaten track, in the back of beyond, godforsaken, inaccessible, cut-off; *informal* in the middle of nowhere, in the sticks; *N. Amer. informal* jerkwater. **2 solitary**, lonely, secluded, reclusive, hermit-like; *N. Amer.* lonesome. **3 unique**, lone, solitary, unusual, exceptional, untypical, freak; *informal* one-off.
- OPPOSITES accessible.

isolation *noun* **1 solitariness**, loneliness, friendlessness. **2 remoteness**, inaccessibility.
- OPPOSITES contact.

issue *noun* **1 matter**, question, point at issue, affair, case, subject, topic, situation. **2 problem**, difficulty, complication, snag, hitch, catch, drawback, pitfall, stumbling block; *informal* headache, hiccup. **3 edition**, number, instalment, copy, impression. **4 issuing**, release, publication, distribution.
● *verb* **1 release**, put out, deliver, publish, broadcast, circulate, distribute. **2 supply**, provide, furnish, arm, equip, fit out, rig out, kit out; *informal* fix up.
□ **take issue with** disagree with, challenge, dispute, (call into) question.

itch *noun* **1 tingling**, irritation, itchiness, prickle. **2** *(informal)* **longing**, yearning, craving, ache, hunger, thirst, urge, hankering; *informal* yen.
● *verb* **1 tingle**, be irritated, be itchy, sting, hurt, be sore. **2** *(informal)* **long**, yearn, ache, burn, crave, hanker for/after, hunger, thirst, be eager, be desperate; *informal* be dying.

item *noun* **1 thing**, article, object, piece, element, constituent, component, ingredient. **2 issue**, matter, affair, case, subject, topic, question, point. **3 report**, story, article, piece, write-up, bulletin, feature, review.

itinerary *noun* **route**, plan, schedule, timetable, programme.

Jj

jab *verb* & *noun* **poke**, prod, dig, elbow, nudge, thrust, stab, push.

jacket *noun* **wrapping**, wrapper, sleeve, cover, covering, sheath.

jagged *adjective* **spiky**, barbed, ragged, rough, uneven, irregular, serrated.
- OPPOSITES smooth.

jail *noun* **prison**, lock-up, detention centre; *N. Amer.* penitentiary, jailhouse; *informal* clink, cooler, the slammer, inside; *Brit. informal* nick; *N. Amer. informal* can, pen, slam, pokey.
● *verb* **imprison**, incarcerate, lock up, put away, detain; *informal* send down, put behind bars, put inside; *Brit. informal* bang up.
- OPPOSITES acquit, release.

jam *verb* **1 stuff**, shove, force, ram, thrust, press, push, wedge, stick, cram. **2 crowd**, pack, pile, press, squeeze, sandwich, cram, throng, mob, fill, block, clog, congest. **3 stick**, become stuck, catch, seize (up).
● *noun* **tailback**, hold-up, queue, congestion, bottleneck; *N. Amer.* gridlock; *informal* snarl-up.

jar[1] *noun* **pot**, container, crock.

jar[2] *verb* **1 jolt**, jerk, shake, vibrate. **2 grate**, set someone's teeth on edge, irritate, annoy, get on someone's nerves. **3 clash**, conflict, contrast, be incompatible, be at variance, be at odds.

jargon *noun* **slang**, idiom, cant, argot, gobbledegook; *informal* lingo, geek-speak, -speak, -ese.

jaunt *noun* **trip**, outing, excursion, tour, drive, ride, run; *informal* spin, junket.

jaws *plural noun* **mouth**, maw, muzzle, mandibles; *informal* chops.

jealous *adjective* **1 envious**, covetous, resentful, grudging, green with envy. **2 suspicious**, distrustful, possessive, proprietorial, overprotective. **3 protective**, vigilant, watchful, mindful, careful.
- OPPOSITES trusting.

jealousy *noun* **envy**, resentment, bitterness; *humorous* the green-eyed monster.

jeer *verb* **taunt**, mock, ridicule, deride, insult, abuse, heckle, catcall (at), boo (at), whistle at, scoff at, sneer at; *Brit.* barrack.
- OPPOSITES applaud, cheer.
● *noun* **taunt**, sneer, insult, shout, jibe, boo, catcall, derision, teasing, scoffing, abuse, scorn, heckling, catcalling; *Brit.* barracking.
- OPPOSITES applause, cheer.

jeopardize *verb* **threaten**, endanger, imperil, risk, compromise, prejudice.
- OPPOSITES safeguard.

jeopardy *noun* **danger**, peril, risk.

jerk *noun* **1 yank**, tug, pull, wrench. **2 jolt**, lurch, bump, judder, jump, bounce, jounce, shake.
● *verb* **1 yank**, tug, pull, wrench, wrest, drag, snatch. **2 jolt**, lurch, bump, judder, bounce, jounce.

jerky *adjective* **convulsive**, spasmodic, fitful, twitchy, shaky.
- OPPOSITES smooth.

jet *noun* **1 stream**, spurt, spray, fountain, rush, spout, gush, surge, burst. **2 nozzle**, head, spout.

jettison *verb* **dump**, drop, ditch, throw out, get rid of, discard, dispose of, scrap.

jetty *noun* **pier**, landing (stage), quay, wharf, dock, breakwater, groyne, mole; *N. Amer.* levee.

jewel *noun* **1 gem**, gemstone, (precious) stone; *informal* sparkler, rock. **2 showpiece**, pride (and joy), cream, crème de la crème, jewel in the crown, prize, pick.

jibe *noun* **taunt**, sneer, jeer, insult, barb; *informal* dig, put-down.

jilt *verb* **leave**, walk out on, throw over, finish with, break up with, stand up, leave at the altar; *informal* chuck, ditch, dump, drop, run out on, give someone the push/elbow, give someone the big E.

jingle *noun* & *verb* **clink**, chink, tinkle, jangle, ring.

jinx *noun* **curse**, spell, the evil eye, black magic, voodoo, bad luck; *N. Amer.* hex.
● *verb* **curse**, cast a spell on; *Austral.* point the bone at; *N. Amer.* hex.

job *noun* **1 position**, post, situation, appointment, occupation, profession, trade, career, work, vocation, calling, métier. **2 task**, piece of work, assignment, mission, project, undertaking, operation, duty, chore, errand, responsibility, charge, role, function; *informal* department.

jobless *adjective* **unemployed**, out of work, unwaged, redundant, laid off; *Brit. informal* on the dole; *Canad. informal* on pogey; *Austral./NZ informal* on the wallaby track.
– OPPOSITES employed.

jog *verb* **1 run**, trot, lope. **2 nudge**, prod, poke, push, bump, jar.

join *verb* **1** *the two parts are joined with clay* **connect**, unite, couple, fix, affix, attach, fasten, stick, glue, fuse, weld, amalgamate, bond, link, yoke, merge, secure, make fast, tie, bind. **2** *the path joins a major road* **meet**, touch, reach. **3** *he joined the search party* **help in**, participate in, get involved in, contribute to, enlist in, join up, sign up, band together, get together, team up.
– OPPOSITES separate, leave.

joint *noun* **join**, junction, intersection, link, connection, weld, seam, coupling.
● *adjective* **common**, shared, communal, collective, mutual, cooperative, collaborative, concerted, combined, united, allied.
– OPPOSITES separate.

jointly *adverb* **together**, in partnership, in cooperation, cooperatively, in conjunction, in combination, mutually, in league.

joke *noun* **1 witticism**, jest, quip, pun; *informal* gag, wisecrack, crack, funny, one-liner. **2 trick**, prank, stunt, hoax, jape; *informal* leg-pull, spoof, wind-up. **3** *(informal)* **laughing stock**, figure of fun, Aunt Sally. **4** *(informal)* **farce**, travesty.
● *verb* **tell jokes**, jest, banter, quip; *informal* wisecrack, josh.

joker *noun* **comedian**, comedienne, comic, humorist, wit, jester, prankster, practical joker, clown.

jolly *adjective* **cheerful**, happy, cheery, good-humoured, jovial, merry, sunny, joyful, light-hearted, in high spirits, buoyant, bubbly, genial; *informal* chipper, chirpy, perky; *literary* blithe.
– OPPOSITES miserable.

jolt *verb* **1 push**, jar, bump, knock, bang, shake, jog. **2 bump**, bounce, jerk, rattle, lurch, shudder, judder, jounce. **3 startle**, surprise, shock, stun, shake; *informal* rock, knock sideways.
● *noun* **bump**, bounce, shake, jerk, lurch, jounce.

jostle *verb* **1 push**, shove, elbow, barge into, bang into, bump against, knock against. **2** *photographers jostled for position* **struggle**, vie, jockey, scramble, fight.

journal *noun* **1 periodical**, magazine, gazette, review, newsletter, newssheet, bulletin, newspaper, paper, daily, weekly, monthly, quarterly. **2 diary**, log, logbook, weblog, blog, chronicle, history, yearbook; *N. Amer.* daybook.

journalist *noun* **reporter**, correspondent, columnist; *Brit.* pressman; *informal* news hound, hack, hackette, stringer, journo.

journey *noun* **trip**, expedition, tour, trek, travels, voyage, cruise, ride, drive, crossing, passage, flight, odyssey, pilgrimage, safari, globetrotting; *old use* peregrinations.
● *verb* **travel**, go, voyage, sail, cruise,

fly, hike, trek, ride, drive, make your way.

jovial *adjective* **cheerful**, jolly, happy, cheery, jocular, good-humoured, convivial, genial, good-natured, affable, outgoing, smiling, merry, sunny; *literary* blithe.
- OPPOSITES miserable.

joy *noun* **delight**, pleasure, jubilation, triumph, exultation, rejoicing, happiness, elation, euphoria, bliss, ecstasy, rapture.
- OPPOSITES misery.

joyful *adjective* **1 cheerful**, happy, jolly, merry, sunny, joyous, cheery, smiling, jovial, mirthful, gleeful, pleased, delighted, thrilled, jubilant, elated, ecstatic; *informal* over the moon, on cloud nine. **2** *joyful news* **pleasing**, happy, good, cheering, gladdening, welcome, gratifying, heart-warming.
- OPPOSITES sad.

jubilant *adjective* **overjoyed**, exultant, triumphant, joyful, cock-a-hoop, elated, thrilled, gleeful, euphoric, ecstatic; *informal* over the moon, on cloud nine.
- OPPOSITES despondent.

jubilee *noun* **anniversary**, commemoration, celebration, festival.

judge *noun* **1 justice**, magistrate, recorder, sheriff; *N. Amer.* jurist; *Brit. informal* beak. **2 adjudicator**, referee, umpire, arbiter, assessor, examiner, moderator, scrutineer.
● *verb* **1 conclude**, decide, consider, believe, think, deduce, infer, gauge, estimate, guess, surmise, conjecture, regard as, rate as, class as; *informal* reckon, figure. **2** *she was judged innocent* **pronounce**, decree, rule, find. **3 adjudicate**, arbitrate, moderate, referee, umpire. **4 assess**, evaluate, appraise, examine, review.

judgement *noun* **1 sense**, discernment, perception, discrimination, understanding, powers of reasoning, reason, logic. **2 opinion**, view, estimate, appraisal, conclusion, diagnosis, assessment, impression, conviction, perception, thinking. **3** *a court judgement* **verdict**, decision, adjudication, ruling, pronouncement, decree, finding, sentence.

judgemental *adjective* **critical**, censorious, disapproving, disparaging, deprecating, negative, overcritical.

judicious *adjective* **wise**, sensible, prudent, shrewd, astute, canny, discerning, sagacious, strategic, politic, expedient.
- OPPOSITES ill-advised.

jug *noun* **pitcher**, ewer, crock, jar, urn, carafe, flask, flagon, decanter; *N. Amer.* creamer.

juice *noun* **liquid**, fluid, sap, extract, concentrate, essence.

juicy *adjective* **1 succulent**, tender, moist, ripe. **2** *(informal)* **sensational**, fascinating, intriguing, exciting, graphic, lurid.
- OPPOSITES dry.

jumble *noun* **heap**, muddle, mess, tangle, confusion, disarray, chaos, hotchpotch; *N. Amer.* hodgepodge; *informal* shambles.
● *verb* **mix up**, muddle up, disorganize, disorder, tangle, confuse.

jump *verb* **1 leap**, spring, bound, vault, hop, skip, caper, dance, prance. **2** *pre-tax profits jumped* **rise**, go up, shoot up, soar, surge, climb, increase; *informal* skyrocket. **3** *the noise made her jump* **start**, jolt, flinch, recoil, shudder.
● *noun* **1 leap**, spring, bound, hop, skip. **2 rise**, leap, increase, upsurge, upswing; *informal* hike. **3 start**, jerk, spasm, shudder.

jumper *noun (Brit.)* **sweater**, pullover, jersey; *informal* woolly.

jumpy *adjective (informal)* **nervous**, on edge, edgy, tense, anxious, restless, fidgety, keyed up, overwrought; *informal* jittery, uptight, het up; *N. Amer. informal* antsy.
- OPPOSITES calm.

junction *noun* **crossroads**, intersection, interchange, T-junction, turn, turn-off, exit; *Brit.* roundabout; *N. Amer.* turnout, cloverleaf.

junior *adjective* **younger**, minor, subordinate, lower, lesser, low-ranking, inferior, secondary.
- OPPOSITES senior, older.

junk *noun (informal)* **rubbish**, clutter, odds and ends, bric-a-brac, refuse, litter, scrap, waste, debris; *N. Amer.* trash.

just *adjective* **1** *a just society* **fair**, fair-minded, equitable, even-handed, impartial, unbiased, objective, neutral, disinterested, unprejudiced, honourable, upright, decent, principled. **2** *a just reward* **deserved**, well deserved, well earned, merited, rightful, due, proper, fitting, appropriate, defensible, justified, justifiable.
- OPPOSITES unfair.
● *adverb* **1 exactly**, precisely, absolutely, completely, totally, entirely, perfectly, utterly, thoroughly; *informal* dead. **2 narrowly**, only just, by a hair's breadth, by the skin of your teeth, barely, scarcely, hardly; *informal* by a whisker.

justice *noun* **1 fairness**, justness, fair play, fair-mindedness, equity, right, even-handedness, honesty, morality. **2** *the justice of his case* **validity**, justification, soundness, well-foundedness, legitimacy. **3 judge**, magistrate, recorder, sheriff; *N. Amer.* jurist.

WORD LINKS
judicial relating to a system of justice

justifiable *adjective* **valid**, legitimate, warranted, well founded, justified, just, reasonable, tenable, defensible, sound, warrantable.
- OPPOSITES unjustifiable, unwarranted.

justification *noun* **grounds**, reason, basis, rationale, premise, vindication, explanation, defence, argument, case.

justify *verb* **1 give grounds for**, give reasons for, explain, account for, defend, vindicate, excuse, exonerate. **2 warrant**, be good reason for.

jut *verb* **stick out**, project, protrude, bulge out, overhang, beetle.

juvenile *adjective* **1 young**, teenage, adolescent, junior. **2 childish**, immature, puerile, infantile, babyish.
- OPPOSITES adult, mature.
● *noun* **child**, youngster, teenager, adolescent, minor, junior; *informal* kid.
- OPPOSITES adult.

Kk

keel *verb*
▫ **keel over 1** capsize, turn turtle, turn upside down, founder, overturn, turn over, tip over. **2** collapse, faint, pass out, black out, swoon.

keen *adjective* **1** *I'm keen to help* **eager**, anxious, intent, impatient, determined; *informal* raring, itching, dying. **2** *a keen birdwatcher* **enthusiastic**, avid, ardent, fervent, conscientious, committed, dedicated, motivated. **3** *a girl he was keen on* **attracted to**, interested in, fond of, taken with, smitten with, enamoured of; *informal* struck on. **4** *a keen mind* **acute**, penetrating, astute, incisive, sharp, perceptive, piercing, razor-sharp, shrewd, discerning, clever, intelligent, brilliant, bright, smart, wise, insightful. **5** *a keen sense of duty* **intense**, acute, fierce, passionate, burning, fervent, strong, powerful.
– OPPOSITES reluctant, unenthusiastic.

keep *verb* **1** *I kept the forms* **retain**, hold on to, save, store, put by/aside, set aside; *informal* hang on to. **2** *keep calm* **remain**, stay. **3** *he keeps going on about it* **persist in**, keep on, carry on, continue, insist on. **4** *keep the rules* **comply with**, obey, observe, conform to, abide by, adhere to, stick to, heed, follow, carry out, act on, make good, honour, keep to, stand by. **5** *keeping the old traditions* **preserve**, keep alive/up, carry on, perpetuate, maintain, uphold. **6** *he stole to keep his family* **provide for**, support, feed, maintain, sustain, take care of, look after. **7** *she keeps rabbits* **breed**, rear, raise, tend, farm, own.
● *noun* **maintenance**, upkeep, sustenance, board (and lodging), food, livelihood.

keeper *noun* **curator**, custodian, guardian, conservator, administrator, overseer, steward, caretaker, attendant, concierge.

keeping *noun* **care**, custody, charge, guardianship, possession, trust, protection.
▫ **in keeping with** consistent with, in harmony with, in accord with, in agreement with, in line with, in character with, compatible with, appropriate to, befitting, suitable for.

key *noun* **1** *the key to the mystery* **answer**, clue, solution, explanation, basis, foundation. **2** *the key to success* **means**, way, route, path, passport, secret, formula.
● *adjective* **crucial**, central, essential, indispensable, pivotal, critical, vital, principal, prime, major, leading, main, important.

kick *verb* **boot**, punt.
● *noun (informal) I get a kick out of driving* **thrill**, excitement, stimulation, tingle, frisson; *informal* buzz, high; *N. Amer. informal* charge.
▫ **kick off** *(informal)* start, commence, begin, get going, get off the ground, get under way, open, set in motion, launch, initiate, introduce, inaugurate.

kid *noun (informal)* **child**, youngster, baby, toddler, tot, infant, boy, girl, minor, juvenile, adolescent, teenager, youth, stripling; *Scottish* bairn; *informal* kiddie, nipper, kiddiewink; *Brit. informal* sprog; *N. Amer. informal* rug rat; *Austral./NZ* ankle-biter; *derogatory* brat.

kidnap *verb* **abduct**, carry off, capture, seize, snatch, take hostage.

kill *verb* **murder**, assassinate, eliminate, terminate, dispatch, execute, slaughter, exterminate, butcher, massacre; *informal* bump off, do away with, do in, top, take out, blow away; *N. Amer. informal* rub out, waste; *literary* slay.

killer *noun* **murderer**, assassin, butcher, gunman, terminator, executioner; *informal* hit man.

killing *noun* **murder**, assassination, homicide, manslaughter, execution, slaughter, massacre, butchery, bloodshed, carnage, extermination, genocide.

kin *noun* **relatives**, relations, family, kith and kin, kindred, kinsfolk, kinsmen, kinswomen, people; *informal* folks.

kind[1] *noun* **sort**, type, variety, style, form, class, category, genre, genus, species.

kind[2] *adjective* **kindly**, good-natured, kind-hearted, warm-hearted, caring, affectionate, loving, warm, considerate, obliging, compassionate, sympathetic, understanding, benevolent, benign, altruistic, unselfish, generous, charitable, philanthropic, helpful, thoughtful, humane; *Brit. informal* decent.
- OPPOSITES unkind.

kindle *verb* **1 light**, ignite, set light to, set fire to; *informal* torch. **2 rouse**, arouse, wake, awaken, stimulate, inspire, stir (up), excite, fire, trigger, activate, spark off.
- OPPOSITES extinguish.

kindly *adjective* **benevolent**, kind, kind-hearted, warm-hearted, generous, good-natured, gentle, warm, compassionate, caring, loving, benign, well meaning, considerate.
- OPPOSITES unkind, cruel.

kindness *noun* **kindliness**, affection, warmth, gentleness, concern, care, consideration, altruism, unselfishness, compassion, sympathy, benevolence, generosity.
- OPPOSITES unkindness.

king *noun* **ruler**, sovereign, monarch, Crown, His Majesty, emperor, prince, potentate.

kingdom *noun* **realm**, domain, dominion, country, empire, land, territory, nation, (sovereign) state, province.

kiss *verb informal* peck, smooch, canoodle, neck, pet; *Brit. informal* snog; *N. Amer. informal* buss; *formal* osculate.
● *noun informal* peck, smack, smacker, smooch; *Brit. informal* snog; *N. Amer. informal* buss.

kit *noun* **1 equipment**, tools, implements, instruments, gadgets, utensils, appliances, gear, tackle, hardware, paraphernalia; *informal* things, stuff; *Military* accoutrements. **2** *(informal)* **clothes**, clothing, garments, outfit, dress, costume, attire, garb, strip; *informal* gear, get-up, rig-out. **3** *a tool kit* **set**, selection, collection, pack.
□ **kit out** equip, fit (out/up), furnish, supply, provide, issue, dress, clothe, attire, rig out, deck out; *informal* fix up.

knack *noun* **1 gift**, talent, flair, instinct, genius, ability, capability, capacity, aptitude, bent, facility, trick; *informal* the hang of something. **2 tendency**, habit, liability, propensity.

knickers *plural noun (Brit.)* **underpants**, briefs; *Brit.* pants; *informal* panties, undies; *Brit. informal* smalls; *dated* drawers; *historical* bloomers.

knife *verb* **stab**, hack, gash, slash, lacerate, cut, bayonet, wound.

knit *verb* **unite**, unify, bond, fuse, coalesce, merge, meld, blend, join, link.

knob *noun* **lump**, bump, protrusion, protuberance, bulge, swelling, knot, nodule, boss.

knock *verb* **1 bang**, tap, rap, thump, pound, hammer, beat, strike, hit; *informal* bash. **2 collide with**, bump into, run into, crash into, smash into, plough into; *N. Amer.* impact.
● *noun* **tap**, rap, rat-tat, knocking, bang, banging, pounding, hammering, thump, thud.
□ **knock down 1** fell, floor, flatten, knock over, rugby-tackle, run over/down. **2** demolish, pull down, tear down, destroy, raze, level, flatten, bulldoze. **knock out** knock unconscious, floor, prostrate; *informal* lay out, KO, fell.

knot *noun a knot of people* **cluster**, group, band, huddle, bunch, circle, ring.
● *verb* **tie**, fasten, secure, bind, do up.

knotted *adjective* **tangled**, matted, snarled, unkempt, tousled; *informal* mussed up.

know *verb* **1** *she doesn't know I'm here* **be aware**, realize, be conscious, be cognizant. **2** *I know the rules* **be familiar with**, be conversant with, be acquainted with, be versed in, have a grasp of, understand, comprehend; *informal* be clued up on. **3** *do you know her?* **be acquainted with**, have met, be familiar with; *Scottish* ken.

know-how *noun (informal)* **expertise**, skill, proficiency, knowledge, understanding, mastery, technique; *informal* savvy.

knowing *adjective* **significant**, meaningful, expressive, suggestive, eloquent, superior.

knowledge *noun* **1 understanding**, comprehension, grasp, command, mastery, familiarity, acquaintance; *informal* know-how. **2 learning**, erudition, education, scholarship, schooling, wisdom. **3 awareness**, consciousness, realization, cognition, apprehension, perception, appreciation, cognizance.
- OPPOSITES ignorance.

WORD LINKS
gnostic relating to knowledge

knowledgeable *adjective* **1 well informed**, learned, well read, (well) educated, erudite, scholarly, cultured, cultivated, enlightened. **2** *he's knowledgeable about art* **conversant with**, familiar with, well acquainted with, au fait with, up on, up to date with, abreast of; *informal* clued up on.
- OPPOSITES ignorant.

known *adjective* **recognized**, well known, widely known, noted, celebrated, notable, notorious, acknowledged.

kudos *noun* **prestige**, cachet, glory, honour, status, standing, distinction, admiration, respect, esteem.

Commonly confused words

There are many words in English which look or sound alike but have quite different meanings. These words are very easy to confuse and most spellcheckers will not be able to help in those situations in which a word is spelled correctly but used in the wrong context. This section provides a quick-reference guide to the differences between those pairs of words that commonly cause problems.

Word 1	Meaning	Word 2	Meaning
accept	to agree to receive or do	except	not including; apart from
access	the means to enter somewhere or opportunity to use something	excess	an amount that is too much
adverse	unfavourable or harmful	averse	strongly disliking or opposed
advice	recommendations about what to do	advise	to recommend something
affect	to change or make a difference to	effect	a result; to bring about a result
aisle	a passage between rows of seats	isle	an island
all together	all in one place or all at once	altogether	in total; completely; on the whole
allusion	an indirect reference	illusion	a false idea or belief
aloud	out loud	allowed	permitted
altar	sacred table in a church	alter	to change
amoral	not concerned with right or wrong	immoral	not following accepted moral standards
ante-	before (e.g. *antedate*)	anti-	against (e.g. *antidepressant*)
appraise	to assess	apprise	to inform someone
assent	approval or agreement	ascent	an act of going up something
augur	to be a sign of a good or bad outcome	auger	a tool for boring holes
aural	relating to the ears or hearing	oral	relating to the mouth; spoken
balmy	pleasantly warm	barmy	crazy
bare	naked; to uncover	bear	to carry; to tolerate
base	the lowest or supporting part; a centre of operations	bass	the lowest male singing voice; the deep low-frequency part of sound
bated	with bated breath (i.e. in great suspense)	baited	taunted

Word 1	Meaning	Word 2	Meaning
bazaar	a Middle Eastern market	bizarre	very strange
berth	a bunk in a ship, train, etc.	birth	the process of being born
blanch	make or become white or pale	blench	flinch through fear or pain
born	having started life	borne	carried
brake	a device for stopping a vehicle; to stop a vehicle	break	to separate into pieces; a pause
breach	a gap in a barrier; an act that breaks a rule or agreement	breech	the back part of a rifle or gun barrel
broach	to raise a subject for discussion	brooch	a piece of jewellery
canvas	a type of strong cloth	canvass	to ask for people's votes
cannon	a large heavy gun	canon	a rule or law; a list of books; a clergyman
censure	to criticize severely	censor	to ban parts of a book or film; an official who does this
chord	a group of musical notes	cord	a length of string; a cord-like body part
climactic	forming a climax	climatic	relating to climate
coarse	rough	course	a direction
complacent	smugly self-satisfied	complaisant	willing to please
complement	to add to so as to improve; an addition that improves something	compliment	to politely congratulate or praise; a polite expression of praise
complementary	combining to form a whole or to improve something	complimentary	praising; given free of charge
council	a group of people who manage or advise	counsel	advice; to advise
councillor	a member of a council	counsellor	a person giving guidance on personal problems
credible	believable; convincing	credulous	too ready to believe things
cue	a signal for action; a wooden rod	queue	a line of people or vehicles
curb	to control or put a limit on; a control or limit	kerb	(in British English) the stone edge of a pavement
currant	a dried grape	current	happening now; a flow of water, air, or electricity
defuse	to make a situation less tense	diffuse	to spread over a wide area
dependant	a person who relies on another for support	dependent	determined; relying on

Word 1	Meaning	Word 2	Meaning
desert	a waterless, empty area	dessert	the sweet course of a meal
discreet	careful not to attract attention or give offence	discrete	separate and distinct
disinterested	impartial	uninterested	not interested
draught	a current of air	draft	a first version of a piece of writing; to write such a version
draw	to produce a picture; to pull; an even score at the end of a game	drawer	a sliding storage compartment
dual	having two parts	duel	a fight or contest between two people
elicit	to draw out a response or reaction	illicit	forbidden by law or rules
emigrant	a person who leaves their country to settle permanently in another	immigrant	a person who has come to live permanently in a foreign country
emotional	showing strong feeling	emotive	arousing strong feeling
empathy	the ability to understand another person's feelings	sympathy	the feeling of being sorry for someone
ensure	to make certain that something will happen	insure	to pay money in order to receive financial compensation if a person dies or property is damaged
envelop	to cover or surround	envelope	a paper container for a letter
exceptional	unusual or unusually good	exceptionable	causing disapproval or offence
exercise	physical activity; to do physical activity	exorcize	to drive out an evil spirit
faint	to lose consciousness; not clearly seen, heard, or smelled	feint	a pretended attacking movement; to make such a movement
fawn	a young deer; light brown	faun	a mythical being, part man, part goat
flair	a natural ability or talent	flare	a brief burst of flame or light; to gradually become wider
flaunt	to display in a way intended to attract attention	flout	to openly fail to follow a rule
flounder	to have trouble doing something	founder	to fail
forbear	to stop yourself from doing something	forebear	an ancestor

Word 1	Meaning	Word 2	Meaning
foreword	an introduction to a book	forward	onwards; ahead
freeze	to turn to ice	frieze	a decoration along a wall
Gallic	French	Gaelic	Celtic
grisly	causing horror or disgust	grizzly	a type of bear
hanger	a person who hangs something, or a frame to hang clothes on	hangar	a building in which aircraft are kept
historic	famous or important in history	historical	relating to history
hoard	a store of money or valuable objects	horde	a large crowd of people
hummus or houmous	a chickpea dip	humus	a substance found in soil
imply	to suggest indirectly	infer	to draw a conclusion about something not directly stated
incredible	impossible to believe	incredulous	unwilling or unable to believe something
internment	imprisonment	interment	burial
its	belonging to it	it's	short for *it is* or *it has*
judicial	relating to a law court or judge	judicious	sensible
lama	a Buddhist monk	llama	an animal related to the camel
licence	a permit to own or do something	license	to grant a licence or authorize something
lightening	getting lighter	lightning	a high-voltage electrical discharge; very quick
loath	reluctant or unwilling	loathe	to hate
loose	to unfasten or set free; not fixed in place	lose	to have something taken away; to be unable to find
meter	a measuring device	metre	a unit of measurement; rhythm in poetry
militate	to make it very difficult for something to happen or exist	mitigate	to make something less severe
muscle	tissue that moves a body part	mussel	a shellfish
omit	to leave out	emit	to give out light, heat, gas, etc.
pain	an unpleasant feeling	pane	a sheet of glass
palate	the roof of the mouth	palette	a board for mixing colours
pedal	a foot-operated lever; to work the pedals of a bicycle	peddle	to sell goods or spread an idea

Word 1	Meaning	Word 2	Meaning
peninsula	piece of land jutting out into the sea	peninsular	relating to a peninsula
perpetrate	to carry out a bad or illegal act	perpetuate	to make something continue for a long time
pole	a long, thin piece of wood; each of the two opposite points of a magnet	poll	the process of voting in an election
pore	a tiny opening; to study or read something closely	pour	to flow in a steady stream
practice	the use of an idea or method; the work or business of a doctor, dentist, etc.	practise	to do something repeatedly to improve your skill; to carry something out regularly
prescribe	to authorize the use of a medicine; to order authoritatively	proscribe	to officially forbid something
principal	most important; the most important person in an organization	principle	a law or theory on which something is based; a belief
prophecy	a prediction of a future event	prophesy	to predict a future event
quiet	making little or no noise	quite	moderately; completely
reign	period that a monarch rules; to rule as a monarch	rein	a strap used to control a horse; also used in the phrase a free rein
role	a part played by an actor	roll	to move by turning over and over; a rolling movement
sceptic	a person who tends to question accepted opinions	septic	infected with bacteria
shear	to cut the wool off a sheep	sheer	nothing but; to change course quickly
sight	the ability to see	site	a location
silicon	an element used in electronics	silicone	a substance used in cosmetic implants
stationary	not moving	stationery	paper and writing materials
storey	a level of a building	story	a tale or account
straight	without a curve or bend	strait	a narrow passage of water; (straits) trouble or difficulty
summary	a brief statement of the main points	summery	typical of summer
swat	to hit or crush	swot	to study hard
tail	the rear or end part	tale	a story

Word 1	Meaning	Word 2	Meaning
team	a group of people playing or working together	teem	to be full of something; to pour down
their	belonging to them	there	in, at, or to that place
titillate	to interest or excite, especially sexually	titivate	to make more attractive
to	in the direction of	too	excessively; in addition
toe	part of the foot; also in toe the line	tow	to pull something along behind a vehicle or boat
tortuous	full of twists and turns; complicated	torturous	full of pain or suffering
vain	having too high an opinion of yourself	vein	a tube that carries blood around the body
venal	open to bribery	venial	(of a sin) slight and able to be forgiven
waive	to choose not to insist on a right	wave	to move to and fro; a ridge of water
who's	short for *who is* or *who has*	whose	belonging to which person
wreath	an arrangement of flowers	wreathe	to surround or encircle
your	belonging to you	you're	short for *you are*

Wordfinder

Contents

Animals 7
Amphibians
Birds
Crustaceans
Dinosaurs
Fish
Insects
Mammals
Reptiles
Shellfish and Other Molluscs
Spiders and Other Arachnids
Male and Female Animals
Young Animals
Collective Names for Animals

Chemical Elements 11

Clothing 12
Clothes
Footwear
Headgear

Food and Drink 13
Bread and Bread Rolls
Cakes, Biscuits, and Desserts
Cheeses
Fruit and Nuts
Pasta
Sweets and Confectionery
Vegetables
Alcoholic Drinks
Non-alcoholic Drinks

Phobias 17

Plants 18
Flowering Plants and Shrubs
Trees and Shrubs

Animals

Amphibians

axolotl
bullfrog
cane toad
fire salamander
flying frog
frog
horned toad
marsh frog
natterjack toad
newt
salamander
toad
tree frog

Birds

albatross
Arctic tern
auk
avocet
barnacle goose
barn owl
Bewick's swan
bird of paradise
bittern
blackbird
blackcap
black swan
bluebird
blue tit
booby
bowerbird
brambling
budgerigar
bullfinch
bunting
bustard
butcher-bird
buzzard
Canada goose
canary
capercaillie
caracara
cassowary
chaffinch
chicken
chiffchaff
chough
coal tit
cockatiel
cockatoo
condor
coot
cormorant
corncrake
crane
crossbill
crow
cuckoo
curlew
dabchick
dipper
dodo
dotterel
dove
duck
dunlin
dunnock
eagle
eagle owl
egret
eider duck
emperor penguin
emu
falcon
fantail
fieldfare
finch
flamingo
flycatcher
fulmar
gannet
goldcrest
golden eagle
goldfinch
goose
goshawk
great tit
grebe
green woodpecker
greenfinch
grouse
guillemot
guineafowl
gull
harrier
hawfinch
hawk
hen
heron
hobby
hoopoe
hornbill
house martin
hummingbird
ibis
jackdaw
jay
kestrel
kingfisher
kite
kittiwake
kiwi
kookaburra
lammergeier
lapwing
lark
linnet
lovebird
lyrebird
macaw
magpie
mallard
martin
merlin

moa
mockingbird
moorhen
mynah bird
nightingale
nightjar
nuthatch
osprey
ostrich
ouzel
owl
oystercatcher
parakeet
parrot
partridge
peacock
peewit
pelican
penguin
peregrine falcon
petrel
pheasant
pigeon
pipit
plover
ptarmigan
puffin
quail
raven
red kite
redpoll
redstart
redwing
rhea
ring ouzel
roadrunner
robin
rook
sandpiper
seagull
shag
shearwater
shelduck
shrike
skua
skylark
snipe
sparrow
sparrowhawk
spoonbill
starling
stonechat
stork
storm petrel
sunbird
swallow
swan
swift
tern
thrush
tit
toucan
turkey
vulture
wagtail
warbler
waxwing
weaver bird
woodcock
woodlark
woodpecker
wren
yellowhammer

Crustaceans

barnacle
crab
crawfish
crayfish
crevette
fiddler crab
ghost crab
goose barnacle
hermit crab
horseshoe crab
king prawn
krill
land crab
langoustine
lobster
prawn
shrimp
spider crab
woodlouse

Dinosaurs

allosaurus
ankylosaur
apatosaurus
brachiosaurus
brontosaurus
carnosaur
coelurosaur
deinonychus
diplodocus
dromaeosaur
duck-billed dinosaur
hadrosaur
iguanodon
megalosaurus
pliosaur
protoceratops
pteranodon
pterodactyl
raptor
saurischian
sauropod
seismosaurus
stegosaurus
theropod
triceratops
tyrannosaurus
velociraptor

Fish

anchovy
angelfish
anglerfish
archerfish
barbel
barracouta
barracuda
basking shark
bass
beluga
blenny
bluefin
boxfish
bream
brill
brisling
bullhead
butterfly fish
carp
catfish
charr
chub
clownfish
cod
coelacanth
coley
conger eel
dab
dace
damselfish
dogfish
dorado
dory
Dover sole
eel
electric eel
electric ray
fighting fish
filefish
flatfish
flathead
flounder
flying fish
garfish
goby
goldfish
gourami
grayling
great white shark
grouper
gudgeon
gulper eel
guppy
gurnard
haddock
hake
halfbeak
halibut
hammerhead
herring
hoki
huss
John Dory
koi carp
lamprey
lanternfish
lemon sole
loach
lumpsucker
lungfish
mackerel
mako
manta
marlin
megamouth
minnow
monkfish
moray eel
mudskipper
mullet
needlefish
nurse shark
oarfish
orfe
parrotfish
perch
pike
pilchard
pilotfish
pipefish
piranha
plaice
pollack
porbeagle
porcupine fish
puffer fish
rabbitfish
rainbow trout
ray
roach
sailfish
salmon
sardine
sawfish
scorpionfish
sea horse
shad
shark
skate
skipjack tuna
skipper
smelt
snapper
sockeye salmon
sole

sprat
stargazer
stickleback
stingray
stonefish
sturgeon
sunfish
surgeonfish
swordfish
swordtail
tench
tetra
thresher
tiger shark
tope
triggerfish
trout
tuna
tunny
turbot
weever
whaler
whale shark
whitebait
whitefish
whiting
wobbegong
wrasse
zander

Insects

ant
ant lion
aphid
assassin bug
bark beetle
bedbug
bee
beetle
blackfly
blowfly
bluebottle
boll weevil
bombardier beetle
borer
botfly
bumblebee
butterfly
caddis fly
carpet beetle
chafer
chigger
cicada
click beetle
cockchafer
cockroach
Colorado beetle
crane fly
cricket
daddy-long-legs
damselfly
death-watch beetle
devil's coach-horse
dragonfly
dung beetle
earwig
firefly
flea
fluke
fly
froghopper
fruit fly
furniture beetle
gadfly
gall wasp
glow-worm
gnat
goliath beetle
grasshopper
greenbottle
greenfly
honeybee
hornet
horsefly
housefly
hoverfly
lacewing
ladybird
leafcutter ant
leafhopper
leaf miner
leatherjacket
leech
locust
louse
mantis
mason bee
May bug
mayfly
mealy bug
midge
mosquito
moth
pond skater
praying mantis
rhinoceros beetle
robber fly
sandfly
sawfly
scale insect
scarab
scorpion fly
sexton beetle
silverfish
springtail
stag beetle
stick insect
stink bug
termite
thrips
thunderbug
thunderfly
tsetse fly
warble fly
wasp
water beetle
water boatman
weevil
whirligig
whitefly
witchetty grub

Mammals

aardvark
alpaca
angora
anteater
antelope
ape
armadillo
ass
aurochs
baboon
badger
baleen whale
Barbary ape
bat
beaked whale
bear
beaver
beluga
bison
blue whale
boar
bobcat
bottlenose dolphin
bottlenose whale
bowhead whale
buffalo
bushbaby
camel
capuchin monkey
capybara
caribou
cat
chamois
cheetah
chimpanzee
chinchilla
chipmunk
civet
coati
colobus
cougar
cow
coyote
coypu
deer
dingo
dog
dolphin
donkey
dormouse
dromedary
duck-billed platypus
dugong
echidna
eland
elephant
elephant seal
elk
ermine
fallow deer
fennec
ferret
fin whale
flying fox
fox
fur seal
gazelle
gemsbok
gerbil
gibbon
giraffe
gnu
goat
gopher
gorilla
grampus
grizzly bear
guinea pig
hamster
hare
harp seal
hartebeest
hedgehog
hippopotamus
hog
horse
howler monkey
humpback whale
hyena
hyrax
ibex
impala
jackal
jaguar
killer whale
kinkajou
Kodiak bear
kudu
langur
laughing hyena
lemming
lemur
leopard
leopard seal
lion
llama
loris
lynx
macaque
manatee
mandrill
margay
marmoset
marsupial
marten
meerkat
mink
minke whale

mole
mongoose
monkey
moose
mouse
mule
muntjac
musk deer
musk ox
narwhal
ocelot
okapi
opossum
orang-utan
orca
oryx
otter
ox
panda
pangolin
panther
peccary
pig
pilot whale
pine marten
pipistrelle
platypus
polar bear
polecat
porcupine
porpoise
possum
potto
puma
rabbit
raccoon
rat
reindeer
rhinoceros
roe deer
rorqual
sea cow
seal
sea lion
serval
sheep
shrew
skunk
sloth
snow leopard
sperm whale
spider monkey
spiny anteater
springbok
squirrel
squirrel monkey
stoat
tapir
tiger
vampire bat
vervet monkey
vole
walrus
wapiti
warthog
waterbuck
water buffalo
weasel
whale
wild boar
wildcat
wildebeest
wolverine
yak
zebra

Reptiles

adder
alligator
anaconda
axolotl
basilisk
boa constrictor
bushmaster
caiman
chameleon
cobra
constrictor
coral snake
corn snake
crocodile
diamondback terrapin
galliwasp
garter snake
gecko
gharial
Gila monster
glass lizard
grass snake
horned toad
iguana
Komodo dragon
leatherback
lizard
loggerhead turtle
mamba
moloch
monitor lizard
pit viper
puff adder
python
rattlesnake
reticulated python
rinkhals
sidewinder
skink
slow-worm
smooth snake
snake
taipan
terrapin
tortoise
turtle
viper
whip snake

Shellfish and Other Molluscs

abalone
argonaut
auger shell
cephalopod
clam
cockle
conch
cowrie
cuttlefish
limpet
mitre
murex
mussel
nautilus
nerite
nudibranch
octopus
ormer
oyster
paua
pearl oyster
periwinkle
piddock
quahog
ramshorn snail
razor shell
scallop
sea slug
slug
snail
squid
triton
whelk
winkle

Spiders and Other Arachnids

bird-eating spider
black widow
camel spider
chigger
crab spider
funnel-web spider
harvestman
harvest mite
jigger
mite
money spider
raft spider
redback
red spider mite
scorpion
spider mite
tarantula
tick
trapdoor spider
whip scorpion
wolf spider

Male and Female Animals

antelope: *buck, doe*
badger: *boar, sow*
bear: *boar, sow*
bird: *cock, hen*
buffalo: *bull, cow*
cat: *tom, queen*
cattle: *bull, cow*
chicken: *cock, hen*
deer: *stag, doe*
dog: *dog, bitch*
donkey: *jackass, jenny*
duck: *drake, duck*
elephant: *bull, cow*
ferret: *jack, gill*
fish: *cock, hen*
fox: *dog, vixen*
goat: *billy goat, nanny*
goose: *gander, goose*
hare: *buck, doe*
horse: *stallion, mare*
kangaroo: *buck, doe*
leopard: *leopard, leopardess*
lion: *lion, lioness*
otter: *dog, bitch*
pheasant: *cock, hen*
pig: *boar, sow*

rabbit: *buck, doe*
seal: *bull, cow*
sheep: *ram, ewe*
swan: *cob, pen*
tiger: *tiger, tigress*
whale: *bull, cow*
wolf: *dog, bitch*
zebra: *stallion, mare*

Young Animals

calf (*antelope, buffalo, camel, cattle, elephant, elk, giraffe, rhinoceros, seal, whale*)
chick (*chicken, hawk, pheasant*)
colt (*male horse*)
cub (*badger, bear, fox, leopard, lion, tiger, walrus, wolf*)
cygnet (*swan*)
duckling (*duck*)
eaglet (*eagle*)
elver (*eel*)
eyas (*hawk*)
fawn (*caribou, deer*)
filly (*female horse*)
foal (*horse, zebra*)
fry (*fish*)
gosling (*goose*)
joey (*kangaroo, wallaby, possum*)
kid (*goat, roe deer*)
kit (*beaver, ferret, fox, mink, weasel*)
kitten (*cat, cougar, rabbit, skunk*)
lamb (*sheep*)
leveret (*hare*)
owlet (*owl*)
parr (*salmon*)
piglet (*pig*)
pup (*dog, rat, seal, wolf*)
puppy (*coyote, dog*)
smolt (*salmon*)
squab (*pigeon*)
tadpole (*frog, toad*)
whelp (*dog, wolf*)

Collective Names for Animals

band (*gorillas*)
bask (*crocodiles*)
bellowing (*bullfinches*)
bevy (*roe deer, quails, larks, pheasants*)
bloat (*hippopotami*)
brood (*chickens*)
bury (*rabbits*)
busyness (*ferrets*)
charm (*finches*)
cloud (*gnats*)
covey (*partridges*)
crash (*rhinoceros*)
cry (*hounds*)
descent (*woodpeckers*)
down (*hares*)
drove (*bullocks*)
exaltation (*larks*)
flight (*birds*)
flock (*sheep*)
gaggle (*geese on land*)
herd (*cattle, elephants*)
hive (*bees*)
hover (*trout*)
kennel (*dogs*)
kindle (*kittens*)
knot (*toads*)
labour (*moles*)
leap (*leopards*)
litter (*kittens, pigs*)
mob (*kangaroos*)
murder (*crows*)
murmuration (*starlings*)
muster (*peacocks, penguins*)
obstinacy (*buffalo*)
pack (*hounds, grouse*)
pandemonium (*parrots*)
parade (*elephants*)
parliament (*owls*)
pod (*seals*)
pride (*lions*)
rookery (*rooks*)
safe (*ducks*)
school (*whales, dolphins, porpoises*)
shoal (*fish*)
shrewdness (*apes*)
siege (*herons*)
skein (*geese in flight*)
skulk (*foxes*)
sloth (*bears*)
span (*mules*)
stare (*owls*)
string (*horses*)
stud (*mares*)
swarm (*bees, flies*)
tiding (*magpies*)
trip (*goats*)
troop (*baboons*)
turmoil (*porpoises*)
turn (*turtles*)
unkindness (*ravens*)
watch (*nightingales*)
yoke (*oxen*)
zeal (*zebras*)

Chemical Elements

***Metal**

*actinium (Ac)
*aluminium (Al)
*americium (Am)
*antimony (Sb)
argon (Ar)
arsenic (As)
astatine (At)
*barium (Ba)
*berkelium (Bk)
*beryllium (Be)
*bismuth (Bi)
bohrium (Bh)
boron (B)
bromine (Br)
*cadmium (Cd)
*caesium (Cs)
*calcium (Ca)
*californium (Cf)
carbon (C)
*cerium (Ce)
chlorine (Cl)
*chromium (Cr)
*cobalt (Co)
*copper (Cu)
*curium (Cm)
darmstadtium (Ds)
dubnium (Db)
*dysprosium (Dy)
einsteinium (Es)
*erbium (Er)
*europium (Eu)
*fermium (Fm)
fluorine (F)
*francium (Fr)
*gadolinium (Gd)
*gallium (Ga)
germanium (Ge)
*gold (Au)
*hafnium (Hf)
hassium (Hs)
helium (He)
*holmium (Ho)
hydrogen (H)
*indium (In)
iodine (I)
*iridium (Ir)
*iron (Fe)
krypton (Kr)
*lanthanum (La)
*lawrencium (Lr)
*lead (Pb)
*lithium (Li)
*lutetium (Lu)
*magnesium (Mg)
*manganese (Mn)
meitnerium (Mt)
*mendelevium (Md)
*mercury (Hg)
*molybdenum (Mo)
*neodymium (Nd)
neon (Ne)
*neptunium (Np)
*nickel (Ni)
*niobium (Nb)
nitrogen (N)
*nobelium (No)
*osmium (Os)
oxygen (O)
*palladium (Pd)
phosphorus (P)
*platinum (Pt)
*plutonium (Pu)
*polonium (Po)
*potassium (K)
*praseodymium (Pr)

*promethium (Pm)
*protactinium (Pa)
*radium (Ra)
radon (Rn)
*rhenium (Re)
*rhodium (Rh)
roentgenium (Rg)
*rubidium (Rb)
*ruthenium (Ru)
rutherfordium (Rf)
*samarium (Sm)
*scandium (Sc)
seaborgium (Sg)
selenium (Se)
silicon (Si)
*silver (Ag)
*sodium (Na)
*strontium (Sr)
sulphur (S)
*tantalum (Ta)
*technetium (Tc)
tellurium (Te)
*terbium (Tb)
*thallium (Tl)
*thorium (Th)
*thulium (Tm)
*tin (Sn)
*titanium (Ti)
*tungsten (W)
*uranium (U)
*vanadium (V)
*xenon (Xe)
*ytterbium (Yb)
*yttrium (Y)
*zinc (Zn)
*zirconium (Zr)

Clothing

Clothes

anorak
apron
ballgown
bandeau
basque
bell-bottoms
belt
Bermuda shorts
bib
bikini
blazer
bloomers
blouse
blouson
boa
bodice
body
body stocking
body warmer
bolero
bomber jacket
bow tie
bra
braces
breeches
burka/burkha/burqa
burnous
cagoule
cape
capri pants
cardigan
cargo pants
carpenter trousers
catsuit
chador
chinos
churidars
coat
combat trousers
cords
corset
cravat
crinoline
crop top
culottes
cummerbund
cut-offs
dashiki
denims
dhoti
dinner jacket
dirndl
djellaba
djibba
dolman
domino
donkey jacket
doublet
dress
dressing gown
dress shirt
duffel coat
dungarees
flannels
flares
fleece
flying jacket
frock coat
gilet
glove
gown
greatcoat
guernsey
gymslip
haik
hair shirt
hipsters
hoody/hoodie
hose
hot pants
housecoat
hula skirt
jacket
jeans
jellaba
jerkin
jersey
jibba
jilbab
jodhpurs
jogging pants
jumper
jumpsuit
kaftan
kagoul
kameez
kilt
kimono
knickers
lederhosen
leggings
leg warmers
leotard
loden
loincloth
lumberjacket
lungi
mac
mackintosh/macintosh
maillot
mandarin jacket
mantilla
mantle
maxi
maxidress
mess jacket
midi
mini
miniskirt
mitt
mitten
morning coat
muff
muffler
nightdress
nightshirt
oilskins
overalls
overcoat
overtrousers
palazzo pants
pantaloons
panties
pants
pantyhose
parka
pedal pushers
peignoir
pencil skirt
peplum
petticoat
pinafore
pinafore dress
plastron
plus fours
polo neck
polo shirt
poncho
pullover
pyjamas
raincoat
reefer jacket
robe
roll-neck
ruff
safari jacket
sailor suit
salopettes
sari
sarong
sash
scarf
serape/sarape
shawl
sheath dress
sheepskin
shell suit
shift
shirt dress
shirtwaister
shorts
skinny-rib
ski pants
skirt
skort
slacks
slip
smock
smoking jacket
sock
stirrup pants
stock
stocking
stole
suit
sundress
suspenders
sweater
sweatpants
sweatshirt
swimming costume
swimming trunks
swimsuit
T-shirt
tabard
tailcoat
tails
tank top
tee
tie
tights
toga
top
topcoat
tracksuit

trench coat
trews
trousers
trouser suit
trunks
tunic
turtleneck
tutu
tux/tuxedo
tweeds
twinset
ulster
underpants
underskirt
veil
vest
V-neck
waistcoat
waterproof
waxed jacket
windcheater
yashmak

Footwear

beetle-crusher
boot
bootee
brogue
carpet slipper
chappal
clog
court shoe
cowboy boot
deck shoe
desert boot
Dr Martens (trademark)
espadrille
flip-flop
galosh
gumboot
half-boot
high-low
hobnail boot
jackboot
jelly shoe
lace-up
loafer
moccasin
moon boot
mukluk
mule
overshoe
Oxford
patten
peep-toe
platform
plimsoll
pump
sabot
sandal
shoe
slingback
slip-on
slipper
sneaker
snow boot
step-in
stiletto
thong
top boot
trainer
wader
walking boot
wedge
wellington boot

Headgear

balaclava
bandeau
baseball cap
beanie
bearskin
beret
biretta
boater
bobble hat
bonnet
bowler
busby
cap
chaplet
circlet
cloche
cloth cap
cocked hat
coif
coolie hat
coronet
cowl
crash helmet
crown
deerstalker
derby
diadem
Dolly Varden
dunce's cap
fedora
fez
flat cap
garland
glengarry
hard hat
headband
headscarf
helmet
hijab
homburg
hood
jester's cap
jockey cap
Juliet cap
keffiyeh
kepi
mantilla
mitre
mob cap
mortar board
nightcap
panama
pillbox hat
pixie hat
pork-pie hat
sailor hat
skullcap
slouch hat
snood
sola topi
sombrero
sou'wester
Stetson (trademark)
stovepipe hat
sun hat
tam-o'-shanter
tarboosh
ten-gallon hat
tiara
top hat
topi
topper
toque
tricorne
trilby
turban
veil
wimple
wreath
zucchetto

Food and Drink

Bread and Bread Rolls

bagel
baguette
bannock
bap
bloomer
bridge roll
brioche
bun
chapatti
ciabatta
cob
cornbread
cottage loaf
crumpet
damper
farl
farmhouse loaf
flatbread
focaccia
French stick
fruit loaf
granary bread (trademark)
hoagie
malt loaf
matzo
milk loaf
muffin
nan/naan
panettone
panino
paratha
petit pain
pikelet
pitta
pone
poppadom
pumpernickel
puri
rye
soda bread
sourdough
split tin
stollen

Cakes, Biscuits, and Desserts

angel cake
apfelstrudel
baba
baked Alaska
Bakewell tart
baklava
banana split
banoffi/ banoffee pie
Bath bun
Bath Oliver
Battenberg
beignet
biscotti
Black Forest gateau
blancmange
bombe
bourbon
brack
brandy snap
bread pudding
bread-and-butter pudding
Brown Betty
brownie
bun
butterfly cake
cabinet pudding
cassata
charlotte
charlotte russe
cheesecake
chocolate chip
clafoutis
cobbler
compote
cookie
cream cracker
cream puff
crème brûlée
crème caramel
crêpe
crêpe Suzette
crispbread
croquembouche
crumble
crumpet
cupcake
custard cream
custard pie
custard tart
Danish pastry
devil's food cake
digestive
doughnut
drop scone
dumpling
Dundee cake
Eccles cake
eclair
egg custard
Eskimo pie (trademark)
Eve's pudding
fairy cake
fancy
flapjack
Florentine
flummery
fool
fortune cookie
frangipane
fruit cocktail
fruit salad
garibaldi
gateau
gelato
Genoa cake
gingerbread
ginger nut
ginger snap
granita
halwa
hot cross bun
ice cream
jelly
junket
Knickerbocker Glory
kulfi
lady's finger
langue de chat
lardy cake
macaroon
Madeira cake
madeleine
maid of honour
marble cake
matzo
meringue
milk pudding
millefeuille
mince pie
Mississippi mud pie
mousse
muffin
Nice biscuit
oatcake
pancake
panettone
panforte
parfait
parkin
pavlova
peach Melba
petit four
plum duff
plum pudding
popover
pound cake
profiterole
queen of puddings
ratafia
rice pudding
rock cake
roly-poly
rusk
Sachertorte
sago pudding
Sally Lunn
sandwich
savarin
scone
seed cake
semolina pudding
shortbread
shortcake
simnel cake
sorbet
soufflé
sponge
sponge pudding
spotted dick
steamed pudding
stollen
streusel
strudel
summer pudding
sundae
Swiss roll
syllabub
tapioca pudding
tart
tarte Tatin
tartlet
tartufo
tipsy cake
tiramisu
torte
treacle tart
trifle
turnover
tutti-frutti
upside-down cake
Victoria sponge
waffle
water biscuit
water ice
whip
yogurt
yule log
zabaglione

Cheeses

asiago
Bel Paese (trademark)
blue vinny
Boursin (trademark)
Brie
Caerphilly
Camembert
Chaumes
Cheddar
Cheshire
chèvre
cottage cheese
cream cheese
crowdie/ crowdy
curd cheese
Danish blue
Derby
Dolcelatte (trademark)
Double Gloucester
Dunlop
Edam
Emmental
feta/fetta
fontina
fromage blanc
fromage frais
Gloucester
Gorgonzola
Gouda
Gruyère
halloumi
havarti
Jarlsberg (trademark)
Lancashire
Leicester
Limburger
Manchego
mascarpone
Monterey Jack
mozzarella
paneer/panir
Parmesan
Parmigiano Reggiano
pecorino
Port Salut
provolone
quark
Red Leicester
ricotta
Romano
Roquefort (trademark)
sage Derby
scamorza
Stilton
taleggio
Tilsit
Wensleydale

Fruit and Nuts

almond
apple
apricot
avocado
banana
betel nut
bilberry
blackberry
blackcurrant
blueberry

boysenberry
Brazil nut
breadfruit
butternut
cantaloupe
Cape gooseberry
carambola
cashew
cherimoya
cherry
chestnut
Chinese gooseberry
citron
clementine
cloudberry
cobnut
coconut
cola nut
cowberry
crab apple
cranberry
currant
damson
date
elderberry
fig
filbert
galia melon
gooseberry
gourd
grape
grapefruit
greengage
groundnut
guava
hazelnut
honeydew melon
huckleberry
jackfruit
jujube
kiwi fruit
kumquat
lemon
lime
loganberry
loquat
lychee
macadamia
mandarin
mango
melon
minneola
monkey nut
mulberry
nectarine
olive
orange
ortanique
papaya
passion fruit
pawpaw
peach
peanut
pear
pecan
persimmon
pineapple
pine nut
pistachio
plum
pomegranate
pomelo
prickly pear
pumpkin
quince
rambutan
raspberry
redcurrant
salmonberry
sapodilla
satsuma
serviceberry
sharon fruit
sloe
star anise
starfruit
strawberry
tamarillo
tangerine
tayberry
tiger nut
Ugli fruit (trademark)
walnut
water chestnut
watermelon
whortleberry

Pasta

agnolotti
angel hair
cannelloni
capelli
capellini
cappelletti
conchiglie
ditalini
farfalle
farfalline
fettuccine
fusilli
lasagne
linguine
macaroni
noodles
orecchiette
orzo
pappardelle
penne
pipe
radiatori
ravioli
rigatoni
spaghetti
spaghettini
strozzapreti
tagliatelle
tagliolini
tortelli
tortellini
tortelloni
tortiglioni
vermicelli
ziti

Sweets and Confectionery

aniseed ball
barley sugar
bonbon
brittle
bullseye
butterscotch
candy
candyfloss
caramel
chew
chocolate
coconut ice
comfit
cracknel
crystallized fruit
dolly mixtures
dragée
Easter egg
fondant
fruit drop
fruit gum
fruit pastille
fudge
gobstopper
gulab jamun
gumdrop
halva
humbug
jalebi
jelly
jelly baby
jelly bean
jujube
Kendal mint cake
laddu
liquorice
liquorice allsort
lollipop
lolly
marshmallow
marzipan
mint
nougat
pastille
pear drop
peppermint
peppermint cream
Pontefract cake
praline
rock
sherbet
sugared almond
toffee
toffee apple
truffle
Turkish delight
walnut whip
wine gum

Vegetables

aduki/adzuki bean
alfalfa
artichoke
asparagus
aubergine
bamboo shoots
bean
beet
beetroot
black bean
black-eyed bean
borlotti bean
breadfruit
broad bean
broccoli
Brussels sprout
butter bean
butternut squash
cabbage
calabrese
cannellini bean
capsicum
carrot
cassava
cauliflower
celeriac
celery
chard
chervil
chickpea
chicory
Chinese leaves
corn on the cob
cos lettuce
courgette
cress
cucumber
curly kale
eggplant
endive
fennel
flageolet bean
French bean
garlic

gherkin
globe artichoke
gourd
haricot bean
Jerusalem artichoke
kale
kidney bean
kohlrabi
leek
lentil
lettuce
lima bean
lollo rosso
mangetout
marrow
marrowfat pea
mooli
mung bean
mushroom
mustard
okra
onion
pak choi
parsnip
pea
pepper
petits pois
pimiento
pinto bean
plantain
potato
pumpkin
radicchio
radish
rocket
runner bean
salsify
samphire
savoy cabbage
shallot
snow pea
soybean
spinach
spinach beet
spring greens
spring onion
squash
string bean
sugar pea
sugar snap pea
swede
sweetcorn
sweet pepper
sweet potato
tomato
turnip
vegetable spaghetti
water chestnut
watercress
waxpod
yam
zucchini

Alcoholic Drinks

absinthe
advocaat
alcopop
ale
amaretto
amontillado
aquavit
Armagnac
barley wine
beer
bitter
bock
bourbon
brandy
brown ale
burgundy
Calvados
cassis
cava
champagne
chartreuse
cherry brandy
cider
claret
cocktail
cognac
crème de menthe
curaçao
fine champagne
fino
genever
gin
ginger wine
grappa
hock
ice beer
Irish coffee
Irish whiskey
kirsch
kümmel
kvass
lager
Liebfraumilch
light ale
liqueur
Madeira
malmsey
malt
malt whisky
manzanilla
maraschino
Marsala
mead
mescal
mild
milk stout
moscato
muscat
muscatel
oloroso
ouzo
pale ale
palm wine
pastis
perry
Pils
Pilsner/Pilsener
port
porter
poteen
raki
ratafia
retsina
rosé
rum
rye
sack
sake
schnapps
Scotch whisky
scrumpy
Sekt
shandy
sherry
single malt
slivovitz
sloe gin
Spumante
stout
tequila
Tia Maria
triple sec
vermouth
vinho verde
vodka
whiskey
whisky
wine

Non-alcoholic Drinks

barley water
bitter lemon
buttermilk
cafe au lait
caffè latte
caffè macchiato
camomile tea
cappuccino
cherryade
citron pressé
club soda (trademark)
cocoa
coffee
cola
cordial
cream soda
crush
dandelion and burdock
decaf
decaffeinated coffee
drinking chocolate
Earl Grey
espresso
filter coffee
fruit juice
fruit tea
ginger ale
ginger beer
green tea
gunpowder tea
herbal tea
horchata
hot chocolate
iced tea
Indian tea
infusion
isotonic drink
jasmine tea
lassi
latte
lemon tea
lemonade
limeade
malted milk
maté

milkshake
mineral water
mint tea
mocha
mochaccino
orangeade
peppermint tea
prairie oyster
pressé
robusta
root beer
rosehip tea
sarsaparilla
seltzer
sherbet
smoothie
soda water
soya milk
sports drink
spring water
squash
St Clements
tea
tisane
tonic water
yerba maté

Phobias

air travel: *aerophobia*
American people and things: *Americophobia*
animals: *zoophobia*
beards: *pogonophobia*
beating: *mastigophobia*
bed: *clinophobia*
bees: *apiphobia*
birds: *ornithophobia*
blood: *haemophobia*
blushing: *erythrophobia*
bridges: *gephyrophobia*
burial alive: *taphephobia*
cancer: *carcinophobia*
cats: *ailurophobia*
childbirth: *tocophobia*
children: *paedophobia*
Chinese people and things: *Sinophobia*
clouds: *nephophobia*
cold: *cheimaphobia*
colour: *chromophobia*
computers: *cyberphobia*
corpses: *necrophobia*
crowds: *demophobia*
dampness: *hygrophobia*
darkness: *scotophobia*
dawn: *eosophobia*
death: *thanatophobia*
depth: *bathophobia*
dirt: *mysophobia*
disease: *pathophobia*
dogs: *cynophobia*
dreams: *oneirophobia*
drink: *potophobia*
dust: *koniophobia*
electricity: *electrophobia*
English people and things: *Anglophobia*
everything: *panophobia, pantophobia*
faeces: *coprophobia*
feathers: *pteronophobia*
fever: *febriphobia*
fire: *pyrophobia*
fish: *ichthyophobia*
flesh: *selaphobia*
floods: *antlophobia*
flowers: *anthophobia*
food: *cibophobia, sitophobia*
foreigners: *xenophobia*
French people and things: *Francophobia, Gallophobia*
fur: *doraphobia*
German people and things: *Germanophobia, Teutophobia*
germs: *spermophobia*
ghosts: *phasmophobia*
God: *theophobia*
gold: *aurophobia, chrysophobia*
hair: *trichophobia*
heat: *thermophobia*
heaven: *uranophobia*
hell: *hadephobia, stygiophobia*
high buildings: *batophobia*
high places: *hypsophobia*
home: *oikophobia*
homosexuals: *homophobia*
horses: *hippophobia*
ice: *cryophobia*
idleness: *thassophobia*
illness: *nosophobia*
imperfection: *atelophobia*
infinity: *apeirophobia*
insanity: *lyssophobia, maniphobia*
insects: *entomophobia*
insect stings: *cnidophobia*
Italian people and things: *Italophobia*
lakes: *limnophobia*
light: *photophobia*
lightning: *astrapophobia*
loneliness: *autophobia, ermitophobia*
machinery: *mechanophobia*
magic: *rhabdophobia*
marriage: *gametophobia*
men: *androphobia*
metal: *metallophobia*
mice: *musophobia*
microbes: *bacillophobia*
mites: *acarophobia*
mobs: *ochlophobia*
motion: *kinetophobia*
music: *musicophobia*
needles: *belonephobia*
new things: *neophobia*
night: *nyctophobia*
nudity: *gymnophobia*
open places: *agoraphobia*
pain: *algophobia*
pins: enetophobia
pleasure: *hedonophobia*
poison: *toxiphobia*
poverty: *peniaphobia*
precipices: *cremnophobia*
priests: *hierophobia*
punishment: *poinephobia*
religious works of art: *iconophobia*
responsibility: *hypegiaphobia*
rivers: *potamophobia*
robbers: *harpaxophobia*
ruin: *atephobia*
Russian people and things: *Russophobia*
Satan: *Satanophobia*
scabies: *scabiophobia*
Scottish people and things: *Scotophobia*
sex: *erotophobia*
shadows: *sciophobia*
sharpness: *acrophobia*
shock: *hormephobia*
sin: *hamartophobia*
sleep: *hypnophobia*
slime: *blennophobia*
small things: *microphobia*
smell: *olfactophobia, osmophobia*
smothering: *pnigerophobia*

snakes: *ophidiophobia*
snow: *chionophobia*
solitude: *eremophobia*
sourness: *acerophobia*
speech: *glossophobia, phonophobia*
speed: *tachophobia*
spiders: *arachnophobia*
stars: *siderophobia*
stealing: *kleptophobia*
stuttering: *laliophobia, lalophobia*
sun: *heliophobia*
swallowing: *phagophobia*
taste: *geumatophobia*
technology: *technophobia*
thunder: *brontophobia, keraunophobia, tonitrophobia*
time: *chronophobia*
touch: *haptophobia*
travel: *hodophobia*
venereal disease: *syphilophobia*
voids: *kenophobia*
vomiting: *emetophobia*
water: *hydrophobia*
waves: *cymophobia*
weakness: *asthenophobia*
wind: *anemophobia*
women: *gynophobia*
words: *logophobia*
work: *ergophobia*
writing: *graphophobia*

Plants

Flowering Plants and Shrubs

acacia
acanthus
aconite
African violet
agapanthus
aloe
alstroemeria
alyssum
amaranth
amaryllis
anemone
aquilegia
arrowgrass
arum lily
asphodel
aspidistra
aster
astilbe
aubretia
avens
azalea
balsam
banksia
bedstraw
begonia
belladonna
bellflower
bergamot
betony
bilberry
bindweed
bird's-foot trefoil
black-eyed Susan
blackthorn
bleeding heart
bluebell
boneset
borage
bougainvillea
bramble
broom
bryony
buddleia
bugloss
bulrush
burdock
burnet
busy Lizzie
buttercup
cactus
calceolaria
calendula
camellia
camomile
campanula
campion
candytuft
Canterbury bell
carnation
catmint
ceanothus
celandine
chickweed
chicory
Chinese lantern
chives
choisya
chokeberry
Christmas cactus
Christmas rose
chrysanthemum
cicely
cinquefoil
clematis
clove pink
clover
cockscomb
coltsfoot
columbine
comfrey
convolvulus
coreopsis
cornflower
corydalis
cotoneaster
cottonweed
cow parsley
cowslip
cranesbill
crocus
crown imperial
crown of thorns
cuckoo pint
cyclamen
daffodil
dahlia
daisy
damask rose
dandelion
daphne
deadly nightshade
delphinium
dianthus
dill
dittany
dock
dog rose
duckweed
echinacea
edelweiss
eglantine
elder
evening primrose
eyebright
feverfew
figwort
firethorn
flax
forget-me-not
forsythia
foxglove
frangipani
freesia
fritillary
fuchsia
furze
gardenia
gentian
geranium
gladiolus
glory-of-the-snow
gloxinia
golden rod
gorse
grape hyacinth
groundsel
guelder rose
gypsophila
harebell
hawkweed
hawthorn
heartsease
heather
hebe
helianthemum
helianthus
heliotrope
hellebore
hemlock
heuchera
hibiscus
hogweed
holly
hollyhock
honesty
honeysuckle
hosta
hyacinth
hydrangea
iris
jacaranda
japonica
jasmine
jonquil
kingcup
knapweed
knotgrass
laburnum
lady's mantle
lady's tresses
larkspur
lavatera
lavender
lemon balm
lilac
lily
lily of the valley
lobelia
London pride
loosestrife
lords and ladies
lotus
lovage
love-in-a-mist
love-lies-bleeding
lungwort
lupin
madonna lily
magnolia

mahonia
mallow
mandrake
marguerite
marigold
marshwort
may
mayflower
meadow rue
meadow saffron
meadowsweet
Michaelmas daisy
milfoil
mimosa
mint
mistletoe
mock orange
montbretia
morning glory
musk rose
myrtle
narcissus
nasturtium
nettle
nicotiana
nigella
night-scented stock
nightshade
old man's beard
oleander
orchid
ox-eye daisy
oxlip
pansy
Parma violet
parsley
pasque flower
passion flower
pelargonium
pennyroyal
penstemon
peony
peppermint
periwinkle
petunia
phlox
pimpernel
pink
pitcher plant
plantain
plumbago
poinsettia
polyanthus
poppy
potentilla
prickly pear
primrose
primula
privet
pulsatilla
pyracantha
pyrethrum
ragwort
ramsons
red-hot poker
rhododendron
rock rose
rose
rosebay willowherb
rose of Sharon
safflower
St John's wort
salvia
samphire
saxifrage
scabious
scarlet pimpernel
scilla
sedum
shamrock
shrimp plant
snapdragon
snow-in-summer
snowdrop
soapwort
sorrel
speedwell
spikenard
spiraea
spurge
spurrey
squill
starwort
stock
stonecrop
streptocarpus
sunflower
sweet pea
sweet william
tansy
teasel
thistle
thrift
toadflax
tradescantia
trefoil
tulip
valerian
Venus flytrap
verbena
veronica
vervain
vetch
viburnum
violet
viper's bugloss
wallflower
water lily
willowherb
winter jasmine
wintergreen
wisteria
witch hazel
wolfsbane
woodruff
wormwood
yarrow
yucca
zinnia

Trees and Shrubs

acacia
acer
alder
almond
apple
apricot
araucaria
ash
aspen
azalea
balsa
balsam fir
bamboo
banksia
banyan
baobab
basswood
bay tree
beech
beefwood
bergamot
birch
blackthorn
bottlebrush
bottle tree
bo tree
box
box elder
bristlecone pine
broom
buckeye
buckthorn
butternut
cacao
calabash
camellia
camphor tree
candelabra tree
candleberry
candlenut
carambola
carob
cassava
cassia
casuarina
cedar
cherimoya
cherry
chestnut
cinnamon
citron
coco de mer
coconut palm
cola
coolibah
copper beech
cork oak
coromandel
crab apple
cypress
dogwood
dragon tree
ebony
elder
elm
eucalyptus
euonymus
ficus
fig
filbert
fir
firethorn
flame tree
frangipani
fuchsia
gean
ginkgo
gorse
grapefruit
greengage
guava
gum tree
hawthorn
hazel
hemlock fir
hickory
holly
holm oak
honeysuckle
hornbeam
horse chestnut
hydrangea
ilex
iroko
ironbark
ironwood
jacaranda
jackfruit
jack pine
japonica
jasmine
juniper
kalmia
kapok
kermes oak
laburnum
larch
laurel
lemon
Leyland cypress
leylandii
lilac
lime
linden
liquidambar
locust
lodgepole pine
logwood
macadamia
magnolia
mahogany
maidenhair tree
mango
mangosteen
mangrove
maple
mastic
may
mimosa
mirabelle
monkey puzzle
mountain ash
mulberry
myrtle
nutmeg
nux vomica
oak
oleaster
olive
osier

pagoda tree
palm
papaya
paper mulberry
paperbark
pawpaw
pear
persimmon
pine
pistachio
pitch pine
plane
plum
pomegranate
pomelo
poplar
privet
pussy willow
quassia
quince
rambutan
red cedar
redwood
rhododendron
robinia
rosewood
rowan
rubber plant
rubber tree
sallow
sandalwood
sapele
sapodilla
sassafras
satinwood
senna
sequoia
service tree
silver birch
Sitka cypress
slippery elm
smoke tree
soapberry
spindle
spruce
star anise
stinkwood
storax
sumac
sycamore
tallow tree
tamarind
tamarisk
tea
teak
tea tree
thuja
tulip tree
tulipwood
umbrella tree
viburnum
walnut
weeping willow
wellingtonia
whitebeam
willow
witch hazel
wych elm
yew

L

label *noun* **1 tag**, ticket, tab, sticker, marker, docket. **2 description**, designation, name, epithet, nickname, sobriquet, title.
● *verb* **1 tag**, ticket, mark, stamp. **2 categorize**, classify, class, describe, designate, identify, mark, stamp, brand, call, name, term, dub.

laborious *adjective* **1 arduous**, hard, heavy, difficult, strenuous, gruelling, punishing, exacting, tough, onerous, challenging, painstaking, time-consuming. **2 laboured**, strained, forced, stiff, stilted, unnatural, artificial, ponderous.
- OPPOSITES easy, effortless.

labour *noun* **1 work**, toil, exertion, effort, industry, drudgery; *informal* slog, grind; *old use* travail. **2 workers**, employees, labourers, workforce, staff. **3 childbirth**, birth, delivery; *technical* parturition.
● *verb* **work (hard)**, toil, slave (away), struggle, strive, exert yourself, endeavour, try hard; *informal* slog away, plug away.

laboured *adjective* **1** *laboured breathing* **strained**, difficult, forced, laborious. **2** *a laboured metaphor* **contrived**, forced, unconvincing, unnatural, artificial, overdone.
- OPPOSITES natural, easy.

labourer *noun* **workman**, worker, manual worker, blue-collar worker, (hired) hand, roustabout, drudge, menial; *Austral./NZ* rouseabout; *dated* navvy.

labyrinthine *adjective* **1 maze-like**, winding, twisting, serpentine, meandering. **2 complicated**, intricate, complex, involved, tortuous, convoluted, elaborate, confusing, puzzling, mystifying, bewildering, baffling.

lace *verb* **1 fasten**, do up, tie up, secure, knot. **2 flavour**, mix, blend, fortify, strengthen, season, spice (up), liven up, doctor, adulterate; *informal* spike.

laceration *noun* **gash**, cut, wound, injury, tear, slash, scratch, scrape, abrasion, graze.

lack *noun* **absence**, want, need, deficiency, dearth, shortage, shortfall, scarcity, paucity.
- OPPOSITES abundance.
● *verb* **be without**, be in need of, be short of, be deficient in, be low on, be pressed for, need; *informal* be strapped for.

lacklustre *adjective* **uninspired**, uninspiring, unimaginative, dull, humdrum, colourless, bland, insipid, flat, dry, lifeless, tame, prosaic, dreary, tedious.
- OPPOSITES inspired.

lad *noun (informal)* **1 boy**, schoolboy, youth, youngster, juvenile, stripling; *informal* kid, nipper; *Scottish informal* laddie; *derogatory* brat. **2 (young) man**, fellow; *informal* guy, geezer; *Brit. informal* chap, bloke; *N. Amer. informal* dude, hombre.

laden *adjective* **loaded**, burdened, weighed down, overloaded, piled high, full, packed, stuffed, crammed; *informal* chock-full, chock-a-block.

lady *noun* **1 woman**, female, girl; *Scottish & N. English* lass, lassie; *N. Amer. informal* dame, broad; *Austral. informal* sheila. **2 noblewoman**, aristocrat, duchess, countess, peeress, viscountess, baroness.

ladylike *adjective* **genteel**, polite, refined, well bred, cultivated, polished, decorous, proper, respectable, well mannered, cultured, sophisticated, elegant; *Brit. informal* posh.

lag *verb* **fall behind**, trail, bring up the rear, dawdle, hang back, delay, loiter, linger, dally, straggle.

laid-back *adjective (informal)* **relaxed**, easy-going, free and easy, casual,

nonchalant, blasé, cool, calm, unconcerned, leisurely, unhurried; *informal* unflappable, chilled.
- OPPOSITES uptight.

lake *noun* **pool**, pond, tarn, reservoir, lagoon, waterhole; *Scottish* loch; *Anglo-Irish* lough; *N. Amer.* bayou.

lame *adjective* **1 limping**, hobbling, crippled, disabled, incapacitated; *informal* gammy. **2 feeble**, weak, thin, flimsy, poor, unconvincing, implausible, unlikely.

lament *verb* **1 mourn**, grieve, sorrow, weep, cry, wail, keen. **2 complain about**, bewail, bemoan, deplore.
- OPPOSITES celebrate, welcome.

lamentable *adjective* **deplorable**, regrettable, terrible, awful, wretched, woeful, dire, disastrous, desperate, grave, appalling, dreadful, pitiful, shameful, unfortunate; *formal* egregious.
- OPPOSITES wonderful.

land *noun* **1 dry land**, terra firma, coast, coastline, shore. **2 grounds**, fields, property, acres, acreage, estate, real estate. **3 country**, nation, state, realm, kingdom, province, region, territory, area, domain.
● *verb* **1 disembark**, go ashore, debark, alight, get off, berth, dock, moor, (drop) anchor, tie up, put in, touch down, come to rest. **2** *(informal)* **get**, obtain, acquire, secure, gain, net, win, achieve, attain, bag, carry off.
- OPPOSITES embark, take off.

WORD LINKS
terrestrial relating to land

landlord, **landlady** *noun* **1 owner**, proprietor, lessor, householder, landowner. **2 licensee**, innkeeper, hotelier; *Brit.* publican; *humorous* mine host.
- OPPOSITES tenant.

landmark *noun* **1 feature**, sight, monument, building. **2** *a landmark in Indian history* **turning point**, milestone, watershed.

landscape *noun* **scenery**, country, countryside, topography, terrain, view, panorama.

landslide *noun* **1 landslip**, rockfall, mudslide, avalanche. **2 decisive victory**, runaway victory, overwhelming majority; *informal* whitewash.

lane *noun* **road**, street, track, trail, alley, alleyway, passage, path.

language *noun* **1 speech**, speaking, talk, discourse, communication, words, vocabulary. **2 tongue**, mother tongue, native tongue, dialect, patois; *informal* lingo, geekspeak. **3 wording**, phrasing, phraseology, style, vocabulary, terminology, expressions, turn of phrase, parlance.

WORD LINKS
linguistic relating to language

languish *verb* **1 deteriorate**, decline, go downhill, wither, droop, wilt, fade. **2 waste away**, rot, be abandoned, be neglected, be forgotten, suffer.
- OPPOSITES thrive.

lap[1] *verb* **1 drink**, lick up, sup, swallow, slurp, gulp. **2 splash**, wash, swish, slosh, break, plash; *literary* purl.
□ **lap up** relish, revel in, savour, delight in, wallow in, glory in, enjoy.

lap[2] *noun* **circuit**, leg, circle, round, stretch.

lapse *noun* **1 failure**, slip, error, mistake, blunder, fault, omission; *informal* slip-up. **2 decline**, fall, deterioration, degeneration, backsliding, regression. **3 interval**, gap, pause, interlude, lull, hiatus, break.
● *verb* **1 expire**, run out, (come to an) end, cease, stop, terminate. **2 revert**, relapse, drift, slide, slip, sink.

large *adjective* **big**, great, sizeable, substantial, considerable, huge, extensive, voluminous, vast, cosmic, prodigious, massive, immense, enormous, colossal, king-size(d), heavy, mammoth, gigantic, giant, fat, stout, strapping, bulky, burly; *informal* jumbo, mega, whopping.
- OPPOSITES small.

largely *adverb* **mostly**, mainly, to a large/great extent, chiefly, predominantly, primarily, principally, for the most part, in the main, on the whole.

lash *verb* **1 beat against**, dash against, pound, batter, hammer against, strike, hit, drum. **2 fasten**, bind, tie (up), tether, hitch, knot, rope.
□ **lash out 1** criticize, attack, condemn, censure; *informal* lay into, dis; *Brit. informal* slag off, have a go at. **2** hit out at, strike, let fly at, take a swing at, set on, turn on, round on, attack; *informal* lay into, pitch into.

last[1] *adjective* **1 final**, closing, concluding, end, ultimate, terminal, later, latter. **2 rearmost**, hindmost, endmost, furthest (back). **3 previous**, preceding, prior, former, latest, most recent.
– OPPOSITES first, next.

last[2] *verb* **1** *the hearing lasted for six days* **continue**, go on, carry on, keep on/going, take. **2** *he won't last long as manager* **survive**, endure, hold on/out, keep going, persevere, persist, stay, remain; *informal* stick it out, hang on, go the distance.
– OPPOSITES end.

lasting *adjective* **enduring**, long-lasting, long-lived, abiding, continuing, long-term, permanent, durable, stable, secure, long-standing, eternal, undying, everlasting, unending, never-ending.
– OPPOSITES passing, ephemeral.

late *adjective* **1 behind schedule**, tardy, overdue, delayed, belated, behindhand. **2 dead**, departed, lamented, passed on/away; *formal* deceased. **3 recent**, fresh, new, up to date, latter-day, current.
– OPPOSITES punctual, early.

lately *adverb* **recently**, not long ago, of late, latterly, in recent times.

latent *adjective* **dormant**, untapped, undiscovered, hidden, concealed, undeveloped, unrealized, unfulfilled, potential.

later *adjective* **subsequent**, following, succeeding, future, upcoming, to come, ensuing, next.
– OPPOSITES earlier, preceding.
● *adverb* **subsequently**, eventually, then, next, later on, afterwards, at a later date, in the future, in due course, by and by, in a while, in time; *formal* thereafter.

latest *adjective* **most recent**, newest, up to the minute, current, state-of-the-art, cutting-edge; *informal* in, with it, trendy, hip, hot, happening, cool.
– OPPOSITES old.

latitude *noun* **freedom**, scope, leeway, (breathing) space, flexibility, liberty, independence, free rein, licence.
– OPPOSITES restriction.

latter *adjective* **1 later**, closing, end, concluding, final. **2 last-mentioned**, second, last, final.
– OPPOSITES earlier, former.

laudable *adjective* **praiseworthy**, commendable, admirable, worthy, deserving, creditable, estimable, exemplary.
– OPPOSITES shameful.

laugh *verb* **chuckle**, chortle, guffaw, giggle, titter, snigger, roar, split your sides; *informal* be in stitches, be rolling in the aisles, crease up, fall about, crack up; *Brit. informal* kill yourself.
● *noun* **1 chuckle**, chortle, guffaw, giggle, titter, snigger, roar, shriek. **2** *(informal)* **joke**, prank, jest; *informal* lark, hoot, scream.
□ **laugh at** ridicule, mock, deride, scoff at, jeer at, sneer at, jibe at, make fun of, poke fun at, taunt, tease; *informal* take the mickey out of. **laugh off** dismiss, make a joke of, make light of, shrug off, brush aside; *informal* pooh-pooh.

laughter *noun* **1 laughing**, chuckling, chortling, guffawing, giggling, tittering, sniggering. **2 amusement**, entertainment, humour, mirth, merriment, gaiety, hilarity, jollity, fun.

launch *verb* **1 propel**, fire, shoot, throw, hurl, fling, pitch, lob, let fly; *informal* chuck, heave, sling. **2 start**, begin, initiate, put in place, set up, inaugurate, introduce; *informal* kick off.

lavatory *noun* **toilet**, WC, convenience, privy, latrine; *Brit.* cloakroom; *N. Amer.* washroom, bathroom, rest room, men's/ladies' room, comfort station; *Brit. informal* loo, bog, the Ladies, the Gents, khazi; *N. Amer. informal* can, john; *Austral./NZ informal* dunny.

lavish *adjective* **1 sumptuous**, luxurious, gorgeous, costly, expensive, opulent, grand, splendid, rich, fancy; *informal* posh, bling-bling. **2 generous**, liberal, bountiful, unstinting, unsparing, free, munificent, extravagant, abundant, copious, plentiful, prolific, excessive, wasteful, prodigal; *literary* plenteous.
- OPPOSITES meagre, frugal.
● *verb* **shower**, heap, pour, deluge, throw at, squander, dissipate.
- OPPOSITES begrudge, stint.

law *noun* **1 regulation**, statute, act, bill, decree, edict, rule, ruling, dictum, command, order, directive, dictate, diktat, fiat, by-law; (**laws**) legislation, constitution, code; *N. Amer. formal* ordinance. **2 principle**, rule, precept, commandment, belief, creed, credo, maxim, tenet, doctrine, canon.

WORD LINKS
legal, **legislative** relating to laws

lawful *adjective* **legitimate**, legal, licit, permissible, permitted, allowable, allowed, rightful, sanctioned, authorized, warranted; *informal* legit.
- OPPOSITES illegal.

lawyer *noun* solicitor, barrister, advocate, counsel, Queen's Counsel, QC; *N. Amer.* attorney, counselor(-at-law); *informal* brief, legal eagle.

lax *adjective* **slack**, slipshod, negligent, remiss, careless, sloppy, slapdash, offhand, casual.
- OPPOSITES strict.

lay[1] *verb* **1 put (down)**, place, set (down), deposit, rest, position, shove; *informal* stick, dump, park, plonk; *Brit. informal* bung. **2** *we laid plans for the voyage* **devise**, arrange, prepare, work out, hatch, design, plan, scheme, plot, conceive, put together, draw up, produce, develop, formulate; *informal* cook up. **3** *I'd lay money on it* **bet**, wager, gamble, stake.
□ **lay down 1** relinquish, surrender, give up, abandon. **2** formulate, set down, draw up, frame, ordain, dictate, decree, enact, pass, decide, determine. **lay in** stock up with, stockpile, store (up), amass, hoard, put aside/away/by, garner, squirrel away; *informal* salt away, stash away. **lay off 1** make redundant, dismiss, let go, discharge, give notice to; *informal* sack, fire. **2** *(informal)* give up, stop, refrain from, abstain from, desist from, cut out; *informal* pack in, leave off, quit. **lay on** provide, supply, furnish, line up, organize, prepare, produce, make available; *informal* fix up.

lay[2] *adjective* **1** *a lay preacher* **non-ordained**, non-clerical. **2** *science books for a lay audience* **non-expert**, non-professional, non-specialist, non-technical, amateur, unqualified, untrained.

layer *noun* **sheet**, stratum, level, tier, seam, coat, coating, film, covering, blanket, skin.

layout *noun* **arrangement**, design, plan, formation, format, configuration, composition, organization, geography, structure.

laze *verb* **relax**, unwind, loaf around/about, lounge around/about, loll around/about, lie around/about, take it easy, idle; *informal* hang around, chill (out), veg (out).

lazy *adjective* **1 idle**, indolent, slothful, bone idle, work-shy, shiftless. **2 slow**, slow-moving, languid, leisurely, lethargic, sluggish, torpid.
- OPPOSITES industrious.

lead *verb* **1 guide**, conduct, show (the way), usher, escort, steer, shepherd, accompany, see, take. **2** *what led you to believe him?* **cause**, induce, prompt, move, persuade, drive, make. **3 control**, preside over, head, command, govern, run, manage, rule, be in charge of; *informal* head up. **4 be ahead**, be winning, be in front, be in the lead,

be first, outrun, outstrip, outpace, leave behind, outdo, outclass, beat. **5** *I want to lead a normal life* **live**, have, spend, follow, pass, enjoy.
- OPPOSITES follow.
● *noun* **1 first place**, winning position, vanguard. **2** *a 3–0 lead* **margin**, advantage, gap, edge. **3 example**, model, pattern, standard, guidance, direction, role model. **4 leading role**, starring role, title role, principal role. **5 leash**, tether, rope, chain. **6 clue**, pointer, hint, tip, tip-off, suggestion, indication.
● *adjective* **leading**, first, top, foremost, front, pole, head, chief, principal, premier.
□ **lead to** result in, cause, bring on/about, give rise to, create, produce, occasion, effect, generate, contribute to, promote, provoke, stir up, spark off.

leader *noun* **chief**, head, principal, commander, captain, controller, superior, chairman, chair, director, manager, superintendent, supervisor, overseer, master, mistress, prime minister, president, premier, governor, ruler, monarch, sovereign; *informal* boss, skipper, gaffer, guv'nor, number one.
- OPPOSITES follower, supporter.

leadership *noun* **1** *the leadership of the Party* **control**, rule, command, dominion, headship, directorship, premiership, chairmanship, governorship, captaincy. **2** *firm leadership* **guidance**, direction, authority, management, supervision, government.

leading *adjective* **main**, chief, top, front, major, prime, principal, foremost, key, central, dominant, greatest, pre-eminent, star.
- OPPOSITES subordinate, minor.

leaf *noun* **1** (**leaves**) **foliage**, greenery. **2 page**, sheet, folio.
● *verb I leafed through a magazine* **flick**, flip, thumb, skim, browse, glance, riffle, scan, run your eye over, peruse.

leaflet *noun* **pamphlet**, booklet, brochure, handbill, circular, flyer, handout; *N. Amer.* folder, dodger.

league *noun* **1 alliance**, confederation, confederacy, federation, union, association, coalition, consortium, affiliation, cooperative, partnership, fellowship, syndicate. **2 class**, group, category, level, standard.
□ **in league** collaborating, cooperating, in alliance, allied, conspiring, hand in glove; *informal* in cahoots.

leak *verb* **1 seep**, escape, ooze, drip, dribble, drain, run. **2 disclose**, divulge, reveal, make public, tell, expose, release, let slip.
● *noun* **1 hole**, opening, puncture, perforation, gash, slit, break, crack, chink, fissure, rupture, tear. **2 escape**, leakage, discharge, seepage. **3 disclosure**, revelation, exposé.

lean[1] *verb* **1 rest**, recline, be propped. **2 slant**, incline, bend, tilt, slope, tip, list. **3** (**lean towards**) **tend towards**, incline towards, gravitate towards, favour, prefer, have a preference for, have an affinity with. **4** (**lean on**) **depend on**, rely on, count on, bank on, trust in, have faith in.

lean[2] *adjective* **1 thin**, slim, slender, skinny, spare, angular, spindly, wiry, lanky. **2 meagre**, sparse, poor, mean, inadequate, insufficient, paltry.
- OPPOSITES fat, abundant.

leaning *noun* **inclination**, tendency, bent, propensity, penchant, preference, predisposition, predilection, proclivity.

leap *verb* **1 jump**, vault, spring, bound, hop, clear. **2 rise**, soar, rocket, skyrocket, shoot up, escalate.
● *noun* **rise**, surge, upsurge, escalation, upswing, upturn.

learn *verb* **1 master**, grasp, take in, absorb, assimilate, digest, familiarize yourself with; *informal* get the hang of. **2 memorize**, learn by heart, learn parrot-fashion, get off pat. **3 discover**, find out, become aware, be informed, hear, understand, gather; *informal* get wind of.

learned *adjective* **scholarly**, erudite, knowledgeable, widely read, cultured, intellectual, academic, literary,

bookish, highbrow; *informal* brainy, genius.
- OPPOSITES ignorant.

learner *noun* **beginner**, novice, starter, trainee, apprentice, pupil, student, fledgling, neophyte, tyro; *informal* rookie, greenhorn.
- OPPOSITES expert, veteran.

learning *noun* **study**, knowledge, education, schooling, tuition, teaching, scholarship, erudition, understanding, wisdom.
- OPPOSITES ignorance.

lease *verb* **rent (out)**, hire (out), charter (out), let (out), sublet.

leave[1] *verb* **1 go away**, depart, withdraw, retire, take your leave, pull out, quit, decamp, flee, escape, abandon, desert, vacate; *informal* vamoose, push off, shove off, clear out/off, split, make tracks, do a bunk. **2 set off**, set sail, get going. **3 abandon**, desert, jilt, leave in the lurch, leave high and dry, throw over; *informal* dump, ditch, walk/run out on. **4 resign**, retire, step down, give up, drop out; *informal* quit, jack in. **5 leave behind**, forget, lose, mislay. **6 entrust**, hand over, pass on, refer, delegate. **7 bequeath**, will, endow, hand down.
- OPPOSITES arrive.
▫ **leave out** miss out, omit, overlook, forget, skip, exclude, drop, pass over.

leave[2] *noun* **1 permission**, consent, authorization, sanction, dispensation, approval, clearance, blessing, agreement, assent; *informal* the go-ahead, the green light. **2 holiday**, vacation, break, furlough, sabbatical, leave of absence; *informal* vac.

lecherous *adjective* **lustful**, licentious, lascivious, libidinous, lewd, salacious, prurient; *informal* randy; *formal* concupiscent.

lecture *noun* **1 speech**, talk, address, discourse, presentation, oration. **2 reprimand**, scolding, rebuke, reproach; *informal* dressing-down, telling-off, talking-to, tongue-lashing.
● *verb* **1 talk**, speak, discourse, hold forth, teach; *informal* spout, sound off. **2 reprimand**, scold, rebuke, reproach, take to task, berate, upbraid, remonstrate with, castigate; *informal* tell off, bawl out; *Brit. informal* tick off, carpet.

leeway *noun* **freedom**, scope, latitude, space, room, liberty, flexibility, licence, free hand, free rein.

left *adjective* **left-hand**, sinistral; *Nautical* port; *Heraldry* sinister.
- OPPOSITES right.

left-wing *adjective* **socialist**, communist, leftist, Labour; *informal* Commie, lefty, red, pinko.
- OPPOSITES right-wing, conservative.

leg *noun* **1 limb**, member, shank; *informal* pin, peg.. **2 part**, stage, section, phase, stretch, lap.

legacy *noun* **bequest**, inheritance, endowment, gift, birthright, estate, heirloom.

legal *adjective* **1 lawful**, legitimate, legalized, valid, permissible, permitted, sanctioned, authorized, licensed, allowed, allowable, above board, acceptable, constitutional; *informal* legit. **2** *the legal system* **judicial**, juridical, forensic.
- OPPOSITES illegal.

legend *noun* **1 myth**, saga, epic, folk tale, folk story, fable; (**legends**) lore, folklore, mythology. **2 celebrity**, star, superstar, icon, phenomenon, luminary, giant, hero; *informal* celeb, megastar. **3 caption**, inscription, dedication, slogan, heading, title.

legendary *adjective* **1 fabled**, mythical, traditional, fairy-tale, storybook, mythological, fictional, fictitious. **2 famous**, celebrated, famed, renowned, acclaimed, illustrious, esteemed, honoured, exalted, venerable, eminent, distinguished, great.

legion *noun* **horde**, throng, multitude, crowd, mass, mob, gang, swarm, flock, herd, army.

legislation *noun* **law**, rules, rulings, regulations, acts, bills, statutes; *N. Amer. formal* ordinances.

legislature *noun* **parliament**, senate, congress, council, chamber, house.

legitimate *adjective* **1** *the legitimate use of such weapons* **legal**, lawful, authorized, permitted, sanctioned, approved, licensed; *informal* legit. **2** *the legitimate heir* **rightful**, lawful, genuine, authentic, real, true, proper; *informal* kosher. **3** *a legitimate excuse* **valid**, sound, admissible, acceptable, well founded, justifiable, reasonable, sensible, just, fair, bona fide.
- OPPOSITES illegal, invalid.

leisure *noun* **free time**, spare time, time off, rest, recreation, relaxation, R & R.
- OPPOSITES work.

leisurely *adjective* **unhurried**, relaxed, easy, gentle, sedate, comfortable, restful, undemanding, slow.
- OPPOSITES hurried.

lend *verb* **1 loan**, advance; *Brit. informal* sub. **2 add**, impart, give, bestow, confer, provide, supply, furnish, contribute.
- OPPOSITES borrow.

length *noun* **1 extent**, distance, span, reach, area, expanse, range. **2 period**, duration, stretch, span, term. **3** *a length of silk* **piece**, strip, section, swatch.
□ **at length 1** in detail, in depth, thoroughly, for a long time, for ages, for hours, interminably, endlessly. **2** eventually, in time, finally, at (long) last, in the end, ultimately.

lengthen *verb* **extend**, elongate, increase, prolong, draw out, protract, spin out.
- OPPOSITES shorten.

lengthy *adjective* **(very) long**, long-lasting, protracted, extended, long-drawn-out, prolonged, interminable, time-consuming, long-winded.
- OPPOSITES short.

lenient *adjective* **merciful**, forgiving, forbearing, tolerant, charitable, humane, indulgent, magnanimous, clement.
- OPPOSITES severe.

lessen *verb* **1 reduce**, decrease, minimize, moderate, diminish, allay, assuage, alleviate, dull, deaden, take the edge off. **2 decrease**, decline, subside, slacken, abate, fade, die down, let up, ease off, tail off, drop (off/away), dwindle, ebb, wane, recede.
- OPPOSITES increase.

lesser *adjective* **1 less important**, minor, secondary, subsidiary, peripheral. **2 subordinate**, inferior, second-class, subservient, lowly, humble.
- OPPOSITES greater, superior.

lesson *noun* **1 class**, session, seminar, tutorial, lecture, period. **2 warning**, deterrent, caution, example, message, moral.

let *verb* **1 allow**, permit, give permission to, give leave to, authorize, license, empower, enable, entitle; *informal* give the go-ahead to, OK. **2 rent (out)**, lease, hire (out), sublet.
- OPPOSITES prevent, prohibit.
□ **let down** fail, disappoint, disillusion, abandon, desert, leave in the lurch. **let go** release, loose your hold on, relinquish. **let off 1** detonate, discharge, explode, set off, fire (off), launch. **2** *(informal)* pardon, forgive, acquit, absolve, exonerate, clear, vindicate; *informal* let someone off the hook. **3** excuse, exempt, spare. **let out 1** release, liberate, (set) free, let go, discharge, set/turn loose. **2** utter, emit, give (vent to), produce, issue, express, voice, release. **3** reveal, make known, tell, disclose, mention, divulge, let slip, give away, let it be known, blurt out. **let up** *(informal)* **1** lessen, decrease, subside, abate, ease, moderate, die down, diminish, tail off. **2** relax, ease up, slow down, pause, break (off), take a break, rest, stop.

let-down *noun* **disappointment**, anticlimax, comedown, non-event, fiasco; *informal* washout, damp squib.

lethal *adjective* **fatal**, deadly, mortal, terminal, life-threatening, murderous, poisonous, toxic, noxious, venomous, dangerous.
- OPPOSITES harmless, safe.

lethargic *adjective* **sluggish**, inert, inactive, slow, lifeless, languid, listless,

apathetic, weary, tired, fatigued, enervated.
- OPPOSITES energetic.

letter *noun* **1 character**, sign, symbol, figure. **2 message**, note, line, missive, dispatch, communication; *formal* epistle; (**letters**) correspondence, post, mail.

WORD LINKS
epistolary relating to letter-writing

level *adjective* **1** *a level surface* **flat**, smooth, even, uniform, plane, flush, horizontal. **2** *a level voice* **steady**, even, uniform, regular, constant, unchanging. **3** *the scores were level* **equal**, even, drawn, tied, all square, neck and neck, level pegging, on a par, evenly matched; *informal* even-stevens, nip and tuck.
- OPPOSITES uneven, unequal.
● *noun* **1 rank**, position, degree, grade, stage, standard, class, group, set, classification. **2** *a high level of employment* **quantity**, amount, extent, measure, degree, volume.
● *verb* **1 even off**, even out, flatten, smooth (out). **2 raze (to the ground)**, demolish, flatten, bulldoze, destroy. **3 equalize**, equal, even (up), make level. **4 aim**, point, direct, train, focus, turn.
□ **on the level** *(informal)* genuine, straight, honest, above board, fair, true, sincere, straightforward; *informal* upfront; *N. Amer. informal* on the up and up.

lever *noun* **handle**, arm, switch, crowbar, bar, jemmy.
● *verb* **prise**, force, wrench; *N. Amer.* pry; *informal* jemmy.

leverage *noun* **1 force**, purchase, grip, hold, anchorage. **2** *more leverage in negotiations* **influence**, power, authority, weight, sway, pull, control, say, advantage, pressure; *informal* clout, muscle, teeth.

levy *verb* **impose**, charge, exact, raise, collect.
● *noun* **tax**, tariff, toll, excise, duty.

liability *noun* **1 responsibility**, accountability. **2** (**liabilities**) **obligations**, debts, arrears, dues, commitments. **3** *he became a liability on and off the field* **hindrance**, handicap, nuisance, inconvenience, embarrassment, impediment, disadvantage, millstone, encumbrance, burden.
- OPPOSITES asset.

liable *adjective* **1 responsible**, accountable, answerable, blameworthy, at fault. **2 likely**, inclined, tending, apt, prone, given, subject, susceptible, vulnerable, exposed, in danger of, at risk of.

liaise *verb* **cooperate**, collaborate, communicate, network, interface, link up; *informal* hook up.

liaison *noun* **1 cooperation**, contact, association, connection, collaboration, communication, alliance, partnership. **2 love affair**, relationship, romance, attachment, fling.

liar *noun* **fibber**, deceiver, perjurer, dissembler, faker, hoaxer, impostor.

libel *noun* **defamation (of character)**, character assassination, calumny, misrepresentation, scandalmongering, slur, smear; *informal* mud-slinging.
● *verb* **defame**, malign, blacken someone's name, sully someone's reputation, smear, cast aspersions on, drag someone's name through the mud/mire, denigrate, traduce; *N. Amer.* slur.

libellous *adjective* **defamatory**, denigratory, disparaging, derogatory, false, untrue, insulting, scurrilous.

liberal *adjective* **1 tolerant**, unprejudiced, broad-minded, open-minded, enlightened, permissive, free (and easy), easy-going, libertarian, indulgent, lenient. **2** *a liberal social agenda* **progressive**, advanced, modern, forward-looking, forward-thinking, enlightened, reformist, radical; *informal* go-ahead. **3** *a liberal interpretation of the law* **flexible**, broad, loose, rough, free, non-literal. **4 abundant**, copious, ample, plentiful, lavish, generous, open-handed, unsparing, unstinting, free, munificent.

– OPPOSITES reactionary, strict.

liberate *verb* **(set) free**, release, let out, let go, set loose, save, rescue, emancipate; *historical* enfranchise.
– OPPOSITES imprison, enslave.

liberty *noun* **freedom**, independence, immunity, self-determination, autonomy, emancipation, sovereignty, self-government, self-rule, civil liberties, human rights.
– OPPOSITES slavery.
□ **at liberty 1** free, loose, on the loose, at large, on the run, out. **2** able, free, entitled, permitted.

licence *noun* **1 permit**, certificate, document, documentation, authorization, warrant, credentials, pass, papers. **2 franchise**, consent, sanction, warrant, charter, concession. **3 freedom**, liberty, free rein, latitude, independence, scope, carte blanche; *informal* a blank cheque.

license *verb* **permit**, allow, authorize, give authority to, give permission to, certify, accredit, empower, entitle, enable, sanction.
– OPPOSITES ban.

lid *noun* **cover**, top, cap, covering, stopper.

lie[1] *noun* **untruth**, falsehood, fib, fabrication, deception, invention, (piece of) fiction, falsification, white lie; *informal* tall story, whopper; *humorous* terminological inexactitude.
– OPPOSITES truth.
● *verb* **tell a lie**, fib, dissemble, perjure yourself.

WORD LINKS
mendacious telling lies

lie[2] *verb* **1** *he was lying on the bed* **recline**, lie down, be recumbent, be prostrate, be supine, be prone, be stretched out, sprawl, rest, repose, lounge, loll. **2** *her bag lay on the chair* **be**, be situated, be positioned, be located, be placed, be found, be sited, be arranged, rest.
– OPPOSITES stand.

life *noun* **1 existence**, being, living, animation, sentience, creation, viability. **2 living creatures**, fauna, flora, the ecosystem, the biosphere, the ecosphere. **3 way of life**, lifestyle, situation, fate, lot. **4 lifetime**, lifespan, days, time (on earth), existence. **5 vitality**, animation, liveliness, vivacity, verve, high spirits, exuberance, zest, enthusiasm, energy, vigour, dynamism, elan, gusto, bounce, spirit, fire. **6 biography**, autobiography, history, chronicle, account, memoirs, diary.
– OPPOSITES death.

WORD LINKS
animate, **vital** having life

lifeless *adjective* **1 dead**, stiff, cold, inert, inanimate; *formal* deceased. **2 barren**, sterile, bare, desolate, stark, bleak, arid, infertile, uninhabited. **3 lacklustre**, apathetic, lethargic, uninspired, dull, colourless, characterless, wooden.
– OPPOSITES alive, lively.

lifelike *adjective* **realistic**, true to life, faithful, detailed, vivid, graphic, natural, naturalistic, representational.

lifestyle *noun* **way of life**, life, situation, conduct, behaviour, ways, habits, mores.

lifetime *noun* **lifespan**, life, days, time (on earth), existence, career.

lift *verb* **1 raise**, hoist, heave, haul up, heft, elevate, hold high, pick up, grab, take up, winch up, jack up; *informal* hump. **2** *the fog had lifted* **clear**, rise, disperse, dissipate, disappear, vanish, dissolve. **3** *the ban has been lifted* **cancel**, remove, withdraw, revoke, rescind, end, stop, terminate.
● *noun the goal will give his confidence a lift* **boost**, fillip, impetus, encouragement, spur, push; *informal* shot in the arm.
□ **lift off** take off, become airborne, be launched, take to the air, blast off.

light[1] *noun* **1 illumination**, brightness, shining, gleam, brilliance, radiance, luminosity, luminescence, incandescence, blaze, glare, glow, lustre; *literary* refulgence, effulgence. **2 lamp**,

lantern, torch, beacon, candle, bulb. **3 daylight**, daytime, day, sunlight.
- OPPOSITES darkness.
● *adjective* **1 bright**, well lit, sunny. **2 pale**, pastel, delicate, subtle, faded, bleached.
- OPPOSITES dark.
● *verb* **1 set fire to**, ignite, kindle. **2 illuminate**, irradiate, floodlight; *literary* illumine.

WORD LINKS
optics study of the behaviour of light

light[2] *adjective* **1 lightweight**, portable, underweight. **2 flimsy**, thin, lightweight, floaty, gauzy, diaphanous, filmy. **3** *a light dinner* **small**, modest, simple, insubstantial, frugal. **4** *light duties* **easy**, simple, undemanding, untaxing; *informal* cushy. **5** *a light touch* **gentle**, delicate, dainty, soft, faint, careful, sensitive, subtle. **6** *light entertainment* **undemanding**, middle-of-the-road, mainstream, lightweight, lowbrow, mass-market, superficial, frivolous, trivial.
- OPPOSITES heavy.

lighten[1] *verb* **1 brighten**, light up, illuminate, irradiate; *literary* illumine. **2 bleach**, whiten, blanch.
- OPPOSITES darken.

lighten[2] *verb* **1 reduce**, lessen, decrease, diminish, ease, alleviate, relieve. **2 cheer (up)**, brighten, gladden, lift, boost, buoy (up), revive, restore, revitalize.
- OPPOSITES increase.

light-hearted *adjective* **carefree**, cheerful, cheery, happy, merry, glad, playful, blithe, bright, entertaining, amusing, diverting; *informal* upbeat; *dated* gay, sportive.
- OPPOSITES miserable.

lightly *adverb* **1 softly**, gently, faintly, delicately. **2 sparingly**, sparsely, moderately, slightly, subtly. **3 carelessly**, airily, readily, heedlessly, uncaringly, unthinkingly, thoughtlessly, flippantly.

lightweight *adjective* **1 thin**, light, filmy, flimsy, insubstantial, summery. **2 trivial**, insubstantial, superficial, shallow, undemanding, frivolous.
- OPPOSITES heavy, serious.

like[1] *verb* **1 be fond of**, have a soft spot for, care about, think well/highly of, admire, respect; be attracted to, fancy, be keen on, be taken with; *informal* rate. **2 enjoy**, have a taste for, care for, be partial to, take pleasure in, be keen on, appreciate, love, adore, relish; *informal* have a thing about, be into, be mad about, be hooked on. **3** *feel free to say what you like* **choose**, please, wish, want, see/think fit, care to, will.
- OPPOSITES hate.

like[2] *preposition* **1 similar to**, the same as, identical to, akin to, resembling. **2 in the manner of**, in the same way/manner as, in a similar way to. **3 such as**, for example, for instance, namely, in particular, viz.. **4 characteristic of**, typical of, in character with.
- OPPOSITES unlike.

likeable *adjective* **pleasant**, friendly, agreeable, affable, amiable, genial, personable, nice, good-natured, engaging, appealing, endearing, convivial, congenial.
- OPPOSITES unpleasant.

likelihood *noun* **probability**, chance, prospect, possibility, odds, risk, threat, danger, hope, promise.

likely *adjective* **1 probable**, possible, odds-on, expected, anticipated; *informal* on the cards. **2 plausible**, reasonable, feasible, acceptable, believable, credible, tenable. **3 suitable**, promising, appropriate.
- OPPOSITES unlikely, implausible.

liken *verb* **compare**, equate, set beside.
- OPPOSITES contrast.

likeness *noun* **1 resemblance**, similarity, similitude, correspondence. **2 representation**, image, depiction, portrayal, picture, drawing, sketch, painting, portrait, photograph, study.
- OPPOSITES dissimilarity.

likewise *adverb* **1 also**, equally, in addition, too, as well, to boot, besides, moreover, furthermore. **2 the same**, similarly, correspondingly.

liking *noun* **fondness**, love, affection, penchant, soft spot, attachment, taste, passion, preference, partiality, predilection, weakness.
- OPPOSITES dislike.

limb *noun* **1 arm**, **leg**, wing, appendage; *old use* member. **2 branch**, bough.

limelight *noun* **attention**, interest, scrutiny, the public eye, publicity, prominence, the spotlight, fame, celebrity.
- OPPOSITES obscurity.

limit *noun* **1 boundary (line)**, border, frontier, bound, edge, perimeter, margin. **2 maximum**, ceiling, cap, cut-off point.
● *verb* **restrict**, curb, cap, (hold in) check, restrain, circumscribe, regulate, control, govern, ration.

limitation *noun* **1 restriction**, curb, restraint, control, check. **2 imperfection**, flaw, defect, failing, shortcoming, weak point, deficiency, frailty, weakness.
- OPPOSITES strength.

limited *adjective* **restricted**, circumscribed, finite, small, tight, slight, in short supply, short, meagre, scanty, sparse, inadequate, insufficient, paltry, poor, minimal.
- OPPOSITES limitless, ample.

limp[1] *verb* **hobble**, hop, lurch, stagger, shuffle, totter, shamble.

limp[2] *adjective* **soft**, flaccid, loose, slack, lax, floppy, drooping, droopy, sagging.
- OPPOSITES firm.

line *noun* **1 stroke**, dash, score, underline, underscore, slash, stripe, strip, band, belt; *Brit.* oblique. **2 wrinkle**, furrow, crease, crinkle, crow's foot. **3** *the Bentley's classic lines* **contour**, outline, configuration, shape, design, profile, silhouette. **4** *the county line* **boundary**, limit, border, frontier, touchline, margin, perimeter. **5 cord**, rope, cable, wire, thread, string. **6 file**, rank, column, string, train, procession, row, queue; *Brit. informal* crocodile. **7 course**, direction, route, track, path, trajectory.
● *verb* **1 furrow**, wrinkle, crease, score. **2 border**, edge, fringe, bound.
□ **in line 1** in a queue, in a row, in a file. **2** in agreement, in accord, in accordance, in harmony, in step, in compliance. **3** level, aligned, alongside, abreast, side by side. **line up** assemble, get together, organize, prepare, arrange, fix up, lay on, book, schedule, timetable.

lineage *noun* **ancestry**, family, parentage, birth, descent, extraction, genealogy, roots, origins.

lined *adjective* **1 ruled**, feint, striped, banded. **2 wrinkled**, wrinkly, furrowed, wizened.

line-up *noun* **1 cast**, bill, programme. **2 team**, squad, side, configuration.

linger *verb* **1 wait (around)**, stand (around), remain, loiter; *informal* stick around, hang around. **2 persist**, continue, remain, stay, endure, carry on, last.

lining *noun* **backing**, facing, padding, insulation.

link *noun* **connection**, relationship, association, linkage, tie-up, tie, bond, attachment, affiliation.
● *verb* **1 join**, connect, fasten, attach, bind, secure, fix, tie, couple, yoke. **2** *the evidence linking him with the body* **associate**, connect, relate, bracket.
- OPPOSITES separate.

lion *noun*

> WORD LINKS
> **leonine** relating to lions

lip *noun* **edge**, rim, brim, border, verge, brink.

liquid *noun* **fluid**, moisture, solution, liquor, juice, sap.
● *adjective* **fluid**, liquefied, melted, molten, thawed, dissolved, runny.
- OPPOSITES solid.

liquor *noun* **1 alcohol**, spirits, drink; *informal* booze, the hard stuff, hooch, moonshine. **2 stock**, broth, bouillon, juice, liquid.

list[1] *noun* **catalogue**, inventory, record, register, roll, file, index, directory, checklist.
● *verb* **record**, register, enter, itemize, enumerate, catalogue, file, log, minute, categorize, inventory, classify, group, sort, rank, index.

list[2] *verb* **lean (over)**, tilt, tip, heel (over), pitch, incline, slant, slope, bank, careen, cant.

listen *verb* **1 pay attention**, be attentive, attend, concentrate, keep your ears open, prick up your ears; *informal* be all ears. **2 heed**, take heed of, take notice/note of, bear in mind, take into consideration/account.

listless *adjective* **lethargic**, lifeless, enervated, languid, inactive, inert, sluggish, apathetic, passive, supine, indifferent, uninterested, impassive.
- OPPOSITES energetic.

literal *adjective* **1 strict**, technical, original, true. **2 word for word**, verbatim, exact, accurate, faithful.
- OPPOSITES figurative.

literary *adjective* **1 artistic**, poetic, dramatic. **2 scholarly**, intellectual, academic, bookish, erudite, well read, cultured.

literate *adjective* **(well) educated**, well read, widely read, scholarly, learned, knowledgeable, cultured, cultivated.
- OPPOSITES ignorant.

literature *noun* **1 writing**, poetry, drama, plays, prose. **2 publications**, reports, studies, material, documentation, leaflets, pamphlets, brochures, handouts, publicity, advertising; *informal* bumf.

lithe *adjective* **agile**, graceful, supple, flexible, lissom, loose-limbed, nimble.
- OPPOSITES clumsy.

litigation *noun* **legal proceedings**, legal action, case, lawsuit, suit, prosecution, indictment.

litter *noun* **rubbish**, refuse, junk, waste, debris, detritus; *N. Amer.* trash, garbage.
● *verb* **cover**, clutter up, mess up, be scattered/strewn around.

little *adjective* **1 small**, compact, miniature, tiny, minute, minuscule, toy, fun-size, baby, undersized, dwarf, midget; *Scottish* wee; *informal* teeny-weeny; *Brit. informal* titchy, dinky; *N. Amer. informal* vest-pocket. **2 short**, small, slight, petite, diminutive, tiny, elfin; *Scottish* wee; *informal* pint-sized. **3 young**, younger, baby. **4 brief**, short, quick, hasty, cursory. **5 minor**, unimportant, insignificant, trivial, trifling, petty, paltry, inconsequential, negligible.
- OPPOSITES big, large, elder, major.
● *adverb* **1 hardly**, barely, scarcely, not much, only slightly. **2 rarely**, seldom, infrequently, hardly (ever), scarcely ever, not much.
- OPPOSITES well, often.
□ **a little 1** some, a bit of, a touch of, a dash of, a taste of, a spot of, a hint of, a dribble of, a splash of, a pinch of, a sprinkling of, a speck of; *informal* a smidgen of, a tad of. **2** a short time, a while, a bit, an interval, a short period, a minute, a moment, a second, an instant; *informal* a sec, a mo, a jiffy. **3** slightly, somewhat, a little bit, quite, to some degree.

live[1] *verb* **1 exist**, be alive, be, have life, breathe, draw breath, walk the earth. **2 reside**, have your home, lodge, inhabit, occupy; *Scottish* stay; *formal* dwell; *old use* abide, bide. **3** *she had lived a difficult life* **experience**, spend, pass, lead, have, go through, undergo. **4** *he lived by scavenging* **survive**, make a living, eke out a living, subsist, support yourself, sustain yourself, make ends meet, keep body and soul together.
- OPPOSITES die.

live[2] *adjective* **1 living**, alive, conscious, animate, vital. **2** *a live rail* **electrified**, charged, powered up, active, switched on. **3** *a live grenade* **unexploded**, explosive, active, primed. **4** *a live issue* **topical**, current, controversial, hot, burning, pressing, important, relevant.
- OPPOSITES dead, inanimate.

livelihood *noun* **(source of) income**, living, subsistence, bread and butter, job, work, employment, occupation.

lively *adjective* **1 energetic**, active, animated, dynamic, full of life, outgoing, spirited, sprightly, high-spirited, vivacious, enthusiastic, vibrant, buoyant, exuberant, boisterous, effervescent, cheerful; *informal* chirpy, full of beans. **2 busy**, crowded, bustling, hectic, buzzing, vibrant, colourful. **3** *a lively debate* **stimulating**, interesting, vigorous, animated, spirited, heated.
- OPPOSITES quiet, dull.

livid *adjective (informal)* **furious**, enraged, very angry, infuriated, irate, incensed, fuming, ranting, raving, seething, beside yourself, outraged; *informal* hopping mad, wild.

living *noun* **1 livelihood**, (source of) income, subsistence, keep, daily bread, bread and butter, job, work, employment, occupation. **2 way of life**, lifestyle, life, conduct, behaviour, activities, habits.
● *adjective* **1 alive**, live, animate, sentient, breathing, existing. **2** *a living language* **current**, contemporary.
- OPPOSITES dead, extinct.

load *noun* **1 cargo**, freight, consignment, delivery, shipment, goods, pack, bundle, parcel. **2** *a heavy teaching load* **commitment**, responsibility, duty, obligation, burden, onus.
● *verb* **1 fill (up)**, pack, stock, stack, stow, store, bundle, place, put, deposit, pile, stuff, cram; *old use* lade. **2 burden**, weigh down, saddle, oppress, charge, overburden, overwhelm, encumber, tax, strain, trouble, worry. **3** *he loaded the gun* **prime**, charge, set up, prepare. **4** *load the cassette into the camcorder* **insert**, put, place, slot, slide.

loaded *adjective* **1 full**, filled, laden, packed, stuffed, crammed, brimming, stacked; *informal* chock-full, chock-a-block. **2** *a politically loaded word* **charged**, emotive, sensitive, delicate.

loaf *verb* **laze**, lounge, loll, idle; *informal* hang around; *Brit. informal* hang about, mooch about/around; *N. Amer. informal* bum around.

loan *noun* **credit**, advance, mortgage, overdraft; *Brit. informal* sub.
● *verb* **lend**, advance.

loath *adjective* **reluctant**, unwilling, disinclined, averse, opposed, resistant.
- OPPOSITES eager, willing.

loathe *verb* **hate**, detest, abhor, despise, abominate, not be able to bear/stand, execrate.
- OPPOSITES love.

loathing *noun* **hatred**, hate, detestation, abhorrence, abomination, antipathy, aversion, dislike, disgust, repugnance.

loathsome *adjective* **hateful**, detestable, abhorrent, repulsive, odious, repugnant, repellent, disgusting, revolting, sickening, nauseating, abominable, despicable, contemptible, reprehensible, vile, horrible, nasty, obnoxious, gross, foul, execrable; *informal* horrid; *literary* noisome.

lobby *noun* **1 entrance (hall)**, hallway, hall, vestibule, foyer, reception. **2** *the anti-hunt lobby* **pressure group**, interest group, movement, campaign, crusade, faction, camp, ginger group.
● *verb* **1 approach**, contact, petition, appeal to, pressurize, importune. **2 campaign**, crusade, press, push, ask, call, demand, promote, advocate, champion.

local *adjective* **1** *the local council* **district**, regional, town, municipal, provincial, parish. **2** *a local restaurant* **neighbourhood**, nearby, near, at hand, close by, handy, convenient. **3** *a local infection* **confined**, restricted, contained, localized.
- OPPOSITES national, widespread.
● *noun* **resident**, native, inhabitant, parishioner.
- OPPOSITES outsider.

locate *verb* **1 find**, pinpoint, track down, unearth, sniff out, smoke out, search out, uncover, run to earth. **2 situate**, site, position, place, base, put, build, establish, station.

location *noun* **position**, place, situation, site, locality, locale, spot, whereabouts, scene, setting, area, environment, venue, address; *technical* locus.

lock[1] *noun* **bolt**, catch, fastener, clasp, hasp, latch.
● *verb* **1 bolt**, fasten, secure, padlock, latch, chain. **2 join**, interlock, link, engage, combine, connect, couple. **3 become stuck**, stick, jam, seize. **4 clasp**, clench, grasp, embrace, hug, squeeze.
- OPPOSITES unlock, open.
□ **lock up** imprison, jail, incarcerate, intern, send to prison, put behind bars, put under lock and key, cage, pen, coop up; *informal* send down, put away, put inside.

lock[2] *noun* **strand**, tress, curl, ringlet, hank, tuft, wisp, coil, tendril.

locker *noun* **cupboard**, cabinet, chest, safe, box, case, coffer, storeroom.

lodge *noun* **1 gatehouse**, cottage, house, cabin, hut. **2** *a Masonic lodge* **section**, branch, wing, group; *N. Amer.* chapter.
● *verb* **1 submit**, register, enter, put forward, advance, lay, present, tender, proffer, put on record, record, table, file. **2** *the bullet lodged in his back* **become embedded**, get stuck, stick, catch, get caught, wedge. **3 reside**, board, stay, live, stop; *N. Amer.* room; *literary* sojourn. **4 deposit**, put, bank, stash, store, stow, put away.

lodging *noun* **accommodation**, rooms, chambers, living quarters, a roof over your head, housing, shelter; *informal* digs; *N. Amer. informal* crib; *formal* residence, dwelling, abode.

lofty *adjective* **1 tall**, high, towering. **2** *lofty ideals* **noble**, exalted, high, high-minded, worthy, grand, fine, elevated. **3** *lofty disdain* **haughty**, arrogant, disdainful, supercilious, condescending, patronizing, scornful, contemptuous, self-important, conceited, snobbish; *informal* stuck-up, snooty; *Brit. informal* toffee-nosed.
- OPPOSITES low, short.

log *noun* **record**, register, logbook, journal, diary, minutes, ledger, account, tally.
● *verb* **1 register**, record, note, write down, put in writing, enter, file. **2** *the pilot had logged 95 hours* **attain**, achieve, chalk up, make, do, go, cover, clock up.

logic *noun* **1 reason**, judgement, rationality, wisdom, sense, good sense, common sense, sanity. **2** *the logic of their argument* **reasoning**, rationale, argument.

logical *adjective* **1 reasoned**, rational, sound, cogent, valid, coherent, clear, systematic, orderly, methodical, analytical, consistent. **2** *the logical outcome* **natural**, reasonable, sensible, understandable, predictable, unsurprising, likely.
- OPPOSITES illogical.

logo *noun* **design**, symbol, emblem, trademark, motif, monogram.

loiter *verb* **linger**, wait, skulk, loaf, lounge, idle; *informal* hang about/around; *Brit. informal* mooch about/around.

lone *adjective* **1 solitary**, single, solo, unaccompanied, sole, isolated. **2** *a lone parent* **single**, unmarried, separated, divorced, widowed.

loneliness *noun* **1 isolation**, friendlessness, abandonment, rejection; *N. Amer.* lonesomeness. **2 solitariness**, solitude, aloneness, separation, seclusion.

lonely *adjective* **1 isolated**, alone, friendless, with no one to turn to, abandoned, rejected, unloved, unwanted; *N. Amer.* lonesome. **2 deserted**, uninhabited, desolate, solitary, isolated, remote, out of the way, off the beaten track, secluded, in the back of beyond, godforsaken; *informal* in the middle of nowhere.

long[1] *adjective* **lengthy**, extended, prolonged, protracted, long-lasting, drawn-out, endless, lingering, interminable.
- OPPOSITES short, brief.

long[2] *verb I longed for the holidays* **yearn**, pine, ache, hanker for/after, hunger, thirst, itch, be eager, be desperate, crave, dream of; *informal* be dying.

longing *noun* **yearning**, craving, ache, burning, hunger, thirst, hankering, desire, wish, hope, aspiration; *informal* yen, itch.

long-standing *adjective* **well established**, time-honoured, traditional, abiding, enduring.
– OPPOSITES new, recent.

long-suffering *adjective* **patient**, forbearing, tolerant, uncomplaining, philosophical, stoical, forgiving.

long-winded *adjective* **verbose**, wordy, lengthy, long, prolix, interminable, rambling, tortuous, meandering, repetitious, repetitive; *Brit. informal* waffly.
– OPPOSITES concise, succinct.

look *verb* **1 glance**, gaze, stare, gape, peer, peep, peek, watch, observe, view, regard, examine, inspect, eye, scan, scrutinize, survey, study, contemplate, take in, ogle, leer at; *informal* take a gander, rubberneck, get a load of; *Brit. informal* gawp; *N. Amer. informal* eyeball. **2 seem (to be)**, appear (to be), come across/over as.
● *noun* **1 glance**, examination, study, inspection, scrutiny, peep, peek, glimpse; *informal* eyeful, once-over, squint; *Brit. informal* dekko, butcher's, shufti. **2 expression**, mien, countenance. **3 appearance**, air, style, effect, ambience, impression, aspect, manner, demeanour.
□ **look after** take care of, care for, attend to, minister to, tend, mind, keep an eye on, keep safe, guard, supervise, be responsible for, protect, nurse, babysit. **look down on** disdain, scorn, look down your nose at, sneer at, despise. **look for** search for, hunt, try to find, seek, cast about/around for, forage for. **look into** investigate, enquire into, go into, probe, explore, follow up, research, study, examine; *informal* check out; *N. Amer. informal* scope out. **look like** resemble, bear a resemblance to, look similar to, take after; *informal* be the (spitting) image of, be a dead ringer for. **look out** beware, watch out, mind out, be on your guard, be alert, be wary, be vigilant, be careful, take care, be cautious, pay attention, keep your eyes open/peeled, keep an eye out, watch your step. **look over** inspect, examine, scrutinize, cast an eye over, take stock of, vet, view, peruse, read through; *informal* give something a/the once-over; *N. Amer.* check out; *N. Amer. informal* eyeball. **look up** improve, get better, pick up, come along/on, progress, make progress, make headway, perk up, rally, take a turn for the better. **look up to** admire, think highly of, hold in high regard, respect, esteem, venerate, revere, idolize.

lookalike *noun* **double**, twin, clone, living image, doppelgänger, replica; *informal* spitting image, dead ringer.

lookout *noun* **1 watchman**, watch, guard, sentry, sentinel, observer. **2** *(Brit. informal) that's your lookout* **problem**, concern, business, affair, responsibility, worry; *informal* pigeon.

loom *verb* **1 emerge**, appear, materialize, take shape. **2 be imminent**, be on the horizon, impend, threaten, brew, be just around the corner.

loop *noun* **coil**, ring, circle, noose, spiral, curl, bend, curve, arc, twirl, whorl, twist, helix.
● *verb* **1 coil**, wind, twist, snake, spiral, curve, bend, turn. **2 fasten**, tie, join, connect, knot, bind.

loophole *noun* **flaw**, discrepancy, inconsistency, ambiguity, omission, excuse, escape clause; *Brit.* get-out.

loose *adjective* **1 not secure**, unsecured, unattached, untied, detached, wobbly, unsteady, dangling, free. **2 free**, at large, at liberty, on the loose. **3 baggy**, roomy, oversized, voluminous, shapeless, sloppy. **4** *a loose interpretation* **vague**, imprecise, approximate, broad, general, rough, liberal.
– OPPOSITES secure, tight.

● *verb* **1 free**, let loose, release, untie, unchain, unfasten, unleash, relax. **2 relax**, slacken, loosen.
- OPPOSITES confine, tighten.

loosen *verb* **1 undo**, slacken, unfasten, detach, release, disconnect. **2 weaken**, relax, slacken, loose, let go.
- OPPOSITES tighten.

loot *noun* **booty**, spoils, plunder, haul; *informal* swag, boodle.
● *verb* **plunder**, pillage, ransack, sack, rifle, rob, strip, gut.

lopsided *adjective* **crooked**, askew, awry, off-centre, uneven, out of true, asymmetrical, tilted, at an angle, slanting; *Scottish* agley; *informal* cockeyed; *Brit. informal* skew-whiff, wonky.
- OPPOSITES even, level.

lord *noun* **1 noble**, nobleman, peer, aristocrat. **2 master**, ruler, leader, chief, superior, monarch, sovereign, king, emperor, prince, governor, commander.

lorry *noun* **truck**, wagon, van, juggernaut, trailer, HGV; *dated* pantechnicon.

lose *verb* **1 mislay**, misplace, be unable to find, lose track of. **2 escape from**, evade, elude, dodge, avoid, give someone the slip, shake off, throw off, leave behind, outdistance, outrun. **3 waste**, squander, let pass, miss; *informal* pass up, blow. **4 be defeated**, be beaten; *informal* come a cropper, go down.
- OPPOSITES find, seize, win.

loser *noun (informal)* **failure**, underachiever, dead loss, write-off, has-been; *informal* also-ran, non-starter, no-hoper.

loss *noun* **1 mislaying**, deprivation, forfeiture, erosion, reduction, depletion. **2 death**, demise, passing away, bereavement. **3 casualty**, fatality, victim, death toll. **4 deficit**, debit, debt.
- OPPOSITES recovery, profit.
□ **at a loss** baffled, mystified, puzzled, perplexed, bewildered, confused, stumped, stuck; *informal* flummoxed, beaten.

lost *adjective* **1 missing**, mislaid, misplaced, gone astray. **2 stray**, off course, going round in circles, adrift, at sea. **3** *a lost opportunity* **missed**, wasted, squandered, gone by the board; *informal* down the drain. **4** *lost traditions* **bygone**, past, former, old, vanished, forgotten, dead. **5** *lost species and habitats* **extinct**, died out, defunct, vanished, gone, destroyed, wiped out, exterminated. **6** *lost in thought* **engrossed**, absorbed, rapt, immersed, deep, intent, engaged, wrapped up.

lot *pronoun* (**a lot/lots**) **a large amount**, a good/great deal, an abundance, a wealth, a profusion, plenty, many, a great many, a large number, a considerable number; *informal* hundreds, loads, masses, heaps, piles, stacks, tons, oodles; *Brit. informal* lashings.
● *adverb* (**a lot**) **a great deal**, a good deal, much, often, frequently, regularly.
● *noun* **1** *(informal)* **group**, crowd, circle, crew; *informal* bunch, gang, mob. **2** *an auction lot* **item**, article, batch, group, bundle, parcel. **3** *his lot in life* **fate**, destiny, fortune, situation, circumstances, plight, predicament.

lotion *noun* **ointment**, cream, balm, rub, moisturizer, lubricant, embrocation, liniment, salve, unguent.

lottery *noun* **raffle**, (prize) draw, sweepstake, sweep, tombola, lotto, pools.

loud *adjective* **1 noisy**, blaring, booming, roaring, thunderous, resounding, sonorous, powerful, stentorian, deafening, ear-splitting, piercing, shrill, raucous; *Music* forte, fortissimo. **2 vociferous**, clamorous, insistent, vehement, emphatic. **3 garish**, gaudy, lurid, showy, flamboyant, ostentatious, vulgar, tasteless; *informal* flashy.
- OPPOSITES quiet.

loudly *adverb* **at the top of your voice**, noisily, stridently, vociferously, shrilly.

lounge *verb* **laze**, lie, loll, recline, relax, rest, take it easy, sprawl, slump, slouch, loaf, idle.
● *noun* **living room**, sitting room, front room, drawing room; *dated* parlour.

lout *noun* **hooligan**, ruffian, thug, boor, oaf, rowdy; *informal* tough, bruiser;

Brit. informal yob, yobbo.

lovable *adjective* **adorable**, dear, sweet, cute, charming, lovely, likeable, engaging, endearing, winning, winsome.
- OPPOSITES hateful, loathsome.

love *noun* **1 adoration**, devotion, affection, fondness, tenderness, attachment, warmth, passion, desire, lust, yearning, infatuation, besottedness. **2 liking**, taste, zeal, zest, enthusiasm, keenness, fondness, weakness, partiality, predilection, penchant. **3 compassion**, care, regard, concern, altruism, unselfishness, philanthropy, benevolence, humanity. **4 beloved**, loved one, dearest, darling, sweetheart, sweet, angel, honey.
- OPPOSITES hatred.
● *verb* **1 be in love with**, adore, be devoted to, be infatuated with, be smitten with, be besotted with, idolize, worship, think the world of, dote on, care for, hold dear, cherish; *informal* be mad/crazy about, carry a torch for. **2 like**, delight in, relish, enjoy, have a soft spot for, have a weakness for, be addicted to, be taken with; *informal* have a thing about, be hooked on, get a kick out of.
- OPPOSITES hate.

WORD LINKS
amatory relating to love

love affair *noun* **relationship**, affair(e), romance, liaison, fling, amour, entanglement, involvement, intrigue; *Brit. informal* carry-on.

lovely *adjective* **1 beautiful**, pretty, attractive, good-looking, handsome, adorable, charming, engaging, enchanting, gorgeous, alluring, ravishing, glamorous; *Scottish & N. English* bonny; *informal* tasty, stunning, drop-dead gorgeous; *Brit. informal* fit; *N. Amer. informal* cute, foxy; *old use* comely. **2 delightful**, marvellous, magnificent, stunning, splendid, wonderful, superb, pleasant, enjoyable; *informal* terrific, fabulous, heavenly, divine, amazing, glorious.
- OPPOSITES ugly, horrible.

lover *noun* **1 boyfriend**, **girlfriend**, beloved, sweetheart, inamorato/a, mistress, partner, gigolo; *informal* bit on the side, fancy man, fancy woman; *dated* beau; *literary* swain; *old use* paramour. **2 devotee**, admirer, fan, enthusiast, aficionado; *informal* buff, nut.

loving *adjective* **affectionate**, fond, devoted, adoring, doting, caring, tender, warm, close, amorous, passionate.
- OPPOSITES cold, cruel.

low *adjective* **1 short**, small, little, squat, stubby, stunted. **2 cheap**, economical, moderate, reasonable, affordable, modest, bargain, bargain-basement, rock-bottom. **3 scarce**, scant, meagre, sparse, few, little, reduced, depleted, diminished. **4 inferior**, substandard, poor, low-grade, unsatisfactory, inadequate, second-rate. **5 quiet**, soft, faint, gentle, muted, subdued, muffled, hushed. **6 bass**, low-pitched, deep, rumbling, booming, sonorous. **7 depressed**, dejected, despondent, downhearted, downcast, down, miserable, dispirited, gloomy, glum, flat; *informal* fed up, down in the dumps, blue.
- OPPOSITES high, expensive, loud.

lower[1] *adjective* **1 subordinate**, inferior, lesser, junior, minor, secondary, subsidiary, subservient. **2** *her lower lip* **bottom**, nether, bottommost, under.
- OPPOSITES upper.

lower[2] *verb* **1 let down**, take down, drop, let fall. **2 soften**, modulate, quieten, hush, tone down, muffle, turn down, mute. **3 reduce**, decrease, lessen, bring down, cut, slash.
- OPPOSITES raise, increase.

low-key *adjective* **restrained**, modest, understated, muted, subtle, quiet, low-profile, inconspicuous, unobtrusive, discreet.
- OPPOSITES ostentatious, obtrusive.

lowly *adjective* **humble**, low, low-ranking, common, ordinary, plain, modest, simple, obscure.
- OPPOSITES aristocratic, exalted.

loyal *adjective* **faithful**, true, true-blue, devoted, constant, steadfast, staunch, dependable, reliable, trustworthy, trusty, patriotic, unswerving.
- OPPOSITES disloyal, treacherous.

loyalty *noun* **allegiance**, faithfulness, fidelity, obedience, adherence, devotion, steadfastness, staunchness, dedication, commitment, patriotism; *old use* fealty.
- OPPOSITES disloyalty, treachery.

lucid *adjective* **1 clear**, crystal-clear, intelligible, comprehensible, cogent, coherent, articulate. **2 rational**, sane, in possession of your faculties, compos mentis, clear-headed, sober; *informal* all there.
- OPPOSITES confused.

luck *noun* **1 good fortune**, good luck, stroke of luck, fluke; *informal* lucky break. **2 fortune**, fate, serendipity, chance, accident, a twist of fate.
- OPPOSITES bad luck, misfortune.

luckily *adverb* **fortunately**, happily, providentially, by good fortune, as luck would have it, mercifully, thankfully.

lucky *adjective* **1 fortunate**, in luck, favoured, charmed, successful; *Brit. informal* jammy. **2 providential**, fortunate, timely, opportune, serendipitous, chance, fortuitous, accidental.
- OPPOSITES unlucky.

lucrative *adjective* **profitable**, gainful, remunerative, moneymaking, well paid, rewarding, worthwhile.
- OPPOSITES unprofitable.

ludicrous *adjective* **absurd**, ridiculous, farcical, laughable, risible, preposterous, mad, insane, idiotic, stupid, asinine, nonsensical; *informal* crazy.
- OPPOSITES sensible.

luggage *noun* **baggage**, bags, suitcases, cases.

lukewarm *adjective a lukewarm response* **indifferent**, cool, half-hearted, apathetic, tepid, unenthusiastic, uninterested, non-committal.
- OPPOSITES warm.

lull *verb* **soothe**, calm, quiet, still, assuage, allay, ease, quell.
● *noun* **1 pause**, respite, interval, break, suspension, breathing space, hiatus; *informal* let-up, breather. **2** *the lull before the storm* **calm**, stillness, quiet, tranquillity, peace, silence, hush.

lumber[1] *verb* **trundle**, stump, clump, plod, stumble, shamble, shuffle, trudge.

lumber[2] *verb (Brit. informal)* **burden**, saddle, encumber, land.

lumbering *adjective* **clumsy**, awkward, slow, blundering, bumbling, ponderous, ungainly; *informal* clodhopping.
- OPPOSITES nimble, agile.

luminous *adjective* **shining**, bright, brilliant, radiant, dazzling, coruscating, glowing, luminescent, phosphorescent, fluorescent, incandescent.
- OPPOSITES dark.

lump *noun* **1 chunk**, hunk, piece, block, wedge, slab, ball, knob, pat, clod, clump, nugget, gobbet. **2 swelling**, bump, bulge, protuberance, protrusion, growth, nodule, tumour.
● *verb* **combine**, put, group, bunch, throw.

lunatic *noun* **maniac**, psychopath, madman, madwoman, idiot; *informal* loony, nutcase, headcase, psycho; *Brit. informal* nutter; *N. Amer. informal* screwball.
● *adjective* **stupid**, foolish, idiotic, insane, absurd, ridiculous, ludicrous, preposterous, asinine; *informal* crazy, mad; *Brit. informal* barmy, daft.

lung *noun*

WORD LINKS
pulmonary relating to the lungs

lunge *noun Darren made a lunge at his attacker* **thrust**, dive, rush, charge, grab.
● *verb he lunged at her with a knife* **thrust**, dive, spring, launch yourself, rush.

lurch *verb* **1 stagger**, stumble, sway, reel, roll, totter. **2 swing**, list, roll, pitch, veer, swerve.

lure *verb* **tempt**, entice, attract, induce, coax, persuade, inveigle, seduce, beguile, draw.
- OPPOSITES deter, put off.
● *noun* **temptation**, attraction, pull, draw, appeal, inducement, allure, fascination, interest, glamour.

lurid *adjective* **1 bright**, vivid, glaring, fluorescent, gaudy, loud. **2** *lurid details* **sensational**, colourful, salacious, graphic, explicit, prurient, shocking, gruesome, gory, grisly; *informal* juicy.

lurk *verb* **skulk**, loiter, lie in wait, hide.

lush *adjective* **1 profuse**, abundant, luxuriant, flourishing, rich, riotous, vigorous, dense, thick, rampant. **2 luxurious**, sumptuous, palatial, opulent, lavish, elaborate, extravagant, fancy; *informal* plush, posh, swanky, bling-bling; *Brit. informal* swish; *N. Amer. informal* swank.
- OPPOSITES sparse, austere.

lust *noun* **1 desire**, longing, passion, libido, sex drive, sexuality, lecherousness, lasciviousness; *Brit. informal* randiness. **2 greed**, desire, craving, eagerness, longing, yearning, hunger, thirst, appetite, hankering.
□ **lust for/after** crave, desire, want, long for, yearn for, dream of, hanker for/after, hunger for, thirst for, ache for.

luxurious *adjective* **opulent**, sumptuous, grand, palatial, magnificent, extravagant, fancy, de luxe, expensive; *Brit.* upmarket; *informal* plush, posh, classy, swanky, bling-bling; *Brit. informal* swish; *N. Amer. informal* swank.
- OPPOSITES plain, basic.

luxury *noun* **1 opulence**, sumptuousness, grandeur, magnificence, splendour, luxuriousness, affluence. **2 indulgence**, extravagance, treat, extra, frill.
- OPPOSITES simplicity, necessity.

lying *noun* **dishonesty**, fabrication, fibbing, perjury, untruthfulness, mendacity, misrepresentation, deceit, duplicity.
- OPPOSITES honesty.
● *adjective* **dishonest**, untruthful, false, mendacious, deceitful, duplicitous, double-dealing, two-faced.
- OPPOSITES honest.

lyrical *adjective* **1 expressive**, emotional, deeply felt, personal. **2 enthusiastic**, effusive, rapturous, ecstatic, euphoric, passionate, impassioned.
- OPPOSITES unenthusiastic.

Mm

machine *noun* **1 device**, appliance, apparatus, engine, gadget, mechanism, tool, instrument, contraption. **2** *an efficient publicity machine* **organization**, system, structure, machinery; *informal* set-up.

machinery *noun* **1 equipment**, apparatus, plant, hardware, gear, gadgetry, technology. **2** *the machinery of local government* **workings**, organization, system, structure; *informal* set-up.

macho *adjective* **manly**, male, masculine, virile, red-blooded; *informal* butch, laddish.

mad *adjective* **1 insane**, crazy, out of your mind, deranged, demented, crazed, lunatic, unbalanced, unhinged, psychotic, non compos mentis; *Brit.* sectionable; *informal* mental, off your head, round the bend, nuts, nutty, off your rocker, bonkers, loony, loopy, batty, cuckoo; *Brit. informal* barmy, crackers, barking (mad), potty, round the twist. **2** *(informal)* **angry**, furious, infuriated, enraged, fuming, incensed, beside yourself; *informal* livid, spare; *N. Amer. informal* sore. **3** *a mad scheme* **foolish**, insane, stupid, lunatic, idiotic, foolhardy, absurd, ludicrous, silly, asinine, wild, crackbrained, senseless, preposterous; *informal* crazy, crackpot; *Brit. informal* daft. **4** *(informal) he's mad about her* **passionate**, fanatical, ardent, fervent, devoted, infatuated; *informal* crazy, dotty, nuts, wild, hooked; *Brit. informal* potty; *N. Amer. informal* nutso. **5** *a mad dash to get ready* **frenzied**, frantic, frenetic, feverish, hysterical, wild, hectic, manic.
- OPPOSITES sane, sensible.

madden *verb* **infuriate**, exasperate, irritate, incense, anger, enrage, provoke, make someone see red, inflame; *informal* aggravate, make someone's blood boil; *Brit. informal* nark; *N. Amer. informal* tee off, tick off.
- OPPOSITES calm.

madman, **madwoman** *noun* **lunatic**, maniac, psychotic, psychopath; *informal* loony, nut, nutcase, head case, psycho; *Brit. informal* nutter; *N. Amer. informal* screwball.

madness *noun* **1 insanity**, mental illness, dementia, derangement, lunacy, mania, psychosis. **2 folly**, foolishness, idiocy, stupidity, foolhardiness. **3 bedlam**, mayhem, chaos, pandemonium, uproar, turmoil.
- OPPOSITES sanity.

magazine *noun* **journal**, periodical, supplement, fanzine; *informal* glossy, mag.

magic *noun* **1 sorcery**, witchcraft, wizardry, necromancy, enchantment, the supernatural, occultism, the occult, black magic, the black arts, voodoo, hoodoo. **2 conjuring (tricks)**, sleight of hand, legerdemain, illusion; *formal* prestidigitation. **3 allure**, excitement, fascination, charm, glamour.

magical *adjective* **1 supernatural**, magic, mystical, other-worldly. **2 enchanting**, entrancing, spellbinding, bewitching, fascinating, captivating, alluring, enthralling, charming, lovely, delightful, beautiful, amazing; *informal* heavenly, gorgeous.

magician *noun* **1 sorcerer**, sorceress, witch, wizard, warlock, enchanter, enchantress, necromancer; *formal* thaumaturge. **2 conjuror**, illusionist; *formal* prestidigitator.

magnanimous *adjective* **generous**, charitable, benevolent, beneficent, big-hearted, open-handed, munificent, philanthropic, noble, unselfish, altruistic.
- OPPOSITES mean.

magnetic *adjective* **attractive**, irresistible, seductive, charismatic, hypnotic, alluring, fascinating, captivating.

magnificent *adjective* **1 splendid**, spectacular, impressive, striking, glorious, superb, majestic, awe-inspiring, breathtaking, sublime, resplendent, sumptuous, grand, imposing, monumental, palatial, opulent, luxurious, lavish, rich, dazzling, coruscating, beautiful. **2 excellent**, outstanding, marvellous, brilliant, wonderful, virtuoso, fine, superb.
– OPPOSITES uninspiring, ordinary.

magnify *verb* **enlarge**, increase, augment, extend, expand, boost, enhance, maximize, amplify, intensify; *informal* blow up.
– OPPOSITES reduce, minimize.

magnitude *noun* **1 size**, extent, immensity, vastness, hugeness, enormity. **2 importance**, import, significance, consequence.

mail *noun* **post**, letters, correspondence, email.
● *verb* **send**, post, dispatch, forward, ship, email.

maim *verb* **injure**, wound, cripple, disable, incapacitate, mutilate, disfigure, mangle.

main *adjective* **principal**, chief, head, leading, foremost, most important, major, dominant, central, focal, key, prime, primary, first, fundamental, predominant, pre-eminent, paramount.
– OPPOSITES subsidiary, minor.

mainly *adverb* **mostly**, for the most part, in the main, on the whole, largely, by and large, to a large extent, predominantly, chiefly, principally, primarily.

maintain *verb* **1 preserve**, conserve, keep, retain, keep going, prolong, perpetuate, sustain, carry on, continue. **2 look after**, service, care for, take care of, support, provide for, keep. **3 insist**, declare, assert, protest, affirm, profess, avow, claim, contend, argue; *formal* aver.
– OPPOSITES discontinue.

maintenance *noun* **1 preservation**, conservation, prolongation, continuation. **2 servicing**, service, repair, running repairs, care. **3 support**, upkeep, alimony, allowance.

majestic *adjective* **stately**, dignified, distinguished, magnificent, grand, splendid, glorious, impressive, regal, noble, awe-inspiring, monumental, palatial, imposing.
– OPPOSITES modest.

majesty *noun* **stateliness**, dignity, magnificence, pomp, grandeur, splendour, glory, impressiveness, nobility.

major *adjective* **1 greatest**, best, finest, most important, chief, main, prime, principal, leading, foremost, outstanding, pre-eminent. **2 crucial**, vital, important, big, significant, considerable, weighty, serious, key, utmost, great, paramount, prime.
– OPPOSITES minor, trivial.

majority *noun* **1 most**, bulk, mass, best part, lion's share, (main) body, preponderance, predominance. **2 coming of age**, age of consent, adulthood, seniority.
– OPPOSITES minority.

make *verb* **1 construct**, build, erect, assemble, put together, manufacture, produce, fabricate, create, form, forge, fashion, model, improvise. **2 force**, compel, coerce, press, drive, dragoon, pressurize, oblige, require; *informal* railroad, steamroller. **3 cause**, create, bring about, produce, generate, give rise to, effect. **4** *they made him chairman* **appoint**, designate, name, nominate, select, elect, vote in. **5** *he's made a lot of money* **acquire**, obtain, gain, get, secure, win, earn. **6** *he made the tea* **prepare**, concoct, cook, whip up, brew; *informal* fix.
– OPPOSITES destroy.
● *noun* **brand**, marque, label, type, sort, kind, variety.
□ **make for** contribute to, produce, promote, facilitate, foster. **make off** run away, run off, take to your heels, flee, take off, take flight, bolt; *informal*

clear off, beat it, split, scram; *Brit. informal* scarper, do a runner. **make out 1** see, discern, distinguish, detect, observe, recognize. **2** understand, grasp, follow, work out, interpret, decipher, make head or tail of, catch. **make peace** make up, bury the hatchet, forgive and forget, shake hands. **make up 1** comprise, form, compose, constitute, account for. **2** invent, fabricate, concoct, think up; *informal* cook up. **make up for** offset, counterbalance, counteract, cancel out, compensate for, atone for, make amends for.

make-believe *noun* **fantasy**, pretence, daydreaming, invention, fabrication, charade, play-acting, masquerade. ● *adjective* **imaginary**, imagined, made-up, fanciful, fictitious; *informal* pretend.
- OPPOSITES real, actual.

maker *noun* **creator**, manufacturer, constructor, builder, producer.

makeshift *adjective* **temporary**, provisional, stopgap, standby, rough and ready, improvised, ad hoc.

make-up *noun* **1 cosmetics**, greasepaint; *informal* warpaint, slap. **2 composition**, constitution, structure, configuration, arrangement. **3 character**, nature, temperament, personality, mentality, persona.

makings *plural noun* **qualities**, characteristics, ingredients, potential, capacity, capability, stuff.

maladjusted *adjective* **disturbed**, unstable, neurotic, dysfunctional; *informal* mixed up, screwed up.

male *adjective* **masculine**, manly, virile, macho.
- OPPOSITES female.

malfunction *verb* **break down**, fail, stop working, crash, go down; *informal* conk out, go kaput; *Brit. informal* play up, pack up.

malice *noun* **spite**, malevolence, ill will, vindictiveness, vengefulness, malignity, animus, enmity, rancour.
- OPPOSITES benevolence.

malicious *adjective* **spiteful**, malevolent, vindictive, vengeful, resentful, malign, nasty, hurtful, cruel, catty, venomous, poisonous, barbed; *informal* bitchy.
- OPPOSITES benevolent.

maltreat *verb* **ill-treat**, mistreat, abuse, ill-use, mishandle, misuse, persecute, harm, hurt, injure.

man *noun* **1 male**, gentleman, fellow, youth; *informal* guy, gent, geezer; *Brit. informal* bloke, chap, lad; *N. Amer. informal* dude, hombre. **2 human being**, human, person, mortal, individual, soul. **3 the human race**, Homo sapiens, humankind, humanity, human beings, humans, people, mankind. ● *verb* **1 staff**, crew, occupy. **2 operate**, work, use.

WORD LINKS
male, **masculine**, **virile** relating to men

manage *verb* **1 be in charge of**, run, head, direct, control, preside over, lead, govern, rule, command, supervise, oversee, administer; *informal* head up. **2 accomplish**, achieve, carry out, perform, undertake, deal with, cope with, get through. **3 cope**, get along/on, make do, survive, get by, muddle through/along, make ends meet; *informal* make out, hack it.

manageable *adjective* **1 achievable**, doable, practicable, feasible, reasonable, attainable, viable. **2 compliant**, tractable, pliant, biddable, docile, amenable, accommodating, acquiescent.

management *noun* **1 administration**, running, managing, organization, direction, leadership, control, governance, rule, command, supervision, guidance, operation. **2 managers**, employers, directors, board, directorate, executive, administration; *informal* bosses, top brass.
- OPPOSITES employees.

manager *noun* **executive**, head, supervisor, principal, director, superintendent, foreman, forewoman, overseer, organizer, administrator; *informal* boss, chief, governor; *Brit. informal* gaffer, guv'nor, honcho.

mandate *noun* **1 authority**, approval, ratification, endorsement, sanction, authorization. **2 instruction**, directive, decree, command, order, injunction.

mandatory *adjective* **obligatory**, compulsory, binding, required, requisite, necessary.
- OPPOSITES optional.

mania *noun* **obsession**, compulsion, fixation, fetish, fascination, preoccupation, passion, enthusiasm, desire, urge, craving, craze, fad, rage; *informal* thing.

maniac *noun* **lunatic**, madman, madwoman, psychopath; *informal* loony, nutcase, nut, head case, headbanger, psycho, sicko; *Brit. informal* nutter; *N. Amer. informal* screwball.

manifest *verb* **display**, show, exhibit, demonstrate, betray, present, reveal; *formal* evince.
- OPPOSITES hide.
● *adjective* **obvious**, clear, plain, apparent, evident, patent, distinct, definite, blatant, overt, glaring, transparent, conspicuous, undisguised.

manifestation *noun* **1 display**, demonstration, show, exhibition, presentation. **2 sign**, indication, evidence, symptom, testimony, proof, mark, reflection, example, instance.

manipulate *verb* **1 operate**, work, handle, turn, pull, push, twist, slide. **2 control**, influence, use to your advantage, exploit, twist.

mankind *noun* **the human race**, humankind, humanity, human beings, humans, Homo sapiens, people, man, men and women.

manly *adjective* **virile**, masculine, strong, all-male, red-blooded, muscular, muscly, strapping, well built, rugged, tough, powerful, brawny; *informal* hunky.
- OPPOSITES effeminate.

man-made *adjective* **artificial**, synthetic, manufactured, imitation, ersatz, simulated, mock, fake, faux.
- OPPOSITES natural, real.

manner *noun* **1 way**, fashion, mode, means, method, methodology, system, style, approach, technique, procedure, process. **2** *her unfriendly manner* **behaviour**, attitude, demeanour, air, aspect, mien, bearing, conduct. **3** (**manners**) **social graces**, politeness, Ps and Qs, etiquette, protocol, decorum, propriety, civility.

mannerism *noun* **idiosyncrasy**, quirk, oddity, foible, trait, peculiarity, habit, characteristic.

manoeuvre *verb* **1 steer**, guide, drive, negotiate, jockey, navigate, pilot, direct, move, work. **2 manipulate**, contrive, manage, engineer, fix, organize, arrange, orchestrate, choreograph, stage-manage; *informal* wangle, pull strings.
● *noun* **1 operation**, exercise, move, movement, action. **2 stratagem**, tactic, gambit, ploy, trick, dodge, ruse, scheme, device, plot, machination, artifice, subterfuge, intrigue.

mansion *noun* **country house**, stately home, hall, manor house; *informal* pile.
- OPPOSITES hovel.

manual *noun* **handbook**, instructions, guide, companion, ABC, guidebook, vade mecum; *informal* bible.
● *adjective* **physical**, labouring, blue-collar, hand.

manufacture *verb* **1 make**, produce, mass-produce, build, construct, assemble, put together, turn out, process. **2 make up**, invent, fabricate, concoct, hatch, dream up, think up, contrive; *informal* cook up.
● *noun* **production**, making, manufacturing, mass production, construction, building, assembly.

manufacturer *noun* **maker**, producer, builder, constructor, industrialist.

many *determiner* & *adjective* **numerous**, a lot of, plenty of, countless, innumerable, scores of, untold, copious, abundant; *informal* lots of, umpteen, loads of, masses of, stacks of, heaps of,

oodles of, a slew of; *literary* myriad.
- OPPOSITES few.

map *noun* **plan**, chart, A to Z, atlas.
● *verb* **chart**, plot, draw, record.

WORD LINKS
cartography making of maps

mar *verb* **spoil**, impair, detract from, disfigure, blemish, scar, deface, ruin, damage, wreck, taint, tarnish.
- OPPOSITES enhance.

march *verb* **1 stride**, walk, troop, step, pace, tread, slog, tramp, hike, trudge, parade, file. **2 stalk**, strut, flounce, storm, stomp, sweep.
● *noun* **1 walk**, trek, slog, route march, hike. **2 parade**, procession, cortège, demonstration; *informal* demo.

margin *noun* **1 edge**, side, verge, border, perimeter, brink, brim, rim, fringe, boundary, periphery, extremity. **2 leeway**, latitude, scope, room, space, allowance.

marginal *adjective* **slight**, small, tiny, minute, insignificant, minimal, negligible.
- OPPOSITES considerable.

marine *adjective* **1 seawater**, sea, saltwater, aquatic. **2 maritime**, nautical, naval, seafaring, seagoing, ocean-going.

mariner *noun* **sailor**, seaman, seafarer; *informal* matelot, sea dog, old salt; *dated* tar.

marital *adjective* **matrimonial**, conjugal, married, wedded, nuptial.

maritime *adjective* **naval**, marine, nautical, seafaring, seagoing, sea, ocean-going, oceanic, coastal.

mark *noun* **1 blemish**, streak, spot, fleck, blot, stain, smear, speck, smudge, blotch, bruise, scratch, scar, dent, chip, nick; *informal* splodge. **2 sign**, token, symbol, emblem, badge, indication, characteristic, feature, trait, attribute, quality, hallmark, indicator, symptom, proof. **3 grade**, grading, rating, score, percentage.
● *verb* **1 discolour**, stain, smear, smudge, streak, dirty, scratch, scar, dent; *informal* splodge. **2 label**, identify, flag, tag, initial, highlight, name, brand. **3 celebrate**, observe, recognize, acknowledge, keep, honour, commemorate, remember, solemnize. **4 represent**, signify, indicate, herald. **5 characterize**, distinguish, identify, typify. **6 assess**, evaluate, appraise, correct; *N. Amer.* grade.

marked *adjective* **noticeable**, pronounced, decided, distinct, striking, clear, unmistakable, obvious, conspicuous, notable.
- OPPOSITES imperceptible.

market *noun* **shopping centre**, marketplace, bazaar, souk, fair; *N. Amer.* mart.
● *verb* **sell**, retail, merchandise, trade, advertise, promote.

maroon *verb* **strand**, cast away, cast ashore, abandon, desert, leave behind, leave.

marriage *noun* **1 matrimony**, wedlock, wedding, nuptials, union, match. **2** *a marriage of jazz, pop, and gospel* **union**, fusion, mixture, mix, blend, amalgamation, combination, hybrid.
- OPPOSITES divorce, separation.

WORD LINKS
marital, **matrimonial**, **nuptial**, **conjugal** relating to marriage

marry *verb* **1 get married**, wed, become man and wife; *informal* tie the knot, walk down the aisle, get spliced, get hitched. **2** *the show marries poetry with art* **join**, unite, combine, fuse, mix, blend, merge, amalgamate.
- OPPOSITES divorce, separate.

marsh *noun* **swamp**, marshland, bog, morass, mire, quagmire, slough, fen.

marshal *verb* **assemble**, gather (together), collect, muster, call together, draw up, line up, array, organize, group, arrange, deploy, position, summon, round up.

martial *adjective* **military**, soldierly, warlike, fighting, militaristic; *informal* gung-ho.

marvel *verb* **be amazed**, be astonished, be in awe, wonder; *informal*

be gobsmacked.
● *noun* **wonder**, miracle, sensation, spectacle, phenomenon, prodigy.

marvellous *adjective* **excellent**, splendid, wonderful, magnificent, superb, sensational, glorious, sublime, lovely, delightful; *informal* super, great, amazing, fantastic, terrific, tremendous, fabulous, cracking, awesome, divine, ace, wicked; *Brit. informal* smashing, brilliant.
– OPPOSITES commonplace, awful.

masculine *adjective* **1 virile**, macho, manly, male, muscular, muscly, strong, strapping, well built, rugged, robust, brawny, powerful, red-blooded, vigorous; *informal* hunky, laddish. **2 mannish**, unfeminine, unladylike; *informal* butch.
– OPPOSITES feminine, effeminate.

mash *verb* **pulp**, crush, purée, cream, pound, beat.

mask *noun* **pretence**, semblance, veil, screen, front, facade, veneer, disguise, cover, cloak, camouflage.
● *verb* **hide**, conceal, disguise, cover up, obscure, screen, cloak, camouflage.

mass *noun* **1** *a mass of fallen leaves* **pile**, heap, accumulation, aggregation, mat, tangle. **2** *a mass of cyclists* **crowd**, horde, throng, host, troop, army, herd, flock, swarm, mob, pack, flood, multitude. **3** *the mass of the population* **majority**, most, preponderance, greater part, best/better part, bulk, body.
● *adjective* **widespread**, general, extensive, large-scale, wholesale, universal, indiscriminate.
● *verb* **assemble**, gather together, collect, rally.

massacre *noun* **slaughter**, mass murder, mass execution, ethnic cleansing, genocide, holocaust, annihilation, liquidation, extermination, carnage, butchery, bloodbath, bloodletting.
● *verb* **slaughter**, butcher, murder, kill, annihilate, exterminate, execute, liquidate, eliminate, mow down.

massage *noun* **rub**, rub-down, kneading.
● *verb* **1 rub**, knead, manipulate, pummel, work. **2 alter**, tamper with, manipulate, doctor, falsify, juggle, fiddle with, tinker with, distort, rig; *informal* cook, fiddle.

massive *adjective* **huge**, enormous, vast, immense, mighty, great, colossal, tremendous, gigantic, mammoth, monumental, giant, mountainous; *informal* monster, whopping, astronomical, mega; *Brit. informal* whacking, ginormous.
– OPPOSITES tiny.

master *noun* **1** *(historical)* **lord**, liege, ruler, sovereign, monarch. **2 expert**, genius, maestro, virtuoso, authority; *informal* ace, wizard, whizz, hotshot, pro; *Brit. informal* dab hand; *N. Amer. informal* maven, crackerjack. **3 teacher**, schoolteacher, schoolmaster, tutor, instructor. **4 guru**, teacher, leader, guide, mentor.
– OPPOSITES servant, pupil.
● *verb* **1 overcome**, conquer, beat, quell, suppress, control, triumph over, subdue, vanquish, subjugate, curb, check, defeat, get the better of; *informal* lick. **2** *he'd mastered the technique* **learn**, become proficient in, pick up, grasp, understand; *informal* get the hang of.
● *adjective* **expert**, adept, proficient, skilled, skilful, deft, dexterous, adroit, practised, experienced, masterly, accomplished; *informal* crack, ace; *N. Amer. informal* crackerjack.
– OPPOSITES amateur.

masterful *adjective* **commanding**, powerful, imposing, magisterial, authoritative.
– OPPOSITES weak.

masterly *adjective* **expert**, adept, skilful, skilled, adroit, proficient, deft, dexterous, accomplished, polished, consummate.
– OPPOSITES inept.

mastermind *noun* **genius**, intellect; *informal* brain(s).
● *verb* **plan**, control, direct, be in charge of, run, conduct, organize,

arrange, preside over, orchestrate, stage-manage, engineer, manage, coordinate.

masterpiece *noun* **magnum opus**, chef-d'œuvre, masterwork, pièce de résistance, tour de force, classic.

mastery *noun* **1 proficiency**, ability, capability, knowledge, understanding, comprehension, command, grasp. **2 control**, domination, command, supremacy, superiority, power, authority, jurisdiction, dominion, sovereignty.

mat *noun* **rug**, carpet, doormat, runner.

match *noun* **1 contest**, competition, game, tournament, tie, fixture, meet, friendly, (local) derby, bout, fight; *Brit.* clash. **2** *an exact match* **lookalike**, double, twin, duplicate, mate, companion, counterpart, pair, replica, copy, doppelgänger; *informal* spitting image, dead ringer.

● *verb* **1 go with**, coordinate with, complement, suit, set off. **2 correspond**, tally, agree, coincide, square. **3 equal**, compare with, be in the same league as, touch, rival, compete with; *informal* hold a candle to.

matching *adjective* **corresponding**, equivalent, parallel, analogous, complementary, paired, twin, identical, alike.
- OPPOSITES different, clashing.

mate *noun* **1** *(Brit. informal)* **friend**, companion, schoolmate, classmate, workmate; *informal* pal, chum; *N. Amer. informal* buddy, amigo, compadre. **2 partner**, husband, wife, spouse, consort, lover; *informal* better half, other half. **3** *a plumber's mate* **assistant**, helper, apprentice.

● *verb* **breed**, couple, copulate, pair.

material *noun* **1 matter**, substance, stuff, constituents. **2 fabric**, cloth, textiles. **3 information**, data, facts, facts and figures, statistics, evidence, details, particulars, background; *informal* info.

● *adjective* **1 physical**, corporeal, fleshly, bodily, tangible, mundane, worldly, earthly, secular, temporal, concrete, real. **2** *information material to the enquiry* **relevant**, pertinent, applicable, germane, vital, essential, key.
- OPPOSITES spiritual.

materialize *verb* **1 happen**, occur, come about, take place, transpire; *informal* come off; *literary* come to pass. **2 appear**, turn up, arrive, emerge, surface, pop up; *informal* show up, fetch up.

maternal *adjective* **motherly**, protective, caring, nurturing, maternalistic.

matrimonial *adjective* **marital**, conjugal, married, wedded, nuptial; *literary* connubial.

matted *adjective* **tangled**, knotted, tousled, dishevelled, uncombed, unkempt, ratty.

matter *noun* **1 material**, stuff, substance. **2 affair**, business, situation, concern, incident, episode, subject, topic, issue, question, point at issue, case.

● *verb* **be important**, make any difference, be of consequence, be relevant, count, signify.

matter-of-fact *adjective* **unemotional**, practical, down-to-earth, sensible, realistic, unsentimental, pragmatic, businesslike, commonsensical, level-headed, hard-headed, no-nonsense, straightforward.

mature *adjective* **1 adult**, of age, fully grown, in your prime. **2 grown-up**, sensible, responsible, adult. **3 ripe**, ripened, mellow, seasoned, ready.
- OPPOSITES immature.

● *verb* **1 grow up**, come of age, reach adulthood. **2 ripen**, mellow, age. **3 develop**, grow, bloom, blossom, evolve.

maturity *noun* **1 adulthood**, coming of age, manhood, womanhood. **2 responsibility**, sense, wisdom.

maul *verb* **savage**, attack, claw, scratch, lacerate, mangle, tear.

maverick *noun* **individualist**, nonconformist, free spirit, original, eccentric, rebel, dissenter, dissident.
- OPPOSITES conformist.

maxim *noun* **saying**, adage, aphorism, proverb, motto, saw, axiom, dictum, precept, epigram.

maximum *adjective* **greatest**, highest, biggest, largest, top, most, utmost, supreme.
● *noun* **upper limit**, limit, utmost, greatest, most, peak, pinnacle, height, ceiling, top.
– OPPOSITES minimum.

maybe *adverb* **perhaps**, possibly, for all you know; *N. English* happen; *literary* perchance.

mayhem *noun* **chaos**, havoc, bedlam, pandemonium, uproar, turmoil, a riot, anarchy; *informal* a madhouse.

maze *noun* **labyrinth**, network, warren, web, tangle, confusion, jungle.

meadow *noun* **field**, paddock, pasture; *literary* lea, mead.

meagre *adjective* **inadequate**, scant, paltry, limited, restricted, sparse, negligible, skimpy, slender, pitiful, miserly, niggardly; *informal* measly, stingy.
– OPPOSITES abundant.

meal *noun* snack, feast, banquet; *informal* spread, blowout; *Brit. informal* nosh-up; *formal* repast.

WORD LINKS
prandial relating to meals

mean[1] *verb* **1 signify**, denote, indicate, convey, designate, show, express, spell out, stand for, represent, symbolize, imply, suggest, intimate, portend. **2 intend**, aim, plan, have in mind, set out, want. **3** *this will mean war* **entail**, involve, necessitate, lead to, result in, give rise to, bring about, cause, engender, produce.

mean[2] *adjective* **1 miserly**, niggardly, parsimonious, penny-pinching, cheese-paring; *informal* tight-fisted, stingy, tight; *N. Amer. informal* cheap. **2 unkind**, nasty, unpleasant, spiteful, malicious, unfair, shabby, horrible, despicable, contemptible, obnoxious, vile, loathsome, base, low; *informal* rotten.
– OPPOSITES generous, kind.

meaning *noun* **1 significance**, sense, signification, import, gist, thrust, drift, implication, message. **2 definition**, sense, explanation, interpretation, connotation.

WORD LINKS
semantic relating to meaning

meaningful *adjective* **1 significant**, relevant, important, telling, expressive, eloquent, pointed, pregnant, revealing, suggestive. **2 sincere**, deep, serious, earnest, significant, important.

meaningless *adjective* **unintelligible**, incomprehensible, incoherent, senseless, pointless.

means *plural noun* **1 method**, way, manner, course, agency, channel, avenue, procedure, process, methodology, expedient, solution. **2 money**, resources, capital, income, finance, funds, cash, the wherewithal, deep pockets, assets, wealth, riches, affluence, fortune.

meanwhile, **meantime** *adverb* **1 for now**, for the moment, for the present, for the time being, in the meanwhile, in the meantime, in the interim. **2 at the same time**, simultaneously, concurrently.

measure *verb* **quantify**, gauge, size, count, weigh, evaluate, assess, determine, calculate, compute.
● *noun* **1 action**, act, course of action, deed, procedure, step, expedient, initiative, programme. **2 statute**, act, bill, law. **3 ruler**, tape measure, gauge, meter, scale. **4** *sales are a measure of their success* **yardstick**, test, standard, barometer, touchstone, benchmark.

measured *adjective* **1 regular**, steady, even, rhythmic, unfaltering, slow, dignified, stately, sedate, leisurely, unhurried. **2 careful**, thoughtful, considered, reasoned, calculated.

measurement *noun* **1 quantification**, evaluation, assessment, calculation, computation, mensuration. **2 size**, dimension, proportions, value, amount, quantity.

meat *noun* **flesh**.

WORD LINKS
carnivorous meat-eating

mechanical *adjective* **1 mechanized**, machine-driven, automated, automatic. **2 automatic**, knee-jerk, unthinking, instinctive, habitual, routine, unemotional, unfeeling.
- OPPOSITES manual.

mechanism *noun* **1 apparatus**, machine, machinery, appliance, device, instrument, tool, contraption, gadget; *informal* gizmo. **2** *a complaints mechanism* **procedure**, process, system, method, means, solution, medium, channel.

meddle *verb* **1 interfere**, intrude, intervene, pry; *informal* poke your nose in. **2 fiddle**, interfere, tamper, mess about; *Brit. informal* muck about.

mediate *verb* **arbitrate**, conciliate, moderate, make peace, intervene, intercede, act as an intermediary, negotiate, liaise, referee.

m

mediation *noun* **arbitration**, conciliation, reconciliation, intervention, intercession, negotiation, shuttle diplomacy.

mediator *noun* **arbitrator**, arbiter, negotiator, conciliator, peacemaker, go-between, middleman, intermediary, moderator, honest broker, liaison officer, umpire, referee, adjudicator, judge.

medicinal *adjective* **curative**, healing, remedial, therapeutic, restorative, health-giving.

medicine *noun* **medication**, drug, prescription, treatment, remedy, cure, nostrum, panacea, cure-all.

WORD LINKS
pharmaceutical relating to medicines

mediocre *adjective* **average**, ordinary, undistinguished, uninspired, indifferent, unexceptional, unexciting, unremarkable, run-of-the-mill, pedestrian, prosaic, lacklustre, forgettable, amateurish; *informal* so-so.
- OPPOSITES excellent.

meditate *verb* **contemplate**, think, consider, ponder, muse, reflect, deliberate, ruminate, brood, mull over.

medium *noun a medium of expression* **means**, method, avenue, channel, vehicle, organ, instrument, mechanism.
● *adjective* **average**, middling, medium-sized, middle-sized, moderate, normal, standard.

meek *adjective* **submissive**, obedient, compliant, tame, biddable, acquiescent, timid, quiet, mild, gentle, docile, shy, diffident, unassuming, self-effacing.
- OPPOSITES assertive.

meet *verb* **1 encounter**, come face to face with, run into, run across, come across/upon, chance on, happen on, stumble across; *informal* bump into. **2 get to know**, be introduced to, make the acquaintance of. **3 assemble**, gather, congregate, convene; *formal* foregather. **4 converge**, connect, touch, link up, intersect, cross, join.

meeting *noun* **1 gathering**, assembly, conference, congregation, convention, forum, summit, rally, consultation, audience, interview, conclave; *informal* get-together. **2 encounter**, contact, appointment, assignation, rendezvous; *literary* tryst. **3** *the meeting of land and sea* **convergence**, confluence, conjunction, union, intersection, crossing. **4** *an athletics meeting* **event**, tournament, meet, rally, competition, match, game, contest.

melancholy *adjective* **sad**, sorrowful, unhappy, gloomy, despondent, dejected, disconsolate, downcast, downhearted, woebegone, glum, miserable, morose, depressed, dispirited, mournful, doleful, lugubrious; *informal* down in the dumps, blue.
- OPPOSITES cheerful.
● *noun* **sadness**, sorrow, unhappiness, depression, despondency, dejection, gloom, misery; *informal* the blues.
- OPPOSITES happiness.

mellow *adjective* **1 sweet-sounding**, dulcet, melodious, mellifluous, soft, smooth, rich. **2 genial**, affable, amiable, good-humoured, good-natured, pleasant, relaxed, easy-going.
- OPPOSITES harsh, rough.

melodious *adjective* **tuneful**, melodic, musical, mellifluous, dulcet, sweet-sounding, harmonious, euphonious, lyrical.
- OPPOSITES discordant.

melodramatic *adjective* **exaggerated**, histrionic, extravagant, overdramatic, overdone, sensationalized, over-emotional, theatrical, stagy; *informal* hammy.

melody *noun* **tune**, air, strain, theme, song, refrain.

melt *verb* **1 liquefy**, thaw, defrost, soften, dissolve; *technical* deliquesce. **2 vanish**, disappear, fade, evaporate.
- OPPOSITES freeze, solidify.

member *noun* **subscriber**, associate, fellow, representative.

memento *noun* **souvenir**, keepsake, reminder, remembrance, token, memorial.

memoir *noun* **1 account**, history, record, chronicle, narrative, story, portrayal, depiction, portrait, profile. **2** (**memoirs**) **autobiography**, life story, journal, diary.

memorable *adjective* **unforgettable**, momentous, significant, historic, remarkable, notable, noteworthy, important, outstanding, arresting, indelible, catchy, haunting.

memorial *noun* **1 monument**, cenotaph, mausoleum, statue, plaque, cairn, shrine, tombstone. **2 tribute**, testimonial, remembrance, memento.

memorize *verb* **commit to memory**, remember, learn (by heart), become word-perfect in, get/have off pat.

memory *noun* **1 recollection**, remembrance, reminiscence, recall. **2 commemoration**, remembrance, honour, tribute, recognition, respect.

WORD LINKS
mnemonic helping the memory

menace *noun* **1 threat**, intimidation, malevolence, oppression. **2 danger**, peril, risk, hazard, threat. **3 nuisance**, pest, troublemaker, mischief-maker.
● *verb* **1 threaten**, endanger, put at risk, jeopardize, imperil. **2 intimidate**, threaten, terrorize, frighten, scare, terrify.

menacing *adjective* **threatening**, ominous, intimidating, frightening, forbidding, hostile, sinister, baleful.
- OPPOSITES friendly.

mend *verb* **repair**, fix, restore, sew (up), stitch, darn, patch, renew, renovate; *informal* patch up.
- OPPOSITES break.

menial *adjective* **unskilled**, lowly, humble, low-grade, low-status, humdrum, routine, boring, dull.

mental *adjective* **1 intellectual**, cerebral, cognitive, rational. **2 psychiatric**, psychological, behavioural.
- OPPOSITES physical.

mentality *noun* **way of thinking**, mind set, mind, psychology, attitude, outlook, make-up, disposition, character.

mentally *adverb* **psychologically**, intellectually, in your mind, in your head, inwardly, internally.

mention *verb* **1 allude to**, refer to, touch on, bring up, raise, broach. **2 state**, say, observe, remark, indicate, disclose, divulge, reveal.
● *noun* **reference**, allusion, comment, citation; *informal* namecheck, plug.

mentor *noun* **adviser**, counsellor, guide, guru, consultant, confidant(e), trainer, teacher, tutor, instructor.

menu *noun* **bill of fare**, tariff, carte du jour, set menu, table d'hôte.

mercenary *adjective* **grasping**, greedy, acquisitive, avaricious, materialistic, venal; *informal* money-grubbing.

merchandise *noun* **goods**, wares, stock, commodities, produce, products.

merchant *noun* **trader**, tradesman, dealer, wholesaler, broker, agent, seller, retailer, supplier, buyer, vendor, distributor.

merciful *adjective* **forgiving**, compassionate, pitying, forbearing, lenient, humane, mild, kind, soft-hearted, tender-hearted, sympathetic, humanitarian, liberal, generous, magnanimous.
- OPPOSITES cruel.

merciless *adjective* **ruthless**, remorseless, pitiless, unforgiving, implacable, inexorable, relentless, inhumane, inhuman, unfeeling, severe, cold-blooded, hard-hearted, stony-hearted, heartless, harsh, callous, cruel, brutal.
- OPPOSITES compassionate.

mercy *noun* **pity**, compassion, leniency, clemency, charity, forgiveness, forbearance, kindness, sympathy, indulgence, tolerance, generosity, magnanimity.
- OPPOSITES ruthlessness, cruelty.

merely *adverb* **only**, purely, solely, simply, just, but.

m

merge *verb* **1 join (together)**, join forces, unite, affiliate, team up. **2 amalgamate**, bring together, join, consolidate, conflate, unite, unify, combine, incorporate, integrate. **3 mingle**, blend, fuse, mix, intermix, intermingle, coalesce.
- OPPOSITES separate.

merger *noun* **amalgamation**, combination, union, fusion, coalition, affiliation, unification, incorporation, consolidation, link-up, alliance.
- OPPOSITES split.

merit *noun* **1 excellence**, quality, calibre, worth, value, distinction, eminence. **2 good point**, strong point, advantage, benefit, value, asset, plus.
- OPPOSITES fault, disadvantage.
● *verb* **deserve**, warrant, justify, earn, rate, be worthy of, be entitled to, have a right to, have a claim to.

merry *adjective* **cheerful**, cheery, in high spirits, sunny, smiling, light-hearted, lively, carefree, joyful, joyous, jolly, convivial, festive, gleeful, happy, laughing; *informal* chirpy.
- OPPOSITES miserable.

mesh *noun* **netting**, net, grille, screen, lattice, gauze.
● *verb* **1 engage**, connect, lock, interlock. **2 harmonize**, fit together, match, dovetail, connect, interconnect.

mess *noun* **1 untidiness**, disorder, disarray, clutter, muddle, jumble, chaos; *informal* shambles; *Brit. informal* tip, omnishambles. **2 plight**, predicament, tight spot, tight corner, difficulty, trouble, quandary, dilemma, problem, muddle, mix-up; *informal* jam, fix, pickle, hole.
□ **mess about/around** potter about, fiddle about/around, play about/around, fool about/around, fidget, toy, trifle, tamper, tinker, interfere, meddle, monkey about/around; *Brit. informal* muck about/around. **mess up 1** dirty, clutter up, jumble, dishevel, rumple; *N. Amer. informal* muss up. **2** bungle, spoil, make a mess of, ruin; *informal* botch, make a hash of, muck up, foul up, screw up, muff.

message *noun* **1 communication**, news, note, memo, email, letter, missive, report, bulletin, communiqué, dispatch. **2** *the message of his teaching* **meaning**, sense, import, idea, point, thrust, moral, gist, essence, implication.

messenger *noun* **courier**, postman, runner, dispatch rider, envoy, emissary, agent, go-between.

messy *adjective* **1 dirty**, filthy, grubby, soiled, grimy, mucky, muddy, stained, smeared, smudged, dishevelled, scruffy, unkempt, rumpled, matted, tousled. **2 untidy**, disordered, in a muddle, chaotic, confused, disorganized, in disarray, cluttered, in a jumble; *informal* like a bomb's hit it; *Brit. informal* shambolic. **3** *a messy legal battle* **complex**, tangled, confused, convoluted, unpleasant, nasty, bitter, acrimonious.
- OPPOSITES clean, tidy.

metaphor *noun* **figure of speech**, image, trope, analogy, comparison, symbol.

method *noun* **1 procedure**, technique, system, practice, routine, modus operandi, process, strategy, tactic, approach, way, manner, mode. **2** *there's no method in his approach* **order**, organization, structure, form, system, logic, planning, design, consistency.
- OPPOSITES disorder.

methodical *adjective* **orderly**, well ordered, well organized, well planned, efficient, businesslike, systematic, structured, logical, disciplined, consistent, scientific.

meticulous *adjective* **careful**, conscientious, diligent, scrupulous, punctilious, painstaking, thorough, studious, rigorous, detailed, perfectionist, fastidious.
- OPPOSITES careless.

midday *noun* **noon**, twelve noon, high noon, noonday.
- OPPOSITES midnight.

middle *noun* **1 centre**, midpoint, halfway point, dead centre, hub, eye, heart, core, kernel. **2 midriff**, waist, belly, stomach; *informal* tummy.
- OPPOSITES edge.
● *adjective* **central**, mid, mean, medium, median, midway, halfway, equidistant.

might *noun* **strength**, force, forcefulness, power, vigour, energy, brawn.

mighty *adjective* **powerful**, forceful, strong, hard, heavy, violent, vigorous, hefty.
- OPPOSITES feeble.

migrant *noun* **immigrant**, **emigrant**, nomad, itinerant, traveller, transient, wanderer, drifter.
● *adjective* **travelling**, wandering, drifting, nomadic, itinerant, transient.

mild *adjective* **1 gentle**, tender, soft, sympathetic, peaceable, good-natured, quiet, placid, docile, meek. **2** *a mild punishment* **lenient**, light. **3 warm**, balmy, temperate, clement. **4 bland**, tasteless, insipid.
- OPPOSITES harsh, strong, severe.

militant *adjective* **hard-line**, extreme, extremist, committed, zealous, fanatical, radical.
● *noun* **activist**, extremist, partisan, radical, zealot.

military *adjective* **fighting**, service, army, armed, defence, martial.
- OPPOSITES civilian.
● *noun* **(armed) forces**, services, militia, army, navy, air force, marines.

militate *verb*
□ **militate against** work against, hinder, discourage, be prejudicial to, be detrimental to.

milk *verb* **exploit**, take advantage of, suck dry; *informal* bleed, squeeze, fleece.

WORD LINKS
lactic relating to milk

mill *noun* **factory**, plant, works, workshop, shop, foundry.
● *verb* **grind**, pulverize, powder, granulate, pound, crush, press.
□ **mill around/about** wander, drift, swarm, crowd, fill, pack, throng.

mimic *verb* **imitate**, copy, impersonate, do an impression of, ape, caricature, parody; *informal* send up, take off.
● *noun* **impersonator**, impressionist; *informal* copycat.

mince *verb* **grind**, chop up, cut up, dice, crumble; *N. Amer.* hash.

mind *noun* **1 brain**, intelligence, intellect, brains, brainpower, wits, understanding, reasoning, judgement, sense, head; *informal* grey matter; *N. Amer. informal* smarts. **2 attention**, thoughts, concentration. **3 sanity**, mental faculties, senses, wits, reason, reasoning, judgement. **4 intellect**, thinker, brain, scholar, genius.
● *verb* **1 object**, care, be bothered, be annoyed, be upset, take offence, disapprove, look askance; *informal* give/care a damn. **2 be careful of**, watch out for, look out for, beware of. **3 look after**, take care of, keep an eye on, watch, attend to, care for.

WORD LINKS
mental relating to the mind

mindless *adjective* **1 stupid**, idiotic, brainless, asinine, witless, empty-headed; *informal* dumb, dopey, dim, half-witted, fat-headed, boneheaded. **2 unthinking**, thoughtless, senseless, gratuitous, wanton, indiscriminate. **3 mechanical**, routine, tedious, boring, monotonous, mind-numbing.

mine *noun* **1 pit**, colliery, excavation, quarry. **2** *a mine of information* **store**, storehouse, reservoir, repository, gold mine, treasure house, treasury.
● *verb* **quarry**, excavate, dig, extract.

mingle *verb* **1 mix**, blend, intermingle, intermix, interweave, interlace, combine, merge, fuse, unite, join, amalgamate. **2 socialize**, circulate, associate, fraternize, get together; *informal* hobnob.
- OPPOSITES separate.

miniature *adjective* **small**, mini, little, small-scale, baby, toy, fun-size, pocket, diminutive; *informal* pint-sized; *Scottish* wee; *N. Amer.* vest-pocket.
- OPPOSITES giant.

minimal *adjective* **very little**, very small, minimum, the least (possible), nominal, token, negligible.
- OPPOSITES maximum.

minimize *verb* **1 keep down**, keep to a minimum, reduce, decrease, cut (down), lessen, curtail, prune; *informal* slash. **2 belittle**, make light of, play down, underrate, downplay, undervalue.
- OPPOSITES maximize, exaggerate.

minimum *noun* **lowest level**, lower limit, rock bottom, least, lowest.
● *adjective* **minimal**, least, smallest, least possible, slightest, lowest.
- OPPOSITES maximum.

minister *noun* **1 member of the government**, member of the cabinet, Secretary of State. **2 clergyman**, clergywoman, cleric, pastor, vicar, rector, priest, parson, curate; *informal* reverend, padre.
● *verb doctors ministered to the injured* **tend**, care for, take care of, look after, nurse, treat, attend to, see to, help.

ministry *noun* **1 department**, bureau, agency, office. **2 the priesthood**, holy orders, the church.

minor *adjective* **1 slight**, small, unimportant, insignificant, inconsequential, negligible, trivial, trifling, paltry, petty; *N. Amer.* nickel-and-dime; *informal* piffling. **2** *a minor poet* **little known**, unknown, lesser, unimportant, obscure; *N. Amer.* minor-league; *informal* small-time; *N. Amer. informal* two-bit.
- OPPOSITES major, important.
● *noun* **child**, infant, youth, adolescent, teenager, boy, girl; *informal* kid.
- OPPOSITES adult.

mint *verb* **coin**, stamp, strike, cast, make, manufacture.

minute[1] *noun* **1 moment**, short time, little while, second, instant; *informal* sec, jiffy; *Brit. informal* tick, mo, two ticks. **2 (minutes) record(s)**, proceedings, log, notes, transcript, summary.

minute[2] *adjective* **1 tiny**, minuscule, microscopic, miniature; *Scottish* wee; *informal* teeny, teeny-weeny; *Brit. informal* titchy, tiddly. **2** *minute detail* **exhaustive**, painstaking, meticulous, rigorous, thorough.
- OPPOSITES huge.

miracle *noun* **wonder**, marvel, sensation, phenomenon.

miraculous *adjective* **amazing**, astounding, remarkable, extraordinary, incredible, unbelievable, sensational, phenomenal, inexplicable.

mirror *noun* **looking glass**; *Brit.* glass.
● *verb* **reflect**, match, reproduce, imitate, copy, mimic, echo, parallel.

misbehave *verb* **behave badly**, be naughty, be disobedient, get up to mischief, get up to no good, be rude; *informal* carry on, act up.

miscellaneous *adjective* **various**, varied, different, assorted, mixed, sundry, diverse, disparate, heterogeneous.

mischief *noun* **naughtiness**, bad behaviour, misbehaviour, misconduct, disobedience, wrongdoing; *informal* monkey business, shenanigans.

mischievous *adjective* **1 naughty**, bad, badly behaved, troublesome, disobedient, rascally. **2 playful**, wicked, impish, roguish.
- OPPOSITES well behaved.

misconduct *noun* **1 wrongdoing**, criminality, unprofessionalism, malpractice, negligence, impropriety; *formal* maladministration. **2 misbehaviour**, bad behaviour, mischief, misdeeds, naughtiness.

miser *noun* **penny-pincher**, Scrooge; *informal* skinflint, cheapskate; *N. Amer. informal* tightwad.
- OPPOSITES spendthrift.

miserable *adjective* **1 unhappy**, sad, sorrowful, melancholy, dejected, depressed, downhearted, downcast, despondent, disconsolate, wretched, glum, gloomy, forlorn, woebegone, mournful; *informal* blue, down in the dumps. **2** *their miserable surroundings* **dreary**, dismal, gloomy, drab, wretched, depressing, grim, cheerless, bleak, desolate.
- OPPOSITES cheerful, lovely.

miserly *adjective* **mean**, parsimonious, close-fisted, penny-pinching, cheeseparing, grasping, niggardly; *informal* stingy, tight, tight-fisted; *N. Amer. informal* cheap.
- OPPOSITES generous.

misery *noun* **unhappiness**, distress, wretchedness, suffering, angst, anguish, anxiety, torment, pain, grief, heartache, heartbreak, despair, despondency, dejection, depression, gloom, sorrow; *informal* the blues.
- OPPOSITES contentment, pleasure.

misfortune *noun* **problem**, difficulty, setback, trouble, adversity, (stroke of) bad luck, misadventure, mishap, blow, failure, accident, disaster, trial, tribulation.

misguided *adjective* **unwise**, foolish, ill-advised, ill-judged, ill-considered, injudicious, imprudent, unsound, mistaken, misplaced.
- OPPOSITES wise.

mislay *verb* **lose**, misplace, be unable to find.
- OPPOSITES find.

mislead *verb* **deceive**, delude, take in, lie to, fool, hoodwink, misinform; *informal* lead up the garden path, take for a ride; *N. Amer. informal* give someone a bum steer.

misleading *adjective* **deceptive**, confusing, deceiving, equivocal, false.
- OPPOSITES clear, straightforward.

miss *verb* **1 go wide of**, fall short of, pass, overshoot. **2 avoid**, beat, evade, escape, dodge, sidestep, elude, circumvent, bypass. **3 pine for**, yearn for, ache for, long for. **4 fail to attend**, be absent from, play truant from, cut, skip, omit; *Brit. informal* skive off.
- OPPOSITES hit, catch.
▫ **miss out** leave out, exclude, miss (off), fail to mention, pass over, skip, omit, ignore.

missing *adjective* **1 lost**, mislaid, misplaced, absent, gone (astray), unaccounted for. **2 absent**, lacking, wanting.
- OPPOSITES present.

mission *noun* **1 assignment**, commission, expedition, journey, trip, undertaking, operation, project. **2** *her mission in life* **vocation**, calling, goal, aim, quest, purpose, function, task, job, labour, work, duty.

missionary *noun* **evangelist**, apostle, proselytizer, preacher.

mist *noun* **haze**, fog, smog, murk, cloud, vapour, steam, spray, condensation.

mistake *noun* **error**, fault, inaccuracy, omission, slip, blunder, miscalculation, misunderstanding, oversight, misinterpretation, gaffe, faux pas, solecism; *informal* slip-up, boo-boo, howler; *Brit. informal* boob, clanger; *N. Amer. informal* goof.
▫ **make a mistake** make an error, go wrong, err, blunder, miscalculate.

mistake for confuse with, mix up with, take for.

mistaken *adjective* **1 inaccurate**, wrong, erroneous, incorrect, off beam, false, fallacious, unfounded, misguided. **2 misinformed**, wrong, in error, under a misapprehension, barking up the wrong tree.
- OPPOSITES correct.

mistimed *adjective* **ill-timed**, badly timed, inopportune, inappropriate, untimely.

mistreat *verb* **ill-treat**, maltreat, abuse, knock about/around, hit, beat, molest, injure, harm, hurt, misuse.

mistrust *verb* **be suspicious of**, be sceptical of, be wary of, be chary of, distrust, have doubts about, have misgivings about, have reservations about, suspect.

misty *adjective* **hazy**, foggy, cloudy, blurred, vague, indistinct.
- OPPOSITES clear.

m

misunderstand *verb* **misapprehend**, misinterpret, misconstrue, misconceive, mistake, misread, be mistaken, get the wrong idea; *informal* get (hold of) the wrong end of the stick.

misunderstanding *noun* **1 misinterpretation**, misreading, misapprehension, misconception, false impression. **2 disagreement**, difference (of opinion), dispute, falling-out, quarrel, argument, clash.

misuse *verb* **put to wrong use**, misapply, misemploy, abuse, squander, waste, dissipate, misappropriate, embezzle.

mix *verb* **1 blend**, mingle, combine, jumble, fuse, unite, join, amalgamate, incorporate, meld, homogenize; *technical* admix; *literary* commingle. **2 associate**, socialize, keep company, consort, mingle, circulate; *Brit.* rub shoulders; *N. Amer.* rub elbows; *informal* hang out/around, hobnob.
- OPPOSITES separate.
● *noun* **mixture**, blend, combination, compound, fusion, union, amalgamation, medley, selection, assortment, variety.

mixed *adjective* **1 assorted**, varied, variegated, miscellaneous, disparate, diverse, diversified, motley, sundry, jumbled, heterogeneous. **2** *mixed reactions* **ambivalent**, equivocal, contradictory, conflicting, confused, muddled.
- OPPOSITES homogeneous.

mixture *noun* **1 blend**, mix, brew, combination, concoction, composition, compound, alloy, amalgam. **2 assortment**, miscellany, medley, blend, variety, mixed bag, mix, diversity, collection, selection, hotchpotch, ragbag; *N. Amer.* hodgepodge.

mix-up *noun* **confusion**, muddle, misunderstanding, mistake, error.

moan *verb* **1 groan**, wail, whimper, sob, cry. **2 complain**, grouse, grumble, whine, carp; *informal* gripe, grouch, bellyache, bitch, beef, whinge.

mob *noun* **crowd**, horde, multitude, rabble, mass, throng, gathering, assembly.
● *verb* **surround**, crowd round, besiege, jostle.

mobile *adjective* **1 able to move**, able to walk, walking; *informal* up and about. **2** *a mobile library* **travelling**, transportable, portable, movable, itinerant, peripatetic.
- OPPOSITES immobile.

mobilize *verb* **1** *mobilize the troops* **marshal**, deploy, muster, rally, call up, assemble, mass, organize, prepare. **2** *mobilizing support for the party* **generate**, arouse, awaken, excite, stimulate, stir up, encourage, inspire, whip up.

mock *verb* **ridicule**, jeer at, sneer at, deride, make fun of, laugh at, scoff at, tease, taunt; *informal* take the mickey out of; *N. Amer. informal* goof on, rag on.
● *adjective* **imitation**, artificial, man-made, simulated, synthetic, ersatz, fake, reproduction, pseudo, false, spurious; *informal* pretend.
- OPPOSITES genuine.

mocking *adjective* **sneering**, derisive, contemptuous, scornful, sardonic, ironic, sarcastic, satirical.

mode *noun* **1 manner**, way, means, method, system, style, approach. **2** *the camera is in manual mode* **function**, position, operation, setting, option.

model *noun* **1 replica**, copy, representation, mock-up, dummy, imitation, duplicate, reproduction, facsimile. **2 prototype**, archetype, type, paradigm, version, mould, template, framework, pattern, design, blueprint. **3 fashion model**, supermodel, mannequin; *informal* clothes horse. ● *adjective* **1 replica**, toy, miniature, dummy, imitation, duplicate, reproduction, facsimile. **2 ideal**, perfect, exemplary, classic, flawless, faultless, nonpareil.

moderate *adjective* **1 average**, modest, medium, middling, tolerable, passable, adequate, fair; *informal* OK, so-so, bog-standard, fair-to-middling. **2** *moderate prices* **reasonable**, within reason, acceptable, affordable, inexpensive, fair, modest. **3** *moderate views* **middle-of-the-road**, non-extremist, liberal, pragmatic.
- OPPOSITES immoderate, extreme.
● *verb* **1 die down**, abate, let up, calm down, lessen, decrease, diminish, recede, weaken, subside. **2 curb**, control, check, temper, restrain, subdue, tame, lessen, decrease, lower, reduce, diminish, alleviate, allay, appease, ease, soothe, calm, tone down.
- OPPOSITES increase.

moderately *adverb* **somewhat**, quite, fairly, reasonably, comparatively, relatively, to some extent, tolerably, adequately; *informal* pretty.

modern *adjective* **1 present-day**, contemporary, present, current, twenty-first-century, latter-day, recent. **2 fashionable**, up to date, trendsetting, stylish, chic, à la mode, the latest, new, newest, newfangled, advanced; *informal* trendy, cool, in, funky.
- OPPOSITES past, old-fashioned.

modernize *verb* **update**, bring up to date, streamline, rationalize, overhaul, renovate, remodel, refashion, revamp.

modest *adjective* **1 humble**, self-deprecating, self-effacing, unassuming, shy, diffident, reserved, bashful. **2** *modest success* **moderate**, fair, limited, tolerable, passable, adequate, satisfactory, acceptable, unexceptional. **3** *a modest house* **small**, ordinary, simple, plain, humble, inexpensive, unostentatious, unpretentious. **4** *her modest dress* **demure**, decent, seemly, decorous, proper.
- OPPOSITES conceited, grand, indecent.

modesty *noun* **humility**, self-effacement, shyness, bashfulness, self-consciousness, reserve.

modification *noun* **change**, adjustment, alteration, adaptation, refinement, revision, amendment; *informal* tweak.

modify *verb* **1 change**, alter, adjust, adapt, amend, revise, refine; *informal* tweak. **2 moderate**, temper, soften, tone down, qualify.

moist *adjective* **1 damp**, steamy, humid, muggy, clammy, dank, wet, soggy, sweaty, sticky. **2 succulent**, juicy, soft, tender.
- OPPOSITES dry.

moisten *verb* **dampen**, wet, damp, water, humidify.

moisture *noun* **wetness**, wet, water, liquid, condensation, steam, vapour, dampness, damp, humidity.

moment *noun* **1 little while**, short time, bit, minute, instant, (split) second; *informal* sec, jiffy; *Brit. informal* tick, mo, two ticks. **2 point (in time)**, stage, juncture, instant, time, hour, second, minute, day.

momentary *adjective* **brief**, short, short-lived, fleeting, passing, transitory, transient, ephemeral.
- OPPOSITES lengthy.

momentous *adjective* **important**, significant, historic, critical, crucial, decisive, pivotal, consequential, far-reaching; *informal* earth-shattering.
- OPPOSITES insignificant.

momentum *noun* **impetus**, energy, force, driving force, power, strength, thrust, speed, velocity.

monarch *noun* **sovereign**, ruler, Crown, crowned head, potentate, king, queen, emperor, empress, prince, princess.

monastery *noun* friary, abbey, priory, cloister.

monetary *adjective* **financial**, fiscal, pecuniary, money, cash, capital, economic, budgetary.

money *noun* **cash**, hard cash, means, wherewithal, deep pockets, funds, capital, finances, notes, coins, change, currency, specie; *informal* dough, bread, loot; *Brit. informal* dosh, brass, lolly, spondulicks, the readies; *N. Amer. informal* dinero.

monitor *noun* **1 detector**, scanner, recorder, sensor, security camera, CCTV. **2** *UN monitors* **observer**, watchdog, overseer, supervisor, scrutineer. **3** *a computer monitor* **screen**, display, VDU.
● *verb* **observe**, watch, track, keep an eye on, keep under surveillance, record, note, oversee; *informal* keep tabs on.

monkey *noun* **simian**, primate, ape.
▫ **monkey with** tamper with, fiddle with, interfere with, meddle with, tinker with, play with; *informal* mess with; *Brit. informal* muck about with.

monotonous *adjective* **tedious**, boring, uninteresting, unexciting, dull, repetitive, repetitious, unvarying, unchanging, mechanical, mind-numbing, soul-destroying; *informal* deadly.
– OPPOSITES interesting.

monster *noun* **1 giant**, mammoth, demon, dragon, colossus, leviathan. **2 fiend**, animal, beast, devil, demon, barbarian, savage, brute; *informal* swine.

monstrous *adjective* **1 grotesque**, hideous, ugly, ghastly, gruesome, horrible, horrific, horrifying, grisly, disgusting, repulsive, dreadful, frightening, terrible, terrifying. **2 appalling**, wicked, abominable, terrible, horrible, dreadful, vile, outrageous, unspeakable, despicable, vicious, savage, barbaric, inhuman.
– OPPOSITES beautiful, humane.

monument *noun* **memorial**, statue, pillar, cairn, column, obelisk, cross, cenotaph, tomb, mausoleum, shrine.

monumental *adjective* **1 huge**, enormous, gigantic, massive, colossal, mammoth, immense, tremendous, mighty, stupendous. **2 significant**, important, majestic, memorable, remarkable, noteworthy, momentous, grand, awe-inspiring, heroic, epic.
– OPPOSITES tiny.

mood *noun* **1 frame of mind**, state of mind, humour, temper. **2 bad mood**, temper, bad temper, sulk, low spirits, the doldrums, the blues; *Brit. informal* paddy. **3 atmosphere**, feeling, spirit, ambience, aura, character, flavour, feel, tone.

moody *adjective* **temperamental**, emotional, volatile, capricious, erratic, bad-tempered, petulant, sulky, sullen, morose.
– OPPOSITES cheerful.

moon *verb* **1 waste time**, loaf, idle; *Brit. informal* mooch. **2 mope**, pine, brood, daydream.

WORD LINKS
lunar relating to the moon

moor[1] *verb* **tie (up)**, secure, make fast, berth, dock.

moor[2] *noun* **upland**, heath, moorland; *Brit.* fell, wold.

mop *noun a tousled mop of hair* **shock**, mane, tangle, mass.

moral *adjective* **1 ethical**, good, virtuous, righteous, upright, upstanding, high-minded, principled, honourable, honest, just, noble. **2** *moral support* **psychological**, emotional, mental.
– OPPOSITES immoral, unethical.
● *noun* **1 lesson**, message, meaning, significance, import, point, teaching. **2** *he's got no morals* **moral code**, code of ethics, values, principles, standards, (sense of) morality, scruples.

morale *noun* **confidence**, self-confidence, self-esteem, spirit(s), team spirit, esprit de corps, motivation.

morality *noun* **1 ethics**, rights and wrongs, whys and wherefores. **2 virtue**, good behaviour, righteousness, uprightness, morals, standards, principles, honesty, integrity, propriety, honour, decency.

morbid *adjective* **ghoulish**, macabre, unhealthy, gruesome, unwholesome; *informal* sick.
- OPPOSITES wholesome.

more *determiner* **extra**, further, added, additional, supplementary, increased, new.
- OPPOSITES less, fewer.

moreover *adverb* **besides**, furthermore, what's more, in addition, also, as well, too, to boot, additionally, on top of that, into the bargain.

morning *noun* **1 before lunch**, a.m.; *literary* morn; *Nautical & N. Amer.* forenoon. **2 dawn**, daybreak, sunrise, first light; *N. Amer.* sunup.

mortal *adjective* **1** *all men are mortal* **perishable**, physical, bodily, corporeal, human, fleshly, earthly, impermanent, transient, ephemeral. **2** *a mortal blow* **fatal**, lethal, deadly, death-dealing, murderous, terminal. **3** *mortal enemies* **deadly**, sworn, irreconcilable, bitter, implacable, unrelenting, remorseless.
- OPPOSITES eternal.
● *noun* **human (being)**, person, man, woman, earthling.

mortuary *noun* **morgue**, funeral parlour; *Brit.* chapel of rest.

mostly *adverb* **1 mainly**, for the most part, on the whole, in the main, largely, chiefly, predominantly, principally, primarily. **2 usually**, generally, in general, as a rule, ordinarily, normally, customarily, typically, most of the time, almost always.

mother *noun* matriarch, materfamilias; *informal* ma; *Brit. informal* mum, mummy; *N. Amer. informal* mom, mommy; *Brit. informal, dated* mater.
● *verb* **look after**, care for, take care of, nurse, protect, tend, raise, rear, pamper, coddle, cosset, fuss over.

WORD LINKS
maternal relating to a mother
matricide killing of your mother

motherly *adjective* **maternal**, maternalistic, protective, caring, loving, affectionate, nurturing.

motif *noun* **1 design**, pattern, decoration, figure, shape, device, emblem. **2 theme**, idea, concept, subject, topic, leitmotif.

motion *noun* **1 movement**, locomotion, progress, passage, transit, course, travel, orbit. **2 gesture**, movement, signal, sign, indication, wave, nod, gesticulation. **3 proposal**, proposition, recommendation.
● *verb* **gesture**, signal, direct, indicate, wave, beckon, nod.

WORD LINKS
kinetic relating to motion

motivate *verb* **prompt**, drive, move, inspire, stimulate, influence, activate, impel, propel, push, spur (on), encourage, incentivize.

motivation *noun* **motive**, motivating force, incentive, stimulus, stimulation, inspiration, inducement, incitement, spur.

motive *noun* **reason**, motivation, motivating force, rationale, grounds, cause, basis.

motto *noun* **slogan**, maxim, saying, proverb, aphorism, adage, saw, axiom, formula, catchphrase.

mould *noun* **1 cast**, die, matrix, form, shape, template, pattern, frame. **2** *an actress in the Hollywood mould* **pattern**, form, type, style, tradition, school.
● *verb* **1 shape**, form, fashion, model, work, construct, make, create, sculpt, cast. **2 determine**, direct, control, guide, influence, shape, form, fashion, make.

mound *noun* **1 heap**, pile, stack, mountain. **2 hillock**, hill, knoll, rise, hummock, hump; *Scottish* brae.

mount *verb* **1 go up**, ascend, climb (up), scale. **2** *mount a horse* **get on to**, bestride, climb on to, leap on to, hop on to. **3** *mount an exhibition* **put on**, present, install, organize, stage, set up, prepare, launch, set in motion. **4 increase**, grow, rise, escalate, soar, spiral, shoot up, rocket, climb, accumulate, build up, multiply.
- OPPOSITES descend, dismount, fall.
● *noun* **setting**, backing, support, mounting, frame, stand.

mountain *noun* **1 peak**, summit; (**mountains**) range, massif, sierra; *Scottish* ben. **2 lot**; *informal* heap, pile, stack, slew, lots, loads, tons, masses.

mourn *verb* **1 grieve for**, sorrow over, lament for, weep for. **2 deplore**, bewail, bemoan, rue, regret.

mourning *noun* **grief**, grieving, sorrowing, lamentation.

mouth *noun* **1 lips**, jaws, muzzle; *informal* trap, chops, kisser; *Brit. informal* gob; *N. Amer. informal* puss. **2 entrance**, opening. **3 estuary**, delta, firth, outlet, outfall.

WORD LINKS
oral relating to the mouth

move *verb* **1 go**, walk, step, proceed, progress, advance, budge, stir, shift, change position. **2 carry**, transfer, shift, push, pull, lift, slide. **3 progress**, advance, develop, evolve, change, happen. **4 act**, take steps, do something, take measures; *informal* get moving. **5 relocate**, move house, move away/out, change address, go (away), decamp. **6 affect**, touch, impress, shake, upset, disturb. **7 inspire**, prompt, stimulate, motivate, provoke, influence, rouse, induce, incite. **8 propose**, submit, suggest, advocate, recommend, urge.
● *noun* **1 movement**, motion, action, gesture. **2 relocation**, change of house/address, transfer, posting. **3 initiative**, step, action, measure, manoeuvre, tactic, stratagem. **4 turn**, go; *Scottish* shot.

movement *noun* **1 motion**, move, gesture, sign, signal, action. **2 transportation**, shifting, conveyance, moving, transfer. **3 group**, party, faction, wing, lobby, camp. **4 campaign**, crusade, drive, push, initiative.

WORD LINKS
kinetic relating to movement

movie *noun* **film**, picture, motion picture, feature film; *informal* flick.

moving *adjective* **1 in motion**, operating, operational, working, on the move, active, movable, mobile. **2 touching**, poignant, heart-warming, heart-rending, affecting, emotional, inspiring, inspirational, stimulating, stirring.
- OPPOSITES stationary, fixed.

mow *verb* **cut**, trim, crop, clip, shear.

much *determiner* **a lot of**, a great/good deal of, a great/large amount of, plenty of, ample, abundant, plentiful; *informal* lots of, loads of, heaps of, masses of, tons of, stacks of.
- OPPOSITES little.
● *adverb* **1 greatly**, a great deal, a lot, considerably, appreciably. **2 often**, frequently, many times, regularly, habitually, routinely, usually, normally, commonly.
● *pronoun* **a lot**, a great/good deal, plenty; *informal* lots, loads, heaps, masses, tons.

muck *noun* **1 dirt**, grime, filth, mud, mess; *Brit. informal* gunge. **2 dung**, manure, excrement, droppings, ordure.

mud *noun* **dirt**, sludge, ooze, silt, clay, mire, soil.

muddle *verb* **1 confuse**, mix up, jumble (up), disarrange, disorganize, disorder, mess up. **2 bewilder**, confuse, bemuse, perplex, puzzle, baffle, mystify.
● *noun* **mess**, confusion, jumble, tangle, chaos, disorder, disarray, disorganization; *informal* shambles; *Brit. informal* omnishambles.

muddy *adjective* **1 marshy**, boggy, swampy, waterlogged, squelchy, squishy, mucky, slimy, wet, soft. **2 dirty**, filthy, mucky, grimy, soiled.

3 murky, cloudy, turbid.
- OPPOSITES clean, clear.

muffle *verb* **1 wrap (up)**, swathe, enfold, envelop, cloak. **2 deaden**, dull, dampen, mute, soften, quieten, mask, stifle, smother.

mug *noun* **beaker**, cup, tankard, glass, stein.
● *verb* **assault**, attack, set upon, beat up, rob; *informal* jump.

muggy *adjective* **humid**, close, sultry, sticky, oppressive, airless, stifling, suffocating, stuffy.
- OPPOSITES fresh.

mull *verb*
□ **mull over** ponder, consider, think over/about, reflect on, contemplate, chew over; *formal* cogitate on.

multicoloured *adjective* **kaleidoscopic**, psychedelic, colourful, many-hued, jazzy, variegated.
- OPPOSITES monochrome.

multiple *adjective* **numerous**, many, various, different, diverse, several, manifold.
- OPPOSITES single.

multiply *verb* **increase**, grow, accumulate, proliferate, mount up, mushroom, snowball.
- OPPOSITES decrease.

mumble *verb* **mutter**, murmur, talk under your breath.

mundane *adjective* **humdrum**, dull, boring, tedious, monotonous, tiresome, unexciting, uninteresting, uneventful, unremarkable, routine, ordinary.
- OPPOSITES extraordinary.

municipal *adjective* **civic**, civil, metropolitan, urban, city, town, borough, council.

murder *noun* **killing**, homicide, assassination, extermination, execution, slaughter, butchery, massacre, manslaughter; *literary* slaying.
● *verb* **kill**, put to death, assassinate, execute, butcher, slaughter, massacre, wipe out; *informal* bump off; *N. Amer. informal* ice, waste; *literary* slay.

murderer *noun* **killer**, assassin, serial killer, butcher; *informal* hit man, hired gun.

murderous *adjective* **homicidal**, brutal, violent, savage, ferocious, fierce, vicious, bloodthirsty, barbarous, barbaric, fatal, lethal, deadly.

murky *adjective* **1 dark**, gloomy, grey, leaden, dull, dim, overcast, cloudy, clouded, sunless, dismal, dreary, bleak. **2 dirty**, muddy, cloudy, turbid.
- OPPOSITES bright, clear.

murmur *noun* **1 whisper**, mutter, mumble, undertone. **2 hum**, buzz, drone.
● *verb* **mutter**, mumble, whisper, talk under your breath, talk sotto voce.

muscle *noun* **1 strength**, power, brawn; *informal* beef, beefiness. **2** *financial muscle* **influence**, power, strength, might, force, forcefulness, weight; *informal* clout.
□ **muscle in** *(informal)* interfere, force your way in, impose yourself, encroach; *informal* horn in.

muscular *adjective* **strong**, brawny, muscly, well built, burly, strapping, sturdy, powerful, athletic; *informal* hunky, beefy.

muse *verb* **ponder**, consider, think over/about, mull over, reflect on, contemplate, turn over in your mind, chew over.

musical *adjective* **tuneful**, melodic, melodious, harmonious, sweet-sounding, dulcet, euphonious, mellifluous.
- OPPOSITES discordant.

must *verb* **ought to**, should, have (got) to, need to, be obliged to, be required to, be compelled to.

muster *verb* **1 assemble**, mobilize, rally, raise, summon, gather, call up, call to arms, recruit, conscript; *US* draft. **2 congregate**, assemble, gather (together), come together, collect, convene, mass, rally. **3** *she mustered her courage* **summon (up)**, screw up, call up, rally.

mutation *noun* **1 alteration**, change, transformation, metamorphosis, transmutation. **2 mutant**, freak (of nature), deviant, monstrosity, monster.

mute *adjective* **1 silent**, speechless, dumb, unspeaking, tight-lipped, taciturn; *informal* mum. **2 wordless**, silent, dumb, unspoken.

– OPPOSITES voluble, spoken.

muted *adjective* **1 muffled**, faint, indistinct, quiet, soft, low, distant, faraway. **2 subdued**, pastel, delicate, subtle, understated, restrained.

mutilate *verb* **1 disfigure**, maim, mangle, dismember, slash, hack up. **2 vandalize**, damage, slash, deface, violate, desecrate.

mutinous *adjective* **rebellious**, insubordinate, subversive, seditious, insurgent, insurrectionary, disobedient, restive.

mutiny *noun* **insurrection**, rebellion, revolt, riot, uprising, insurgence, insubordination.

● *verb* **rise up**, rebel, revolt, riot, strike.

mutter *verb* **1 murmur**, talk under your breath, talk sotto voce, mumble, whisper. **2 grumble**, complain, grouse, carp, whine; *informal* moan, whinge.

mutual *adjective* **reciprocal**, reciprocated, requited, returned, common, joint, shared.

mysterious *adjective* **1 puzzling**, strange, peculiar, curious, funny, odd, weird, queer, bizarre, mystifying, inexplicable, baffling, perplexing, arcane, esoteric, cryptic, obscure. **2 secretive**, inscrutable, impenetrable, enigmatic, reticent, evasive.

mystery *noun* **1 puzzle**, enigma, conundrum, riddle, secret, paradox, question mark, closed book. **2 secrecy**, obscurity, uncertainty.

mystic, **mystical** *adjective* **spiritual**, religious, transcendental, paranormal, other-worldly, supernatural, occult, metaphysical.

mystify *verb* **bewilder**, puzzle, perplex, baffle, confuse, confound, bemuse, throw; *informal* flummox, stump, bamboozle.

myth *noun* **1 folk tale**, folk story, legend, fable, saga, lore, folklore. **2 misconception**, fallacy, old wives' tale, fairy story, fiction; *informal* cock and bull story.

Nn

nadir *noun* **low point**, all-time low, bottom, rock bottom; *informal* the pits.
- OPPOSITES zenith.

nag *verb* **1 harass**, keep on at, go on at, badger, chivvy, hound, plague, criticize, find fault with, moan at, grumble at, henpeck; *informal* hassle; *N. Amer. informal* ride. **2 trouble**, worry, bother, torment, niggle, prey on your mind; *informal* bug.

nail *noun* **tack**, pin, brad, hobnail, spike, staple, rivet.
● *verb* **fasten**, fix, attach, secure, affix, pin, tack, hammer.

naive *adjective* **innocent**, unsophisticated, artless, inexperienced, unworldly, trusting, gullible, credulous, immature, callow, raw, green; *informal* wet behind the ears.
- OPPOSITES worldly.

naked *adjective* **nude**, bare, in the nude, stark naked, stripped, unclothed, undressed; *informal* without a stitch on, in your birthday suit, in the raw/buff, in the altogether; *Brit. informal* starkers; *N. Amer. informal* buck naked.
- OPPOSITES dressed.

name *noun* **title**, designation, tag, nickname, sobriquet, epithet, label, honorific; *informal* moniker, handle; *formal* appellation, denomination, cognomen.
● *verb* **1 call**, dub, label, style, term, title, baptize, christen. **2 nominate**, designate, select, pick, decide on, choose.

WORD LINKS
onomastic relating to names

namely *adverb* **that is (to say)**, to be specific, specifically, viz., to wit, in other words.

nap *noun* **sleep**, catnap, siesta, doze, lie-down, rest; *informal* snooze, forty winks, shut-eye; *Brit. informal* kip, zizz.

narcotic *noun* **drug**, sedative, opiate, painkiller, analgesic, palliative.
● *adjective* **soporific**, sedative, calming, painkilling, pain-relieving, analgesic, anodyne.

narrate *verb* **tell**, relate, recount, recite, describe, chronicle, report, present.

narrative *noun* **account**, chronicle, history, description, record, report, story, tale.

narrator *noun* **storyteller**, chronicler, commentator, presenter, author.
- OPPOSITES listener, audience.

narrow *adjective* **1 slender**, slim, small, slight, attenuated, tapering, thin, tiny. **2 confined**, cramped, tight, restricted, limited, constricted, small, tiny, inadequate, insufficient.
- OPPOSITES wide, broad.
● *verb* **reduce**, restrict, limit, decrease, diminish, taper, contract, shrink, constrict.
- OPPOSITES widen.

narrowly *adverb* **(only) just**, barely, scarcely, hardly, by a hair's breadth; *informal* by a whisker.

narrow-minded *adjective* **intolerant**, illiberal, reactionary, conservative, parochial, provincial, insular, small-minded, petty, blinkered, inward-looking, hidebound, prejudiced, bigoted.
- OPPOSITES tolerant.

nasty *adjective* **1 unpleasant**, disagreeable, disgusting, vile, foul, abominable, revolting, repulsive, repellent, horrible, obnoxious, unsavoury, loathsome, noxious, foul-smelling, smelly, stinking, rank, fetid, malodorous; *informal* ghastly, horrid, yucky; *N. Amer. informal* lousy; *literary* noisome. **2 unkind**, unpleasant, unfriendly, disagreeable, rude, spiteful, malicious, mean, vicious, malevolent, hurtful. **3** *a nasty accident* **serious**, dangerous, bad, awful,

dreadful, terrible, severe, painful.
- OPPOSITES nice, pleasant.

nation *noun* **country**, state, land, realm, kingdom, republic, people, race, tribe.

national *adjective* **1** *national politics* **state**, public, federal, governmental. **2** *a national strike* **nationwide**, countrywide, general, widespread.
- OPPOSITES local, international.
● *noun* **citizen**, subject, native, resident, inhabitant, voter, passport holder.

nationalism *noun* **patriotism**, allegiance, xenophobia, chauvinism, jingoism, flag-waving.

nationwide *adjective* **national**, countrywide, state, general, widespread, extensive.
- OPPOSITES local.

native *noun* **inhabitant**, resident, local, citizen, national, countryman.
- OPPOSITES foreigner.
● *adjective* **1** *native species* **indigenous**, original, local, domestic. **2** *native wit* **innate**, inborn, natural, inherent, intrinsic.

n

natural *adjective* **1 unprocessed**, organic, pure, unrefined, additive-free, green, GM-free. **2** *a natural occurrence* **normal**, ordinary, everyday, usual, regular, common, commonplace, typical, routine, standard, logical, understandable, (only) to be expected, predictable. **3** *a natural leader* **born**, instinctive, congenital, pathological. **4** *his natural instincts* **innate**, inborn, inherent, native, inherited, hereditary. **5** *she seemed very natural* **unaffected**, spontaneous, uninhibited, relaxed, unselfconscious, genuine, open, artless, guileless, unpretentious, unstudied.
- OPPOSITES abnormal, artificial, affected.

naturally *adverb* **of course**, as might be expected, needless to say, obviously, clearly, it goes without saying.

nature *noun* **1 the natural world**, the environment, Mother Earth, the universe, the cosmos, wildlife, the countryside, the land. **2 character**, personality, disposition, temperament, make-up, psyche. **3 kind**, sort, type, variety, category, class, genre, order, quality, complexion; *N. Amer.* stripe.

naughty *adjective* **1 badly behaved**, disobedient, bad, wayward, defiant, unruly, insubordinate, wilful, delinquent, undisciplined, refractory, disruptive, attention-seeking, mischievous, impish. **2 indecent**, risqué, rude, racy, vulgar, dirty, filthy, smutty, crude, coarse.
- OPPOSITES well behaved, clean.

nausea *noun* **sickness**, biliousness, queasiness, vomiting, retching.

nautical *adjective* **maritime**, marine, naval, seafaring, seagoing, sailing.

navigate *verb* **steer**, pilot, guide, direct, captain; *informal* skipper.

navy *noun* **fleet**, flotilla, armada.

near *adjective* **1 close**, nearby, (close/near) at hand, a stone's throw away, neighbouring, within reach, accessible, handy, convenient; *informal* within spitting distance. **2 imminent**, in the offing, on its way, coming, impending, looming.
- OPPOSITES far, distant.

nearby *adjective* **not far away**, not far off, close at hand, close by, near, within reach, neighbouring, local, accessible, convenient, handy.
- OPPOSITES distant.

nearly *adverb* **almost**, just about, more or less, practically, virtually, all but, as good as, not far off, to all intents and purposes, not quite; *informal* pretty well.

neat *adjective* **1 tidy**, orderly, well ordered, in (good) order, spick and span, uncluttered, shipshape, straight, trim. **2 smart**, spruce, dapper, trim, well groomed, well turned out; *informal* natty. **3** *his neat footwork* **skilful**, deft, dexterous, adroit, adept, expert, nimble, elegant, graceful, accurate; *informal* nifty. **4** *a neat solution* **clever**, ingenious, inventive, imaginative. **5** *neat gin* **undiluted**, straight, pure.
- OPPOSITES untidy.

necessarily *adverb* **as a consequence**, as a result, automatically, as a matter of course, certainly, incontrovertibly, inevitably, unavoidably, inescapably, of necessity.

necessary *adjective* **1 obligatory**, required, requisite, compulsory, mandatory, imperative, needed, essential, vital, indispensable, de rigueur; *formal* needful. **2** *a necessary consequence* **inevitable**, unavoidable, inescapable, inexorable.

necessity *noun* **1 essential**, prerequisite, requisite, sine qua non; *informal* must-have. **2** *political necessity forced him to resign* **force of circumstance**, obligation, need, exigency.

need *verb* **require**, be in need of, want, be crying out for, demand, call for, necessitate, entail, involve, lack, be without, be short of.
● *noun* **1** *there's no need to apologize* **necessity**, requirement, call, demand. **2** *basic human needs* **requirement**, necessity, want, requisite, prerequisite, desideratum. **3** *my hour of need* **difficulty**, trouble, distress, crisis, emergency, urgency, extremity.

needed *adjective* **necessary**, required, called for, wanted, desired, lacking.
– OPPOSITES optional.

needless *adjective* **unnecessary**, unneeded, uncalled for, gratuitous, pointless, superfluous, redundant, excessive.
– OPPOSITES necessary.

needy *adjective* **poor**, deprived, disadvantaged, underprivileged, in need, hard up, poverty-stricken, impoverished, destitute, penniless; *informal* broke, strapped (for cash); *Brit. informal* skint; *dated* needful.
– OPPOSITES wealthy.

negative *adjective* **1 pessimistic**, defeatist, gloomy, critical, cynical, fatalistic, dismissive, unenthusiastic, apathetic, unresponsive. **2 harmful**, bad, adverse, damaging, detrimental, unfavourable, disadvantageous.
– OPPOSITES positive, optimistic, favourable.

neglect *verb* **1 fail to look after**, leave alone, abandon, ignore, pay no attention to, let slide, not attend to, be remiss about, be lax about, shirk. **2 fail**, omit, forget.
– OPPOSITES cherish, remember.
● *noun* **1 disrepair**, dilapidation, shabbiness, abandonment, disuse. **2 negligence**, dereliction (of duty), carelessness, laxity, slackness, irresponsibility.
– OPPOSITES care.

neglected *adjective* **1** *neglected animals* **uncared for**, abandoned, mistreated, maltreated. **2** *a neglected cottage* **derelict**, dilapidated, tumbledown, ramshackle, untended. **3** *a neglected masterpiece* **disregarded**, forgotten, overlooked, ignored, unrecognized, unnoticed, unsung, underrated.

negligent *adjective* **neglectful**, remiss, careless, lax, irresponsible, inattentive, thoughtless, uncaring, unmindful, forgetful, slack, sloppy; *N. Amer.* derelict.
– OPPOSITES dutiful.

negligible *adjective* **trivial**, trifling, insignificant, unimportant, of no account, minor, inconsequential, minimal, small, slight, infinitesimal, minuscule.
– OPPOSITES significant.

negotiate *verb* **1 discuss (terms)**, talk, consult, confer, debate, compromise, bargain, haggle. **2 arrange**, broker, work out, thrash out, complete, close, conclude, agree on. **3 get round**, get past, get over, clear, cross, surmount, overcome, deal with, cope with.

negotiation *noun* **1 discussion(s)**, talks, conference, debate, dialogue, consultation. **2 arrangement**, brokering, settlement, conclusion, completion.

negotiator *noun* **mediator**, arbitrator, moderator, go-between, middleman, intermediary, representative, spokesperson, broker.

neighbourhood *noun* **1 district**, area, locality, locale, quarter, community; *informal* neck of the woods; *N. Amer. informal* hood. **2 vicinity**, environs.

neighbouring *adjective* **adjacent**, adjoining, bordering, connecting, next-door, nearby, in the vicinity.
- OPPOSITES remote.

neighbourly *adjective* **obliging**, helpful, friendly, kind, considerate, amicable, sociable, hospitable, companionable, civil, cordial.
- OPPOSITES unfriendly.

nerve *noun* **1 confidence**, assurance, courage, bravery, determination, will power, spirit, grit; *informal* guts; *Brit. informal* bottle; *N. Amer. informal* moxie. **2 audacity**, cheek, effrontery, gall, temerity, presumption, impudence, impertinence, arrogance; *informal* face, front, brass neck, chutzpah. **3** (**nerves**) **anxiety**, tension, nervousness, stress, worry, cold feet, apprehension; *informal* butterflies (in your stomach), collywobbles, jitters, the heebie-jeebies.

n

WORD LINKS
neural relating to nerves in the body

nervous *adjective* **anxious**, worried, apprehensive, on edge, edgy, tense, stressed, agitated, uneasy, restless, worked up, keyed up, overwrought, jumpy, on tenterhooks, highly strung, nervy, excitable, neurotic; *informal* jittery, twitchy, in a state, uptight, wired, trepidatious; *N. Amer. informal* squirrelly.
- OPPOSITES relaxed, calm.

nestle *verb* **snuggle**, cuddle, huddle, nuzzle, settle, burrow.

net[1] *noun* **netting**, mesh, tulle, fishnet, lace, openwork.
● *verb* **catch**, capture, trap, snare; *informal* nab, bag, collar, bust; *Brit. informal* nick.

net[2] *adjective* **after tax**, after deductions, take-home, final.
- OPPOSITES gross.
● *verb* **earn**, make, clear, take home, bring in, pocket, realize.

network *noun* **web**, lattice, net, matrix, mesh, criss-cross, grid, maze, labyrinth, warren, tangle.

neurotic *adjective* **highly strung**, oversensitive, nervous, tense, paranoid, obsessive, fixated, hysterical, overwrought, irrational.
- OPPOSITES stable, calm.

neutral *adjective* **1 impartial**, unbiased, unprejudiced, objective, open-minded, non-partisan, even-handed, disinterested, dispassionate, detached, non-aligned, unaffiliated, uninvolved. **2 inoffensive**, bland, unobjectionable, unexceptionable, anodyne, uncontroversial, safe, harmless, innocuous. **3 pale**, light, colourless, indeterminate, drab, insipid, nondescript, dull.
- OPPOSITES biased, provocative.

neutralize *verb* **counteract**, offset, counterbalance, balance, cancel out, nullify, negate.

never-ending *adjective* **incessant**, continuous, ceaseless, constant, continual, perpetual, uninterrupted, unbroken, steady, unremitting, relentless, persistent, interminable, non-stop, endless, unending.

nevertheless *adverb* **nonetheless**, even so, however, still, yet, in spite of that, despite that, be that as it may, notwithstanding.

new *adjective* **1 recent**, up to date, the latest, current, state-of-the-art, contemporary, advanced, cutting-edge, modern, avant-garde. **2 unused**, brand new, pristine, fresh. **3 different**, another, alternative, additional, extra, supplementary, further, unfamiliar, unknown, strange. **4 reinvigorated**, restored, revived, improved, refreshed, regenerated.
- OPPOSITES old, second-hand.

newcomer *noun* **1 incomer**, immigrant, settler, stranger, outsider, foreigner, alien; *informal* new kid on the block, johnny-come-lately; *Austral. informal* blow-in. **2 beginner**, novice, learner, trainee, apprentice, probationer; *informal* rookie, newbie; *N. Amer. informal* tenderfoot.

newly *adverb* **recently**, only just, lately, freshly, not long ago.

news *noun* **report**, story, account, announcement, press release, communication, communiqué, bulletin, intelligence, information, word, revelation, disclosure, exposé; *Brit.* stop press; *informal* scoop; *literary* tidings.

newspaper *noun* **paper**, journal, gazette, news-sheet, tabloid, broadsheet, periodical; *Brit.* red top; *informal* rag.

next *adjective* **1 following**, succeeding, subsequent, ensuing, upcoming, to come. **2 neighbouring**, adjacent, adjoining, next-door, bordering, connected, closest, nearest; *formal* contiguous, proximate.
- OPPOSITES previous.
● *adverb* **afterwards**, after, then, later, subsequently; *formal* thereafter.

nice *adjective* **1** *have a nice time* **enjoyable**, pleasant, agreeable, good, pleasurable, satisfying, entertaining, amusing; *informal* lovely, great; *N. Amer. informal* neat. **2** *nice people* **pleasant**, likeable, agreeable, personable, good-natured, congenial, amiable, affable, genial, friendly, charming, delightful, engaging, sympathetic, polite, courteous, well mannered, civil, kind, obliging, helpful. **3** *nice weather* **fine**, dry, sunny, warm, mild, clement. **4** *a nice distinction* **subtle**, fine, slight, delicate, precise.
- OPPOSITES unpleasant, nasty.

niche *noun* **1 recess**, alcove, nook, cranny, hollow, bay, cavity, pigeonhole. **2 position**, slot, place, vocation, calling, métier, station, job, level.

nick *noun* **cut**, scratch, incision, notch, chip, dent, indentation.
● *verb* **cut**, scratch, graze, chip, dent.

nickname *noun* **pet name**, diminutive, endearment, tag, label, sobriquet, epithet; *informal* handle, moniker.

night *noun* **night-time**, (hours of) darkness, dark.
- OPPOSITES day.

WORD LINKS
nocturnal occurring or active at night

nightfall *noun* **sunset**, sundown, dusk, twilight, evening, dark; *literary* eventide.
- OPPOSITES dawn.

nightmare *noun* **ordeal**, trial, hell, misery, agony, torture, murder, purgatory, disaster; *informal* the pits.

nil *noun* **nothing**, none, nought, zero; *Tennis* love; *Cricket* a duck.

nimble *adjective* **1 agile**, light, quick, lithe, skilful, deft, dexterous, adroit, sprightly, spry; *informal* nippy. **2** *a nimble mind* **quick**, alert, lively, astute, perceptive, penetrating, discerning, shrewd, sharp, intelligent, bright, smart, clever, brilliant; *informal* quick on the uptake.
- OPPOSITES clumsy.

nip *verb* & *noun* **bite**, nibble, peck, pinch, tweak.

no *adverb* **absolutely not**, of course not, under no circumstances, not at all, never; *informal* nope, no way, not a chance, not on your life; *Brit. informal* no fear; *old use* nay.
- OPPOSITES yes.

noble *adjective* **1 aristocratic**, blue-blooded, patrician, high-born, titled. **2 worthy**, righteous, good, honourable, virtuous, upright. **3 magnificent**, splendid, grand, impressive, stately, imposing, dignified, proud, striking, majestic.
- OPPOSITES humble, lowly.
● *noun* **aristocrat**, nobleman, noblewoman, lord, lady, peer (of the realm), peeress, patrician; *informal* aristo.
- OPPOSITES commoner.

nod *verb* **1 incline**, bob, bow, dip. **2 signal**, gesture, gesticulate, motion, sign, indicate.

noise *noun* **sound**, din, hubbub, clamour, racket, uproar, tumult, commotion, pandemonium; *Brit.* row; *informal* hullabaloo.
- OPPOSITES silence.

noisy *adjective* **1 raucous**, rowdy, strident, clamorous, vociferous, boisterous. **2 loud**, blaring, booming, deafening, thunderous, ear-splitting, piercing, cacophonous, tumultuous.
- OPPOSITES quiet, soft.

nominal *adjective* **1 in name only**, titular, formal, official, theoretical, supposed, ostensible, so-called, self-styled. **2 token**, symbolic, minimal; *Brit.* peppercorn.
- OPPOSITES real, considerable.

nominate *verb* **1 propose**, put forward, put up, submit, present, recommend, suggest. **2 appoint**, choose, decide on, select, designate, assign.

nonchalant *adjective* **calm**, composed, unconcerned, cool, imperturbable, casual, blasé, offhand, insouciant; *informal* laid-back.
- OPPOSITES anxious.

non-committal *adjective* **evasive**, equivocal, guarded, circumspect, reserved; *informal* cagey.

nonconformist *noun* **dissenter**, protester, rebel, freethinker, individualist, free spirit, maverick, renegade, schismatic, apostate, heretic.

nondescript *adjective* **undistinguished**, unremarkable, featureless, unmemorable, ordinary, average, run-of-the-mill, mundane, uninteresting, uninspiring, colourless, bland.
- OPPOSITES distinctive.

non-existent *adjective* **imaginary**, imagined, unreal, fictional, fictitious, made up, invented, fanciful, mythical, illusory.
- OPPOSITES real.

nonsense *noun* **1 rubbish**, gibberish, claptrap, balderdash, garbage; *informal* baloney, bosh, tripe, drivel, gobbledegook, mumbo-jumbo, poppycock, twaddle, guff, tosh, bilge, hogwash, piffle; *Brit. informal* cobblers, codswallop, double Dutch, rot. **2 mischief**, misbehaviour; *informal* tomfoolery, monkey business, shenanigans, malarkey; *Brit. informal* monkey tricks, jiggery-pokery.
- OPPOSITES sense.

non-stop *adjective* **continuous**, constant, continual, incessant, ceaseless, uninterrupted, unbroken, never-ending, perpetual, round-the-clock, persistent, steady, unremitting, relentless, interminable.
- OPPOSITES intermittent, occasional.
● *adverb* **continuously**, continually, incessantly, ceaselessly, all the time, constantly, perpetually, persistently, steadily, relentlessly, interminably; *informal* 24-7.

noon *noun* **midday**, twelve o'clock, twelve hundred hours, high noon, noonday.

norm *noun* **standard**, convention, criterion, yardstick, benchmark, touchstone, rule, formula, pattern.
□ **the norm** normal, usual, the rule, standard, typical, average, par for the course, expected.

normal *adjective* **1 usual**, standard, ordinary, customary, conventional, habitual, accustomed, typical, common, regular, routine, traditional, commonplace, everyday. **2 ordinary**, average, run-of-the-mill, middle-of-the-road, conventional, mainstream; *N. Amer.* garden-variety; *Brit. informal* common or garden, bog-standard. **3 sane**, in your right mind, right in the head, of sound mind, compos mentis; *informal* all there.
- OPPOSITES unusual, insane.

normally *adverb* **1 naturally**, conventionally, properly, like everyone else. **2 usually**, ordinarily, as a rule, generally, in general, mostly, on the whole, typically, habitually.

nose *noun* **snout**, muzzle, proboscis, trunk; *informal* beak, conk, schnozz, hooter.
● *verb* **1 pry**, enquire, poke about/around, interfere (in), meddle (in), stick/poke your nose in; *informal* snoop; *Austral./NZ informal* stickybeak. **2 ease**, inch, edge, move, manoeuvre, steer, guide.

WORD LINKS
nasal relating to the nose

nostalgic *adjective* **wistful**, sentimental, emotional, homesick, regretful, dewy-eyed, maudlin.

nosy *adjective (informal)* **prying**, inquisitive, curious, spying, eavesdropping, intrusive; *informal* snooping.

notable *adjective* **1 noteworthy**, remarkable, outstanding, important, significant, memorable, marked, striking, impressive, momentous, uncommon. **2 prominent**, well known, famous, famed, noted, of note.
- OPPOSITES unremarkable, unknown.
● *noun* **celebrity**, VIP, dignitary, luminary, star, big name, personage; *informal* celeb, bigwig.

notably *adverb* **1 in particular**, particularly, especially, primarily, principally, chiefly. **2 remarkably**, especially, exceptionally, singularly, particularly, peculiarly, distinctly, significantly, unusually, uncommonly, conspicuously.

notch *noun* **nick**, cut, incision, score, scratch, slit, snick, slot, groove.

note *noun* **1 record**, entry, reminder, comment, jotting. **2 message**, letter, line, missive; *informal* memo; *formal* memorandum, epistle. **3 annotation**, footnote, marginalia. **4** *(Brit.)* **banknote**; *N. Amer.* bill; *US informal* greenback. **5** *the note of hopelessness in her voice* **tone**, hint, indication, sign, element, suggestion, sense.
● *verb* **1 bear in mind**, be mindful of, consider, take notice of, register, be aware, take in, notice, observe, see, perceive. **2 write down**, put down, jot down, take down, scribble, enter, mark, record, register, pencil in.

notebook *noun* **notepad**, exercise book, register, logbook, log, diary, journal, record; *Brit.* jotter, pocketbook; *trademark* Filofax.

noted *adjective* **famous**, famed, well known, renowned, prominent, notable, important, eminent, great, acclaimed, celebrated, distinguished.
- OPPOSITES unknown.

noteworthy *adjective* **notable**, interesting, significant, important, remarkable, striking, memorable, unique, special, unusual.
- OPPOSITES unexceptional.

nothing *noun* **1 not a thing**, zero; *N. English* nowt; *informal* zilch, sweet FA, not a dicky bird; *N. Amer. informal* zip, nada, diddly-squat. **2 zero**, nought, nil, 0; *Tennis* love; *Cricket* a duck.

notice *verb* **observe**, note, see, discern, detect, spot, perceive, make out; *Brit. informal* clock.
- OPPOSITES overlook.
● *noun* **1 sign**, announcement, advertisement, poster, placard, bill, handbill, flyer. **2 attention**, observation, awareness, consciousness, perception, regard, consideration, scrutiny; *formal* cognizance. **3** *advance notice of the price increase* **notification**, warning, information, news, word.

noticeable *adjective* **obvious**, evident, apparent, manifest, plain, clear, conspicuous, perceptible, discernible, detectable, observable, visible, appreciable, unmistakable, patent.
- OPPOSITES imperceptible.

notify *verb* **inform**, tell, let someone know, advise, apprise, alert, warn.

notion *noun* **idea**, impression, belief, opinion, view, concept, conception, understanding, feeling, suspicion, intuition, inkling.

notorious *adjective* **infamous**, scandalous, disreputable, of ill repute.

nought *noun* **nil**, zero, nothing; *Tennis* love; *Cricket* a duck; *informal* zilch; *N. Amer. informal* zip, nada.

nourish *verb* **feed**, sustain, provide for, care for, nurture.

nourishing *adjective* **nutritious**, wholesome, good for you, nutritive, healthy, health-giving, beneficial.
- OPPOSITES unhealthy.

nourishment *noun* **food**, nutriment, nutrients, nutrition, sustenance.

novel[1] *noun* **story**, tale, narrative, romance, novella.

novel[2] *adjective* **new**, original, unusual, unconventional, unorthodox, different,

fresh, imaginative, innovative, unfamiliar, surprising.
- OPPOSITES traditional.

novelty *noun* **1 originality**, newness, freshness, unconventionality, innovation, unfamiliarity. **2 knick-knack**, trinket, bauble, toy, trifle, ornament; *N. Amer.* kickshaw.

novice *noun* **beginner**, learner, newcomer, fledgling, trainee, probationer, student, pupil, apprentice, tyro, neophyte; *informal* rookie, newbie; *N. Amer. informal* tenderfoot, greenhorn.
- OPPOSITES expert, veteran.

now *adverb* **1 at the moment**, at present, presently, at this moment in time, currently, nowadays, these days, today, in this day and age. **2 at once**, straight away, right away, this minute, this instant, immediately, instantly, directly; *informal* pronto, asap.

noxious *adjective* **poisonous**, toxic, deadly, harmful, dangerous, environmentally unfriendly, polluting, unhealthy, unpleasant.
- OPPOSITES innocuous.

n

nuance *noun* **distinction**, shade, gradation, refinement, degree, subtlety, nicety.

nucleus *noun* **core**, centre, heart, kernel, nub, hub, middle, focus.

nude *adjective* **naked**, stark naked, bare, unclothed, undressed, stripped; *informal* without a stitch on, in your birthday suit, in the raw/buff, in the altogether; *Brit. informal* starkers; *N. Amer. informal* buck naked.
- OPPOSITES dressed.

nudge *verb* **prod**, elbow, dig, poke, jab, jog, push, touch.
● *noun* **prod**, dig (in the ribs), poke, jab, push.

nuisance *noun* **annoyance**, inconvenience, bore, bother, irritation, trial, burden, pest; *informal* pain (in the neck), hassle, bind, drag, headache.

nullify *verb* **annul**, render null and void, invalidate, repeal, reverse, rescind, revoke, cancel, neutralize, negate, counteract.

numb *adjective* **1 without feeling**, without sensation, dead, numbed, desensitized, frozen, anaesthetized, insensible, insensate. **2 dazed**, stunned, stupefied, paralysed, immobilized.
● *verb* **1 deaden**, desensitize, anaesthetize, immobilize, freeze. **2 daze**, stun, stupefy, paralyse, immobilize.

number *noun* **1 numeral**, integer, figure, digit, character. **2 quantity**, total, aggregate, tally, quota. **3 song**, piece, tune, track, dance.
● *verb* **1 add up to**, amount to, total, come to. **2 include**, count, reckon, deem.

WORD LINKS
numerical relating to numbers

numerous *adjective* **many**, a number of, a lot of/lots of, several, plenty of, countless, copious, an abundance of, frequent; *informal* umpteen.
- OPPOSITES few.

nurse *verb* **1 care for**, take care of, look after, tend, minister to. **2** *they nursed old grievances* **harbour**, foster, bear, have, hold (on to), retain.

nurture *verb* **1 bring up**, care for, take care of, look after, tend, rear, raise. **2** *he nurtured my love of art* **encourage**, promote, stimulate, develop, foster, cultivate, boost, strengthen, fuel.
- OPPOSITES neglect.

nut *noun (informal)* **1 maniac**, lunatic, madman, madwoman; *informal* loony, nutcase, head case; *Brit. informal* nutter; *N. Amer. informal* screwball. **2 enthusiast**, fan, devotee, aficionado; *informal* freak, fanatic, addict, buff.

nutritious *adjective* **nourishing**, nutritive, wholesome, good for you, healthy, health-giving, beneficial.

Oo

oath *noun* **1 vow**, pledge, promise, affirmation, word (of honour), guarantee. **2 swear word**, expletive, profanity, four-letter word, dirty word, obscenity, curse; *formal* imprecation.

obedient *adjective* **compliant**, biddable, acquiescent, good, law-abiding, deferential, governable, docile, submissive.
– OPPOSITES rebellious.

obey *verb* **1 do as you are told**, defer to, submit to, bow to. **2** *he refused to obey the order* **carry out**, perform, act on, execute, discharge, implement. **3** *rules have to be obeyed* **comply with**, adhere to, observe, abide by, act in accordance with, conform to, respect, follow, keep to, stick to.
– OPPOSITES defy, ignore.

object *noun* **1 thing**, article, item, entity, device, gadget. **2 target**, butt, focus, recipient, victim. **3 objective**, aim, goal, target, purpose, end, plan, point, ambition, intention, idea.
● *verb they objected to the scheme* **protest about**, oppose, take exception to, take issue with, take a stand against, argue against, quarrel with, condemn, draw the line at, demur at, mind, complain about.
– OPPOSITES approve of, accept.

objection *noun* **protest**, protestation, complaint, opposition, demurral, counter-argument, disagreement, disapproval, dissent.

objective *adjective* **1 impartial**, unbiased, unprejudiced, non-partisan, disinterested, neutral, uninvolved, even-handed, fair, dispassionate, detached. **2 factual**, actual, real, empirical, verifiable.
– OPPOSITES subjective, emotional.
● *noun* **aim**, intention, purpose, target, goal, object, end, idea, plan, ambition.

objectively *adverb* **impartially**, without bias/prejudice, even-handedly, fairly, dispassionately, with an open mind, without fear or favour.

obligation *noun* **1 commitment**, duty, responsibility, function, task, job, charge, onus, liability, requirement, debt. **2** *a sense of obligation* **duty**, compulsion, indebtedness, necessity, pressure, constraint.

obligatory *adjective* **compulsory**, mandatory, prescribed, required, statutory, enforced, binding, requisite, necessary, imperative, de rigueur.
– OPPOSITES optional.

oblige *verb* **1 compel**, force, require, make, bind, constrain. **2 do someone a favour**, accommodate, help, assist, indulge, humour.

obliged *adjective* **thankful**, grateful, appreciative, beholden, indebted, in someone's debt.

obliging *adjective* **helpful**, accommodating, cooperative, agreeable, amenable, generous, kind; *Brit. informal* decent.

obliterate *verb* **1 destroy**, wipe out, annihilate, demolish; *informal* zap. **2 hide**, obscure, blot out, block, cover, screen.

oblivious *adjective* **unaware**, unconscious, heedless, unmindful, insensible, ignorant, blind, deaf, impervious.
– OPPOSITES conscious.

obscene *adjective* **1 pornographic**, indecent, smutty, dirty, filthy, X-rated, explicit, lewd, rude, vulgar, coarse, scatological; *informal* blue; *euphemistic* adult. **2 scandalous**, shocking, outrageous, immoral.

obscure *adjective* **1 unclear**, uncertain, unknown, mysterious, hazy, vague, indeterminate. **2 abstruse**, oblique, opaque, cryptic, arcane, enigmatic, puzzling, perplexing, baffling, incomprehensible, impenetrable, elliptical.

3 little known, unknown, unheard of, unsung, minor, unrecognized, forgotten.
- OPPOSITES clear, plain, famous.
● *verb* **1 hide**, conceal, cover, veil, shroud, screen, mask, cloak, block, obliterate, eclipse. **2 confuse**, complicate, obfuscate, cloud, blur, muddy.
- OPPOSITES reveal, clarify.

observant *adjective* **alert**, sharp-eyed, eagle-eyed, attentive, watchful; *informal* beady-eyed, on the ball.
- OPPOSITES inattentive.

observation *noun* **1 monitoring**, watching, scrutiny, survey, surveillance, attention, study. **2 remark**, comment, opinion, impression, thought, reflection.

observe *verb* **1 notice**, see, note, perceive, discern, spot. **2 watch**, look at, contemplate, view, survey, regard, keep an eye on, scrutinize, keep under surveillance, monitor; *informal* keep tabs on. **3 remark**, comment, say, mention, declare, announce, state; *formal* opine. **4 comply with**, abide by, keep, obey, adhere to, heed, honour, fulfil, respect, follow, consent to, accept.

observer *noun* **spectator**, onlooker, watcher, fly on the wall, viewer, witness.

obsessed *adjective* **fixated**, possessed, haunted, consumed, infatuated, besotted; *informal* smitten, hung up.

obsession *noun* **fixation**, passion, mania, compulsion, fetish, preoccupation, infatuation, hobby horse, phobia, complex, neurosis; *informal* bee in your bonnet, hang-up, thing.

obsessive *adjective* **consuming**, all-consuming, compulsive, controlling, fanatical, neurotic, excessive; *informal* pathological.

obsolete *adjective* **out of date**, outdated, outmoded, old-fashioned, passé, antiquated, antediluvian, anachronistic, superannuated, archaic, ancient, fossilized, extinct, defunct; *informal* out of the ark; *Brit. informal* past its sell-by date.
- OPPOSITES current, modern.

obstacle *noun* **barrier**, hurdle, stumbling block, obstruction, bar, block, impediment, hindrance, snag, catch, drawback, hitch, fly in the ointment, handicap, difficulty, problem, disadvantage; *Brit.* spanner in the works.
- OPPOSITES advantage, aid.

obstinate *adjective* **stubborn**, pig-headed, mulish, self-willed, unyielding, inflexible, unbending, intransigent, intractable; *old use* contumacious.
- OPPOSITES compliant.

obstruct *verb* **1 block (up)**, clog (up), cut off, bung up, choke, dam up; *technical* occlude. **2 impede**, hinder, interfere with, hamper, block, interrupt, hold up, stand in the way of, frustrate, slow down, delay, bring to a standstill, stop, halt.
- OPPOSITES clear, facilitate.

obstruction *noun* **obstacle**, barrier, stumbling block, impediment, hindrance, difficulty, check, restriction, blockage, stoppage, congestion, bottleneck, hold-up.

obtain *verb* **get**, acquire, come by, secure, procure, pick up, gain, earn, achieve, attain; *informal* get hold of, lay your hands on, land.

obtainable *adjective* **available**, to be had, in circulation, on the market, on offer, in season, at your disposal, accessible; *informal* up for grabs, on tap.

obvious *adjective* **clear**, plain, evident, apparent, patent, manifest, conspicuous, pronounced, prominent, distinct, noticeable, unmistakable, perceptible, visible, palpable; *informal* sticking out a mile.
- OPPOSITES imperceptible.

occasion *noun* **1 time**, instance, juncture, point, moment, experience, case. **2 event**, affair, function, celebration, party, get-together, gathering; *informal* do, bash.
● *verb* **cause**, give rise to, bring about, result in, lead to, prompt, create, engender.

occasional *adjective* **infrequent**, intermittent, irregular, periodic, sporadic,

odd; *N. Amer.* sometime.
- OPPOSITES regular, frequent.

occasionally *adverb* **sometimes**, from time to time, (every) now and then, (every) now and again, at times, every so often, (every) once in a while, on occasion, periodically.
- OPPOSITES often.

occult *adjective* **supernatural**, magic, magical, satanic, mystical, unearthly, esoteric, psychic.
□ **the occult** the supernatural, magic, black magic, witchcraft, necromancy, the black arts, occultism.

occupant *noun* **resident**, inhabitant, owner, householder, tenant, leaseholder, lessee; *Brit.* occupier, owner-occupier.

occupation *noun* **1 job**, profession, work, line of work, trade, employment, business, career, métier, calling. **2 pastime**, activity, hobby, pursuit, interest, entertainment, recreation. **3 conquest**, capture, invasion, seizure, annexation, colonization, subjugation.

occupied *adjective* **1 busy**, working, at work, active; *informal* tied up, hard at it, on the go. **2 in use**, full, engaged, taken.

occupy *verb* **1 live in**, inhabit, lodge in, tenant, move into, people, populate, settle; *Scottish* stay in. **2 engage**, busy, distract, absorb, engross, hold, interest, involve, entertain. **3** *the region was occupied by Japan* **capture**, seize, conquer, invade, colonize, annex, subjugate.

occur *verb* **1 happen**, take place, come about, transpire; *N. Amer. informal* go down. **2 be found**, be present, exist, appear, develop, manifest itself.
□ **occur to** enter your head, cross your mind, come/spring to mind, strike, dawn on, suggest itself.

occurrence *noun* **1 event**, incident, happening, phenomenon, circumstance, episode. **2 existence**, instance, appearance, frequency, incidence, prevalence, rate; *Statistics* distribution.

odd *adjective* **1 strange**, peculiar, queer, funny, bizarre, eccentric, unconventional, outlandish, unusual, weird, curious, abnormal, puzzling, mystifying, baffling, unaccountable; *informal* wacky. **2** *odd jobs* **occasional**, casual, irregular, isolated, sporadic, periodic, miscellaneous, various, varied, sundry. **3** *an odd shoe* **mismatched**, unmatched, unpaired, single, lone, solitary, extra, leftover, spare.
- OPPOSITES normal, ordinary, regular.

odds *plural noun* **likelihood**, probability, chances.
□ **odds and ends** bits and pieces, bits and bobs, stuff, paraphernalia, sundries, bric-a-brac, knick-knacks, oddments; *informal* junk; *Brit. informal* odds and sods, clobber, gubbins.

odour *noun* **smell**, stench, stink, reek, aroma, bouquet, scent, perfume, fragrance; *Brit. informal* pong, whiff, niff; *N. Amer. informal* funk; *literary* redolence.

WORD LINKS
olfactory relating to odour

odyssey *noun* **journey**, voyage, trip, trek, travels, quest, crusade, pilgrimage.

off *adjective* **1 away**, absent, off duty, on holiday/leave; *N. Amer.* on vacation. **2 cancelled**, postponed, called off. **3 rotten**, bad, stale, mouldy, sour, rancid, turned, spoiled.

offence *noun* **1 crime**, illegal act, misdemeanour, felony, infringement, violation, wrongdoing, sin. **2 annoyance**, resentment, indignation, displeasure, bad feeling, animosity.

offend *verb* **1 upset**, give offence to, affront, hurt someone's feelings, insult, hurt, wound, slight. **2 break the law**, commit a crime, do wrong.

offender *noun* **wrongdoer**, criminal, lawbreaker, crook, villain, miscreant, felon, delinquent, malefactor, culprit, guilty party.

offensive *adjective* **1 insulting**, rude, derogatory, disrespectful, personal,

hurtful, upsetting, wounding, abusive. **2 unpleasant**, disagreeable, nasty, distasteful, objectionable, off-putting, dreadful, frightful, obnoxious, abominable, disgusting, repulsive, repellent, vile, foul, horrible, sickening, nauseating; *informal* ghastly, horrid, gross; *Brit. informal* beastly. **3 hostile**, attacking, aggressive, invading, incursive, combative, threatening, martial, warlike, belligerent, bellicose.
- OPPOSITES complimentary, pleasant, defensive.
● *noun* **attack**, assault, onslaught, invasion, push, thrust, charge, raid, incursion, blitz, campaign.

offer *verb* **1 put forward**, proffer, give, present, come up with, suggest, propose, advance, submit, tender. **2 volunteer**, step/come forward, show willing. **3 bid**, tender, put in a bid/offer of.
- OPPOSITES withdraw, refuse.
● *noun* **1 proposal**, proposition, suggestion, submission, approach, overture. **2 bid**, tender, bidding price.

offering *noun* **contribution**, donation, gift, present, sacrifice, tribute.

offhand *adjective* **casual**, careless, uninterested, indifferent, cool, nonchalant, blasé, insouciant, cavalier, glib, perfunctory, cursory, dismissive.

office *noun* **1 place of work**, workplace, workroom. **2** *the company's Paris office* **branch**, division, section, bureau, department. **3** *the office of President* **post**, position, appointment, job, occupation, role, situation, function.

officer *noun* **official**, functionary, executive.

official *adjective* **1 authorized**, approved, validated, authenticated, certified, accredited, endorsed, sanctioned, licensed, recognized, legitimate, legal, lawful, valid, bona fide, proper; *informal* kosher. **2 ceremonial**, formal, solemn, bureaucratic.
- OPPOSITES unauthorized, informal.
● *noun* **officer**, executive, functionary, administrator, bureaucrat, mandarin, representative, agent; *derogatory* apparatchik.

officious *adjective* **self-important**, bumptious, self-assertive, overbearing, interfering, intrusive, meddlesome, meddling; *informal* bossy.

offset *verb* **counteract**, balance (out), even out/up, counterbalance, compensate for, make up for, neutralize, cancel (out).

offspring *noun* **children**, family, progeny, young, brood, descendants, heirs, successors; *informal* kids; *Brit. informal* sprogs, brats.

often *adverb* **frequently**, many times, a lot, repeatedly, again and again, time after time, regularly, commonly, generally, ordinarily; *N. Amer.* oftentimes.
- OPPOSITES seldom.

oily *adjective* **greasy**, fatty, buttery, rich, oleaginous.

ointment *noun* **lotion**, cream, salve, liniment, embrocation, rub, gel, balm, emollient, unguent.

OK, **okay** *(informal) adjective* **1 satisfactory**, all right, acceptable, competent, adequate, tolerable, passable, reasonable, decent, fair, not bad, average, middling, moderate, unremarkable, unexceptional; *informal* so-so, fair-to-middling. **2 permissible**, allowable, acceptable, all right, in order, permitted, fitting, suitable, appropriate.
- OPPOSITES unsatisfactory.
● *noun* **authorization**, (seal of) approval, agreement, consent, assent, permission, endorsement, ratification, sanction, blessing, leave; *informal* the go-ahead, the green light, the thumbs up, say-so.

old *adjective* **1** *old people* **elderly**, aged, older, senior, venerable, in your dotage, past your prime, long in the tooth, grizzled, ancient, decrepit, doddery, senescent, senile; *informal* getting on, past it, over the hill. **2** *old clothes* **worn**, shabby, threadbare, frayed, patched, tattered, moth-eaten, ragged; *informal* tatty. **3** *the old days* **bygone**, olden, past, prehistoric, primitive. **4** *old cars*

antique, veteran, vintage, classic. **5** *an old girlfriend* **former**, previous, earlier, past, ex-, one-time, sometime, erstwhile; *formal* quondam.
- OPPOSITES young, new, modern, current.

WORD LINKS
geriatric relating to old people

old-fashioned *adjective* **out of date**, outdated, dated, out of fashion, outmoded, unfashionable, passé, outworn, behind the times, antiquated, antediluvian, archaic, obsolescent, obsolete, superannuated; *informal* out of the ark, old hat, clunky.
- OPPOSITES modern.

omen *noun* **portent**, sign, signal, token, forewarning, warning, harbinger, presage, indication; *literary* foretoken.

ominous *adjective* **threatening**, menacing, baleful, forbidding, foreboding, fateful, sinister, black, dark, gloomy.
- OPPOSITES promising.

omission *noun* **1 exclusion**, leaving out, deletion, elimination. **2 negligence**, neglect, dereliction, oversight, lapse, failure.

omit *verb* **1 leave out**, exclude, miss out, miss, cut, drop, skip. **2 forget**, neglect, overlook, fail.
- OPPOSITES include, remember.

once *adverb* **1 on one occasion**, one time. **2 formerly**, previously, in the past, once upon a time, in days/times gone by, in the (good) old days, long ago.
● *conjunction* **as soon as**, the moment, when, after.
□ **at once 1** immediately, right away, right now, straight away, instantly, directly, forthwith, without delay, without further ado. **2** at the same time, (all) together, simultaneously, as a group, in unison.

one-sided *adjective* **1 biased**, prejudiced, partisan, partial, slanted, distorted, unfair. **2 unequal**, uneven, unbalanced.
- OPPOSITES impartial, equal.

ongoing *adjective* **in progress**, under way, going on, continuing, proceeding.

onlooker *noun* **eyewitness**, witness, observer, spectator, bystander; *informal* rubberneck.

only *adverb* **1 at most**, at best, just, no more than, hardly, barely, scarcely. **2 exclusively**, solely, purely.
● *adjective* **sole**, single, one (and only), solitary, lone, unique, exclusive.

onset *noun* **start**, beginning, commencement, arrival, appearance, inception, day one, outbreak; *informal* kick-off.
- OPPOSITES end.

onslaught *noun* **attack**, assault, offensive, advance, charge, blitz, bombardment, barrage.

onus *noun* **burden**, responsibility, obligation, duty, weight, load.

ooze *verb* **seep**, discharge, flow, exude, trickle, drip, dribble, drain, leak.

opaque *adjective* **1 non-transparent**, cloudy, filmy, blurred, smeared, misty. **2 obscure**, unclear, unfathomable, incomprehensible, unintelligible, impenetrable; *informal* as clear as mud.
- OPPOSITES transparent, clear.

open *adjective* **1 unlocked**, unlatched, off the latch, ajar, gaping, yawning. **2** *open countryside | open spaces* **unenclosed**, rolling, sweeping, wide open, exposed, spacious, uncrowded, uncluttered, undeveloped. **3** *the position is still open* **available**, free, vacant, unfilled; *informal* up for grabs. **4** *open to abuse* **vulnerable**, subject, susceptible, liable, exposed, an easy target for. **5** *she was very open* **frank**, candid, honest, forthcoming, communicative, forthright, direct, unreserved, plain-spoken, outspoken, blunt; *informal* upfront. **6** *open hostility* **overt**, manifest, conspicuous, plain, undisguised, unconcealed, clear, naked, blatant, flagrant, barefaced, brazen.
- OPPOSITES shut, closed.
● *verb* **1 unfasten**, unlock, unbolt, throw wide. **2 unwrap**, undo, untie. **3 spread out**, unfold, unfurl, unroll,

straighten out. **4 begin**, start, commence, initiate, set in motion, get going, get under way, get off the ground; *informal* kick off.
- OPPOSITES close, shut.

WORD LINKS
agoraphobia fear of open spaces

open-air *adjective* **outdoor**, out-of-doors, outside, alfresco.

opening *noun* **1 hole**, gap, aperture, space, orifice, vent, crack, slit, chink, fissure, cleft, crevice, interstice. **2 beginning**, start, commencement, outset; *informal* kick-off. **3 vacancy**, position, post, job, opportunity.
● *adjective* **first**, initial, introductory, preliminary, maiden, inaugural.
- OPPOSITES final, closing.

openly *adverb* **1 publicly**, blatantly, flagrantly, overtly. **2 frankly**, candidly, explicitly, honestly, sincerely, forthrightly, freely.

open-minded *adjective* **unbiased**, unprejudiced, neutral, objective, disinterested, tolerant, liberal, permissive, broad-minded.
- OPPOSITES prejudiced, narrow-minded.

operate *verb* **1 work**, run, use, handle, control, manage, drive, steer, manoeuvre, function, go, perform. **2 direct**, control, manage, run, handle, be in control/charge of.

operation *noun* **1 functioning**, working, running, performance, action. **2** *a military operation* **action**, exercise, undertaking, enterprise, manoeuvre, campaign. **3 business**, enterprise, company, firm.

operational *adjective* **running**, up and running, working, functioning, operative, in operation, in use, in action, in working order, serviceable, functional.

operative *adjective* **running**, up and running, working, functioning, operational, in operation, in use, in action, in effect.
● *noun* **1 machinist**, operator, mechanic, engineer, worker, workman, (factory) hand. **2 agent**, secret/undercover agent, spy, mole, plant; *N. Amer. informal* spook.

opinion *noun* **belief**, thought(s), idea, way of thinking, feeling, mind, view, point of view, viewpoint, standpoint, assessment, estimation, judgement, conviction.

opponent *noun* **1 rival**, adversary, competitor, enemy, antagonist, combatant, contender, challenger; *literary* foe. **2 critic**, objector, dissenter.
- OPPOSITES ally, supporter.

opportunity *noun* **chance**, time, occasion, moment, opening, option, window, possibility, scope, freedom; *informal* shot, break, look-in.

oppose *verb* **be against**, object to, be hostile to, disagree with, disapprove of, resist, take a stand against, put up a fight against, fight, counter, challenge, take issue with.
- OPPOSITES support.

opposed *adjective*
□ **opposed to** against, dead set against, averse to, hostile to, antagonistic to, antipathetic to; *informal* anti.

opposing *adjective* **1 conflicting**, contrasting, opposite, incompatible, irreconcilable, contradictory, clashing, at variance, at odds, opposed. **2 rival**, opposite, enemy, competing.
- OPPOSITES similar, allied.

opposite *adjective* **1 facing**, face to face with, across from. **2 conflicting**, contrasting, incompatible, irreconcilable, contradictory, at variance, at odds, differing. **3 rival**, opposing, competing, enemy.
● *noun* **reverse**, converse, antithesis, contrary.
- OPPOSITES same.

opposition *noun* **1 resistance**, hostility, antagonism, antipathy, objection, dissent, disapproval. **2 opponent(s)**, opposing side, competition, rival(s), adversary.
- OPPOSITES agreement.

oppress *verb* **persecute**, tyrannize, crush, repress, subjugate, subdue, keep down, rule with a rod of iron.

oppression *noun* **persecution**, abuse, ill-treatment, tyranny, repression, suppression, subjugation, cruelty, brutality, injustice.
- OPPOSITES freedom.

oppressive *adjective* **1 harsh**, cruel, brutal, repressive, tyrannical, despotic, draconian, ruthless, merciless, pitiless. **2 muggy**, close, heavy, hot, humid, sticky, airless, stuffy, stifling, sultry.
- OPPOSITES lenient, fresh.

opt *verb* **choose**, select, pick, decide, elect; (**opt for**) go for, settle on, plump for.

optimistic *adjective* **1 positive**, confident, hopeful, sanguine, bullish, buoyant, upbeat. **2 encouraging**, promising, reassuring, favourable.
- OPPOSITES pessimistic, depressing.

optimum *adjective* **best**, most favourable, most advantageous, ideal, perfect, prime, optimal.

option *noun* **choice**, preference, alternative, selection, possibility.

optional *adjective* **voluntary**, non-compulsory, elective, discretionary.
- OPPOSITES compulsory.

opulent *adjective* **luxurious**, sumptuous, palatial, lavishly appointed, rich, splendid, magnificent, grand, fancy; *informal* plush; *Brit. informal* swish; *N. Amer. informal* swank.
- OPPOSITES spartan.

oral *adjective* **spoken**, verbal, unwritten, vocal, uttered.
- OPPOSITES written.

orbit *noun* **circuit**, course, path, track, trajectory, rotation, revolution.
● *verb* **circle**, go round, revolve round, travel round, circumnavigate.

orchestra *noun* **ensemble**, group; *informal* band, combo.

orchestrate *verb* **organize**, arrange, plan, set up, mobilize, mount, stage, mastermind, coordinate, direct.

ordain *verb* **1 confer holy orders on**, admit to the priesthood, appoint, anoint, consecrate. **2 determine**, predestine, preordain, predetermine, prescribe, designate.

ordeal *noun* **trial**, hardship, suffering, nightmare, trauma, hell, torture, torment, agony.

order *noun* **1** *alphabetical order* **sequence**, arrangement, organization, codification, classification, system, series, succession. **2** *some semblance of order* **tidiness**, neatness, orderliness, method, symmetry, uniformity, regularity, routine. **3** *the police managed to keep order* **peace**, control, law and order, calm. **4** *in good order* **condition**, state, repair, shape, situation; *Brit. informal* nick. **5** *I had to obey orders* **command**, instruction, directive, direction, decree, edict, injunction, dictate. **6** *the lower orders of society* **class**, level, rank, grade, caste. **7** *a religious order* **community**, brotherhood, sisterhood. **8** *the Orange Order* **organization**, association, society, fellowship, fraternity, lodge, guild, league, union, club.
- OPPOSITES chaos.
● *verb* **1 instruct**, tell, command, direct, charge, require, enjoin, ordain, decree, rule. **2 request**, apply for, book, reserve, requisition. **3 organize**, arrange, sort out, lay out, group, classify, categorize, catalogue.

orderly *adjective* **1 neat**, tidy, well ordered, in order, trim, in apple-pie order, shipshape. **2 organized**, efficient, methodical, systematic, coherent, structured, logical. **3 well behaved**, law-abiding, disciplined, peaceful, peaceable.
- OPPOSITES untidy, unruly.

ordinary *adjective* **1 usual**, normal, standard, typical, common, customary, habitual, everyday, regular, routine, day-to-day, quotidian. **2 average**, run-of-the-mill, typical, middle-of-the-road, conventional, humdrum, unremarkable, unexceptional, pedestrian, prosaic, workday; *informal* bog-standard; *Brit. informal* common or garden; *N. Amer. informal* garden-variety.
- OPPOSITES unusual.

organ *noun* **newspaper**, paper, journal, periodical, magazine, voice, mouthpiece.

organic *adjective* **1** *organic matter* **living**, live, animate, biological. **2** *organic vegetables* **natural**, chemical-free, pesticide-free, bio-. **3** *an organic whole* **structured**, organized, coherent, integrated, coordinated, ordered, harmonious.

organism *noun* **living thing**, being, creature, animal, plant, life form.

organization *noun* **1 planning**, arrangement, coordination, organizing, running, management. **2 structure**, arrangement, plan, pattern, order, form, format, framework, composition. **3 institution**, body, group, company, concern, firm, business, corporation, conglomerate, consortium, syndicate, agency, association, society; *informal* outfit.

organize *verb* **1 order**, arrange, sort, assemble, marshal, put straight, group, classify, collate, categorize, catalogue, codify. **2 arrange**, coordinate, sort out, put together, fix up, set up, lay on, orchestrate, see to, mobilize.

orient, **orientate** *verb* **1** *you need time to orient yourself* **acclimatize**, familiarize, adjust, accustom, find your feet, get your bearings. **2 aim**, direct, pitch, design, intend. **3 align**, place, position, arrange.

origin *noun* **1 beginning**, start, genesis, birth, dawning, dawn, emergence, creation, source, basis, cause, root(s), derivation, provenance. **2 descent**, ancestry, parentage, pedigree, lineage, line (of descent), heritage, birth, extraction, family, roots.

original *adjective* **1 indigenous**, aboriginal, native, first, earliest, early, ur-. **2 authentic**, genuine, actual, true, bona fide. **3 innovative**, creative, imaginative, inventive, new, novel, fresh, unusual, unconventional, unorthodox, groundbreaking, disruptive, pioneering, unique, distinctive; *informal* edgy. ● *noun* **prototype**, source, master.

originally *adverb* **at first**, in the beginning, to begin with, initially, in the first place, at the outset.

originate *verb* **1 arise**, have its origin, begin, start, stem, spring, emerge, emanate. **2 invent**, create, devise, think up, dream up, conceive, formulate, form, develop, produce, mastermind, pioneer.

ornament *noun* **1 knick-knack**, trinket, bauble, gewgaw; *N. Amer. informal* kickshaw. **2 decoration**, adornment, embellishment, ornamentation, trimming, accessories, frills.

ornamental *adjective* **decorative**, fancy, ornate, ornamented, attractive.

ornate *adjective* **elaborate**, decorated, embellished, adorned, ornamented, rococo, fancy, fussy, ostentatious, showy; *informal* flashy.
– OPPOSITES plain.

orthodox *adjective* **1 conventional**, mainstream, conformist, established, traditional, traditionalist, prevalent, popular, conservative, received. **2** *an orthodox Muslim* **observant**, devout, strict.
– OPPOSITES unconventional.

oscillate *verb* **1 swing to and fro**, swing back and forth, sway. **2 waver**, swing, fluctuate, alternate, see-saw, yo-yo, vacillate.

ostentatious *adjective* **showy**, conspicuous, flamboyant, gaudy, brash, vulgar, loud, extravagant, fancy, ornate, rococo; *informal* flash, flashy, bling-bling, over the top, OTT, glitzy.
– OPPOSITES restrained.

ostracize *verb* **exclude**, shun, spurn, cold-shoulder, reject, ignore, snub, cut dead, blackball, blacklist; *Brit.* send to Coventry; *informal* freeze out; *Brit. informal* blank.

other *adjective* **1 alternative**, different, distinct, separate, various. **2 more**, further, additional, extra, fresh, new, added, supplementary.

oust *verb* **expel**, drive out, force out, eject, get rid of, depose, topple, unseat, overthrow, bring down, overturn, dismiss, dislodge.

outbreak *noun* **1 eruption**, flare-up, upsurge, rash, wave, spate, burst, flurry. **2 start**, beginning, commencement, onset.

outburst *noun* **eruption**, explosion, flare-up, storm, outpouring, burst, surge, fit, paroxysm, spasm.

outcome *noun* **result**, end result, net result, consequence, upshot, conclusion, end product; *informal* pay-off.

outcry *noun* **protest**, protestation, complaints, objections, furore, hue and cry, fuss, uproar, opposition, dissent; *informal* hullabaloo, ructions, stink.

outdated *adjective* **old-fashioned**, out of date, outmoded, out of fashion, unfashionable, dated, passé, old, behind the times, antiquated; *informal* out, old hat, square, clunky.
- OPPOSITES modern.

outdo *verb* **surpass**, outshine, overshadow, eclipse, outclass, outmanoeuvre, put in the shade, upstage, exceed, transcend, top, cap, beat, better; *informal* be a cut above.

outdoor *adjective* **open-air**, out-of-doors, outside, alfresco.
- OPPOSITES indoor.

outer *adjective* **1 outside**, outermost, outward, exterior, external, surface. **2 outlying**, distant, remote, faraway, far-flung, furthest.
- OPPOSITES inner.

outfit *noun* **1 costume**, suit, uniform, ensemble, clothes, clothing, dress, garb; *informal* get-up, gear; *Brit. informal* kit. **2** *(informal)* **organization**, enterprise, company, firm, business, group, body, team; *informal* set-up.

outgoing *adjective* **1 extrovert**, uninhibited, unreserved, demonstrative, affectionate, warm, sociable, gregarious, convivial, lively, expansive. **2 departing**, retiring, leaving.
- OPPOSITES introverted, incoming.

outgoings *plural noun* **expenses**, expenditure, spending, outlay, payments, costs, overheads.

outing *noun* **trip**, excursion, jaunt, expedition, day out, tour, drive, ride, run; *informal* spin, junket.

outlaw *noun* **fugitive**, bandit, robber.
● *verb* **ban**, bar, prohibit, forbid, make illegal, proscribe.
- OPPOSITES permit.

outlet *noun* **1 vent**, way out, outfall, opening, channel, conduit, duct. **2 market**, shop, store.

outline *noun* **1 silhouette**, profile, shape, contours, form, lines. **2 rough idea**, thumbnail sketch, rundown, summary, synopsis, résumé, precis, gist, bare bones.
● *verb* **rough out**, sketch out, draft, summarize, precis.

outlook *noun* **1 point of view**, viewpoint, way of thinking, perspective, attitude, standpoint, stance, frame of mind. **2 view**, vista, prospect, panorama. **3 prospects**, future, expectations, prognosis.

out of date *adjective* **1 old-fashioned**, outmoded, outdated, dated, old, passé, behind the times, obsolete, antiquated, anachronistic, antediluvian; *informal* old hat, clunky. **2 expired**, lapsed, invalid, void.
- OPPOSITES fashionable, valid, current.

output *noun* **production**, yield, product, productivity, work, result.

outrage *noun* **1 indignation**, fury, anger, rage, wrath, annoyance; *literary* ire. **2 scandal**, offence, insult, affront, disgrace, atrocity.
● *verb* **enrage**, infuriate, incense, anger, scandalize, offend, affront, shock.

outrageous *adjective* **1 shocking**, disgraceful, scandalous, atrocious, appalling, dreadful, insufferable, intolerable. **2 exaggerated**, improbable, preposterous, ridiculous, unwarranted.

outright *adverb* **1 completely**, entirely, wholly, totally, categorically, absolutely, utterly, flatly, unreservedly, out of hand. **2 explicitly**, directly, frankly, candidly, bluntly, plainly, to someone's

face; *Brit. informal* straight up.
3 instantly, instantaneously, immediately, at once, straight away, then and there, on the spot.
● *adjective* **1 complete**, absolute, out-and-out, downright, utter, sheer, categorical. **2 definite**, unequivocal, unmistakable, clear.

outset *noun* **start**, starting point, beginning, inception; *informal* the word go.
- OPPOSITES end.

outside *noun* **exterior**, case, skin, shell, covering, facade.
● *adjective* **1 exterior**, external, outer, outdoor, out-of-doors. **2 independent**, freelance, consultant, external.
● *adverb* **outdoors**, out of doors, alfresco.
- OPPOSITES inside.

outsider *noun* **stranger**, visitor, foreigner, alien, interloper, immigrant, incomer, newcomer.

outskirts *plural noun* **edges**, fringes, margins, suburbs, suburbia, environs, borders, periphery.

outspoken *adjective* **forthright**, direct, candid, frank, straightforward, open, straight from the shoulder, plain-spoken, blunt.

outstanding *adjective* **1 excellent**, marvellous, fine, magnificent, superb, wonderful, superlative, exceptional, pre-eminent, renowned, celebrated; *informal* great, terrific, tremendous, super; *Brit. informal* brilliant; *N. Amer. informal* neat. **2 to be done**, undone, unfinished, incomplete, remaining, pending. **3 unpaid**, unsettled, owing, owed, to be paid, payable, due, overdue; *N. Amer.* delinquent.

outward *adjective* **external**, surface, superficial, seeming, apparent, ostensible.
- OPPOSITES inward.

outweigh *verb* **be greater than**, exceed, be superior to, prevail over, override, supersede, offset, cancel out, outbalance, compensate for.

outwit *verb* **outsmart**, outmanoeuvre, steal a march on, trick, get the better of; *informal* pull a fast one on, put one over on.

ovation *noun* **applause**, round of applause, cheers, bravos, acclaim, standing ovation; *informal* (big) hand.

over *preposition* **1 above**, on top of, atop, covering. **2 more than**, above, in excess of, upwards of.
- OPPOSITES under.
● *adverb* **1 overhead**, past, by. **2 at an end**, finished, ended, no more, a thing of the past; *informal* finito.

overall *adjective* **total**, all-inclusive, gross, final, inclusive, complete, entire, blanket.
● *adverb* **generally (speaking)**, in general, altogether, all in all, on balance, on average, for the most part, in the main, on the whole, by and large.

overbearing *adjective* **domineering**, dominating, autocratic, tyrannical, despotic, high-handed; *informal* bossy.

overcast *adjective* **cloudy**, sunless, dark, grey, black, leaden, heavy, dull, murky.
- OPPOSITES bright.

overcome *verb* **conquer**, defeat, beat, prevail over, control, get/bring under control, master, get the better of; *informal* lick, best; *US informal* own.
● *adjective she was overcome with excitement* **overwhelmed**, moved, affected, speechless.

overdue *adjective* **1 late**, behind schedule, behind time, delayed, tardy. **2 unpaid**, unsettled, owing, owed, payable, due, outstanding, undischarged; *N. Amer.* delinquent.
- OPPOSITES early, punctual.

overflow *verb* **spill over**, flow over, brim over, well over, flood.
● *noun* **surplus**, excess, extra, remainder, overspill.

overhaul *verb* **service**, maintain, repair, mend, fix up, rebuild, renovate, recondition, refit, refurbish.

overlook *verb* **1 fail to notice**, fail to spot, miss. **2 disregard**, neglect, ignore, pass over, forget, take no notice of, make allowances for, turn a blind eye to, excuse, pardon, forgive. **3 have a view of**, look over/across, look on to, look out on.

overpower *verb* **overwhelm**, get the better of, overthrow, subdue, suppress, subjugate, repress, bring someone to their knees.

overpowering *adjective* **overwhelming**, oppressive, unbearable, unendurable, intolerable, shattering.

override *verb* **1 disallow**, overrule, countermand, veto, quash, overturn, overthrow, cancel, reverse, rescind, revoke, repeal. **2 outweigh**, supersede, take precedence over, take priority over, cancel out, outbalance.

overriding *adjective* **most important**, top, first (and foremost), predominant, principal, primary, paramount, chief, main, major, foremost, central, key.

overrule *verb* **countermand**, cancel, reverse, rescind, repeal, revoke, disallow, override, veto, quash, overturn, overthrow.

overrun *verb* **invade**, storm, occupy, swarm into, surge into, inundate, overwhelm.

overshadow *verb* **outshine**, eclipse, surpass, exceed, outclass, outstrip, outdo, upstage; *informal* be head and shoulders above.

overt *adjective* **undisguised**, unconcealed, plain (to see), clear, conspicuous, obvious, noticeable, manifest, patent, open, blatant.
- OPPOSITES covert.

overtake *verb* **1 pass**, go past, pull ahead of; *Brit.* overhaul. **2 outstrip**, surpass, overshadow, eclipse, outshine, outclass, exceed, top, cap. **3 befall**, happen to, come upon, hit, strike, overwhelm, overcome.

overthrow *verb* **oust**, remove, bring down, topple, depose, displace, unseat, defeat, conquer.
● *noun* **removal**, ousting, defeat, fall, collapse, demise.

overture *noun* **1 preliminary**, prelude, introduction, lead-in, precursor, start, beginning. **2 opening move**, approach, advances, feeler, signal.

overturn *verb* **1 capsize**, turn turtle, keel over, tip over, topple over, upset, turn over, knock over, upend. **2 cancel**, reverse, rescind, repeal, revoke, countermand, disallow, override, overrule, veto, quash, overthrow.

overweight *adjective* **fat**, obese, stout, plump, portly, chubby, pot-bellied, flabby; *informal* tubby; *Brit. informal* podgy.

overwhelm *verb* **1 trounce**, rout, beat hollow, conquer, crush; *informal* thrash, lick, wipe the floor with; *US informal* own. **2 overcome**, move, stir, affect, touch, strike, dumbfound, shake, leave speechless; *informal* bowl over, knock sideways; *Brit. informal* knock/hit for six.

overwhelming *adjective* **1 very large**, enormous, immense, inordinate, massive, huge. **2 very strong**, powerful, uncontrollable, irrepressible, irresistible, overpowering, compelling.

owe *verb* **be in debt (to)**, be indebted (to), be in arrears (to), be under an obligation (to).

owing *adjective* **unpaid**, to be paid, payable, due, overdue, undischarged, owed, outstanding, in arrears; *N. Amer.* delinquent.
□ **owing to** because of, as a result of, on account of, due to, as a consequence of, thanks to, in view of.

own *adjective* **personal**, individual, particular, private, personalized, unique.
● *verb* **possess**, keep, hold, be the owner of, have to your name.
□ **own up** confess, admit, acknowledge; *informal* come clean.

owner *noun* **possessor**, holder, proprietor, homeowner, freeholder, landlord, landlady.

ownership *noun* **possession**, freehold, proprietorship, title.

Pp

pace *noun* **1 step**, stride. **2 gait**, walk, march, tread. **3 speed**, rate, velocity, tempo.
● *verb* **walk**, step, stride, march, pound.

pacify *verb* **placate**, appease, calm (down), conciliate, propitiate, assuage, mollify, soothe.
- OPPOSITES enrage.

pack *noun* **1 packet**, container, package, box, carton, parcel. **2 group**, herd, troop, crowd, mob, band, party, set, gang, rabble, horde, throng, huddle, mass, assembly, gathering, host; *informal* crew, bunch.
● *verb* **1 fill**, load, stow, store, bundle, stuff, cram. **2 wrap (up)**, package, parcel, swathe, swaddle, encase, envelop, bundle. **3 throng**, crowd, fill, cram, jam, squash into, squeeze into.

package *noun* **1 parcel**, packet, box, carton. **2 collection**, bundle, combination, range, complement, raft, platform.
● *verb* **wrap**, gift-wrap, pack, box, seal.

packed *adjective* **crowded**, full, filled (to capacity), crammed, jammed, solid, teeming, seething, swarming; *informal* jam-packed, chock-full, chock-a-block, full to the gunwales, bursting/bulging at the seams.

packet *noun* **pack**, carton, container, case, package.

pact *noun* **agreement**, treaty, entente, protocol, deal, settlement, armistice, truce.

pad[1] *noun* **1 dressing**, pack, wad. **2 notebook**, notepad, writing pad, jotter; *N. Amer.* scratch pad.

pad[2] *verb* **creep**, sneak, steal, tiptoe, pussyfoot.

padded *adjective* **cushioned**, insulated, lined, quilted, stuffed, lagged.

padding *noun* **1 wadding**, cushioning, stuffing, packing, filling, lining. **2 verbiage**, wordiness; *Brit. informal* waffle.

paddle[1] *noun* **oar**, scull.
● *verb* **row**, pull, scull.

paddle[2] *verb* **splash (about)**, dabble, wade.

pagan *noun* & *adjective* **heathen**, infidel, non-Christian.

page[1] *noun* **folio**, sheet, side, leaf.

page[2] *noun* **1 errand boy**, messenger boy; *N. Amer.* bellboy, bellhop. **2 attendant**, pageboy, train-bearer.
● *verb* **call (for)**, summon, send for.

pageant *noun* **parade**, procession, cavalcade, tableau, spectacle, extravaganza, show.

pageantry *noun* **spectacle**, display, ceremony, magnificence, pomp, splendour, grandeur, show; *informal* razzle-dazzle, razzmatazz.

pain *noun* **1 suffering**, agony, torture, torment. **2 ache**, aching, soreness, throbbing, sting, twinge, stab, pang, discomfort, irritation. **3 sorrow**, grief, heartache, heartbreak, sadness, unhappiness, distress, misery, despair, agony, torment, torture. **4** *he took pains to hide his feelings* **care**, effort, bother, trouble.
● *verb* **sadden**, grieve, distress, trouble, perturb, oppress, cause anguish to.

WORD LINKS
analgesic pain-relieving drug
anaesthetic drug that stops you feeling pain

painful *adjective* **1 sore**, hurting, tender, aching, throbbing. **2 disagreeable**, unpleasant, nasty, distressing, upsetting, sad, traumatic, miserable, heartbreaking, agonizing, harrowing.

painfully *adverb* **distressingly**, disturbingly, uncomfortably, unpleasantly, dreadfully.

painless *adjective* **1 pain-free**, without pain. **2 easy**, trouble-free, straightforward, simple, uncomplicated; *informal* child's play.
- OPPOSITES painful, difficult.

painstaking *adjective* **careful**, meticulous, thorough, assiduous, attentive, conscientious, punctilious, scrupulous, rigorous.
- OPPOSITES slapdash.

paint *noun* **colouring**, colour, tint, dye, stain, pigment, emulsion, gloss.
● *verb* **1 colour**, decorate, whitewash, airbrush, daub, smear. **2 portray**, picture, paint a picture/portrait of, depict, represent.

painting *noun* **picture**, illustration, portrayal, depiction, representation, image, artwork, canvas, oil, watercolour.

pair *noun* **set**, brace, couple, duo, two.
● *verb* **match**, put together, couple, combine.

palace *noun* **castle**, chateau, mansion, stately home, schloss.

palatable *adjective* **1 edible**, tasty, appetizing, delicious, mouth-watering, toothsome, succulent; *informal* scrumptious, yummy, scrummy, moreish. **2 pleasant**, acceptable, agreeable, to your liking.
- OPPOSITES disagreeable.

palatial *adjective* **luxurious**, magnificent, sumptuous, splendid, grand, opulent, lavish, stately, fancy; *Brit.* upmarket; *informal* plush, swanky, posh, ritzy; *Brit. informal* swish.
- OPPOSITES modest.

pale *adjective* **1 white**, pallid, pasty, wan, colourless, anaemic, washed out, peaky, ashen, sickly; *informal* like death warmed up. **2 light**, pastel, muted, subtle, soft, faded, bleached, washed out. **3 dim**, faint, weak, feeble.
- OPPOSITES ruddy, dark.
● *verb* **turn white**, turn pale, blanch, lose colour.

palpable *adjective* **1 tangible**, touchable. **2 perceptible**, visible, noticeable, discernible, detectable, observable, unmistakable, transparent, obvious, clear, plain (to see), evident, apparent, manifest, staring you in the face, written all over someone.
- OPPOSITES imperceptible.

paltry *adjective* **small**, meagre, trifling, insignificant, negligible, inadequate, insufficient, derisory, pitiful, pathetic, miserable, niggardly, beggarly; *informal* measly, piddling, poxy.
- OPPOSITES considerable.

pamper *verb* **spoil**, indulge, overindulge, cosset, mollycoddle, coddle, baby, wait on someone hand and foot.

pamphlet *noun* **brochure**, leaflet, booklet, circular; *N. Amer.* mailer, folder.

pan[1] *noun* **saucepan**, pot, bowl, frying pan, skillet.

pan[2] *verb* **swing (round)**, sweep, move, turn.

panache *noun* **flamboyance**, confidence, self-assurance, style, flair, elan, dash, verve, zest, spirit, brio, vivacity, gusto, liveliness, vitality, energy; *informal* pizzazz, oomph, zip, zing.

panel *noun* **1 console**, dashboard, instruments, controls, dials. **2 group**, team, body, committee, board.

panic *noun* **alarm**, anxiety, fear, fright, trepidation, dread, terror, hysteria, apprehension; *informal* flap, fluster, cold sweat.
- OPPOSITES calm.
● *verb* **1 be alarmed**, be scared, be afraid, take fright, be hysterical, lose your nerve, get worked up; *informal* run around like a headless chicken. **2 frighten**, alarm, scare, unnerve; *Brit. informal* put the wind up.

panorama *noun* **view**, vista, prospect, scenery, landscape, seascape, cityscape, skyline.

panoramic *adjective* **sweeping**, wide, extensive, scenic, commanding.

pant *verb* **breathe heavily**, breathe hard, puff and blow, huff and puff, gasp, heave, wheeze.

pants *plural noun* **1** *(Brit.)* **underpants**, briefs, boxer shorts, boxers, knickers; *N. Amer.* shorts, undershorts; *informal* panties; *dated* drawers, bloomers. **2** *(N. Amer.)* **trousers**, slacks; *Brit. informal* trews, strides, kecks; *Austral. informal* daks.

paper *noun* **1 newspaper**, journal, gazette, periodical, tabloid, broadsheet, daily, weekly; *informal* rag. **2 exam**, examination, test. **3 essay**, article, monograph, thesis, work, dissertation, treatise, study, report, analysis; *N. Amer.* theme. **4 document**, certificate, letter, file, deed, record, archive; (**papers**) paperwork, documentation. **5** *they asked us for our papers* **identification**, identity card, ID, credentials.

parable *noun* **allegory**, moral tale, fable.

parade *noun* **1 procession**, march, cavalcade, motorcade, spectacle, display, pageant, review, tattoo; *Brit.* march past. **2 promenade**, walkway, esplanade, mall; *N. Amer.* boardwalk; *Brit. informal* prom.
● *verb* **1 march**, process, file, troop. **2 strut**, swagger, stride; *N. Amer.* sashay. **3 display**, exhibit, make a show of, flaunt, show (off), demonstrate.

paradise *noun* **1 heaven**, the promised land, the Elysian Fields. **2 Utopia**, Shangri-La, Eden, idyll. **3 bliss**, heaven (on earth), ecstasy, delight, joy, happiness.
- OPPOSITES hell.

paradox *noun* **contradiction**, self-contradiction, inconsistency, incongruity, conflict, enigma, puzzle, conundrum.

paragraph *noun* **section**, division, part, portion, segment, passage, clause.

parallel *adjective* **1 aligned**, side by side, equidistant. **2 similar**, analogous, comparable, corresponding, like, equivalent, matching.
- OPPOSITES divergent, different.
● *noun* **1 counterpart**, analogue, equivalent, match, twin, duplicate, mirror. **2 similarity**, likeness, resemblance, analogy, correspondence, comparison, equivalence, symmetry.
- OPPOSITES divergence, difference.

paralyse *verb* **1 disable**, cripple, immobilize, incapacitate; (**paralysed**) *Medicine* paraplegic, quadriplegic. **2 bring to a standstill**, immobilize, bring to a halt, freeze, cripple, disable.

paralysis *noun* **1 immobility**, powerlessness, incapacity; *Medicine* paraplegia, quadriplegia. **2 shutdown**, immobilization, stoppage, gridlock, standstill, blockage.

parameter *noun* **framework**, variable, limit, boundary, limitation, restriction, criterion, guideline.

paramount *adjective* **most important**, supreme, chief, overriding, predominant, foremost, prime, primary, principal, main, key, central; *informal* number-one.

paranoid *adjective* **suspicious**, mistrustful, anxious, fearful, insecure, obsessive.

paraphrase *verb* **reword**, rephrase, express differently, rewrite, gloss.

parasite *noun* **hanger-on**, cadger, leech, passenger; *informal* freeloader, sponger, scrounger; *N. Amer. informal* mooch; *Austral./NZ informal* bludger.

parcel *noun* **package**, packet, pack, bundle, box, case, bale.
● *verb* **pack (up)**, package, wrap (up), gift-wrap, tie up, bundle up.

parched *adjective* **1 (bone) dry**, dried up/out, arid, desiccated, dehydrated, baked, burned, scorched, withered, shrivelled. **2 dehydrated**, dry; *informal* gasping.

pardon *noun* **1 forgiveness**, absolution. **2 reprieve**, amnesty, exoneration, release, acquittal, discharge.
● *verb* **1 forgive**, absolve. **2 exonerate**, acquit, reprieve; *informal* let off.
- OPPOSITES blame, punish.

parentage *noun* **origins**, extraction, birth, family, ancestry, lineage, heritage, pedigree, descent, blood, stock, roots.

parish *noun* **1 district**, community. **2 parishioners**, churchgoers, congregation, fold, flock, community.

WORD LINKS
parochial relating to a parish

park *noun* **1 public garden**, recreation ground, playground. **2 parkland**, grassland, woodland, garden(s), lawns, grounds, estate.
● *verb* **1 leave**, position, stop, pull up. **2** *(informal)* **put (down)**, place, deposit, leave, stick, shove, dump; *informal* plonk; *Brit. informal* bung.

parliament *noun* **legislature**, assembly, chamber, house, congress, senate, diet.

parliamentary *adjective* **legislative**, law-making, governmental, congressional, democratic, elected.

parochial *adjective* **narrow-minded**, small-minded, provincial, small-town, conservative; *N. Amer. informal* jerkwater.
- OPPOSITES broad-minded.

parody *noun* **1 satire**, burlesque, lampoon, pastiche, caricature, imitation; *informal* spoof, take-off, send-up. **2 distortion**, travesty, misrepresentation, perversion, corruption.

parry *verb* **1** *he parried the blow* **ward off**, fend off, deflect, block. **2** *I parried her questions* **evade**, sidestep, avoid, dodge, field.

parson *noun* **priest**, minister, clergyman, vicar, rector, cleric, chaplain, pastor, curate; *informal* reverend, padre.

part *noun* **1 piece**, amount, portion, proportion, percentage, fraction; *informal* slice, chunk. **2 component**, bit, constituent, element, module, unit. **3 organ**, limb, member. **4 section**, division, volume, chapter, act, scene, instalment. **5 district**, neighbourhood, quarter, section, area, region. **6 role**, character. **7 involvement**, role, function, hand, responsibility, capacity, participation, contribution; *informal* bit.
- OPPOSITES whole.
● *verb* **1 separate**, divide, split, move apart. **2 leave each other**, part company, say goodbye/farewell, say your goodbyes/farewells, go your separate ways, take your leave.
- OPPOSITES join, meet.
□ **part with** give away, give up, relinquish, forgo, surrender, hand over. **take part** participate, join in, get involved, enter, play a part, play a role, be a participant, contribute, have a hand; *informal* get in on the act.

partial *adjective* **1 incomplete**, limited, qualified, imperfect, fragmentary, unfinished. **2 biased**, prejudiced, partisan, one-sided, slanted, skewed, coloured, unbalanced.
- OPPOSITES complete, unbiased.
□ **be partial to** like, love, enjoy, be fond of, be keen on, have a soft spot for, have a taste for, have a penchant for.

partially *adverb* **somewhat**, to a limited extent, to a certain extent, partly, in part, up to a point, slightly.
- OPPOSITES wholly.

participant *noun* **participator**, contributor, party, member, entrant, competitor, player, contestant, candidate.

participate *verb* **take part**, join, engage, get involved, share, play a part, play a role, contribute, partake, have a hand in.

participation *noun* **involvement**, part, contribution, association.

particle *noun* **(tiny) bit**, (tiny) piece, speck, spot, fragment, sliver, splinter.

particular *adjective* **1 specific**, individual, certain, distinct, separate, definite, precise. **2 special**, exceptional, unusual, uncommon, notable, noteworthy, remarkable, unique. **3 fussy**, fastidious, finicky, discriminating, selective; *informal* pernickety, choosy, picky; *Brit. informal* faddy.
- OPPOSITES general, indiscriminate.
● *noun* **detail**, item, point, element, fact, circumstance, feature.

particularly *adverb* **1 especially**, specially, exceptionally, unusually, remarkably, outstandingly, uncommonly, uniquely. **2 specifically**, explicitly, expressly, in particular, especially, specially.

parting *noun* **farewell**, leave-taking, goodbye, adieu, departure.

partisan *noun* **guerrilla**, freedom fighter, resistance fighter, underground fighter, irregular.
● *adjective* **biased**, prejudiced, one-sided, discriminatory, partial, sectarian, factional.
- OPPOSITES neutral.

partition *noun* **1 division**, partitioning, separation, break-up. **2 screen**, divider, dividing wall, barrier, panel.
● *verb* **1 divide**, separate, split up, break up. **2 subdivide**, divide (up), separate, section off, screen off.

partly *adverb* **in part**, partially, somewhat, a little, up to a point, in some measure, slightly, to some extent.
- OPPOSITES wholly.

partner *noun* **1 colleague**, associate, co-worker, fellow worker, collaborator, comrade, teammate. **2 accomplice**, confederate, accessory, collaborator, fellow conspirator, helper; *informal* sidekick. **3 spouse**, husband, wife, lover, girlfriend, boyfriend, fiancé, fiancée, significant other, live-in lover, mate; *Brit. informal* other half.

partnership *noun* **1 cooperation**, association, collaboration, coalition, alliance, union, affiliation, connection. **2 company**, association, consortium, syndicate, firm, business, organization.

party *noun* **1 social gathering**, function, get-together, celebration, reunion, festivity, reception, soirée, social; *informal* bash, do. **2 group**, company, body, gang, band, crowd, pack, contingent; *informal* bunch, crew, load. **3 faction**, group, bloc, camp, caucus, alliance.

pass *verb* **1 go**, proceed, move, progress, make your way, travel. **2 overtake**, go past/by, pull ahead of, leave behind. **3 elapse**, go by, advance, wear on, roll by, tick by. **4** *he passed the time reading* **occupy**, spend, fill, use (up), employ, while away. **5 hand**, let someone have, give, reach. **6** *her estate passed to her grandson* **be transferred**, go, be left, be bequeathed, be handed down/on, be passed on; *Law* devolve. **7 happen**, occur, take place. **8 come to an end**, fade (away), blow over, run its course, die out/down, finish, end, cease. **9 be successful in**, succeed in, get through; *informal* sail through, scrape through. **10 approve**, vote for, accept, ratify, adopt, agree to, authorize, endorse, legalize, enact; *informal* OK.
- OPPOSITES fail, reject.
● *noun* **permit**, warrant, authorization, licence.
□ **pass out** faint, lose consciousness, black out. **pass up** turn down, reject, refuse, decline, give up, forgo, let pass, miss (out on); *informal* give something a miss.

passable *adjective* **1 adequate**, all right, acceptable, satisfactory, not (too) bad, average, tolerable, fair, mediocre, middling, ordinary, indifferent, unremarkable, unexceptional; *informal* OK, so-so. **2 navigable**, traversable, negotiable, open, clear.

passage *noun* **1 journey**, voyage, crossing, transit, trip. **2 passing**, progress, advance, course, march, flow. **3 corridor**, hall, hallway. **4 alley**, alleyway, passageway, lane, path, footpath, track, thoroughfare; *N. Amer.* areaway. **5 extract**, excerpt, quotation, quote.

passenger *noun* **traveller**, commuter, fare-payer, rider, fare.

passing *adjective* **1 fleeting**, transient, transitory, ephemeral, brief, short-lived, temporary, momentary. **2 hasty**, rapid, hurried, brief, quick, cursory, superficial, casual, perfunctory, desultory.
● *noun* **1 passage**, course, progress, advance. **2 death**, demise, passing away, end, loss.

passion *noun* **1 intensity**, enthusiasm, fervour, eagerness, zeal, vigour, fire, energy, spirit, fanaticism. **2 love**, desire, ardour, lust, lasciviousness, lustfulness. **3 fascination**, love, mania,

obsession, preoccupation, fanaticism, fixation, compulsion, appetite, addiction; *informal* thing.
- OPPOSITES apathy.

passionate *adjective* **1 intense**, impassioned, ardent, fervent, vehement, fiery, heated, emotional, heartfelt, excited. **2 very keen**, very enthusiastic, addicted; *informal* mad, crazy, hooked. **3 amorous**, ardent, hot-blooded, loving, sexy, sensual, erotic, lustful; *informal* steamy, hot, turned on.
- OPPOSITES apathetic, cool.

passive *adjective* **1 inactive**, non-active, non-participative, uninvolved. **2 submissive**, acquiescent, unresisting, compliant, docile.
- OPPOSITES active, resistant.

past *adjective* **1 gone by**, bygone, former, previous, old, of old, olden, long-ago. **2 last**, recent, preceding. **3 previous**, former, foregoing, erstwhile, one-time, sometime, ex-, as was.
- OPPOSITES present, future.
● *noun* **history**, background, past life, life story.

paste *noun* **1 purée**, pulp, mush, spread, pâté. **2 adhesive**, glue, gum; *N. Amer.* mucilage.
● *verb* **stick**, glue, gum, fix, affix.

pastel *adjective* **pale**, soft, light, delicate, muted.
- OPPOSITES dark, bright.

pastime *noun* **hobby**, leisure activity, leisure pursuit, recreation, game, amusement, diversion, entertainment, interest.

pastor *noun* **priest**, minister, parson, clergyman, cleric, chaplain, vicar, rector, curate; *informal* reverend, padre.

pastoral *adjective* **1 rural**, country, rustic, agricultural, bucolic; *literary* Arcadian. **2 priestly**, clerical, ecclesiastical, ministerial.
- OPPOSITES urban, lay.

pasture *noun* **grassland**, grass, grazing, meadow, field; *literary* lea.

pat *verb* & *noun* **tap**, clap, touch, stroke.

patch *noun* **1 blotch**, mark, spot, smudge, smear, stain, streak, blemish; *informal* splodge. **2 plot**, area, piece, strip, tract, parcel, bed; *Brit.* allotment; *N. Amer.* lot. **3** *(Brit. informal)* **period**, time, spell, phase, stretch.
● *verb* **mend**, repair, sew up, stitch up, cover, reinforce.

patent *adjective* **1 obvious**, clear, plain, evident, manifest, conspicuous, blatant, barefaced, flagrant. **2 proprietary**, patented, licensed, branded.

path *noun* **1 footpath**, pathway, track, trail, bridle path, lane, towpath. **2 route**, way, course, direction, orbit, trajectory. **3 course of action**, route, road, avenue, line, approach, tack.

pathetic *adjective* **1 pitiful**, piteous, moving, touching, poignant, plaintive, wretched, heart-rending, sad. **2** *(informal)* **feeble**, woeful, sorry, poor, weak, pitiful, lamentable, deplorable, contemptible.

pathological *adjective* **1 morbid**, diseased. **2** *(informal)* **compulsive**, obsessive, inveterate, habitual, persistent, chronic, hardened, confirmed.

patience *noun* **1 forbearance**, tolerance, restraint, equanimity, understanding, indulgence. **2 perseverance**, persistence, endurance, tenacity, application, doggedness, staying power.

patient *adjective* **1 forbearing**, uncomplaining, long-suffering, resigned, stoical, calm, imperturbable, tolerant, accommodating, indulgent. **2 persevering**, persistent, tenacious, dogged, determined.
- OPPOSITES impatient.

patriotic *adjective* **nationalistic**, loyalist, loyal, chauvinistic, jingoistic, flag-waving.
- OPPOSITES traitorous.

patrol *noun* **1** *ships on patrol in the straits* **guard**, watch, vigil. **2 squad**, detachment, party, force.
● *verb* **guard**, keep watch on, police, make the rounds of, stand guard (over), defend, safeguard.

patron *noun* **1 sponsor**, backer, benefactor, contributor, subscriber, donor, philanthropist, promoter, friend, supporter; *informal* angel. **2 customer**, client, consumer, user, visitor, guest; *informal* regular.

patronage *noun* **1 sponsorship**, backing, funding, financing, assistance, support. **2 custom**, trade, business.

patronize *verb* **1 talk down to**, look down on, condescend to, treat like a child. **2 use**, buy from, shop at, be a customer/client of, deal with, frequent, support.

patronizing *adjective* **condescending**, supercilious, superior, imperious, scornful; *informal* uppity, high and mighty.

pattern *noun* **1 design**, decoration, motif, device, marking. **2 system**, order, arrangement, form, method, structure, scheme, plan, format. **3 model**, example, blueprint, criterion, standard, norm, yardstick, touchstone, benchmark.

pause *noun* **break**, interruption, lull, respite, breathing space, gap, interlude, adjournment, rest, wait, hesitation; *informal* let-up, breather.
● *verb* **stop**, break off, take a break, adjourn, rest, wait, hesitate; *informal* take a breather.

pave *verb* **surface**, floor, cover, tile, flag.

pavement *noun* **footpath**, walkway; *N. Amer.* sidewalk.

pay *verb* **1 reward**, reimburse, recompense, remunerate. **2 spend**, pay out; *informal* lay out, shell out, fork out, cough up; *N. Amer. informal* ante up, pony up. **3 discharge**, settle, pay off, clear. **4 be profitable**, make money, make a profit. **5 be advantageous to**, benefit, be of advantage to, be beneficial to. **6** *he will pay for his mistakes* **suffer**, be punished, atone, pay the penalty/price.
● *noun* **salary**, wages, payment, earnings, remuneration, fee, reimbursement, income, revenue, stipend, emolument.
□ **pay back 1** get your revenge on, get back at, get even with, settle the score. **2** repay, pay off, give back, return, reimburse, refund. **pay off** pay (in full), settle, discharge, clear, liquidate.

payable *adjective* **due**, owed, owing, outstanding, unpaid, overdue; *N. Amer.* delinquent.

payment *noun* **1 remittance**, settlement, discharge, clearance. **2 instalment**, premium. **3 salary**, wages, pay, earnings, fees, remuneration, reimbursement, income, stipend, emolument.

peace *noun* **1 quiet**, silence, peace and quiet, hush, stillness, still. **2 serenity**, peacefulness, tranquillity, calm, calmness, composure, ease, contentment, rest, repose. **3 treaty**, truce, ceasefire, armistice.
– OPPOSITES noise, war.

peaceful *adjective* **1 tranquil**, calm, restful, quiet, still, relaxing, serene, composed, placid, at ease, untroubled, unworried. **2 harmonious**, on good terms, amicable, friendly, cordial, non-violent.
– OPPOSITES noisy.

peacemaker *noun* **arbitrator**, arbiter, mediator, negotiator, conciliator, go-between, intermediary.

peak *noun* **1 summit**, top, crest, pinnacle, cap. **2 mountain**, hill, height. **3 height**, high point, pinnacle, summit, top, climax, culmination, apex, zenith, acme.
● *verb* **reach its height**, climax, culminate.
● *adjective* **maximum**, greatest, busiest, highest.

peculiar *adjective* **1 strange**, unusual, odd, funny, curious, bizarre, weird, eccentric, queer, abnormal, unconventional, outlandish, anomalous, out of the ordinary, unexpected, offbeat. **2** *customs peculiar to the area* **distinctive**, exclusive, unique, characteristic, distinct, individual, typical, special.
– OPPOSITES ordinary.

pedant *noun* **dogmatist**, purist, literalist, formalist, quibbler, hair-splitter;

informal nit-picker.

pedantic *adjective* **finicky**, fussy, fastidious, dogmatic, purist, hair-splitting, quibbling; *informal* nit-picking, pernickety.

peddle *verb* **sell**, hawk, tout, trade, deal in, traffic in.

pedestal *noun* **plinth**, base, support, mount, stand, pillar, column.
□ **put on a pedestal** idealize, look up to, hold in high regard, think highly of, admire, esteem, revere, worship.

pedestrian *noun* **walker**, person on foot.
● *adjective* **dull**, boring, tedious, monotonous, unremarkable, uninspired, unimaginative, unexciting, routine, commonplace, ordinary, everyday, run-of-the-mill, mundane, humdrum; *informal* bog-standard.
- OPPOSITES exciting.

pedigree *noun* **ancestry**, lineage, line, descent, genealogy, extraction, parentage, bloodline, family tree.
● *adjective* **pure-bred**, full-blooded, thoroughbred.

peek *verb* **1 peep**, look; *informal* take a gander, have a squint; *Brit. informal* have a dekko, take a butcher's, take a shufti. **2 appear**, show, peep (out).
● *noun* **look**, peep, glance, glimpse.

peel *verb* **1 pare**, skin, hull, shell. **2 flake (off)**, come off, fall off, strip off.
● *noun* **rind**, skin, covering, zest.

peep *verb* **peek**, look, sneak a look, glance; *informal* squint.
● *noun* **peek**, look, glance; *informal* squint, dekko.

peer[1] *verb* **look closely**, squint, gaze.

peer[2] *noun* **1 aristocrat**, lord, lady, noble, nobleman, noblewoman.
2 equal, fellow, contemporary.

peeve *verb (informal)* **irritate**, annoy, vex, anger, irk, gall, pique, put out, nettle; *informal* aggravate, rile, needle, get to, bug, hack off, get someone's goat, get/put someone's back up; *N. Amer. informal* tee off, tick off.

peg *noun* **pin**, nail, dowel.
● *verb* **1 fix**, pin, attach, fasten, secure.
2 set, hold, fix, limit, freeze, keep down, hold down.

pen[1] *verb* **write**, compose, draft, dash off, scribble.

pen[2] *noun* **enclosure**, fold, pound, compound, stockade, sty, coop; *N. Amer.* corral.
● *verb* **confine**, coop, cage, shut, box, lock, trap, kettle, imprison, incarcerate.

penalize *verb* **1 punish**, discipline.
2 handicap, disadvantage, discriminate against.
- OPPOSITES reward.

penalty *noun* **punishment**, sanction, fine, forfeit, sentence.
- OPPOSITES reward.

penance *noun* **atonement**, expiation, amends, punishment, penalty.

penchant *noun* **liking**, fondness, preference, taste, appetite, partiality, love, passion, weakness, inclination, bent, proclivity, predilection, predisposition.

pending *adjective* **1 unresolved**, undecided, unsettled, up in the air, ongoing, outstanding; *informal* on the back burner. **2 imminent**, impending, about to happen, forthcoming, on the way, coming, approaching, looming, near, on the horizon, in the offing.

penetrate *verb* **1 pierce**, puncture, enter, perforate, stab, gore. **2 permeate**, pervade, fill, imbue, suffuse, seep through, saturate. **3 register**, sink in, become clear, fall into place; *informal* click.

penetrating *adjective* **1 cold**, cutting, biting, keen, sharp, harsh, raw, freezing, chill, bitter. **2 shrill**, strident, piercing, ear-splitting. **3 intent**, searching, piercing, probing, sharp, keen.
4 perceptive, insightful, keen, sharp, intelligent, clever, smart, incisive, trenchant, astute.
- OPPOSITES mild, soft.

pension *noun* **old-age pension**, superannuation, allowance, benefit, support, welfare.

pensioner *noun* **retired person**, old-age pensioner, OAP, senior citizen; *N. Amer.* senior, retiree, golden ager.

people *plural noun* **1 human beings**, persons, individuals, humans, mortals, living souls, personages, {men, women, and children}; *informal* folk. **2 citizens**, subjects, electors, voters, taxpayers, residents, inhabitants, public, citizenry, nation, population, populace. **3 the common people**, the proletariat, the masses, the populace, the rank and file; *derogatory* the hoi polloi; *informal, derogatory* the proles, the plebs. **4 family**, parents, relatives, relations, folk, kinsfolk, flesh and blood, nearest and dearest; *informal* folks. **5** *(singular)* **race**, ethnic group, tribe, clan, nation.
● *verb* **populate**, settle (in), colonize, inhabit, live in, occupy.

WORD LINKS
ethnic relating to a people
anthropology study of people

pepper *verb* **1 sprinkle**, fleck, dot, spot, stipple. **2 bombard**, pelt, shower, rain down on, strafe, rake, blitz.

perceive *verb* **1 see**, discern, detect, catch sight of, spot, observe, notice; *literary* espy. **2 regard**, look on, view, consider, think of, judge, deem.

p

perception *noun* **1 impression**, idea, conception, notion, thought, belief. **2 insight**, perceptiveness, understanding, intelligence, intuition, incisiveness.

perceptive *adjective* **insightful**, discerning, sensitive, intuitive, observant, penetrating, intelligent, clever, canny, keen, sharp, astute, shrewd, quick, smart, acute; *informal* on the ball; *N. Amer. informal* heads-up.
- OPPOSITES obtuse.

perch *verb* **1 sit**, rest, alight, settle, land, roost. **2 put**, place, set, rest, balance.

perennial *adjective* **lasting**, enduring, abiding, long-lasting, long-lived, perpetual, continuing, continual, recurring.
- OPPOSITES ephemeral.

perfect *adjective* **1 ideal**, model, faultless, flawless, consummate, exemplary, best, ultimate, copybook. **2 flawless**, mint, as good as new, pristine, immaculate, optimum, prime, peak; *informal* tip-top, A1. **3 exact**, precise, accurate, faithful, true; *Brit. informal* spot on; *N. Amer. informal* on the money. **4 absolute**, complete, total, real, out-and-out, thorough, downright, utter; *Brit. informal* right; *Austral./NZ informal* fair.
● *verb* **improve**, polish (up), hone, refine, brush up, fine-tune.

perfection *noun* **the ideal**, a paragon, the last word, the ultimate; *informal* the tops, the bee's knees.

perform *verb* **1 carry out**, do, execute, discharge, conduct, implement; *informal* pull off. **2 function**, work, operate, run, go, respond, behave, act. **3 stage**, put on, present, mount, act, produce. **4 play**, sing, appear.

performance *noun* **1 show**, production, showing, presentation, staging, concert, recital; *informal* gig. **2 rendition**, interpretation, playing, acting. **3 carrying out**, execution, discharge, completion, fulfilment. **4 functioning**, working, operation, running, behaviour, response.

performer *noun* **actor**, **actress**, artiste, artist, entertainer, trouper, player, musician, singer, dancer, comic, comedian, comedienne.

perfume *noun* **1 scent**, fragrance, eau de toilette, toilet water, cologne, eau de cologne. **2 smell**, scent, fragrance, aroma, bouquet, nose.

perhaps *adverb* **maybe**, for all you know, it could be, it may be, it's possible, possibly, conceivably; *N. English* happen.

peril *noun* **danger**, jeopardy, risk, hazard, menace, threat.
- OPPOSITES safety.

perimeter *noun* **boundary**, border, limits, bounds, edge, margin, fringe(s), periphery.
- OPPOSITES centre.

period *noun* **1 time**, spell, interval, stretch, term, span, phase, bout; *Brit. informal* patch. **2 era**, age, epoch, aeon, time, days, years.

periodic *adjective* **regular**, at fixed intervals, recurrent, recurring, repeated, cyclical, seasonal, occasional, intermittent, sporadic, odd.

periodical *noun* **journal**, magazine, newspaper, paper, review, newsletter, digest, gazette, organ; *informal* mag, glossy.

peripheral *adjective* **secondary**, subsidiary, incidental, tangential, marginal, minor, unimportant, ancillary.
- OPPOSITES central.

perish *verb* **1 die**, lose your life, be killed, fall, be lost; *informal* buy it. **2 go bad**, spoil, rot, decay, decompose.

perk *noun* **fringe benefit**, advantage, bonus, extra, plus; *informal* freebie.

permanent *adjective* **lasting**, enduring, indefinite, continuing, constant, perpetual, indelible, irreparable, irreversible, lifelong, perennial, established, standing, long-term, stable, secure.
- OPPOSITES temporary.

permanently *adverb* **1 forever**, for all time, for good, irreversibly, incurably, irreparably, indelibly; *informal* for keeps. **2 continually**, constantly, perpetually, always.

permission *noun* **authorization**, consent, leave, authority, sanction, licence, dispensation, assent, agreement, approval, blessing, clearance; *informal* the go-ahead, the green light, say-so.
- OPPOSITES ban.

permit *verb* **allow**, let, authorize, give permission, sanction, grant, license, consent to, assent to, agree to; *informal* give the go-ahead to, give the green light to.
- OPPOSITES forbid.
● *noun* **authorization**, licence, pass, ticket, warrant, passport, visa.

perpetual *adjective* **1 constant**, permanent, uninterrupted, continuous, unremitting, unending, everlasting, eternal, unceasing, without end, persistent, lasting, abiding. **2 interminable**, incessant, ceaseless, endless, relentless, unrelenting, persistent, continual, continuous, non-stop, never-ending, repeated, unremitting, round-the-clock, unabating; *informal* eternal.
- OPPOSITES temporary, intermittent.

perpetuate *verb* **keep alive**, keep going, preserve, conserve, sustain, maintain, continue, extend.

perplex *verb* **puzzle**, baffle, mystify, bemuse, bewilder, confound, confuse, nonplus, disconcert; *informal* flummox.

perplexing *adjective* **puzzling**, baffling, mystifying, mysterious, bewildering, confusing, disconcerting, worrying.

persecute *verb* **1 oppress**, abuse, victimize, ill-treat, mistreat, maltreat, torment, torture. **2 harass**, hound, plague, badger, harry, intimidate, pick on, pester; *informal* hassle.

persecution *noun* **1 oppression**, victimization, ill-treatment, mistreatment, abuse, discrimination. **2 harassment**, hounding, intimidation, bullying.

persevere *verb* **persist**, continue, carry on, go on, keep on, keep going, struggle on, hammer away, be persistent, keep at it, not take no for an answer, be tenacious, plod on, plough on; *informal* soldier on, hang on, plug away, stick to your guns, stick it out, hang in there.
- OPPOSITES give up.

persist *verb* **1** *he persisted with his questioning* **persevere**, continue, carry on, go on, keep on, keep going, hammer away, keep at it; *informal* soldier on, plug away. **2** *the dry weather persists* **continue**, hold, carry on, last, keep on, remain, linger, stay, endure.
- OPPOSITES give up, stop.

persistence *noun* **perseverance**, tenacity, determination, staying power, endurance, doggedness, stamina; *informal* stickability; *formal* pertinacity.

persistent *adjective* **1 tenacious**, determined, resolute, dogged, tireless, indefatigable, insistent, unrelenting; *formal* pertinacious. **2 constant**, continuous,

continuing, continual, non-stop, never-ending, steady, uninterrupted, unbroken, interminable, incessant, endless, unending, unrelenting. **3** *a persistent cough* **chronic**, nagging, frequent, repeated, habitual.
- OPPOSITES irresolute, intermittent.

person *noun* **human being**, individual, man, woman, human, being, living soul, mortal, creature; *informal* type, sort, beggar, cookie.
□ **in person** physically, in the flesh, personally, yourself.

personal *adjective* **1 distinctive**, characteristic, unique, individual, idiosyncratic. **2 in person**, in the flesh, actual, live, physical. **3 private**, intimate. **4 derogatory**, disparaging, belittling, insulting, rude, disrespectful, offensive, pejorative.

personality *noun* **1 character**, nature, disposition, temperament, make-up, psyche. **2 charisma**, magnetism, character, charm, presence. **3 celebrity**, VIP, star, superstar, big name, somebody, leading light, luminary, notable; *informal* celeb.

personally *adverb* **1 in person**, yourself. **2 for my part**, for myself, as far as I am concerned, from my own point of view, subjectively.

personification *noun* **embodiment**, incarnation, epitome, quintessence, essence, type, symbol, soul, model, exemplification, exemplar, image, representation.

personnel *noun* **staff**, employees, workforce, workers, labour force, manpower, human resources.

perspective *noun* **outlook**, view, viewpoint, point of view, standpoint, position, stand, stance, angle, slant, attitude.

persuade *verb* **1 prevail on**, talk into, coax, convince, get, induce, win over, bring round, influence, sway; *informal* sweet-talk. **2 cause**, lead, move, dispose, incline.
- OPPOSITES dissuade, deter.

persuasion *noun* **1 coaxing**, urging, inducement, encouragement; *informal* sweet-talking. **2 group**, grouping, sect, denomination, party, camp, side, faction, school of thought, belief, creed, faith.

persuasive *adjective* **convincing**, compelling, effective, telling, forceful, powerful, eloquent, impressive, sound, cogent, valid, strong, plausible, credible.
- OPPOSITES unconvincing.

pertain *verb* **1** *developments pertaining to the economy* **concern**, relate to, be connected with, be relevant to, apply to, refer to, have a bearing on, affect, involve, touch on. **2 exist**, be the case, prevail.

pertinent *adjective* **relevant**, to the point, apposite, appropriate, suitable, applicable, material, germane.
- OPPOSITES irrelevant.

perturb *verb* **worry**, upset, disturb, unsettle, concern, trouble, disquiet, disconcert, discomfit, unnerve, alarm, bother; *informal* rattle.
- OPPOSITES reassure.

pervade *verb* **permeate**, spread through, fill, suffuse, imbue, penetrate, filter through, infuse, inform.

pervasive *adjective* **prevalent**, pervading, extensive, ubiquitous, omnipresent, universal, widespread, general.

perverse *adjective* **1 awkward**, contrary, difficult, unreasonable, uncooperative, unhelpful, obstructive, stubborn, obstinate; *Brit. informal* bloody-minded, bolshie. **2 illogical**, irrational, wrong-headed.

perversion *noun* **1 distortion**, misrepresentation, travesty, twisting, corruption, misuse. **2 deviance**, abnormality, depravity.

pervert *verb* **distort**, warp, corrupt, subvert, twist, bend, abuse, divert.
● *noun* **deviant**, degenerate; *informal* perv, dirty old man, sicko.

perverted *adjective* **unnatural**, deviant, warped, twisted, abnormal, unhealthy, depraved, perverse, aberrant, debased, degenerate; *informal* sick, kinky.

pessimist *noun* **defeatist**, fatalist, prophet of doom, alarmist, cynic, sceptic, misery, killjoy, Cassandra; *informal* doom (and gloom) merchant, wet blanket.
– OPPOSITES optimist.

pessimistic *adjective* **gloomy**, negative, cynical, defeatist, downbeat, bleak, fatalistic, depressed.
– OPPOSITES optimistic.

pest *noun* **nuisance**, annoyance, irritant, thorn in your flesh/side, trial, menace, trouble, problem, worry, bother; *informal* pain in the neck, headache.

pester *verb* **badger**, hound, harass, plague, annoy, bother, harry, worry; *informal* hassle, bug.

pet *adjective* **1 tame**, domesticated, companion; *Brit.* house-trained; *N. Amer.* housebroken. **2 favourite**, favoured, cherished, particular, special, personal.
● *verb* **1 stroke**, caress, fondle, pat, tickle. **2 cuddle**, embrace, caress, kiss; *informal* canoodle, neck, smooch; *Brit. informal* snog; *N. Amer. informal* make out.

peter *verb*
□ **peter out** fizzle out, fade (away), die away/out, dwindle, diminish, taper off, tail off, trail away/off, wane, ebb, melt away, evaporate, disappear.

petition *noun* **appeal**, round robin, letter, request, entreaty, application, plea.
● *verb* **appeal to**, request, ask, call on, entreat, beg, implore, plead with, apply to, press, urge.

petrified *adjective* **1 terrified**, horrified, scared/frightened out of your wits, scared/frightened to death. **2 ossified**, fossilized, calcified.

petty *adjective* **1 trivial**, trifling, minor, insignificant, paltry, unimportant, inconsequential, footling, negligible; *informal* piffling. **2 small-minded**, mean, shabby, spiteful.
– OPPOSITES important, magnanimous.

petulant *adjective* **peevish**, bad-tempered, querulous, pettish, fretful, irritable, sulky, tetchy, crotchety, testy, fractious; *informal* grouchy; *Brit. informal* ratty; *N. English informal* mardy; *N. Amer. informal* cranky.
– OPPOSITES good-humoured.

phantom *noun* **ghost**, apparition, spirit, spectre, wraith; *informal* spook.

phase *noun* **stage**, period, chapter, episode, part, step.

phenomenal *adjective* **remarkable**, exceptional, extraordinary, marvellous, miraculous, wonderful, outstanding, unprecedented; *informal* fantastic, terrific, tremendous, stupendous.

phenomenon *noun* **1 occurrence**, event, happening, fact, situation, circumstance, experience, case, incident, episode. **2 marvel**, sensation, wonder, prodigy.

philanderer *noun* **womanizer**, Casanova, Don Juan, Lothario, flirt, ladies' man, playboy; *informal* stud, ladykiller.

philanthropic *adjective* **charitable**, generous, benevolent, humanitarian, public-spirited, altruistic, magnanimous, unselfish, kind.
– OPPOSITES selfish, mean.

philistine *adjective* **uncultured**, lowbrow, uncultivated, uncivilized, uneducated, unenlightened, commercial, materialist, bourgeois, ignorant, crass, boorish, barbarian.
● *noun* **barbarian**, boor, yahoo, materialist.

philosopher *noun* **thinker**, theorist, theoretician, scholar, intellectual, sage.

philosophical *adjective* **1 theoretical**, metaphysical. **2 thoughtful**, reflective, pensive, meditative, contemplative, introspective. **3 stoical**, self-possessed, serene, dispassionate, phlegmatic, long-suffering, resigned.

philosophy *noun* **1 thinking**, thought, reasoning, logic. **2 beliefs**, credo, ideology, ideas, thinking, theories, doctrine, principles, views, outlook.

phobia *noun* **fear**, dread, horror, terror, aversion, antipathy, revulsion; *informal* hang-up.

phone *noun* **telephone**, mobile; *N. Amer.* cellphone, cell; *Brit. informal* blower.
● *verb* **call**, telephone; *Brit.* ring, give someone a ring; *informal* call up, give someone a buzz; *Brit. informal* give someone a bell.

phoney *(informal) adjective* **bogus**, false, fake, fraudulent, counterfeit, forged, imitation, affected, insincere; *informal* pretend; *Brit. informal* cod.
– OPPOSITES authentic.
● *noun* **1 impostor**, sham, fake, fraud, charlatan; *informal* con artist. **2 fake**, imitation, counterfeit, forgery.

photocopy *noun* **copy**, duplicate, reproduction, facsimile; *trademark* Xerox, photostat.
● *verb* **copy**, duplicate, xerox, photostat, reproduce.

photograph *noun* **picture**, photo, snap, snapshot, shot, print, still, transparency.

photographic *adjective* **1 pictorial**, graphic, in photographs. **2 detailed**, exact, precise, accurate, vivid.

phrase *noun* **expression**, construction, term, turn of phrase, idiom, saying.
● *verb* **express**, put into words, put, word, formulate, couch, frame.

physical *adjective* **1 bodily**, corporeal, corporal, carnal, fleshly, non-spiritual. **2 manual**, labouring, blue-collar. **3 material**, concrete, tangible, palpable, solid, substantial, real, actual, visible.
– OPPOSITES mental, spiritual.

physician *noun* **doctor**, medical practitioner, general practitioner, GP, clinician, specialist, consultant; *informal* doc, medic, quack.

pick *verb* **1 harvest**, gather (in), collect, pluck. **2 choose**, select, single out, opt for, plump for, elect, decide on, settle on, fix on, name, nominate, identify. **3** *pick a fight* **provoke**, start, cause, incite, instigate, prompt.
● *noun* **best**, finest, choice, choicest, cream, flower, crème de la crème, elite.
□ **pick on** bully, victimize, torment, persecute, taunt, tease; *informal* get at, needle. **pick out** see, make out, distinguish, discern, spot, perceive, detect, notice, recognize, identify, catch sight of, glimpse. **pick up 1** improve, recover, rally, bounce back, perk up, look up, take a turn for the better, turn the corner, be on the mend, make headway, make progress. **2** lift, take up, raise, hoist, scoop up, gather up, snatch up. **3** arrest, apprehend, detain, take into custody, seize; *informal* nab, run in; *Brit. informal* nick. **4** *he picked up the story in the 1950s* resume, take up, start again, recommence, continue, carry/go on with.

picket *noun* **1 demonstrator**, striker, protester. **2 demonstration**, picket line, blockade, boycott, strike.

pickup *noun* **improvement**, recovery, revival, upturn, upswing, rally, resurgence, renewal, turnaround.

picture *noun* **1 painting**, **drawing**, sketch, watercolour, print, canvas, portrait, illustration, depiction, likeness, representation, image. **2 photograph**, photo, snap, snapshot, shot, frame, exposure, still, print. **3 concept**, idea, impression, image, vision, visualization, notion. **4 personification**, embodiment, epitome, essence, quintessence, soul, model.
● *verb* **1 depict**, portray, show, represent, draw, sketch, photograph, paint. **2 visualize**, see (in your mind's eye), imagine, remember.

picturesque *adjective* **attractive**, pretty, beautiful, lovely, scenic, charming, quaint, pleasing, delightful.
– OPPOSITES ugly.

piece *noun* **1 bit**, slice, chunk, segment, section, lump, hunk, wedge, slab, block, cake, bar, stick, length. **2 component**, part, bit, constituent, element, section, unit, module. **3 item**, article, specimen. **4 share**, portion, slice, quota, part, percentage, amount, quantity, ration, fraction; *Brit. informal* whack. **5 work (of art)**, artwork, artefact, composition, opus. **6 article**, item, story, report, essay, feature, review, column.

pier *noun* **jetty**, quay, wharf, dock, landing stage.

pierce *verb* **penetrate**, puncture, perforate, prick, spike, stab, drill, bore.

piercing *adjective* **1 shrill**, ear-splitting, high-pitched, penetrating, strident. **2 searching**, probing, penetrating, sharp, keen, shrewd.

pig *noun* **hog**, boar, sow, porker, swine, piglet.

WORD LINKS
porcine relating to pigs

pigment *noun* **colouring**, colour, tint, dye, stain.

pile[1] *noun* **1 heap**, stack, mound, pyramid, mass, collection, accumulation, assemblage, stockpile, hoard. **2** *(informal)* **lot**, mountain, reams, abundance; *informal* load, heap, mass, slew, stack, ton, oodles.
● *verb* **1 heap**, stack, load, fill, charge. **2 crowd**, clamber, pack, squeeze, scramble, struggle.
□ **pile up** accumulate, amass, grow, mount up, build up, multiply, escalate, soar, spiral, rocket, increase.

pile[2] *noun* **nap**, fibres, threads.

pile-up *noun* **crash**, collision, smash, accident; *Brit.* RTA; *N. Amer.* wreck; *Brit. informal* shunt.

pilgrim *noun* **traveller**, wayfarer, worshipper, devotee, believer; *Islam* haji; *old use* palmer.

pilgrimage *noun* **journey**, expedition, mission, hajj, visit, trek, trip, odyssey.

pill *noun* **tablet**, capsule, pellet, lozenge, pastille.

pillar *noun* **1 column**, post, support, upright, pier, pile, prop, stanchion, obelisk. **2 stalwart**, mainstay, bastion, leading light, worthy, backbone, supporter, upholder, champion.

pilot *noun* **1 airman**, **airwoman**, flyer, captain; *informal* skipper; *dated* aviator. **2 navigator**, helmsman, steersman, coxswain. **3 trial**, sample, experiment.
● *adjective* **experimental**, exploratory, trial, test, sample, preliminary.
● *verb* **navigate**, guide, manoeuvre, steer, control, direct, captain, fly, drive, sail; *informal* skipper.

pin *noun* **1 tack**, safety pin, nail, staple, fastener. **2 bolt**, peg, rod, rivet, dowel. **3 badge**, brooch.
● *verb* **1 attach**, fasten, affix, fix, join, secure, clip, nail. **2 hold**, press, pinion.
□ **pin down** confine, trap, hem in, corner, close in, shut in, pen in. **pin on** blame for, hold responsible for, attribute to, ascribe to, lay something at someone's door; *informal* stick on.

pinch *verb* **nip**, tweak, squeeze, grasp, compress.
● *noun* **1 nip**, tweak, squeeze. **2 bit**, touch, dash, spot, trace, soupçon, speck, taste; *informal* smidgen, tad.

pine *verb* **fade**, waste away, weaken, decline, languish, wilt, sicken.
□ **pine for** long for, yearn for, ache for, sigh for, hunger for, thirst for, itch for, carry a torch for, miss, mourn.

pink *adjective* **rose**, rosy, rosé, pale red, salmon, coral, flushed, blushing.

pinnacle *noun* **1 height**, peak, high point, top, apex, zenith, acme. **2 peak**, needle, crag, tor.
– OPPOSITES nadir.

pinpoint *adjective pinpoint accuracy* **precise**, exact, strict, absolute, complete, scientific.
● *verb* **identify**, determine, distinguish, discover, find, locate, detect, track down, spot, diagnose, recognize, pin down, home in on.

pioneer *noun* **1 settler**, colonist, colonizer, frontiersman, explorer. **2 developer**, innovator, trailblazer, groundbreaker, founding father, architect, creator.
● *verb* **introduce**, develop, launch, instigate, initiate, spearhead, institute, establish, found.

pious *adjective* **religious**, devout, God-fearing, churchgoing, holy, godly, saintly, reverent, righteous.
- OPPOSITES irreligious.

pipe *noun* **tube**, conduit, hose, main, duct, line, channel, pipeline, drain.
● *verb* **feed**, siphon, channel, run, convey.

piquant *adjective* **1** *a piquant sauce* **spicy**, tangy, peppery, hot, tasty, flavoursome, savoury, pungent, sharp, tart, zesty, strong, salty. **2** *a piquant story* **intriguing**, stimulating, interesting, fascinating, colourful, exciting, lively, spicy, provocative, racy; *informal* juicy.
- OPPOSITES bland, dull.

pirate *noun* **raider**, hijacker, freebooter, marauder; *historical* privateer, buccaneer; *old use* corsair.
● *verb* **steal**, copy, plagiarize, poach, appropriate, bootleg; *informal* crib, lift, rip off.

pit *noun* **1 hole**, trough, hollow, excavation, cavity, crater, pothole. **2 coal mine**, colliery, quarry, shaft.
● *verb* **mark**, pockmark, pock, scar, dent, indent.

pitch *noun* **1 playing field**, ground, sports field, stadium; *Brit.* park. **2 tone**, key, modulation, frequency. **3 gradient**, slope, slant, angle, tilt, incline. **4 level**, intensity, point, degree, height, extent. **5 patter**, talk; *informal* spiel, line.
● *verb* **1 throw**, toss, fling, hurl, cast, lob, flip; *informal* chuck, sling, heave, bung. **2 fall**, tumble, topple, plunge, plummet. **3 put up**, set up, erect, raise. **4 lurch**, toss, plunge, roll, reel, sway, rock, list.

pitfall *noun* **hazard**, danger, risk, peril, difficulty, catch, snag, stumbling block, drawback, issue.

pitiful *adjective* **1 distressing**, sad, piteous, pitiable, pathetic, heart-rending, moving, touching, tear-jerking, plaintive, poignant, forlorn, poor, sorry, wretched, miserable. **2 paltry**, miserable, meagre, trifling, negligible, pitiable, derisory; *informal* pathetic, measly; *Brit. informal* poxy. **3 dreadful**, awful, terrible, appalling, lamentable, hopeless, feeble, pitiable, woeful, inadequate, deplorable, laughable; *informal* pathetic, useless, lousy, abysmal, dire.

pitiless *adjective* **merciless**, unmerciful, ruthless, cruel, heartless, remorseless, hard-hearted, cold-hearted, harsh, callous, severe, unsparing, unforgiving, unfeeling, uncaring, unsympathetic, uncharitable.
- OPPOSITES merciful.

pity *noun* **1 compassion**, commiseration, condolence, sympathy, fellow feeling, understanding. **2** *it's a pity you can't go* **shame**, misfortune.
- OPPOSITES indifference.
● *verb* **feel sorry for**, feel for, sympathize with, empathize with, commiserate with, take pity on, be moved by, bleed for.

pivot *noun* **fulcrum**, axis, axle, swivel, pin, shaft, hub, spindle, hinge, kingpin.
● *verb* **1 rotate**, turn, swivel, revolve, spin. **2** *it all pivoted on his response* **depend**, hinge, turn, centre, hang, rely, rest, revolve around.

placate *verb* **pacify**, calm, appease, mollify, soothe, win over, conciliate, propitiate, make peace with, humour.
- OPPOSITES provoke.

place *noun* **1 location**, site, spot, setting, position, situation, area, region, locale, venue. **2 country**, state, area, region, town, city. **3 home**, house, flat, apartment, pied-à-terre, accommodation, property, rooms, quarters; *informal* pad; *formal* residence, abode, dwelling. **4 situation**, position, circumstances. **5 seat**, chair, space. **6 job**, position, post, appointment, situation, employment. **7 status**, position, standing, rank, niche. **8 responsibility**, duty, job, task, role, function, concern, affair, charge.
● *verb* **1 put (down)**, set (down), lay, deposit, position, plant, rest, stand, station, situate, leave; *informal* stick, dump, bung, park, plonk, pop; *N. Amer.*

informal plunk. **2 rank**, order, grade, class, classify, put. **3 identify**, recognize, remember, put a name to, pin down, locate, pinpoint.
□ **out of place 1** inappropriate, unsuitable, unseemly, improper, untoward, out of keeping, unbecoming. **2** incongruous, out of your element, like a fish out of water, uncomfortable, uneasy. **take place** happen, occur, come about, go on, transpire; *N. Amer. informal* go down. **take the place of** replace, stand in for, substitute for, act for, fill in for, cover for, relieve.

placid *adjective* **1 even-tempered**, calm, tranquil, equable, unexcitable, serene, mild, composed, self-possessed, poised, easy-going, level-headed, steady, unruffled, unperturbed, phlegmatic; *informal* unflappable. **2 quiet**, calm, tranquil, still, peaceful, undisturbed, restful, sleepy.
– OPPOSITES excitable.

plagiarize *verb* **copy**, pirate, steal, poach, appropriate; *informal* rip off, crib; *Brit. informal* pinch, nick.

plague *noun* **1 pandemic**, epidemic, disease, sickness; *dated* contagion; *old use* pestilence. **2 infestation**, invasion, swarm.
● *verb* **1 afflict**, trouble, torment, beset, dog, curse, bedevil. **2 pester**, harass, badger, bother, torment, harry, hound, trouble, nag, molest; *informal* hassle, bug.

plain *adjective* **1 obvious**, clear, evident, apparent, manifest, unmistakable. **2 intelligible**, comprehensible, understandable, clear, lucid, simple, straightforward, user-friendly. **3 candid**, frank, outspoken, forthright, direct, honest, truthful, blunt, bald, unequivocal; *informal* upfront. **4 simple**, ordinary, unadorned, homely, basic, modest, unsophisticated, restrained. **5 unattractive**, unprepossessing, ugly, ordinary; *N. Amer.* homely; *Brit. informal* no oil painting. **6 sheer**, pure, downright, out-and-out.
– OPPOSITES obscure, fancy, attractive.
● *noun* **grassland**, flatland, prairie, savannah, steppe, tundra, pampas, veld, plateau.

plaintive *adjective* **mournful**, sad, pathetic, pitiful, melancholy, sorrowful, unhappy, wretched, woeful, forlorn.

plan *noun* **1 scheme**, idea, proposal, proposition, project, programme, system, method, strategy, stratagem, solution, formula, recipe. **2 intention**, aim, idea, objective, object, goal, target, ambition. **3 map**, diagram, chart, blueprint, drawing, sketch, impression; *N. Amer.* plat.
● *verb* **1 organize**, arrange, work out, outline, map out, prepare, formulate, frame, develop, devise. **2 intend**, aim, propose, mean, hope. **3 design**, draw up a plan for, sketch out, map out; *N. Amer.* plat.

plane[1] *noun* **level**, degree, standard, stratum, dimension.
● *verb* **skim**, glide.

plane[2] *noun* **aircraft**, airliner, jet, flying machine; *Brit.* aeroplane; *N. Amer.* airplane, ship.

WORD LINKS
aeronautics science of flight

plant *noun* **1 flower**, vegetable, herb, shrub, bush, weed; (**plants**) vegetation, greenery, flora. **2 spy**, informant, informer, secret agent, mole, infiltrator, operative; *N. Amer. informal* spook. **3 factory**, works, facility, refinery, mill. **4 machinery**, machines, equipment, apparatus, appliances, gear.
● *verb* **1 sow**, scatter. **2 place**, put, set, position, situate, settle; *informal* plonk. **3 instil**, implant, put, place, introduce, fix, establish, lodge.

WORD LINKS
botany study of plants
herbivorous plant-eating

plaster *verb* **1 spread**, smother, smear, cake, coat, bedaub. **2 flatten (down)**, smooth down, slick down.

plastic *adjective* **1 soft**, pliable, pliant, flexible, malleable, workable, mouldable; *informal* bendy. **2 artificial**, false, fake, bogus, insincere; *informal* phoney, pretend.

plate *noun* **1 dish**, platter, salver; *historical* trencher; *old use* charger. **2 plateful**, helping, portion, serving. **3 panel**, sheet, slab. **4 plaque**, sign, tablet. **5 picture**, print, illustration, photograph, photo.
● *verb* **cover**, coat, overlay, laminate, gild.

plateau *noun* **upland**, mesa, highland, tableland.

platform *noun* **1 stage**, dais, rostrum, podium, stand. **2 programme**, manifesto, policies, principles, party line.

platitude *noun* **cliché**, truism, commonplace, old chestnut, banality.

platter *noun* **plate**, dish, salver, tray; *old use* charger.

plausible *adjective* **credible**, believable, reasonable, likely, possible, conceivable, imaginable, convincing, persuasive.
– OPPOSITES unlikely.

play *verb* **1 amuse yourself**, entertain yourself, enjoy yourself, have fun, relax, occupy yourself, frolic, romp, cavort; *informal* mess about/around. **2 take part in**, participate in, be involved in, compete in, do. **3 compete against**, take on, meet. **4 act the part of**, take the role of, appear as, portray, perform.
● *noun* **1 amusement**, relaxation, recreation, diversion, leisure, enjoyment, pleasure, fun. **2 drama**, theatrical work, piece, comedy, tragedy, production, performance.
□ **play down** make light of, make little of, gloss over, downplay, understate, soft-pedal, diminish, trivialize. **play up** *(Brit. informal)* **1** misbehave, be bad, be naughty. **2** malfunction, not work, be defective, be faulty; *informal* be on the blink, act up.

player *noun* **1 participant**, contestant, competitor, contender, sportsman, sportswoman. **2 musician**, performer, artist, virtuoso, instrumentalist. **3 actor**, **actress**, performer, thespian, entertainer, artiste, trouper.

playful *adjective* **1 frisky**, lively, full of fun, frolicsome, high-spirited, exuberant, mischievous, impish; *informal* full of beans. **2 light-hearted**, jokey, teasing, humorous, jocular, facetious, frivolous, flippant.
– OPPOSITES serious.

plea *noun* **appeal**, entreaty, supplication, petition, request, call.

plead *verb* **claim**, use as an excuse, assert, allege, argue.
□ **plead with** beg, implore, entreat, appeal to, ask.

pleasant *adjective* **1 enjoyable**, pleasurable, nice, agreeable, entertaining, amusing, delightful, charming; *informal* lovely, great. **2 friendly**, charming, agreeable, amiable, nice, delightful, sweet, genial, cordial, good-natured, personable, hospitable, polite.

please *verb* **1 make happy**, give pleasure to, delight, charm, amuse, entertain, divert, satisfy, gratify, humour. **2 like**, want, wish, desire, see fit, think fit, choose, will, prefer.
– OPPOSITES annoy.

pleased *adjective* **happy**, glad, delighted, gratified, grateful, thankful, content, contented, satisfied, thrilled; *informal* over the moon, on cloud nine; *Brit. informal* chuffed; *N. English informal* made up; *Austral. informal* wrapped.
– OPPOSITES unhappy.

pleasing *adjective* **1 good**, agreeable, pleasant, pleasurable, satisfying, gratifying, great. **2 friendly**, amiable, pleasant, agreeable, affable, nice, genial, likeable, charming, engaging, delightful; *informal* lovely.

pleasure *noun* **happiness**, delight, joy, gladness, glee, satisfaction, gratification, contentment, enjoyment, amusement, fun, entertainment, relaxation, recreation, diversion.

pledge *noun* **promise**, vow, undertaking, word, commitment, assurance, oath, guarantee.
● *verb* **promise**, vow, undertake, swear, commit yourself, declare, affirm.

plentiful *adjective* **abundant**, copious, ample, profuse, rich, lavish, generous, bountiful, bumper, prolific; *informal* galore.
- OPPOSITES scarce.

plenty *pronoun* **a lot of**, many, a great deal of, a plethora of, enough and to spare, no lack of, a wealth of; *informal* loads of, heaps of, stacks of, masses of, oodles of.
● *noun* **prosperity**, affluence, wealth, opulence, comfort, luxury, abundance.

plethora *noun* **excess**, abundance, superabundance, surplus, glut, surfeit, profusion, enough and to spare.
- OPPOSITES dearth.

pliable *adjective* **1 flexible**, pliant, bendable, supple, workable, plastic; *informal* bendy. **2 malleable**, impressionable, flexible, adaptable, biddable, pliant, tractable, suggestible, persuadable.
- OPPOSITES rigid.

plight *noun* **predicament**, difficult situation, dire straits, trouble, difficulty, bind; *informal* tight corner, tight spot, hole, pickle, jam, fix.

plod *verb* **trudge**, walk heavily, clump, stomp, tramp, lumber, slog.

plot *noun* **1 conspiracy**, intrigue, stratagem, plan, machinations. **2 storyline**, story, scenario, action, thread, narrative. **3 piece of ground**, patch, area, tract, acreage; *Brit.* allotment; *N. Amer.* lot, plat.
● *verb* **1 plan**, scheme, arrange, organize, contrive. **2 conspire**, scheme, intrigue, connive. **3 mark**, chart, map.

plough *verb* **1 till**, furrow, harrow, cultivate, work. **2 crash**, smash, career, plunge, bulldoze, hurtle, cannon.

ploy *noun* **ruse**, tactic, move, device, stratagem, scheme, trick, gambit, plan, manoeuvre, dodge, subterfuge; *Brit. informal* wheeze.

pluck *verb* **1 remove**, pick, pull, extract. **2 pull**, tug, clutch, snatch, grab, catch, tweak, jerk; *informal* yank. **3 strum**, pick, thrum, twang.
● *noun* **courage**, bravery, nerve, daring, spirit, grit; *informal* guts; *Brit. informal* bottle; *N. Amer. informal* moxie.

plug *noun* **1 stopper**, bung, cork; *N. Amer.* stopple. **2** *(informal)* **advertisement**, promotion, commercial, recommendation, mention, good word; *informal* hype, push, puff.
● *verb* **1 stop**, seal, close, block, fill. **2** *(informal)* **publicize**, promote, advertise, mention, bang the drum for, draw attention to; *informal* hype, push.

plumb *verb* **explore**, probe, delve into, search, examine, investigate, fathom, penetrate, understand.
● *adverb (informal)* **right**, exactly, precisely, directly, dead, straight; *informal* (slap) bang.

plummet *verb* **plunge**, dive, drop, fall, hurtle, nosedive, tumble.
- OPPOSITES soar.

plump *adjective* **fat**, chubby, rotund, ample, round, stout, portly, overweight; *informal* tubby, roly-poly, pudgy; *Brit. informal* podgy; *N. Amer. informal* zaftig, corn-fed.
- OPPOSITES thin.

plunder *verb* **1 pillage**, loot, rob, raid, ransack, rifle, strip, sack. **2 steal**, seize, thieve, pilfer, embezzle.
● *noun* **booty**, loot, stolen goods, spoils, ill-gotten gains; *informal* swag.

plunge *verb* **1 dive**, jump, throw yourself, immerse yourself. **2 plummet**, nosedive, drop, fall, tumble, descend. **3 charge**, hurtle, career, plough, tear; *N. Amer. informal* barrel. **4 thrust**, stab, sink, stick, ram, drive, push, shove, force.

plus *preposition* **as well as**, together with, along with, in addition to, and, added to, not to mention.
- OPPOSITES minus.
● *noun* **advantage**, good point, asset, pro, benefit, bonus, attraction; *informal* perk.
- OPPOSITES disadvantage.

plush *adjective (informal)* **luxurious**, luxury, de luxe, sumptuous, opulent, magnificent, rich, expensive, fancy; *Brit.* upmarket; *informal* posh, classy;

Brit. informal swish; *N. Amer. informal* swank.
- OPPOSITES austere.

ply *verb* **1 engage in**, carry on, pursue, conduct, practise. **2 travel**, shuttle, go back and forth. **3** *she plied me with scones* **provide**, supply, shower. **4** *he plied her with questions* **bombard**, assail, pester, plague, harass; *informal* hassle.

pocket *noun* **1 pouch**, compartment. **2 area**, patch, region, cluster.
● *adjective* **small**, little, miniature, mini, fun-size, compact, concise, abridged, portable.
● *verb* **1 acquire**, obtain, gain, get, secure, win, make, earn. **2 steal**, appropriate, purloin, misappropriate, embezzle.

pod *noun* **shell**, husk, hull, case; *N. Amer.* shuck.

podium *noun* **platform**, stage, dais, rostrum, stand.

poem *noun* **verse**, rhyme, lyric, piece of poetry.

poetic *adjective* **expressive**, figurative, symbolic, flowery, artistic, imaginative, creative.

poetry *noun* **poems**, verse, versification, rhyme.

poignant *adjective* **touching**, moving, sad, affecting, pitiful, pathetic, plaintive.

point *noun* **1 tip**, (sharp) end, extremity, prong, spike, tine, nib, barb. **2 pinpoint**, dot, spot, speck. **3 place**, position, location, site, spot. **4 time**, stage, juncture, period, phase. **5 level**, degree, stage, pitch, extent. **6 detail**, item, fact, thing, argument, consideration, factor, element, subject, issue, topic, question, matter. **7 heart of the matter**, essence, nub, core, crux; *informal* nitty-gritty. **8 purpose**, aim, object, objective, goal, intention, use, sense, value, advantage. **9 attribute**, characteristic, feature, trait, quality, property, aspect, side.
● *verb* **aim**, direct, level, train, focus.
□ **point out** identify, show, draw attention to, indicate, specify, detail, mention. **point to** indicate, suggest, evidence, signal, signify, denote.

pointed *adjective* **1 sharp**, spiky, spiked, tapering, barbed. **2 cutting**, biting, incisive, trenchant, acerbic, caustic, scathing, venomous, sarcastic.

pointer *noun* **1 indicator**, needle, arrow, hand. **2 indication**, indicator, clue, hint, sign, signal, evidence. **3 tip**, hint, suggestion, guideline, recommendation.

pointless *adjective* **senseless**, futile, useless, hopeless, unavailing, unproductive, aimless, idle, worthless, valueless.
- OPPOSITES valuable.

poise *noun* **1 grace**, gracefulness, elegance, balance, control. **2 composure**, equanimity, self-possession, aplomb, self-assurance, self-control, sangfroid, dignity, presence of mind; *informal* cool.

poised *adjective* **1 balanced**, suspended, motionless, hanging, hovering. **2 prepared**, ready, braced, geared up, all set, standing by.

poison *noun* **toxin**, venom.
● *verb* **pollute**, contaminate, infect, taint, spoil.

WORD LINKS
toxicology study of poisons

poisonous *adjective* **1 venomous**, deadly. **2 toxic**, noxious, deadly, fatal, lethal, mortal, environmentally unfriendly, polluting. **3 malicious**, malevolent, hostile, spiteful, bitter, venomous, malign.
- OPPOSITES harmless.

poke *verb* **1 prod**, jab, dig, elbow, nudge, shove, jolt, stab, stick. **2** *leave the cable poking out* **stick out**, jut out, protrude, project, extend.
● *noun* **prod**, jab, dig, elbow, nudge.

poky *adjective* **small**, little, tiny, cramped, confined, restricted, boxy.
- OPPOSITES spacious.

pole *noun* **post**, pillar, stanchion, stake, support, prop, stick, paling, staff.

police *noun* **police force**, police service, police officers, policemen, policewomen; *Brit.* constabulary; *informal* the cops, the fuzz, the law, the boys in blue; *Brit. informal* the (Old) Bill; *N. Amer. informal* the heat.
● *verb* **1 guard**, watch over, protect, defend, patrol. **2 enforce**, regulate, oversee, supervise, monitor, observe, check.

police officer *noun* **policeman**, **policewoman**; *Brit.* constable; *N. Amer.* patrolman, trooper, roundsman; *informal* cop; *Brit. informal* copper, rozzer, bobby; *N. Amer. informal* uniform.

policy *noun* **plans**, approach, code, system, guidelines, theory, line, position, stance.

polish *verb* **1 shine**, wax, buff, rub up/down, gloss, burnish. **2** *polish up your essay* **perfect**, refine, improve, hone, enhance, brush up, revise, edit, correct, rewrite, go over, touch up.
● *noun* **sophistication**, refinement, urbanity, suaveness, elegance, style, grace, finesse; *informal* class.

polished *adjective* **1 shiny**, glossy, gleaming, lustrous, glassy, waxed, buffed, burnished. **2 expert**, accomplished, masterly, skilful, adept, adroit, dexterous, consummate, superlative, superb.
– OPPOSITES dull, inexpert.

polite *adjective* **1 well mannered**, civil, courteous, respectful, well behaved, well bred, gentlemanly, ladylike, genteel, gracious, tactful, diplomatic. **2 civilized**, refined, cultured, sophisticated, urbane.
– OPPOSITES rude.

politic *adjective* **wise**, prudent, sensible, shrewd, astute, judicious, expedient, advantageous, beneficial, profitable.
– OPPOSITES unwise.

political *adjective* **governmental**, government, constitutional, ministerial, parliamentary, diplomatic, legislative, administrative.

politician *noun* **legislator**, Member of Parliament, MP, representative, minister, statesman, stateswoman, senator, congressman, congresswoman; *informal* politico.

poll *noun* **1 vote**, ballot, show of hands, referendum, plebiscite, election. **2 survey**, opinion poll, market research, census.
● *verb* **1 canvass**, survey, ask, question, interview, ballot. **2 get**, gain, register, record, return.

pollute *verb* **contaminate**, taint, poison, foul, dirty, soil, infect.
– OPPOSITES purify.

pollution *noun* **contamination**, impurity, dirt, filth, infection.

pomp *noun* **ceremony**, solemnity, ritual, display, spectacle, pageantry, show, ostentation, splendour, grandeur, magnificence, majesty, stateliness, glory; *informal* razzmatazz.

pompous *adjective* **self-important**, overbearing, sententious, grandiose, affected, pretentious, puffed up, haughty, proud, conceited, supercilious, condescending, patronizing.

ponder *verb* **think about**, contemplate, consider, review, reflect on, mull over, meditate on, muse on, dwell on.

pontificate *verb* **hold forth**, expound, declaim, preach, lay down the law, sound off, lecture; *informal* mouth off.

pool[1] *noun* **puddle**, pond, lake; *literary* mere.

pool[2] *noun* **1 supply**, reserve(s), reservoir, fund, store, bank, stock, cache. **2 fund**, reserve, kitty, pot, bank, purse.
● *verb* **combine**, group, join, unite, merge, share.

poor *adjective* **1 poverty-stricken**, penniless, impoverished, impecunious, needy, destitute; *Brit.* on the breadline; *informal* hard up, strapped, on your uppers; *formal* penurious. **2 substandard**, bad, deficient, defective, faulty, imperfect, inferior, unsatisfactory, shoddy, crude, inadequate, unacceptable; *informal* crummy, rotten; *Brit. informal* duff. **3 meagre**, scanty, scant, paltry, reduced, modest, sparse, spare,

deficient, insubstantial, skimpy, lean; *informal* measly, stingy. **4 unfortunate**, unlucky, unhappy, hapless, wretched, luckless, ill-fated, ill-starred.
– OPPOSITES rich.

poorly *adverb* **badly**, imperfectly, incompetently, crudely, shoddily, inadequately.
● *adjective* **ill**, unwell, not very well, ailing, indisposed, out of sorts, under par, peaky; *Brit.* off colour; *informal* under the weather, rough; *Brit. informal* ropy, grotty; *Scottish informal* wabbit; *Austral./NZ informal* crook.

pop *verb* **1 go bang**, go off, crack, snap, burst, explode. **2 go**; *informal* tootle, whip; *Brit. informal* nip. **3 put**, place, slip, throw, slide, stick, set, lay, position.
● *noun* **bang**, crack, snap, explosion, report.

populace *noun* **population**, inhabitants, residents, natives, community, country, (general) public, people, nation, common people, masses, multitude, rank and file; *Brit. informal* Joe Public; *derogatory* hoi polloi, common herd, rabble, riff-raff.

popular *adjective* **1 well liked**, sought-after, in demand, commercial, marketable, fashionable, in vogue, all the rage, hot; *informal* in, cool, big. **2 non-specialist**, non-technical, amateur, lay person's, general, middle-of-the-road, accessible, simplified, understandable, mass-market. **3 widespread**, general, common, current, prevailing, standard, ordinary, conventional.

populate *verb* **inhabit**, occupy, people, settle, colonize.

population *noun* **inhabitants**, residents, people, citizens, public, community, populace, society, natives, occupants.

pornographic *adjective* **obscene**, indecent, dirty, smutty, filthy, erotic, titillating, sexy, risqué, X-rated, adult.

porous *adjective* **permeable**, penetrable, absorbent, spongy.
– OPPOSITES impermeable.

port *noun* **harbour**, docks, marina, haven, seaport.

portable *adjective* **transportable**, movable, mobile, wireless, lightweight, compact, handy, convenient.

portend *verb* **presage**, augur, foreshadow, foretell, prophesy, be a sign, warn, be an omen, indicate, herald, signal, bode, promise, threaten, signify, spell, denote.

porter[1] *noun* **carrier**, bearer; *N. Amer.* redcap, skycap.

porter[2] *noun (Brit.)* **doorman**, doorkeeper, commissionaire, gatekeeper, concierge, security officer.

portion *noun* **1 part**, piece, bit, section, segment. **2 share**, quota, ration, allocation, tranche; *Brit. informal* whack. **3 helping**, serving, plateful, slice, piece.

portrait *noun* **1 picture**, likeness, painting, drawing, photograph, image. **2 description**, portrayal, representation, depiction, impression, account, profile.

portray *verb* **1 paint**, draw, sketch, picture, depict, represent, illustrate, render, show. **2 describe**, depict, characterize, delineate, put into words. **3 play**, act the part of, take the role of, represent, appear as.

portrayal *noun* **description**, representation, characterization, depiction, delineation, evocation, interpretation.

pose *verb* **1 constitute**, present, offer. **2 raise**, ask, put, submit, advance, propose. **3 posture**, attitudinize, put on airs; *informal* show off, ponce about.
● *noun* **1 posture**, position, stance, attitude. **2 act**, affectation, show, display, front, airs.
□ **pose as** pretend to be, impersonate, pass yourself off as, masquerade as; *formal* personate.

poser[1] *noun* **difficult question**, problem, puzzle, mystery, riddle, conundrum; *informal* dilemma.

poser[2] *noun* **exhibitionist**, poseur; *informal* show-off, pseud.

posh *adjective* **1** *(informal)* **smart**, stylish, fancy, high-class, fashionable, chic, luxurious, luxury, exclusive; *Brit.* upmarket; *informal* classy, plush, flash; *Brit. informal* swish; *N. Amer. informal* swank, tony. **2** *(Brit. informal)* **upper-class**, aristocratic.

position *noun* **1 location**, place, situation, spot, site, locality, setting, area, whereabouts, bearings. **2 posture**, stance, attitude, pose. **3 situation**, state, condition, circumstances, predicament, plight. **4 status**, place, level, rank, standing, stature, prestige, reputation. **5 job**, post, situation, appointment, opening, vacancy, placement. **6 viewpoint**, opinion, outlook, attitude, stand, standpoint, stance, perspective, thinking, policy, feelings.
● *verb* **put**, place, locate, situate, set, site, stand, station, plant, stick; *informal* plonk, park.

positive *adjective* **1 affirmative**, favourable, good, enthusiastic, supportive, constructive, useful, productive, helpful, worthwhile, beneficial. **2 optimistic**, hopeful, confident, cheerful, sanguine, buoyant; *informal* upbeat. **3** *positive economic signs* **good**, promising, favourable, encouraging, heartening, propitious, auspicious. **4 definite**, certain, reliable, concrete, tangible, clear-cut, explicit, firm, decisive, real, actual. **5 convinced**, sure, confident, satisfied.
– OPPOSITES negative, pessimistic.

positively *adverb* **1 confidently**, definitely, firmly, categorically, with certainty, conclusively. **2 absolutely**, utterly, downright, simply, virtually; *informal* plain.

possess *verb* **1 own**, have (to your name), be in possession of. **2 have**, be blessed with, be endowed with, enjoy, boast. **3 take control of**, take over, bewitch, enchant, enslave.

possession *noun* **1 ownership**, control, hands, keeping, care, custody, charge. **2** *she packed her possessions* **belongings**, things, property, worldly goods, goods and chattels, personal effects, stuff, bits and pieces; *informal* gear, junk; *Brit. informal* clobber.

possessive *adjective* **proprietorial**, overprotective, controlling, dominating, jealous, clingy.

possibility *noun* **1 chance**, likelihood, probability, potentiality, hope, risk, hazard, danger, fear. **2 option**, alternative, choice, course of action, solution. **3 potential**, promise, prospects.

possible *adjective* **1 feasible**, practicable, viable, attainable, achievable, workable, within reach; *informal* on, doable. **2 likely**, plausible, imaginable, believable, potential, probable, credible, tenable.
– OPPOSITES impossible, unlikely.

possibly *adverb* **1 perhaps**, maybe, it is possible, for all you know. **2 conceivably**, under any circumstances, by any means.

post[1] *noun* **pole**, stake, upright, shaft, prop, support, picket, strut, pillar, stanchion, baluster.
● *verb* **1 affix**, attach, fasten, display, pin up, put up, stick up. **2 announce**, report, make known, publish.

post[2] *noun (Brit.)* **1 mail**; *informal* snail mail. **2 letters**, correspondence, mail.

post[3] *noun* **1 job**, position, appointment, situation, place, vacancy, opening. **2 assigned position**, station, place, base.
● *verb* **1 send**, assign, dispatch, consign. **2 put on duty**, mount, station.

poster *noun* **notice**, placard, bill, sign, advertisement, playbill.

postpone *verb* **put off**, put back, delay, defer, hold over, reschedule, adjourn, shelve; *informal* put on ice, put on the back burner.

posture *noun* **1 position**, pose, attitude, stance, carriage, bearing, comportment; *Brit.* deportment. **2 attitude**, standpoint, point of view, viewpoint, opinion, position, stance.
● *verb* **pose**, strike an attitude, attitudinize, strut; *informal* show off.

potent *adjective* **1 powerful**, strong, mighty, formidable, influential, dominant. **2 forceful**, convincing, cogent, compelling, persuasive, powerful, strong.
- OPPOSITES weak.

potential *adjective* **possible**, likely, prospective, future, probable.
● *noun* **possibilities**, potentiality, prospects, promise, capability, capacity.

potion *noun* **concoction**, mixture, brew, elixir, drink, medicine, tonic, philtre.

potter *verb* **amble**, wander, meander, stroll, saunter; *informal* mosey, tootle, toddle; *N. Amer. informal* putter.

pottery *noun* **ceramics**, crockery, earthenware, terracotta, stoneware, china, porcelain.

pouch *noun* **bag**, purse, sack, sac, pocket; *Scottish* sporran.

pounce *verb* **jump**, spring, leap, dive, lunge, swoop, attack.

pound[1] *verb* **1 beat**, strike, hit, batter, thump, pummel, punch, rain blows on, belabour, hammer; *informal* bash, clobber, wallop. **2 beat against**, crash against, batter, dash against, lash, buffet. **3 bombard**, bomb, shell. **4 crush**, grind, pulverize, mash, pulp. **5 stomp**, stamp, clomp, clump, tramp, lumber. **6 throb**, thump, thud, hammer, pulse, race.

pound[2] *noun* **enclosure**, compound, pen, yard, corral.

pour *verb* **1 stream**, flow, run, gush, course, jet, spurt, surge, spill. **2 tip**, splash, spill, decant; *informal* slosh, slop. **3 rain hard**, teem down, pelt down, tip down, rain cats and dogs; *informal* be chucking it down; *Brit. informal* bucket down; *N. Amer. informal* rain pitchforks. **4 crowd**, throng, swarm, stream, flood.

poverty *noun* **1 pennilessness**, destitution, penury, impoverishment, neediness, hardship, impecuniousness, indigence. **2 scarcity**, deficiency, dearth, shortage, paucity, absence, lack, inadequacy.
- OPPOSITES wealth, abundance.

powdery *adjective* **fine**, dry, fine-grained, powder-like, dusty, chalky, floury, sandy, crumbly, friable.

power *noun* **1 ability**, capacity, capability, potential, potentiality, faculty. **2 control**, command, authority, dominance, supremacy, ascendancy, mastery, influence, sway, leverage; *informal* clout, teeth. **3 authority**, right, authorization. **4 state**, country, nation. **5 strength**, might, force, vigour, energy; *Brit. informal* welly. **6 forcefulness**, powerfulness, strength, force, cogency, persuasiveness. **7 driving force**, horsepower, acceleration, torque; *informal* oomph, poke. **8 energy**, electricity.
- OPPOSITES weakness.

WORD LINKS
megalomania obsession with power

powerful *adjective* **1 strong**, muscular, muscly, sturdy, strapping, robust, brawny, burly, athletic, manly, well built, solid; *informal* beefy. **2 intoxicating**, hard, strong, stiff, potent. **3 violent**, forceful, hard, mighty. **4 intense**, keen, fierce, strong, irresistible, overpowering, overwhelming. **5 influential**, strong, important, dominant, commanding, formidable. **6 cogent**, compelling, convincing, persuasive, forceful, potent.
- OPPOSITES weak, gentle.

powerless *adjective* **impotent**, helpless, ineffectual, ineffective, useless, defenceless, vulnerable.

practicable *adjective* **realistic**, feasible, possible, viable, reasonable, sensible, workable, achievable; *informal* doable.

practical *adjective* **1 empirical**, hands-on, actual. **2 feasible**, practicable, realistic, viable, workable, possible, reasonable, sensible; *informal* doable. **3 functional**, sensible, utilitarian. **4 realistic**, sensible, down-to-earth, businesslike, commonsensical, hard-headed, no-nonsense; *informal* hard-nosed.
- OPPOSITES theoretical.

practically *adverb* **1 almost**, very nearly, virtually, just about, all but, more or less, as good as, to all intents and purposes; *informal* pretty well. **2 realistically**, sensibly, reasonably, rationally, matter-of-factly.

practice *noun* **1 application**, exercise, use, operation, implementation, execution. **2 custom**, procedure, policy, convention, tradition. **3 training**, rehearsal, repetition, preparation, dummy run, run-through; *informal* dry run. **4 profession**, career, business, work. **5 business**, firm, office, company; *informal* outfit.

practise *verb* **1 rehearse**, run through, go over/through, work on/at, polish, perfect, refine. **2 train**, rehearse, prepare, go through your paces. **3 carry out**, perform, observe, follow. **4 work in**, pursue a career in, engage in.

practised *adjective* **expert**, experienced, seasoned, skilled, skilful, accomplished, proficient, talented, able, adept.

pragmatic *adjective* **practical**, matter-of-fact, sensible, down-to-earth, commonsensical, businesslike, hard-headed, no-nonsense; *informal* hard-nosed.
- OPPOSITES impractical.

praise *verb* **commend**, applaud, pay tribute to, speak highly of, compliment, congratulate, sing the praises of, rave about.
- OPPOSITES criticize.
● *noun* **approval**, acclaim, admiration, approbation, plaudits, congratulations, commendation, accolade, compliment, a pat on the back, eulogy; *N. Amer. informal* kudos.
- OPPOSITES criticism.

praiseworthy *adjective* **commendable**, admirable, laudable, worthy (of admiration), meritorious, estimable, excellent, exemplary.

prance *verb* **cavort**, dance, jig, trip, caper, jump, leap, spring, bound, skip, hop, frisk, romp, frolic.

prank *noun* **(practical) joke**, trick, escapade, stunt, caper, jape, game, hoax; *informal* lark, leg-pull.

preach *verb* **1 give a sermon**, sermonize, evangelize, spread the gospel. **2 proclaim**, teach, spread, propagate, expound. **3 advocate**, recommend, advise, urge, teach, counsel.

WORD LINKS
homiletic relating to preaching

precarious *adjective* **insecure**, uncertain, unpredictable, risky, hazardous, dangerous, parlous, unsafe, unstable, unsteady, shaky; *informal* dicey, iffy; *Brit. informal* dodgy.
- OPPOSITES safe.

precaution *noun* **safeguard**, preventive measure, safety measure, insurance; *informal* backstop.

precede *verb* **1 go before**, come before, lead up to, pave the way for, herald, introduce, usher in. **2 go ahead of**, go in front of, lead the way.
- OPPOSITES follow.

precedence *noun* **seniority**, superiority, ascendancy, supremacy.
□ **take precedence over** take priority over, outweigh, prevail over, come before.

precedent *noun* **model**, exemplar, example, pattern, paradigm, criterion, yardstick, standard.

precinct *noun* **district**, zone, sector, quarter, area.

precious *adjective* **1 valuable**, costly, expensive, invaluable, priceless. **2 valued**, cherished, treasured, prized, favourite, dear, beloved, special. **3 affected**, pretentious; *informal* la-di-da; *Brit. informal* poncey.

precipitate *verb* **bring about**, bring on, cause, lead to, give rise to, instigate, trigger, spark off, touch off, provoke, hasten, speed up, accelerate.
● *adjective* **hasty**, overhasty, rash, hurried, rushed, impetuous, impulsive, precipitous, incautious, imprudent, injudicious, ill-advised, reckless.

precipitous *adjective* **1 steep**, sheer, perpendicular, abrupt, sharp, vertical. **2 sudden**, rapid, swift, abrupt, headlong, speedy, quick, fast.

precise *adjective* **1 exact**, accurate, correct, specific, detailed, explicit, careful, meticulous, strict, rigorous. **2** *at that precise moment* **exact**, particular, actual, specific, distinct.
- OPPOSITES inaccurate.

precisely *adverb* **1 exactly**, sharp, on the dot, promptly; *informal* bang (on); *Brit. informal* spot on; *N. Amer. informal* on the button. **2 just**, exactly, in all respects; *informal* to a T.

precision *noun* **exactness**, accuracy, exactitude, correctness, care, meticulousness, scrupulousness, punctiliousness, rigour.

preclude *verb* **prevent**, make it impossible for, rule out, stop, prohibit, debar, bar, hinder, impede, inhibit, exclude.

preconception *noun* **preconceived idea**, presupposition, assumption, presumption, prejudgement, prejudice.

predatory *adjective* **1 predacious**, carnivorous, hunting. **2 exploitative**, wolfish, rapacious, manipulative.

predecessor *noun* **1 forerunner**, precursor, antecedent. **2 ancestor**, forefather, forebear, antecedent.
- OPPOSITES successor, descendant.

predicament *noun* **difficulty**, mess, plight, quandary, muddle, dilemma; *informal* hole, fix, jam, pickle.

predict *verb* **forecast**, foretell, prophesy; *old use* augur.

predictable *adjective* **foreseeable**, to be expected, anticipated, likely, foreseen, unsurprising, reliable; *informal* inevitable.

prediction *noun* **forecast**, prophecy, prognosis, prognostication.

predisposition *noun* **1 susceptibility**, proneness, tendency, liability, inclination, vulnerability. **2 preference**, predilection, inclination, leaning, bent.

predominantly *adverb* **mainly**, mostly, for the most part, chiefly, principally, primarily, in the main, on the whole, largely, by and large, typically, generally, usually.

preface *noun* **introduction**, foreword, preamble, prologue, prelude, front matter; *informal* intro.
● *verb* **precede**, introduce, begin, open, start.

prefer *verb* **like better**, would rather (have), would sooner (have), favour, be more partial to, choose, select, pick, opt for, go for, plump for.

preferable *adjective* **better**, best, more desirable, more suitable, advantageous, superior, preferred, recommended.

preferably *adverb* **ideally**, if possible, for preference, from choice.

preference *noun* **1 liking**, partiality, fondness, taste, inclination, leaning, bent, penchant, predisposition. **2 priority**, favour, precedence, preferential treatment.

pregnant *adjective* **1 expecting**, expectant, carrying a child, with child; *informal* in the family way. **2 meaningful**, significant, suggestive, expressive, charged.

prejudice *noun* **1 preconceived idea**, preconception. **2 bigotry**, bias, partiality, intolerance, discrimination, unfairness, inequality.
● *verb* **1 bias**, influence, sway, predispose, make partial, colour. **2 damage**, be detrimental to, be prejudicial to, injure, harm, hurt, spoil, impair, undermine, compromise.

prejudiced *adjective* **biased**, bigoted, discriminatory, partisan, intolerant, narrow-minded, unfair, unjust, inequitable.
- OPPOSITES impartial.

preliminary *adjective* **preparatory**, introductory, initial, opening, early, exploratory.
- OPPOSITES final.
● *noun* **introduction**, preamble, preface, opening remarks, formalities.

prelude *noun* **preliminary**, overture, opening, preparation, introduction, lead-in, precursor.

premature *adjective* **1 untimely**, too early, before time, unseasonable. **2 rash**, overhasty, hasty, precipitate, impulsive, impetuous; *informal* previous.
– OPPOSITES overdue.

premier *adjective* **leading**, foremost, chief, principal, head, top-ranking, top, prime, primary, first, highest, pre-eminent, senior, outstanding; *N. Amer.* ranking.
● *noun* **head of government**, prime minister, PM, president, chancellor.

premiere *noun* **first performance**, first night, opening night, debut.

premise *noun* **proposition**, assumption, hypothesis, thesis, presupposition, supposition, presumption, assertion.

premises *plural noun* **building(s)**, property, site, office, establishment.

premium *noun* **1 (regular) payment**, instalment. **2 surcharge**, additional payment, extra.
□ **at a premium** scarce, in great demand, hard to come by, in short supply, thin on the ground, like gold dust.

preoccupation *noun* **obsession**, fixation, concern, passion, enthusiasm, hobby horse; *informal* bee in your bonnet.

preoccupied *adjective* **lost in thought**, deep in thought, oblivious, pensive, distracted, absorbed, engrossed, involved, wrapped up, concerned.

preparation *noun* **1** *preparations for the party* **arrangements**, planning, plans, groundwork, spadework, provision. **2 devising**, drawing up, construction, composition, development. **3 mixture**, compound, concoction, solution, medicine, potion.

prepare *verb* **1 get ready**, put together, draw up, produce, arrange, assemble, construct, compose, formulate. **2 cook**, make, get, concoct; *informal* fix, rustle up; *Brit. informal* knock up. **3 get ready**, make preparations, arrange things, make provision. **4 train**, get into shape, practise, get ready, warm up, limber up. **5** *prepare yourself for a shock* **brace**, ready, tense, steel, steady.

prepared *adjective* **1 ready**, (all) set, equipped, primed, waiting, poised. **2 willing**, ready, disposed, (favourably) inclined, of a mind, minded.

prescribe *verb* **1 advise**, recommend, advocate, suggest. **2 stipulate**, lay down, dictate, order, direct, specify, determine.

presence *noun* **1 existence**, being. **2 attendance**, appearance. **3 aura**, charisma, personality, magnetism.
– OPPOSITES absence.
□ **presence of mind** composure, self-possession, level-headedness, self-assurance, calmness, alertness, quick-wittedness; *informal* cool, unflappability.

present[1] *adjective* **1 in attendance**, here, there, near, nearby, at hand, available. **2 in existence**, detectable, occurring, existing, extant, current.
– OPPOSITES absent.
● *noun* **now**, today, the present time, the here and now, modern times.
– OPPOSITES past, future.
□ **at present** at the moment, just now, right now, at the present time, currently, at this moment in time.

present[2] *verb* **1 hand over**, give (out), confer, bestow, award, grant, accord. **2 submit**, set forth, put forward, offer, tender, table. **3 introduce**, make known, acquaint someone with. **4 host**, introduce, compère; *N. Amer. informal* emcee. **5 represent**, describe, portray, depict.

present[3] *noun* **gift**, donation, offering, contribution, gratuity, tip, handout; *informal* prezzie.

presentation *noun* **1 awarding**, presenting, bestowal, granting. **2 appearance**, arrangement, packaging, layout. **3 demonstration**, talk, lecture, address, speech, show, exhibition, display, introduction, launch, unveiling.

presently *adverb* **1 soon**, shortly, quite soon, in a short time, in a little while, at any moment/minute/second; before long; *N. Amer.* momentarily; *Brit. informal* in a mo. **2 at present**, currently, at the/this moment.

preservation *noun* **1 conservation**, protection, care. **2 continuation**, conservation, maintenance, upholding, sustaining, perpetuation.

preserve *verb* **1 conserve**, protect, maintain, care for, look after. **2 continue (with)**, conserve, keep going, maintain, uphold, sustain, perpetuate, prolong. **3 guard**, protect, keep, defend, safeguard, shelter, shield.
- OPPOSITES attack, abandon.
● *noun* **1** *jobs which are no longer the preserve of men* **domain**, area, field, sphere, orbit, realm, province, territory; *informal* turf, bailiwick. **2 sanctuary**, (game) reserve, reservation.

preside *verb*
▫ **preside over** be in charge of, be responsible for, head, manage, administer, control, direct, chair, conduct, officiate at, lead, govern, rule, command, supervise, oversee; *informal* head up.

press *verb* **1 push (down)**, depress, hold down, force, thrust, squeeze, compress. **2 iron**, smooth out, flatten. **3 clasp**, hold close, hug, cuddle, squeeze, clutch, grasp, embrace. **4 cluster**, gather, converge, congregate, flock, swarm, crowd. **5 plead**, urge, advance, present, submit, put forward. **6 urge**, put pressure on, pressurize, force, push, coerce, dragoon, steamroller, browbeat; *informal* lean on, put the screws on, twist someone's arm, railroad, bulldoze. **7** *they pressed for a ban* **call**, ask, clamour, push, campaign, demand.
● *noun* **the media**, the newspapers, journalism, reporters, the fourth estate; *Brit. dated* Fleet Street.

pressing *adjective* **1 urgent**, critical, crucial, acute, desperate, serious, grave, life-and-death. **2 important**, high-priority, critical, crucial, unavoidable.

pressure *noun* **1 force**, load, stress, thrust, compression, weight. **2 persuasion**, intimidation, coercion, compulsion, duress, harassment, nagging, badgering. **3 strain**, stress, tension, trouble, difficulty, burden; *informal* hassle.
● *verb* **coerce**, push, persuade, force, bulldoze, hound, nag, badger, browbeat, bully, intimidate, dragoon, twist someone's arm; *informal* railroad, lean on; *N. Amer. informal* hustle.

pressurize *verb* **coerce**, pressure, push, persuade, force, bulldoze, hound, nag, badger, browbeat, bully, bludgeon, intimidate, dragoon, twist someone's arm; *informal* railroad, lean on; *N. Amer. informal* hustle.

prestige *noun* **status**, standing, kudos, cachet, stature, reputation, repute, renown, honour, esteem, importance, prominence, distinction.

prestigious *adjective* **reputable**, distinguished, respected, high-status, esteemed, eminent, highly regarded, renowned, influential.
- OPPOSITES disreputable, obscure.

presume *verb* **1 assume**, suppose, surmise, imagine, take it, expect. **2 dare**, venture, have the effrontery, be so bold as, go so far as, take the liberty of.

pretence *noun* **1 make-believe**, acting, faking, play-acting, posturing, deception, trickery. **2 show**, semblance, affectation, appearance, outward appearance, impression, guise, facade.
- OPPOSITES honesty.

pretend *verb* **put on an act**, act, play-act, put it on, dissemble, sham, feign, fake, dissimulate, make believe, put on a false front, posture, go through the motions, make as if.
● *adjective (informal)* **mock**, fake, sham, simulated, artificial, false, pseudo; *informal* phoney.

pretty *adjective* **attractive**, good-looking, nice-looking, personable, fetching, prepossessing, appealing, charming,

delightful, cute; *Scottish & N. English* bonny; *old use* fair, comely.
- OPPOSITES plain, ugly.
● *adverb (informal)* **quite**, rather, somewhat, fairly.

prevail *verb* **1 win**, triumph, be victorious, carry the day, come out on top, succeed, rule, reign. **2 exist**, be present, be the case, occur, be prevalent, be in force.

prevailing *adjective* **current**, existing, prevalent, usual, common, general, widespread.

prevalent *adjective* **widespread**, frequent, usual, common, current, popular, general.
- OPPOSITES rare.

prevent *verb* **stop**, avert, nip in the bud, foil, inhibit, thwart, prohibit, forbid.
- OPPOSITES allow.

previous *adjective* **1 preceding**, foregoing, prior, past, last. **2 former**, preceding, old, earlier, ex-, past, last, sometime, one-time, erstwhile, as was; *formal* quondam.
- OPPOSITES next.

previously *adverb* **formerly**, earlier (on), before, hitherto, at one time, in the past.

prey *noun* **1 quarry**, kill. **2 victim**, target, dupe; *informal* sucker; *Brit. informal* mug.
- OPPOSITES predator.

price *noun* **1 cost**, charge, fee, fare, amount, sum; *informal* damage. **2 consequence**, result, cost, penalty, toll, sacrifice, downside, drawback, disadvantage, minus.

priceless *adjective* **invaluable**, beyond price, irreplaceable, expensive, costly.
- OPPOSITES worthless, cheap.

prick *verb* **pierce**, puncture, stab, perforate, spike, penetrate, jab.
● *noun* **jab**, sting, pinprick, stab, pinhole, wound.

prickly *adjective* **spiky**, spiked, thorny, barbed, spiny, bristly.

pride *noun* **1 self-esteem**, dignity, honour, self-respect. **2 pleasure**, joy, delight, gratification, fulfilment, satisfaction, sense of achievement. **3 arrogance**, vanity, self-importance, hubris, conceitedness, egotism, snobbery.
- OPPOSITES shame, humility.

priest *noun* **clergyman**, clergywoman, minister, cleric, pastor, vicar, rector, parson, churchman, churchwoman, father, curate; *N. Amer.* dominie; *informal* reverend, padre.

WORD LINKS
clerical, **sacerdotal** relating to priests

primarily *adverb* **1 first and foremost**, firstly, essentially, in essence, fundamentally, principally, predominantly. **2 mostly**, for the most part, chiefly, mainly, in the main, on the whole, largely, principally, predominantly.

primary *adjective* **main**, chief, key, prime, central, principal, foremost, first, most important, predominant, paramount; *informal* number-one.
- OPPOSITES secondary.

prime[1] *adjective* **1 main**, chief, key, primary, central, principal, foremost, first, most important, paramount, major; *informal* number-one. **2 top-quality**, top, best, first-class, superior, choice, select, finest; *informal* tip-top, A1.
- OPPOSITES secondary, inferior.
● *noun* **heyday**, peak, pinnacle, high point/spot, zenith, flower, bloom, flush.

prime[2] *verb* **brief**, fill in, prepare, advise, instruct, coach, drill, train.

primitive *adjective* **1 ancient**, earliest, first, prehistoric, primordial, primeval. **2 crude**, simple, rough (and ready), basic, rudimentary, makeshift.
- OPPOSITES modern, sophisticated.

prince *noun* **ruler**, sovereign, monarch, crowned head.

principal *adjective* **main**, chief, primary, leading, foremost, first, most important, predominant, dominant, pre-eminent, highest, top; *informal* number-one.
- OPPOSITES minor.

● *noun* **head teacher**, headmaster, headmistress, head, dean, rector, master, mistress, chancellor, vice chancellor, president, provost, warden.

principally *adverb* **mainly**, mostly, chiefly, for the most part, in the main, on the whole, largely, predominantly, primarily.

principle *noun* **1 truth**, concept, idea, theory, fundamental, essential, precept, rule, law. **2 doctrine**, belief, creed, credo, code, ethic. **3 morals**, morality, ethics, ideals, standards, integrity, virtue, probity, honour, decency, conscience, scruples.
□ **in principle 1** in theory, theoretically, on paper, ideally. **2** in general, in essence, on the whole, in the main.

print *verb* **1 publish**, issue, release, circulate, run off, copy, reproduce. **2 imprint**, impress, stamp, mark.
● *noun* **1 type**, printing, letters, lettering, characters, typeface, font. **2 impression**, handprint, fingerprint, footprint. **3 picture**, engraving, etching, lithograph, woodcut. **4 photograph**, photo, snap, snapshot, picture, still, enlargement, reproduction, copy.

prior *adjective* **earlier**, previous, preceding, advance, pre-existing.
– OPPOSITES subsequent.
□ **prior to** before, until, up to, previous to, preceding, earlier than, in advance of.

priority *noun* **1 prime concern**, main consideration, most important thing. **2 precedence**, preference, pre-eminence, predominance, primacy.

prison *noun* **jail**, penal institution; *N. Amer.* jailhouse, penitentiary, correctional facility; *informal* clink, slammer; *Brit. informal* nick; *N. Amer. informal* can, pen.
□ **in prison** behind bars; *informal* inside, doing time; *Brit. informal* doing porridge.

prisoner *noun* **1 convict**, detainee, inmate; *informal* jailbird, con; *Brit. informal* lag; *N. Amer. informal* yardbird. **2 prisoner of war**, POW, internee, captive, hostage.

pristine *adjective* **immaculate**, perfect, in mint condition, as new, spotless, unspoilt.
– OPPOSITES dirty, spoilt.

privacy *noun* **seclusion**, solitude, isolation.

private *adjective* **1 personal**, own, special, exclusive. **2 confidential**, secret, classified, privileged, unofficial, off the record; *informal* hush-hush. **3 intimate**, personal, secret, innermost, undisclosed, unspoken, unvoiced. **4 reserved**, introverted, self-contained, reticent, retiring, unsociable, withdrawn, solitary, reclusive, secretive. **5 secluded**, undisturbed, out of the way, remote, isolated. **6 independent**, non-state, privatized, commercial, private-enterprise.
– OPPOSITES public, open, official.
● *noun* **private soldier**, trooper; *Brit.* sapper, gunner; *US* GI; *Brit. informal* Tommy, squaddie.
□ **in private** in secret, secretly, privately, behind closed doors, in camera, sub rosa.

privilege *noun* **1 advantage**, benefit, prerogative, entitlement, right, concession, freedom, liberty. **2 honour**, pleasure.

privileged *adjective* **1 wealthy**, rich, affluent, prosperous, elite, advantaged. **2 confidential**, private, secret, restricted, classified, not for publication, off the record, inside; *informal* hush-hush.
– OPPOSITES underprivileged, disadvantaged.

prize *noun* **award**, reward, trophy, medal, cup, winnings, purse, honour.
● *adjective* **1 champion**, award-winning, top, best. **2 utter**, complete, total, absolute, real, perfect; *Brit. informal* right.

probability *noun* **likelihood**, prospect, expectation, chance(s), odds, possibility.

probable *adjective* **likely**, odds-on, expected, anticipated, predictable; *informal* on the cards, a safe bet.

– OPPOSITES unlikely.

probably *adverb* **in all likelihood**, in all probability, as likely as not, ten to one, the chances are, doubtless.

probation *noun* **trial**, trial period, apprenticeship, training.

probe *noun* **investigation**, enquiry, examination, inquest, study.
● *verb* **1 prod**, poke, dig into, delve into, explore, feel around in, examine. **2 investigate**, enquire into, look into, go into, study, examine, explore.

problem *noun* **1 difficulty**, worry, complication, snag, hitch, drawback, stumbling block, obstacle, hiccup, setback, issue, catch, dilemma, quandary; *informal* headache, fly in the ointment. **2 nuisance**, bother; *informal* drag, pain, hassle. **3 puzzle**, question, poser, riddle, conundrum; *informal* brain-teaser.

problematic *adjective* **difficult**, troublesome, tricky, awkward, controversial, ticklish, complicated, complex, knotty.
– OPPOSITES easy, straightforward.

procedure *noun* **course of action**, method, system, strategy, way, approach, formula, solution, mechanism, technique, routine, drill, practice.

proceed *verb* **1 begin**, make a start, get going, move. **2 go**, make your way, advance, move, progress, carry on, continue, press on, push on.
– OPPOSITES stop.

proceedings *plural noun* **1 events**, activities, action, happenings, goings-on. **2 report**, transactions, minutes, account, story, record(s). **3 legal action**, litigation, suit, lawsuit, case, prosecution.

proceeds *plural noun* **profits**, earnings, receipts, returns, takings, income, revenue, profit, yield; *Sport* gate (money); *N. Amer.* take.

process *noun* **1 procedure**, operation, action, activity, exercise, business, job, task, undertaking. **2** *a new manufacturing process* **method**, system, technique, means.
● *verb* **deal with**, attend to, see to, sort out, handle, take care of.

procession *noun* **parade**, march, march past, cavalcade, motorcade, cortège, column, file; *Brit. informal* crocodile.

proclaim *verb* **declare**, announce, pronounce, state, make known, give out, advertise, publish, broadcast, trumpet.

prod *verb* **1 poke**, jab, stab, dig, nudge, elbow. **2 spur**, stimulate, prompt, push, galvanize, persuade, urge, chivvy, remind.

prodigal *adjective* **wasteful**, extravagant, spendthrift.
– OPPOSITES thrifty.

prodigy *noun* **genius**, mastermind, virtuoso, wunderkind; *informal* whizz-kid, whizz.

produce *verb* **1 manufacture**, make, construct, build, fabricate, put together, assemble, turn out, create, mass-produce. **2 yield**, grow, give, supply, provide, furnish, bear. **3 give birth to**, bear, deliver, bring forth, bring into the world. **4 create**, fashion, turn out, compose, write, pen, paint. **5 pull out**, extract, fish out, present, offer, proffer, show. **6 cause**, bring about, give rise to, occasion, generate, lead to, result in, provoke, precipitate, spark off, trigger. **7 stage**, put on, mount, present, exhibit.
● *noun* **food**, foodstuff(s), products, crops, harvest.

producer *noun* **1 manufacturer**, maker, builder, constructor. **2 grower**, farmer. **3 impresario**, manager, administrator, promoter, director.

product *noun* **1 artefact**, commodity; (**products**) goods, ware(s), merchandise, produce. **2 result**, consequence, outcome, effect, upshot.

production *noun* **1 manufacture**, making, construction, building, fabrication, assembly, creation, mass production. **2 creation**, origination, fashioning, composition, writing. **3 output**, yield, productivity. **4 performance**, staging, presentation, show, piece, play.

productive *adjective* **1 prolific**, inventive, creative. **2 useful**, constructive, profitable, fruitful, valuable, effective, worthwhile, helpful. **3 fertile**, fruitful, rich, fecund.

productivity *noun* **efficiency**, work rate, output, yield, production.

profess *verb* **1 declare**, announce, proclaim, assert, state, affirm, maintain, protest, avow. **2 claim**, pretend, purport, affect, make out.

professed *adjective* **1 claimed**, supposed, ostensible, self-styled, apparent, pretended, purported. **2 declared**, sworn, confirmed, self-confessed.

profession *noun* **career**, occupation, calling, vocation, métier, line of work, job, business, trade, craft.

professional *adjective* **1 white-collar**, non-manual, graduate, qualified, chartered. **2 paid**, salaried. **3 expert**, accomplished, skilful, masterly, fine, polished, skilled, proficient, competent, able, businesslike, deft. **4** *he always behaved in a professional way* **appropriate**, fitting, proper, honourable, ethical.
- OPPOSITES amateur, amateurish.
● *noun* **expert**, virtuoso, old hand, master, maestro, past master; *informal* pro, ace.

profile *noun* **1 outline**, silhouette, side view, contour, shape, form, lines. **2 description**, account, study, portrait, rundown, sketch, outline.

profit *noun* **1 financial gain**, return(s), yield, proceeds, earnings, winnings, surplus; *informal* pay dirt, bottom line. **2 advantage**, benefit, value, use, good; *informal* mileage.
- OPPOSITES loss, disadvantage.
● *verb* **1 make money**, earn; *informal* rake it in, clean up, make a killing; *N. Amer. informal* make a fast buck. **2 benefit**, be advantageous to, be of use to, do someone good, help, be of service to, serve.
- OPPOSITES lose.

profitable *adjective* **1 moneymaking**, profit-making, paying, lucrative, commercial, successful, money-spinning, gainful. **2 beneficial**, useful, advantageous, valuable, productive, worthwhile, rewarding, fruitful, illuminating, informative, well spent.

profound *adjective* **1 heartfelt**, intense, keen, extreme, acute, severe, sincere, earnest, deep, deep-seated, overpowering, overwhelming. **2 far-reaching**, radical, extensive, sweeping, exhaustive, thoroughgoing. **3 wise**, learned, intelligent, scholarly, discerning, penetrating, perceptive, astute, thoughtful, insightful.
- OPPOSITES superficial.

programme *noun* **1 schedule**, agenda, calendar, timetable, order (of the day), line-up. **2 scheme**, plan, package, strategy, initiative, proposal. **3 broadcast**, production, show, presentation, transmission, performance, telecast, videocast, podcast. **4 course**, syllabus, curriculum.
● *verb* **arrange**, organize, schedule, plan, map out, timetable, line up; *N. Amer.* slate.

progress *noun* **1 (forward) movement**, advance, going, headway, passage. **2 development**, advance, advancement, headway, step forward, improvement, growth.
● *verb* **1 go**, make your way, move, proceed, advance, go on, continue, make headway, work your way. **2 develop**, make progress, advance, make headway, move on, get on, gain ground, improve, get better, come on, come along, make strides.
- OPPOSITES regress.
□ **in progress** under way, going on, ongoing, happening, occurring, taking place, proceeding, continuing.

progression *noun* **1 progress**, advancement, movement, passage, development, evolution, growth. **2 succession**, series, sequence, string, stream, chain, train, row, cycle.

progressive *adjective* **1 continuing**, continuous, ongoing, gradual, step-by-step, cumulative. **2 modern**, liberal, advanced, forward-thinking,

enlightened, pioneering, reforming, reformist, radical; *informal* go-ahead.
- OPPOSITES conservative.

prohibit *verb* **1 forbid**, ban, bar, proscribe, make illegal, outlaw, disallow, veto. **2 prevent**, stop, rule out, preclude, make impossible.
- OPPOSITES allow.

prohibition *noun* **ban**, bar, veto, embargo, boycott, injunction, moratorium, interdict.

project *noun* **1 scheme**, plan, programme, enterprise, undertaking, venture, proposal, idea, concept. **2 assignment**, piece of work, task.
● *verb* **1 forecast**, predict, expect, estimate, calculate, reckon. **2 stick out**, jut (out), protrude, extend, stand out, bulge out. **3 cast**, throw, send, shed, shine.

projection *noun* **1 forecast**, prediction, prognosis, expectation, estimate. **2 outcrop**, outgrowth, overhang, ledge, shelf, prominence, protrusion, protuberance.

proliferate *verb* **increase**, grow, multiply, rocket, mushroom, snowball, burgeon, spread, expand, run riot.
- OPPOSITES decrease, dwindle.

prolific *adjective* **1 plentiful**, abundant, bountiful, profuse, copious, luxuriant, rich, lush, fruitful. **2 productive**, fertile, creative, inventive.
- OPPOSITES meagre.

prolong *verb* **lengthen**, extend, drag out, draw out, protract, spin out, carry on, continue, keep up, perpetuate.
- OPPOSITES shorten.

prominence *noun* **1 fame**, celebrity, eminence, importance, distinction, greatness, prestige, stature, standing. **2** *the press gave prominence to the reports* **wide coverage**, importance, precedence, weight, a high profile, top billing.

prominent *adjective* **1 important**, well known, leading, eminent, distinguished, notable, noteworthy, noted, illustrious, celebrated, famous, renowned; *N. Amer.* major-league. **2 jutting (out)**, protruding, projecting, protuberant, standing out, sticking out, proud, bulging. **3 conspicuous**, noticeable, obvious, unmistakable, eye-catching, pronounced, salient, striking, dominant, obtrusive.
- OPPOSITES unimportant, inconspicuous.

promise *noun* **1 word (of honour)**, assurance, pledge, vow, guarantee, oath, bond, undertaking, agreement, commitment, contract. **2 potential**, ability, talent, aptitude, possibility.
● *verb* **1 give your word**, swear, pledge, vow, undertake, give an undertaking, guarantee, warrant, contract, give an assurance, commit yourself. **2 indicate**, lead someone to expect, point to, be a sign of, betoken, give hope of, augur, herald, portend, presage.

promising *adjective* **1 good**, encouraging, favourable, hopeful, auspicious, propitious, bright, rosy, heartening. **2 talented**, gifted, budding, up-and-coming, rising, coming, in the making.
- OPPOSITES unfavourable.

promote *verb* **1 upgrade**, give promotion to, elevate, advance, move up. **2 encourage**, further, advance, foster, develop, contribute to, boost, stimulate. **3 advertise**, publicize, give publicity to, beat/bang the drum for, market, merchandise; *informal* push, plug, hype.
- OPPOSITES demote, obstruct.

promotion *noun* **1 upgrading**, preferment, elevation, advancement, step up (the ladder). **2 encouragement**, furtherance, furthering, advancement, contribution to, fostering, boosting, stimulation. **3 advertising**, marketing, publicity, propaganda; *informal* hard sell, plug, hype, puff.

prompt *verb* **1 induce**, make, move, motivate, lead, dispose, persuade, incline, encourage, stimulate, prod, impel, spur on, inspire. **2 give rise to**, bring about, cause, occasion, result in, lead to, elicit, produce, precipitate, trigger, spark off, provoke. **3 remind**,

cue, feed, help out, jog someone's memory.
- OPPOSITES deter.
● *adjective* **quick**, swift, rapid, speedy, fast, expeditious, direct, immediate, instant, early, punctual, in good time, on time.
- OPPOSITES slow, late.
● *adverb* **exactly**, precisely, sharp, on the dot, dead, punctually; *informal* bang on; *N. Amer. informal* on the button, on the nose.

promptly *adverb* **1 punctually**, on time; *informal* on the dot, bang on; *Brit. informal* spot on; *N. Amer. informal* on the button, on the nose. **2 without delay**, straight/right away, at once, immediately, now, as soon as possible, quickly, swiftly, rapidly, speedily, fast; *informal* pronto, asap.
- OPPOSITES late.

prone *adjective* **1 susceptible**, vulnerable, subject, open, liable, given, predisposed, likely, disposed, inclined, apt. **2 lying face down**, on your stomach/front, lying flat, lying down, horizontal, prostrate.

pronounce *verb* **1 say**, enunciate, articulate, utter, voice, sound, vocalize, get your tongue round. **2 declare**, proclaim, judge, rule, decree, ordain.

pronounced *adjective* **noticeable**, marked, strong, conspicuous, striking, distinct, prominent, unmistakable, obvious.
- OPPOSITES slight.

proof *noun* **evidence**, verification, corroboration, demonstration, authentication, confirmation, certification, documentation.
● *adjective* **resistant**, immune, unaffected, impervious.

prop *noun* **1 pole**, post, support, upright, brace, buttress, stay, strut. **2 mainstay**, pillar, anchor, support, cornerstone.
● *verb* **lean**, rest, stand, balance.
□ **prop up 1** hold up, shore up, buttress, support, brace, underpin. **2** subsidize, underwrite, fund, finance.

propaganda *noun* **information**, promotion, advertising, publicity, disinformation; *informal* hype.

propel *verb* **1 move**, power, push, drive. **2 throw**, thrust, toss, fling, hurl, pitch, send, shoot.

proper *adjective* **1 real**, genuine, actual, true, bona fide; *informal* kosher. **2 right**, correct, accepted, conventional, established, official, regular, acceptable, appropriate, suitable, apt. **3 formal**, conventional, correct, orthodox, polite, respectable, seemly.
- OPPOSITES wrong, improper.

property *noun* **1 possessions**, belongings, things, effects, stuff, goods; *informal* gear. **2 building(s)**, premises, house(s), land; *N. Amer.* real estate. **3 quality**, attribute, characteristic, feature, power, trait, hallmark.

prophecy *noun* **prediction**, forecast, prognostication, prognosis, divination.

prophesy *verb* **predict**, foretell, forecast, foresee, prognosticate.

prophet, **prophetess** *noun* **forecaster**, seer, soothsayer, fortune teller, clairvoyant, oracle.

proportion *noun* **1 part**, portion, amount, quantity, bit, piece, percentage, fraction, section, segment, share. **2 ratio**, distribution, relative amount/number, relationship. **3 balance**, symmetry, harmony, correspondence, correlation, agreement. **4** *men of huge proportions* **size**, dimensions, magnitude, measurements, mass, volume, bulk, expanse, extent.

proportional, **proportionate** *adjective* **corresponding**, comparable, in proportion, pro rata, commensurate, equivalent, consistent.
- OPPOSITES disproportionate.

proposal *noun* **scheme**, plan, idea, project, programme, motion, proposition, suggestion, submission.

propose *verb* **1 put forward**, suggest, submit, advance, offer, present, move, come up with, nominate, recommend. **2 intend**, mean, plan, have in mind, aim.

proposition *noun* **1 proposal**, scheme, plan, project, idea, programme. **2 task**, job, undertaking, venture, activity, affair.

proprietor, **proprietress** *noun* **owner**, possessor, holder, householder, master, mistress, landowner, landlord, landlady, shopkeeper.

prosecute *verb* **charge**, take to court, take legal action against, sue, try, bring to trial, put on trial, put in the dock, indict; *N. Amer.* impeach.
- OPPOSITES defend.

prospect *noun* **likelihood**, hope, expectation, chance, odds, probability, possibility, promise, outlook, lookout. ● *verb* **search**, look, explore, survey, scout, hunt, dowse.

prospective *adjective* **potential**, possible, probable, likely, future, eventual, -to-be, soon-to-be, in the making, intending, aspiring, would-be.

prospectus *noun* **brochure**, syllabus, curriculum, catalogue, programme, list, schedule.

prosper *verb* **flourish**, thrive, do well, bloom, blossom, burgeon, progress, do all right for yourself, get ahead, get on (in the world), be successful; *informal* go places.
- OPPOSITES fail.

prosperity *noun* **success**, affluence, wealth, ease, plenty.
- OPPOSITES hardship, failure.

prosperous *adjective* **thriving**, flourishing, successful, strong, vigorous, profitable, lucrative, expanding, booming, burgeoning, **affluent**, wealthy, rich, moneyed, well off, well-to-do; *informal* in the money.
- OPPOSITES ailing, poor.

prostitute *noun* whore, sex worker, call girl, courtesan; *informal* working girl; *N. Amer. informal* hooker, hustler. ● *verb* **betray**, sacrifice, sell, sell out, debase, degrade, demean, devalue, cheapen, lower, shame, misuse.

protect *verb* **keep safe**, keep from harm, guard, defend, shield, save, safeguard, preserve, cushion, insulate, shelter, screen, keep, look after.
- OPPOSITES expose, harm.

protection *noun* **1 defence**, security, safeguard, safety, sanctuary, shelter, refuge, immunity, indemnity. **2 safe keeping**, care, charge, guardianship, support, aegis, patronage. **3 barrier**, buffer, shield, screen, cushion, bulwark, armour, insulation.

protective *adjective* **1 protecting**, covering, insulated, impermeable, -proof, -resistant. **2 solicitous**, careful, caring, defensive, paternal, maternal, overprotective, possessive.

protector *noun* **1 defender**, preserver, guardian, champion, patron, custodian. **2 guard**, shield, buffer, cushion, pad, screen.

protest *noun* **1 objection**, complaint, challenge, dissent, demurral, remonstration, fuss, outcry. **2 demonstration**, rally, vigil, sit-in, occupation, work-to-rule, stoppage, strike, walkout, mutiny, picket, boycott; *informal* demo. ● *verb* **1 object**, express opposition, dissent, take issue, take a stand, put up a fight, take exception, complain, express disapproval, disagree, make a fuss, speak out; *informal* kick up a fuss. **2 insist on**, maintain, assert, affirm, announce, proclaim, declare, profess, avow.

protocol *noun* **etiquette**, convention, formalities, custom, the rules, procedure, ritual, decorum, the done thing.

prototype *noun* **original**, master, template, pattern, sample.

protract *verb* **prolong**, lengthen, extend, draw out, drag out, spin out, stretch out, string out.
- OPPOSITES curtail, shorten.

protracted *adjective* **prolonged**, extended, long-drawn-out, lengthy, long.
- OPPOSITES short.

proud *adjective* **1 pleased**, glad, happy, delighted, thrilled, satisfied, gratified. **2** *a proud moment* **pleasing**, gratifying, satisfying, cheering, heart-warming,

happy, glorious. **3 arrogant**, conceited, vain, self-important, full of yourself, overbearing, bumptious, presumptuous, overweening, haughty, high and mighty; *informal* big-headed, too big for your boots, stuck-up.
- OPPOSITES ashamed, humble.

prove *verb* **show (to be true)**, demonstrate, substantiate, corroborate, verify, validate, authenticate, confirm.
- OPPOSITES disprove.

proverb *noun* **saying**, adage, saw, maxim, axiom, motto, aphorism, epigram.

provide *verb* **1 supply**, give, come up with, produce, deliver, donate, contribute; *informal* fork out, lay out. **2** *he was provided with tools* **equip**, furnish, issue, supply, fit out, rig out, kit out, arm, provision; *informal* fix up. **3 offer**, present, afford, give, add, bring, yield, impart, lend.
▫ **provide for** feed, nurture, nourish, support, maintain, keep, sustain.

provided, **providing** *conjunction* **if**, on condition that, provided that, presuming (that), assuming (that), as long as, with/on the understanding that.

provider *noun* **supplier**, donor, giver, contributor, source.

p

province *noun* **1 territory**, region, state, department, canton, area, district, sector, zone, division. **2** (**the provinces**) **the regions**, the rest of the country, rural areas/districts, the countryside; *informal* the sticks, the middle of nowhere; *N. Amer. informal* the boondocks. **3 domain**, area, department, responsibility, sphere, world, realm, field, discipline, territory; *informal* bailiwick.

provincial *adjective* **1 local**, small-town, rural, country, outlying, backwoods; *informal* one-horse. **2 unsophisticated**, parochial, insular, narrow-minded, inward-looking, suburban, small-town; *N. Amer. informal* corn-fed.
- OPPOSITES cosmopolitan, sophisticated.

provision *noun* **1** *limited provision for young children* **facilities**, services, amenities, resource(s), arrangements. **2** (**provisions**) **supplies**, food and drink, stores, groceries, foodstuff(s), rations. **3 term**, requirement, specification, stipulation.

provisional *adjective* **interim**, temporary, transitional, changeover, stopgap, short-term, fill-in, acting, working.
- OPPOSITES permanent, definite.

provocation *noun* **goading**, prodding, incitement, harassment, pressure, teasing, taunting, torment; *informal* hassle, aggravation.

provocative *adjective* **annoying**, irritating, maddening, galling, insulting, offensive, inflammatory, incendiary, like a red rag to a bull; *informal* aggravating.

provoke *verb* **1 arouse**, produce, evoke, cause, give rise to, excite, spark off, touch off, kindle, generate, engender, instigate, result in, lead to, bring on, precipitate, prompt, trigger. **2 goad**, spur, prick, sting, prod, incite, rouse, stimulate. **3 annoy**, anger, enrage, irritate, madden, nettle; *Brit.* rub up the wrong way; *informal* aggravate, rile, needle, get/put someone's back up; *Brit. informal* wind up.
- OPPOSITES allay, appease.

prowess *noun* **skill**, expertise, mastery, ability, capability, capacity, talent, aptitude, dexterity, proficiency, finesse; *informal* know-how.
- OPPOSITES inability, ineptitude.

prowl *verb* **steal**, slink, skulk, sneak, stalk, creep; *informal* snoop.

proxy *noun* **deputy**, representative, substitute, delegate, agent, surrogate, stand-in, go-between.

prudent *adjective* **1 wise**, well judged, sensible, politic, judicious, shrewd, sage, sagacious, far-sighted, canny. **2 cautious**, careful, provident, circumspect, thrifty, economical.
- OPPOSITES unwise, extravagant.

prudish *adjective* **puritanical**, priggish, prim, moralistic, censorious, strait-laced, Victorian, stuffy; *informal* goody-goody.

- OPPOSITES permissive.

prune *verb* **1 cut back**, trim, clip, shear, shorten, thin, shape. **2 reduce**, cut (back/down), pare (down), slim down, trim, downsize, axe, shrink; *informal* slash.
- OPPOSITES increase.

pry *verb* **be inquisitive**, poke about/around, ferret about/around, spy, be a busybody; *informal* stick/poke your nose in/into, be nosy, snoop; *Austral./NZ informal* stickybeak.

pseudonym *noun* **pen name**, nom de plume, assumed name, alias, sobriquet, stage name, nom de guerre.

psychiatrist *noun* **psychotherapist**, psychoanalyst, analyst; *informal* shrink.

psychic *adjective* **1 supernatural**, paranormal, other-worldly, metaphysical, extrasensory, magic(al), mystic(al), occult. **2 clairvoyant**, telepathic.
● *noun* **clairvoyant**, fortune teller, medium, spiritualist, telepath, mind-reader.

psychological *adjective* **1 mental**, emotional, inner, cognitive. **2 (all) in the mind**, psychosomatic, emotional, subjective, subconscious, unconscious.
- OPPOSITES physical.

psychology *noun* **mind**, mindset, thought processes, way of thinking, mentality, psyche, attitude(s), make-up, character, temperament; *informal* what makes someone tick.

pub *noun (Brit.)* **bar**, inn, tavern, hostelry; *Brit.* public house; *informal* watering hole; *Brit. informal* local, boozer; *N. Amer. historical* saloon.

puberty *noun* **adolescence**, pubescence, youth, teenage years, teens.

public *adjective* **1 state**, national, constitutional, civic, civil, official, social, municipal, nationalized. **2 popular**, general, common, communal, collective, shared, joint, universal, widespread. **3 prominent**, well known, important, leading, eminent, distinguished, celebrated, household, famous; *N. Amer.* major-league. **4 open (to the public)**, communal, available, free, unrestricted.
- OPPOSITES private, secret.
● *noun* **1 people**, citizens, subjects, electors, electorate, voters, taxpayers, residents, inhabitants, citizenry, population, populace, community, society, country, nation. **2 audience**, spectators, concertgoers, theatregoers, followers, following, fans, devotees, admirers.

WORD LINKS
agoraphobia fear of public places

publication *noun* **1 book**, volume, title, opus, tome, newspaper, paper, magazine, periodical, newsletter, bulletin, journal, report. **2 issuing**, publishing, printing, distribution.

publicity *noun* **1 public attention**, media attention, exposure, glare, limelight, spotlight. **2 promotion**, advertising, propaganda, boost, push; *informal* hype, ballyhoo, puff, build-up, plug.

publicize *verb* **1 make known**, make public, announce, broadcast, spread, promulgate, disseminate, circulate, air. **2 advertise**, promote, build up, talk up, push, beat the drum for, boost; *informal* hype, plug, puff (up).
- OPPOSITES conceal, suppress.

publish *verb* **1 issue**, bring out, produce, print. **2 make known**, make public, publicize, announce, broadcast, issue, put out, distribute, spread, promulgate, disseminate, circulate, air.

pudding *noun* **dessert**, sweet, last course; *Brit. informal* afters, pud.

puerile *adjective* **childish**, immature, infantile, juvenile, babyish, silly, inane, fatuous, foolish.
- OPPOSITES mature.

puff *noun* **1 gust**, blast, flurry, rush, draught, waft, breeze, breath. **2 pull**; *informal* drag, toke.
● *verb* **1 breathe heavily**, pant, blow, gasp. **2 smoke**, draw on, drag on, inhale.

pugnacious *adjective* **combative**, aggressive, antagonistic, belligerent,

quarrelsome, argumentative, hostile, truculent.
- OPPOSITES peaceable.

pull *verb* **1 tug**, haul, drag, draw, tow, heave, jerk, wrench; *informal* yank. **2 strain**, sprain, wrench, tear. **3 attract**, draw, bring in, pull in, lure, seduce, entice, tempt.
- OPPOSITES push.
● *noun* **1 tug**, jerk, heave; *informal* yank. **2 gulp**, draught, drink, swallow, mouthful, slug; *informal* swig. **3 puff**; *informal* drag, toke. **4 attraction**, draw, lure, magnetism, fascination, appeal, allure.
□ **pull off** achieve, fulfil, succeed in, accomplish, bring off, carry off, clinch, fix. **pull out** withdraw, resign, leave, retire, step down, bow out, back out, give up; *informal* quit. **pull through** get better, get well again, improve, recover, rally, come through, recuperate.

pulp *noun* **1 mush**, mash, paste, purée, slop, slush, mulch. **2 flesh**, marrow, meat.
● *verb* **mash**, purée, cream, crush, press, liquidize.

pulse *noun* **1 heartbeat**, heart rate. **2 rhythm**, beat, tempo, pounding, throb, throbbing, thudding, drumming.
● *verb* **throb**, pulsate, vibrate, beat, pound, thud, thump, drum, reverberate, echo.

pump *verb* **1 force**, drive, push, inject, suck, draw. **2 inflate**, blow up, fill up, swell, enlarge, distend, expand, dilate, puff up. **3 spurt**, spout, squirt, jet, surge, spew, gush, stream, flow, pour, spill, well, cascade.

punch[1] *verb* **hit**, strike, thump, jab, smash; *informal* sock, slug, biff, bop; *Brit. informal* stick one on, slosh; *N. Amer. informal* boff, bust; *Austral./NZ informal* quilt.
● *noun* **blow**, hit, knock, thump, box, jab, clip; *informal* sock, slug, biff, bop; *N. Amer. informal* boff, bust.

punch[2] *verb* **perforate**, puncture, pierce, prick, hole, spike, skewer.

punctual *adjective* **on time**, prompt, on schedule, in (good) time; *informal* on the dot.
- OPPOSITES late.

punctuate *verb* **break up**, interrupt, intersperse, pepper, sprinkle, scatter.

puncture *noun* **1 hole**, perforation, rupture, cut, gash, slit, leak. **2 flat tyre**; *informal* flat.
● *verb* **prick**, pierce, stab, rupture, perforate, cut, slit, deflate.

pungent *adjective* **strong**, powerful, pervasive, penetrating, sharp, acid, sour, biting, bitter, tart, vinegary, tangy, aromatic, spicy, piquant, peppery, hot, garlicky.
- OPPOSITES bland, mild.

punish *verb* **discipline**, penalize, correct, sentence, teach someone a lesson; *informal* come down on (like a ton of bricks); *dated* chastise.

punishing *adjective* **arduous**, demanding, taxing, strenuous, rigorous, stressful, trying, heavy, difficult, tough, exhausting, tiring, gruelling.
- OPPOSITES easy.

punishment *noun* **penalty**, sanction, penance, discipline, forfeit, sentence.

WORD LINKS
penal, **punitive** relating to punishment

punitive *adjective* **penal**, disciplinary, corrective.

puny *adjective* **1 small**, weak, feeble, slight, undersized, stunted, underdeveloped; *informal* weedy. **2 pitiful**, pitiable, miserable, sorry, meagre, paltry; *informal* pathetic, measly.
- OPPOSITES sturdy.

pupil *noun* **1 student**, scholar, schoolchild, schoolboy, schoolgirl. **2 disciple**, follower, student, protégé, apprentice, trainee, novice.
- OPPOSITES teacher.

puppet *noun* **1 marionette**, glove puppet, finger puppet. **2 pawn**, tool, instrument, cat's paw, poodle, mouthpiece, stooge.

purchase *verb* **buy**, acquire, obtain, pick up, procure, pay for, invest in; *informal* get hold of, score.
- OPPOSITES sell.
● *noun* **1 acquisition**, buy, investment, order. **2 grip**, grasp, hold, foothold, toehold, anchorage, support, traction, leverage.
- OPPOSITES sale.

pure *adjective* **1 unadulterated**, undiluted, sterling, solid, unalloyed. **2 clean**, clear, fresh, sparkling, unpolluted, uncontaminated, untainted. **3 virtuous**, moral, good, righteous, honourable, reputable, wholesome, clean, honest, upright, upstanding, exemplary, innocent, chaste, unsullied, undefiled; *informal* squeaky clean. **4 sheer**, utter, absolute, out-and-out, complete, total, perfect.
- OPPOSITES impure, polluted.

purely *adverb* **entirely**, wholly, exclusively, solely, only, just, merely.

purge *verb* **1 cleanse**, clear, purify, rid, empty, strip, scour. **2 remove**, get rid of, eliminate, clear out, sweep out, expel, eject, evict, dismiss, sack, oust, axe, depose, root out, weed out.
● *noun* **removal**, elimination, expulsion, ejection, exclusion, eviction, dismissal.

purify *verb* **clean**, cleanse, refine, decontaminate, filter, clear, freshen, deodorize, sanitize, disinfect, sterilize.

puritanical *adjective* **moralistic**, puritan, strait-laced, stuffy, prudish, prim, priggish, narrow-minded, censorious, austere, severe, ascetic, abstemious; *informal* goody-goody, starchy.
- OPPOSITES permissive.

purity *noun* **1 cleanness**, freshness, cleanliness. **2 virtue**, morality, goodness, righteousness, piety, honour, honesty, integrity, innocence.

purpose *noun* **1 motive**, motivation, grounds, occasion, reason, point, basis, justification. **2 intention**, aim, object, objective, goal, plan, ambition, aspiration. **3 function**, role, use. **4 determination**, resolution, resolve, steadfastness, single-mindedness, enthusiasm, ambition, motivation, commitment, conviction, dedication.
□ **on purpose** deliberately, intentionally, purposely, wilfully, knowingly, consciously.

purposeful *adjective* **determined**, resolute, steadfast, single-minded, committed.
- OPPOSITES aimless.

purposely *adverb* **deliberately**, intentionally, on purpose, wilfully, knowingly, consciously.

purse *noun* **1 wallet**; *N. Amer.* change purse, billfold. **2** *(N. Amer.)* **handbag**, shoulder bag, clutch bag; *N. Amer.* pocketbook. **3 prize**, reward, winnings, stake(s).
● *verb* **press together**, compress, tighten, pucker, pout.

pursue *verb* **1 follow**, run after, chase, hunt, stalk, track, trail, hound. **2 strive for**, work towards, seek, search for, aim at/for, aspire to. **3 engage in**, be occupied in, practise, follow, conduct, ply, take up, undertake, carry on with, continue, proceed with, apply oneself to.

pursuit *noun a range of leisure pursuits* **activity**, hobby, pastime, diversion, recreation, amusement, occupation.

push *verb* **1 shove**, thrust, propel, send, drive, force, prod, poke, nudge, elbow, shoulder, ram, squeeze, jostle. **2 press**, depress, hold down, squeeze, operate, activate. **3 urge**, press, pressure, pressurize, force, coerce, dragoon, browbeat; *informal* lean on, twist someone's arm.
- OPPOSITES pull.
● *noun* **1 shove**, thrust, nudge, bump, jolt, prod, poke. **2** *the army's eastward push* **advance**, drive, thrust, charge, attack, assault, onslaught, onrush, offensive.

pushy *adjective* **assertive**, overbearing, domineering, aggressive, forceful, forward, thrusting, ambitious, driven, overconfident, cocky; *informal* bossy.

put *verb* **1 place**, set, lay, deposit, position, leave, plant, locate, situate,

settle, install; *informal* stick, dump, park, plonk, pop; *N. Amer. informal* plunk. **2 express**, word, phrase, frame, formulate, render, convey, state.
▫ **put across/over** communicate, convey, get across/over, explain, make clear, spell out. **put off 1** deter, discourage, dissuade, daunt, unnerve, intimidate, scare off; *informal* turn off. **2** postpone, defer, delay, put back, adjourn, hold over, reschedule, shelve; *N. Amer.* table; *informal* put on ice, put on the back burner. **put out 1** annoy, anger, irritate, offend, displease, irk, gall, upset; *informal* rile, miff. **2** inconvenience, trouble, bother, impose on. **3** extinguish, quench, douse, smother, blow out, snuff out. **4** issue, publish, release, bring out, circulate, publicize, post. **put up 1** accommodate, house, take in, give someone a roof over their head. **2** nominate, propose, put forward, recommend. **3** build, construct, erect, raise. **4** display, pin up, stick up, hang up, post. **5** provide, supply, furnish, give, contribute, donate, pledge, pay; *informal* cough up, shell out; *N. Amer. informal* ante up, pony up. **put up with** tolerate, take, stand (for), accept, stomach, swallow, endure, bear; *informal* abide, lump it; *Brit. informal* stick; *formal* brook.

puzzle *verb* **baffle**, perplex, bewilder, confuse, bemuse, mystify, nonplus; *informal* flummox, stump, beat.
● *noun* **enigma**, mystery, paradox, conundrum, poser, riddle, problem.

puzzling *adjective* **baffling**, perplexing, bewildering, confusing, complicated, unclear, mysterious, enigmatic.

Qq

quaint *adjective* **1 picturesque**, charming, sweet, attractive, old-fashioned, old-world; *Brit.* twee. **2 unusual**, curious, eccentric, quirky, bizarre, whimsical, unconventional; *informal* offbeat.
- OPPOSITES ugly.

quake *verb* **shake**, tremble, quiver, shudder, sway, rock, wobble, move, heave, convulse.

qualification *noun* **1 certificate**, diploma, degree, licence, document, warrant. **2 modification**, limitation, reservation, stipulation, alteration, amendment, revision, moderation, mitigation, condition, proviso, caveat.

qualified *adjective* **1 certified**, certificated, chartered, licensed, professional. **2 limited**, conditional, restricted, contingent, circumscribed, guarded, equivocal, modified, adapted, amended, adjusted, moderated, reduced.
- OPPOSITES wholehearted.

qualify *verb* **1 be eligible**, meet the requirements, be entitled, be permitted. **2 be certified**, be licensed, pass, graduate, succeed. **3 authorize**, empower, allow, permit, license. **4 modify**, limit, restrict, make conditional, moderate, temper, modulate, mitigate.

quality *noun* **1 standard**, grade, class, calibre, condition, character, nature, form, rank, value, level. **2 excellence**, superiority, merit, worth, value, virtue, calibre, distinction. **3 feature**, trait, attribute, characteristic, point, aspect, facet, side, property.

quantity *noun* **amount**, total, aggregate, sum, quota, mass, weight, volume, bulk.

quarrel *noun* **argument**, disagreement, squabble, fight, dispute, wrangle, clash, altercation, feud, vendetta; *Brit.* row; *informal* tiff, slanging match, run-in, spat; *Brit. informal* bust-up.
- OPPOSITES agreement.
● *verb* **argue**, fight, disagree, fall out, differ, be at odds, bicker, squabble, cross swords; *Brit.* row.
- OPPOSITES agree.
□ **quarrel with** fault, criticize, object to, oppose, take exception to, attack, take issue with, impugn, contradict, dispute, controvert; *informal* knock.

quarrelsome *adjective* **argumentative**, disputatious, confrontational, captious, pugnacious, combative, antagonistic, bellicose, belligerent, cantankerous, choleric; *Brit. informal* stroppy.
- OPPOSITES peaceable.

quarry *noun* **prey**, victim, object, goal, target, kill, game, prize.

quarter *noun* **1 district**, area, region, part, side, neighbourhood, precinct, locality, sector, zone, ghetto, community, enclave. **2 source**, direction, place, location. **3** *the servants' quarters* **accommodation**, lodgings, rooms, chambers, home; *informal* pad, digs; *formal* abode, residence, domicile. **4** *riot squads gave no quarter* **mercy**, leniency, clemency, compassion, pity, charity, sympathy, tolerance.
● *verb* **accommodate**, house, board, lodge, put up, take in, install, shelter; *Military* billet.

quash *verb* **1 cancel**, reverse, rescind, repeal, revoke, retract, countermand, withdraw, overturn, overrule. **2 stop**, put an end to, stamp out, crush, put down, check, curb, nip in the bud, squash, suppress, stifle.

queasy *adjective* **nauseous**, bilious, sick, ill, unwell, poorly, green about the gills; *Brit.* off colour.

queen *noun* **monarch**, sovereign, ruler, head of state, Crown, Her Majesty.

queer *adjective* **odd**, strange, unusual, funny, peculiar, curious, bizarre, weird, uncanny, freakish, eerie, unnatural, abnormal, anomalous; *informal* spooky.
- OPPOSITES normal.

quell *verb* **1 put an end to**, put a stop to, crush, put down, check, crack down on, curb, nip in the bud, squash, quash, subdue, suppress, overcome. **2 calm**, soothe, pacify, settle, quieten, silence, allay, assuage, mitigate, moderate.

query *noun* **1 question**, enquiry. **2 doubt**, uncertainty, question (mark), reservation.
● *verb* **1 ask**, enquire, question; *Brit. informal* quiz. **2 challenge**, question, dispute, doubt, have suspicions about, distrust.
- OPPOSITES accept.

quest *noun* **1 search**, hunt, pursuance. **2 expedition**, journey, voyage, trek, travels, odyssey, adventure, exploration, search, crusade, mission, pilgrimage.

question *noun* **1 enquiry**, query, interrogation. **2 doubt**, dispute, argument, debate, uncertainty, reservation. **3 issue**, matter, topic, business, problem, concern, debate, argument, dispute, controversy.
- OPPOSITES answer, certainty.
● *verb* **1 interrogate**, cross-examine, cross-question, quiz, interview, debrief, examine; *informal* grill, pump. **2 query**, challenge, dispute, cast aspersions on, doubt, suspect.
□ **out of the question** impossible, impracticable, unfeasible, unworkable, inconceivable, unimaginable, unrealizable, unsuitable; *informal* not on.

WORD LINKS
interrogative relating to questions

questionable *adjective* **suspicious**, suspect, dubious, irregular, odd, strange, murky, dark, unsavoury, disreputable; *informal* funny, fishy, shady, iffy; *Brit. informal* dodgy.

queue *noun* **row**, column, file, chain, string, procession, waiting list; *N. Amer.* line, wait list.

quick *adjective* **1 fast**, swift, rapid, speedy, brisk, smart, lightning, whirlwind, whistle-stop, breakneck; *informal* nippy, zippy; *literary* fleet. **2 hasty**, hurried, cursory, perfunctory, desultory, superficial, brief. **3 sudden**, instantaneous, instant, immediate, abrupt, precipitate. **4 intelligent**, bright, clever, gifted, able, astute, sharp-witted, smart, alert, sharp, perceptive; *informal* brainy, on the ball, genius.
- OPPOSITES slow, long.

quicken *verb* **1 speed up**, accelerate, step up, hasten, hurry (up). **2 stimulate**, excite, arouse, rouse, stir up, activate, whet, inspire, kindle.

quickly *adverb* **1 fast**, swiftly, briskly, rapidly, speedily, at full tilt, at a gallop, at the double, post-haste, hotfoot; *informal* like (greased) lightning, hell for leather, like blazes, like the wind; *Brit. informal* like the clappers, like billy-o; *N. Amer. informal* lickety-split. **2 immediately**, directly, at once, straight away, right away, instantly, forthwith; *N. Amer.* momentarily; *informal* like a shot, asap, p.d.q., pronto. **3 briefly**, fleetingly, briskly, hastily, hurriedly, cursorily, perfunctorily.

quiet *adjective* **1 silent**, still, hushed, noiseless, soundless, mute, dumb, speechless. **2 soft**, low, muted, muffled, faint, hushed, whispered, suppressed. **3 peaceful**, sleepy, tranquil, calm, still, restful.
- OPPOSITES loud, busy.
● *noun* **silence**, still, hush, restfulness, calm, tranquillity, serenity, peace.

quietly *adverb* **1 silently**, noiselessly, soundlessly, inaudibly. **2 softly**, faintly, in a low voice, in a whisper, in a murmur, under your breath, in an undertone, sotto voce.

quilt *noun* **duvet**, cover(s); *Brit.* eiderdown; *N. Amer.* comforter; *Austral. trademark* Doona.

quirk *noun* **1 idiosyncrasy**, peculiarity, oddity, eccentricity, foible, whim, vagary, habit, characteristic, trait, fad. **2 chance**, fluke, freak, anomaly, twist.

quirky *adjective* **eccentric**, idiosyncratic, unconventional, unorthodox, unusual, strange, bizarre, peculiar, zany; *informal* wacky, way-out, offbeat.
- OPPOSITES conventional.

quit *verb* **1 leave**, vacate, exit, depart from. **2** *(informal)* **resign from**, leave, give up, hand in your notice; *informal* chuck, pack in. **3** *(informal)* **give up**, stop, discontinue, drop, abandon, abstain from; *informal* pack in, leave off.

quite *adverb* **1 completely**, entirely, totally, wholly, absolutely, utterly, thoroughly, altogether. **2 fairly**, rather, somewhat, relatively, comparatively, moderately, reasonably; *informal* pretty.

quiz *noun* **competition**, test of knowledge.
● *verb* **question**, interrogate, cross-examine, cross-question, interview; *informal* grill, pump.

quota *noun* **share**, allocation, allowance, ration, portion, slice, percentage; *Brit. informal* whack.

quotation *noun* **1 extract**, quote, citation, excerpt, passage; *N. Amer.* cite. **2 estimate**, quote, price, tender, bid, costing.

quote *verb* **1 recite**, repeat, reproduce, retell, echo. **2 mention**, cite, refer to, name, instance, allude to, point out.
● *noun* see **quotation**.

Rr

race[1] *noun* **1 contest**, competition, event, fixture, heat, trial(s). **2** *the race for naval domination* **rivalry**, competition, contention, quest.
● *verb* **1 compete**, contend, run, be pitted against. **2 hurry**, dash, rush, run, sprint, bolt, charge, career, shoot, hurtle, hare, fly, speed, zoom; *informal* tear, belt.

race[2] *noun* **1 ethnic group**, origin, bloodline, stock. **2 people**, nation.

racial *adjective* **ethnic**, ethnological, race-related, cultural, national, tribal, genetic.

rack *noun* **frame**, framework, stand, holder, trestle, support, shelf.
● *verb* **torment**, afflict, torture, agonize, harrow, plague, persecute, trouble, worry.

racket *noun* **1 noise**, din, hubbub, clamour, uproar, tumult, commotion, rumpus, pandemonium; *Brit.* row; *informal* hullabaloo. **2** *(informal)* **fraud**, swindle, sharp practice; *informal* scam, rip-off.

radiant *adjective* **1 shining**, bright, illuminated, brilliant, gleaming, glowing, ablaze, luminous, lustrous, incandescent, dazzling, coruscating, shimmering. **2 joyful**, elated, thrilled, overjoyed, jubilant, rapturous, ecstatic, euphoric, in seventh heaven, on cloud nine, delighted, very happy; *informal* on top of the world, over the moon.
- OPPOSITES dark, gloomy.

radiate *verb* **1 emit**, give off, discharge, diffuse, scatter, shed, cast. **2 shine**, beam, emanate, pour. **3 fan out**, spread out, branch out/off, extend, issue.

radical *adjective* **1 thorough**, complete, total, comprehensive, exhaustive, sweeping, far-reaching, wide-ranging, extensive, profound, major. **2 fundamental**, basic, deep-seated, essential, structural. **3 revolutionary**, progressive, reformist, revisionist, progressivist, extreme, fanatical, militant.
- OPPOSITES superficial, minor, conservative.

raffle *noun* **lottery**, (prize) draw, sweepstake, sweep, tombola; *N. Amer.* lotto.

rage *noun* **1 fury**, anger, wrath, outrage, indignation, temper, spleen; *formal* ire. **2 craze**, passion, fashion, taste, trend, vogue, fad, mania; *informal* thing.
● *verb* **be angry**, be furious, be enraged, be incensed, seethe, be beside yourself, rave, storm, fume, spit; *informal* be livid, be wild, be steamed up.

ragged *adjective* **1 tattered**, torn, ripped, frayed, worn (out), threadbare, scruffy, shabby; *informal* tatty. **2 jagged**, craggy, rugged, uneven, rough, irregular, indented.

raid *noun* **1 attack**, assault, descent, blitz, incursion, sortie, onslaught, storming. **2 robbery**, burglary, hold-up, break-in, ram raid; *informal* smash-and-grab, stick-up; *N. Amer. informal* heist.
● *verb* **1 attack**, assault, set upon, descend on, swoop on, storm, rush. **2 rob**, hold up, break into, plunder, steal from, pillage, loot, ransack; *informal* stick up.

raider *noun* **robber**, burglar, thief, housebreaker, plunderer, pillager, looter, marauder, attacker, assailant, invader.

railing *noun* **fence**, fencing, rail(s), palisade, balustrade, banister.

rain *noun* **1 rainfall**, precipitation, raindrops, drizzle, mizzle, shower, rainstorm, cloudburst, torrent, downpour, deluge, storm. **2** *a rain of hot ash* **shower**, deluge, flood, torrent, avalanche, flurry, storm, hail.

● *verb* **1 pour (down)**, pelt down, tip down, teem down, beat down, lash down, drizzle, spit; *informal* be chucking it down; *Brit. informal* bucket down. **2** *bombs rained on the city* **fall**, hail, drop, shower.

WORD LINKS
pluvial relating to rain

rainy *adjective* **wet**, showery, drizzly, damp, inclement.
- OPPOSITES dry, fine.

raise *verb* **1 lift (up)**, hold aloft, elevate, uplift, hoist, haul up, hitch up; *Brit. informal* hoick up. **2 increase**, put up, push up, up, mark up, inflate; *informal* hike (up), jack up, bump up. **3 amplify**, louden, magnify, intensify, boost, lift, increase. **4 get**, obtain, acquire, accumulate, amass, collect, fetch, net, make. **5 bring up**, air, present, table, propose, submit, advance, suggest, put forward. **6 give rise to**, occasion, cause, produce, engender, elicit, create, result in, lead to, prompt. **7 bring up**, rear, nurture, educate.
- OPPOSITES lower, reduce.

rake *verb* **1 scrape**, collect, gather. **2 smooth (out)**, level, even out, flatten, comb. **3 rummage**, search, hunt, sift, rifle.

rally *verb* **1 regroup**, reassemble, re-form, reunite, convene, mobilize. **2 recover**, improve, get better, pick up, revive, bounce back, perk up, look up, turn a corner.
● *noun* **1 (mass) meeting**, gathering, assembly, demonstration, march; *informal* demo. **2 recovery**, upturn, improvement, comeback, resurgence.

ram *verb* **1 force**, thrust, plunge, stab, push, sink, dig, stick, cram, jam, stuff. **2 hit**, strike, crash into, collide with, impact, smash into, butt.

ramble *verb* **1 walk**, hike, tramp, trek, backpack. **2 chatter**, babble, prattle, blather, gabble, jabber, twitter, rattle; *Brit. informal* witter, chunter, rabbit.

rambling *adjective* **1 long-winded**, verbose, wordy, prolix, disjointed, disconnected. **2 sprawling**, spreading, labyrinthine, maze-like.
- OPPOSITES concise, compact.

ramification *noun* **consequence**, result, aftermath, outcome, effect, upshot, development, implication.

ramp *noun* **slope**, bank, incline, gradient, rise, drop.

rampage *verb* **riot**, run amok, go berserk, storm, charge, tear.
□ **go on the rampage** riot, go berserk, get out of control, run amok; *N. Amer. informal* go postal.

rampant *adjective* **uncontrolled**, unrestrained, unchecked, unbridled, out of control, out of hand, widespread, rife, spreading.
- OPPOSITES controlled.

random *adjective* **unsystematic**, unmethodical, arbitrary, unplanned, chance, casual, indiscriminate, non-specific, haphazard, stray, erratic, hit-or-miss.
- OPPOSITES systematic.

range *noun* **1 extent**, limit, reach, span, scope, compass, sweep, area, field, orbit, ambit, horizon, latitude. **2 row**, chain, sierra, ridge, massif. **3 assortment**, variety, diversity, mixture, collection, array, selection, choice.
● *verb* **1 vary**, fluctuate, differ, extend, stretch, reach, go, run, cover. **2 roam**, wander, travel, journey, rove, traverse, walk, hike, trek.

rank[1] *noun* **1 position**, level, grade, echelon, class, status, standing. **2 high standing**, blue blood, high birth, nobility, aristocracy. **3 row**, line, file, column, string, train, procession.
● *verb* **1 classify**, class, categorize, rate, grade, bracket, group, designate, list. **2 line up**, align, order, arrange, dispose, set out, array, range.

rank[2] *adjective* **1 abundant**, lush, luxuriant, dense, profuse, vigorous, overgrown; *informal* jungly. **2 offensive**, nasty, revolting, sickening, obnoxious, foul, fetid, rancid, putrid. **3** *rank stupidity* **downright**, utter, out-and-out, absolute, complete, sheer, blatant, arrant, thorough, unqualified.

rankle *verb* **annoy**, upset, anger, irritate, offend, affront, displease, provoke, irk, vex, pique, nettle, gall; *informal* rile, miff, peeve, aggravate, hack off; *Brit. informal* nark; *N. Amer. informal* tick off.

ransack *verb* **1 plunder**, pillage, raid, rob, loot, sack, strip, despoil, ravage, devastate. **2** scour, rifle through, comb, search, turn upside down.

ransom *noun* **pay-off**, payment, sum, price.

rant *verb* **shout**, sound off, hold forth, go on, fulminate, spout, bluster; *informal* mouth off.

rap *verb* **hit**, knock, strike, smack, bang; *informal* whack, thwack, bash, wallop.

rapid *adjective* **quick**, fast, swift, speedy, express, expeditious, brisk, lightning, meteoric, whirlwind, sudden, instantaneous, instant, immediate.
- OPPOSITES slow.

rapport *noun* **affinity**, close relationship, (mutual) understanding, bond, empathy, sympathy, accord.

rare *adjective* **1 infrequent**, scarce, sparse, few and far between, occasional, limited, isolated, odd, unaccustomed. **2 unusual**, recherché, uncommon, thin on the ground, like gold dust, unfamiliar, atypical. **3 exceptional**, outstanding, unparalleled, peerless, matchless, unique, unrivalled, beyond compare.
- OPPOSITES common, commonplace.

rarely *adverb* **seldom**, infrequently, hardly (ever), scarcely.
- OPPOSITES often.

raring *adjective* **eager**, keen, enthusiastic, impatient, longing, desperate; *informal* dying, itching.

rarity *noun* **1 infrequency**, scarcity. **2 curiosity**, oddity, collector's item, rare bird, wonder, nonpareil, one of a kind; *Brit. informal* one-off.

rash[1] *noun* **1 spots**, eruption, nettle-rash, hives. **2** *a rash of articles in the press* **series**, succession, spate, wave, flood, deluge, torrent, outbreak, epidemic, flurry.

rash[2] *adjective* **reckless**, impulsive, impetuous, hot-headed, daredevil, madcap, hasty, foolhardy, incautious, precipitate, careless, heedless, thoughtless, unthinking, imprudent, foolish.
- OPPOSITES prudent.

rate *noun* **1 percentage**, ratio, proportion, scale, standard. **2 charge**, price, cost, tariff, fare, fee, remuneration, payment. **3 speed**, pace, tempo, velocity.
● *verb* **1 assess**, evaluate, appraise, judge, weigh up, estimate, gauge. **2 merit**, deserve, warrant, be worthy of.

rather *adverb* **1 sooner**, by preference, by choice, more readily. **2 quite**, a bit, a little, fairly, slightly, somewhat, relatively, comparatively; *informal* pretty.

ratify *verb* **confirm**, approve, sanction, endorse, agree to, accept, uphold, authorize, formalize, sign.

rating *noun* **grade**, classification, ranking, position, category, assessment, evaluation, mark, score.

ratio *noun* **proportion**, relationship, rate, percentage, fraction, correlation.

ration *noun* **1 allowance**, allocation, quota, share, portion, helping. **2** *the garrison ran out of rations* **supplies**, provisions, food, stores.
● *verb* **control**, limit, restrict, conserve.

rational *adjective* **logical**, reasoned, sensible, reasonable, realistic, cogent, intelligent, shrewd, common-sense, sane, sound.

rationale *noun* **reason(s)**, thinking, logic, grounds, sense.

rationalize *verb* **1 justify**, explain (away), account for, defend, vindicate, excuse. **2 streamline**, reorganize, modernize, update, trim, hone, simplify, downsize, prune.

rattle *verb* **1 clatter**, clank, knock, clunk, clink, jangle, tinkle. **2 unnerve**, disconcert, disturb, fluster, shake, perturb, throw, discomfit; *informal* faze.

raucous *adjective* **1 harsh**, strident, screeching, piercing, shrill, grating, discordant, dissonant, noisy, loud,

cacophonous. **2 rowdy**, noisy, boisterous, roisterous, wild.
- OPPOSITES soft, quiet.

ravage *verb* **lay waste**, devastate, ruin, destroy, wreak havoc on.

rave *verb* **1 rant**, rage, lose your temper, storm, fume, shout; *informal* fly off the handle, hit the roof; *Brit. informal* go spare; *N. Amer. informal* flip your wig. **2 enthuse**, go into raptures, wax lyrical, rhapsodize, sing the praises of, acclaim, eulogize, extol; *N. Amer. informal* ballyhoo.
- OPPOSITES criticize.

raw *adjective* **1 uncooked**, fresh, natural. **2 unprocessed**, untreated, unrefined, crude, natural. **3 inexperienced**, new, untrained, untried, untested, callow, green; *informal* wet behind the ears. **4 sore**, red, painful, tender, chafed.
- OPPOSITES cooked, processed.

ray *noun* **beam**, shaft, stream, streak, flash, glimmer, flicker, spark.

raze *verb* **destroy**, demolish, tear down, pull down, knock down, level, flatten, bulldoze, wipe out, lay waste.

reach *verb* **1 extend**, stretch, outstretch, thrust, stick, hold. **2 arrive at**, get to, come to, end up at. **3** *the temperature reached 75°* **attain**, get to, rise to, fall to, sink to, drop to; *informal* hit. **4** *ministers reached an agreement* **achieve**, work out, draw up, put together, negotiate, thrash out, hammer out. **5 contact**, get in touch with, get through to, get, speak to; *informal* get hold of.
● *noun* **1 grasp**, range, stretch, capabilities, capacity. **2 jurisdiction**, authority, influence, power, scope, range, compass, ambit.

react *verb* **respond**, act in response, reply, answer, behave.

reaction *noun* **1 response**, answer, reply, rejoinder, retort, riposte; *informal* comeback. **2 backlash**, counteraction.

reactionary *adjective* **right-wing**, conservative, traditionalist, conventional, diehard.
- OPPOSITES radical, progressive.

read *verb* **1 peruse**, study, scrutinize, look through, pore over, run your eye over, cast an eye over, leaf through, scan. **2 understand**, make out, make sense of, decipher, interpret, construe. **3 register**, record, display, show, indicate.

WORD LINKS
literacy ability to read
illiteracy inability to read

readable *adjective* **1 legible**, decipherable, clear, intelligible, comprehensible. **2 enjoyable**, entertaining, interesting, absorbing, gripping, enthralling, engrossing; *informal* unputdownable.
- OPPOSITES illegible.

readily *adverb* **1 willingly**, unhesitatingly, ungrudgingly, gladly, happily, eagerly. **2 easily**, without difficulty.

readiness *noun* **willingness**, eagerness, keenness, enthusiasm, alacrity.
□ **in readiness** (at the) ready, prepared, available, on hand, accessible, handy.

reading *noun* **1 perusal**, study, scanning. **2 learning**, scholarship, education, erudition. **3 recital**, recitation, performance. **4 lesson**, passage, excerpt. **5 interpretation**, understanding, explanation, analysis, construction.

ready *adjective* **1 prepared**, equipped, all set, organized, primed; *informal* fit, psyched up, geared up. **2 completed**, finished, prepared, organized, done, arranged, fixed. **3** *he's always ready to help* **willing**, prepared, pleased, inclined, disposed, eager, keen, happy, glad; *informal* game. **4** *a ready supply of food* **(easily) available**, accessible, handy, close/near at hand, to/on hand, convenient, within reach, near, at your fingertips; *informal* on tap. **5** *a ready answer* **prompt**, quick, swift, speedy, fast, immediate, unhesitating.
● *verb* **prepare**, organize, gear up; *informal* psych up.

real *adjective* **1 actual**, true, factual, non-fictional, historical, material,

physical, tangible, concrete. **2 genuine**, authentic, bona fide, proper, true; *informal* pukka, kosher. **3 sincere**, genuine, true, unfeigned, heartfelt. **4 complete**, utter, thorough, absolute, total, prize, perfect; *Brit. informal* right, proper.
- OPPOSITES imaginary, false.

realism *noun* **1 pragmatism**, practicality, common sense, level-headedness. **2 authenticity**, accuracy, fidelity, truthfulness, verisimilitude.

realistic *adjective* **1 practical**, pragmatic, matter-of-fact, down-to-earth, sensible, commonsensical, rational, level-headed; *informal* no-nonsense. **2 achievable**, attainable, feasible, practicable, reasonable, sensible, workable; *informal* doable. **3 authentic**, accurate, true to life, lifelike, truthful, faithful, natural, naturalistic.
- OPPOSITES unrealistic.

reality *noun* **1 the real world**, real life, actuality, corporeality. **2 fact**, actuality, truth. **3 authenticity**, verisimilitude, fidelity, truthfulness, accuracy.
- OPPOSITES fantasy.

realization *noun* **1 awareness**, understanding, comprehension, consciousness, appreciation, recognition, discernment. **2 fulfilment**, achievement, accomplishment, attainment.

realize *verb* **1 register**, perceive, understand, grasp, comprehend, see, recognize, take in; *informal* tumble to; *Brit. informal* twig. **2 fulfil**, achieve, accomplish, make happen, bring to fruition, bring about/off, actualize. **3 make**, clear, gain, earn, return, produce. **4 be sold for**, fetch, go for, make, net.

really *adverb* **1 in (actual) fact**, actually, in reality, in truth. **2 genuinely**, truly, certainly, honestly, undoubtedly, unquestionably.

realm *noun* **1 kingdom**, country, land, state, nation, territory, dominion, empire, monarchy, principality. **2** *the realm of academia* **domain**, sphere, area, field, world, province.

reap *verb* **1 harvest**, cut, pick, gather, garner. **2 receive**, obtain, get, derive, acquire, secure, realize.

rear[1] *noun* **back (part)**, hind part, end, tail (end), back (end); *Nautical* stern.
● *adjective* **back**, end, rearmost, hind, last.
- OPPOSITES front.

rear[2] *verb* **1 bring up**, care for, look after, nurture, parent; *N. Amer.* raise. **2 breed**, raise, keep, grow, cultivate. **3** *houses reared up on either side* **rise**, tower, soar, loom.

reason *noun* **1 cause**, ground(s), basis, rationale, motive, explanation, justification, defence, vindication, excuse, apologia. **2 rationality**, logic, cognition, reasoning, intellect, thought, understanding; *formal* ratiocination. **3 sanity**, mind, mental faculties, senses, wits; *informal* marbles.
● *verb* **calculate**, conclude, reckon, think, judge, deduce, infer, surmise; *informal* figure.
□ **reason out** work out, think through, make sense of, get to the bottom of, puzzle out; *informal* figure out.
reason with talk round, bring round, persuade, prevail on, convince.

WORD LINKS
rational relating to reason

reasonable *adjective* **1 sensible**, rational, logical, fair, just, equitable, intelligent, wise, level-headed, practical, realistic, sound, valid, commonsensical, tenable, plausible, credible, believable. **2 practicable**, sensible, appropriate, suitable. **3 fairly good**, acceptable, satisfactory, average, adequate, fair, tolerable, passable; *informal* OK. **4 inexpensive**, affordable, moderate, low, cheap, within your means.

reassure *verb* **put someone's mind at rest**, encourage, hearten, buoy up, cheer up, comfort, soothe.
- OPPOSITES alarm.

rebate *noun* **partial refund**, partial repayment, discount, deduction, reduction.

rebel *noun* **1 revolutionary**, insurgent, insurrectionist, mutineer, guerrilla, terrorist, freedom fighter. **2 nonconformist**, dissenter, dissident, maverick.
- OPPOSITES loyalist, conformist.
● *verb* **revolt**, mutiny, riot, rise up, take up arms.
● *adjective* **1 rebellious**, insurgent, revolutionary, mutinous. **2 defiant**, disobedient, insubordinate, subversive, rebellious, nonconformist, maverick.
- OPPOSITES loyal, obedient.
□ **rebel against** defy, disobey, kick against, challenge, oppose, resist.

rebellion *noun* **1 revolt**, uprising, insurrection, mutiny, revolution, insurgence. **2 defiance**, disobedience, insubordination, subversion, resistance.
- OPPOSITES compliance.

rebellious *adjective* **1 rebel**, insurgent, mutinous, revolutionary. **2 defiant**, disobedient, insubordinate, unruly, mutinous, obstreperous, recalcitrant, intractable; *Brit. informal* bolshie.
- OPPOSITES loyal, obedient.

rebound *verb* **1 bounce (back)**, spring back, ricochet, boomerang. **2 backfire**, misfire, come back on.

rebuff *verb* **reject**, turn down, spurn, refuse, decline, snub, slight, dismiss, brush off.
- OPPOSITES accept.
● *noun* **rejection**, snub, slight, refusal, spurning; *informal* brush-off, kick in the teeth, slap in the face.

rebuke *verb* **reprimand**, reproach, scold, admonish, reprove, chastise, upbraid, berate, take to task; *informal* tell off; *Brit. informal* tick off; *N. Amer. informal* chew out; *formal* castigate.
● *noun* **reprimand**, reproach, scolding, admonition; *informal* telling-off, dressing-down; *Brit. informal* ticking-off.
- OPPOSITES praise.

recalcitrant *adjective* **uncooperative**, intractable, insubordinate, defiant, rebellious, wilful, wayward, headstrong, self-willed, contrary, perverse, difficult, awkward; *Brit. informal* bloody-minded, bolshie, stroppy; *formal* refractory.
- OPPOSITES amenable.

recall *verb* **1 remember**, recollect, call to mind, think back on/to, reminisce about. **2 remind someone of**, bring to mind, call up, conjure up, evoke. **3 call back**, order home, withdraw.
- OPPOSITES forget.
● *noun* **recollection**, remembrance, memory.

recede *verb* **1 retreat**, go back/down/away, withdraw, ebb, subside. **2 diminish**, lessen, dwindle, fade, abate, subside.
- OPPOSITES advance, grow.

receive *verb* **1 be given**, be presented with, be awarded, be sent, be in receipt of, get, obtain, gain, acquire, be paid. **2 hear**, listen to, respond to, react to. **3 experience**, sustain, undergo, meet with, suffer, bear.
- OPPOSITES give, send.

recent *adjective* **new**, the latest, current, fresh, modern, late, contemporary, up to date, up to the minute.
- OPPOSITES old.

recently *adverb* **not long ago**, a little while back, just now, newly, freshly, of late, lately, latterly.

reception *noun* **1 response**, reaction, treatment. **2 party**, function, social occasion, celebration, get-together, gathering, soirée; *N. Amer.* levee; *informal* do.

receptive *adjective* **open-minded**, responsive, amenable, well disposed, flexible, approachable, accessible.
- OPPOSITES unresponsive.

recess *noun* **1 alcove**, bay, niche, nook, corner. **2 break**, adjournment, interlude, interval, rest, holiday, vacation.

recession *noun* **downturn**, depression, slump, slowdown.
- OPPOSITES boom.

recipe *noun a recipe for success* **formula**, prescription, blueprint.

reciprocal *adjective* **mutual**, common, shared, give-and-take, joint, corresponding, complementary.

reciprocate *verb* **requite**, return, give back.

recital *noun* **1 performance**, concert, recitation, reading. **2 report**, account, listing, catalogue, litany.

recite *verb* **1 quote**, say, speak, read aloud, declaim, deliver, render. **2 recount**, list, detail, reel off, relate, enumerate.

reckless *adjective* **rash**, careless, thoughtless, heedless, precipitate, impetuous, impulsive, irresponsible, foolhardy, devil-may-care.
– OPPOSITES cautious.

reckon *verb* **1 calculate**, compute, work out, figure, count (up), add up, total, tally; *Brit.* tot up. **2 include**, count, regard as, look on as, consider, judge, think of as, deem, rate. **3 think**, believe, be of the opinion, suppose, assume.
□ **reckon on/with** take into account, take into consideration, bargain for/on, anticipate, foresee, be prepared for, consider.

reckoning *noun* **calculation**, estimation, computation, working out, addition, count.

reclaim *verb* **1 get back**, claim back, recover, retrieve, recoup. **2 save**, rescue, redeem, salvage.

recline *verb* **lie**, lie down/back, lean back, relax, loll, lounge, sprawl, stretch out.

recluse *noun* **hermit**, ascetic, eremite, loner, lone wolf; *historical* anchorite.

recognition *noun* **1 identification**, recollection, remembrance. **2 acknowledgement**, acceptance, admission, confession. **3 appreciation**, gratitude, thanks, congratulations, credit, commendation, acclaim, acknowledgement.

recognize *verb* **1 identify**, place, know, put a name to, remember, recall, recollect; *Scottish & N. English* ken. **2 acknowledge**, accept, admit, concede, confess, realize. **3 pay tribute to**, appreciate, be grateful for, acclaim, commend.

recoil *verb* **1 draw back**, jump back, pull back, flinch, shy away, shrink (back), blench. **2 feel revulsion**, feel disgust, shrink from, wince at.

recollect *verb* **remember**, recall, call to mind, think of, think back to, reminisce about.
– OPPOSITES forget.

recollection *noun* **memory**, recall, remembrance, impression, reminiscence.

recommend *verb* **1 advocate**, endorse, commend, suggest, put forward, propose, nominate, put up, speak favourably of, put in a good word for, vouch for; *informal* plug. **2 advise**, counsel, urge, exhort, enjoin, prescribe, argue for, back, support.

recommendation *noun* **1 advice**, counsel, guidance, suggestion, proposal. **2 commendation**, endorsement, good word, testimonial, tip; *informal* plug.

reconcile *verb* **1 reunite**, bring (back) together, pacify, appease, placate, mollify; *formal* conciliate. **2** *reconciling his religious beliefs with his career* **make compatible**, harmonize, square, make congruent, balance. **3 settle**, resolve, sort out, smooth over, iron out, mend, remedy, heal, rectify; *informal* patch up. **4** *they had to reconcile themselves to drastic losses* **accept**, resign yourself to, come to terms with, learn to live with, get used to, make the best of.

reconnoitre *verb* **survey**, explore, scout (out), find out the lie of the land, investigate, examine, scrutinize, inspect, observe, take a look at, patrol; *informal* recce, check out.

reconsider *verb* **rethink**, review, revise, re-evaluate, reassess, have second thoughts, change your mind.

reconstruct *verb* **rebuild**, remake, recreate, restore, reassemble, remodel, revamp, renovate.

record *noun* **1 account**, document, data, file, dossier, evidence, report, annals, archive, chronicle, minutes,

transactions, proceedings, transcript, certificate, deed, register, log. **2 disc**, recording, album, LP, single.
● *verb* **1 write down**, take down, note, jot down, put down on paper, document, enter, log, minute, register. **2 indicate**, register, show, display. **3 film**, photograph, tape, tape-record, video-record, videotape.

recount *verb* **tell**, relate, narrate, describe, report, relay, convey, communicate, impart.

recover *verb* **1 get better**, improve, rally, recuperate, convalesce, revive, be on the mend, get back on your feet, pick up, heal, bounce back, pull through. **2 retrieve**, regain, get back, recoup, reclaim, repossess, recapture. **3 salvage**, save, rescue, retrieve.
- OPPOSITES deteriorate.

recovery *noun* **1 improvement**, recuperation, convalescence, rally, revival. **2 retrieval**, repossession, reclamation, recapture.
- OPPOSITES relapse.

recreation *noun* **1 pleasure**, leisure, relaxation, fun, enjoyment, entertainment, amusement, diversion. **2 pastime**, hobby, leisure activity.
- OPPOSITES work.

recruit *verb* **1 enlist**, call up, conscript; *US* draft. **2 muster**, form, raise, mobilize. **3 hire**, employ, take on, enrol, sign up, engage.
- OPPOSITES demobilize.
● *noun* **1 conscript**; *US* draftee; *N. Amer. informal* yardbird. **2 newcomer**, trainee, initiate, joiner, beginner, novice.

rectify *verb* **correct**, (put) right, sort out, deal with, amend, remedy, repair, fix, make good, resolve, settle; *informal* patch up.

recur *verb* **happen again**, reoccur, repeat (itself), come back, return, reappear.

recycle *verb* **reuse**, reprocess, reclaim, recover, salvage.

red *adjective* **1 scarlet**, vermilion, ruby, cherry, cerise, cardinal, carmine, crimson, maroon, magenta, burgundy, claret. **2 flushed**, blushing, pink, rosy, florid, ruddy. **3** auburn, Titian, chestnut, carroty, ginger.

redeem *verb* **1 save**, deliver from sin, absolve. **2 retrieve**, regain, recover, get back, reclaim, repossess, buy back. **3 exchange**, convert, trade in, cash in.

redolent *adjective* **evocative**, suggestive, reminiscent.

redress *verb* **rectify**, correct, right, compensate for, make amends for, remedy, make good.
● *noun* **compensation**, reparation, restitution, recompense, repayment, amends.

reduce *verb* **1 lessen**, make smaller, lower, decrease, diminish, minimize, shrink, narrow, cut, curtail, contract, shorten, downsize; *informal* chop. **2 bring down**, make cheaper, lower, mark down, slash, discount. **3** *he reduced her to tears* **bring to**, bring to the point of, drive to.
- OPPOSITES increase.

reduction *noun* **1 lessening**, lowering, decrease, diminution, cut, cutback, downsizing. **2 discount**, deduction, cut.

redundancy *noun* **dismissal**, lay-off, sacking, discharge, unemployment.

redundant *adjective* **unnecessary**, not required, unneeded, surplus (to requirements), superfluous.
□ **make redundant** dismiss, lay off, discharge, give someone their notice; *informal* sack, fire.

reel *verb* **1 stagger**, lurch, sway, rock, stumble, totter, wobble, teeter. **2 go round (and round)**, whirl, spin, revolve, swirl, twirl, turn, swim.

refer *verb* **pass**, direct, hand on/over, send on, transfer, entrust, assign.
□ **refer to 1** mention, allude to, touch on, speak of/about, talk of/about, write about, comment on, point out, call attention to. **2** apply to, relate to, pertain to, be relevant to, concern, be connected with. **3** consult, turn to, look at, have recourse to.

referee *noun* **umpire**, judge, adjudicator, arbitrator; *informal* ref.

reference *noun* **1 mention**, allusion, quotation, comment, remark. **2 source**, citation, authority, credit. **3 testimonial**, recommendation, character reference, credentials.

referendum *noun* **(popular) vote**, ballot, poll, plebiscite.

refine *verb* **1 purify**, filter, distil, process, treat. **2 improve**, perfect, polish (up), hone, fine-tune.

refined *adjective* **1 purified**, processed, treated. **2 cultivated**, cultured, polished, elegant, sophisticated, urbane, polite, gracious, well bred. **3 discriminating**, discerning, fastidious, exquisite, impeccable, fine.
- OPPOSITES crude, coarse.

reflect *verb* **1 mirror**, send back, throw back, echo. **2 indicate**, show, display, demonstrate, be evidence of, evince, reveal, betray. **3 think**, consider, review, mull over, ponder, contemplate, deliberate, ruminate, meditate, muse, brood; *formal* cogitate.

reflection *noun* **1 image**, likeness. **2 indication**, display, demonstration, manifestation, expression, evidence. **3 thought**, consideration, contemplation, deliberation, pondering, rumination, meditation, musing; *formal* cogitation.

reform *verb* **1 improve**, better, ameliorate, correct, rectify, restore, revise, refine, adapt, revamp, redesign, reconstruct, reorganize. **2 mend your ways**, change for the better, turn over a new leaf.
● *noun* **improvement**, amelioration, refinement, rectification, restoration, adaptation, revision, redesign, revamp, reconstruction, reorganization.

refrain *verb* **abstain**, desist, hold back, stop yourself, forbear, avoid; *informal* swear off.

refresh *verb* **1 reinvigorate**, revitalize, revive, rejuvenate, restore, energize, enliven, perk up, brace, freshen, wake up, breathe new life into; *informal* buck up. **2** *refresh your memory* **jog**, stimulate, prompt, prod.

refreshing *adjective* **1 invigorating**, revitalizing, reviving, bracing, fortifying, enlivening, stimulating, exhilarating, energizing. **2** *a refreshing change of direction* **welcome**, stimulating, fresh, new, imaginative, innovative.

refreshment *noun* **food and drink**, snacks, titbits; *informal* nibbles.

refuge *noun* **1 shelter**, protection, safety, security, asylum, sanctuary. **2 place of safety**, shelter, haven, sanctuary, sanctum, retreat, bolt-hole, hiding place.

refugee *noun* **asylum seeker**, fugitive, displaced person, exile, émigré.

refund *verb* **repay**, give back, return, pay back, reimburse, compensate, recompense.
● *noun* **repayment**, reimbursement, compensation, rebate.

refurbish *verb* **renovate**, recondition, rehabilitate, revamp, overhaul, restore, redecorate, upgrade, refit; *informal* do up.

refusal *noun* **non-acceptance**, no, rejection, rebuff; *informal* knock-back, thumbs down.

refuse[1] *verb* **1 decline**, turn down, say no to, reject, spurn, rebuff; *informal* pass up, knock back. **2 withhold**, deny.
- OPPOSITES accept.

refuse[2] *noun* **rubbish**, waste, litter; *N. Amer.* garbage, trash; *informal* dreck, junk.

refute *verb* **1 disprove**, prove wrong, rebut, explode, debunk, discredit, invalidate; *informal* shoot full of holes. **2 deny**, reject, repudiate, rebut, contradict.

regain *verb* **recover**, get back, win back, recoup, retrieve, repossess, take back, retake, recapture, reconquer.

regal *adjective* **royal**, kingly, queenly, princely, majestic.

regard *verb* **1 consider**, look on, view, see, think of, judge, deem, estimate,

assess, reckon, rate. **2 look at**, contemplate, eye, gaze at, stare at, observe, view, study, scrutinize.
● *noun* **1 consideration**, care, concern, thought, notice, heed, attention. **2** *doctors are held in high regard* **esteem**, respect, admiration, approval, honour, estimation. **3 (fixed) look**, gaze, stare, observation, contemplation, study, scrutiny. **4** *he sends his regards* **best wishes**, greetings, respects, compliments.

regarding *preposition* **concerning**, as regards, with/in regard to, with respect to, with reference to, relating to, respecting, re, about, apropos, on the subject of, in connection with, vis-à-vis.

regardless *adverb* **anyway**, anyhow, in any case, nevertheless, nonetheless, despite everything, even so, all the same, in any event, come what may.
□ **regardless of** irrespective of, without reference to, without consideration of, discounting, ignoring, notwithstanding, no matter.

regime *noun* **1 government**, administration, leadership, rule, authority, control, command. **2 system**, arrangement, scheme, policy, method, course, plan, programme.

region *noun* **district**, province, territory, division, area, section, sector, zone, belt, quarter.

regional *adjective* **1 geographical**, territorial. **2 local**, provincial, district, parochial, zonal.
– OPPOSITES national.

register *noun* **1 list**, roll, roster, index, directory, catalogue, inventory. **2 record**, chronicle, log, ledger, archive, annals, files.
● *verb* **1 record**, enter, file, lodge, write down, submit, report, note, minute, log. **2 enrol**, put your name down, enlist, sign on/up, apply. **3 indicate**, read, record, show. **4 display**, show, express, exhibit, betray, reveal.

regret *verb* **1 be sorry about**, feel contrite about, feel remorse for, rue, repent of. **2 mourn**, grieve for/over, weep over, sigh over, lament, bemoan.
– OPPOSITES welcome.
● *noun* **1 remorse**, contrition, repentance, compunction, ruefulness, self-reproach, pangs of conscience. **2 sadness**, sorrow, disappointment, unhappiness, grief.

regrettable *adjective* **unfortunate**, unwelcome, sorry, woeful, disappointing, reprehensible, deplorable, disgraceful.

regular *adjective* **1 uniform**, even, consistent, constant, unchanging, unvarying, fixed. **2 frequent**, repeated, continual, recurrent, periodic, constant, perpetual, numerous. **3 usual**, normal, customary, habitual, routine, typical, accustomed, established.
– OPPOSITES erratic, occasional, unusual.

regulate *verb* **1 control**, adjust, balance, set, synchronize. **2 police**, supervise, monitor, be responsible for, control, manage, direct, govern.

regulation *noun* **1 rule**, order, directive, act, law, by-law, statute, dictate, decree. **2 control**, policing, supervision, superintendence, monitoring, governance, management, administration, responsibility.

rehabilitate *verb* **1 reintegrate**, readapt; *N. Amer. informal* rehab. **2 reinstate**, restore, bring back, pardon, absolve, exonerate, forgive; *formal* exculpate. **3 recondition**, restore, renovate, refurbish, revamp, overhaul, redevelop, rebuild, reconstruct.

rehearsal *noun* **practice**, trial performance, read-through, run-through, drill, training, coaching; *informal* dry run.

rehearse *verb* **1 prepare**, practise, read through, run through/over, go over. **2 train**, drill, prepare, coach. **3 list**, enumerate, itemize, detail, spell out, catalogue, recite, repeat, go over, run through, recap.

reign *verb* **1 be king/queen**, sit on the throne, wear the crown, be supreme, rule. **2** *chaos reigned* **prevail**, exist, be present, be the case, occur, be rife,

be rampant, be the order of the day.
● *noun* **rule**, sovereignty, monarchy, dominion, control.

rein *verb* **restrain**, check, curb, constrain, hold back/in, keep under control, regulate, restrict, control, curtail, limit.
□ **free rein** freedom, a free hand, leeway, latitude, flexibility, liberty, independence, licence, room to manoeuvre, carte blanche. **keep a tight rein on** regulate, discipline, control, keep in line.

reinforce *verb* **1 strengthen**, fortify, bolster up, shore up, buttress, prop up, underpin, brace, support, boost. **2 augment**, increase, add to, supplement, boost, top up.

reinforcement *noun* **1 strengthening**, fortification, bolstering, shoring up, buttressing. **2** *we need reinforcements* **additional troops**, auxiliaries, reserves, support, backup, help.

reinstate *verb* **restore**, put back, bring back, reinstitute, reinstall, re-establish.

reiterate *verb* **repeat**, restate, recapitulate, recap, go over, rehearse.

reject *verb* **1 turn down**, refuse, decline, say no to, spurn; *informal* pass up, give the thumbs down to. **2 rebuff**, spurn, shun, snub, cast off/aside, discard, abandon, desert, turn your back on, cold-shoulder; *informal* give someone the brush-off.
- OPPOSITES accept, welcome.
● *noun* **second**, discard, misshape, faulty item, cast-off.

rejoice *verb* **be happy**, be glad, be delighted, celebrate, make merry; *informal* be over the moon.
- OPPOSITES mourn.
□ **rejoice in** delight in, enjoy, revel in, glory in, relish, savour.

rejoin *verb* **return to**, be reunited with, join again, reach again, regain.

rejuvenate *verb* **revive**, revitalize, regenerate, breathe new life into, revivify, reanimate, resuscitate, refresh, reawaken; *informal* give a shot in the arm to, pep up, buck up.

relapse *verb* **deteriorate**, degenerate, lapse, slip back, slide back, regress, revert, retrogress.
- OPPOSITES improve.

relate *verb* **tell**, recount, narrate, report, describe, recite, rehearse.
□ **relate to 1** connect with, associate with, link with, ally with, couple with. **2** apply to, concern, pertain to, have a bearing on, involve. **3** identify with, get on (well) with, feel sympathy with, have a rapport wit, empathize with, understand; *informal* hit it off with.

related *adjective* **connected**, interconnected, associated, linked, allied, corresponding, analogous, parallel, comparable, equivalent.

relation *noun* **1 connection**, relationship, association, link, tie-in, correlation, correspondence, parallel. **2 relative**, family member, kinsman, kinswoman; (**relations**) family, kin, kith and kin, kindred. **3** *our relations with Europe* **dealings**, communication, relationship, connections, contact, interaction.

relationship *noun* **1 connection**, relation, association, link, correlation, correspondence, parallel. **2 family ties**, kinship, affinity, common ancestry. **3 romance**, affair, love affair, liaison, amour, fling.

relative *adjective* **1 comparative**, respective, comparable. **2 proportionate**, in proportion, commensurate, corresponding.
- OPPOSITES disproportionate.
● *noun* **relation**, member of the family, kinsman, kinswoman; (**relatives**) family, kin, kith and kin, kindred.

relax *verb* **1 rest**, loosen up, ease up/off, slow down, de-stress, unbend, unwind, put your feet up, take it easy; *informal* chill (out); *N. Amer. informal* hang loose, decompress. **2 loosen**, slacken, unclench, weaken, lessen. **3 moderate**, temper, ease, loosen, lighten, dilute, weaken, reduce, decrease; *informal* let up on.
- OPPOSITES tense, tighten.

relaxation *noun* **recreation**, enjoyment, amusement, entertainment, fun, pleasure, leisure.

relay *noun* **broadcast**, transmission, showing, feed.
● *verb* **pass on**, hand on, transfer, repeat, communicate, send, transmit, circulate.

release *verb* **1 free**, set free, turn loose, let go/out, liberate, discharge. **2 untie**, undo, unfasten, loose, let go, unleash. **3 make public**, make known, issue, put out, publish, broadcast, circulate, launch, distribute.
- OPPOSITES imprison.

relegate *verb* **downgrade**, demote, lower, put down, move down.
- OPPOSITES upgrade, promote.

relent *verb* **1 change your mind**, do a U-turn, back-pedal, back down, give way/in, capitulate; *Brit.* do an about-turn. **2 ease**, slacken, let up, abate, drop, die down, lessen, decrease, subside, weaken, tail off.

relentless *adjective* **1 persistent**, unfaltering, unremitting, unflagging, untiring, unwavering, dogged, single-minded, tireless, indefatigable. **2 harsh**, cruel, remorseless, unrelenting, merciless, pitiless, implacable, inexorable, unforgiving, unbending, unyielding.

relevant *adjective* **pertinent**, applicable, apposite, material, apropos, to the point, germane.

reliable *adjective* **dependable**, trustworthy, good, safe, authentic, faithful, genuine, sound, true, loyal, unfailing; *humorous* trusty.
- OPPOSITES unreliable.

reliance *noun* **1 dependence**, need. **2 trust**, confidence, faith, belief, conviction.

relic *noun* **artefact**, historical object, antiquity, remnant, vestige, remains.

relief *noun* **1 respite**, remission, interruption, variation, diversion; *informal* let-up. **2 alleviation**, relieving, palliation, soothing, easing, lessening, mitigation. **3 help**, aid, assistance, charity, succour. **4 replacement**, substitute, deputy, reserve, cover, stand-in, supply, locum, understudy.

relieve *verb* **1 alleviate**, mitigate, ease, counteract, dull, reduce. **2 replace**, take over from, stand in for, fill in for, substitute for, deputize for, cover for. **3 free**, release, exempt, excuse, absolve, let off.
- OPPOSITES aggravate.

relieved *adjective* **glad**, thankful, grateful, pleased, happy, easy/easier in your mind, reassured.
- OPPOSITES worried.

religion *noun* **faith**, belief, worship, creed, church, sect, denomination, cult.

WORD LINKS
divinity, **theology** study of religion

religious *adjective* **1 devout**, pious, reverent, godly, God-fearing, churchgoing. **2 spiritual**, theological, scriptural, doctrinal, ecclesiastical, church, holy, divine, sacred. **3 scrupulous**, conscientious, meticulous, punctilious, strict, rigorous.
- OPPOSITES atheistic, secular.

relinquish *verb* **1 renounce**, resign, give up/away, hand over, let go of. **2 leave**, resign from, stand down from, bow out of, give up; *informal* quit, chuck.
- OPPOSITES retain.

relish *noun* **1 enjoyment**, gusto, delight, pleasure, glee, appreciation, enthusiasm. **2 condiment**, sauce, dressing.
- OPPOSITES distaste.
● *verb* **enjoy**, delight in, love, adore, take pleasure in, rejoice in, appreciate, savour, revel in, luxuriate in, glory in.
- OPPOSITES dislike.

reluctance *noun* **unwillingness**, disinclination, hesitation, wavering, vacillation, doubts, second thoughts, misgivings.

reluctant *adjective* **unwilling**, disinclined, unenthusiastic, resistant,

opposed, hesitant, loath.
– OPPOSITES willing, eager.

rely *verb*
▫ **rely on** depend on, count on, bank on, be confident of, be sure of, have faith in, trust in; *informal* swear by; *N. Amer. informal* figure on.

remain *verb* **1 continue**, endure, last, abide, carry on, persist, stay around, survive, live on. **2 stay**, stay behind, stay put, wait behind, be left, hang on; *informal* hang around/round. **3** *he remained calm* **continue to be**, stay, keep.

remainder *noun* **rest**, balance, residue, others, remnant(s), leftovers, surplus, extra, excess.

remains *plural noun* **1 remainder**, residue, rest, remnant(s), leftovers, scraps, debris, detritus. **2 antiquities**, relics, artefacts. **3 corpse**, body, carcass, bones; *Medicine* cadaver.

remark *verb* **comment**, say, observe, mention, reflect; *formal* opine.
● *noun* **comment**, statement, utterance, observation, reflection.

remarkable *adjective* **extraordinary**, exceptional, outstanding, notable, striking, memorable, unusual, conspicuous, momentous.
– OPPOSITES ordinary.

remedy *noun* **1 treatment**, cure, medicine, medication, medicament, drug. **2 solution**, answer, cure, fix, antidote, panacea.
● *verb* **put right**, set right, rectify, solve, sort out, straighten out, resolve, correct, repair, mend, fix.

remember *verb* **1 recall**, call to mind, recollect, think of, reminisce about, look back on. **2 memorize**, retain, learn off by heart, get off pat. **3 bear in mind**, be mindful of, take into account. **4 commemorate**, pay tribute to, honour, salute, pay homage to.
– OPPOSITES forget.

remembrance *noun* **1 recollection**, reminiscence, recall. **2 commemoration**, memory, recognition.

remind *verb* **jog someone's memory**, prompt.
▫ **remind someone of** make someone think of, cause someone to remember, put someone in mind of, call to mind, evoke.

reminiscent *adjective* **similar to**, comparable with, evocative of, suggestive of, redolent of.

remiss *adjective* **negligent**, neglectful, irresponsible, careless, thoughtless, heedless, lax, slack, slipshod, lackadaisical; *N. Amer.* derelict; *informal* sloppy.
– OPPOSITES careful.

remit *noun* **area of responsibility**, sphere, orbit, scope, ambit, province, brief, instructions, orders; *informal* bailiwick.
● *verb* **1 send**, dispatch, forward, hand over, pay. **2 pardon**, forgive, excuse.

remnant *noun* **remains**, remainder, leftovers, offcut, residue, rest.

remonstrate *verb* **protest**, complain, object, take issue, argue, expostulate..

remorse *noun* **regret**, guilt, contrition, repentance, shame.

remorseful *adjective* **sorry**, regretful, contrite, repentant, penitent, guilt-ridden, conscience-stricken, chastened, self-reproachful.
– OPPOSITES unrepentant.

remote *adjective* **1 isolated**, far-off, faraway, distant, out of the way, off the beaten track, secluded, lonely, inaccessible; *N. Amer.* in the backwoods; *informal* in the middle of nowhere. **2** *a remote possibility* **unlikely**, improbable, doubtful, dubious, faint, slight, slim, small, slender. **3 aloof**, distant, detached, withdrawn, unforthcoming, unapproachable, unresponsive, unfriendly, unsociable, introspective, introverted; *informal* stand-offish.
– OPPOSITES close.

removal *noun* **1 taking away**, withdrawal, abolition. **2 dismissal**, ejection, expulsion, ousting, deposition; *informal* sacking, firing. **3 move**, transfer, relocation.

remove *verb* **1 take off**, take away, move, take out, pull out, withdraw, detach, undo, unfasten, disconnect. **2 dismiss**, discharge, get rid of, eject, expel, oust, depose, unseat; *informal* sack, fire, kick out. **3 abolish**, withdraw, eliminate, get rid of, do away with, stop, cut; *informal* axe.
- OPPOSITES attach, insert.

renaissance *noun* **revival**, renewal, resurrection, reawakening, re-emergence, rebirth, reappearance, resurgence.

render *verb* **1 make**, cause to be/become, leave, turn. **2 give**, provide, supply, furnish, contribute. **3 act**, perform, play, depict, portray, interpret, represent, draw, paint, execute.

rendezvous *noun* **meeting**, appointment, assignation; *informal* date; *literary* tryst.
● *verb* **meet**, come together, gather, assemble.

renegade *noun* **traitor**, defector, deserter, turncoat, rebel, mutineer.
● *adjective* **1 treacherous**, traitorous, disloyal, treasonous, rebel, mutinous. **2 apostate**, heretic, heretical, dissident.
- OPPOSITES loyal.

renege *verb* **default on**, fail to honour, go back on, break, back out of, withdraw from, retreat from, backtrack on, break your word/promise.
- OPPOSITES honour.

renew *verb* **1 resume**, return to, take up again, come back to, begin again, restart, recommence, continue (with), carry on (with). **2 reaffirm**, repeat, reiterate, restate. **3 revive**, regenerate, revitalize, reinvigorate, restore, resuscitate. **4 renovate**, restore, refurbish, revamp, remodel, modernize; *informal* do up; *N. Amer. informal* rehab.

renounce *verb* **1 give up**, relinquish, abandon, surrender, waive, forego, desist from, keep off; *informal* say goodbye to. **2 reject**, repudiate, deny, abandon, wash your hands of, turn your back on, disown, spurn, shun.

renovate *verb* **modernize**, restore, refurbish, revamp, recondition, rehabilitate, update, upgrade, refit; *informal* do up; *N. Amer. informal* rehab.

renown *noun* **fame**, distinction, eminence, illustriousness, prominence, repute, reputation, prestige, acclaim, celebrity, notability.

renowned *adjective* **famous**, well known, celebrated, famed, eminent, distinguished, acclaimed, illustrious, prominent, great, esteemed.
- OPPOSITES unknown.

rent *noun* **hire charge**, rental, payment.
● *verb* **1 hire**, lease, charter. **2 let (out)**, lease (out), hire (out), charter (out).

repair *verb* **1 mend**, fix (up), put/set right, restore (to working order), overhaul, renovate; *informal* patch up. **2 rectify**, make good, (put) right, correct, make up for, make amends for, compensate for, redress.
● *noun* **1 restoration**, mending, overhaul, renovation. **2 mend**, darn, patch. **3** *in good repair* **condition**, working order, state, shape, fettle; *Brit. informal* nick.

repay *verb* **1 reimburse**, refund, pay back, recompense, compensate, remunerate, settle up with. **2** *he repaid her kindness* **reciprocate**, return, requite, reward.

repeal *verb* **cancel**, abolish, reverse, rescind, revoke, annul, quash.
- OPPOSITES enact.
● *noun* **cancellation**, abolition, reversal, rescinding, annulment.

repeat *verb* **1 say again**, restate, reiterate, go/run through again, recapitulate, recap. **2 recite**, quote, parrot, regurgitate, echo; *informal* trot out. **3 do again**, redo, replicate, duplicate.
● *noun* **repetition**, replication, duplicate.

repeated *adjective* **recurrent**, frequent, persistent, continual, incessant, constant, regular, periodic, numerous, (very) many.
- OPPOSITES occasional.

repeatedly *adverb* **frequently**, often, again and again, over and over (again), time and (time) again, many times, persistently, recurrently, constantly, continually, regularly; *N. Amer.* oftentimes.

repel *verb* **1 fight off**, repulse, drive back, force back, beat back, hold off, ward off, fend off, keep at bay; *Brit.* see off. **2 revolt**, disgust, repulse, sicken, nauseate, turn someone's stomach; *informal* turn off; *N. Amer. informal* gross out.
- OPPOSITES attract.

repellent *adjective* **1 revolting**, repulsive, disgusting, repugnant, sickening, nauseating, stomach-turning, vile, nasty, foul, awful, horrible, dreadful, terrible, obnoxious, loathsome, offensive, objectionable, abhorrent, despicable, reprehensible, contemptible, odious, hateful; *N. Amer.* vomitous; *informal* ghastly, horrid, gross; *literary* noisome. **2 impermeable**, impervious, resistant, -proof.

repent *verb* **feel remorse**, regret, be sorry, rue, reproach yourself, be ashamed, feel contrite, be penitent, be remorseful.

repentant *adjective* **penitent**, contrite, regretful, rueful, remorseful, apologetic, chastened, ashamed, shamefaced.
- OPPOSITES impenitent.

repercussion *noun* **consequence**, result, effect, outcome, reverberation, backlash, aftermath, fallout, footprint.

repertoire *noun* **collection**, range, repertory, list, store, stock, repository, supply.

repetition *noun* **1 reiteration**, restatement, retelling. **2 repetitiousness**, repetitiveness, tautology.

repetitive, **repetitious** *adjective* **recurring**, recurrent, repeated, unvaried, unchanging, routine, mechanical, automatic, monotonous, boring; *informal* samey.
- OPPOSITES varied.

replace *verb* **1 put back**, return, restore. **2 take the place of**, succeed, take over from, supersede, stand in for, substitute for, deputize for; *informal* step into someone's shoes/boots. **3 substitute**, exchange, change, swap.

replacement *noun* **substitute**, stand-in, fill-in, locum, understudy, relief, cover, proxy, surrogate.

replenish *verb* **1 refill**, top up, fill up, recharge; *N. Amer.* freshen. **2 stock up**, restock, restore, replace.
- OPPOSITES empty.

replica *noun* **copy**, model, duplicate, reproduction, dummy, imitation, facsimile.

reply *verb* **respond**, answer, write back, rejoin, retort, riposte, counter, come back.
● *noun* **answer**, response, rejoinder, retort, riposte; *informal* comeback.

report *verb* **1 communicate**, announce, divulge, disclose, reveal, relay, describe, narrate, delineate, detail, document, give an account of, make public, publish, broadcast, proclaim, publicize. **2 inform on**; *informal* shop, tell on, squeal on, rat on; *Brit. informal* grass on. **3** *I reported for duty* **present yourself**, arrive, turn up, clock in; *informal* show up.
● *noun* **1 account**, record, minutes, proceedings, transcript. **2 news**, information, word, intelligence. **3 story**, account, article, piece, item, column, feature, bulletin, dispatch, communiqué. **4 rumour**, whisper; *informal* buzz. **5 bang**, crack, explosion, boom.

reporter *noun* **journalist**, correspondent, newsman, newswoman, columnist; *Brit.* pressman; *informal* hack, stringer, journo.

reprehensible *adjective* **deplorable**, disgraceful, discreditable, despicable, blameworthy, culpable, wrong, bad, shameful, dishonourable, inexcusable, unforgivable, indefensible, unjustifiable.
- OPPOSITES praiseworthy.

represent *verb* **1 stand for**, symbolize, personify, epitomize, typify, embody, illustrate, exemplify. **2 depict**, portray, render, picture, delineate, show, illustrate. **3 appear for**, act for, speak on behalf of.

representation *noun* **1 portrayal**, depiction, delineation, presentation, rendition. **2 likeness**, painting, drawing, picture, illustration, sketch, image, model, figure, statue.

representative *adjective* **1 typical**, archetypal, characteristic, illustrative, indicative. **2 symbolic**, emblematic.
- OPPOSITES atypical.
● *noun* **1 spokesperson**, spokesman, spokeswoman, agent, official, mouthpiece. **2 salesman**, commercial traveller, agent, negotiator; *informal* rep. **3 deputy**, substitute, stand-in, proxy, delegate, ambassador, emissary.

repress *verb* **1 suppress**, quell, quash, subdue, put down, crush, extinguish, stamp out, defeat, contain. **2 oppress**, subjugate, keep down, tyrannize. **3 restrain**, hold back/in, suppress, keep in check, control, curb, stifle, bottle up; *informal* button up, keep the lid on.
- OPPOSITES express.

repression *noun* **1 suppression**, quashing, subduing, crushing, stamping out. **2 oppression**, subjugation, suppression, tyranny, authoritarianism, despotism. **3 restraint**, suppression, control, curbing, stifling.

repressive *adjective* **oppressive**, authoritarian, despotic, tyrannical, dictatorial, fascist, autocratic, totalitarian, undemocratic.

reprieve *verb* **pardon**, spare, amnesty; *informal* let off (the hook).
● *noun* **pardon**, stay of execution, amnesty.

reprimand *verb* **rebuke**, reproach, scold, admonish, reprove, chastise, upbraid, berate, take to task, castigate; *informal* tell off; *Brit. informal* tick off; *N. Amer. informal* chew out.
- OPPOSITES praise.
● *noun* **rebuke**, reproach, scolding, admonition; *informal* telling-off, dressing-down, carpeting; *Brit. informal* ticking-off.

reprisal *noun* **retaliation**, counter-attack, comeback, revenge, vengeance, retribution, requital; *informal* a taste of your own medicine.

reproachful *adjective* **disapproving**, reproving, critical, censorious, disparaging, withering, accusatory, admonitory.
- OPPOSITES approving.

reproduce *verb* **1 copy**, duplicate, replicate, photocopy, xerox, photostat, print. **2 repeat**, replicate, recreate, redo, simulate, imitate, emulate, mimic. **3 breed**, procreate, propagate, multiply, proliferate.

reproduction *noun* **1 print**, copy, reprint, duplicate, facsimile, photocopy; *trademark* Xerox. **2 breeding**, procreation, propagation, proliferation.

repudiate *verb* **1 reject**, renounce, disown, abandon, give up, turn your back on, cast off, lay aside, wash your hands of; *formal* forswear; *literary* forsake. **2 deny**, refute, contradict, controvert, rebut, dispute, dismiss, brush aside; *formal* gainsay.
- OPPOSITES embrace.

repugnant *adjective* **abhorrent**, revolting, repulsive, repellent, disgusting, offensive, objectionable, vile, foul, nasty, loathsome, sickening, nauseating, hateful, detestable, execrable, abominable, monstrous, appalling, unsavoury, unpalatable.
- OPPOSITES pleasant.

repulsive *adjective* **disgusting**, revolting, foul, nasty, obnoxious, sickening, nauseating, stomach-churning, vile; *informal* ghastly, gross, horrible; *literary* noisome.
- OPPOSITES attractive.

reputable *adjective* **well thought of**, highly regarded, respected, respectable, of (good) repute, prestigious, established, reliable, dependable, trustworthy.
- OPPOSITES untrustworthy.

reputation *noun* **name**, good name, character, repute, standing, stature, position, renown, esteem, prestige.

request *noun* **1 appeal**, entreaty, plea, petition, application, demand, call, solicitation. **2 requirement**, wish, desire, choice.
● *verb* **ask for**, appeal for, call for, seek, solicit, plead for, beg for, apply for, put in for, demand, petition for, sue for, implore, entreat; *literary* beseech.

require *verb* **1 need**, have need of, be short of, want, desire, lack, miss. **2 necessitate**, demand, call for, involve, entail, take. **3 demand**, insist on, call for, ask for, expect. **4 order**, instruct, command, enjoin, oblige, compel, force.

requirement *noun* **need**, necessity, prerequisite, stipulation, demand, want, essential.

requisition *noun* **1 order**, request, call, application, claim, demand; *Brit.* indent. **2 appropriation**, commandeering, seizure, confiscation, expropriation.
● *verb* **1 commandeer**, appropriate, take over, take possession of, occupy, seize, confiscate, expropriate. **2 request**, order, call for, demand.

rescue *verb* **1 save**, free, set free, release, liberate, deliver. **2 retrieve**, recover, salvage.
● *noun* **saving**, rescuing, release, freeing, liberation, deliverance.

research *noun* **investigation**, experimentation, testing, analysis, fact-finding, examination, scrutiny.
● *verb* **investigate**, study, enquire into, look into, probe, explore, analyse, examine, scrutinize.

resemblance *noun* **similarity**, likeness, similitude, correspondence, congruence, conformity, comparability, parallel.
– OPPOSITES dissimilarity.

resemble *verb* **look like**, be similar to, remind someone of, take after, approximate to, smack of, correspond to, echo, mirror, parallel.
– OPPOSITES differ from.

resent *verb* **begrudge**, feel aggrieved at/about, feel bitter about, grudge, be resentful of, take exception to, object to, take amiss, take offence at.
– OPPOSITES welcome.

resentful *adjective* **aggrieved**, indignant, irritated, piqued, put out, in high dudgeon, dissatisfied, disgruntled, discontented, offended, bitter, jaundiced, envious, jealous; *informal* miffed, peeved; *Brit. informal* narked; *N. Amer. informal* sore.

resentment *noun* **bitterness**, indignation, irritation, pique, dissatisfaction, disgruntlement, discontentment, acrimony, rancour.

reservation *noun* **1 doubt**, qualm, scruple; (**reservations**) misgivings, scepticism, unease, hesitation, objection. **2 reserve**, enclave, sanctuary, territory, homeland.

reserve *verb* **1 put aside**, set aside, keep (back), save, hold back, keep in reserve, earmark, retain. **2 book**, order, arrange for, secure, engage, hire.
● *noun* **1 stock**, store, supply, stockpile, pool, hoard, cache, fund. **2 reinforcements**, extras, auxiliaries. **3 national park**, sanctuary, preserve, reservation. **4 shyness**, diffidence, timidity, taciturnity, inhibition, reticence, detachment, aloofness, distance, remoteness. **5** *she trusted him without reserve* **reservation**, qualification, condition, limitation, hesitation, doubt.
● *adjective* **substitute**, stand-in, relief, replacement, fallback, spare, extra.

reserved *adjective* **1 uncommunicative**, reticent, unforthcoming, aloof, cool, undemonstrative, unsociable, unfriendly, quiet, silent, taciturn, withdrawn, secretive, shy, retiring, diffident, timid, introverted; *informal* stand-offish. **2 booked**, taken, spoken for, prearranged.
– OPPOSITES outgoing.

reservoir *noun* **1 lake**, pool, pond, basin. **2 receptacle**, container, holder, tank. **3 stock**, store, stockpile, reserve(s), supply, bank, pool.

reside *verb* **1 live**, lodge, stay, occupy, inhabit; *formal* dwell, be domiciled. **2** *power resides with the president* **be vested in**, be bestowed on, be conferred on, be in the hands of.

residence *noun* **home**, house, address, quarters, lodgings; *informal* pad; *formal* dwelling, abode, domicile.

resident *noun* **inhabitant**, local, citizen, native, householder, homeowner, occupier, tenant; *humorous* denizen.

residue *noun* **remainder**, rest, remnant(s), surplus, extra, excess, remains, leftovers.

resign *verb* **1 leave**, give notice, stand down, step down; *informal* quit, pack in. **2 give up**, leave, vacate, renounce, relinquish, surrender.

resignation *noun he accepted his fate with resignation* **patience**, forbearance, stoicism, fortitude, fatalism, acceptance.

resigned *adjective* **patient**, long-suffering, uncomplaining, forbearing, stoical, philosophical, fatalistic.

resilient *adjective* **1 flexible**, pliable, supple, durable, hard-wearing, stout, strong, sturdy, tough. **2 strong**, tough, hardy, quick to recover, buoyant, irrepressible.

resist *verb* **1 withstand**, be proof against, combat, weather, endure, be resistant to, keep out. **2 oppose**, fight against, object to, defy, kick against, obstruct. **3 refrain from**, abstain from, forbear from, desist from, not give in to, restrain yourself from.

resistance *noun* **1 opposition**, hostility, struggle, fight, battle, stand, defiance. **2 immunity**, defences.

resistant *adjective* **1 impervious**, immune, invulnerable, proof, unaffected. **2 opposed**, averse, hostile, inimical, against; *informal* anti.
- OPPOSITES vulnerable.

resolute *adjective* **determined**, purposeful, resolved, adamant, single-minded, firm, unswerving, unwavering, steadfast, staunch, stalwart, unfaltering, indefatigable, tenacious, strong-willed, unshakeable.
- OPPOSITES half-hearted.

resolution *noun* **1 intention**, decision, intent, aim, plan, commitment, pledge, promise. **2 motion**, proposal, proposition. **3 determination**, purpose, purposefulness, resolve, single-mindedness, firmness, will power, strength of character. **4 solution**, answer, end, settlement, conclusion.

resolve *verb* **1 settle**, sort out, solve, fix, straighten out, deal with, put right, rectify; *informal* hammer out, thrash out. **2 determine**, decide, make up your mind. **3 vote**, rule, decide formally, agree.
● *noun* **determination**, purpose, resolution, single-mindedness; *informal* guts.

resort *noun* **option**, alternative, choice, possibility, hope, measure, step, recourse, expedient.
□ **resort to** fall back on, have recourse to, turn to, make use of, use, avail yourself of.

resound *verb* **echo**, reverberate, ring, boom, thunder, rumble, resonate.

resounding *adjective* **1 reverberating**, resonating, echoing, ringing, sonorous, deep, rich. **2** *a resounding success* **enormous**, huge, very great, tremendous, terrific, colossal, emphatic, outstanding, remarkable, phenomenal.

resource *noun* **1 facility**, amenity, aid, help, support, solution. **2 initiative**, resourcefulness, enterprise, ingenuity, inventiveness. **3** *we lack resources* **assets**, funds, wealth, money, capital, supplies, materials, stores, stocks, reserves, deep pockets.

resourceful *adjective* **ingenious**, enterprising, inventive, creative, clever, talented, able, capable.

respect *noun* **1 esteem**, regard, high opinion, admiration, reverence, deference, honour. **2** *the report was accurate in every respect* **aspect**, regard, feature, way, sense, particular, point, detail.

3 (**respects**) **regards**, compliments, greetings, best/good wishes.
- OPPOSITES contempt.
● *verb* **1 esteem**, admire, think highly of, have a high opinion of, look up to, revere, honour. **2 show consideration for**, have regard for, observe, be mindful of, be heedful of. **3 abide by**, comply with, follow, adhere to, conform to, act in accordance with, obey, observe, keep (to).
- OPPOSITES despise, disobey.

respectable *adjective* **1 reputable**, upright, honest, honourable, trustworthy, decent, good, well bred, clean-living. **2 fairly good**, decent, fair-sized, reasonable, moderately good, large, sizeable, considerable.
- OPPOSITES disreputable.

respectful *adjective* **deferential**, reverent, dutiful, polite, well mannered, civil, courteous, gracious.
- OPPOSITES rude.

respective *adjective* **separate**, personal, own, particular, individual, specific, special.

respite *noun* **rest**, break, breathing space, interval, lull, pause, time out, relief; *informal* breather, let-up.

respond *verb* **1 answer**, reply, write back, come back, rejoin, retort, riposte, counter. **2 react**, reciprocate, retaliate.

response *noun* **1 answer**, reply, rejoinder, retort, riposte; *informal* comeback. **2 reaction**, reply, retaliation; *informal* comeback.
- OPPOSITES question.

responsibility *noun* **1 duty**, task, function, job, role, onus; *Brit. informal* pigeon. **2 blame**, fault, guilt, culpability, liability, accountability, answerability. **3 trustworthiness**, (common) sense, maturity, reliability, dependability. **4** *managerial responsibility* **authority**, control, power, leadership.

responsible *adjective* **1 in charge of**, in control of, at the helm of, accountable for, liable for. **2 accountable**, answerable, to blame, guilty, culpable, blameworthy, at fault, in the wrong. **3 trustworthy**, sensible, mature, reliable, dependable, level-headed, stable.
- OPPOSITES irresponsible.

responsive *adjective* **reactive**, receptive, open to suggestions, amenable, flexible, forthcoming.

rest[1] *verb* **1 relax**, ease up/off, let up, slow down, have/take a break, unbend, unwind, take it easy, put your feet up; *informal* take five, have/take a breather, chill (out). **2** *her hands rested on the rail* **lie**, be laid, repose, be placed, be positioned, be supported by. **3 support**, prop (up), lean, lay, set, stand, position, place, put.
● *noun* **1 relaxation**, repose, leisure, time off; *informal* lie-down. **2 break**, breathing space, interval, interlude, intermission, time off/out, respite, lull, pause; *informal* breather. **3 stand**, base, holder, support, rack, frame, shelf.

rest[2] *noun* **remainder**, residue, balance, others, remnant(s), surplus, excess.

restful *adjective* **relaxing**, quiet, calm, tranquil, soothing, peaceful, leisurely, undisturbed, untroubled.
- OPPOSITES exciting.

restless *adjective* **1 uneasy**, ill at ease, fidgety, edgy, tense, worked up, nervous, nervy, agitated, anxious; *informal* jumpy, jittery, twitchy, uptight. **2** *a restless night* **sleepless**, wakeful, fitful, broken, disturbed, troubled, unsettled.

restoration *noun* **1 reinstatement**, reinstitution, re-establishment, reimposition, return. **2 repair**, renovation, mending, refurbishment, reconditioning, rehabilitation, rebuilding, reconstruction; *N. Amer. informal* rehab.

restore *verb* **1 reinstate**, bring back, reinstitute, reimpose, reinstall, re-establish. **2** *he restored it to its rightful owner* **return**, give back, hand back. **3 repair**, fix, mend, refurbish, recondition, rehabilitate, renovate, revamp, rebuild; *informal* do up; *N. Amer. informal* rehab. **4 reinvigorate**, revitalize, revive, refresh, energize, freshen.

restrain *verb* **control**, check, hold in check, curb, suppress, repress, contain, rein back/in, smother, stifle, bottle up; *informal* keep the lid on.

restrained *adjective* **1 self-controlled**, sober, steady, unemotional, undemonstrative. **2 muted**, soft, discreet, subtle, quiet, unobtrusive, unostentatious, understated, tasteful.
- OPPOSITES impetuous.

restraint *noun* **1 constraint**, check, control, restriction, limitation, curtailment, rein, brake, deterrent. **2 self-control**, self-discipline, control, moderation, judiciousness. **3 subtlety**, taste, discretion, discrimination.

restrict *verb* **1 limit**, keep within bounds, regulate, control, moderate, cut down, curtail. **2 hinder**, interfere with, impede, hamper, obstruct, block, check, curb.

restricted *adjective* **1 cramped**, confined, constricted, small, narrow, tight. **2 limited**, controlled, regulated, reduced.

restriction *noun* **limitation**, constraint, control, regulation, check, curb, reduction, diminution, curtailment.

result *noun* **consequence**, outcome, upshot, sequel, effect, reaction, repercussion, footprint.
- OPPOSITES cause.
● *verb* **follow**, ensue, develop, stem, spring, arise, derive, proceed; (**result from**) be caused by, be brought about by, be produced by, originate in.
□ **result in** end in, culminate in, lead to, trigger, cause, bring about, occasion, effect, give rise to, produce.

resume *verb* **restart**, recommence, begin again, start again, reopen, renew, return to, continue with, carry on with.
- OPPOSITES suspend, abandon.

résumé *noun* **summary**, precis, synopsis, abstract, outline, abridgement, overview.

resumption *noun* **restart**, recommencement, reopening, continuation, renewal, return, revival.

resurgence *noun* **renewal**, revival, renaissance, recovery, comeback, reawakening, resurrection, reappearance, re-emergence.

resurrect *verb* **revive**, restore, regenerate, revitalize, breathe new life into, reinvigorate, resuscitate, rejuvenate, re-establish, relaunch.

retain *verb* **keep (possession of)**, keep hold of, hang on to, maintain, preserve, conserve.

retaliate *verb* **fight back**, hit back, respond, react, reply, reciprocate, counter-attack, get back at someone, pay someone back; *informal* get your own back.

retaliation *noun* **revenge**, vengeance, reprisal, retribution, repayment, response, reaction, reply, counter-attack.

retard *verb* **delay**, slow down/up, hold back/up, postpone, detain, decelerate, hinder, impede, check.
- OPPOSITES accelerate.

reticent *adjective* **uncommunicative**, unforthcoming, unresponsive, tight-lipped, quiet, taciturn, silent, reserved.
- OPPOSITES expansive.

retire *verb* **1 give up work**, stop work, be pensioned off; *informal* be put out to grass. **2 withdraw**, go away, exit, leave, take yourself off, absent yourself. **3 go to bed**, call it a day; *informal* turn in, hit the hay/sack.

retiring *adjective* **1 departing**, outgoing. **2 shy**, diffident, self-effacing, unassuming, unassertive, reserved, reticent, quiet, timid, modest.
- OPPOSITES incoming, outgoing.

retort *verb* **answer**, reply, respond, return, counter, riposte, retaliate.
● *noun* **answer**, reply, response, counter, rejoinder, riposte, retaliation; *informal* comeback.

retract *verb* **1 pull in**, pull back, draw in. **2 take back**, withdraw, recant, disavow, disclaim, repudiate, renounce, reverse, revoke, rescind, go back on, backtrack on, row back on; *formal* abjure.

retreat *verb* **withdraw**, retire, draw back, pull back/out, fall back, give way, give ground.
- OPPOSITES advance.
● *noun* **1 withdrawal**, retirement, pullback, flight. **2 refuge**, haven, sanctuary, hideaway, hideout, hiding place; *informal* hidey-hole.

retribution *noun* **punishment**, penalty, your just deserts, revenge, reprisal, requital, retaliation, vengeance, an eye for an eye (and a tooth for a tooth), tit for tat, nemesis.

retrieve *verb* **get back**, bring back, recover, recapture, regain, recoup, salvage, rescue.

retrograde *adjective* **for the worse**, regressive, retrogressive, negative, downhill, backward(s), unwelcome.

retrospect *noun*
□ **in retrospect** looking back, on reflection, in/with hindsight.

return *verb* **1 go back**, come back, arrive back, come home. **2 recur**, reoccur, repeat itself, reappear. **3 give back**, hand back, pay back, repay, restore, put back, replace, reinstall, reinstate.
- OPPOSITES leave.
● *noun* **1 recurrence**, reoccurrence, repeat, reappearance. **2 replacement**, restoration, reinstatement, restitution. **3 yield**, profit, gain, revenue, interest, dividend.

r

revamp *verb* **renovate**, redecorate, refurbish, remodel, refashion, redesign, restyle; *informal* do up, give something a facelift, give something a makeover, vamp up; *Brit. informal* tart up.

reveal *verb* **1 disclose**, make known, make public, broadcast, publicize, circulate, divulge, tell, let slip/drop, give away/out, blurt out, release, leak, bring to light, lay bare, unveil; *informal* let on. **2 show**, display, exhibit, unveil, uncover.
- OPPOSITES conceal, hide.

revel *verb* **celebrate**, make merry; *informal* party, live it up, whoop it up, paint the town red.
● *noun* **celebration**, festivity, jollification, merrymaking, party; *informal* rave, shindig, bash; *Brit. informal* rave-up; *N. Amer. informal* wingding, blast.
□ **revel in** enjoy, delight in, love, like, adore, take pleasure in, relish, lap up, savour; *informal* get a kick out of.

revelation *noun* **disclosure**, announcement, report, admission, confession, divulging, giving away/out, leak, betrayal, publicizing.

revelry *noun* **celebration(s)**, parties, festivity, jollification, merrymaking, carousal, roistering, fun and games; *informal* partying.

revenge *noun* **retaliation**, retribution, vengeance, reprisal, recrimination, an eye for an eye (and a tooth for a tooth), redress.
- OPPOSITES forgiveness.
● *verb* **avenge**, exact retribution for, take reprisals for, get redress for, make someone pay for; *informal* get your own back for.

revenue *noun* **income**, takings, receipts, proceeds, earnings, profit(s), gain, yield.
- OPPOSITES expenditure.

reverberate *verb* **resound**, echo, resonate, ring, boom, rumble.

revere *verb* **respect**, admire, think highly of, esteem, venerate, look up to, be in awe of.
- OPPOSITES despise.

reverence *noun* **high esteem**, high regard, great respect, honour, veneration, homage, admiration, appreciation, deference.
- OPPOSITES scorn.

reverent *adjective* **reverential**, respectful, admiring, devoted, devout, awed, deferential.

reversal *noun* **1 turnaround**, turnabout, about-face, volte-face, change of heart, U-turn, rowback, backtracking; *Brit.* about-turn. **2 swap**, exchange, change, interchange, switch. **3 alteration**, overturning, overthrow, disallowing, overriding, overruling, veto, revocation. **4 setback**, upset, failure, misfortune, mishap, disaster, blow, disappointment, adversity, hardship, affliction, vicissitude, defeat.

reverse *verb* **1 back**, move back/backwards. **2 turn upside down**, turn over, upend, invert, turn back to front. **3 swap (round)**, change (round), exchange, switch (round), transpose. **4 alter**, change, overturn, overthrow, disallow, override, overrule, veto, revoke, row back on.
● *adjective* **backward(s)**, inverted, transposed, opposite.
● *noun* **1 opposite**, contrary, converse, inverse, antithesis. **2 setback**, reversal, upset, failure, misfortune, mishap, disaster, blow, disappointment, adversity, hardship, affliction, vicissitude, defeat. **3 other side**, back, underside, flip side.
– OPPOSITES front.

revert *verb* **return**, go back, change back, default, relapse.

review *noun* **1 analysis**, evaluation, assessment, appraisal, examination, investigation, enquiry, probe, inspection, study. **2 reconsideration**, reassessment, re-evaluation, reappraisal. **3 criticism**, critique, write-up, assessment, commentary.
● *verb* **1 survey**, study, research, consider, analyse, examine, scrutinize, explore, look into, probe, investigate, inspect, assess, evaluate, appraise, weigh up; *informal* size up. **2 reconsider**, re-examine, reassess, re-evaluate, reappraise, rethink.

reviewer *noun* **critic**, commentator, judge.

revise *verb* **1 reconsider**, review, re-examine, reassess, re-evaluate, reappraise, rethink, change, alter, modify. **2 amend**, correct, edit, rewrite, redraft, rephrase, rework. **3** *(Brit.)* **go over**, reread, memorize, cram; *informal* bone up on; *Brit. informal* swot up (on), mug up (on).

revision *noun* **1 alteration**, adaptation, editing, rewriting, redrafting, correction, updating. **2 reconsideration**, review, re-examination, reassessment, re-evaluation, reappraisal, rethink, change, modification.

revitalize *verb* **reinvigorate**, re-energize, boost, regenerate, revive, revivify, rejuvenate, reanimate, resuscitate, refresh, stimulate, breathe new life into; *informal* give a shot in the arm to, pep up, buck up.

revival *noun* **1 improvement**, rallying, turn for the better, upturn, upswing, resurgence. **2 comeback**, re-establishment, reintroduction, restoration, reappearance, resurrection, rebirth.
– OPPOSITES downturn.

revive *verb* **1 resuscitate**, bring round, bring back to consciousness; *informal* give the kiss of life to. **2 reinvigorate**, revitalize, refresh, energize, reanimate. **3** *reviving old traditions* **reintroduce**, re-establish, restore, resurrect, bring back.

revoke *verb* **cancel**, repeal, rescind, reverse, annul, nullify, void, invalidate, countermand, retract, withdraw, overrule, override; *formal* abrogate.

revolt *verb* **1 rebel**, rise up, take to the streets, riot, mutiny. **2 disgust**, sicken, nauseate, turn someone's stomach, put off, offend; *informal* turn off; *N. Amer. informal* gross out.
● *noun* **rebellion**, revolution, insurrection, mutiny, uprising, riot, insurgence, coup (d'état).

revolting *adjective* **disgusting**, sickening, nauseating, stomach-turning, repulsive, repugnant, hideous, nasty, foul, offensive; *N. Amer.* vomitous; *informal* ghastly, horrid, gross.
– OPPOSITES attractive, pleasant.

revolution *noun* **1 rebellion**, revolt, insurrection, mutiny, uprising, rising, riot, insurgence, coup (d'état). **2 dramatic change**, sea change, metamorphosis, transformation, innovation, reorganization, restructuring; *informal* shake-up; *N. Amer. informal* shakedown. **3 turn**, rotation, circle, spin, orbit, circuit, lap.

revolutionary *adjective* **1 rebellious**, rebel, insurgent, rioting, mutinous, renegade. **2 new**, novel, original, unusual,

unconventional, unorthodox, newfangled, innovatory, disruptive, modern, state-of-the-art, futuristic, pioneering; *informal* edgy.
● *noun* **rebel**, insurgent, mutineer, insurrectionist, agitator.

revolutionize *verb* **transform**, shake up, turn upside down, restructure, reorganize, transmute, metamorphose; *humorous* transmogrify.

revolve *verb* **1 go round**, turn round, rotate, spin. **2 circle**, travel, orbit.

revulsion *noun* **disgust**, repulsion, abhorrence, repugnance, nausea, horror, aversion, abomination, distaste.
- OPPOSITES delight.

reward *noun* **award**, honour, decoration, bonus, premium, bounty, present, gift, payment, recompense, prize; *informal* pay-off.
● *verb* **recompense**, pay, remunerate.
- OPPOSITES punish.

rewarding *adjective* **satisfying**, gratifying, pleasing, fulfilling, enriching, illuminating, worthwhile, productive, fruitful.

rhetoric *noun* **1 oratory**, eloquence, command of language, way with words. **2 wordiness**, verbosity, grandiloquence, bombast, pomposity, extravagant language, purple prose, turgidity; *informal* hot air.

rhetorical *adjective* **1** *a rhetorical device* **stylistic**, oratorical, linguistic, verbal. **2 extravagant**, grandiloquent, high-flown, bombastic, grandiose, pompous, pretentious, overblown, turgid, flowery; *informal* highfalutin.

rhyme *noun* **poem**, verse, ode; (**rhymes**) poetry, doggerel.

rhythm *noun* **1 beat**, cadence, tempo, time, pulse. **2 metre**, measure, pattern.

rich *adjective* **1 wealthy**, affluent, moneyed, well off, well-to-do, prosperous; *informal* loaded, well heeled, made of money. **2 sumptuous**, opulent, luxurious, lavish, gorgeous, splendid, magnificent, costly, expensive, fancy, palatial; *informal* plush; *Brit. informal* swish; *N. Amer. informal* swank. **3** *a garden rich in flowers* **well stocked**, well provided, abounding, crammed, packed, teeming, bursting. **4** *a rich supply* **plentiful**, abundant, copious, ample, profuse, lavish, liberal, generous. **5 fertile**, productive, fruitful, fecund. **6 creamy**, fatty, heavy, full-flavoured. **7** *rich colours* **strong**, deep, full, intense, vivid, brilliant.
- OPPOSITES poor, plain.

riches *plural noun* **money**, wealth, funds, cash, means, assets, capital, resources, deep pockets; *informal* bread, loot; *Brit. informal* dosh, brass, lolly; *N. Amer. informal* bucks.

richly *adverb* **1 sumptuously**, opulently, luxuriously, lavishly, gorgeously, splendidly, magnificently. **2** *the reward she richly deserves* **fully**, amply, well, thoroughly, completely, wholly, totally, entirely, absolutely, utterly.

rid *verb* **clear**, free, purge, empty, strip.
□ **get rid of** dispose of, throw away/out, clear out, discard, scrap, dump, bin, jettison, expel, eliminate; *informal* chuck (away), ditch, junk; *Brit. informal* get shot of; *N. Amer. informal* trash.

riddle *noun* **puzzle**, conundrum, brain-teaser, problem, question, poser, enigma, mystery.

ride *verb* **1 sit on**, mount, control, manage, handle. **2 travel**, move, proceed, drive, cycle, trot, canter, gallop.
● *noun* **trip**, journey, drive, run, excursion, outing, jaunt, lift; *informal* spin.

ridicule *noun* **mockery**, derision, laughter, scorn, scoffing, jeering.
- OPPOSITES respect.
● *verb* **mock**, deride, laugh at, heap scorn on, jeer at, make fun of, scoff at, satirize, caricature, parody.

ridiculous *adjective* **laughable**, absurd, ludicrous, risible, comical, funny, hilarious, amusing, farcical, silly, stupid, idiotic, preposterous.
- OPPOSITES sensible.

rife *adjective* **widespread**, general, common, universal, extensive, ubiquitous, endemic, inescapable.

rifle *verb* **1 rummage**, search, hunt, forage. **2 burgle**, rob, steal from, loot, raid, plunder, ransack.

rift *noun* **1 crack**, split, breach, fissure, fracture, cleft, crevice, opening. **2 disagreement**, estrangement, breach, split, schism, quarrel, falling-out, conflict, feud; *Brit.* row; *Brit. informal* bust-up.

rig[1] *verb* **1 equip**, kit out, fit out, supply, furnish, provide, arm. **2 dress**, clothe, attire, robe, garb, get up; *informal* doll up. **3** *he will rig up a shelter* **set up**, erect, assemble, put together, whip up, improvise, contrive; *Brit. informal* knock up.

rig[2] *verb* **manipulate**, engineer, distort, misrepresent, pervert, tamper with, falsify, fake; *informal* fix; *Brit. informal* fiddle.

right *adjective* **1 just**, fair, equitable, proper, good, upright, righteous, virtuous, moral, ethical, principled, honourable, honest, lawful, legal. **2 correct**, unerring, accurate, exact, precise, valid; *Brit. informal* spot on. **3 suitable**, appropriate, fitting, apposite, apt, correct, proper, desirable, preferable, ideal. **4 opportune**, advantageous, favourable, convenient, good, lucky, fortunate. **5 right-hand**; *Nautical* starboard; *Heraldry* dexter.

- OPPOSITES wrong, left.

● *adverb* **1 completely**, fully, totally, absolutely, utterly, thoroughly, quite. **2 exactly**, precisely, directly, immediately, just, squarely, dead; *informal* (slap) bang, smack, plumb. **3 correctly**, accurately, perfectly.

- OPPOSITES wrong, badly.

● *noun* **1 goodness**, righteousness, virtue, integrity, propriety, probity, morality, truth, honesty, honour, justice, fairness, equity. **2 entitlement**, prerogative, privilege, liberty, authority, power, licence, permission, dispensation, leave, due.

- OPPOSITES wrong.

● *verb* **remedy**, rectify, retrieve, fix, resolve, sort out, settle, square, straighten out, correct, repair, mend, redress.

□ **right away** at once, straight away, (right) now, this (very) minute, this instant, immediately, instantly, directly, forthwith, without further ado, promptly, quickly, without delay, asap, as soon as possible; *N. Amer.* in short order; *informal* straight off, pronto.

righteous *adjective* **good**, virtuous, upright, upstanding, decent, ethical, principled, moral, honest, honourable, blameless.

- OPPOSITES wicked.

rightful *adjective* **1 legal**, lawful, real, true, proper, correct, recognized, genuine, authentic, acknowledged, approved, valid, bona fide; *informal* legit, kosher. **2 deserved**, merited, due, just, right, fair, proper, fitting, appropriate, suitable.

- OPPOSITES wrongful.

right-wing *adjective* **conservative**, rightist, reactionary, traditionalist, conventional.

- OPPOSITES left-wing.

rigid *adjective* **1 stiff**, hard, taut, firm, inflexible, unbendable, unyielding, inelastic. **2** *a rigid routine* **fixed**, set, firm, inflexible, invariable, hard and fast, cast-iron, strict, stringent, rigorous, uncompromising, intransigent.

- OPPOSITES flexible.

rigorous *adjective* **1 meticulous**, conscientious, punctilious, careful, scrupulous, painstaking, exact, precise, accurate, particular, strict. **2 strict**, stringent, rigid, inflexible, draconian, intransigent, uncompromising. **3** *rigorous conditions* **harsh**, severe, bleak, extreme, demanding.

- OPPOSITES slapdash, lax.

rim *noun* **edge**, brim, lip, border, side, margin, brink, boundary, perimeter, circumference, limits, periphery.

rind *noun* **skin**, peel, zest, integument.

ring[1] *noun* **1 circle**, band, halo, disc. **2 arena**, enclosure, amphitheatre, bowl. **3 gang**, syndicate, cartel, mob, band, circle, organization, association, society, alliance, league.

● *verb* **surround**, circle, encircle, enclose, hem in, confine, seal off.

ring[2] *verb* **1 chime**, sound, peal, toll, clang, bong; *literary* knell. **2 resound**, reverberate, resonate, echo. **3 telephone**, phone (up), call (up); *informal* give someone a buzz; *Brit. informal* give someone a bell, get on the blower to.

rinse *verb* **wash (out)**, clean, cleanse, bathe, dip, drench, splash, swill, sluice.

riot *noun* **disorder**, disturbance, lawlessness, upheaval, uproar, commotion, free-for-all, uprising, insurrection.
● *verb* **(go on the) rampage**, run wild, run amok, run riot, go berserk; *informal* raise hell.

riotous *adjective* **1 unruly**, rowdy, disorderly, uncontrollable, unmanageable, undisciplined, uproarious, tumultuous, violent, wild, lawless, anarchic. **2 boisterous**, lively, loud, noisy, unrestrained, uninhibited, uproarious; *Brit. informal* rumbustious.
– OPPOSITES peaceful.

rip *verb* **tear**, pull, wrench, snatch, drag, pluck; *informal* yank.

ripe *adjective* **1 mature**, full grown, fully developed. **2** *ripe for development* **ready**, fit, suitable, right. **3** *the time is ripe* **opportune**, advantageous, favourable, auspicious, good, right.
– OPPOSITES immature.

ripen *verb* **mature**, mellow, develop.

riposte *noun* **retort**, counter, rejoinder, sally, return, answer, reply, response; *informal* comeback.

rise *verb* **1 climb**, come up, arise, ascend, mount, soar. **2 loom**, tower, soar. **3 go up**, increase, soar, shoot up, surge, leap, jump, rocket, escalate, spiral. **4 get higher**, grow, increase, become louder, swell, intensify. **5 stand up**, get to your feet, get up, jump up, leap up, stir, bestir yourself.
– OPPOSITES fall, descend, drop.
● *noun* **1 increase**, hike, leap, upsurge, upswing, climb. **2 raise**, increase, increment. **3 slope**, incline, hill, elevation, acclivity.

risk *noun* **1 chance**, uncertainty, unpredictability, instability, insecurity. **2 possibility**, chance, probability, likelihood, danger, peril, threat, menace, prospect.
● *verb* **endanger**, jeopardize, imperil, hazard, gamble (with), chance, put at risk, put on the line.

risky *adjective* **dangerous**, hazardous, perilous, unsafe, insecure, precarious, touch-and-go, treacherous, uncertain, unpredictable; *informal* dicey.

rite *noun* **ceremony**, ritual, ceremonial, custom, service, observance, liturgy, worship, office.

ritual *noun* **ceremony**, rite, act, practice, custom, tradition, convention, formality, protocol.
● *adjective* **ceremonial**, prescribed, set, conventional, traditional, formal.

rival *noun* **opponent**, opposition, challenger, competitor, contender, adversary, antagonist, enemy, nemesis; *literary* foe.
– OPPOSITES ally.
● *verb* **match**, compare with, compete with, vie with, equal, emulate, measure up to, touch; *informal* hold a candle to.
● *adjective rival candidates* **competing**, opposing, in competition.

rivalry *noun* **competition**, contention, opposition, conflict, feuding; *informal* keeping up with the Joneses.

river *noun* **1 stream**, brook, watercourse, rivulet, tributary; *Scottish & N. English* burn; *N. English* beck; *S. English* bourn; *N. Amer. & Austral./NZ* creek. **2** *a river of molten lava* **stream**, torrent, flood, deluge, cascade.

WORD LINKS
fluvial relating to rivers

riveting *adjective* **fascinating**, gripping, engrossing, intriguing, absorbing, captivating, enthralling, compelling, spellbinding, mesmerizing; *informal* unputdownable.
– OPPOSITES boring.

road *noun* **1 street**, thoroughfare, roadway, highway, lane; *Brit.* motorway.

2 *the road to recovery* **way**, path, route, course.

roam *verb* **wander**, rove, ramble, drift, walk, traipse, range, travel, tramp, trek; *informal* cruise.

roar *verb* **bellow**, yell, shout, thunder, bawl, howl, scream, cry, bay; *informal* holler.

roaring *adjective* **blazing**, burning, flaming.

rob *verb* **1 burgle**, steal from, hold up, break into, raid, loot, plunder, pillage; *informal* mug; *N. Amer.* burglarize. **2 cheat**, swindle, defraud; *informal* do out of, con out of.

robber *noun* **burglar**, thief, housebreaker, mugger, shoplifter, raider, looter.

robbery *noun* **burglary**, theft, stealing, housebreaking, shoplifting, embezzlement, fraud, hold-up, raid; *informal* mugging, smash-and-grab, stick-up; *N. Amer. informal* heist.

robe *noun* **1 cloak**, kaftan, djellaba, wrap, mantle, cape; *N. Amer.* wrapper. **2** *ceremonial robes* **garb**, vestments, regalia, finery.

robot *noun* **machine**, automaton, android; *informal* bot, droid.

robust *adjective* **1 strong**, vigorous, sturdy, tough, powerful, solid, rugged, hardy, strapping, healthy, (fighting) fit, hale and hearty. **2 durable**, resilient, tough, hard-wearing, long-lasting, sturdy, strong.
- OPPOSITES frail, fragile.

rock[1] *noun* **boulder**, stone, pebble.

rock[2] *verb* **1 move to and fro**, sway, see-saw, roll, pitch, plunge, toss, lurch. **2 stun**, shock, stagger, astonish, startle, surprise, shake, take aback, throw, unnerve, disconcert.

rocky[1] *adjective* **stony**, pebbly, shingly, rough, bumpy, craggy, mountainous.

rocky[2] *adjective* **unsteady**, shaky, unstable, wobbly, tottery, rickety.
- OPPOSITES steady, stable.

rod *noun* **bar**, stick, pole, baton, staff, shaft, strut, rail, spoke.

rogue *noun* **scoundrel**, rascal, good-for-nothing, wretch, villain, criminal, lawbreaker; *informal* crook.

role *noun* **1 part**, character. **2 capacity**, position, function, job, post, office, duty, responsibility.

roll *verb* **1 turn over and over**, spin, rotate, revolve, wheel, trundle, bowl. **2 flow**, run, course, stream, pour, trickle. **3 wind**, coil, fold, curl, twist. **4 rock**, sway, reel, list, pitch, plunge, lurch, toss.
● *noun* **1 cylinder**, tube, scroll, reel, spool, bobbin. **2 turn**, rotation, revolution, spin, whirl. **3 list**, register, directory, record, file, index, catalogue, inventory. **4** *a roll of thunder* **rumble**, reverberation, echo, boom, clap, crack.

romance *noun* **1 love affair**, relationship, liaison, courtship, attachment, amour. **2 story**, tale, legend, fairy tale. **3 mystery**, glamour, excitement, exoticism, mystique, appeal, allure, charm.

romantic *adjective* **1 loving**, amorous, passionate, tender, affectionate; *informal* lovey-dovey. **2 sentimental**, hearts-and-flowers; *informal* slushy, schmaltzy; *Brit. informal* soppy. **3 idyllic**, picturesque, fairy-tale, beautiful, lovely, charming, pretty. **4 idealistic**, unrealistic, fanciful, impractical, head-in-the-clouds, starry-eyed, utopian, rose-tinted.
- OPPOSITES unsentimental, realistic.
● *noun* **idealist**, sentimentalist, dreamer, fantasist.
- OPPOSITES realist.

romp *verb* **play**, frolic, frisk, gambol, skip, prance, caper, cavort.

room *noun* **1 space**, headroom, legroom, area, expanse, extent. **2** *there's very little room for manoeuvre* **scope**, opportunity, capacity, leeway, latitude, freedom.

roomy *adjective* **spacious**, capacious, sizeable, generous, big, large, extensive, voluminous, ample; *formal* commodious.
- OPPOSITES cramped.

root *noun* **1 source**, origin, cause, reason, basis, foundation, bottom, seat. **2** *his Irish roots* **origins**, beginnings, family, birth, heritage.
● *verb* **rummage**, hunt, search, rifle, delve, forage, dig, poke.
□ **root out** eradicate, eliminate, weed out, destroy, wipe out, stamp out, abolish, end, put a stop to.

rope *noun* **cord**, cable, line, hawser, string.

roster *noun* **schedule**, list, register, agenda, calendar; *Brit.* rota.

rosy *adjective* **1 pink**, roseate, reddish, glowing, healthy, fresh, radiant, blooming, blushing, flushed, ruddy. **2 promising**, optimistic, auspicious, hopeful, encouraging, favourable, bright, golden.
- OPPOSITES pale, bleak.

rot *verb* **1 decay**, decompose, disintegrate, crumble, perish. **2 go bad**, go off, spoil, moulder, putrefy, fester. **3 deteriorate**, degenerate, decline, decay, go to seed, go downhill; *informal* go to pot, go to the dogs.
● *noun* **decay**, decomposition, mould, mildew, blight, canker.

rotate *verb* **1 revolve**, go round, turn (round), spin, gyrate, whirl, twirl, swivel, circle, pivot. **2 alternate**, take turns, change, switch, interchange, exchange, swap.

rotation *noun* **1 revolving**, turning, spinning, gyration, circling. **2 turn**, revolution, orbit, spin. **3 sequence**, succession, alternation, cycle.

rotten *adjective* **1 decaying**, mouldy, bad, off, decomposing, spoiled, putrid, rancid, festering, fetid. **2 corrupt**, unprincipled, dishonest, dishonourable, unscrupulous, untrustworthy, immoral; *informal* crooked; *Brit. informal* bent.
- OPPOSITES fresh.

rough *adjective* **1 uneven**, irregular, bumpy, stony, rocky, rugged, rutted, pitted. **2 coarse**, bristly, scratchy, prickly, shaggy, hairy, bushy. **3 dry**, leathery, weather-beaten, chapped, calloused, scaly. **4 gruff**, hoarse, harsh, rasping, husky, throaty, gravelly. **5 violent**, aggressive, belligerent, pugnacious, boisterous, rowdy, disorderly, unruly, riotous. **6 boorish**, loutish, oafish, brutish, coarse, crude, uncouth, vulgar, unrefined, unladylike, ungentlemanly, uncultured. **7 turbulent**, stormy, squally, tempestuous, violent, heavy, choppy. **8 preliminary**, hasty, quick, sketchy, cursory, basic, crude, rudimentary, raw, unpolished, incomplete, unfinished. **9 approximate**, inexact, imprecise, vague, estimated; *N. Amer. informal* ballpark.
- OPPOSITES smooth, gentle, calm, exact.
● *noun* **sketch**, draft, outline, mock-up.

round *adjective* **circular**, spherical, globular, cylindrical.
● *noun* **1 ball**, sphere, globe, orb, circle, disc, ring, hoop. **2** *a policeman on his rounds* **circuit**, beat, route, tour. **3 stage**, level, heat, game, bout, contest. **4 succession**, sequence, series, cycle.
● *verb* **go round**, travel round, skirt, circumnavigate, orbit.
□ **round off** complete, finish off, crown, cap, top, conclude, close, end. **round up** gather together, herd together, muster, marshal, rally, assemble, collect, group; *N. Amer.* corral.

roundabout *adjective* **circuitous**, indirect, meandering, serpentine, tortuous, oblique, circumlocutory.
- OPPOSITES direct.

roundly *adverb* **1 vehemently**, emphatically, fiercely, forcefully, severely, plainly, frankly, candidly. **2 utterly**, completely, thoroughly, decisively, conclusively, heavily, soundly.

rouse *verb* **1 wake (up)**, awaken, arouse; *Brit. informal* knock up. **2 wake up**, awake, come to, get up, rise, bestir yourself. **3 stir up**, excite, galvanize, electrify, stimulate, inspire, move, inflame, agitate, goad, provoke, prompt, whip up.

rousing *adjective* **stirring**, inspiring, exciting, stimulating, moving, electrifying, invigorating, energizing, exhilarating.

rout *noun* **defeat**, beating, retreat, flight; *informal* licking, hammering, thrashing, pasting, drubbing.
- OPPOSITES victory.
● *verb* **defeat**, beat, conquer, vanquish, crush, put to flight, drive off, scatter; *informal* lick, hammer, clobber, thrash; *US informal* own.

route *noun* **way**, course, road, path, direction.

routine *noun* **1 procedure**, practice, pattern, drill, regime, programme, schedule, plan. **2 act**, performance, number, turn, piece; *informal* spiel, patter.
● *adjective* **1 standard**, regular, customary, normal, usual, ordinary, typical, everyday. **2 boring**, tedious, monotonous, humdrum, run-of-the-mill, pedestrian, predictable, hackneyed, unimaginative, unoriginal, banal, trite.
- OPPOSITES unusual.

row[1] *noun* **1 line**, column, file, queue, procession, chain, string, succession; *informal* crocodile. **2 tier**, line, rank, bank.
□ **in a row** consecutively, in succession, running, straight; *informal* on the trot.

row[2] *(Brit.) noun* **1 argument**, quarrel, squabble, fight, dispute, altercation, falling-out; *informal* tiff, run-in, slanging match, spat; *Brit. informal* bust-up. **2 din**, noise, racket, uproar, hubbub, rumpus; *informal* hullabaloo.
● *verb* **argue**, quarrel, squabble, bicker, fight, fall out, disagree, have words; *informal* scrap.

rowdy *adjective* **unruly**, disorderly, riotous, undisciplined, uncontrollable, ungovernable, disruptive, obstreperous, out of control, rough, wild, boisterous, uproarious, noisy, loud; *Brit. informal* rumbustious.
- OPPOSITES peaceful.

royal *adjective* **regal**, kingly, queenly, princely, sovereign.

rub *verb* **1 massage**, knead, stroke, pat. **2 apply**, smear, spread, work in. **3 chafe**, scrape, pinch.
□ **rub out** erase, delete, remove, obliterate, expunge.

rubbish *noun* **1 refuse**, waste, litter, scrap, detritus, debris, dross; *N. Amer.* garbage, trash; *informal* dreck, junk. **2 nonsense**, gibberish, claptrap, garbage; *informal* baloney, tripe, drivel, bilge, bunk, piffle, twaddle, poppycock, gobbledegook; *Brit. informal* codswallop, cobblers, tosh.

rude *adjective* **1 ill-mannered**, bad-mannered, impolite, discourteous, uncivil, impertinent, insolent, impudent, disparaging, abusive, curt, brusque, offhand. **2 vulgar**, coarse, smutty, dirty, filthy, crude, lewd, obscene, risqué; *informal* blue; *Brit. informal* near the knuckle.
- OPPOSITES polite.

rudimentary *adjective* **1 basic**, elementary, fundamental, essential. **2 primitive**, crude, simple, unsophisticated, rough (and ready), makeshift. **3 vestigial**, undeveloped, incomplete.

rudiments *plural noun* **basics**, fundamentals, essentials, first principles, foundations; *informal* nuts and bolts, ABC.

rueful *adjective* **regretful**, apologetic, sorry, remorseful, shamefaced, sheepish, hangdog, contrite, repentant, penitent, conscience-stricken, self-reproachful, sorrowful, sad.

ruffle *verb* **1 disarrange**, tousle, dishevel, rumple, mess up; *N. Amer. informal* muss up. **2 disconcert**, unnerve, fluster, agitate, upset, disturb, discomfit, put off, perturb, unsettle; *informal* faze, throw, get to.
- OPPOSITES smooth.

rugged *adjective* **1 rough**, uneven, bumpy, rocky, stony, pitted. **2 robust**, durable, sturdy, strong, tough, resilient. **3 well built**, burly, strong, muscular, muscly, brawny, strapping, tough, hardy, robust, sturdy, solid; *informal* hunky. **4** *his rugged features* **strong**,

craggy, rough-hewn, manly, masculine.
– OPPOSITES smooth, delicate.

ruin *noun* **1 disintegration**, decay, disrepair, dilapidation, destruction, demolition, devastation. **2** *the ruins of a church* **remains**, remnants, fragments, rubble, debris, wreckage. **3 downfall**, collapse, defeat, undoing, failure. **4 bankruptcy**, insolvency, penury, destitution, poverty.
● *verb* **1 spoil**, wreck, blight, shatter, dash, scotch, mess up, sabotage; *informal* screw up; *Brit. informal* scupper. **2 bankrupt**, make insolvent, impoverish, pauperize, wipe out, break, cripple, bring someone to their knees. **3 destroy**, devastate, lay waste, ravage, raze, demolish, wreck, wipe out, flatten.

ruined *adjective* **derelict**, dilapidated, tumbledown, ramshackle, decrepit, falling to pieces, crumbling, decaying, disintegrating, in ruins.

ruinous *adjective* **1 disastrous**, devastating, catastrophic, calamitous, crippling, crushing, damaging, destructive, harmful, costly. **2 extortionate**, exorbitant, excessive, sky-high, outrageous, inflated; *Brit.* over the odds; *informal* steep.

rule *noun* **1 regulation**, ruling, directive, order, law, statute, ordinance. **2 procedure**, practice, protocol, convention, norm, routine, custom, habit. **3 principle**, precept, standard, axiom, truth, maxim. **4 government**, jurisdiction, command, power, dominion, control, administration, sovereignty, leadership.
● *verb* **1 govern**, preside over, control, lead, dominate, run, head, administer. **2 reign**, be on the throne, be in power, govern. **3 decree**, order, pronounce, judge, adjudge, ordain, decide, determine, find.
□ **as a rule** usually, in general, normally, ordinarily, customarily, for the most part, on the whole, by and large, in the main, mostly, commonly, typically. **rule out** exclude, eliminate, disregard, preclude, prohibit, prevent, disallow.

ruler *noun* **leader**, sovereign, monarch, potentate, king, queen, emperor, empress, prince, princess, crowned head, head of state, president, premier, governor.
– OPPOSITES subject.

ruling *noun* **judgement**, decision, adjudication, finding, verdict, pronouncement, resolution, decree, injunction.
● *adjective* **1 governing**, controlling, commanding, supreme. **2 main**, chief, principal, major, dominating, consuming; *informal* number-one.

rummage *verb* **search**, hunt, root about/around, ferret about/around, fish about/around, dig, delve, go through, explore, sift through, rifle through.

rumour *noun* **gossip**, hearsay, talk, tittle-tattle, speculation, word, report, story, whisper; *informal* the grapevine, the word on the street, the buzz.

run *verb* **1 sprint**, race, dart, rush, dash, hasten, hurry, scurry, scamper, gallop, jog, trot. **2 flee**, take flight, make off, take off, take to your heels, bolt, make your getaway, escape; *informal* beat it, clear off/out, scram, leg it; *Brit. informal* scarper. **3 extend**, stretch, reach, continue. **4 flow**, pour, stream, gush, flood, cascade, roll, course, glide, spill, trickle, drip, dribble, leak. **5 be in charge of**, manage, direct, control, head, govern, supervise, superintend, oversee, organize, coordinate. **6** *it's expensive to run a car* **maintain**, keep, own, possess, have, use, operate. **7** *I left the engine running* **operate**, function, work, go.
● *noun* **1 jog**, sprint, dash, gallop, trot. **2 route**, journey, circuit, round, beat. **3 drive**, ride, turn, trip, excursion, outing, jaunt; *informal* spin, tootle. **4 series**, succession, sequence, string, streak, spate. **5 enclosure**, pen, coop. **6** *a ski run* **slope**, track, piste; *N. Amer.* trail.
□ **run down 1** run over, knock down/over, hit. **2** criticize, denigrate, belittle, disparage, deprecate, find fault with; *informal* put down, knock, bad-mouth; *Brit. informal* rubbish, slag off. **run into 1** collide with, hit, strike, crash into,

smash into, plough into, ram. **2** meet (by chance), run across, chance on, stumble on, happen on; *informal* bump into. **3** experience, encounter, meet with, be faced with, be confronted with. **run out 1** be used up, dry up, be exhausted, be finished, peter out. **2** expire, end, terminate, finish, lapse. **run over 1** overflow, spill over, brim over. **2** exceed, go over, overshoot, overreach. **3** review, repeat, run through, go over, reiterate, recapitulate, look over, read through; *informal* recap on. **4** run down, knock down/over, hit.

runaway *noun* **fugitive**, refugee, truant, absconder, deserter.

rundown *noun* **summary**, synopsis, precis, run-through, recap, review, overview, briefing, sketch, outline; *informal* low-down.

run down *adjective* **1 dilapidated**, tumbledown, ramshackle, derelict, crumbling, neglected, uncared-for. **2 unwell**, ill, poorly, unhealthy, peaky, tired, drained, exhausted, worn out, below par, washed out; *Brit.* off colour; *informal* under the weather; *Brit. informal* off; *Austral./NZ informal* crook.

runner *noun* **1 athlete**, sprinter, hurdler, racer, jogger. **2 messenger**, courier, errand boy; *informal* gofer.

running *noun* **1 administration**, management, organization, coordination, orchestration, handling, direction, control, supervision. **2 operation**, working, function, performance.
● *adjective* **1 flowing**, gushing, rushing, moving. **2 in succession**, in a row, in sequence, consecutively, straight, together; *informal* on the trot.

runny *adjective* **liquid**, liquefied, fluid, melted, molten, watery, thin.
– OPPOSITES solid, thick.

rupture *noun* & *verb* **break**, fracture, crack, burst, split, fissure, breach.

rural *adjective* **country**, rustic, bucolic, pastoral, agricultural, agrarian.
– OPPOSITES urban.

ruse *noun* **ploy**, stratagem, tactic, scheme, trick, gambit, dodge, subterfuge, machination, wile; *Brit. informal* wheeze.

rush *verb* **1 hurry**, dash, run, race, sprint, bolt, dart, gallop, career, charge, shoot, hurtle, hare, fly, speed, zoom, scurry, scuttle, scamper, hasten; *informal* tear, belt, pelt, scoot, zip, whip, hotfoot it; *Brit. informal* bomb. **2 gush**, pour, surge, stream, course, cascade. **3 attack**, charge, storm.
● *noun* **1 dash**, run, sprint, dart, bolt, charge, scramble. **2 hustle and bustle**, commotion, hubbub, hurly-burly, stir. **3 charge**, onslaught, attack, assault.

rushed *adjective* **hasty**, fast, speedy, quick, swift, rapid, hurried.

rust *verb* **corrode**, oxidize, tarnish.

rustic *adjective* **1 rural**, country, pastoral, bucolic, agricultural, agrarian; *literary* Arcadian. **2 plain**, simple, homely, unsophisticated, rough, crude.
– OPPOSITES urban.
● *noun* **peasant**, countryman, countrywoman, bumpkin, yokel, country cousin; *N. Amer. informal* hillbilly, hayseed, hick.

rustle *verb* **1 swish**, whoosh, whisper, sigh. **2 steal**, thieve, take, abduct, kidnap.

rut *noun* **1 furrow**, groove, trough, ditch, hollow, pothole, crater. **2 boring routine**, humdrum existence, groove, dead end.

ruthless *adjective* **merciless**, pitiless, cruel, heartless, hard-hearted, cold-hearted, cold-blooded, harsh, callous.
– OPPOSITES merciful.

Ss

sabotage *noun* **vandalism**, wrecking, destruction, damage, obstruction, disruption; *Brit. informal* a spanner in the works.
● *verb* **vandalize**, wreck, damage, destroy, incapacitate, obstruct, disrupt, spoil, ruin, undermine; *Brit. informal* throw a spanner in the works.

sack *noun* **bag**, pouch, pocket, pack.
● *verb (informal)* **dismiss**, discharge, lay off, make redundant, let go, throw out; *informal* fire, give someone the sack; *Brit. informal* give someone their cards.
□ **the sack** *(informal)* dismissal, discharge, redundancy; *informal* the boot, the axe, the heave-ho, the push.

sacred *adjective* **1 holy**, hallowed, blessed, consecrated, sanctified. **2 religious**, spiritual, devotional, church, ecclesiastical.
– OPPOSITES secular, profane.

sacrifice *noun* **1 offering**, gift, oblation. **2 surrender**, giving up, abandonment, renunciation, forfeiture.
● *verb* **1 offer up**, immolate. **2 give up**, forgo, abandon, renounce, relinquish, cede, surrender, forfeit.

sacrilege *noun* **desecration**, profanity, blasphemy, irreverence, disrespect.

sad *adjective* **1 unhappy**, sorrowful, depressed, downcast, miserable, down, despondent, wretched, glum, gloomy, doleful, melancholy, mournful, woebegone, forlorn, heartbroken; *informal* blue, down in the mouth, down in the dumps. **2 tragic**, unhappy, miserable, wretched, sorry, pitiful, pathetic, heartbreaking, heart-rending. **3 unfortunate**, regrettable, sorry, deplorable, lamentable, pitiful, shameful, disgraceful.
– OPPOSITES happy, cheerful.

sadden *verb* **depress**, dispirit, deject, dishearten, grieve, discourage, upset, get down.

saddle *verb* **burden**, encumber, lumber, land, impose something on.

sadness *noun* **unhappiness**, sorrow, dejection, depression, misery, despondency, wretchedness, gloom, gloominess, melancholy.

safe *adjective* **1 secure**, protected, sheltered, guarded, out of harm's way. **2 unharmed**, unhurt, uninjured, unscathed, all right, fine, well, in one piece, out of danger, safe and sound. **3 cautious**, circumspect, prudent, careful, unadventurous, conservative. **4 harmless**, innocuous, non-toxic, non-poisonous.
– OPPOSITES dangerous, harmful.

safeguard *noun* **protection**, defence, buffer, provision, security, cover, insurance.
● *verb* **protect**, preserve, conserve, save, secure, shield, guard, keep safe.
– OPPOSITES jeopardize.

safety *noun* **1 welfare**, well-being, protection, security. **2 shelter**, sanctuary, refuge.

sag *verb* **1 sink**, slump, loll, flop, crumple. **2 dip**, droop, bulge, bag.

saga *noun* **1 epic**, legend, (folk) tale, romance, narrative, myth. **2 story**, tale, yarn.

sage *noun* **wise man/woman**, philosopher, scholar, guru, prophet, mystic.

sail *verb* **1 voyage**, travel, navigate, cruise. **2 set sail**, put to sea, leave, weigh anchor. **3 steer**, pilot, captain; *informal* skipper. **4 glide**, drift, float, flow, sweep, skim, coast, flit, scud.

sailor *noun* **seaman**, seafarer, mariner, yachtsman, yachtswoman, hand; *informal* old salt, matelot, Jack Tar.

saintly *adjective* **holy**, godly, pious, religious, devout, spiritual, virtuous, righteous, good, pure.
– OPPOSITES ungodly.

sake *noun* **1** *for the sake of clarity* **purpose(s)**, reason(s). **2** *for her son's sake* **benefit**, advantage, good, well-being, welfare.

salary *noun* **pay**, wages, earnings, payment, remuneration, fee(s), stipend, income.

sale *noun* **1 selling**, dealing, trading. **2 deal**, transaction, bargain.
- OPPOSITES purchase.

salty *adjective* **salt**, salted, saline, briny, brackish.

salubrious *adjective* **pleasant**, agreeable, nice, select, high-class; *Brit.* upmarket; *informal* posh, classy; *Brit. informal* swish.

salute *noun* **tribute**, testimonial, homage, honour, celebration (of), acknowledgement (of).
● *verb* **pay tribute to**, pay homage to, honour, celebrate, acknowledge, take your hat off to.

salvage *verb* **rescue**, save, recover, retrieve, reclaim.

salvation *noun* **1 redemption**, deliverance. **2 lifeline**, means of escape, saviour.
- OPPOSITES damnation, ruin.

same *adjective* **1 identical**, selfsame, very same. **2 matching**, identical, alike, carbon-copy, twin, indistinguishable, interchangeable, corresponding, equivalent, parallel, like, comparable, similar, homogeneous.
- OPPOSITES another, different.
□ **the same** unchanging, unvarying, unvaried, consistent, uniform.

sample *noun* **1 specimen**, example, snippet, swatch, taste, taster. **2 cross section**, sampling, selection.
● *verb* **try (out)**, taste, test, put to the test, appraise, evaluate; *informal* check out.

sanctimonious *adjective* **self-righteous**, holier-than-thou, pious, moralizing, smug, superior, priggish, hypocritical, insincere; *informal* goody-goody.

sanction *noun* **1 penalty**, punishment, deterrent, restriction, embargo, ban, prohibition, boycott. **2 authorization**, consent, leave, permission, authority, dispensation, assent, acquiescence, agreement, approval, endorsement, blessing; *informal* the thumbs up, the OK, the green light.
- OPPOSITES prohibition.
● *verb* **authorize**, permit, allow, endorse, approve, accept, back, support; *informal* OK.
- OPPOSITES prohibit.

sanctuary *noun* **1 refuge**, haven, oasis, shelter, retreat, bolt-hole, hideaway. **2 safety**, protection, shelter, immunity, asylum. **3 reserve**, wildlife reserve, park.

sane *adjective* **1 of sound mind**, in your right mind, compos mentis, lucid, rational, balanced, normal; *informal* all there. **2 sensible**, practical, realistic, prudent, reasonable, rational, level-headed, commonsensical.
- OPPOSITES mad, foolish.

sanguine *adjective* **optimistic**, hopeful, buoyant, positive, confident, cheerful, bullish; *informal* upbeat.
- OPPOSITES gloomy.

sanity *noun* **1 mental health**, reason, rationality, stability, lucidity, sense, wits, mind. **2 sense**, good sense, common sense, wisdom, prudence, rationality.

sap *noun* **juice**, secretion, fluid, liquid.
● *verb* **erode**, wear away/down, deplete, reduce, lessen, undermine, drain, bleed.

sarcasm *noun* **irony**, derision, mockery, ridicule, scorn.

sarcastic *adjective* **ironic**, sardonic, derisive, scornful, contemptuous, mocking, caustic, scathing, trenchant, acerbic.

sardonic *adjective* **mocking**, cynical, scornful, derisive, sneering, scathing, caustic, trenchant, cutting, acerbic.

satanic *adjective* **diabolical**, fiendish, devilish, demonic, ungodly, hellish, infernal, wicked, evil, sinful.
- OPPOSITES godly.

satire *noun* **parody**, burlesque, caricature, irony, lampoon, skit; *informal* spoof, take-off, send-up.

satirical *adjective* **mocking**, ironic, sardonic, critical, irreverent, disparaging, disrespectful.

satirize *verb* **mock**, ridicule, deride, make fun of, parody, lampoon, caricature, take off, criticize; *informal* send up, take the mickey out of.

satisfaction *noun* **contentment**, content, pleasure, gratification, fulfilment, enjoyment, happiness, pride.

satisfactory *adjective* **adequate**, all right, acceptable, good enough, sufficient, reasonable, competent, fair, decent, average, passable, fine, in order, up to scratch, up to the mark.

satisfy *verb* **1 fulfil**, gratify, meet, fill, indulge, appease, assuage, quench, slake, satiate. **2 convince**, assure, reassure, put someone's mind at rest. **3 comply with**, meet, fulfil, answer, conform to, measure up to, come up to.
- OPPOSITES frustrate.

saturate *verb* **1 soak**, drench, wet through. **2 flood**, glut, oversupply, overfill, overload.

saturated *adjective* **1 soaked**, soaking (wet), wet through, sopping (wet), sodden, dripping, wringing wet, drenched, soaked to the skin. **2 waterlogged**, flooded, boggy, awash.
- OPPOSITES dry.

sauce *noun* **relish**, condiment, ketchup, dip, dressing, jus, coulis, gravy.

saunter *verb* **stroll**, amble, wander, meander, walk; *informal* mosey, tootle; *formal* promenade.

savage *adjective* **1 vicious**, brutal, cruel, sadistic, ferocious, fierce, violent, barbaric, bloodthirsty, merciless, pitiless. **2 untamed**, wild, feral, undomesticated. **3** *a savage attack on the government* **fierce**, blistering, scathing, searing, stinging, devastating, withering, virulent, vitriolic.
- OPPOSITES mild, tame.
● *noun* **brute**, beast, monster, barbarian, sadist, animal.
● *verb* **maul**, attack, lacerate, claw, bite, tear to pieces.

save *verb* **1 rescue**, set free, free, liberate, deliver, redeem. **2 preserve**, keep, protect, safeguard, salvage, retrieve, reclaim, rescue. **3 put aside**, set aside, put by, keep, conserve, retain, store, hoard, stockpile; *informal* squirrel away. **4 prevent**, avoid, forestall, spare, stop, obviate, avert.

saving *noun* **1 reduction**, cut, decrease, economy. **2** (**savings**) **nest egg**, capital, assets, funds, resources, reserves.

saviour *noun* **rescuer**, liberator, deliverer, champion, protector, redeemer.

savour *verb* **relish**, enjoy, appreciate, delight in, revel in, luxuriate in.
● *noun* **smell**, aroma, fragrance, scent, perfume, bouquet, taste, flavour, tang, smack.

savoury *adjective* **salty**, spicy, tangy, piquant.
- OPPOSITES sweet.
● *noun* **canapé**, hors d'oeuvre, appetizer, titbit.

say *verb* **1 speak**, utter, voice, pronounce. **2 declare**, state, announce, remark, observe, mention, comment, note, add. **3 recite**, repeat, utter, deliver, perform. **4 indicate**, show, read.
● *noun* **influence**, sway, weight, voice, input.

saying *noun* **proverb**, maxim, aphorism, axiom, expression, phrase, formula, slogan, catchphrase.

scale *noun* **1 hierarchy**, ladder, ranking, pecking order, order, spectrum. **2 ratio**, proportion. **3 extent**, size, scope, magnitude, dimensions, range, breadth, degree.
● *verb* **climb**, ascend, clamber up, scramble up, shin (up), mount; *N. Amer.* shinny (up).

scaly *adjective* **dry**, flaky, scurfy, rough, scabrous.

scan *verb* **1 study**, examine, scrutinize, inspect, survey, search, scour, sweep, watch. **2 glance through**, look through, have a look at, run your eye over, cast your eye over, flick through, browse through, leaf through, thumb through.

scandal *noun* **1 gossip**, rumour(s), slander, libel, aspersions, muckraking; *informal* dirt. **2** *it's a scandal that the hospital has closed* **disgrace**, outrage, sin, (crying) shame.

scandalous *adjective* **1 disgraceful**, shocking, outrageous, monstrous, criminal, wicked, shameful, appalling, deplorable, inexcusable, intolerable, unforgivable, unpardonable. **2 discreditable**, disreputable, dishonourable, improper, unseemly, sordid. **3 scurrilous**, malicious, slanderous, libellous, defamatory.

scant *adjective* **little**, little or no, minimal, limited, negligible, meagre, insufficient, inadequate.
- OPPOSITES abundant, ample.

scanty *adjective* **1 meagre**, scant, minimal, limited, modest, restricted, sparse, tiny, small, paltry, negligible, scarce, in short supply, thin on the ground, few and far between; *informal* measly, piddling, mingy, pathetic. **2 skimpy**, revealing, short, brief, low-cut.
- OPPOSITES ample, plentiful.

scapegoat *noun* **whipping boy**, Aunt Sally; *informal* fall guy; *N. Amer. informal* patsy.

scar *noun* **1 mark**, blemish, disfigurement, discoloration, pockmark, pit, lesion, cicatrix. **2** *psychological scars* **trauma**, damage, injury.
● *verb* **disfigure**, mark, blemish, discolour, mar, spoil.

scarce *adjective* **in short supply**, scant, scanty, inadequate, lacking, meagre, sparse, hard to come by, at a premium, few and far between, thin on the ground, rare.
- OPPOSITES plentiful.

scarcely *adverb* **1 hardly**, barely, only just. **2 rarely**, seldom, infrequently, not often, hardly ever; *informal* once in a blue moon.

scarcity *noun* **shortage**, dearth, lack, undersupply, insufficiency, paucity, poverty, deficiency, inadequacy, unavailability, absence.

scare *verb* **frighten**, startle, alarm, terrify, unnerve, worry, intimidate, terrorize, cow; *informal* freak out; *Brit. informal* put the wind up; *N. Amer. informal* spook.
● *noun* **fright**, shock, start, turn, jump.

scared *adjective* **frightened**, afraid, fearful, nervous, panicky, terrified; *informal* in a cold sweat; *N. Amer. informal* spooked.

scary *adjective (informal)* **frightening**, terrifying, hair-raising, spine-chilling, blood-curdling, eerie, sinister; *informal* creepy, spine-tingling, spooky.

scathing *adjective* **withering**, blistering, searing, devastating, fierce, ferocious, savage, severe, stinging, biting, cutting, virulent, vitriolic, scornful, bitter, harsh.
- OPPOSITES mild.

scatter *verb* **1 spread**, sprinkle, distribute, strew, disseminate, sow, throw, toss, fling. **2 disperse**, break up, disband, separate, dissolve.
- OPPOSITES gather, assemble.

scavenge *verb* **search**, hunt, look, forage, rummage, root about/around, grub about/around.

scenario *noun* **1 plot**, outline, storyline, framework, screenplay, script. **2 situation**, chain of events, course of events.

scene *noun* **1 location**, site, place, position, spot, locale. **2 background**, setting, context, milieu, backdrop. **3 incident**, event, episode, happening, proceeding. **4 view**, vista, outlook, panorama, landscape, scenery. **5** *she made a scene* **fuss**, exhibition of yourself, performance, tantrum, commotion, disturbance, row; *informal* to-do; *Brit. informal* carry-on. **6** *the political scene* **arena**, stage, sphere, world, milieu, realm. **7 clip**, section, segment, part, sequence, extract.

scenery *noun* **1 landscape**, countryside, country, terrain, setting, surroundings, environment. **2 set**, setting, backdrop.

scenic *adjective* **picturesque**, pretty, attractive, beautiful, charming, impressive, striking, spectacular, breathtaking, panoramic.

scent *noun* **1 smell**, fragrance, aroma, perfume, savour, odour. **2 perfume**, fragrance, eau de toilette, toilet water, eau de cologne. **3 spoor**, trail, track.
● *verb* **smell**, nose out, detect, pick up, sense.

scented *adjective* **perfumed**, fragranced, fragrant, sweet-smelling, aromatic.

sceptic *noun* **cynic**, doubter, unbeliever, doubting Thomas.

sceptical *adjective* **dubious**, doubtful, doubting, cynical, distrustful, suspicious, disbelieving, unconvinced.
– OPPOSITES certain, convinced.

scepticism *noun* **doubt**, a pinch of salt, disbelief, cynicism, distrust, suspicion, incredulity.

schedule *noun* **plan**, programme, timetable, scheme, agenda, diary, calendar, itinerary.
● *verb* **arrange**, organize, plan, programme, timetable, set up, line up; *N. Amer.* slate.

scheme *noun* **1 plan**, project, programme, strategy, stratagem, tactic; *Brit. informal* wheeze. **2 plot**, intrigue, conspiracy, ruse, ploy, stratagem, manoeuvre, subterfuge, machinations; *informal* racket, scam.
● *verb* **plot**, conspire, intrigue, connive, manoeuvre, plan.

scheming *adjective* **cunning**, crafty, calculating, devious, conniving, wily, sly, tricky, artful.
– OPPOSITES ingenuous, honest.

schism *noun* **division**, split, rift, breach, rupture, break, separation, severance, chasm, gulf, disagreement.

scholar *noun* **academic**, intellectual, learned person, man/woman of letters, authority, expert; *informal* egghead; *N. Amer. informal* pointy-head.

scholarly *adjective* **learned**, educated, erudite, academic, well read, intellectual, literary, highbrow.
– OPPOSITES uneducated, illiterate.

scholarship *noun* **1 learning**, knowledge, erudition, education, academic study. **2 grant**, award, endowment; *Brit.* bursary.

school *noun* **1 college**, academy, alma mater. **2 department**, faculty, division. **3 tradition**, approach, style, way of thinking, persuasion, creed, credo, doctrine, belief, opinion, point of view.
● *verb* **train**, teach, tutor, coach, instruct, drill.

WORD LINKS
scholastic relating to schools

science *noun the science of criminology* **subject**, discipline, field, branch of knowledge, body of knowledge, area of study.

scientific *adjective* **1 technological**, technical, evidence-based, empirical. **2 systematic**, methodical, organized, ordered, rigorous, exact, precise, accurate, mathematical.

scintillating *adjective* **brilliant**, dazzling, coruscating, exciting, exhilarating, stimulating, sparkling, lively, vivacious, vibrant, animated, effervescent, witty, clever.
– OPPOSITES dull, boring.

scoff *verb* **sneer**, jeer, laugh; (**scoff at**) mock, deride, ridicule, dismiss, belittle; *informal* pooh-pooh.

scoop *noun* **spoon**, ladle, dipper.
□ **scoop out 1** hollow out, gouge out, dig, excavate. **2** remove, take out, spoon out, scrape out. **scoop up** pick up, gather up, lift, take up, snatch up, grab.

scope *noun* **1 extent**, range, breadth, reach, sweep, span, area, sphere, realm, compass, orbit, ambit, terms of reference, remit. **2 opportunity**, freedom, latitude, leeway, capacity, room (to manoeuvre).

scorch *verb* **1 burn**, sear, singe, char, blacken, discolour. **2 dry up**, parch, wither, shrivel, desiccate.

scorching *adjective* **hot**, red-hot, blazing, flaming, fiery, burning, blistering, searing; *informal* boiling, baking, sizzling.
- OPPOSITES freezing, mild.

score *noun* **1 result**, outcome, total, tally, count. **2 rating**, grade, mark, percentage.
● *verb* **1 get**, gain, chalk up, achieve, make, record, rack up, notch up; *informal* bag, knock up. **2 arrange**, set, adapt, orchestrate, write, compose. **3 scratch**, cut, notch, incise, scrape, nick, gouge.
□ **score out/through** cross out, strike out, delete, put a line through, obliterate.

scorn *noun* **contempt**, derision, disdain, mockery, sneering.
- OPPOSITES admiration, respect.
● *verb* **1 deride**, treat with contempt, mock, scoff at, sneer at, jeer at, laugh at. **2 spurn**, rebuff, reject, ignore, shun, snub.
- OPPOSITES admire, respect.

scornful *adjective* **contemptuous**, derisive, withering, mocking, sneering, jeering, scathing, snide, disparaging, supercilious, disdainful.
- OPPOSITES admiring.

scour[1] *verb* **scrub**, rub, clean, polish, buff, shine, burnish, grind, abrade.

scour[2] *verb* **search**, comb, hunt through, rummage through, look high and low in, ransack, turn upside-down.

scourge *noun* **affliction**, bane, curse, plague, menace, evil, misfortune, burden, blight, cancer, canker.

scout *noun* **1 lookout**, outrider, spy. **2 reconnaissance**, reconnoitre, survey, exploration, search; *informal* recce; *Brit. informal* shufti.
● *verb* **1** *I scouted around for some logs* **search**, look, hunt, ferret around, root around. **2** *a patrol was sent to scout out the area* **reconnoitre**, explore, inspect, investigate, spy out, survey, scan, study; *informal* check out, case.

scowl *verb* **glower**, frown, glare, grimace, lour, look daggers.
- OPPOSITES smile.

scramble *verb* **1 clamber**, climb, crawl, claw your way, scrabble, struggle; *N. Amer.* shinny. **2 muddle**, confuse, mix up, jumble (up), disarrange, disorganize, disorder, disturb, mess up.
● *noun* **1 clamber**, climb. **2** *the scramble for a seat* **struggle**, jostle, scrimmage, scuffle, tussle, free-for-all, jockeying, competition, race.

scrap *noun* **1 fragment**, piece, bit, snippet, oddment, remnant, morsel, sliver. **2** *not a scrap of evidence* **bit**, shred, speck, iota, particle, ounce, jot. **3 waste**, rubbish, refuse, debris; *N. Amer.* garbage, trash; *informal* junk.
● *verb* **1 throw away**, throw out, dispose of, get rid of, discard, dispense with, bin, decommission, break up, demolish; *informal* chuck (away/out), ditch, dump, junk; *Brit. informal* get shot of; *N. Amer. informal* trash. **2 abandon**, drop, abolish, withdraw, do away with, put an end to, cancel, axe; *informal* ditch, dump, junk.
- OPPOSITES keep.

scrape *verb* **1 rub**, scratch, scour, grind, sand, sandpaper, abrade, file. **2 grate**, creak, rasp, scratch. **3 graze**, scratch, scuff, rasp, skin, cut, lacerate, bark, chafe.
● *noun* **1 grating**, creaking, rasp, scratch. **2 graze**, scratch, abrasion, cut, laceration, wound.

scratch *verb* **scrape**, abrade, graze, score, scuff, skin, cut, lacerate, bark, chafe.
● *noun* **abrasion**, graze, scrape, cut, laceration, wound, mark, line.
□ **up to scratch** good enough, up to the mark, up to standard, up to par, satisfactory, acceptable, adequate, passable, sufficient, all right; *informal* OK.

scream *verb* & *noun* **shriek**, screech, yell, howl, bawl, yelp, squeal, wail, squawk.

screen *noun* **1 partition**, divider, windbreak. **2 display**, monitor, visual display

unit. **3 mesh**, net, netting. **4 buffer**, protection, shield, shelter, guard.
● *verb* **1 partition**, divide, separate, curtain. **2 conceal**, hide, veil, shield, shelter, shade, protect. **3** *all blood is screened for the virus* **check**, test, examine, investigate, vet; *informal* check out. **4 show**, broadcast, transmit, televise, put out, air.

screw *noun* **1 bolt**, fastener. **2 propeller**, rotor.
● *verb* **1 tighten**, turn, twist, wind. **2 fasten**, secure, fix, attach. **3** *(informal)* **extort**, force, extract, wrest, wring, squeeze; *informal* bleed.
□ **screw up 1** wrinkle, pucker, crumple, crease, furrow, contort, distort, twist. **2** *(informal)* wreck, ruin, destroy, damage, spoil, mess up; *informal* louse up, foul up, scupper.

scribble *verb* **scrawl**, scratch, dash off, jot (down), doodle, sketch.
● *noun* **scrawl**, squiggle(s), jottings, doodle, doodlings.

script *noun* **1 handwriting**, writing, hand. **2 text**, screenplay, libretto, score, lines, dialogue, words.

scrounge *verb* **beg**, borrow; *informal* cadge, sponge, bum, touch someone for; *N. Amer. informal* mooch; *Austral./NZ informal* bludge.

scrounger *noun* **beggar**, parasite, cadger; *informal* sponger, freeloader; *N. Amer. informal* mooch; *Austral./NZ informal* bludger.

scrub *verb* **1 brush**, scour, rub, clean, cleanse, wash. **2** *(informal)* **abandon**, scrap, drop, cancel, call off, axe; *informal* ditch, dump, junk.

scruffy *adjective* **shabby**, worn, down at heel, ragged, tattered, mangy, dirty, untidy, unkempt, bedraggled, messy, dishevelled, ill-groomed; *informal* tatty.
– OPPOSITES smart.

scruples *plural noun* **qualms**, compunction, hesitation, reservations, second thoughts, doubt(s), misgivings, uneasiness, reluctance.

scrupulous *adjective* **careful**, meticulous, painstaking, thorough, assiduous, sedulous, attentive, conscientious, punctilious, searching, close, rigorous, strict.
– OPPOSITES careless.

scrutinize *verb* **examine**, inspect, survey, study, look at, peruse, investigate, explore, probe, enquire into, go into, check.

sculpture *noun* **carving**, statue, statuette, figure, figurine, effigy, bust, head, model.

scum *noun* **film**, layer, covering, froth, filth, dross, dirt.

scupper *verb (Brit. informal)* **ruin**, wreck, destroy, sabotage, torpedo, spoil.

scurrilous *adjective* **defamatory**, slanderous, libellous, scandalous, insulting, offensive, abusive, malicious; *informal* bitchy.

sea *noun* **1 ocean**, waves; *informal* the drink; *Brit. informal* the briny; *literary* the deep. **2** *a sea of roofs* **expanse**, stretch, area, tract, sweep, carpet, mass.
● *adjective* **marine**, ocean, oceanic, maritime, naval, nautical.
□ **at sea** confused, perplexed, puzzled, baffled, mystified, bemused, bewildered, nonplussed, dumbfounded, at a loss, lost; *informal* flummoxed, fazed.

seal *noun* **1 sealant**, adhesive, mastic. **2 emblem**, symbol, insignia, badge, crest.
● *verb* **1 stop up**, seal up, cork, stopper, plug, make watertight. **2 clinch**, secure, settle, conclude, complete, finalize, confirm.
□ **seal off** close off, shut off, cordon off, fence off, isolate.

seam *noun* **1 join**, stitching, joint. **2 layer**, stratum, vein, lode.

seaman *noun* **sailor**, seafarer, mariner, boatman, hand, merchant seaman.
– OPPOSITES landlubber.

sear *verb* **1 scorch**, burn, singe, char, dry up, wither. **2 flash-fry**, seal, brown.

search *verb* **1 hunt**, look, seek, forage, look high and low, ferret about, root about, rummage. **2** *he searched the house* **look through**, scour, go

through, sift through, comb, turn upside down, ransack, rifle through; *Austral./NZ informal* fossick through. **3 examine**, inspect, check, frisk.
● *noun* **hunt**, look, quest, examination, exploration.

searching *adjective* **penetrating**, piercing, probing, keen, shrewd, sharp, intent.

seaside *noun* **coast**, shore, seashore, beach, sand, sands.

season *noun* **period**, time, time of year, spell, term.
● *verb* **flavour**, add salt/pepper to, spice.

seasoned *adjective* **experienced**, practised, well versed, knowledgeable, established, veteran, hardened.
- OPPOSITES inexperienced.

seasoning *noun* **flavouring**, salt and pepper, herbs, spices, condiments.

seat *noun* **1 chair**, bench, stool; (**seats**) seating. **2 headquarters**, base, centre, nerve centre, hub, heart, location, site. **3 residence**, ancestral home, mansion.
● *verb* **1 position**, put, place, ensconce, install, settle. **2 have room for**, contain, take, sit, hold, accommodate.

secluded *adjective* **sheltered**, private, concealed, hidden, unfrequented, sequestered, tucked away, remote, isolated, off the beaten track.

second[1] *adjective* **1 next**, following, subsequent. **2 additional**, extra, alternative, another, spare, backup; *N. Amer.* alternate. **3 secondary**, subordinate, subsidiary, lesser, inferior.
- OPPOSITES first.
● *noun* **assistant**, attendant, helper, aide, supporter, auxiliary, second in command, number two, deputy, understudy; *informal* sidekick.
● *verb* **support**, vote for, back, approve, endorse.

second[2] *noun* **moment**, bit, little while, instant, flash; *informal* sec, jiffy; *Brit. informal* mo, tick.

secondary *adjective* **1 less important**, subordinate, lesser, minor, peripheral, incidental, subsidiary, ancillary. **2 accompanying**, attendant, concomitant, consequential, resulting, resultant.
- OPPOSITES primary, main.

second-hand *adjective* **used**, old, worn, pre-owned, nearly new, handed-down, hand-me-down, cast-off.
- OPPOSITES new, direct.
● *adverb* **indirectly**; *informal* on the grapevine.
- OPPOSITES directly.

secondly *adverb* **furthermore**, also, moreover, second, in the second place, next.

secrecy *noun* **confidentiality**, privacy, mystery, concealment, stealth.

secret *adjective* **1 confidential**, top secret, classified, undisclosed, unknown, private, under wraps; *Military* black; *informal* hush-hush. **2 hidden**, concealed, disguised, camouflaged. **3 clandestine**, covert, undercover, underground, surreptitious, stealthy, cloak-and-dagger, furtive, conspiratorial.
- OPPOSITES public, open.
□ **in secret** secretly, in private, behind closed doors, under cover, furtively, stealthily, on the quiet, covertly; *formal* sub rosa.

secretive *adjective* **uncommunicative**, secret, unforthcoming, playing your cards close to your chest, reticent, tight-lipped.
- OPPOSITES open, communicative.

secretly *adverb* **in secret**, in private, privately, behind closed doors, under cover, furtively, stealthily, on the quiet, covertly.

sect *noun* **group**, cult, denomination, order, splinter group, faction, camp.

sectarian *adjective* **factional**, separatist, partisan, doctrinaire, dogmatic, illiberal, intolerant, bigoted, narrow-minded.

section *noun* **1 part**, bit, portion, segment, compartment, module, element, unit. **2 passage**, subsection, chapter, subdivision, clause. **3 department**, area, division.

sector *noun* **1 part**, branch, arm, division, area, department, field, sphere. **2 district**, quarter, section, zone, region, area, belt.

secular *adjective* **non-religious**, lay, temporal, civil, worldly, earthly, profane.
- OPPOSITES sacred, religious.

secure *adjective* **1 fastened**, fixed, secured, done up, closed, shut, locked. **2 safe**, protected, safe and sound, out of harm's way, in safe hands, invulnerable, undamaged, unharmed. **3** *his position as leader was secure* **certain**, assured, settled, stable, not at risk. **4 unworried**, at ease, relaxed, happy, confident.
- OPPOSITES loose, insecure.
● *verb* **1 fasten**, close, shut, lock, bolt, chain, seal. **2 obtain**, acquire, gain, get, get hold of, come by; *informal* land.

security *noun* **1 safety**, protection. **2 safety measures**, safeguards, surveillance, defence, policing. **3 guarantee**, collateral, surety, pledge, bond.

sedate[1] *verb* **tranquillize**, put under sedation, drug.

sedate[2] *adjective* **1 slow**, steady, dignified, unhurried, relaxed, measured, leisurely, slow-moving, easy, gentle. **2 calm**, placid, tranquil, quiet, uneventful, staid, boring, dull.
- OPPOSITES fast, exciting.

sediment *noun* **dregs**, grounds, lees, residue, deposit, silt.

S

seduce *verb* **1 attract**, allure, lure, tempt, entice, beguile, inveigle, manipulate. **2 have your (wicked) way with**, take advantage of.

seductive *adjective* **tempting**, inviting, enticing, alluring, beguiling, attractive.

see *verb* **1 discern**, detect, perceive, spot, notice, catch sight of, glimpse, make out, pick out, distinguish, spy; *informal* clap eyes on, clock; *literary* behold, espy, descry. **2 watch**, look at, view, catch. **3 inspect**, view, look round, tour, survey, examine, scrutinize. **4 understand**, grasp, comprehend, follow, realize, appreciate, recognize, work out, fathom; *informal* get, latch on to, tumble to, figure out; *Brit. informal* twig, suss (out). **5** *see what he's up to* **find out**, discover, learn, ascertain, determine, establish. **6** *see that no harm comes to him* **ensure**, make sure/certain, see to it, take care, mind. **7** *I see trouble ahead* **foresee**, predict, forecast, prophesy, anticipate, envisage. **8 consult**, confer with, talk to, have recourse to, call in, turn to. **9 go out with**, date, take out, be involved with; *informal* go steady with; *dated* court.
□ **see to** attend to, deal with, see about, take care of, look after, sort out, organize, arrange.

seed *noun* **pip**, stone, kernel.

seek *verb* **1 search for**, try to find, look for, be after, hunt for. **2 ask for**, request, solicit, call for, appeal for, apply for. **3 try**, attempt, endeavour, strive, work, do your best.

seem *verb* **appear (to be)**, have the appearance/air of being, give the impression of being, look, sound, come across as, strike someone as.

seep *verb* **ooze**, trickle, exude, drip, dribble, flow, leak, drain, bleed, filter, percolate, soak.

seethe *verb* **1 teem**, swarm, boil, swirl, churn, surge, bubble, heave. **2 be angry**, be furious, be enraged, rage, be incensed, be beside yourself, boil, rant, fume; *informal* be livid, foam at the mouth.

segment *noun* **piece**, bit, section, part, portion, division, slice, wedge.

segregate *verb* **separate**, set apart, keep apart, isolate, quarantine, partition, divide, discriminate against.
- OPPOSITES integrate.

seize *verb* **1 grab**, grasp, snatch, take hold of, clutch, grip. **2 capture**, take, overrun, occupy, conquer, take over. **3 confiscate**, impound, commandeer, requisition, appropriate, expropriate, sequestrate. **4 kidnap**, abduct, take captive, take prisoner, take hostage,

hijack; *informal* snatch.
- OPPOSITES release.

seizure *noun* **1 capture**, takeover, annexation, invasion, occupation. **2 confiscation**, appropriation, expropriation, sequestration. **3 kidnap**, abduction, hijack. **4 convulsion**, fit, spasm, paroxysm.

seldom *adverb* **rarely**, infrequently, hardly (ever), scarcely (ever); *informal* once in a blue moon.
- OPPOSITES often.

select *verb* **choose**, pick (out), single out, opt for, decide on, settle on, sort out, take, adopt.
● *adjective* **1 choice**, prime, hand-picked, top-quality, first-class, A-list; *informal* top-flight. **2 exclusive**, elite, privileged, wealthy; *informal* posh.
- OPPOSITES inferior.

selection *noun* **1 choice**, pick, option, preference. **2 range**, array, diversity, variety, assortment, mixture. **3 anthology**, assortment, collection, assemblage, miscellany, medley.

selective *adjective* **discerning**, discriminating, exacting, demanding, particular; *informal* choosy, picky.
- OPPOSITES indiscriminate.

self-centred *adjective* **egocentric**, egotistic, self-absorbed, self-obsessed, self-seeking, self-serving, narcissistic, vain, inconsiderate, thoughtless; *informal* looking after number one.

self-confidence *noun* **self-assurance**, assurance, confidence, composure, aplomb, poise, sangfroid.

self-conscious *adjective* **embarrassed**, uncomfortable, uneasy, ill at ease, nervous, awkward, shy, diffident, timid.
- OPPOSITES confident.

selfish *adjective* **egocentric**, egotistic, self-centred, self-absorbed, self-obsessed, self-seeking, wrapped up in yourself, mean, greedy; *informal* looking after number one.
- OPPOSITES unselfish, altruistic.

selfless *adjective* **unselfish**, altruistic, considerate, compassionate, kind, noble, generous, magnanimous, ungrudging.
- OPPOSITES selfish, inconsiderate.

self-righteous *adjective* **sanctimonious**, holier-than-thou, pious, self-satisfied, smug, priggish, complacent, moralizing, superior, hypocritical; *informal* goody-goody.
- OPPOSITES humble.

sell *verb* **put up for sale**, put on the market, auction (off), trade in, deal in, retail, market, traffic in, peddle, hawk.
- OPPOSITES buy.

seller *noun* **vendor**, dealer, retailer, trader, merchant, agent, hawker, pedlar, purveyor, supplier, stockist.
- OPPOSITES buyer.

semblance *noun* **(outward) appearance**, air, show, facade, front, veneer, guise, pretence.

seminar *noun* **1 conference**, symposium, meeting, convention, forum, summit. **2 study group**, workshop, tutorial, class.

send *verb* **1 dispatch**, post, mail, email, consign, forward, transmit, convey, communicate, broadcast, radio. **2 propel**, project, eject, deliver, discharge, spout, fire, shoot, release, throw, fling, cast, hurl. **3** *you're sending me crazy* **make**, drive, turn.
- OPPOSITES receive.
□ **send for** call, summon, ask for, request, order. **send up** *(informal)* satirize, ridicule, make fun of, parody, lampoon, mock, caricature, imitate, ape; *informal* take off, spoof, take the mickey out of.

send-off *noun* **farewell**, goodbye, adieu, leave-taking, departure.

senior *adjective* **1 older**, elder. **2 superior**, higher-ranking, more important; *N. Amer.* ranking.
- OPPOSITES junior, subordinate.

sensation *noun* **1 feeling**, sense, perception, impression. **2 commotion**, stir, uproar, furore, scandal, impact; *informal* splash, to-do.

sensational *adjective* **1 shocking**, scandalous, fascinating, exciting, thrilling, interesting, dramatic, momentous, historic, newsworthy. **2 overdramatized**, melodramatic, exaggerated, sensationalist, graphic, explicit, lurid; *informal* shock-horror, juicy. **3** *(informal)* **gorgeous**, stunning, wonderful, superb, excellent, first-class; *informal* great, terrific, tremendous, fantastic, fabulous, out of this world; *Brit. informal* smashing.
- OPPOSITES dull, unremarkable.

sense *noun* **1 feeling**, faculty, awareness, sensation, recognition, perception. **2 appreciation**, awareness, understanding, comprehension. **3 wisdom**, common sense, wit, reason, intelligence, judgement, brain(s), sagacity; *informal* gumption, nous, horse sense, savvy; *N. Amer. informal* smarts. **4 purpose**, point, use, value, advantage, benefit. **5 meaning**, definition, denotation, nuance, drift, gist, thrust, tenor, message.
- OPPOSITES stupidity.
● *verb* **detect**, feel, observe, notice, recognize, pick up, be aware of, distinguish, make out, perceive, discern, divine, intuit; *informal* catch on to.

senseless *adjective* **pointless**, futile, useless, needless, meaningless, absurd, foolish, insane, stupid, idiotic, mindless, illogical.
- OPPOSITES wise.

sensible *adjective* **practical**, realistic, responsible, reasonable, commonsensical, rational, logical, sound, no-nonsense, level-headed, down-to-earth, wise.
- OPPOSITES foolish.

sensitive *adjective* **1** *she's sensitive to changes in temperature* **responsive to**, reactive to, sensitized to, aware of, conscious of, susceptible to, affected by, vulnerable to. **2 delicate**, fragile, tender, sore. **3 tactful**, careful, thoughtful, diplomatic, delicate, subtle, kid-glove. **4 touchy**, oversensitive, hypersensitive, easily offended, thin-skinned, defensive, paranoid, neurotic. **5 difficult**, delicate, tricky, awkward, problematic, ticklish, controversial, emotive.
- OPPOSITES insensitive, resilient.

sensitivity *noun* **1 responsiveness**, sensitiveness, reactivity, susceptibility. **2 tact**, diplomacy, delicacy, subtlety, understanding, soft skills. **3 touchiness**, oversensitivity, hypersensitivity, defensiveness. **4 delicacy**, trickiness, awkwardness, ticklishness.

sensual *adjective* **1 physical**, carnal, bodily, fleshly, animal. **2 passionate**, sexual, physical, tactile, hedonistic.
- OPPOSITES spiritual.

sensuous *adjective* **1 rich**, sumptuous, luxurious. **2 voluptuous**, sexy, seductive, luscious, lush, ripe.

sentence *noun* **1 judgement**, ruling, decision, verdict. **2** *a long sentence* **punishment**, prison term; *informal* time, stretch.
● *verb* **condemn**, doom, punish, convict.

sentiment *noun* **1 view**, feeling, attitude, thought, opinion, belief. **2 sentimentality**, emotion, tenderness, softness; *informal* schmaltz; *Brit. informal* soppiness.

sentimental *adjective* **1 nostalgic**, emotional, affectionate, loving, tender. **2 mawkish**, overemotional, romantic, hearts-and-flowers; *Brit.* twee; *informal* schmaltzy, corny; *Brit. informal* soppy; *N. Amer. informal* sappy.

separate *adjective* **1 unconnected**, unrelated, different, distinct, discrete, detached, divorced, disconnected, independent. **2 set apart**, detached, cut off, segregated, isolated, free-standing, self-contained.
● *verb* **1 disconnect**, detach, disengage, uncouple, split, sunder, sever. **2 partition**, divide, stand between, come between, keep apart, isolate, section off. **3 part (company)**, go their separate ways, split up, disperse, scatter. **4 split up**, break up, part, become estranged, divorce.
- OPPOSITES unite, join.

separately *adverb* **individually**, one by one, one at a time, singly, severally, apart, independently, alone, by yourself, on your own.

separation *noun* **1 disconnection**, splitting, division, breaking-up. **2 break-up**, split, estrangement, divorce; *Brit. informal* bust-up.

septic *adjective* **infected**, festering, suppurating, putrid, putrefying, poisoned; *Medicine* purulent.

sequel *noun* **continuation**, further episode, follow-up.

sequence *noun* **1 succession**, order, course, series, chain, train, progression, chronology, pattern, flow. **2 excerpt**, clip, extract, section.

serene *adjective* **calm**, composed, tranquil, peaceful, placid, untroubled, relaxed, at ease, unperturbed, unruffled, unworried; *chiefly US* centred; *informal* together, unflappable, chilled.
– OPPOSITES agitated.

series *noun* **succession**, sequence, string, chain, run, round, spate, wave, rash, course, cycle, row.

serious *adjective* **1 solemn**, earnest, grave, sombre, unsmiling, stern, grim, humourless, stony, dour, poker-faced, long-faced. **2 important**, significant, momentous, weighty, far-reaching, consequential. **3 intellectual**, highbrow, heavyweight, deep, profound, literary, learned, scholarly; *informal* heavy. **4** *a serious injury* **severe**, grave, bad, critical, acute, terrible, dire, dangerous, grievous. **5 sincere**, earnest, genuine, wholehearted, committed, resolute, determined.
– OPPOSITES light-hearted, trivial, minor.

sermon *noun* **address**, homily, talk, speech, lecture.

servant *noun* **attendant**, domestic, maid, housemaid, retainer, flunkey, minion, slave, lackey, drudge; *informal* skivvy.

serve *verb* **1 work for**, obey, do the bidding of. **2** *this job serves the community* **benefit**, help, assist, aid, make a contribution to. **3** *he served a six-month apprenticeship* **carry out**, perform, do, fulfil, complete, discharge, spend. **4 present**, give out, distribute, dish up, provide, supply. **5 attend to**, deal with, see to, assist, help, look after. **6** *a saucer serving as an ashtray* **act as**, function as, do duty.

service *noun* **1 work**, employment, labour. **2** *he has done us a service* **favour**, kindness, good turn, helping hand. **3 ceremony**, ritual, rite, sacrament. **4 overhaul**, check, maintenance, servicing, repair. **5** *a range of local services* **amenity**, facility, resource, utility, solution. **6 (armed) forces**, military, army, navy, air force.
● *verb* **overhaul**, check, go over, maintain, repair.

serviceable *adjective* **1 in working order**, working, functioning, operational, usable, workable, viable. **2 functional**, utilitarian, sensible, practical, hard-wearing, durable, tough, robust.

session *noun* **1 meeting**, sitting, assembly, conclave; *N. Amer. & NZ* caucus. **2 period**, time, term.

set[1] *verb* **1 put (down)**, place, lay, deposit, position, settle, leave, stand, plant; *informal* stick, dump, park, plonk, pop. **2 fix**, embed, insert, mount. **3** *set the table* **lay**, prepare, arrange. **4** *he set us some work* **assign**, allocate, give, allot. **5 arrange**, schedule, fix (on), decide on, settle on, choose, agree on, determine, designate, appoint, name, specify, stipulate. **6 adjust**, regulate, synchronize, calibrate, put right, correct. **7 solidify**, harden, stiffen, thicken, gel, cake, congeal, coagulate, clot.
□ **set off/out** set out, start out, sally forth, leave, depart, embark, set sail; *informal* hit the road. **set up 1** erect, put up, construct, build. **2** establish, start, begin, institute, found, create. **3** arrange, organize, fix (up), schedule, timetable, line up.

set[2] *noun* **1 series**, collection, group, batch, arrangement, array, assortment, selection. **2 group**, circle, crowd, crew, band, fraternity, company, ring, camp, school, clique, faction; *informal* gang, bunch.

set[3] *adjective* **1 fixed**, established, scheduled, specified, appointed, arranged, settled, decided, agreed, predetermined, hard and fast, unvarying, unchanging, invariable, rigid, inflexible. **2 ready**, prepared, organized, equipped, primed; *informal* geared up, psyched up.
- OPPOSITES variable, unprepared.

setback *noun* **problem**, difficulty, hitch, issue, complication, upset, blow; *informal* glitch, hiccup.
- OPPOSITES breakthrough.

setting *noun* **surroundings**, position, situation, environment, background, backdrop, spot, place, location, locale, site, scene.

settle *verb* **1 resolve**, sort out, clear up, end, fix, work out, iron out, set right, reconcile; *informal* patch up. **2 put in order**, sort out, tidy up, arrange, organize, order, clear up, straighten out. **3 decide on**, set, fix, agree on, name, establish, arrange, choose, pick. **4** *I've settled the bill* **pay**, square, clear. **5 make your home**, set up home, take up residence, put down roots, establish yourself, live, move to. **6** *a drink will settle your nerves* **calm**, quieten, quiet, soothe, relax. **7 land**, come to rest, alight, perch.

settlement *noun* **1 agreement**, deal, arrangement, conclusion, resolution, understanding, pact. **2 community**, colony, outpost, encampment, post, village.

settler *noun* **colonist**, frontiersman, pioneer, immigrant, newcomer, incomer.

sever *verb* **1 cut off**, chop off, detach, separate, amputate. **2 cut (through)**, rupture, split, pierce. **3 break off**, discontinue, suspend, end, cease, dissolve.
- OPPOSITES join.

several *adjective* **some**, a number of, a few, various, assorted.

severe *adjective* **1 acute**, very bad, serious, grave, critical, dire, dangerous, life-threatening. **2** *severe storms* **fierce**, violent, strong, powerful, intense, forceful. **3 cold**, freezing, icy, arctic, harsh, bitter. **4** *severe criticism* **harsh**, scathing, sharp, strong, fierce, savage, devastating, withering. **5** *a severe expression* **stern**, dour, grim, forbidding, disapproving, unsmiling, unfriendly, sombre, stony, cold, frosty. **6 plain**, simple, austere, spartan, unadorned, stark, clinical, uncluttered, minimalist, functional.
- OPPOSITES minor, gentle, mild.

sew *verb* **stitch**, tack, seam, hem, embroider.

sex *noun* **1 sexual intercourse**, lovemaking, making love, sexual relations, mating, copulation; *formal* fornication, coitus. **2 gender**.

WORD LINKS
carnal relating to sexual activity

sexuality *noun* **1 sensuality**, sexiness, seductiveness, eroticism, physicality, sexual appetite, passion, desire, lust. **2 sexual orientation**, sexual preference, leaning, persuasion.

sexy *adjective* **1 sexually attractive**, seductive, desirable, alluring; *informal* fanciable, hot; *Brit. informal* fit; *N. Amer. informal* foxy. **2 erotic**, sexually explicit, titillating, naughty, X-rated, rude, pornographic, crude; *informal* raunchy, steamy; *euphemistic* adult.

shabby *adjective* **1 run down**, scruffy, dilapidated, in disrepair, ramshackle, tumbledown, dingy; *Brit. informal* grotty. **2 scruffy**, old, worn out, threadbare, ragged, frayed, tattered, battered, faded, moth-eaten, the worse for wear; *informal* tatty; *N. Amer. informal* raggedy. **3 mean**, unkind, unfair, shameful, shoddy, unworthy, contemptible, despicable, discreditable, ignoble; *informal* rotten.
- OPPOSITES smart.

shack *noun* **hut**, cabin, shanty, lean-to, shed, hovel; *Scottish* bothy.

shackle *verb* **1 chain**, fetter, manacle, secure, tie (up), bind, tether, hobble, put in chains, clap in irons, handcuff. **2 restrain**, restrict, limit, constrain, handicap, hamstring, hamper, hinder, impede, obstruct, inhibit.

shade *noun* **1 shadow**, shadiness, shelter, cover. **2 colour**, hue, tone, tint, tinge. **3 nuance**, gradation, degree, difference, variation, variety, nicety, subtlety, undertone, overtone. **4 little**, bit, trace, touch, modicum, tinge; *informal* tad, smidgen. **5 blind**, curtain, screen, cover, covering, awning, canopy.
- OPPOSITES light.
● *verb* **cast a shadow over**, shadow, shelter, cover, screen.

shadow *noun* **1 silhouette**, outline, shape, contour, profile. **2 shade**, darkness, twilight, gloom.
● *verb* **follow**, trail, track, stalk, pursue; *informal* tail, keep tabs on.

shady *adjective* **1 shaded**, shadowy, dim, dark, sheltered, leafy. **2** *(informal)* **suspicious**, suspect, questionable, dubious, irregular, underhand; *informal* fishy, murky; *Brit. informal* dodgy; *Austral./NZ informal* shonky.
- OPPOSITES bright, honest.

shaft *noun* **1 pole**, stick, rod, staff, shank, handle, stem. **2** *a shaft of light* **ray**, beam, gleam, streak, pencil. **3 tunnel**, passage, hole, bore, duct, well, flue, vent.

shake *verb* **1 vibrate**, tremble, quiver, quake, shiver, shudder, judder, wobble, rock, sway, convulse. **2 jiggle**, joggle, jerk, agitate; *informal* wiggle, waggle. **3 brandish**, wave, flourish, swing wield. **4 upset**, distress, disturb, unsettle, disconcert, discompose, unnerve, throw off balance, agitate, fluster, shock, alarm, scare, worry; *informal* rattle.
● *noun* **judder**, trembling, quivering, quake, tremor, shiver, shudder, wobble.

shaky *adjective* **1 unsteady**, unstable, rickety, wobbly; *Brit. informal* wonky. **2 faint**, dizzy, light-headed, giddy, weak, wobbly, in shock. **3 unreliable**, untrustworthy, questionable, dubious, doubtful, tenuous, suspect, flimsy, weak; *informal* iffy; *Brit. informal* dodgy.
- OPPOSITES steady, stable.

shallow *adjective* **superficial**, trivial, facile, insubstantial, lightweight, empty, trifling, surface, skin-deep, frivolous, foolish, silly.
- OPPOSITES profound.

sham *noun* **pretence**, fake, act, simulation, fraud, lie, counterfeit, humbug.
● *adjective* **fake**, pretended, feigned, simulated, false, artificial, bogus, insincere, affected, make-believe; *informal* pretend, put-on, phoney.
- OPPOSITES genuine.
● *verb* **pretend**, fake, malinger; *informal* put it on; *Brit. informal* swing the lead.

shambles *noun* **1 chaos**, muddle, jumble, confusion, disorder, havoc; *Brit. informal* omnishambles. **2 mess**, pigsty; *informal* disaster area; *Brit. informal* tip.

shame *noun* **1 guilt**, remorse, contrition. **2 humiliation**, embarrassment, indignity, loss of face, mortification, disgrace, dishonour, discredit, ignominy, disrepute, infamy, scandal. **3** *it's a shame she never married* **pity**, sad thing, bad luck; *informal* crime, sin.
- OPPOSITES pride, honour.
● *verb* **1 disgrace**, dishonour, discredit, blacken, drag through the mud. **2 humiliate**, embarrass, humble, take down a peg or two, cut down to size, show up.
- OPPOSITES honour.

shamefaced *adjective* **ashamed**, abashed, sheepish, guilty, contrite, sorry, remorseful, repentant, penitent, regretful, rueful, apologetic; *informal* with your tail between your legs.
- OPPOSITES unrepentant.

shameful *adjective* **1 disgraceful**, deplorable, despicable, contemptible, discreditable, unworthy, reprehensible, shabby, shocking, scandalous, outrageous, abominable, atrocious, appalling, inexcusable, unforgivable. **2 embarrassing**, mortifying, humiliating, ignominious.
- OPPOSITES admirable.

shameless *adjective* **flagrant**, blatant, barefaced, overt, brazen, undisguised, unconcealed, unabashed, unashamed, unblushing, unrepentant.

shape *noun* **1 form**, appearance, configuration, structure, contours, lines, outline, silhouette, profile. **2 guise**, likeness, semblance, form, appearance, image. **3 condition**, health, trim, fettle, order; *Brit. informal* nick.
● *verb* **1 form**, fashion, make, mould, model. **2** *events which shaped the course of her life* **determine**, form, influence, affect.

shapeless *adjective* **1 formless**, amorphous, unformed, indefinite. **2 baggy**, saggy, ill-fitting, oversized, unstructured, badly cut.

shapely *adjective* **well proportioned**, curvaceous, voluptuous, full-figured, attractive, sexy; *informal* curvy.

share *noun* **portion**, part, division, quota, allowance, ration, allocation; *informal* cut, slice; *Brit. informal* whack.
● *verb* **1 split**, divide, go halves on; *informal* go fifty-fifty on. **2 apportion**, divide up, allocate, portion out, measure out, carve up; *Brit. informal* divvy up. **3 participate**, take part, play a part, be involved, have a hand.

sharp *adjective* **1 keen**, razor-edged, sharpened, well honed. **2 intense**, acute, severe, agonizing, excruciating, stabbing, shooting, searing. **3 tangy**, piquant, acidic, acid, sour, tart, pungent, vinegary. **4 cold**, chilly, icy, bitter, biting, brisk, keen, penetrating. **5 harsh**, bitter, cutting, caustic, scathing, barbed, spiteful, hurtful, unkind, cruel, malicious. **6** *a sharp increase* **sudden**, abrupt, unexpected, rapid, steep. **7 astute**, intelligent, bright, incisive, keen, quick-witted, shrewd, canny, perceptive, smart, quick; *informal* on the ball, quick on the uptake, genius; *N. Amer. informal* heads-up.
– OPPOSITES blunt, mild.
● *adverb* **precisely**, exactly, prompt, promptly, punctually; *informal* on the dot; *N. Amer. informal* on the button.

sharpen *verb* **hone**, whet, strop, grind, file.

shatter *verb* **1 smash**, break, splinter, crack, fracture, fragment, disintegrate. **2 destroy**, wreck, ruin, dash, crush, devastate, demolish, torpedo, scotch; *informal* do for, put paid to; *Brit. informal* scupper.

shave *verb* **1 cut off**, crop, trim, barber. **2 plane**, pare, whittle, scrape, shear.

sheath *noun* **covering**, cover, case, casing, sleeve, scabbard.

shed[1] *noun* **hut**, lean-to, outhouse, outbuilding, cabin, shack.

shed[2] *verb* **1 drop**, scatter, spill. **2 throw off**, cast off, discard, slough off, moult. **3 take off**, remove, discard, climb out of, slip out of; *Brit. informal* peel off. **4** *the moon shed a faint light* **cast**, radiate, emit, give out.

sheen *noun* **shine**, lustre, gloss, patina, burnish, polish, shimmer.

sheer *adjective* **1 utter**, complete, absolute, total, thorough, pure, downright, out-and-out, unqualified, unmitigated, unalloyed. **2 steep**, abrupt, sharp, precipitous, vertical. **3 thin**, fine, gauzy, diaphanous, transparent, see-through, flimsy, filmy, translucent.

sheet *noun* **1 layer**, covering, blanket, coat, film, veneer, crust, skin, surface, stratum. **2 pane**, panel, slab, plate, piece. **3 page**, leaf, folio. **4** *a sheet of water* **expanse**, area, stretch, sweep.

shell *noun* **1 pod**, hull, husk. **2 body**, case, casing, framework, hull, fuselage, hulk.
● *verb* **1 pod**, hull, husk; *N. Amer.* shuck. **2 bombard**, fire on, attack, bomb, blitz.

shelter *noun* **1 protection**, cover, shade, safety, security, refuge. **2 sanctuary**, refuge, home, haven, safe house.
– OPPOSITES exposure.
● *verb* **1 protect**, shield, screen, cover, shade, defend, cushion, guard, insulate, cocoon. **2 take shelter**, take refuge, take cover; *informal* hole up.
– OPPOSITES expose.

sheltered *adjective* **1 shady**, shaded, protected, still, tranquil. **2 protected**, cloistered, isolated, secluded, cocooned, insulated, secure, safe, quiet.

shelve *verb* **postpone**, put off, delay, defer, put back, reschedule, hold over/off, put to one side, suspend, stay, mothball; *N. Amer.* put over, table; *informal* put on ice, put on the back burner.

shepherd *verb* **usher**, steer, herd, lead, take, escort, guide, conduct, marshal, walk.

shield *noun* **protection**, guard, defence, cover, screen, shelter.
● *verb* **protect**, guard, defend, cover, screen, shade, shelter.
– OPPOSITES expose.

shift *verb* **1 move**, transfer, transport, switch, relocate, reposition, rearrange. **2** *the wind shifted* **veer**, alter, change, turn.
● *noun* **1 change**, alteration, adjustment, variation, modification, revision, reversal, rowback, U-turn. **2 stint**, stretch, spell.

shimmer *verb* **glint**, glisten, twinkle, sparkle, flash, gleam, glow, glimmer, wink.
● *noun* **glint**, twinkle, sparkle, flash, gleam, glow, glimmer, lustre, glitter.

shine *verb* **1 beam**, gleam, radiate, glow, glint, glimmer, sparkle, twinkle, glitter, glisten, shimmer, flash. **2 polish**, burnish, buff, rub up, brush, clean. **3 excel**, stand out
● *noun* **polish**, gleam, gloss, lustre, sheen, patina.

shiny *adjective* **glossy**, bright, glassy, polished, gleaming, satiny, lustrous.
– OPPOSITES matt.

ship *noun* **boat**, vessel, craft.
● *verb* **deliver**, send, dispatch, transport, carry, distribute.

WORD LINKS
maritime, nautical relating to ships

shirk *verb* **evade**, dodge, avoid, get out of, sidestep, shrink from, shun, skip, neglect; *informal* duck (out of), cop out of; *Brit. informal* skive off; *N. Amer. informal* cut.

shiver *verb* **tremble**, quiver, shake, shudder, quake.
● *noun* **shudder**, twitch, start.

shock[1] *noun* **1 blow**, upset, surprise, revelation, bolt from the blue, rude awakening, eye-opener. **2 fright**, scare, start; *informal* turn. **3 trauma**, collapse, breakdown, post-traumatic stress disorder. **4 vibration**, reverberation, shake, jolt, impact, blow.
● *verb* **appal**, horrify, outrage, scandalize, disgust, traumatize, distress, upset, disturb, stun, rock, shake.
– OPPOSITES delight.

shock[2] *noun* **mass**, mane, mop, thatch, head, bush, tangle, cascade, halo.

shocking *adjective* **appalling**, horrifying, horrific, dreadful, awful, terrible, scandalous, outrageous, disgraceful, abominable, atrocious, disgusting, distressing, upsetting, disturbing, startling.

shoddy *adjective* **poor-quality**, inferior, second-rate, tawdry, jerry-built, cheapjack, gimcrack; *informal* tatty.

shoot *verb* **1 gun down**, mow down, pick off, hit, wound, injure, kill. **2 fire**, open fire, snipe, let fly, bombard, shell, discharge, launch. **3 race**, speed, flash, dash, rush, hurtle, streak, whizz, zoom, career, fly; *informal* belt, tear, zip, whip; *Brit. informal* bomb; *N. Amer. informal* hightail it, barrel. **4 film**, photograph, record.
● *noun* **sprout**, bud, runner, tendril, offshoot, cutting.

shop *noun* **store**, retail outlet, boutique, emporium, department store, supermarket, hypermarket, superstore, chain store; *N. Amer.* mart.

shore *noun* **seashore**, beach, sand(s), shoreline, coast; *literary* littoral.

short *adjective* **1 small**, little, petite, tiny, diminutive, elfin; *Scottish* wee; *informal* pint-sized, knee-high to a grasshopper. **2 concise**, brief, succinct, to the point, compact, pithy, abridged,

abbreviated, condensed. **3 brief**, fleeting, short-lived, momentary, passing, lightning, quick, rapid, cursory. **4 scarce**, scant, meagre, sparse, insufficient, deficient, inadequate, lacking. **5 curt**, sharp, abrupt, blunt, brusque, terse, offhand.
- OPPOSITES tall, long, plentiful.
● *adverb she stopped short* **abruptly**, suddenly, sharply, all of a sudden, unexpectedly, without warning.
□ **short of** deficient in, lacking, in need of, low on, short on, missing; *informal* strapped for, pushed for, minus.

shortage *noun* **scarcity**, dearth, poverty, insufficiency, deficiency, inadequacy, famine, lack, deficit, shortfall.
- OPPOSITES abundance.

shortcoming *noun* **fault**, defect, flaw, imperfection, deficiency, limitation, failing, drawback, weakness, weak point.
- OPPOSITES strength.

shorten *verb* **abbreviate**, abridge, condense, contract, compress, reduce, shrink, diminish, cut (down), trim, pare (down), prune, curtail, truncate.
- OPPOSITES lengthen.

shortly *adverb* **soon**, presently, in a little while, at any moment, in a minute, in next to no time, before long, by and by; *N. Amer.* momentarily; *informal* anon, any time now, in a jiffy; *Brit. informal* in a mo.

shot *noun* **1 report**, crack, bang, blast; (**shots**) gunfire, firing. **2** *the winning shot* **stroke**, hit, strike, kick, throw. **3 marksman**, markswoman, shooter. **4 photograph**, photo, snap, snapshot, picture, print, slide, still.

shoulder *verb* **1 take on (yourself)**, undertake, accept, assume, bear, carry. **2 push**, shove, thrust, jostle, force, bulldoze, bundle.

shout *verb* **yell**, cry (out), call (out), roar, howl, bellow, bawl, raise your voice; *informal* holler.
- OPPOSITES whisper.
● *noun* **yell**, cry, call, roar, howl, bellow, bawl; *informal* holler.

shove *verb* **push**, thrust, propel, drive, force, ram, knock, elbow, shoulder, jostle.

show *verb* **1 be visible**, be seen, be in view, be obvious. **2 display**, exhibit, put on show, put on display, put on view. **3** *he showed his frustration* **manifest**, exhibit, reveal, convey, communicate, make known, express, make plain, make obvious, disclose, evince, betray. **4 demonstrate**, explain, describe, illustrate, teach, instruct. **5 prove**, demonstrate, confirm, substantiate, corroborate, verify, bear out. **6** *she showed them to their seats* **escort**, accompany, take, conduct, lead, usher, guide, direct.
- OPPOSITES conceal.
● *noun* **1 display**, array, sight, spectacle. **2 exhibition**, display, fair, exposition, festival, parade; *N. Amer.* exhibit. **3 programme**, broadcast, presentation, production. **4 appearance**, outward appearance, image, pretence, (false) front, guise, pose, affectation, semblance.
□ **show off 1** *(informal)* put on airs, put on an act, swank, strut, grandstand, posture, draw attention to yourself. **2** display, show to advantage, exhibit, demonstrate, parade, draw attention to, flaunt. **show up 1** be visible, be obvious, be seen, be revealed, appear. **2** *(informal)* turn up, appear, arrive, come, get here/there, put in an appearance, materialize. **3** *(informal)* humiliate, embarrass, shame, put someone to shame, mortify. **4** expose, reveal, make obvious, highlight, emphasize, draw attention to.

showdown *noun* **confrontation**, clash, face-off.

shower *noun* **1 fall**, drizzle, sprinkling, flurry. **2 volley**, hail, salvo, barrage.
● *verb* **1 rain**, fall, hail. **2 deluge**, flood, inundate, swamp, overwhelm, snow under.

show-off *noun (informal)* **exhibitionist**, extrovert, poser, poseur, swaggerer, self-publicist.

showy *adjective* **ostentatious**, flamboyant, gaudy, garish, brash, vulgar, loud, fancy, ornate; *informal* flash, flashy.
- OPPOSITES restrained.

shred *noun* **1 tatter**, ribbon, rag, fragment, sliver, snippet, remnant. **2 scrap**, bit, speck, particle, ounce, jot, crumb, fragment, grain, drop, trace.
● *verb* **grate**, cut up, tear up.

shrewd *adjective* **astute**, sharp, smart, intelligent, clever, canny, perceptive; *informal* on the ball.
- OPPOSITES stupid.

shriek *verb* & *noun* **scream**, screech, squeal, squawk, roar, howl, shout, yelp; *informal* holler.

shrill *adjective* **high-pitched**, piercing, high, sharp, ear-piercing, ear-splitting, penetrating.

shrink *verb* **1 get smaller**, contract, diminish, lessen, reduce, decrease, dwindle, decline, fall off. **2 recoil**, shy away, flinch, be averse, be afraid, hesitate.
- OPPOSITES expand, increase.

shrivel *verb* **wither**, shrink, wilt, dry up, dehydrate, parch, frazzle.

shroud *noun* **covering**, cover, cloak, mantle, blanket, layer, cloud, veil, winding sheet.
● *verb* **cover**, envelop, veil, cloak, blanket, screen, conceal, hide, mask, obscure.

shudder *verb* **shake**, shiver, tremble, quiver, judder.
● *noun* **shake**, shiver, tremor, trembling, quivering, judder, vibration.

shuffle *verb* **1 shamble**, hobble, limp, drag your feet. **2 mix (up)**, rearrange, jumble (up), reorganize.

shun *verb* **avoid**, steer clear of, give a wide berth to, have nothing to do with; *informal* freeze out; *Brit. informal* send to Coventry.
- OPPOSITES welcome.

shut *verb* **close**, pull to, push to, slam, fasten, put the lid on, lock, secure.
- OPPOSITES open.
□ **shut down** close (down), cease trading; *informal* fold, flatline. **shut up** be quiet, keep quiet, stop talking, hold your tongue; *informal* keep mum, pipe down, belt up; *N. Amer. informal* can it.

shuttle *verb* **commute**, run, ply, go/travel back and forth, ferry.

shy *adjective* **bashful**, diffident, timid, reserved, introverted, retiring, self-effacing, withdrawn.
- OPPOSITES confident.
□ **shy away from** flinch, recoil, hang back, be loath, be reluctant, baulk at, be unwilling, be disinclined, hesitate.

sick *adjective* **1 ill**, unwell, poorly, ailing, indisposed, out of sorts; *informal* under the weather, laid up; *Austral./NZ informal* crook. **2 nauseous**, queasy, bilious, green about the gills. **3** *I'm sick of this music* **fed up**, bored, tired, weary, jaded. **4** *(informal)* **macabre**, tasteless, ghoulish, morbid, black, gruesome, perverted, cruel.
- OPPOSITES well.
□ **be sick** *(Brit.)* vomit, heave, retch; *informal* puke (up), throw up, spew (up); *N. Amer. informal* barf, upchuck.

sicken *verb* **1 nauseate**, make sick, turn someone's stomach, disgust, revolt, repel, appal; *N. Amer. informal* gross out. **2 fall ill**, become infected, be stricken.

sickening *adjective* **nauseating**, stomach-turning, repulsive, revolting, disgusting, offensive, off-putting, distasteful, obscene, gruesome, grisly; *N. Amer.* vomitous; *informal* gross.

sickly *adjective* **1 unhealthy**, in poor health, delicate, frail, weak. **2 pale**, wan, pasty, sallow, pallid, ashen, anaemic. **3 sentimental**, mawkish, cloying, sugary, syrupy, saccharine; *informal* slushy, schmaltzy, cheesy, corny; *Brit. informal* soppy.
- OPPOSITES healthy.

sickness *noun* **1 illness**, disease, ailment, infection, malady, infirmity; *informal* bug, virus; *Brit. informal* lurgy. **2 nausea**, biliousness, queasiness, vomiting, retching; *informal* throwing up, puking.

side *noun* **1 edge**, border, verge, boundary, margin, rim, fringe(s), flank, bank, perimeter, extremity, periphery, limit(s). **2 district**, quarter, area, region, part, neighbourhood, sector, zone. **3 surface**, face. **4 point of view**, viewpoint, perspective, opinion, standpoint, position, outlook, slant, angle, aspect, facet. **5 faction**, camp, bloc, party, wing. **6 team**, squad, line-up.
- OPPOSITES centre, end.
● *adjective* **1 lateral**, wing, flanking. **2 subordinate**, secondary, minor, peripheral, incidental, subsidiary.
- OPPOSITES front, central.
□ **side with** support, take someone's part, stand by, back, be loyal to, defend, champion, ally yourself with.

sidetrack *verb* **distract**, divert, deflect, draw away.

sideways *adverb* **1 to the side**, laterally. **2 edgewise**, edgeways, side first, end on.
● *adjective* **1 lateral**, sideward, on the side, side to side. **2 indirect**, oblique, sidelong, surreptitious, furtive, covert, sly.

sift *verb* **1 sieve**, strain, screen, filter. **2** *we sift out unsuitable applications* **separate out**, filter out, sort out, weed out, get rid of, remove. **3** *sifting through the data* **search**, look, examine, inspect, scrutinize.

sigh *verb* **1 breathe (out)**, exhale, groan, moan. **2 rustle**, whisper, murmur.

S

sight *noun* **1 eyesight**, vision, eyes. **2 view**, glimpse, glance, look. **3 landmark**, place of interest, monument, spectacle, marvel, wonder.
● *verb* **glimpse**, catch sight of, see, spot, spy, make out, pick out, notice, observe.

WORD LINKS
optical, **visual** relating to sight

sign *noun* **1 indication**, signal, symptom, pointer, suggestion, intimation, mark, manifestation, demonstration, token. **2 warning**, omen, portent, threat, promise. **3 notice**, board, placard, signpost. **4 symbol**, figure, emblem, device, logo, character.
● *verb* **1 write your name on**, autograph, initial, countersign. **2 endorse**, validate, agree to, approve, ratify, adopt. **3 write**, inscribe, pen.

signal *noun* **1 gesture**, gesticulation, sign, wave, cue, indication, warning, prompt, reminder. **2 indication**, sign, symptom, hint, pointer, clue, demonstration, evidence, proof.
● *verb* **1 gesture**, gesticulate, sign, indicate, motion, wave, beckon, nod. **2** *his death signals the end of an era* **mark**, signify, mean, indicate, be a sign of, be evidence of.

significance *noun* **importance**, import, consequence, seriousness, gravity, weight, magnitude.

significant *adjective* **1 notable**, noteworthy, remarkable, important, of consequence, momentous. **2 large**, considerable, sizeable, appreciable, conspicuous, obvious, sudden. **3 meaningful**, expressive, eloquent, suggestive, knowing, telling.

signify *verb* **mean**, denote, designate, represent, symbolize, stand for.

silence *noun* **1 quietness**, quiet, still, stillness, hush, tranquillity, peace, peacefulness. **2 failure to speak**, dumbness, muteness, reticence, taciturnity.
- OPPOSITES noise, loquacity.
● *verb* **1 quieten**, quiet, hush, still, muffle. **2 gag**, muzzle, censor.

silent *adjective* **1 quiet**, still, hushed, noiseless, soundless, inaudible. **2 speechless**, quiet, unspeaking, dumb, mute, taciturn, uncommunicative, tight-lipped. **3 unspoken**, wordless, tacit, unvoiced, unexpressed, implied, implicit, understood.
- OPPOSITES audible, loquacious.

silhouette *noun* **outline**, contour(s), profile, form, shape.
● *verb* **outline**, define.

silly *adjective* **1 foolish**, stupid, inane, feather-brained, bird-brained, frivolous,

immature, childish, empty-headed, scatterbrained; *informal* dotty, scatty. **2 unwise**, imprudent, thoughtless, foolish, stupid, unintelligent, rash, reckless, foolhardy, irresponsible, hare-brained; *informal* crazy, barmy; *Brit. informal* daft. **3** *he brooded about silly things* **trivial**, trifling, petty, small, insignificant, unimportant.
- OPPOSITES sensible.

similar *adjective* **alike**, like, much the same, comparable, corresponding, equivalent, parallel, analogous, kindred; *informal* much of a muchness.
- OPPOSITES different, dissimilar.

similarity *noun* **resemblance**, likeness, comparability, correspondence, parallel, equivalence, uniformity.

similarly *adverb* **likewise**, comparably, correspondingly, in the same way, by the same token.

simmer *verb* **1 boil gently**, cook gently, bubble, stew, poach. **2 seethe**, fume, smoulder.

simple *adjective* **1 straightforward**, easy, uncomplicated, uninvolved, undemanding, elementary; *informal* child's play, a cinch, a piece of cake, like falling off a log. **2 clear**, plain, lucid, straightforward, unambiguous, understandable, comprehensible, accessible; *informal* user-friendly. **3 plain**, unadorned, basic, unsophisticated, no-frills, classic, understated, uncluttered, restrained. **4 unpretentious**, unsophisticated, ordinary, unaffected, unassuming, natural, straightforward.
- OPPOSITES difficult, complex, ornate.

simplicity *noun* **1 straightforwardness**, ease. **2 clarity**, plainness, lucidity, intelligibility, comprehensibility, accessibility. **3 austerity**, plainness, spareness, clean lines. **4 plainness**, modesty, naturalness.
- OPPOSITES complexity.

simplify *verb* **make simpler**, clarify, put into words of one syllable, streamline; *informal* dumb down.
- OPPOSITES complicate.

simply *adverb* **1 straightforwardly**, directly, clearly, plainly, intelligibly, lucidly, unambiguously. **2 plainly**, soberly, unfussily, without clutter, classically. **3 merely**, just, purely, solely, only.

simulate *verb* **1 feign**, pretend, fake, affect, put on. **2 replicate**, reproduce, imitate, mimic.

simultaneous *adjective* **concurrent**, happening at the same time, contemporaneous, coinciding, coincident, synchronized.
- OPPOSITES separate.

simultaneously *adverb* **at the same time**, at one and the same time, at once, concurrently, (all) together, in unison, in concert, in chorus.

sin *noun* **1 wrong**, act of wickedness, transgression, crime, offence, misdeed; *old use* trespass. **2 wickedness**, wrongdoing, evil, immorality, iniquity, vice, crime.
- OPPOSITES virtue.
● *verb* **transgress**, do wrong, misbehave, err, go astray; *old use* trespass.

sincere *adjective* **1 heartfelt**, wholehearted, profound, deep, true, honest, earnest, fervent. **2 honest**, genuine, truthful, direct, frank, candid; *informal* straight, on the level, upfront; *N. Amer. informal* on the up and up.

sincerely *adverb* **genuinely**, honestly, really, truly, truthfully, wholeheartedly, earnestly.

sincerity *noun* **genuineness**, honesty, truthfulness, integrity, directness, openness, candour.

sinful *adjective* **immoral**, wicked, (morally) wrong, evil, bad, iniquitous, ungodly, irreligious, sacrilegious.
- OPPOSITES virtuous.

sing *verb* **1 chant**, trill, intone, croon, chorus. **2 trill**, warble, chirp, chirrup, cheep.

singe *verb* **scorch**, burn, sear, char.

singer *noun* **vocalist**, songster, songstress, soloist, chorister, cantor.

single *adjective* **1 sole**, one, lone, solitary, unaccompanied, alone. **2 individual**, separate, particular, distinct. **3 unmarried**, unwed, unattached, free.
- OPPOSITES double, multiple.
□ **single out** select, pick out, choose, decide on, target, earmark, mark out, separate out, set apart.

single-handed *adverb* **by yourself**, alone, on your own, solo, unaided, unassisted, without help.

single-minded *adjective* **determined**, committed, unswerving, unwavering, resolute, purposeful, devoted, dedicated, uncompromising, tireless, tenacious, persistent, dogged.
- OPPOSITES half-hearted.

singly *adverb* **one by one**, one at a time, one after the other, individually, separately.
- OPPOSITES together.

sinister *adjective* **1 menacing**, threatening, forbidding, baleful, frightening, alarming, disturbing, ominous. **2 evil**, wicked, criminal, nefarious, villainous; *informal* shady.
- OPPOSITES innocent.

sink *verb* **1 submerge**, founder, capsize, go down, be engulfed. **2 scuttle**; *Brit.* scupper. **3 fall**, drop, descend, plunge, plummet, slump. **4 embed**, insert, drive, plant.
- OPPOSITES float, rise.

sinner *noun* **wrongdoer**, evil-doer, transgressor, miscreant, offender, criminal; *old use* trespasser.

S

sip *verb* **drink**, taste, sample, nip.
● *noun* **mouthful**, swallow, drink, drop, dram, nip; *informal* swig.

sit *verb* **1 take a seat**, sit down, be seated, perch, ensconce yourself, flop; *informal* take the load off your feet; *Brit. informal* take a pew. **2 be placed**, be positioned, be situated, be set, rest, stand, perch. **3 be in session**, meet, be convened. **4** *she sits on the tribunal* **serve on**, have a seat on, be a member of.
- OPPOSITES stand.

site *noun* **location**, place, position, situation, locality, whereabouts.
● *verb* **place**, put, position, situate, locate.

situation *noun* **1 circumstances**, state of affairs, affairs, state, condition, case, predicament, plight. **2 location**, position, spot, site, setting, environment. **3 post**, position, job, employment.

size *noun* **dimensions**, measurements, proportions, magnitude, largeness, area, expanse, breadth, width, length, height, depth.
□ **size up** *(informal)* assess, appraise, get the measure of, judge, take stock of, evaluate; *Brit. informal* suss out.

sizeable *adjective* **large**, substantial, considerable, respectable, significant, goodly.
- OPPOSITES small.

sizzle *verb* **crackle**, fizzle, sputter, hiss, spit.

sketch *noun* **drawing**, outline, draft, diagram, design, plan; *informal* rough.
● *verb* **draw**, make a drawing of, pencil, rough out, outline.

sketchy *adjective* **incomplete**, patchy, fragmentary, scrappy, cursory, perfunctory, scanty, vague, inadequate, insufficient.
- OPPOSITES detailed.

skilful *adjective* **expert**, accomplished, skilled, masterly, talented, deft, dexterous, handy; *informal* mean, crack, ace, genius; *N. Amer. informal* crackerjack.
- OPPOSITES incompetent.

skill *noun* **expertise**, accomplishment, skilfulness, mastery, talent, deftness, dexterity, prowess, competence, artistry.
- OPPOSITES incompetence.

skim *verb* **1** *skim off the fat* **remove**, scoop off, separate. **2 glide**, move lightly, slide, sail, skate. **3** *she skimmed through the paper* **glance**, flick, flip, leaf, thumb, scan, run your eye over.

skin *noun* **1 hide**, pelt, fleece. **2 peel**, rind. **3 film**, layer, membrane, crust, covering, coating.

● *verb* **1 peel**, pare. **2 graze**, scrape, abrade, bark, rub raw, chafe.

WORD LINKS
cutaneous relating to the skin
dermatology branch of medicine concerning the skin

skinny *adjective* **thin**, underweight, scrawny, bony, gaunt, emaciated, skeletal, wasted, pinched, spindly, gangly; *informal* anorexic.

skip *verb* **1 caper**, prance, trip, dance, bound, bounce, gambol. **2 omit**, leave out, miss out, dispense with, pass over, skim over, disregard; *informal* give something a miss.

skirt *verb* **1 go round**, walk round, circle. **2 border**, edge, flank, line. **3** *he skirted round the subject* **avoid**, evade, sidestep, dodge, pass over, gloss over; *informal* duck.

skull *noun* cranium.

WORD LINKS
cranial relating to the skull

sky *noun literary* the heavens, the firmament, the ether, the (wide) blue yonder.

WORD LINKS
celestial relating to the sky

slab *noun* **piece**, block, hunk, chunk, lump, cake, tablet, brick, panel, plate, sheet.

slack *adjective* **1 limp**, loose. **2 sagging**, flabby, flaccid, loose, saggy. **3 sluggish**, slow, quiet, slow-moving, flat, depressed, stagnant. **4 lax**, negligent, careless, slapdash, slipshod; *informal* sloppy.
- OPPOSITES taut, firm.
● *verb (Brit. informal)* **idle**, shirk, be lazy, be indolent, waste time, lounge about; *Brit. informal* skive; *N. Amer. informal* goof off.

slam *verb* **bang**, thump, crash, smash, plough, run, bump, collide with, hit, strike, ram; *N. Amer.* impact.

slanderous *adjective* **defamatory**, denigratory, disparaging, libellous, pejorative, false, misrepresentative, scurrilous, scandalous, malicious.

slant *verb* **1 slope**, tilt, incline, be at an angle, tip, lean, dip, pitch, shelve, list, bank. **2 bias**, distort, twist, skew, weight.
● *noun* **1 slope**, incline, tilt, gradient, pitch, angle, camber. **2 point of view**, viewpoint, standpoint, stance, angle, perspective, approach, view, attitude, position, bias, spin.

slap *verb* **smack**, strike, hit, cuff, clip, spank; *informal* whack.
● *noun* **smack**, blow, cuff, clip, spank; *informal* whack.

slash *verb* **1 cut**, gash, slit, lacerate, knife. **2** *(informal)* **reduce**, cut, lower, bring down, mark down.
● *noun* **cut**, gash, slit, laceration, incision, wound.

slaughter *verb* **1 kill**, butcher, cull, put down. **2 massacre**, murder, butcher, kill, exterminate, wipe out, put to death, execute; *literary* slay.
● *noun* **massacre**, (mass) murder, (mass) killing, (mass) execution, extermination, carnage, bloodshed, bloodletting, bloodbath; *literary* slaying.

slave *noun* **servant**, lackey, drudge; *Brit. informal* skivvy, dogsbody; *historical* serf, vassal.
- OPPOSITES master.
● *verb* **toil**, labour, sweat, work like a Trojan/dog, work your fingers to the bone; *informal* sweat blood, slog away; *Brit. informal* graft.

WORD LINKS
servile like a slave

slavery *noun* **enslavement**, servitude, serfdom, bondage, captivity.
- OPPOSITES freedom.

sleazy *adjective* **1 corrupt**, immoral, ignoble, dishonourable. **2 squalid**, seedy, seamy, sordid, insalubrious.

sleek *adjective* **1 smooth**, glossy, shiny, shining, lustrous, silken, silky. **2 streamlined**, elegant, graceful.
- OPPOSITES scruffy.

sleep *noun* **nap**, doze, siesta, catnap; *informal* snooze, forty winks, shut-eye; *Brit. informal* kip; *literary* slumber.
● *verb* **be asleep**, doze, take a siesta, take a nap, catnap; *informal* snooze, get some shut-eye; *Brit. informal* kip; *literary* slumber.
- OPPOSITES wake up.
□ **go to sleep** fall asleep, get to sleep; *informal* drop off, nod off, drift off, crash out, flake out; *N. Amer. informal* sack out.

WORD LINKS
sedative, **soporific** causing sleep

sleepy *adjective* **1 drowsy**, tired, somnolent, heavy-eyed; *informal* dopey. **2 quiet**, peaceful, tranquil, placid, slow-moving, dull, boring.
- OPPOSITES awake, alert.

slender *adjective* **1 slim**, lean, willowy, svelte, lissom, graceful, slight, thin, skinny. **2 faint**, remote, tenuous, fragile, slim, small, slight.
- OPPOSITES plump, strong.

slice *noun* **1 piece**, portion, slab, wedge, rasher, sliver, wafer. **2 share**, part, portion, tranche, percentage, proportion, allocation; *informal* cut, whack.
● *verb* **cut**, carve, divide.

slick *adjective* **1 efficient**, smooth, smooth-running, polished, well organized, well run, streamlined. **2 glib**, polished, assured, self-assured, smooth-talking, plausible; *informal* smarmy.
● *verb* **smooth**, plaster, sleek, grease, oil, gel.

slide *verb* **glide**, slip, slither, skim, skate, skid, slew.

slight *adjective* **1 small**, tiny, minute, negligible, insignificant, minimal, remote, slim, faint. **2 slim**, slender, delicate, dainty, fragile.
- OPPOSITES large, plump.
● *verb* **insult**, snub, rebuff, spurn, give someone the cold shoulder, cut (dead), take no notice of, scorn, ignore.
● *noun* **insult**, affront, snub, rebuff; *informal* put-down, slap in the face.

slightly *adverb* **a little**, a bit, somewhat, faintly, vaguely, a shade.
- OPPOSITES very.

slim *adjective* **1 slender**, lean, thin, willowy, sylphlike, svelte, lissom, slight, trim. **2** *a slim chance* **slight**, small, slender, faint, remote.
- OPPOSITES fat.
● *verb* **lose weight**, diet, go on a diet; *N. Amer.* slenderize.

slimy *adjective* **slippery**, slithery, greasy, sticky, viscous; *informal* slippy.

sling *verb* **1 hang**, suspend, string, swing. **2** *(informal)* **throw**, toss, fling, hurl, cast, pitch, lob, flip; *informal* chuck, heave, bung.

slip *verb* **1 slide**, skid, slither, fall (over), lose your balance, lose your footing, tumble. **2 creep**, steal, sneak, slide, sidle, slope, slink, tiptoe.
● *noun* **1 false step**, slide, skid, fall, tumble. **2 mistake**, error, blunder, gaffe, oversight, miscalculation, omission, lapse; *informal* slip-up, boo-boo, howler; *Brit. informal* boob, clanger, bloomer; *N. Amer. informal* goof, blooper.
□ **slip up** *(informal)* make a mistake, blunder, get something wrong, miscalculate, make an error, err; *informal* make a boo-boo; *Brit. informal* boob, drop a clanger; *N. Amer. informal* goof up.

slippery *adjective* **1 slithery**, greasy, oily, icy, glassy, smooth, slimy, wet; *informal* slippy. **2 sneaky**, sly, devious, crafty, cunning, tricky, evasive, scheming, unreliable, untrustworthy; *informal* shady, shifty; *Brit. informal* dodgy; *Austral./NZ informal* shonky.

slit *noun* **1 cut**, incision, split, slash, gash. **2 opening**, gap, chink, crack, aperture, slot.
● *verb* **cut**, slash, split open, slice open.

slither *verb* **slide**, slip, glide, wriggle, crawl, skid.

sliver *noun* **splinter**, shard, chip, flake, shred, scrap, shaving, paring, piece, fragment.

slobber *verb* **drool**, slaver, dribble, salivate.

slogan *noun* **catchphrase**, catchline, motto, jingle; *N. Amer. informal* tag line.

slope *noun* **tilt**, pitch, slant, angle, gradient, incline, inclination, fall, camber; *N. Amer.* grade.
● *verb* **tilt**, slant, incline, lean, drop/fall away, descend, shelve, camber, rise, ascend, climb.

sloping *adjective* **slanting**, leaning, inclined, angled, cambered, tilted.
- OPPOSITES level.

sloppy *adjective* **1 runny**, watery, liquid, mushy; *informal* gloopy. **2 careless**, slapdash, slipshod, disorganized, untidy, slack, slovenly; *informal* slap-happy.

slot *noun* **1 aperture**, slit, crack, hole, opening. **2 time**, spot, period, niche, space; *informal* window.
● *verb* **insert**, slide, fit, put, place.

slovenly *adjective* **1 scruffy**, untidy, messy, unkempt, ill-groomed, dishevelled, bedraggled, rumpled, frowzy. **2 careless**, slapdash, slipshod, haphazard, hit-or-miss, untidy, messy, negligent, lax, lackadaisical, slack; *informal* sloppy, slap-happy.
- OPPOSITES tidy, careful.

slow *adjective* **1 unhurried**, leisurely, steady, sedate, measured, ponderous, sluggish, plodding. **2 lengthy**, time-consuming, long-drawn-out, protracted, prolonged, gradual. **3 stupid**, unintelligent, obtuse; *informal* dense, dim, thick, slow on the uptake, dumb, dopey; *Brit. informal* dozy.
- OPPOSITES fast, quick.
● *verb* **1 reduce speed**, go slower, decelerate, brake. **2 hold back**, hold up, delay, retard, set back, check, curb.
- OPPOSITES accelerate.

slowly *adverb* **1 unhurriedly**, without hurrying, steadily, at a leisurely pace, at a snail's pace. **2 gradually**, bit by bit, little by little, slowly but surely, step by step.
- OPPOSITES quickly.

sluggish *adjective* **lethargic**, listless, lacking in energy, lifeless, inactive, slow, torpid, enervated.
- OPPOSITES vigorous.

slum *noun* **hovel**; (**slums**) ghetto, shanty town.

slump *verb* **1 sit heavily**, flop, collapse, sink; *informal* plonk yourself. **2 fall**, plummet, tumble, collapse, drop; *informal* crash, nosedive.
● *noun* **1 fall**, drop, tumble, downturn, downswing, slide, decline, decrease; *informal* nosedive. **2 recession**, decline, depression, slowdown.
- OPPOSITES rise, boom.

slur *verb* **mumble**, speak unclearly, garble.
● *noun* **insult**, slight, slander, smear, allegation, imputation.

sly *adjective* **1 cunning**, crafty, clever, wily, artful, tricky, scheming, devious, underhand, sneaky. **2 roguish**, mischievous, impish, playful, wicked, arch, knowing. **3 surreptitious**, furtive, stealthy, covert.
- OPPOSITES open, straightforward.

smack *noun* **slap**, blow, cuff, clip, spank; *informal* whack.
● *verb* **slap**, strike, hit, cuff, clip, spank; *informal* whack.
● *adverb (informal)* **exactly**, precisely, straight, right, directly, squarely, dead, plumb; *informal* slap, bang; *N. Amer. informal* smack dab.

small *adjective* **1 little**, tiny, short, petite, diminutive, elfin, miniature, mini, minute, toy, baby, undersized, poky, cramped; *Scottish* wee; *informal* teeny, tiddly, pint-sized; *Brit. informal* titchy. **2 slight**, minor, unimportant, trifling, trivial, insignificant, inconsequential, negligible, inappreciable; *informal* piffling.
- OPPOSITES big, large.

smarmy *adjective (informal)* **unctuous**, ingratiating, slick, oily, greasy, obsequious, sycophantic, fawning; *informal* slimy.

smart *adjective* **1 well dressed**, well turned out, stylish, chic, fashionable, modish, elegant, dapper; *N. Amer.* trig; *informal* natty, snappy. **2** *a smart restaurant* **fashionable**, stylish, high-class, exclusive, chic, fancy; *Brit.* upmarket; *N. Amer.* high-toned; *informal* trendy, classy, swanky; *Brit. informal* swish; *N. Amer. informal* swank. **3** *(informal)* **clever**, bright, intelligent, quick-witted, shrewd, astute, perceptive; *informal* brainy, quick on the uptake, genius. **4** *a smart pace* **brisk**, quick, fast, rapid, lively, energetic, vigorous; *informal* cracking.

- OPPOSITES scruffy, stupid.

● *verb* **1 sting**, burn, tingle, prickle, hurt. **2** *she smarted at the accusation* **feel hurt**, feel upset, take offence, feel aggrieved, feel indignant, be put out.

smash *verb* **1 break**, shatter, splinter, crack; *informal* bust. **2** *he smashed into a wall* **crash**, smack, slam, plough, run, bump, hit, strike, ram, collide with; *N. Amer.* impact.

● *noun* **crash**, collision, accident; *N. Amer.* wreck; *informal* pile-up; *Brit. informal* shunt.

smattering *noun* **bit**, little, modicum, touch, soupçon, rudiments, basics; *informal* smidgen, smidge, tad.

smear *verb* **1 spread**, rub, daub, slap, cover, coat, smother, plaster. **2 smudge**, streak, mark. **3 sully**, tarnish, blacken, drag through the mud, damage, defame, malign, slander, libel; *N. Amer.* slur.

● *noun* **1 streak**, smudge, daub, dab, spot, patch, blotch, mark; *informal* splodge. **2 accusation**, lie, untruth, slur, slander, libel, defamation.

smell *noun* **1 odour**, aroma, fragrance, scent, perfume, bouquet, nose. **2 stink**, stench, reek; *Brit. informal* pong, whiff.

● *verb* **1 scent**, sniff, get a sniff of, detect. **2 stink**, reek; *Brit. informal* pong, hum.

WORD LINKS
olfactory relating to the sense of smell

smelly *adjective* **foul-smelling**, stinking, reeking, rank, fetid, malodorous, pungent; *literary* noisome.

smile *verb* **beam**, grin (from ear to ear), smirk, simper, leer.

- OPPOSITES frown.

● *noun* **beam**, grin, smirk, simper, leer.

smirk *verb* **sneer**, simper, snigger, leer, grin.

smitten *adjective* **1 struck down**, laid low, suffering, affected, afflicted. **2 infatuated**, besotted, in love, obsessed, head over heels, enamoured, captivated, enchanted, under someone's spell; *informal* bowled over, swept off your feet.

smoke *verb* **1 smoulder**; *old use* reek. **2 puff on**, draw on, pull on, inhale; *informal* drag on.

● *noun* **fumes**, exhaust, gas, vapour, smog.

smoky *adjective* **smoke-filled**, sooty, smoggy, hazy, foggy, murky, thick; *Brit. informal* fuggy.

smooth *adjective* **1 even**, level, flat, plane, unwrinkled, glassy, glossy, silky, polished. **2 creamy**, fine, velvety. **3 calm**, still, tranquil, undisturbed, unruffled, even, flat, like a millpond. **4 steady**, regular, uninterrupted, unbroken, easy, effortless, trouble-free. **5 suave**, urbane, sophisticated, polished, debonair, courteous, gracious, persuasive, glib, slick, smooth-tongued; *informal* smarmy.

- OPPOSITES uneven, rough.

● *verb* **1 flatten**, level (out/off), even out/off, press, roll, iron, plane. **2 ease**, facilitate, expedite, help, assist, aid, pave the way for.

- OPPOSITES roughen, hinder.

smother *verb* **1 suffocate**, asphyxiate, stifle, choke. **2 extinguish**, put out, snuff out, douse, stamp out. **3 smear**, daub, spread, cover, plaster. **4** *she smothered a giggle* **stifle**, muffle, strangle, suppress, hold back, fight back, swallow, conceal.

smudge *noun* **streak**, smear, mark, stain, blotch, blob, dab; *informal*

splotch, splodge.
● *verb* **streak**, mark, dirty, soil, blotch, blacken, smear, blot, daub, stain; *informal* splotch, splodge.

smug *adjective* **self-satisfied**, conceited, complacent, superior, pleased with yourself.

snack *noun* **light meal**, sandwich, refreshments, nibbles, titbit(s); *informal* bite (to eat).

snag *noun* **complication**, difficulty, catch, hitch, obstacle, pitfall, problem, issue, setback, disadvantage, drawback.
● *verb* **catch**, hook, tear.

snake *noun* serpent.
● *verb the road snakes inland* **twist**, wind, meander, zigzag, curve.

snap *verb* **1 break**, fracture, splinter, split, crack; *informal* bust. **2 bark**, snarl, growl, retort; *informal* jump down someone's throat.
● *noun* **photograph**, picture, photo, shot, snapshot, print, slide.

snare *noun* **trap**, gin, wire, net, noose.
● *verb* **trap**, catch, net, bag, ensnare, hook.

snatch *verb* **1 grab**, seize, take hold of, take, pluck, grasp at, clutch at. **2 steal**, take, thieve, make off with; *informal* swipe, nab, lift; *Brit. informal* nick, pinch, whip. **3 kidnap**, abduct, take as hostage.

sneak *verb* **creep**, slink, steal, slip, slide, sidle, tiptoe, pad.

sneaking *adjective* **1 secret**, private, hidden, concealed, unvoiced, unexpressed. **2** *a sneaking suspicion* **niggling**, nagging, insidious, lingering, persistent.

sneaky *adjective* **sly**, crafty, cunning, wily, scheming, devious, deceitful, underhand.

sneer *verb* **1 smirk**, snigger, curl your lip. **2 scoff**, laugh, scorn, disdain, be contemptuous, mock, ridicule, deride, jeer, jibe.
● *noun* **1 smirk**, snigger. **2 jeer**, jibe, insult; *informal* dig.

sniff *verb* **1 inhale**, snuffle. **2 smell**, scent, get a whiff of.
● *noun* **1 snuffle**, snort. **2 smell**, scent, whiff, lungful.
□ **sniff out** *(informal)* detect, find, discover, bring to light, track down, dig up, root out, uncover, unearth.

snigger *verb* & *noun* **giggle**, titter, snicker, chortle, laugh, sneer, smirk.

snippet *noun* **piece**, bit, scrap, fragment, particle, shred, excerpt, extract.

snivel *verb* **sniffle**, snuffle, whimper, whine, weep, cry; *Scottish* greet; *informal* blubber; *Brit. informal* grizzle.

snobbish, **snobby** *adjective* **elitist**, superior, supercilious, arrogant, condescending, pretentious, affected; *informal* snooty, high and mighty, la-di-da, stuck-up; *Brit. informal* toffee-nosed.

snoop *verb (informal)* **pry**, spy, be a busybody, poke your nose into, root about, ferret about; *informal* be nosy; *Austral. informal* stickybeak.

snub *verb* **rebuff**, spurn, cold-shoulder, cut (dead), ignore, insult, slight; *informal* freeze out; *N. Amer. informal* stiff.
● *noun* **rebuff**, slap in the face; *informal* brush-off, put-down.

snug *adjective* **1 cosy**, comfortable, warm, sheltered, secure; *informal* comfy. **2 tight**, skintight, close-fitting, figure-hugging.
– OPPOSITES loose.

snuggle *verb* **nestle**, curl up, huddle (up), cuddle up, nuzzle, settle; *N. Amer.* snug down.

soak *verb* **1 dip**, immerse, steep, submerge, douse, marinate, souse. **2 drench**, wet through, saturate. **3** *water soaked through the carpet* **permeate**, penetrate, impregnate, percolate, seep, spread. **4 absorb**, suck up, blot, mop up.

soaking *adjective* **drenched**, wet (through), soaked (through), sodden, soggy, waterlogged, saturated, sopping, dripping, wringing.
– OPPOSITES parched.

soar *verb* **1 rise**, ascend, climb. **2 glide**, plane, float, hover. **3 increase**, escalate, shoot up, spiral, rocket; *informal* go through the roof, skyrocket.
- OPPOSITES plummet.

sob *verb* **weep**, cry, snivel, whimper; *Scottish* greet; *informal* blubber; *Brit. informal* grizzle.

sober *adjective* **1 clear-headed**, teetotal, abstinent, dry; *informal* on the wagon. **2 serious**, solemn, sensible, staid, sedate, quiet, dignified, grave, level-headed, down-to-earth. **3 sombre**, subdued, restrained, austere, severe, drab, plain, dark.
- OPPOSITES drunk.

so-called *adjective* **supposed**, alleged, presumed, inappropriately named, ostensible, reputed, self-styled.

sociable *adjective* **friendly**, amicable, affable, companionable, gregarious, cordial, warm, genial.
- OPPOSITES unfriendly.

social *adjective* **1 communal**, community, collective, general, popular, civil, public, civic. **2 recreational**, leisure, entertainment.
● *noun* **party**, gathering, function, get-together, celebration; *informal* do.

socialize *verb* **interact**, converse, be sociable, mix, mingle, get together, meet, fraternize, consort; *informal* hobnob, hang out.

society *noun* **1 the community**, the (general) public, the people, the population, civilization, humankind, mankind, the world at large. **2** *an industrial society* **culture**, community, civilization, nation. **3 high society**, polite society, the upper classes, the gentry, the elite, the smart set, the beau monde; *informal* the upper crust. **4 club**, association, group, circle, institute, guild, lodge, league, union, alliance. **5 company**, companionship, fellowship, friendship.

WORD LINKS
sociology study of society

S

sofa *noun* **settee**, couch, divan, chaise longue, chesterfield.

soft *adjective* **1 mushy**, squashy, pulpy, squishy, doughy, spongy, springy, elastic, pliable, pliant; *informal* gooey; *Brit. informal* squidgy. **2 swampy**, marshy, boggy, muddy, squelchy. **3 smooth**, velvety, fleecy, downy, furry, silky, silken. **4 dim**, low, faint, subdued, muted, subtle. **5 quiet**, low, gentle, faint, muted, subdued, muffled, hushed, whispered. **6 lenient**, easy-going, tolerant, forgiving, forbearing, indulgent, liberal, lax.
- OPPOSITES hard, firm, harsh.

soften *verb the compensation should soften the blow* **ease**, alleviate, relieve, soothe, take the edge off, cushion, lessen, diminish, blunt, deaden.

soggy *adjective* **mushy**, squashy, pulpy, slushy, squelchy, swampy, marshy, boggy, soaking, wet, saturated, drenched; *Brit. informal* squidgy.

soil[1] *noun* **1 earth**, dirt, clay, ground, loam. **2 territory**, land, region, country, domain, dominion.

soil[2] *verb* **dirty**, stain, smear, smudge, spoil, foul.

soldier *noun* **fighter**, trooper, serviceman/woman, warrior; *US* GI; *Brit. informal* squaddie.

WORD LINKS
military relating to soldiers

sole *adjective* **only**, one, single, solitary, lone, unique, exclusive.

solely *adverb* **only**, simply, purely, just, merely, uniquely, exclusively, entirely, wholly, alone.

solemn *adjective* **1 dignified**, ceremonial, stately, formal, majestic, imposing, splendid, magnificent, grand. **2 serious**, grave, sober, sombre, unsmiling, stern, grim, dour, humourless. **3 sincere**, earnest, honest, genuine, firm, heartfelt, wholehearted, sworn.
- OPPOSITES frivolous, light-hearted.

solicit *verb* **1 ask for**, request, seek, apply for, put in for, call for, beg for, plead for. **2 ask**, approach, appeal to, lobby, petition, importune, call on, press.

solid *adjective* **1 hard**, rock-hard, rigid, firm, solidified, set, frozen, compact, compressed, dense. **2** *solid gold* **pure**, unadulterated, genuine. **3 well built**, sound, substantial, strong, sturdy, durable, stout. **4 well founded**, valid, sound, logical, authoritative, convincing, cogent. **5** *solid support* **unanimous**, united, consistent, undivided.
– OPPOSITES liquid, flimsy, untenable.

solidarity *noun* **unanimity**, unity, agreement, team spirit, accord, harmony, consensus; *formal* concord.

solidify *verb* **harden**, set, thicken, stiffen, congeal, cake, freeze, ossify, fossilize, petrify.
– OPPOSITES liquefy.

solitary *adjective* **1 lonely**, unaccompanied, by yourself, on your own, alone, friendless, unsociable, withdrawn, reclusive; *N. Amer.* lonesome. **2 isolated**, remote, lonely, out of the way, in the back of beyond, outlying, off the beaten track, secluded; *N. Amer.* in the backwoods. **3 single**, lone, sole, only, one, individual.
– OPPOSITES sociable.

solitude *noun* **loneliness**, solitariness, isolation, seclusion, privacy, peace.

solution *noun* **1 answer**, result, resolution, key, explanation. **2 mixture**, blend, emulsion, compound.

solve *verb* **answer**, resolve, work out, puzzle out, fathom, decipher, decode, clear up, straighten out, get to the bottom of, unravel, explain; *informal* figure out, crack; *Brit. informal* suss out.

sombre *adjective* **1 dark**, drab, dull, dingy, restrained, sober, funereal. **2 solemn**, earnest, serious, grave, sober, unsmiling, gloomy, sad, mournful, melancholy, lugubrious, cheerless.
– OPPOSITES bright, cheerful.

somehow *adverb* **one way or another**, no matter how, by fair means or foul, by hook or by crook, come what may.

sometimes *adverb* **occasionally**, from time to time, now and then, every so often, once in a while, on occasion, at times, off and on.

song *noun* **air**, strain, ditty, chant, number, track, melody, tune.

sonorous *adjective* **resonant**, rich, full, round, booming, deep, clear, mellow, strong, resounding, reverberant.

soon *adverb* **shortly**, presently, in the near future, before long, in a little while, in a minute, in a moment; *Brit. informal* in a tick.

sooner *adverb* **1 earlier**, before now. **2 rather**, preferably, given the choice.

soothe *verb* **1 calm (down)**, pacify, comfort, hush, quiet, settle (down), appease, mollify; *Brit.* quieten (down). **2 ease**, alleviate, relieve, take the edge off, allay, lessen, reduce.
– OPPOSITES agitate, aggravate.

soothing *adjective* **relaxing**, restful, calm, calming, tranquil, peaceful.

sophisticated *adjective* **1 advanced**, state-of-the-art, the latest, up-to-the-minute, cutting-edge, complex. **2 worldly**, worldly-wise, experienced, cosmopolitan, urbane, cultured, cultivated, polished, refined.
– OPPOSITES crude, naive.

sophistication *noun* **worldliness**, experience, urbanity, culture, polish, refinement, elegance, style, poise, finesse, savoir faire.

sordid *adjective* **1 sleazy**, seedy, seamy, unsavoury, tawdry, cheap, disreputable, discreditable, ignominious, shameful, wretched, despicable. **2 squalid**, slummy, dirty, filthy, shabby, scummy; *informal* scuzzy; *Brit. informal* grotty.
– OPPOSITES respectable.

sore *adjective* **1 painful**, hurting, aching, throbbing, smarting, stinging, inflamed, sensitive, tender, raw, wounded, injured. **2** *(N. Amer. informal)* **upset**, angry, annoyed, cross, disgruntled, dissatisfied, irritated; *informal* aggravated, miffed, peeved; *Brit. informal* narked, not best pleased; *N. Amer. informal* ticked off.

sorrow *noun* **1 sadness**, unhappiness, misery, despondency, regret, despair, desolation, heartache, grief. **2** *the sorrows of life* **trouble**, difficulty, problem, woe, affliction, trial, tribulation, misfortune.
- OPPOSITES joy.

sorry *adjective* **1 regretful**, apologetic, remorseful, contrite, repentant, rueful, penitent, guilty, shamefaced, ashamed. **2** *he felt sorry for her* **full of pity**, sympathetic, compassionate, moved, concerned. **3** *I was sorry to hear about the accident* **sad**, sorrowful, distressed.
- OPPOSITES glad, unrepentant.

sort *noun* **type**, kind, variety, class, category, style, form, genre, species, breed, make, model, brand.
● *verb* **1 classify**, class, group, organize, arrange, order, grade, catalogue. **2** *the problem was soon sorted out* **resolve**, settle, solve, fix, work out, straighten out, deal with, put right, set right, rectify, iron out.

soul *noun* **1 spirit**, psyche, (inner) self. **2 feeling**, emotion, passion, animation, intensity, warmth, energy, vitality, spirit.

sound[1] *noun* **1 noise**, din, racket, row, resonance, reverberation. **2 utterance**, cry, word, noise, peep.
- OPPOSITES silence.
● *verb* **1 make a noise**, resonate, resound, reverberate, go off, ring, chime, ping. **2** *sound the horn* **blow**, blast, toot, ring, use, operate, activate, set off. **3 appear**, look (like), seem, give every indication of being, strike someone as.

WORD LINKS
acoustic, **sonic** relating to sound

sound[2] *adjective* **1 healthy**, in good condition/shape, fit, hale and hearty, in fine fettle, undamaged, unimpaired. **2 well built**, solid, substantial, strong, sturdy, durable, stable, intact. **3 well founded**, valid, reasonable, logical, weighty, authoritative, reliable. **4 reliable**, dependable, trustworthy, fair, good. **5 solvent**, debt-free, in the black, in credit, creditworthy, secure. **6 deep**, undisturbed, uninterrupted, untroubled, peaceful.
- OPPOSITES unhealthy, unsafe.

sour *adjective* **1 acid**, acidic, tart, bitter, sharp, vinegary, pungent. **2 bad**, off, turned, curdled, rancid, high, fetid. **3 embittered**, resentful, jaundiced, bitter, cross, crabby, crotchety, cantankerous, bad-tempered, disagreeable, unpleasant; *informal* grouchy.
- OPPOSITES sweet, fresh.
● *verb* **spoil**, mar, damage, harm, impair, upset, poison, blight.

source *noun* **1 spring**, wellspring, wellhead, origin. **2 origin**, derivation, starting point, start, beginning, fountainhead, root, author, originator.

souvenir *noun* **memento**, keepsake, reminder, memorial, trophy.

sovereign *noun* **ruler**, monarch, potentate, overlord, king, queen, emperor, empress, prince, princess.
● *adjective* **autonomous**, independent, self-governing, self-determining, non-aligned, free.

sovereignty *noun* **1 power**, rule, supremacy, dominion, jurisdiction, ascendancy, domination, authority, control. **2 autonomy**, independence, self-rule, self-government, home rule, self-determination, freedom.

sow *verb* **plant**, scatter, disperse, strew, broadcast, seed.

space *noun* **1 room**, capacity, latitude, margin, leeway, play, elbow room, clearance. **2 area**, expanse, stretch, sweep, tract, footprint. **3 gap**, interval, opening, aperture, cavity, niche, interstice. **4 blank**, gap, box. **5 period**, span, time, duration, stretch, course, interval, gap. **6 outer space**, deep space, the universe, the galaxy, the solar system.
● *verb* **position**, arrange, range, array, spread, lay out, set.

spacious *adjective* **roomy**, capacious, commodious, voluminous, sizeable, generous.
- OPPOSITES cramped.

span *noun* **1 extent**, length, width, reach, stretch, spread, distance, range. **2 period**, space, time, duration, course, interval.
● *verb* **1 bridge**, cross, traverse, pass over. **2 last**, cover, extend, spread over.

spare *adjective* **1 extra**, supplementary, additional, second, other, alternative, emergency, reserve, backup, relief, substitute; *N. Amer.* alternate. **2 surplus**, superfluous, excess, leftover, redundant, unnecessary, unwanted; *informal* going begging. **3** *your spare time* **free**, leisure, unoccupied. **4 slender**, lean, willowy, svelte, lissom, thin, skinny, gaunt, lanky, spindly.
● *verb* **1 afford**, manage, part with, give, provide, do without. **2 pardon**, let off, forgive, have mercy on, reprieve, release, free.

sparing *adjective* **thrifty**, economical, frugal, careful, prudent, cautious.
- OPPOSITES lavish, extravagant.

spark *noun* **flash**, glint, twinkle, flicker, flare.
● *verb the arrest sparked off riots* **cause**, give rise to, occasion, bring about, start, precipitate, prompt, trigger (off), provoke, stimulate, stir up.

sparkle *verb* & *noun* **glitter**, glint, glisten, twinkle, flicker, flash, shimmer.

sparkling *adjective* **1 effervescent**, fizzy, carbonated, aerated. **2 brilliant**, dazzling, scintillating, coruscating, exciting, exhilarating, stimulating, invigorating, vivacious, lively, vibrant.
- OPPOSITES still, dull.

sparse *adjective* **scant**, scanty, scattered, scarce, infrequent, few and far between, meagre, paltry, limited, in short supply.
- OPPOSITES abundant.

spartan *adjective* **austere**, harsh, hard, frugal, rigorous, strict, severe, ascetic, self-denying, abstemious, bleak, bare, plain.
- OPPOSITES luxurious.

spate *noun* **series**, succession, run, cluster, string, rash, epidemic, outbreak, wave, flurry.

speak *verb* **1 talk**, converse, communicate, chat, have a word, gossip, commune, say something; *informal* chew the fat. **2 say**, utter, state, declare, voice, express, pronounce, articulate, enunciate, verbalize. **3 give a speech**, talk, lecture, hold forth; *informal* spout, sound off.

speaker *noun* **speech-maker**, lecturer, talker, orator, spokesperson, spokesman/woman, reader, commentator, broadcaster, narrator.

special *adjective* **1 exceptional**, unusual, remarkable, out of the ordinary, outstanding, unique. **2 distinctive**, distinct, individual, particular, specific, peculiar. **3 momentous**, significant, memorable, important, historic, red-letter.
- OPPOSITES ordinary, general.

specialist *noun* **expert**, authority, pundit, professional, connoisseur, master, maestro; *informal* buff.

speciality *noun* **strength**, strong point, forte, métier, strong suit, party piece, pièce de résistance, claim to fame.

species *noun* **type**, kind, sort, breed, strain, variety, class, classification, category.

specific *adjective* **1 particular**, specified, fixed, set, determined, distinct, definite. **2 detailed**, explicit, express, clear-cut, unequivocal, precise, exact.
- OPPOSITES general, vague.

specification *noun a shelter built to their specifications* **instruction**, guideline, parameter, stipulation, requirement, condition, order, detail.

specify *verb* **state**, name, identify, define, set out, itemize, detail, list, enumerate, spell out, stipulate, lay down.

specimen *noun* **sample**, example, model, instance, illustration, demonstration.

spectacle *noun* **1 display**, show, pageantry, performance, exhibition, pomp and circumstance, extravaganza, spectacular. **2 sight**, vision, scene, prospect, picture.

spectacular *adjective* **impressive**, magnificent, splendid, dazzling, sensational, stunning, dramatic, outstanding, memorable, unforgettable, striking, picturesque, eye-catching, breathtaking, glorious; *informal* out of this world.
- OPPOSITES dull, unimpressive.

spectator *noun* **watcher**, viewer, observer, onlooker, bystander, witness.

spectre *noun* **ghost**, phantom, apparition, spirit, wraith, presence; *informal* spook.

speculate *verb* **1 conjecture**, theorize, hypothesize, guess, surmise, wonder, muse. **2 gamble**, venture, wager, invest, play the market.

speculative *adjective* **1 conjectural**, suppositional, theoretical, hypothetical, tentative, unproven, unfounded, groundless, unsubstantiated. **2 risky**, hazardous, unsafe, uncertain, unpredictable; *informal* chancy.

speech *noun* **1 speaking**, talking, verbal communication, conversation, dialogue, discussion. **2 diction**, elocution, articulation, enunciation, pronunciation, delivery, words. **3 talk**, address, lecture, discourse, oration, presentation, sermon. **4 language**, parlance, tongue, idiom, dialect, vernacular; *informal* lingo.

WORD LINKS
oral, **phonetic**, **phonic** relating to speech

S

speechless *adjective* **lost for words**, dumbstruck, struck dumb, tongue-tied, inarticulate, mute, dumb, voiceless, silent.

speed *noun* **1 rate**, pace, tempo, momentum, velocity; *informal* lick. **2 rapidity**, swiftness, promptness, alacrity, briskness, haste, hurry; *old use* celerity.
- OPPOSITES slowness.
● *verb* **1 hurry**, rush, dash, race, sprint, career, shoot, hurtle, hare, fly, zoom, hasten; *informal* tear, belt, pelt; *Brit. informal* bomb. **2** *a holiday will speed his recovery* **hasten**, accelerate, advance, further, promote, boost, stimulate, aid, assist, facilitate.
- OPPOSITES slow, hinder.
□ **speed up** hurry up, accelerate, go faster, get a move on, put a spurt on, pick up speed; *informal* step on it.

speedy *adjective* **fast**, swift, quick, rapid, expeditious, prompt, immediate, brisk, hasty, hurried, precipitate, rushed.
- OPPOSITES slow.

spell[1] *verb* **signal**, signify, mean, amount to, add up to, constitute.
□ **spell out** explain, make clear, clarify, specify, detail.

spell[2] *noun* **1 charm**, incantation, magic formula, curse; *N. Amer.* hex; (**spells**) magic, sorcery, witchcraft. **2 influence**, charm, magnetism, charisma, magic.
□ **put a spell on** bewitch, enchant, entrance, curse, jinx; *N. Amer.* hex.

spell[3] *noun* **1 period**, time, interval, season, stretch, run; *Brit. informal* patch. **2 bout**, fit, attack.

spellbound *adjective* **enthralled**, fascinated, rapt, riveted, transfixed, gripped, captivated, bewitched, enchanted, mesmerized, hypnotized.

spend *verb* **1 pay out**, expend, disburse; *informal* lay out, blow, splurge. **2 pass**, occupy, fill, take up, while away.

sphere *noun* **1 globe**, ball, orb, bubble. **2** *his sphere of influence* **area**, field, compass, orbit, range, scope, extent. **3 domain**, realm, province, field, area, territory, arena, department.

spice *noun* **1 seasoning**, flavouring, condiment. **2 excitement**, interest, colour, piquancy, zest, an edge.

spicy *adjective* **hot**, tangy, peppery, piquant, spiced, highly seasoned, pungent.
- OPPOSITES bland.

spike *noun* **prong**, pin, barb, point, skewer, stake, spit.

spill *verb* **1 knock over**, tip over, upset, overturn. **2 overflow**, brim over, run over, pour, slop, slosh, splash, leak.

spin *verb* **1 revolve**, rotate, turn, go round, whirl, twirl, gyrate. **2** *she spun round to face him* **whirl**, wheel, turn, swing, twist, swivel, pivot.
● *noun* **1 rotation**, revolution, turn, whirl, twirl, gyration. **2 slant**, angle, twist, bias. **3 trip**, jaunt, outing, excursion, journey, drive, ride, run, turn; *informal* tootle.

spine *noun* **1 backbone**, spinal column, back. **2 needle**, quill, bristle, barb, spike, prickle, thorn.

WORD LINKS
vertebral relating to the spine

spiral *adjective* **coiled**, helical, curling, winding, twisting.
● *noun* **coil**, curl, twist, whorl, scroll, helix, corkscrew.
● *verb smoke spiralled up* **coil**, wind, swirl, twist, snake.

spirit *noun* **1 soul**, psyche, inner self, mind. **2 ghost**, phantom, spectre, apparition, presence. **3 mood**, frame/state of mind, humour, temper, morale, esprit de corps. **4 ethos**, essence, atmosphere, mood, feeling, climate. **5 enthusiasm**, energy, verve, vigour, dynamism, dash, sparkle, exuberance, gusto, fervour, zeal, fire, passion; *informal* get-up-and-go.
– OPPOSITES body, flesh.

spirited *adjective* **lively**, energetic, enthusiastic, vigorous, dynamic, passionate; *informal* feisty, gutsy; *N. Amer. informal* peppy.
– OPPOSITES apathetic, lifeless.

spiritual *adjective* **1 inner**, mental, psychological, incorporeal, non-material. **2 religious**, sacred, divine, holy, devotional.
– OPPOSITES physical, secular.

spit *verb* **expectorate**, hawk; *Brit. informal* gob.
● *noun* **spittle**, saliva, sputum, slobber, dribble.

spite *noun* **malice**, malevolence, ill will, vindictiveness, meanness, nastiness; *informal* bitchiness, cattiness.
● *verb* **upset**, hurt, wound.
– OPPOSITES please.
□ **in spite of** despite, notwithstanding, regardless of, in defiance of, in the face of.

spiteful *adjective* **malicious**, malevolent, vindictive, vengeful, mean, nasty, hurtful, mischievous, cruel, unkind; *informal* bitchy, catty.
– OPPOSITES benevolent.

splash *verb* **1 sprinkle**, spatter, splatter, spray, shower, wash, squirt, slosh, slop. **2 wash**, break, lap, pound. **3 paddle**, wade, wallow.

splendid *adjective* **1 magnificent**, sumptuous, grand, imposing, superb, spectacular, resplendent, rich, lavish, ornate, gorgeous, glorious, dazzling, handsome, beautiful; *informal* plush; *Brit. informal* swish. **2** *(informal)* **excellent**, wonderful, marvellous, superb, glorious, lovely, delightful, first-class; *informal* super, great, amazing, fantastic, terrific, tremendous; *Brit. informal* smashing, brilliant.
– OPPOSITES simple, modest, inferior.

splendour *noun* **magnificence**, sumptuousness, grandeur, resplendence, richness, glory, majesty.
– OPPOSITES simplicity.

splinter *noun* **sliver**, chip, shard, fragment, shred; *Scottish* skelf.
● *verb* **shatter**, smash, break into smithereens, fracture, split, crack, disintegrate.

split *verb* **1 break**, cut, burst, snap, crack, splinter, fracture, rupture, come apart. **2 tear**, rip, slash, slit. **3 share**, divide up, distribute, dole out, parcel out, carve up, slice up, apportion. **4 fork**, divide, branch, diverge. **5** *the band split up last year* **break up**, separate, part, part company, go their separate ways.
– OPPOSITES join, unite, converge.
● *noun* **1 crack**, fissure, cleft, crevice, break, fracture, breach. **2 rip**, tear, cut, rent, slash, slit. **3 division**, rift, breach, schism, rupture, separation, estrangement. **4 break-up**, split-up, separation, parting, estrangement, rift.
– OPPOSITES merger.

spoil *verb* **1 damage**, ruin, impair, blemish, disfigure, blight, deface, harm, destroy, wreck. **2** *rain spoiled my plans* **upset**, mess up, ruin, wreck, undo, sabotage, scotch, torpedo; *informal* muck up, screw up, do for; *Brit. informal* scupper. **3 overindulge**, pamper, indulge, mollycoddle, cosset, wait on someone hand and foot. **4 go bad**, go off, go rancid, turn, go sour, rot, decompose, decay, perish.
- OPPOSITES improve, enhance.

spoilsport *noun* **killjoy**, dog in the manger, misery; *informal* wet blanket, party-pooper.

spoken *adjective* **verbal**, oral, vocal, unwritten, word-of-mouth.

spokesperson, **spokesman**, **spokeswoman** *noun* **representative**, voice, mouthpiece, agent, official; *informal* spin doctor.

sponsor *noun* **backer**, patron, promoter, benefactor, supporter, contributor.
● *verb* **finance**, fund, subsidize, back, promote, support, contribute to; *N. Amer. informal* bankroll.

spontaneous *adjective* **1 unplanned**, unpremeditated, impulsive, impromptu, spur-of-the-moment, unprompted; *informal* off-the-cuff. **2 natural**, uninhibited, relaxed, unselfconscious, unaffected.

sporadic *adjective* **occasional**, infrequent, irregular, periodic, scattered, patchy, isolated, odd, intermittent, spasmodic, fitful, desultory, erratic, unpredictable.
- OPPOSITES frequent, continuous.

sport *noun* **game**, physical recreation.
● *verb* **wear**, have on, dress in, show off, parade, flaunt.

sporting *adjective* **sportsmanlike**, generous, considerate, fair; *Brit. informal* decent.

sporty *adjective (informal)* **athletic**, fit, active, energetic.

spot *noun* **1 mark**, patch, dot, fleck, smudge, smear, stain, blotch, splash; *informal* splotch, splodge. **2 pimple**, pustule, blackhead, boil, blemish; *informal* zit; *Scottish informal* plook; (**spots**) acne, rash. **3 place**, site, position, situation, setting, location, venue.
● *verb* **see**, notice, observe, catch sight of, detect, make out, discern, recognize, identify, locate; *Brit. informal* clock; *literary* espy, descry.

spotless *adjective* **clean**, pristine, immaculate, shining, shiny, gleaming, spick and span.
- OPPOSITES filthy.

spotlight *noun* **attention**, glare of publicity, limelight, public eye.

spotted *adjective* **spotty**, dotted, polka-dot, freckled, mottled.

spotty *adjective* **1 polka-dot**, spotted, dotted. **2** *(Brit.)* **pimply**, pimpled, acned; *Scottish informal* plooky.

spouse *noun* **partner**, husband, wife, mate, consort; *informal* better half; *Brit. informal* other half.

sprawl *verb* **stretch out**, lounge, loll, slump, flop, slouch.

spray *noun* **1 shower**, sprinkle, jet, squirt, mist, spume, foam, froth, spindrift. **2 aerosol**, vaporizer, atomizer, sprinkler.
● *verb* **1 sprinkle**, dribble, drizzle, water, soak, douse, drench. **2 spout**, jet, gush, spurt, shoot, squirt.

spread *verb* **1 lay out**, open out, unfurl, unroll, roll out, straighten out, fan out, stretch out, extend. **2** *the landscape spread out below* **extend**, stretch, sprawl. **3 scatter**, strew, disperse, distribute. **4 circulate**, broadcast, put about, publicize, propagate, repeat. **5 travel**, move, be borne, sweep, diffuse, reproduce, be passed on, be transmitted. **6 smear**, daub, plaster, apply, rub.
● *noun* **1 expansion**, proliferation, dissemination, diffusion, transmission, propagation. **2 span**, width, extent, stretch, reach.

spree *noun* **bout**, orgy; *informal* binge, splurge.

spring *verb* **leap**, jump, bound, vault, hop.
● *noun* **springiness**, bounce, resilience, elasticity, flexibility, stretch, stretchiness, give.
□ **spring from** originate from, have its origins in, derive from, arise in, stem from, emanate from, evolve from.

WORD LINKS
vernal relating to the season of spring

sprinkle *verb* **splash**, trickle, drizzle, spray, shower, drip, scatter, strew, dredge, dust.

sprint *verb* **run**, race, rush, dash, bolt, fly, charge, shoot, speed; *informal* hotfoot it, leg it.
- OPPOSITES stroll.

sprout *verb* **1 germinate**, put/send out shoots, bud. **2 spring**, come up, grow, develop, appear.

spruce *adjective* **neat**, well groomed, well turned out, well dressed, smart, trim, dapper; *informal* natty, snazzy.
- OPPOSITES dishevelled.
□ **spruce up** smarten up, tidy up, clean, groom; *informal* do up, titivate; *Brit. informal* tart up; *N. Amer. informal* gussy up.

spur *noun* **stimulus**, incentive, encouragement, inducement, impetus, motivation.
- OPPOSITES disincentive.
● *verb* **stimulate**, encourage, prompt, prod, impel, motivate, move, galvanize, inspire, drive.
- OPPOSITES discourage.

spurious *adjective* **bogus**, fake, false, fraudulent, sham, artificial, imitation, simulated, feigned; *informal* phoney.
- OPPOSITES genuine.

spurn *verb* **reject**, rebuff, scorn, turn down, treat with contempt, disdain, look down your nose at; *informal* turn your nose up at.
- OPPOSITES welcome, accept.

spurt *verb* **squirt**, shoot, jet, erupt, gush, pour, stream, pump, surge, spew, course, well, spring, burst, spout.
● *noun* **squirt**, jet, gush, stream, rush, surge, flood, cascade, torrent.

spy *noun* **agent**, mole, plant; *N. Amer. informal* spook.
● *verb* **notice**, observe, see, spot, sight, catch sight of, glimpse, make out, discern, detect.
□ **spy on** observe, keep under surveillance, eavesdrop on, watch, bug.

spying *noun* **espionage**, intelligence gathering, surveillance, infiltration.

squabble *noun* **quarrel**, disagreement, row, argument, dispute, wrangle, clash, altercation; *informal* tiff, set-to, run-in, scrap, dust-up; *Brit. informal* barney, ding-dong.
● *verb* **quarrel**, row, argue, bicker, disagree; *informal* scrap.

squad *noun* **1 team**, crew, gang, force. **2 detachment**, detail, unit, platoon, battery, troop, patrol, squadron, commando.

squalid *adjective* **1 dirty**, filthy, dingy, grubby, grimy, wretched, miserable, mean, seedy, shabby, sordid, insalubrious; *Brit. informal* grotty. **2 improper**, sordid, unseemly, unsavoury, sleazy, cheap, base, low, corrupt, dishonest, dishonourable, disreputable, discreditable, contemptible, shameful.
- OPPOSITES clean.

squander *verb* **waste**, throw away, misuse, misspend, fritter away, spend like water; *informal* blow, run through, splurge, pour down the drain.
- OPPOSITES save.

square *noun* **piazza**, plaza, quadrangle.
● *adjective* **level**, even, drawn, equal, tied, level pegging; *informal* even-steven(s).

squash *verb* **1 crush**, squeeze, mash, pulp, flatten, compress, distort, pound, trample. **2 force**, ram, thrust, push, cram, jam, stuff, pack, squeeze, wedge.

squeak *noun* & *verb* **peep**, cheep, squeal, tweet, yelp, whimper.

squeeze *verb* **1 compress**, press, crush, squash, pinch, nip, grasp, grip, clutch. **2 extract**, press, force, express.

3 force, thrust, cram, ram, jam, stuff, pack, wedge, press, push, squash, crush, crowd, force your way.
● *noun* **1 press**, pinch, nip, grasp, grip, clutch, hug. **2 crush**, jam, squash, congestion.

squirm *verb* **1 wriggle**, wiggle, writhe, twist, slither, fidget, twitch, toss and turn. **2 wince**, shudder.

squirt *verb* **1 spurt**, shoot, spray, jet, erupt, gush, rush, pump, surge, stream, spew, well, issue, emanate. **2 splash**, spray, shower, sprinkle.

stab *verb* **knife**, run through, skewer, spear, gore, spike, impale.
● *noun* **1** *a stab of pain* **twinge**, pang, throb, spasm, cramp, prick. **2** *(informal)* **attempt**, try, endeavour, effort; *informal* go, shot, crack, bash.

stability *noun* **1 firmness**, solidity, steadiness. **2 balance (of mind)**, (mental) health, sanity, reason. **3 strength**, durability, lasting nature, permanence.

stable *adjective* **1 firm**, solid, steady, secure. **2 well balanced**, well adjusted, of sound mind, compos mentis, sane, normal, rational, reasonable, sensible. **3** *a stable relationship* **secure**, solid, strong, steady, firm, sure, steadfast, established, enduring, lasting.
- OPPOSITES unstable.

stack *noun* **heap**, pile, mound, mountain, pyramid, tower.
● *verb* **1 heap (up)**, pile (up), assemble, put together, collect. **2 load**, fill (up), pack, charge, stuff, cram, stock.

S

staff *noun* **1 employees**, workers, workforce, personnel, human resources, manpower, labour. **2 stick**, stave, pole, rod.
● *verb* **man**, people, crew, work, operate.

stage *noun* **1 phase**, period, juncture, step, point, level. **2 part**, section, portion, stretch, leg, lap, circuit. **3 platform**, dais, stand, rostrum, podium.

stagger *verb* **1 lurch**, reel, sway, teeter, totter, stumble. **2 amaze**, astound, astonish, surprise, stun, confound, daze, take aback; *informal* flabbergast; *Brit. informal* knock for six.

stagnant *adjective* **1 still**, motionless, standing, stale, dirty, brackish. **2 inactive**, sluggish, slow-moving, static, flat, depressed, moribund, dead, dormant.
- OPPOSITES flowing.

staid *adjective* **sedate**, respectable, serious, steady, conventional, traditional, unadventurous, set in your ways, sober, formal, stuffy, stiff; *informal* starchy, stick-in-the-mud.
- OPPOSITES frivolous.

stain *verb* **1 discolour**, soil, mark, spot, spatter, splatter, smear, splash, smudge, begrime. **2 colour**, tint, dye, paint.
● *noun* **1 mark**, spot, blotch, smudge, smear. **2 blemish**, taint, blot, smear, slur, stigma.

stake[1] *noun* **post**, pole, stick, spike, upright, support, cane.

stake[2] *noun* **1 bet**, wager, ante. **2 share**, interest, investment, involvement, concern.
● *verb* **bet**, wager, lay, put on, gamble, risk.

stale *adjective* **1 old**, past its best, off, dry, hard, musty, mouldy, rancid. **2 stuffy**, musty, fusty, stagnant. **3 overused**, hackneyed, tired, worn out, overworked, threadbare, banal, clichéd, trite, unimaginative, uninspired, flat; *informal* old hat; *N. Amer.* played out.
- OPPOSITES fresh.

stalemate *noun* **deadlock**, impasse, stand-off, gridlock.

stalk *verb* **1 trail**, follow, shadow, track, go after, hunt; *informal* tail. **2 strut**, stride, march, flounce, storm, stomp, sweep.

stall *noun* **1 stand**, table, counter, booth, kiosk. **2 pen**, coop, sty, corral, enclosure, compartment.
● *verb* **1 delay**, play for time, procrastinate, hedge, drag your feet, filibuster, stonewall. **2 hold off**, stave off, keep at bay, evade, avoid.

stalwart *adjective* **staunch**, loyal, faithful, committed, devoted, dedicated, dependable, reliable.
– OPPOSITES disloyal.

stamina *noun* **endurance**, staying power, energy, toughness, determination, tenacity, perseverance, grit.

stammer *verb* **stutter**, stumble over your words, hesitate, falter, pause, splutter.

stamp *verb* **1 trample**, step, tread, tramp, stomp, stump, clump, crush, squash, flatten. **2 imprint**, print, impress, punch, inscribe, emboss.
● *noun* **mark**, hallmark, sign, seal, sure sign, smack, savour, air.
□ **stamp out** put an end to, end, stop, crush, put down, curb, quell, suppress, extinguish, stifle, abolish, get rid of, eliminate, eradicate, destroy, wipe out.

stance *noun* **1 posture**, body position, pose, attitude. **2 attitude**, opinion, standpoint, position, approach, policy, line.

stand *verb* **1 rise**, get to your feet, get up, pick yourself up. **2 be situated**, be located, be positioned, be sited. **3 put**, set, erect, place, position, prop, install, arrange; *informal* park. **4 remain in force**, remain in operation, hold, hold good, apply, be the case, exist, prevail. **5 withstand**, endure, bear, put up with, take, cope with, handle, sustain, resist, stand up to. **6** *(informal)* **put up with**, endure, tolerate, accept, take, abide, stand for, support, countenance; *formal* brook.
– OPPOSITES sit, lie down.
● *noun* **1 attitude**, stance, opinion, standpoint, position, approach, policy, line. **2 opposition**, resistance. **3 base**, support, platform, stage, dais, rest, plinth, tripod, rack, trivet. **4 stall**, counter, booth, kiosk.
□ **stand by 1** wait, be prepared, be ready for action, be on full alert, wait in the wings. **2** support, stick with/by, remain loyal to, stand up for, back up, defend, stick up for. **3** abide by, keep (to), adhere to, hold to, stick to, observe, comply with. **stand for** mean, be short for, represent, signify, denote, symbolize. **stand in** deputize, act, substitute, fill in, take over, cover, hold the fort, step into the breach, replace, relieve. **stand out** be noticeable, be visible, be obvious, be conspicuous, stick out, attract attention; *informal* stick/stand out a mile, stick/stand out like a sore thumb.

standard *noun* **1 quality**, level, calibre, merit, excellence. **2 guideline**, norm, yardstick, benchmark, gauge, measure, criterion, guide, touchstone, model, pattern. **3 principle**, ideal; (**standards**) morals, code of behaviour, ethics. **4 flag**, banner, ensign, colour(s).
● *adjective* **1 normal**, usual, average, typical, stock, common, ordinary, customary, conventional, established. **2 definitive**, classic, recognized, accepted, approved, authoritative.
– OPPOSITES unusual, special.

standing *noun* **1 status**, ranking, position, reputation, stature. **2 prestige**, rank, eminence, seniority, repute, stature, esteem, importance, account.

staple *adjective* **main**, principal, chief, major, primary, leading, foremost, first, most important, predominant, dominant, basic, prime; *informal* number-one.

star *noun* **1 heavenly body**, celestial body. **2 principal**, leading lady/man, lead, hero, heroine. **3 celebrity**, superstar, famous name, household name, leading light, VIP, personality, luminary; *informal* celeb, big shot, megastar.
● *adjective* **1 outstanding**, exceptional. **2 top**, leading, greatest, foremost, major, pre-eminent.

WORD LINKS
astral, **stellar** relating to stars
astronomy study of stars

stare *verb* **gaze**, gape, goggle, glare, ogle, peer; *informal* gawk; *Brit. informal* gawp.

stark *adjective* **1 sharp**, sharply defined, crisp, distinct, clear, clear-cut.

2 desolate, bare, barren, empty, bleak, dreary, depressing, grim.
- OPPOSITES indistinct, ornate.
● *adverb stark naked* **completely**, totally, utterly, absolutely, entirely, wholly, fully, quite, altogether, thoroughly.

start *verb* **1 begin**, commence, get under way, get going, go ahead, make a start; *informal* kick off, get the ball rolling, get the show on the road. **2 come into being**, begin, arise, originate, develop. **3 establish**, set up, found, create, bring into being, institute, initiate, inaugurate, introduce, open, launch. **4 activate**, switch/turn on, start up, fire up, boot up. **5 flinch**, jerk, jump, twitch, wince.
- OPPOSITES end, finish, stop.
● *noun* **1 beginning**, commencement, inception, onset, inauguration, dawn, birth, emergence; *informal* kick-off. **2 lead**, head start, advantage. **3 jerk**, twitch, spasm, jump.
- OPPOSITES end.

startle *verb* **surprise**, frighten, scare, alarm, shock, give someone a fright, make someone jump.

starving *adjective* **hungry**, undernourished, malnourished, starved, ravenous, famished.
- OPPOSITES full.

state[1] *noun* **1 condition**, shape, position, situation, circumstances, state of affairs, predicament, plight. **2 country**, nation, land, kingdom, realm, power, republic. **3 government**, parliament, administration, regime. **4 state of anxiety**, panic, fluster; *informal* flap, tizzy.

state[2] *verb* **express**, voice, utter, put into words, declare, announce, make known, put across/over, communicate, air.

stately *adjective* **dignified**, majestic, ceremonious, courtly, imposing, solemn, regal, grand.
- OPPOSITES undignified.

statement *noun* **declaration**, expression, affirmation, assertion, announcement, utterance, communication, bulletin, communiqué.

static *adjective* **1 unchanged**, fixed, stable, steady, unchanging, unvarying, constant. **2 stationary**, motionless, immobile, unmoving, still, at a standstill.
- OPPOSITES variable, dynamic.

station *noun* **1 establishment**, base, camp, post, depot, mission, site, facility, installation. **2 office**, depot, base, headquarters. **3 channel**, wavelength.
● *verb* **base**, post, establish, deploy, garrison.

stationary *adjective* **static**, parked, motionless, immobile, still, stock-still, at a standstill, at rest.
- OPPOSITES moving.

stature *noun* **1 height**, size, build. **2 reputation**, repute, standing, status, position, prestige, distinction, eminence, prominence, importance.

status *noun* **1 standing**, rank, position, level, place. **2 prestige**, kudos, cachet, standing, stature, esteem, image, importance, authority, fame.

staunch[1] *adjective* **stalwart**, loyal, faithful, committed, devoted, dedicated, reliable.
- OPPOSITES disloyal, unfaithful.

staunch[2] *verb* **stem**, stop, halt, check, curb; *N. Amer.* stanch.

stay *verb* **1 remain (behind)**, wait, linger, stick, be left, hold on, hang on; *informal* hang around; *Brit. informal* hang about; *old use* tarry. **2 continue (to be)**, remain, keep, carry on being. **3 visit**, stop (off/over), holiday, lodge; *N. Amer.* vacation.
- OPPOSITES leave.
● *noun* **visit**, stop, stopover, break, holiday; *N. Amer.* vacation; *literary* sojourn.

steady *adjective* **1 stable**, firm, fixed, secure. **2 still**, motionless, static, stationary, unmoving. **3** *a steady gaze* **fixed**, intent, unwavering, unfaltering. **4** *steady breathing* **constant**, consistent, regular, even, rhythmic. **5 continuous**, continual, unceasing, ceaseless,

perpetual, unremitting, endless. **6 regular**, settled, firm, committed, long-term.
- OPPOSITES unstable, shaky, fluctuating.
● *verb* **1 stabilize**, hold steady, brace, support, balance, rest. **2 calm**, soothe, quieten, compose, settle, subdue, quell.

steal *verb* **1 take**, thieve, help yourself to, pilfer, embezzle; *informal* swipe, lift, filch; *Brit. informal* nick, pinch, knock off; *N. Amer. informal* heist. **2 plagiarize**, copy, pirate; *informal* rip off, lift, pinch, crib; *Brit. informal* nick. **3 creep**, sneak, slink, slip, glide, tiptoe, slope.

WORD LINKS
kleptomania compulsion to steal

stealth *noun* **furtiveness**, secretiveness, secrecy, surreptitiousness.

stealthy *adjective* **furtive**, secretive, secret, surreptitious, sneaky, sly; *Military* black.
- OPPOSITES open.

steep *adjective* **1 sheer**, precipitous, abrupt, sharp, perpendicular, vertical. **2** *a steep increase* **sharp**, sudden, dramatic, precipitate.
- OPPOSITES gentle, gradual.

steeped *adjective*
□ **steeped in** imbued with, filled with, permeated with, suffused with, soaked in, pervaded by.

steer *verb* **guide**, direct, manoeuvre, drive, pilot, navigate.

stem[1] *noun* **stalk**, shoot, trunk.
□ **stem from** come from, arise from, originate from, have its origins in, spring from, derive from.

stem[2] *verb* **stop**, staunch, halt, check, curb; *N. Amer.* stanch.

stench *noun* **stink**, reek; *Brit. informal* niff, pong, whiff; *N. Amer. informal* funk; *literary* miasma.

step *noun* **1 pace**, stride, footstep, footfall, tread, tramp. **2 stair**, tread; (**steps**) stairs, staircase, flight of stairs. **3 action**, act, course of action, measure, move, operation, procedure. **4 advance**, development, move, movement, breakthrough. **5 stage**, level, grade, rank, degree, phase.
● *verb* **walk**, move, tread, pace, stride.
□ **step down** resign, stand down, give up your post/job, bow out, abdicate; *informal* quit. **step in** intervene, become involved, intercede. **step up** increase, intensify, strengthen, escalate, speed up, accelerate; *informal* up, crank up.

stereotype *noun* **conventional idea**, standard image, cliché, formula.
● *verb* **typecast**, pigeonhole, conventionalize, categorize, label, tag.

sterile *adjective* **1 unproductive**, infertile, unfruitful, barren. **2 hygienic**, clean, pure, uncontaminated, sterilized, disinfected, germ-free, antiseptic.
- OPPOSITES fertile.

sterilize *verb* **1 disinfect**, fumigate, decontaminate, sanitize, clean, cleanse, purify. **2 neuter**, castrate, spay, geld; *N. Amer. & Austral.* alter; *Brit. informal* doctor.
- OPPOSITES contaminate.

stern *adjective* **1 unsmiling**, frowning, serious, severe, forbidding, grim, unfriendly, austere, dour. **2 strict**, severe, stringent, harsh, drastic, hard, tough, extreme, draconian.
- OPPOSITES genial, lax.

stick[1] *noun* **1 branch**, twig, switch. **2 walking stick**, cane, staff, crutch. **3 post**, pole, cane, stake, rod.

stick[2] *verb* **1 thrust**, push, insert, jab, poke, dig, plunge. **2 pierce**, penetrate, puncture, prick, stab. **3 adhere**, cling. **4** *stick the stamp there* **attach**, fasten, affix, fix, paste, glue, gum, tape. **5 jam**, get jammed, catch, get caught, get trapped. **6** *(Brit. informal)* **tolerate**, put up with, take, stand, stomach, endure, bear, abide.
□ **stick out 1** protrude, jut (out), project, stand out, extend, poke out, bulge. **2** be conspicuous, be obvious, stand out, leap out; *informal* stick out a mile. **stick to** abide by, keep, adhere to, hold to, comply with, fulfil, stand by. **stick up for** support, take someone's

side, take someone's part, side with, stand by, stand up for, defend.

sticky *adjective* **1 adhesive**, self-adhesive, gummed. **2 tacky**, gluey, gummy, treacly, glutinous, viscous; *informal* gooey. **3 humid**, muggy, close, sultry, steamy, sweaty, sweltering, oppressive. **4 awkward**, difficult, tricky, ticklish, delicate, embarrassing, sensitive; *informal* hairy.
- OPPOSITES dry, fresh, cool.

stiff *adjective* **1 rigid**, hard, firm, inelastic, unyielding, brittle. **2 thick**, firm, viscous, semi-solid. **3 aching**, achy, painful, arthritic; *informal* creaky. **4 formal**, reserved, wooden, forced, strained, stilted; *informal* starchy, uptight. **5** *stiff penalties* **harsh**, severe, heavy, stringent, drastic, draconian; *Brit.* swingeing. **6** *they put up a stiff resistance* **vigorous**, determined, strong, spirited, resolute, tenacious, dogged, stubborn. **7 difficult**, hard, arduous, tough, strenuous, laborious, exacting, tiring, demanding. **8 strong**, potent, alcoholic.
- OPPOSITES flexible, soft, limp.

stifle *verb* **1 smother**, check, restrain, keep back, hold back, hold in, withhold, choke back, muffle, suppress, curb. **2 suppress**, quash, quell, put an end to, put down, stop, extinguish, stamp out, crush, subdue, repress. **3 suffocate**, smother, asphyxiate, choke.

stigma *noun* **shame**, disgrace, dishonour, ignominy, humiliation, stain, taint.
- OPPOSITES honour.

S

still *adjective* **1 motionless**, unmoving, stock-still, immobile, rooted to the spot, transfixed, static, stationary. **2 quiet**, silent, calm, peaceful, serene, windless, noiseless, undisturbed, flat, smooth, like a millpond.
- OPPOSITES moving, noisy.

● *adverb* **1 even now**, yet. **2 nevertheless**, nonetheless, all the same, even so, but, however, despite that, in spite of that.

● *verb* **quieten**, quiet, silence, hush, calm, settle, pacify, subdue.

stimulate *verb* **encourage**, prompt, motivate, trigger, spark, spur on, galvanize, fire, inspire, excite; *N. Amer.* light a fire under.
- OPPOSITES discourage.

stimulating *adjective* **thought-provoking**, interesting, inspiring, inspirational, lively, exciting, provocative.
- OPPOSITES uninspiring, boring.

stimulus *noun* **motivation**, encouragement, impetus, prompt, spur, inducement, incentive, inspiration, fillip; *informal* shot in the arm.
- OPPOSITES deterrent.

sting *noun* **1 prick**, wound, injury. **2 pain**, pricking, smarting, soreness, hurt, irritation.

● *verb* **1 prick**, wound. **2 smart**, burn, hurt, be irritated, be sore. **3** *the criticism stung her* **upset**, wound, hurt, distress, pain, mortify.

stink *verb* **reek**, smell.

● *noun* **stench**, reek; *Brit. informal* pong; *N. Amer. informal* funk.

stint *noun* **spell**, stretch, turn, session, term, time, shift, tour of duty.

stipulate *verb* **specify**, set out, lay down, demand, require, insist on.

stir *verb* **1 mix**, blend, beat, whip, whisk, fold in; *N. Amer.* muddle. **2 move**, get up, get out of bed, rise, rouse yourself, bestir yourself. **3 disturb**, rustle, shake, move, agitate. **4** *the war stirred him to action* **spur**, drive, rouse, prompt, propel, motivate, encourage, urge, impel, provoke, goad.

● *noun* **commotion**, disturbance, fuss, excitement, sensation; *informal* to-do, hoo-ha.

stock *noun* **1 merchandise**, goods, wares. **2 store**, supply, stockpile, reserve, hoard, cache, bank. **3 animals**, livestock, beasts, flocks, herds. **4 descent**, ancestry, origin(s), lineage, birth, extraction, family, blood, pedigree.

● *adjective* **usual**, routine, predictable, set, standard, staple, customary, familiar, conventional, traditional, stereotyped, clichéd, hackneyed,

unoriginal, formulaic.
- OPPOSITES unusual, original.
● *verb* **sell**, carry, keep (in stock), offer, supply, provide, furnish.

stockpile *noun* **stock**, store, supply, collection, reserve, hoard, cache; *informal* stash.
● *verb* **store up**, amass, accumulate, stock up on, hoard, cache, collect, lay in, put away, put/set aside, put by, stow away, save; *informal* salt away, stash away.

stocky *adjective* **thickset**, sturdy, heavily built, chunky, burly, strapping, brawny, solid, heavy, hefty, beefy.
- OPPOSITES slender.

stomach *noun* **1 abdomen**, middle, belly, gut, paunch; *informal* tummy, insides, pot, spare tyre. **2 appetite**, taste, inclination, desire, wish.
● *verb* **tolerate**, put up with, take, stand, endure, bear; *informal* hack, abide; *Brit. informal* stick.

WORD LINKS
gastric relating to the stomach

stone *noun* **1 rock**, pebble, boulder. **2 gem**, gemstone, jewel; *informal* rock, sparkler. **3 kernel**, seed, pip, pit.

WORD LINKS
lapidary relating to stone

stoop *verb* **bend**, lean, crouch, bow, duck.

stop *verb* **1 end**, halt, finish, terminate, wind up, bring to a stop/halt, discontinue, cut short, interrupt, nip in the bud, shut down. **2** *he stopped smoking* **cease**, refrain from, discontinue, desist from, break off, give up, abandon, cut out; *informal* quit, pack in; *Brit. informal* jack in. **3 pull up**, draw up, come to a stop/halt, come to rest, pull in/over. **4** *the music stopped* **come to an end**, draw to a close, end, cease, halt, finish, be over, conclude. **5 prevent**, obstruct, impede, block, bar, preclude, dissuade from.
- OPPOSITES start, begin, continue.
● *noun* **1 halt**, end, finish, cessation, close, conclusion, termination, standstill. **2 break**, stopover, stop-off, stay, visit; *literary* sojourn. **3 stopping place**, station, halt.

store *noun* **1 stock**, supply, stockpile, hoard, cache, reserve, bank, pool; *informal* stash. **2 storeroom**, storehouse, repository, stockroom, depot, depository, warehouse. **3** *ship's stores* **supplies**, provisions, stocks, food, rations, materials, equipment, hardware. **4 shop**, emporium, (retail) outlet, boutique, department store, supermarket, hypermarket, superstore, megastore; *N. Amer.* mart.
● *verb* **keep**, stockpile, stock up with, lay in, set aside, put aside, put away/by, save, collect, accumulate, amass, hoard; *informal* squirrel away, salt away, stash.
- OPPOSITES use, discard.

storehouse *noun* **warehouse**, depository, repository, store, storeroom, depot.

storm *noun* **1 tempest**, squall, gale, hurricane, tornado, cyclone, typhoon, thunderstorm, rainstorm, monsoon, hailstorm, snowstorm, blizzard. **2 uproar**, outcry, fuss, furore, rumpus, trouble; *informal* to-do, hoo-ha, ructions, stink; *Brit. informal* row.
● *verb* **1 stride**, march, stomp, stamp, stalk, flounce, fling. **2 attack**, charge, rush, swoop on.

stormy *adjective* **1 blustery**, squally, windy, gusty, blowy, thundery, wild, violent, rough, foul. **2 angry**, heated, fierce, furious, passionate, acrimonious.
- OPPOSITES calm, peaceful.

story *noun* **1 tale**, narrative, account, history, anecdote, saga; *informal* yarn. **2 plot**, storyline, scenario. **3 news**, report, item, article, feature, piece. **4 rumour**, whisper, allegation, speculation, gossip.

stout *adjective* **1 fat**, big, plump, portly, rotund, dumpy, corpulent, thickset, burly, bulky; *informal* tubby; *Brit. informal* podgy; *N. Amer. informal* zaftig, corn-fed. **2 strong**, sturdy, solid, robust, tough, durable, hard-wearing.

3 determined, vigorous, forceful, spirited, committed, brave, fearless, valiant, gallant, bold, plucky; *informal* gutsy.
- OPPOSITES thin, flimsy.

straight *adjective* **1 direct**, linear, unswerving, undeviating. **2 level**, even, in line, aligned, square, vertical, upright, perpendicular, horizontal. **3 in order**, tidy, neat, shipshape, spick and span, orderly, organized, arranged, sorted out, straightened out. **4 honest**, direct, frank, candid, truthful, sincere, forthright, straightforward, plain-spoken, blunt, unambiguous; *informal* upfront. **5 undiluted**, neat, pure; *N. Amer. informal* straight up.
- OPPOSITES winding, crooked.
● *adverb* **1 right**, directly, squarely, full; *informal* smack, (slap) bang; *N. Amer. informal* smack dab. **2 frankly**, directly, candidly, honestly, forthrightly, plainly, point-blank, bluntly, flatly; *Brit. informal* straight up. **3 logically**, rationally, clearly, lucidly, coherently, cogently.
□ **straight away** at once, right away, (right) now, this/that (very) minute, this/that instant, immediately, instantly, directly, forthwith, then and there; *N. Amer.* in short order; *informal* straight off, pronto; *N. Amer. informal* lickety-split.

straighten *verb* **1 put straight**, adjust, put in order, arrange, rearrange, tidy, neaten. **2** *we must straighten things out with him* **put right**, sort out, clear up, settle, resolve, rectify, remedy; *informal* patch up.

S

straightforward *adjective* **1 uncomplicated**, easy, simple, plain sailing, elementary, undemanding. **2 honest**, frank, candid, open, truthful, sincere, on the level, forthright, plain-speaking, direct; *informal* upfront; *N. Amer. informal* on the up and up.
- OPPOSITES complicated, devious.

strain[1] *verb* **1 overtax**, overwork, overextend, overreach, overdo it, exhaust, wear out; *informal* knacker, knock yourself out. **2 injure**, damage, pull, wrench, twist, sprain. **3 sieve**, sift, filter, screen.
● *noun* **1 tension**, tightness, tautness. **2 injury**, sprain, wrench, twist. **3 pressure**, demands, burdens, stress; *informal* hassle. **4 stress**, (nervous) tension, exhaustion, fatigue, pressure, overwork.

strain[2] *noun* **variety**, kind, type, sort, breed, genus.

strained *adjective* **1 awkward**, tense, uneasy, uncomfortable, edgy, difficult, troubled. **2 forced**, unnatural, artificial, insincere, false, affected, put-on.

strait *noun* **1 channel**, sound, narrows, stretch of water. **2** (**straits**) **difficulty**, trouble, crisis, mess, predicament, plight; *informal* hot water, jam, hole, fix, scrape.

strand *noun* **thread**, filament, fibre, length.

stranded *adjective* **1 shipwrecked**, wrecked, marooned, grounded, aground, beached. **2 helpless**, abandoned, forsaken, left high and dry, left in the lurch.

strange *adjective* **1 unusual**, odd, curious, peculiar, funny, queer, bizarre, weird, uncanny, surprising, unexpected, anomalous, atypical; *informal* fishy. **2 unfamiliar**, unknown, new, novel.
- OPPOSITES ordinary, familiar.

stranger *noun* **newcomer**, new arrival, visitor, guest, outsider, foreigner.

strangle *verb* **throttle**, choke, garrotte, asphyxiate.

strap *noun* **belt**, tie, band, thong.
● *verb* **tie**, lash, secure, fasten, bind, make fast, truss.

strapping *adjective* **big**, strong, well built, brawny, burly, muscular; *informal* beefy.

strategic *adjective* **planned**, calculated, deliberate, tactical, judicious, prudent, shrewd.

strategy *noun* **plan**, grand design, game plan, policy, programme, scheme.

stray *verb* **1 wander off**, go astray, get separated, get lost, drift away. **2 digress**, deviate, wander, get sidetracked, go off at a tangent, get off the subject.
● *adjective* **1 homeless**, lost, abandoned, feral. **2** *a stray bullet* **random**, chance, freak, unexpected, isolated.

streak *noun* **1 band**, line, strip, stripe, vein, slash, ray, smear. **2 element**, vein, strain, touch. **3 period**, spell, stretch, run; *Brit. informal* patch.
● *verb* **1 stripe**, band, fleck, smear, mark. **2 race**, speed, flash, shoot, dash, rush, hurtle, whizz, zoom, career, fly; *informal* belt, tear, zip, whip; *Brit. informal* bomb; *N. Amer. informal* barrel.

stream *noun* **1 brook**, rivulet, tributary; *Scottish & N. English* burn; *N. English* beck; *S. English* bourn; *N. Amer. & Austral./NZ* creek. **2 jet**, flow, rush, gush, surge, torrent, flood, cascade. **3 succession**, series, string.
● *verb* **1 flow**, pour, course, run, gush, surge, flood, cascade, spill. **2 pour**, surge, flood, swarm, pile, crowd.

streamlined *adjective* **1 aerodynamic**, smooth, sleek, elegant. **2 efficient**, smooth-running, well run, well oiled, slick.

street *noun* **road**, thoroughfare, avenue, drive, boulevard, lane; *N. Amer.* highway.

strength *noun* **1 power**, muscle, might, brawn, muscularity, robustness, sturdiness, vigour, stamina. **2 fortitude**, resilience, spirit, backbone, courage, bravery, pluck, grit; *informal* guts. **3** *strength of feeling* **intensity**, vehemence, force, depth. **4** *the strength of their argument* **force**, weight, power, persuasiveness, soundness, cogency, validity. **5 strong point**, advantage, asset, forte, aptitude, talent, skill, speciality.
– OPPOSITES weakness.

strengthen *verb* **1 make strong**, make stronger, build up, harden, toughen. **2 grow strong**, grow stronger, gain strength, intensify, pick up. **3 reinforce**, support, back up, bolster, authenticate, confirm, substantiate, corroborate.
– OPPOSITES weaken.

strenuous *adjective* **1 difficult**, arduous, hard, tough, taxing, demanding, exacting, exhausting, tiring, gruelling, back-breaking; *Brit. informal* knackering. **2 vigorous**, energetic, forceful, strong, spirited, intense, determined, resolute, dogged.
– OPPOSITES easy, half-hearted.

stress *noun* **1 strain**, pressure, (nervous) tension, worry, anxiety, trouble, difficulty; *informal* hassle. **2 emphasis**, importance, weight, accent, accentuation.
● *verb* **1 emphasize**, draw attention to, underline, underscore, point up, highlight, accentuate. **2 overstretch**, overtax, pressurize, pressure, push to the limit, worry, harass; *informal* hassle.
– OPPOSITES play down.

stressful *adjective* **demanding**, trying, taxing, difficult, hard, tough, fraught, traumatic, tense, frustrating.
– OPPOSITES relaxing.

stretch *verb* **1 expand**, give, be elastic, be stretchy, be tensile. **2 pull (out)**, draw out, extend, lengthen, elongate, expand. **3 bend**, strain, distort, exaggerate, embellish. **4** *she stretched out her arm* **reach out**, hold out, extend, straighten (out). **5** *I stretched out on the sofa* **lie down**, recline, lean back, sprawl, lounge, loll. **6 extend**, spread, continue, go on.
– OPPOSITES shorten, contract.
● *noun* **1 expanse**, area, tract, belt, sweep, extent. **2 period**, time, spell, run, stint, session, shift.

strict *adjective* **1 precise**, exact, literal, faithful, accurate, careful, scrupulous, meticulous, punctilious. **2 stringent**, rigorous, severe, harsh, hard, stern, rigid, tough, uncompromising, authoritarian, firm. **3** *in strict confidence* **absolute**, utter, complete, total.
– OPPOSITES loose, liberal.

stride *verb* & *noun* **step**, pace, march.

strife *noun* **conflict**, friction, discord, disagreement, dissension, dispute, argument, quarrelling.
- OPPOSITES peace.

strike *verb* **1 hit**, slap, smack, thump, punch, beat, bang; *informal* clout, wallop, belt, whack, thwack, bash, clobber, bop, biff; *Austral./NZ informal* quilt. **2 crash into**, collide with, hit, run into, bump into, smash into; *N. Amer.* impact. **3 occur to**, come to (mind), dawn on someone, hit, spring to mind, enter your head. **4** *you strike me as intelligent* **seem to**, appear to, give someone the impression of being. **5 take industrial action**, go on strike, down tools, walk out.
● *noun* **1 industrial action**, walkout. **2 attack**, assault, bombing.

striking *adjective* **1 noticeable**, obvious, conspicuous, visible, distinct, marked, unmistakable, strong, remarkable. **2 impressive**, imposing, magnificent, spectacular, breathtaking, marvellous, wonderful, stunning, sensational, dramatic.
- OPPOSITES unremarkable.

string *noun* **1 twine**, cord, yarn, thread. **2 series**, succession, chain, sequence, run, streak. **3 queue**, procession, line, file, column, convoy, train, cavalcade. **4 (strings) conditions**, qualifications, provisions, provisos, caveats, stipulations, riders, limitations, restrictions; *informal* catches.
● *verb* **hang**, suspend, sling, stretch, run, thread, loop, festoon.

S

stringent *adjective* **strict**, firm, rigid, rigorous, severe, harsh, tough, tight, exacting, demanding.
- OPPOSITES lax.

strip[1] *verb* **1 undress**, strip off, take your clothes off, disrobe. **2 dismantle**, disassemble, take to bits/pieces, take apart. **3 empty**, clear, clean out, plunder, rob, burgle, loot, pillage, ransack, sack.

strip[2] *noun* **(narrow) piece**, band, belt, ribbon, slip, shred, stretch.

strive *verb* **try (hard)**, attempt, endeavour, aim, make an effort, exert yourself, struggle, do your best, do all you can, do your utmost, labour, work, toil, strain; *informal* go all out, give it your best shot.

stroke *noun* **1 blow**, hit, slap, smack, thump, punch. **2 movement**, action, motion. **3 mark**, line. **4 thrombosis**, embolism, seizure; *dated* apoplexy.
● *verb* **caress**, fondle, pat, pet, touch, rub, massage, soothe.

stroll *verb* & *noun* **walk**, amble, wander, meander, ramble, promenade, saunter; *informal* mosey.

strong *adjective* **1 powerful**, sturdy, robust, athletic, fit, tough, rugged, strapping, well built, muscular, brawny, lusty, healthy. **2 forceful**, determined, spirited, assertive, self-assertive, tough, formidable, strong-minded, redoubtable; *informal* gutsy, feisty. **3 secure**, solid, well built, durable, hard-wearing, heavy-duty, tough, sturdy, well made, long-lasting. **4** *a strong supporter* **keen**, passionate, fervent, zealous, enthusiastic, eager, dedicated, loyal. **5** *strong feelings* **intense**, vehement, passionate, ardent, fervent, deep-seated. **6 forceful**, compelling, powerful, convincing, persuasive, sound, valid, cogent, well founded. **7 intense**, bright, brilliant, vivid, vibrant, dazzling, glaring. **8 highly flavoured**, mature, ripe, piquant, tangy, spicy. **9 concentrated**, undiluted. **10 alcoholic**, intoxicating, hard, stiff.
- OPPOSITES weak, gentle, mild.

stronghold *noun* **1 fortress**, fort, castle, citadel, garrison. **2** *a Tory stronghold* **bastion**, centre, hotbed.

structure *noun* **1 building**, edifice, construction, erection. **2 construction**, organization, system, arrangement, framework, form, formation, shape, composition, anatomy, make-up.
● *verb* **arrange**, organize, design, shape, construct, build.

struggle *verb* **1 strive**, try hard, endeavour, make every effort, exert yourself, do your best, do your utmost. **2 fight**, battle, grapple, wrestle, scuffle.

● *noun* **1 striving**, endeavour, effort, exertion, campaign, battle, drive, push. **2 fight**, scuffle, brawl, tussle, fracas; *informal* bust-up, set-to. **3** *a power struggle* **contest**, competition, fight, clash, rivalry, friction, feuding, conflict.

strut *verb* **swagger**, prance, parade, stride, sweep, flounce; *N. Amer. informal* sashay.

stubborn *adjective* **1 obstinate**, headstrong, wilful, strong-willed, pig-headed, mulish, inflexible, uncompromising, unbending, unyielding, obdurate, intractable, recalcitrant; *informal* stiff-necked. **2 indelible**, permanent, persistent, tenacious, resistant.

stuck *adjective* **1 fixed**, fastened, attached, glued, pinned. **2 jammed**, immovable. **3 baffled**, beaten, at a loss; *informal* stumped, up against a brick wall.

student *noun* **1 undergraduate**, scholar, pupil, schoolchild, schoolboy, schoolgirl. **2 trainee**, apprentice, probationer, novice, learner.

studio *noun* **workshop**, workroom, atelier.

studious *adjective* **scholarly**, academic, bookish, intellectual, erudite, learned, donnish; *informal* brainy.

study *noun* **1 learning**, education, schooling, scholarship, tuition, research. **2 investigation**, enquiry, research, examination, analysis, review, survey. **3 office**, workroom, studio.
● *verb* **1 work**, revise; *informal* swot, cram, mug up. **2 learn**, read up on, be taught. **3 investigate**, research, inquire into, look into, examine, analyse, survey. **4 scrutinize**, examine, inspect, consider, regard, look at, observe, watch, survey.

stuff *noun* **1 material**, substance, fabric, matter. **2 items**, articles, objects, goods, belongings, possessions, effects, paraphernalia; *informal* gear, kit, things, bits and pieces, odds and ends; *Brit. informal* clobber.
● *verb* **1 fill**, pack, pad, upholster. **2 shove**, thrust, push, ram, cram, squeeze, force, jam, pack, pile.

stuffing *noun* **padding**, wadding, filling, packing.

stuffy *adjective* **1 airless**, close, musty, stale, unventilated. **2 staid**, sedate, sober, priggish, strait-laced, conformist, conservative, old-fashioned; *informal* straight, starchy, fuddy-duddy.
– OPPOSITES airy.

stumble *verb* **1 trip**, lose your balance, lose your footing, slip. **2 stagger**, totter, blunder, hobble.
□ **stumble across/on** find, chance on, happen on, light on, come across/upon, discover, unearth, uncover; *informal* dig up.

stump *verb (informal)* **baffle**, perplex, puzzle, confound, defeat, put at a loss; *informal* flummox, fox, throw, floor.

stun *verb* **1 daze**, stupefy, knock out, lay out. **2 astound**, amaze, astonish, dumbfound, stupefy, stagger, shock, take aback; *informal* flabbergast, knock sideways.

stunning *adjective* **beautiful**, lovely, glorious, wonderful, marvellous, magnificent, superb, sublime, spectacular, fine, delightful; *informal* fantastic, terrific, tremendous, sensational, heavenly, divine, gorgeous, fabulous, awesome.
– OPPOSITES ordinary.

stunt *noun* **feat**, exploit, trick.

stunted *adjective* **small**, undersized, underdeveloped, diminutive.

stupid *adjective* **1 unintelligent**, dense, obtuse, foolish, idiotic, slow, simple-minded, brainless, mindless; *informal* thick, dim, dumb, dopey, dozy, moronic, cretinous; *Brit. informal* daft. **2 foolish**, silly, senseless, idiotic, ill-advised, ill-considered, unwise, nonsensical, ludicrous, ridiculous, laughable, fatuous, asinine, lunatic; *informal* crazy, half-baked, cockeyed, hare-brained, crackbrained; *Brit. informal* potty.
– OPPOSITES intelligent, sensible.

sturdy *adjective* **1 strapping**, well built, muscular, strong, hefty, brawny,

powerful, solid, burly; *informal* beefy. **2 robust**, strong, well built, solid, stout, tough, durable, long-lasting, hard-wearing.
- OPPOSITES feeble.

stutter *verb* **stammer**, stumble, falter, hesitate.

style *noun* **1 manner**, way, technique, method, methodology, approach, system, mode. **2 flair**, elegance, stylishness, chic, taste, grace, poise, polish, sophistication, suavity, urbanity; *informal* class. **3 kind**, type, variety, sort, design, pattern, genre. **4 fashion**, trend, vogue, mode.
● *verb* **design**, fashion, tailor, cut.

stylish *adjective* **fashionable**, modern, up to date, modish, smart, sophisticated, elegant, chic, dapper, dashing; *informal* trendy, natty; *N. Amer. informal* kicky, tony.
- OPPOSITES unfashionable.

subdue *verb* **conquer**, defeat, vanquish, overcome, overwhelm, crush, beat, subjugate, suppress.

subdued *adjective* **1 sombre**, downcast, sad, dejected, depressed, gloomy, despondent. **2 hushed**, muted, quiet, low, soft, faint, muffled, subtle, indistinct, dim, unobtrusive.
- OPPOSITES cheerful, loud, bright.

subject *noun* **1 theme**, subject matter, topic, issue, thesis, question, concern. **2 branch of study**, discipline, field. **3 citizen**, national, resident, taxpayer, voter.
● *verb* **expose to**, submit to, treat with, put through.
□ **subject to** conditional on, contingent on, dependent on.

subjective *adjective* **personal**, individual, emotional, biased, intuitive.
- OPPOSITES objective.

submerge *verb* **1 go under (water)**, dive, sink, plunge, plummet. **2 immerse**, dip, plunge, duck, dunk. **3** *the farmland was submerged* **flood**, deluge, swamp, overwhelm, inundate.

submission *noun* **1 yielding**, capitulation, surrender, resignation, acceptance, consent, compliance, acquiescence, obedience, subjection, subservience, servility. **2 proposal**, suggestion, proposition, tender, presentation. **3 argument**, assertion, contention, statement, claim, allegation.
- OPPOSITES defiance.

submissive *adjective* **compliant**, yielding, acquiescent, passive, obedient, dutiful, docile, pliant, tractable, biddable, malleable, meek, unassertive; *informal* under someone's thumb.

submit *verb* **1 yield**, give in/way, back down, cave in, capitulate, surrender, acquiesce. **2** *he refused to submit to their authority* **be governed by**, abide by, comply with, accept, be subject to, agree to, consent to, conform to. **3 put forward**, present, offer, tender, propose, suggest, enter, put in, send in. **4 contend**, assert, argue, state, claim, allege.
- OPPOSITES resist.

subordinate *adjective* **inferior**, junior, lower-ranking, lower, supporting.
● *noun* **junior**, assistant, second (in command), number two, deputy, aide, underling, minion.
- OPPOSITES superior, senior.

subscribe *verb* **contribute**, donate, give, pay.
□ **subscribe to** support, endorse, agree with, accept, go along with.

subscription *noun* **membership fee**, dues, annual payment, charge.

subsequent *adjective* **following**, ensuing, succeeding, later, future, coming, to come, next.
- OPPOSITES previous.

subsequently *adverb* **later (on)**, at a later date, afterwards, in due course, following this/that, eventually; *formal* thereafter.

subside *verb* **1 abate**, let up, quieten down, calm, slacken (off), ease (up), relent, die down, diminish, decline. **2 recede**, ebb, fall, go down, get lower. **3 sink**, settle, cave in, collapse, give way.
- OPPOSITES intensify, rise.

subsidiary *adjective* **subordinate**, secondary, subservient, supplementary, peripheral, auxiliary.
- OPPOSITES principal.
● *noun* **branch**, division, subdivision, derivative, offshoot.

subsidize *verb* **finance**, fund, support, contribute to, give money to, underwrite, sponsor; *informal* shell out for; *N. Amer. informal* bankroll.

subsidy *noun* **finance**, funding, backing, support, grant, sponsorship, allowance, contribution, handout.

substance *noun* **1 material**, compound, matter, stuff. **2 significance**, importance, import, validity, foundation. **3 content**, subject matter, theme, message, essence. **4 wealth**, fortune, riches, affluence, prosperity, money, means.

substantial *adjective* **1 considerable**, real, significant, important, major, valuable, useful, sizeable, appreciable. **2 sturdy**, solid, stout, strong, well built, durable, long-lasting, hard-wearing.
- OPPOSITES insubstantial.

substitute *noun* **replacement**, deputy, relief, proxy, reserve, surrogate, cover, stand-in, understudy; *informal* sub.
● *verb* **1 exchange**, swap, use instead of, use as an alternative to, use in place of, replace with. **2** *I found someone to substitute for me* **deputize for**, stand in for, cover for, fill in for, take over from.

subtle *adjective* **1 understated**, muted, subdued, delicate, soft, low-key, toned-down. **2 gentle**, slight, gradual. **3** *a subtle distinction* **fine**, fine-drawn, nice, tenuous.
- OPPOSITES gaudy, crude.

suburban *adjective* **1 residential**, commuter-belt. **2 dull**, boring, uninteresting, conventional, ordinary, unsophisticated, provincial, parochial, bourgeois, middle-class.

subversive *adjective* **disruptive**, troublemaking, insurrectionary, seditious, dissident.
● *noun* **troublemaker**, dissident, agitator, renegade.

succeed *verb* **1 triumph**, achieve success, be successful, do well, flourish, thrive; *informal* make it, make the grade. **2 be successful**, turn out well, work (out), be effective; *informal* come off, pay off. **3 replace**, take over from, follow, supersede.
- OPPOSITES fail, precede.

success *noun* **1 victory**, triumph. **2 prosperity**, affluence, wealth, riches, opulence. **3 best-seller**, sell-out, winner, triumph; *informal* hit, smash, sensation.
- OPPOSITES failure.

successful *adjective* **1 prosperous**, affluent, wealthy, rich, famous, eminent, top, respected. **2 flourishing**, thriving, booming, buoyant, profitable, moneymaking, lucrative.

succession *noun* **sequence**, series, progression, chain, string, train, line, run.

successive *adjective* **consecutive**, in a row, sequential, in succession, running; *informal* on the trot.

succinct *adjective* **concise**, short (and sweet), brief, compact, condensed, crisp, laconic, terse, to the point, pithy.
- OPPOSITES verbose.

succulent *adjective* **juicy**, moist, luscious, soft, tender, choice, mouth-watering, appetizing, flavoursome, tasty, delicious; *informal* scrumptious, scrummy.
- OPPOSITES dry.

succumb *verb* **yield**, give in/way, submit, surrender, capitulate, cave in, fall victim.
- OPPOSITES resist.

suck *verb* **sip**, sup, slurp, drink, siphon.

sudden *adjective* **unexpected**, unforeseen, immediate, instantaneous, instant, precipitous, abrupt, rapid, swift, quick.

suddenly *adverb* **all of a sudden**, all at once, abruptly, swiftly, unexpectedly, without warning, out of the blue.
- OPPOSITES gradually.

sue *verb* **take legal action**, go to court, take to court, litigate.

suffer *verb* **1 hurt**, ache, be in pain, be in distress, be upset, be miserable. **2** *he suffers from asthma* **be afflicted by**, be affected by, be troubled with, have. **3 undergo**, experience, be subjected to, receive, sustain, endure, face, meet with.

suffering *noun* **hardship**, distress, misery, adversity, pain, agony, anguish, trauma, torment, torture, hurt, affliction.
- OPPOSITES pleasure, joy.

sufficient *adjective* & *determiner* **enough**, adequate, plenty of, ample.
- OPPOSITES inadequate.

suggest *verb* **1 propose**, put forward, recommend, advocate, advise. **2 indicate**, lead someone to the belief, give the impression, demonstrate, show. **3 hint**, insinuate, imply, intimate.

suggestion *noun* **1 proposal**, proposition, recommendation, advice, counsel, hint, tip, clue, idea. **2 hint**, trace, touch, suspicion, ghost, semblance, shadow, glimmer. **3 insinuation**, hint, implication.

suggestive *adjective* **1 redolent**, evocative, reminiscent, characteristic, indicative, typical. **2 provocative**, titillating, sexual, sexy, risqué, **indecent**, indelicate, improper, unseemly, smutty, dirty.

suit *noun* **1 outfit**, ensemble. **2 legal action**, lawsuit, (court) case, action, (legal/judicial) proceedings, litigation. ● *verb* **1 look attractive on**, look good on, become, flatter. **2 be convenient for**, be acceptable to, be suitable for, meet the requirements of; *informal* fit. **3** *recipes suited to students* **be appropriate**, tailor, fashion, adjust, adapt, modify, fit, gear, design.

suitable *adjective* **1 acceptable**, satisfactory, convenient. **2 appropriate**, apposite, apt, fitting, fit, suited, tailor-made, in keeping, ideal; *informal* right up someone's street. **3 proper**, right, seemly, decent, appropriate, fitting, correct, due.
- OPPOSITES unsuitable.

suite *noun* **apartment**, flat, rooms.

sullen *adjective* **surly**, sulky, morose, resentful, moody, grumpy, bad-tempered, unsociable, uncommunicative, unresponsive.
- OPPOSITES cheerful.

sum *noun* **1 amount**, quantity, price, charge, fee, cost. **2 total**, sum total, grand total, tally, aggregate. **3 entirety**, totality, total, whole, beginning and end. **4 calculation**, problem; (**sums**) arithmetic, mathematics; *Brit. informal* maths; *N. Amer. informal* math. ◻ **sum up** summarize, make/give a summary of, encapsulate, put in a nutshell, precis, outline, recapitulate, review, recap.

summarize *verb* **sum up**, abridge, condense, outline, put in a nutshell, precis.

summary *noun* **synopsis**, precis, résumé, abstract, outline, rundown, summing-up, overview.

summit *noun* **1 (mountain) top**, peak, crest, crown, apex, tip, cap, hilltop. **2 meeting**, conference, talk(s).
- OPPOSITES base.

summon *verb* **1 send for**, call for, request the presence of, ask, invite. **2 convene**, call, assemble, rally, muster, gather together. **3 summons**, subpoena.

sumptuous *adjective* **lavish**, luxurious, opulent, magnificent, resplendent, gorgeous, splendid; *informal* plush; *Brit. informal* swish.
- OPPOSITES plain.

sun *noun* **sunshine**, sunlight, daylight, light, warmth.

> WORD LINKS
> **solar** relating to the sun

sundry *adjective* **various**, varied, miscellaneous, assorted, mixed, diverse, diversified, several, numerous, many, manifold, multifarious, multitudinous; *literary* divers.

sunny *adjective* **1 bright**, sunlit, clear, fine, cloudless. **2 cheerful**, cheery, happy, bright, merry, bubbly, jolly,

good-natured, good-tempered, optimistic, upbeat.
- OPPOSITES dull, cloudy.

sunrise *noun* **dawn**, crack of dawn, daybreak, break of day, first light, early morning; *N. Amer.* sunup.

sunset *noun* **nightfall**, twilight, dusk, evening; *N. Amer.* sundown.

superb *adjective* **excellent**, first-class, outstanding, marvellous, wonderful, splendid, admirable, fine, exceptional, glorious; *informal* great, fantastic, fabulous, terrific, super, awesome, ace; *Brit. informal* brilliant, smashing.
- OPPOSITES poor, unimpressive.

supercilious *adjective* **arrogant**, haughty, conceited, disdainful, overbearing, pompous, condescending, superior, patronizing, imperious, proud, snobbish, smug, scornful, sneering; *informal* high and mighty, snooty, stuck-up.

superficial *adjective* **1 surface**, exterior, external, outer, slight. **2 cursory**, perfunctory, casual, sketchy, desultory, token, slapdash, offhand, rushed, hasty, hurried. **3 apparent**, seeming, outward, ostensible, cosmetic, slight. **4 facile**, shallow, flippant, empty-headed, trivial, frivolous, silly, inane.
- OPPOSITES deep, thorough.

superfluous *adjective* **surplus**, redundant, unneeded, unnecessary, excess, extra, (to) spare, remaining, unused, left over, waste.
- OPPOSITES necessary.

superhuman *adjective* **extraordinary**, phenomenal, prodigious, stupendous, exceptional, immense, heroic, Herculean.

superior *adjective* **1 senior**, higher-ranking, higher. **2 better**, finer, higher quality, top-quality, choice, select, prime, excellent. **3 condescending**, supercilious, patronizing, haughty, disdainful, lordly, snobbish; *informal* high and mighty, snooty, toffee-nosed.
- OPPOSITES junior, inferior.
● *noun* **manager**, chief, supervisor, senior, controller, foreman; *informal* boss.
- OPPOSITES subordinate.

superiority *noun* **supremacy**, advantage, lead, dominance, primacy, ascendancy, eminence.

supernatural *adjective* **1 paranormal**, psychic, magic, magical, occult, mystic, mystical. **2 ghostly**, phantom, spectral, other-worldly, unearthly.

supersede *verb* **replace**, take the place of, take over from, succeed, supplant.

supervise *verb* **oversee**, be in charge of, superintend, preside over, direct, manage, run, look after, be responsible for, govern, keep an eye on, observe, monitor, mind.

supervisor *noun* **manager**, director, overseer, controller, superintendent, governor, chief, head, foreman; *informal* boss; *Brit. informal* gaffer.

supple *adjective* **1 lithe**, lissom, willowy, flexible, agile, acrobatic, nimble. **2 pliable**, flexible, soft, bendy, workable, stretchy, springy.
- OPPOSITES stiff, rigid.

supplement *noun* **1 extra**, add-on, accessory, adjunct. **2 surcharge**, addition, increase, increment. **3 appendix**, addendum, postscript, addition, coda. **4 pull-out**, insert.
● *verb* **add to**, augment, increase, boost, swell, amplify, enlarge, top up.

supplementary *adjective* **additional**, supplemental, extra, more, further, add-on, subsidiary, auxiliary, ancillary.

supply *verb* **1 provide**, give, furnish, equip, contribute, donate, grant, confer, dispense. **2 satisfy**, meet, fulfil, cater for.
● *noun* **1 stock**, store, reserve, reservoir, stockpile, hoard, cache, fund, bank. **2** *we're running out of supplies* **provisions**, stores, rations, food, necessities.

support *verb* **1 hold up**, bear, carry, prop up, keep up, brace, shore up, underpin, buttress, reinforce. **2 provide for**, maintain, sustain, keep,

take care of, look after. **3 stand by**, defend, back, stand/stick up for, take someone's side, side with. **4 back up**, substantiate, bear out, corroborate, confirm, verify. **5 help**, aid, assist, contribute to, back, subsidize, fund, finance; *N. Amer. informal* bankroll. **6 back**, champion, favour, be in favour of, advocate, encourage, promote, endorse, espouse.
- OPPOSITES contradict, oppose.
● *noun* **1 pillar**, post, prop, upright, brace, buttress, foundation, underpinning. **2 encouragement**, friendship, backing, endorsement, help, assistance, comfort. **3 contributions**, donations, money, subsidy, funding, funds, finance, capital.

supporter *noun* **1 advocate**, backer, adherent, promoter, champion, defender, upholder, campaigner. **2 contributor**, donor, benefactor, sponsor, backer, patron, subscriber, well-wisher. **3 fan**, follower, enthusiast, devotee, admirer.

supportive *adjective* **encouraging**, caring, sympathetic, reassuring, understanding, concerned, helpful.

suppose *verb* **1 assume**, presume, surmise, expect, imagine, dare say, take it, take as read, suspect, guess, conjecture. **2 hypothesize**, postulate, posit.

supposed *adjective* **alleged**, reputed, rumoured, claimed, purported.

supposition *noun* **belief**, conjecture, speculation, assumption, presumption, inference, theory, hypothesis, feeling, idea, notion, guesswork.

suppress *verb* **1 subdue**, crush, quell, quash, squash, stamp out, crack down on, clamp down on, put an end to. **2 restrain**, repress, hold back, control, stifle, smother, check, keep in check, curb, contain, bottle up. **3 censor**, redact, keep secret, conceal, hide, hush up, gag, withhold, cover up, stifle.
- OPPOSITES encourage, reveal.

supremacy *noun* **control**, power, rule, sovereignty, dominance, superiority, predominance, primacy, dominion, authority, mastery, ascendancy.

supreme *adjective* **1 highest**, chief, head, top, foremost, principal, superior, premier, first, prime. **2 extraordinary**, remarkable, phenomenal, exceptional, outstanding, incomparable, unparalleled. **3** *the supreme sacrifice* **ultimate**, greatest, highest, extreme, final, last.
- OPPOSITES subordinate.

sure *adjective* **1 certain**, positive, convinced, confident, definite, satisfied, persuaded, assured, free from doubt. **2 guaranteed**, unfailing, infallible, unerring, foolproof, certain, reliable, dependable, trustworthy, trusty; *informal* sure-fire.
- OPPOSITES uncertain, unlikely.

surface *noun* **1 outside**, exterior, top, side, finish. **2 outward appearance**, facade, veneer.
- OPPOSITES inside, interior.
● *verb* **1 come to the surface**, come up, rise. **2 emerge**, arise, appear, come to light, crop up, materialize, spring up.

surge *noun* **1 gush**, rush, outpouring, stream, flow. **2** *a surge in demand* **increase**, rise, growth, upswing, upsurge, escalation, leap.
● *verb* **1 gush**, rush, stream, flow, burst, pour, cascade, spill, sweep, roll. **2 increase**, rise, grow, leap.

surly *adjective* **sullen**, sulky, moody, morose, unfriendly, unpleasant, scowling, unsmiling, bad-tempered, grumpy, gruff, churlish, ill-humoured.
- OPPOSITES friendly.

surmise *verb* **guess**, conjecture, suspect, deduce, infer, conclude, theorize, speculate, assume, presume, suppose, understand, gather.

surmount *verb* **overcome**, prevail over, triumph over, beat, vanquish, conquer, get the better of.

surpass *verb* **excel**, exceed, transcend, outdo, outshine, outstrip, outclass, eclipse, improve on, top, trump, cap, beat, better, outperform.

surplus *noun* **excess**, surfeit, superfluity, oversupply, glut, remainder, residue, remains, leftovers.

- OPPOSITES dearth.
● *adjective* **excess**, leftover, unused, remaining, extra, additional, spare, superfluous, redundant, unwanted, unneeded, dispensable.
- OPPOSITES insufficient.

surprise *noun* **1 astonishment**, amazement, wonder, bewilderment, disbelief. **2 shock**, bolt from the blue, bombshell, revelation, rude awakening, eye-opener.
● *verb* **1 astonish**, amaze, startle, astound, stun, stagger, shock, take aback; *informal* bowl over, floor, flabbergast; *Brit. informal* knock for six. **2 take by surprise**, catch unawares, catch off guard, catch red-handed.

surprised *adjective* **astonished**, amazed, astounded, startled, stunned, staggered, nonplussed, shocked, taken aback, dumbfounded, speechless, thunderstruck; *informal* bowled over, flabbergasted.

surprising *adjective* **unexpected**, unforeseen, astonishing, amazing, startling, astounding, staggering, incredible, extraordinary.

surrender *verb* **1 give up**, give yourself up, give in, cave in, capitulate, concede (defeat), submit, lay down your arms/weapons. **2 give up**, relinquish, renounce, cede, abdicate, forfeit, sacrifice, hand over, turn over, yield.
- OPPOSITES resist.
● *noun* **1 capitulation**, submission, yielding. **2 relinquishing**, renunciation, abdication, resignation.

surreptitious *adjective* **secret**, secretive, stealthy, clandestine, sneaky, sly, furtive, covert; *Military* black.
- OPPOSITES blatant.

surround *verb* **encircle**, enclose, encompass, ring, hem in, confine, cut off, besiege, trap.

surrounding *adjective* **neighbouring**, enclosing, nearby, near, local, adjoining, adjacent.

surroundings *plural noun* **environment**, setting, background, backdrop, vicinity, locality, habitat.

surveillance *noun* **observation**, scrutiny, watch, view, inspection, supervision, spying, espionage.

survey *verb* **1 look at**, look over, view, contemplate, regard, gaze at, stare at, eye, scrutinize, examine, inspect, scan, study, assess, appraise, take stock of; *informal* size up. **2 interview**, question, canvass, poll, investigate, research.
● *noun* **1 study**, review, overview, examination, inspection, assessment, appraisal. **2 poll**, investigation, enquiry, study, probe, questionnaire, census, research.

survive *verb* **1 remain alive**, live, sustain yourself, pull through, hold out, make it. **2 continue**, remain, persist, endure, live on, persevere, abide, go on, carry on. **3 outlive**, outlast, remain alive after.

susceptible *adjective* **impressionable**, credulous, gullible, innocent, ingenuous, naive, easily led, defenceless, vulnerable.
□ **susceptible to** liable to, prone to, subject to, inclined to, predisposed to, open to, vulnerable to, an easy target for.

suspect *verb* **1 have a suspicion**, have a feeling, feel, be inclined to think, fancy, reckon, guess, conjecture, surmise, have a hunch, fear. **2 doubt**, distrust, mistrust, have misgivings about, have qualms about, be suspicious of, be sceptical about.
● *adjective* **suspicious**, dubious, doubtful, untrustworthy; *informal* fishy, funny; *Brit. informal* dodgy.

suspend *verb* **1 adjourn**, interrupt, break off, cut short, discontinue; *N. Amer.* table. **2 exclude**, debar, remove, expel, eject, rusticate. **3 hang**, sling, string, swing, dangle.

suspense *noun* **tension**, uncertainty, doubt, anticipation, excitement, anxiety, strain.

suspicion *noun* **1 intuition**, feeling, impression, inkling, hunch, fancy, notion, idea, theory, premonition; *informal* gut feeling. **2 misgiving**,

doubt, qualm, reservation, hesitation, scepticism.
- OPPOSITES trust.

suspicious *adjective* **1 doubtful**, unsure, dubious, wary, chary, sceptical, mistrustful. **2 suspect**, dubious, unsavoury, disreputable; *informal* shifty, shady; *Brit. informal* dodgy. **3** *suspicious circumstances* **strange**, odd, questionable, irregular, funny, doubtful, mysterious; *informal* fishy.
- OPPOSITES trusting, innocent.

sustain *verb* **1 comfort**, help, assist, encourage, support, give strength to, buoy up. **2 continue**, carry on, keep up, keep alive, maintain, preserve. **3 nourish**, feed, nurture, keep alive. **4 suffer**, experience, undergo, receive. **5 confirm**, corroborate, substantiate, bear out, prove, authenticate, back up, uphold.

sustained *adjective* **continuous**, ongoing, steady, continual, constant, prolonged, persistent, non-stop, perpetual, relentless.
- OPPOSITES sporadic.

sustenance *noun* **nourishment**, food, nutrition, provisions, rations; *informal* grub, chow; *Brit. informal* scoff; *literary* viands; *dated* victuals.

swagger *verb* **strut**, parade, stride, prance; *informal* sashay.

swallow *verb* **eat**, drink, gulp down, consume, devour, put away, quaff, slug; *informal* swig, swill, down; *Brit. informal* scoff.

S

swamp *noun* **marsh**, bog, fen, quagmire, morass.
● *verb* **1 flood**, inundate, deluge, fill. **2** *fans swamped her website with messages* **overwhelm**, engulf, snow under, overload, inundate, deluge.

swap *verb* **exchange**, trade, barter, switch, change, replace.

swarm *noun* **1 hive**, flock. **2 crowd**, horde, mob, throng, mass, army, herd, pack.
● *verb* **flock**, crowd, throng, surge, stream.

swathe *verb* **wrap**, envelop, bandage, cover, shroud, drape, wind, enfold.

sway *verb* **1 swing**, shake, undulate, move to and fro. **2 stagger**, wobble, rock, lurch, reel, roll. **3 influence**, affect, manipulate, bend, mould.
● *noun* **1 swing**, roll, shake, undulation. **2 power**, rule, government, sovereignty, dominion, control, jurisdiction, authority.

swear *verb* **1 promise**, vow, pledge, give your word, undertake, guarantee. **2 insist**, declare, proclaim, assert, maintain, emphasize, stress. **3 curse**, blaspheme, use bad language; *informal* cuss, eff and blind.

swearing *noun* **bad language**, cursing, blaspheming, obscenities, expletives, swear words; *informal* effing and blinding, four-letter words.

sweat *verb* **1 perspire**, drip with sweat. **2 work**, labour, toil, slog, slave, work your fingers to the bone.

WORD LINKS
sudorific causing sweating

sweep *verb* **brush**, clean (up), clear (up).

sweeping *adjective* **1 extensive**, wide-ranging, broad, comprehensive, far-reaching, thorough, radical. **2 wholesale**, blanket, general, unqualified, indiscriminate, oversimplified.
- OPPOSITES limited.

sweet *adjective* **1 sugary**, sweetened, sugared, honeyed, syrupy, sickly, cloying. **2 fragrant**, aromatic, perfumed. **3 musical**, melodious, dulcet, tuneful, soft, harmonious, silvery, mellifluous. **4 likeable**, appealing, engaging, amiable, pleasant, agreeable, kind, nice, thoughtful, considerate, delightful, lovely. **5 cute**, lovable, adorable, endearing, charming, winsome.
- OPPOSITES sour, savoury, disagreeable.
● *noun (Brit.)* **1 confectionery**, bonbon; *N. Amer.* candy; *old use* sweetmeat. **2 dessert**, pudding; *Brit. informal* afters, pud.

sweeten *verb* **1 make sweet**, add sugar to, sugar. **2 mollify**, placate, soothe, soften up, pacify, appease, win over.

sweetheart *noun* **lover**, love, girlfriend, boyfriend, beloved, beau; *informal* steady, squeeze; *literary* swain.

swell *verb* **1 expand**, bulge, distend, inflate, dilate, bloat, blow up, puff up, balloon, fatten, fill out. **2 grow**, enlarge, increase, expand, rise, escalate, multiply, proliferate, snowball, mushroom.
- OPPOSITES shrink, decrease.

swelling *noun* **bump**, lump, bulge, protuberance, protrusion, distension.

swerve *verb* **veer**, deviate, diverge, weave, zigzag, change direction; *Sailing* tack.

swift *adjective* **fast**, rapid, quick, speedy, expeditious, prompt, brisk, immediate, instant, hasty, hurried, sudden, abrupt.
- OPPOSITES slow, leisurely.

swindle *verb* **defraud**, cheat, trick, dupe, deceive, fool, hoax, hoodwink, bamboozle; *informal* fleece, do, con, diddle, rip off, take for a ride, pull a fast one on, put one over on; *N. Amer. informal* stiff.
● *noun* **fraud**, trick, deception, cheat, racket, sharp practice; *informal* con, fiddle, diddle, rip-off.

swindler *noun* **fraudster**, fraud, (confidence) trickster, cheat, rogue, charlatan, impostor, hoaxer; *informal* con man, shark, hustler, phoney, crook.

swing *verb* **1 sway**, move back and forth, oscillate, wave, rock, swivel, pivot, turn, rotate. **2 brandish**, wave, flourish, wield. **3 curve**, bend, veer, turn, bear, wind, twist, deviate, slew. **4 change**, fluctuate, waver, see-saw.
● *noun* **1 oscillation**, sway, wave. **2 change**, move, turnaround, turnabout, reversal, fluctuation, variation.

swirl *verb* **whirl**, eddy, billow, spiral, twist, twirl, circulate, revolve, spin.

switch *noun* **1 button**, lever, control. **2 change**, move, shift, transition, transformation, reversal, turnaround, rowback, U-turn, changeover, transfer, conversion.
● *verb* **1 change**, shift; *informal* chop and change. **2 exchange**, swap, interchange, change round, rotate.

swollen *adjective* **distended**, bulging, inflated, dilated, bloated, puffed up, puffy, tumescent, inflamed.

swoop *verb* **dive**, descend, pounce, sweep down, plunge, drop down.

sycophant *noun* **toady**, creep, flatterer; *informal* bootlicker, yes-man.

sycophantic *adjective* **obsequious**, servile, subservient, grovelling, toadying, fawning, ingratiating, unctuous; *informal* smarmy, bootlicking.

symbol *noun* **1 representation**, token, sign, emblem, figure, image, metaphor, allegory. **2 sign**, character, mark, letter. **3 logo**, emblem, badge, stamp, trademark, crest, insignia, coat of arms, seal, device, monogram, hallmark, motif.

symbolic *adjective* **1 emblematic**, representative, typical, characteristic, symptomatic. **2 figurative**, metaphorical, allegorical.
- OPPOSITES literal.

symbolize *verb* **represent**, stand for, be a sign of, denote, signify, mean, indicate, convey, express, embody, epitomize, encapsulate, personify.

symmetrical *adjective* **regular**, uniform, consistent, even, equal, balanced, proportional.

sympathetic *adjective* **1 compassionate**, caring, concerned, understanding, sensitive, supportive, empathetic, kind-hearted, warm-hearted. **2 likeable**, pleasant, agreeable, congenial, companionable.
- OPPOSITES unsympathetic.

sympathize *verb* **commiserate**, show concern, offer condolences; (**sympathize with**) pity, feel sorry for, feel for, identify with, understand, relate to.

sympathy *noun* **compassion**, care, concern, commiseration, pity, condolence.
- OPPOSITES indifference.

symptom *noun* **indication**, indicator, manifestation, sign, mark, feature, trait, clue, hint, warning, evidence, proof.

symptomatic *adjective* **indicative**, characteristic, suggestive, typical, representative, symbolic.

synthesis *noun* **combination**, union, amalgam, blend, mixture, compound, fusion, composite, alloy.

synthetic *adjective* **artificial**, fake, imitation, mock, simulated, man-made, manufactured; *informal* pretend.
- OPPOSITES natural.

system *noun* **1 structure**, organization, arrangement, order, network; *informal* set-up. **2 method**, methodology, modus operandi, technique, procedure, means, way, scheme, plan, policy, programme, formula, solution, routine. **3** (**the system**) **the establishment**, the administration, the authorities, the powers that be, bureaucracy, officialdom.

systematic *adjective* **structured**, methodical, organized, orderly, planned, regular, routine, standardized, standard, logical, coherent, consistent.
- OPPOSITES disorganized.

Tt

table *noun* **chart**, diagram, figure, graphic, graph, plan, list.

tablet *noun* **1 slab**, stone, panel, plaque, plate, sign. **2 pill**, capsule, lozenge, pastille, drop. **3 bar**, cake, slab, brick, block.

taboo *noun* **prohibition**, proscription, veto, ban, interdict.
● *adjective* **forbidden**, prohibited, vetoed, banned, proscribed, outlawed, off limits, beyond the pale, unmentionable, unspeakable; *informal* no go.
- OPPOSITES acceptable.

tacit *adjective* **implicit**, understood, implied, inferred, hinted, suggested, unspoken, unstated, unsaid, unexpressed, unvoiced, taken for granted, taken as read.
- OPPOSITES explicit.

tack *noun* **pin**, nail, staple, rivet.
● *verb* **pin**, nail, staple, fix, fasten, attach, secure.
□ **tack something on** add, append, attach, join on, tag on.

tackle *noun* **1 equipment**, apparatus, kit, implements, paraphernalia; *informal* gear, clobber. **2 interception**, challenge, block, attack.
● *verb* **1 deal with**, take care of, attend to, see to, handle, manage, get to grips with, address. **2 confront**, face up to, take on, challenge, attack, grab, struggle with, intercept, block, stop, bring down, floor, fell, rugby-tackle; *informal* have a go at.

tacky[1] *adjective* **sticky**, wet, gluey, viscous, gummy; *informal* gooey.

tacky[2] *adjective* **tawdry**, tasteless, kitsch, vulgar, crude, garish, gaudy, trashy, cheap; *informal* cheesy; *Brit. informal* naff.
- OPPOSITES tasteful.

tactful *adjective* **diplomatic**, discreet, considerate, sensitive, understanding, thoughtful, delicate, judicious, subtle.

tactic *noun* **1 scheme**, plan, manoeuvre, method, trick, ploy. **2** (**tactics**) **strategy**, policy, campaign, game plan, planning, manoeuvres, logistics.

tactical *adjective* **calculated**, planned, strategic, prudent, politic, diplomatic, judicious, shrewd.

tactless *adjective* **insensitive**, inconsiderate, thoughtless, indelicate, undiplomatic, indiscreet, unsubtle, inept, gauche, blunt.

tag *noun* **label**, ticket, badge, mark, tab, sticker, docket.
● *verb* **label**, mark, ticket, identify, flag, indicate.

tail *noun* **rear**, end, back, extremity, bottom.
- OPPOSITES head, front.
● *verb (informal)* **follow**, shadow, stalk, trail, track, keep under surveillance.

tailor *noun* **outfitter**, couturier, costumier, dressmaker, fashion designer.
● *verb* **customize**, adapt, adjust, modify, change, convert, alter, mould, gear, fit, shape, tune.

WORD LINKS
sartorial relating to tailoring

taint *verb* **1 contaminate**, pollute, adulterate, infect, blight, spoil, soil, ruin. **2 tarnish**, sully, blacken, stain, blot, damage.

take *verb* **1** *she took his hand* **grasp**, get hold of, grip, clasp, clutch, grab. **2** *he took an envelope from his pocket* **remove**, pull, draw, withdraw, extract, fish. **3 capture**, seize, catch, arrest, apprehend, take into custody, carry off, abduct. **4 steal**, remove, appropriate, make off with, pilfer, purloin; *informal* filch, swipe, snaffle; *Brit. informal* pinch, nick. **5** *take four from the total* **subtract**, deduct, remove, discount; *informal* knock off, minus. **6 occupy**, use, utilize, fill, hold, reserve, engage; *informal* bag. **7 write**, note (down), jot (down), scribble, scrawl, record, register, document, minute. **8 bring**, carry, bear, transport, convey, move, transfer, shift, ferry; *informal* cart, tote. **9 escort**, accompany, help, assist, show, lead, guide, see, usher, convey. **10 travel on/by**, journey on, go via, use. **11** *I can't take much more* **endure**, bear, tolerate, stand, put up with, abide, stomach, accept, allow, countenance, support, shoulder; *formal* brook.

- OPPOSITES give, add.

□ **take after** resemble, look like, remind someone of. **take apart** dismantle, take to pieces, disassemble, break up. **take in 1** deceive, delude, hoodwink, mislead, trick, dupe, fool, cheat, defraud, swindle; *informal* con. **2** comprehend, understand, grasp, follow, absorb; *informal* get. **take off 1** become airborne, take to the air, leave the ground, lift off, blast off. **2** succeed, do well, become popular, catch on, prosper, flourish. **take on 1** compete against, oppose, challenge, confront, face. **2** engage, hire, employ, sign up. **3** undertake, accept, assume, shoulder, acquire. **take over** assume control of, take charge of, take command of, seize, hijack, commandeer. **take up 1** begin, start, commence, engage in, practise. **2** consume, fill, absorb, use, occupy. **3** resume, recommence, restart, carry on, continue, pick up, return to. **4** accept, say yes to, agree to, adopt.

t

takeover *noun* **buyout**, purchase, acquisition, amalgamation, merger.

takings *plural noun* **proceeds**, returns, receipts, earnings, winnings, pickings, spoils, profit, gain, income, revenue.

tale *noun* **story**, narrative, anecdote, account, history, legend, fable, myth, saga; *informal* yarn.

talent *noun* **flair**, aptitude, facility, gift, knack, technique, bent, ability, forte, genius, brilliance.

talented *adjective* **gifted**, skilful, accomplished, brilliant, expert, consummate, able, proficient; *informal* ace.

- OPPOSITES inept.

talk *verb* **1 speak**, chat, chatter, gossip, jabber, prattle; *informal* yak; *Brit. informal* natter, rabbit. **2** *they were able to talk in peace* **converse**, communicate, speak (to one another), confer, consult, negotiate, parley; *informal* have a confab.

● *noun* **1 chatter**, gossip, prattle, jabbering; *informal* yak; *Brit. informal* nattering. **2 conversation**, chat, discussion, tête-à-tête, heart-to-heart, dialogue; *informal* confab, gossip; *Austral. informal* convo. **3** (**talks**) **negotiations**, discussions, conference, summit, meeting, consultation, dialogue. **4 lecture**, speech, address, discourse, oration, presentation, report, sermon.

talkative *adjective* **chatty**, garrulous, loquacious, voluble, communicative; *informal* mouthy.

- OPPOSITES taciturn.

tall *adjective* **1** *a tall man* **big**, large, huge, giant, lanky, gangling. **2** *tall buildings* **high**, big, lofty, towering, sky-high, gigantic, colossal.

- OPPOSITES short, low.

tally *noun* **running total**, count, record, reckoning, register, account, roll.

● *verb* **correspond**, agree, accord, concur, coincide, match, fit, be consistent, conform, equate, parallel; *informal* square.

- OPPOSITES disagree.

tame *adjective* **1 domesticated**, docile, trained, gentle, mild, pet. **2 unexciting**, uninteresting, uninspiring, uninspired, dull, bland, flat, pedestrian, humdrum, boring.

- OPPOSITES wild.

● *verb* **1 domesticate**, break in, train. **2** *she learned to tame her emotions* **subdue**, curb, control, calm, master, moderate, discipline, overcome.

tamper *verb* **interfere**, meddle, monkey around, tinker, fiddle; *informal* mess about; *Brit. informal* muck about.

tangible *adjective* **real**, actual, physical, solid, palpable, material, substantial, concrete, visible, definite, perceptible, discernible.
- OPPOSITES abstract, theoretical.

tangle *verb* **entangle**, snarl, catch, entwine, twist, knot, mat.
● *noun* **1 snarl**, mass, knot, mesh. **2 muddle**, jumble, mix-up, confusion, shambles.

tank *noun* **container**, receptacle, vat, cistern, repository, reservoir, basin.

tantalize *verb* **tease**, torment, torture, tempt, entice, lure, beguile, excite, fascinate, titillate, intrigue.

tantrum *noun* **fit of temper**, fit of rage, outburst, pet, paroxysm, frenzy; *informal* paddy, wobbly; *N. Amer. informal* hissy fit.

tap[1] *noun* **valve**, stopcock; *N. Amer.* faucet, spigot.
● *verb* **1 bug**, wiretap, monitor, eavesdrop on. **2 draw on**, exploit, milk, mine, use, utilize, turn to account.

tap[2] *verb* **knock**, rap, strike, beat, pat, drum.

tape *noun* **1 binding**, ribbon, string, braid, band. **2 cassette**, recording, video.
● *verb* **1 bind**, stick, fix, fasten, secure, attach. **2 record**, tape-record, video.

taper *verb* **narrow**, thin (out), come to a point, attenuate.
- OPPOSITES thicken.
□ **taper off** decrease, lessen, dwindle, diminish, reduce, decline, die down, peter out, wane, ebb, slacken (off), fall off, let up, thin out.

target *noun* **1 objective**, goal, aim, mark, end, plan, intention, aspiration, ambition. **2 victim**, butt, recipient, focus, object, subject.
● *verb* **1 pick out**, single out, earmark, fix on, attack, aim at, fire at. **2** *a product targeted at women* **aim**, direct, level, intend, focus.

tariff *noun* **1 tax**, duty, toll, excise, levy, charge, rate, fee. **2 price list**, menu.

tarnish *verb* **1 discolour**, rust, oxidize, corrode, stain, dull, blacken. **2 sully**, blacken, stain, blemish, ruin, disgrace, mar, damage, harm, drag through the mud.
● *noun* **discoloration**, oxidation, rust, verdigris.

tart[1] *noun* **pastry**, flan, quiche, tartlet, vol-au-vent, pie.

tart[2] *(informal) verb* **1 dress up**, smarten up; *informal* doll yourself up, titivate yourself. **2 decorate**, renovate, refurbish, redecorate, smarten up; *informal* do up, fix up.

tart[3] *adjective* **1 sour**, sharp, acidic, zesty, tangy, piquant. **2 scathing**, sharp, biting, cutting, sarcastic, hurtful, spiteful.
- OPPOSITES sweet, kind.

task *noun* **job**, duty, chore, charge, assignment, detail, mission, engagement, occupation, undertaking, exercise.

taste *noun* **1 flavour**, savour, relish, tang, smack. **2 mouthful**, morsel, drop, bit, sip, nip, touch, soupçon, dash. **3** *a taste for adventure* **liking**, love, fondness, fancy, desire, penchant, partiality, inclination, appetite, stomach, palate, thirst, hunger. **4** *his first taste of opera* **experience**, impression, exposure to, contact with, involvement with. **5 judgement**, discrimination, discernment, refinement, elegance, grace, style. **6 sensitivity**, decorum, propriety, etiquette, nicety, discretion.
● *verb* **1** *I tasted the wine* **sample**, test, try, savour. **2** *he could taste blood* **perceive**, discern, make out, distinguish.

WORD LINKS
gustatory relating to the sense of taste

tasteful *adjective* **stylish**, refined, cultured, elegant, smart, chic, exquisite.
- OPPOSITES tasteless.

tasteless *adjective* **1 flavourless**, bland, insipid, unappetizing, watery, weak, thin. **2 vulgar**, crude, tawdry, garish, gaudy, loud, trashy, showy, ostentatious, cheap;

informal flash, tacky, kitsch; *Brit. informal* naff. **3 crude**, indelicate, uncouth, crass, tactless, undiplomatic, indiscreet, inappropriate, offensive.
- OPPOSITES tasty, tasteful.

tasty *adjective* **delicious**, palatable, luscious, mouth-watering, delectable, appetizing, tempting; *informal* yummy, scrumptious, moreish.
- OPPOSITES bland.

taunt *noun* **jeer**, jibe, sneer, insult, barb; *informal* dig, put-down; (**taunts**) teasing, provocation, goading, derision, mockery.
● *verb* **jeer at**, sneer at, scoff at, poke fun at, make fun of, get at, insult, tease, torment, ridicule, deride, mock; *N. Amer.* ride; *informal* rib, needle.

taut *adjective* **tight**, stretched, rigid, flexed, tensed.
- OPPOSITES slack.

tawdry *adjective* **gaudy**, flashy, showy, garish, loud, tasteless, vulgar, trashy, cheapjack, shoddy, shabby, gimcrack; *informal* rubbishy, tacky, kitsch.
- OPPOSITES tasteful.

tax *noun* **duty**, excise, customs, dues, levy, tariff, toll, tithe, charge.
● *verb* **strain**, stretch, overburden, overload, overwhelm, try, wear out, exhaust, sap, drain, weary, weaken.

WORD LINKS
fiscal relating to tax

teach *verb* **educate**, instruct, school, tutor, inform, coach, train, drill.

WORD LINKS
educational relating to teaching

teacher *noun* **educator**, tutor, instructor, schoolteacher, master, mistress, schoolmarm, governess, coach, trainer, lecturer, professor, don, guide, mentor, guru.

team *noun* **group**, squad, company, party, crew, troupe, band, side, line-up; *informal* bunch, gang.
● *verb ankle boots teamed with jeans* **match**, coordinate, complement, pair up.
□ **team up** join (forces), collaborate, work together, unite, combine, cooperate, link, ally, associate, club together.

tear *verb* **1 rip**, split, slit, pull apart, pull to pieces, shred, rupture, sever. **2 lacerate**, cut (open), gash, slash, scratch, hack, pierce, stab. **3 snatch**, grab, seize, rip, wrench, wrest, pull, pluck; *informal* yank.
● *noun* **rip**, hole, split, slash, slit, ladder, snag.

tearful *adjective* **1 close to tears**, emotional, upset, distressed, sad, unhappy, in tears, crying, weeping, sobbing, snivelling; *informal* weepy, blubbing; *formal* lachrymose. **2 emotional**, upsetting, distressing, sad, heartbreaking, sorrowful, poignant, moving, touching, tear-jerking.
- OPPOSITES cheerful.

tease *verb* **make fun of**, laugh at, deride, mock, ridicule, guy, make a monkey (out) of, taunt, bait, goad, pick on; *informal* take the mickey out of, rag, have on, pull someone's leg; *Brit. informal* wind up.

technical *adjective* **1 practical**, scientific, technological, high-tech. **2 specialist**, specialized, scientific, complex, complicated, esoteric.

technique *noun* **1 method**, approach, procedure, system, way, manner, means, strategy, solution. **2 skill**, ability, proficiency, expertise, artistry, craftsmanship, adroitness, deftness, dexterity.

tedious *adjective* **boring**, dull, monotonous, repetitive, unrelieved, unvaried, uneventful, lifeless, uninteresting, unexciting, uninspiring, lacklustre, dreary, soul-destroying; *informal* deadly; *N. Amer. informal* dullsville.
- OPPOSITES exciting.

teenager *noun* **adolescent**, youth, young person, minor, juvenile; *informal* teen.

teetotal *adjective* **abstinent**, abstemious, sober, dry; *informal* on the wagon.

telephone *noun* **phone**, handset, receiver; *informal* blower; *N. Amer.*

informal horn.
● *verb* **phone**, call, dial; *Brit.* ring (up); *informal* call up, give someone a buzz, get on the blower to; *Brit. informal* give someone a bell, give someone a tinkle; *N. Amer. informal* get someone on the horn.

television *noun* **TV**; *informal* the small screen; *Brit. informal* telly, the box; *N. Amer. informal* the tube.

tell *verb* **1** *why didn't you tell me?* **inform**, notify, let know, make aware, acquaint with, advise, put in the picture, brief, fill in, alert, warn; *informal* clue in/up. **2** *she told the story slowly* **relate**, recount, narrate, report, recite, describe, sketch. **3 instruct**, order, command, direct, charge, enjoin, call on, require. **4** *it was hard to tell what he meant* **ascertain**, determine, work out, make out, deduce, discern, perceive, see, identify, recognize, understand, comprehend; *informal* figure out; *Brit. informal* suss out. **5** *he couldn't tell one from the other* **distinguish**, differentiate, discriminate. **6** *the strain began to tell on him* **take its toll**, leave its mark, affect.

telling *adjective* **revealing**, significant, weighty, important, meaningful, influential, striking, potent, powerful, compelling.
– OPPOSITES insignificant.

temper *noun* **1** *he walked out in a temper* **rage**, fury, fit of pique, tantrum, bad mood, pet, sulk, huff; *Brit. informal* strop, paddy; *N. Amer. informal* hissy fit. **2** *a display of temper* **anger**, fury, rage, annoyance, irritation, pique, petulance; *Brit. informal* stroppiness. **3** *she struggled to keep her temper* **composure**, self-control, self-possession, calm, good humour; *informal* cool.
● *verb their idealism is tempered with realism* **moderate**, modify, modulate, mitigate, alleviate, reduce, weaken, lighten, soften.
□ **lose your temper** get angry, fly into a rage, erupt; *informal* go mad, go bananas, have a fit, see red, fly off the handle, blow your top, hit the roof, lose your rag; *Brit. informal* go spare, throw a wobbly.

temperament *noun* **character**, nature, disposition, personality, make-up, constitution, temper.

temperamental *adjective* **volatile**, excitable, emotional, unpredictable, hot-headed, quick-tempered, impatient, touchy, moody, sensitive, highly strung.
– OPPOSITES placid.

tempestuous *adjective* **turbulent**, wild, stormy, violent, emotional, passionate, impassioned, fiery, intense, uncontrolled, unrestrained.
– OPPOSITES calm.

temple *noun* **place of worship**, shrine, sanctuary, church, cathedral, mosque, synagogue, mandir, gurdwara.

temporarily *adverb* **1 for the time being**, for the moment, for now, for the present, provisionally, pro tem, in the interim. **2 briefly**, for a short time, momentarily, fleetingly.
– OPPOSITES permanently.

temporary *adjective* **1 provisional**, short-term, interim, makeshift, stopgap, acting, fill-in, stand-in, caretaker. **2 brief**, short-lived, momentary, fleeting, passing, ephemeral.
– OPPOSITES permanent, lasting.

tempt *verb* **entice**, persuade, convince, inveigle, induce, cajole, coax, lure, attract, appeal to, tantalize, whet the appetite of, seduce; *informal* sweet talk.
– OPPOSITES discourage, deter.

temptation *noun* **1 desire**, urge, itch, impulse, inclination. **2 lure**, allure, enticement, attraction, draw, pull.

tempting *adjective* **enticing**, alluring, attractive, appealing, inviting, seductive, beguiling, fascinating, mouth-watering.
– OPPOSITES uninviting.

tenable *adjective* **defensible**, justifiable, supportable, sustainable, arguable, able to hold water, reasonable, rational, sound, viable, plausible, credible,

believable, conceivable.
- OPPOSITES untenable.

tenacious *adjective* **persevering**, persistent, determined, dogged, strong-willed, indefatigable, tireless, resolute, patient, purposeful, unflagging, staunch, steadfast, untiring, unwavering, unswerving, unshakeable; *formal* pertinacious.

tenant *noun* **occupant**, resident, inhabitant, leaseholder, lessee, lodger; *Brit.* occupier.

tend[1] *verb* **be inclined**, be apt, be disposed, be prone, be liable, be likely, have a tendency.

tend[2] *verb* **look after**, take care of, minister to, attend to, see to, watch over, keep an eye on, mind, protect, guard.
- OPPOSITES neglect.

tendency *noun* **inclination**, propensity, proclivity, proneness, aptness, likelihood, bent, leaning, liability.

tender[1] *adjective* **1** *a gentle, tender man* **caring**, kind, kind-hearted, soft-hearted, compassionate, sympathetic, warm, gentle, mild, benevolent. **2** *a tender kiss* **affectionate**, fond, loving, romantic, emotional; *informal* lovey-dovey. **3 soft**, succulent, juicy, melt-in-the-mouth. **4 sore**, sensitive, inflamed, raw, painful, hurting, aching, throbbing. **5** *the tender age of fifteen* **young**, youthful, impressionable, inexperienced; *informal* wet behind the ears.
- OPPOSITES hard-hearted, callous, tough.

tender[2] *verb* **offer**, proffer, put forward, present, propose, suggest, advance, submit, hand in.
● *noun* **bid**, offer, quotation, quote, estimate, price.

tense *adjective* **1 taut**, tight, rigid, stretched, strained, stiff. **2 anxious**, nervous, on edge, edgy, strained, stressed, ill at ease, uneasy, restless, worked up, keyed up, overwrought, jumpy, nervy; *informal* a bundle of nerves, jittery, twitchy, uptight. **3 nerve-racking**, stressful, anxious, worrying, fraught, charged, strained, nail-biting.
- OPPOSITES relaxed, calm.
● *verb* **tighten**, tauten, flex, contract, brace, stiffen.
- OPPOSITES relax.

tension *noun* **1 tightness**, tautness, rigidity, pull. **2 strain**, stress, anxiety, pressure, worry, nervousness, jumpiness, edginess, restlessness, suspense, uncertainty. **3 strained relations**, strain, ill feeling, friction, antagonism, antipathy, hostility.

tentative *adjective* **1** *a tentative arrangement* **provisional**, unconfirmed, preliminary, exploratory, experimental. **2** *a few tentative steps* **hesitant**, uncertain, cautious, timid, hesitating, faltering, shaky, unsteady, halting.
- OPPOSITES definite, confident.

tenuous *adjective* **slight**, insubstantial, flimsy, weak, doubtful, dubious, questionable, suspect, vague, nebulous, hazy.
- OPPOSITES convincing.

tepid *adjective* **1 lukewarm**, warmish. **2 unenthusiastic**, apathetic, half-hearted, indifferent, cool, lukewarm, uninterested.

term *noun* **1 word**, expression, phrase, name, title, designation, label, description. **2** *the terms of the contract* **condition**, stipulation, specification, provision, proviso, restriction, qualification. **3 period**, length of time, spell, stint, duration, stretch, run, session.
● *verb* **call**, name, entitle, title, style, designate, describe as, dub, label, tag.

terminal *adjective* **1 incurable**, untreatable, inoperable, fatal, lethal, mortal, deadly. **2 final**, last, concluding, closing, end.
● *noun* **1 station**, last stop, end of the line, depot; *Brit.* terminus. **2 workstation**, VDU, visual display unit.

terminate *verb* **bring to an end**, end, bring to a close, close, conclude, finish, stop, wind up, discontinue, cease, cut short, abort, axe; *informal* pull the plug on.
- OPPOSITES begin.

terminology *noun* **phraseology**, terms, expressions, words, language, parlance, vocabulary, nomenclature, usage, idiom, jargon; *informal* lingo, geekspeak.

terrain *noun* **land**, ground, territory, topography, landscape, countryside, country.

terrestrial *adjective* **earthly**, worldly, mundane, earthbound.

terrible *adjective* **1** *a terrible crime* **dreadful**, awful, appalling, horrific, horrible, horrendous, atrocious, monstrous, sickening, heinous, vile, gruesome, unspeakable. **2** *terrible pain* **severe**, extreme, intense, excruciating, agonizing, unbearable. **3** *a terrible film* **very bad**, dreadful, awful, frightful, atrocious, execrable; *informal* pathetic, pitiful, useless, lousy, appalling; *Brit. informal* chronic.
- OPPOSITES minor, slight, excellent.

terrific *adjective* **1 tremendous**, huge, massive, gigantic, colossal, mighty, considerable; *informal* mega, whopping; *Brit. informal* ginormous. **2** *(informal)* **marvellous**, wonderful, sensational, outstanding, superb, excellent, first-rate, dazzling, out of this world, breathtaking; *informal* great, fantastic, fabulous, super, ace, wicked, awesome; *Brit. informal* brilliant.

terrify *verb* **frighten**, horrify, petrify, scare, strike terror into, paralyse, transfix.

territory *noun* **1 region**, area, enclave, country, state, land, dependency, colony, dominion. **2** *mountainous territory* **terrain**, land, ground, countryside.

terror *noun* **fear**, dread, horror, fright, alarm, panic, shock.

terrorize *verb* **persecute**, victimize, torment, tyrannize, intimidate, menace, threaten, bully, browbeat, scare, frighten, terrify, petrify; *Brit. informal* put the frighteners on.

terse *adjective* **brief**, short, to the point, concise, succinct, crisp, pithy, incisive, laconic, elliptical, brusque, abrupt, curt, clipped, blunt.
- OPPOSITES long-winded, polite.

test *noun* **1 trial**, experiment, check, examination, assessment, evaluation, appraisal, investigation. **2 exam**, examination; *N. Amer.* quiz.
● *verb* **try out**, trial, put through its paces, experiment with, check, examine, assess, evaluate, appraise, investigate, sample.

testify *verb* **swear**, attest, give evidence, state on oath, declare, assert, affirm.

testimonial *noun* **reference**, letter of recommendation, commendation.

testimony *noun* **evidence**, sworn statement, attestation, affidavit, statement, declaration, assertion.

testing *adjective* **difficult**, challenging, tough, hard, demanding, taxing, stressful.
- OPPOSITES easy.

text *noun* **1 book**, work, textbook. **2** *the pictures relate well to the text* **words**, content, body, wording, script, copy.

textiles *plural noun* **fabrics**, cloths, materials.

texture *noun* **feel**, touch, appearance, finish, surface, grain, consistency.

thank *verb* **express your gratitude to**, say thank you to, show your appreciation to.

thankful *adjective* **grateful**, relieved, pleased, glad.

thankless *adjective* **unenviable**, difficult, unpleasant, unrewarding, unappreciated, unrecognized, unacknowledged.
- OPPOSITES rewarding.

thanks *plural noun* **gratitude**, appreciation, acknowledgement, recognition, credit.
□ **thanks to** as a result of, owing to, due to, because of, through, on account of, by virtue of.

thaw *verb* **melt**, unfreeze, defrost, soften, liquefy.
- OPPOSITES freeze.

theatre *noun* **1 playhouse**, auditorium, amphitheatre. **2 acting**, the stage, drama, dramaturgy, show business; *informal* showbiz. **3** *a lecture theatre* **hall**, room, auditorium.

theatrical *adjective* **1 stage**, dramatic, thespian, show-business; *informal* showbiz. **2 exaggerated**, ostentatious, stagy, melodramatic, showy, affected, overdone; *informal* hammy.

theft *noun* **robbery**, stealing, larceny, shoplifting, burglary, embezzlement, raid, hold-up; *informal* smash-and-grab; *N. Amer. informal* heist.

theme *noun* **1 subject**, topic, argument, idea, thrust, thread, motif, keynote. **2 melody**, tune, air, motif, leitmotif.

theoretical *adjective* **hypothetical**, speculative, academic, conjectural, suppositional, notional, unproven.
– OPPOSITES actual.

theory *noun* **1 hypothesis**, thesis, conjecture, supposition, speculation, postulation, proposition, premise, opinion, view, belief, contention. **2** *modern economic theory* **ideas**, concepts, philosophy, ideology, thinking, principles.

therapeutic *adjective* **healing**, curative, remedial, medicinal, restorative, health-giving.

therapist *noun* **psychologist**, psychotherapist, analyst, psychoanalyst, psychiatrist, counsellor; *informal* shrink.

therapy *noun* **1 treatment**, remedy, cure. **2** *he's currently in therapy* **psychotherapy**, psychoanalysis, counselling.

therefore *adverb* **consequently**, because of that, for that reason, that being the case, so, as a result, hence, accordingly.

thesis *noun* **1 theory**, contention, argument, proposal, proposition, premise, assumption, supposition, hypothesis. **2 dissertation**, essay, paper, treatise, composition, study; *N. Amer.* theme.

thick *adjective* **1 broad**, wide, deep, stout, bulky, hefty, chunky, solid, plump. **2** *the station was thick with people* **crowded**, full, packed, teeming, seething, swarming, crawling, crammed, thronged, bursting at the seams, solid, overflowing; *informal* jam-packed, chock-a-block, stuffed; *Austral./NZ informal* chocker. **3 plentiful**, abundant, profuse, luxuriant, bushy, rich, riotous, exuberant, rank, rampant, dense; *informal* jungly. **4 semi-solid**, firm, stiff, heavy, viscous, gelatinous. **5** *thick fog* **dense**, heavy, opaque, impenetrable, soupy, murky.
– OPPOSITES thin, slender, sparse.

thicken *verb* **stiffen**, condense, solidify, set, gel, congeal, clot, coagulate.

thief *noun* **robber**, burglar, housebreaker, shoplifter, pickpocket, mugger, kleptomaniac; *informal* crook.

thieve *verb* **steal**, take, purloin, help yourself to, snatch, pilfer, embezzle, misappropriate; *informal* rob, swipe, nab, lift; *Brit. informal* nick, pinch, knock off; *N. Amer. informal* heist.

thin *adjective* **1 narrow**, fine, attenuated. **2 lightweight**, light, fine, delicate, flimsy, diaphanous, gauzy, gossamer, sheer, filmy, transparent, see-through. **3 slim**, lean, slender, willowy, svelte, sylphlike, spare, slight, skinny, underweight, scrawny, scraggy, bony, gaunt, emaciated, skeletal, lanky, spindly, gangly; *informal* anorexic. **4 watery**, weak, runny, sloppy.
– OPPOSITES thick, broad, fat.
● *verb* **1 dilute**, water down, weaken. **2** *the crowds thinned out* **disperse**, dissipate, scatter.
– OPPOSITES thicken.

thing *noun* **1 object**, article, item, artefact, commodity; *informal* doodah, whatsit; *Brit. informal* gubbins. **2 (things) belongings**, possessions, stuff, property, worldly goods, goods and chattels, effects, paraphernalia, bits and pieces, luggage, baggage; *informal* gear, junk; *Brit. informal* clobber. **3 (things) equipment**, apparatus, gear, kit, tackle, stuff, implements, tools, utensils, impedimenta, accoutrements.

think *verb* **1 believe**, be of the opinion, be of the view, be under the impression, expect, imagine, anticipate, suppose, guess, fancy; *informal* reckon, figure. **2** *his family was thought to be rich* **consider**, judge, hold, reckon, deem, presume, estimate, regard as, view as. **3 ponder**, reflect, deliberate, consider, meditate, contemplate, muse, ruminate, brood; *formal* cogitate. **4** *she thought of all the visits she had made* **recall**, remember, recollect, call to mind, imagine, picture, visualize, envisage.
▫ **think up** devise, dream up, come up with, invent, create, concoct, make up, hit on; *informal* cook up.

thinker *noun* **intellectual**, philosopher, scholar, sage, ideologist, theorist, intellect, mind; *informal* brain.

thinking *adjective* **intelligent**, sensible, reasonable, rational, logical, analytical, thoughtful.
● *noun* **reasoning**, idea(s), theory, thoughts, philosophy, beliefs, opinion(s), view(s).

thirst *noun his thirst for knowledge* **craving**, desire, longing, yearning, hunger, hankering, eagerness, lust, appetite; *informal* yen, itch.
▫ **thirst for** crave, want, covet, desire, hunger for, lust after, hanker after, wish for, long for.

thirsty *adjective* **longing for a drink**, dry, dehydrated; *informal* parched, gasping.

thorn *noun* **prickle**, spike, barb, spine.

thorny *adjective* **1 prickly**, spiky, barbed, spiny, sharp. **2 problematic**, tricky, ticklish, delicate, controversial, awkward, difficult, knotty, tough, complicated, complex, involved, intricate, vexed; *informal* sticky.

thorough *adjective* **1** *a thorough investigation* **rigorous**, in-depth, exhaustive, minute, detailed, close, meticulous, methodical, careful, complete, comprehensive. **2** *he's slow but thorough* **meticulous**, scrupulous, assiduous, conscientious, painstaking, punctilious, methodical, careful. **3 utter**, downright, absolute, complete, total, out-and-out, real, perfect, proper; *Brit. informal* right; *Austral./NZ informal* fair.
– OPPOSITES superficial, cursory.

thought *noun* **1 idea**, notion, opinion, view, impression, feeling, theory. **2 thinking**, contemplation, musing, pondering, consideration, reflection, rumination, deliberation, meditation; *formal* cogitation. **3** *have you no thought for others?* **consideration**, understanding, regard, sensitivity, care, concern, compassion, sympathy.

thoughtful *adjective* **1 pensive**, reflective, contemplative, musing, meditative, ruminative, introspective, philosophical, preoccupied, in a brown study. **2 considerate**, caring, attentive, understanding, sympathetic, solicitous, concerned, helpful, obliging, accommodating, kind, compassionate.
– OPPOSITES thoughtless.

thoughtless *adjective* **1 inconsiderate**, uncaring, insensitive, uncharitable, unkind, tactless, undiplomatic, indiscreet, careless. **2 unthinking**, heedless, careless, unmindful, absent-minded, injudicious, ill-advised, ill-considered, imprudent, unwise, foolish, silly, stupid, reckless, rash, precipitate, negligent, neglectful, remiss.
– OPPOSITES thoughtful.

thrash *verb* **1 hit**, beat, strike, batter, thump, hammer, pound; *informal* belt. **2** *he was thrashing around in pain* **flail**, writhe, thresh, jerk, toss, twist, twitch.

thread *noun* **1 cotton**, yarn, fibre, filament. **2 train of thought**, drift, direction, theme, tenor.
● *verb she threaded her way through the tables* **weave**, inch, squeeze, navigate, negotiate.

threadbare *adjective* **worn**, old, holey, moth-eaten, mangy, ragged, frayed, tattered, decrepit, shabby, scruffy; *informal* tatty, the worse for wear.

threat *noun* **1 threatening remark**, warning, ultimatum. **2** *a possible threat to aircraft* **danger**, peril, hazard, menace, risk. **3** *the company faces the threat of liquidation* **possibility**, chance, probability, likelihood, risk.

threaten *verb* **1 menace**, intimidate, browbeat, bully, terrorize. **2 endanger**, jeopardize, imperil, put at risk. **3 herald**, bode, warn of, presage, foreshadow, indicate, point to, be a sign of, signal.

threshold *noun* **1 doorstep**, entrance, entry, gate, portal. **2 start**, beginning, commencement, brink, verge, dawn, inception, day one, opening, debut.

thrifty *adjective* **frugal**, economical, sparing, careful with money, provident, prudent, abstemious, parsimonious, penny-pinching.
- OPPOSITES extravagant.

thrill *noun* **excitement**, stimulation, pleasure, tingle; *informal* buzz, kick; *N. Amer. informal* charge.
- OPPOSITES boredom.
● *verb* **excite**, stimulate, arouse, rouse, inspire, delight, exhilarate, intoxicate, stir, electrify, move; *informal* give someone a buzz/kick; *N. Amer. informal* give someone a charge.
- OPPOSITES bore.

thrilling *adjective* **exciting**, stimulating, stirring, action-packed, rip-roaring, gripping, electrifying, riveting, fascinating, dramatic, hair-raising.
- OPPOSITES boring.

thrive *verb* **flourish**, prosper, burgeon, bloom, blossom, do well, advance, succeed, boom.
- OPPOSITES decline, wither.

thriving *adjective* **flourishing**, prospering, growing, developing, blooming, healthy, successful, booming, profitable; *informal* going strong.
- OPPOSITES declining.

throb *verb* **pulsate**, beat, pulse, palpitate, pound, thud, thump, drum, judder, vibrate, quiver.
● *noun* **pulsation**, beat, pulse, palpitation, pounding, thudding, thumping, drumming, juddering, vibration, quivering.

throng *noun* **crowd**, horde, mass, army, herd, flock, drove, swarm, sea, troupe, pack; *informal* bunch, gaggle, gang.
● *verb* **1** *pavements thronged with tourists* **fill**, crowd, pack, cram, jam. **2** *visitors thronged round him* **flock**, crowd, cluster, mill, swarm, congregate, gather.

throttle *verb* **choke**, strangle, garrotte.

through *preposition* **1 by means of**, by way of, by dint of, via, using, thanks to, by virtue of, as a result of, as a consequence of, on account of, owing to. **2 throughout**, for the duration of, until/to the end of, all.

throughout *preposition* **1 all over**, in every part of, everywhere in. **2 all through**, for the duration of, for the whole of, until the end of, all.

throw *verb* **1 hurl**, toss, fling, pitch, cast, lob, launch, bowl; *informal* chuck, heave, sling, bung. **2** *he threw the door open* **push**, thrust, fling, bang. **3 cast**, send, give off, emit, radiate, project. **4 disconcert**, unnerve, fluster, ruffle, put off, throw off balance, unsettle, confuse; *informal* rattle, faze.
● *noun* **lob**, toss, pitch, bowl.
□ **throw away/out** discard, dispose of, get rid of, scrap, dump, jettison; *informal* chuck (away/out), ditch, bin, junk; *Brit. informal* get shot of. **throw out** expel, eject, evict, drive out, force out, oust, remove, get rid of, depose, topple, unseat, overthrow; *informal* boot out, kick out; *Brit. informal* turf out.

thrust *verb* **1 shove**, push, force, plunge, stick, drive, ram, lunge. **2** *fame had been thrust on him* **force**, foist, impose, inflict.
● *noun* **1 shove**, push, lunge, poke. **2 advance**, push, drive, attack, assault, onslaught, offensive. **3 force**, propulsion, power, impetus. **4 gist**, substance, drift, message, import, tenor.

thug *noun* **ruffian**, hooligan, bully boy, hoodlum, gangster, villain; *informal* tough, bruiser, heavy; *Brit. informal* rough, bovver boy; *N. Amer. informal* hood, goon.

thump *verb* **1 hit**, beat, punch, strike, smack, batter, pummel; *informal* whack, wallop, bash, biff, clobber, clout; *Brit. informal* slosh; *N. Amer. informal* slug. **2 throb**, pound, beat, thud, hammer.

thunder *noun* **rumble**, boom, roar, pounding, crash, reverberation.
● *verb* **1 rumble**, boom, roar, pound, crash, resound, reverberate. **2** *'Answer me!' he thundered* **shout**, roar, bellow, bark, bawl.

thwart *verb* **foil**, frustrate, forestall, stop, check, block, prevent, defeat, impede, obstruct, derail, snooker; *informal* put paid to, do for, stymie; *Brit. informal* scupper.
– OPPOSITES help.

ticket *noun* **1 pass**, authorization, permit, token, coupon, voucher. **2 label**, tag, sticker, tab, slip, docket.

tickle *verb* **1 stroke**, pet. **2 stimulate**, interest, appeal to, amuse, entertain, divert, please, delight.

tide *noun* **1 current**, flow, stream, ebb. **2** *the tide of history* **course**, movement, direction, trend, current, drift, run.

tidy *adjective* **1** *a tidy room* **neat**, orderly, in good order, well kept, in apple-pie order, shipshape, spick and span, spruce, uncluttered, straight. **2** *a tidy person* **organized**, neat, methodical, meticulous, systematic.
– OPPOSITES untidy.
● *verb* **put in order**, clear up, sort out, straighten (up), clean up, spruce up, smarten up.

tie *verb* **1 bind**, tie up, tether, hitch, strap, truss, fetter, rope, make fast, moor, lash. **2 do up**, lace, knot. **3 restrict**, restrain, limit, tie down, constrain, cramp, hamper, handicap, hamstring, encumber, shackle. **4 link**, connect, couple, relate, join, marry. **5 draw**, be equal, be even.
● *noun* **1 lace**, string, cord, fastening. **2 bond**, connection, link, relationship, attachment, affiliation. **3 restriction**, constraint, curb, limitation, restraint, hindrance, encumbrance, handicap, obligation, commitment. **4 draw**, dead heat.

tier *noun* **1 row**, rank, bank, line, layer, level. **2 grade**, gradation, echelon, rung on the ladder.

tight *adjective* **1 firm**, secure, fast. **2 taut**, rigid, stiff, tense, stretched, strained, clenched. **3 close-fitting**, narrow, figure-hugging, skintight; *informal* sprayed on. **4** *a tight mass of fibres* **compact**, compressed, dense, solid. **5 small**, tiny, narrow, limited, restricted, confined, cramped, constricted. **6** *tight security* **strict**, rigorous, stringent, tough.
– OPPOSITES slack, loose.

tighten *verb* **1 stretch**, tauten, strain, stiffen, tense. **2 strengthen**, increase, make stricter.
– OPPOSITES loosen, slacken.

tilt *verb* **slope**, tip, lean, list, bank, slant, incline, pitch, cant, angle.
● *noun* **slope**, list, camber, gradient, bank, slant, incline, pitch, cant, bevel, angle.

timber *noun* **1 wood**; *N. Amer.* lumber. **2 beam**, spar, plank, batten, lath, board, joist, rafter.

time *noun* **1 moment**, point (in time), occasion, instant, juncture, stage. **2** *he worked there for a time* **while**, spell, stretch, stint, interval, period, length of time, duration, phase. **3 era**, age, epoch, aeon, period, years, days.
● *verb* **schedule**, arrange, set, organize, fix, book, line up, timetable, plan; *N. Amer.* slate.
□ **all the time** constantly, around the clock, day and night, {morning, noon, and night}, {day in, day out}, always, without a break, ceaselessly, endlessly, incessantly, perpetually, permanently, continuously, continually, eternally; *informal* 24-7. **at times** occasionally, sometimes, from time to time, now and then, every so often, once in a while, on occasion, off and on, at intervals, periodically.

WORD LINKS
chronological, **temporal** relating to time

timeless *adjective* **lasting**, enduring, classic, ageless, permanent, perennial, abiding, unchanging, unvarying, never-changing, eternal, everlasting.
- OPPOSITES ephemeral.

timely *adjective* **opportune**, well timed, convenient, appropriate, expedient, seasonable, propitious.
- OPPOSITES ill-timed.

timetable *noun* **schedule**, programme, agenda, calendar, diary.
● *verb* **schedule**, arrange, programme, organize, fix, time, line up; *Brit.* diarize; *N. Amer.* slate.

timid *adjective* **fearful**, afraid, faint-hearted, timorous, nervous, scared, frightened, shy, diffident.
- OPPOSITES bold.

tinge *verb* **tint**, colour, stain, shade, wash.
● *noun* **1 tint**, colour, shade, tone, hue. **2 trace**, note, touch, suggestion, hint, flavour, element, streak, suspicion, soupçon.

tingle *verb* **prickle**, prick, sting, itch, tickle.
● *noun* **prickle**, pricking, tingling, sting, itch, pins and needles.

tinker *verb* **fiddle**, play about, mess about, adjust, try to mend; *Brit. informal* muck about.

tint *noun* **1 shade**, colour, tone, hue, tinge, cast, flush, blush. **2 dye**, colourant, colouring, wash.
● *verb* **dye**, colour, tinge.

tiny *adjective* **minute**, minuscule, microscopic, very small, mini, diminutive, miniature, baby, toy, fun-size, dwarf; *Scottish* wee; *informal* teeny, tiddly; *Brit. informal* titchy.
- OPPOSITES huge.

tip[1] *noun* **1 point**, end, extremity, head, spike, prong, nib. **2 peak**, top, summit, apex, crown, crest, pinnacle.
● *verb* **cap**, top, crown, surmount.

tip[2] *verb* **1 overturn**, turn over, topple (over), fall (over), keel over, capsize, roll over. **2 lean**, tilt, list, slope, bank, slant, incline, pitch, cant. **3 pour**, empty, drain, dump, discharge, decant.
● *noun (Brit.)* **dump**, rubbish dump, landfill site.

tip[3] *noun* **1 gratuity**, baksheesh, present, gift, reward. **2 piece of advice**, suggestion, word of advice, pointer, hint; *informal* wrinkle.

tirade *noun* **diatribe**, harangue, rant, attack, polemic, broadside, fulmination, tongue-lashing; *informal* blast.

tire *verb* **1 get tired**, weaken, flag, droop. **2 fatigue**, tire out, exhaust, wear out, drain, weary, enervate; *informal* knock out, take it out of; *Brit. informal* knacker.

tired *adjective* **1 exhausted**, worn out, weary, fatigued, ready to drop, drained, enervated; *informal* all in, dead beat, shattered, done in; *Brit. informal* knackered, whacked; *N. Amer. informal* pooped, tuckered out; *Austral./NZ informal* stonkered. **2** *I'm tired of him* **fed up with**, weary of, bored with/by, sick (and tired) of; *informal* up to here with. **3 hackneyed**, overused, stale, clichéd, predictable, unimaginative, unoriginal, dull, boring; *informal* corny.
- OPPOSITES energetic, fresh.

tiresome *adjective* **1 wearisome**, laborious, wearing, tedious, boring, monotonous, dull, uninteresting, unexciting, humdrum, routine. **2 troublesome**, irksome, vexatious, irritating, annoying, exasperating, trying; *informal* aggravating, pesky.
- OPPOSITES interesting, pleasant.

tiring *adjective* **exhausting**, wearying, taxing, draining, hard, arduous, strenuous, onerous, gruelling; *informal* killing; *Brit. informal* knackering.

title *noun* **1 heading**, label, inscription, caption, subheading, legend. **2 name**, designation, form of address, rank, office, position; *informal* moniker, handle. **3** *an Olympic title* **championship**, crown, first place.

toast *verb* **drink (to) the health of**, salute, honour, pay tribute to; *old use* pledge.

toddle *verb* **totter**, teeter, wobble, falter, waddle, stumble.

together *adverb* **1 with each other**, in conjunction, jointly, in cooperation, in collaboration, in partnership, in combination, in league, side by side; *informal* in cahoots. **2 simultaneously**, at the same time, at once, concurrently, as a group, in unison, in chorus.
- OPPOSITES separately.
● *adjective (informal)* **level-headed**, well adjusted, sensible, practical, realistic, mature, stable, full of common sense, well organized, efficient, methodical, self-confident, self-assured; *informal* unflappable.

toil *verb* **1 work**, labour, slave, strive; *informal* slog, beaver; *Brit. informal* graft. **2 struggle**, drag yourself, trudge, slog, plod; *N. Amer. informal* schlep.
● *noun* **hard work**, labour, exertion, slaving, drudgery, effort, {blood, sweat, and tears}; *informal* slog, elbow grease; *Brit. informal* graft; *old use* travail.

toilet *noun* **lavatory**, WC, (public) convenience, cloakroom, powder room, latrine, privy, urinal; *N. Amer.* bathroom, washroom, rest room, men's/ladies' room, comfort station; *Brit. informal* loo, bog, the Ladies, the Gents; *N. Amer. informal* can, john; *Austral./NZ informal* dunny.

token *noun* **1 symbol**, sign, emblem, badge, representation, indication, mark, expression, demonstration. **2 memento**, souvenir, keepsake, reminder. **3 voucher**, coupon, note.
● *adjective token resistance* **symbolic**, nominal, perfunctory, slight, minimal, superficial.

tolerable *adjective* **1 bearable**, endurable, supportable, acceptable. **2 fairly good**, fair, passable, adequate, all right, acceptable, satisfactory, average, run-of-the-mill, mediocre, middling, ordinary, unexceptional; *informal* OK, so-so, no great shakes.
- OPPOSITES intolerable.

tolerance *noun* **1 toleration**, acceptance, open-mindedness, broad-mindedness, forbearance, patience, charity, understanding, lenience. **2 endurance**, resilience, resistance, immunity.

tolerant *adjective* **open-minded**, forbearing, broad-minded, liberal, unprejudiced, unbiased, patient, long-suffering, understanding, charitable, lenient, easy-going, indulgent, permissive.

tolerate *verb* **1 allow**, permit, condone, accept, swallow, countenance; *formal* brook. **2** *he couldn't tolerate her moods any longer* **endure**, put up with, bear, take, stand, support, stomach, abide; *Brit. informal* stick.

toll[1] *noun* **1 charge**, fee, payment, levy, tariff, tax. **2 number**, count, tally, total, sum. **3** *the toll on the environment has been high* **harm**, damage, injury, detriment, adverse effect, cost, price, loss.

toll[2] *verb* **ring**, sound, clang, chime, strike, peal.

tomb *noun* **burial chamber**, vault, crypt, catacomb, sepulchre, mausoleum, grave.

WORD LINKS
sepulchral relating to a tomb

tone *noun* **1 sound**, timbre, voice, colour, tonality, intonation, inflection, modulation. **2 mood**, air, feel, flavour, note, attitude, character, spirit, vein. **3 shade**, colour, hue, tint, tinge.
● *verb* **harmonize**, go, blend, coordinate, team, match, suit, complement.
□ **tone down** moderate, modify, temper, soften, modulate, lighten, subdue.

tonic *noun* **stimulant**, boost, restorative, refresher, fillip; *informal* shot in the arm, pick-me-up, bracer.

too *adverb* **1 excessively**, overly, unduly, immoderately, inordinately, unreasonably, extremely, very. **2 also**, as well, in addition, into the bargain, besides, furthermore, moreover.

tool *noun* **implement**, utensil, instrument, device, apparatus, gadget, appliance, machine, contrivance, contraption; *informal* gizmo.

tooth *noun* **fang**, tusk; *informal* gnasher.

WORD LINKS
dental relating to teeth

top *noun* **1 summit**, peak, pinnacle, crest, crown, brow, head, tip, apex, apogee. **2 lid**, cap, cover, stopper, cork. **3** *he was at the top of his career* **height**, peak, pinnacle, zenith, culmination, climax, prime.
- OPPOSITES bottom, base.
● *adjective* **1 highest**, topmost, uppermost. **2 foremost**, chief, leading, principal, pre-eminent, greatest, best, finest, elite, premier, prime, superior, select, five-star, grade A, A-list. **3 maximum**, greatest, utmost.
- OPPOSITES lowest, minimum.
● *verb* **1 exceed**, surpass, go beyond, better, beat, outstrip, outdo, outshine, eclipse, transcend. **2 lead**, head, be at the top of. **3** *mousse topped with cream* **cover**, cap, coat, finish, garnish.
□ **top up** fill, refill, refresh, freshen, replenish, recharge, resupply.

topic *noun* **subject**, theme, issue, matter, point, question, concern, argument, thesis.

topical *adjective* **current**, up to date, up to the minute, contemporary, recent, relevant, in the news.
- OPPOSITES out of date.

topple *verb* **1 fall**, tumble, tip, overbalance, overturn, keel over, lose your balance. **2 knock over**, upset, push over, tip over, upend. **3 overthrow**, oust, unseat, overturn, bring down, defeat, get rid of, dislodge, eject.

torment *noun* **agony**, suffering, torture, pain, anguish, misery, distress, trauma.
● *verb* **1 torture**, afflict, rack, harrow, plague, haunt, distress, agonize. **2 tease**, taunt, bait, provoke, harass, bother, persecute; *informal* needle.

torn *adjective* **1 ripped**, rent, cut, slit, ragged, tattered. **2 wavering**, vacillating, irresolute, dithering, uncertain, unsure, undecided, in two minds.

tornado *noun* **whirlwind**, cyclone, typhoon, storm, hurricane; *N. Amer. informal* twister.

torrent *noun* **1** *a torrent of water* **flood**, deluge, spate, cascade, rush. **2** *a torrent of abuse* **outburst**, outpouring, stream, flood, volley, barrage, tide.
- OPPOSITES trickle.

tortuous *adjective* **1 twisting**, winding, zigzag, sinuous, snaky, meandering, serpentine. **2 convoluted**, complicated, complex, labyrinthine, involved, Byzantine, lengthy.
- OPPOSITES straight.

torture *noun* **1 abuse**, ill-treatment, mistreatment, maltreatment, persecution, cruelty, atrocity. **2 torment**, agony, suffering, pain, anguish, misery, distress, heartbreak, trauma.
● *verb* **1 abuse**, ill-treat, mistreat, maltreat, persecute. **2 torment**, rack, afflict, harrow, plague, distress, trouble.

toss *verb* **1 throw**, hurl, fling, sling, pitch, lob, launch; *informal* heave, chuck, bung. **2** *he tossed a coin* **flip**, flick, spin. **3 pitch**, lurch, rock, roll, plunge, reel, sway.

total *adjective* **1 entire**, complete, whole, full, combined, aggregate, gross, overall. **2 utter**, complete, absolute, thorough, perfect, downright, out-and-out, outright, sheer, unmitigated, unqualified, unalloyed.
- OPPOSITES partial.
● *noun* **sum**, aggregate, whole, entirety, totality.
● *verb* **1 add up to**, amount to, come to, run to, make. **2** *he totalled up his score* **add**, count, reckon, tot up, compute, work out.

totalitarian *adjective* **autocratic**, undemocratic, one-party, dictatorial, tyrannical, despotic, fascist, oppressive, authoritarian, absolutist.
- OPPOSITES democratic.

totally *adverb* **completely**, entirely, wholly, thoroughly, fully, utterly, absolutely, perfectly, unreservedly,

unconditionally, downright.
- OPPOSITES partly.

touch *verb* **1 contact**, meet, brush, graze, come up against, be in contact with, border, abut. **2 feel**, pat, tap, stroke, fondle, caress, pet, handle. **3** *sales touched £20,000* **reach**, attain, come to, make, rise to, soar to; *informal* hit. **4 compare with**, be on a par with, equal, match, rival, measure up to, better, beat; *informal* hold a candle to. **5 handle**, hold, pick up, move, use, meddle with, play about with, fiddle with, interfere with, tamper with, disturb. **6 affect**, move, stir, make an impression on.
● *noun* **1 tap**, pat, contact, stroke, caress. **2 skill**, expertise, dexterity, deftness, adroitness, adeptness, ability, talent, flair, facility, proficiency, knack. **3 trace**, bit, suggestion, suspicion, hint, scintilla, tinge, dash, taste, spot, drop, dab, soupçon. **4** *the gas lights are a nice touch* **detail**, feature, point, element, addition. **5** *are you in touch with him?* **contact**, communication, correspondence.
□ **touch on** refer to, mention, comment on, remark on, bring up, raise, broach, allude to, cover, deal with.

WORD LINKS
tactile relating to touch

touching *adjective* **moving**, affecting, heart-warming, emotional, emotive, poignant, sad, tear-jerking.

touchy *adjective* **1 sensitive**, oversensitive, hypersensitive, easily offended, thin-skinned, highly strung, tense, irritable, tetchy, testy, crotchety, peevish, querulous, bad-tempered, petulant; *informal* snappy, ratty; *N. Amer. informal* cranky. **2 delicate**, sensitive, tricky, ticklish, embarrassing, awkward, difficult, contentious, controversial.

tough *adjective* **1 durable**, strong, resilient, sturdy, rugged, solid, stout, robust, hard-wearing, long-lasting, heavy-duty, well built, made to last. **2 chewy**, leathery, gristly, stringy, fibrous. **3 strict**, stern, severe, stringent, rigorous, hard, firm, hard-hitting, uncompromising. **4** *the training was pretty tough* **difficult**, hard, strenuous, onerous, gruelling, exacting, arduous, demanding, taxing, tiring, exhausting, punishing. **5** *tough questions* **difficult**, hard, knotty, thorny, tricky.
- OPPOSITES weak, lenient, easy.
● *noun* **ruffian**, thug, hoodlum, hooligan, bully boy; *informal* heavy, bruiser; *Brit. informal* yob.

toughen *verb* **1 strengthen**, fortify, reinforce, harden, temper, anneal. **2** *measures to toughen up discipline* **make stricter**, make more severe, stiffen, tighten up.

tour *noun* **1 trip**, excursion, journey, expedition, jaunt, outing, trek. **2** *a tour of the factory* **visit**, inspection, walkabout.
● *verb* **travel round**, visit, explore, holiday in, go round.

tourist *noun* **holidaymaker**, traveller, sightseer, visitor, backpacker, globe-trotter, tripper; *N. Amer.* vacationer.
- OPPOSITES local.

tournament *noun* **competition**, contest, championship, meeting, event.

tow *verb* **pull**, haul, drag, draw, tug, lug.

tower *verb* **soar**, rise, rear, overshadow, overhang, hang over, dominate.

town *noun* **city**, metropolis, conurbation, municipality; *Brit.* borough; *Scottish* burgh.
- OPPOSITES country.

WORD LINKS
urban, municipal relating to towns

toxic *adjective* **poisonous**, dangerous, harmful, injurious, noxious, pernicious, deadly, lethal, environmentally unfriendly, polluting.
- OPPOSITES harmless.

toy *noun* **plaything**, game.
● *adjective* **model**, imitation, replica, miniature.
□ **toy with 1** think about, consider, flirt with, entertain the possibility of; *informal* kick around. **2** fiddle with, play

with, fidget with, twiddle, finger.

trace *verb* **1 track down**, find, discover, detect, unearth, turn up, hunt down, ferret out, run to ground. **2 draw**, outline, mark.
● *noun* **1 sign**, mark, indication, evidence, clue, vestige, remains, remnant. **2 bit**, touch, hint, suggestion, suspicion, shadow, dash, tinge; *informal* smidgen, tad.

track *noun* **1 path**, footpath, lane, trail, route, way. **2 course**, racecourse, racetrack, velodrome; *Brit.* circuit. **3** *the tracks of a fox* **traces**, marks, prints, footprints, trail, spoor. **4** *the railway tracks* **rail**, line. **5 song**, recording, number, piece.
● *verb* **follow**, trail, pursue, shadow, stalk; *informal* tail.
□ **track down** discover, find, detect, hunt down, unearth, uncover, turn up, dig up, ferret out, run to ground.

trade *noun* **1 dealing**, buying and selling, commerce, traffic, business. **2 occupation**, work, craft, job, career, profession, business, line (of work), métier.
● *verb* **1 deal**, do business, bargain, negotiate, traffic, buy and sell, merchandise. **2** *I traded the car for a newer model* **swap**, exchange, barter, part-exchange.

WORD LINKS
mercantile relating to trade

trader *noun* **dealer**, merchant, buyer, seller, vendor, purveyor, supplier, trafficker.

tradition *noun* **custom**, practice, convention, ritual, observance, way, usage, habit, institution, unwritten law; *formal* praxis.

traditional *adjective* **customary**, long-established, time-honoured, classic, wonted, accustomed, standard, regular, normal, conventional, habitual, ritual, age-old.

tragedy *noun* **disaster**, calamity, catastrophe, cataclysm, misfortune, adversity.

tragic *adjective* **1 disastrous**, calamitous, catastrophic, cataclysmic, devastating, terrible, dreadful, awful, appalling, horrendous, fatal. **2 sad**, unhappy, pathetic, moving, distressing, painful, harrowing, heart-rending, sorry.
– OPPOSITES fortunate, happy.

trail *noun* **1** *a trail of clues* **series**, string, chain, succession, sequence. **2 track**, spoor, path, scent, traces, marks, signs, prints, footprints. **3 path**, way, footpath, track, route.
● *verb* **1 drag**, sweep, be drawn, dangle. **2** *roses trailed over the banks* **hang**, droop, fall, spill, cascade. **3 follow**, pursue, track, shadow, stalk, hunt; *informal* tail. **4 lose**, be down, be behind, lag behind.

train *verb* **1 instruct**, teach, coach, tutor, school, educate, prime, drill, ground. **2 study**, learn, prepare, take instruction. **3 exercise**, work out, get into shape, practise. **4 aim**, point, direct, level, focus.
● *noun* **chain**, string, series, set, sequence, succession, course.

trainer *noun* **coach**, instructor, teacher, tutor, handler.

trait *noun* **characteristic**, attribute, feature, quality, habit, mannerism, idiosyncrasy, peculiarity.

traitor *noun* **betrayer**, back-stabber, double-crosser, renegade, Judas, quisling, fifth columnist, turncoat, defector; *informal* snake in the grass.

tramp *verb* **trudge**, plod, stamp, trample, lumber, trek, walk, slog, hike; *informal* traipse; *N. Amer. informal* schlep.
● *noun* **1 vagrant**, vagabond, homeless person, down-and-out, traveller, drifter; *N. Amer.* hobo; *N. Amer. informal* bum. **2 tread**, step, footstep, footfall. **3 trek**, walk, hike, slog, march, roam, ramble; *N. Amer. informal* schlep.

trample *verb* **tread**, stamp, walk, squash, crush, flatten.

trance *noun* **daze**, stupor, hypnotic state, dream, reverie.

tranquil *adjective* **peaceful**, calm, restful, quiet, still, serene, relaxing, undisturbed.
- OPPOSITES busy, excitable.

tranquillizer *noun* **sedative**, barbiturate, calmative, narcotic, opiate; *informal* downer.
- OPPOSITES stimulant.

transaction *noun* **deal**, bargain, agreement, undertaking, arrangement, negotiation, settlement.

transcend *verb* **go beyond**, rise above, exceed, surpass, excel, outstrip.

transfer *verb* **move**, take, bring, shift, convey, remove, carry, transport, relocate.

transform *verb* **change**, alter, convert, revolutionize, overhaul, reconstruct, rebuild, reorganize, rearrange, rework.

transformation *noun* **change**, alteration, conversion, metamorphosis, revolution, overhaul, reconstruction, rebuilding, reorganization, rearrangement, reworking.

transient *adjective* **transitory**, temporary, short-lived, short-term, ephemeral, impermanent, brief, short, momentary, fleeting, passing.
- OPPOSITES permanent.

transition *noun* **change**, passage, move, transformation, conversion, metamorphosis, alteration, changeover, shift, switch.

transitional *adjective* **1** *a transitional period* **intermediate**, interim, changeover, changing, fluid, unsettled. **2** *a transitional government* **interim**, temporary, provisional, pro tem, acting, caretaker.

translate *verb* **interpret**, convert, render, put, change, express, decipher, reword, decode, gloss, explain.

translation *noun* **interpretation**, rendition, conversion, change, alteration, adaptation.

transmission *noun* **1 transfer**, communication, passing on, conveyance, dissemination, spread, circulation, relaying. **2 broadcasting**, televising, airing. **3 broadcast**, programme, show, telecast, videocast, podcast.

transmit *verb* **1 transfer**, communicate, pass on, hand on, convey, impart, channel, carry, relay, dispatch, disseminate, spread, circulate. **2 broadcast**, send out, air, televise, telecast, videocast, podcast.

transparent *adjective* **1 clear**, translucent, limpid, crystal clear, crystalline, pellucid. **2 see-through**, sheer, filmy, gauzy, diaphanous. **3 obvious**, blatant, unambiguous, unequivocal, clear, plain, apparent, unmistakable, manifest, conspicuous, patent.
- OPPOSITES opaque, obscure.

transport *verb* **convey**, carry, take, transfer, move, shift, send, deliver, bear, ship, ferry; *informal* cart.
● *noun* **conveyance**, carriage, delivery, shipping, freight, shipment, haulage.

trap *noun* **1 snare**, net, mesh, gin; *N. Amer.* deadfall. **2 trick**, ploy, ruse, deception, subterfuge; *informal* set-up.
● *verb* **1 snare**, entrap, capture, catch, ambush. **2 confine**, cut off, corner, shut in, pen in, hem in, imprison. **3 trick**, dupe, deceive, fool, hoodwink.

trash *noun* **1** *(N. Amer.)* **rubbish**, refuse, waste, litter, junk; *N. Amer.* garbage. **2** *(informal)* **nonsense**, rubbish, trivia, pulp fiction, pap; *informal* drivel.

trauma *noun* **1 shock**, upheaval, distress, stress, strain, pain, anguish, suffering, upset, ordeal. **2 injury**, damage, wound.

traumatic *adjective* **disturbing**, shocking, distressing, upsetting, painful, agonizing, hurtful, stressful, devastating, harrowing.

travel *verb* **journey**, tour, take a trip, voyage, go sightseeing, globetrot, backpack, trek.
● *noun* **travelling**, journeys, expeditions, trips, tours, excursions, voyages, treks, wanderings, jaunts.

traveller *noun* **tourist**, tripper, holidaymaker, sightseer, globetrotter, backpacker, passenger, commuter; *N. Amer.* vacationer.

treacherous *adjective* **1 traitorous**, disloyal, unfaithful, duplicitous, deceitful, false, back-stabbing, double-crossing, two-faced, untrustworthy, unreliable, apostate, renegade. **2 dangerous**, hazardous, perilous, unsafe, precarious, risky; *informal* dicey, hairy.
- OPPOSITES loyal, faithful.

tread *verb* **1 walk**, step, stride, pace, march, tramp, plod, stomp, trudge. **2 crush**, flatten, press down, squash, trample on, stamp on.
● *noun* **step**, footstep, footfall, tramp.

treason *noun* **treachery**, disloyalty, betrayal, sedition, subversion, mutiny, rebellion.

treasure *noun* **1 riches**, valuables, jewels, gems, gold, silver, precious metals, money, cash, wealth, fortune. **2 masterpiece**, gem, pearl, jewel.
● *verb* **cherish**, hold dear, prize, set great store by, value greatly.

treasury *noun* **storehouse**, repository, treasure house, exchequer, fund, mine, bank, coffers, purse.

treat *verb* **1 behave towards**, act towards, use, deal with, handle. **2** *police are treating the fires as arson* **regard**, consider, view, look on, put down as. **3 deal with**, tackle, handle, discuss, explore, investigate. **4 tend**, nurse, attend to, give medical attention to. **5 cure**, heal, remedy. **6** *he treated her to lunch* **buy**, take out for, stand, give, pay for, entertain, wine and dine; *informal* foot the bill for. **7** *the crowd was treated to a superb display* **entertain with**, regale with, fete with.
● *noun* **1 celebration**, entertainment, amusement, surprise. **2 present**, gift, titbit, delicacy, luxury, indulgence, extravagance; *informal* goody. **3 pleasure**, delight, thrill, joy.

treatment *noun* **1 behaviour**, conduct, handling, management, dealings. **2 medical care**, therapy, nursing, ministrations, medication, medicament, drugs. **3 discussion**, handling, investigation, exploration, consideration, study, analysis.

treaty *noun* **agreement**, settlement, pact, deal, entente, concordat, accord, protocol, compact, convention; *formal* concord.

tree *noun*

WORD LINKS
arboreal relating to trees

trek *noun* **journey**, trip, expedition, safari, hike, march, tramp, walk.

tremble *verb* **shake**, quiver, shudder, judder, vibrate, wobble, rock, move, sway.

tremendous *adjective* **1 huge**, enormous, immense, colossal, massive, cosmic, prodigious, stupendous; *informal* whopping, astronomical; *Brit. informal* ginormous. **2 excellent**, first-class, outstanding, marvellous, wonderful, splendid, superb, admirable; *informal* great, fantastic, fabulous, terrific, super, awesome, ace; *Brit. informal* brilliant, smashing.

trench *noun* **ditch**, channel, trough, excavation, furrow, rut, conduit.

trend *noun* **1 tendency**, movement, drift, swing, shift, course, current, direction, inclination, leaning. **2 fashion**, vogue, style, mode, craze, mania, rage; *informal* fad, thing.

trespass *verb* **intrude**, encroach, invade, enter without permission.

trial *noun* **1 case**, lawsuit, hearing, tribunal, litigation, proceedings. **2 test**, experiment, pilot study, examination, check, assessment, audition, evaluation, appraisal; *informal* dry run. **3 trouble**, affliction, ordeal, tribulation, difficulty, problem, misfortune, mishap.

tribe *noun* **ethnic group**, people, family, clan, race, dynasty, house, nation.

tribunal *noun* **court**, board, panel, committee.

tribute *noun* **accolade**, praise, commendation, salute, testimonial, homage, congratulations, compliments, plaudits.
- OPPOSITES criticism.

trick *noun* **1 stratagem**, ploy, ruse, scheme, device, manoeuvre, dodge, subterfuge, swindle, fraud; *informal* con, set-up, scam, sting. **2 practical joke**, hoax, prank; *informal* leg-pull, spoof, put-on. **3 knack**, skill, technique, secret, art.
● *verb* **deceive**, delude, hoodwink, mislead, take in, dupe, fool, gull, cheat, defraud, swindle; *informal* con, diddle, take for a ride, pull a fast one on; *N. Amer. informal* sucker.

trickle *verb* **dribble**, drip, ooze, leak, seep, spill, exude, percolate.
- OPPOSITES pour, gush.
● *noun* **dribble**, drip, thin stream, rivulet.

tricky *adjective* **1 difficult**, awkward, problematic, delicate, ticklish, sensitive; *informal* sticky. **2 cunning**, crafty, wily, devious, sly, scheming, calculating, deceitful.
- OPPOSITES straightforward.

trifle *noun* **triviality**, thing of no consequence, bagatelle, inessential, nothing, technicality; (**trifles**) trivia, minutiae.

trifling *adjective* **trivial**, unimportant, insignificant, inconsequential, petty, minor, of no account, footling, incidental; *informal* piffling.
- OPPOSITES important.

trigger *verb* **start**, set off, initiate, spark (off), activate, touch off, provoke, precipitate, prompt, stir up, cause, give rise to, lead to, set in motion, bring about.

trim *verb* **1 cut**, crop, bob, shorten, clip, snip, shear, dock, lop off, prune, shave, pare. **2 decorate**, adorn, ornament, embellish, edge, border, fringe.
● *noun* **1 decoration**, ornamentation, adornment, embellishment, border, edging, piping, fringe, frill. **2 haircut**, cut, clip, snip.
● *adjective* **1 neat**, tidy, orderly, uncluttered, well kept, well maintained, immaculate, spick and span, spruce, dapper. **2 slim**, slender, lean, sleek, willowy.
- OPPOSITES untidy.
□ **in trim** fit, in good health, in fine fettle, slim, in shape.

trimming *noun* **1 decoration**, ornamentation, adornment, borders, edging, piping, fringes, frills. **2** (**trimmings**) **accompaniments**, extras, frills, accessories, accoutrements, trappings, paraphernalia.

trio *noun* **threesome**, three, triumvirate, triad, troika, trinity, trilogy.

trip *verb* **1 stumble**, lose your footing, catch your foot, slip, fall (down), tumble. **2 skip**, dance, prance, bound, spring, scamper.
● *noun* **1 excursion**, outing, jaunt, holiday, break, visit, tour, journey, expedition, voyage, drive, run; *informal* spin. **2 stumble**, slip, fall, misstep.

triple *adjective* **threefold**, tripartite, three-way, three times, treble.

triumph *noun* **1 victory**, win, conquest, success, achievement. **2 jubilation**, exultation, elation, delight, joy, happiness, glee, pride, satisfaction.
- OPPOSITES defeat, disappointment.
● *verb* **win**, succeed, come first, be victorious, carry the day, prevail.
- OPPOSITES lose.
□ **triumph over** defeat, beat, conquer, trounce, vanquish, overcome, overpower, overwhelm, get the better of; *informal* lick; *US informal* own.

triumphant *adjective* **1 victorious**, successful, winning, conquering. **2 jubilant**, exultant, celebratory, elated, joyful, delighted, gleeful, proud, cock a hoop.
- OPPOSITES defeated, despondent.

trivial *adjective* **unimportant**, insignificant, inconsequential, minor, of no account, of no importance, petty, trifling, footling, negligible; *informal* piffling.
- OPPOSITES important, significant.

troop *noun* **1 group**, party, band, gang, body, company, troupe, crowd, squad, unit. **2** (**troops**) **soldiers**, armed forces, soldiery, servicemen, servicewomen.
● *verb* **walk**, march, file, flock, crowd, throng, stream, swarm.

trophy *noun* **1 cup**, medal, prize, award. **2 souvenir**, memento, keepsake, spoils, booty.

tropical *adjective* **hot**, sweltering, humid, sultry, steamy, sticky, oppressive, stifling.
- OPPOSITES cold.

trot *verb* **run**, jog, scuttle, scurry, bustle, scamper.

trouble *noun* **1 difficulty**, problems, issues, bother, inconvenience, worry, anxiety, distress, stress, agitation, harassment, unpleasantness; *informal* hassle. **2** *she poured out all her troubles* **problem**, misfortune, difficulty, trial, tribulation, woe, grief, heartache, misery, affliction, suffering. **3** *he's gone to a lot of trouble* **bother**, inconvenience, fuss, effort, exertion, work, labour. **4 nuisance**, bother, inconvenience, irritation, problem, trial, pest; *informal* headache, pain, drag. **5** *you're too gullible, that's your trouble* **shortcoming**, weakness, failing, fault. **6 disease**, illness, sickness, ailment, complaint, problem, disorder, disability. **7 malfunction**, failure, breakdown. **8 disturbance**, disorder, unrest, fighting, scuffles, breach of the peace.
● *verb* **1 worry**, bother, concern, disturb, upset, agitate, distress, perturb, annoy, nag, prey on someone's mind; *informal* bug. **2 afflict**, burden, suffer from, be cursed with. **3** *I'm sorry to trouble you* **inconvenience**, bother, impose on, disturb, put out, disoblige; *informal* hassle.

troublesome *adjective* **1 annoying**, irritating, exasperating, maddening, infuriating, bothersome, tiresome, nagging, difficult, awkward; *N. Amer. informal* pesky. **2 difficult**, awkward, uncooperative, rebellious, unmanageable, unruly, obstreperous, disruptive, disobedient, naughty, attention-seeking, recalcitrant.

truant *noun* **absentee**; *Brit. informal* skiver; *Austral./NZ informal* wag.
□ **play truant** stay away from school, truant; *Brit. informal* skive (off), bunk off; *N. Amer. informal* play hookey; *Austral./NZ informal* play the wag.

truce *noun* **ceasefire**, armistice, cessation of hostilities, peace.

true *adjective* **1 correct**, truthful, accurate, right, verifiable, the case; *formal* veracious. **2 genuine**, authentic, real, actual, bona fide, proper, legitimate; *informal* kosher. **3 sincere**, genuine, real, unfeigned, heartfelt. **4 loyal**, faithful, constant, devoted, trustworthy, reliable, dependable, staunch. **5** *a true reflection* **accurate**, faithful, telling it like it is, realistic, factual, lifelike.
- OPPOSITES false, untrue.

trumpet *verb* **proclaim**, announce, declare, noise abroad, shout from the rooftops.

trunk *noun* **1 stem**, bole, stock, stalk. **2 torso**, body. **3 proboscis**, nose, snout. **4 chest**, box, crate, coffer, case, portmanteau.

trust *noun* **confidence**, belief, faith, certainty, assurance, conviction, credence, reliance.
● *verb* **1 have faith in**, have (every) confidence in, believe in, pin your hopes/faith on. **2 rely on**, depend on, bank on, count on, be sure of. **3 hope**, expect, take it, assume, presume. **4 entrust**, consign, commit, give, hand over, turn over, assign.
- OPPOSITES distrust, mistrust.

trusting *adjective* **trustful**, unsuspecting, unquestioning, naive, innocent, childlike, ingenuous, wide-eyed, credulous, gullible, easily taken in.
- OPPOSITES distrustful, suspicious.

trustworthy *adjective* **reliable**, dependable, honest, as good as your word, above suspicion; *informal* on the level.
- OPPOSITES unreliable.

truth *noun* **1 accuracy**, correctness, authenticity, veracity, verity, truthfulness. **2 fact(s)**, reality, real life, actuality.
- OPPOSITES lies, fiction, falsehood.

truthful *adjective* **true**, accurate, correct, factual, faithful, reliable.
- OPPOSITES deceitful, untrue.

try *verb* **1 attempt**, endeavour, make an effort, exert yourself, strive, do your best, do your utmost, aim, seek; *informal* have a go/shot/crack/stab, go all out. **2 test**, put to the test, sample, taste, inspect, investigate, examine, appraise, evaluate, assess; *informal* check out. **3** *she tried his patience* **tax**, strain, test, stretch, sap, drain, exhaust, wear out.
● *noun* **attempt**, effort, endeavour; *informal* go, shot, crack, stab, bash.

trying *adjective* **1 stressful**, taxing, demanding, difficult, challenging, frustrating, fraught; *informal* hellish. **2 annoying**, irritating, exasperating, maddening, infuriating, tiresome, troublesome, irksome, vexatious.

tuck *verb* **push**, insert, slip, thrust, stuff, stick, cram; *informal* pop.

tug *verb* **1** *he tugged at her sleeve* **pull**, pluck, tweak, twitch, jerk, catch hold of; *informal* yank. **2 drag**, pull, lug, draw, haul, heave, tow, trail.

tuition *noun* **instruction**, teaching, coaching, tutoring, tutelage, lessons, education, schooling, training.

tumble *verb* **1 fall over**, fall down, topple over, go head over heels, lose your balance, take a spill, trip (up), stumble. **2** *oil prices tumbled* **plummet**, plunge, dive, nosedive, drop, slump, slide; *informal* crash.
– OPPOSITES rise.

tumour *noun* **cancer**, growth, lump, malignancy; *Medicine* carcinoma, sarcoma.

WORD LINKS
oncology branch of medicine concerning tumours

tune *noun* **melody**, air, strain, theme, song, jingle, ditty.
● *verb* **attune**, adapt, adjust, regulate.

tunnel *noun* **underground passage**, underpass, subway, shaft, burrow, hole, warren, labyrinth.
● *verb* **dig**, burrow, mine, bore, drill.

turbulent *adjective* **tempestuous**, stormy, unstable, unsettled, tumultuous, chaotic, anarchic, lawless.
– OPPOSITES peaceful.

turmoil *noun* **confusion**, upheaval, turbulence, tumult, disorder, disturbance, ferment, chaos, mayhem.
– OPPOSITES peace, order.

turn *verb* **1 go round**, revolve, rotate, spin, roll, circle, wheel, whirl, twirl, gyrate, swivel, pivot. **2 change direction**, change course, make a U-turn, turn about/round, wheel round. **3 bend**, curve, wind, twist, meander, snake, zigzag. **4** *he turned pale* **become**, go, grow, get. **5 (go) sour**, go off, curdle, become rancid, go bad, spoil.
● *noun* **1 rotation**, revolution, spin, whirl, twirl, gyration, swivel. **2 bend**, corner, junction, twist, dog-leg; *Brit.* hairpin bend. **3 opportunity**, chance, say, stint, time, try; *informal* go, shot, stab, crack. **4** *she did me some good turns* **service**, deed, act, favour, kindness.
□ **turn down 1** reject, spurn, rebuff, refuse, decline. **2** reduce, lower, decrease, lessen, mute. **turn into 1** become, develop into, turn out to be, be transformed into, change into, metamorphose into. **2** convert, change, transform, make, adapt, modify. **turn off/out** switch off, shut off, put off, extinguish, deactivate; *informal* kill, cut. **turn on** switch on, put on, start up, activate, trip. **turn out 1** come, be present, attend, appear, turn up, arrive, assemble, gather; *informal* show up. **2** transpire, emerge, come to light, become apparent. **3** happen, occur, come about, develop, work out, come out, end up; *informal* pan out. **turn up 1** be found, be discovered, be located, reappear. **2** arrive, appear, present yourself; *informal* show (up). **3** present itself, occur, happen, crop up. **4** increase, raise, amplify, intensify. **5** discover, uncover, unearth, find, dig up, expose.

turning *noun* **junction**, turn-off, side road, exit; *N. Amer.* turnout.

turning point *noun* **watershed**, critical moment, decisive moment, moment of truth, crossroads, crisis.

turnout *noun* **1 attendance**, audience, house, congregation, crowd, gate, gathering. **2 outfit**, clothing, dress, garb, attire, ensemble; *informal* get-up.

turnover *noun* **1 gross revenue**, income, yield, sales, business. **2** *staff turnover* **rate of replacement**, change, movement.

tutor *noun* **teacher**, instructor, coach, educator, lecturer, trainer, mentor.
● *verb* **teach**, instruct, educate, school, coach, train, drill.

twig *noun* **stick**, sprig, shoot, offshoot, stem, branchlet.

twilight *noun* **1 dusk**, sunset, sundown, nightfall, evening, close of day. **2 half-light**, semi-darkness, gloom.

WORD LINKS
crepuscular resembling twilight

twin *noun* **duplicate**, double, carbon copy, likeness, mirror image, replica, lookalike, clone, match, pair; *informal* spitting image, dead ringer.
● *adjective* **1 matching**, identical, paired. **2 twofold**, double, dual, related, linked, connected, parallel, complementary.
● *verb* **combine**, join, link, couple, pair.

twinge *noun* **pain**, spasm, ache, throb, cramp, stitch, pang.

twinkle *verb* & *noun* **glitter**, sparkle, shine, glimmer, shimmer, glint, gleam, glisten, flicker, flash, wink.

twist *verb* **1 crumple**, crush, buckle, mangle, warp, deform, distort, contort. **2 sprain**, wrench, turn, rick, crick. **3** *she twisted her hair round her finger* **wind**, twirl, coil, curl, wrap. **4** *the wires were twisted together* **intertwine**, interlace, weave, plait, braid, coil, wind. **5** *the road twisted and turned* **wind**, bend, curve, turn, meander, weave, zigzag, snake.
● *noun* **bend**, curve, turn, zigzag, dog-leg.

twitch *verb* **jerk**, convulse, have a spasm, quiver, tremble, shiver, shudder.
● *noun* **spasm**, convulsion, quiver, tremor, shiver, shudder, tic.

tycoon *noun* **magnate**, mogul, businessman, captain of industry, industrialist, financier, entrepreneur; *informal, derogatory* fat cat.

type *noun* **1 kind**, sort, variety, class, category, set, genre, species, order, breed, ilk. **2 print**, typeface, characters, lettering, font; *Brit.* fount.

typical *adjective* **1 representative**, characteristic, classic, quintessential, archetypal. **2 normal**, average, ordinary, standard, regular, routine, run-of-the-mill, conventional, unremarkable; *informal* bog-standard.
– OPPOSITES unusual, exceptional.

typify *verb* **epitomize**, exemplify, characterize, embody, be representative of, personify, symbolize.

tyranny *noun* **despotism**, absolute power, autocracy, dictatorship, totalitarianism, fascism, oppression, repression, subjugation, enslavement.

tyrant *noun* **dictator**, despot, autocrat, authoritarian, oppressor, slave-driver, martinet, bully.

Uu

ubiquitous *adjective* **everywhere**, omnipresent, all over the place, all-pervasive, universal, worldwide, global.
– OPPOSITES rare.

ugly *adjective* **1 unattractive**, unsightly, ill-favoured, hideous, plain, unprepossessing, horrible, ghastly, repellent, grotesque; *N. Amer.* homely; *Brit. informal* no oil painting. **2 unpleasant**, nasty, disagreeable, alarming, dangerous, perilous, threatening, menacing, hostile, ominous, sinister.
– OPPOSITES beautiful.

ulterior *adjective* **underlying**, undisclosed, undivulged, concealed, hidden, covert, secret, unapparent.
– OPPOSITES overt.

ultimate *adjective* **1 eventual**, final, concluding, terminal, end. **2 fundamental**, basic, primary, elementary, absolute, central, crucial, essential. **3 best**, ideal, greatest, quintessential, supreme.

ultimately *adverb* **1 eventually**, in the end, in the long run, at length, finally, in time, one day. **2 fundamentally**, basically, primarily, essentially, at heart, deep down.

umpire *noun* **referee**, judge, line judge, linesman, adjudicator, arbitrator, moderator; *informal* ref.

unable *adjective* **incapable**, powerless, impotent, inadequate, incompetent, unqualified, unfit.

unacceptable *adjective* **unsatisfactory**, inadmissible, inappropriate, unsuitable, undesirable, unreasonable, insupportable, intolerable, objectionable, distasteful; *informal* out of order.
– OPPOSITES satisfactory.

unanimous *adjective* **in agreement**, of one mind, in accord, united, undivided, with one voice.
– OPPOSITES split.

unarmed *adjective* **defenceless**, unprotected, unguarded.

unassuming *adjective* **modest**, self-effacing, humble, meek, reserved, diffident, unobtrusive, unostentatious, unpretentious, unaffected, natural.

unauthorized *adjective* **unofficial**, unsanctioned, unaccredited, unlicensed, unwarranted, unapproved, disallowed, prohibited, banned, forbidden, outlawed, illegal, illicit, proscribed.
– OPPOSITES official.

unaware *adjective* **ignorant**, oblivious, unconscious, unwitting, unsuspecting, uninformed, unenlightened, innocent; *informal* in the dark.
– OPPOSITES aware.

unbelievable *adjective* **incredible**, inconceivable, unthinkable, unimaginable, unconvincing, far-fetched, implausible, improbable; *informal* hard to swallow.

unbiased *adjective* **impartial**, unprejudiced, neutral, non-partisan, disinterested, detached, dispassionate, objective, even-handed, fair.

unborn *adjective* **expected**, embryonic, fetal, in utero.

unbroken *adjective* **1 undamaged**, unharmed, unscathed, untouched, sound, intact, whole. **2 uninterrupted**, continuous, endless, constant, unremitting, ongoing. **3 unbeaten**, undefeated, unsurpassed, unrivalled, unmatched, supreme.

uncanny *adjective* **1 eerie**, unnatural, unearthly, other-worldly, ghostly, strange, abnormal, weird; *informal* creepy, spooky. **2** *an uncanny resemblance* **striking**, remarkable, extraordinary, exceptional, incredible.

uncertain *adjective* **1** *the effects are uncertain* **unknown**, debatable, open

to question, in doubt, in the balance, up in the air, unpredictable, unforeseeable, undetermined; *informal* iffy. **2** *he was uncertain about the decision* **unsure**, doubtful, dubious, undecided, irresolute, hesitant, vacillating, vague, unclear, ambivalent, in two minds.
- OPPOSITES certain, sure.

unclear *adjective* **uncertain**, unsure, unsettled, up in the air, in doubt, ambiguous, equivocal, indefinite, vague, mysterious, obscure, hazy, nebulous.
- OPPOSITES clear, evident.

uncomfortable *adjective* **1 painful**, awkward, lumpy, confining, cramped. **2 uneasy**, ill at ease, awkward, nervous, tense, edgy, restless, embarrassed, anxious; *informal* rattled, twitchy.
- OPPOSITES comfortable, relaxed.

uncommon *adjective* **unusual**, abnormal, rare, atypical, exceptional, unconventional, unfamiliar, strange, extraordinary, peculiar, scarce, few and far between, isolated, infrequent.

unconditional *adjective* **unquestioning**, unqualified, unreserved, unlimited, unrestricted, wholehearted, complete, total, entire, full, absolute, unequivocal.

unconscious *adjective* **1 knocked out**, senseless, comatose, inert, stunned; *informal* out cold, out for the count. **2 subconscious**, instinctive, involuntary, uncontrolled, subliminal; *informal* gut. **3 unaware**, oblivious, ignorant, in ignorance, heedless.
- OPPOSITES aware.

uncouth *adjective* **uncivilized**, uncultured, rough, coarse, crude, loutish, boorish, rude, discourteous, disrespectful, bad-mannered, ill-bred.
- OPPOSITES civilized.

uncover *verb* **1 expose**, reveal, lay bare, unwrap, unveil, strip. **2 discover**, detect, come across, stumble on, chance on, find, turn up, unearth, dig up.

under *preposition* **1 below**, beneath, underneath. **2 less than**, lower than, below. **3 subordinate to**, answerable to, responsible to, subject to, junior to, inferior to.
- OPPOSITES above, over.

undercover *adjective* **secret**, covert, clandestine, underground, surreptitious, furtive, cloak-and-dagger, stealthy; *Military* black; *informal* hush-hush.
- OPPOSITES overt.

underestimate *verb* **underrate**, undervalue, miscalculate, misjudge, do an injustice to.
- OPPOSITES overestimate.

undergo *verb* **experience**, go through, submit to, face, be subjected to, receive, endure, brave, bear, withstand, weather.

underground *adjective* **1 subterranean**, buried, sunken. **2 secret**, clandestine, surreptitious, covert, undercover, closet, cloak-and-dagger, resistance, subversive; *Military* black. ● *noun* **metro**; *N. Amer.* subway; *Brit. informal* tube.

underline *verb* **1 underscore**, mark, pick out, emphasize, highlight. **2 emphasize**, stress, highlight, accentuate, accent, focus on, spotlight.

underlying *adjective* **fundamental**, basic, primary, central, essential, principal, elementary, initial.

undermine *verb* **weaken**, diminish, reduce, impair, mar, spoil, ruin, damage, sap, shake, threaten, subvert, compromise, sabotage.
- OPPOSITES strengthen.

understand *verb* **1 comprehend**, grasp, take in, see, apprehend, follow, make sense of, fathom; *informal* work out, figure out, make head or tail of, get; *Brit. informal* twig, suss. **2 know**, realize, recognize, acknowledge, appreciate, be aware of, be conscious of. **3 believe**, gather, take it, hear (tell), notice, see, learn.

understandable *adjective* **1 comprehensible**, intelligible, clear, plain, unambiguous, transparent, straightforward, explicit, coherent. **2 unsurprising**, expected, predictable, inevitable,

reasonable, acceptable, logical, rational, normal, natural, justifiable, excusable, pardonable, forgivable.
- OPPOSITES incomprehensible.

understanding *noun* **1 comprehension**, grasp, mastery, appreciation, knowledge, awareness, skill, expertise, proficiency; *informal* know-how. **2 intellect**, intelligence, brainpower, judgement, insight, intuition, acumen, sagacity, wisdom; *informal* nous. **3 belief**, perception, view, conviction, feeling, opinion, intuition, impression. **4 sympathy**, compassion, pity, feeling, concern, consideration, kindness, sensitivity, decency, goodwill. **5 agreement**, arrangement, deal, bargain, settlement, pledge, pact.
- OPPOSITES ignorance.
● *adjective* **sympathetic**, compassionate, sensitive, considerate, kind, thoughtful, tolerant, patient, forbearing, lenient, forgiving.

understate *verb* **play down**, underrate, underplay, trivialize, minimize, diminish, downgrade, brush aside, gloss over.
- OPPOSITES exaggerate.

undertake *verb* **1 set about**, embark on, go about, engage in, take on, be responsible for, get down to, get to grips with, tackle, attempt; *informal* have a go at. **2 promise**, pledge, vow, give your word, swear, guarantee, contract, give an assurance, commit yourself.

undertaker *noun* **funeral director**; *N. Amer.* mortician.

undertaking *noun* **1 enterprise**, venture, project, campaign, scheme, plan, operation, endeavour, effort, task. **2 promise**, pledge, agreement, oath, covenant, vow, commitment, guarantee, assurance.

underwater *adjective* **submerged**, sunken, undersea, submarine.

underwear *noun* **underclothes**, undergarments, underthings, lingerie; *informal* undies; *Brit. informal* smalls.

underwrite *verb* **sponsor**, support, back, insure, indemnify, subsidize, pay for, finance, fund; *N. Amer. informal* bankroll.

undesirable *adjective* **unpleasant**, disagreeable, nasty, unwelcome, unwanted, unfortunate.
- OPPOSITES pleasant.

undo *verb* **1 unfasten**, unbutton, unhook, untie, unlace, unlock, unbolt, loosen, detach, free, open. **2 cancel**, reverse, overrule, overturn, repeal, rescind, countermand, revoke, annul, invalidate, negate. **3 ruin**, undermine, overturn, scotch, sabotage, spoil, impair, mar, destroy, wreck; *informal* blow; *Brit. informal* scupper.
- OPPOSITES fasten.

undoubtedly *adverb* **doubtless**, indubitably, unquestionably, indisputably, undeniably, incontrovertibly, without (a) doubt, clearly.

undue *adjective* **excessive**, immoderate, intemperate, inordinate, disproportionate, uncalled for, unnecessary, unwarranted, unjustified, unreasonable, inappropriate, unmerited, unsuitable, improper.
- OPPOSITES appropriate.

unearth *verb* **1 dig up**, excavate, exhume, disinter, root out. **2** *I unearthed an interesting fact* **discover**, find, come across, hit on, bring to light, expose, turn up.

uneasy *adjective* **1 worried**, anxious, troubled, disturbed, nervous, nervy, tense, edgy, on edge, apprehensive, fearful, uncomfortable, unsettled, ill at ease; *informal* jittery. **2** *an uneasy peace* **tense**, awkward, strained, fraught, precarious, unstable, insecure.
- OPPOSITES calm.

unemployed *adjective* **jobless**, out of work, unwaged, redundant, laid off, on benefit; *Brit.* signing on; *N. Amer.* on welfare; *Brit. informal* on the dole, resting.

uneven *adjective* **1 bumpy**, rough, lumpy, stony, rocky, rutted. **2 irregular**, crooked, lopsided, askew, asymmetrical. **3 inconsistent**, variable,

fluctuating, irregular, erratic, patchy, fitful.
- OPPOSITES flat, regular.

unfair *adjective* **1 unjust**, prejudiced, biased, discriminatory, one-sided, unequal, uneven, unbalanced, partisan. **2 undeserved**, unmerited, unreasonable, unjustified; *Brit. informal* out of order. **3 unsporting**, dirty, underhand, dishonourable, dishonest.
- OPPOSITES just, justified.

unfasten *verb* **undo**, open, disconnect, untie, unbutton, unzip, loosen, free, unlock, unbolt.

unfit *adjective* **1** *the film is unfit for children* **unsuitable**, inappropriate, not designed. **2** *unfit for duty* **incapable of**, not up to, not equal to, unequipped, inadequate, unprepared; *informal* not cut out for. **3 unhealthy**, out of condition/shape, debilitated.
- OPPOSITES suitable, healthy.

unfold *verb* **1 open out**, spread out, flatten, straighten out, unroll, unfurl. **2 develop**, evolve, happen, take place, occur.

unfortunate *adjective* **1 unlucky**, hapless, ill-starred, star-crossed, wretched, poor, pitiful; *informal* down on your luck. **2 unwelcome**, disadvantageous, unfavourable, unlucky, adverse, unpromising, inauspicious. **3 regrettable**, inappropriate, unsuitable, tactless, injudicious.
- OPPOSITES lucky.

unfriendly *adjective* **hostile**, disagreeable, antagonistic, aggressive, unpleasant, surly, uncongenial, inhospitable, unneighbourly, unwelcoming, unsociable, cool, cold, aloof, distant; *informal* stand-offish.

u

ungainly *adjective* **awkward**, clumsy, graceless, inelegant, gawky, gauche, uncoordinated.
- OPPOSITES graceful.

unhappy *adjective* **1 sad**, miserable, sorrowful, dejected, despondent, disconsolate, morose, heartbroken, down, dispirited, downhearted, depressed, melancholy, mournful, gloomy, glum; *informal* down in the mouth, fed up, blue. **2** *I was very unhappy with the service* **dissatisfied**, displeased, discontented, disappointed, disgruntled; *Brit. informal* narked, not best pleased. **3 unfortunate**, unlucky, ill-starred, ill-fated, doomed; *informal* jinxed.
- OPPOSITES happy, pleased.

unhealthy *adjective* **1 harmful**, detrimental, destructive, injurious, damaging, noxious, poisonous. **2 sick**, poorly, ill, unwell, unfit, ailing, weak, frail, infirm, washed out, run down. **3 abnormal**, morbid, macabre, twisted, unwholesome, warped, depraved, unnatural; *informal* sick.

uniform *adjective* **1 constant**, consistent, steady, invariable, unchanging, stable, static, regular, fixed, even. **2 identical**, matching, similar, equal, same, like, consistent.
- OPPOSITES variable.
● *noun* **costume**, outfit, suit, ensemble, livery, regalia; *informal* get-up, rig, gear.

unify *verb* **unite**, combine, bring together, join, merge, fuse, amalgamate, coalesce, consolidate.
- OPPOSITES separate.

uninteresting *adjective* **boring**, dull, unexciting, tiresome, tedious, dreary, lifeless, humdrum, colourless, bland, insipid, banal, dry.
- OPPOSITES exciting.

union *noun* **1 unification**, joining, merger, fusion, amalgamation, coalition, combination, synthesis, blend. **2 association**, league, guild, confederation, federation.
- OPPOSITES separation.

unique *adjective* **1 distinctive**, individual, special, particular, specific, idiosyncratic, single, sole, lone, unrepeated, solitary, exclusive; *informal* one-off. **2 remarkable**, special, notable, unequalled, unparalleled, unmatched, unsurpassed, incomparable.
- OPPOSITES common.

unit *noun* **1 component**, part, section, segment, element, module, constituent, subdivision. **2 quantity**, measure, denomination. **3 group**, detachment, contingent, division, cell, faction, department, office, branch.

unite *verb* **1 unify**, join, link, connect, combine, amalgamate, fuse, weld, bond, bring together. **2 join together**, join forces, combine, band together, ally, cooperate, collaborate, work together, team up. **3 merge**, mix, blend, mingle, combine.
- OPPOSITES divide.

unity *noun* **1 union**, unification, integration, amalgamation, coalition, federation, confederation. **2 harmony**, accord, cooperation, collaboration, agreement, consensus, solidarity. **3 oneness**, singleness, wholeness, uniformity, homogeneity.
- OPPOSITES disunity.

universal *adjective* **general**, common, widespread, ubiquitous, comprehensive, global, worldwide, international.

universally *adverb* **always**, without exception, by everyone, in all cases, everywhere, worldwide, globally, internationally, commonly, generally.

universe *noun* **cosmos**, macrocosm, space, infinity, nature, all existence.

WORD LINKS
cosmic relating to the universe

unkind *adjective* **unpleasant**, disagreeable, nasty, mean, cruel, vicious, spiteful, malicious, callous, unsympathetic, uncharitable, harsh, hard-hearted, heartless, cold-hearted; *informal* bitchy, catty.

unknown *adjective* **1 undisclosed**, unrevealed, secret, undetermined, undecided. **2 unexplored**, uncharted, unmapped, undiscovered, untravelled. **3 unidentified**, unnamed, anonymous, nameless. **4 obscure**, unfamiliar, unheard of, unsung, minor, undistinguished.
- OPPOSITES familiar.

unlikely *adjective* **improbable**, doubtful, dubious, questionable, unconvincing, implausible, far-fetched, unrealistic, incredible, unbelievable, inconceivable.
- OPPOSITES probable, likely.

unload *verb* **unpack**, empty, clear, remove, offload.

unlucky *adjective* **1 unfortunate**, hapless, luckless, down on your luck, unsuccessful, ill-fated, ill-starred, jinxed. **2 unfavourable**, inauspicious, unpropitious, ominous.
- OPPOSITES lucky, fortunate.

unnatural *adjective* **1 abnormal**, unusual, uncommon, extraordinary, strange, unorthodox, exceptional, irregular, untypical. **2 artificial**, man-made, synthetic. **3 affected**, artificial, stilted, forced, false, fake, insincere, contrived, mannered, self-conscious; *informal* put on, phoney.
- OPPOSITES natural.

unnecessary *adjective* **unneeded**, inessential, not required, uncalled for, unwarranted, dispensable, optional, extraneous, expendable, redundant.

unpleasant *adjective* **1** *an unpleasant situation* **disagreeable**, distressing, nasty, horrible, terrible, awful, dreadful, invidious, objectionable. **2** *an unpleasant man* **unlikeable**, unlovable, disagreeable, bad-tempered, unfriendly, rude, impolite, obnoxious, nasty, spiteful, mean, objectionable, annoying, irritating. **3 unappetizing**, unpalatable, unsavoury, unappealing, disgusting, revolting, nauseating, sickening.
- OPPOSITES pleasant, agreeable.

unpopular *adjective* **disliked**, friendless, unloved, unwelcome, avoided, ignored, rejected, shunned, out of favour.

unravel *verb* **1 untangle**, disentangle, separate out, unwind, untwist. **2 solve**, resolve, clear up, puzzle out, get to the bottom of, explain, clarify; *informal* figure out.
- OPPOSITES entangle.

unreal *adjective* **imaginary**, fictitious, pretend, make-believe, made-up, dreamed-up, mock, false, illusory, mythical, fanciful, hypothetical, theoretical; *informal* phoney.

unrest *noun* **disturbance**, trouble, turmoil, disruption, disorder, chaos, anarchy, dissatisfaction, dissent, strife, agitation, protest, rebellion, uprising, rioting.
- OPPOSITES peace.

unsafe *adjective* **1 dangerous**, risky, hazardous, high-risk, treacherous, insecure, unsound, harmful, injurious, toxic. **2 unreliable**, open to doubt, questionable, doubtful, dubious, suspect; *informal* iffy; *Brit. informal* dodgy.
- OPPOSITES safe.

unsatisfactory *adjective* **disappointing**, displeasing, inadequate, unacceptable, poor, bad, substandard, weak, mediocre, not up to par, defective, deficient; *informal* leaving a lot to be desired.

unscrupulous *adjective* **dishonest**, deceitful, devious, underhand, unethical, immoral, shameless, exploitative, corrupt, unprincipled, dishonourable, disreputable; *informal* crooked, shady.

unsettle *verb* **disturb**, disconcert, unnerve, upset, disquiet, perturb, alarm, dismay, trouble, bother, agitate, fluster, ruffle, shake (up), throw; *informal* rattle, faze.

unsightly *adjective* **unattractive**, ugly, unprepossessing, hideous, horrible, repulsive, revolting, offensive, grotesque.
- OPPOSITES attractive.

unsociable *adjective* **unfriendly**, uncongenial, unneighbourly, unapproachable, introverted, reserved, withdrawn, retiring, aloof, distant, remote, detached; *informal* stand-offish.

unstable *adjective* **1 unsteady**, rocky, wobbly, rickety, shaky, unsafe, insecure, precarious. **2 changeable**, volatile, variable, fluctuating, irregular, unpredictable, erratic. **3 unbalanced**, of unsound mind, mentally ill, deranged, demented, disturbed, unhinged; *Brit.* sectionable.
- OPPOSITES steady, firm.

unsuccessful *adjective* **1 failed**, abortive, ineffective, fruitless, profitless, unproductive, vain, futile. **2 unprofitable**, loss-making.

unsuitable *adjective* **1 inappropriate**, ill-suited, inapposite, inapt, unacceptable, unfitting, incompatible, out of place, out of keeping, incongruous, unseemly. **2** *an unsuitable moment* **inopportune**, badly timed, unfortunate, difficult, infelicitous.
- OPPOSITES appropriate.

unsure *adjective* **1 undecided**, uncertain, irresolute, dithering, in two minds, in a quandary, dubious, doubtful, sceptical, unconvinced. **2 unconfident**, unassertive, insecure, hesitant, diffident, anxious, apprehensive.
- OPPOSITES sure, certain.

untangle *verb* **disentangle**, unravel, unsnarl, straighten out, untwist, unknot, sort out.

unthinkable *adjective* **unimaginable**, inconceivable, unbelievable, incredible, implausible, out of the question, impossible, unconscionable, unreasonable.

untidy *adjective* **1 disordered**, messy, disorganized, cluttered, in chaos, haywire, in disarray, disorderly, topsy-turvy, at sixes and sevens, jumbled; *informal* higgledy-piggledy. **2 scruffy**, dishevelled, unkempt, messy, rumpled, bedraggled.
- OPPOSITES neat, tidy.

untoward *adjective* **unexpected**, unforeseen, surprising, unusual, inappropriate, inconvenient, unwelcome, unfavourable, adverse, unfortunate, infelicitous.

untrue *adjective* **false**, invented, made up, fabricated, concocted, trumped up, erroneous, wrong, incorrect, inaccurate.
- OPPOSITES true, correct.

unusual *adjective* **1** *an unusual sight* **uncommon**, abnormal, atypical, unexpected, surprising, unfamiliar, different, strange, odd, curious, extraordinary, unorthodox, unconventional, peculiar, queer, unwonted; *informal* weird,

offbeat. **2** *a man of unusual talent* **remarkable**, extraordinary, exceptional, particular, outstanding, notable, noteworthy, distinctive, striking, significant, special, unique, unparalleled, prodigious.
- OPPOSITES common.

unwarranted *adjective* **1 unjustified**, indefensible, inexcusable, unforgivable, unpardonable, uncalled for, unnecessary, unjust, groundless. **2 unauthorized**, unsanctioned, unapproved, uncertified, unlicensed, illegal, unlawful, illicit, illegitimate, criminal, actionable.
- OPPOSITES justified.

unwieldy *adjective* **awkward**, unmanageable, unmanoeuvrable, cumbersome, clumsy, massive, heavy, hefty, bulky.

unwilling *adjective* **1 reluctant**, unenthusiastic, hesitant, resistant, grudging, involuntary, forced. **2** *he was unwilling to go* **disinclined**, reluctant, averse, loath, not in the mood; (**be unwilling to do something**) baulk at, demur at, shy away from, flinch from, shrink from, have qualms about, have misgivings about, have reservations about.
- OPPOSITES willing.

upbeat *adjective* **cheerful**, optimistic, cheery, positive, confident, hopeful, sanguine, bullish, buoyant.
- OPPOSITES pessimistic.

upbringing *noun* **childhood**, early life, formative years, teaching, instruction, rearing.

update *verb* **1 modernize**, upgrade, improve, overhaul. **2 brief**, bring up to date, inform, fill in, tell, notify, keep posted; *informal* clue in, put in the picture, bring/keep up to speed.

upgrade *verb* **improve**, modernize, update, reform.
- OPPOSITES downgrade.

upheaval *noun* **disturbance**, disruption, trouble, turbulence, disorder, confusion, turmoil.

uphill *adjective* **1 upward**, rising, ascending, climbing. **2 difficult**, hard, tough, demanding, arduous, taxing, exacting, stiff, gruelling, onerous.
- OPPOSITES downhill.

uphold *verb* **1 confirm**, endorse, sustain, approve, support, back (up). **2 maintain**, sustain, continue, preserve, protect, keep, hold to, keep alive, keep going.
- OPPOSITES oppose.

upkeep *noun* **1 maintenance**, repair(s), servicing, care, preservation, conservation, running. **2 (financial) support**, maintenance, keep, subsistence, care.

uplifting *adjective* **inspiring**, stirring, inspirational, rousing, moving, touching, affecting, cheering, heartening, encouraging.

upper *adjective* **1 higher**, superior, top. **2 senior**, superior, higher-level, higher-ranking, top.
- OPPOSITES lower.

upper-class *adjective* **aristocratic**, noble, patrician, titled, blue-blooded, high-born, elite; *Brit.* county; *informal* upper-crust, top-drawer; *Brit. informal* posh.

upright *adjective* **1 vertical**, perpendicular, plumb, straight (up), erect, on end, on your feet. **2 honest**, honourable, upstanding, respectable, high-minded, law-abiding, worthy, righteous, decent, good, virtuous, principled.
- OPPOSITES flat, horizontal.

uprising *noun* **rebellion**, revolt, insurrection, mutiny, revolution, insurgence, rioting, coup.

uproar *noun* **1 commotion**, disturbance, rumpus, disorder, confusion, chaos, tumult, mayhem, pandemonium, bedlam, noise, din, clamour, hubbub, racket; *Brit.* row; *informal* hullabaloo. **2 outcry**, furore, fuss, commotion, hue and cry, rumpus; *Brit.* row; *informal* hullabaloo, stink, ructions.
- OPPOSITES calm.

upset *verb* **1 distress**, trouble, perturb, dismay, sadden, grieve, disturb, unsettle, disconcert, disquiet, worry, bother, agitate, fluster, throw, ruffle, unnerve,

shake. **2 knock over**, overturn, upend, tip over, topple, spill. **3 disrupt**, interfere with, disturb, throw into confusion, mess up.
- OPPOSITES calm.
● *noun* **1 distress**, trouble, dismay, disquiet, worry, bother, agitation, hurt, grief. **2** *a stomach upset* **disorder**, complaint, ailment, illness, sickness; *informal* bug; *Brit. informal* lurgy.
● *adjective* **1 distressed**, troubled, perturbed, dismayed, disturbed, unsettled, disconcerted, worried, bothered, anxious, agitated, flustered, ruffled, unnerved, shaken, saddened, grieved; *informal* cut up, choked; *Brit. informal* gutted. **2** *an upset stomach* **disturbed**, unsettled, queasy, bad, poorly; *informal* gippy.
- OPPOSITES calm.

upside down *adjective* **1 upturned**, upended, wrong side up, overturned, inverted, capsized. **2 in disarray**, in disorder, jumbled up, in a muddle, untidy, disorganized, in chaos, in confusion, topsy-turvy, at sixes and sevens; *informal* higgledy-piggledy.

up to date *adjective* **1 modern**, contemporary, the latest, state-of-the-art, new, up-to-the-minute, advanced. **2 informed**, up to speed, in the picture, in touch, au fait, conversant, familiar, knowledgeable, acquainted.
- OPPOSITES out of date, old-fashioned.

urban *adjective* **town**, city, municipal, metropolitan, built-up, inner-city, suburban.
- OPPOSITES rural.

urge *verb* **1 encourage**, exhort, press, entreat, implore, call on, appeal to, beg, plead with. **2 advise**, counsel, advocate, recommend.
● *noun his urge to travel* **desire**, wish, need, compulsion, longing, yearning, hankering, craving, hunger, thirst; *informal* yen, itch.

urgent *adjective* **pressing**, acute, dire, desperate, critical, serious, grave, intense, crying, burning, compelling, extreme, high-priority, life-and-death.

usage *noun* **1** *energy usage* **consumption**, use. **2** *the usage of equipment* **use**, utilization, operation, manipulation, running, handling. **3 language**, expression, phraseology, parlance, idiom.

use *verb* **1 utilize**, employ, avail yourself of, work, operate, wield, ply, apply, put into service. **2 exercise**, employ, bring into play, practise, apply. **3 take advantage of**, exploit, manipulate, take liberties with, impose on, abuse, capitalize on, profit from, trade on, milk; *informal* cash in on, walk all over. **4** *we have used up our funds* **consume**, get/go through, exhaust, deplete, expend, spend.
● *noun* **1 utilization**, application, employment, operation, manipulation. **2 exploitation**, manipulation, abuse. **3** *what is the use of that?* **advantage**, benefit, good, point, object, purpose, sense, reason, service, utility, help, gain, avail, profit, value, worth.

used *adjective* **second-hand**, pre-owned, nearly new, old, worn, hand-me-down, cast-off.
□ **used to** accustomed to, no stranger to, familiar with, at home with, in the habit of, experienced in, versed in, conversant with, acquainted with.

useful *adjective* **1** *a useful tool* **functional**, practical, handy, convenient, utilitarian, serviceable, of service; *informal* nifty. **2** *a useful experience* **beneficial**, advantageous, helpful, worthwhile, profitable, rewarding, productive, constructive, valuable, fruitful.
- OPPOSITES useless.

useless *adjective* **1 futile**, pointless, to no avail, vain, to no purpose, unavailing, hopeless, ineffectual, fruitless, unprofitable, unproductive, abortive. **2** *(informal)* **incompetent**, inept, ineffective, incapable, inadequate, hopeless, bad; *informal* a dead loss.
- OPPOSITES useful, beneficial.

usher *verb* **escort**, accompany, take, show, see, lead, conduct, guide.
● *noun* **guide**, attendant, escort.

usual *adjective* **normal**, customary, accustomed, wonted, habitual, routine, regular, standard, typical, established, set, stock, conventional, traditional, expected, familiar.
- OPPOSITES exceptional.

usually *adverb* **normally**, generally, habitually, customarily, routinely, typically, ordinarily, commonly, as a rule, in general, more often than not, mainly, mostly.

utensil *noun* **implement**, tool, instrument, device, apparatus, gadget, appliance, contrivance, contraption; *informal* gizmo.

utility *noun* **usefulness**, use, benefit, value, advantage, help, practicality, effectiveness, service.

utilize *verb* **use**, employ, avail yourself of, press into service, bring into play, deploy, draw on, exploit.

utmost *adjective* **greatest**, highest, maximum, most, extreme, supreme, paramount.

utter[1] *adjective* **complete**, total, absolute, thorough, perfect, downright, out-and-out, outright, sheer, arrant, positive, prize, pure, unmitigated, unadulterated, unqualified, unalloyed.

utter[2] *verb* **say**, speak, voice, mouth, express, articulate, pronounce, enunciate, emit, let out, give, produce.

utterance *noun* **remark**, comment, statement, observation, declaration, pronouncement.

Vv

vacancy *noun* **opening**, position, post, job, opportunity.

vacant *adjective* **1 empty**, unoccupied, not in use, free, available, unfilled, uninhabited, untenanted; *informal* up for grabs. **2 blank**, expressionless, unresponsive, emotionless, impassive, vacuous, empty, glazed.
- OPPOSITES full, occupied.

vacate *verb* **1 leave**, move out of, evacuate, quit, depart from. **2 resign from**, leave, stand down from, give up, bow out of, relinquish, retire from; *informal* quit.
- OPPOSITES occupy.

vacation *noun* **holiday**, trip, tour, break, leave, time off, recess.

vagrant *noun* **tramp**, drifter, down-and-out, beggar, itinerant, wanderer; *N. Amer.* hobo; *N. Amer. informal* bum.

vague *adjective* **1 indistinct**, indefinite, indeterminate, unclear, ill-defined, hazy, fuzzy, misty, blurry, out of focus, shadowy, obscure. **2 imprecise**, rough, approximate, inexact, non-specific, ambiguous, hazy, uncertain. **3 absent-minded**, forgetful, dreamy, abstracted; *informal* with your head in the clouds, scatty, not with it.
- OPPOSITES clear, definite.

vaguely *adverb* **1 slightly**, a little, a bit, somewhat, rather, in a way, faintly, obscurely; *informal* sort of, kind of. **2 absent-mindedly**, abstractedly, vacantly.

vain *adjective* **1 conceited**, narcissistic, proud, arrogant, boastful, cocky, egotistical, immodest; *informal* big-headed. **2 futile**, useless, pointless, ineffective, unavailing, fruitless, unproductive, unsuccessful, failed, abortive.
- OPPOSITES modest, successful.
□ **in vain** unsuccessfully, to no avail, to no purpose, fruitlessly.

valiant *adjective* **brave**, courageous, plucky, intrepid, heroic, gallant, bold, fearless, daring, unflinching, unafraid, undaunted, doughty, indomitable, stout-hearted; *informal* game, gutsy.
- OPPOSITES cowardly.

valid *adjective* **1 well founded**, sound, reasonable, rational, logical, justifiable, defensible, cogent, credible, forceful. **2 legally binding**, lawful, official, in force, in effect.

validate *verb* **ratify**, endorse, approve, agree to, accept, authorize, legalize, legitimize, warrant, license, certify, recognize.

valley *noun* **dale**, vale, hollow, gully, gorge, ravine, canyon, rift; *Brit.* combe; *Scottish* glen.

valuable *adjective* **1 precious**, costly, high-priced, expensive, dear, priceless. **2 useful**, helpful, beneficial, advantageous, invaluable, productive, worthwhile, worthy, important.
- OPPOSITES worthless.

valuables *plural noun* **precious items**, costly items, prized possessions, treasures.

value *noun* **1 price**, cost, worth, market price. **2 worth**, usefulness, advantage, benefit, gain, profit, good, help. **3** (**values**) **principles**, ethics, morals, standards, code of behaviour.
● *verb* **1 evaluate**, assess, estimate, appraise, price. **2 think highly of**, have a high opinion of, rate highly, esteem, set great store by, respect.
- OPPOSITES despise.

vanish *verb* **disappear**, be lost to sight, become invisible, recede from view, fade (away), evaporate, melt away, end, cease to exist.
- OPPOSITES appear.

vanity *noun* **conceit**, narcissism, self-love, self-admiration, egotism, pride,

arrogance, boastfulness, cockiness; *informal* big-headedness.
- OPPOSITES modesty.

variable *adjective* **changeable**, shifting, fluctuating, irregular, inconstant, inconsistent, fluid, unstable; *informal* up and down.
- OPPOSITES constant.

variant *noun* **variation**, version, form, alternative, adaptation, alteration, modification.
● *adjective* **alternative**, other, different, divergent.

variation *noun* **1** *regional variations* **difference**, dissimilarity, disparity, contrast, discrepancy, imbalance. **2** *there was little variation from the pattern* **deviation**, variance, divergence, departure, fluctuation, change, alteration, modification.

varied *adjective* **diverse**, assorted, miscellaneous, mixed, sundry, wide-ranging, disparate, heterogeneous, motley.

variety *noun* **1 diversity**, variation, diversification, change, difference. **2 assortment**, miscellany, range, array, collection, selection, mixture, medley. **3 sort**, kind, type, class, category, style, form, make, model, brand, strain, breed.
- OPPOSITES uniformity.

various *adjective* **diverse**, different, differing, varied, assorted, mixed, sundry, miscellaneous, disparate, heterogeneous, motley.

varnish *noun* & *verb* **lacquer**, shellac, japan, enamel, glaze, polish.

vary *verb* **1 differ**, be dissimilar, disagree, be at variance. **2 fluctuate**, rise and fall, go up and down, change, alter, shift, swing.

vast *adjective* **huge**, extensive, broad, wide, boundless, enormous, immense, great, massive, colossal, gigantic, mammoth, giant, mountainous; *informal* mega, whopping.
- OPPOSITES tiny.

vault[1] *noun* **1 cellar**, basement, crypt, undercroft, catacomb, burial chamber. **2 strongroom**, safe deposit.

vault[2] *verb* **jump**, leap, spring, bound, clear.

veer *verb* **turn**, swerve, swing, weave, wheel, change direction, change course, deviate.

vehement *adjective* **passionate**, forceful, ardent, impassioned, heated, spirited, urgent, fervent, fierce, strong, forcible, powerful, emphatic, vigorous, intense, earnest, keen, enthusiastic, zealous.
- OPPOSITES mild.

vehicle *noun* **1 means of transport**, transportation, conveyance. **2 channel**, medium, means, agent, instrument, mechanism, organ, apparatus.

WORD LINKS
automotive relating to vehicles

veil *noun* **covering**, screen, curtain, mantle, cloak, mask, blanket, shroud, canopy, cloud, pall.
● *verb* **cover**, surround, swathe, enfold, envelop, conceal, hide, obscure, screen, shield, cloak, blanket, shroud.

vein *noun* **1 blood vessel**, capillary. **2 layer**, seam, lode, stratum, deposit.

WORD LINKS
vascular, **venous** relating to veins

velocity *noun* **speed**, pace, rate, tempo, rapidity.

veneer *noun* **1 surface**, lamination, layer, overlay, facing, covering, finish, exterior. **2 facade**, front, show, outward display, appearance, impression, semblance, guise, mask, pretence, cover, camouflage.

vengeance *noun* **revenge**, retribution, retaliation, requital, reprisal, an eye for an eye.
- OPPOSITES forgiveness.

venomous *adjective* **poisonous**, toxic, dangerous, deadly, lethal, fatal.
- OPPOSITES harmless.

vent *noun* **outlet**, **inlet**, opening, aperture, hole, gap, orifice, space, duct, flue, shaft, well, passage, airway.
● *verb* **let out**, release, pour out, utter, express, air, voice.

ventilate *verb* **air**, aerate, oxygenate, freshen, cool.

venture *noun* **enterprise**, undertaking, project, scheme, operation, endeavour, speculation.
● *verb* **1 put forward**, advance, proffer, offer, air, suggest, volunteer, submit, propose. **2 dare**, be so bold as, presume, have the audacity, have the nerve, take the liberty of.

verbal *adjective* **oral**, spoken, word-of-mouth, stated, said, unwritten.

verbose *adjective* **wordy**, loquacious, garrulous, talkative, voluble, long-winded, lengthy, prolix, circumlocutory, rambling.
- OPPOSITES succinct.

verdict *noun* **judgement**, adjudication, decision, finding, ruling, sentence.

verge *noun* **1 edge**, border, margin, side, brink, rim, lip, fringe, boundary, perimeter. **2** *I was on the verge of tears* **brink**, threshold, edge, point.
□ **verge on** approach, border on, be close/near to, resemble, be tantamount to, tend towards, approximate to.

verify *verb* **confirm**, prove, substantiate, corroborate, back up, bear out, justify, support, uphold, testify to, validate, authenticate.
- OPPOSITES refute.

versatile *adjective* **1** *a versatile player* **adaptable**, flexible, all-round, multi-talented, resourceful. **2** *a versatile device* **adjustable**, adaptable, multi-purpose, all-purpose.

V

verse *noun* **1 poetry**, lyrics. **2 poem**, lyric, rhyme, ditty, limerick. **3 stanza**, canto.

version *noun* **1 account**, report, statement, description, record, story, rendering, interpretation, explanation, understanding, reading, impression, side. **2 edition**, translation, impression. **3 type**, sort, kind, form, equivalent, variety, variant, design, model, style.

vertical *adjective* **upright**, erect, perpendicular, plumb, on end, standing.
- OPPOSITES flat, horizontal.

very *adverb* **extremely**, exceedingly, exceptionally, extraordinarily, tremendously, immensely, acutely, singularly, decidedly, highly, remarkably, really; *informal* awfully, terribly, seriously, mega, ultra; *Brit. informal* well, dead, jolly; *N. Amer. informal* real, mighty.
- OPPOSITES slightly.

vessel *noun* **1 boat**, ship, craft. **2 container**, receptacle, basin, bowl, pan, pot, jug.

vestige *noun* **remnant**, fragment, relic, echo, trace, mark, legacy, reminder.

vet *verb* **check up on**, screen, investigate, examine, scrutinize, inspect, look over, assess, evaluate, appraise; *informal* check out.

veteran *noun* **old hand**, past master, doyen, doyenne; *informal* old-timer; *N. Amer. informal* vet.
- OPPOSITES novice.
● *adjective* **long-serving**, seasoned, old, hardened, practised, experienced; *informal* battle-scarred.

veto *noun* **rejection**, dismissal, prohibition, proscription, embargo, ban, interdict.
● *verb* **reject**, turn down, throw out, dismiss, prohibit, forbid, proscribe, disallow, embargo, ban, rule out; *informal* kill, give the thumbs down to.
- OPPOSITES approve.

viable *adjective* **feasible**, workable, practicable, practical, realistic, achievable, attainable; *informal* doable.
- OPPOSITES impracticable.

vibrant *adjective* **1 spirited**, lively, energetic, vigorous, dynamic, passionate, fiery; *informal* feisty. **2 vivid**, bright, striking, brilliant, glowing, strong, rich.
- OPPOSITES lifeless, pale.

vibrate *verb* **shake**, tremble, shiver, quiver, shudder, throb, pulsate.

vice *noun* **1 immorality**, wrongdoing, wickedness, evil, iniquity, villainy, corruption, misconduct, sin, depravity. **2 fault**, failing, flaw, defect, shortcoming, weakness, deficiency, foible, frailty.
- OPPOSITES virtue.

vicious *adjective* **1 brutal**, ferocious, savage, violent, ruthless, merciless, heartless, callous, cruel, cold-blooded, inhuman, barbaric, bloodthirsty. **2 malicious**, spiteful, vindictive, venomous, cruel, bitter, acrimonious, hostile, nasty; *informal* catty.
- OPPOSITES gentle.

victim *noun* **sufferer**, injured party, casualty, fatality, loss, survivor.

victimize *verb* **persecute**, pick on, bully, abuse, discriminate against, exploit, take advantage of; *informal* have it in for.

victorious *adjective* **triumphant**, conquering, vanquishing, winning, champion, successful.
- OPPOSITES unsuccessful.

victory *noun* **success**, triumph, conquest, win, coup; *informal* walkover.
- OPPOSITES defeat, loss.

vie *verb* **compete**, contend, struggle, fight, battle, jockey.

view *noun* **1 outlook**, prospect, panorama, vista, scene, scenery, landscape. **2 opinion**, viewpoint, belief, judgement, thinking, notion, idea, conviction, persuasion, attitude, feeling, sentiment. **3** *the church came into view* **sight**, perspective, vision, visibility.
● *verb* **1 look at**, observe, eye, gaze at, contemplate, regard, scan, survey, inspect, scrutinize; *informal* check out; *N. Amer. informal* eyeball. **2 consider**, regard, look on, see, perceive, judge, deem, reckon.

viewer *noun* **watcher**, spectator, onlooker, observer; (**viewers**) audience, crowd.

vigilant *adjective* **watchful**, observant, attentive, alert, eagle-eyed, on the lookout, on your guard; *informal* beady-eyed.
- OPPOSITES inattentive.

vigorous *adjective* **1 robust**, healthy, hale and hearty, strong, sturdy, fit, hardy, tough, energetic, lively, active. **2 strenuous**, powerful, forceful, spirited, determined, aggressive, passionate; *informal* punchy, feisty.
- OPPOSITES weak, feeble.

vigorously *adverb* **strenuously**, strongly, powerfully, forcefully, energetically, heartily, all out, fiercely, hard; *informal* like mad; *Brit. informal* like billy-o.

vigour *noun* **health**, strength, robustness, energy, life, vitality, spirit, passion, determination, dynamism, drive; *informal* oomph, get-up-and-go.
- OPPOSITES lethargy.

vile *adjective* **foul**, nasty, unpleasant, bad, horrid, repulsive, disgusting, hateful, nauseating; *informal* gross.
- OPPOSITES pleasant.

villain *noun* **criminal**, lawbreaker, offender, felon, miscreant, wrongdoer, rogue, scoundrel, reprobate; *informal* crook, baddy.

vindicate *verb* **1 acquit**, clear, absolve, exonerate; *informal* let off. **2 justify**, warrant, substantiate, confirm, corroborate, prove, defend, support, back, endorse.
- OPPOSITES incriminate.

vintage *adjective* **1 high-quality**, quality, choice, select, superior. **2 classic**, ageless, timeless, old, antique, historic.

violate *verb* **1 contravene**, breach, infringe, break, transgress, disobey, defy, flout, disregard, ignore. **2 desecrate**, profane, defile, degrade, debase, damage, vandalize, deface, destroy.
- OPPOSITES respect.

violation *noun* **1 contravention**, breach, infringement, transgression, defiance, flouting, disregard. **2 desecration**, defilement, damage, vandalism, destruction.

violence *noun* **1 brutality**, savagery, cruelty, barbarity. **2 force**, power, strength, might, ferocity, intensity, vehemence.

violent *adjective* **1 brutal**, vicious, savage, rough, aggressive, threatening, fierce, ferocious, bloodthirsty. **2 powerful**, forceful, hard, sharp, smart, strong, vigorous, mighty, hefty. **3 intense**, extreme, strong, powerful, fierce, unbridled, uncontrollable, ungovernable, consuming, passionate.
- OPPOSITES gentle, mild.

virtual *adjective* **effective**, near (enough), essential, practical, to all intents and purposes, in all but name, implied, unacknowledged.

virtually *adverb* **effectively**, all but, more or less, practically, almost, nearly, close to, verging on, just about, as good as, essentially, to all intents and purposes.

virtue *noun* **1 goodness**, righteousness, morality, integrity, dignity, rectitude, honour, probity. **2 good point**, good quality, strong point, asset, forte, attribute, strength, merit, advantage, benefit; *informal* plus.
- OPPOSITES vice.

visible *adjective* **observable**, perceptible, noticeable, detectable, discernible, in sight, in view, on display, evident, apparent, manifest, plain.

vision *noun* **1 eyesight**, sight, observation, eyes, view, perspective. **2 apparition**, spectre, phantom, ghost, wraith, manifestation, hallucination, illusion, mirage. **3 dream**, reverie, plan, hope, fantasy, pipe dream. **4 imagination**, creativity, inventiveness, inspiration, intuition, perception, insight.

WORD LINKS
visual, **optic** relating to vision

visit *verb* **call on**, go to see, look in on, stay with, holiday with, stop by, drop by; *informal* pop/drop in on, look up.
● *noun* **(social) call**, stay, stopover, trip, holiday, vacation; *literary* sojourn.

visitor *noun* **1 guest**, caller, company. **2 tourist**, traveller, holidaymaker, tripper, vacationer, sightseer.

vista *noun* **view**, scene, prospect, panorama, sight, scenery, landscape.

visual *adjective* **1 optical**, ocular. **2 visible**, observable, perceptible, discernible.

visualize *verb* **envisage**, conjure up, picture, call to mind, see, imagine, dream up.

vital *adjective* **1 essential**, critical, crucial, indispensable, all-important, imperative, mandatory, high-priority, key, life-and-death. **2 lively**, energetic, active, sprightly, spirited, vivacious, exuberant, dynamic, vigorous; *informal* full of beans.
- OPPOSITES unimportant.

vitality *noun* **life**, energy, spirit, vivacity, exuberance, dynamism, vigour, passion, drive; *informal* get-up-and-go.

vivid *adjective* **1 bright**, colourful, brilliant, radiant, vibrant, strong, bold, deep, intense, rich, warm. **2 graphic**, realistic, lifelike, faithful, authentic, striking, evocative, arresting, colourful, dramatic, memorable, powerful, stirring, moving, haunting.
- OPPOSITES dull, vague.

vocal *adjective* **1 spoken**, said, voiced, uttered, articulated, oral. **2 vociferous**, outspoken, forthright, plain-spoken, blunt, frank, candid, passionate, vehement, vigorous.

vocation *noun* **calling**, life's work, mission, purpose, profession, occupation, career, job, employment, trade, craft, line (of work).

vogue *noun* **fashion**, trend, fad, fancy, craze, rage, enthusiasm, passion.

voice *noun* **opinion**, view, feeling, wish, desire, vote.
● *verb* **express**, communicate, declare, state, vent, utter, say, speak, articulate, air; *informal* come out with.

WORD LINKS
vocal relating to the human voice

void *noun* **vacuum**, emptiness, nothingness, blankness, (empty) space, gap, cavity, chasm, gulf.
● *adjective* **1 empty**, vacant, blank, bare, clear, free. **2 invalid**, null (and

void), ineffective, worthless.
- OPPOSITES full, valid.

volatile *adjective* **1 unpredictable**, temperamental, capricious, fickle, impulsive, emotional, excitable, turbulent, erratic, unstable. **2** *a volatile situation* **tense**, strained, fraught, uneasy, uncomfortable, charged, explosive, inflammatory, turbulent.
- OPPOSITES stable.

volley *noun* **barrage**, cannonade, battery, bombardment, salvo, burst, storm, hail, shower, deluge, torrent.

volume *noun* **1 book**, publication, tome, work, title. **2 capacity**, mass, bulk, extent, size, dimensions. **3 quantity**, amount, mass, bulk, measure. **4 loudness**, sound, amplification.

voluntarily *adverb* **of your own free will**, of your own volition, by choice, by preference, spontaneously, willingly, readily, freely.

voluntary *adjective* **1 optional**, discretionary, at your discretion, elective, non-compulsory. **2 unpaid**, unsalaried, for free, honorary.
- OPPOSITES compulsory.

volunteer *verb* **1 offer**, tender, proffer, put forward, put up, venture. **2 offer your services**, present yourself, make yourself available, come forward.

vomit *verb* **be sick**, spew, heave, retch, gag; *informal* throw up, puke; *N. Amer. informal* barf.

vote *noun* **1 ballot**, poll, election, referendum, plebiscite, show of hands. **2** (**the vote**) **suffrage**, franchise, voting rights.

WORD LINKS
psephology study of trends in voting

voucher *noun* **coupon**, token, ticket, pass, chit, slip, stub, docket; *Brit. informal* chitty.

vow *noun* **promise**, pledge, oath, bond, covenant, commitment, word (of honour).
● *verb* **promise**, pledge, swear, undertake, make a commitment, give your word, guarantee.

voyage *noun* **journey**, trip, cruise, passage, sail, crossing, expedition, odyssey.

vulgar *adjective* **1 rude**, crude, dirty, filthy, smutty, naughty, indecent, obscene, coarse, risqué; *informal* blue. **2 tasteless**, crass, tawdry, ostentatious, flamboyant, showy, gaudy, garish; *informal* flash, tacky. **3 impolite**, ill-mannered, boorish, uncouth, unsophisticated, unrefined.
- OPPOSITES tasteful.

vulnerable *adjective* **1 in danger**, in peril, in jeopardy, at risk, unprotected, undefended, unguarded, open to attack, exposed, defenceless, an easy target. **2 helpless**, weak, sensitive, thin-skinned.
- OPPOSITES invulnerable.

Ww

waddle *verb* **toddle**, totter, wobble, shuffle.

wag *verb* **1 swing**, swish, switch, sway, shake; *informal* waggle. **2 shake**, wave, wiggle, flourish, brandish.

wage *noun* **pay**, salary, stipend, fee, remuneration, income, earnings.
● *verb* **engage in**, carry on, conduct, execute, pursue, prosecute, proceed with.

wail *noun* & *verb* **howl**, cry, bawl, moan, groan, yowl, whine, lament.

wait *verb* **1** *we waited in the airport* **stay (put)**, remain, rest, stop, linger, loiter; *informal* stick around; *old use* tarry. **2** *she had to wait until her bags arrived* **stand by**, hold back, bide your time, mark time, kill time, waste time, kick your heels, twiddle your thumbs; *informal* hold on, hang around, sit tight.
● *noun* **delay**, hold-up, interval, interlude, pause, break, suspension, stoppage, halt, interruption, lull, gap.

waiter, **waitress** *noun* **server**, steward, stewardess, attendant, butler, servant; *N. Amer.* waitperson.

waive *verb* **1 give up**, abandon, renounce, relinquish, surrender, sacrifice, turn down. **2 disregard**, ignore, overlook, set aside, forgo.

wake[1] *verb* **awake**, waken, wake up, stir, come to, come round, rouse.
● *noun* **vigil**, watch, funeral.

wake[2] *noun* **backwash**, slipstream, trail, path, track.
□ **in the wake of** in the aftermath of, after, subsequent to, following, as a result of, as a consequence of, on account of, because of.

walk *verb* **1 stroll**, saunter, amble, trudge, plod, hike, tramp, trek, march, stride, troop, wander, ramble, promenade, traipse; *informal* mosey, hoof it. **2 accompany**, escort, guide, show, see, take, usher.
● *noun* **1 ramble**, hike, tramp, march, stroll, promenade, constitutional, turn. **2 gait**, step, stride, tread. **3 path**, pathway, footpath, track, walkway, promenade, footway, pavement, trail, towpath.

walker *noun* **rambler**, hiker, trekker, stroller, pedestrian.

wall *noun* **fortification**, rampart, barricade, bulwark, partition.

wallet *noun* **purse**, case, pouch, holder; *N. Amer.* billfold, pocketbook.

wallow *verb* **1 roll**, loll about, lie around, splash about. **2 luxuriate**, bask, take pleasure, take satisfaction, indulge (yourself), delight, revel, glory.

wan *adjective* **pale**, ashen, white, grey, anaemic, colourless, waxen, pasty, peaky, sickly, washed out, ghostly.

wander *verb* **1 stroll**, amble, saunter, walk, potter, ramble, meander, roam, range, drift; *informal* traipse, mosey. **2 stray**, depart, diverge, deviate, digress, drift, get sidetracked.

wane *verb* **decline**, diminish, decrease, dwindle, shrink, tail off, ebb, fade, lessen, peter out, fall off, recede, slump, weaken, wither, evaporate, die out.
– OPPOSITES grow.

want *verb* **desire**, wish for, hope for, fancy, care for, like, long for, yearn for, crave, hanker after, hunger for, thirst for, cry out for, covet; *informal* have a yen for, be dying for.
● *noun* **1 lack**, absence, non-existence, dearth, deficiency, inadequacy, insufficiency, paucity, shortage, scarcity. **2 need**, austerity, privation, deprivation, poverty, destitution. **3** *her wants would be taken care of* **wish**, desire, demand, longing, fancy, craving, need, requirement; *informal* yen.

wanting *adjective* **deficient**, inadequate, lacking, insufficient, imperfect, flawed, unsound, substandard, inferior, second-rate.

wanton *adjective* **deliberate**, wilful, malicious, gratuitous, unprovoked, motiveless, arbitrary, unjustifiable, senseless.

war *noun* **1 conflict**, warfare, combat, fighting, action, bloodshed, fight, campaign, hostilities. **2 campaign**, crusade, battle, fight, struggle.
- OPPOSITES peace.
● *verb* **fight**, battle, combat, wage war, take up arms, feud, quarrel, struggle, contend, wrangle, cross swords.

WORD LINKS
martial relating to war
belligerent engaged in a war

ward *noun* **1 room**, department, unit, area. **2 district**, constituency, division, quarter, zone, parish. **3 dependant**, charge, protégé.

warden *noun* **1 superintendent**, caretaker, porter, steward, custodian, watchman, concierge, doorman, commissionaire. **2 prison officer**, guard, jailer, warder, keeper; *informal* screw.

warehouse *noun* **storeroom**, depot, depository, stockroom; *informal* lock-up.

wares *plural noun* **goods**, merchandise, products, produce, stock, commodities.

warfare *noun* **fighting**, war, combat, conflict, action, hostilities.

warm *adjective* **1** *a warm kitchen* **hot**, cosy, snug. **2** *a warm day* **balmy**, summery, sultry, hot, mild, temperate. **3** *warm water* **tepid**, lukewarm, heated. **4** *a warm sweater* **thick**, chunky, thermal, woolly. **5** *a warm welcome* **friendly**, cordial, amiable, genial, kind, pleasant, fond, welcoming, hospitable, hearty.
- OPPOSITES cold, chilly.

warmth *noun* **1 heat**, cosiness, snugness. **2 friendliness**, amiability, geniality, cordiality, kindness, tenderness, fondness.

warn *verb* **1 inform**, notify, tell, alert, apprise, make someone aware, remind; *informal* tip off. **2 advise**, exhort, urge, counsel, caution.

warning *noun* **1 (advance) notice**, alert, hint, signal, sign, alarm bells; *informal* a tip-off. **2 caution**, notification, information, exhortation, advice. **3 omen**, premonition, foreboding, prophecy, prediction, forecast, token, portent, signal, sign. **4** *his sentence is a warning to other drunk drivers* **example**, deterrent, lesson, caution, message, moral. **5 reprimand**, caution, remonstrance, admonition, censure; *informal* dressing-down, talking-to, telling-off.

warp *verb* **1 buckle**, twist, bend, distort, deform, curve, bow, contort. **2 corrupt**, twist, pervert, deprave.

warrant *noun* **1 authorization**, order, writ, mandate, licence, permit, summons. **2 voucher**, chit, slip, ticket, coupon, pass.
● *verb* **1 justify**, deserve, vindicate, call for, sanction, permit, authorize, excuse, account for, legitimize, support, license, merit, qualify for, rate. **2 guarantee**, promise, affirm, swear, vouch, vow, pledge, undertake, declare, testify.

warranty *noun* **guarantee**, assurance, promise, commitment, undertaking, pledge, agreement, covenant.

warrior *noun* **fighter**, soldier, serviceman, combatant.

wary *adjective* **1 cautious**, careful, circumspect, on your guard, chary, alert, on the lookout, attentive, heedful, watchful, vigilant, observant. **2** *we are wary of strangers* **suspicious**, chary, leery, careful, distrustful.
- OPPOSITES inattentive, trustful.

wash *verb* **1 clean yourself**, bathe, shower. **2 clean**, cleanse, scrub, wipe, shampoo, launder, lather, sluice, swill, douse, swab, disinfect. **3** *she washed off the blood* **remove**, expunge, eradicate, sponge off, scrub off, wipe off, rinse off.

4 splash, lap, dash, break, beat, surge, ripple, roll.
● *noun* **1 laundry**, washing. **2 backwash**, wake, trail, path.
□ **wash away** erode, abrade, wear away, eat away.

waste *verb* **1 squander**, misspend, misuse, fritter away, throw away, lavish, dissipate; *informal* blow, splurge. **2** *she is wasting away* **grow weak**, grow thin, wilt, fade, deteriorate.
- OPPOSITES conserve.
● *adjective* **1 unwanted**, excess, superfluous, left over, scrap, unusable, unprofitable. **2 uncultivated**, barren, desert, arid, bare, desolate.
● *noun* **1 misuse**, misapplication, abuse, extravagance, lavishness. **2 rubbish**, refuse, litter, debris, junk, sewage, effluent; *N. Amer.* garbage, trash. **3** (**wastes**) **desert**, wasteland, wilderness, emptiness, wilds.

wasteful *adjective* **prodigal**, profligate, uneconomical, extravagant, lavish, excessive, imprudent, improvident, spendthrift.
- OPPOSITES frugal.

watch *verb* **1 observe**, view, look at, eye, gaze at, peer at, contemplate, inspect, scrutinize, scan; *informal* check out, get a load of, recce, eyeball. **2 spy on**, keep in sight, keep under surveillance, track, monitor, tail; *informal* keep tabs on, stake out. **3 guard**, mind, protect, look after, keep an eye on, take care of, shield, defend.
- OPPOSITES ignore.
● *noun* **1 wristwatch**, timepiece, chronometer. **2 guard**, vigil, lookout, observation, surveillance.

watchdog *noun* **ombudsman**, monitor, scrutineer, inspector, supervisor.

watchful *adjective* **observant**, alert, vigilant, attentive, aware, sharp-eyed, eagle-eyed, on the lookout, wary, cautious, careful.

water *verb* **1 sprinkle**, moisten, dampen, wet, spray, splash, hose, douse. **2 salivate**, become wet, moisten.
□ **water down 1** dilute, thin (out), weaken, adulterate. **2** tone down, temper, mitigate, moderate, soften, tame.

WORD LINKS
aquatic, **aqueous** relating to water

waterfall *noun* **falls**, cascade, cataract, rapids.

watertight *adjective* **1 impermeable**, impervious, (hermetically) sealed, waterproof. **2 indisputable**, unquestionable, incontrovertible, irrefutable, unassailable, foolproof, sound, flawless, conclusive.
- OPPOSITES leaky.

wave *verb* **1 flap**, wag, shake, swish, swing, brandish, flourish, wield. **2 ripple**, flutter, undulate, stir, flap, sway, shake, quiver. **3 gesture**, signal, beckon, motion.
● *noun* **1 signal**, sign, motion, gesture. **2 breaker**, roller, comber, boomer, ripple; (**waves**) swell, surf. **3** *a wave of planning applications* **spate**, surge, flow, flood, stream, torrent. **4** *a wave of emotion* **surge**, rush, tide, upsurge, sudden feeling.

waver *verb* **1** *the candlelight wavered* **flicker**, quiver. **2** *his voice wavered* **falter**, wobble, tremble, quaver. **3 hesitate**, dither, be irresolute, be undecided, vacillate, blow hot and cold; *Brit.* haver, hum and haw; *informal* shilly-shally, sit on the fence.

way *noun* **1 method**, process, procedure, technique, system, plan, strategy, scheme, solution, means, mechanism, approach. **2 manner**, style, fashion, mode. **3** *I've changed my ways* **practice**, wont, habit, custom, convention, routine, trait, attribute, peculiarity, idiosyncrasy, conduct, behaviour. **4 route**, course, direction, track, path, access, gate, exit, entrance, door. **5 distance**, length, stretch, journey. **6** *April is a long way away* **time**, stretch, term, span, duration. **7 direction**, bearing, course, orientation, line, tack. **8** *in some ways, he may be better off* **respect**, regard, aspect, facet, sense, detail, point, particular. **9** *the country is in a bad way*

state, condition, situation, circumstances, position, predicament, plight; *informal* shape.
□ **give way 1** yield, back down, surrender, concede defeat, give in, submit; *informal* throw in the towel/sponge, cave in. **2** collapse, give, cave in, fall in, come apart, crumple.

waylay *verb* **1 ambush**, hold up, attack, pounce on; *informal* mug. **2 accost**, detain, intercept; *informal* buttonhole.

wayward *adjective* **wilful**, headstrong, stubborn, obstinate, perverse, contrary, disobedient, undisciplined, rebellious, defiant, recalcitrant, unruly, wild; *formal* refractory.

weak *adjective* **1 feeble**, frail, delicate, fragile, infirm, ailing, debilitated, decrepit, exhausted, enervated; *informal* weedy. **2 inadequate**, poor, defective, faulty, deficient, imperfect, substandard. **3 unconvincing**, tenuous, implausible, unsatisfactory, poor, inadequate, lame, feeble, flimsy, hollow; *informal* pathetic. **4** *a weak bridge* **fragile**, rickety, insubstantial, wobbly, unstable, ramshackle, jerry-built, shoddy. **5 spineless**, craven, cowardly, timid, irresolute, indecisive, ineffectual, meek, tame, soft, faint-hearted; *informal* yellow, gutless. **6** *a weak voice* **indistinct**, muffled, muted, hushed, faint, low. **7 watery**, dilute, diluted, watered down, thin, tasteless.
– OPPOSITES strong.

weaken *verb* **1 enfeeble**, debilitate, incapacitate, sap, tire, exhaust.
2 decrease, dwindle, diminish, wane, ebb, subside, peter out, fizzle out, tail off, decline, falter. **3 impair**, undermine, compromise, lessen.
– OPPOSITES strengthen, bolster.

weakness *noun* **1 frailty**, feebleness, fragility, delicacy, debility, incapacity, decrepitude; *informal* weediness.
2 fault, flaw, defect, deficiency, failing, shortcoming, imperfection, Achilles heel. **3** *a weakness for champagne* **fondness**, liking, partiality, love, penchant, predilection, inclination, taste.
4 timidity, cravenness, cowardliness, indecision, irresolution, ineffectuality, ineffectiveness, impotence.

wealth *noun* **1 affluence**, prosperity, riches, means, fortune, money, cash, capital, treasure, finance, wherewithal, deep pockets; *informal* dough, bread.
2 abundance, profusion, plethora, mine, store; *informal* lot, load, mountain, stack, ton; *Brit. informal* shedload.
– OPPOSITES poverty, dearth.

wealthy *adjective* **rich**, affluent, moneyed, well off, well-to-do, prosperous; *informal* well heeled, rolling in it, made of money, loaded, flush.
– OPPOSITES poor.

wear *verb* **1 be dressed in**, be clothed in, have on, sport. **2 bear**, show, display, exhibit, give, put on, assume. **3 erode**, abrade, rub away, grind away, wash away, crumble (away), eat away (at). **4 last**, endure, hold up, bear up.
● *noun* **1 use**, service, value; *informal* mileage. **2 clothes**, garments, dress, attire, garb, wardrobe; *informal* get-up, gear, togs; *Brit. informal* kit, clobber.
3 damage, friction, abrasion, erosion.
□ **wear off** fade, diminish, lessen, dwindle, decrease, wane, peter out, fizzle out, pall, disappear, vanish. **wear out 1** deteriorate, become worn, fray, become threadbare. **2** tire out, fatigue, weary, exhaust, drain, sap, enervate; *informal* whack, poop, shatter, do in; *Brit. informal* knacker.

wearing *adjective* **tiring**, exhausting, wearying, fatiguing, enervating, draining, sapping, demanding, exacting, taxing, gruelling, punishing.

weary *adjective* **1 tired**, worn out, exhausted, fatigued, sapped, spent, drained; *informal* done in, ready to drop, shattered, bushed; *Brit. informal* knackered, whacked; *N. Amer. informal* pooped. **2 tiring**, exhausting, fatiguing, enervating, draining, sapping, demanding, taxing, arduous, gruelling.
– OPPOSITES energetic.

weather *noun* **conditions**, climate, elements, forecast, outlook.

● *verb* **survive**, come through, ride out, pull through, withstand, endure, rise above; *informal* stick out.

weave[1] *verb* **1 entwine**, lace, twist, knit, braid, plait. **2 invent**, make up, fabricate, construct, create, spin.

weave[2] *verb he had to weave his way through the crowds* **thread**, wind, wend, dodge, zigzag.

web *noun* **1 mesh**, net, lattice, lacework, gauze, gossamer. **2 network**, nexus, complex, tangle, chain.

wedded *adjective* **1 married**, matrimonial, marital, conjugal, nuptial. **2** *he is wedded to his work* **dedicated**, devoted, attached, fixated.

wedding *noun* **marriage (service)**, nuptials, union.

wedge *noun* **triangle**, segment, slice, section, chunk, lump, slab, hunk, block, piece.
● *verb* **squeeze**, cram, jam, ram, force, push, shove; *informal* stuff, bung.

weep *verb* **cry**, shed tears, sob, snivel, whimper, wail, bawl, keen; *Scottish* greet; *informal* boohoo, blub.

weigh *verb* **1 measure the weight of**, put on the scales. **2 have a weight of**, tip the scales at. **3** *he weighed up the possibilities* **consider**, contemplate, think about, mull over, chew over, reflect on, ruminate about, muse on, assess, examine, review, explore, take stock of. **4** *they need to weigh benefit against risk* **balance**, evaluate, compare, juxtapose, contrast.

weight *noun* **1 mass**, heaviness, load, burden. **2 influence**, force, leverage, sway, pull, power, authority; *informal* clout. **3 burden**, load, millstone, trouble, worry. **4** *the weight of the evidence is against him* **most**, bulk, majority, preponderance, body, lion's share.

W

weird *adjective* **1 uncanny**, eerie, unnatural, supernatural, unearthly, other-worldly, ghostly, mysterious, strange, abnormal, unusual; *informal* creepy, spooky, freaky. **2 bizarre**, odd, curious, strange, quirky, outlandish, eccentric, unconventional, unorthodox, idiosyncratic, surreal, crazy, absurd, grotesque, peculiar; *informal* wacky, freaky; *N. Amer. informal* wacko.
– OPPOSITES normal, conventional.

welcome *noun* **greeting**, salutation, reception, hospitality, the red carpet.
● *verb* **1 greet**, salute, receive, meet, usher in. **2 be pleased by**, be glad about, approve of, applaud, appreciate, embrace.
– OPPOSITES resent.
● *adjective* **pleasing**, good, agreeable, encouraging, gratifying, heartening, promising, favourable, pleasant.

weld *verb* **fuse**, bond, stick, join, attach, seal, splice, melt, solder.

welfare *noun* **1 well-being**, health, comfort, security, safety, protection, success, interest, good. **2 social security**, benefit, public assistance, pension, credit, support, sick pay, unemployment benefit; *Brit. informal* the dole.

well[1] *adverb* **1 satisfactorily**, nicely, correctly, properly, fittingly, suitably, appropriately. **2 skilfully**, ably, competently, proficiently, adeptly, deftly, expertly, excellently. **3** *they speak well of him* **admiringly**, highly, approvingly, favourably, appreciatively, warmly, enthusiastically, in glowing terms.
– OPPOSITES badly.
● *adjective* **1 healthy**, fine, fit, robust, strong, vigorous, blooming, thriving, in fine fettle; *informal* in the pink. **2 satisfactory**, all right, fine, in order, as it should be, acceptable; *informal* OK, hunky-dory.
– OPPOSITES unwell, unsatisfactory.
□ **as well** too, also, in addition, into the bargain, besides, furthermore, moreover, to boot.

well[2] *noun* **borehole**, spring, waterhole, shaft.
● *verb* **flow**, spill, stream, gush, roll, cascade, flood, spout, burst, issue.

well built *adjective* **sturdy**, strapping, brawny, burly, hefty, muscular, strong, rugged; *informal* hunky, beefy.
– OPPOSITES puny.

well known *adjective* **1 familiar**, popular, common, everyday, established. **2 famous**, famed, prominent, notable, renowned, distinguished, eminent, illustrious, acclaimed.
- OPPOSITES unknown.

wet *adjective* **1 damp**, moist, soaked, drenched, saturated, sopping, dripping, soggy, waterlogged, squelchy. **2 rainy**, pouring, teeming, showery, drizzly. **3 sticky**, tacky.
● *verb* **dampen**, moisten, sprinkle, spray, splash, soak, saturate, flood, douse, drench.
- OPPOSITES dry.

wharf *noun* **quay**, pier, dock, berth, landing, jetty, harbour, dockyard.

wheel *verb* **1 push**, trundle, roll. **2** *gulls wheeled overhead* **turn**, go round, circle, orbit.

wheeze *verb* **gasp**, whistle, hiss, rasp, croak, pant, cough.

whereabouts *noun* **location**, position, site, situation, spot, point, home, address, neighbourhood.

while *noun we chatted for a while* **time**, spell, stretch, stint, span, interval, period; *Brit. informal* patch.
● *verb tennis helped to while away the time* **pass**, spend, occupy, use up, kill.

whim *noun* **impulse**, urge, notion, fancy, inclination, caprice, vagary.

whimper *verb* **whine**, cry, sob, moan, snivel, wail, groan; *Brit. informal* grizzle.

whimsical *adjective* **fanciful**, playful, mischievous, waggish, quaint, curious, droll, eccentric, quirky, idiosyncratic, unconventional.

whine *verb* **1 wail**, whimper, cry, mewl, moan, howl, yowl; *informal* grizzle. **2 complain**, grouse, grouch, grumble, moan, carp; *informal* gripe, bellyache, whinge.

whip *noun* **lash**, scourge, strap, belt.
● *verb* **1 flog**, lash, flagellate, cane, belt, thrash, beat; *informal* tan someone's hide. **2 whisk**, beat. **3 rouse**, stir up, excite, galvanize, electrify, stimulate, inspire, fire up, inflame, provoke.

whirl *verb* **rotate**, circle, wheel, turn, revolve, orbit, spin, twirl, pirouette, gyrate.

whirlpool *noun* **eddy**, vortex, maelstrom.

whirlwind *noun* **tornado**, hurricane, typhoon, cyclone, vortex; *N. Amer. informal* twister.
● *adjective* **rapid**, lightning, headlong, impulsive, breakneck, meteoric, sudden, swift, fast, quick, speedy.

whisk *verb* **1 speed**, hurry, rush, sweep, hurtle, shoot. **2 pull**, snatch, pluck, tug, jerk; *informal* whip, yank. **3 whip**, beat, mix.
● *noun an egg whisk* **beater**, mixer, blender.

whisper *verb* **murmur**, mutter, mumble, speak softly, breathe, say sotto voce.
● *noun* **1 murmur**, mutter, mumble, low voice, undertone. **2 rumour**, story, report, gossip, speculation, suggestion, hint; *informal* buzz.
- OPPOSITES shout.

white *adjective* **pale**, pallid, wan, ashen, chalky, pasty, peaky, washed out, ghostly, deathly.

whole *adjective* **1 entire**, complete, full, unabridged, uncut. **2 intact**, in one piece, unbroken, undamaged, flawless, unmarked, perfect.
- OPPOSITES incomplete.
● *noun* **1 entity**, unit, body, ensemble. **2** *the whole of the year* **all**, every part, the lot, the sum.
□ **on the whole** overall, all in all, all things considered, for the most part, in the main, in general, by and large, normally, usually, almost always, typically, ordinarily.

wholehearted *adjective* **unqualified**, unreserved, unconditional, complete, full, total, absolute.
- OPPOSITES half-hearted.

wholesale *adjective* **extensive**, widespread, large-scale, wide-ranging, comprehensive, total, mass, indiscriminate, sweeping.
- OPPOSITES partial.

wholesome *adjective* **1 healthy**, health-giving, good, nutritious, nourishing, natural, organic. **2 moral**, ethical, good, clean, virtuous, pure, innocent, chaste, uplifting, edifying.

wholly *adverb* **completely**, totally, absolutely, entirely, fully, thoroughly, utterly, downright, in every respect; *informal* one hundred per cent.

wicked *adjective* **1 evil**, sinful, immoral, wrong, bad, iniquitous, corrupt, base, vile, villainous, criminal, nefarious; *informal* crooked. **2 mischievous**, playful, naughty, impish, roguish, puckish, cheeky.
- OPPOSITES virtuous.

wide *adjective* **1 broad**, extensive, spacious, vast, spread out. **2 comprehensive**, ample, broad, extensive, wide-ranging, large, exhaustive, all-inclusive, expansive, all-embracing, encyclopedic, catholic. **3 off target**, off the mark, inaccurate.
- OPPOSITES narrow.

widen *verb* **broaden**, open up/out, expand, extend, enlarge.

widespread *adjective* **general**, extensive, universal, common, global, worldwide, omnipresent, ubiquitous, across the board, predominant, prevalent, rife, broad.
- OPPOSITES limited.

width *noun* **breadth**, thickness, span, diameter, girth.

wield *verb* **1 brandish**, flourish, wave, swing, use, employ, handle. **2** *he wields enormous power* **exercise**, exert, hold, maintain, command, control.

wife *noun* **spouse**, partner, mate, consort, bride; *informal* better half, missus; *Brit. informal* other half.

WORD LINKS
uxorious very fond of your wife

W

wild *adjective* **1 untamed**, undomesticated, feral, fierce, ferocious, savage. **2 uncultivated**, native, indigenous. **3 uninhabited**, unpopulated, uncultivated, rugged, rough, inhospitable, desolate, barren. **4 stormy**, squally, tempestuous, turbulent, blustery. **5 uncontrolled**, unrestrained, undisciplined, attention-seeking, unruly, rowdy, disorderly, riotous, out of control, unbridled. **6** *a wild scheme* **foolish**, ridiculous, ludicrous, stupid, foolhardy, idiotic, madcap, absurd, silly, impractical, impracticable, unworkable; *informal* crazy, crackpot. **7** *a wild guess* **random**, arbitrary, haphazard, uninformed.
- OPPOSITES tame, cultivated, calm, disciplined.

wilderness *noun* **wilds**, wastes, desert, wasteland.

wiles *plural noun* **tricks**, ruses, ploys, schemes, dodges, manoeuvres, subterfuges, guile, artfulness, cunning.

wilful *adjective* **1 deliberate**, intentional, premeditated, planned, conscious, calculated. **2 headstrong**, strong-willed, obstinate, stubborn, pig-headed, recalcitrant; *Brit. informal* bloody-minded, bolshie.
- OPPOSITES accidental.

will *noun* **1 determination**, strength of character, resolve, single-mindedness, drive, commitment, dedication, doggedness, tenacity, staying power. **2** *they stayed against their will* **desire**, wish, preference, inclination, intention. **3** *it was God's will* **wish**, desire, decision, choice, decree, command.
● *verb* **1 want**, wish, please, see fit, think fit/best, like, choose, prefer. **2 decree**, order, ordain, command.

willing *adjective* **1 ready**, prepared, disposed, inclined, minded, happy, glad, pleased, agreeable, amenable; *informal* game. **2 readily given**, ungrudging.
- OPPOSITES reluctant.

willingly *adverb* **voluntarily**, of your own free will, of your own accord, readily, without reluctance, ungrudgingly, cheerfully, happily, gladly, with pleasure.
- OPPOSITES reluctantly.

willingness *noun* **readiness**, inclination, will, wish, desire.
- OPPOSITES reluctance.

wilt *verb* **1 droop**, sag, become limp, flop. **2 languish**, flag, droop, become listless, fade.
- OPPOSITES flourish.

wily *adjective* **shrewd**, clever, sharp, astute, canny, smart, crafty, cunning, artful, sly, scheming, calculating, devious; *informal* foxy.
- OPPOSITES naive.

win *verb* **1 come first**, be victorious, carry/win the day, come out on top, succeed, triumph, prevail. **2 earn**, gain, secure, collect, pick up, walk away/off with, carry off; *informal* land, net, bag, scoop.
- OPPOSITES lose.
● *noun* **victory**, triumph, conquest.
- OPPOSITES defeat.

wince *verb* **grimace**, pull a face, flinch, blench, start.

wind[1] *noun* **1 breeze**, current of air, gale, hurricane, gust, draught; *informal* blow; *literary* zephyr. **2 breath**; *informal* puff.

wind[2] *verb* **1 twist (and turn)**, bend, curve, loop, zigzag, weave, snake. **2 wrap**, furl, entwine, lace. **3 coil**, roll, twist, twine.
□ **wind up 1** conclude, bring to an end/close, terminate; *informal* wrap up. **2** close (down), dissolve, put into liquidation.

windfall *noun* **bonanza**, jackpot, pennies from heaven, godsend.

windy *adjective* **breezy**, blowy, fresh, blustery, gusty, wild, stormy, squally.
- OPPOSITES still.

wing *noun* **1 part**, section, side, annexe, extension. **2 faction**, camp, caucus, arm, branch, group, section, set.
● *verb* **1 fly**, glide, soar. **2 wound**, graze, hit.

wink *verb* **1 blink**, flutter, bat. **2 sparkle**, twinkle, flash, glitter, gleam, shine, scintillate.

winner *noun* **victor**, champion, conqueror, medallist; *informal* champ, top dog.
- OPPOSITES loser.

winning *adjective* **1 victorious**, successful, triumphant, undefeated, conquering, first, top. **2 engaging**, charming, appealing, endearing, sweet, cute, winsome, attractive, prepossessing, fetching, disarming, captivating.

winnings *plural noun* **prize money**, gains, booty, spoils, proceeds, profits, takings, purse.

wintry *adjective* **bleak**, cold, chilly, frosty, freezing, icy, snowy, arctic, glacial, bitter, raw; *informal* nippy; *Brit. informal* parky.
- OPPOSITES warm.

wipe *verb* **1 rub**, mop, sponge, swab, clean, dry, polish. **2** *he wiped off the marks* **rub off**, clean off, remove, erase, efface.

wisdom *noun* **1 understanding**, intelligence, sagacity, sense, common sense, shrewdness, astuteness, judgement, prudence, circumspection, logic, rationale, soundness, advisability. **2 knowledge**, learning, erudition, scholarship, philosophy, lore.
- OPPOSITES folly.

wise *adjective* **sage**, sagacious, intelligent, clever, learned, knowledgeable, enlightened, astute, smart, shrewd, sharp-witted, canny, knowing, sensible, prudent, discerning, perceptive.
- OPPOSITES foolish.

wish *verb* **want**, desire, feel inclined, feel like, care, choose, please, think fit.
● *noun* **1 desire**, longing, yearning, whim, craving, hunger, hope, aspiration, aim, ambition, dream; *informal* hankering, yen. **2** *her parents' wishes* **request**, requirement, bidding, instruction, direction, demand, order, command, want, desire, will.
□ **wish for** desire, want, hope for, covet, dream of, long for, yearn for, crave, hunger for, aspire to, set your heart on, seek, fancy, hanker after; *informal* have a yen for.

wistful *adjective* **nostalgic**, yearning, longing, forlorn, melancholy, sad, mournful, pensive, reflective, contemplative.

wit *noun* **1** *he needed all his wits to escape* **intelligence**, shrewdness, astuteness, cleverness, canniness, sense, judgement, acumen, insight, brains, mind; *informal* nous. **2 wittiness**, humour, drollery, repartee, badinage, banter, wordplay, jokes, witticisms, quips, puns. **3 comedian**, humorist, comic, joker; *informal* wag.

witch *noun* **sorceress**, enchantress, hex.

witchcraft *noun* **sorcery**, (black) magic, wizardry, spells, incantations, necromancy, Wicca.

withdraw *verb* **1 remove**, extract, pull out, take out, take back. **2 abolish**, cancel, lift, set aside, end, stop, remove, reverse, revoke, rescind, repeal, annul. **3 retract**, take back, go back on, recant, repudiate, renounce, back down, climb down, backtrack, back-pedal, do a U-turn, row back, eat your words. **4 retreat**, pull out of, evacuate, quit, leave. **5 retire**, retreat, adjourn, decamp, leave, depart, absent yourself; *formal* repair.
- OPPOSITES insert, enter.

withdrawal *noun* **1 removal**, abolition, cancellation, discontinuation, termination, elimination. **2 departure**, pull-out, exit, exodus, evacuation, retreat.

withdrawn *adjective* **introverted**, unsociable, inhibited, uncommunicative, unforthcoming, quiet, reticent, reserved, retiring, private, reclusive, distant, shy, timid.
- OPPOSITES outgoing.

wither *verb* **1 shrivel (up)**, dry up, wilt, droop, go limp, fade, perish. **2 waste (away)**, shrivel (up), shrink, atrophy. **3 diminish**, dwindle, shrink, lessen, fade, wane, evaporate, disappear.
- OPPOSITES thrive.

withering *adjective* **scornful**, contemptuous, scathing, stinging.

withhold *verb* **1 hold back**, keep back, refuse to give, retain, hold on to, hide, conceal, keep secret; *informal* sit on. **2 suppress**, repress, hold back, fight back, choke back, control, check, restrain, contain.
- OPPOSITES release.

withstand *verb* **resist**, weather, survive, endure, cope with, stand, tolerate, bear, defy, brave, hold out against.

witness *noun* **observer**, onlooker, eyewitness, spectator, viewer, watcher, bystander, passer-by.
● *verb* **1 see**, observe, watch, view, notice, spot, be present at, attend. **2 countersign**, sign, endorse, validate.

witty *adjective* **humorous**, amusing, droll, funny, comic, jocular, sparkling, scintillating, entertaining, clever, quick-witted.

wizard *noun* **1 sorcerer**, warlock, magus, (black) magician, enchanter. **2 genius**, expert, master, virtuoso, maestro, marvel; *informal* hotshot, whizz-kid; *Brit. informal* dab hand; *N. Amer. informal* maven.

wobble *verb* **1 rock**, sway, see-saw, teeter, jiggle, shake. **2 teeter**, totter, stagger, lurch, waddle. **3** *her voice wobbled* **tremble**, shake, quiver, quaver, waver.

wobbly *adjective* **1 unsteady**, unstable, shaky, rocky, rickety, unsafe, precarious; *informal* wonky. **2 shaky**, quivery, weak, unsteady; *informal* like jelly.
- OPPOSITES stable.

woe *noun* **1 misery**, sorrow, distress, sadness, unhappiness, heartache, heartbreak, despair, adversity, misfortune, disaster, suffering, hardship. **2** *financial woes* **trouble**, difficulty, problem, trial, tribulation, misfortune, setback, reverse.
- OPPOSITES joy.

woeful *adjective* **1 sad**, unhappy, sorrowful, miserable, gloomy, doleful, plaintive, wretched. **2 dreadful**, awful, terrible, atrocious, disgraceful, deplorable, hopeless, lamentable; *informal* rotten, appalling, pathetic, pitiful, lousy, abysmal, dire; *Brit. informal* duff, chronic.
- OPPOSITES cheerful, excellent.

woman *noun* **lady**, female; *Scottish & N. English* lass; *Irish* colleen; *informal* chick; *N. Amer. informal* sister, dame, broad; *Austral./NZ informal* sheila; *literary* damsel.

WORD LINKS
female, **feminine** relating to women
gynaecology branch of medicine concerning women
misogyny hatred of women

womanly *adjective* **1 feminine**, female. **2 voluptuous**, curvaceous, shapely, ample, buxom, full-figured; *informal* curvy, busty.
– OPPOSITES manly, boyish.

wonder *noun* **1 awe**, admiration, fascination, surprise, astonishment, amazement. **2** *the wonders of nature* **marvel**, miracle, phenomenon, sensation, spectacle, beauty, curiosity.
● *verb* **1 ponder**, think about, meditate on, reflect on, muse on, speculate about, conjecture, be curious about. **2 marvel**, be amazed, be astonished, stand in awe, be dumbfounded; *informal* be flabbergasted.

wonderful *adjective* **marvellous**, magnificent, superb, glorious, sublime, lovely, delightful; *informal* super, great, fantastic, terrific, tremendous, sensational, fabulous, awesome, magic, wicked; *Brit. informal* smashing, brilliant; *N. Amer. informal* peachy, dandy, neat; *Austral./NZ informal* beaut, bonzer.

woo *verb* **1 pay court to**, pursue, chase; *dated* court, romance, seek the hand of. **2 seek**, pursue, curry favour with, try to win, try to attract, try to cultivate. **3 entice**, tempt, coax, persuade, wheedle, seduce; *informal* sweet-talk.

wood *noun* **1 timber**, planks, logs; *N. Amer.* lumber. **2 forest**, woodland, trees, copse, coppice, grove; *Brit.* spinney.

WORD LINKS
ligneous relating to wood

wooded *adjective* **forested**, afforested, tree-covered; *literary* sylvan.

wooden *adjective* **1 wood**, timber. **2 stilted**, stiff, unnatural, awkward, flat, clumsy, graceless, inelegant. **3 expressionless**, impassive, poker-faced, emotionless, blank, vacant, unresponsive, lifeless.

wool *noun* **fleece**, hair, coat.

woolly *adjective* **1 woollen**, wool. **2 fleecy**, shaggy, hairy, fluffy. **3 vague**, ill-defined, hazy, unclear, fuzzy, indefinite, confused, muddled.

word *noun* **1 term**, name, expression, designation. **2 remark**, comment, observation, statement, utterance. **3 script**, lines, lyrics, libretto. **4** *I give you my word* **promise**, assurance, guarantee, undertaking, pledge, vow, oath, bond. **5 talk**, conversation, chat, tête-à-tête, heart-to-heart, one-to-one, discussion; *informal* confab. **6** *there's no word from the hospital* **news**, information, communication, intelligence, message, report, communiqué, dispatch, bulletin; *literary* tidings.
● *verb* **phrase**, express, put, couch, frame, formulate, style.

WORD LINKS
verbal, **lexical** relating to words

wording *noun* **phrasing**, phraseology, language, words, expression, terminology.

wordy *adjective* **long-winded**, verbose, lengthy, rambling, garrulous, voluble; *informal* windy; *Brit. informal* waffly.
– OPPOSITES succinct.

work *noun* **1 labour**, toil, slog, drudgery, exertion, effort, industry; *informal* grind, sweat; *Brit. informal* graft; *old use* travail. **2 employment**, job, post, position, situation, occupation, profession, career, vocation, calling. **3 tasks**, jobs, duties, assignments, projects, chores. **4 composition**, piece, creation, opus; (**works**) oeuvre, canon.
– OPPOSITES leisure.
● *verb* **1 labour**, toil, exert yourself, slave (away); *informal* slog (away), beaver away; *Brit. informal* graft. **2 be employed**, have a job, earn your living, do business. **3 function**, go, run, operate. **4 operate**, use, handle, control,

run, manipulate. **5 succeed**, turn out well, go as planned, get results, be effective; *informal* come off, pay off, do the trick. **6 achieve**, accomplish, bring about, produce, perform.
- OPPOSITES rest, fail.
□ **work out 1** calculate, compute, reckon up, determine. **2** understand, comprehend, puzzle out, sort out, make sense of, get to the bottom of, make head or tail of, unravel, decipher, decode; *informal* figure out; *Brit. informal* suss out. **3** devise, formulate, draw up, put together, develop, construct, arrange, organize, contrive, concoct.

worker *noun* **employee**, member of staff, workman, labourer, hand, operator, operative, agent, wage-earner, breadwinner, proletarian.

workshop *noun* **1 workroom**, studio, factory, works, plant, industrial unit. **2 study group**, discussion group, seminar, forum, class.

world *noun* **1 earth**, globe, planet, sphere. **2 sphere**, society, circle, arena, milieu, province, domain, preserve, realm, field. **3 (the world) everyone**, people, mankind, humankind, humanity, the public, all and sundry.

worldly *adjective* **1 earthly**, terrestrial, temporal, mundane, mortal, human, material, physical. **2 sophisticated**, experienced, worldly-wise, knowledgeable, knowing, enlightened, mature, seasoned, cosmopolitan, urbane, cultured.
- OPPOSITES spiritual, naive.

worldwide *adjective* **global**, international, intercontinental, universal, ubiquitous.
- OPPOSITES local.

worn *adjective* **shabby**, worn out, threadbare, in tatters, falling to pieces, ragged, frayed, moth-eaten, scruffy, having seen better days.
- OPPOSITES new, smart.

worried *adjective* **anxious**, troubled, bothered, concerned, uneasy, fretful, agitated, nervous, edgy, tense, apprehensive, fearful, afraid, frightened; *Brit. informal* in a stew, in a flap.
- OPPOSITES carefree.

worry *verb* **1 be anxious**, be concerned, fret, agonize, brood, panic, lose sleep, get worked up; *informal* get in a flap, get in a state. **2 trouble**, bother, make anxious, disturb, distress, upset, concern, unsettle, perturb, scare, prey on someone's mind; *informal* bug, get to.
● *noun* **1 anxiety**, distress, concern, unease, disquiet, nerves, agitation, edginess, tension, apprehension, fear, misgiving. **2 problem**, cause for concern, nuisance, pest, trial, trouble, bane, bugbear; *informal* pain, headache, hassle.

worsen *verb* **1 aggravate**, add to, intensify, increase, compound, magnify, heighten, inflame, exacerbate. **2 deteriorate**, degenerate, decline; *informal* go downhill.
- OPPOSITES improve.

worship *noun* **1 reverence**, veneration, adoration, glorification, exaltation, devotion, praise, thanksgiving, homage, honour. **2 service**, rite, prayer, praise, devotion, observance.
● *verb* **1 revere**, pray to, pay homage to, honour, adore, venerate, praise, glorify, exalt. **2 love**, cherish, treasure, hold dear, esteem, adulate, idolize, deify, hero-worship, lionize; *informal* put on a pedestal.

worth *noun* **1 value**, price, cost, valuation, estimate. **2 benefit**, good, advantage, use, value, virtue, desirability, sense.

worthless *adjective* **1 valueless**, of no value; *informal* trashy. **2 useless**, pointless, meaningless, senseless, inconsequential, ineffective, ineffectual, fruitless, unproductive, unavailing, valueless. **3 good-for-nothing**, ne'er-do-well, useless, despicable, contemptible, degenerate; *informal* no-good, lousy.
- OPPOSITES valuable, useful.

worthwhile *adjective* **valuable**, useful, of service, beneficial, rewarding, advantageous, positive, helpful, profitable, gainful, fruitful, productive, constructive, effective.

worthy *adjective* **good**, righteous, virtuous, moral, ethical, upright, respectable, upstanding, high-minded, principled, reputable, decent.
- OPPOSITES disreputable.
● *noun* **dignitary**, personage, grandee, VIP, notable, pillar of society, luminary, leading light; *informal* bigwig.

would-be *adjective* **aspiring**, budding, promising, prospective, potential, hopeful, keen, eager, ambitious; *informal* wannabe.

wound *noun* **1 injury**, cut, gash, laceration, graze, scratch, abrasion, puncture, lesion; *Medicine* trauma. **2 insult**, blow, slight, offence, affront, hurt, damage, injury.
● *verb* **1 injure**, hurt, harm, lacerate, cut, graze, gash, stab, slash. **2** *her words wounded him* **hurt**, offend, affront, distress, grieve, pain.

wrap *verb* **1 enclose**, enfold, envelop, encase, cover, fold, wind, swathe, bundle, swaddle. **2 pack**, package, parcel up, bundle (up), gift-wrap.
● *noun* **shawl**, stole, cloak, cape, mantle, scarf.

wrath *noun* **anger**, rage, temper, fury, outrage, spleen, resentment, (high) dudgeon, indignation; *literary* ire.
- OPPOSITES happiness.

wreath *noun* **garland**, circlet, chaplet, crown, festoon, lei, ring, loop, circle.

wreathe *verb* **1 festoon**, qarland, drape, cover, deck, decorate, ornament, adorn. **2 spiral**, coil, loop, wind, curl, twist, snake.

wreck *noun* **1 shipwreck**, sunken ship, hull. **2 wreckage**, debris, ruins, remains, burnt-out shell.
● *verb* **1 destroy**, break, demolish, crash, smash up, write off; *N. Amer. informal* trash, total. **2 ruin**, spoil, disrupt, undo, put a stop to, frustrate, blight, crush, dash, destroy, scotch, shatter, devastate, sabotage; *informal* mess up, screw up, put paid to, stymie; *Brit. informal* scupper.

wrench *verb* **1 tug**, pull, jerk, wrest, heave, twist, force, prise; *N. Amer.* pry; *informal* yank. **2 sprain**, twist, turn, strain, rick, crick.

wrestle *verb* **grapple**, fight, struggle, scuffle, tussle, brawl; *informal* scrap.

wretched *adjective* **1 miserable**, unhappy, sad, heartbroken, grief-stricken, distressed, desolate, devastated, disconsolate, downcast, dejected, depressed, melancholy, forlorn. **2 harsh**, hard, grim, difficult, poor, pitiful, piteous, pathetic, tragic, miserable, bleak, cheerless, hopeless, sorry, sordid; *informal* crummy.
- OPPOSITES cheerful, comfortable.

wriggle *verb* **squirm**, writhe, wiggle, thresh, flounder, flail, twitch, twist and turn, snake, worm.
□ **wriggle out of** avoid, shirk, dodge, evade, sidestep, escape; *informal* duck.

wrinkle *noun* **crease**, fold, pucker, line, crinkle, furrow, ridge, groove; *informal* crow's feet.
● *verb* **crease**, pucker, gather, crinkle, crumple, rumple, ruck up, scrunch up.

write *verb* **1 put in writing**, put down, jot down, note (down), take down, record, inscribe, sign, scribble, scrawl, pen, pencil. **2 compose**, draft, think up, formulate, compile, pen, dash off, produce. **3 correspond**, communicate, get in touch, keep in contact; *informal* drop someone a line.

writer *noun* **author**, wordsmith; *informal* scribbler, scribe, pen-pusher, hack.

writhe *verb* **squirm**, wriggle, thrash, flail, toss, twist.

writing *noun* **1 handwriting**, hand, script, calligraphy, lettering, print, printing; *informal* scribble, scrawl. **2 written work**, compositions, books, publications, papers, articles, essays, oeuvre.

WORD LINKS
graphology study of handwriting

wrong *adjective* **1 incorrect**, mistaken, erroneous, inaccurate, wide of the mark, inexact, imprecise; *informal* off beam, out. **2 inappropriate**, unsuitable, ill-advised, ill-considered, ill-judged, unwise, infelicitous; *informal* out of order. **3 bad**, dishonest, illegal, unlawful, illicit, criminal, corrupt, unethical, immoral, wicked, sinful, iniquitous, nefarious, reprehensible; *informal* crooked. **4 amiss**, awry, out of order, not right, defective, faulty.

- OPPOSITES right, correct.

● *adverb* **incorrectly**, wrongly, inaccurately, erroneously, mistakenly.

● *noun* **1 immorality**, sin, wickedness, evil, illegality, unlawfulness, crime, corruption, villainy, dishonesty, injustice, misconduct, transgression. **2 misdeed**, offence, injury, crime, transgression, sin, injustice, outrage, atrocity.

- OPPOSITES right.

● *verb* **mistreat**, ill-use, ill-treat, do an injustice to, abuse, harm, hurt, injure.

wrongdoer *noun* **offender**, lawbreaker, criminal, felon, delinquent, villain, culprit, evil-doer, sinner, transgressor, malefactor, miscreant, rogue, scoundrel; *informal* crook, wrong 'un.

Yy

yank *verb* & *noun (informal)* **jerk**, pull, tug, wrench.

yardstick *noun* **standard**, measure, gauge, scale, guide, guideline, indicator, test, touchstone, barometer, criterion, benchmark.

yarn *noun* **thread**, cotton, wool, fibre, filament.

yawning *adjective* **gaping**, wide, cavernous, deep, huge, vast.

yearly *adverb* **annually**, once a year, per annum, each/every year.

yearn *verb* **long**, pine, crave, desire, want, wish, hanker, covet, hunger, thirst, ache; *informal* itch.

yell *verb* **shout**, cry out, howl, wail, scream, shriek, screech, yelp, squeal, roar, bawl; *informal* holler.

yellow *adjective* golden, gold, blonde, fair, flaxen, lemon, primrose, mustard.

yes *adverb* **certainly**, very well, of course, by all means, sure, all right, absolutely, indeed, affirmative, agreed, roger; *Scottish & N. English* aye; *informal* yeah, yep; *Brit. informal* righto.
- OPPOSITES no.

yield *verb* **1 produce**, bear, give, provide, afford, return, bring in, earn, realize, generate, deliver, pay out. **2 surrender**, capitulate, submit, admit defeat, back down, give in, cave in, raise the white flag, throw in the towel, give up the struggle.
- OPPOSITES withhold, resist.
● *noun* **profit**, gain, return, dividend, earnings.

yob, **yobbo** *noun (Brit. informal)* **lout**, thug, hooligan, tearaway, vandal, ruffian, troublemaker; *Austral.* larrikin; *informal* tough, bruiser, yahoo; *Brit. informal* lager lout; *Scottish informal* ned.

yokel *noun* **rustic**, bumpkin, peasant, provincial; *N. Amer. informal* hayseed, hillbilly, hick.

young *adjective* **1 youthful**, juvenile, junior, adolescent, teenage, in your salad days. **2 immature**, childish, inexperienced, naive, green, wet behind the ears. **3** *a young industry* **new**, fledgling, developing, budding, in its infancy, emerging, in the making.
- OPPOSITES old, mature.
● *noun* **offspring**, progeny, family, babies, litter, brood.

youngster *noun* **child**, teenager, adolescent, youth, juvenile, minor, junior, boy, girl; *Scottish & N. English* lass, lassie; *informal* lad, kid, whippersnapper, teen.

youth *noun* **1 early years**, teens, adolescence, boyhood, girlhood, childhood, minority. **2 young man**, boy, juvenile, teenager, adolescent, junior, minor; *informal* lad, kid.

youthful *adjective* **young**, boyish, girlish, fresh-faced, young-looking, spry, sprightly, vigorous, active.
- OPPOSITES elderly.

Zz

zany *adjective* **eccentric**, odd, unconventional, bizarre, weird, mad, crazy, comic, madcap, quirky, idiosyncratic; *informal* wacky, oddball, off the wall; *Brit. informal* daft; *N. Amer. informal* kooky.
- OPPOSITES conventional.

zeal *noun* **enthusiasm**, passion, ardour, fervour, fervency, fire, devotion, gusto, vigour, energy, vehemence, intensity, eagerness, fanaticism.
- OPPOSITES apathy.

zealot *noun* **fanatic**, enthusiast, extremist, radical, diehard, activist, militant.

zealous *adjective* **ardent**, fervent, passionate, impassioned, enthusiastic, devoted, committed, dedicated, eager, keen, avid, vehement, intense, fierce, fanatical.
- OPPOSITES apathetic.

zenith *noun* **high point**, crowning point, height, top, acme, peak, pinnacle, apex, apogee, crown, crest, summit, culmination, climax.
- OPPOSITES nadir.

zero *noun* **nought**, nothing, nil, 0; *informal* zilch; *old use* naught.

zest *noun* **enthusiasm**, gusto, relish, appetite, eagerness, keenness, zeal, passion, energy, liveliness.

zigzag *verb* **twist**, meander, snake, wind, weave, swerve.

zone *noun* **area**, sector, section, belt, stretch, region, territory, district, quarter, neighbourhood.

zoom *verb (informal)* **hurry**, rush, dash, race, speed, sprint, career, shoot, hurtle, hare, fly; *informal* tear, belt, whizz; *Brit. informal* bomb.

Oxford Paperback Reference

The Concise Oxford Companion to English Literature
Dinah Birch and Katy Hooper

Based on the best-selling *Oxford Companion to English Literature*, this is an indispensable guide to all aspects of English literature.

Review of the parent volume
'the foremost work of reference in its field'

Literary Review

A Dictionary of Shakespeare
Stanley Wells

Compiled by one of the best-known international authorities on the playwright's works, this dictionary offers up-to-date information on all aspects of Shakespeare, both in his own time and in later ages.

The Oxford Dictionary of Literary Terms
Chris Baldick

A best-selling dictionary, covering all aspects of literature, this is an essential reference work for students of literature in any language.

A Dictionary of Critical Theory
Ian Buchanan

The invaluable multidisciplinary guide to theory, covering movements, theories, and events.

'an excellent gateway into critical theory' *Literature and Theology*

OXFORD

Oxford Companions

'Opening such books is like sitting down with a knowledgeable friend. Not a bore or a know-all, but a genuinely well-informed chum ... So far so splendid.'

Sunday Times [of *The Oxford Companion to Shakespeare*]

For well over 60 years Oxford University Press has been publishing Companions that are of lasting value and interest, each one not only a comprehensive source of reference, but also a stimulating guide, mentor, and friend. There are between 40 and 60 Oxford Companions available at any one time, ranging from music, art, and literature to history, warfare, religion, and wine.

Titles include:

The Oxford Companion to English Literature
Edited by Dinah Birch
'No guide could come more classic.'

Malcolm Bradbury, *The Times*

The Oxford Companion to Music
Edited by Alison Latham
'probably the best one-volume music reference book going'

Times Educational Supplement

The Oxford Companion to Theatre and Performance
Edited by Dennis Kennedy
'A work that everyone who is serious about the theatre should have at hand'

British Theatre Guide

The Oxford Companion to Food
Alan Davidson
'the best food reference work ever to appear in the English language'

New Statesman

The Oxford Companion to Wine
Edited by Jancis Robinson
'the greatest wine book ever published'

Washington Post

OXFORD

More Literature titles from OUP

The Oxford Companion to Charles Dickens
edited by Paul Schlicke

Reissued to celebrate the bicentenary of Charles Dickens's birth, this companion draws together an unparalleled diversity of information on one of Britain's greatest writers; covering his life, his works, his reputation, and his cultural context.

Reviews from previous edition:
'comes about as close to perfection as humanly possible'
Dickens Quarterly

'will prove invaluable to scholars, readers and admirers of Dickens'
Peter Ackroyd, *The Times*

The Oxford Companion to the Brontës
Christine Alexander and Margaret Smith

This Companion brings together a wealth of information about the fascinating lives and writings of the Brontë sisters.

'This book is a must ... a treasure trove of a book'
Irish Times

The Oxford Companion to Classical Literature
edited by M. C. Howatson

A broad-ranging and authoritative guide to the classical world and its literary heritage.

Reviews from previous edition:
'a volume for all seasons ... indispensable'
Times Educational Supplement

'A necessity for any seriously literary household.' *History Today*

OXFORD

Oxford Paperback Reference

The Kings and Queens of Britain
John Cannon and Anne Hargreaves

A detailed, fully-illustrated history ranging from mythical and pre-conquest rulers to the present House of Windsor, featuring regional maps and genealogies.

A Dictionary of World History

Over 4,000 entries on everything from prehistory to recent changes in world affairs. An excellent overview of world history.

A Dictionary of British History
Edited by John Cannon

An invaluable source of information covering the history of Britain over the past two millennia. Over 3,000 entries written by more than 100 specialist contributors.

Review of the parent volume
'the range is impressive ... truly (almost) all of human life is here'
Kenneth Morgan, *Observer*

The Oxford Companion to Irish History
Edited by S. J. Connolly

A wide-ranging and authoritative guide to all aspects of Ireland's past from prehistoric times to the present day.

'packed with small nuggets of knowledge' *Daily Telegraph*

The Oxford Companion to Scottish History
Edited by Michael Lynch

The definitive guide to twenty centuries of life in Scotland.
'exemplary and wonderfully readable'
Financial Times

OXFORD

Oxford Paperback Reference

A Dictionary of Chemistry

Over 4,700 entries covering all aspects of chemistry, including physical chemistry and biochemistry.

'It should be in every classroom and library ... the reader is drawn inevitably from one entry to the next merely to satisfy curiosity.'

School Science Review

A Dictionary of Physics

Ranging from crystal defects to the solar system, 4,000 clear and concise entries cover all commonly encountered terms and concepts of physics.

A Dictionary of Biology

The perfect guide for those studying biology — with over 5,500 entries on key terms from biology, biochemistry, medicine, and palaeontology.

'lives up to its expectations; the entries are concise, but explanatory'

Biologist

'ideally suited to students of biology, at either secondary or university level, or as a general reference source for anyone with an interest in the life sciences'

Journal of Anatomy

OXFORD

Oxford Paperback Reference

The Concise Oxford Dictionary of Quotations
SIXTH EDITION
Edited by Susan Ratcliffe

Now based on the highly acclaimed seventh edition of *The Oxford Dictionary of Quotations*, this new edition maintains its extensive coverage of literary and historical quotations, and contains completely up-to-date material. A fascinating read and an essential reference tool.

Oxford Dictionary of Quotations by Subject
Edited by Susan Ratcliffe

The ideal place to discover what's been said about what, the dictionary presents quotations on nearly 600 areas of special interest and concern in today's world.

The Oxford Dictionary of Humorous Quotations
Edited by Ned Sherrin

From the sharply witty to the downright hilarious, this sparkling collection will appeal to all senses of humour.

The Oxford Dictionary of Political Quotations
Edited by Antony Jay

This lively and illuminating dictionary from the writer of 'Yes Minister' presents a vintage crop of over 4,000 political quotations. Ranging from the pivotal and momentous to the rhetorical, the sincere, the bemused, the tongue-in-cheek, and the downright rude, examples include memorable words from the old hands as well as from contemporary politicians.

'funny, striking, thought-provoking and incisive ... will appeal to those browsing through it as least as much as to those who wish to use it as a work of reference'
Observer

Oxford Dictionary of Modern Quotations
Edited by Elizabeth Knowles

The answers to all your quotation questions lie in this delightful collection of over 5,000 of the twentieth century's most famous quotations.

'Hard to sum up a book so useful, wayward and enjoyable' *Spectator*

OXFORD